An Accounting Thesaurus
500 Years of Accounting

An Accounting Thesaurus

500 Years of Accounting

R. J. Chambers

Pergamon

UK	Elsevier Science Ltd, The Boulevard, Langford Lane, Kidlington, Oxford, OX5 1GB, UK
USA	Elsevier Science Inc., 660 White Plains Road, Tarrytown, New York 10591-5153, USA
JAPAN	Elsevier Science Japan, Tsunashima Building Annex, 3-20-12 Yushima, Bunkyo-ku, Tokyo 113, Japan

First edition 1995

Library of Congress Cataloging in Publication Data

A catalog record for this book is available from the Library of Congress

British Library Cataloguing in Publication Data

A catalogue record for this book is available from the British Library

ISBN 0 08 042573 9 (Hardcover)

The publisher gratefully acknowledges the support of The Accounting Foundation within The University of Sydney in the publication of this book

Printed at Redwood Books, Trowbridge, Wiltshire.

Acknowledgements

The work and I are in debt to many –

To the authors, editors and publishers of books, periodicals and other material acknowledged in the Source Index.

To the collections of national, regional, professional association and university libraries, at home and abroad, and to helpful librarians.

To colleagues and associates who have drawn attention to some useful sources, and given access to material in their own collections.

To those who kindly offered opinions on the scope and the utility of the work.

To The University of Sydney, for physical means and an environment congenial to the preparation of the work.

To The Accounting Foundation within The University of Sydney, for a subvention towards the costs of preparation and publication.

To Elsevier Science and its editors, for undertaking publication of a volume without precedent in its field.

To Murray Wells, for mediation and aid in negotiation with the Publisher.

To Graeme Dean, for providing help in a variety of ways in processing the material from raw to publishable form.

To Margaret, for abiding patience, especially over the past decade of my preoccupation with the work.

R. J. Chambers
December 1994

Contents

Preface

For some thousands of years, records have been kept of the property and debts of persons and social institutions. Those records began to assume some of the features of modern commercial accounting about 700 years ago. The earliest treatment in print of its functions and rules appeared in a mathematical treatise of Luca Pacioli, published in 1494. Since then, the growth in trade and commerce, and the growing variety of trusts, partnerships, and public and private corporations serving individual and collective wants, have turned what was once a largely private matter into the business of a widespread and populous profession and the concern of a numerous public.

Like all serviceable arts, accounting has been influenced by shifts in the ideas of its practitioners and teachers, and by the exigencies of those served by it. It has been hailed as an instrument of prudent, fair and equitable dealing. It has been assailed for the part it has seemed to play in the schemes of crafty promoters and financial manipulators. Its ideals are unquestionable; but, like other arts, its practice has recurrently been found to fall short of those ideals.

This collection of dicta is drawn from the English-language literature of the past 500 years, especially of the last 150 years, the period of the greatest growth, stress and diversification in doctrine and practice. It illustrates the antiquity and the merit of some ideas, and the transience of others; the cohesion of some and the conflict of others. Its object is to give an historical perspective and an up to date conspectus of what accounting and its products have been, and are, and do. It is not a handbook or a textbook, but a complement and companion to any and all such works.

Much of the wisdom and the folly of the past is now little known, for its sources are scattered or remote. Reliable knowledge pertinent to accounting – economics, law, psychology, mathematics, administration, and so on – is often disregarded, for its sources, too, are diverse and have seldom attracted the close attention of those who have shaped the present common style of accounting, and may shape its future.

The justification of this selection, from diverse ages and fields of inquiry and practice, lies in a belief in its potential, as irritant or stimulus, for advancing the development of a demonstrably rigorous and serviceable accounting in a world that cannot do without it.

R. J. Chambers
December 1994

Introduction

Counting, weighing and measuring have long been among the means by which people have striven to accommodate themselves to the world about them. The powerful products of human invention could not have been devised or controlled without instruments of great diversity and increasingly powerful discrimination. Accounting is one such instrument. Its roots are embedded in the matrix of ideals, customs, laws and understandings that nurture the orderly, fair and just conduct of commercial and other financial affairs. Its branches reach out to the management of households, business corporations, charitable and cultural associations, and nation states.

Financial matters are only one element of the ends we seek. But the ebb and flow of rights in money and money's worth have become so central a part of social interaction and interrelation that observers and historians have assigned to accounting a major role in the development of social and economic institutions.

The concern of accounting with the wealth and income of individuals and institutions is shared with significant sections of legal studies, economic studies and other studies of individual and social behavior. The products of accounting, periodical statements of wealth, debt and income, are expected, and generally intended, to convey to financially interested parties the factual outcomes of extended and varied operations and events. They are communications on the truth and intelligibility of which depend the furtherance and protection of the interests of those parties. The processes of accounting – the recording, classification, aggregation and relation of dated money amounts – are, ideally, disciplined by the common rules of mathematics and logical reasoning. These associations with contributory branches of knowledge provide the foundations for a systematic art or technology. Some of those foundations have influenced the rules and principles governing practice.

But today's practices have emerged from a wide and conflicting array of demands and circumstances. The rising need in commerce for systematic bookkeeping from the 15th century onwards; the foreign engagements of European venturers from the 16th century; the growth in size and diversity of firms, and the growing investment in durable and costly equipment, in the 18th and 19th centuries arising out of the industrial revolution; the emergence of large partnerships and corporations as the dominant form of business in the 19th and 20th centuries; the growth in personal investment in corporate securities, and of public regulation of their issue, over the same period; the drive for recognition of accounting as a profession from the mid-19th century; the introduction of the study and teaching of accounting to the institutions of higher learning, and the rise of a largely descriptive literature in the 20th century – these all have left their marks on 20th century doctrine and practice.

Introduction

Rules of practice, originally few and simple, have become numerous and complex; their justifications often arbitrary, diverse and contradictory; expedients and conventions have at many points taken the place of disciplined reasoning. Trade, commerce and finance have survived the influence on accounting of these things, largely through the ever-necessary recourse of merchants and business people to immediate knowledge of market conditions and market prices and the means at their disposal. But countless individual corporations, and the hopes of their investors and creditors, have not escaped the consequences of faulty financial instrumentation. The profession has been, for decades, uneasy about the effects of the flexibility of its rules of practice.

However, seldom is more than passing attention given in manuals, textbooks and instruction in accounting to the dicta and practices of the past, their origins and their consequences; or to seminal ideas from other fields of scholarship that could aid in the resolution of past debates and present dilemmas. Yet, without knowledge of the origins and associations of what are now called traditional or conventional practices, we can neither understand them nor wisely shape the future of accounting. Hence this thesaurus – a view of the past with an eye to the future.

The dicta here gathered present the main ideas, precepts and proposals that have commanded endorsement, at some stage over the past half-millennium, by accounting practitioners and teachers and others having interests in financial affairs. It is not a dictionary, indicative of the common usages of words and phrases. It is not an encyclopedia, abstracting all there is to know about accounting. It is not a selection of the most elegant expressions of what accountants have believed or done, or now believe or do. Parts of the collection deal with technical minutiae, parts with ideals and general maxims. Parts draw on the work of scholars and practitioners in other fields that have some bearing on accounting work and thought.

Many of the judgments and conclusions represented are antithetical. The collection as a whole, then, does not represent or highlight any school of specialist thought or the work of any author or institution. It is a product of random influences and deliberate inquiries over many years under different exigencies and circumstances. Its scope and content have been dictated by the many interests and concerns of practitioners, scholars, research workers, regulators and students of accounting and related fields of knowledge and expertise.

Arrangement

The material is arranged in sections, subsections and captions, numbered for reference on a decimal system. There are ten sections:

000   Accounting in general
100   The economic background of accounting
200   The psychological and social background of accounting
300   General characteristics of accounting
400   Financial position and its elements
500   Dated valuation of assets and equities

600 Income and income calculation
700 Accounting systems
800 Systematic inquiry and knowledge
900 Accounting beliefs and knowledge

The content of the subsections and the reference numbers of sections and captions are given in the Outline. The focal points of the collection are ideas, not words. The captions are thus more frequently phrases or quasi-sentences than simple terms. Where captions refer to postulation, endorsement or criticism of ideas, these words are intended to be neutrally descriptive; they are not to be taken as judgments of the compiler. There are many points at which, in general discourse, ideas become interlocked or juxtaposed. Items and subsections, then, might occur in one section as properly as in another. Cross references in the text and the Subject Index make some of these connections. Cross references and the Source and Subject Indexes use reference numbers, not page numbers, for location.

Sources

Items on accounting ideas have been drawn from professional and scholarly journals and the financial press; from treatises, monographs and textbooks; from the edicts or pronouncements of legislative, regulatory and investigative agencies, the courts and professional and commercial organizations. The selection relates largely to the mainstream of thought and practice. The greater part is drawn from the English language literature on commercial accounting over the last 150 years.

Parts of the material, particularly in sections 100, 200 and 800, are drawn from the literatures of economics, psychology, management and administration, the physical and biological sciences, and the history and philosophy of disciplined inquiry – but from those fields only insofar as they seem to bear on accounting thought or practice.

Most items are taken from primary sources – original or subsequent editions and reprints; secondary sources where used are given in the Source Index. Source references in the main text are sufficient to enable the source to be found in that index, and the quotation thence to be traced to the source. For some items dual dates are given, such as 1918/1962. The latter date refers to the source used. The former date is the date of an earlier version of a work which may or may not have contained the material cited, or the date given in secondary sources. The earlier date is given as indicative of the time when an idea under reference could have come to the notice of others. Items under each caption are generally arranged chronologically.

Practices and expositions in the English language countries of sources have differed in some respects. In some cases these differences are identified; otherwise countries of origin or application are deducible from the domicile of authors or from places of publication.

Editorial discretion

Some liberties have been taken in reproducing extracts from source material, but with care to ensure that the substance is not misrepresented.

Abbreviations. Some items have been reduced in size to focus on points under observation. The usual conventions are followed; three points, . . . , mark an omission within a sentence; four points, ... , mark an omission that includes the end of a sentence. Square brackets enclose added words; round brackets enclose parenthetical words or phrases in the source. Where appropriate, minor changes have been made in punctuation.

Capital letters, bold face, italics and quotation marks appearing in sources have often been varied or eliminated. Their original use may have been dictated by the style of authors or publishers, or the habits of the times; they are not usually pertinent beyond the context of the source.

Only family names of authors are given in the text, and only initials of given names are used in the Source Index. Where co-authors exceed two, the text reference is of the form, Jones & others; the Source Index gives the names of all joint authors. The names of publishers are frequently abbreviated. A list is given of other abbreviations commonly used.

Orthography. Many words now spelled differently from the customary form of several hundred years ago have been given their modern form. The spelling of words that now have optional forms has been standardized. With few exceptions, words ending in –ise or –ize, and their derivatives, are given the z-form; words ending in –or or –our are given the –or form

Abbreviations

AA	*The Australian Accountant* (ASA, ASCPA)
AAA	American Accounting Association
AARF	Australian Accounting Research Foundation
AAS	(with number), Australian Accounting Standard
AASB	Australian Accounting Standards Board
Abacus	twice-yearly, (AFUS)
ABR	*Accounting and Business Research* (UK)
AccHor	*Accounting Horizons* (AAA)
Accountant, Acct	*The Accountant* (UK)
AccRes	*Accounting Research* (UK)
Accy	*Accountancy* (UK)
AEA	American Economic Association
AER	*American Economic Review*
AFUS	Accounting Foundation within the University of Sydney (formerly AFFUS)
AHJ	*The Accounting Historians Journal*
AIA	American Institute of Accountants (precursor of AICPA)
AICPA	American Institute of Certified Public Accountants
AISG	Accountants International Study Group
Anon	Author unknown
AOS	*Accounting, Organizations and Society* (UK)
APB	Accounting Principles Board (AICPA)
APBO	with number, Accounting Principles Board Opinion (AICPA)
APBS	with number, Accounting Principles Board Statement (AICPA)
AR	*The Accounting Review* (AAA)
ARB	with number, Accounting Research Bulletin (of AIA, AICPA)
ARM	with number, Accounting Research Monograph (AICPA)
ARS	with number, Accounting Research Study (of AICPA)
AR Supp	*The Accounting Review Supplement*
ASA	Australian Society of Accountants (precursor of ASCPA)
ASC	Accounting Standards Committee (UK)
ASCPA	Australian Society of Certified Practising Accountants
ASR	with number, Accounting Series Release (of SEC)
ASRB	Accounting Standards Review Board (Australia)
ASRC	Accounting Standards Review Committee (New South Wales)
ASSC	Accounting Standards Steering Committee (precursor of ASC)
ATB	with number, Accounting Terminology Bulletin (AIA, AICPA)
attr	attributed to
AU	with number, Statements on auditing (AIA, AICPA)

Abbreviations

BPP	*British Parliamentary Papers*
Bull	Bulletin
c with date,	*circa*, about
CAA	*The Chartered Accountant in Australia*, (ICAA)
CAMag	*The Chartered Accountants Magazine*, (CICA)
CanCA	*The Canadian Chartered Accountant*, (CICA)
CAP	Committee on Accounting Procedure (AIA, AICPA)
CCA	Current cost accounting
CCAB	Consultative Committee of Accountancy Bodies (UK)
CertAcc	*The Certified Accountant* (UK)
Charter	successor to *CAA* (Australia)
CICA	Canadian Institute of Chartered Accountants
CIERA	Center for International Education and Research in Accounting, U of Illinois
CoCoA	Continuously contemporary accounting
CUP	Cambridge University Press
EC	Englewood Cliffs, New Jersey
ed	edition
(ed), (eds),	editor, editors
ED	with number, exposure draft
EJ	*The Economic Journal* (UK)
ERA	*Empirical Research in Accounting* (U of Chicago)
FASB	Financial Accounting Standards Board (USA)
FTC	Federal Trade Commission (USA)
GAAP	Generally accepted accounting principles
HBR	*Harvard Business Review*
HMSO	Her (His) Majesty's Stationery Office (UK)
IAS	with number, International Accounting Standard (IASC)
IASC	International Accounting Standards Committee
IASG	Inflation Accounting Study Group (UK, Ref ED18)
ICAA	The Institute of Chartered Accountants in Australia
ICAEW	The Institute of Chartered Accountants in England and Wales
ICAS	The Institute of Chartered Accountants of Scotland
ICRA	International Centre for Research in Accounting, Lancaster
ICWA	Institute of Cost and Works Accountants (UK)
IJAER	*International Journal of Accounting, Education and Research* (U of Illinois)
J	*Journal*
JA	*The Journal of Accountancy* (AIA, AICPA)
JAPP	*Journal of Accounting and Public Policy*
JAR	*Journal of Accounting Research* (USA)
JBF	*Journal of Business Finance*, precursor of *JBFA*
JBFA	*Journal of Business Finance and Accounting*
J Bus	*Journal of Business*
JPE	*Journal of Political Economy*
LCP	*Law and Contemporary Problems* (Duke University)
MIT	Massachusetts Institute of Technology

Abbreviations

N	with number, Recommendation of ICAEW
NAA	National Association of Accountants (USA)
NACA	National Association of Cost Accountants (USA)
n.d.	no date given
n.p.	no place given
NY	New York
NYCPA	*New York Certified Public Accountant*
NYSE	New York Stock Exchange
NZSA	New Zealand Society of Accountants
OUP	Oxford University Press
P	Press (of publishers)
QJE	*Quarterly Journal of Economics*
repr	reproduced in or reprinted by
rev	revised, revised by
RPA	Replacement price (or cost) accounting
SAB	with number, Staff Accounting Bulletin (of SEC)
SAC	with number, Statement of Accounting Concepts (AARF)
s.c.	source cited
SEC	Securities and Exchange Commission (USA)
SFAC	with number, Statement of Financial Accounting Concepts (FASB)
SFAS	with number, Statement of Financial Accounting Standards (FASB)
SSAP	Statement of Standard Accounting Practice (UK)
Supp	Supplement
TAJ	*The Accountants Journal* (NZSA)
TAM	*The Accountant's Magazine* (ICAS)
TIMS	The Institute of Management Sciences (US)
trans	translated by
U	University
UCP	University of Chicago Press
UGD	with number, Archives of the University of Glasgow
USARC	University of Sydney Research Centre, adjunct of AFUS
USGPO	United States Government Printing Office

OUTLINE

000 Accounting in General

001 Pot Pourri

010 The Domain of Accounting – 011 Documents, records and like artifacts – 012 The financial domain of accounting – 013 The art of bookkeeping – 014 Accounting as monetary calculation – 015 Accounting as abstraction – 016 A suprafinancial domain postulated

020 Accounting as Art, Technology, Science – 021 Accounting as a practical art – 022 Accounting described as a science – 023 Accounting – science and art

030 Accounting as Representation – 031 Accounting as representation of wealth and changes in wealth – 032 – as representation of financial position and results – 033 – as representation of transactions and affairs – 034 – as representation of information on economic affairs, events and resources – 035 – as representation of performance – 036 Accounting as information processing – 037 Accounting as periodical allocation – 038 Accounting as communication

040 The Subject of an Accounting – 041 The subject of an accounting an identified entity – 042 The accounting entity regarded as distinct from proprietors, stockholders and other parties – 043 Corporations as entities – 044 Interests of corporation and stockholder – 045 Entities regarded as co-proprietorships – 046 Entity and proprietary foci, differential aspects – 047 Agglomerations of entities held to constitute other entities – 048 Agglomerations of entities held not to constitute other entities – 049 Subdivisions as entities

050 Functions of Accounting – 051 Accounting related to decision making – 052 Accounting and resource allocation – 053 Accounting as (aid to) memory – 054 Accounting as instrumentation – 055 Accounting as a tool – 056 Accounting information as feedback – 057 Accounting information and prediction; prediction not an accounting function – 058 Accounting information as aid in forming expectations – 059 Limited function of accounting information

060 Users and Uses of Accounting Information – 061 Parties having interests in financial information – 062 Common interests of diverse parties in financial information – 063 Accounting information as mediating conflicts of interest – 064 Accounting and the public interest – 065 Variety of uses of accounting information – 066

Monofunctional and multifunctional information – 067 Internal and external information to be based on the same principles – 068 Required financial information said to be unknown

070 Accounting and Accountability – 071 A custodial function of accounting – 072 Accounting and accountability (stewardship) – 073 Books of account required to be kept – 074 Accounts to be available for inspection – 075 Accounts expected to be truthful

080 Auditing – 081 Audit – 082 Audit as authentication or verification – 083 Audit as safeguard against error and fraud – 084 A conformity function – 085 A credibility endowment function – 086 Independent evidence, verification – 087 Statutory prescription of audit

090 Auditor and Audit Report – 091 The role of the auditor – 092 Qualifications of an auditor – 093 Independence – of mind; – of self-interest and other interests – 094 Internal control and internal check – 095 The audit report – 096 Audit reports – examples – 097 Qualified audit reports – 098 The audit gap – 099 Comment on auditing practice

100 The Economic Background of Accounting

101 Economics and Accounting

110 Money and the Money Unit – 111 Money and the money symbol – 112 Money as a medium of exchange – 113 Money as general purchasing power – 114 The money unit as the common denominator of prices – 115 The money unit as unit of account; as special accounting unit – 116 The dated general purchasing power of money – 117 The general purchasing power of nonmoney goods

120 The Variable Purchasing Power of Money – 121 A money unit of invariant purchasing power contemplated – 122 A money unit of invariant dimension not essential – 123 The variable purchasing power of the money unit – 124 The value of money and the general price level reciprocally related – 125 Inflation and deflation – 126 Money not neutral in economic calculation and action – 127 Differential impacts of changes in the purchasing power of money; personalization of purchasing power – 128 Stable value of the money unit assumed in certain accounting – 129 The assumption of monetary stability rejected

130 Exchanges and Prices – 131 Exchanges, transactions – 132 Exchange said to entail inequality of [subjective] valuations – 133 Exchange said to entail equality of valuations – 134 Cost taken, in accounting, as equal to value at purchase date – 135 Price and prices – 136 Prices as signals – 137 Price variations – 138 Significance of current values or prices of assets – 139 Markets; isolated exchanges

140 Value and Valuation – 141 Diverse meanings of value – 142 Dated value as value in exchange (in economics) – 143 Dated value as value in exchange (in accounting) – 144 Subjective (personal) value and valuation – 145 Valuation of a prospect – 146 Prospective (*ex ante*, capitalized) value of an asset – 147 Prospective value and dated wealth treated as cognate, or alternatives – 148 Value in use

150 Wealth and Capital – 151 Wealth as potentially exchangeable means – 152 Wealth as dated purchasing power – 153 Wealth held to exclude inherent or intrinsic properties – 154 Wealth said to subsist in expectations or to be subjective – 155 Capital as income- or product-yielding wealth – 156 Capital as purchasing power – 157 Capital as a financial concept – 158 Capital as capital goods – 159 Capital and income in social (aggregative) and individual settings

160 Income, Profit – 161 Nominal income – 162 Income as periodical increment in general purchasing power – 163 Periodical income (*ex post*) defined with reference to an opening capital – 164 Economic income said to be based on the present (discounted) value of expected net receipts – 165 Past (*ex post*) profit and expected (*ex ante*) profit necessarily different

170 Choice, Decision Making – 171 Decision – 172 Scarcity a precondition of choice – 173 Volatility of the context of choice – 174 Uncertainty as to the future – 175 Decision making said to be continuous – 176 Group decision

180 Premises of Choice – 181 Factual premises – knowledge of the past – 182 Factual premises – knowledge of present state – 183 Expectations – 184 Predictions – 185 Valuation as preference ordering – 186 Opportunity costs – 187 Probability and choice – 188 Multivaluational choice – 189 Decisions as syntheses from factual, expectational and valuational premises

190 Financial Desiderata of Choice – 191 Rate of return – on capital; – on assets; calculation of rate of return (or return on investment) – 192 Short run solvency or liquidity; current and quick ratios; working capital – 193 Cash flows – 194 The composition of assets and equities – 195 The debt to equity relationship – 196 Financial flexibility – 197 The financial feasibility of options – 198 Maintenance of capital as managerial policy

200 The Psychological and Social Background of Accounting

200 Belief and Action – 201 Actions and beliefs – 202 Knowledge – 203 Commonsense and science – 204 Grounds of belief – habit, inertia, tenacity – 205 Grounds of belief – tradition, authority – 206 Education and acculturation – 207 Truth and falsity

210 Observation and Inference – 211 Impressions and ideas – 212 Discrimination and assimilation – 213 Selective perception – 214 Memory – 215 Reasoning – 216 Logic – 217 Limited data processing capacity of the mind

220 Signs, Symbols, Language – 221 Signs; symbols – 222 Words as signs – 223 Dated terms – 224 Ambiguity, inexactitude and equivocation – 225 Reification – 226 Language; jargon; degeneration of language – 227 Accounting as language – 228 Vernacular and technical languages – 229 Use of abstractions

230 Information and Communication – 231 Information and information content – 232 Variety of communications – 233 Data processing – 234 The communication process – 235 Communication dependent on shared understandings – 236 Communication dependent on source of signals – 237 Impediments to communication at the source – 238 Communication dependent on recipient of signals – 239 Noise and other impediments to communication

240 Measurement and Measuring – 241 Objects of measurement – 242 The utility of measurements – 243 Measurement as quantification of properties – 244 Measurement as outcome of observation or experience; measurements and predictions distinguished – 245 Measurable properties – 246 Direct and indirect (fundamental and derived) measurement – 247 Additive or extensive properties – 248 Aggregative (additive) measurement – 249 Units and scales; ratio scales

250 Measurement in Accounting – 251 Accounting described as measurement – 252 Measurement used of past, present and future magnitudes; accounting measurement said to be future-dependent; measurement not descriptive of, nor dependent on, future magnitudes – 253 The money unit as common denominator in accounting – 254 The money unit as the unit of measurement; dated purchasing power as the unit of measurement – 255 An identified attribute (property) to be measured; the attribute said to be cost; – service potential; – money equivalent or value in exchange; –value; no singular attribute specified – 256 Aggregative measurement – 257 The fallacy of heterogeneous aggregation; of heteroscalar aggregation – 258 Accuracy and approximation – 259 Derived measurement; scalar adjustments; ratios

260 Law and Order – 261 Law and laws – 262 Functions of laws – 263 Custom and convention – 264 Property and property rights – 265 Law and accounting – 266 The interpretation of statutes – words of popular and technical meanings; – interpretation and intent – 267 Commercial morality – 268 Groups and group behavior; group morality – 269 Ethics

270 Firms and Organizations – 271 Organizations – 272 Organizational equilibrium and survival – 273 Firms as systems – 274 The firm as an adaptive concern – 275 The conventional accounting view of the firm as a going concern – 276 Communication essential to organizations; organizational memory – 277 Feedback; responses to feedback – 278 Company directors and managers as agents; as fiduciaries – 279 The subordinate position of shareholders

280 Financial Publicity – 281 Secrecy – 282 Privacy or secrecy in financial matters; private or secret accounts – 283 Financial publicity by companies as *quid pro quo* – 284 Financial disclosure, in principle – 285 Disclosure held not to be inimical

400 Financial Position and its Elements

reference to spending or debt-paying power – 434 Assets as unamortized outlays – 435 Assets as service potentials – 436 Treatment of assets as costs or service potentials challenged

440 Asset Classes – 441 Current, circulating or floating assets – 442 Liquid (quick) assets – 443 Fixed or noncurrent assets – 444 Fixed assets indeterminate – 445 Intangible and fictitious assets – 446 Goodwill, as potential or expectation – 447 Goodwill – other aspects – 448 Dubious financial significance of intangibles; intangibles as offset to equity – 449 Monetary and nonmonetary items

450 Liabilities – 451 Liabilities described as dated debts – 452 Liabilities described with reference to future settlement; liability provisions – 453 Liabilities described otherwise – 454 Liabilities described as capital – 455 Current liabilities – 456 Fixed, long term or deferred liabilities – 457 Contingent liabilities – 458 Executory contracts – 459 Accounting for long term leases

460 Equity, Ownership, Proprietorship, Capital – 461 Equities generally as rights or claims – 462 Equities (or proprietorship) as interests or rights in or claims against the assets of firms – 463 Owners' equity as paid in or legal capital; –as capital and surplus – 464 Capital as equity of owners or stockholders in business assets – 465 Capital as a liability – 466 The amount of capital as the amount of net assets – 467 Capital as aggregate assets – 468 Retained earnings, undivided profits, surplus

470 Reserves – 471 Reserves generally – 472 Reserve accounts or funds – 473 Variety of "reserves" – 474 Secret, hidden or undisclosed reserves – 475 Posited objects of secret reserves – 476 Objections to secret reserves – 477 Ambivalent attitudes towards secret reserves

480 Group Accounts – 481 Legal entities and groups – 482 Combinations as purchases and poolings of interests – 483 Accounting for combinations as purchases; purchased goodwill; negative goodwill – 484 Accounting for combinations as poolings of interests; fair value pooling – 485 Group accounting alternatives – 486 Objects of consolidated financial statements; criteria for inclusion in a group – 487 Eliminations on consolidation; minority interests; goodwill on consolidation – 488 Comment on consolidated statements – 489 Equity accounting

490 Funds Statements – 491 Funds statements described – 492 The rationale of funds statements – 493 Variants of the funds statement – 494 General publication of funds statements endorsed – 495 Comment on funds statements – 496 Cash flow – interpretation – 497 Posited utility of cash flow information – 498 Cash flow statements – 499 Cautions on use of cash flow information

580 Annual and Occasional Valuation – 581 Periodical valuation – 582 Accounting for asset appreciation – 583 Asset revaluation – 584 Upward revaluation rejected – 585 Quasi-reorganization

590 Heterogeneous Valuations – 591 Grounds for a single (uniform) valuation rule – 592 The utility of a single valuation rule rejected – 593 Heterogeneous valuations and their aggregation tolerated – 594 Heterogeneous and heterotemporal aggregation illustrated

600 Income and Income Calculation

600 Income Concepts – 601 Vagueness of the notion of income – 602 Income said to be a subjective or conventional notion – 603 A single concept of income contemplated – 604 Enterprise net income and income to financial supporters – 605 A single concept of income not desirable or not possible

610 Income or Profit – 611 Income as gain – 612 Income or profit as increment in wealth; – as increment in net assets; – as increment in owners' equity – 613 Income calculation from periodical asset valuations – 614 Capital maintenance a condition of the emergence of income – 615 Varied interpretations of capital maintenance – 616 Capital erosion – 617 Whole life income alone considered determinate – 618 Conjecture in periodical income determination – 619 Identification of income components said to be desirable

620 Receipts and Revenues – 621 Revenue – 622 Capital receipts – 623 Revenue recognition – 624 Realization as event or process – 625 Point of revenue realization – 626 Comment on the realization test

630 Expenditures and Expenses – 631 Revenue expenditures – 632 Capital expenditures – 633 Expenditure on durables considered as prepaid expenses – 634 Revenue and capital expenditures indistinguishable – 635 Capitalization of expenditures – 636 Deferred revenue expenditure – 637 Expenses – 638 Expenses as expired costs

640 Matching, Allocation and Amortization in Income Calculation – 641 Income as resultant of effort and accomplishment – 642 Periodical income calculation; – as matching costs with revenues; – as matching costs with realized revenues – 643 Matching costs with revenues challenged – 644 Allocation – 645 Temporal allocation – 646 Product and process allocation – 647 Allocation defended – 648 Allocation said to be unnecessary or misleading – 649 Amortization

650 Inventory Charges – 651 Cost flow assumptions – 652 Identified (actual) cost – 653 Average cost – 654 First in first out (fifo) – 655 Base stock – 656 Last in first out (lifo); lifo and the cost rule; posited merits of lifo; critical comment on lifo – 657 Other methods

660 Depreciation and Appreciation – 661 Causes of depreciation – 662 Depreciation as decline in market price or value in exchange; – as decline in value or wealth; depreciation not used, in accounting, of decline in value; depreciation accounting as cost amortization – 663 Depreciation charges related to nominal capital maintenance – related to maintenance of "real capital" – 664 Depreciation charges said to be related to replacement; depreciation and replacement as distinct phenomena – 665 Depreciation distinguished from price fluctuation; price fluctuations to be disregarded – 666 Formal methods of charging or providing for depreciation – 667 Conventional depreciation methods conjectural and arbitrary – 668 Appreciation – 669 Appreciation regarded as gain or profit; objection to treatment of appreciation as gain or profit

670 Losses and Gains from Inflation and Deflation – 671 Accounting for inflation and deflation necessary – 672 Inflation accounting said to be related to tangible assets only – 673 Purchasing power gains and losses associated with monetary items only – 674 Purchasing power gain or loss on long term debt – 675 Purchasing power gains and losses said to be associated with all items – 676 Realized and unrealized gains and losses of purchasing power

680 Transfer Payments and Quasi-expenses – 681 Transfer payments (in economics) – 682 Grants received – 683 Income taxes held not to be in the nature of expenses – 684 Income taxes held to be in the nature of expenses; timing differences – 685 Tax allocation endorsed – 686 Tax allocation rejected – 687 Tax allocation "assets" and "liabilities" – 688 Amortization of intangibles including goodwill; –systematic; - *ad hoc*

690 Classification of Gains and Losses – 691 Operating gains and losses; – distinction between operating and nonoperating items questioned – 692 Capital gains and losses – 693 Holding gains and losses; operating and holding gains said to be undistinguishable – 694 Realized and unrealized income or profits; unrealized increments not to be counted as income or profit; critical comment on realization as income desideratum – 695 Extraordinary items – 696 Prior period adjustments – 697 Comprehensive or all-inclusive income – 698 Divisible income or profit – 699 The income (profit and loss) statement

700 Accounting Systems

710 Cost based Systems Generally – 711 Origin and persistence of cost based accounting – 712 Justifications of cost based accounting – 713 The alleged objectivity of conventional accounting; the subjectivity of conventional accounting; the role of estimate, judgment and opinion – 714 Capital maintenance as maintenance of nominal capital – 715 The irrelevance of cost based accounting – 716 Other comment on cost based accounting – 717 Posited effects of cost based accounting on the trade cycle

720 Practice under Generally Accepted Accounting Principles (conventional, initial cost based accounting) – 721 Practices having substantial support – 722 Generally accepted accounting principles described – 723 Generally accepted accounting principles said to be unspecified – 724 Interpretation of acceptable, accepted, and generally accepted – 725 General acceptance an inadequate criterion for principles

730 Features of Practice under Generally Accepted Principles – 731 Inconsistency in principle and practice – 732 Diversity, ambiguity and variability of conventional accounting – 733 Manipulation and smoothing of reported income – 734 Comment on conventional income calculation – 735 Creative or cosmetic accounting – 736 Uniformity of accounting said to be undesirable or impossible; potential variation in accounting outputs illustrated; diversity of practices criticized – 737 Posited functional unfitness of products of conventional accounting; irrelevance to decision; lack of correspondence with reality – 738 Audit of conventional accounts – 739 Accounting and corporate misdemeanors

740 Index adjusted Historical Cost (CPP) Accounting – 741 CPP accounting described – 742 General object of CPP accounting – 743 Posited merits of CPP accounting – 744 Capital maintenance under CPP accounting – 745 Index adjusted historical cost (CPP) income – 746 CPP income calculation components – depreciation – 747 CPP income components – purchasing power gains and losses – 748 Adjustment information sources – 749 Critical comment on CPP accounting

750 Replacement Price (Cost) Accounting – 751 Replacement price accounting (RPA) described – 752 Posited functions or objects of RPA – 753 Capital maintenance as maintenance of substantive property; – as maintenance of productive capacity or operating capability – 754 Critical comment on physical capital maintenance – 755 Replacement cost income – 756 Replacement cost income components –depreciation; – backlog depreciation – 757 Posited objections to replacement cost income – 758 Sources of replacement cost information – 759 Critical comment on replacement cost valuation; appraisal of replacement price accounting

760 Current Cost Accounting (CCA) – 761 Current cost accounting described – 762 Objects of current cost accounting – 763 Posited merits of CCA – 764 Asset valuation under CCA – 765 Current cost income – 766 CCA income calculation components – 767 Valuation adjustments and their disposition under CCA – 768 Adjustment information sources – 769 Appraisal of current cost accounting

770 Current Money Equivalent Accounting – 771 Current money equivalent accounting (CoCoA) described – 772 Object – a purchasing power accounting – 773 Posited merits of current money equivalent accounting – 774 Capital maintenance as maintenance of general purchasing power – 775 Real (current purchasing power) income – 776 Real income calculation components – 777 Treatment of the effects of inflation and deflation – 778 Accessibility of market selling prices –

800 Systematic Inquiry and Knowledge

860 Testability and Testing – 861 The testability of hypotheses, laws and theories – 862 Verification, confirmation – 863 Testing of hypotheses and theories – 864 Experiment – 865 Mathematics and mathematical reasoning; mathematics as abstraction; mathematics and statistics in economic and scientific inquiry – 866 Convergence – 867 The explanatory power of theories – 868 The predictive power of theories; prediction and retrodiction – 869 Abandonment of theories

870 Description and Prescription – 871 Theory and practice – 872 Positive and imperative (normative) propositions – 873 The positive, the normative, and action – 874 Skill

880 Advancement of Knowledge – 881 The growth of knowledge – 882 Rate of change of knowledge and art – 883 Impediments to the endorsement of new knowledge – 884 Conditioned thinking and fixation – 885 Vested interests and conservatism – 886 Fear of novelty – 887 Disputation – 888 Obscurantism – 889 Diversions and distractions

890 Science, Art, Technology and Philosophy – 891 Science as art – 892 Science and technology – 893 Science and philosophy – 894 Inquiry and practice

900 Accounting Beliefs and Knowledge

910 Accounting Practices, Procedures and Rules – 911 Accounting procedures said to be based on practical considerations or opinions – 912 Accounting principles said to be derived from experience – 913 Rules and ritual – 914 Accounting principles as rules – 915 Practices described as accounting policies – 916 Diverse influences on accounting rules and procedures – 917 Accounting development said to be evolutionary – 918 Tradition

920 Guiding Dicta – 921 An accounting viewpoint posited – 922 Principles and accounting principles; dicta or ideas described as principles – 923 Accounting doctrines; dicta or ideas described as doctrines – 924 Accounting said to be conventional; – conventions and accounting conventions; dicta or ideas described as conventions – 925 Accounting postulates, assumptions, axioms; dicta or ideas described as assumptions or postulates – 926 Dicta or ideas described as basic concepts or features – 927 Diversity of descriptions of dominant ideas

930 Variance, Flexibility and Conflict of Principles – 931 The mutability and flexibility of principles – 932 Rules said to be subject to exceptions and variations in application – 933 Conflicts of principle, doctrine and convention – 934 Terminological propriety; inexactitude in discourse; obscurity in financial communications – 935 Recourse to fictions – 936 Education of investors advanced as antidote to accounting limitations – 937 Accounting theory as rationalization – 938 Accounting thought said to lack systematic development – 939 A unified theory said to be unattainable

000 ACCOUNTING IN GENERAL

001 Pot Pourri

The first appearance of the double entry system of accounting in Europe coincided with the introduction of algebra during the early 13th century . . . mathematicians . . . may well have developed the concept of double entry accounting which, after all, is based on an equation.

Hain, 1970, 240

It is, I think, quite clear from [evidence cited] . . . that collections of little tracts on letter writing, conveyancing, accounting and elementary legal procedure circulated in England, at least from the earlier part of Henry III's reign [1216–1272], and that they had their origin in Oxford . . . . From early in the reign of Edward I [1272–1307] there comes . . . a treatise on accounting with the date 1274 . . . . With the reign of Edward III [1327–1377] we come to Thomas Sampson . . . . Sampson's main profession was to train young men in business methods – to write letters, to keep accounts and to do miscellaneous legal work for landowners of substance . . . . He did not take part in any of the teaching of the university which led to a degree; but he was one of the class known as grammar masters . . . . who undertook instruction in practical business methods, as applied, of course, to the great business of medieval England – agriculture.

Richardson, 1939, 451ff

Up to the beginning of the fourteenth century merchants had mostly kept rough and ready accounts, which were often little more than memorandums of entries of credit, without any record of cash transactions . . . .

Origo, 1963, 115

The most ancient double entry books known to exist are those of the Massari of the Commune of Genoa, dating from the year 1340.

Peragallo, 1938, 3

On the first page of Datini's [14 century] great ledgers stood the words, "In the name of God and of profit", and these were the only goals to which these merchants aspired: profit in this world or in the next, as if the whole of life were one vast counting-house – and at its end, the final Day of Accounting.

Origo, 1963, 9

The pen is an instrument so noble and excellent that it is absolutely necessary not only to merchants but also in any art, whether liberal, mercantile or mechanical. And when you see a merchant to whom the pen is a burden or who is inept with the pen, you may say that he is not a merchant. And [a good merchant] not only must be skilled in writing but also must keep his accounts methodically.

Cotrugli, 1458/1955, 375

By summing the debit and credit entries to this account, the profit or loss will be known .... From the capital account ... you may learn the entire value of your property.

Pacioli, 1494/1963, 96

At the end of each annual account [of the Sidney Ironworks] the "clear gain" was reckoned by totalling the market value of the increases in stocks of raw and semi-finished materials over the previous year, and the market value of the iron produced .... in 1548 the cost of producing a ton of bar iron appears to have been £4 4s 5d, compared with the valuation of £7 in the stock accounts. The stock valuation can be taken as approximately the price the market would bear .... The stock valuations can be used at each stage of the process to test whether any operations were endangering profitability and should have been replaced by buying in.

Crossley (ed), 1975, 27–29

Polonius:
Neither a borrower nor a lender be;
For loan oft loses both itself and friend,
And borrowing dulls the edge of husbandry.
This above all, to thine own self be true,
And it must follow, as the night the day,
Thou canst not then be false to any man.

Shakespeare, *Hamlet*, I:iii

Iago: "Certes", says he [Othello],
"I have already chose my officer."
And what was he?
Forsooth, a great arithmetician,
One Michael Cassio, a Florentine, ...
That never set a squadron in the field,
Nor the division of a battle knows
More than a spinster; ...
... mere prattle, without practice,
Is all his soldiership. But he, sir, had the election:
And I, of whom his eyes had seen the proof
At Rhodes, at Cyprus and on other grounds
Christian and heathen, must be be-lee'd and calm'd
By debitor and creditor: this counter-caster
He, in good time, must his lieutenant be.

Shakespeare, *Othello*, I:i

Iago:
Who steals my purse steal trash; 'tis something, nothing;
'Twas mine, 'tis his, and has been slave to thousands;
Shakespeare, Othello, III:iii

Flavius:
If you suspect my husbandry or falsehood
Call me before the exactest auditors
And set me on the proof.
Shakespeare, Timon of Athens, II:ii

[A perfect merchant] ought to be a good penman, a good arithmetician, and a good accountant, by that noble order of debtor and creditor, which is used only amongst merchants ...
Mun, 1664/1949, 1

I and my wife up to her closet ... to examine her kitchen accounts, and there I took occasion to fall out with her for her buying a laced handkercher and pinner without my leave. Though the thing is not much, yet I would not permit her begin to do so, lest worse should follow. From this we began both to be angry, and so continued till bed, and did not sleep friends.
Pepys, 1666/1930, Aug 12

. . . .
For here as in a mirror they may view
What's due to them, and what themselves are due.
This was the famed and quick invention which
Made Venice, Genoa and Florence rich:
. . . .
Which noble art (when it augments our store)
This shall admire, and the next age adore.
[Encomium on Colinson's *Idea rationaria*]
Patterson, 1683

. . .
Euclid, Archimedes, had they surviv'd
To view this method which thou hast contriv'd
Would into such encomiums break forth
As would extend over this ball of Earth ...
["In commendation ..." of John Hawkins' *Clavis commercii*]
Hatton, 1689

Merchants' accounts, tho' a science not likely to help a gentleman to get an estate, yet possibly there is not any thing of more use and efficacy to make him preserve the estate he has .... I would therefore advise all gentlemen to learn perfectly merchants' accounts, and not to think it is a skill that belongs not to them, because it has received its name from, and has been chiefly practised by, men of traffic.
Locke, 1693/1970, 250

I do not know that any art practised among men is come up to a positive *ne plus ultra*, but that of accounting.

North, 1714/1986, 2

Stocks and stock-jobbing, a mystery born in this age. That which is in law called a corporation, to take and to grant, is a political essence, distinct from human nature, and contrived . . . for no purpose but cheating. For corporate acts however knavish, charge no literal knave to make amends in his private capacity, tho' his head and hands contrived, and acted the cheat. For this reason fraud hath ever been zealously in love with a corporate capacity . . . . the way [of corporations] is to cast the interest in the stock, and profit in proportion, into shares, which are called stocks, such as the Bank, Indian Company, Sword Blade Company, South Sea, &c. which shares in stocks are vendible, as in a market, and have a nation of brokers, that live upon them, who are to knaves, as pimps to whores. And the whole influence of this invisible traffic is secret confederacy, and no truth, or what they call intrinsic, governs anything.

North, 1714/1986, Vocabulary

A tradesman without his books, in case of a lawsuit for a debt, is like a married woman without her certificate . . . . Next to being prepared for death, with respect to heaven and his soul, a tradesman should be always in a state of preparation for death, with regard to his books.

Defoe, 1726, 345

Sir Isaac Newton, though so deep in algebra and fluxions, could not readily make up a common account: and, when he was Master of the Mint, used to get somebody to make up his accounts for him.

Spence, c1735/1964, 118

Every prudent person that has but the least regard to his own estate . . . must acknowledge it to be very convenient to keep some sort of books or other . . . and . . . to enter every article in so fair, plain and intelligible a manner, [and] . . . to make them up in so just and true a manner, as to show, at any time, whether the owner's circumstances are in an ebbing or flowing way, and how, and in what posture, at all times, his affairs do lie, in relation to his estate.

Hayes, 1741, 1

The counting house of an accomplished merchant is a school of method where the great science may be learned of ranging particulars under generals, of bringing the different parts of a transaction together and of showing at one view a long series of dealing and exchange. Let no man venture into large business while he is ignorant of the method of regulating books; never let him imagine that any degree of natural abilities will enable him to supply this deficiency, or preserve multiplicity of affairs from inextricable confusion.

Johnson, 1761, preface

Ladies in the general course of their education have been debarred by custom from a necessary knowledge of accounts; as if their sex prohibited them from being endowed with so reasonable an accomplishment, as to know the real state of their own affairs; notwithstanding the incontrovertible reasons why they should share in the great benefits accruing from it: . . . .

Quin, 1776, 68

Johnson: Keeping accounts, Sir, is of no use when a man is spending his own money, and has nobody to whom he is to account. You won't eat less beef today, because you have written down what it cost yesterday. . . . *Boswell*: I maintained that keeping an account has this advantage, that it satisfies a man that his money has not been lost or stolen, which he might sometimes be apt to imagine, were there no written state of his expense; and besides, a calculation of economy so as not to exceed one's income, cannot be made without a view of the different articles in figures, that one may see how to retrench in some particulars less necessary than others.

Boswell, 1783/1867, 436

Whoever considers the business of a merchant, with respect to its variety, extent, or importance, must see that a faithful register of all his transactions, disposed and arranged in that order . . . by which a real state of the whole, or any particular branch, may be at once discovered and laid open . . . is absolutely necessary, not only to the welfare and prosperity, but to the very being of his trade.

Gordon, 1787/1986, 13

What a panorama is . . . provided for us by the orderliness in which we pursue our business! It lets us have a conspectus of the whole at any time without our needing to be confused by detail. What advantages are conferred on the trader by double-entry bookkeeping! It is one of the finest inventions of the human spirit, and every good manager should introduce it in his administration.

von Goethe, 1795/1977, 40

double entry, being more complex and obscure [than the method by single entry], admits of greater secrecy in case of fraud, and is more capable of being converted into a cloak for the vilest statements that designing ingenuity can fabricate. A man may defraud his partner, or a bookkeeper his employer, if they be so disposed, without ever being detected; or else, how comes it that we often see such opposite changes in the circumstances of men belonging to the same concern? The rich man becomes poor, and the poor man becomes rich! Co-partners in a concern become insolvent. The one, whose fortune had originally supported the trade, is reduced almost to want; while the other, who was originally poor, and, being insolvent, ought still to be so, makes a pompous appearance in the world, immediately enters into trade again, and finds a capital sufficient to answer every new demand. It is possible to account for this in a favorable way; but a change so extraordinary wears a very suspicious appearance.

Jones, 1796/1978, 12

what is poetry to one, may be bookkeeping to another.

Scott, 1816, 32

[The South Sea House] With what reverence have I paced thy great bare rooms and courts at eventide! They spoke of the past: the shade of some dead accountant, with visionary pen in ear, would flit by me, stiff as in life. Living accounts and accountants puzzle me. I have no skill in figuring. But thy great dead tomes . . . with their old fantastic flourishes, and decorative rubric interlacings – their sums in triple columniations, set down with formal superfluity of cyphers – with pious sentences at the beginning, without which our religious ancestors never ventured to open a book of business, or bill of lading – the costly vellum covers of some of them almost persuading us that we are got into some better library, are very agreeable and edifying spectacles.

Lamb, 1820/1963, 52

Of quite another stamp was the then accountant, John Tipp. He neither pretended to high blood, nor in good truth cared one fig about the matter. He "thought an accountant the greatest character in the world, and himself the greatest accountant in it" . . . . The striking of the annual balance in the company's books (which perhaps differed from the balance of last year in the sum of £25 1s 6d) occupied his days and nights for a month previous . . . . but to a genuine accountant the difference in proceeds is as nothing. The fractional farthing is as dear to his heart as the thousands which stand before it . . . . With Tipp form was everything. His life was formal. His actions seemed ruled with a ruler . . . . Tipp never mounted the box of a stage coach in his life, or leaned against the rails of a balcony; . . . or looked down a precipice; or let off a gun; or went upon a water party; . . . neither was it recorded of him. that for lucre, or for intimidation, he ever forsook friend or principle.

Lamb, 1820/1963, 54–56

If my nephew is steady, cautious, fond of sedentary life and quiet pursuits, and at the same time proficient at arithmetic and with a disposition towards the prosecution of its higher branches, he cannot follow a better line than that of an accountant. [Letter of July 23, 1820]

Scott, 1820/1934

The system of bookkeeping by double entry is one of consummate beauty . . .

Jackson, 1827/1896, 29

When the numerous and irrational rules shall cease to be resorted to by the ignorant, and discarded from the institutions of learning by the wise, then will bookkeeping advance to a station among the first branches of necessary knowledge, and be taught with the first.

Marsh, 1835/1988, 186

it astonishes us that anyone living in London and having any intercourse with practical men, should have been found to lay the least stress on the publication of balance sheets, or accounts of assets and obligations. They are worse than worthless, being eminently calculated to deceive and mislead .... Even though the parties were perfectly honest, the publication of a balance sheet would be good for nothing.

McCulloch, 1836/1936, 433

[In the mid-1840s] railway shareholders were so bewildered and mystified by cooked accounts, manipulated figures, partial statements, and delusive representations of railway property, that they actually regarded the payment of dividends out of capital as a legitimate practice. [155–6]

Wang, 1918/1985, 26

Annual income twenty pounds, annual expenditure nineteen nineteen six, result happiness. Annual income twenty pounds, annual expenditure twenty pounds ought and six, result misery. [Micawber to Copperfield]

Dickens, *David Copperfield*, 1850,
ch XII

To the mercantile system of accounts we attach the highest value. As a science it comes to us with the powerful recommendation, not only of long experience, but of high authority, of those engaged in the active pursuits of life, and of those who have surveyed its concerns with the eye of philosophy. The Italian method of book-keeping (i.e. double entry) affords unquestionable valuable facilities for unravelling and elucidating intricate accounts; and we are satisfied that no person without a knowledge of it can be a good accountant.

UK Government *Report on Public
Accounts*, c1850/1862, vii

The system of bookkeeping by double entry is perhaps the most beautiful one in the wide domain of literature and science. Were it less common it would be the admiration of the learned world.

Freedley, 1852/1954, 12

Ages ago a savage method of keeping accounts on notched sticks was introduced into the Court of Exchequer, and the accounts were kept, much as Robinson Crusoe kept his calendar on the desert island .... a multitude of accountants, bookkeepers and actuaries were born, and died. Still official routine inclined to these notched sticks, as if they were pillars of the constitution, and still the Exchequer accounts continued to be kept on certain splints of elm wood called "tallies". In the reign of George III an inquiry was made by some revolutionary spirit, whether pens, ink and paper, slates and pencils, being in existence, this obstinate adherence to an obsolete custom ought to be continued, and whether a change ought not to be effected. All the red tape in the country grew redder at the bare mention of this bold and original conception, and it took till 1826 to get these stocks abolished.

Dickens, 1855, 463

Good accounts are troublesome things to keep, and occasionally cause trouble to the parties of whose affairs they are registers. The true chandler's shop system is to keep no books at all. A cross for a halfpenny, a down stroke for a penny, a little

O for sixpence, and a larger for a shilling, all in chalk, on a board or cupboard door, constitute the accounts of many a money-getting shopkeeper; and, we doubt not, would suit well the purposes of some of the railways. Chalk is easily rubbed out and put in again; ink is a permanent nuisance. One great company is reported, at one time, to have used pencils for their figures, in preference to ink, which, we presume, must have been for the sake of convenience. [Press comment on discovery of ways in which accounts of railway companies were cooked under the chairmanship of George Hudson, c.1840]

Evans, 1859/1968, 19

The science of bookkeeping, the theory of which is founded on simple mathematical truths and governed by clear and invariable rules, is esteemed, by those at least who understand it, as a complete and beautiful system for exhibiting the state or condition arising out of monetary affairs, or, of owning and being owed.

Marsh, 1864, 5

Once invested with full powers, Mr Holwell spared no labor in his task of cleansing this Augean stable of foul accountancy. [said, in fiction, of the successor of a deceptive agent of the East India Company].

Braddon, 1872, 124

There is perhaps scarcely anything more deceptive than a balance sheet, except to really practised eyes.

Accountant, editorial, 1875, 2

Before the science of accounts rose into a distinct profession, it was generally practised by solicitors, with the aid of more or less qualified clerks; and a pretty muddle they made of it between them.

Accountant, editorial, 1876, 4

the notion that any form of account will prevent fraud is quite delusive. Anybody who has had any experience of these things knows that a rogue will put false figures into an account, or cook it, as the phrase is, whatever form of account you prescribe .... I have an utter distrust of these pieces of paper called balance sheets. [before Select Committee on the Companies Acts, 1862 and 1867. #2192, 2253]

Jessel, 1877, *BPP, 1877*

Bookkeeping ... is purely a branch of mathematics, and as such entitled to the favor and consideration of scientific men, yet at no period of its history has it ranked in the estimation of scholars with the more complex and abstract sciences. It is lamentably true that men will grow enthusiastic over the solution of a problem in Euclid, or the effect of a combination of movements upon a chess board, who are ignorant of the first principles of this the most beautiful and practical of sciences ...

Packard & Bryant, 1878/1970, 56

for years the management of the [City of Glasgow] Bank had been issuing false balance sheets. Their falsification had begun not later than 1873 .... Without these false balance sheets the Bank would have failed in 1873, if not earlier, and, though a loss was inevitable, it would have been far less than the £6.2 million of October 1878.

Tyson, 1974, 130

The rapid growth of the railroad interest has developed everywhere embryo accountants in more or less profusion, whose greatest delight seems to have been to introduce in connection with the property with which they were identified all the new and strange forms and observances that occurred to them. In the progress of their work what was before luminous such men make wholly incomprehensible; with them the dawn is ever succeeded by eternal darkness .... disregarding that which is, they exercise their circumscribed minds in producing something that does not exist and that ought not to exist. This something that they create they claim as their own, and herein lies their pride; here rests their individuality. It does not matter that that which they have created is to all but them a monstrosity, a pulseless, inanimate and boneless thing, imperfectly conceived, unduly developed, projected into the world before its time. As the authors of this strange and nebulous substance and its *accoucheurs*, they discern in it something inexpressibly beautiful and attractive; their form trembles as they contemplate it .... To all but its victim, the shapeless mass that we have hinted at rather than described, that has neither color nor life, is repulsive and incomplete in the extreme. But to its author it is a thing of exceeding beauty, and in the depths of the sublime egotism that animates him he contemplates it without questioning its utility.

Kirkman, 1880, 2:32–33

Bookkeeping gives a mental discipline equal to that gained from the study of any other branch, and superior to that realized from the study of most branches. Double entry bookkeeping, while a science, deserves to rank among the fine arts. It challenges the admiration of lovers of the beautiful and the true. It cultivates the judicial powers of the mind. It quickens and strengthens the love of justice and equity. It promotes fair dealing among men. It contributes to private and public virtue. It leads to economy and thrift in private and public affairs. Its general study and practice will reduce pauperism and crime, and promote frugality and virtue.

Mayhew, 1884/1959, 63

The biggest swindles in the financial world have always produced balance sheets duly audited by well known firms of accountants.

Manchester City News, 1892/1972, 269

During the last year or so, the continent of Australasia has certainly enjoyed quite its fair share of disastrous failures and gigantic frauds; and accordingly, Australian accountants have had, of late, ample cause for reflection upon the duties of auditors generally, and the possibility of the performance of those duties tending to diminish future such disasters in particular.

Accountant, editorial, 1892, 486

Commerce is like war; its result is patent. Do you make money or do you not make it? There is as little appeal from figures as from battle.

Bagehot, 1894, 116

[One] of the two greatest and newest intellectual agencies of our time . . . . is business. We see so much of the material fruits of commerce, that we forget its mental fruits. It begets a mind desirous of things, careless of ideas, not acquainted with the niceties of words. In all labor there should be profit, is its motto. It is not only true that we have "left swords for ledgers", but war itself is made as much by the ledger as by the sword.

Bagehot, 1894, 248

The principles of bookkeeping by double entry constitute a theory which is mathematically by no means uninteresting; it is in fact like Euclid's theory of ratios an absolutely perfect one, and it is only its extreme simplicity which prevents it from being as interesting as it would otherwise be.

Cayley, 1894, Preface

The profession of accountancy is open to anyone who chooses to adopt it, and there is nothing to prevent any incompetent person from practising it.

Worthington, 1895, 1

Mr. Justice Quain . . . in 1875 . . . said from the bench: The whole affairs in bankruptcy have been handed over to an ignorant set of men called accountants, which was one of the greatest abuses ever introduced into law.

Worthington, 1895, 72

Scientific accountancy is the hub of the universe of commerce, trade and finance . . . .

Haskins, 1900, 1010

Double entry bookkeeping is born of the same spirit as the systems of Galileo and Newton, like the teachings of modern physics and chemistry . . . . Double entry bookkeeping is a simple way of representing the cosmos of economic, or more precisely capitalistic, affairs, in the same way as, later, the great naturalists mastered the cosmos of the heavens and the processes of physiological systems. Double entry bookkeeping is based on the principle of treating all phenomena simply as quantities, the principle of quantification which has brought to light all the wonders of scientific knowledge, and which, here, for the first time in human history, is made the underlying principle of a system. With little imagination one may detect in double entry bookkeeping the seminal form of the ideas of gravity, the circulation of the blood, the conservation of energy, and other notions which have so greatly advanced knowledge of the natural world.

Sombart, 1902/1917, II:119

A man who manages badly finds himself in a fog; he does not like to correlate the entries to see what he owes. On the other hand, nothing can be more acceptable to a good manager than to examine every day the amounts of his growing fortune. Even a loss, if it annoys him and surprises him, does not perturb him, for he knows at once what profits he has gained to set on the other side. [Robertson, 1933]

Sombart, 1902/1933, II, 118

The question of depreciation is one upon which so many articles have been written, and so many opinions expressed, that there would not appear to be much more which could profitably be said upon the subject.

Armstrong, 1903, 1014

Cost of production. A phrase much used in economics, to signify the sum total of all the services requisite to make an article and bring it to market or place it in the hands of the consumer. These services fall under three heads:– labor, endurance, and abstinence.

Bithell, 1903, 80

I wished him [Ernest Pontifex] to understand bookkeeping by double entry. I had myself, as a young man, been compelled to master this not very difficult art: having acquired it, I have become enamored of it, and consider it the most necessary branch of any young man's education after reading and writing.

Butler, *The way of all flesh*, 1903/1976, #84

Bookkeeping ... as a science is most beautiful and as a practice most valuable.

Soulé, 1903/1976, 19

in this march of progress, the system of account-keeping has progressed from knots in strings, notches in reeds, and pebbles in chests, to the perfect equilibrium system of double entry bookkeeping which, today, in its manifold forms, holds trade and commerce in their orbits, and maintains in harmonious revolution the financial values of the business world.

Soulé, 1903/1976, 201

Accounting is not a matter of arithmetic, or of mathematics of any kind.

Dicksee, 1905a, 147

Bookkeeping is the art of keeping a clear and correct account of one's pecuniary affairs. It enables a business man to ascertain, at any time, the true condition of his business; shows him the exact amount of his income; how much he has gained or lost, and how such gain or loss has arisen. It prevents him from inadvertently exceeding his means; it regulates the amount of his purchases and sales; and it enables him to calculate to a nicety whether his expenses are in proportion to his profits.

Anon, c1910, 1

Left alone, a business man seems to love to fool himself; so he goes along, year after year, overstating his assets, overlooking depreciation, and forgetting his liabilities. A correct balance sheet made up by a professional auditor brings him sharply to time.

Montgomery, 1912/1976, 18

Goethe calls this [the invention of double entry bookkeeping] in *Wilhelm Meister* "one of the finest discoveries of the human intellect", and indeed its author [said by Spengler to be Pacioli, 1494] may without hesitation be ranked with his contemporaries Columbus and Copernicus .... Double entry bookkeeping is a pure analysis of the space of values, referred to a coordinate system, of which the origin is "the firm".

Spengler, (1917)/1946, II:490

"To succeed," Kreuger went on ..., "one must understand our times and the people populating them. This is the key. In the end, you depend on little men, your accountants .... Every period in history has its own gods, its own high priests, its own holy days. It's been true of politics, religion and war. Now it's true of economics. We've created something new, Reis, men like you and I. Instead of being fighting men, as in days of old, we're all in business; our high priests are called accountants. They too have a holy day – the thirty-first of December – on which we're supposed to confess. In olden times, the princes would go to confession because it was the thing to do, whether they believed or not. Today the world demands balance sheets, profit and loss statements once a year. But if you're working on great ideas ...." [attr to Ivar Kreuger, c1920, in an historical novel]

Gifford, 1978, 286

The contempt for accounting is not limited to university circles, but is well-nigh universal. It is evidenced by ignorance of the subject, by condescension towards its devotees, by their exclusion from polite literature .... Let us boldly raise the question whether accounting, the late claimant for recognition as a profession, is not entitled to some respect, or must it consort with crystal-gazing, sociology, chiropractic, pedagogy and palm-reading.

Hatfield, 1924, 241, 243

More men have led themselves blindly into the bankruptcy court by their system of bookkeeping than any one other thing. [per District Judge Dickinson]

Ellett v Klein, 1927

nowhere has the rational element entered more strongly into economic activity than through accountancy – it is a necessary condition of the separation of the firm from the individuals of which it consists and therefore of the growth of large joint stock businesses – and the slow spread of scientific bookkeeping was one of the chief causes of the persistence of traditional and unbusinesslike methods of ordering affairs throughout the Middle Ages.

Robertson, 1933, 55

When I say you are an economist I mean it in a special, private sense. Disguised as a professor of accounting, you go prying into people's secrets. You peep into their account books. You ferret out the kind of things men use for information in their affairs. You stare rudely at their less than algebraic reasoning about simultaneous impossibilities. It would be bad enough if you had kept all this to yourself. But you did not. Ten years ago you published 474 pages of shameless gossip about it. You even called attention to the innumerable contradictions in it. You excused this by saying "The student may thus get a broader view of the subject . . .". You held out the solemn nonsense of judicial opinions, commission rulings, and statutory provisions so that anyone could see the intellectual sores and scar tissue. You referred to them as "these somewhat carefully prepared statements". You called the book *Accounting: Its Principles and Problems* instead of *Follies in Economic Behavior*. Problems, yes: but principles, no. Could anything be more unprincipled? [letter of J B Canning to H R Hatfield on the latter's retirement from the University of California, 1937; in S A Zeff, Foreword to Scholars Book Co reprint (1971) of Hatfield's *Accounting: its principles and problems*]

Canning, 1937/1971

At its worst chartered accountancy will break the average university man's heart with its rigid monotony, its pettiness, . . . its concentration on the trees and ignorance of the wood as a whole, and by its parasitical derivation of life from other men's dishonesty and incompetence.

Accountant, Anon, 1938, 218

The accounting profession in the United States enjoys something less of assured recognition and authority than is the case in England. The idea that accounting is what accountants say it is is not a generally accepted tenet in America. On the contrary, all sorts of people, government officials, lawyers, economists, legislators, business men, emboldened perhaps by a course taken in elementary accounting in the schools have no hesitation in telling accountants what accounting ought to be.

Sanders, 1939a, 536

The extreme importance of the techniques of accountancy lies in the fact that it works in the most nearly universal medium available for the expression of facts, so that facts of great diversity can be represented in the same picture.

Renold, 1948, 434

In . . . periods of great inflation, every reckless fool can become a great financier.

Samuelson, 1948, 281

The notion of the firm came into general European practice in the sixteenth and early seventeenth centuries; its importance lay in its implication that the business enterprise conducted by partners was a legal entity apart from their persons . . . Legal separation was supported (or perhaps led) by the notion of the business as a separate accounting entity. The books of the firm are not the accounts of the partners as individuals. As the system of double entry spread in use it developed to include the notion of the firm's balance sheet (first introduced about 1608) – a recurring statement of the assets and liabilities of the group . . . . No longer is the merchant just a merchant pursuing a trade for his livelihood. He has become at once the owner and the servant of an abstract collection of expectancies reduced to an arithmetical form. His daily income comes from "drawings"; the increase in his wealth is ascertained arithmetically in the abstract at recurring intervals, and is reduced to an increase in capital values. The notion of profit is no longer only the profit on a single sale, but the increase, over a period, of the "capital stock" of the business.

> Cooke, 1950, 48

The hardship of accounting
> Never ask of money spent
> Where the spender thinks it went.
> Nobody was ever meant
> To remember or invent
> What he did with every cent.

> Frost, 1951/1967, 338

An asset is what a leading firm of chartered accountants will certify as an asset.
> Lyttleton, 1953, 603

Reader, if you ever have to start a computing laboratory, be warned by me and do not take as a computer an accountant, no matter how honest and efficient. Your computer must work to so and so many places of accuracy. This means so and so many significant figures, whether the significance of the digits begins six places before or six places after the decimal point. Your accountant works to cents, and he will work to cents till hell freezes over. Whatever numbers our accountant computed he kept at all stages to exactly two places after the decimal point, whether they were numbers in the millions, where even the first place to the left of the decimal point was of no possible significance, or numbers which begin only five places after the decimal point.

> Wiener, 1956, 248

It is an enormous advantage to be able to find your way about in a balance sheet and a profit and loss account. It must be most disconcerting never to know whether to look on the left or the right and to be continually surprised to find a trading loss included among the assets. [reported]

> Mr Justice Salmon, 1959, 429

According to [Sombart, 1902], it is double entry bookkeeping which endows the economic world with accuracy, knowledge and system. It provided the idea of quantification, of maximizing incomes instead of providing a living, of increasing the value of a capital sum, irrespective of its material composition, and of separating the entrepreneur from the capital, creating the enterprise as an independent concern.

> Pollard, 1963, 75

an accountant, trained in a narrow and often spurious exactitude, can easily fail to recognize the distinction between, first, a historical record of stewardship, and, second, a clear statement of the current standing of a company in wealth and profitability and in comparison with previous periods, and other companies.

Economist, 1964, 805

Both in time and in intellectual outlook, the progress of accounting is closely linked with ... scientific and technological progress. The essence of scientific method is accurate measurement, systematic classification, and logical deduction, and these are just the processes which accounting brings to bear on economic life .... the development of a money measure of costs and benefits has been among the most powerful forces transforming traditional craft societies into the modern industrial state.

Morgan, 1965, 55

Numbers imply precision, so it is a bit hard to get used to the idea that a company's net profit could vary by 100 per cent depending on which bunch of accountants you call in .... Some companies value their inventories last in first out. Some companies charge their research costs as they incur them, some amortize them over several years. Some companies amortize their unfunded pension costs; some do not amortize them at all. Some companies make provisions for the taxes on the profits of subsidiaries as these profits are earned; some make no provision until the subsidiary remits a dividend to the parent .... The accountants have my sympathy. But not much of it.

"Adam Smith", 1967/1969, 155, 157, 159

Recreations: reading who dunnits and balance sheets, light music.

Lord Thomson of Fleet, 1972

Accounting was born without notice and reared in neglect.

Sterling, 1979, ix

accounting performs the same function in a modern society which witchcraft performed in a more primitive one.

Gambling, 1987, 319

Increasingly, City institutions, staffed as they are by a considerable number of people who have had accounting training or who understand the flexibility that exists in the rules, are alert to the demand for creative accounting and are able to tailor transactions so that they will have the desired accounting effects. Deals can therefore be put together, not on the basis of the underlying business reality but according to how they will look in the accounts. Finance directors are also aware of the facilities that are available in the City whether the transactions proposed are really in the interests of their company.

Jameson, 1988, 79

010 The Domain of Accounting

011 Documents, records and like artifacts

counting was not, as formerly assumed, subservient to writing but, on the contrary, writing emerged from counting.
Schmandt-Besserat, 1992, 7

Writing began in Sumer as a symbolic accountancy, used to keep records of goods brought into or despatched from temple storehouses . . . . Writing was used primarily for temple accounts, secondarily to record economic contracts between individuals, and scarcely at all for other purposes.
McNeill, 1965, 69

The first design of those who invented hieroglyphics was to preserve the memory of events, and to record openly and plainly their laws, policies and whatever else relates to civil matters.
de Condillac, 1756, 275

The common mode of examining books, kept by this [double entry] system, is for one person to read over the transactions in the day book, while a second refers to the different accounts in the ledger, to see if each entry be correctly posted, at the same time giving his assent by saying "right" or some such word. But it is very common for the tongue to acquire, from frequent use, such an aptitude for this expression, that the reply "right" may be given, when no real examination has taken place – the mind being diverted from its proper object by fatigue, some trifling occurrence, or a natural aversion to such dry exercises.
Jones, 1796/1978, 12

The necessity of some record of property must have been felt in the earliest ages of society . . . . Long before the invention of figures, men began to designate their simple possessions by collections of pebbles and shells, in which size or color represents the kind of property, and number its extent . . . . Another contrivance for this purpose consisted of notches cut on rods or canes . . . . To the age of notches must obviously be referred the invention of tallies. It was truly an ingenious device to split the stick, so that, by uniting its halves to receive the common indenture, each party might possess a proof as well as a record of the transaction. Tallies were rude accounts current, the conformity of which was ascertained at every new transaction; and they exhibit the first conception of a check on numerical records. The practice of scoring presents us with a third class of expedients for registering accounts. Of these primitive modes of recording transactions we possess various testimonies, among which language is not the least observable. The word *calculate* is derived from *calculus*, the Latin term for pebble; when accounts disagree, we still say they do not *tally*; and when we have paid a debt, that we have rubbed out our *scores*.
Foster, 1852/1976, 5

Symbolization constitutes objects not constituted before, objects which would not exist except for the context of social relationships wherein symbolization occurs.
Mead, 1934/1962, 78

any source may be tainted: this writer prejudiced, that misinformed; this inscription misread by a bad epigraphist, that blundered by a careless stonemason; this potsherd placed out of its context by an incompetent excavator, that by a blameless rabbit. The critical historian has to discover and correct all these and many other kinds of falsification. He does it, and can only do it, by considering whether the picture of the past to which the evidence leads him is a coherent and continuous picture, one which makes sense.
Collingwood, 1946, 245

Information in the scientist's sense is always an instrumental record. This means that in order to understand the nature of information we must examine the nature of instruments and the nature of records.
Meredith, 1966, 114

012 The financial domain of accounting

Bookkeeping .... is a science absolutely necessary for all accountants, but especially for merchants, whether their trade be great or small .... a merchant of ordinary capacity ... in one instant can see (as doth his person in a mirror) his whole estate and in what posture it is at any time. If he be fortunate and acquire much, it directs him the way to employ it to the best advantage, if he be unfortunate it satisfies the world of his just dealing, and is the fairest and best apology of his innocence and honesty to the world ... and often proves the great cause to bring him to a most favorable composition with his creditors .... he who knows not true bookkeeping and the necessary arithmetic, let him not assume the name of a merchant.
Colinson, 1683, 1

it is indispensably required of every prudent man to know exactly the computed value and condition of his estate, in order to the well governing himself in the management of his worldly affairs: for without that knowledge, he cannot make any one step in them with certainty; but must grope blindly in the dark, and by chance sink or swim; which is a hazard no wise man would willingly trust his fortune to. But it is not sufficient at one time only to understand his circumstances; but he ought always and at all times to be acquainted completely through the many revolutions of them; he must be able to trace them from the first to the present period, in a chain of consequences, or he never can judge of the present circumstances exactly; whether he has not lost by oversight of his own, or imposition of his neighbors; he cannot make any judgment of the future from the past, or justly reflect upon his own former conduct, whether good or bad.
Stephens, 1735, 4

Bookkeeping by double entry . . . is the art of keeping our accounts in such a manner, as will not only exhibit to us our net gain or loss upon the whole, but our particular gain or loss upon each article we deal in, by which we are instructed what branches to pursue, and which to decline; a piece of knowledge so very essential to every man in business, that without it a person can only be said to deal at random, or at best can be called but guessed work.

Thompson, 1777, II:1

Bookkeeping . . . . As a method susceptible of harmony and system, it owes its origin to the invention of money. Without this universal symbol of property, book-keeping would be merely a series of memoranda, incapable of that beautiful harmony between the whole and the parts, which now entitles it to rank amongst the exact sciences. Without the relation of money, a man might keep accounts of various kinds of property and even of personal debts; but he could not collect the different parts into one whole, nor state his real wealth by any other method than an enumeration of all his possessions and debts. Neither could he accurately calculate his profit or loss from year to year . . . .

Cronhelm, 1818/1978, 1

To the affluent it [bookkeeping] yields a satisfaction that often amounts to protection. It presents to them a true picture of their pecuniary circumstances; it bestows the ability to substantiate their claims, to preserve their property, to shield their honor as merchants and gentlemen; and at dissolution, the consolation of rendering to their friends or relations testimony whereby their rights as heirs, debtors or creditors may not be obscurely seen through the windings of suspicion and fraud, and left to the avarice of humanity.

Marsh, 1835/1988, 186

Capital accounting is the valuation and verification of opportunities for profit and of the success of profit making activity. It involves the valuation of the total assets of the enterprise, whether these consist in goods in kind or in money, at the beginning of a period of activity; and the comparison of this with a similar valuation of the assets still present or newly acquired, at the end of the process. In the case of a profit making organization operating continuously, it is a matter of accounting periods.

Weber, c1920/1947, 176

The antecedents of double entry [are] the art of writing . . . . arithmetic . . . . private property . . . . money . . . . credit . . . . commerce . . . . capital . . . .

Littleton, 1927, 140

The significance of systematic bookkeeping for the development of capitalism, that is, for the rational pursuit of unlimited profits, can hardly be exaggerated . . . . It reduced the gain idea to an abstraction by putting the profit in a specific form, a definite sum of money in contrast to the natural aim of subsistence which was in the forefront of the medieval business man's mental attitude. It was this abstraction of profit that first made the concept possible . . . . Systematic accounting made it possible for the capitalistic entrepreneur to formulate his aim, to recognize the degree to which he was attaining it, to determine the plans for his future activity. Notions like fixed capital and cost of production were practically impossible without account-ing.

Nussbaum, 1937, 159

The importance of the double entry system of keeping books lies not in its arith-metic, but in its metaphysics. To create a capital fund which can be shown as in debit or in credit towards its owners was to do the same thing in terms of finance that the lawyers did in terms of law. The lawyers created, for essentially practical purposes, the legal entity of the corporation, a legal person separate and distinct from its members, linked with them by rights and duties. The business men created the financial entity of the business, a fund separate and distinct from its subscribers, linked with them by debits and credits. The most common corporate form of the twentieth century, the joint stock company, is descended from these two inventions.

Cooke, 1950, 185

Accounting is a discipline concerned with the quantitative description and projec-tion of the income circulation and of wealth aggregates by means of a method based on [18 assumptions, including the assumption of a set of additive values expressed in a monetary unit].

Mattessich, 1964, 19

Accounting is a systematic method of retrospective and contemporary monetary calculation the purpose of which is to provide a continuous source of financial information as a guide to future action in markets.

Chambers, 1966a, 102

See also 031, 032

013 The art of bookkeeping

The art of bookkeeping is a methodical way of recording the transactions of the man of business; enabling him, at any time, to ascertain not only the state of every person's account with whom he has any concern or connection in trade, but also the true situation of his own affairs.

Jones, 1796/1978, 21

Bookkeeping .... is an art that teaches to record the several transactions of our affairs, in so exact and regular a manner, that, at any time, we may know the true state of each particular branch of our dealings, or of the whole, with ease and dispatch.

Jackson, 1809, 1

Double entry bookkeeping is a systematic exhibition of the transactions of business, for the purpose of ascertaining all that we owe, and all that owes us.

Marsh, 1835/1988, 193

the aim of all bookkeeping should be:- ... To exhibit at a glance the state of every account ... To embrace such a plan as shall obviate the liability to error ... To show accurately, the profit and loss in trade ... To collate past results for future guidance in management.

Sawyer, 1862, ix

Bookkeeping .... is the science of accounts ....

Soulé, 1903/1976, 19

Bookkeeping may be defined as the art of recording business transactions and showing their effect upon wealth.

Lisle, 1903–04, I:408

Perhaps the easiest way of stating the difference between bookkeeping and accounting is to say that the purpose of bookkeeping is to show debts, both those due by the owner of the business and those due to him, and the purpose of accounting is to show profits, losses and valuations.

Cole, 1908, 69

Bookkeeping bears somewhat the same relation to accounting that the operation of a machine bears to the invention and design of the machine. The product of bookkeeping constitutes the raw data which the accountant must interpret and arrange for presentation.

Porter & Fiske, 1935, 8

Double entry bookkeeping is a skill based on a knowledge of how to record financial data. It does not presuppose a knowledge of the character, meaning, interpretability or functional fitness of those data.

Wolnizer, 1987, 165

014 Accounting as monetary calculation

accounting in modern times deals directly and primarily with the value representations of things; the use of physical facts in accounting statistics is entirely subordinate.

Paton & Stevenson, 1917, 3

The modern accountant is .... one who is competent to design and control the systems of accounts required to record the immense volume of transactions that take place every day in the world of industry, trade and finance, [and] to marshall such records, so as to convey, by means of figures, an intelligible expression of the experience, at all times and stages, of the business or industry, in terms of money and money's worth.

Lightband, 1920, 605

All of [the consequences of the widespread use of money] are dependent on . . . the most important fact of all, the possibility of money calculation; that is, the possibility of assigning money values to all goods and services which in any way might enter into transactions of purchase and sale . . . . money is the most efficient means of economic accounting. That is, it is formally the most rational means of orienting economic activity. Accounting in terms of money, and not its actual use, is thus the specific means of rational, economic provision.

Weber, c1920/1947, 165, 171

comparison is important in many ways; upon it . . . depends the estimation of profit and loss, which is the guiding principle of capitalist enterprise. The process of comparison is made possible by thinking in terms of value; it could not be effected extensively in any other way. For these considerations of value we depend upon the unit of account.

Coulborn, 1938, 19

Accounting is not at all, or only incidentally and in subsidiary records, concerned with weight or superficies or number, but only with values, i.e. the number of monetary units attributed to the item.

Hatfield, 1942/1947, 36

capitalist practice turns the unit of money into a tool of rational cost-profit calculations, of which the towering monument is double entry bookkeeping . . . . by crystallizing and defining numerically, it powerfully propels the logic of enterprise.

Schumpeter, 1947, 123

Monetary calculation reaches its full perfection in capital accounting. It establishes the money prices of the available means and confronts this total with the changes brought about by action and by the operation of other factors. This confrontation shows what changes occurred in the state of the acting man's affairs, and the magnitude of those changes; it makes success and failure, profit and loss ascertainable.

von Mises, 1949, 231

The trader's maximand is utility. The *raison d'être* of the enterprise is to maximize the trader's maximand. Utility varies in the same direction as the ability to command goods and services. Money is the appropriate expression of the ability to command goods. Therefore, the prime maximand of the enterprise is money (or ability to command money), and the correct valuing agent is money.

Sterling, 1970a, 34

015 Accounting as abstraction

Accountancy is, like all mathematical sciences which assume a correspondence between number and material things, essentially abstract. It chooses to neglect all aspects and qualities of the material things with which it deals, except the mere correspondence to money value. In the same way, the science of celestial mechanics neglects every quality of its objects except forces of attraction exerted at physical points.

Dewing, 1920, 453

Accounting is a method of description which chooses, as all methods of description must, a particular aspect of a complete and complicated phenomenon. The aspect chosen is the financial one . . . .

Peloubet, 1945, 393

Accounts have to be compiled in money and so can only deal with values that can be measured in money. There are many of the most important values in life which clearly cannot be measured in this way . . . . Where decisions involve both economic and noneconomic values, accounting cannot tell the full facts, but at least it can tell how much measurable gain or loss there is to set against changes in other values which cannot be measured.

Morgan, 1965, 52

accountancy is structured upon a process of abstracting numerical equivalents from real world qualities, many of which are nonquantifiable.

Fertakis, 1969, 688

Wealth, or net worth, refers to real things – land, machines, securities, cash, etc. Assignment of monetary values to these real things is an abstraction, and the summation of these values is a further abstraction from reality.

Anderson & others, 1974, 25

Accounting is an art and technique by which the real world of economic events is abstracted into numbers that can be grouped by periods through arithmetical addition and subtraction, and compared with the numbers of the same economic entity for different periods and with the numbers of other entities for the same and different periods.

Kripke, 1979, 143

See also 229, 843

016 A suprafinancial domain postulated

The whole process of measurement and communication constitutes the accounting function.

Bevis, 1962, 28

To tie accounting irrevocably to financial occurrences is too restrictive and not in accordance with the facts of accounting procedures as they are carried out at present.

Goldberg, 1965, 89

There is no *prima facie* reason why a narrow economic significance should be the only attribute measured by accounting, although it is no doubt the most important. There is also no reason why the only measure applied should be value in terms of dollars. It is entirely conceivable that accounting should deal with various measures .... Finally, there is no reason why a single number – a point value or deterministic measure – must always be used.

AAA, 1966, 12

Accounting is a discipline which provides financial and other information essential to the efficient conduct and evaluation of the activities of any organization .... The data may be expressed in monetary or other quantitative terms, or in symbolic or verbal forms.

AICPA, 1966b, 61

the province of accounting should embrace any type of information needed for decision making regarding entities, i.e. retrospective, contemporary and anticipatory; monetary and nonmonetary; economic and noneconomic; quantitative and nonquantitative; information should be provided depending on the needs of decision makers.

Iselin, 1972, 297

The time has come to move the accounting discipline beyond financial information generated by organization operations. Information useful in strategy formulation and implementation and in tactical planning and controls needs to be developed and distributed by accountants in addition to that derived by summarizing, disaggregating, and analyzing the day to day operating transactions of an organization. There are practical day to day issues that press for this expansion of the accounting discipline into a much more comprehensive information development and distribution function in society.

Bedford, 1988, 209

020 Accounting as Art, Technology, Science

021 Accounting as a practical art

[Accounting principles] ... are merely the classified results of the accumulated experiences of business men.

Couchman, 1924, 4

[Accountancy] can not attain any high degree of mystery, for its methods and principles must be practical and understandable and in step with the progress of industry and people.

Andersen, 1935, 332

The Committee on Accounting Procedure has emphasized the fact that accounting rules and principles are founded not on abstract theories or logic, but on utility . . . . There is a demand for the development of a harmonious body of accounting rules or principles.

May, 1942, 35

accounting (measuring and communicating as it does economic forces in financial terms) is an art and not a science . . . .

Yorston & others, 1947, 1

accounting is a highly complex technology . . . .

Littleton, 1953, 170

Accounting has been created and developed to accomplish various desired objectives and, therefore, it is not based on fundamental laws or absolute precepts . . . .

Catlett, 1960b, 44

The development of financial statements has essentially been by trial and error . . . . In the pursuit of consistency (early recognized as a vital factor) and to systematize its procedures, certain rules were evolved that might be dignified with the description accounting theory. But theoretical reasoning weighs lightly in accounting . . . .

Ross, 1966, 19

[The term technology meant the application of scientific principles to a particular case. A doctor was a technologist, so was a lawyer and even a priest.] So are you. [reported speech to accountants]

Wolfenden, 1969, 665

See also 911, 941

022 Accounting as a science

The books of merchants accounts are kept in a certain method that, from the style and form of the entries, is called Debtor and Creditor; which method is so comprehensive and perfect, as makes it worthy to be put among the sciences, and to be understood by all virtuosi, whether they ever intend to make use of it or no, but even for pure speculation, curiosity, or rather admiration . . . .

North, 1714/1986, 1

Bookkeeping . . . . is a science whose principles are so simple and solid; its conclusions so natural, certain and evident; and the symmetry of its several parts so complete and harmonious, that the very speculation is no less pleasing than the practice is profitable.

Jackson, 1809, 1

Accountancy ... is a science, an erudition; and not, as some have seemed to suppose, a mere collection of approximative and hardly certain rules indicated by observation and intuition, and to be applied with tact and wariness. It thinks out, and thus finds out, with logical and mathematical accuracy, the condition of affairs of any business enterprise; ....
Haskins, 1900, 1010

Accounting is that science which treats of the methods of recording transactions in business and interprets the statements recorded in books and documents so that the layman may have a clear conception of the exact financial and managerial standing of the firm or enterprise both in parts and as a whole.
Duncan, 1909, 281

In a broad sense, accounting is the science which attempts to present and classify the statistics of the property and property rights in the business enterprise.
Paton & Stevenson, 1917, 1

Statements having content, i.e. statements, as is usually said, expressing some state of affairs, belong to the field of empirical sciences.
Carnap, 1934, 34

accounting is a social science.
Mautz, 1963, 318

Accounting is not an exact science. It is predominantly a social science .... its concepts are, of necessity, rooted in the value system of the society in which it operates, and, moreover, these concepts are socially determined and socially expressed.
Bernstein, 1965, 34

See also 942

023 Accounting – science and art

No theory of accounting was devised from the time of Pacioli down to the opening of the nineteenth century .... Authors .... were chiefly engaged in the solution of practical problems and in getting examples to demonstrate how entries should be made in books. The result was that, instead of a gradual formation of a body of theory ... there grew up a great mass of rules applicable to particular cases.
Peragallo, 1938, 92

Bookkeeping is the science and art of correctly recording in books of account all those business transactions that result in the transfer of money and money's worth .... the art of keeping accounts in such a manner that a man may know the true state of his business and property by an inspection of his books.
Carter, 1923, 1

By calling accounting a science, attention is directed to the orderly classifications used as the accountant's framework, and to the known body of facts which in a given case are fitted into this framework. The committee would not ignore these aspects of accounting, but would emphasize rather the creative skill and ability which the accountant brings to the application of his knowledge to a given problem. Webster and the Standard [dictionaries] agree that in part art is science, and that art adds the skill and experience of the artist to science. In this sense the committee would call accounting an art . . . . Every art must work according to a body of applicable rules, but it also reserves the right to depart from the rules whenever it can thereby achieve a better result. It is desirable that the accountant conceive of his work as a complex problem to be solved, of his statements as creative works of art, and that he reserve to himself the freedom to do his work with the canons of the art constantly in mind, and as his skill, knowledge and experience best enable him.

AIA, 1940c, ARB7

[Accounting] is an art only in the same general sense that the practice of law or the practice of medicine is an art . . . . Accounting is also a science in the same sense that law, government and economics are sciences. It can achieve the objective validity which we so much wish for it only in the same way that they achieve objective validity.

Scott, 1941, 349

The theoretical aspect of accounting is that which views it as a science, albeit not an exact science (because of the human element), and the theories of accounting are nothing but principles expressing the result of the scientific analysis of the significance of the financial condition or the operating results of a business enterprise and of the methods needed in order that they may be properly expressed and interpreted. The practical aspect of accounting is that which views it as an art, viz. the practical application of the theories of accounting to the solution of the problems of business.

Oehler, 1942, 278

accounting is a technical art . . . accounting is also a science, not dissimilar in its elements to medicine, economics . . . .

Irish, 1950, 215

accounting is the science of which accountancy is the art.

Eaton, 1955, 46

Accounting is the science of describing and measuring in terms of money, and the art of interpreting, the exchange events to which a particular entity is a party.

Schrader & others, 1988, 11

See also 890, 942

030 Accounting as Representation

031 Accounting as representation of wealth and changes in wealth

The method of keeping books by way of debtor and creditor, or (as some call it) after the Italian manner, is so regular and precise that at any time the merchant can be resolved what he gaineth or loseth by every particular person he dealeth with, or merchandise he dealeth in, and consequently what he is worth to a farthing.

Hatton, 1695, 137

The system of bookkeeping enables a man at any time to know his exact worth, the nature of his assets and liabilities, the gains or losses in detail, and how they arise . . . ; he can compare his expenditures for similar objects during different periods, and he can analyse the results.

Battersby, 1878, 4

Accounting is the science which treats of the methods of recording transactions entered into in connection with the production and exchange of wealth, and which shows their effect upon its production, distribution and exchange.

Lisle, 1899, 1

Accounting . . . is essentially an attempt to present . . . . an exhibit . . . of the wealth owned and the debts for which the proprietor is liable . . . . and how his wealth increases or decreases from time to time.

Hatfield, 1927/1971, 1

Accumulated wealth used in the creation of new wealth is called capital. To report the wealth (capital) being used in this process, and the increase in that wealth (income) over time periods, is the function of accounting.

Marple, 1962, 58

The details of the change in wealth during each period are revealed in the income statement; the details of the composition of wealth appear in the balance sheet.

Corbin, 1964, 26

Financial statements are vehicles for conveying information concerning the wealth of a business entity.

Andersen & Co, 1972, 13

The job of accounting is to provide measures of wealth, show how it increases or decreases over an accounting period and report to interested parties.

Skinner, 1972b, 377

The balance sheet is traditionally thought of as a report of the wealth of the enterprise at a specific time. The income statement . . . is traditionally conceived of as a report of the change in wealth resulting from economic activities for a period of time.

Anderson & others, 1974, 21

One of the accountant's main tasks is to keep track of wealth; he has to measure both wealth at a given time (e.g. in the balance sheet), and changes in wealth between given times (e.g. in the income statement).

Baxter, 1975, 17

032 Accounting as representation of financial position and results

Merchants accounts is the art of bookkeeping, in such a methodical decorum of debtor and creditor . . . as that at any time or times, whensoever the accountant or owner pleaseth, he shall or may know how his estate standeth (in every respect) to a penny, and how the same increaseth or decreaseth; as likewise, how much he hath gained or lost, by any one particular commodity that he dealeth in, from the beginning of such his account, to the end of any term or time afterwards, through the whole course of his dealing.

Hawkins, 1689, 1

A tradesman's books are his repeating clock, which upon all occasions are to tell him how he goes on, and how things stand with him in the world; there he will know when 'tis time to give over; and upon his regular keeping, and fully acquainting himself with his books, depends at least the comport of his trade, if not the very trade itself.

Defoe, 1726, 18

One of the chief objects of keeping accounts at all is to be able to ascertain the financial position of affairs from time to time.

Dicksee, 1903b, 470

Bookkeeping is the science and art of recording in books pecuniary transactions, so unremittingly and so accurately, that you are able at any time to ascertain (1) the result during a given period, (2) the exact state of your financial affairs at the end of the period, or any portion of them, with clearness and expedition, and to prove their accuracy.

Fieldhouse & Fieldhouse, 1929, 11

the primary objects of bookkeeping and accounting [include] . . . to keep day by day and to preserve a permanent record of the transactions of a business . . . . to enable accounts to be prepared periodically, showing the results of trading and the liabilities and assets of the business . . . . to have reliable figures available, if occasion arises for the sale or amalgamation of the business or for the raising of bank loans, further capital, etc. . . .

Moore, 1937, 2

Accounting should make available all material information of a financial nature relating to (a) the financial condition or status of the business, (b) its progress in earning income.

Sanders & others, 1938, 113

The primary purpose . . . of modern accounting is to record the changes in financial position or economic status . . . in a manner that permits the determination, from the record, of the new financial position at some subsequent date and the results of operations during the period . . . ended on that date.

Moonitz & Jordan, 1963, I:16

Accounting in its broadest sense is concerned with the measurement of transactions (usually involving money as the medium of exchange, but occasionally resulting from barter), transformations (the conversion, usually through the process of production, of goods from one form to another) and events (all other economic occurrences, external and internal, that affect the position or performance of the entity).

CICA, 1980, 23

See also 423

033 Accounting as representation of transactions and affairs

accounts are nothing else than the expression in writing of the proper order of your affairs: you will know all about your business and whether or not it is going well.

Pacioli, 1494/1963, 75

The end aimed at in bookkeeping is to represent distinctly the true state of one's affairs; that is, to record a man's dealings and transactions; and withal, to range and dispose the accounts in such order, that the books may exhibit a plain, full, and exact account of the condition and circumstances of each part of his business; and to put the man in case at all times to satisfy both himself and others with respect to the state and posture of his affairs.

Mair, 1793, 1

Accounting . . . is scientific analysis and record of business transactions. It attempts to tell about every transaction everything that can be of service when known.

Cole, 1908, 4

The primary function of accounting is to accumulate and communicate information essential to an understanding of the activities of an enterprise, whether large or small, corporate or noncorporate, profit or nonprofit, public or private.

AAA, 1957a/1957b, 1

Accounting is a systematic method of measuring and reporting business transactions.

Vatter, 1971, 1

Financial reporting should provide information about how an enterprise obtains and spends cash, about its borrowing and repayment of borrowing, about its capital transactions, including cash dividends and other distributions of enterprise resources to owners, and about other factors that may affect an enterprise's liquidity or solvency.
                                                     FASB, 1978, SFAC1

034 Accounting as representation of information on economic affairs, events and resources

What is accounting, in the broadest sense of the term? . . . . a synthesis of concepts, rules and techniques designed to facilitate understanding and control of economic activity.
                                                     Paton, 1939/1943, 87

The accounting function deals with the measurement and communication of financial and other economic data . . . . to do with the whole or any part of any type of organization – profit, nonprofit, private, or governmental.
                                                     AICPA, 1959a, 71

The major purpose of accounting is to provide information to interested parties regarding the nature and significance of economic transactions.
                                                     Mathews, 1962, 4

Accounting is a system for communicating the economic events of an entity . . . . [including] not only internal events . . . but also external events that affect the economic activities of the entity . . . . we shall use the term economic events of an entity to mean the economic status of an entity as well as its changes.
                                                     Ijiri, 1967, 3

When . . . accounts are summarized in the form of financial statements, they compactly present figure-pictures of the economic results of transaction decisions affecting the enterprise concerned.
                                                     Littleton, 1970, 476

Accounting information is intended in a very broad sense as economic information.
                                                     AAA, 1972, 23

The overall purpose of financial statements is, in our opinion, to communicate information concerning the nature and value of the economic resources of a business enterprise, the interests of creditors and the equity of owners in the economic resources, and the changes in the nature and value of those resources from period to period.
                                                     Andersen & Co, 1972, 15

the fundamental objective of corporate reports is to communicate economic measurements of and information about the resources and performance of the reporting entity useful to those having reasonable rights to such information.

ASSC, 1975a, 31

The purpose of accounting is to provide information about the economic affairs of an organization. It is a means of recording facts or forecasts about the economic aspects of an organization's activities and translating them into a useful form for further action. [per G Sh]

Enc Britannica, 1981, I:36

035 Accounting as representation of performance

accounting reports are generally regarded as regular, written, financial summaries of economic performance.

Goldberg, 1947, 99

the major objectives to be achieved by accounting methodology are but two; namely (1) furnishing dependable and relevant financial information as an aid in the management of an enterprise's operations; and (2) determining the efficiency and accountability of such management.

Campfield, 1958, 115

Accounting measures and communicates data that is not only in terms of money symbols, but also in nonmonetary units, such as material, labor and time. Accounting, therefore, embraces that part of the control function of management which utilizes . . . data regarding acquisition, disposition, and exhaustion, of material and human resources, and the efficiency of their utilization.

AICPA, 1959a, 71

Implicit in the choice of [the income statement and the balance sheet] for financial reporting is the assumption that the efficiency of management's actions can be determined from a study of the economic data the statements reveal.

Birnberg & Dopuch, 1963, 57

the only income concept of importance to accountants would seem to be that concerned with measuring the efforts and accomplishments of a business enterprise.

DeMaris, 1963, 37

Accounting data and reports . . . . provide guidance respecting management effectiveness in directing the utilization of scarce resources.

Illinois, 1964, 3

in the economics game accountants . . . belong in the umpire-scorekeeper group . . . . [dedicated] to the financial facts as they are, not as the players wish them to be . . . . By far the core function of the independent umpire-scorekeeper is to ascertain the correct score for each ball game as it actually was played . . . . being an impartial historian.

> Fagerberg, 1971, 82

The primary focus of financial reporting is information about an enterprise's performance provided by measures of earnings and its components . . . . Financial reporting . . . usually cannot and does not separate management performance from enterprise performance.

> FASB, 1978, SFAC1

financial accounting is concerned with the ways in which organizations communicate information about their performance to the outside world.

> Arnold & others, 1985, 1

036 Accounting as information processing

Accounting is the art of recording, classifying and summarizing in a significant manner and in terms of money, transactions and events which are, in part at least, of a financial character, and the results thereof.

> AIA, 1940c, ARB7

Accounting is the science of recording and classifying business transactions and events, primarily of a financial character, and the art of making significant summaries, analyses and interpretations of those transactions and events and communicating the results to persons who must make decisions or form judgments.

> Smith & Ashburne, 1960, 2

The function of accounting is (1) to measure the resources held by specific entities; (2) to reflect the claims against and the interests in those entities; (3) to measure the changes in those resources, claims and interests; (4) to assign the changes to specifiable periods of time; and (5) to express the foregoing in terms of money as a common denominator.

> Moonitz, 1961, 23

The elements of the accounting function have to do with the observing, measuring, recording, classifying, summarizing, interpreting, reporting and inspecting (auditing) of economic data.

> Carey (ed), 1962, 16

Accounting involves the systematic recording, summarizing and interpreting of economic transactions and activities.

> Mathews, 1962, 3

Accounting is an information system .... The subfunctions of accounting include data collection, processing and control, summarization, distribution and interpretation.
Buckley & Lightner, 1973, 4

Accounting is an information system that measures, processes and communicates information, primarily financial in nature, about an identifiable economic entity for the purpose of making economic decisions.
Needles & others, 1984, 21

See also 350, 360, 370

037 Accounting as periodical allocation

the cost of the consumption of machinery and other erections must be attributed to the whole term ["life"] assumed.
Guthrie, 1883, 7

Accounting is ... not essentially a process of valuation, but the allocation of historical costs and revenues to the current and succeeding fiscal periods.
AAA, 1936/1957b, 61

Accounting is essentially the allocation of historical costs and revenues to the current and succeeding fiscal periods.
Byrne, 1937, 372

The third [balance sheet] convention ... is that the original basis of fixed asset values is cost. Subsequent valuation of them is a process of apportioning their original cost over their useful lives.
Sanders & others, 1938, 57

Financial statements are the result of allocations – of receipts, payments, accruals and various other financial events and transactions. Many of the allocations are necessarily based on assumptions, but no one suggests that allocations based on imperfect criteria should be abandoned ....
AIA, 1944, ARB23

The basis of the accounts of a business undertaking is the allocation of costs and revenues .... Whilst figures of assets are ascertained and put into the balance sheet each year, ... these figures are costs incurred, and not values.
Norris, 1945c, 127

firm rejection of accounting as a valuation process in favor of accounting as an allocation process was the fundamental axiom on which all [American Accounting]

Association statements, including the Paton and Littleton monograph, were specifically based [prior to 1957].

Storey, 1964, 44

See also 640

038 Accounting as communication

Accounting strives to measure economic forces in financial terms and to communicate the results of such measurement to interested parties.

Paton, 1939/1943, 87

Now accounting is an indispensable medium of communication between business enterprises and the many diverse interests concerned. In many ways the large American corporation is a huge venture in cooperation. The cooperation exists between workers receiving wages and salaries, investors receiving dividends and interest, government receiving tax revenues, consumers receiving goods and services. The more complex these interrelations become, the more need there is for dependable accounting information.

Littleton, 1953, 7

the degree of success with which the accounting process fulfills its purpose depends to a large extent on the effectivenesss of the financial statements in transmitting useful information . . . .

Owen, 1958, 66

accounting is a branch of statistics and statistics a branch of information. Our task is communication and our objective should be to make that communication as clear and as useful as possible.

Cannon, 1962, 44

Even if they are prepared simply and solely as an *aide memoire*, as the equivalent of a diary of events, and even if they are used only by the person who prepares them, they [accounting records] are just as much an example of communication as the most elaborate and widely disseminated report.

Goldberg, 1965, 348

The purpose of accounting is to communicate economic messages as the results of business decisions and events, in so far as they can be expressed in terms of quantifiable data, in such a way as to achieve maximum understanding and correspondence of the messages with economic reality.

Jordan, 1969/1970, 139

our whole object is to provide decision makers (who have no opportunity of contact with economic realities) with reports which give them as clear a picture as possible of what is going on.

Ross, 1969, 4

See also 060, 227, 280, 290

040 The Subject of an Accounting

041 The subject of an accounting an identified entity

It is as a rule the financial facts of the "business", not those pertaining to the individual as such, that the accountant must consider it his task to report.

Paton, 1924, 6

we cannot begin to shape accounts until we have conceived either the unit of organized activity, or the transactor whose history and condition we wish to measure and portray in financial terms .... it must have a real existence, and it must be significant for .... the measurement of periodic income and the measurement of wealth.

Bray, 1953, 4

A business entity is a formal or informal unit of enterprise .... The business entity concept provides a basis for identifying economic resources and activities with specific enterprises, and thus for defining the area of coverage appropriate to a given set of records and reports.

AAA, 1957a/1957b, 2

each accounting system is designed for a single business entity .... Every situation is considered from its point of view and all transactions are analyzed in terms of their effect upon it.

Mason & others, 1959, 19

An economic entity ... is an aggregate of assets, directed by human intelligence and effort, committed to and engaged in an economic undertaking.

Raby, 1959, 453

The accounting records kept and the reports rendered are those of a rather specifically circumscribed entity of experience .... Commonly, the experiences of a given business undertaking constitute the entity ....

Husband, 1960, 12

the accounting process is primarily concerned with the enterprise as a productive economic unit and is only secondarily concerned with the investor as a claimant of the assets . . . . revenues and expenses of any enterprise are viewed as affecting the business assets and liabilities, not the owners' assets and liabilities.

Noble & Niswonger, 1961, 328

An accounting entity is simply a bundle of wealth which is being accounted for . . . . A wide variety of accounting entities exist in practice: businesses, municipalities, estates, countries – in short, anything to which anyone wants to attribute and measure wealth and income.

Sands, 1963, 39

Economic activity is engaged in by identifiable enterprises, and these enterprises constitute units of accountability and centers of interest for accounting analysis and reports.

Illinois, 1964, 8

We create [an artificial] person every time we install a self-contained system of accounts. Even an individual who keeps a double entry record of his personal assets and expenses creates an artificial person by so doing.

Kohler, 1965a, 35

Accounting information pertains to entities, which are circumscribed areas of interest. In financial accounting the entity is the specific business enterprise.

AICPA, 1970c, APBS4

See also 270

042 The accounting entity *per se* regarded as distinct from proprietors, stockholders and other parties

In these general relations of debtors and creditors [debit amd credit balances] the estate or concern itself is abtracted from its proprietor, and becomes a whole, of which the stock or proprietor's account is now also one of the component parts . . . . when we thus abstract a concern from its proprietor . . . the concern itself is constantly neutral, consisting of a mass of relations between debtors and creditors in perpetual and necessary equilibrium. The concern thus abstracted is always a cypher . . . .

Cronhelm, 1818/1978, 7

The mercantile notion of a partnership is simply that it is a kind of corporation. The firm is always regarded as a kind of impersonification . . . . the accounts of the partnership are always the accounts of the firm itself, and never of the partners . . . . the accounts of the individual partners [would be dealt with] as if they were simply debtors or creditors of the firm.

Cory, 1839, 71

The accounting records of a business organization are operated from the viewpoint of the organization as an entity apart from the people who own it.
Couchman, 1924, 12

The business undertaking is generally conceived of as an entity or institution in its own right, separate and distinct from the parties who furnish the funds, and . . . the business accounts and statements are those of the entity rather than those of the proprietor, partners, investors, or other parties or groups concerned.
Paton & Littleton, 1940, 8

A business, as an accounting unit, is separate from its owners.
Blough, 1956, 13

the accounting process is deliberately designed to account for the affairs of a single entity [that is regarded as] distinct and separate from its owner or owners.
Owen, 1958, 68

the entity is not . . . merely an "agent" for the stockholders. From the transaction viewpoint . . . no one owns an economic entity. Instead of owners, there are various sources of entity assets, there are various persons who are party to different types of related transactions with the entity.
Raby, 1959, 454

According to the entity concept, the business or other unit being accounted for must be considered as entirely apart from the shareholders or other owners . . . . the entity is conceived of as having a separate existence – an arm's-length relationship with its owners.
Lorig, 1964, 566

Accounting treats the business as a complete unit, or entity, apart from its owners, creditors, employees, and other persons.
Black & others, 1967, 13

Under the entity theory, the firm and its owners are separate beings. The assets belong to the firm itself while both liability and equity holders are investors in those assets with different rights and claims against them.
Wolk & others, 1984, 127

043 Corporations as entities

[In England, by the seventeenth century] . . . the common law forms of corporation and partnership were solidly established. A business could not be separated from its owners in the Italian manner unless it had unequivocal corporate form. So for the unincorporated business, other devices had to be brought into play. One such device was the creation of an accounting officer, the purser of ships and cost book

companies . . . . [Another was] the device of the trust . . . . [which, unlike incorporation by charter,] was a private affair. [But whether a person was a member of a chartered corporation] or the shareholder of a trust operating a joint stock fund mattered little. In either instance he had a claim or an obligation . . . . And in either instance he had something which could be sold, whether it was the stock of an incorporated company or the share of and in a trust . . . . All through the eighteenth century the unincorporated joint stock company continued to flourish under the protection of Chancery, covered by the mantle of the trust . . . . by 1800 it is firmly established that the unincorporated company with a carefully drafted deed of association can conduct its affairs with all the advantages of incorporation.
Cooke, 1950, 185–7

If any general rule can be laid down in the present state of authority, it is that a corporation will be looked upon as a legal entity as a general rule and until sufficient reason to the contrary appears; but when the notion of legal entity is used to defeat public convenience, justify wrong, protect frauds or defend crime, the law will regard the corporation as an association of persons. [per Judge Sanborn]
U S v Milwaukee Refrigerator
Corporation, 1905

Technically the stockholders are not the owners of the corporate business, since the corporation is itself a legal entity, and the ownership of the business vests in it. The corporation is, however, owned by the stockholders, the ownership of each being fixed by the ratio of his shares to the total number of shares outstanding . . . .
Bentley, 1911, 43

in the case of the corporation . . . . there is no element corresponding closely to the sole proprietor or partner. The stockholder is not the owner; he has merely an equity. The same can be said of the other investors. The managerial view, a conception of the corporation as a legal and economic entity operating a mass of properties in the interest of a whole body of investors of various classes, is the proper starting point.
Paton, 1922/1962, 84

The shareholders, as such, are proprietors of their shares only – they have mere contracts with the corporation in which certain beneficial interests . . . are granted . . . to subscribers and their successors.
Canning, 1929a, 55

Their Lordships . . . . believe that the distinction should be clearly marked, observed and maintained between an incorporated company's legal entity and its actions, assets, rights and liabilities on the one hand, and the individual shareholders and their actions, assets, rights and liabilities on the other. [per Lord Russell]
E B M Co Ltd v Dominion Bank, 1937

Conclusions based upon the *situs* of legal title are logically consistent with the entity theory: the corporation is its own proprietor, assets are the property of the corporation, all income earned is the income of the corporate entity until declared in dividends, surplus is the equity of the corporate entity and ought not to be added to the capital stock in computing the book value of the stockholders' equity, the latter should be regarded as a species of liability.

Husband, 1938, 244

The corporation .... is a distinct entity, not by any means an association of equity shareholders. It has its own life, its own greatness, ... and, most important, it has its own interest to be served. The entrepreneur may say, and believe, when he speaks at the company meeting and is reported in *The Times*, that the interests of the company are the interests of the shareholders, but his ordinary thoughts do not run along these lines.

Keirstead, 1953, 57

Entity theory stems from the legal fiction of the corporate enterprise as a person in its own right. The assets and debts are those of the corporate entity ....

Vatter, 1955, 365

044 Interests of corporation and stockholder

The concern owns its going business in the sense that it owns the liberty to continue in business through access to markets, and it owns its gross income in the sense that its board of directors have power to acquire, use and dispose of the gross income.

Commons, 1924/1959, 162

A stockholder has no present interest in the physical property of an unliquidated corporation.

Kaufman v Société Internationale, 1952

The stockholder's claim against corporate assets .... [is exercisable only upon] .... the dissolution and liquidation of the company .... [But] economic and accounting analysis has as a basic premise the going concern concept .... From this current viewpoint – representing the truer and more accurate state of affairs – the stockholder's enforceable claim against his share of corporate retained earnings is essentially nil.

Seidman, 1956, 66

business capital supplied by stockholders to the corporation does not represent the equity of the former, but rather that of the latter.

Li, 1960, 261

Resources which have been committed to an economic entity, say, a proprietorship by its legal owner, are ... regarded as the entity's own assets.

Edwards & others, 1979, 67

Shareholders funds [a term commonly used in company balance sheets] are not funds of shareholders .... The terms, shareholders funds and stockholders equity, are misnomers.

Chambers, 1991, 187

See also 278, 279

045 Entities regarded as co-proprietorships

We cannot separate a firm from its members nor a company from its stockholders; the members are the firm and the stockholders are the company. The words firm and company are simply what the grammarians call collective nouns, the one meaning the partners collectively, the other meaning the stockholders collectively .... When we speak of the assets and liabilities of a company we mean the assets and liabilities of the stockholders collectively .... as proprietors of the business whose accounts we are keeping.

VanCleve, 1913, 426

The business entity as such, whether incorporated or not, has assets but no capital, the net worth of which (i.e. assets minus other liabilities) is the capital of the collective investors. The so-called capital of a corporation is at most a quasi, fictitious or pseudo capital, created by and corresponding to the legal fiction of the separate corporate entity. The corporation owns the assets but the shareholders own the capital .... The corporation owes the capital, it does not own it. The shareholders own it.

Fetter, 1937, 9

the principal aim of accounts is to determine the net worth and income of the proprietors.

Edwards, 1938b, 81

The proprietor is a natural person or a group of natural persons who undertake a business adventure .... He is the owner of the business .... he owns all the assets and owes all the liabilities; the excess of his assets over his liabilities measures his net interest or proprietorship in the business.

Chow, 1942, 157

accounting theory would be more realistically hinged to economic reality if the corporation were assumed to be an agency organization .... [From this] point of view the earnings of the enterprise constitute earnings to the stockholders at the moment of their realization.

Husband, 1954b, 554, 557

Under proprietary theory, the proprietor is the center of accounting, and all accounting concepts and processes relate to the basic notion of the proprietor's interests.

The assets are the property of the proprietor, liabilities are the debts of the proprietor .... [The] proprietor's total assets, minus the total of his debts equals his net worth at any time .... Income is the change in net worth.
                                                            Vatter, 1955, 362

The proprietary theory of accounting requires that the corporation be viewed as an association of individual owners.
                                                            Sprouse, 1958, 48

According to the proprietary theory, the business or other organization being accounted for belongs to one or more persons thought of as proprietors or owners, and their viewpoint is reflected in the accounting. The assets are regarded as their assets and the liabilities as their liabilities.
                                                            Lorig, 1964, 564

According to the proprietary theory, the assets of the enterprise are owned effectively by the stockholders (or other owners), and the liabilities are considered as liabilities of the stockholders.
                                                            Bedford & others, 1967, 12

the proprietorship or ownership theory of accounting .... proposed that the proprietor or owner of a business was the focus of accounting procedures. Assets were either things owned by or benefits accruing to the owner, liabilities were amounts owed by the owner, revenues were received by the owner and expenses were incurred by the owner. Transactions were interpreted from the owner's viewpoint. The proprietorship or capital account was a control account for all other accounts in the ledger and showed the firm's worth to its owner.
                                                            Henderson & Peirson, 1983, 52

Under proprietary theory the assets belong to the firm's owners and the liabilities are their obligations. The balance sheet equation would be:
$$\text{Assets} - \text{Liabilities} = \text{Owners' equities}$$
                                                            Wolk & others, 1984, 127

046 Entity and proprietorship foci – differential aspects

[Where P = so-called proprietorship theory; E = so-called entity theory] Primary purpose of accounting: [P] accounting by the owner ... for his own property; [E] accounting to outsiders (owners and creditors). [P] Proprietor owns all the assets but owes certain amounts to creditors; [E] the entity owns all the assets; both liabilities and proprietorship are claims against the assets .... [P] Liabilities are negative assets. [E] Liabilities considered to be capital sources as much as so-called proprietary investments .... [P] Assets are objects or realizable claims .... Assets are essentially debt-paying media. [E] Most of the assets are outlays which have been made for productive reasons . . . . Center of attention [P] Balance sheet values, particularly short-term realizable values. [E] Association of costs and returns from costs . . . . Going concern valuation concepts . . . .

Newlove & Garner, 1951, I:21

The importance of the controversy over the choice between proprietary theory and entity theory has been greatly exaggerated . . . . some writers envisage the choice of an orientation postulate as affecting vitally the core of accounting theory. Some make it appear as though the choice . . . implies the use of an entirely different concept of asset valuation . . . . Such is not the case . . . .

Zeff, 1961/1978, 216

From the entity point of view, the important thing about income is the amount of income generated by the various assets without regard to the manner in which that income is distributed . . . ; interest payments are not an expense to be deducted in determining income. From the proprietary point of view, the important thing about income is the amount of it that the entity is successful in generating for its proprietors; interest expense is an expense in determining the stockholders' share of income from corporate activities. From the entity viewpoint, return on assets is the relevant form of the return on capital computation; whereas from the proprietary viewpoint, the relevant form is return on equity. The income used in the calculation is, of course, before deducting interest expense in the case of the entity viewpoint, and after deducting interest in the proprietary case.

Coughlan, 1965, 159

Most textbooks written since 1922 [the date of Paton's *Accounting Theory*] have been influenced by both the proprietary and entity concepts. The presentations, however, cannot generally be classified as purely either one or the other approach.

Hendriksen, 1970, 32

Under the entity theory, owners' equity is generally acknowledged to be an obligation or a liability of the enterprise to its owners . . . . proprietary theory disavows that owners' equity is in any sense a liability or an obligation of an enterprise to its owners.

Bird & others, 1974, 234

The entity theory entails accounting for the activities of an enterprise through the eyes of the entity itself; the proprietary theory accounts for an entity's activities through the eyes of the proprietors . . . . both the entity and proprietary theories are employed in conventional accounting, leading to numerous ambiguities and inconsistencies.

Stamp, 1977, 92

See also 604

047 Agglomerations of entities held to constitute other entities

the directors of the subsidiary company are necessarily the nominees of the holding company, and . . . consequently the whole group of subsidiary companies is in effect managed as if they were integral parts of the organization of the holding company without the legal fiction of separate companies.

Dickinson, 1906, 488

The principle underlying consolidated statements is that . . . companies, which may be separate entities legally, constitute practically a single entity. The consolidated statements present the financial position and operations of the corporate group as they would appear if the group were in fact merged into a single entity.

Staub, 1929, 656

Combined financial statements portray the joint position or operating results of two or more business or other units as though but one existed. They are secondary rather than primary in character, and, as enlargements of the financial statements of a common controlling interest, they assist in explaining the relationships of that interest to the outside world.

Kohler, 1938, 63

any number of corporate or other forms of enterprises that are established as separate funds for some purposes may be combined (with appropriate adjustments) into larger funds to meet [some] purposes.

Vatter, 1947, 95

The presentation of consolidated statements is in order whenever there exists an economic or business entity composed of two or more legal units . . . subject to a common control based primarily on powers conferred by share ownership . . . . Consolidation through stockholdings performs functions similar to consolidation through merger or fusion; consequently consolidated statements should reflect the status and operations of the affiliated group as though it were fused in the legal as well as in the economic sense. At the same time certain legal relationships, for example, creditors' rights and dividend limits, will probably be determined on the basis of existing legal entities; consequently the statements of each legal entity involved may not be discarded as superficial or redundant.

Moonitz, 1951/1978, 20, 12

Insofar as practicable, the consolidated data should reflect the underlying assumption that they represent the operations, resources, and equities of a single entity.

AAA, 1954a/1957b, 42

A corporation may own one or more other corporations; each is a separate accounting entity and legal entity. The accountant, however, can prepare statements to show the family of corporations as if it were a single entity.

Smith & Ashburne, 1960, 48

[One] school of thought considers that an economic entity exists when ... : 1. A dominant central financial interest in two or more companies exists and is accompanied by administrative control of their activities and resources. 2. The operations of the allied companies are integrated.

Gagnon, 1962, 50

Consolidated statements are prepared for the purpose of reporting the position and activities of a group of companies operated under a common control. They are intended to reflect the facts with respect to an economic rather than a legal unit.

Wixon (ed), 1962, 23.1

The boundaries of the accounting entity may not be the same as those of the legal entity, for example, a parent corporation and its subsidiaries treated as a single business enterprise.

AICPA, 1970c, APBS 4

See also 481, 486

048 Agglomerations of entities held not to constitute other entities

I am not sure that I really understand what is meant by an amalgamated or consolidated balance sheet. The incorporation in a statement purporting to be the balance sheet of a holding company of the assets and liabilities of other legal entities .... would be a conglomeration of figures futile as an aid to any person desirous of understanding the true position, and ... misleading .... The prevailing sound practice in accountancy is to base statements of figures on facts. The observance of the legal independence of separate entities as the basis for published accounts is, in my view, fundamentally necessary .... [letter to Company Law Amendment Committee]

Cooper, 1925/1980, 112

the law looks upon each corporation as a separate entity .... the law abandons such a view in philosophy, perhaps, in dealing with monopolies and restraint of trade, but such cases seem to be the exception. Certainly the law does not give any legal sanction to the concept of business enterprise which is behind the consolidated balance sheet.

Jones, 1933, 255

The holding company and its subsidiaries do not constitute any common unit of responsibility. In the realm of contracts and torts, employees and customers, investors and the general public, corporations are usually allowed to define their duties and liabilities strictly in terms of separate corporate entities, largely irrespective of intercorporate relationships. By defining the real business unit on a consolidated basis for affiliated companies, the Federal tax laws accepted a unit of responsibility which was practically non-existent elsewhere in corporate relationships.

Hynning, 1941/1951, 52

assets and equities . . . can only have a sensible meaning in relation to some legal entity which can own properties and incur obligations. The only entities of this kind are natural persons and corporations. A holding company and its subsidiaries, as a complex, is not an entity of this kind . . . . for the above reason consolidated balance sheets and consolidated profit and loss accounts are not balance sheets and profit and loss accounts in any ordinary sense of those terms.

Chambers, 1968a, 89–92

Only legal entities can own assets, owe liabilities, issue capital stock, earn revenues, enjoy gains and incur expenses and losses. A group of companies cannot do these things. So the elements of consolidated financial statements are the elements of the financial statements of the members of the consolidated group of companies.

Rosenfield & Rubin, 1985, 4

See also 481, 488

049 Subdivisions as entities

departmental, territorial, or commodity areas may be defined for certain purposes and reported on without reference to personal or legal relationships.

Vatter, 1947, 95

entity: a division of the activities of a natural person, partnership, corporation, or other organization, separate and complete in form, usually distinguished from a larger identity such as a head office, controlling corporation, or other more inclusive economic unit; . . . .

Kohler, 1952, 167

The product line is . . . an entity; it is an area of economic interest as defined by management.

AAA, 1965b, 362

A subdivision or department of a corporation cannot be a reporting entity.

Grady, 1965, 26

separate financial statements may be prepared for divisions of a single corporation, when such divisions are operated as distinct profit centers.

Meigs & others, 1978, 13

a branch of a business may be a separate accounting entity but usually is not a legal entity separate from the business as a whole.

Henderson & Peirson, 1983, 79

050 Functions of Accounting

051 Accounting related to decision making

It is not without good reason that most people of business and ingenuity are desirous to be masters of this art, if we consider the satisfaction that naturally arises from an account well kept; the pleasure that accrues to a person by seeing what he gains by each species of goods he deals in, and his whole profit by a year's trade; and thereby also, to know the true state of his affairs and circumstances; so that he may, according to his discretion, retrench or enlarge his expenses, etc. as he shall think fit. [126]

Anon, 1737/1984, 41

from it [double entry bookkeeping] . . . we can in a few hours, and with very little trouble, at any time, know the exact state of our affairs, viz, what goods of every sort we have in hand; what payments we have to make, and what cash we can command; by which means we are timely apprized to prepare for any demands which can be made upon us, and can extend or curtail our trade as we find our capital will admit of, or the nature of our affairs require.

Thompson, 1777, 2:2

Q 1884. Do you think that, upon those accounts which are generally rendered by railway companies, there is sufficient knowledge communicated to capitalists to enable them to judge by the mere accounts themselves of the expediency or inexpediency of investing their capital in one railway in preference to another? *Russell*: I think there are much greater facilities to attain that knowledge with respect to railway accounts than with respect to any analogous mode of investment . . . .

Russell, 1849

It is not too much to assert, that very many of the bankruptcies which occur are owing primarily to the neglect of bookkeeping; and secondly, as a natural sequence, to the uncertainty and recklessness engendered by such neglect. Can it be imagined, in the case of any honorable minded trader, who is anxious to maintain his standing and reputation, and who possesses books which yearly exhibit a true result of his business, that he will not contract his expenditure to a sum warranted by existing circumstances? that the experience of a disastrous year will not forearm him with greater discretion and increased prudence for the succeeding one?

Sawyer, 1862, viii

accounts are mainly valuable to [an investor] in so far as they afford guidance in determining which of these courses [retaining, increasing or disposing of his investment] he shall pursue.

AIA, 1932

the only important use of this [accounting] information is to facilitate the making of decisions and the formulation of judgments.

Graham, 1949, 17

[The job of accounting is to present] these quantitative data in a way that leads to sound and realistic economic decisions.

Mason & others, 1959, 1

In Counsel's view the object of annual accounts is to assist shareholders in exercising their control of the company by enabling them to judge how its affairs have been conducted . . . . the purpose for which annual accounts are normally prepared is not to enable individual shareholders to take investment decisions. [Statement of Council of ICAEW]

ICAEW, 1965, 164

accounting . . . the process of identifying, measuring and communicating economic information to permit informed judgments and decisions by users of the information.

AAA, 1966, 1

Accounting is a service activity. Its function is to provide quantitative information, primarily financial in nature, about economic entities that is intended to be useful in making economic decisions.

AICPA, 1970c, APBS4

accounting is concerned with decision making.

Arnold & others, 1985, 11

Before the advent of modern technology and communication, decision making was simpler in one critical respect – direct observation provided the basis for most judgments . . . . complexity gave rise to financial reporting since abstractions (or surrogates) became necessary to summarize events and to provide information for more complex analyses . . . . Today virtually all financial decisions in both the private and the public sectors use accounting surrogates rather than directly observed events as the basis for action.

Revsine, 1991, 16

See also 054, 181, 182

052 Accounting and resource allocation

Capital should flow into those industries which serve the public interest, and within an industry into those enterprises in which the management is capable of using capital effectively . . . . The social importance of accounting therefore is clear . . .

since dependable information about earning power can be an important aid to the flow of capital into capable hands and away from unneeded industries.

Paton & Littleton, 1940, 3

In a free economy, resources are guided to their most fruitful uses (in the main) by the decisions of individuals. If the economy is to work efficiently, these decisions must be based on adequate information. Investors should have available the fullest and clearest data on the working of the various sectors. Guided by such data, they will put new resources into sectors where likely returns are highest – thus helping to give the consumer what he wants, and to reduce abnormally high profit rates to the competitive level . . . . This is the main argument for disclosure. [Memorandum to Company Law (Jenkins) Committee]

Baxter, 1960/1980, 298

If accountants do not provide the data necessary for measuring performance, resources are misallocated and both business firms and the community at large suffer as a consequence.

Edwards & Bell, 1961, 271

The information the auditor reports as true and fair is the basis of making a market in securities, of taking individual investment decisions to buy and sell and thereby ultimately of determining to which companies in the national economy funds will flow . . . .

Marley, 1970, 11

the ratio of net income to net equity . . . . can provide a basis for comparing dissimilar enterprises and is, accordingly, an important factor in determining the distribution of scarce financial means.

van Bruinessen, 1972, 46

An economy is organized to strive for efficient allocation of resources. This allocation is affected by government action and by private actions in the marketplace, or some combination of the two. Both kinds of actions involve economic decisions and require financial information.

AICPA, 1973, 14

the more relevant information that is published and reflected in the share price . . . the more likely will capital be allocated efficiently between one company and another.

Keane, 1977, 83

The effectiveness of individuals, enterprises, markets, and government in allocating scarce resources among competing uses is enhanced if those who make economic decisions have information that reflects the relative standing and performance of business enterprises to assist them in evaluating alternative courses of action and the expected returns, costs, and risks of each.

FASB, 1978, SFAC1

In order for our capital markets to function effectively and for our economy to allocate resources efficiently, it is essential that business enterprises report accurately and fairly to investors and that investors perceive that they do so. Our economy needs both the fact and the appearance of credible financial reporting – of reporting free from fraud and error.

Cook, 1987, 96

053 Accounting as (aid to) memory

[Records] not only preserve and keep in the memory [all] transactions, but they also are a means to avoid many litigations, quarrels, and scandals . . . . Mercantile records are the means to remember all that a man does, and from whom he must have, and to whom he must give, and the costs of wares, and the profits, and the losses, and every other transaction on which the merchant is at all dependent . . . . And undoubtedly a merchant must not rely upon memory, for such reliance has caused many persons to err.

Cotrugli, 1458/1955, 375

The fundamental reasons for the necessity of recording financial transactions lie first, in the fallibility of human memory and human nature, secondly, in the need for evidential data in case of differences, and thirdly, in the division of labor.

Goldberg, 1939/1948, 17

accounts are used as aids to memory . . . .

Hatfield & others, 1940, 4

Accounting was useful to assist the memory in the regulation of credit dealings, and in the control of property.

Yamey, 1940, 336

accounting . . . began long ago as the making of a simple record to aid businessmen in remembering their financial obligations and to help partners to account to each other for their actions . . . .

Littleton, 1953, 7

Early merchants, finding that they could not conveniently remember the details of all the transactions concerning them, began to make written memoranda . . . . These memory aids were supposed to be useful, and a very high degree of emphasis on usefulness has colored accounting activities down to the present day.

Stanley, 1965, 1

See also 276

054 Accounting as instrumentation

The reason for the art is best seen in the operation of it ... – it shows a perfect reason for the increase and decrease in one's estate; ... he who daily sees his accounts fairly and duly kept, knows how to steer the fly-boat of his expenses, to hoist or lower his sails of outgoing, according to wisdom: whereas the ungrounded young merchant reckons at random, goes on and sees not the labyrinth he runs himself into, but at haphazard spends prodigally, according to his vain surmise on the one side, of profit where little or none is; on the other side, of small expenses where they are thick and threefold.
Monteage, 1682, Preface

if the necessary regularity in keeping accounts is observed; as a man can tell at one view whether his manner of living is suited to his fortune, he will consequently be enabled to form a proper medium for adjusting his expenses to his income, by which means he may be guarded against extravagance, and the evil consequences of intemperance; from which flow so many vices, destructive of domestic tranquility.
Quin, 1779/1963, 11

having the net gain or loss for the week, month, quarter, or other period of time, [and] the gain per cent on the different lines of business .... compound judgment and mature deliberation [are possible] to the end that the business may be properly managed or directed. This work may be termed taking observations to determine the financial latitude and longitude of the business. If they are not often taken, the ship of business is not safe from the winds of adversity or from the rocks of bankruptcy.
Soulé, 1903/1976, 564

Accounting .... is the barometer of the business.
Duncan, 1909, 281

Accounting activities – This group is the visual organ of business. It must throw up at any moment, present position and future trend, must afford accurate, clear and precise information about the economic position of the concern. An efficient accounting system, clear and simple, giving an accurate idea of the firm's condition is a powerful managerial instrument.
Fayol, 1916/1949, 5

financial statements, including balance sheets and income statements, are in reality expressions of fundamental business relationships .... [Ratios] .... are barometers of the relationships and business conditions within the organization.
Bliss, 1923, 35, 37

From the managerial point of view, accounting is an instrument designed to promote the rational administration of business activity. Similarly, from the standpoint of the industrial community as a whole, accounting is the principal statistical means for controlling and facilitating economic production.

Paton, 1924, 18

accounts have developed into a position of importance as an instrument of administrative control.

Scott, 1931/1973, 207

Without a knowledge of the facts management is in the position of a ship's captain without a compass in a fog. Both can only grope about blindly and hope to avoid disaster. Data regarding resources and obligations are necessary to maintain solvency. Dividends should not be declared without information both as to cash position and as to earnings . . . . Funds cannot be borrowed without submission of facts concerning financial condition. Plans for the future cannot be made wisely except upon the basis of knowledge of the past.

Porter & Fiske, 1935, 3

A company is a complex operating system or machine. It has many parts, some at a considerable distance from points of regulation. It has many variable properties . . . . To each of these there is a special form of instrumentation . . . . Company accounts are one such form of instrumentation. Their function is to indicate what is happening financially. They have no other function . . . . like other instruments, company accounts must be isomorphic. If financial changes occur they should become apparent from looking at the accounts. The singular fallacy of company accounting, as it is now done, is that it does not operate, and is not designed to operate, as an isomorphic instrument.

Chambers, 1964d, 29

Accounting has developed into one of man's most powerful instruments, both as a means of control and a guide to rational behavior, over a large range of activities.

Morgan, 1965, 48

055 Accounting as a tool

Accounting is a tool for use in the control of economic activity.

Rorem, 1928, 3

The tool by which the accountant gathers the factual data needed for satisfactory control of the business enterprise is bookkeeping . . . . An adequate records system . . . . must be designed for its purpose as carefully as any machine.

Porter & Fiske, 1935, 77

accounting serves as a tool of management . . . . The use of accounting as a tool of management is the forgotten objective of accounting.

Goetz, 1939, 151, 157

accounting systems are tools of rational choice and action for the undertaking, ...
Potter, 1951, 312

To [a security] analyst, financial statements represent the most important tool in appraising whether or not a given security represents a good or poor value . . . .
Smith, 1959, 37

the tool of analysis that we call accounting . . . .
Littleton & Zimmerman, 1962, 46

accounting practice . . . . is an instrument of decision making . . . . a tool of business management . . . .
Williams & Griffin, 1964, 2

Accountants are still . . . far from recognizing the potential of their role as precision-tool makers for management . . . .
Economist, 1964, 805

Accounting . . . serves as a tool for the present and future.
Patillo, 1965, 47

056 Accounting information as feedback

[From your accounts] you will know all about your business and whether it is going well . . . . According to the state of your business, you will be able to remedy that which is required.
Pacioli, 1494/1963, 75

Financial accounting is . . . primarily historical in character . . . having for its most important function the extraction and presentation of the essence of the financial experience of businesses, so that decisions affecting the present and the future may be taken in the light of the past.
May, 1943, vii

Accounting has a major role to play in calling management's attention to troubles that need managerial investigation and action.
Goetz & Klein, 1960, 411

a principal function of accounting is to serve as a fundamental tool in the evaluation of past decisions . . . .
Edwards & Bell, 1961, 3

From [the periodical financial summary] a manager or owner can compare what is earned with the expenses of earning it. He can consider whether or not some of the expenses are too large and take steps to reduce them. He can find what activity is profitable and expand it, or what is not and curtail it.

Vance, 1961, 3

The primary role of the financial statements, the role peculiar to them, is to test the soundness of the general policies the owner has been following .... If the statements indicate that the business is doing poorly, the owner questions his policies, searches for new ones, and the result is that his decisions and the future receipts of the firm are different than they otherwise would have been.

Gordon, 1964, 257

What, then, do we chief executives expect nowadays of our information systems? First, continual and sensitive checks on our present progress. We need to know at once when we are off target. We need to identify where we have gone astray, so that we can take the necessary action quickly.

Keith, 1969, 642

The relevance of such numbers [as appear in externally reported financial statements] to management hardly lies in their predictive power, but rather in their feedback power, i.e. the degree to which they validly measure the effect of decisions which the management has made ....

Greenball, 1971, 2

As all investors can benefit from feedback, reporting objectives should place more emphasis on feedback than on prediction.

Peasnell, 1974, 74

Feedback value – The quality of information that enables users to confirm or correct prior expectations.

FASB, 1980a, SFAC2, Glossary

See also 277

057 Accounting information and prediction

Accountants are essentially engaged in economic forecasting. Their schedules are statements of opinion about the future of the enterprise; they are not assertions about things that are known to exist.

Nelson, 1935, 316

The measurement and reporting of current income should provide a basis for prediction of future earnings.

AAA, 1964a, 693

The primary purpose of the measurement of last year's income reported to investors is to provide a basis for predicting future years' income. Such predictions have obvious relevance to all investors . . . .

Sprouse, 1966b, 106

The criterion [of predictive ability has been used with reference to predictions of] . . . the market value of the firm . . . . future annual earnings . . . . bond rating changes and ratings on newly issued bonds . . . . bankruptcy and bond default.

Beaver & others, 1968, 49

One normative function of external accounting reports is to provide information which will be useful to decision makers in generating estimates of the future levels of relevant variables. The reporting objective which follows from this belief is commonly called the predictive ability criterion.

Revsine, 1971, 480

An objective of financial statements is to provide information useful to investors and creditors for predicting, comparing and evaluating potential cash flows to them in terms of amount, timing and related uncertainty.

AICPA, 1973, 20

Information provided as a guide for decisions can be useful only if it predicts those future events which can be influenced by the decisions.

Carsberg & others, 1974, 166

See also 184, 187

Prediction not an accounting function

The training . . . and the experience of a chartered accountant . . . do not properly equip him to foretell the future. Anyone who attempts to do so is in our judgment a mere charlatan, but there can be no doubt that an estimate of future profits subscribed to by a chartered accountant would attract far more attention than a similar estimate made by the promoter of the company, and it is for this reason that a certain class of promoter is willing to pay for estimates of this description. He can afford to pay for them because they produce applications for shares. The practice is accordingly wholly indefensible in that it borders upon a fraud. If it were to be permitted, the Council of the Institute might be criticized as tacitly subscribing to the fraud, and the standing of the whole profession would suffer in consequence.

A Chartered Accountant, 1927, 45

it is certainly no part of the work of the accountant to make estimates for the future; so that if he is to make any contribution at all to the knowledge of the investor, it must be in the form of a report on what has taken place in the past.

May, 1933, 36

Observation, analysis and projection should be aimed at decision-making. This implies a view of the past and present that permits and facilitates decisions, without making them.

Vatter, 1963, 197

A stockholder should bear in mind at all times that financial statements are not designed to predict the future, but to report on the past and present.

Bevis, 1965, 68

Since the concept of predictive ability seems applicable only to a person, a prediction model, or a scientific hypothesis, and an accounting method is none of these, we must conclude that there is no such thing as the predictive ability of an accounting method.

Greenball, 1971, 5

while financial statements should be presented in a manner to assist as much as possible in assessing the future, the role of financial statements is not to provide predictions or interpretations about the future. Prediction is at the heart of risk taking and is the function of the investor and other users of financial statements.

Andersen & Co, 1972, 10

058 Accounting information as aid in forming expectations

The importance of bookkeeping lies not only in the study of the past activities of an enterprise, but also in the indications which it furnishes for future direction. From the observation and study of events that are over it provides the possibility of forejudging future activity and finding sure bases for reasoning out the actions to come.

Gomberg, 1901/1933, 55

Until the science [of bookkeeping] had been perfected there was no continuous systematic utilization of capital, and no widespread diffusion of forms of organization having for their object the profitable employment of definite capitals. The use of exact accounts made it possible not only to know at any given time exactly how a business stood, but also to employ rational plans for extensive future operations.

Robertson, 1933, 55

The past . . . is primarily important as it foreshadows the future. The accountant . . . must thus stand, like the Roman god Janus, looking two ways at once.

Raby, 1959, 452

Accountants must become more conscious that it is the future that matters, and that their concern with the past must increasingly be only as a basis for forecasting the future.

Stewart, 1962, 487

if one adopts the view that accounting is "a method of monetary calculation designed to provide a continuous source of financial information as a guide to future action in markets", the emphasis shifts almost entirely from the past to the future.

Bonham (ed), 1964, 59

there cannot be a report on wealth and progress which is simply an account of the past and has no reference to the future, and there cannot be a report on wealth and progress which embodies specific assumptions about future uses of assets. There can be only one report on the amount and composition of wealth at any time, and, for fruitful use, it must be equally serviceable as a point of departure for analyzing the past and as a point of departure for constructing, with imagination, the shape of possible futures.

Chambers, 1974a, 3

See also 182, 183

059 Limited function of accounting information

The accounts furnish some of the fundamental data for the determination of business policy, but they cannot furnish all of the necessary elements; they must be supplemented by much additional data and by the intelligence and business acumen of our industrial, commercial and financial chiefs.

Wasserman, 1931, 32

Many factors elude the pecuniary calculus.

Goetz & Klein, 1960, 419

[Economic] decisions involve the identification of the alternative lines of action that are open, the determination of the consequences which will flow from each line of action, and the selection of the action which will in fact be taken. Financial reports can supply some of the data needed to make these decisions.

Moonitz, 1961, 26

An investor makes his decision about the desirability of a stock based on the historical record of the firm, its risk characteristics and his risk preferences, and forecasts of the financial future of the firm, of its stock prices, and of the economy. All these factors are combined to form a value for the stock which is then compared to the stock price and to alternative investments. The accounting information is only a small part of the evaluation process.

Bierman, 1974, 560

There ... is a quite definite limit to the aid accounting may give to decision-makers. It aids diagnosis and prognosis, that is all. And it aids these only if the figures which describe wealth and progress correspond closely – and, in terms of the passage of time, continuously – with the financial consequences of events and transactions.

Chambers, 1974a, 3

Accounting information must be seen as only a part of a competitive market in information which is both available to and used by investors as a group.

Hopwood, 1974, 176

[It is a myth] that financial statements play a dominant role in making decisions about investments . . . . financial statements have limited usefulness in making investment decisions. They serve to confirm or refute our prior predictions of future events. In this sense they become one factor among many other types of information which we take into account in our forecasts.

Olson, 1977, 69

It is the responsibility of financial reporting to provide some of the information that aids in prediction. (Much will come from other sources – e.g. data on the state of the economy.) Financial reporting is concerned with past events and transactions. It nevertheless will aid prediction if it captures the economic reality of, or "faithfully represents", the financial consequences of the activities engaged in by the reporting entity.

Skinner, 1982, 124

060 Users and Uses of Accounting Information

061 Parties having interests in financial information

[After the Civil War], shortening in mercantile terms of sale brought about an equally revolutionary change in banking practice . . . . James Buell [bank president] . . . proceeded in the 1870s to show his depositors the distinct advantages of borrowing funds upon their own credit standing and using these funds to pay for merchandise purchases on discount terms. This revolution in lending technique was predicated upon the borrower's giving to the banker a current balance sheet and such other financial information as the banker felt he needed to analyze the condition of the borrower.

Foulke, 1945, 13

Accounting . . . is a service. Its function is to supply information to executives and managers which will enable them to handle their business in the most effective and advantageous manner.

Bliss, 1923, 218

Executives and employees, directors, stockholders, bank creditors, merchandise creditors, and governmental agencies are those for whom the balance sheet renders the most important service.

McKinsey, 1925, 155

[The] analytical and interpretive functions [of accounting] are of two kinds ... to afford aid to management in the conduct of business ... [and to present] statements relating to the financial position and results of operations of a business for the guidance of directors, stockholders, credit grantors, and others.

May, 1943, 1

Obvious users of business income measurements are – managers .... investors or potential investors .... employees .... creditors .... suppliers and customers .... government ....

Finnie, 1968a, 281

The groups ... having a reasonable right to information and whose information needs should be recognized by corporate reports are .... the equity investor group .... the loan creditor group .... the employee group .... the analyst-adviser group .... the business contact group .... the government .... the public ....

ASSC, 1975a, 17

Among the potential users [of financial reports] are owners, lenders, suppliers, potential investors and creditors, employees, management, directors, customers, financial analysts and advisers, brokers, underwriters, stock exchanges, lawyers, economists, taxing authorities, regulatory authorities, legislators, financial press and reporting agencies, labor unions, trade associations, business researchers, teachers and students, and the public.

FASB, 1978, SFAC1

[External users of financial reports include] shareholders .... potential shareholders .... creditors .... analysts and advisers .... employees .... non-executive directors .... customers .... suppliers .... industry groups .... labor unions .... government departments .... the public .... regulatory agencies .... other companies .... standard setters, academic researchers, etc.

CICA, 1980, 43

062 Common interests of diverse parties in financial information

there is a common interest by the four parties to the balance sheet [management, creditors, owners and the public] in the proper indication of the following two factors of financial position: 1. the position as to solvency – debt-paying ability, and 2. the position as to progress – the earning power of a business.

Kester, 1946, 37

There is a common body of accounting information which can be useful to all interests in an enterprise. This takes the form of an analytical report of what has happened, the activities of an enterprise, and the results of those activities.

Illinois, 1964, 3

Can . . . one set of statements satisfy so many different groups? . . . . Yes. The reason is that . . . what all of them want to know is: Is the company in good shape? Thus they all want to know what the company's assets and liabilities are currently and, seeing that the strongest position can deteriorate rapidly if the company's operations are unsatisfactory, they also must know the trend of operations.

Ross, 1966, 32

investors, creditors, employees, customers, and managers significantly share a common interest in an enterprise's ability to generate favorable cash flows.

FASB, 1978, SFAC1

Interested outsiders (investors, creditors, labor unions, government regulatory bodies) may or may not be privy to the firm's plans. But they clearly have the same interest as the managers in ascertaining objective events – in measuring actual performance . . . .

Edwards & others, 1979, 456

All those who have an interest in, or are affected by, the activities of a business . . . are interested in its performance and financial situation . . . . Whether they are investors, employees, customers, government agencies or whoever, they want to know about the wealth of the entity and changes in this wealth.

Macve, 1981, 25

Financial reports . . . . must serve many purposes for a wide variety of users, including present and potential stockholders, creditors, financial analysts, and regulatory agency officials. Though each of these users has different needs, there is a common body of financial information about an entity that suits all of their purposes. This information is contained in the financial statements.

Skousen & others, 1981, 32

both parties [shareholder and lender] must be interested in the operating profitability and solvency of the entity because, in the last analysis, both their interests depend upon ability to pay.

Skinner, 1982, 125

063 Accounting information as mediating conflicts of interest

The principles of accounting, principles of law, accounting technique and the machinery of the market are all mixed up together in the process by which conflicting interests are adjusted. Lines drawn between [them] . . . are arbitrary. All are closely related parts of the current economic structure.

Scott, 1931/1973, 202

[Accounting] is vitally concerned with human rights and relationships, as is the law.
Paton, 1939/1943, 87

Every decision made by the accountant is a valuation decision fraught with possibilities of justice or injustice to some economic interest. Only if his decisions are guided by accounting principles that have validity and meaning in relation to contemporary society will they serve to meet this vital protective function.
Odmark, 1954, 638

In any deliberate competition, the parties work against one another and subject to the rules of the game. So it is with firms. As in any other competition, there is need for a scoring device which indicates how well the competitors are doing as the game proceeds. The competitors need such a device themselves so that in the light of the latest cumulative score they may devise their own tactics for the next step. And if their capacity to compete depends on what others think of the score, they will want a scoring device which does equal justice to their respective performances up to any time. They will want a neutral, factual, scoring device.
Chambers, 1967b, 17

accountants must develop and operate an accounting system in the most objective, consistent and unambiguous manner since the data they provide directly affect the way in which conflicting interests are solved . . . .
Ijiri, 1967, 67

Financial statements must be fair to all users and should provide the basis for resolving these conflicting interests [. . . creditors versus stockholders, one class of stockholders versus another, consumers versus labor . . .] in a manner that recognizes lawfully established economic rights and interests.
Andersen & Co, 1972, 8

Accounting is essentially about the use of financial measurements in arbitrating and resolving potential conflicts between the many users of published financial reports.
Stamp, 1981a, 240

064 Accounting and the public interest

The accountant's duty to the public may well be deemed to be his paramount duty, the non-observance of which would inevitably prevent accountancy from ever obtaining general recognition as a profession.
Nau, 1924, 5

The primary purpose which lay behind the British legislation in the nineteenth century requiring the appointment of auditors for every company was the protection of the

shareholding investors against fraudulent promotions and directors' mismanagement. Parliament could hardly be said to have had any motives for such statutes
than the public welfare.

AR, editorial, 1931, 231

The test of the corporate system and of the special phase of it represented by corporate
accounting ultimately lies in the results which are produced. These results must be
judged from the standpoint of society as a whole – not from that of any one group
of interested parties.

AIA, 1939a, ARB1

The accounting profession has a duty to the public. Its body of accounting principles must be tinged with the public interest else its procedures and utterances will
be accorded no greater significance than that given those of the servants of its
clients.

Colbert, 1943, 362

[The affairs of large scale business enterprise] are matters of public, as well as
private, concern. Public accounting must, therefore, assume a full responsibility for
the preparation of sound and informative reports on the operations of business, or
await the time when the alternative of rigid governmental control of such matters
will become an established fact.

Foulke, 1945, 603

the accountant's responsibility as auditor is mainly to the public – to all those people
who may rely on the financial statements the CPA approves.

Trueblood, 1970, 38

The accountant occupies a crucial spot in the US business and financial system.
Essentially his job is to keep the game honest.

Business week, 1971, 86

See also 986

065 Variety of uses of accounting information

A man who does not keep books properly, so that he really knows how his business
stands and whether or not he is actually making a profit, is not entitled to credit
and should not get it. Credit should always be based on an intelligible and accurate
balance sheet. Those who grant credit can do a good deal to enforce adequate bookkeeping.

Saturday evening post, editorial,
1916/1963, 60

[The functions of accounting] are to locate responsibility, to prevent fraud, to guide
industry, to determine equities, to solve the all-essential conundrum of business:

What are my profits? ; to facilitate the government in its fiscal operations, to guide the business manager in the attempt to secure efficiency.

Hatfield, 1924, 253

the major uses of financial accounts. We can recognize at least ten distinguishable uses: 1. as a report of stewardship; 2. as a basis for fiscal policy; 3. to determine the legality of dividends; 4. as a guide to wise dividend action; 5. as a basis for the granting of credit; 6. as information for prospective investors in an enterprise; 7. as a guide to the value of investments already made; 8. as an aid to government supervision; 9. as a basis for price or rate regulation; 10. as a basis for taxation.

May, 1943, 3

Accounting data and reports have validity and usefulness for widely differing purposes . . . . Thus, the data . . . provide an analytical record of past events and a basis for predicting future events, and are used by interested parties to evaluate past or present economic activities of an enterprise for many decision-making purposes.

Illinois, 1964, 8

[Users of financial statements need the information they provide for] assessment of overall performance . . . . assessment of managerial quality . . . . estimating future prospects . . . . assessing financial strength and stability . . . . assessing solvency . . . . assessing liquidity . . . . assessing risk and uncertainty . . . . aid to resource allocation . . . . making comparisons with past performance, with other entities, with industry and economy as a whole . . . . valuation of debt and equity holdings in the company . . . . assessing adaptive ability . . . . determining compliance with law or regulations . . . . assessing entity's contribution to society, national goals, etc.

CICA, 1980, 48

Accounting reports . . . are now called upon to give a realistic view of current economic performance, to provide early warning of financial difficulties, to provide a simple comparative guide to investors in corporate securities and to form the basis of a reliable forecast of future economic performance in terms of cash flows and other features.

Carrington & Howitt, 1983, 111

066 Monofunctional and multifunctional information

there are different kinds of problems for which we need information about costs, and . . . the particular information we need differs from one problem to another.

Clark, 1923, 35

Just why the public accountants have, in the main, fought shy of organizing balance sheets freely with respect to their clients' principal need for information, and have tended, on the whole, to prepare all-purpose balance sheets, is impossible to determine

.... it is illusory to hope that any all-purpose balance sheet can ever be well suited to each legitimate class of use ....

Canning, 1929a, 86

it should be obvious that it is not possible to get one form of account or one statement which will serve equally well the purposes of regulation, taxation, annual reporting and a security issue.

May, 1937, 17

The same financial statement, in varying degrees of detail, is prepared for the management, the owner, the prospective investor, the trade creditor, the banker, and the like. But each of these groups have different needs because the decision or decisions which they are endeavoring to make rest upon particular factors, aspects, or elements of the company's operations .... single purpose statements appear to be a means of achieving a noteworthy advance in the furtherance of the admitted objectives.

Brink, 1940, 285, 291

It is not possible for accounts to be prepared upon a multi-purpose basis. The purpose governs the particular conventions to be applied in each particular case. For example, the basic conventions will vary in important particulars when calculating revenue results for: (a) showing the profits available for distribution as dividend; (b) calculating costs for the purpose of testing the profitability of selling prices; (c) calculating results for taxation purposes; (d) calculating results for prospectus purposes.

de Paula, 1948, 442

Different users of information need different information, and it is impossible for the accounting profession to give specialized service to all interested parties.

Devine, 1963, 129

The different purposes of [financial] calculations entail that the inputs to and the outputs of each of them shall be different in kind. The prospective purchase (or replacement) price of an asset is serviceable in budgetary calculations; as an indication of prospective commitments, not as indicating resources available. It has nothing to do with reporting the consequences of past transactions and events. The net present values of possible future projects are serviceable in choosing between them; but they are not serviceable in the construction of budgets, and they have nothing to do with reporting the consequences of past transactions and events. The actual costs of assets and operations are indicative of the actual cash outlays made; but they are only one-half of the inputs to profit calculations, and they have nothing to do with the subsequent representation of a company's financial position. That some actual or proposed accounting standards endorse the use in [periodical] accounts of original costs, replacement prices and net present values (capitalized values), is evidence of the failure to identify these magnitudes with the particular purposes of the calculations in which they occur.

ASRC, 1978, 48

Financial statements are needed for various purposes. Legally oriented needs cover such matters as tax assessment, legality of dividend distribution, remuneration by share of profit, pooling of profit and restriction of borrowing by reference to profit and asset valuations . . . . Decision oriented needs . . . include investment analysis . . . judgments on lending, wage negotiations . . . price control . . . . the performance of management . . . . [For these varied purposes] all purpose accounts will not do . . . . if the basic accounts are to be all-purpose, they must be based on an acceptable model, the rules for which are understood widely, which is susceptible of interpretation and audit, and which gives the legal type data required. Such a model is unlikely to be ideal for decision oriented purposes . . . . it is impossible to encapsulate the whole financial state of an undertaking and its future potential into a single figure. Decisions need multiple data.

Edey, 1978, 108, 109

the idea of different costs for different purposes has been misinterpreted because the authors have taken it to mean different kinds of costs for different purposes . . . . But a manager's area of control is only a subdivision of the firm as a whole. Logically, therefore, the costs used in the review of a manager's performance should be a subdivision of those used to review the performance of the firm as a whole. The costs are not different; they represent simply a lower or a higher level of aggregation.

Wells, 1978, 23

accountants must cease to believe that all of the financial complexities of a modern public corporation can be captured and portrayed by one set of figures prepared on what would necessarily be an arbitrarily selected measurement basis.

CICA, 1980, 72

Different users will have different needs for accounting information depending on the situations and decisions they face, their level of understanding and the alternative sources of information available to them.

Macve, 1981, 11

there is no universally correct model [of accounting] which will serve all uses and users in all circumstances.

Whittington, 1983a/1986, 208

See also 595, 791

067 Internal and external information to be based on the same principles

More detail is given in the balance sheet presented to the management of a business than is published . . . but the same general principles are applicable both to the detailed and abridged versions.

Moore, 1937, 29

In the ultimate analysis the shareholder is interested in the same kind of financial information as the director, ... [Memorandum to Company Law (Jenkins) Committee]

Edey, 1960/1980, 194

There is really no distinction, except perhaps in the extent of detail desirable, between what the shareholder and the manager ought to know.

Stewart, 1962, 488

Internal and external reporting must be coordinated in a single accounting system .... Neither is more important than the other.

Spacek, 1971, 89

There is to be no substantive difference in financial reports or information issued for different purposes.

Tietjen, 1971, 72

the internal and external reports may in principle differ only with regard to specificness, to the degree of detail and to frequency. The same reasoning applies to reporting within the company: the higher the level to which a report is directed, the fewer the details.

Louwers, 1972, 533

Management ... generally needs the same kinds of information about ... [assets, liabilities, earnings and related elements] as external users.

FASB, 1978, SFAC1

068 Required financial information said to be unknown

No one really knows what [financial or accounting information] individuals or any organization wants, or what they should want ....

AAA, 1966, 69

Relatively little is known about the way in which information is used in decision making .... until we know more about the conditions that affect perceived relevance of accounting information for decision making, and until we know more about the conceptions of accounting held by users, we do not have adequate bases on which to reduce diversity in accounting or to increase it selectively.

Bruns, 1968, 469, 479

it is very difficult to know which information gives the investor a clear picture of the value of an investment. Truth and prognostication are inextricably mixed, and the process of separation is thwarted by an underlay of historical accounting data.

Demsetz, 1969, 17

It is so difficult to choose [between alternative systems of accounting] because we really do not know the decision models of users.

Horngren, 1970, 4

The basic objective of financial statements is to provide information useful for making economic decisions .... Users' needs for information, however, are not known with any degree of certainty. No study has been able to identify precisely the specific role financial statements play in the economic decision-making process.

AICPA, 1973, 13

little is currently known about the detailed information needs of various categories of users.

Revsine, 1973, 19

we remain almost entirely ignorant about the rational (and often irrational) mental processes that users go through in reaching their decisions .... we will therefore never be able to define exactly what information ought to be supplied to legitimate users [of accounting information].

CICA, 1980, 48

Users need accounting information about the economic activities and status of an entity, but the type of information they need is not precisely known.

Anthony, 1983, 44

Little is known about users' decision models and their information requirements.

Ma & others, 1987, 141

070 Accounting and Accountability

071 A custodial function of accounting

What are the objects of keeping accounts? .... The first object is information; the second object is protection.

Sprague, 1901/1984, #1

It is the function of the accounting records to display at all times ... the condition of these values under the custodianship of the business organization and ... the responsibility for these values to creditors and to proprietorship.

Couchman, 1924, 12

the whole purpose of ancient [Roman] accounting was not to measure the rate of profit or loss but to keep accurate records of acquisitions and outgoings, in money and kind, and to expose any losses due to dishonesty or negligence.

de Ste Croix, 1956, 38

The origins of accounting and indeed of written records are probably to be found in the need of an accounting officer to render a statement of money and other assets received in his charge on behalf of his employer, or disbursed on his behalf. There was a need for a check on the honesty and reliability of subordinates.

Yamey, 1962, 15

The historical role of accounting is that of stewardship: the prevention of fraud, waste, and gross inefficiency. The owner's assets are to be protected against the unscrupulous or incapable manager.

Churchill & Stedry, 1966, 29

the function of accounting in controlling the resources of a firm is the most fundamental one. . .

Ijiri, 1971, 5

A principal use of accounting data and the double entry bookkeeping system from which these data are derived is the establishment of control over resources . . . . the system enables the managers and owners of enterprises to determine responsibility for resources, thereby reducing opportunities for fraud and misallocations.

Benston, 1982, 212

072 Accounting and accountability (stewardship)

all and every such clerk . . . shall, upon oath when thereunto required [by the Commissioners] . . . give . . . a true, exact, and perfect account in writing under their respective hands, with proper vouchers of all moneys . . . received, paid or disbursed, by virtue of this Act . . .

Fen Lands Act, 1773

Periodical accounts, if honestly made and fairly audited, cannot fail to excite attention to the real state of a concern; and by means of improved remedies, parties to mismanagement may be made more amenable for acts of fraud and illegality.

Gladstone Committee, 1844, *BPP, 1844*

Every officer and servant appointed or employed under this Act by a local authority shall . . . make out and deliver to them a true and perfect account in writing of all moneys received by him for the purposes of this Act . . . and shall, together with such account, deliver the vouchers or receipts for all payments made by him, and pay over to the treasurer all moneys owing by him on the balance of accounts.

UK *Public Health Act, 1875*

The science of accounting . . . arises primarily out of the need that accounting parties should from time to time render to those to whom they are responsible an account of their stewardship . . . .

Dicksee, 1905a, 147

Corporate financial statements are usually prepared as an accounting by the management for its stewardship of the stockholders' property, and as a periodical report on progress.

Broad, 1944, 190

financial stewardship is the paramount objective ... of accounting.

Irish, 1950, 216

The primary purpose of the annual accounts of a business is to present information to the proprietors, showing how their funds have been utilized and the profits derived from such use.

ICAEW, 1952, N15

Scorekeeping, or ... the accounting element of stewardship ... historically ... was the earliest stage in the development of the accounting profession. It is the most basic of accounting functions.

Firmin, 1957, 569

Predominant in shaping the framework assumptions ... [of] financial accounting is the stewardship view of the business undertaking. Investors commit their funds to employment in the business with the end purpose in mind of deriving an income. Those entrusted with the care and use of the invested funds need to report periodically upon the financial status of the commitment ... and the success achieved in its use.

Husband, 1960, 477

Owners entrust funds to management and management is expected to use these funds wisely. Periodically, management must report to the owners the results of management's actions. Financial statements are one of the principal means whereby management fulfils this reporting responsibility.

Hawkins, 1971, 58

British company law envisages a situation where the board of directors is entrusted with the stewardship of the shareholders' investment.

Anderson, 1976, 284

Financial reporting should provide information about how management of an enterprise has discharged its stewardship responsibility to owners (stockholders) .... for the custody and safekeeping of enterprise resources but also for their efficient and profitable use ....

FASB, 1978, SFAC1

General purpose financial reporting ... provides a mechanism to enable managements and governing bodies to discharge their accountability. Managements and governing bodies are accountable to those who provide resources to the entity for planning and controlling the operations of the entity.

AARF & ASRB, 1990a, SAC2

073 Books of account required to be kept

[The named partners] bind and oblige themselves to keep exact and regular mercantile account books of the whole transactions of the said company ... the day book ... shall contain a true and faithful record and narrative of the whole transactions of the company ... [the] books ... shall be brought to a regular balance ... yearly ... which balance ... [when approved by the partners] shall be deemed and taken as complete legal evidence in every question which may afterwards arise among the partners. [Contract of copartnery]

Gilmour Rankin & Company, 1812

exact and regular books of the company's business and transactions shall be kept and ... balanced annually ... [which books shall be] signed by the partners and binding on each of them .... To which books and inventory and valuation and to all the papers belonging to the concern each of the partners shall have free access at all times and occasions for inspection. [Contract of copartnery]

St Rollox Foundry Co, 1830

exact and regular books of the company's business and transactions shall be kept ... and on no account whatever be allowed to fall behind .... And the books when so balanced ... shall be signed by each of the partners and binding upon them. [Partnership contract]

Newton Bernie & Company, 1837

That the said partners shall keep, or cause to be kept, proper accounts in writing. That each of the said partners shall, in the said accounts, make true, plain and perfect entries of all the monies, goods, effects, credits, and other things received, purchased, sold, or contracted for .... That ... each year ... a general account and rest in writing shall be taken and made of all the stock, credits and effects, debts and liabilities ... and a just valuation or appraisement shall be made of all the particulars included in such account. And the said general account ... shall ... be signed and subscribed ... by each of the said partners ... [who shall be] bound and concluded by every such account respectively .... [Model articles of partnership]

Pulling, 1850, 149–153

The said copartnership shall keep regular and distinct books containing entries of all the affairs and transactions of the said joint trade ... and the company's books shall be brought to a balance at least once in every year .... [Partnership contract]

Denny and Company, 1862

The directors shall cause true accounts to be kept of the stock in trade of the company; of the sums of money received and expended by the company, and the matter in respect of which such receipt and expenditure takes place; and of the credits and liabilities of the company .... [First Schedule, Table A. The provisions of Table

A were binding on companies except to the extent that their articles of association excluded or modified any such provision.]

UK *Companies Act*, 1862

The directors shall cause true accounts to be kept of the sums of money received and expended by the company and the matter in respect of which such receipt and expenditure takes place, and of the assets and liabilities of the company. [Schedule I, Table A]

UK *Companies (Consolidation) Act, 1908*

074 Accounts to be available for inspection

the book or books in which the accounts . . . shall be stated and settled . . . shall be deposited under the care and custody of [appointed persons] . . . and every proprietor . . . at reasonable times, shall have free access to such book and books, for his, her, or their inspection.

Plate Glass Manufacturers Act, 1773

such accounts . . . shall be fairly entered in two distinct and separate books . . . one of which books to be kept by the treasurer . . . ; and the other . . . shall be deposited in [an appointed place where it] may be inspected and perused at all reasonable times by or at the request of any person or persons rated or taxed by virtue of this Act, on paying sixpence for perusing the same.

Fen Lands Act, 1773

it is expedient that the accounts of every such [registered joint stock] company be open to the inspection of the shareholders; and that the annual balance sheet, together with the reports of the auditors thereon, be registered.

Gladstone Committee, 1844, *BPP, 1844*

the books of any such company wherein the proceedings of the company are recorded shall . . . at all reasonable times . . . be open to the inspection of any shareholder of the company . . . . (s 33) . . . during the space of fourteen days previously to such ordinary meeting [of shareholders], and also during one month thereafter, every shareholder of the company may . . . inspect the books of account and the balance sheet of the company and take copies thereof and extracts therefrom . . . . (s 37)

UK *Joint Stock Companies Act*, 1844

no member (not being a director) shall have any right of inspecting any account or book of account of the company except as conferred by statute or authorized by the directors or by the company in general meeting. [Order dated July 30 1906 substituting a new Table A – regulations for management of a company limited by shares – for that contained in the Companies Act, 1862]

UK Board of Trade, 1906

Incidental to the right of stockholders to hold directors responsible for their actions is the right to inspect the main books of account. This is a common law right of the stockholder, independent of any statute .... In practice, this right is usually taken care of by an annual audit of the books; ....

Dewing, 1953, II:88

Any stockholder, in person or by attorney or other agent, shall, upon written demand under oath stating the purpose thereof, have the right during the normal hours of business to inspect for any proper purpose the corporation's stock ledger, a list of its stockholders, and its other books and records, and to make copies or extracts therefrom. A proper purpose shall mean a purpose reasonably related to such person's interest as a stockholder.

Delaware Corporation Laws, 1974,
#220(b)

075 Accounts expected to be truthful

First of all, he who will render the [estate] account ought to swear that he will render true account and that he will charge himself with as many of the goods belonging to his lord as he has received; and that he will spend them honestly and will not enter anything on his account roll except what he spent, honestly, and to the lord's advantage. The clerk also ought to swear that he has faithfully entered on his roll all the goods belonging to the lord which his master had received and that nothing has been entered on his roll as expenses except what he understands to have been spent faithfully and to the lord's advantage.

Anon, The husbandry, c1300/1971, 419

although it is possible to make false or imperfect accounts; and some have done it ... yet ... that person who is guilty of it is to all merchants and tradesmen detestable to the last degree; ... so sacred a thing is it to keep books of accounts in time, and with the utmost rigor of truth and justice, in the manner and form of them.

North, 1714/1986, 45

The directors shall cause true accounts to be kept – of the stock in trade of the company; of the sums of money received and expended by the company and the matter in respect of which such receipt and expenditure takes place; and, of the creditors and liabilities of the company. Such accounts shall be kept upon the principle of double entry, in a cash book, journal and ledger. [Table B, Model articles of association]

UK Joint Stock Companies Act, 1856

if any clerk, officer or servant ... shall wilfully, and with intent to defraud, destroy, alter, mutilate or falsify any book, paper, writing, valuable security, or account which belongs to or is in possession of his employer ... the person so offending shall be guilty of a misdemeanor, and be liable to be kept in penal servitude for a term not exceeding seven years, or to be imprisoned with or without hard labor for any term not exceeding two years.

UK *Falsification of Accounts Act,* 1875

the fundamental principle of truthfulness in accounting . . . .

Hatfield, 1909, 170

Accounting is nothing but sublimated common sense applied to finding and telling the truth about business.

Cole, 1915, vi

Now, the success of the whole system of business depends upon the truthfulness of reports. The truthfulness of reports depends mainly on the truthfulness of accounting.

Sweeney, 1936/1964, xliii

since reliable information is the main objective of an income statement . . . no considerations of policy should prevent a true showing of the facts.

Sanders & others, 1938, 26

no part of the function of accounting can be useful unless it is truthful.

Wilcox & Hassler, 1941, 311

See also 072, 073, 331

080 Auditing

081 Audit

no system of accounts is secure from the designs of the fraudulent or the consequences of carelessness – from intentional neglect or accidental perversion. The fundamental principles of double entry are as infallible in their application as their application is extensive; but in practice they are exposed to all the moral and mental imperfections of the accountant.

Foster, 1843, I:37

an audit is an effort to discover whether or not the financial statements do actually portray the financial position and the results of operations of the company or institution under examination.

Mautz, 1954/1964, 3

In the distant past audits no doubt had their origin in the natural distrust felt by one man for another in matters where the handling of money or other valuables was at stake. The function of the auditor then was to obtain an account of a man's stewardship and to assure himself that no misappropriation of funds had taken place.

With the passage of time, as businesses grew and developed into complex organizations, this original concept of the auditor's function became impracticable and
outdated . . . . The detection of fraud should not [now] . . . be regarded as the main
purpose, or even as one of the purposes, of an audit.

Smith, 1960, 525, 526

The essential features of an audit are: (a) to make a critical review of the system
of bookkeeping, accounting and internal control (b) to make such tests and inquiries
as the auditors consider necessary to form an opinion as to the reliability of the
records as a basis for the preparation of accounts (c) to compare the profit and loss
account and balance sheet with the underlying records in order to see whether they
are in accordance therewith . . . .

ICAEW, 1961, U1

the disclosure philosophy, . . . as the fundamental principle of investor protection,
only works if the information disclosed can be safely taken as accurate. Unless
checked by some independent authority this cannot be relied on; so far as the accounts
are concerned the auditors are this independent (and usually reliable) authority.

Gower, 1969, 468

Using financial statements prepared by management . . . without the statements having
first been subjected to an independent review would be comparable to having a
judge hear a case in which he was a litigant . . . . Nevertheless, management is
logically assigned to "keep the score" because it needs similar information for its
own use in guiding the affairs of the business.

Stettler, 1970, 1

Auditing is a systematic process of objectively obtaining and evaluating evidence
regarding assertions about economic actions and events to ascertain the degree of
correspondence between those assertions and established criteria and communicating the results to interested users.

AAA, 1973, SAR6

The audit of accounts is a kind of quality control, control of the quality of the
information on which managers, investors and creditors will make judgments about
the performance and prospects of companies.

Chambers, 1973, 144

082 Audit as authentication or verification

What is required is an intelligent examination of the books, with the object of determining whether they really tally with facts.

Accountant, editorial, 1878, 5

it is the auditor's duty to conscientiously employ every faculty and exercise every
precaution in protecting the honest rights of his clients, to arrive at the true facts

and results disclosed by his examination of the accounts he is employed to audit and to report thereon impartially respecting all essential particulars.

Broaker & Chapman, 1897/1978, 45

[Formerly] students were taught that the chief objects of an audit were: (1) the detection or prevention of fraud; (2) the detection or prevention of errors .... We must [now relegate these] to a subordinate position .... [the major object now being] to ascertain the actual financial condition and earnings of an enterprise for its proprietors ... its executives ... bankers or investors ....

Montgomery, 1912/1976, 9

the original purpose of an audit was principally confined to ascertaining whether the accounting party had properly accounted for all receipts and payments on behalf of his principal, and was in fact merely a cash audit; .... [A modern audit may] be said to be such an examination of the books, accounts and vouchers of a business, as shall enable an auditor to satisfy himself whether or not the balance sheet is properly drawn up so as to exhibit a true and correct view of the state of affairs of the business, ...

Spicer & Pegler, 1914, 4

The scope of a balance sheet audit for a fiscal year ... of an industrial or mercantile corporation or firm comprises a verification of the assets and liabilities, a general examination of the profit and loss account, and, incidental thereto, an examination of the essential features of the accounting.

Federal Reserve Board (US), 1917, 271

The function of the independent certified public accountant [as auditor] is to examine a concern's accounting records and supporting data, in certain matters to obtain outside confirmations, and to require and consider supplementary explanations and information from the management and employees, to the extent necessary to enable him to form an opinion as to whether or not the financial statements as submitted present fairly the position and results of periodic operations.

AIA, 1939b, 342

The auditor's general aims may be compactly indicated by such verbs as understand, report, recommend, certify. Before he can carry out these aims he must inquire, examine, authenticate.

Littleton, 1953, 103

Originally, audits were directed primarily toward the accountability of individuals ... for money or property entrusted to them, with perhaps the most important objective the discovery of errors and irregularities. With the growing magnitude and complexity of corporations ..., the audit ... has perforce had to direct itself ... primarily to reporting upon the financial statements ... as an accounting for the business and assets entrusted to it by the owners; upon the adequacy and fairness of disclosures made in such statements; and upon whether or not accounting principles have been applied in a manner which will fairly disclose the position and results of operations.

The discovery of error and irregularities is still an objective, but not the primary one.

Broad, 1955, 38

the term, attest function (the root of which means to bear witness), seems particularly descriptive of the independent auditor's relationship to data communication.

Bevis, 1962, 28

In principle an auditor is really in no different position from any skilled inquirer. To the inquirer in any field to know by direct examination is surer proof than to believe on the hearsay of others or by inference. [per Moffitt J]

Pacific Acceptance Corporation Ltd
v Forsyth & others, 1970

See also 086, 862

083 Audit as safeguard against error and fraud

An audit, to be effectual, that is to enable the auditor to certify as to the accuracy of the accounts presented, may for practical purposes be divided into three parts, namely, to guard against (1) errors of omission; (2) errors of commission; and (3) errors of principle.

Pixley, 1881/1976, 92

The object of an audit is a two-fold one, the detection of fraud where it has been committed, and its prevention by imposing such safeguards and devising such means as will make it extremely difficult of accomplishment, even if the inclination is in that direction.

Bourne, 1887, 330

The object of the auditor should be, in the main, threefold: (1) detection of fraud, (2) discovery of errors of principle, (3) verification of the mechanical accuracy of the accounts.

Staub, 1904/1943, 91

The object of an audit may be said to be threefold: 1. the detection of fraud; 2. the detection of technical errors; 3. the detection of errors of principle.

Dicksee, 1909a, 7

The two principal reasons for which an audit may be instituted are :- (a) the detection of fraud [defalcations and fraudulent manipulation of accounts not involving defalcation], (b) the detection of errors, and coincident with these the prevention of fraud and errors by reason of the deterrent and moral effect of the audit.

Spicer & Pegler, 1914, 5

the objects of an audit are to discover errors for the purpose of ensuring that the books will show the financial position and the final results as accurately as it is possible to ascertain . . . . [The auditor] will be on the lookout for . . . clerical errors, errors due to ignorance and errors intentionally committed with the object of covering fraud.

Barton, 1923, 2

The primary function of the investigation [audit] is to enable the auditor to report on the financial statement presented to him, but the secondary objects may be stated as (a) the confirmation of the statement; (b) the detection of errors and fraud; and (c) the prevention of errors and fraud.

Taylor & Perry, 1952, 4

I take the main objective of an audit to be to enable [the auditor] to express . . . an opinion for the guidance and protection of proprietors; the detection and prevention of fraud or error may be incidental results of the audit but are not, in my opinion, objectives in themselves.

Stewart, 1957, 217

In the early days of public accounting, the audit function was primarily a police function: its objective was to detect fraud and error.

Porter & Burton, 1970, 610

the expectations gap should be met . . . by accountants providing the audit that the public wants and apparently thinks it is getting already . . . . Fraud detection must become a primary objective, not an incidental byproduct, of the audit.

Kaplan, 1987, 4

084 A conformity function

That normal function [which the independent certified public accountant has declared himself competent to serve, is] . . . to satisfy himself by generally accepted auditing standards that the representations of management appearing in related financial statements are set forth fairly and in conformity with generally accepted accounting principles consistently applied . . . . the ordinary examination of financial statements . . . precludes responsibility for the detection of defalcations because that type of examination is not sufficiently extensive for the purpose.

Stempf, 1943, 52

The extent of the responsibility assumed by the auditor is limited to (a) performing an audit in accordance with authoritative auditing standards considered appropriate in relation to existing internal controls; (b) determining whether the financial statements are prepared in conformity with accounting principles and practices having substantial authoritative support; and (c) establishing that such accounting principles and practices have been consistently applied.

AISG, 1969, 830

The primary objective of an audit examination . . . is the expression of an opinion on the fairness with which the financial statements . . . present the financial position and results of operations of the client company in accordance with principles generally accepted by the accounting profession.

Porter & Burton, 1970, 610

The objective of the ordinary examination of financial statements by the independent auditor is the expression of an opinion on the fairness with which they present financial position, results of operations and changes in financial position in conformity with generally accepted accounting principles.

AICPA, 1972c, AU110.01

Management is responsible for presenting financial statements that reflect underlying events and transactions in conformity with generally accepted accounting principles. The existing accounting framework encompasses notions such as matching, realization, and historical cost. Some criticisms of auditors' judgments are, in fact, criticisms of the accounting framework. However, preparers of financial statements and independent auditors should not be expected to make the judgment that a departure from the existing accounting framework should be made . . . . Judgment should always be exercised within the existing accounting framework, not independently of it.

Cohen Commission, 1978, 14

085 A credibility endowment function

Independence is an essential auditing standard because the opinion of the independent accountant is furnished for the purpose of adding justified credibility to financial statements which are primarily the representations of management.

Wilcox, 1952, #13:8

The possibility of error, misrepresentation, fraud in the accounts leaves the statistical creditability (figure accuracy) of the financial statements open to doubt unless the transaction sources and amounts have been tested by appropriate audit procedures.

Littleton, 1953, 177

The attest function results in the expression of an opinion by an independent expert that a communication of economic data by one party to another is fairly presented. Discharge of the function lends credibility to the representation and increases reliance upon it.

Bevis, 1962, 28

Company auditing is concerned with the creation of belief and confidence in the financial accounting information which describes the use made of economic resources

within a company over a stated period of time .... the auditor attests to the ... credibility [of the annual financial accounts] ....
$$\text{Lee, 1970, 292}$$

no one would deny that the function of the auditor, in lending credibility to financial statements, has been growing in importance, rapidly and steadily, over the last fifty years .... The role of the auditor, in lending credibility to these financial statements, is vital in establishing and maintaining confidence in the capital markets.
$$\text{Stamp, 1970a, 168}$$

The purpose of the audit is to give an independent judgment of the financial condition of a business enterprise for presentation to the client and/or to one or more interested third parties .... This opinion lends credibility to and reliance on the financial reports ....
$$\text{Montagna, 1974, 26}$$

organizations must issue stewardship reports on resource administration .... A primary function of the public accounting profession is to render independent and expert opinions on the fairness of presentation of these stewardship reports .... this function – called the attest function – fulfils the role of adding to the credibility of representations on resource stewardship .... This examination [is] called an audit.
$$\text{Willingham \& Carmichael, 1975, 3}$$

the principal purpose of independent financial auditing is to lend credibility to financial assertions and representations made by management ....
$$\text{Robertson, 1979, 68}$$

086 Independent evidence, verification

Proof should be sought outside the books in the statements of debtors and creditors themselves for comparison with the books ....
$$\text{Greer, 1882/1951, 4}$$

Verification: The act of proving any statement to be true.
$$\text{AIA, 1931a, 125}$$

When do we call a sentence true? We demand ... that the symbols should be in a certain correspondence to their objects .... Verification, therefore, is an act of comparison between the objects and the symbols.
$$\text{Reichenbach, 1938/1961, 31}$$

[Evidence] Any knowable fact or group of facts, not a legal or a logical principle, considered with a view toward its being offered before a legal tribunal for the purpose of producing a persuasion, positive or negative, on the part of the tribunal, as to the truth of a proposition, not of law or logic, on which the determination of the tribunal is to be asked.

Wigmore, 1940, I:3

Evidence is always a relative term. It signifies a relation between two facts, the *factum probandum*, or proposition to be established, and the *factum probans*, or material evidencing the proposition. The former is necessarily to be conceived of as hypothetical; it is that which the one party affirms and the other denies .... The latter is brought forward as a reality for the purpose of convincing the tribunal that the former is also a reality.

Wigmore, 1940, I:6

Anything is evidence which enables you to answer your question – the question you are asking now .... nothing is evidence except in relation to some definite question.

Collingwood, 1946, 281

Sufficient competent evidential matter is to be obtained through inspection, observation, inquiries and confirmations to afford a reasonable basis for an opinion regarding the financial statements under examination.

AIA, 1947d

the substantiation of an entry [in the books] under the date on which it is made does not prove the existence of the related asset or liability at the date of the balance sheet, nor is the value or amount of such asset or liability necessarily the same as on the date of the original entry. The auditor has the ... duty of substantiating the existence and value of such items as at the date of the balance sheet, and this work is known as verification.

Taylor & Perry, 1952, 101

Audit evidence includes any factual matter available to an auditor from which he may know or infer the relative truth or falsity of the assertions in financial statements. Competent evidential matter includes: (a) real evidence – actual examination by the auditor of the thing in question; (b) testimonial evidence – oral or written statements by people; (c) indirect evidence – documents, books and records, actions and events, and any other fact that the auditor uses in forming an opinion on financial statements.

Mautz, 1958, 46

If an auditor finds a financial statement proposition to be in accord with business facts as they appear to him at the time of examination, he can accept the proposition as true.

Mautz, 1959, 42

Once it is accepted that the auditor's duty requires him to go behind the books and determine the true financial position of the company, and so to examine the accord or otherwise of the financial position of the company, the books and the balance sheet, it follows that the possible causes to the contrary, namely, error, fraud, or unsound accounting, are the auditor's concern. [per Moffitt J]

Pacific Acceptance Corporation Ltd v.
Forsyth & others, 1970

verification is always a backward-looking procedure . . . . all evidence comes from the past.

Sterling, 1970a, 127, 149

While the Commission [SEC] does not suggest that management representations are not a significant source of evidence, it is apparent that if the independent professionalism inherent in the auditor's role is to be maintained, evidence beyond these assertions must be obtained in significant audit areas.

SEC, 1975, ASR173

the attestor [auditor] must make an examination of the objective evidence underlying the data reported . . . . The auditor . . . . attempts to satisfy himself that the data which are summarized in the statements are in fact the data and only the data which the organization actually experienced.

Willingham & Carmichael, 1975, 3, 71

by its nature evidence just cannot be defined with precision. It is simply anything that influences the auditor.

Willingham & Carmichael, 1975, 102

The effectiveness of the auditing process is not only dependent upon the attributes of the auditors . . . , but also upon the extent to which the financial information on which an audit opinion is given has been independently derived and is capable of verification.

Wolnizer, 1978, 51

The experience and wisdom of the scientific enterprise is that the most reliable facts are those that are attested to by several independent witnesses or by material evidence, such as a photograph that has been generated under identical circumstances by independent research workers.

Ziman, 1978, 56

See also 862

087 Statutory prescription of audit

the said directors . . . are hereby empowered to appoint one or more honest and able accountant or accountants which . . . shall take his corporal oath . . . to well and truly according to the best of his or their skill examine the books deeds and papers and accounts relating and belonging to the said company to see if the said accounts are fairly and regularly entered and justly made up and properly vouched and to fairly and impartially lay before the next general meeting . . . the true state of the company's accounts with such observations and informations thereon as may to him or them seem just and reasonable . . . .

Mine Adventurers Act, 1710

every joint stock company . . . shall annually at a general meeting appoint one or more auditors of the accounts of the company . . . . (s 38) . . . the auditors shall receive from the directors such accounts and balance sheet and examine the same. (s 39) . . . the auditors shall either confirm such accounts, and report generally thereon, or shall, if they do not see proper to confirm such accounts, report specially thereon, and deliver such accounts and balance sheet to the directors of the company. (s 41)

UK Joint Stock Companies Act, 1844

Once at least in every year the accounts of every banking company registered after the passing of this Act as a limited company shall be examined by an auditor or auditors, who shall be elected annually by the company in general meeting. A director or officer of the company shall not be capable of being elected as auditor. The auditor or auditors shall make a report to the members on the accounts examined . . . ; and . . . shall state whether, in his or their opinion, the balance sheet referred to in the report is a full and fair balance sheet properly drawn up, so as to exhibit a true and correct view of the state of the company's affairs, as shown by the books of the company . . . .

UK Companies Act, 1879

The auditors shall make a report to the shareholders on the accounts examined by them, and on every balance sheet laid before the company in general meeting during their tenure of office, and the report shall state (a) whether or not they have obtained all the information and explanations they have required, and (b) whether, in their opinion, the report is properly drawn up so as to exhibit a true and correct view of the state of the company's affairs according to the best of their information and the explanations given to them, and as shown by the books of the company.

UK Companies (Consolidation) Act, 1908

The expression "as shown by the books of the company" [in the report to be made by auditors under the Companies Act, 1929] does not confine the matter to a mere verification of the balance sheet by the entries in the books, but is introduced to relieve the auditors from responsibility for matters kept out of the books and concealed from them.

Buckley, 1930, 294

090 Auditor and Audit Report

091 The role of the auditor

The whole duty of an auditor may be summed up in a very few words – it is that of verifying balance sheets.

Accountant, editorial, 1881, 5

[The auditor's] business is to ascertain and state the true financial position of the company at the time of the audit . . . . A person whose duty it is to convey information to others does not discharge that duty by simply giving them so much information as is calculated to induce them, or some of them, to ask for more. Information and means of information are by no means equivalent terms . . . . an auditor who gives shareholders means of information instead of information in respect of a company's financial position does so at his peril and runs the very serious risk of being held judicially to have failed to discharge his duty. [per Lindley L J]

London & General Bank Ltd, Re, 1895

An auditor is not bound to be a detective . . . . He is a watchdog, not a bloodhound. He is justified in believing tried servants of the company . . . . He is entitled to assume that they are honest and to rely upon their representations, provided he takes reasonable care. [per Lopes L J]

Kingston Cotton Mill Co. (no.2), Re, 1896

An auditor is the critical representative of the stockholders, the reviewer of the work of the financial officers, and the supervisor of the board of directors, in case they have neglected their duties or intentionally prepared erroneous accounts or statements to be presented to their stockholders . . . . From all parts of our country, evidence is being constantly produced of the incompetency, the mismanagement, the misrepresentation and the misstatements of the directors or management of corporations. Hence, in strict justice to the honestly conducted corporations, as well as to the shareholders of the others, we hold that the qualifications and the functions of auditors should be increased.

Soulé, 1903/1976, 560

financial accounts . . . . are audited not with a view to detecting mistakes but with a view to demonstrating that there are no mistakes; and that the accounts are not merely correct in themselves, but in accordance with actual facts.

Accountant, editorial, 1907, 602

the auditor should carefully check . . . all the various figures relating to the stock . . . with the object of satisfying himself that such figures fairly represent the then market or realizable value of the stock.

Parfitt, 1907, 155

the function of the auditor is primarily to safeguard the interests of the creditor and stockholder.

JA, editorial, 1912, 360

An auditor is not to be confined to the mechanics of checking vouchers and making arithmetical computations. He is not to be written off as a professional adder-upper and subtractor. His vital task is to take care to see that errors are not made, be they errors of computation, or errors of omission or commission, or downright untruths. [per Lord Denning]

Fomento (Sterling Area) Ltd v Selsdon Fountain Pen Co Ltd, 1958

The potential conflict of interest between an entity's management and users of its financial information makes audits necessary. Audits are designed to assure the integrity of the financial information prepared by management and help safeguard the assets entrusted by shareholders and creditors. Thus audits both affect financial information and improve the entity's accountability.

Cohen Commission, 1977, xvii

The role of the independent auditor for publicly owned corporations is analogous to that of an umpire in sports. Like the umpire, an auditor must perform his or her responsibilities in a manner which assures all interested parties that the opinion given is competent and unbiased.

Metcalf Report, 1977b, 7

092 Qualifications of an auditor

Prior to 1844, the general body of proprietors tended to elect two groups of representatives. The one, designated as managers, operated the enterprise; the other, called the auditors, ascertained that the results of the managerial activities were properly reported back to the main body of proprietors. Both groups were ordinarily selected from the members of the company.

Hein, 1963, 508

One of the advantages of auditors selected from those who are interested in the property [railway companies] is that they may, if they see fit, reasonably institute an inquiry into the prudence and propriety of every charge; an auditor appointed by the government could have no right to apply any other than a mere technical audit; to inquire, is the charge legal, or is it illegal; the audit of an auditor elected by the shareholders is of a much more general character . . . .

Russell, 1849, #1920

The auditors may be members of the company; but no person is eligible as an auditor who is interested otherwise than as a member in any transaction of the company; and no director or other officer of the company is eligible during his continuance in office. [First Schedule, Table A]

UK *Companies Act*, 1862

One of the most absurd qualifications, and yet the one most frequently put forward by a candidate [for election as an auditor] is the fact of his being a shareholder, and for this reason alone most incompetent persons are frequently selected to fulfil the office . . . . those thus elected . . . . are amateurs pitted against professionals, the

bookkeeper and manager being from the nature of their occupation the latter, while auditors of the above description must most certainly be classed among amateurs.
Pixley, 1881/1976, 152

A director or officer of the company shall not be capable of being appointed auditor of the company.
UK *Companies (Consolidation) Act,* 1908

A person shall not be qualified for appointment as auditor of a company unless either (a) he is a member of a body of accountants established in the United Kingdom and for the time being recognized for the purposes of this provision by the Board of Trade; or (b) he is for the time being authorized by the Board of Trade to be so appointed either as having similar qualifications obtained outside the United Kingdom or as having adequate knowledge and experience in the course of his employment by a member of a body of accountants recognized ... or as having before [6 August 1947] practised in Great Britain as an accountant ....
UK *Companies Act,* 1948

093 Independence – of mind

a review by an independent accountant not only contemplates integrity and an independent state of mind on the part of the accountant, but also that the accountant not be connected with the company being audited or with its management or have any relationship which might give rise to a conflict of interest.
Barr, 1962, 34

Independence is an attitude of mind which goes deeper than any formal rules or standards. It is an honest disinterestedness and absolute impartiality in the expression of an opinion on the fairness of the financial statements, and connotes an unbiased and objective judgment by the auditor in the performance of his examination and in consideration of the facts which underlie the opinion ....
Newman, 1964, 148

In all matters relating to the assignment, an independence of mental attitude is to be maintained by the auditor or auditors .... To be independent, the auditor must be intellectually honest; to be recognized as independent, he must be free from any obligation to or interest in the client, its management, or its owners.
AICPA, 1972d, AU220

Independence is the essential characteristic of an auditor which provides the basis for public confidence in the integrity of his or her professional opinion. The auditor must be independent in both fact and appearance.
Metcalf Report, 1977b, 7

Professional independence . . . . is essentially an attitude of mind characterized by integrity and an objective approach to professional work. A member in public practice should be, and be seen to be, free . . . of any interest which might detract from objectivity.

CCAB, Statement 1, 1979

Independence is first and foremost a state of mind.

Mednick, 1990, 87

Independence of self-interest and other interests

an accountant cannot be deemed to be independent if he is, or has been during the period under review, an officer or director of the registrant or if he holds an interest in the registrant that is significant with respect to its total capital or his own personal fortune.

SEC, 1937, ASR2

If an audit is to be effective and reliable, it must be performed by someone who is sufficiently independent of the people whose work is under examination that he will not be either so impressed by their position, sympathetic to their point of view, or intimidated by their power to influence his own security that his procedures or conclusions will be in any way affected.

Mautz, 1954/1964, 6

Independence involves freedom from control or domination by another party and the absence of a personal interest which might improperly affect decisions to be made.

Berryman, 1960, 73

There are actually two kinds of independence which a CPA must have – independence in fact . . . the quality of not being influenced by regard to personal advantage . . . and independence in appearance . . . freedom from potential conflicts of interest which might tend to shake public confidence in his independence in fact.

Higgins, 1962, 31

The modern accountant, American or British . . . . Although theoretically he is hired by the stockholders, this usually amounts to no more than rubber-stamping a management decision. For most practical purposes, the management is the client, and the client has the leverage in the relationship. He can always get another auditor, while the auditor may not be able to get another client.

Business week, 1971, 87

The cohabitation of an accountant with the board [APB] and with his firm, company or industry is an incestuous relationship.

Trueblood, 1971, 87

The existence of conflict of interest between the preparer and user [of financial statements] makes it mandatory that the audit function be performed by one who is independent of the preparer and his interests.

AAA, 1972, 31

Because an independent audit is intended to determine the reliability of management's representations of its stewardship the audit should be performed by persons who are independent of management.

Holmes & Overmyer, 1972, 2

Many audit failures would never have happened if the accountants saw themselves as "public watchdogs", as the Supreme Court has described them (*United States v Arthur Young & Co*, 1984). Instead, far too many accountants seem to shun the unglamorous role of skeptical guardian of the public for the more charismatic posture of business advisor and confidante. They apparently see themselves as assisting corporate management, not monitoring them.

Kaplan, 1987, 6

See also 984

094 Internal control and internal check

Such a system [of internal check] implies that the accounting records, methods and details generally of an establishment are so laid out that no part of the accounts or procedure is under the absolute and independent control of any one person; that, on the contrary, the work of one employee is complementary to that of another; and that a continuous audit is made of the details of the business.

Montgomery, 1927, 67

Internal control comprises the plan of organization and all of the coordinate methods and measures adopted within a business to safeguard its assets, check the accuracy and reliability of its accounting data, promote operational efficiency, and encourage adherence to prescribed managerial policies. [modified, 1958, to deal separately with accounting controls and administrative controls]

AICPA, 1949c/1986, AU320.09

the work must be so arranged that the work of one employee serves as a check on the work of another. When possible, no single employee should be allowed to handle all or several phases of a transaction.

Easton & Newton, 1958, 116

By internal control is meant the whole system of controls, both financial and otherwise, established by the management in order to secure as far as possible the accuracy and reliability of the company's records and to safeguard its assets.

Cooper, 1966, 11

Persons having the custody or control of assets should not also be responsible for the accounting in respect of those assets. When this is unavoidable, there should be frequent independent checks of the accounting records.

Cooper, 1966, 13

In general, no one department should be responsible for handling all phases of a transaction, and, if possible, the division of responsibility should keep operations and custodianship separate from accounting.

Stettler, 1977, 56

Reliance on internal control and internal check

The auditor will do well to create, as far as possible, a system of internal checks, by which his work may be materially assisted, or even lessened. By allowing one department to have the checking of the accounts of another, a sufficiently reliable safeguard of accuracy is produced . . . .

Harvey, 1897, 374

The ordinary examination of financial statements, leading to the issuance of the standard short form of . . . [audit] report, precludes responsibility for the detection of defalcations because that type of examination is not sufficiently extensive for the purpose. The independent certified public accountant is on guard for evidence of collusive fraud but relies upon the integrity of the client's organization unless circumstances arouse doubt, in which event he extends his sampling and testing to clear the suspicion.

Stempf, 1943, 52

The prevention and detection of error and fraud is not regarded as a primary purpose of the audit [in respect of very large businesses].

Stewart, 1959, 15

In recent years there has been a growing recognition of the fact that the overriding purpose of an audit is the expression by the auditors of an independent opinion as to the truth and fairness of accounts examined by them, and not the detection of defalcations and errors. This has required a change of emphasis in auditing procedures. The verification of large numbers of detailed transactions and balances should give way to a review and assessment of the systems of internal control undertaken with the object of determining the extent to which the auditor can rely on it in framing his audit procedures.

Smith, 1960, 525

095 The audit report

the auditors . . . shall fully examine into the state of the accounts and affairs of the corporation, and shall make a just, true, and faithful report thereon . . . and shall

make a declaration . . . that such report is, to the best of their several and respective knowledge and belief, a just, true, and faithful report and statement of the accounts and affairs of the company, and that the same is made by them after diligent and careful examination into the state of such accounts and affairs . . . .
BNSW Act, 1850

A certificate in its simplest form may be described as a written declaration of some fact or facts. Accountants' certificates are usually written declarations made upon accounts which accountants are called upon to examine into and verify. They are as important in relation to what they may be made to omit to disclose, as they are in relation to what they are made to purport or reveal. What, clearly, they are required to make known is truth; what to omit, falsity.
Whitehill, 1897, 14

The certificate of the auditor or auditing committee is a simple statement of the correctness of the books and reports. It is attached to the report, and about as follows: We, the undersigned, have audited the books of the association and find them correct, and the above statement is in accordance therewith.
Bennett, 1912, 18

[Proposed form] I have audited the accounts of Blank & Co. for the period from . . . . . . to . . . . . . and I certify that the above balance sheet and statement of profit and loss have been made in accordance with the plan suggested and advised by the Federal Reserve Board and in my opinion set forth the financial condition of the firm at . . . . . . and the results of its operations for the period. (Signed)
Federal Reserve Board (US), 1917, 283

It would be desirable to hear no more of the foolish expression, "I certify that in my opinion", and the equally ridiculous, "I certify that the balance sheet and the profit and loss account are in accordance with the books", and a score of other archaic expressions. Instead it would be well to have a single straightforward statement to the client that "I or we, the accountant or accountants, have examined the records of the company both in the books and elsewhere and as a result of our investigation we believe that the condition of affairs of the company is correctly shown in the accompanying statements".
JA, editorial, 1931b, 87

The form of audit certificate suggested in 1929 [by an AIA committee] was as follows: I have examined the accounts of the . . . . company for the period from . . . . to . . . . I certify that the accompanying balance sheet and statement of profit and loss, in my opinion, set forth the financial condition of the company at . . . . and the results of operations for the period.
Carey, 1969, 160

The ultimate objective might be for the auditor's unqualified report, on publicly held companies, to contain only the following points: (1) that the report is an opinion, as contrasted with a certification of facts; (2) explicit identification of the statements reported upon; (3) a concise evaluation of the financial statements, such as that they are "fair and reasonable". An example of such a simplified auditor's report, along the lines of that presently used in the UK, follows: To the shareholders of X Co: In our opinion, the accompanying balance sheet of X Co at .... and the related statements of income (earnings), retained earnings, and source and application of funds for the year then ended are fair and reasonable.

AISG, 1969, 830

The auditors' report should state whether in their opinion: (a) the auditors have received all the information and explanations required by them. (b) the accounting procedures followed by the company are appropriate to its business. (c) the financial statements and the notes thereon have disclosed to management the results from trading for the year and the state of the company's affairs. (d) the published statements are identical with those produced to management. (e) the statements and the notes thereon do not include any items which are false or which would mislead those who read them.

Danby, 1970, 361

we cannot conceal our surprise that eleven distinguished accountants [a committee] should have concurred in perpetuating the hoary error of describing the audit report as a certificate.

Accountant, editorial, 1973, 131

Section 2500.08 of the CICA Handbook addresses itself to the auditor's opinion: "The auditors should express an opinion, or report that they are unable to express an opinion, as to whether: (a) the financial statements present fairly the financial position of the enterprise, the results of its operations and, where applicable, the source and application of its funds, and (b) the financial statements were prepared in accordance with generally accepted accounting principles applied on a basis consistent with that of the preceding period". The concept of the two part opinion is now a well established and deliberate part of the pronouncements of the CICA.

Eckel, 1973, 40

096 Audit reports - examples

Audit certificate (Aberdeen, 1586) "Heard, seen, considerit, calculat and allowit by the auditors"

s.c. Hain, 1965, 315

We the subscribers having examined and audited the accounts of William Prentis under the name of himself and company to the 25th of November last do find the same rightly stated, and that the stock of said company has been well and truly managed by him the said William Prentis and therefore we acquit and discharge him, his heirs, executors and administrators of all his past intromissions with the said stock. [Colonial Virginia]

> William Prentis and Company, c1750/ 1974, 34

We have duly examined the books and accounts of the company, and certify that the balance sheet is a fair and true statement of the assets and liabilities of the company.

> Wigan Coal and Iron Co Ltd, 1876/ 1982

I certify the above to be a true statement of the liabilities and assets of the company, according to the books, which I have examined.

> Bryant & May, 1885/1937, 916

In accordance with the Companies Act, 1900, we certify that all our requirements as auditors have been complied with. We report that, having examined the foregoing balance sheet and profit and loss account, and compared them with the books, accounts and vouchers of the company, such balance sheet is, in our opinion, properly drawn up so as to exhibit a true and correct view of the state of the company's affairs, as shown by the books of the company. [Price Waterhouse & Co]

> Barclay Perkins & Co, 1903/1981, 131

The balance sheet [of United States Steel Corporation] of 1902 carried the notation "Audited and found correct" over the auditors' signature. In the following year, this on-the-face certification was changed to read: "We have audited the above balance sheet, and certify that in our opinion it is properly drawn up so as to show the true financial position of the United States Steel Corporation and its subsidiary companies on December 31, 1903." The same wording was used on each balance sheet thereafter until 1921 when the reference to "true" was deleted.

> Claire, 1945, 45

We have audited the above balance sheet and have obtained all the information and explanations we have required. In our opinion, such balance sheet is properly drawn up so as to exhibit a true and correct view of the state of the company's affairs according to the best of our information and the explanations given to us, and as shown by the books of the company.

> Finlay & Co Ltd, 1941, 112

097 Qualified audit reports

It is a mere truism to say that the value of loans and securities depends on their realization. We are told that a statement to that effect is so unusual that the mere presence of those words is enough to excite suspicion. But . . . the duty of an auditor is to convey information, not to arouse inquiry, and although an auditor might infer from an unusual statement that something was seriously wrong, it by no means follows that ordinary people would have their suspicions aroused by a similar statement if, as in this case, its language expresses no more than any ordinary person would infer without it. [per Lindley L J]

London and General Bank Ltd, Re, 1895

[The word, accepting,] should imply that, while the accountant is not in a position to verify the statement to which it relates, yet he has no reason to believe that it is inaccurate in any respect; while the expression, subject to, should imply that the accountant is not satisfied with the conditions disclosed, and is prepared only to certify to the accuracy of the statement, excluding the item to which he takes exception.

Dickinson, 1914, 239

We have audited the balance sheet and here is our report:
The cash is overstated, the cashier being short;
The customers' receivables are very much past due,
If there are any good ones, they are very, very few;
The inventories are out of date and practically junk,
And the method of their pricing is very largely bunk;
According to our figures the enterprise is wrecked . . .
But subject to these comments, the balance sheet's correct.

AR, Anon, 1951, 197

It is not enough for auditors simply to qualify their report as [the auditors] did in 1962–64 with Associated Fire Alarms: "true and fair view, dependent on the bases of valuation referred on page . . . .". As it turned out some of the bases of valuation used . . . were ludicrous. If the auditors were not satisfied, why did they not say so, instead of sheltering behind general words of warning, and leaving it for a firm of stockbrokers to ferret out the truth.

Economist, 1966, 54

A pet hate of mine is the audit report which begins "Subject to . . . ." and ends up by failing to make clear whether the auditor's qualification is a minor reservation or a matter of real significance.

Holmes, 1974a, 60

most of today's audit reports addressed to shareholders mumble rather than proclaim, and the standardization of wording may possess the advantage of uniformity - but that is hardly an advantage when no one outside the profession really knows what the report is saying. Meaningless references to the accounting conventions used; subtle distinctions between an "except" opinion and a "subject to" opinion; a readiness to disclaim (i.e. provide a non-opinion) at the least excuse; these and other contemporary reporting quirks combine to suggest to impartial observers that, like the lemmings, auditors are motivated by nothing so much as a desire for their own extinction.

Woolf, 1979, 122

The function of qualified audit reports is often assumed to be the provision of information for shareholders .... however, the results of empirical research do not unambiguously support this presumption .... While it may have been the case prior to the 1970s that a qualification was regarded with concern by auditors and managers, the proliferation of qualifications and the survival of companies which, year after year, have suffered qualifications, may well have removed any stigma that once attached to qualified audit reports.

Craswell, 1984, 199, 216

098 The audit (expectation) gap

It is typical rather than exceptional to find that conventionally labeled institutions do not in fact perform the function that the label implies.

Lasswell, 1960, 97

Bankers, investors and the general public view the auditor's responsibilities in a far broader context than does the accounting profession .... Some auditors seem to see themselves as nonquestioning reporters working within the confines of "generally accepted accounting principles". [under caption, "The audit gap"]

Laeri, 1966, 58

The expectation gap is at the heart of the criticism of the profession. Only when this gap is narrowed and responsible levels of expectation are established as guidelines for professional conduct will the litigious environment in which we exist be sharply narrowed.

Liggio, 1974a/1977, 56

[The Commission on Auditors' Responsibilities] should consider whether a gap may exist between what the public expects or needs and what auditors can and should reasonably expect to accomplish. If such a gap does exist, it needs to be explored to determine how the disparity may be resolved. [Charge to the Commission]

Cohen Commission, 1977, xi

One of the central issues faced by the profession is the extent to which expectations of auditors and other members of the financial community are compatible as they relate to the former's obligation to detect and disclose corporate irregularities and illegal acts .... the survey data demonstrates an expectation gap between auditors and other segments of the financial community about the duty to discover deliberate material falsification of the financial statements.

Baron & others, 1977, 56–58

Essentially, the public's doubts about the profession's auditing performance result from unsatisfied expectations that the audit mission, no excuses accepted, is to prevent the publication of misleading financial statements [and] expectations that the financial reporting system will warn the public of impending business failure.

Connor, 1986, 77

divergence in outlook [between accountants and the potential users of audited statements] is customarily denominated "the expectations gap" .... Accountants typically regard as satisfactory as long as it was conducted in accordance with generally accepted auditing standards or GAAS. But who determines auditing standards and who establishes when they are generally accepted? Accountants, of course. Moreover, in many situations, the precise procedures are not codified in some public promulgation but are applied by the auditors in any given situation as they deem appropriate. Is it really surprising, then, that nonaccountants regard this GAAS-oriented definition of a satisfactory audit as rather heavy-handed, if not downright arrogant. The idea that accountants may dictate their own standards ... seems like professional hubris to investors, creditors, surety bond issuers and other laypeople - a pool of likely plaintiffs. To them, an audit failure is any audit that did not discover, or reveal, losses in major assets, understated liabilities, exaggerated profits, or any other financial deception, whether it was inflicted upon, or perpetuated by, the company and its management.

Kaplan, 1987, 1–3

There's a difference between what the public and financial statement users believe accountants and auditors are responsible for and what the accountants and auditors themselves believe they're responsible for ... the expectation gap. The public and financial statement users believe the auditor should assume more responsibility for the detection and reporting of fraud and illegal acts .... improve detection of material misstatements .... communicate ... more useful information ... including early warnings about the possibility of business failure. [In the light of this, the AICPA auditing standards board has reissued nine revised statements of auditing standards.]

Guy & Sullivan, 1988, 36

the audit expectation gap has two major components: (i) a gap between what the public expects of external auditors and the duties which auditors may reasonably be expected to perform (the feasibility gap); (ii) a gap between the duties which may reasonably be expected of auditors and auditors' performance (the performance gap).

Porter, 1990, 50

A few years ago, spokesmen for the [Australian accounting] profession started to promote the idea of a gap between the expectations of the public and the views of auditors about the nature of audit. In its simplest form, the expectation gap argument reflects the fact that accounting reports do not always reflect present market values - although many think they do.

Walker, 1991, 60

099 Comment on auditing practice

The innocent shareholder ... probably reads no more than the statement of the dividend, or the absence of a dividend, and the dignified sentence in which the auditors certify their examination of the company's accounts, and testify to their correctness. The auditors . . . . may have made the searching investigation which it was their duty to make; . . . they may have estimated each asset at its real and not its nominal value, or they may have gone through their task in a perfunctory manner . . . . If [the auditor] considers himself, as he, in fact, is, the delegate of the shareholders, chosen to protect them and to act entirely in their interests, if he looks upon officials as his natural enemies and pursues his task of investigation with fearless thoroughness, no harm can arise . . . , but many insolvent companies would be exposed before they had time to do much mischief, and investors, apart from pecuniary saving, would be more at ease in their mind in knowing the worst at once, and have the satisfaction of reflecting that there had been no opportunities for crafty knaves to reap a harvest by reading between the lines of an apparently cheering balance sheet. [reproduced also under "Fifty years ago" in *Accountant*, February 7, 1925]

Accountant, editorial, 1875, 2

auditing as carried on under the present system, is of no practical value as evidence of the true financial position of a company . . . . auditors' certificates . . . . merely certify that the balance sheet is correctly copied from the books, sometimes with the addition that the auditors have counted the cash and inspected the bill case and the security box. Audits under such conditions are a delusion and a snare.

Vanity Fair, Oct 6 1883

What is an auditor? . . . . Turning to authorities various definitions are given, such as "an officer who overlooks accounts" . . . . There is a suspicion of that definition having been taken too literally, as recent revelations in our criminal courts have testified to. [contributor to *Sydney Daily Telegraph*]

Accountant, Anon, 1892, 477

The duties of an auditor at present consist of comparing the final statement with the books supplied him, and in satisfying himself that the books are kept properly . . . . No valuation whatever is made of the assets; indeed, they may consist of mere book entries as far as he is aware. He has to accept the valuation made by the directors. To allow the directors alone to fix the value of the assets is most objectionable, as they are frequently liable to adopt values based upon their own convictions, which others would consider, at least, illusionary.

Pall Mall Gazette, Jan 17, 1894

The auditor was the shareholders' watchdog, but nowadays in many cases his other preoccupations (tax consultancy, computer or management adviser) have claimed so much of his attention that he has forgotten how to bark even, let alone bite.

Robinson, 1970, 191

Fundamentally, [the *Pacific Acceptance* case] warns the auditor in terms of the Psalmist's lament (*) and subjects to critical analysis some of the professional doctrines whose lack of logic has provided no bar to their acceptance.

*They have mouths and speak not: eyes have they and see not. They have ears, and hear not: noses have they, and smell not. They have hands and handle not; feet have they, and walk not: neither speak they through their throat. Psalm cxv, 5

Samuels, 1971, 9

Audit has changed remarkably during the past century. Auditors once examined every transaction. Later they reviewed only a sample of transactions. Then they decided it was more appropriate to concentrate on the systems used by an organization to ensure that transactions were appropriately approved and documented. An audit of a big company in the 1990s will probably involve a detailed review of only a handful of transactions.

Walker, 1991, 60

See also 986

100 THE ECONOMIC BACKGROUND OF ACCOUNTING

101 Economics and Accounting

behind the art of bookkeeping lies the science of economics.

Accountant, Anon, 1900, 353

The science of accountancy makes inquiry into the laws determining the money results of business operations. It deals with the same phenomena as economics, but it has a different end in view. It is entirely concerned with prices, with money wages and with money costs, and not at all with exchange values and with real wages or with real costs.

JA, editorial, 1909, 238

Not only are the professional origins [of economics and accountancy] different, but also from the beginning the two groups have had important diverse interests. At no time can either's field of learning be looked upon as including the other's; nor is either calling an offshoot of the other.

Canning, 1929a, 310

Both professions [accountancy and economics] . . . deal with the conduct of men in gaining a livelihood . . . but with a difference. The accountant is concerned with those activities almost exclusively as they manifest themselves in those actual, particular institutions which we call enterprises. His unit group is the business enterprise . . . . the economist, on the contrary, devotes no attention at all to real individuals or to real enterprises . . . . [To the economist,] laborers, or capitalists, or managers, or landlords . . . are functional groupings invested by the economist with standard sets of motives, aims, interests and opportunities . . . . the economist passes freely from this large group standardized in his imagination, to the hypothetical individual within the group. He describes the conduct of this imaginary individual in an imaginary market situation. The older economists were content to discuss broad qualitative type-differences almost exclusively. The accountants have always dealt in classified individual differences of a quantitative character . . . . The economist looks upon social benefit, the accountant upon individual profit, upon that which can be acquired and appropriated by certain individuals.

Canning, 1929b, 2

Economics and accounting treat of similar subject matter. Both are concerned with property and with human activities relating to . . . this property . . . . Economics

treats of society as a whole, of wealth in general . . . . Accounting sets up individual units, the property of each unit . . . . Economics is general; accounting is specific.
McKinsey & Noble, 1935, 9

in the past few years . . . . The economist, supported by a growing body of accounting opinion, was contending that conventional accounting based upon historical costs failed to represent the economic profit or loss, that when costs, incurred at various price levels, were brought together as though they were homogeneous units the results were deceptive . . . . accounting must make up its mind in the near future whether it is primarily concerned with historical monetary arithmetic or with constructive business economics. [attributed]
Alban, 1949a, 3

the underlying conceptual conflict between economists and accountants concerns futurity. Economic ideas of income, assets and net worth all look to the future for their meaning, while the corresponding financial accounts are all histories of past transactions.
Dean, 1951, 26

The urge to change the valuation basis . . . . appears to have been generated by a group of economists whose interest has been not in balance sheets but in the advancement of techniques yielding components of national income. Their point of view has been concerned with the national economy and not the individual enterprise.
Kohler, 1953, 52

the accountant on the whole is interested in what is or what has been, whereas the economist is interested in what might be . . . . Their concepts are often different because the purposes for which they are used are different.
Boulding, 1962, 50, 55

in respect of economic behavior, accounting and anticipatory analysis serve two distinctive functions, complementary functions. There can be no deliberate behavior without anticipatory calculation; the economics of the firm concerns itself with this. But there can be no valid anticipatory calculation without a foundation in the contemporary facts of the firm, its financial position at a point of time which it is the business of accounting to discover: . . . . Any attempt simply to translate the terms of economics into accounting analogues is therefore beside the point and misleading. The processes of choice and of discovery require different concepts and different viewpoints. But the processes and concepts of the two must be at least compatible, for the one depends on the other. In this lies the complementarity of accounting and economics.
Chambers, 1965a, 85

it is the expectation of profits that provides the impulse to economic activity. Thus, in economic analysis, an individual is continually being faced with alternative activities, of which he has to choose one, the basis of his choice being his assessment of the likely resulting profit. In his function of recording, the accountant, on the other hand, has no alternative to consider; his task is to measure the result of activities previously chosen and already undertaken; . . . . Each course of action actually undertaken is unique, and the accounting process is directed towards measuring a unique set of activities. This is a fundamentally different attitude from that of the economist . . . . What people do depends on what they think; the economist is concerned with what they think; the accountant is concerned with measuring the results of what they have done.

Goldberg, 1965, 251

accountants and economists analyze economic phenomena from different viewpoints. Economists wish to describe how scarce resources are allocated, and, since expectations concerning the future determine this, economists are directly concerned with such expectations. Financial accountants are concerned with describing the firm's past economic history. Hence they report the current effects of past decisions rather than describing the current expectations of decision makers. The past, then, which is irrelevant to the economist . . . is relevant to the financial accountant. The future which is irrelevant to the financial accountant . . . is relevant to the economist. The accountant in drawing upon the methodology and wisdom of the economist must ensure that the subtle differences between economics and accounting are not obscured by superficial similarities between the two disciplines.

Shwayder, 1967, 35

See also 159

110 Money and the Money Unit

111 Money and the money symbol

Money is indeed the most important thing in the world; and all sound and successful personal and national morality should have this fact for its basis.

Shaw, 1905, x

The first and most perfect instrument of economic liberty is money . . . . although within the limits of the amount of money possessed and the number of alternatives accessible.

Commons, 1924/1959, 271

The reality behind the money symbol is doctrinal, mental, and one of the most precious characteristics of mankind. But it must be used properly; that is, with proper understanding of its structure and ways of functioning. It constitutes a grave danger when misused.

Korzybski, 1933/1958, 76

no element in business is more difficult really to understand than money.

Littleton, 1934, 346

[The word, money,] may stand for (1) pieces of money (substantial reference); (2) the medium of exchange and/or store of value as such (functional reference); (3) purchasing power – conceived quantitatively; (4) liquid or short term capital (the "financial" meaning); (5) (liquid) resources in general (the "popular" meaning); (6) units of value (the "abstract" meaning).

Fraser, 1937/1947, 156

in the modern world the prime function which money as such carries out is to act as a denominator of value or unit of account, with money in a physical form performing in addition the functions of a medium of exchange. Money in a modern community thus consists of the various categories of media of exchange . . . which are referred to as purchasing power.

Gregory, 1948, X:601

112 Money as a medium of exchange

money has become in all civilized nations the universal instrument of commerce, by the intervention of which goods of all kinds are bought and sold, or exchanged for one another.

Smith, 1776/1937, I:24

Money never bears interest except in the sense of creating convenience in the process of exchange. This convenience is the special service of money and offsets the apparent loss of interest in keeping it in one's pocket instead of investing.

Fisher, 1912, 9

Money-making . . . means securing the means for the achievement of *all* those ends which are capable of achievement by the aid of purchasable commodities. Money *as such* is obviously merely a means – a medium of exchange, an instrument of calculation.

Robbins, 1935/1969, 31

Money, as money rather than a commodity, is wanted not for its own sake but for the things it will buy . . . . There are two distinct functions of money: as a medium of exchange and as a standard unit of value.

Samuelson, 1948, 55, 57

Money is the thing which serves as the generally accepted and commonly used medium of exchange. This is its only function.

von Mises, 1949, 398

money is an embodied power of choice, a medium by whose use the individual is enabled to specialize and to benefit by the specialities of others . . . . It is a medium of exchange, acceptable by anyone in any transaction – that is what constitutes its liquidity.

Croome, 1956, 6, 8

The use of money as a medium of exchange removes [the problem of a double coincidence of wants of the parties to exchanges] .... with money as a medium of exchange, everyone is free to specialize ....

Lipsey, 1972, 542

113 Money as general purchasing power

any commodity which may be required can be obtained by money. When, therefore, an individual exchanges a commodity for money, he obtains that which will give him the power of purchasing any article which he may require; ....

Fawcett, 1883, 348

money is general purchasing power, and is sought as a means to all kinds of ends ....

Marshall, 1890/1920, 22

A shilling represents to me the same power of drawing on the circle of exchange, that is the same power of securing cooperation towards the accomplishment of my purposes, whether it comes from the purse of a millionaire or a pauper; ....

Wicksteed, 1910, 189

We think of [the dollar] as a unit of value .... What it buys is the vital question .... The dollar is what the dollar buys.

Fisher, 1929, 17

A man does not value money for its own sake, but for its purchasing power – that is to say, for what it will buy. Therefore his demand is not for units of money as such, but for units of purchasing power. Since, however, there is no means of holding general purchasing power except in the form of money, his demand for purchasing power translates itself into a demand for an equivalent quantity of money.

Keynes, 1930, I:53

What is money? The simple answer is that money is what buys things – purchasing power. For it is above all of the power to buy things that most men think when the idea of money comes into their minds.

Cole, 1933, 21

the unique characteristic of money is general purchasing power.

Jones, 1956, 3

Misers apart, the value of a given quantity of money in nominal terms is determined by the quantity of goods it can purchase. It is not demanded for its own sake. At any moment of time the possession of a nominal quantity of money constitutes a certain command over goods and services and the extent of this command will depend on the general price level.

Ball, 1964, 28

114 The money unit as the common denominator of prices

Currency [money], then, by making things commensurate as a measure does, equalizes them; for there would be no association without exchange, no exchange without equality, no equality without commensurability. And so, though things so different cannot become commensurate in reality, they can become commensurate enough in relation to our needs. Hence there must be some single unit fixed . . . by a stipulation. This is why it is called currency; for this makes everything commensurate, since everything is measured in currency.

Aristotle, 4c BC/1985, #1133b

Money itself, namely that by delivery of which debt contracts and price contracts are discharged, and in the shape of which a store of general purchasing power is held, derives its character from the relationship to the money of account, since the debts and prices must first have been expressed in terms of the latter.

Keynes, 1930, I:1

Nothing but prices can . . . be expressed by evaluating things in terms of monetary units. It cannot be said that the monetary unit makes things comparable that are not logically comparable. No such magic trick is feasible. What really takes place is that things are replaced by prices for the purposes of comparison and calculation. The comparison refers to the prices, not directly to the objects themselves; the calculations are calculations with prices.

Olivecrona, 1957, 159

There persists a view that firms are concerned with particular collections of assets and therefore with the level of prices of such collections; . . . . But . . . a steel manufacturer does not receive or spend "steel money"; a food manufacturer does not pay its dividends in "food money"; a brewer does not pay wages in "beer money". If a plastic goods manufacturer wants to purchase a new machine, he cannot calculate how much "plastic money" he must pay to acquire a machine the price of which is expressed in "machinery money". Money is money to all and sundry. What they do with it is their own affair. What they do will certainly be influenced by the prices of different things – but prices expressed in the one unit common alike at any time to all buyers and sellers from housewives to tycoons.

Chambers, 1969, 642

115 The money unit as unit of account

Money, which I call of account, is no more than an arbitrary scale of equal parts, invented for measuring the respective value of things vendible. Money of account therefore is quite a different thing from money-coin, and might exist, although there was no such thing in the world as any substance which could become an adequate and proportional equivalent for every commodity.

Steuart, 1805/1966, II:408

[In an exchange economy,] a unit for the measurement of debts is indispensable .... The money of account provides a unit for the measurement of debts. It must also provide a unit for the measurement of prices .... the unit for the measurement of prices is inevitably the unit for the measurement of values.
Hawtrey, 1919, 2, 5

Money-of-account, namely that in which debts and prices and general purchasing power are expressed, is the primary concept of a theory of money .... Perhaps we may elucidate the distinction between money and money-of-account by saying that the money-of-account is the description or title and the money is the thing which answers to the description. Now if the same thing always answered to the same description, the distinction would have no practical interest. But if the thing can change, whilst the description remains the same, then the distinction can be highly significant.
Keynes, 1930, I:1, 3

the money of account in any community is an institution with an existence independent of that of the coin or currency which provides the medium for the payment of debts. The two are linked by the law which makes the coin legal tender to a value denominated in terms of the money of account.
Hawtrey, 1940, 15

let us ask what an inch is. Can an inch be picked up and handled? An inch is a distance, a creation of the mind, an idea; it can be thought of, or represented by strokes and numbers on a ruler, but itself it is intangible, invisible and insubstantial. So is the abstract side of money, the ... unit of account. We reckon in pounds, use them to compute the value of miscellaneous things; we juggle mathematically with them .... The unit of account is the vehicle of our thoughts of value, price and worth. Without it we should remain pedestrian in the economic section of the mind.
Coulborn, 1950/1957, 117

[The existence of money] makes possible the keeping of accounts and meaningful economic records and the making of economic estimates; thus it constitutes a unit of account.
Croome, 1956, 8

The terms used for the unit are – besides money of account – ideal unit, unit of account, unit of value, and monetary unit. Some authors prefer simply to use the word money for money of account. This terminology is based on the idea that the money of account is the real and true money.
Olivecrona, 1957, 77

The money unit said to be a special accounting unit

The truthfulness of accounting depends largely on the truthfulness of the dollar – and the dollar is a liar! For it says one thing and means another.
Sweeney, 1936/1964, xliii

The dollar symbol which represents an asset in the accounting equation theoretically remains unchanged as long as the physical asset itself remains unchanged. Where the quantity of that asset ... is actually reduced, then the financial symbol is proportionately reduced.
Gilman, 1939, 248

The money symbol as used in accounting should never be read as a measure of current value. It is nothing more than a special unit of accounting measurement .... It is a technical measuring device.
Irish, 1950, 217

The dollar sign (... before each amount in the financial statement) does not mean today's dollar.
Littleton, 1970, 478

See also 253, 254

116 The dated general purchasing power of money

At the same time and place, ... money is the exact measure of the real exchangeable value of all commodities. It is so, however, at the same time and place only.
Smith, 1776/1937, I:32

let us suppose that ... a government department .... having ascertained the prices of all important commodities, would publish from time to time the amount of money required to give the same general purchasing power as, say, one pound had at the beginning of 1887 .... The standard unit of purchasing power might be called ... the unit .... [All contracts and undertakings could be written in terms of the unit.] ....The public .... dislike of it even at first would be less than was their dislike of coal fires, of railways, and of gas. Ere long the currency would, I believe, be restricted to the function for which it is well fitted, of measuring and settling transactions that are completed shortly after they are begun.
Marshall, 1887/1966, 197, 199

The general purchasing power of money should properly be measured by reference to the retail prices paid by the ultimate consumers of finished goods.
Marshall, 1923, 30

the money-of-account is the term in which units of purchasing power are expressed. Money is the form in which units of purchasing power are held. The index number of the price of the composite commodity representative of consumption is the standard in which units of purchasing power are measured.
Keynes, 1930, I:55

A dollar (or a number of dollars) can be used to purchase any good or service or to liquidate any debt .... To be useful in these (and other) ways, the dollar must have a common meaning or significance to payers and receivers and holders of it. At any time that meaning is its general purchasing power at that time. If anything, a purchasing power unit is simply a dated dollar.

Chambers, 1975b, 60

117 The general purchasing power of nonmoney goods

What then is it possible to do in the way of measuring value? .... All that is practicable appears to be simply this: if I know the value of A in relation to B, and the value of B in relation to C, I can tell the value of A and C in relation to each other, and consequently their comparative power of purchasing all other commodities.

[Bailey], 1825/1967, 96

People are not usually said to buy or sell money. This, however, is merely an accident of language, In point of fact money is bought and sold like other things, whenever other things are bought and sold for money.

Mill, 1848/1940, 490

all commodities at any given time and place stand in some definite relation to each other, i.e. have certain amounts of purchasing power which are capable of numerical expression ....

Kitson, 1903, 94

The exchange value of a thing is its purchasing power or its command over other things, quite irrespective of the reasons for the existence of that power.

Laughlin, 1903, 4

when commodity values are expressed in money terms what is meant is simply that they are expressed quantitatively (or numerically) as containing so many units of purchasing power.

Fraser, 1937/1947, 149

Because the exchange values of goods are expressed in units of money we can, conversely, express the exchange value of money by the amount of goods which can be exchanged for the unit of money.

Halm, 1946, 93

If the price of goods in terms of money is the number of dollars that must be given up to obtain the goods, then the price of dollars is the amount of goods that must be given up to obtain one dollar.

Rogers, 1971, 110

if money can be used to purchase physical goods and services, clearly those goods and services can be used to purchase money .... [Goods and services exchangeable for money] entail purchasing power in no less a manner than does an amount of coins and notes, etc. equal to their selling prices.

Clarke, 1976, 394

120 The Variable Purchasing Power of Money

121 A money unit of invariant purchasing power contemplated

a commodity, which is itself continually varying in its own value, can never be an accurate measure of the value of other commodities.

Smith, 1776/1937, I:28

As nothing can be a real measure of magnitude and quantity, which is subject to variations in its own dimensions, so nothing can be a real measure of the value of other commodities, which is constantly varying in its own value.

Lauderdale, 1804/1825, 243

A standard, by reference to which we may ascertain the fluctuation in the exchangeable power of other things, must itself possess an exchangeable value fixed and unalterable.

Torrens, 1821/1965, 56

It is evidently desirable that the currency should not be subject to fluctuations of value. The ratios in which money exchanges for other commodities should be maintained as nearly as possible invariable on the average .... The whole incitement to industry and commerce and the accumulation of capital depends upon the expectation of enjoyment thence arising, and every variation of the currency tends in some degree to frustrate such expectation and to lessen the motives for exertion.

Jevons, 1875, 38, 39

Accounting reports should be based on a stable measuring unit.

Moonitz, 1961, 50

the principal criteria for a unit of measurement underlying an accounting system [include] .... the unit should represent a constant value through time.

Sandilands, 1975, 43

122 A money unit of invariant dimension not essential

Money, strictly and philosophically speaking, is ... an ideal scale of equal parts. If it be demanded what ought to be the standard value of one part? I answer, by putting another question; What is the standard length of a degree, minute or second [of arc]? It has none, and there is no necessity of its having any other than what by convention mankind think to give it.

Steuart, 1805/1966, II:411

It is . . . indispensable that the instrument employed as a measure remain unaltered, or be altered in a known degree, during its successive applications to the objects measured, in order to give us their relations to one common object.

[Bailey], 1825/1967, 107

Since [the dollar] must serve as a medium of exchange and be itself affected by the very transactions whose magnitude it measures, an abstract unit for the measurement of value will be necessary . . . . Such a unit we may call a standard dollar, which is merely the dollar of some selected period in terms of which the dollars of other periods may be evaluated.

Jones, 1935, 175

familiar objections to the use of index numbers [in income determination] . . . have not prevented their use in labor negotiations and . . . in other important ways . . . . the real question . . . is whether the imperfections of index numbers are greater or less than those of current accounting practices which ignore fluctuations in the price level.

May, 1950a, 505

we can at least present a reasonably accurate account of the results of a year in terms of the average value of the pound in that year, with appropriations [out of profits of past years or the current year] to make good previous years, and in so doing . . . preventing an overstatement of real profit.

Hartley, 1953, 139

If money is to serve as a satisfactory standard of value it is essential that its own value should be stable . . . . a unit of money which itself fluctuates widely in value is . . . useless as a measure of value . . . . In practice changes in the value of money are measured by means of index numbers which show average current prices as percentages of those of a base period . . . . a properly constructed index can give a fairly accurate measure of price changes over a moderate period of time.

Morgan, 1965, 48–50

123 The variable purchasing power of the money unit

The significance of the money unit – the accountant's yardstick – is constantly changing . . . . The value of the dollar – its general purchasing power – is subject to serious change over a period of years, and the fluctuation in a single year is not always negligible.

Paton, 1922/1962, 426

Of . . . the liability to variation of the value of money . . . the merchant, the accountant, and the commercial court, are alike unsuspicious. They hold money to be a measure of price and value, and they reckon as freely in monetary units as in units of length, area, capacity and weight.

von Mises, 1934, 204

the actual purchasing power involved in a given transaction is more important than the number of monetary units, yet it is the peculiar aptitude of accounting to record only the number of units without regard to their purchasing power.

Jones, 1935, 176

The value of money is not stable over time. By the value of money we mean what it will purchase; the value of money is the reciprocal, or inverse, of all prices. We think of the value (price) of other things as changing, but the value of money most people think of as fixed and unaltering . . . . But the value of money changes only slowly, while the prices of most other things have changed, during their history, often rapidly and by wide margins . . . .

Coulborn, 1938, 24

The first essential [to accounting for inflation] is a yardstick and the only one which is applicable to all types of assets and liabilities is the general purchasing power of money.

Wilk, 1960, 35

the dollar, as a measuring device, is unstable or elastic . . . . If the change [in the general purchasing power of the dollar] is material, the dollar at two points of time cannot, for most purposes, be added, subtracted or otherwise compared with any expectation of getting meaningful or useful results.

AICPA, 1963a, 23

It is well recognized, even by the staunchest supporters of historical accounting, that dollars of different time vintages are not of equal purchasing power.

Grady, 1965, 30

Our fundamental problem is that the laws of physical measurement and of economic measurement are very different.

Baxter, 1972, 388

The basis for using money as a unit of measure is its meaning as an index or unit of command over quantities (and varieties) of goods and services . . . . When prices generally go up or down, that power changes proportionately for everyone, quite apart from individual tastes and preferences.

May & others, 1975, 191

107

124 The value of money and the general price level reciprocally related

the purchasing power of money is the reciprocal of the level of prices . . . .
Fisher, 1912, 14

economists and statisticians . . . . have computed index numbers of prices which are trustworthy measures of the purchasing power of the dollar at various times. These numbers are measures in the inverse sense, however, for the higher prices go and the higher the price index, the lower the purchasing power of money.
Middleditch, 1918, 115

The reciprocal of a general index of prices, in a very real sense, measures the market value of dollars, ...
Jones, 1956, 28

When . . . general movements in prices occur they automatically involve changes in the value of money. If we say that prices have doubled we are implying that money has lost half its value; each unit of money will go only half as far. We can either look at the change in terms of the price level or turn it round the other way and put it in terms of the value of money.
Cairncross, 1960, 451

The general purchasing power of money and the general price level are reciprocals.
AICPA, 1969, APBS3

the value of money as an asset varies inversely with the general price level . . . . wealth held in the form of money will be decreased for individuals and the economy as a whole with increases in the price level, and increased with decreases in the price level.
Rogers, 1971, 151

A change in the money scale is reflected by a reciprocal change in the general price level.
Goldschmidt & Admon, 1977, 8

125 Inflation and deflation

By inflation we mean a period of generally rising prices. By deflation we mean a period in which most prices are falling. The root cause of inflation and deflation is a change in total money spending relative to the flow of goods offered for sale . . . . Neither in inflation nor in deflation do all prices move in the same direction or in exactly the same proportion.
Samuelson, 1948, 280

inflation is a state in which the value of money is falling, i.e. prices are rising. Deflation then becomes a state in which the value of money is rising, i.e. prices are falling.

Crowther, 1949, 107

A long term upward price trend such as we are forecasting, ... represents not a break with all past history but rather the resumption of a movement which can be traced back to classical antiquity. It is the century and a quarter [1815–1940] of prices fluctuating around a horizontal trend, beginning after the battle of Waterloo in 1815, which becomes a hiatus in the history of rising prices .... During this "stable price" period ... price declines constantly threatened, and might conceivably have eventuated except for the effects of gold discoveries and innovations in economizing the use of precious metals .... The conditions of 1815–1940, more particularly the limiting influence of the gold standard or sound money "religion", are dead and gone, perhaps forever.

Bronfenbrenner, 1950, 103–104

I am proposing to use it [the term inflation] simply as an equivalent for "a rise in the general price level" or "a fall in the value, or purchasing power, of money".

Shackle, 1966, 203

The general purchasing power of the dollar – its command over goods and services in general – varies often significantly from time to time. Changes in the general purchasing power of money are known as inflation or deflation.

AICPA, 1969, APBS3

In the 1540s Henry VIII of England debased the coinage to pay for his French wars so that prices rose, causing a sterling devaluation and much social unrest. A few years later the old coinage was replaced, and one new penny was made to equal two old ones. The economy entered a period of stagflation ... and there was more social unrest .... during the Napoleonic wars and the first half of the nineteenth century there was inflation at a decreasing rate, and in the second half of that century there was a period of deflation. In our own century we have had inflation during and immediately after the two wars, but whereas in the 'thirties it was followed by a longish period of deflation, in the period since the last war there has been continuous inflation.

Pearcy, 1971, 350

The average level of money prices is called the price level. If all money prices double, we say that the price level has doubled. An increase in the price level is called an inflation, a decrease is called a deflation.

Lipsey, 1972, 153

Inflation ... is the decline in the purchasing power of money as the general price level of goods and services rises ....

ASSC, 1974c, PSSAP7

The all time inflation record holder is 1946 Hungary which issued 100,000,000,000,000,000,000 pengo bills worth about $10US. Before World War II a pengo had been worth 20 cents. Germany between World Wars I and II suffered 4 trillion per cent inflation, and Germans pushing wheelbarrows of money often valued the wheelbarrow more highly than the currency inside.

Time, 1980, 64

inflation ... refers not to specific price changes but to a general fall in the value of money as a medium of exchange .... There is no defensible reason why rates [of inflation] applied to businesses should differ from those applied to housewives for, whatever the money affected may be, in the final analysis its worth is always measured by the same yardstick, i.e. in terms of its value in alternative uses .... there is only one rate of inflation, the rate which measures increases in the general cost of living shown in the upward movement in the general index of retail prices.

Greener, 1982, 77

126 Money not neutral in economic calculation and action

The more the evidence ... is studied, the deeper will grow the public conviction that our shifting dollar is responsible for colossal social wrongs .... our dollar is the great pickpocket, robbing first one set of persons and then another ... of billions of dollars a year, confounding business calculations, convulsing trade, stirring up discontent, fanning the flames of class hatred, perverting policies and, withal, keeping its sinister operations out of sight and unsuspected ....

Fisher, 1920, 123

money can never be merely a harmless unit of accounting or of calculation so long as it is money. Its valuation is always, in very complex ways, dependent ... on its scarcity or, in the case of inflation, on its over-abundance.

Weber, c1920/1947, 164

By a continuing process of inflation, governments can confiscate, secretly and unobserved, an important part of the wealth of their citizens. By this method they not only confiscate, but they confiscate arbitrarily; and while the process impoverishes many, it actually enriches some .... Lenin was certainly right. There is no subtler, no surer means of overturning the existing basis of society than to debauch the currency. The process engages all the hidden forces of economic law on the side of destruction, and does it in a manner that not one man in a million is able to diagnose.

Keynes, 1920, 220

both inflation and deflation bring about injustice ... both disappoint reasonable expectations ....

Coulborn, 1938, 188

Most people do not think of money holding as a speculation, because there is then no chance of making a capital loss or gain. But this is important only if we reckon gains and losses in terms of money, as most of us – because of indoctrination since childhood – have got into the habit of doing. By this fallacious reasoning, a widow who keeps her money in a stocking during the years when inflation is wiping out the value of her wealth is holding her own; when, actually, she is frittering away her inheritance.

Samuelson, 1948, 302

A serious blunder . . . was the assumption that the medium of exchange is a neutral factor only . . . . [People] tacitly assumed that changes in purchasing power occur with respect to all goods and services at the same time and to the same extent. This is, of course, what the fable of money's neutrality implies.

von Mises, 1949, 203

[Inflation] depreciates the value of the monetary unit, raises everybody's cost of living, imposes what is in effect a tax on the poorest (without exemptions) at as high a rate as the tax on the richest, wipes out the value of past earnings, redistributes wealth and income wantonly . . . . every inflation affects different persons and different prices unequally and at different times.

Hazlitt, 1960/1965, 18, 144

The variety of ways in which inflation disturbs the calculations and affairs of business is enormous. It is enough to say that inflation acts on prices and costs, and on profits and taxes. It undermines the basis on which past commitments were made, creates current and urgent pressures, and it clouds expectations about the future. It disturbs relations with customers, labor, suppliers, financial institutions, and governmental agencies, and internal relations within business firms.

Fabricant, 1976, 51

127 Differential impacts of changes in the purchasing power of money

debtors benefit and creditors suffer from a depreciation of the monetary unit, while the converse is true of monetary appreciation.

Hargreaves, 1933, 451

a company financed in large part by fixed debt has a substantial hedge against the effect of an inflation, since the creditors are being repaid in a depreciating currency.

Moonitz, 1948, 138

Inflation tends to favor debtors and profit receivers at the expense of creditors and fixed income receivers, while the effects of inflation are the opposite.

Samuelson, 1948, 280

Inflation . . . affects the real distribution of wealth away from those who hold liquid assets towards those who hold assets which are rising in price . . . . Similarly, a

deflation redistributes wealth towards those who simply sit tight with liquid assets, ...
Boulding, 1962, 54

holders of cash and similar assets always lose general purchasing power during a period of inflation, but holders of other assets may or may not lose general purchasing power during a period of inflation.
AICPA, 1969, APBS3

The person who borrows money gains from unexpected inflation because the sacrifice in terms of goods and services in repaying the debt is reduced, whereas the person who has loaned money loses because the real value of the money returned is less than the real value of the money originally given up.
Lipsey, 1972, 154

Changes in the purchasing power of the dollar affect individual enterprises differently, depending on the amount of the change and the age and composition of the enterprise's assets and equities. For example, during periods of inflation, those who hold monetary assets . . . suffer a loss in purchasing power represented by those monetary assets . . . . debtors gain because their liabilities are able to be repaid in dollars having less purchasing power.
FASB, 1974, 8

if money or the equivalent is held during a period of inflation, there will inevitably be losses in purchasing power. Conversely, there are very definite benefits to be obtained by getting into debt in a period of inflation, as the amount eventually repaid will not have the same purchasing power as the amount originally borrowed.
Kirkman, 1974, 86

the impact [of inflation] does not fall equally on either businesses or on classes of assets or costs within a business . . . . The company that is able to raise its selling prices promptly . . . is able to reflect this fact in increasing revenue figures while the company faced with competitive factors or government controls . . . must report lower revenues.
Burton, 1975, 69

Personalization of purchasing power

Money has different values in the hands of different people and different companies. In each case it depends on the use these people and companies have for this money . . . . One general index of prices designed to show changes in the value of money can have no meaning to any one person or company.
Gynther, 1962, 562

Strictly speaking there is an index of dollar purchasing power for each participant in the market process.
Paton & Paton, 1971, 334

If I wish to maintain my purchasing power, there must be an index specific to me. A general index can not – and should not be expected to – do it.
Walsh, 1973, 6

Just as a general index of prices is of little practical use to any particular individual or entity so a general index of the purchasing power of money is unlikely to be helpful. Such an index would be related to the pattern of purchases made by all individuals and all entities and would reflect the price changes experienced by an individual over a period only by chance. Just as general price changes in the abstract cannot be quantified, so no precise meaning can be attached to the concept of the general purchasing power of money in the abstract. The purchasing power of money is not an attribute of money quantifiable without a knowledge of what the money is spent on . . . . The rate of inflation will vary for different individuals and entities in the country according to the selection of goods and services which they buy.
Sandilands, 1975, 12

There are two ways of looking at inflation. In one view it is seen as an erosion in the value of the monetary unit, a decline in the currency's purchasing power. In the other view it is seen as individual changes in the specific prices affecting a firm's operations, its capital and its cash flow. These are the changes in price of the specific items and services a firm buys, makes or sells. The aggregate of these individual changes for a specific firm is not necessarily equal to the general inflation rate for the total economy.
Alexander, 1981, 8:4

Inflation, as a personalized phenomenon, contradicts all the established uses of the term . . . . it is not inflation, but how different individuals fare under inflation, which is individualistic.
Clarke, 1984, 84

See also 116

128 Stable purchasing power of the money unit assumed in certain accounting

[The accountant assumes] that the measuring unit, the dollar, is of constant value . . . . This assumption at times causes misstatement in the values of assets especially durables held over a long period of time.
Rorem, 1928, 291

Accounting . . . assumes a stable measuring unit.
Paton & Littleton, 1940, 23

the monetary unit is generally assumed to be substantially constant in value, but at times this assumption of stability has to be abandoned with the result that accounting conventions have to be modified.
May, 1943, 7

The monetary postulate . . . . Fluctuations in the value of the monetary unit, which is the accounting symbol, may properly be ignored.

AIA, 1952, 20

Ignore fluctuations of price levels as an excuse for altering data already recorded in enterprise accounts, because price changes are usually irrelevant to the objectively determined facts lodged in the accounts until the changes are particularized by actual transactions of the given enterprise.

Littleton, 1953, 196

Changes in the purchasing power of the monetary unit are not important . . . dollars of cost are intermingled in the accounts as though they were of equal purchasing power at the time incurred, although, as a matter of fact, it is well recognized that they are not. Dollars of revenue are treated as the equivalent of dollars of cost allocated to the same period regardless of any material changes in the purchasing power of the dollar between the time the costs were incurred and the time they are matched against revenues.

Blough, 1956, 13

Accounting assumes that the economic value or significance of the monetary measuring unit remains unchanged. However it is generally recognized that this never has been true and never will be.

Dilley, 1960, 542

Fluctuations in the purchasing power of the dollar, or present value of assets, are ignored in financial accounting as being irrelevant to an accounting for funds committed to, or obtained by, the accounting entity . . . . If financial accounting is supposed to account for present value, disregard of changes in purchasing power cannot be excused. But when accounting for acquisition value is the only task assumed, disregard of purchasing power –either of dollars or noncash assets – is entirely logical.

Smith & Ashburne, 1960, 52

The use of the monetary unit as the common denominator . . . assumes a stability of the measurement unit . . . . The instability of the purchasing power of the dollar is well-known . . . . Accounting records and reports are based on verifiable objective evidence and the use of subjective estimates or opinions should be avoided. It is for this reason that accounting treats all dollars alike.

Noble & Niswonger, 1961, 330

For accounting purposes, it is assumed that fluctuations in the purchasing power of the dollar will be insignificant and hence may be ignored; . . . accountants use the dollar as though it were a unit of measurement having constant dimensions.

Finney & Miller, 1968, 239

Changes through time in the general purchasing power of money may be ignored.

Lee, 1973, 14

The value of the dollar changes . . . . But at present the assumption of stability is accepted by accountants for practical reasons and should be recognised by users as a possible limitation of financial reports.

Needles & others, 1984, 28

129 The assumption of monetary stability rejected

The significance of the dollar . . . is constantly changing . . . . The units of physical science are always the same; and hence direct comparisons of situations and phenomena arising at different times can be made in this field. Accountants deal with an unstable, untrustworthy index; and, accordingly, comparisons of unadjusted accounting statements prepared at different periods are always more or less unsatisfactory and are often positively misleading.

Paton, 1920, 2

among the securely known facts of psychology, as touches the conduct of business, is the ingrained persuasion that the money unit is stable . . . . This persuasion or presumption prevails wherever the price system has gone fully into effect . . . . It affects not only the business men, properly speaking, but the underlying population as well. It is known not to accord with fact, but still it remains a principle of conduct. It has something like an instinctive force, or perhaps rather, it is something like a tropismatic reaction, in that the presumption is acted upon even when it is known to be misleading.

Veblen, 1923/1964, 179

ordinary accounting procedure is not complete because it does not include all the kinds of realized and unrealized profit and loss from changes in the value of money.

Sweeney, 1936/1964, 24

In a world of fluctuating currencies and durable equipment accountants must be prepared to face the fact that the unit in which they are measuring is unstable and, therefore, imperfect.

Edwards, 1938a, 571

In drawing up profit and loss accounts and balance sheets, the pound sterling is treated as being the stable factor in a changing world . . . . such a treatment is just as incorrect as treating dollars and pounds as the same unit.

Humphreys, 1940, 644

One of the basic assumptions of accounting is the stability of the dollar. It just isn't so.

Montgomery & others, 1949, iv

when the value of money is changing as progressively as it has done in recent years, then there is great difficulty in interpreting the published accounts of public companies so as to measure changes in capital. This difficulty arises from the use, in a long period of rising prices, of accounting methods which assume a stable value of money.

FBI, 1951

An acceptance of the assumption that the monetary unit is stable . . . under present conditions amounts to sticking one's head in the sand . . . . .

Paton & Paton, 1955, 527

When the general level of prices is rising . . . revenues are made up entirely of small current dollars while both expenses and invested capital are stated at least in part in older and larger dollars. This . . . creates a strong upward bias in nominal or apparent rates of return.

Jones, 1956, 1

130 Exchanges and Prices

131 Exchanges, transactions

Exchange of wealth . . . means the mutual and voluntary transfer of wealth between two owners, each transfer being in consideration of the other.

Fisher, 1906/1965, 11

the actual choice made by any person who actually exchanges upon the market is a choice . . . between only the actual and the next best of the potential exchanges which he has the option of making at the moment of exchange.

Commons, 1924/1959, 65

Action is an attempt to substitute a more satisfactory state of affairs for a less satisfactory one. We call such a wilfully induced alteration an exchange.

von Mises, 1949, 97

Typically, the initial appearance of an asset . . . is the result of an exchange transaction . . . supported by documents and market data. This tends to make the transaction unambiguous and objective, and the requirements for measurement are met clearly and directly . . . . Bargained price is the objective . . . result of a completed transaction.

AAA, 1957a/1957b, 3

From an accounting viewpoint a transaction is any occurrence, process, condition or decision that results in an immediate change in the asset or equity elements of an enterprise. Thus a decision to purchase an asset some time in the future is not a transaction; even the placing of an order is not a transaction.

Paton & Dixon, 1958, 61

Exchanges are reciprocal transfers of resources or obligations between the enterprise and other entities in which the enterprise either sacrifices resources or incurs obligations in order to obtain other resources or satisfy other obligations.
AICPA, 1970c, APBS4

132 Exchange said to entail inequality of [subjective] valuations

The value of what you have got is not affected by the value of what you have relinquished or forgone in order to get it . . . . You have the thing you bought, not the price you paid for it; and the thing is worth its own value, not the value of something else that you might have got instead of it but did not.
Wicksteed, 1910, 89

Subjective value must always exceed cost at the time of a purchase, otherwise no consumer's surplus would exist to provide a motive for the purchase.
MacNeal, 1939, 201

Unless Mrs Jones feels that she wants two pounds of butter more than she wants $1.60, and unless the storekeeper feels that he wants $1.60 more than two pounds of butter, the exchange will not take place . . . . An exchange, therefore, is not so much an equality (two pounds of butter = $1.60) as two inequalities.
Boulding, 1941/1955, 21

Nor does he [the consumer] benefit at the expense of the seller. In a swap, one party does not lose what the other gains. Unlike energy, which cannot be created or destroyed, the well-being of all participants is increased by trade.
Samuelson, 1948, 483

The basis of modern economics is the cognition that it is precisely the disparity in the value attached to the objects exchanged that results in their being exchanged. People buy and sell only because they appraise the things they give up less than those received.
von Mises, 1949, 205

Since both parties to an act of barter or sale must necessarily gain by it . . . there can be no equivalence between the subjective or utility values of the goods exchanged or between the good and the money paid or received for it.
Schumpeter, 1954/1967, 61

If there is to be a bargain, both parties must regard the future position as more favorable to him than the present one. Exchange presupposes difference. The idea that exchange requires "equality of value" dissolves when confronted with the facts. For each party the question is only which position he prefers: the actual one or the one expected as a result of the proposed deal.
Olivecrona, 1957, 155

An actual price . . . says nothing very precise about personal evaluations or utilities of goods. An actual price merely expresses the fact that one party is or was willing to forgo the title to units of money, and the other was willing to forgo the title to goods, at the stated price . . . . If the vendor did not value so much money more highly than so many goods, he would not engage in the transaction; for the opposite reason neither would the buyer.

> Chambers, 1966a, 73

no exchange transaction will take place in the market unless both parties to it expect it to be beneficial to them.

> Bourn, 1969a, 78

Exchanges occur if each party to the transaction values that which he will receive more than that which he must give up and if the particular exchange is evaluated as preferable to alternative actions.

> AICPA, 1970c, APBS4

See also 144

133 Exchange said to entail equality of valuations

In all business transactions there is a coequal receiving and giving of values.

> Folsom, 1873/1976, 17

A business transaction consists of an exchange of equal values . . . . every contract of a firm based upon value carries with it an exchange of equal values, though the result may be a gain or a loss.

> Soulé, 1903/1976, 21

It is the usual accounting convention to value purchases at the price paid for them, i.e. it is assumed that equal values are exchanged . . . .

> Boulding, 1950/1962, 30

Exchange is a double sided affair establishing an equality of inputs and outputs, the genesis of double entry recording.

> Bray, 1953, 74

every transaction involves a value given and a value received, and these values are assumed to be equal.

> Goetz & Klein, 1960, 126

In all business transactions equal values are exchanged. If Smith buys furniture for 400 pounds, he gives 400 pounds in cash and receives furniture to that value.

> Garbutt (ed), 1969, 0103

134 Cost taken, in accounting, as equal to value at purchase date

The accountant ... assumes that cost gives actual value for purposes of initial statement.

Paton, 1922/1962, 489

In the normal case, the acquisition of inventories and fixed assets is the result of a market transaction conducted by two parties, each acting in terms of his own self-interest. As a result, we may accept cost as the best available measure of value at the date of purchase.

Moonitz & Jordan, 1963, I:168

When plant assets are acquired the price paid – their cost – is generally regarded for accounting purposes as a fair valuation of the future benefits . . . .

Trumbull, 1963, 51

Under normal conditions, cost is a reliable indication of value at the date the [purchase] transaction is completed, because, as a general rule, a seller would not sell an asset for an amount less than its worth, nor would a purchaser pay more than an asset is worth.

Finney & Miller, 1968, 8

The initial value imputed to any newly acquired asset, other than money or a fixed claim thereto, shall be the amount of money paid or payable in exchange for it, or the money value imputed to the resources given up or transformed in producing it.

Lee, 1973, 15

135 Price and prices

In practical life, if I say that the value of a horse is 31 pounds, I am either speaking from the point of view of a buyer, . . . or . . . from the point of view of a seller . . . but I cannot mean both, for notoriously (if all the conditions remain the same) the buying and selling prices are never identical.

Wicksteed, 1888/1955, 80

The treatment of values as money prices enables the accountant to apply to the analysis and synthesis of the highly complex phenomena of production and consumption those powerful instruments of thought which are called the rules of arithmetic – for values in becoming prices take on the form of arithmetical quantities . . . . price does, as a matter of fact, tend more and more to be restricted in its use to expressing the money equivalent of the current market unit of a particular kind of commodity or service.

Branford, 1903–04, I:27, 30

Price: The consideration in money given for the purchase of a thing. It is not synonymous with value.

Bouvier's law dictionary, 1914, 2683

the independence of cost and selling price . . . . With [some] exceptions, cost and price are for any particular business man at a particular time determined by independent transactions with unrelated elements of business society.

Cole, 1921, 277

money values [prices] unavoidably constitute the base line to which transactions are finally referred, and by . . . measurements upon which they are ultimately checked, controlled, adjusted and accounted for.

Veblen, 1923/1964, 179

Prices . . . render possible the rational control of economic activity by accounting; for accounting is based upon the plan of representing all the unlike commodities, services and rights with which an enterprise is concerned as buyer or seller in terms of a money price. Most important of all for the present purpose, the margins between different prices within the system hold out that prospect of money profit which is the motive power that drives our business world.

Mitchell, 1928, 116

We call the price of a good the number of units of money which is given in exchange for one unit of it, i.e. its exchange value in terms of money; . . .

Roll, 1937, 94

price serves the purpose of a unit and a scale for adding and subtracting the importance of collections of various quantities of various things. Price, or market value, enables us to measure production.

Shackle, 1970, 14

136 Prices as signals

Prices are signs which are read by the enterpriser and which markedly affect his actions with respect to direction and volume of production . . . . It is the task of the accountant to follow market prices as, attached to specific property items, they become affected by the business process.

Paton, 1922/1962, 8, 9

the actions of the individual will be influenced by changes in current market value – in fact, the working of our economy depends on this!

Edwards, 1938b, 326

in a general way a high price will encourage production and discourage consumption, while a low price will discourage production and encourage consumption.

Boulding, 1941/1955, 109

The movement of prices on a free market establishes sensitive and continuous communication between . . . rival buyers and rival sellers through which each continually responds to the others.

Vickers, 1955, 76

company directors who ignore the signals of the market do so at their peril . . . . in the long run a market economy substitutes entrepreneurs who can read the signs of the times for those who cannot.

Lachmann, 1956, 71

price constitutes the all-important guide to production in every business enterprise.

Yang, 1959, 446

Prices . . . . transmit information effectively and efficiently; they provide an incentive to users of resources to be guided by this information; and they provide an incentive to owners of resources to follow this information.

Friedman, 1962/1968, 10

Perhaps the most outstanding feature of the market system is that its value systems and information systems are essentially the same thing. The same messages simultaneously communicate information and motivation. The main information is that of prices . . . .

Kuhn, 1963, 583

no market can adjust in isolation. A change in conditions in one market will be communicated to others; indeed, this is the social purpose of price changes, for price changes disseminate economic intelligence from the points where it originates to the points where it is needed.

Dorfman, 1964, 107

if producers allow themselves to be guided by self interest and price signals, a production packet will result that tallies exactly with the consumers' optimum.

Pen, 1966, 31

Under a system of division of labor and decentralized decision-making . . . resources, technological knowledge and wants . . . are coordinated by means of market values. Prices on the market perform as signals . . . to resource owners . . . . to ultimate purchasers of commodities . . . . [and to] entrepreneurs . . . . Changes in resources, wants or technology will affect . . . decisions [of these parties] through the effect on the market signals.

Rothenberg, 1966, 222

137 Price variations

while there is and must be a connection between present prices and anticipations of future prices, there is no necessary connection or significant value relationship

121

between present prices and past prices . . . . There is a fundamental asymmetry in price relationships through time. The future – the apparent future, that is to say – affects the present, but the past is irrelevant.
Robbins, 1935/1969, 62

In the pricing process . . . we have . . . to distinguish two different, though closely interrelated, price movements. There are, first, the relative price movements which indicate, e.g. that the consumers care more for A's than for B's product, whereupon A will be induced to expand production, to hire more men, to pay . . . higher wages, and to borrow loanable funds. These are the price movements that regulate production and distribution. But secondly there are general price movements, caused by an increase or decrease in total monetary demand, provided that the change in demand is not exactly compensated by a proportional change in total supply. These general price movements . . . are bound to disturb the structure of relative prices . . . .
Halm, 1946, 6

for goods in trade there are two types of price changes – one . . . being change in the value of money, and the other being change in the value of goods, such as might be brought about by change in the means of creating the goods or of making them available for sale.
Blackie, 1948, 1363

though the majority of prices tend to move in the same direction at the same time, it must not be thought that they all move to the same extent . . . . The prices that move most rapidly are those of certain raw materials that are traded on speculative markets . . . . The prices of manufactured goods fluctuate less than those of raw materials . . . . Wages are even slower to move . . . . At the other end of the range of volatility . . . are prices and payments that are fixed by contract.
Crowther, 1949, 91

Price changes are fundamentally of two kinds: general and specific. They reflect markedly different economic phenomena, and although it is often well nigh impossible to measure precisely one apart from the other, they must nonetheless be kept separate at the conceptual level . . . . A general price level change is a shifting in the economy-wide exchange value of the monetary unit . . . . Specific, or individual, price level changes refer to the movement in the prices of single, particular assets – presumably in response to shifting demand and supply functions.
Zeff, 1962, 612

In considering price changes, it is most important to distinguish between two different types of changes which reflect completely different aspects based on discernible influences, price level changes and relative price changes. Price level changes purport to reflect changes in the value of money . . . . The income determined . . . with data from different price levels is a composite consisting of elements with materially different meanings. The sense of financial accounting is fully destroyed .... individual price changes .... result from the state of markets .... Only these price changes can be regarded as true price changes.

Kosiol, 1966, 3

See also 173

138 Significance of current values or prices of assets

labor once spent has no influence on the future value of any article: it is gone and lost for ever. In commerce, bygones are for ever bygones; and we are always starting clear at each moment, judging the values of things with a view of future utility. Industry is essentially prospective, not retrospective ....

Jevons, 1871, 159

the cost of materials already bought is one of those matters of ancient history which has nothing to do with the question [of filling a present order] .... the sacrifice now involved in putting these materials into a given order is really represented by what the concern could realize on these materials if it did not make them up and sell them to this particular customer. This sacrifice is measured by the market price of the materials and not by their original cost.

Clark, 1923, 197

it is the present market value which expresses that competitive significance which makes property an asset.

Scott, 1929, 222

In general the prices which motivate conduct throughout the business field are those currently in effect rather than those of an earlier period.

Paton, 1941, 324

prices of the market are the ultimate fact for economic calculation .... Acting man is faced with the problem of how to take best advantage of the available supply of goods .... The actual sacrifices made and the time absorbed in their production are beside the point. These belong to the dead past.

von Mises, 1949, 217, 491

The difference between the value at the time of exchange and the proceeds of the goods is the spendable income, but the value of the goods exchanged is not in any way determined by the price originally paid for the goods or for the means of their production. No matter what the original expenditure may represent it is certainly not the value of the goods at the time of the exchange.

Goudeket, 1952, 74

As far as planning whether or not to use services previously acquired, the only monetary sacrifice involved in using them would be their selling price . . . the cash forgone by using the services rather than selling them.

Bedford, 1957, 13

a rational market decision model specifies the following prices: (1) The present selling prices of all assets held because (a) when compared to (2), they define the feasible market alternatives and (b) they completely define the investment required to maintain the *status quo*. (2) The present purchase prices of all assets not held because (a) when compared to (1), they define the feasible market alternatives, and (b) they completely define the investment required for new projects. (3) The future purchase and selling prices associated with [each] given alternative because when compared to the required investment (1b or 2b) they permit a rational decision.

Sterling, 1972, 205

139 Markets

In a competitive economic system . . . . valuations are placed upon the services of men and of other factors of production by the free play of competing interests meeting in the market . . . . the machinery of the market controls economic activity, determines incomes and adjusts conflicts of economic interests between different classes and individuals of society. The market is thus the focal point of economic organization in a competitive society.

Scott, 1925, 191

[Citing the emergence of monopolies and state regulation] fluctuating prices and instability of operating conditions which have accompanied a rapid development of large scale production have tended to create a popular conviction that regulation by competition is not working well . . . . that, as a rule, big business dominates its markets rather than is controlled by them.

Scott, 1931/1973, 71

The primary purpose of a market is to bring the intending buyers and the intending sellers of any commodity into communication with one another, so that at a given time and place no buyer need pay a higher price than any other and no seller need accept a lower price than any other. In other words, buyers and sellers compete with one another, and the market aims at ensuring to both buyers and sellers sufficient knowledge of one another's operations, and of the opportunities thereby offered, to make the competition effective.

Hawtrey, 1940, 11

In a real dynamic process one would not expect information to be diffused through the market, or to be acted upon, instantaneously. Rather, knowledge would be diffused slowly and imperfectly like an innovation in the Schumpeterian process. Time is apt to be required for those who discover information to reap their rewards, and

only gradually as it spreads to other traders will their profit opportunities be eliminated.

Baumol, 1965b, 44

All in all, one cannot escape the impression that, at best, the allocative function [of
the stock market] is performed rather imperfectly as measured by the criteria of the
welfare economist. The oligopolistic position of those who operate the market, the
brokers, the floor traders and the specialists; the random patterns which characterize
the behavior of stock prices; the apparent unresponsiveness of supply to price changes
and management's efforts to avoid the market as a source of funds, all raise some
questions about the perfection of the regulatory operations of the market.

Baumol, 1965b, 83

The market system in all its complexity of detail and simplicity of principle is
nothing but a vast information dispenser. It gathers from all persons, businesses and
nations information concerning the buying and selling propensities of all sources of
action, computes their resultant in the form of a price and re-transmits this guiding
datum to them so that, substituting it for the unknown in their action equations,
they can decide what to do.

Shackle, 1966, x

An efficient market is one in which the common price of a security reflects all
relevant information about its value . . . . In an efficient market, prices will adjust
immediately to the disclosure of previously unavailable, relevant information.

Benston, 1969, 26

Markets governed by general laws of behavior create the environment in which
accountants operate. Markets determine the values that accountants measure, classify,
record, and even . . . predict.

Mosso, 1980, 132

Isolated exchanges

the problem of isolated exchanges is indeterminate, i.e. . . . . there are many possible
ratios (within certain limits) at which exchange may take place. The determination
of the ratio in practice will depend on many circumstances, the most important of
which are the relative astuteness, perseverance, and bargaining power of the two
parties . . . . In earlier times certain goods, such as land, were legally excluded from
general exchange and could, therefore, not obtain a place on the objective scale
[market price or value in exchange]. Goods that are rare and are only infrequently
the object of exchange (certain precious stones, or old masters, for example) do not
appear on the objective scale at all . . . .

Roll, 1937, 68, 95

bargaining is a face to face contest. It is essential to disguise from the other party,
as far as you can, what you are ultimately willing to do. The bargaining situation

thus stands at the opposite pole from that of the equilibrating market, where, because of his insignificance, each individual is content to contribute his own mite of undissembled truth (his willingness to buy or supply such and such a quantity at such and such a price) and accept the solutions distilled from the combining of all such mites by the great market computer.

Shackle, 1970, 142

140 Value and Valuation

141 Diverse meanings of value

Hector: Brother, she is not worth what she doth cost the holding.
Troilus: What is aught, but as 'tis valued?

Shakespeare, *Troilus and Cressida*, II:ii

The word value . . . has two different meanings, and sometimes expresses the utility of some particular object, and sometimes the power of purchasing other goods which the possession of that object conveys. The one may be called value in use; the other value in exchange.

Smith, 1776/1937, 24

Cecil Graham: What is a cynic?
Lord Darlington: A man who knows the price of everything and the value of nothing.
Cecil Graham: And a sentimentalist, my dear Darlington, is a man who sees an absurd value in everything and doesn't know the market price of any single thing.

Wilde, 1893, *Lady Windermere's Fan*, III

Anyone who appreciates the complications of modern commerce must also appreciate that assets in business can no longer be considered as having only one value at a given time. In considering forced realization, as in bankruptcy, a certain value may be correct. In valuing for purposes of replacement, an entirely different amount may rightly be found. For purposes of determining a base for fair return in rate-making, the just value may be yet another amount. The proper value for a balance sheet may be different from any of these. The purpose to be served must determine the method to be used.

Couchman, 1924, 43

the value of a given object may be any one of the four following values: particular use value; general use value; particular exchange value; general exchange value . . . . it is apparent that money value is not an inherent quality of an object; that it is not absolute, but relative; and that it is not objective, but subjective.

Gundelfinger, 1924, 336

Value . . . may signify one of several different monetary amounts, even in the case of a single asset: cost, cost of replacement, depreciated cost . . . , selling price . . . , forced sale value ..., scrap value ..., and so forth. All these values are used in accounting under different circumstances.

Kohler & Morrison, 1926, 20

If I remember aright there was an Act of Parliament relating to finance, passed in this country [UK] some years ago, with regard to which it was said, with what truth I have not concerned myself to ascertain, that it contained twenty-seven definitions of the word value. In any event, it will be generally agreed, I think, that the word is susceptible of various shades of meaning.

Wyon, 1933, 135

The report of the special committee on accounting terminology of the American Institute of Accountants gives definitions of thirty-one different sorts of value which are met in accounting or financial transactions.

Peloubet, 1935, 205

[There are] no less than four senses in which the word [value] may be used in ordinary speech .... cost-value, exchange value, use-value and esteem-value .... So far as works on economic theory are concerned ... value means either exchange value or esteem value.

Fraser, 1937/1947, 59

At least five different meanings of the term value can be distinguished: moral good, aesthetic merit, utility, exchange value, and ideal exchange value .... In economics, value is sometimes used to mean exchange value, and sometimes to mean utility or value in use.

Cairncross, 1960, 217

142 Dated value as value in exchange (in economics)

For what's the worth of any thing?
But just as much as it will bring.

Postlethwayt, 1757, I:386

Value is a relation between contemporary commodities, because such only admit of being exchanged for each other; ....

[Bailey], 1825/1967, 72

The word value, when used without an adjunct, always means, in political economy, value in exchange ... or exchangeable value .... By the price of a thing therefore, we shall henceforth understand its value in money; by the value or exchange value of a thing, its general purchasing power; the command which its possession gives over purchasable commodities in general.

Mill, 1848/1940, 437

The value of a commodity is always supposed to mean its exchange value, for unless it has some exchange value it is not, in political economy, considered to have any value at all.
                                                                    Fawcett, 1883, 347

Value is power in exchange . . . . Where money is used, price commonly expresses power-in-exchange-for-money. Where nothing to the contrary is intimated, the price of an article is understood to be the value of that article in terms of money – the amount of money it will command in exchange.
                                                                    Walker, 1887, 5, 131

Value: The utility of an object. The worth of an object in purchasing other goods. The first may be called value in use; the latter, value in exchange. When applied without qualification to property of any description, it necessarily means the price which it will command in the market.
                                                                    Bouvier's law dictionary, 1914, 3387

Jevons in his day very wisely dispensed with the word "value", which from being stretched in this, that, and every direction, and from having countless meanings, ended by having no meaning at all; and he proposed a new term, "rate of exchange", to which he gave an exact definition. [#117]
                                                                    Pareto, 1916/1963, 62

The value of a commodity means in economics its power of commanding other commodities in exchange. It means the rate at which the commodity exchanges for others . . . . its value in exchange.
                                                                    Taussig, 1925, 111–112

Value depends upon utility, since nothing could have value unless it had the power to satisfy some want or gratify some desire . . . ; yet value is not the power to satisfy that want or to gratify that desire, but only the power to purchase other things.
                                                                    Carver, 1926, 3

any of these [durable use] goods has, in ordinary practice, two sorts of values: (1) its capital value, the value at which it could be sold outright; (2) its annual value, the price which would be paid for the right to use it during a year . . . . For the purpose of calculating the national capital, the values which are used are capital values . . . .
                                                                    Hicks, 1942/1948, 101

The values in value theory refer to market values – the market values of productive services or what embodies them and of commodities. These market values are anonymous, impersonal entities. But they are not abstract; they are concrete. They have their representation as market prices . . . . They stipulate the terms on which a commodity can be exchanged on a market.
                                                                    Rothenberg, 1966, 221

143 Dated value as value in exchange (in accounting)

Value, in the sense of political economy, means generally value in exchange, or exchangeable value .... [Commercial value] is the exchange value treated of in political economy.

Folsom, 1873/1976, 2

Value is the ratio or unit of measure of wealth existing between different commodities with reference to an exchange. It is the sole condition of wealth and the universal name given to the inherent quality or power of one thing to command another in exchange.

Soulé, 1903/1976, 21

when we try to measure the value of anything we mean the number of pounds that will be given in exchange for it – that is, its exchange value, its general purchasing power, the command which its possession gives over purchasable commodities in general. We cannot think of value apart from exchange, or from buying and selling .... the value of a thing is what it will fetch or its market value.

Carter, 1910b, 561

The value of anything is sometimes defined as that which it will fetch; and in the sale of a factory, the price at any particular time will, if there be freedom on both sides, depend .... on the supply and demand.

Matheson, 1910, 147

the layman ... inevitably associates the word "value" with exchange value ....

Smails, 1927, 105

Value may be defined as the general purchasing power of a commodity, while price is such value expressed in relation to money. The value of a thing is the amount of other commodities for which that thing can be exchanged ....

Fieldhouse & Fieldhouse, 1929, 914

I think ... that to the ordinary person not specially versed in the technicalities of business, the word "value" as applied to a thing means what that thing could be sold for.

Wyon, 1933, 135

the economic value of anything is its power in exchange which, measured in money, is its market price .... the price at which it is being bought and sold.

MacNeal, 1939, 87

The value of anything is its worth in exchange or in use at a given time and is determined normally by the acts of buyers and sellers.

Kester, 1946, 29

profit depends upon the value placed on wealth . . . this value is in the end quite fixed and definite, being the selling price of the product, for in one way or another all wealth produced is sold to consumers, including capital equipment, and its value is fixed as it, in effect, crosses the counter.

Briscoe, 1951, 41

The price (i.e. the value in exchange) of a unit of any good or service is an expression of the "bundle of things in general" which can be obtained in exchange for it.

AICPA, 1963a, 8

See also 540

144 Subjective (personal) value and valuation

Fundamentally, value resides in some one's mind, and is attributed to or read into an article, rather than residing inherently within it . . . . Value varies with individuals and according to circumstances for the same individual; . . . differential preference among men for the same things is the principal element which makes trading possible . . . . An article, therefore, . . . could conceivably have as many different values as there are individuals tentatively appraising it for themselves and as there are differing purposes actuating the individuals.

Littleton, 1929, 148

The reason primitive man preserved stores of fuel, flint or bones was because he thought that in the future they would be useful to him. In other words, he decided in his own mind that they had a value to him. Value was thus a subjective idea, and the basic concept of value has never changed from that day to this.

Peloubet, 1935, 201

The value that consists in the relation of an object – particularly of behavior – to the wish or will of an individual can be designated a subjective value, in contradistinction to the value that consists in the relation of a behavior to an objectively valid norm that can be designated as objective value . . . . Value in the subjective sense . . . is distinguished from value in the objective sense . . . by the fact that the subjective value can have various degrees. For the wish or will of an individual is capable of different degrees of intensity. But a graduation of an objective value is not possible because a behavior can only conform or not conform with an objectively valid norm, but cannot do so more or less.

Kelsen, 1960/1967, 20

The subjective value of an item . . . is that value which an individual attaches to that item according to his own special circumstances. This value naturally varies from person to person, and is the result of an individual's taste, desire and well-being. It is further influenced by time, place and circumstance.

Kollaritsch, 1965, 57

Knowledge is always retrospective .... Science is a kind of knowledge .... But values are different from knowledge; they do not come to us from the world, but they go from us to the world; they refer not to what is or was the case, but to what will or may be the case. They are, therefore, always prospective or future referential.

Caws, 1967, 49, 54

the economic worth of a set of resources is not single-valued but many-valued, there are as many such values as there are possible uses of those resources; ....

Lowe, 1970, 6

All value is subjective, existing only in the mind of the valuer. There can therefore be an infinite number of valuation models ....

Most, 1977b, 148

the market price of an asset is the result of the consensus of all market participants who assign different discounted values to the asset and have alternative uses for the asset.

Sterling, 1982b, 47

See also 132, 185

145 Valuation of a prospect

If one could approximate the whole future series of money outgoes and money receipts of an enterprise, one could find, given a rate of discount, a direct capital value of that enterprise.

Canning, 1929a, 207

Income is derived from capital goods. But the value of the income is not derived from the value of the capital goods. On the contrary, the value of the capital is derived from the value of the income. Valuation is a human process in which foresight enters. Coming events cast their shadows before. Our values are always anticipations.

Fisher, 1930a, 14

earning capacity is the fact of crucial importance in the valuation of an industrial enterprise.

AIA, 1932

what the investor or speculator is interested in is the value of the business as a whole, and that is dependent mainly on what it will produce in the future and is not determinable by any purely accounting process.

May, 1936, 19

The only way of estimating the value of the business as a whole is to estimate future receipts and future payments and discount them.

> Edwards, 1938b, 83

Value-propositions of the distinctive sort exist whenever things are appraised as to their suitability and serviceability as means, for such propositions are not about things or events that have occurred or that already exist . . . , but are about things to be brought into existence.

> Dewey, 1939/1960, 51

Earning power – not cost price, not replacement price, not sale or liquidation price – is the significant basis of enterprise value.

> Paton & Littleton, 1940, 10

Those who seek to determine the present value of a business enterprise as a going concern would do better to concentrate their attention on its earnings statements and prospects rather than its balance sheet.

> Dohr, 1941, 202

The accountants grant that the capitalized earning power is the only proper basis for valuing equity for purchase or sale . . . .

> Alexander, 1950, 40

The earning power of an enterprise is more significant than the market value of its individual assets in judging the overall worth of a business.

> Noble & Niswonger, 1961, 330

To serve as an effective resource allocator it would appear that the [stock] market should value a stock in some manner on the basis of the capitalized value of the company's expected future earnings as determined by the investment opportunities available to it.

> Baumol, 1965b, 6

It is the prospect of future earnings which determines the current value of a business. Any valuation would, therefore, be based on a speculation as to future earnings.

> Nelson, 1966, 45

When the total discounted value of any given series of conjectured [periodical] sums, to be earned by the tool in future years, has been reckoned, that total . . . , being based on conjectures, is itself a conjecture.

> Shackle, 1972, 19

146 Prospective (*ex ante*, capitalized) value of an asset

The real basis of value ... which generally guides a purchaser, is the estimated earning power, or the net revenue, past, present and prospective, as far as it can be ascertained.

Matheson, 1910, 148

The economic theorist ... will tell us that a capital instrument ... derives its value from the value of the [instrument's] future services and disservices – that the true valuation of the machine is determined by capitalizing its future money-valued service and disservice series. But unless the latter consists in bringing in a sale price either for the lathe itself or for a separately sold schedule of its technical services no series of future services independently valued in money can exist outside the imagination.

Canning, 1929b, 5

Capital, in the sense of capital value, is simply future income discounted or, in other words, capitalized. The value of any property, or rights to wealth, is its value as a source of income and is found by discounting that expected income.

Fisher, 1930b, 12

resources have value to the enterprise solely because they may be employed to yield valuable services through future time. And the amount of value to be attached to the resources at any time must necessarily be a derivative from the prospective stream of returns as now computed on the basis of information now available.

Buchanan, 1940, 211

Let us assume that the future receipts associated with the asset are known with certainty ... and that the general price level remains constant .... Then, to measure the value of any asset, we need merely capitalize its future receipts; that is, find the sum of the present values of those future receipts.

Alexander, 1950, 26

The value of an asset is the money equivalent of its service potentials .... the sum of the future market prices of all streams of service to be derived, discounted by probability and interest factors to their present worths.

AAA, 1957a/1957b, 4

Because the value of assets ... depends upon the future economic services they are capable of rendering to the business enterprise, the dollar amounts identified with the assets should be related to those anticipated benefits.

Sprouse & Moonitz, 1962, 23

Simply stated, the value of an asset in economic theory is the discounted value of its future income stream (future net cash inflow).

Corbin, 1964, 224

Let us define the investment value of a stock as the present worth of all the dividends to be paid upon it. Likewise let us define the investment value of a bond as the present worth of its future coupons and principal. In both cases, dividends, or coupons and principal, must be adjusted for expected changes in the purchasing power of money . . . . To appraise the investment value, then, it is necessary to estimate the future payments. The annuity of payments, adjusted for changes in the value of money itself, may then be discounted at the pure interest rate demanded by the investor.

Williams, 1964, 55

The value of an economic resource is, in the final analysis, the amount of future economic benefit that can be derived from it . . . . The value of an asset now is, therefore, the discounted value of net future cash receipts from the property . . . . In short, the value of an economic resource is essentially a subjective estimate.

Anderson & others, 1974, 25

The traditional approach of the economist towards the valuation problem has been to suggest that the present value of the assets of a business should be based on the streams of expected cash receipts produced by these assets, suitably discounted at an appropriate rate of interest.

Kirkman, 1974, 31

Economists measure utility in terms of cash because, being the medium of exchange, it can be exchanged at a very low transactions cost for other goods and services. Thus the value of an asset is measured in terms of the net cash flow (the monetary value of utility) it is expected to yield its owner as long as the owner expects to keep it.

Benston, 1982, 163

See also 550

147 Prospective value and dated wealth treated as cognate (or alternatives)

we call a stock, store, or accumulation of existing instruments of wealth, each instrument being measured in its own unit, capital instruments, or capital-wealth, and we call the value of this stock, when all articles are measured in a common unit, capital-value . . . . [if it is assumed that the future income is foreknown with certainty, and that the rate of interest – the ratio between income and capital – is constant] it is very simple to derive the capital-value of the income to be yielded by any article of wealth or item of property; in other words, to derive the value of that wealth or property. That value is simply the present worth of the future income from the specified capital.

Fisher, 1906/1965, 66, 202

There are two methods for computing the value of an enterprise. First, we can start with the present day cost prices of all parts of the assets of the date on the balance sheet and sum them up; second, there is the possibility of computing the earning value of an enterprise from the earnings.

Schmidt, 1930/1982, 503

For ordinary valuation purposes the future productivity concept [of capital] is the soundest in theory, but the most arbitrary and difficult in practice. On the other hand, the economic, past cost-of-production concept, which, more closely than does any other, approximates the usual, original cost valuation view so prevalent throughout the business world, is one of the weakest in theory under actual dynamic conditions of fluctuating price levels, but one of the least arbitrary and difficult in practice.

Sweeney, 1933a, 198

An asset is worth the capital value of what it produces or what a willing buyer will pay a willing seller . . . .

Anderson, 1961, 332

while some assets can be valued by reference to prices established in the market, other assets . . . such as fixed assets, work in process, etc. are not in marketable form. Therefore they must be valued by reference to the future income anticipated from their use . . . . very much a matter of highly subjective, personal opinion.

Skinner, 1961, 57

Valuation involves (i) determining the relevant concept of value for the purpose in question, and (ii) finding a method of measuring this value. There is no essential difference between the evaluation of an investment project and of assets already owned . . . . both must reflect what we intend to do with the asset(s).

Amey, 1970, 572

Where the value of the firm as a whole is the issue, there are perhaps two main concepts . . . . One concept is forward-looking, and equates the firm's value with the present value of the firm's net receipts . . . . The second concept is more down-to-earth. It finds the firm's wealth by summing values of all the separate assets (for example, in a balance sheet).

Baxter, 1971, 28

See also 553

148 Value in use

the value in use and the value in exchange of any commodity are two distinct, but connected, functions of the quantity of the commodity possessed by the persons or the community to whom it is valuable.

Wicksteed, 1888/1955, 1

it is wholly impossible to express in figures the use value of individual assets and it is therefore quite impossible to reflect such values in a balance sheet.
Weigmann, 1932, 104

once dollars have been turned into other tangible and intangible assets, the money value invested therein, the cost, ceases to have any direct bearing on their value. Value thenceforth is determined by their ability to produce income.
Daniels, 1934/1980, 33

value in exchange is essentially subjective and fleeting at best. It would seem therefore that accountants would have a direct responsibility for correctly disclosing value in use (original cost prices) but very little responsibility for exhibiting an estimate of value for exchange (replacement or market prices).
Littleton, 1935b, 270

Use-value in the objective sense is the relation between a thing and the effect it has the capacity to bring about . . . . Subjective use-value is not always based on objective use-value. There are things to which subjective use-value is attached because people erroneously believe that they have the power to bring about a desired effect.
von Mises, 1949, 120–1

Use value – the discounted present worth of future net receipts . . . .
Stanley, 1965, 44

There are many concepts of value. Value in use (user value) is the only true basis for assessing the value of a going concern.
Backer, 1973, 3

Value in use . . . of assets: resources on hand (tangible and executory contracts) measured by discounted present value of expected future cash flows adjusted for uncertainty . . . . of liabilities: discounted present value of expected future use of resources adjusted for uncertainty.
Abdel-khalik, 1992, 49

150 Wealth and Capital

151 Wealth as potentially exchangeable means

we ought to absolutely identify the sense of the word "wealth" with that which is presented to us by the words "exchangeable values."
Cournot, 1838/1963, 6

In common discourse, wealth is always expresed in money . . . . To an individual anything is wealth, which, though useless in itself, enables him to claim from others a part of their stock of things useful or pleasant . . . . Wealth, then, may be defined [as] all useful or agreeable things which possess exchangeable value . . . .

Mill, 1848/1940, 3, 7, 9

Wealth may be defined to consist of every commodity which has an exchange value . . . . exchange value is the characteristic which stamps a commodity with the attribute of wealth.

Fawcett, 1883, 6

Wealth may . . . be defined as consisting of all potentially exchangeable means of satisfying human needs.

Keynes, 1890/1930, 95

a man's wealth . . . is to be taken to be his stock of two classes of goods . . . . those material goods to which he has (by law or custom) private rights of property and which are therefore transferable and exchangeable . . . . [and] . . . . those immaterial goods which belong to him, are external to him, and serve directly as the means of enabling him to acquire material goods.

Marshall, 1890/1920, 56

By wealth (in its more restricted sense) we mean material objects owned by man and external to the owner.

Fisher, 1906/1965, 5

There is nothing in existence to represent capital except tangible things, i.e. exchangeable materials and commodities . . . . All exchangeable values other than materials and commodities, consist of personal rights of individuals which are always set off by duties to be performed by other individuals.

Leake, 1929a, 3, 4

To have economic value, an element of wealth must . . . have exchangeability. Exchangeability means that an economic resource is separable from a business as a whole and that it has value in and of itself . . . .

Andersen & Co, 1972, 14

152 Wealth as dated purchasing power

Wealth . . . is power . . . . The power which that possession [of a fortune] immediately and directly conveys to him [the possessor] is the power of purchasing: a certain command over all the labor, or over all the produce of labor, which is then in the market.

Smith, 1776/1937, 26

It is true that in the inventory of a person's fortune are included, not only the money in his actual possession, or due to him, but all other articles of value. These, however, enter not in their own character, but in virtue of the sums of money which they would sell for; and if they would sell for less, their owner is reputed less rich, though the things themselves are precisely the same.

Mill, 1848/1940, 3

this aggregate [of wealth, things valuable and transferable at a certain price] is suitably measured by its exchange value; the common standard of value, money, being taken for convenience sake. Our object in such estimates is to compare the potential control of any one individual, here and now, over purchasable commodities, with that of any other individual.

Sidgwick, 1887, 68

The value of a given quantity of wealth is found by multiplying the quantity by the [unit] price . . . . what price the article would or should fetch.

Fisher, 1906/1965, 12

Common usage in the present day confines the term "wealth" to things capable of being bought and sold, measuring the amount of wealth they represent by the quantity of money they would fetch in the market.

Hobson, 1911/1914, 9

153 Wealth held to exclude inherent or intrinsic properties

The exclusion of human qualities and capacities from the wealth category is on the whole in accordance with scientific convenience, as well as with popular thought and speech, which . . . broadly distinguishes between the able man and the wealthy man, between what a man is and what he has.

Keynes, 1890/1930, 98

[A man's wealth] excludes all his own personal qualities and faculties, even those which enable him to earn his living; because they are internal . . . . This use of the term wealth is in harmony with the usage of ordinary life . . . .

Marshall, 1890/1920, 57

The term "wealth" is used in this book to signify material objects owned by human beings . . . . [Attributes of an object] enter economic science as giving characterization to that particular kind of wealth . . . . swift horses are wealth, but not their swiftness; . . . .

Fisher, 1906/1965, 3, 39

The personality of the proprietor, his skill, his experience, though important elements of his capital, can never be brought into his balance sheets. They cannot be bought nor sold and they only make themselves manifest through the services which he does sell.

Sprague, 1907/1972, 36

In the consideration of personal accounting, that which really belongs to a person intrinsically – the intangible but inherently most valuable qualities, such as wisdom, learning, health, conscience, personality – cannot form the substance of accounting, not merely because they cannot be measured, whether in money or otherwise, but because they *are* the entity to whom the accounting must be made.

Goldberg, 1939/1948, 52

See also 151

154 Wealth said to subsist in expectations or to be subjective

we may say that those parts of the material universe which are at any time under the dominion of man constitute his capital; its ownership, his capital property; its value, his capital value; its desirability, his subjective capital. But capital in any of these senses stands for anticipated income, which consists of a stream of services or its value.

Fisher, 1906/1965, 328

Capital values are . . . by definition nothing more than future expected income multiplied by the reciprocal of the rate of interest.

Edey, 1949, 76

Wealth . . . consists of expectations of future benefit . . . . In principle, the most satisfactory measurements of wealth and profit are based on assessments of the present value of the firm and of its constituent parts.

Bourn, 1969a/1969b, 96

For decades economists have realized that income and wealth – concepts that are fundamental to accounting – are value judgments. That is, in accounting as well as in economics, concepts of income and wealth are not descriptive, but normative; not objective, but subjective; and not unique, but manifold.

Gerboth, 1973, 478

economic income . . . . is an *ex ante* concept, where wealth or capital at a point of time is given by the present value of expected future cash flows.

Ma & others, 1987, 479

See also 144, 145, 146

155 Capital as income- or product-yielding wealth

Capital is a mercantile word for their [merchants'] real effects in money or goods which actually subsist, in contradistinction to the profit that is or should be running upon them; . . . .

North, 1714/1986, Vocabulary

[When a man] possesses stock sufficient to maintain him for months or years, he naturally endeavors to derive a revenue from the greater part of it . . . . That part which, he expects, is to afford him this revenue, is called his capital.
Smith, 1776/1937, I:243

The wealth which has been accumulated with the object of assisting production is termed capital.
Fawcett, 1883, 17

the language of the market place commonly regards a man's capital as that part of his wealth which he devotes to acquiring an income in the form of money.
Marshall, 1890/1920, 71

the word capital implies a measure of wealth, and the words profit and loss imply increase of wealth and diminution of wealth.
Cooper, 1894, 1038

One can define capital straight away as the wealth set aside for gain comprehended by means of double entry bookkeeping.
Sombart, 1902/1933, 54

Capital is defined by economists as that portion of wealth which is set aside for the production of additional wealth.
Sprague, 1907/1972, 47

Capital is any wealth devoted to production.
Cole, 1921, 288

Capital is wealth committed to productive use.
Marple, 1964, 112

156 Capital as purchasing power

Capital can exist only in exchangeable value.
Leake, 1912/1976, 18

[Real capital] consists in the general purchasing power that the original investment [in an asset] represented . . . . real capital is the kind of capital that stabilized accounting endeavors to preserve. For it deducts the current expression of the real capital that was originally invested from the net amount of general purchasing power currently owned.
Sweeney, 1936/1964, 48

Capital should be defined to mean the monetary summation and expression of enterpriser's purchasing power.
Fetter, 1937, 9

Capital is the sum of the money equivalent of all assets minus the sum of the money equivalent of all liabilities as dedicated at a definite date to the conduct of the operations of a definite business unit.

von Mises, 1949, 262

[Under the purchasing power definition of capital] the capital of a corporation is viewed as being a stock of purchasing power, expressed in monetary terms, received from all sources. Thus the value of any resource would equal the current purchasing power given in exchange for it.

Ladd, 1963, 53

The firm's fortune at any moment comprises the market value at that moment of all the material objects and legal rights which it then possesses, plus the money it has, plus the debts owed to it less those it owes to others.

Shackle, 1970, 28

See also 142, 143

157 Capital as a financial concept

What then is his [a manufacturer's] capital? Precisely that part of his possessions, whatever it be, which is to constitute his fund for carrying on fresh production.

Mill, 1848/1940, 55

Capital is the sum of money in terms of which the means of profit making which are available to the enterprise are valued.

Weber, c1920/1947, 176

Capital in the original sense of the principal of a money loan, later expanded to include the worth of any kind of business asset or investment, is a purely financial conception; .... Capital .... is essentially a financial concept, relating to business investment, and includes the present market valuation of all legal rights to income possessed by natural persons.

Fetter, 1937, 6, 9

Capital is the sum of exchangeable values which serves as the basis for capitalistic enterprise. It may be money, or credit; it may be commodities.

Nussbaum, 1937, 294

In [the] value sense ... the capital of a business enterprise is no more than the sum total value of all its assets.

Buchanan, 1940, 31

It must be borne in mind, when dealing with money values, that the capital that must be kept intact is a money capital.

Davis, 1953, 17

The word capital had been part of legal and business terminology long before economists found employment for it. With the Roman jurists and their successors, it denoted
the principal of a loan . . . . it later came to denote the sums of money or their
equivalents brought by partners into a partnership or company, the sum total of a
firm's assets, and the like. Thus the concept was essentially monetary, meaning
either actual money, or claims to money, or some goods evaluated in money . . . .
What a mass of confused, futile and downright silly controversies it would have
saved us, if economists had had the sense to stick to those monetary and accounting
meanings of the term instead of trying to deepen them.

Schumpeter, 1954/1967, 322

158 Capital as capital goods

capital in the sense of a man's stock or substance is essentially a physical goods
conception.

Fetter, 1937, 6

three distinct sorts of capital: 1. real capital, a stock of goods at a point of time . . . ;
2. nominal capital, which means the contemporary value of an amount of real capital;
3. what we may call legal capital . . . which is the amount on which companies pay
fixed interest and dividends.

Coulborn, 1938, 6

The concept of capital in the sense of capital goods, or what is sometimes called
real capital, means simply (man made) instruments used for further production.

Buchanan, 1940, 30

Capital . . . consists of all those goods, existing at a particular time, which can be
used in any way so as to satisfy wants during the subsequent period.

Hicks, 1942/1948, 73

The economists' "capital" comprises fixed assets, excluding all forms of financial
investment plus inventories and deferred charges; all these the economists regard
as capital in the sense of productive power independent of any financial claims that
may be associated with them. Economists regard the whole community as beginning
an accounting period with a store of "real" assets which are the source of production during the period . . . . The store at the beginning is not regarded as a money
value . . . but as a real item consisting of physical goods . . . . An economists' balance
sheet for the whole community would be similar in form to [an accountants' balance
sheet], except that the total equity ceases to represent a proprietary interest and
becomes the community's store of assets . . . .

ICAEW & NIESR, 1951, 26

To the economist, the terms capital and investment do not refer to quantities of
money or their use in purchasing stocks and bonds. Rather, he takes them to denote

"real" assets – factories, raw materials, machinery, inventories of finished and half-finished goods (goods in process), etc. Capital, in sum, is any previously produced input or asset of a business firm or any other producer. Investment refers to the production or acquisition of any such real capital asset.

Baumol, 1965a, 408

Capital consists of goods that are used to produce other goods.

Rogers, 1971, 93

159 Capital and income in social (aggregative) and individual settings

the gain of a merchant and the gain of a nation are sometimes different; for a merchant may have a distinct interest from that of his country; and may thrive by a trade which may prove its ruin. [under "Gain"]

Rolt's *Dictionary*, 1761

In the language of business the word capital stands for a single, clear conception; in the language of economic science it stands for two unlike conceptions, and is unconsciously applied now to the one and now to the other .... Ask a manufacturer, "What is your capital?" and he will probably express his answer in dollars. Ask him, "In what is your capital invested?" and he will specify the buildings, machines, land, materials, etc. in which his productive fund now chances to be embodied. The concrete things will figure in his thought as the containers of his capital; while the content itself will appear to him to be a value, an abstract quantum of wealth .... This abstract conception of capital is employed in business a hundred times where the concrete conception is employed once. For the purposes of a scientific study of modern problems it is the primary notion of capital .... The actual practice of economic science has been to first define capital in the concrete, and then in the problems connected with it, to tacitly substitute again and again the abstract conception.

Clark, 1888/1988, 9, 11

Capital [in macroeconomics] consists at any given moment of a definite inventory of physical things .... an unambiguous physical collection. In order that capital may be kept intact, if any object embraced in this collection becomes worn out or is thrown out (scrapped), it must be replaced by equivalent objects .... From the joint work of the whole mass of productive factors there comes an (annual) inflowing stream of output. This is gross real income. When what is required to maintain capital intact is subtracted from this, there is left net real income.

Pigou, 1941, 271

In economics the capital of a community consists in the stock of goods of all sorts possessed by the community ... at a particular moment of time .... When we are considering the personal capital of particular people, we have to regard the debts owing to them as part of their capital, and the debts which they owe as deductions from their capital. This is the reason for the distinction between capital in its economic sense (capital goods) and capital in its business sense (when it may mean nothing but pieces of paper acknowledging claims).

Hicks, 1942/1948, 37, 87

in the stock of real capital [of a community] we do not include bonds, mortgages, stock shares and other paper titles to capital. Also we must be careful to exclude, from real capital formation, all capital gains or losses resulting from the writing up or down of prices.

Samuelson, 1948, 236

From the viewpoint of society the structure of debts and credits so characteristic of modern economies cancels out . . . and therefore the relevant concept of capital is the sum total of physical assets. But for the individual firm the position is not the same . . . . Footnote . . . . the distinction between rival concepts of income and capital should perhaps be drawn in respect of social income on the one hand and personal and business income on the other . . . .

Prest, 1950, 390

160 Income, Profit

161 Nominal income

When a man is engaged in business, his profits for the year are the excess of his receipts from his business during the year over his outlay for his business; the difference between the value of his stock and plant at the end and at the beginning of the year being taken as part of his receipts or as part of his outlay, according as there has been an increase or a decrease of value.

Marshall, 1890/1920, 74

We may say that a man's money income in any period is equal to the money value of his consumption plus the increase in the money value of his capital assets. For the sum of these two is the amount which he could have spent on consumption while maintaining the money value of his capital stock intact.

Meade & Stone, 1941, 219

In statics . . . . A person's income can be taken without qualification as equal to his receipts . . . . If a person expects no change in economic conditions, and expects to receive a constant flow of receipts, the same amount in every future week as he receives this week, it is reasonable to say that that amount is his income.

Hicks, 1946/1953, 172

162 Income as periodical increment in general purchasing power

Though we frequently . . . express a person's revenue by the metal pieces which are annually paid to him, it is because the amount of those pieces regulates the extent of his power of purchasing, or the value of the goods which he can annually afford to consume. We still consider his revenue as consisting in this power of purchasing or consuming, and not in the pieces which convey it.

Smith, 1776/1937, 255

[Income is] the increase or accretion in one's power to satisfy his wants in a given period in so far as that power consists of (a) money itself, or, (b) anything susceptible of valuation in terms of money. More simply stated, the definition which the economist offers is this: Income is the money value of the net accretion in one's economic power between two points of time.

Haig, 1921/1959, 59

What concerns us is the total wealth or purchasing power which a given income represents . . . the total wealth accruing to him as measured and expressed in terms of a standard of value.

Fraser, 1937/1947, 332

In order to attract purchasing power a business has to convince the owner of a purchasing power that it will yield him net advantages . . . greater than the net advantages . . . offered by any alternative investment. The net advantages will usually include an expected stream of inflowing purchasing power . . . .

Edwards, 1938b, 13

Personal income connotes, broadly, the exercise of control over the use of society's scarce resources . . . . it implies estimate of consumption and accumulation . . . . [It] may be defined as the algebraic sum of (1) the market value of rights exercised in consumption and (2) the change in the value of the store of property rights between the beginning and the end of the period in question . . . . The essential connotation of income . . . is gain to someone during a specified period and measured according to objective market standards.

Simons, 1938, 49

The significance to [any person] of the units in which his income is calculated is their purchasing power in the market over every kind of wealth.

Hawtrey, 1940, 15

the economist regards income as the change in the recipient's entire command over goods and services over a given period . . . . A man's economic income . . . can . . . be defined as the net increase in the wealth available for his consumption in a given period. An equivalent definition . . . is his consumption of wealth . . . plus [the increment in his wealth during the period, wealth being based on the market value of each item of wealth in his possession].

Alexander, 1950, 8, 13

163 Periodical income (*ex post*) defined with reference to an opening capital

The gross revenue of all the inhabitants of a great country comprehends the whole annual produce of their land and labor; the net revenue, what remains free to them after deducting the expense of maintaining – first, their fixed, and secondly, their circulating capital; or what, without encroaching on their capital, they can place in their stock reserved for immediate consumption, or spend upon their subsistence, convenience and amusements.

Smith, 1776/1937, 251

no profits can be earned unless the capital, both fixed and circulating, is maintained intact.

Dickinson, 1914, 73

It is an axiom of economics that the maintenance of invested capital is a prerequisite to the showing of profit, that a business enterprise must deduct from its gross income for any given period of time the amount of all assets consumed and all values expired in the earning of income before a figure of net income or net loss for the period can be determined.

Mason, 1937/1939, 199

a man's income may be defined as the value of his expenditure on consumption plus the value of any increase in the real amount of his capital assets. For the sum of these two is the amount he could have spent while maintaining the real amount of his capital stock intact.

Meade & Stone, 1941, 219

The purpose of income calculations in practical affairs is to give people an indication of the amount which they can consume without impoverishing themselves. Following out this idea, it would seem that we ought to define a man's income as the maximum value which he can consume during a week, and still expect to be as well off at the end of the week as he was at the beginning ... the income *ex post* of any individual is ... an objective magnitude ... [it] equals consumption plus capital accumulation.

Hicks, 1946/1953, 172, 179

the term, as well off, means as well off in terms of purchasing power or command over real, physical wealth.

Skinner, 1961, 57

The classic definition of income from economic literature states: Income is the amount of wealth that a person or other entity can dispose of during a time period and be as well off at the end of the period as at the beginning.

Anderson & others, 1974, 22

The definition of profit or income used by economists is: The income of an individual for a period is the amount that the individual can consume (spend) during that period and still be as well off at the end of the period as he was at the beginning.

Carscallen, 1977, 36

See also 613

164 Economic income said to be based on the present (discounted) value of expected net receipts

the concept of income in economics as forward looking and the concept of income in accounting as backward looking.

Buchanan, 1940, 219

The very basis of economic income is the present value of future receipts . . . . future receipts although unknown are the most important measure of the value of an asset, and so the most appropriate basis for the determination of income.

Alexander, 1950, 59

This concept of business income [the difference between dated estimates of net present value of an expected income stream] is an unattainable ideal, but it shows the importance of future flows in income measurement and it is the right arbiter in choosing the most proximate accounting treatment of specific costs and revenues.

Dean, 1951, 14

The economists, in general, seem to conceive income as an accretion to economic power between two points of time; a concept that would have to be implemented by discounting expectations; a concept that could not possibly be implemented by accounting means.

May, 1957, 36

it seems fair to describe economic income as being based on the present value of future receipts. Thus the theoretically correct way to place a value on an asset (or on a business as a whole) is to compute the present value of the expected receipts (dividends) that will be derived from it. Income for a period is equal to the net receipts of the period adjusted for the change in asset values . . . . any attempts to measure income on this basis must be highly subjective . . . .

Philips, 1963a, 16

The net worth of the concern at any point of time is the present value of . . . future revenue flows. The profit of a period is then the difference between the present values of the revenue expectations of the concern at the beginning and at the end of the period.

Bourn, 1966, 151

A company's profit for the year may ... be defined in economic terms as: The discounted net present value of all future net cash flows at the end of the year, less the discounted net present value of the future net cash flows at the beginning of the year, plus the net cash flow arising within the year after making adjustments for the introduction of new capital during the year.

Sandilands, 1975, 29

For the owner of assets, net income for a period is the difference between the economic value [sum of the expected net receipts] of the assets owned at the end of the period [and] their economic value [in real terms] at the beginning of the period, ... [adjusted] for assets added or withdrawn during the period ... [by the owner and other parties].

Benston, 1982, 165

See also 145, 146

165 Past (*ex post*) profit and expected (*ex ante*) profit necessarily different

Both kinds of income measurement [estimates made by accountants *ex post* and by economists *ex ante*] are important to management, but substituting one for the other is more misleading than is commonly supposed.

Dean, 1951, 16

a flow of income and a change in the value of expectations would seem to differ in essential characteristics sufficiently to make their treatment in separate categories desirable ....

AIA, 1952, 9

Past profit is known, a recorded fact; expected profit is a creation of the mind, in essence no more than a conjecture, however subtle and exhaustive the comparisons which the enterpriser has made between the circumstances of past success or failure and his apparent situation at the moment of deciding .... but these two meanings of the word [profit] are essentially and radically different.

Shackle, 1959/1962, 111

Accounting income is *ex post*; it ... is based on market transactions and events that have actually occurred in the past .... Economic income is *ex ante*; it evaluates expectations of future income and refers to transactions that have not yet occurred .... Each concept refers to a different period of time and set of transactions.

Barton, 1974, 672

a concern with performance implies *ex post* measures of profit and financial position; economic income and present value are *ex ante* and thus cannot throw light on performance.

Gee & Peasnell, 1976, 242

The two kinds of calculation [*ex post* and *ex ante*] are clearly related, yet their nature is quite different. The former are factual, involve measures, and may be verified. The latter are expectations, entirely subjective, and nonverifiable. To argue against some aspect of one (for example, *ex post* profit measurements) from the point of view of the other (for example, *ex ante* decision data) is to argue beside the point.

Wells, 1978, 131

170 Choice, Decision Making

171 Decision

The principle of marginal adjustments . . . runs through all the administration of our resources . . . . Terms upon which alternatives are offered and declining marginal significances as supplies increase are the universal regulators of our choice between alternatives.

Wicksteed, 1910, 114

the most essential aspect of economic action for practical purposes is the prudent choice between alternative ends . . . . Economic action is primarily oriented to the problem of choosing the end to which a thing shall be applied; technology, to the problem, given the end, of choosing the appropriate means.

Weber, c1920/1947, 147, 149

Administrative man recognizes that the world he perceives is a drastically simplified model of the buzzing, blooming confusion that constitutes the real world . . . . He makes his choices using a simple picture of the situation that takes into account just a few of the factors that he regards as most relevant and crucial.

Simon, 1949, xxv

The characteristic of human action is that it is a choice at each step between what are conceived to be several alternative courses open to us . . . . action is directed towards the future. Men are conscious of this direction, and choose one action rather than another in the conscious hope that it will lead to one rather than another kind of future.

Bronowski, 1960, 109

Decision . . . is not a mere application of logic, it is not the solving of a problem in the restricted sense of the finding of that which is known to exist uniquely though concealed. It is an act of origination, requiring something to be supplied which is not present in the evidence, the essentially and eternally insufficient evidence offered by the present about the future.

Shackle, 1961/1969, 296

a decision is the selection of a response. It is an act of adaptive behavior when the stimulus situation, the motives, and/or the possible responses are complex. The occasion for a decision arises when a change occurs at one or more stages of adaptive behavior, with the result that what was previously deemed satisfactory is now deemed unsatisfactory.

Kuhn, 1963, 304

Economics has been defined as the logic of choice. Amongst what, then, are men free to choose? Not amongst situations or events which exist or occur in some objective reality, for when something is actual the time is too late for choosing something else. Not amongst perfectly specified situations or events whose occurrence in some future time is somehow guaranteed, for there is no such perfect knowledge and no such guarantee. Men choose amongst their own imaginations of what rival policies will bring them . . . . almost none of them [economists] have said that their subject is concerned with imagination.

Shackle, 1966, ix

there can be no question of finding absolute optima of behavior – either for men or companies – because all the alternatives cannot be examined. It is, by the laws of nature, fundamentally impossible.

Beer, 1972, 65

To take a decision is to choose between branching paths into the future, in the light of their imagined or calculated end points.

Ziman, 1978, 107

any [public policy] decision maker starts with on-going activities and gradually begins to define his objective in the light of his experience with policies. In other words, decision makers do not try to get what they want; rather they learn to want by appraising what they get. Means and ends are indissolubly related, and evaluation of past decisions, or technical advice about future decisions, searches in vain for a social preference function that is not there.

Blaug, 1980/1984, 150

Choice is future-oriented, and never fully expressed in present action. It requires what is most distinctive about human reasoning – the capacity to envisage and to compare future possibilities, to make estimates, sometimes to take indirect routes to a goal or to wait.

Bok, 1983/1989, 22

172 Scarcity a precondition of choice

in every economy needs have to be restricted, demands have to be cut short, so far that they can be satisfied by aid of the available means. This is the principle of scarcity.

Cassel, 1925, 83

wealth is not wealth because of its substantial qualities. It is wealth because it is scarce . . . . Scarcity of means to satisfy ends of varying importance is an almost ubiquitous condition of human behavior. Here, then, is the unity of subject of economic science, the forms assumed by human behavior in disposing of scarce means . . . .
Robbins, 1935/1969, 47, 15

the practical man . . . must know whether what he wants to achieve will be an improvement when compared with the present state of affairs and with the advantages to be expected from other technically realizable projects which cannot be put into execution if the project he has in mind absorbs the available means. Such comparisons can only be made by the use of money prices.
von Mises, 1949, 209

Decision can take place only when several distinct and mutually exclusive acts appear to an individual to be available to him.
Shackle, 1961/1969, 4

Whether they choose to or not, human beings must choose . . . . A basic fact of life is that we cannot have everything we want.
Kuhn, 1963, 253, 262

Effective management involves timely and well-informed decisions concerning [the] scarce resources available to an enterprise . . . . [The value of assets] arises from the fact of scarcity.
Bedford & others, 1967, 4, 6

173 Volatility of the context of choice

Profit is so very fluctuating that the person who carries on a particular trade cannot always tell you himself what is the average of his annual profit. It is affected not only by every variation of price in the commodities which he deals in, but by the good or bad fortune both of his rivals and of his customers, and by a thousand other accidents to which goods . . . are liable. It varies, therefore, not only from year to year, but from day to day, and almost from hour to hour.
Smith, 1776/1937, I:78

Past valuations become obsolete because of changes in price levels, changes in technology, changes in the institutional matrix, and changes in the attitudes and beliefs of people.
Goetz & Klein, 1960, 416

Because of the vast interconnectedness of the price system . . . and the fact that it is almost impossible to change one price without setting off a vast reverberation among other prices, the ultimate effects of the change of a single price may be very different from its immediate effects.
Boulding, 1963, 195

Most firms operate in economic environments which are subject to more or less continual change – in factor supply prices, technology, products, prices, competitors' actions, expectations, and so on. They are relatively ignorant of the future course of events; they do not have perfect knowledge of what is going to happen in the future.

Barton, 1974, 677

Companies cannot and do not stand still. They grow or wither. They have no natural right to survival or existence. Every shift in customers' tastes, every strike or boycott, every interruption in the supply of power or fuel or credit, every change in the style of private or governmental spending, every change in overseas markets and foreign exchange rates – these and scores of other human, technical and financial shifts threaten the survival of some companies and provide opportunities for others. The effects of most of these shifts and changes are to raise or lower the net cash flows of companies, to increase or to reduce their wealth and progress.

Chambers, 1974a, 1

See also 123, 137

174 Uncertainty as to the future

The only risk which leads to a profit is a unique uncertainty resulting from an exercise of ultimate responsibility which in its very nature cannot be insured nor capitalized nor salaried. Profit arises out of the inherent, absolute unpredictability of things, out of the sheer brute fact that the results of human activity cannot be anticipated and then only in so far as even a probability calculation in regard to them is impossible and meaningless.

Knight, 1921/1940, 310

[Value has been said by Taussig, an economist, to be] "determined in the long run by cost to the marginal producer. . ." . . . Let us ask each of [a number of manufacturers of a claw hammer of given design and specification]: What has it cost you in past years to put this tool on the market? What do you expect it to cost you next year, or five years from now? Have you been, are you, or do you expect to be, a marginal producer? . . . . professional students of cost analysis . . . . will be aware of that intricate and ever changing condition of joint costs that prevails in modern enterprise, and that runs through from expenses of site, of housing, of purchasing materials and supplies, of operating technical equipment, of advertising, of selling, and of collecting accounts, to expenses of general administration. They will be aware too that this rationally unanalyzable mass of joint costs will be shot through and through with the variables of idle time and inadequate use of men and things and the variable prices to be paid. They will be aware too of the difficulty of writing the schedules of future prices for these hammers and the schedules of the future sales volume in them. [They] can be trusted to view with the utmost scepticism not merely what the manufacturers of these hammers may say about their costs but also the proposition of the economist about normal value or price. They will know that the information and the supporting evidence upon which the economist supposes the manufacturer to act doesn't exist. They will know that the figure representing the economist's cost of production exists only in his imagination. They will know that if a marginal producer exists at all he exists by accident. No one can pick out the marginal producers either by observing their entrance into, or withdrawal from, the market or by any other reliable objective evidence.

Canning, 1929b, 4

The outstanding fact is the extreme precariousness of the basis of knowledge on which our estimates of prospective yield have to be made. Our knowledge of the factors which will govern the yield of an investment some years hence is usually very slight and often negligible. If we speak frankly, we have to admit that our basis of knowledge for estimating the yield ten years hence of a railway, a copper mine, a textile factory, the goodwill of a patent medicine, an Atlantic liner, a building in the City of London amounts to little and sometimes to nothing; or even five years hence.

Keynes, 1936/1942, 149

The businessman never knows exactly how, for instance, a change in price or selling cost will affect sales, nor does he know exactly how much his costs will change if he increases his output . . . . the data on which he works are subject to so many errors of estimate that his decisions belong rather to the nature of an art than of a science.

Boulding, 1941/1955, 780

the future is not there to be discovered, but must be created.

Shackle, 1961/1969, 16

forecasting over the period of time for which most [security] stocks are held is at best an extremely hazardous and at worst a totally hopeless business.

Baumol, 1965b, 40

> A trend is a trend is a trend
> But the question is, will it bend?
> Will it alter its course
> Through some unforeseen force
> And come to a premature end?

Cairncross, 1969, 797

Knowledge is about the past, but decision is about the future . . . . Like all humans, the businessman is the prisoner of time. If the act of decision or choice contributes in any true sense to the making of history, if it is an act of origination, then there can be no knowing for certain what will be the consequence of any course of action which he may now begin.

Shackle, 1970, 20

Uncertainty about the future will never be resolved. All that management can hope to do is to make intelligent forecasts, and, from them, to appraise the risks and possible rewards of alternative plans of action. To look ahead intelligently, however, requires a firm present base . . . .
Isbister, 1977, 13

See also 187

175 Decision making said to be continuous

[In a society characterized by uncertainty] a condition of perfect equilibrium is no longer possible. Since productive arrangements are made on the basis of anticipations and the results actually achieved do not coincide with these as a usual thing, the oscillations will not settle down to zero . . . . The experiments by which alone the value of human judgment is determined involve a proportion of failures or errors, are never complete, and in view of human mortality have constantly to be recommenced at the beginning.
Knight, 1921/1940, 272

You maintain that you are free to take either the right- or the left-hand fork in the road. I defy you to set up a single objective criterion by which you can prove after you have made the turn that you might have made the other . . . . we must be continually prepared to find that our solutions are only partially successful . . . .
Bridgman, 1936/1964, 12, 17

repeated decisions involving constant determination of new strategic factors are necessary for the accomplishment of broad purposes or any purpose not of immediate attainment . . . . the process of decision is one of successive approximations – constant refinement of purpose, closer and closer discriminations of fact – in which the march of time is essential. Hence those who make general decisions can only envisage conditions in general and vaguely.
Barnard, 1938, 206

those in charge of the enterprise are constantly revising their expectations and their plans of operations . . . . because of a change in the relative prices of factors of production, the appearance of a new technique of production, a shift in consumers' tastes, or merely a revision of the expectations of the managers concerning any or all of these matters . . . . the plans are always in the process of gradual modification as new knowledge becomes available.
Buchanan, 1940, 186

Since circumstances, values and possible policies change constantly, the analyst knows that to attempt to solve a problem is to run the risk of achieving tomorrow a solution to yesterday's problem. He copes more successfully with fluidity therefore by attending to those changing social ills that a series of steps may remedy than by postulating more positive goals and aspiring to more fully conceived solutions.

He does not imagine that his analytical work is anything more than a continuing problem-solving process, itself fluid in nature.

                              Braybrooke & Lindblom, 1963/1970,
                              121

The basic structure of a feedback system is a loop within which the system condition provides the input to a decision process that generates action which modifies the system condition. It is a continuously circulating process. Every decision – personal, corporate, national, international, or in nature – occurs with such a context.

                              Forrester, 1968, 402

decisions must be made continuously. Some of these decisions are of a long term nature . . . . Others concern daily business operations such as hiring new personnel, ordering materials, establishing selling prices . . . .

                              Bakker, 1977, 15

Plans keep about as well as dead fish . . . .

                              Stevenson, 1980, 49

176 Group decision

the whole idea that sovereignty can be vested in a number of people is a fiction: the will of a group is always changing, never really one; its commands are really compromises, never actually the will of anyone.

                              Hall, 1956/1966, 326

At least six major defects in decision making contribute to failures to solve problems adequately [by group action]. First, the group's discussions are limited to a few alternative courses of action (often only two) without a survey of the full range of alternatives. Second, the group fails to reexamine the course of action initially preferred by the majority of members from the standpoint of nonobvious risks and drawbacks that had not been considered when it was originally evaluated. Third, the members neglect courses of action initially evaluated as unsatisfactory by the majority of the group . . . . Fourth, members make little or no attempt to obtain information from experts who can supply sound estimates of losses and gains to be expected from alternative courses of actions. Fifth, selective bias is shown in the way the group reacts to factual information and relevant judgments from experts, the mass media and outside critics . . . . Sixth, the members spend little time deliberating about how the chosen policy might be hindered by bureaucratic inertia, sabotaged by political opponents, or temporarily derailed by the common accidents that happen to the best of well laid plans.

                              Janis, 1972, 10

Normally, the advantages of group decision making are undermined by powerful psychological pressures resulting from members working closely together and sharing the same set of values . . . . Members of groups formed to make decisions show a tendency to be lenient in their judgment of the ideas of their leader or fellow members for fear of being ostracized or disciplined. They go so far as being unnecessarily strict with themselves, placing controls on their own freedom of thought . . . . there is a strong urge on the part of each member to avoid rocking the boat and this can be instrumental in persuading the individual to accept whatever proposals are promoted by the leader or a majority of the group members.

McKenna, 1978, 49

committees, though often useful for collecting facts or deciding on joint action, may not be good at finding ideas: members may think best in solitude; and, sitting in committee, they may be hampered by the need for tact and compromise, or by pressure from outside.

Baxter, 1979, 34

Secrecy can diminish the sense of personal responsibility for joint decisions and facilitate all forms of skewed or careless judgment, including that exhibited in taking needless risks. It offers participants a shield against outside criticism, and can obscure the possibilities of failure – especially if the decision makers come to think that the situation resembles a game.

Bok, 1983/1989, 109

[Groupthink] . . . comes about when well-meaning people become too close and cohesive to challenge assumptions, to check out facts, to explore new options, or to risk too much argument.

Handy, 1989, 159–160

See also 268, 825

180 Premises of Choice

181 Factual premises – knowledge of the past

we have absolutely no other means of preparing for the future except on the basis of what has already happened to us.

Bridgman, 1936/1964, 16

Statements concerning past events assume importance for actions only in so far as they lead to statements concerning the future, i.e. in so far as they furnish a basis for a determination of the weight of statements.

Reichenbach, 1938/1961, 70

the accountant has no more interest in the past than anyone else. But the past is considered for what it may teach us, and to help us in dealing with the future.

Dohr, 1953, 169

It is only by obtaining accurate information about the effects of our own behavior that we can correct and modify our own behavior.

Leavitt, 1964, 81

Facts, as far as they can be ascertained or foretold, and the inferences to be drawn from them by general reasoning and statistical analysis, provide the foundation of a good corporate plan. There is no room at all for fictions whether they are fabricated in support of the chairman's pet theory or because fabrication is easier than making an effort to discover the truth.

Broster, 1969, 293

Without a knowledge of the past, the basis for prediction will usually be lacking. Without an interest in the future, knowledge of the past is sterile.

FASB, 1980a, SFAC2

If we can obtain an accurate explanation of the past, we have identified the causal factors that will aid us in controlling the future. Surely controlling the future makes information useful; even if it does not permit it to be forecasted.

Sterling, 1982a, 73

See also 051

182 Factual premises – knowledge of present state

To realize the full measure of satisfaction that the resources at our command would enable us to secure .... we must know what we want and must distinguish the presence of things themselves from a mere assurance or conventional indication that they are there. There are people who seem hardly to reckon with any direct perceptions or experiences of their own at all. They regulate their lives, and apparently even their feelings, by symbols and indices rather than facts.

Wicksteed, 1910, 114

Present problems should be worked out with reference to present events. We cannot rule the future. We can only imagine it in terms of the present. And the only way to do that is as thoroughly as possible to know the present.

Frank, 1930/1963, 167

any advance which we undertake is immediately dependent on the data here and now at our disposal.

Schrödinger, 1935/1957, 87

We require such an understanding of the present conditions as may give us some grasp of the novelty which is about to produce a measurable influence on the immediate future.

Whitehead, 1933/1948, 114

It is reasonable . . . to be guided to a considerable degree by the facts about which we feel somewhat confident, even though they may be less decisively relevant to the issue than other facts about which our knowledge is vague and scanty. For this reason the facts of the situation enter, in a sense disproportionately, into the formation of our long term expectations; our usual practice being to take the existing situation and to project it into the future, modified only to the extent that we have more or less definite reasons for expecting a change.

Keynes, 1936/1942, 148

desires arise only when there is something the matter, when there is some trouble in an existing situation. When analyzed, this something the matter is found to spring from the fact that there is something lacking, wanting, in the existing situation as it stands, an absence which produces conflict in the elements that do exist.

Dewey, 1939/1960, 33

Policy analysts [e.g. decision makers] always begin somewhere . . . . They have an idea of present conditions, present policies, and present objectives . . . . they focus on the increments by which the social states that might result from alternative policies differ from the *status quo*.

Braybrooke & Lindblom, 1963/1970, 83

The problem of behavior is enormously complicated by the fact that behavior units have a state, condition, or structure of their own at any moment of time, which is a result of all previous outputs and inputs and may be the principal source of current outputs . . . . A stimulus . . . is a special category of input which has, as it were, a triggering effect on the state of the organization. It is the combination of the trigger plus the state or condition which produces the output or the response.

Boulding, 1970, 54

Rationality is an empty and idle term until the data available to the individual are specified. If they are incorrect, what is the good of his taking action which would be rational if they were correct? If they are essentially incomplete, conduct which assumes them to be sufficient may plunge to disaster through the gaps of knowledge which it has ignored.

Shackle, 1972, 37

The present state . . . . is the starting point for all actions or decisions.

Carrington & Howitt, 1983, 15

See also 429

183 Expectations

We frame our actions in accordance with expectations, and reasonable as well as unreasonable expectations may be falsified by the event.

Wicksteed, 1910, 122

Whether an asset is for sale, or is to be held, is clearly a question of anticipations and these are constantly changing. The owner of the orchard may decide to sell his apples now or later, and the same is true of the orchard. If the orchard is retained it is because the owner takes the view that the present value of receipts from retaining it exceeds the present value of receipts from disposing of it. In making this decision the investor looks at all the expected receipts, not some of them.

Edwards, 1938b, 155

At the beginning of the week the individual possesses a stock of consumption goods, and expects a stream of receipts which will enable him to acquire in the future other consumption goods, perishable or durable. Call this Prospect I. At the end of the week [he will have a similar but different prospect]. Call this Prospect II. Now if Prospect II were available on the first Monday, we may assume that the individual would know whether he preferred I to II on that date; . . . . But to inquire whether I on the first Monday is preferred to II on the second Monday is a nonsense question; the choice between them can never be actual at all; the terms of the comparison are not *in pari materia*.

Hicks, 1946/1953, 176

To expect is to imagine situations and events which this or that available act would make to seem possible. Decision is choice amongst available acts, and this choice is aimed at securing a preferred combination of experiences.

Shackle, 1961/1969, 13

A private judgment of value is, of its nature, essentially and inescapably, a con-jecture of what the valued object or system will be able to do, a conjecture of its potentialities, of its future. Valuation is expectation. What is vital is that expecta-tions are conjectures, let us say figments, resting on elusive, fragmentary and confusing evidence whose interpretation and suggestion can change from moment to moment with no visible cause. Valuation is expectation and expectation is imagination.

Shackle, 1972,

most, if not all, economic decision models require forecasts of one or more of the inputs [to choice].

Sterling, 1979, 90

See also 059

184 Predictions

An amusing book during the depression entitled *Oh Yeah* (Edward Angly, Viking Press, 1931) collected the predictions of the most prominent financiers, monetary experts, and economists and created uproarious laughter, so absurd did those pre-dictions appear in the light of what followed.

Arnold, 1937/1950, 200

When a prediction is offered in the light of information, somewhere in the process a law must be assumed which enables us to use the past in order to advance into the future. The test of whether or not the law is a good one is, or course, pragmatic. The more and the better are one's data on the past, the more chance one has of picking a good law for predicting the future.

Shubik, 1954, 634

All predictions, all estimates of the consequences of contemplated actions, derive from experiences of past events.

Goetz & Klein, 1960, 481

long term prophecies can be derived from scientific conditional predictions only if they apply to systems which can be described as well-isolated, stationary and recurrent. These systems are very rare in nature; and modern society is surely not one of them.

Popper, 1963/1974, 339

Prediction combines a predictor and a functional relationship to estimate attributes at some other point in time or space.

McDonald, 1967, 665

Predictive ability is one criterion for a scientific proposition . . . . However, for prediction to be significant in human affairs it is necessary that propositions be formulated in reference to experienced problems, as potential solutions to those problems. And the income projectability arguments are not supported by such propositions except in the vaguest manner.

Louderback, 1971, 305

What does not yet exist cannot now be known. The future is imagined by each man for himself and this process of the imagination is a vital part of the process of decision. But it does not make the future known.

Shackle, 1972, 3

Predictions, of course, pertain to what has not yet been observed. And they cannot be logically inferred from what has been observed; for what has happened imposes no logical restrictions on what will happen.

Goodman, 1983, 59

See also 057, 058

185 Valuation as preference ordering

A judgment of value does not measure, it arranges in a scale of degrees, it grades. It is expressive of an order of preference and sequence . . . . Only the ordinal numbers can be applied to it, but not the cardinal numbers. It is vain to speak of any calculation of values . . . . The difference between the valuation of two states of affairs is entirely psychical and personal. It is not open to any projection into the external world. It can be sensed only by the individual. It cannot be communicated or imparted to any fellow man. It is an intensive magnitude.

von Mises, 1949, 97

the process of determining preferences among consequences .... may be termed valuation. To each strategy corresponds a unique set of consequences. Rational behavior involves a listing of the consequences [of the possible strategies] in their order of preference, and the choice of that strategy which corresponds to the alternative highest on the list.

Simon, 1949, 73

an ordering [of options, on some scale of preference or value] is all that is necessary in order to pick out the optimum – that combination of quantities which stands higher on the [better-worse, or] up-down scale than any other.

Boulding, 1941/1955, 787

To prefer is to place one good or course of action higher than another in a preference rating (or preference ordering). Preference is the anticipatory mental state which precedes choice .... Value is the relative position of a good in a preference ordering, and the higher its position the greater is its value.

Kuhn, 1963, 265

valuation, the central theme of accounting, is a procedure by which numerals are assigned to objects or events according to rules ... in order to express preferences with regard to particular actions .... The numeral which usually expresses this preference order is called the value.

Mattessich, 1964, 144, 221

A preference ordering arranges a series of objects in the order in which they are preferred. It says something about the person who does the ordering, but it says nothing about the magnitude of any property of the ... objects.

Chambers, 1966b, 110

See also 144, 189

186 Opportunity costs

opportunity or alternative cost. The cost of doing anything consists of the receipts which could have been obtained if that particular decision had not been taken.

Coase, 1938, 560

Opportunity costs take the form of profits from alternative ventures that are forgone by using limited facilities for a particular purpose. Since they represent only sacrificed alternatives, they are never recorded as such in financial accounts.

Dean, 1951, 259

Opportunity costs – values that could currently be realized if assets . . . were sold (without further processing) outside the firm at the best prices immediately obtainable . . . . These values [opportunity costs = dated resale prices of assets] represent the amount which the firm is risking in the succeeding fiscal period.

Edwards & Bell, 1961, 79, 87

Defined internally, cost is the satisfaction denied in the course of achieving other satisfaction. Defined externally, cost is the goods denied in the course of achieving or acquiring other goods.

Kuhn, 1963, 262

The opportunity cost of using a particular input for one purpose rather than another is to be measured in terms of the highest net receipts forgone, i.e. the revenue that would be forgone less the costs that would be avoided by putting the input to the use in question.

Amey, 1968, 451

The opportunity cost of using any factor [of production] is what is currently forgone by using it. With factors obtained from outside the firm this cost is measured by the price paid for their services. With factors already owned by the firm this is usually measured by the amount for which the factors could be leased or sold.

Lipsey, 1972, 209

If the (measured) required sacrifice to acquire project i is less than the discounted value of the (forecasted) cash flows from project i, then (it is forecasted that) one will accumulate more money by acquiring project i than by investing the required sacrifice at the discount rate.

Sterling, 1979, 90

Opportunity cost is the maximum contribution that is forgone by using limited resources for a particular purpose.

Horngren & Foster, 1987, 314

187 Probability and choice

we cannot discover by any possibility a law which will enable us to predict what the distribution of errors will be in any future instance.

Campbell, 1919/1957, 452

A weight is what a degree of probability becomes if it is applied to a single case . . . . The statement about a single case is not uttered by us with any pretence of its being a true statement; it is uttered in the form of . . . a wager . . . . We stand in a similar way before every future event . . . . Any statement concerning the future is uttered in the sense of a wager . . . . we cannot avoid laying wagers because this is the only way to take future events into account.

Reichenbach, 1938/1961, 315

The attempts that have been made to describe uncertain expectations in terms of probability analysis have not been altogether successful, because of the fact that the probability concept involves the idea of a universe of like events, an idea that is not present in the concept of uncertainty.

Boulding, 1950/1962, 47

the approach taken in the theory of games and in statistical decision theory to the problem of rational choice is fundamentally wrong-headed. It is wrong . . . . in ignoring the principle of bounded rationality, in seeking to erect a theory of human choice on the unrealistic assumptions of virtual omniscience and unlimited computational power.

Simon, 1957, 202

But in a great multitude and diversity of matters the individual has no record of a sufficient number of sufficiently similar acts, of his own or other people's, to be able to construct a valid frequency table of the outcomes of acts of this kind. Regarding these acts probabilities are not available to him.

Shackle, 1961/1969, 55

The ineffable diversity and complexity of the conceivable states of the world and their sequence . . . preclude any but a sketchy sampling by the human mind of an unimaginably complex "phase space". It follows that a [probability] cannot serve to express the decision maker's judgments about the hypothetical outcomes of an act of his own, as to whether some particular outcome will or will not, may or may not happen . . . . Probability must be abandoned in favor of possibility, and a means must be sought of defining and expressing degrees of possibility.

Shackle, 1966, 90

conditions of risk, where nonarbitrary numerical probabilities can be ascribed, are rarely met with. We no longer meet with them when we venture out of the casino on to the racecourse; still less do we meet with them in the worlds of business, politics and war.

Watkins, 1970, 193

What is not at all plausible . . . is that the mind subconsciously performs the operation of forming a mathematical expectation . . . . no ordinary business man makes such a calculation consciously (the exception being a few who have learnt a statistical theory of decision making, and consciously apply it): and it stretches credulity too far to suppose that the human mind is so constructed that the mental arithmetic required is done automatically . . . .

Carter, 1972, 31

what conditions must, in a general sense, be satisfied in order to permit probability thought forms to be employed [in decision making] with logical cogency and viability? First, . . . that possible outcomes in the future . . . are generated by a stable, defined, and unvarying structure or mechanism, such that the proportion of instances in which an outcome of a given magnitude can be expected to occur can be firmly specified *a priori* [as in throwing dice] .... Or second, ... that the outcomes are generated by genuinely replicable or repeatable experiments, conducted under uniformly describable conditions .... Unfortunately for the probabilists, ... in the money capital investment case none of these necessary conditions applies, the outcomes are not therefore able to be assumed to be genuinely random, and the conditions necessary for the use of the probability calculus are not satisfied.

Vickers, 1981, 173

See also 174

188 Multivaluational choice

Neither the conception of the economic man nor any other abstraction can suffice as an adequate basis upon which to construct the whole science of economics.

Keynes, 1890/1930, 128

Choice is not a question of isolated alternatives but of selection from endless varieties or combinations of ends.

Scott, 1931/1973, 98

All investors are inevitably influenced by two contradictory desiderata – that of making as large a profit as possible and that of obtaining the greatest measure of security for their capital.

Loveday, 1933, 411

Business men play a mixed game of skill and chance, the average results of which to the players are not known by those who take a hand. If human nature felt no temptation to take a chance, no satisfaction (profit apart) in constructing a factory, a railway, a mine or a farm, there might be not much investment merely as a result of cold calculation.

Keynes, 1936/1942, 150

economists tend to underrate the importance of what may be called the liquidity-solvency motive in business. The fear of bankruptcy and the even more widespread fear of temporary financial embarrassment are probably more powerful drives than the desire for the absolute maximum in profits.

Gordon, 1948, 271

there is no one goal by which an organization can be judged. The bases upon which decisions and appraisals of performance are made involve a host of uneasy compromises of conflicting value demands.

Pfiffner & Sherwood, 1960, 407

there are always things for which businessmen are willing to sacrifice profits, such as security, respectability, liquidity, and so on, which means, of course, that they do not maximize profits.

Boulding, 1962, 51

the two objectives of liquidity and profitability are always in conflict. Economy in the use of assets requires that they be kept in constant use. Yet there is sufficient uncertainty to require that enough excess provision shall be made to handle unexpected contingencies.

Osborn, 1965, 28

The idea that in [private undertakings operating for profit] all governing relations are subservient to and can therefore be resolved into maximizing profit is, I shall suggest, a myth. For even economic criteria are manifold; growth and stability have many dimensions. And apart from these, such undertakings are expected and even expect themselves to maintain a host of other relations, political, social, legal, and moral, in their multiple roles as producer, supplier, employer, land developer, earner of foreign exchange and so on.

Vickers, 1965/1968, 29

The multi-valued choice is a central, inescapable, irreducible fact of life.

Vickers, 1968/1970, 129

an organization may seek to attain several desirable goals simultaneously . . . . high profitability . . . . growth . . . . avoidance of undue risk . . . .

Carrington & Howitt, 1983, 7

189 Decisions as syntheses from factual, expectational and valuational premises

We look before and after;
We pine for what is not:

Shelley (1792–1822), *To a Skylark*

The ideal process of decision is to discriminate the strategic factors and to redefine or change purpose on the basis of the estimate of future results of action in the existing situation, in the light of history, experience, knowledge of the past.

Barnard, 1938, 209

Whether the action is performed or not will depend upon evaluations made; will be determined by reference to anticipated possible experience as something to be desired or something to be avoided. Action attempts to control future experience, so far as may be in our own interest. It has its *terminus a quo* in the situation which is given, its *terminus ad quem* in some experience to which a positive value (or comparative value in relation to alternatives) is assigned. The principal function of empirical knowledge is that of an instrument enabling transition from one to the other; from an actual present to a future which is desired and which the present is believed to signalize as possible . . . the utility of knowledge lies in the control it gives us, through appropriate action, over the quality of our future experience. And such control will be exercised in the interest of realizing that which we value, and of obviating or avoiding what is undesirable.

Lewis, 1946, 4

These . . . are the three groups of causal factors that must in principle be represented in all laws of behavior science: the environmental conditions, on the one hand, and, on the other, the two kinds of state variables, the individual's needs and his knowledge.

Bergmann, 1951, 208

In deciding which of the . . . assets to buy, the investor must first form an opinion about the incomes that he is likely to obtain from them at t_1, t_2, . . . t_n, and also about the prices which the assets will have at t_n. Secondly, he must discount these incomes and prices back to the present . . . . Finally he must compare the discounted values with the present market prices of the . . . assets. He will then choose that asset for which the present value of future incomes up to t_n plus the present value of the price of the asset at t_n minus the present price is greatest.

Lutz & Lutz, 1951, 179

the behavior unit has some image of the state of things of himself and his environment and especially some image of the possible alternative situations or positions that this state might take under various possible lines of behavior. A decision consists of a choice among alternative states. Involved in any decision, then, are two properties of the image. There must be a set of alternatives; that is, there must be some distinction between possible and impossible states of the relevant universe in the mind of the decider. Then there must also be an ordering of these possible states at least adequate to permit identification of the state at the top of the ordering. This best state is, of course, the one that is selected.

Boulding, 1963, 150

Several features of incremental or margin-dependent choice need to be distinguished . . . . only those policies are considered whose known or expected consequent social states differ from each other incrementally . . . . only those policies are considered whose known or expected consequences differ incrementally from the *status quo* . . . . examination of policies proceeds through comparative analysis of no more than the marginal or incremental differences in the consequent social states . . . . choice among policies is made by ranking in order of preference the increments by which social states differ.

Braybrooke & Lindblom, 1963/1970, 85

We used to assume, especially in economic theory, that the [ideal or best solution to a problem having many possible solutions] existed, and that people would look for it; that people would rationally select the one very best alternative from an array of all possible alternatives laid out before them. There are two things wrong with this assumption. The first is that we do not usually have anything like a complete array of alternatives laid out before us . . . . The second thing wrong is the idea that only the best actually satisfies most people most of the time . . . . We usually indulge in a limited amount of search, until we reach a satisfactory rather than an optimal alternative. This model of man as a satisficing problem-solver – as an individual using both his head and his guts with a limited degree of rationality and with large elements of strategic guesswork – is quite a different model from . . . . earlier conceptions of problem solving . . . .

Leavitt, 1964, 85, 88

Fact looks to the past, value to the future; that is the fundamental difference between them. But . . . they meet . . . in this present, which divides what is already part of my cumulative experience from all the future possibilities which await me.

Caws, 1967, 59

The data needed for insight into men's actions are answers to the questions: What do they possess? (in material wealth and personal skills): What do they desire? and What do they know?

Shackle, 1970, 142

[Consider] a business man who has to decide between a number of alternative investments . . . . [each having] a number of possible outcomes . . . . Each set of outcomes is the consequence of a particular set of surrounding circumstances . . . . The first step towards making a decision is the heroic one of ignoring nearly all the possible combinations of surrounding circumstances . . . . the members of the remaining set [will have] attached to them degrees of uncertainty . . . . outcomes [will be related to] rankings of uncertainties of selected relevant events . . . . [There follows] a process of successive simplification (by the discarding of alternatives) until the problem becomes soluble . . . .

Carter, 1972, 34–39

In the economic sciences, to which accounting, of course, belongs, the objects of concern are economic agents capable of making choices. The models that we make of these objects require specification of (1) the resources available, (2) the technological opportunities available for transforming these resources into other quanta, (3) the decisions available, (4) the possible consequences of each choice and their likelihoods, and (5) a value system, consisting either of preference orderings over all relevant consequences . . . or, in some descriptive models, over actions . . . .

Hakansson, 1973, 161

190 Financial Desiderata of Choice

191 Rate of return on capital

In all commercial countries there is a fixed rate of interest, and the merchant's gain should only be estimated by the excess of his gross profits above the interest of his stock . . . . if the profit of his trade be less than his stock would have yielded at common interest, he may properly account it as a losing one.

Hamilton, 1788/1982, 471

So far as the investor . . . is concerned, accountancy, in my opinion, should have but one ultimate objective – to disclose the reasonably prospective net earning power of the enterprise.

Frank, 1939, 297

The best single measure of the success of a business enterprise is the rate of return which it earns on the capital invested in it.

Jones, 1956, 1

The profit/capital employed ratio has its principal value for the management within a business . . . (a) as a check on the operating efficiency of the whole business (b) as an indication of whether and in which direction to develop . . . (c) as a yardstick by which management can examine itself.

ICAEW, 1958b, R3

rate of return on capital is a significant and widely used guide to many types of decisions made by business management.

NAA, 1959, 5

The rate of return on investment is . . . . of central importance for the evaluation of an individual investment project, the financial evaluation of a company's performance, the evaluation of managerial efficiency for a division or a product-line and finally for establishing ceiling prices in the regulated industries.

Solomon, 1966, 232

The ratio of net profit after taxes to net worth measures the productivity of the resources the owners of the firm have committed to the operation of the business. It is the kind of information the owners are desirous of having for determining whether their historical investments have performed better in this outlet than in others.

Weston & Brigham, 1966, 79

The return on capital employed is in wide use as an indicator of management performance, since both the denominator and the numerator are the outcome of management's decisions.

Newbold, 1970, 153

The relationship between profitability and investment is considered the key ratio by many analysts . . . . It is perhaps the most common return on investment figure published by financial services.

Hawkins, 1971, 44

ROI [return on investment] is a pervasive, useful yardstick, and a good measurement system should yield an ROI calculation that permits managers to appraise the effectiveness of their actions to achieve corporate objectives.

Vancil, 1976, 61

Rate of return on assets

From the operating point of view as distinguished from the stockholders' point of view, the real measure of the financial return earned by a business is the percentage of operating profits earned on the total capital used in the conduct of such operations . . . . regardless from what source such capital may have been secured.

Bliss, 1923, 78

The rates of return that are conventionally calculated [include] . . . total profits from all sources (before charging taxation or interest on borrowed funds) expressed as a percentage on average total funds employed (proprietorship funds plus outside liabilities) . . . .

Mathews, 1962, 292

earning power may be expressed as the relation between (1) total net income available to all parties providing funds (including creditors . . .) and (2) the total of all the resources of the enterprise . . . . For the purpose of appraising operating performance, . . . [this] form of earning rate is the more significant.

Paton, 1963, 63

The rate of return on assets . . . [relates] . . . net income to average total assets . . . . This measure shows how efficiently a company is using all its assets.

Needles & others, 1984, 326

Calculation of rate of return (or return on investment)

The surplus net profits earned on the net worth is the real measure of the earning power of a business from its stockholders' point of view. It is the measure of the commercial success of a business . . . . [It should] be stated as the percentage earned per year on the net worth at the beginning of the year.

Bliss, 1923, 57

The rate of return on total stockholders' equity . . . . is computed by dividing the net income of the firm for the year by the average stockholders' equity . . . .

Hendriksen, 1961, 39

[The earning power] ratio has two main forms: (1) the rate of net income realized on total resources employed; (2) the rate earned on the total equity of the stockholders . . . . The first . . . . is especially useful in comparing enterprises having different forms of capitalization . . . . The second type of earning rate expresses the relation of the earnings applicable to the stockholders' equity to the [average] amount of such equity.

Dixon & others, 1966, 357

An investor becomes and remains a stockholder in a company because he believes that dividends and capital gains (increase in the price of the stock) will compare favorably with the rate of return he can earn on alternative investments of comparable risk.

Gordon & Shillinglaw, 1969, 243

The amount to be included in the denominator [of an *ex post* rate of return calculation for the evaluation of management] would appear to be the amount for which the assets could be exchanged ... , because at any point in time the only externally visible alternatives open to management are to sell or not to sell those assets which the corporation already owns .... Net income, the numerator ... should also, by the same line of reasoning, be computed using net realizable value measurements of assets.

Bedford & McKeown, 1972, 334

The rate of return on an investment in stock reflects both dividend payments and the change in the market price of the stock since the date the stock was purchased.

O'Connor, 1973, 340

increased earnings ... results in an increase in the market price of the shares. A more reliable measure of yield [than dividend per share divided by market price per share], therefore, includes not only the dividends received but also the change in the value of the share for the year: [Yield = (Dividends received + Increment in market price per share) divided by Market price per share].

Anderson & others, 1974, 25

The rate of return of any asset during period t is defined as the ratio, [(Net cash receipts of the period + Market price at the end of the period – Market price at the beginning of the period) divided by the Market price at the beginning of the period), where the Market prices are the selling prices of the asset] at the two points of time.

Dopuch & others, 1974, 192

192 Short run solvency or liquidity

In the late nineteenth century, analysts employed the current ratio ... to assess the liquidity of firms .... the use of the current ratio is only meaningful when current assets are stated at their current market values and, strictly, these values should be given by the market resale price.

Ma & others, 1987, 426, 427

If the assets exceed the liabilities, the firm is solvent, that is, able to pay its debts in full. If the total of debts due to creditors ... is greater than the liquid assets ...

the position of the firm may be financially unsound. Where debts are being contracted without sufficient means of payment, the firm is said to be overtrading.
Carter, 1923, 43

If the ratio of current liabilities to current assets is rising, this is a danger sign and may indicate overtrading [excessive dependence on short term debt].
de Paula, 1926/1978, 127

Perhaps the most important information that the balance sheet provides concerns the liquidity of the business . . . . Liquidity is, of course, of vital importance because a business can be forced into bankruptcy if it cannot pay its debts.
Dearden & Shank, 1975, 13

Liquidity refers to the ability of a firm to meet its short run financial obligations when and as they fall due.
Foster, 1978, 28

Liquidity is closely related to solvency. The term, liquidity, is often used in at least two different ways. First, it is used to describe the nature of a company's asset holdings, that is their nearness to cash in some (often unspecified) sense . . . . Second, it is used to describe some relationship between a company's liquid assets and its short term liabilities.
Heath, 1978a, 2

Liquidity means having enough money on hand to (1) pay a company's bills when they are due and (2) take care of unexpected needs for cash. Two measures of liquidity often used are working capital and the current ratio.
Needles & others, 1984, 325

Current and quick ratios

The quick asset, liquid or acid test ratio is . . . an extreme test of the capacity of a business to meet a financial crisis. It is calculated by dividing the total of quick assets [current assets less inventories] by the total of liabilities immediately payable.
Fitzgerald, 1956a, 68

The working capital ratio [current assets to current liabilities] is one of the most important single relationships that can be derived from the balance sheet.
Mathews, 1962, 279

The current ratio is the generally accepted measure of short term solvency, as it indicates the extent to which the claims of short term creditors are covered by assets that are expected to be converted to cash in a period roughly corresponding to the maturity of the claims.
Weston & Brigham, 1966, 70

The acid test or quick ratio [quick assets to current liabilities] measures the ability of a company to use its current assets to immediately extinguish its current liabilities.

Hawkins, 1971, 38

Relative liquidity is expressed by the current ratio, which is the amount of current assets divided by the amount of current liabilities.

Dearden & Shank, 1975, 13

The ratio between a firm's current assets and its current liabilities, known as the current ratio, is generally regarded as one indicator of its financial health .... the firm's ability to make good its obligations and thereby to avoid insolvency and bankruptcy.

Edwards & others, 1979, 74

the use of the current ratio [to assess the liquidity of firms] is only meaningful when current assets are stated at their current market values and, strictly, these values should be given by the market resale price.

Ma & others, 1987, 427

Working capital

In March 1915, the Standard Statistics Service Inc, now known as Standard & Poor's Corporation ... determined the net working capital on its card report on United States Steel Corporation. [By 1922 the practice had been extended to reports on all other important industrial corporations whose securities were held extensively by the public.]

Foulke, 1945, 184

The expression, working capital, has sprung into use within the past few years, from whence no one seems sure; meaning what, no one appears to state definitely; and how to interpret, no one seems to agree with another.

CanCA, editorial, 1919, 132

The working capital of a prospective borrower has always been of prime interest to grantors of credit; and frequently working capital has been the subject, in bond indentures, credit agreements and preferred stock agreements, of provisions restricting corporate actions with respect to its reduction or impairment.

AIA, 1947b, ARB30

It is essential ... for financial stability of any enterprise that its working capital be maintained at a level which will adequately cover its day to day financial needs.

Fitzgerald, 1956a, 62

The most common measure of liquidity is working capital, which is current assets minus current liabilities .... The amount of working capital indicates the protection that a company has against adverse conditions.

Dearden & Shank, 1975, 13

193 Cash flows

If the firm can provide any accounting information which will be of assistance in making a choice between investing and not investing, it must be information related to the times and amounts of the investor's future cash receipts from the investment relationship.

Staubus, 1959, 6

The primary and continuing goal of every commercial enterprise is to increase its monetary wealth so that over time it can return the maximum amount of cash to its owners .... An objective of financial statements is to provide information useful to investors and creditors for predicting, comparing, and evaluating potential cash flows to them in terms of amount, timing, and related uncertainty.

AICPA, 1973, 21, 20

It is the present and near future money flows which should be the continuing concern of businessmen.

Nicholls, 1975a, 121

Cash, current cash equivalents, and cash flows are matters which appear to underlie most of the decision models to which financial reporting is directed – for example, shareholders concerned about dividends; lenders, bankers and creditors concerned about interest and capital repayments; employees concerned about wages and security of employment; and so on.

Lee, 1981b, 164

The key concepts in accounting and business management are now cash flows and debt, and it is the measurement of these concepts which needs to be given pride of place in the financial statements published by companies.

Mathews, 1989, 44

194 The composition of assets and equities

A wise merchant ... will not only avoid insolvency, but also pseudo-insolvency; that is, he will not only keep his assets in excess of his liabilities by a safe margin, but will also see that his assets are invested in the right form so as to enable him to cancel each claim at the time and in the manner agreed upon.

Fisher, 1906/1965, 82

[Business men] may fail for lack of proper balance between fixed and current assets and between current assets and current liabilities . . . . Good management involves preservation of proper balance between all the different groups of items in the balance sheet.
Scott, 1925, 39

total amount of capital, distribution of assets, and kinds and proportions of sources of capital tapped – provide the background in which the company seeks to make profits and to avoid insolvency.
Porter & Fiske, 1935, 33

Managers, creditors and stockholders . . . . want to know the present net worth of the business, i.e. the present value of its net possessions . . . . They desire to know the present value of each of the different classes of assets. They wish to know how much the company owes and, within practical limits, to whom.
MacNeal, 1939, 180

it can reasonably be maintained that many, if not all, firms when faced with a difficult decision ask themselves primarily the effect on the structure of their assets as measured by, for example, the ratio of current assets to current liabilities, or the effect on their relations with their shareholders rather than the effect on income from trading ten years hence.
Prest, 1950, 390

The statement of financial position discloses asset composition and capital structure. Such information is relevant to the appraisal of the firm's stability and the soundness of its financial policies.
AAA, 1964a, 694

Presumably, the asset composition preferred by management is the one which promises to grow in market value most rapidly through its profit-seeking activities.
Edwards & others, 1979, 68

195 The debt to equity relationship

The larger the [ratio of equity to debt] the stronger will be [the stockholders'] position and that of the management set up by them; they will be freer to pursue their plans for the development of the business, unhindered by lack of funds on the one hand and by the interference of creditors on the other.
Hatfield & others, 1940, 357

The equity ratio [total stock equity to total of liabilities, or similar ratios] is a means of focusing attention sharply on the question of long run solvency.
Paton, 1941, 660

Whether it is a rule of economic affairs that "to him that hath shall be given" may be disputed; but there can be no doubt that it is a rule of borrowing and lending that to him that hath shall be lent.

> Hicks, 1942/1948, 89

The financial stability of a company depends first on the maintenance of a satisfactory relation between short term assets and short term liabilities, and secondly on the maintenance of a satisfactory relation between borrowed funds and shareholders' funds.

> Mathews & Grant, 1958, 9

One important function of financial management is to arrive at a happy mean between the extremes of too much debt and too little debt in order to obtain the maximum leverage consistent with safety. [Indicators of debt dependence are the equity ratio, proprietary capital to total assets; and the worth-debt ratio, proprietary capital to total liabilities.]

> Dohr & others, 1964, 35

The purpose of the debt to equity ratio is to derive an idea of the amount of capital supplied to the firm by owners, and . . . the amount of asset cushion available to creditors in the event of liquidation.

> Archer & D'Ambrosio, 1966, 521

The debt ratio [debt to total assets] measures the firm's obligations to creditors in relation to all the funds that have been provided . . . . Creditors prefer moderate debt ratios, since the lower the ratio, the greater the cushion against creditors' losses in the event of liquidation . . . . the owners may seek to use higher leverage either to magnify earnings or because raising new equity will mean giving up some degree of control.

> Weston & Brigham, 1966, 74

The relationship of borrowed funds to ownership funds is an important solvency ratio. Capital from debt and other creditor sources is more risky for a company than equity capital . . . . An excessive amount of ownership capital relative to debt capital may [indicate that . . .] the company may be forgoing opportunities to trade on its equity.

> Hawkins, 1971, 39

Debt to net worth. If the ratio of debt to net worth is one to one, the assets could decline 50 per cent in value before threatening the actual solvency of the business . . . . A debt to net worth ratio that is too high tells the financial manager that his chances of securing additional borrowed funds are slight, or that additional funds will cost more.

> Johnson, 1971, 74

a banker, a credit rating agent, or an institutional investor who is concerned about . . . a firm's financial position . . . . checks cash on hand, the current ratio, and

working capital as indicators of short run ability to pay. He sees the debt-equity ratio and coverage of fixed charges as indicators of the long run risk of insolvency.
Staubus, 1977, 121

the debt to equity ratio .... is computed by dividing total liabilities by owner's equity .... the more debt a company has, the more profit it must earn to protect the payment of interest to the creditors .... the amount of interest that must be paid affects the amount of profit that is left to provide a return on owner's investment. The debt to equity ratio also shows how much expansion may be possible by borrowing additional long term funds.
Needles & others, 1984, 326

196 Financial flexibility

The percentage composition of the assets shows something as to the flexibility of the company. If current assets, and especially if quick assets, are a large part of total assets, the company is in a relatively good position to meet social and technological change .... more able to change its policies quickly with minimum loss.
Goetz & Klein, 1960, 380

flexibility .... is used in reference to capital structure .... the ability to adjust the financial structure if events do not work out as expected. To be flexible in sources of funds is to have more than one alternative by which to deal with an uncertain future.
Donaldson, 1969, 7

Maneuverability .... ability to adjust our sources of funds upwards or downwards in response to major changes in needs for funds .... we seek ... to have as many alternatives as possible open when we need to expand or contract our total funds employed.
Johnson, 1971, 228

Of primary importance for predicting the risk associated with a firm's cash flows ... is the degree of flexibility or maneuverability that the management of the firm possesses in employing its resources .... One readily available alternative for the firm's resources is disposal of them. Market values of the firm's resources quantify this alternative .... Market values also [indicate] .... the convertibility of the resources into flexible means of exchange and the extent to which resources are specialized.
Ronen, 1974, 101

A financially flexible company may be defined as one that can take corrective action that will eliminate an excess of required cash payments over expected cash receipts quickly and with minor adverse effect on present or future earnings or on the market value of its stock.
Heath, 1978a, 20

Financial flexibility is the ability of a firm to obtain cash on short notice in order to meet unforeseen contingencies or to take advantage of favorable opportunities.
Hendriksen, 1982, 246

The ability of the company to generate sufficient amounts of cash to respond to unanticipated needs and opportunities is referred to as its financial flexibility . . . . The statement of cash flows read together with the other statements provides a guide to a company's financial flexibility.
Gaffikin, 1993, 625

197 The financial feasibility of options

All organisms equipped with memory are obliged to govern their expectations in the light of what is attainable in the circumstances in which they find themselves.
Mach, 1908/1960, 268

Insofar as man is treated as a purposive being, attempting rationally to attain ends, he cannot be considered as fully oriented to his situation until, among other things, he has adequate knowledge of the situation in the respects which are relevant to the attainment of the ends in question.
Parsons, 1938/1963, 25

The first step in choosing a future course of action is to eliminate any course which is beyond the means presently available to the firm. If the cost of acquiring [a new asset exceeds the means available, that course] is not financially feasible. The comparison which leads to the elimination . . . is a comparison of present, ascertained or measured amounts of money – [the cost price of the prospective asset, and the sum of the cash available and the resale price of any other asset or assets the firm could sell . . .].
Chambers, 1973/1986, III:409

The sets of feasible actions typically differ [as between persons, and at different dates], for they are sensitive to the level of resources.
Hakansson, 1973, 161

for a market exchange to be classified as a feasible alternative, the entry value of unowned assets must be less than or equal to the available funds. Exit values of owned assets are components of the available funds.
Sterling, 1979, 102

See also 058, 182, 429

198 Maintenance of capital as managerial policy

it is always bad when they [merchants] eat upon the capital.
North, 1714, Vocabulary

The maintenance of true economic capital (from the standpoint of the private enterprise) ... does not insure the preservation of physical capital in the typical case, and the maintenance of physical capital would not in general guarantee the conservation of economic capital. Nevertheless it is clear that, from a managerial point of view, the extent and capacity of plant must be maintained if the volume of production is not to be curtailed, and sound management accordingly demands that adequate provision for replacements be made . . . .

Paton, 1922/1962, 431

The maintenance of capital intact is, of course, not an aim in itself . . . . We are not interested in the magnitude of capital because there is any inherent advantage in any of its conceivable absolute measurements. We are interested in it because, *ceteris paribus*, a change in it will cause a change in the income to be expected from it . . . .

von Hayek, 1941, 298

The maintenance of capital intact, in the sense of preserving the productive capacity of the enterprise, is ... one of the most important responsibilities of management. For the fulfilment of this responsibility only the balance remaining after provision has been made for the maintenance of capital can be regarded as profit . . . .

FBI, 1951

The maintenance of capital is indeed important, but maintenance is an objective of management policy; it cannot be an objective of a statistical methodology like accounting.

Littleton, 1953, 23

See also 753, 754

200 THE PSYCHOLOGICAL AND SOCIAL BACKGROUND OF ACCOUNTING

200 Belief and Action

201 Actions and beliefs

The human intellect is not of the character of a dry light, but receives a tincture from the will and affections which generates "sciences after its own will"; for man more readily believes what he wishes to be true. And so it rejects difficult things, from impatience of inquiry; – sober things, because they narrow hope; – the deeper things of nature, from superstition; – the light of experience, from arrogance and disdain, lest the mind should seem to be occupied with worthless and changing matters; – paradoxes, from a fear of the opinion of the vulgar: – in short, the affections enter and corrupt the intellect in innumerable ways, and these sometimes imperceptible. [Aphorism xlix]

> Bacon, 1620/c1900, 259

Social action, like all action, may be oriented in four ways. It may be (1) instrumentally rational, that is, determined by expectations as to the behavior of objects in the environment and of other human beings . . . . (2) value rational, that is, determined by a conscious belief in the value for its own sake of some ethical, aesthetic, religious or other form of behavior, independently of its prospects of success; (3) affectual (especially emotional), that is, determined by the actor's specific affects and feeling states; (4) traditional, that is, determined by ingrained habituation.

> Weber, 1922/1968, 24

if a statement is to become a basis of actions, it is sufficient if we think it to be true.

> Reichenbach, 1938/1961, 65

Normally the demand for reliability in knowledge . . . . calls upon the knower to face in two directions: he must look backward toward the past through memory for most of his foundation material; and he must also look forward toward the future for the purposes which are to guide him in its selection and use. If he confines himself to the backward look for its own sake, he may become a mere antiquarian, satisfying his curiosity by piling up masses of tested, established, and yet possibly useless data in the form of records of past occurrences. But reliable knowledge is more than embalmed knowledge.

> Larrabee, 1945, 6

An act is rational in so far as (a) it is oriented to a clearly formulated unambiguous goal, or a set of values which are clearly formulated and logically consistent; (b) the means chosen are, according to the best available knowledge, adapted to the realization of the goal.

Parsons, 1947, 13

Acting man believes that the services a thing can render are apt to improve his own well-being, and calls this the utility of the thing concerned . . . . There are things to which subjective use-value is attached because people erroneously believe that they have the power to bring about a desired effect. On the other hand there are things able to produce a desired effect to which no use-value is attached because people are ignorant of this fact.

von Mises, 1949, 120

The principle of rationality. A postulate frequently encountered in theoretical economics and elsewhere in social theory is that the behavior of the individual or group can be described by saying that the individual or group is seeking to maximize some quantity. Thus, in the theory of the firm . . . [the postulated maximand is profit]. In the theory of consumption, it is assumed that among all the combinations of commodities an individual can afford, he chooses that combination which maximises his utility or satisfaction. Behavior of this type is frequently referred to as rational.

Arrow, 1951, 135

So far as human actions are concerned the things *are* what the acting people think they are.

von Hayek, 1955/1964, 27

The relationship between what a person knows and how he acts is not a simple one. By and large, of course, people act in ways which are consistent with what they know . . . . Frequently, however, inconsistencies occur between how a person acts and what he knows . . . . Any time a person has information or an opinion which considered by itself would lead him not to engage in some action, then this information or opinion is dissonant with having engaged in the action. When such dissonance exists, the person will try to reduce it either by changing his actions or by changing his beliefs or opinions. If he cannot change the action, opinion change will ensue.

Festinger, 1963, 17, 18–19

An act may be regarded as rational if (i) it is maximally adequate to a present goal and (ii) both the goal and the means to implement it have been chosen by deliberately employing the best available relevant knowledge . . . . The knowledge underlying rational action may be anywhere in the broad spectrum between common knowledge and scientific knowledge; in any case it must be knowledge proper, not habit or superstition.

Bunge, 1967, II:121

Men have their own purposes and may also, as in their daily jobs, serve the purposes of others. Serving a purpose, their actions also have a function. Tools and machines, having no purposes of their own, only have functions . . . . A man behaves purposefully when he does things that he believes will bring him to a certain goal.
Brodbeck, 1968, 139

202 Knowledge

[The *a priori* method of fixation of beliefs] resembles that by which conceptions of art have been brought to maturity . . . . Systems of this sort have not usually rested upon observed facts, at least not in any great degree. They have been chiefly adopted because their fundamental propositions seemed agreeable to reason . . . . [The method] makes of inquiry something similar to the development of taste; but taste, unfortunately, is always more or less a matter of fashion . . . . This method, therefore, does not differ in a very essential way from that of authority.
Peirce, 1877/1958, 105

human thought has its ultimate source in sense-impressions, beyond which it cannot reach . . . . The term knowledge is meaningless when extended beyond the sphere in which we may legitimately infer consciousness, or when applied to things outside the plane of thought, i.e. to metaphysical terms dignified by the name of conceptions although they do not flow from sense impressions.
Pearson, 1911, 74

Knowledge . . . can only include beliefs of mankind which are true, that is, which agree with reality; in knowledge, belief is in harmony with fact.
Welton, 1915, 62

The belief that one can find out something about real things by speculation alone is one of the most long-lived delusions in human thought. It is the spirit of anti-science which is always trying to lead men away from the study of reality to the spinning of fanciful theories out of their own minds.
Thouless, 1930/1977, 78

Knowledge, as an abstract term, is a name for the product of competent inquiries . . . . The attainment of settled beliefs is a progressive matter; there is no belief so settled as not to be exposed to further inquiry. It is the convergent and cumulative effect of continued inquiry that defines knowledge in its general meaning. In scientific inquiry, the criterion of what is taken to be settled, or to be knowledge, is being so settled that it is available as a resource in further inquiry; not being settled in such a way that it is not to be subject to revision in further inquiry . . . . the term "warranted assertion" is preferred to the terms belief and knowledge.
Dewey, 1938/1966, 8

By reliable knowledge is meant any claim-to-know that is substantiated as trustworthy for a given purpose. The question of the reliability of knowledge is usually raised when the presence of a problem arouses in the knower a demand, not only for something more than mere conjecture, but for something which shall be useful in a given situation and perhaps in other similar situations . . . . strictly speaking, reliable knowledge should be defined as consisting of claims-to-know which can be backed up by overt evidence.

Larrabee, 1945, 5, 6

Incompleteness . . . is the mark of empirical knowledge as opposed to *a priori* knowledge such as mathematics. In fact it is the criterion by which we can distinguish perfectly formalized languages constructed by logicians from natural languages as used in describing reality. In a formalized system, the use of each symbol is governed by a definitive number of rules, and further, all the rules of inference and procedure can be stated completely. In view of the incompleteness which permeates empirical knowledge such a demand cannot be fulfilled by any language we may use to express it.

Waismann, 1951/1965, 135

There are many things which, as Aristotle says, it is better not to know than to know – namely, those things which do not count in controlling the mind's fortunes nor enter into its ideal expression.

Santayana, 1962, 40

no state of affairs is described by such statements as "All bachelors are unmarried", "Anything that is red is colored" . . . . Whether or not it makes sense to speak of empirical verification of such statements, it will be agreed that they do not *require* empirical verification. We can see that they are true by just thinking about the meanings of the terms, without recourse to experience. In this sense they are *a priori* statements, not empirical statements . . . . *A posteriori* knowledge – knowledge based on experience. *A priori* knowledge – knowledge which is independent of experience.

Pap, 1963, 13, 421

knowledge is the body of true belief; we cannot know what is not true. Nor can we characterize a belief as false unless we know what would make it true. In order to know, as we do, that perception sometimes deceives us, we must also know what is really there . . . . Just as we cannot say that something is a lie unless we know the truth, so deception and distortion have no meaning unless we know what is being misperceived or distorted. If social causes are among the causes of false belief, they are also among the causes of the grasp of truth.

Brodbeck, 1968, 81

To say that someone knows something is to say more than that he claims to know it, or that he believes it most strongly. It is to say also, both that it is true, and that he is in a position to know.

Flew, 1975, 28

203 Commonsense and science

The method of scientific investigation is nothing but the expression of the necessary working of the human mind.

Huxley, 1894, 363

Science ... originally took over from common sense laws which had already been elaborated; and although it has greatly refined and elaborated those laws and has added many new types, it has never wholly abandoned the laws of common sense. Modern science depends as much as the crudest common sense on the notion of a substance ... , on the notion of the succession of events in time and the separation of bodies in space and so on.

Campbell, 1921/1952, 92

science is rooted in ... the whole apparatus of commonsense thought .... You may polish up commonsense, you may contradict it in detail, you may surprise it. But ultimately your whole task is to satisfy it.

Whitehead, 1929/1957, 110

this work of science .... consists in the task of introducing order and regularity into the wealth of heterogeneous experiences conveyed by the various fields of the sense world .... this task proves to be fully consistent with the task we are habitually performing in our lives since our earliest infancy, in order to find our way and place in our environment .... Scientific reasoning does not differ from ordinary everyday thinking in kind, but merely in degree of refinement and accuracy ....

Planck, 1950, 88

Science starts from common sense, and from generalizations by induction or imagination one derives science; but the derived principles themselves may be very far from common sense.

Frank, 1957/1962, 46

scientific knowledge can be more easily studied than common sense knowledge. For it is common sense knowledge writ large, as it were. [Preface to 1958 ed of Popper, 1934/1961]

Popper, 1958, 22

intellectual activity anywhere is the same, whether at the frontier of knowledge or in a third grade classroom. What a scientist does at his desk or in his laboratory, what a literary critic does in reading a poem, are of the same order as what anybody else does when he is engaged in like activities – if he is to achieve understanding. The difference is in degree, not in kind.

Bruner, 1960, 14

Economists use terribly complicated jargon: long words, fine definitions, cabalistic mathematical symbols and graphs, complicated statistical techniques. Yet, if they have done their job well, they end up with what is simple common sense.

Samuelson, 1960, 185

We use similar patterns of thought [to those of scientists] in the common affairs of daily life; and, in a sense, the task of science is to extend, improve on, and refine the patterns of expectation we display every day. There is a continual interplay between the two fields.

Toulmin, 1963, 59

204 Grounds of belief – habit, inertia, tenacity

what experience and history teach is this – that peoples and governments never have learned anything from history, or acted on principles deduced from it.

Hegel, 1830/1944, 6

the instinctive dislike of an undecided state of mind, exaggerated into a vague dread of doubt, makes men cling spasmodically to the views they already take. The man feels that if he only holds to his belief without wavering, it will be entirely satisfactory . . . . this method of fixing belief . . . may be called the method of tenacity . . . .

Peirce, 1877/1958, 102

We think so because other people all think so;
Or because – or because – after all, we do think so;
Or because we once thought so, and think we still think so;
Or because, having thought so, we think we will think so.

Sidgwick, –/1945, 56

Our purchases and our general conduct alike are largely determined by mere inertia and tradition. Our action is often guided neither by an estimate of the future nor by a direct impulse, but by mere habit formed on past estimates and impulses.

Wicksteed, 1910, 117

No popular saying is more misleading than that we learn from experience; really the capacity of learning from experience is one of the rarest gifts of genius, attained by humble folk only by long and arduous training . . . . popular beliefs . . . are almost uniformly contradicted by the commonest everyday experience.

Campbell, 1921/1952, 170

The questioning of that which we have been accustomed to accept and on which we have habitually relied is profoundly disturbing. Hence we naturally resist the questioner's challenge and we hold to our primary beliefs with increased vehemence. This is plainly seen when naïve people are confronted with the demand to show the evidence for the views that they regard as certain. They answer, generally, with some emphatic: It is so; I know it is so; I am sure it is so; or: How could it be otherwise?

Cohen, 1931/1964, 47

Habit or inertia makes it easier for us to continue to believe a proposition simply because we have always believed it. Hence, we may avoid doubting it by closing our mind to all contradictory evidence. That frequent verbal reiteration may strengthen beliefs which have been challenged is a truth acted upon by all organized sects or parties.

Cohen & Nagel, 1934/1957, 193

In nearly all matters the human mind has a strong tendency to judge in the light of its own experience, knowledge and prejudices rather than on the evidence presented.

Beveridge, 1950/1957, 144

Man is primarily a creature of habit.

Munn, 1961, 286

The great thing, . . . in all education, is to make our nervous system our ally instead of our enemy. It is to fund and capitalize our acquisitions, and live at ease upon the interest of the fund. For this we must make automatic and habitual, as early as possible, as many useful actions as we can . . . .

James, 1962, 160

The force of habit, the grip of convention, hold us down on the trivial plane; we are unaware of our bondage because the bonds are invisible, their restraints acting below the level of awareness. They are the collective standards of value, which determine the rules of the game, and make most of us run, most of the time in the grooves of habit – reducing us to the status of skilled automata . . . .

Koestler, 1966, 365

A habit is a course of action which we regularly, though not necessarily invariably, pursue but without any sense of obligation or compulsion to do so . . . . Many, if not most, habits never assume a normative character, but remain on the level of personal idiosyncrasy.

Lloyd, 1964, 228, 230

205 Grounds of belief – tradition, authority

the ground of our opinions is far more custom and example than any certain knowledge. And . . . a plurality of suffrages is no guarantee of truth.

Descartes, 1637/1937, 14

Let an institution be created which shall have for its object to keep correct doctrines before the attention of the people, to reiterate them perpetually, and to teach them to the young; having at the same time power to prevent contrary doctrines from being taught, advocated or expressed. Let all possible causes of a change of mind be removed from men's apprehensions. Let them be kept ignorant .... Let their passions be enlisted .... Then, let all men who reject the established belief be terrified into silence .... this method of fixing belief .... may be called the method of authority.

Peirce, 1877/1958, 103

The conceit of authority [*Autoritätsdusel*] is the greatest enemy of truth.

Einstein, 1901/1987, I:177

it is very remarkable how people will go on believing things on authority, when the weight of that authority is quite unknown, and when their belief is flatly contradicted by experience.

Campbell, 1921/1952, 170

The essence of the argument for tradition and authority is the actual inability of any single individual thoroughly to apply the process of reasoning and verification to all the propositions that solicit his attention .... It may well be contended that many errors are eliminated by the attrition of time, so that any belief long held by a large group of people has a fair presumption in its favor. Unfortunately, however, errors also strike deep roots. Legends grow and abuses become so well established that it becomes hopeless to try to eradicate them. The history of long-persistent human error certainly looms large in any fair survey of our past.

Cohen, 1931/1964, 29

The extended reasoning process has litle function in the practical arts .... a practical art ... has no method of discovery other than that of almost purely random trial and error; it has no characteristic method of proof and can assimilate truth only when the prestige of its discoverer is great.

Trotter, 1941/1946, 169

the overwhelming part of our factual beliefs are held at second hand through trusting others; and ... in the great majority of cases our trust is placed in the authority of certain persons, either by virtue of their public office or as our chosen intellectual leaders .... this system of shared beliefs relies on a chain of overlapping areas, within each of which a few authoritative persons can keep watch over each other's integrity and their sense of what is important.

Polanyi, 1958, 240

dogma in institutions ... serves the purpose of ensuring the continued existence of the institution and the belief-disbelief system for which it stands .... A threatening historical situation leads to the convocation of a council; the council formulates doctrines or disciplinary measures which are designed to remove the threat.

Rokeach, 1960, 379

science students accept theories on the authority of teacher and text, not because of evidence. What alternatives have they, or what competence? The applications given in texts are not there as evidence but because learning them is part of learning the paradigm at the base of current practice.

Kuhn, 1962, 80

As far as he [the ordinary man] is concerned all [rational] principles whatever . . . are transcendent; he commands evidence for none of them, but accepts them, as he always has, on authority. To believe something it is enough for him if he knows that it is believed by people he respects, as long as it meets a rough intuitive test of plausibility.

Caws, 1967, 32

The layman . . . . is persuaded to believe in science, not by the weight of evidence in the scientific archives but in the light of the intellectual authority of the scientific expert.

Ziman, 1978, 125

206 Education and acculturation

in the habits and regulations of schools, universities, and the like assemblies, destined for the abode of learned men and the improvement of learning, everything is found to be opposed to the progress of the sciences; for the lectures and exercises are so ordered, that anything out of the common track scarcely enters the thoughts and contemplations of the mind.

Bacon, 1620/1891, 424

One hundred repetitions three nights a week for four years, thought Bernard Marx, who was a specialist in hypnopaedia. Sixty-two thousand four hundred repetitions make one truth. Idiots!

Huxley, *Brave new world*, 1932/1966, 31

a large part of our education consists in unconsciously acquiring the ability to imitate the methods which our companions have found to be successful . . . . A clear-eyed recognition of what actually happens is hindered by most of the mental habits drilled into us by education.

Bridgman, 1936/1964, 3, 5

Learning should not only take us somewhere; it should allow us later to go further more easily . . . . What learning general or fundamental principles does is to ensure that memory loss will not mean total loss, that what remains will permit us to reconstruct the details when needed. A good theory is the vehicle not only for understanding a phenomenon now but also for remembering it tomorrow.

Bruner, 1960, 17, 25

I think that we often tend to exaggerate grossly the value of knowledge as such. The object in education is to train the mind, not to crowd the memory.

Lord Tweedsmuir, 1960, 437

Education, which is a necessary and powerful instrument in promoting the expansion of individual capacities and opportunities, and therefore of increasing individual-ization, is also a powerful instrument in the hands of interested groups for promoting social uniformity.

Carr, 1962, 139

worldly wisdom teaches us to be a little suspicious of knowledge that emanates from a unique, compactly organized and self-regarding social institution, staffed by specially trained and thoroughly indoctrinated personnel using machinery of awesome size and complexity.

Ziman, 1978, 64

207 Truth and falsity

The false means that which is false as a fact . . . . an account is always false when applied to anything of which it is not true . . . . Falsehood consists in saying of that which is that it is not or of that which is not that it is. Truth consists in saying of that which is that it is, or of that which is not that it is not.

Aristotle, 4c BC/1956, 44, 142

> *Antonio*:
> The devil can cite Scripture for his purpose.
> An evil soul producing holy witness
> Is like a villain with a smiling cheek,
> A goodly apple rotten at the heart:
> O, what a goodly outside falsehood hath!
>
> Shakespeare, *The Merchant of Venice*,
> I:iii

it is implied in the very notion of truth that it is essentially the same for all minds.

Sidgwick, 1874/1962, 341

Truthfulness is a condition of any collective undertaking. It is interesting to observe the growing recognition of the need of publicity wherever democratic institutions prevail. Secrecy is a sort of treason. If men are to work together for their common welfare they must be truly in touch with one another; otherwise there is a spy at their councils, an incalculable force that may counterwork their plans.

Perry, 1909/1937, 97

True: That only is true which is conformable to the actual state of things. In that sense, a statement is untrue which does not express things exactly as they are. But in another and broader sense, the word, true, is often used as a synonym of honest, sincere, not fraudulent.

Bouvier's law dictionary, 1914, 3328

Intellectual truth is objective and has a form of validity which is universal; it is the public truth ... [as distinct from] private sentiment .... The idea of intellectual crime presupposes things of intellectual value; and these are truth and truthfulness. And intellectual crime may be defined as any behavior which shows indifference to truth or truthfulness; or is harmful to these. Behavior which is harmful to truth-fulness includes such things as: the starving or ill-using of the minds of others ... ; the professing of a thing to be true and acting as if it were false .... Behavior which is harmful to the truth includes such things as: the disparagement of thought; the neglect or wilful mishandling of knowledge or opinion; ... the coining of judgments on insufficient data; the disparagement of the necessity for verification by fact; the substitution of fantasy, which has individual value only, for knowledge which has universal value; the making of statements that outstrip the evidence.

Chance, 1933, 21, 33

many, perhaps most, human utterances appeal to other tests of truth [than accor-dance with "facts observed and experienced in that world which is common to us all"], appeal to other judges .... Here "truth" depends on accord with something quite unlike our facts, upon ethical principles, religious doctrine, patriotism. "Truth" becomes obedience to authority, loyalty to your faith, harmony with your beliefs. Non-experimental theories are those which are in accord with the sentiments, rather than with the facts.

Homans & Curtis, 1934/1970, 55

We believe that men are not in any genuine sense free to choose unless the fullest possible truth is presented to them. That is to say, freedom is not permission to flout the truth but to regulate your life in knowledge of it.

Harvard Committee, 1946, 105

the ethical cannot be detached from reality, and consequently continual progress in learning to appreciate reality is a necessary ingredient in ethical action. In the question with which we are now concerned ["what is meant by telling the truth?"] action consists of speaking. The real is to be expressed in words. That is what constitutes truthful speech.

Bonhoeffer, 1955, 327

It has frequently been noted that the surest result of brainwashing in the long run is a peculiar kind of cynicism, the absolute refusal to believe in the truth of anything, no matter how well it may be established. In other words, the result of a consistent and total substitution of lies for factual truth is not that the lie will now be accepted as truth, and truth be defamed as lie, but that the sense by which we take our bearings in the real world – and the category of truth versus falsehood is among the mental means to this end – is being destroyed.

Arendt, 1967, 128

A fact is false if it is untrue in fact. It is misleading if it is misstated in such a way that it does not give a true picture of the facts being presented, or if it omits material facts necessary to a proper understanding of the facts presented . . . . Sometimes a half truth is no better than an outright falsehood. Fraud may be effected by half truths calculated to deceive and mislead. A statement, although literally true, is nevertheless false if, when interpreted in the light of the effect it would produce on the minds of those whom it was calculated to influence, it would create a false impression of the true state of affairs.

United States v Simon, 1969

publicity is connected more directly to veracity than to other moral principles. In ethics, publicity without truthfulness is misleading and thus worthless. In addition, lies, inherently secretive, may call for submission to public justification more than openly performed problematic acts. Such acts are more likely to arouse controversy eventually, whereas lies, if they succeed, may never do so.

Bok, 1978/1989, 92

See also 082, 086

210 Observation and Inference

211 Impressions and ideas

To me it seems that all sciences are vain and full of errors that are not born of experience, mother of all certainty, and that are not tested by experience; that is to say, that do not at their origin, middle or end, pass through any of the five senses.

Leonardo, d.1519/1980, 5

all our simple ideas in their first appearance are derived from simple impressions, which are correspondent to them, and which they exactly represent.

Hume, 1739/1960, 4

Without an accurate acquaintance with the visible and tangible properties of things, our conceptions must be erroneous, our inferences fallacious, and our operations unsuccessful . . . . exhaustive observation is an element in all great success.

Spencer, 1861/1976, 50

all sense data come first in wholes and are later analyzed into smaller and smaller wholes . . . . Observation of single isolated things is impossible, for a single object without a contrasting background is invisible. Some kind of whole [or pattern], even though it be so simple as object and background, is invariably essential in either ordinary or scientific observation.

George, 1936, 115

The things and events that occur in the external world act on our sense organs (eyes, ears, etc.), and the mind which receives those sensory signals weaves them into the fabric of a perceived or experienced reality. Since we cannot get out of our own minds, our senses provide our only contact with the external world. The world we see ... has only a subjective or internal reality. We translate this subjective reality into what we think the external world is really like.

Beck, 1962, 87

212 Discrimination and assimilation

discrimination is the simplest and most basic operation performable .... When we attempt to reduce complex operations to simpler and simpler ones, we find in the end that discrimination, or differential response, is the fundamental operation.

Stevens, 1939, 246, 248

Analogy is a sort of similarity. Similar objects agree with each other in some respect, analogous objects agree in certain relations of their respective parts .... Inference by analogy appears to be the most common kind of conclusion, and it is possibly the most essential kind. It yields more or less plausible conjectures which may or may not be confirmed by experience and stricter reasoning.

Polya, 1945/1957, 37, 43

Although no argument by analogy is ever valid, in the sense of having its conclusion follow from its premises with logical necessity, some are more cogent than others .... The first criterion relevant to the appraisal of an analogical argument is the number of entities between which the analogies are said to hold .... A second ... is the number of respects in which the things involved are said to be analogous .... A third ... is the strength of their conclusions relative to their premises .... A fourth ... has to do with the number of disanalogies or points of difference between the instances mentioned in the premises and the instance with which the conclusion is concerned .... Our fifth criterion ... is that the more dissimilar the instances mentioned in the premises, the stronger is the argument .... [The last criterion is relevance.] In an argument by analogy, the relevant analogies are those which deal with causally related properties or circumstances.

Copi, 1953/1964, 343–348

All our knowing has this characteristic: it is a double-edged process, in which we recognize things as being the same in some respects and different in others. It is one and the same process by which we identify or connect things and discriminate or distinguish between them

Latta & Macbeath, 1956, 13

Men are always trying to find similarities between new and familiar situations, to find out the extent to which the former can be explained in terms of accepted concepts.

This habit of mind is the *raison d'être* of metaphor and analogy and their wide-spread use in our ordinary conversation. But it is more than a matter of psychological comfort or convenience, for it plays a vital part in scientific thinking . . . . experimental science depends on the recognition and exploration of analogies, upon the construction of models . . . . How could any experiment be devised with no idea as to what the system under investigation is like?

> Theobald, 1968, 55

Without analogy there might be no knowledge: the perception of analogies is a first step towards classification and generalization . . . . A first role of analogy is to suggest equivalence, without however establishing it.

> Bunge, 1973, 125

See also 835

Classification

classification is a first step that is almost indispensable if one would have an adequate grasp of any great number of differing objects. [#8]

> Pareto, 1916/1963, 7

The limited spans of human attention and memory make it impossible for anyone to think long in purely individual terms . . . . the only way in which a human mind can cope with [numerous and diverse things] in thinking is by grouping individual items into classes to which names or symbols are usually attached . . . .

> Larrabee, 1945, 239

Rules of classification . . . . 1. The classes chosen should fit the material to be classified . . . . Sensations should not be classified as true or false . . . . 2. At each level the classes should have a single basis of classification without overlapping. The constituent species must be mutually exclusive . . . . 3.To avoid inadvertent omissions, a classification should be exhaustive . . . . A classification should cover all the material it purports to classify, and it should allow for the inclusion of new data when discovered.

> Larrabee, 1945, 245

Classificaton and aggregation of items are necessary to protect users of the statements from being submerged in detail. But more important than that, significant statistical relationships within any population cannot be seen until the population has been broken down into relevant classes . . . and aggregates of each class have been arrived at.

> Solomons, 1989, 33–4

See also 382

213 Selective perception

"Pussycat, pussycat, where have you been?"
"I've been up to London to visit the Queen."
"Pussycat, pussycat, what did you there?"
"I saw a little mouse under a chair."
Anon

Verbalism and word magic; fatuous insistence on illusory certainty, continuity and uniformity; wishful intellection which ignores, or tries to obliterate from cognizance, unpleasant circumstances – these are the marks of childish thought and often affect legal thinking.
Frank, 1930/1963, 89

while we learn largely by observation, we observe largely by use of what has previously been learned.
Woodworth, 1935, 452

Perception is functionally selective.
Krech & Crutchfield, 1948, 87

We do not observe anything and everything indiscriminately . . . . We often see just what we look for, and we look for what we have been trained to see, or for what interests us.
Latta & Macbeath, 1956, 300

Self-interest often leads us to refuse to look for evidence that we don't want to face.
Fearnside & Holther, 1959, 107

no observation can be undertaken in all innocence. We always know something already, and this knowledge is intimately involved in what we come to know next, whether by observation or in any other way. We see what we expect to see, what we believe we have every reason for seeing . . . . We do not make proper observations by stripping ourselves of theories – which is impossible in any case – but rather by making use of theories appropriate to the observational context.
Kaplan, 1964, 132

Perception is a part-innate, part-acquired skill of transforming the raw material of vision into the "finished product"; and every period has its conventional formulae and methods of interpretation for doing this. The ordinary mortal thinks most of the time in clichés – and sees most of the time in clichés. His visual schemata are prefabricated for him; he looks at the world through contact lenses without being aware of it.
Koestler, 1966, 379

People can learn to perceive in a set way through familiarity – that is, as a process of learning. Thus, they can start to perceive what they expect or want to perceive rather than what they should perceive; this gives security and avoids anxiety.

Lee, 1976, 63

the idealized anatomist who draws what he sees in a dissection, is strongly prejudiced in practice by what he knows he ought to see.

Ziman, 1978, 90

214 Memory

whatever is present to the memory, striking upon the mind with a vivacity which resembles an immediate impression, must become of considerable moment in all the operations of the mind, and must easily distinguish itself above the mere fictions of the imagination.

Hume, 1739/1960, 107

The mind is so limited that we cannot revive a great number of ideas to render them all at the same time the subject of our reflection.

de Condillac, 1756, 118

Memory . . . is a postulate of knowledge, like apprehension . . . . It is a direct or immediate belief about the past . . . . Memory is an assertion of a past experience, which may be true or false.

Hobhouse, 1896, 71, 76, 80

The gap of time between my present thought and its past object is bridged not by the survival or revival of the object, but only by the power of thought to overleap such a gap; and the thought which does this is memory.

Collingwood, 1946, 293

needs . . . help determine which of all the objects originally perceived will be selected out for retention . . . . the individual . . . will not remember everything he has ever perceived . . . . He will remember only a selected sample . . . . he will retain events in which he was deeply involved, and he will forget others.

Krech & Crutchfield, 1948, 132, 133

Semantic reception [concerned with meaning] demands memory . . . . The semantic receiving apparatus neither receives nor translates the language word by word, but idea by idea, and often still more generally. In a certain sense, it is in a position to call on the whole of past experience in its transformations, ...

Wiener, 1950/1954, 80

Perhaps the most basic thing that can be said about human memory . . . is that unless detail is placed into a structured pattern, it is rapidly forgotten. Detailed material is conserved in memory by the use of simplified ways of representing it . . . . A scientist does not try to remember the distances travelled by falling bodies in different gravitational fields over different periods of time. What he carries in memory instead is a formula that permits him with varying degrees of accuracy to regenerate the details on which the more easily remembered formula is based.

Bruner, 1960, 24

Long before Freud was ever born Darwin made it his practice to write down all objections to his theories the moment he met them. That observant naturalist had noticed that we are all more apt to forget what we have some interest in not remembering.

Flew, 1975, 65

all cognition seems to be affected heavily by memory; but . . . memory is more than simple recall of stored data. Memory seems to involve organized reconstruction of events.

Littlejohn, 1983, 132

Our memory is rigorously selective . . . . we remember what interests us; but we may also perversely conceal or recompose things that are too threatening to face.

Roszak, 1986, 97

215 Reasoning

We think only through the medium of words . . . . The art of reasoning is nothing more than a language well arranged.

de Condillac, 18c, 1960/1967, 168, 169

The conditions of valid reasoning, by the aid of symbols are – 1st, that a fixed interpretation be assigned to the symbols employed in the expression of data; and that the laws of the combination of those symbols be correctly determined from the interpretation. 2nd, that the formal processes of solution or demonstration be conducted throughout in obedience to all the laws determined as above, without regard to the question of the interpretability of the particular results obtained. 3rd, that the final result be interpretable in form, and that it be actually interpreted in accordance with that system of interpretation which has been employed in the expression of the data.

Boole, 1854, 68

Most men of business love a sort of twilight. They have lived all their lives in an atmosphere of probabilities and doubt, where nothing is very clear, where there are some chances for many events, where there is much to be said for several courses, where nevertheless one course must be determinedly chosen and fixedly adhered to. They like to hear arguments suited to this intellectual haze. So far from caution and hesitation in the statement of an argument striking them as an indication of imbecility, it seems to them a sign of practicality.

Bagehot, 1894, 143

All of our ideas are, after all, only inner thought-pictures or, when uttered, combinations of sounds. The task of our thinking, then, is to use and connect concepts in such a way that with their help we always and most easily perform the right actions and also guide others to right actions.
Boltzmann, 1899/1960, 245

Reasoning may be described as mental exploration . . . . It differs from mere trial and error in that it follows clues by thinking them through . . . . It follows them by recall of previously observed facts . . . . Reasoning culminates in inference.
Woodworth, 1935, 464

All reasoning is thinking, but not all thinking is reasoning.
Copi, 1953/1964, 5

Analytic thinking characteristically proceeds a step at a time. Steps are explicit and usually can be adequately reported by the thinker to another individual. Such thinking proceeds with relatively full awareness of the information and operations involved . . . . In contrast to analytic thinking, intuitive thinking characteristically does not advance in careful, well-defined steps . . . . The thinker arrives at an answer, which may be right or wrong, with little if any awareness of the process by which he reached it . . . . Usually intuitive thinking rests on familiarity with the domain of knowledge involved and with its structure, which makes it possible to leap about, skipping steps and employing short cuts in a manner that requires a later rechecking of conclusions by more analytic means, whether deductive or inductive.
Bruner, 1960, 57

Reasoning does not occur unless there is a difficulty, or unless a question has arisen for which there is no ready answer.
Munn, 1961, 485

The relation between laws of any kind and the occurrences to which they relate is one of correspondence rather than of formal logic . . . . A correspondence between two strata of language – the language of laws and the language of occurrences – is the characteristic mark of working logic, of logic in use. Interpretation is the process of establishing this correspondence, of moving from one stratum to another. It functions where formal logic is silent; it connects concepts in logically heterogeneous domains.
Gottlieb, 1968, 68

The subject/motive shift [in argument, moves] from discussing the truth or falsity of some proposition . . . to discussing the quite different questions of what someone's motives might be for asserting or denying, . . . or for wishing to believe or reject the proposition . . . . the word "reason" is itself relevantly ambiguous. When someone is said to have some reason for believing a certain proposition, we may need to ask: whether this reason is a ground for holding that that proposition is actually true; or whether it is a motive for persuading himself of it, whether it is true or not. In the former case we can speak of a reason (ground), in the latter of a reason (motive).

We might also distinguish a third sense. For in the phrase "one reason why" ...
what is referred to is ... a reason (cause).

Flew, 1975, 58

the law of conservation of information .... No process of logical reasoning – no
mere act of mind or computer-programmable operation – can enlarge the information content of the axioms and premises or observation statements from which
it proceeds.

Medawar, 1986, 79

216 Logic

The purpose of logic ... is to make clear and explicit the principles and the character
of valid thought; of thought, that is, which attains knowledge.

Welton, 1915, 68

[Logic deals with] the relation of implication between propositions, that is, with the
relation between premises and conclusions in virtue of which the possible truth and
falsity of one set limits the possible truth and falsity of the other.

Cohen & Nagel, 1934/1957, 27

Logic tells us that nothing is both a bird and not a bird, because it tells us that
whatever A is, nothing is both A and not A .... the specific meaning of "bird" is
irrelevant to the ground on which the truth of [the statement] is logically determinable.

Lewis, 1946, 113

The study of logic is the study of the methods and principles used in distinguishing
correct from incorrect reasoning.

Copi, 1953/1964, 3

logic is the science ... of reasoned discourse or language, discourse which expresses
thought .... as the subject of logic is the intellectual element of discourse, we may
describe logic generally as the science of thought.

Latta & Macbeath, 1956, 1, 3

logic has as its subject matter a normative order that does not have a social character.
For the acts of human thought, which are regulated by the norms of this order, do
not refer to other human beings; one does not think "toward" another man in the
way that one acts toward another man.

Kelsen, 1960/1967, 24

217 Limited data processing capacity of the mind

What renders general ideas so necessary is the limited capacity of the human mind.
de Condillac, 1756, 139

so we learn our first lesson about thought, that to grasp anything at all we must leave out the greater part of it . . . . we must admit that the mind never yet sifted out a grain of truth without letting twenty other grains slip past unnoticed.
Hobhouse, 1896, 6

it is not the quantity of information sent that is important for action, but rather the quantity of information which can penetrate into a communication and storage apparatus sufficiently to serve as the trigger for action.
Wiener, 1950/1954, 94

the span of absolute judgment and the span of immediate memory impose severe limitations on the amount of information we are able to receive, process and remember. By organizing the stimulus input simultaneously into several dimensions and successively into a sequence of chunks, we manage to break (or at least stretch) this informational bottleneck.
Miller, 1956, 95

the principle of bounded rationality: The capacity of the human mind for formulating and solving complex problems is very small compared with the size of the problems whose solution is required for objectively rational behavior in the real world – or even for a reasonable approximation to such objective rationality.
Simon, 1957, 198

an individual's capacity for making sound judgment about a complex situation may be seriously impaired by supplying him with a lot of information which he believes should be relevant but whose influence on the situation is not clear to him.
Millikan, 1960, 164

There are limits to the amount of communication which can be received, coded, and effectively handled by any individual.
Katz & Kahn, 1966/1978, 471

Inability to cope effectively with the surfeit of attractive information inputs [is among] the most potent sources of frustration in our society.
Lipowski, 1971, 470

The brain of the firm, just as man's brain, has more potential states than can ever be analyzed or examined by an enormous factor – an unthinkably large factor. Information, then, has to be thrown away by the billion bits all the time, and without making nonsense of control.
Beer, 1972, 65

In the behavioral sciences . . . we may be the victims of what I call irrelevant variety. Irrelevant variety is generated by the presence of attributes in a situation which have little to do with the phenomena we are studying but which give the impression that what we are studying is very complex . . . . Merely because persons differ along a large number of physical, psychological, and social dimensions, does not mean that all of these differences will make a difference in terms of the phenomena we are studying . . . . it is probably the case that relatively few variables can account for most of the action.

Berger, 1977, 15

The mind thinks with ideas, not with information . . . . An excess of information may actually crowd out ideas, leaving the mind . . . distracted by sterile, disconnected facts, lost among shapeless heaps of data.

Roszak, 1986, 88

See also 793

220 Signs, Symbols, Language

221 Signs

A sign is an arbitrary mark, having a fixed interpretation, and susceptible of combination with other signs in subjection to fixed laws dependent upon their mutual interpretation.

Boole, 1854, 25

all thought is in signs.

Peirce, 1868/1958, 34

a sentential sign present to an organism O is true when, as sign, it promotes behavior which would have been promoted by a situation that exists, if this situation had been present to the organism.

Russell, 1940/1963, 178

The symbol-making function is one of man's primary activities, like eating, looking, or moving about. It is the fundamental process of his mind, and goes on all the time . . . . Because a sign may mean so many things, we are very apt to misinterpret it, especially when it is artificial . . . . The misinterpretation of signs is the simplest form of mistake. It is the most important form, for purposes of practical life, and the easiest to detect; for its normal manifestation is the experience called disappointment. Where we find the simplest form of error, we may expect to find also, as its correlate, the simplest form of knowledge. This is, indeed, the interpretation of signs. It is the most elementary and most tangible sort of intellection; the kind

of knowledge we share with animals, that we acquire entirely by experience, that has obvious biological uses, and equally obvious criteria of truth and falsehood.
Langer, 1942/1969, 40, 59

Human civilization is dependent upon signs and systems of signs, and the human mind is inseparable from the functioning of signs.
Morris, 1955/1962, 79

Another system of signs and rules is money. The coins are signs or tokens; the rules relate pennies to shillings, and shillings to pounds, while somewhat more shifting and flexible rules relate these tokens to the value of goods!
Cherry, 1955, 46

Symbols

a symbol is not, properly speaking, either true or false; it is, rather, something more or less well selected to stand for the reality it represents, and pictures that reality in a more or less precise, a more or less detailed manner.
Duhem, 1914/1962, 168

A true symbol = one which correctly records an adequate reference. It is usually a set of words in the form of a proposition or sentence. It correctly records an adequate reference when it will cause a similar reference to occur in a suitable interpreter. It is false when it records an inadequate reference . . . . If on the other hand the speaker makes a true reference, but uses symbols such that a suitable interpreter, rightly interpreting, makes a false reference, then the symbol is incorrect.
Ogden & Richards, 1923/1960, 102

Man's achievements rest upon the use of symbols . . . . we shall always be ruled by those who rule symbols . . . .
Korzybski, 1933/1958, 76

What is essential to communication is that the symbol should arouse in one's self what it arouses in the other individual. It must have that sort of universality to any person who finds himself in the same situation.
Mead, 1934/1962, 149

Scientific theories are universal statements. Like all linguistic representations they are systems of signs or symbols.
Popper, 1934/1961, 59

Without symbols, human beings could not communicate with each other at all . . . . Language itself is actually nothing else than a symbol for something higher – for thought.
Planck, 1950, 163

222 Words as signs

Here . . . is the first distemper of learning, when men study words and not matter.
Bacon, 1605/1891, 44

Commerce, however necessary, however lucrative, as it depraves the manners, corrupts the language . . . . Of the laborious and mercantile part of the people, the diction is in a great measure casual and mutable; many of their terms are formed for some temporary or local convenience, and, though current at certain times and places, are in others utterly unknown.
Johnson, 1755, Preface

A word designates a concept, and the concept may or may not correspond to a thing. But the correspondence, when it is there, cannot be perfect. [#108] . . . . Literary economists . . . are to this day dilly-dallying with speculations such as "What is value?", "What is capital?" They cannot get it into their heads that things are everything and words nothing, and that they may apply the terms capital and value to any blessed things they please, so only they be kind enough – they never are – to tell us precisely what those things are. [#118]
Pareto, 1916/1963, 57, 62

Words are very useful when they really represent ideas, but are a most terrible danger when they do not. A word represents ideas, in the sense important for the practical applications of science, only when the things which it is used to denote are truly collections of properties or events associated by laws; for it is only then that the word can properly occur in one of the laws on which all those applications depend.
Campbell, 1921/1952, 175

it is perhaps hardly realized how widespread is the habit of using the power of words not only for *bona fide* communications, but also as a method of misdirection; and in the world as it is today the naïve interpreter is likely on many occasions to be seriously misled if the existence of this unpleasant trait – equally prevalent amongst the classes and the masses without distinction of race, creed, sex or colour – is overlooked.
Ogden & Richards, 1923/1960, 19

We live in two different worlds – the world of facts and that of their symbols. In order to acquire knowledge of ourselves, we utilize both observation and scientific abstractions. But the abstract may be mistaken for the concrete. In such an instance, facts are treated as symbols and the individual is likened to the human being. Most of the errors made by educators, physicians, and sociologists come from such confusion.
Carrel, 1935/1948, 219

Language is made up of physical existences; sounds, or marks on paper . . . . But these do not operate or function as mere physical things when they are media of communication. They operate in virtue of their representative capacity or meaning. The particular physical existence which has meaning is, in the case of speech, a conventional matter. But . . . . the meaning which a conventional symbol has is not itself conventional.

Dewey, 1938/1966, 46

Thirty-four meanings of the word "account" were revealed in an inquiry to discover the multiple meanings of words which are most confusing to grammar school pupils and foreigners who are studying English.

Larrabee, 1945, 264

Whenever two or more human beings can communicate with each other, they can, by agreement, make anything stand for anything . . . . [But] the word is not the thing.

Hayakawa, 1952/1965, 24, 28

words are an imperfect instrument for expressing complicated concepts with certainty; only mathematics can be sure of doing that.

Gowers, 1954, 9

words are symbols for perceptual and cognitive events, but they are not the events. They are vehicles of thought, but the vehicle should not be confused with the passengers.

Koestler, 1966, 605

The neurotic sensitivity of the [stock] market might be guessed from the language of stock exchange reports . . . share prices . . . do not fall, but ease, sink back, or lose their shine. The language is an odd compound of the sports ground, the turf, the battlefield and the psychiatrist's couch: shares edge forward, score gains, lose ground, rally, advance and put on spurts; like acrobats they take upward or downward turns, jump or soar; like ships they are bouyant, surge forward or sink. It is difficult to remember that they can really only do two things: go up or go down.

Sampson, 1971, 481

223 Dated terms

$Smith_{1900}$ is quite a different person from $Smith_{1933}$.

Korzybski, 1933/1958, 263

operations are performed by human beings in time and are subject to the essential limitations of the time of our experience – the full meaning of any term involves the addition of a date.

Bridgman, 1936/1964, 41

Accountants insist on dating appraisal values shown on balance sheets; they do not insist on dating cost valuations, as though such values were immutable, timeless, true for eternity.

Goetz, 1939, 153

The pound of 1914 is . . . not the same thing, in its practical aspect, as the pound of 1940.

Humphreys, 1940, 644

I shall give the name, factual premise, to any uninferred proposition which asserts something having a date, and which I believe after critical scrutiny. I do not mean that the date is part of the assertion, but merely that some kind of temporal occurrence is what is involved in the truth of the assertion.

Russell, 1940/1963, 144

in history the general conditions of knowledge are derived from the fundamental principle that the knower is placed in the present, and from the point of view of the present is looking at the past. The first axiom of intuition for history . . . is that every historical event is situated somewhere in past time.

Collingwood, 1946, 109

If I make notes for my subsequent use, then I am practically two different persons, in different places or at different times, one here and now, the other somewhere else in the future.

Whatmough, 1957, 22

Balance sheets bear on the face of them an indication of the date as at which the statements they contain are to be interpreted. They do not say "this balance sheet is dated 31 December 1962, but this item is to be interpreted as for 1952, and that item is to be interpreted as for 1957". If any such statement were made it would be a clear indication of the uselessness of the balance sheet. For firstly, no user can cast his mind back to the setting of 1952 or 1957 for the purpose of interpreting specific statements, however well he may recollect the broad settings of those years. And secondly, it would be pointless to do so; for the purpose of reading the balance sheet is to be informed about the actions he may take now, not about the actions he could have taken years ago.

Chambers, 1965b, 24

Historic cost is a fact . . . . At any given date after acquisition, historic cost is not a reality . . .

Skinner, 1982, 125

See also 311

224 Ambiguity, inexactitude and equivocation

for a long time I have not said what I believed, nor do I ever believe what I say, and if indeed sometimes I do happen to tell the truth, I hide it among so many lies that it is hard to find.

Machiavelli, 1521/1990, xi

[On the rationalization of chemical nomenclature] We must clean house thoroughly, for they have made use of an enigmatical language peculiar to themselves, which in general presents one meaning for the adepts and another meaning for the vulgar, and at the same time contains nothing that is rationally intellectual either for the one or for the other.

Lavoisier, 1782/1957, 74

A widely used method for splitting terms into double meanings is to qualify them with certain epithets, such as "true", "right", "honest", "noble", "good" . . . . The epithet "true" is helpful [to the user] because . . . meaning little or nothing it can be made to mean anything desired. [#1561, 1562]

Pareto, 1916/1963, 1007–8

use of the language of identity for two different things that are in some ways analogous is precisely what constitutes the nature of fiction . . . . The attempt . . . to use old popular words in new senses is always productive of intellectual confusion.

Cohen, 1931/1964, 389

The great enemy of clear language is insincerity. When there is a gap between one's real and one's declared aims, one turns as it were instinctively to long words and exhausted idioms, like a cuttlefish squirting out ink.

Orwell, 1949/1975, 69

When some part of a doctrine is relatively simple, there is a tendency among the faithful to complicate and obscure it. Simple words are made pregnant with meaning and made to look like symbols in a secret message. There is thus an illiterate air about the most literate true believer. He seems to use words as if he were ignorant of their true meaning. Hence, too, his taste for quibbling, hairsplitting and scholastic tortuousness.

Hoffer, 1951, 80

Most words have more than one literal meaning . . . . When we keep these different meanings apart, no difficulty arises. But when we confuse the different meanings a single word or phrase may have, using it in different senses in the same context, we are using it equivocally. If the context happens to be an argument, we commit the fallacy of equivocation.

Copi, 1953/1964, 74

Words are essential tools for formulating and communicating thoughts, and also for putting them into the storage of memory; but words can also become snares, decoys or straitjackets.

Koestler, 1966, 175

Ordinary everyday controversies are always loose and inconclusive; one side or the other finds loopholes, such as ill-defined terms or ambiguities of expression, that allow him to avoid an unpalatable conclusion. That is why legal documents have to be written in a complex, formalized (and ultimately repellent) language. Scientific communications are forced along the same path.

Ziman, 1978, 12

See also 852, 934

225 Reification

It is ... a point of great importance not to realize our abstractions.

de Condillac, 1756, 150

I wish the use of the word, thingified, were more common, since that which it denotes, the tendency to think of relations and operations as things, is one of the most common sources of philosophical error.

Cohen, 1931/1964, 390

To identify them [abstractions, i.e. parts, elements or phases of things, or their relations] with things is a widespread fallacy which may be called reification.

Cohen, 1944/1961, 108

A concept or system of concepts, which critical analysis can show to be abstract, is "reified" when it is used naïvely as though it provided an adequate total description of the concrete phenomenon in question. The fallacy of reification is virtually another name for what Professor Whitehead has called the fallacy of misplaced concreteness.

Parsons, 1947, 94

scientists were constantly committing and still constantly commit [what Whitehead – 1926/1938, 70–74 – called] the fallacy of misplaced concreteness, which makes the mistake of placing theoretical entities in the same world as observable ones.

Caws, 1965, 285

The term, reification, is used to describe the tendency to think that because there are certain words there must necessarily be certain things that correspond to them .... Words like ego, id, collective unconscious, and so on are reified terms when the psychologist sets about to look for things that correspond to those words .... The problems with reification are especially common when the terms are preceded by adjectives like real or pure or true or essential.

Condon, 1966, 44

the repetition of a sentence separates it from the person who uttered it and it acquires its own identity. In short, cut adrift and tossed into the social environment, the image associated with a word or idea comes to be treated as a reality; a conventional reality, of course, but still a reality.

Moscovici, 1981, 200

To reify a concept means to speak of it as if it were a physical thing .... Often accountants ... become so accustomed to viewing real world events through the accounting model that they confuse the model with the events themselves.

Heath, 1987, 2, 3

226 Language

language is an instrument of human reason, and not merely a medium for the expression of thought ....

Boole, 1854, 24

Language is not language unless it not only expresses fairly definite and coherent ideas, but unless it also conveys these ideas to some other living intelligent being, either man or brute, that can understand them.

Butler, 1890/1969, 14–15

[With reference to] the communication of thoughts and feelings .... that language ranks highest which goes farthest in the art of accomplishing much with little means, or in other words, which is able to express the greatest amount of meaning with the simplest mechanism.

Jespersen, 1921/1964, 324

A language, to be most useful, should be similar in its structure to the structure of the events which it is supposed to represent.

Korzybski, 1933/1958, 412

the background linguistic system (in other words, the grammar) of each language is not merely a reproducing system for voicing ideas but rather is itself a shaper of ideas, the program and guide for the individual's mental activity, for his analysis of impressions, for his synthesis of his mental stock in trade.

Whorf, 1956/1989, 212

Language is first and foremost a means of transmitting information, and its study a branch of the study of the signs and objects that they symbolize.

Whatmough, 1957, 22

Thought and language mold each other . . . .
Whyte, 1962/1967, 42

Language enables us to do many things . . . . We can tell people what might be the case, what we feel about whatever is the case, and as scientists what is the case. What enables us to discern and attend to our experiences of the world reliably is that we can make statements about them in a public language.
Theobald, 1968, 29

I have much sympathy with the view . . . that languages and the reaction patterns they involve are not merely instruments for describing events (facts, states of affair), but that they are also shapers of events (facts, states of affair), that their "grammar" contains a cosmology, a comprehensive view of the world, of society, of the situation of man which influences thought, behavior, perception.
Feyerabend, 1975/1982, 223

Jargon

When officials are accused of writing jargon, what is usually meant is that they affect a pompous and flabby verbosity. The Americans have a pleasant word for it – gobbledygook. It cannot be questioned that there is too much of that sort of thing in the general run of present-day writing, both official and other . . . . But there is also a jargon in the strict sense of the word . . . . Technical terms are used – especially conventional phrases invented by a government department – which are understood inside the department, but are unintelligible to outsiders. That is true jargon . . . . using jargon is a dangerous habit; it is easy to forget that the public do not understand it, and to slip into the use of it in explaining things to them.
Gowers, 1951, 75

The proper meaning of "jargon" is writing that employs technical words not commonly intelligible. "Catachresis" for instance is grammarians' jargon for using a word in a wrong sense. When grammarians call writing jargon merely because it is verbose, circumlocutory and flabby, they themselves commit the sin of catachresis that they denounce in others.
Gowers, 1954, 8

"Gobbledegook" was coined by an exasperated Congressman, Maury Maverick of Texas, and means using two, three, or ten words in the place of one, or using a five-syllable word where a single syllable would suffice . . . . Gobbledegook can be defined as squandering words, packing a message with excess baggage and so introducing semantic noise. Or it can be scrambling words in a message so that meaning does not come through.
Chase, 1955, 249, 251

In the original meaning of the term, there is nothing wrong with jargon. All it meant was the special terms of a trade or art . . . . But there is another kind of language . . .

which ought really to be called pseudo-jargon. This second kind . . . has gradually invaded business, the professions and ordinary speech, until it now prevails over plain speaking. It is made up of terms and expressions that purport to be special and indispensable, although they are not technical words. They are pretentious imitations of technicality . . . . area for subject; concept for notion, idea, conception; . . . objective for goal, aim, purpose, intention: . . . .

Barzun & Graff, 1962, 258

[Jargon] contains four essential elements: 1. It reflects a particular profession or occupation. 2. It is pretentious, with only a small kernel of meaning underneath it. 3. It is used mainly by intellectually inferior people, who feel a need to convince the general public of their importance. 4. It is, deliberately or accidentally, mystifying. The best minds in any profession are never guilty of jargon, except when they are tired. Pedestrian minds are drawn towards it automatically and to a most frightening extent. Jargon, one could suggest, is the weapon of highly paid people with very little of any value to say.

Hudson, 1978, 3

Degeneration of language and its uses

Tongues, like governments, have a natural tendency to degeneration.

Johnson, 1755, Preface

> Words strain,
> Crack and sometimes break, under the burden
> Under the tension, slip, slide, perish,
> Decay with imprecision, will not stay in place,
> Will not stay still.

Eliot, 1935/1963, 194

A dictionary definition of jargon is a word applied contemptuously to the language of scholars, the terminology of a science or art, or the cant of a class, sect, trade or profession. When it was confined to that sense, it was a useful word. But it has been handled so promiscuously of recent years that the edge has been taken off it, and now . . . it signifies little more than any speech that a person feels to be inferior to his own.

Gowers, 1951, 75

It is a consequence of the wide diffusion of the public word through the newspapers and the wireless that the essential character and the limits of the various different words are no longer clearly felt and that, for example, the special quality of the personal word is almost entirely destroyed. Genuine words are replaced with idle chatter. Words no longer possess any weight. There is too much talk. And when the limits of the various words are obliterated, when words become rootless and homeless, then the word loses truth, and then indeed there must almost inevitably be lying.

Bonhoeffer, 1955, 329

language can be used to disguise messages as well as to transmit them .... Language is not only the chief means of communication; it is also the most effective way to falsify real communication thereby leading to noncommunication.

Aranguren, 1967, 137, 138

227 Accounting as language

Accounting is the language of finance.

Montgomery, 1938
MacNeal, 1939, 1
Foulke, 1945, 29

accounting as the language in which the results of business operations are interpreted cannot be spoken in a multitude of dialects if it is to serve society well.

JA, editorial, 1947a, 456

The purpose of accounting is to provide information .... It is utilitarian. It is a language and a system of measurement.

Cannon, 1952, 421

accounting is an indispensable medium of communication between business enterprises and the many diverse interests concerned.

Littleton, 1953, 7

Accounting is the language in which most business events are expressed.

Mason & others, 1959, 1

Accounting is a means of communication between corporate managements and properly interested outsiders ....

Ladd, 1963, 38

The state of a business, its wealth and its profitability, cannot be observed directly. It needs to be represented in words, numbers and pictures .... This is the role of accounting. It is a language that describes and communicates aspects of a business to its owners and other interested parties. Like any other language, it has its characteristic rules, nuances and shortcomings.

Jameson, 1988, 8

See also 038, 341

228 Vernacular and technical languages

we shall have three things to distinguish in every physical science: the series of facts that constitute the science; the ideas that call the facts to mind; and the words that express them. The word should give birth to the idea; the idea should depict the fact; they are three impressions of one and the same seal; and as it is the words that preserve and transmit ideas, it follows that the science can never be brought to perfection, if the language be not first perfected, and that however true the facts may be and however correct the ideas to which they give rise, they will still transmit only false impressions, if there are no exact expressions to convey them.

Lavoisier, 18c, 1962, 192

In the physical sciences indeed, whenever it is seen that a group of things have a certain set of qualities in common, and will often be spoken of together, they are formed into a class with a special name; and as soon as a new notion emerges, a new technical term is invented to represent it. But economics cannot venture to follow this example. Its reasonings must be expressed in language that is intelligible to the general public; it must therefore endeavor to conform itself to the familiar terms of everyday life, and so far as possible, must use them as they are commonly used.

Marshall, 1890/1920, 51

the words of the statute are not the statute itself; the law expressed by the words is not the same thing as the words which express it. Thus a person imperfectly acquainted with English may know the words of the statute, but he will not know the law. The same is true in a greater or lesser degree of anyone who comes to the reading of a statute without sufficient legal knowledge . . . . of the meaning of legal technical terms, but also of the whole system of law of which the statute forms a part; . . . .

Geldart, 1911/1933, 13

a living language grows out of common usage . . . even technical terminology must retain a realistic contact with the concrete data to which it is applied. That accounting terminology is best which best serves to promote clear thinking about the concrete problems with which accounting and business management are concerned.

Scott, 1945, 315

In the initial stages of scientific inquiry, descriptions as well as generalizations are stated in the vocabulary of everyday language. The growth of a scientific discipline, however, always brings with it the development of a system of specialized, more or less abstract, concepts and of a corresponding technical terminology.

Hempel, 1952/1960, 1

The semantical rules connect our equations or our calculus with the words of the language of our daily life, at least in physics and, perhaps, elsewhere too. But, in order to avoid any ambiguity, we have to be sure never to apply these words in a wider domain than in the range of their applications in our daily life.

Frank, 1955/1962, 430

Accounting statements are drawn up to be read, for the most part, by people who are not accountants. The terminology of accounting statements is drawn from everyday language, using such words as asset, liability, net worth and income . . . . the meaning which accountants attach to these words should correspond as closely as possible with the meaning given them by the man in the street.

Skinner, 1961, 58

Whatever we can discriminate in the facts we can distinguish in our meanings; we can always call the fuzzy edge a definite fringe. The point is that facts are indefinitely indefinite; however fine a mesh we use, finer differences slip through the conceptual net. And the more discriminations we make the more opportunities we create for borderline cases to arise.

Kaplan, 1964, 65

229 Use of abstractions

The human intellect is by its own nature prone to abstractions, and imagines those things which are variable to be constant. But it is better to dissect nature than to resolve it into abstractions . . . . [Aphorism li]

Bacon, 1620/c1900, 259

Abstract nouns are indispensable in their proper places. But one of the greatest faults of present-day writing is to use them to excess. There are two reasons why this is bad. First, it means that statements are made in a roundabout instead of a direct way, and the meaning is more difficult to grasp . . . . Secondly, abstract nouns have less precision than concrete ones . . . . the very vagueness of abstract words is one of the reasons for their popularity. To express one's thoughts accurately is hard work, and to be precise is sometimes dangerous. We are tempted to prefer the safer obscurity of the abstract.

Gowers, 1951, 1

Relationships which can only be revealed by powerful statistical tools could not have been acted upon perfectly and thereby eliminated completely by investors who are privy to no special information, and whose acquaintance with econometric methods is limited.

Baumol, 1965b, 44

Absolutes are too inhuman and elusive to cope with, unless they are connected with some experience in the tangible world of the finite.

Koestler, 1966, 366

Beware of the lure of the abstract word against the concrete. The abstract is often so attractive just because it is imprecise.

Parsons, 1972, 37

Many of the concepts . . . assets, liabilities, financial position, and particularly income, are at very high levels of abstraction, and highly abstract concepts are tricky things. It is difficult to deposit them in another person's mind and make them stick.

Heath, 1987, 8

See also 015, 843

230 Information and Communication

231 Information and information content

The capacity . . . to secure relevant information, to judge reliability of its authenticity, and to use it intelligently in further inquiry, is essential to the right use of reason in human affairs.

Murphy, 1943, 25

Information is the name for the content of whatever is exchanged with the outer world as we adjust to it, and make our adjustment felt upon it. The process of receiving and using information is the process of our adjusting to the contingencies of the outer environment, and of our living effectively in that environment . . . to live effectively is to live with adequate information . . . . Information cannot be conserved as easily [as tangible commodities] . . . . Just as entropy [the degree of disorganization] tends to increase spontaneously in a closed system, so information tends to decrease; just as entropy is a measure of disorder, so information is a measure of order. Information and entropy are not conserved, and are equally unsuitable to being commodities . . . . The idea that information can be stored in a changing world without an overwhelming depreciation in its value is false.

Wiener, 1950/1954, 17–18, 116, 120

Reports adhere to the following rules: first, they are capable of verification; second, they exclude, as far as possible, inferences and judgments . . . . The extensional meaning of an utterance is that which it points to in the extensional (physical) world . . . . it is that which words stand for . . . . The intensional meaning of a word or expression . . . is that which is suggested (connoted) inside one's head.

Hayakawa, 1952/1965, 38, 58

What is information? We mean by it knowledge communicated by way of transmitting symbols, as distinct from knowledge acquired at first hand. Such information may, of course, be about brute facts – facts which do not call for interpretation. But information as such is something that must be understood, something that must be interpreted. We cannot grasp information as information without performing an act of interpretation, that is, without making a choice among possibilities that can be "good" or "bad". Only a being which can interpret meaning can receive and use information.

Kecskemeti, 1952, 12

It is precisely the meaning attached to and action taken on receipt of a message that is of interest to the social scientist.

Shubik, 1954, 630

it is customary to speak of signals as conveying information, as though information were a kind of commodity. But signals do not convey information as railway trucks carry coal. Rather we should say: signals have an information content by virtue of their potential for making selections. Signals operate upon the alternatives forming the recipient's doubt; they give the power to discriminate amongst, or select from, those alternatives.

Cherry, 1957/1961, 169

We can define content as the material in the message that was selected by the source to express his purpose.

Berlo, 1960, 59

meanings are not found in words, statements, messages. Thus, what the accountant is transmitting to the destination is not meaning, but rather messages about a firm's economic status and progress. For only messages are transferable or transmittable.

Bedford & Baladouni, 1962, 656

communication . . . is the sharing of an orientation toward a set of informational signs. Information, in this sense, . . . is not limited to news or facts or what is taught in the classroom or contained in reference books. It is any content that reduces uncertainty or the number of alternative possibilities in a situation.

Schramm, 1971, 13

The net effect of semantic information (receiving messages) is to reduce the total amount of uncertainty in the situation.

Littlejohn, 1983, 120

Mechanical interpretation of information content

the information given to the machine [e.g. calculating machine] differs in principle from the information received and interpreted by human beings. The former, in fact, may be described as an instruction rather than as information proper. The machine is instructed to perform certain operations according to the tape fed into it; it is not merely informed of a certain state of the world. It cannot help performing the good response if it is properly contructed and if the tape which it is given makes sense in terms of its construction.

Kecskemeti, 1952, 13

the engineer is concerned solely with the correct transmission of signs, not with the truth, value, or usefulness of the messages conveyed.

Cherry, 1955, 52

for the information theorist [following the mechanical or engineering analysis of Shannon], it does not matter whether we are transmitting a fact, a judgment, a shallow cliché, a deep teaching, a sublime truth, or a nasty obscenity. All are information. The word comes to have vast generality, but at a price; the meaning of things communicated comes to be leveled, and so too the value.

Roszak, 1986, 14

232 Variety of communications

We have . . . four basic reasons for social communication, (1) to increase uniformity of information, (2) to increase uniformity of opinion, (3) to change status in the group, and (4) to express emotions.

Miller, 1951/1963, 253

linguistic signs have many other uses than that of communicating confirmable propositions: they may be used in many ways to control the behavior of one's self or of other users of the sign . . . . Commands, questions, entreaties and exhortations are of this sort . . . .

Morris, 1955/1962, 117

Language is not always used with the intention of communicating something to other persons. Language may be used for the purpose of influencing persons, of raising in them certain states of feelings which we want to have produced in them . . . . But the suggestive function of language must be logically separated from its communicative function, i.e. its function of informing other persons about certain facts or relations between facts.

Reichenbach, 1938/1961, 59

[There are] . . . informative uses of language . . . . directive uses of language . . . . affective uses of language . . . .

Hayakawa, 1952/1965, 69, 102, 118

In view of their concern with truth and falsehood, it is natural that philosophers, in giving their accounts of meaning, should have concentrated mainly on the fact-stating use of language . . . . There are very many uses of language, prescriptive, ritualistic, playful, or performative, which are not fact-stating . . . .

Ayer, 1955, 26

[Purposes of communication include] to convey information about what is happening both outside and inside the organization . . . . to imprint rules about how various types of situation should be handled . . . . to form and render effective collective decisions . . . . to move to action . . . . to create, confirm or modify the actions of individuals . . . .

Vickers, 1955, 82

The inform-persuade-entertain distinction causes difficulty if we assume that these can be considered as independent purposes of communication . . . . we communicate to influence – to affect with intent . . . . Too often writers think their job is to write technical reports rather than to affect the behavior of their readers.

Berlo, 1960, 9, 12, 13

The four main types of communication – informational, instructional, persuasive, and entertaining – each require slightly different patterns of information processing . . . .

Schramm, 1971, 34

Any number of appearances and words can mislead us; but only a fraction of them are intended to do so . . . . We must single out, therefore, from the countless ways in which we blunder uninformed through life, that which is done with the intention to mislead; and from the countless partial stabs at truth, those which are intended to be truthful . . . . it is to this question alone that the court addresses itself in its request for "the truth, the whole truth, and nothing but the truth".

Bok, 1978/1989, 8

much of the research literature of science is intended rhetorically – to persuade other scientists of the validity of a new hypothesis or to shatter received opinions . . . . [Every scientist's] communications are intended not only to tell things as he saw them, or as he thinks they are; he is also desperately keen to persuade his readers or his audience.

Ziman, 1978, 7, 12

233 Data processing

It used to be said that facts speak for themselves. This is, of course, untrue. The facts only speak when the historian calls on them; it is he who decides which facts to give the floor, and in what order and context.

Carr, 1962, 5

Selective control of the input is the first stage in the process of extracting information from the chaotic noises and other sensations which bombard the organism's receptors; . . . the most powerful single factor among the many factors which enter into the processing of the visual input: the power of convention as a hidden persuader.

Koestler, 1966, 519, 378

knowledge is always gained by the orderly loss of information, that is, by condensing and abstracting and indexing the great buzzing confusion of information that comes from the world around us into a form which we can appreciate and comprehend.

Boulding, 1970, 2

control in a business is something much more than the interaction of its senior managers. It has to do with information of an extent and complexity beyond the capacity of those senior people to absorb and interpret it. Therefore it has to do with the structure of information flows, with the method of information handling, with techniques for information reduction, and so forth.

Beer, 1972, 106

At an early stage in the communication process there has to be a sifting of the transmitter's knowledge such that only that knowledge which is useful to the receiver filters through to the receiver as information.

Macdonald, 1974a, 31

See also 036, 381

234 The communication process

Meaning as such, i.e. the object of thought, arises in experience through the individual stimulating himself to take the attitude of the other in his reaction toward the object. Meaning is that which can be indicated to others while it is by the same process indicated to the indicating individual.

Mead, 1934/1962, 89

[Language] first has reference to some other person or persons with whom it institutes communication – the making of something common. Hence, to that extent its reference becomes general and objective.

Dewey, 1938/1966, 46

The communication process in society performs three functions: (a) surveillance of the environment, disclosing threats and opportunities affecting the value position of the community and of the component parts within it; (b) correlation of the components of the society in making a response to the environment; (c) transmission of the social inheritance.

Lasswell, 1948/1971, 98–99

When we communicate, one with another, we do not transmit our thoughts; we make signs (spoken, written, gestured) and act on rules.

Cherry, 1955, 49

Communication does not consist of the transmission of meaning. Meanings are not transmittable, not transferable. Only messages are transmittable, and meanings are not in the message, they are in the message-users.

Berlo, 1960, 175

Communication is more than meaning, for it is meaning that is communicated. : . . . Communication is a process in which meaning is conveyed. It is also purposive: it is an intended provoking of response.

Ross, 1962, 155

Our language has derived words such as community and communication from the Latin word, *communis*, meaning common. Communication, then, can mean individuals having something in common, sharing something and being fellow members of a community in one sense or another. A person who is communicating in this frame of reference is really "community making".

Sawatsky, 1962, 493

Communication basically means a process in which there is some predictable relation between the message transmitted and the message received.

Katz & Kahn, 1966/1978, 431

235 Communication dependent on shared understandings

Communication of thought and knowledge . . . depends on the existence of corresponding ideas in different minds.

Welton, 1915, 49

Communication depends upon a common core of signals that all the communicators can encode and decode in the same way.

Miller, 1951/1963, 132

if there has been no common experience . . . then communication is impossible . . . . if the experiences of source and destination [of messages] have been strikingly unlike, then it is going to be very difficult to get an intended meaning across from one to the other.

Schramm, 1954/1971, 16

it is of primary importance that the terms, definitions, and methods of measurement used in accounting be highly consistent and comparable so that what is intended by the speaker or writer will be understood in the same way by the hearer or reader.

Cannon, 1955, 60

A small set of consistently used symbols . . . can be used to carry information to other people . . . . only if speakers and listeners have heard the terms used in similar circumstances, and have derived from these experiences the same relation between the symbols and the recurrent features (or functions) which they represent.

Polanyi, 1958, 204

People can have similar meanings only to the extent that they have had similar experiences, or can anticipate similar experiences.

Berlo, 1960, 184

Thinking always implies a symbol which will call out the same response in another that it calls out in the thinker . . . . For there to be meaning in communication, symbols must mean the same to the speaker and the listener.

Duncan, 1968, 77

The first and most fundamental requirement [of a contractual information system] is that the basic properties of the information system be common knowledge among the contracting parties . . . . [and] . . . . the output of the information system must be verifiable by all the contracting parties.

Butterworth & others, 1981, 20

The goal of communication is to create a similar mental experience in the other, a goal that can be achieved only when the communicators share a certain degree of past experience.

Littlejohn, 1983, 96

The success, or effectiveness, of a neutral communication in accounting might be judged on whether the recipient of the information makes the same response that he would have made had he been given access to all the original information.

Arnold & others, 1985, 30

See also 221

236 Communication dependent on source of signals

it is quite impossible for any interpreter to derive more information from any balance sheet than that measure of information which those who compiled it desired should be extracted. A balance sheet is probably the most diplomatic of all business documents. It may quite frankly be conceded that this is an undesirable state of affairs; . . .

Dicksee, 1930, 805

if we are to avoid confusion we must be sure that the recipient of our ideas can understand what we say.

Werntz, 1941/1968, 51

The basic difficulty in accounting as elsewhere is that terminology is looked upon as a means of expressing one's self, whereas, in point of fact, self-expression is of little importance in the understanding of any subject matter. The traffic officer's signal to "stop" was not developed for the benefit of the officer; it is significant only . . . in that it is intended to induce a certain type of response on the part of the motorist. And so it should be with accounting terms.

Dohr, 1941, 203

Signals possess a potential to communicate, and the information communicated will depend upon the choice of signals in any particular channel of communication with relation to the receiver's expectancies.

Cherry, 1957/1961, 12

Good scientists . . . . use the cunning of language, without particularly meaning to. The language used is a social object, and using language is a social act. It requires cunning (or, if you prefer, consideration), attention to the other minds present when one speaks.

McCloskey, 1985, xvii

the form in which ideas are expressed affects what those ideas will be.

Postman, 1987, 32

237 Impediments to communication at the source

Information does not automatically transmit itself from its point of origin to the rest of the organization; the individual who first obtains it must transmit it. In transmitting it, he will naturally be aware of the consequences its transmission will have for him. When he knows that the boss is going to be "burned up" by the news, the news is very likely to be suppressed.

Simon, 1949, 162

Uncertainty absorption takes place when inferences are drawn from a body of evidence and the inferences, instead of the evidence itself, are then communicated . . . . Through the process of uncertainty absorption, the recipient of a communication is severely limited in his ability to judge its correctness . . . . the recipient must, . . . if he accepts the communication at all, accept it pretty much as it stands.

March & Simon, 1958, 165

the practice of filtering information as it travels through various hierarchical stages. People on the lower echelons deliberately distort messages going up in order (1) to give the boss the information that will please him, and (2) to present their own performances in the best light.

Pfiffner & Sherwood, 1960, 298

One of the difficulties of hierarchical organization is the dependency of the lower members of the hierarchy on the upper members. This dependency almost inevitably tends to distort the information that passes from lower to higher members of the hierarchy. The lower members tend to tell the higher members what they think will be acceptable rather than what they know to be true.

Boulding, 1963, 149

Managers at every level of the corporate pyramid tend to screen information in their possession so that only data favorable to them are passed upward to their superiors. (after G Tullock, undated, unpublished ms)

Monsen & Downs, 1965, 228

People are always smarter than systems and if the system is functioning in such a way that it pays to make figures "look right", instead of doing something about the underlying causes, this is what will happen.

Hofstede, 1969, 212

238 Communication dependent on recipient of signals

Every communication depends for its meaning on much which has previously happened to the receiving mind and itself contributes to the meaning of what will follow . . . .
                                                    Vickers, 1955, 77

the same sign may mean different things to (set up different reactions in) different people, ... The interpretation of a sign, the reaction set up in some individual . . . depends upon the particular accumulation of experiences which that individual comprises.
                                                    Cherry, 1957/1961, 264

The existence of dissonance [inconsistency in beliefs or attitudes and actions], being psychologically uncomfortable, will motivate the person to try to reduce the dissonance and achieve consonance . . . . the person will actively avoid situations and information which would likely increase the dissonance.
                                                    Festinger, 1957/1962, 3

People will always respond to a stimulus [sensation or communication] in light of their own experience.
                                                    Berlo, 1960, 184

people tend to hear what they want to hear and ignore that which they do not want to hear. They even go so far as to devise defensive "noise".
                                                    Pfiffner & Sherwood, 1960, 298

The audience, at least in a democratic society, exposes itself to what it wants to hear; even a captive audience engages in a kind of missing-of-the-point when it finds its prejudgments under fire.
                                                    Katz, 1963, 80

[Cognitive dissonance is a] state of disharmony, inconsistency or conflict between the organized attitudes, beliefs and values within an individual's cognitive system. Dissonance theory suggests that people are motivated to restore balance, equilibrium or consonance by reducing such conflict . . . . [and that] we continually justify and rationalize our actions, even when they appear irrational, inappropriate, or unnecessary.
                                                    O'Sullivan & others, 1983, 39

Dissonance occurs when two cognitive inputs to our mental processes are out of line. The result is a certain amount of psychological discomfort. Action is usually taken to resolve the dissonance and restore balance . . . . [by] downgrading the source of the dissonance; compliance with rather than acceptance of new expectations and ideas; changing one's previous ideas and attitudes; and avoidance of the source of dissonance.
                                                    Watson & Hill, 1984, 60

What we see, conceive or understand depends very much on what we expect to see.
Kohn, 1989, 164

239 Noise and other impediments to communication

whenever the social function [of conferring prestige upon its users and arousing respect and awe in others] of a learned vocabulary becomes more important to its users than its communicative function, communication suffers and jargon proliferates.
Hayakawa, 1952/1965, 287

there may be filtering or distortion at any stage [in the communication process] . . . . if the source does not have adequate or clear information; if the message is not encoded fully, accurately, effectively in transmittable signs; if these are not transmitted fast enough and accurately enough, despite interference and competition, to the desired receiver; if the message is not decoded in a pattern that corresponds to the encoding; and finally, if the destination is unable to handle the decoded message so as to produce the desired response – then, obviously, the system is working at less than top efficiency.
Schramm, 1954/1971, 14

organizational devices have been evolved . . . to meet this functional requirement of visibility [to occupants of authoritative positions] . . . . Few groups, it appears, so fully absorb the loyalties of members that they will readily accept unrestricted observability of their role performance. This attitude is sometimes described as a need for privacy. But . . . . Some measure of leeway in conforming with expectations is presupposed in all groups . . . . Resistance to full visibility of activities is of course accentuated by an assumed or actual cleavage of interests between authoritative strata and governed strata.
Merton, 1949/1968, 396

the process of transmitting information may involve several consecutive stages . . . and between any two of these there will be an act of translation, capable of dissipating information. That information may be dissipated but not gained is . . . the cybernetic form of the second law of thermodynamics.
Wiener, 1950/1954, 78

[Communication considered as an act of imparting, conferring or delivering from one to another] is only a small segment of the communication continuum, whose beginning is the sender's impulse to transmit and whose end is the receiver's ability to understand the message. Between these poles lie countless filters within each person which may expedite or hinder the transmission, send it straight or skew it, or indeed blank it out entirely.
Tsaklanganos, 1978, 146

Noise is any disturbance in the channel that distorts or otherwise masks the signal. The disturbance may be, literally, noise in auditory communication, but any kind of interference is included.

Littlejohn, 1983, 118

Noise: impedance or barrier between the sending and receiving of communication messages . . . . [Physical or technical noise is] any distortion of meaning occurring in the communication process which is not intended by the source . . . . [Semantic level noise is] impedance in terms of codes – linguistic, personal, psychological, cultural. . . .

Watson & Hill, 1984, 117

240 Measurement and Measuring

241 Objects of measurement

One of the outstanding characteristics of the present day administration of business is the development of measuring sticks for the various kinds of business activities which have . . . been thought not possible of satisfactory measurement. The standardization movement is closely related to the development of such measuring sticks.

Kester, 1929/1982, 595

Most philosophers and many scientists regard measurement as a simple look-and-see procedure, requiring at the most a careful description of apparatus and the recording of a number. In doing so they ignore . . . the relevance of the number obtained, its reference to something that is to be measured, and its physical dimension. For the apparatus and the act alone do not tell us that the measured number represents a length, an energy, or a frequency; this identification involves the use of certain rules of correspondence with preformed theoretical constructs which greatly complicate the meaning of measurement.

Margenau, 1959/1962, 164

The purpose of measurement is to represent the content of observations by symbols which are related to each other in the same way that the observed objects, events or properties are or can be. Numbers are the symbols generally used because their inter-relationships have been exhaustively studied in mathematics, and because some of the relationships between them are shared by the observations.

Ackoff with others, 1962, 178

The man who builds an instrument to determine optical wave lengths must not be satisfied with a piece of equipment that merely attributes particular numbers to particular spectral lines. He is not just an explorer or measurer. On the contrary, he must show, by analyzing his apparatus in terms of the established body of optical theory, that the numbers his instrument produces are the ones that enter theory as wave lengths.

Kuhn, 1962, 39

The purpose of the operation of measurement is to discover the proper placement of a given object in a given scale. The general statement of placement is in terms of numerosity of units.

Sterling, 1970a, 80

242 The utility of measurements

The need for standards of measurement is by no means novel. In an earlier day . . . trade . . . was hampered by the existence of diverse monetary media of uncertain value, by uncertain and conflicting systems of weighing and measuring, by dishonest scales and measures and by clipped and base coins . . . . Later the problem of providing these prime essentials was assigned to government, and the outgrowth has been standard coinage and currency, and standard weights, measures and grades.

Werntz, 1940/1968, 424

One aim of the language of measurement is to communicate to as many potential users as possible since this will increase the scope of utilization. Another aim is to enable the user to employ the information when there is need for fine distinctions since this also will increase the scope of utilization.

Churchman, 1959/1962, 85

The value of measurement can perhaps best be appreciated if one realizes that the range of uses to which measurement of a property can be put increases with its exactness. A perfectly exact measurement of a property would make it possible to answer any question or solve any problem involving only that property; and, furthermore, it allows one to do it vicariously.

Ackoff with others, 1962, 205

Measurement . . . is a device for standardization, by which we are assured of equivalences among objects of diverse origin . . . . A second function of measurement . . . is to make possible more subtle discriminations and correspondingly more precise descriptions.

Kaplan, 1964, 173

243 Measurement as quantification of properties

Measurement is the process of assigning numbers to represent qualities; the object of measurement is to enable the powerful weapon of mathematical analysis to be applied to the subject matter of science.

Campbell, 1919/1957, 267

[Measurement is] the assignment of numerals to things so as to represent facts and conventions about them . . . . The problem as to what is and is not measurement . . . reduces to the simple question: What are the rules, if any, under which numerals are assigned? If we can point to a consistent set of rules, we are obviously concerned with measurement of some sort, and we can then proceed to the more interesting question as to the kind of measurement it is.

Stevens, 1946, 680

in measuring A [an object or situation at a given moment] . . . one does not observe A alone, but, rather, certain aspects of a situation (A,B) compounded of A and the yardstick or measuring instrument B . . . . A property (A,B) is a measure of A if and only if it enters, together with other such properties of A (and of other objects), into empirical laws that predict and postdict the behavior, before and after the occurrence of (A,B) of A (or of A in interaction with other objects).

Bergmann, 1947/1953, 478–9

It should be noted that only properties can be measured; the flower itself as an object of experience is not measurable but is the carrier of a number of quantities.

Margenau, 1950, 174

The essential function of measurement . . . is the setting in order of a class of events with respect to its exhibition of a particular property . . . . Measurement is the assignment of particular mathematical characteristics to conceptual entities in such a way as to permit (1) an unambiguous mathematical description of every situation involving the entity and (2) the arrangement of all occurrences of it in a quasi-serial order.

Caws, 1959/1962, 5

Measurement of a property . . . involves the assignment of numbers to systems to represent that property. In order to represent the property, an isomorphism, i.e. a one-to-one relationship, must obtain between certain characteristics of the number system involved and the relations between various quantities (instances) of the property to be measured.

Torgerson, 1958/1967, 14

[Measurement] is a way of obtaining symbols to represent the properties of objects, events or states, which things have the same relevant relationship to each other as do the things which are represented.

Ackoff with others, 1962, 179

A measurement procedure is a set of rules for measuring an attribute.

AAA, 1969, 89

A measurement requires that one consciously decide which attribute is to be measured.

Sterling, 1975a, 43

Measuring an object requires selecting one of its attributes and expressing this attribute in terms of some scale.

Goldschmidt & Admon, 1977, 6

244 Measurement an outcome of observation or experience

In every case of measuring we merely ascertain ratios – the ratio which one thing bears to another.

[Bailey], 1825/1967, 95

measurement involves (1) an object . . . upon which an operation is to be performed; (2) an observable whose value is to be determined; (3) some apparatus by means of which the operation can be carried out.

Margenau, 1950, 369

measurement, defined functionally, is the organization of experiences . . . .

Churchman, 1961, 101

What is given in perceptual experience prior to all measurement is [e.g.] that some objects are longer than others.

Pap, 1963, 127

Quantitative observation is measurement. Whenever numbers are assigned to certain traits on the basis of observation, measurements are being taken . . . . to measure is to assign particular values to the numerical variable(s) of a quantitative concept on the basis of observation.

Bunge, 1967, II:194, 203

Measurement is the systematic assignment of numbers to a set of observations to reflect the status of each member of the set in terms of a variable property.

Upshaw, 1968, 60

Measurements and predictions distinguished

never do we say that we are measuring the value of a quantity at a future time, even though it may be possible to predict that value on the basis of a measurement made at present.

Margenau, 1950, 374

Measurement is the discovery of an extant condition and requires a present act. One cannot measure a magnitude that lies in the future. Instead one predicts such magnitudes and verifies them by a measurement operation when the future becomes the present.

Sterling, 1968a, 498

discounted values are not measurements. Instead, they are mathematically adjusted forecasts. As such, they have no present empirical referent – they are subjective.

Sterling, 1979, 126

245 Measurable properties

we have no common measure by which we can compare the necessities, wants or desires of one man with those of another. We cannot even say that a shilling is worth more to a poor man than to a rich one, if we mean to enunciate a rule that can safely be applied to individual cases. The most we can say is that a shilling is worth more to a man when he is poor than (*ceteris paribus*) to the same man when he is rich.

Wicksteed, 1888/1955, 86

The essential character of any attribute belonging to the category of quantity is . . . the following: Each state of a quantity's magnitude may always be formed through addition by means of other smaller states of the same quantity; each quantity is the union through a commutative and associative operation of quantities smaller than the first but of the same kind as it is, and they are parts of it.

Duhem, 1914/1962, 110

If a property is to be measurable it must be such that (1) two objects which are the same in respect of that property as some third object are the same as each other; (2) by adding objects successively we must be able to make a standard series one member of which will be the same in respect of the property as any other object we want to measure; (3) equals added to equals produce equal sums. In order to make a property measurable we must find some method of judging equality and of adding objects, such that these rules are true.

Campbell, 1921/1952, 117

246 Direct and indirect (fundamental and derived) measurement

[Fundamental measurement] consists of two steps: first, the specification of a comparative concept, which determines a nonmetrical order; and, second, the metrization of that order by the introduction of numerical values.

Hempel, 1952/1960, 58

By derived measurement we understand the determination of a metrical scale by means of criteria which presuppose at least one previous scale of measurement . . . . derived measurement by stipulation . . . consists in defining a "new" quantity by means of others which are readily available; it is illustrated by the definition of the average speed of a point during a certain period of time as the quotient of the distance covered and the length of the period of time. Derived measurement by law, on the other hand, does not introduce a "new" quantity, but rather an alternative way of measuring one that has been previously introduced . . . . by the discovery of some law which represents the magnitude in question as a mathematical function of other quantities for which methods of measurement have likewise been laid down previously.

Hempel, 1952/1960, 69

A fundamental measurement is one which presupposes no others, save those which consist in establishing an order or making a count; a derived measurement is one which is carried out by making use of laws, logical or empirical, relating to fundamental measures.

Kaplan, 1964, 187

A direct measurement is made by comparing the mensurandum with a standard or with the units on a material scale and counting the number of times the unit is contained in the mensurandum . . . . [Indirect measurement is] measurement involving both direct measurement (of something else) and computation [with the help of formulae].

Bunge, 1967, II:232, 234

Since money is the medium is terms of which all other prices are expressed, we have no direct measure (indicator) of these changes [in the relative price of money] . . . . we resort to an indirect measure, namely, the reciprocal of an index of prices generally, the more general the better.

Moonitz, 1970a, 474

a number that is generated directly by quantifying the property of an object [is called a primary measure] and a number that is derived indirectly by an algebraic transformation of a set of numbers which are direct measures of some objects or their attributes [is called a secondary measure].

AAA, 1971, 20

in a simple measurement of latitude, the position of a bright star or the sun must be known with an accuracy considerably better than one minute of arc. Such an accuracy demands not only a refined technique of observation but an understanding of how to correct these observations for a number of quite obscure and complicated effects, such as the aberration of light, the precession of the equinoxes, the nutation of the earth's pole and the refraction of light in the earth's atmosphere.

Brown, 1987, 25

247 Additive or extensive properties

The difference between those [physical] properties which can be measured perfectly, like weight, and those which cannot arises . . . from the possibility or impossibility of finding in connection with these properties a physical significance for the process of addition.

Campbell, 1919/1957, 277

In fundamental measurement, this resemblance . . . [between the property measured and the numerals assigned to represent it] arises from the fact that the property is susceptible to addition following the same rule as that of number, with which numerals are so closely associated.

> Campbell, 1921/1952, 126

although many qualities can be serially ordered and so numbered in accordance with an arbitrary plan, a few of those qualities (and a limited few they are) possess also a capacity for addition which the rest do not. This cleavage between additive or extensive qualities and nonadditive or intensive qualities is of fundamental importance in the philosophy of physical measurement.

> Nagel, 1932/1960, 128

Ultimately, the logic and usefulness of [physical science] measurements depend on the additivity of extensive properties.

> Vickrey, 1970, 738

248 Aggregative (additive) measurement

If individual measures are to be merged by summation or otherwise, the individual things measured should belong to a common population . . . . the unit of measure must have a sensibly common significance throughout the measuring . . . . the unit of measure must either be uniform throughout the measuring, or all units employed must be convertible into the unit in terms of which the measures are merged . . . . the method and circumstances of measuring should be as nearly as possible common to all measures . . . . the degree of error (error per unit of measure likely to occur) should not significantly vary as between one variate and another.

> Canning, 1929a, 199

The rules of arithmetic are the rules for the manipulation of numbers when related to a collection of homogeneous objects . . . . [objects] of the same kind or nature, or consisting of elements of like nature. Now numbers themselves are a collection of homogeneous mental objects or concepts. Obviously such objects are not necessarily of the same kind or nature as physical objects, nor do they necessarily consist of the same elements as physical objects . . . . the processes of arithmetic . . . must be applied to physical objects with care if [they are] not to result in absurdities. The rules of arithmetic . . . can only be applied to physical things when the things are found to be ordered in exactly the same way as numbers. This is correct of all mathematical processes.

> Jones, 1934, 6

One of the most fundamental postulates of mathematical analysis . . . is that the variables of the analysis are homogeneous quantities . . . . The fallacy of aggregation, i.e. of working with aggregates with too significantly heterogeneous a structure, has been a common one in the history of social thought.

> Boulding, 1950/1962, 187

A quantity *s* is additive relatively to a combining operation o if $s(x \circ y) = s(x) + s(y)$ whenever *x, y,* and *x* o *y* belong to the domain in which *s* is defined.

Hempel, 1952/1960, 60

The formal properties of a scale . . . do not describe properties of that which is being measured, but properties of the operations which can be performed on that which is being measured. Thus, to say that the scale of weight is additive is not to say anything about weight itself, but it does say something about what operations can be performed on objects which have weight.

Ackoff with others, 1962, 204

Q is an additive magnitude if there is a physical joining operation such that the value of Q characterizing the join to two objects x and y equals the arithmetic sum of the values of Q that characterize x and y.

Pap, 1963, 130

A particular type of measurement which . . . [enables] us to measure a magnitude in such a way that we can usefully perform whatever arithmetical operations we choose on the numbers assigned . . . . is that known as additive measurement.

Kaplan, 1964, 184

There is an operation of dimensional addition which corresponds to the operation of arithmetical addition. There are two distinct operations in this definition. One, the operation of arithmetical addition, which is the familiar notion of combining numerals according to the rules of arithmetic. Two, the operation of dimensional addition, which is the combination of objects. If the sum of the numbers that are discovered by the operation of measurement on the separate objects is equal to the number that is discovered by performing an operation of measurement on the combined objects, the dimension is said to be additive.

Sterling, 1970a, 101

249 Units and scales

Now the order found to exist among those economic things the economist calls goods, services and money, arises out of those things themselves, and is not merely a matter of thinking. Our problem is to find what known form of mathematical order best describes the order of such things from the economic viewpoint . . . . If the physical order is found to be measurable in terms of some unit of physical magnitude common to all the things at various times and places, then there is some way of expressing this order in terms of this unit.

Jones, 1934, 8

Counting yields a measurement only when things are classified by some common descriptive property . . . . If the property can be divided into units in a specifiable way, then by counting the units we can tell how much of it is present; 2 feet joined to 2 feet make a length of 4 feet, just as 2 + 2=4. It is an empirical law about length that it has this property of additivity. This means that there is an empirical relation, that of being joined together, corrresponding to arithmetical addition, such that after the lengths are joined together, the number assigned to the result is the arithmetic sum of the numbers assigned to its parts. Properties of this kind are called extensive.

Brodbeck, 1968, 575

Measurement requires a unit, a standard thing with which to compare the things to be measured. To serve its purpose this unit must be invariant against change of circumstances, and must mean the same thing to everybody.

Shackle, 1970, 13

Ratio scales

Ratio scales are those most commonly encountered in physics and are possible only when there exist operations for determining all four relations: equality, rank order, equality of intervals, and equality of ratios . . . . Foremost among the ratio scales is the scale of number itself – cardinal number – the scale we use when we count such things as eggs, pennies, and apples. This scale of the numerosity of aggregates is so basic and so common that it is ordinarily not even mentioned in discussions of measurement.

Stevens, 1946, 679

the monetary unit . . . has two functions: that of a standard of payment and that of a measure of value. In both respects we count numbers of monetary units: the debts amount to so and so many units; the value of an object is expresed in terms of such units. We seem to be counting numbers of these units just as we count people, cattle, apples, or anything else; and the counting is, of course, essential for our use of money.

Olivecrona, 1957, 80

A ratio scale is one which provides equal intervals, but with a zero which is . . . [not] arbitrary . . . . ratio scales are isomorphic with the measure of cardinality itself: measurement by a ratio scale has the same structure as counting the number of units to be found in a given magnitude . . . . Measurement with ratio scales constitutes what is called extensive measurement.

Kaplan, 1964, 196

Measurement in monetary terms . . . belongs to the type of metrical or ratio scaling, mathematically expressed by the functional relation $x' = cx$ of similarity transformations, i.e. the hierarchy of scaling classes is order-ranked so that all class intervals are of equal size and so that there is an absolute zero point which is valid for all pertinent scales. Moreover, each value of one scale x can be transformed into the corresponding value of any other scale x' by multiplying x with a constant factor c, the proportionality factor. All possible currency scales are thus interconnected with each other by these constant ratios or coefficients. They represent the exchange rates for any two currencies.

Kosiol, 1966, 1

250 Measurement in Accounting

251 Accounting described as measurement

it is their measured amounts – their values – which give [all items in the balance sheet] their real significance when used to show financial condition.

Kester, 1933, 95

Accounting strives to measure economic forces in financial terms and to communicate the results of such measurement to interested parties.

Paton, 1939/1943, 87

The principal functions in accounting are usually recognized as being those of recording, reporting and interpreting. But underlying all of these is the necessity for measuring. The problem facing the accountant is that of measuring something. He therefore needs concepts which are capable of measurement.

Goldberg, 1955, 484

Accounting is a system for recording and summarizing measurements of business facts, and, as is the case with any measurement, an accounting figure is an approximation rather than a precisely accurate statement.

Anthony, 1960, 6

Accounting is the art of measuring and communicating financial information . . . . acknowledgment that accounting is concerned with measurement is a first necessary step towards a long awaited revolution in accounting.

Bierman, 1963b, 501

Accounting is a measuring process which tries to describe a firm's attainment over a period of time and its position at the end of that period.

Bourn, 1968, 346

accounting is a measurement discipline if and only if at least one extensive economic property is identified which (1) is possessed by accounting phenomena, (2) is measurable in standard monetary units . . . .

Vickrey, 1970, 738

In the sciences the word measurement is used in a very general sense: measurement occurs whenever numerals are assigned to phenomena (objects, events, traits) on

the basis of observation and according to rules. Under this definition, financial accounting is a way of measuring the economic phenomena of individual accounting entities.

Thomas & Basu, 1972, 224

accounting is a measurement discipline.

Buckley & Lightner, 1973, 121

Wealth is the fundamental subject matter of accounting measurement. Accounting
identifies, measures, classifies and reports stocks and flows of wealth so as to provide
information on income, liquidity, risk, and other aspects of wealth.

Staubus, 1985, 73

252 Measurement used of past, present and future magnitudes

Accounting data are based on prices generated by past, present, or future exchanges
which have actually taken place or are expected to.

Moonitz, 1961, 37

accounting measurement is an assignment of numerals to an entity's past, present
or future economic phenomena, on the basis of observation and according to rules.
Under this definition, it should be pointed out, the rules employed need not be good
ones and observations made need not be correct to qualify as accounting measurement.

AAA, 1971, 3

The [accounting] system admits information regarding economic events or transactions generated by past, present, or future exchanges.

Buckley & Lightner, 1973, 60

Accounting measurement said to be future-dependent

Allocations as between years of both charges and credits affecting the determination of net income are, in fact, estimated and conventional and based on assumptions as to future events which may be invalidated by experience.

AIA, 1947c, ARB32

Unless we are prepared to use market values of assets as a criterion, we must necessarily invoke estimates of future earnings when deciding whether capital is being
maintained.

Edey, 1951, 138

the problem of measuring (pricing, valuing) an asset is the problem of measuring
the future services.

Sprouse & Moonitz, 1962, 23

Accounting measurements will always be difficult since they will always involve estimates of the future, . . .

Stamp, 1970c, 629

True examples of reliance upon future exchange prices [include]: (a) estimation of future costs when revenue is recognized on the percentage of completion basis . . . . (b) estimation of salvage value of a depreciable asset. (c) . . . the estimation of future selling price and disposition costs when assets are written down to net realizable value.

Staubus, 1972, 38

We . . . postulate the . . . concept of an objectively quantifiable future benefit . . . . It seems that there has to be some demonstrably objective basis of allocating cost to future periods before it is conventionally respectable to treat it in this way . . . . it has to be a basis that would readily commend itself to anyone else . . . . It is not the certainty, but the general acceptability, both of the hypothesis about the future and the basis of quantification, that distinguishes a quantifiable future benefit.

Morison, 1974, 355

summing up the quality of the financial legacy bequeathed to future years . . . . involves looking into the future and is, therefore, in a large degree judgmental . . . . Judgments or guesses about the future . . . . estimates of the value of intangibles, consideration of the life and earning potential of assets, future realizations and so on, become important [in decision oriented financial statements].

Edey, 1978, 108

Estimates resting on expectations of the future are often needed in financial reporting . . . to measure financial effects of past transactions or events or the present status of an asset or liability.

FASB, 1978, SFAC1

all values reside ultimately in the future, since it is our estimate of the services that we shall derive from an asset in the future . . . that determines its value to its owner today . . . . since income (which is generally thought of as measuring what has happened in the past) depends upon measures of value it becomes impossible to divorce the past from the present and the future when the accountant attempts to measure past performance.

CICA, 1980, 5

We accountants have tended to play down the scientific measurement aspect of our business. We have papered it over with an emphasis on recording transactions. We intimate that recording historical cost on a transaction basis is a recording of hard fact – an anchor to reality. We seldom acknowledge that every [such] recording is a prediction. We predict that an expenditure has acquired a future benefit, and we book it as an asset; or we predict that the benefit has expired, and we book it as an expense. Every time that we prepare a balance sheet, we predict that every asset will generate enough future cash flow at least to recover its booked cost, or else we predict that it will not and reduce the book value. So historical transaction cost, our anchor to reality, turns out to be an anchor made of wood. That leaves us, like it or not, adrift on a sea of prediction.

Mosso, 1980, 133

Accrual accounting, by its very nature, involves looking into the future.

AAA, 1991, 83

See also 328, 618

Measurement not descriptive of, nor dependent on, future magnitudes

Market value .... is the only general conception of value that admits of measurement.

Carter, 1910b, 561

there can be no history of the future. A future event .... cannot directly contradict any strictly historical statement as to what happened in the past.

Cohen, 1931/1964, 100

A speedometer measures the speed of an automobile at the time it is read, not five minutes ago or five minutes hence .... never do we say that we are measuring the value of a quantity at a future time, even though it may be possible to *predict* that value on the basis of a measurement made at present.

Margenau, 1950, 374

we must report the effect of present conditions, uninfluenced by guesswork about anticipated future developments. Financial statements are not designed to present guesses as to the future but should present the facts as to the present.

Spacek, 1968, 61

One is not required to forecast the future in order to make a present measurement. In fact, that is a contradiction in terms. Measurement is the process of discovering a present existing magnitude. It is not a process of allocating past magnitudes to time periods on the basis of forecast future magnitudes.

Sterling, 1975b, 32

253 The money unit as common denominator in accounting

it is impossible to add railroad tracks, buildings, bridges, etc, without reducing all these items to a common denominator.

Paton & Stevenson, 1917, 2

At the close of the fiscal period all of these different assets must be reduced to a common value denominator so that they may properly express the financial condition at that date.

Kester, 1933, 94

The dollar, the pound, the franc or other monetary unit must be used as a common denominator to permit land, buildings, and machinery to be added to inventories, accounts receivable, patents and goodwill. The process of expressing such diverse items in terms of a common unit is known as valuation.

Jones, 1935, 171

The balance sheet includes a heterogeneous group of items each of which may be measured and stated in terms of some standard. In order, however, that these items may be set forth as an aggregate, they must be expressed in terms of a common denominator. The only standard available for this purpose is the money standard.

Dohr, 1941, 203

Monetary calculations do not consist in mathematical operations with abstract numbers; they are concerned with numbers of something: money units.

Olivecrona, 1957, 80

the accountant must deal with capital forms and sources of widely varying characteristics, the only common denominator of which is value . . . . he uses the monetary unit for this purpose.

Hill & Gordon, 1959, 5

Business transactions are of many types . . . . The common denominator in these experiences is money. It therefore constitutes the basis of the accounting record and of the accounting reports . . . . whether the transactions are domestic only or are in part foreign, money of common denomination serves to unify all transactions recorded and reported.

Husband, 1960, 12

the only function of money essential to the accounting problem is its use as a common denominator of value.

Moonitz & Jordan, 1963, I:17

See also 114

254 The money unit as the unit of measurement

When any transaction is recorded in the financial records, the quantitative measurement of it is expressed in the common monetary unit, the dollar.

Kester, 1946, 28

The monetary unit is the principal unit of measure employed in accounting .... It is the simplest and most adaptable common denominator in which business transactions may be expressed and its use facilitates the summarizations and comparisons essential to effective reporting.

AAA, 1957a/1957b, 2

Money is the common denominator in terms of which goods and services including labor, natural resources and capital are measured.

Moonitz, 1961, 22

Throughout ED8 [1973] .... purchasing power was the unit of account .... the Sandilands Committee [1975] ... [chose] money as the unit of account .... ED18 [1976] remained faithful to money as the unit of account. But it also incorporated [a] statement showing the effect of changes in the value of money .... [In] the Hyde guidelines [1977] .... money and purchasing power were mixed as the unit of account .... ED24 [1979] perpetuated this procedure.

Buckley, 1979, 130

Measurement in monetary terms becomes essential only when we have more than one good. Monetary measurement is then a device for translating heterogeneous physical measures into a common unit of measurement, the monetary unit.

Whittington, 1983a/1986, 64

Money is the only factor common to all business transactions, and thus it is the only practical unit of measure that can produce financial data that are alike and can be compared.

Needles & others, 1984, 28

Dated purchasing power as the unit of measurement

Accountants are fully aware of the difference between dollar accounting and a conceivable purchasing power accounting, and would prefer, just as the economists do, a purchasing power accounting.

Canning, 1929a, 196

that balance sheets should use a valuation which will express or reflect the present purchasing power of the dollar or other monetary unit of measure .... is a very important question about which, however, there is a great difference of opinion ....

Kester, 1929/1982, 601

stabilized accounting is primarily concerned with the use of a homogeneous measuring unit .... Stabilized means uniformly expressed in the value of the dollar as of the date represented by [the] balance sheet rather than expressed as a mixture of the dollar values of many different dates and periods.

Sweeney, 1936/1964, 44, 198

In order to attract purchasing power, a business has to convince the owner of the purchasing power that it will yield him net advantages if used in this particular business greater than the net advantages offered by any alternative investment.

Edwards, 1938b, 13

The greatest significance in accounts would be attained if (a) revenues and charges against revenues were stated in terms of units of the same purchasing power, and (b) the treatment of all costs were homogeneous.

May, 1949a, 42

The view point of organized labor today is to express wages in terms of what it will buy. Some labor agreements make provision for the automatic adjustment of money wages to reflect uniform purchasing power . . . . upwards of 3,000,000 workers are known to work under [such] contracts . . . . The purchasing power concept is thus already accepted in certain important economic relationships. It is worth noting, too, that this first general acceptance has occurred in nonprofessional and non-technical circles.

Broad, 1952, 307

balance sheet . . . presentation in terms of a consistent monetary standard . . . can perhaps only be achieved by a complete revaluation each year, which few of us would be prepared to suggest or contemplate.

Hartley, 1953, 139

If we are to account for inflation (or deflation), the first thing to be done at the end of every accounting period is to apply to capital the index which shows the change which has occurred in the purchasing power of accountancy's unit of measurement.

Mutton, 1962, 412

In financial statements, many types of resources . . . are all related to a single resource, money. That single resource may for convenience be called the standard resource . . . . [Some types of accounting use] general purchasing power as the standard resource.

Rosenfield, 1975b, 64

Historical cost can be stated in terms either of the units of money or of the units of general purchasing power that were expended for the object of measurement.

Stickney, 1977, 32:2

To eliminate from the accounts the distorting effects of inflation, the unit of measurement must be one of general, not specific, purchasing power.

Fabricant, 1978, 12

255 An identified attribute (property) to be measured

If one intends ... to make the balance sheet a true picture of the values in an enterprise, one has by all means to apply to all parts of the assets a uniform value, or otherwise it is impossible to find a total value by adding simply several kinds of values.

Schmidt, 1930/1982, 504

The decision as to which attribute we ought to measure must be based on the relevance of the attributes [to a decision model], not on one's being wrong and the other's being right .... Selection of the attribute that ought to be measured requires precise criteria, rigorously applied.

Sterling, 1975a, 44, 50

Before measurement can take place ... the specific attribute to be measured must be selected.

Hendriksen, 1977, 125

Attributes or properties are particular characteristics of objects .... we do not measure objects themselves but rather something that might be termed the dollar numerosity or how-much-ness that relates to a particular attribute of the object.

Wolk & others, 1984, 15

See also 243

The measured attribute said to be cost

Logically considered books of account should be kept so as to reflect cost and not value and this is the theory at the basis of accounting structure.

JA, editorial, 1921, 50

Cost (or adjusted cost) is the natural basis for the accountant's entries; to leave this basis would be to throw open the entire accounting system to a maze of conjecture and uncertainty.

Paton, 1922/1962, 320

The entity, as such, is not concerned with economic measures of valuation but rather symbolizes in terms of money various transactions reflecting a charge and discharge relationship between entity and proprietor .... From the entity viewpoint valuation at cost is natural ....

Gilman, 1939, 55

Every well versed accountant knows that the accounts ... are framed on the basis of monetary cost. Indeed, it is difficult to know what other basis could be used.

Bray, 1943, 27

The accountant . . . is largely concerned with the business enterprise as a going concern. It follows that accounting is generally on a cost basis and that there is and should be a strong presumption in favor of statement in terms of cost.

Dohr, 1944, 195

There should be no departure from the cost basis to reflect the assets of an enterprise at amounts higher than unassigned costs.

AAA, 1948/1957b, 14

With the adoption of the principle of the going concern, fixed assets, inventories, and intangibles are no longer regarded as marketable wealth but rather as deferred costs to be matched against future revenues.

Backer, 1955a/1958b, 215

the basis of recording assets is generally their cost, since the cost of an asset is an objective measure . . . .

Bierman, 1963c, 21

The money convention . . . . under this convention it is held that the function of accounting is not to account for value; rather it is (1) to record dollars invested and dollars borrowed, (2) to trace the various commitments of these dollars of capital . . . , and finally (3) to measure out of gross dollars of revenue the recapture of dollars of capital with any excess being designated as dollars of income.

Pyle & White, 1966, 823

Most accountants accept the use of historical cost as the primary basis of asset valuation.

Kemp, 1970, 58

Generally cost is the attribute of resources which is measured and accepted as an input into the accounting system, although there are exceptions to this . . . .

Carrington & Howitt, 1983, 28

See also 510

The measured attribute said to be service potential

The whole subject of accountancy, if not the whole essence of economics, lies in the study of services. Capital accounts, that is, accounts of assets and liabilities, merely represent the discounted valuation at a particular date of the series of services and disservices or outlays which are expected to be rendered subsequent to that date . . . . No competent accountant would value any asset or liability except by valuing the anticipated future services and outlays.

Fisher, 1930b, 608

The accounting function in relation to capital assets is to measure and record not the fluctuations in their value but the extent to which their usefulness is being exhausted through age or use, and to make proper charges against income in respect of such exhaustion, based on the cost of the property exhausted, with the intent that the property shall stand in the books at its salvage value when the term of its usefulness is ended.

May, 1936, 16

Wealth is ... an aggregation of service potentials .... Commodities, productive agencies, money and other financial claims ... have thus a common significance – they are service potentials, capable of satisfying wants through the processes of business .... assets are service potentials, not physical things, legal rights or money claims.

Vatter, 1947, 16

The aim of all measurements of assets is to state the amount of available service potential in the most objective and realistic terms.

AAA, 1957a/1957b, 5

Money and other resources being economically, in essence, service potentials, the present and future inflows and outgoes of services ... are the actual objects of accounting.

Kafer, 1966, 70

assets may be defined as embodiments of present or future economic benefits or service potentials measurable in terms of monetary units, accruing to an enterprise as a result of economic events, the enjoyment of which by the enterprise is secured by the law.

Lall, 1968, 797

Underlying measurement concept .... the basic attribute [of business resources] is capacity to render valuable services.

Paton & Paton, 1971, 17

See also 435

The measured attribute said to be money equivalent or value in exchange

it is the potential exchange value of assets which an accountant must discover in his measurement of financial status and operations.

Rorem, 1928, 281

To value any asset whatever means to indicate the amount of money current in the particular country, which, at that moment, and under those existent conditions, it is possible to obtain in exchange for the thing valued.

Bottini, 1929, 533

the present value of property is, generally speaking, the measurement of outstanding importance; it indicates . . . what the owner may expect to realize on a sale; it determines his borrowing capacity . . . , it fixes his liability for various forms of taxation; it reflects his earning capacity as owner; . . . it is the basis upon which the property may be insured.

Dohr, 1944, 193

Whatever the method of valuation . . . the meaning of valuation is always the same: it is to discover a dollar equivalent for each physical unit of assets, representing at least a potential rate of transformation of nonliquid into liquid assets.

Boulding, 1950/1962, 28

In the world of economics and accounting, a major attribute of an object is its exchange ability, that is, its value in exchange . . . . Price is . . . the measure of a particular attribute of a given object – its exchange value.

Goldschmidt & Admon, 1977, 7

Valuation to an accountant is simply the process of converting various assets to their cash equivalent.

Ross, 1969, 30

See also 542

The attribute said to be value

Bookkeeping is the art of recording property, so as to show at all times the value of the whole capital and of each component part.

Cronhelm, 1818/1978, 1

Bookkeeping is a history of values.

Sprague, 1880, 2

The data with which accounting deals are values, measured in terms of the money unit.

Paton & Stevenson, 1916/1976, 47

The relevant attribute with which we [accountants] are essentially concerned is that of value; the measurement process in which we are fundamentally engaged may be properly described as valuation.

Sprouse, 1966b, 107

If the accountant declines to treat his asset figures as part of a valuation process, then he divorces these values and costs from the reality that he is striving to measure and reduces them to empty abstractions.

Baxter, 1971, 27

Financial position and the results of operations are stated in terms of prices (values) generated by past, present, or future exchanges which have actually taken place or are expected to. Corollary: hypothetical, arbitrary, and sentimental values are excluded.

Buckley & Lightner, 1973, 67

See also 321, 322

No singular attribute specified

When an accountant refers merely to the measurement of assets he is either consciously avoiding or carelessly omitting specification of the attribute to be measured – surely a crucial factor.

Sprouse, 1966b, 101

Four types of money prices are used in measuring resources in financial accounting. 1. Price in past purchase exchanges of the enterprise .... 2. Price in a current purchase exchange .... 3. Price in a current sale exchange .... 4. Price based on future exchanges.

AICPA, 1970c, APBS4

it is difficult to know exactly what attribute the accounting tradition is attempting to measure. The fundamental unit of measure is variously described as future benefits, service potentials, and utility. In respect to inventories this fundamental unit seems to reduce to dollars that will be received when the inventory items are sold, i.e. a future sales price. Yet they use a past purchase price to value the inventory items unless the present price is less than the past price. Neither the logical nor the empirical connection of a past price to a future price is clear to us, especially when the past price is used to calculate a cost value which is reported on a current or present financial statement.

Sterling, 1970a, 277

Items currently reported in financial statements are measured by different attributes, depending on the nature of the item and the relevance and reliability of the attribute measured. The Board expects the use of different attributes to continue. Five different attributes ... are used in present practice: historical cost (historical proceeds) .... current [replacement] cost .... current market value .... net realizable (settlement) value .... present (or discounted) value of future cash flows ....

FASB, 1984, SFAC5

256 Aggregative measurement

one of the first principles of statistics ... is that valid comparisons can be made between quantitative data only when the data are homogeneous .... yet there are accountants who maintain as an infallible rule of their profession that the value of all assets must be stated in terms of their cost in dollars and that no account may be taken of the changes in the value of money .... Even in physics, the standard measure is standard only at a standard temperature, and corrections are applied accordingly. Is it not ridiculous that accountants, who pretend to a scientific standing, persist in ignoring such a basic fact that their unit of measurement (in this case the dollar) is constantly varying in size?

DuBrul, 1925/1964, 10

The most elementary rule of mathematics requires that in any financial statement or computation, every element of the computation must be stated in dollars of like purchasing power.

Dohr, 1950a, 116

if purchasing power ... the ability of an object to command other objects and services in exchanges, is shown to satisfy the conditions [of additivity of extensive properties] .... Periodic income could be defined as the increase in the residual purchasing power of the accounting entity over a specified period of time .... Financial position could be defined as the ability of the accounting entity to command goods and services in exchanges, ...

Vickrey, 1970, 739

A business measuring unit must permit the addition of things or amounts for reporting purposes; ....

Vatter, 1971, 4

Accounting is concerned with measurement and accounting processes must conform consistently with measurement rules, the most fundamental of which in this context is additivity. The necessary conditions for additivity are, first, that the properties of objects being measured are identical for all objects, and second, that the measurement standard is uniform for all measurements.

Ma & Mathews, 1979, 469

By additivity we mean that all the numbers in a statement, when added together, should have a sum which has the same meaning as each of the numbers taken on its own.

ICAS, 1988, 57

257 The fallacy of heterogeneous aggregation

Many economists are grieved to find that the balance sheet valuations of accountants are of mongrel origin .... They find that cash has been counted (a present valuation); that accounts, bills and notes receivable have been valued at the number of dollars expected to come in (a future valuation); ... that inventories are valued at cost or market (a purely arbitrary index); that items like organization expense, purchased goodwill, etc. having no attributes in common with the assets grouped with them are included (valuation account balances); that fixed assets are valued at an approximation to the cost of the future services expected to become available provided that cost does not exceed the cost of available substitute services (a division of costs into past and future charges). They find, moreover, that these diverse valuations of diverse things are added to find an asset total that, dollar for dollar, cannot possibly have a common significance.

Canning, 1929a, 319

I do not believe it to be the function of accounting to jumble up the prognostications of forecasters with the known facts of the past and present.

Cole, 1936, 9

people who would not dream of adding together a cart-horse and a saw-horse and speaking of the result as two horses, have no compunction at all about adding together a book figure (or, as they call it, a book value) and a market value, and speaking of the result as a value, even in the case of a stock the selling price of which is a mere fraction of that value.

May, 1936, 17

A balance sheet in which one asset is stated at book value, another at replacement value, a third at liquidation value and a fourth at going concern value, and the liabilities at their face value, does not yield a figure that can be described as net worth expressed in a single measure of value any more than one in which were mingled American and Chinese dollars and Mexican and Chilean pesos, all preceded by the same familiar dollar sign, could produce a net worth expressed in any one of those currencies.

May, 1936, 20

it is a universally accepted practice to add the cost value of one asset to the market value of another, and to deduct from the sum the nominal value of a liability to arrive at a net figure . . . . This procedure, although open to obvious criticism of its mathematical propriety, possesses so many practical advantages and is so well established both here and abroad, in accounts subject to regulations as well as in accounts not so subject, that it is not likely to be abandoned.

AIA, 1940c, ARB7

the balance sheet, as a statement of affairs, remains a mixture of historical and current costs, face values, conventional valuations and arithmetical estimates, all of which have to be reconsidered in greater or less degree when it comes to a current assessment of the present value of proprietorship worth.

Accountant, editorial, 1946c, 293

the [historic cost] balance sheet is not additive because it contains amounts representing different properties of the assets . . . . to add a current market value to a written down historic cost, a market value prevailing two years ago and a current market value . . . . must be misleading for analytical purposes.

Martin, 1984, 392

The fallacy of heteroscalar aggregation

As the general price level fluctuates, the dollar is bound to become a unit of different magnitude. To mix these units is like mixing inches and centimeters or measuring a field with a rubber tape line. Would it not be more reasonable in accounts to treat of the various dollars as distinct units of measure rather than to combine them without distinction?

Middleditch, 1918, 114

What do [entries, for purchases over a series of years, on the debit side of a fixed asset account] express in their present form? Nothing except dissimilar amounts. There is no advantage in finding the total. It would be meaningless.

Sweeney, 1927, 189

ordinary accounting procedure combines figures that are not expressed in the same kind of measuring unit, thus violating the basic mathematical axiom that like added to like gives like.

Sweeney, 1936/1964, 24

to measure the distance round the world we would not measure the distance across the United States in statute miles, the distance across the Atlantic in nautical miles, the distance across Europe in kilometers, and so on, and add them together . . . . Yet much the same error is present in income statements when depreciation stated in pre-war dollars is deducted from income in current dollars.

Broad, 1949, 388

there is a fallacy in setting aside from income amounts intended to cover the gradual using up of fixed plant and other wearing assets, unless the deduction is in the same currency as used in recording the income. It is fallacious to set aside deductions in 1939 pounds from income expressed in 1950 pounds; the currencies are not the same.

CSR, 1950

no proper judgments can be formed from data which are intertwined with different measurements occasioned by different price levels brought into use at the same time.

Barrowcliff, 1952, 63

We cannot add incommensurables, yet this is what the constant money value convention of accountants would have us do . . . . On the other hand, if we produce a balance sheet [in which all prices are prices as at balance date] we have a document with some meaning.

Morgan, 1953, 31

the recorded dollars of plant cost . . . over a series of years are dated dollars . . . . The error in dealing with such data arises when the various generations of monetary units are added, averaged, or otherwise combined as if they were all of the same economic potency.

Paton, 1963, 54

By what feat of semantic legerdemain can a balance sheet, consisting of a conglomeration of amounts arrived at on the basis of cost or at a valuation other than cost, each referable to numerous and unspecified points of time, be said to give shareholders, or any other group for that matter, a true and fair view of the state of affairs of the company as at the end of the period to which it relates?

Ryan, 1967, 97

time may be past, present or future. The attempt to combine two or more "vectors" of time in one statement is at the root of much confusion when seeking to measure profit and return on investment.

Risk, 1969, 192

Measurements using different scales . . . cannot be directly compared, added or subtracted. The same is true if the exchange ratio of money has changed between two points of time. Although the measurement unit is denoted by the same name as before, its size has changed . . . . The results of measurements carried out at two different points of time cannot be meaningfully compared, added or subtracted unless they are first transformed (adjusted, restated).

Goldschmidt & Admon, 1979, 6

traditional accounts are in practice a mixture of two different units of measurement. There is the unit of record measure (historical cost, if you like) in which nonmonetary assets are expressed, and the unit of exchange measure in which monetary items are expressed. The first soon ceases to bear any relation to current values, but the second retains its current value significance.

Coad, 1977, 466

In times of inflation, historical cost accounts using money add and subtract heterogeneous units of account. The result is meaningless.

Myddelton, 1981, 93

it is theoretically incorrect to perform any arithmetic operations . . . using amounts expressed in different measurement scales [differently named money units or differently dated money units].

Ma & others, 1987, 493

See also 593, 594

258 Accuracy and approximation

If some goal is to be attained at the end of several or many separate steps, a slight error in the measurement of the size or direction of the various steps is enough to lead us astray. Small errors in several of the numbers of a computation may thus significantly falsify the conclusion.

Mach, 1908/1960, 268

physics progresses by successive approximations . . . . there is every reason to suppose that however far we go, we shall always be dealing with approximations.

D'Abro, 1927/1950, 384

Even if the completely correct calculation of a theoretically defined profit were not possible, we would still have gained a great deal by knowing what was correct; because then we need only strive for better technical methods of approximation, for approximations are always customary in the application of all theoretical knowledge.

Schmidt, 1930, 235

However far we go in the pursuit of accuracy we shall never get anything other than a finite series of discrete results which are *a priori* settled by the nature of the instrument.

Schrödinger, 1935/1957, 73

coincidence [of measurement] does not have to be perfect in order to serve as the basis for wide agreement among observers. Most of the exact measurements of science are advanced, not as final figures which are never to be corrected, but as the latest products of the method of successive approximations . . . . How far the refinement must be advanced in order to be acceptable in any given instance depends upon the demands of the observers.

Larrabee, 1945, 135

The problem of accuracy is the problem of defining the allowable limits in these processes [of control]. These allowable limits must be defined in part in terms of the uses to which the measurement is put.

Churchman, 1961, 127

A significant aspect of measurement, often overlooked in accounting, is its approximating character. Measurement is never any more than approximation.

Larson, 1969, 38

259 Derived measurement

Scalar adjustments

before we can begin to compare real income in different years, we have to solve a similar problem within the single year – we have to reduce the capital stock at the beginning and end of the year into comparable real terms.

Hicks, 1942, 176

[Judgments in two tax cases (*Hutzler Bros Co v Commissioner*, 1947, *8 TC 14*, and *Edgar A Basse et al v Commissioner*, 1948, *10 TC 328*, recognized] the usefulness and practicability of index numbers [in calculation of taxable income when inflation occurred]. In the *Hutzler Bros* case, an index prepared by someone other than the taxpayer was used; in the *Basse* case, however, the taxpayer constructed his own index based on his own experience, and was upheld in its use by the Tax Court. Never again can anyone argue against the use of price indexes to adjust accounting data on the grounds that they are unpractical or unrealistic or beyond the comprehension of the average taxpayer.

Moonitz & Nelson, 1960, 211–2

A desirable feature of any method of adjustment of accounts [for price level changes] would be certainty in its application. This would be one practical reason in favor of the use of a general price index . . . rather than a number of specialized indices.

Skinner, 1961, 59

General price level restatement is the accounting process of changing the standard used to compare diverse resources from units of money to units of general purchasing power.

Rosenfield, 1972, 65

the appropriate procedure [for dealing with the effects of price changes] is to (1) adjust the present statement to current values and (2) adjust the previous statement by a [general] price index. It is important to recognize that both adjustments are necessary and that neither is a substitute for the other.

Sterling, 1975a, 51

In any branch of knowledge, when a unit of measurement is found to be changing, there are two ways of allowing for the change in the calculations which use the unit. One way is to change every quantity which enters the calculation separately . . . . but there is a simpler method. [If a ship is going against the tide, and] if the speed of the tide can be measured separately (e.g. from an anchored ship), it can be simply subtracted from the water speed of any moving ship at the end of the calculation . . . . this analogy [suggests] . . . . a single correction for inflation.

Rudd, 1979, 57

Ratios, trends

In order to interpret the accounts effectively, it is necessary to have the figures for a period of years. The accounts for one year alone will give information, but they will not carry one very far. If, however, the figures are available for a number of years, it is then possible to see the trend or movement, that is to say, whether the position is steady, expanding, contracting or fluctuating.

de Paula, 1926/1978, 124

our work should not be confined to expressions in monetary terms ... use should be made of ratios, percentages, and the like.

Yeabsley, 1949, 293

if the series [of periodical accounts] is to be of any use at all for the purpose of discerning a trend [in any aspect of financial affairs and results], then the underlying accounts must be prepared with an eye to exactness of form in order to preserve identical types of relationship between the intrinsic aggregates which constitute the items in those accounts. Standardized accounts are essential for the investigation of long term trends.

Barrowcliff, 1952, 62

note that ratios can be computed from absolutes but that absolutes cannot be derived from ratios.

Goetz & Klein, 1960, 376

It is not in the absolute terms of dollars of revenues and profits that financial data are useful and viable. It is in their reduction to ratios and use for comparisons that these data come to life.

Cannon, 1962, 43

See also 190

260 Law and Order

261 Law and laws

a multitude of laws often hampers justice, so that a state is best governed where, with few laws, these are rigidly administered ....

Descartes, 1637/1937, 15

Law, in its most general and comprehensive sense, signifies a rule of action, and is applied indiscriminately to all kinds of action, whether animate or inanimate, rational or irrational. Thus we say, the laws of motion, of gravitation, of optics, or mechanics, as well as the laws of nature and of nations.

Blackstone, 1783/1978, 38

A law always consists of a delimitation of possibilities, whether this be conceived as a restriction on our behavior, as an unalterable channel for the course of events, or as a guide for our anticipation of them.

Mach, 1908/1960, 267

Here is the essence of law. It is a process which continually issues imperatives to individuals. An imperative is not a command, it is a rule, a judgment or an opinion. It says "You must do this", or "You should do this". But it is never an indicative

statement that can be shown to be true or false, such as "This book is printed". The activities of men in their day to day affairs are subject to this flow of imperatives.
Cooke, 1950, 189

A normative order that regulates human behavior in its direct or indirect relations to other human beings, is a social order. Morals and laws are such social orders.
Kelsen, 1960/1967, 24

law is the enterprise of subjecting human conduct to governance by rules.
Fuller, 1964/1978, 106

Laws in the broadest connotation fall into two groups: scientific laws and practical laws. Scientific laws are empirical generalizations stating principles of uniformity in the physical universe or human society. Into this category fall, for instance, the laws of physics and chemistry, economic laws and the laws of psychology. Practical laws prescribe a course of action for rational human beings. Into this group fall the laws of the lawyer, of ethics, of honor and etiquette, of bridge and football. The principle of order and regularity which scientific laws describe exists, independent of our wishes. We can make use of scientific laws but cannot break them. Practical laws, on the other hand, do not state what "is", but what we, as rational human beings, "ought" or "ought not" to do – "norms" (from the Latin *norma*, meaning yardstick or rule) . . . . The notion of truth or falsity, applicable to scientific laws, has no place with normative rules.
Hahlo & Kahn, 1968, 3

[There are] two varieties of rules and each has a role to play in resolving coordination problems. First is a summary rule, which merely summarizes what a man does in such and such circumstances. This sort of rule is exemplified by rules of thumb and routines. A second variety is a practice rule, which actually alters behavior. Examples of this sort are moral and legal norms . . . . The content of a social rule, be it moral or legal, is ordinarily such that an individual benefits if and only if others adhere to the rule. His own adherence to the rule does not necessarily benefit him; on the contrary, it usually entails some costs to him. People benefit from being told the truth, not from telling the truth; people benefit from not being assaulted, not from refraining from assaulting others.
Goodin, 1976, 42, 43

See also 844, 913

262 Functions of laws

What, then, is this law business about? It is about the fact that our society is honeycombed with disputes. Disputes actual and potential; disputes to be settled and disputes to be prevented; both appealing to law, both making up the business of the law.
Llewellyn, 1930/1960, 12

the first duty of the law . . . is to know what it wants.The first duty of the legislator or the judge is to make clear, unambiguous statements, which not only experts but the common man of the times will interpret in one way and in one way only.

Wiener, 1950/1954, 110

all social orders designated by the word "law", . . . are orders of human behavior . . . . they are coercive orders . . . . they react against certain events, regarded as undesirable because detrimental to society, especially against human behavior of this kind, with a coercive act; that is to say, by inflicting on the responsible individual an evil – such as deprivation of life, health, liberty or economic values . . . .

Kelsen, 1960/1967, 33

A society cannot remain lawful when many members break the laws. In an orderly society an impostor now and again gains an advantage: but he gains it only so long as imposture remains occasional – so long, that is, as his own practice does not destroy the social order. The counterfeiter can exploit the confidence of society in the value of money only so long as he himself does not sap this confidence by swamping the market with counterfeits; only so long, that is, as good money remains the norm. Destroy this, and Gresham's law really takes its revenge. The society falls apart to suspicion and barter.

Bronowski, 1964, 59

each society has a pattern of legal norms directed to maintaining a stable order conforming with its basic postulates . . . . the success of a society in maintaining such stability will depend upon the degree of integration which it has succeeded in achieving, and this in turn will be reflected in the degree to which its basic ideology commands general assent . . . . [The legal system] is a normative system within whose framework, linguistic though it may be, human behavior is rendered intelligible . . . . The law is therefore concerned to classify and regulate types of transaction which recur in real life.

Lloyd, 1964, 238, 287, 289

A law [statute] is an unequivocal declaration of public policy. A law gives support to those who do not wish to discriminate, but who feel compelled to do so by social pressure. A law gives protection and redress to minority groups. A law thus provides for the peaceful and orderly adjustment of grievances and the release of tensions. A law reduces prejudice by discouraging the behavior in which prejudice finds expression.

Race Relations Board (UK), 1967/1976, 65

263 Custom and convention

The term convention will be employed to designate that part of the custom followed within a given social group which is recognized as binding and protected against violation by sanctions of disapproval . . . . it is not enforced by a functionally specialized agency.

Weber, c1920/1947, 116

practices which continue to be observed over a long period tend, especially if they appear to possess a distinct social function or utility, to be norm-creating. That is to say that the "done thing" eventually proves to be the thing that ought to be, and perhaps ultimately, must be done . . . . Custom may result from deliberate innovations instituted by the ruling class or the example of some authoritative or highly reverenced personage in a community.

Lloyd, 1964, 230

The special feature . . . of conventional behavior is that while particular individuals may feel themselves bound to observe it, it is not regarded as generally binding, and the individual may largely please himself whether he conforms or not.

Lloyd, 1964, 230

Within [certain] limits . . . the courts are bound to apply those rules that originate independently from statute or precedent from the custom of the land or a particular locality . . . . Custom must be distinguished from conventional usage which is not a legal source. A conventional usage is a term customarily included in a particular type of contract. The important point is that, if the parties to the contract neither expressly include or exclude such a term, the courts will presume that the parties intended to contract on the basis of the usage, which accordingly becomes an implied term.

Newton, 1972/1977, 113, 115

See also 918, 924

264 Property and property rights

A property right is the right to the chance of obtaining some or all of the future services of one or more articles of wealth . . . . Property is thus always a right to the chance of a future benefit.

Fisher, 1906/1965, 22, 34

Property is an interest, recognized and protected by law, which entitles the person in whom it is vested, not as a matter of fact, but as a matter of right, to the full and complete enjoyment of the subject over which it is exercised . . . . For what do we understand by property? Is it not that interest, in tangible things which can be bought and sold, taken in execution for debt, left to descend to one's heirs, or disposed of by will? These are the very essentials of our notion of property . . . .

Jenks, 1913, 189, 237–238

Property is a requisite antecedent to bookkeeping, of course; without the right to possess, enjoy and dispose of articles of property there would be little reason indeed to keep books.

Littleton, 1933/1966, 14

Property. That which is peculiar or proper to any person; that which belongs exclusively to one; in the strict legal sense, an aggregate of rights which are guaranteed and protected by the government .... More specifically, ownership; the unrestricted and exclusive right to a thing; the right to dispose of a thing in every legal way, to possess it, to use it, and to exclude every one else from interfering with it .... The word is also commonly used to denote ... everything that has an exchangeable value or which goes to make up wealth or estate.

Black's law dictionary, 1951, 1382

Practically every entry made in the accounts of a business entity rests on [recognition of private property rights].

Grady, 1965, 25

[By statutory definition] property includes any thing in action and any interest in real or personal property. There must be a definite interest; a mere expectancy as distinguished from a conditional interest is not a subject of property.

Jowitt's dictionary of English law, 1977, 2:1447

See also 431

265 Law and accounting

any attempt at defining the terms used by accountants that does not take into consideration the legal aspect of the undertaking is doomed at the outset to fail of its true purpose.

Gerstenberg, 1910, 201

in certain directions, the progress of the law is through accounting .... we [lawyers] need the accountant quite as much for our own enlightenment and evolution as for his own peculiar contribution. But we need the cross-fertilization as a schematic, systematic body of doctrine; and that is to be had only by guarding the manner of its growth.

Berle, 1938, 15

the process by which the principles and practices evolved in business or general affairs are drawn upon for the solution of questions presented to courts of law almost inevitably leads to a development in the law itself. For, under our system of precedent, a decision adopting or resorting to any given accounting principle or application of

principle is almost bound to settle for the future the rule to be observed and the rule thus comes to look very like a proposition of law. [per Dixon J]
Carden's case, 1938

Accounting practices are much influenced by laws and must follow such laws as affect them . . . .
Hatfield & others, 1940, 14

where accounting concepts differ from legal concepts, there must be substantial grounds to support the departure, something more than mere definition.
Broad, 1942, 29

Most of the transactions of business flow from legal contracts, express or implied. It is an important function of accounting to show the legal status of the business unit in relation to its contracts.
Kester, 1942, 532

Obviously, accounting principles and rules dare not run counter to established legal principles.
Kester, 1946, 5

Accounting operates within a framework of legal principles and institutions. Business operations, and the corresponding accounting procedures, could not be carried on if the law did not provide for such things as private property, enforceable contracts and various kinds of business organizations such as partnerships and corporations.
Mason & Davidson, 1953, 14

records and reports should give recognition to the legal position of the parties to whom the accounts refer. Nevertheless, . . . it is frequently necessary to frame accounts in a manner that does not precisely display the legal position.
Carrington & Battersby, 1963, 44

In the United States, nearly every accounting entry assumes that the property rights of those involved are legally enforceable. Also accounting assumes that society and government will continue to recognize that individuals have the right to invest and enjoy their property rights, as long as they do not interfere with the rights of others or the public interest.
Hawkins, 1971, 57–8

Sometimes . . . there is conflicting evidence; and sometimes there is evidence of two parallel but conflicting principles of commercial accounting. In such cases, the courts must do the best they can without evidence, or choose beween the conflicting evidence, or decide which is the most appropriate principle of commercial accounting to adopt. Where, however, there is evidence which is accepted by the court as establishing a sound commercial accounting practice conflicting with no statute, that normally is the end of the matter. The court adopts the practice, applies it and decides the case accordingly. [per Salmon L J, on appeal]

Odeon Associated Theatres Ltd v Jones,
1972

266 The interpretation of statutes – words of popular and technical meanings

a statute [containing language which is capable of being construed in a popular sense] is not to be construed according to the strict or technical meaning of the language contained in it, but is to be construed in its popular sense, meaning of course by the words "popular sense" that sense which people conversant with the subject matter with which the statute is dealing would attribute to it. [per Pollock]

Grenfell v Inland Revenue, 1876

The first and most elementary rule of construction is, that it is assumed that the words and phrases are used in their technical meaning if they have acquired one, and in their popular meaning if they have not, and that the phrases and sentences are to be construed according to the rules of grammar; and from this presumption it is not allowable to depart, unless adequate grounds are found, either in the context or in the consequences which would result from the literal interpretation, for concluding that that interpretation does not give the real intention of the legislature .... the language of a statute, as of every other writing, is to be construed in the sense which it bore at the period when it was passed.

Maxwell, 1883, 2, 75

Where two or more words, susceptible of analogous meaning, are coupled together ... they are understood to be used in their cognate sense. They take, as it were, their color from each other; that is, the more general is restricted in a sense analogous to the less general.

Maxwell, 1883, 398

It is a rule of law (... the plain meaning rule) that where, in relation to the facts of the instant case, (a) the enactment under inquiry is grammatically capable of one meaning only, and (b) on an informed interpretation of that enactment the interpretive criteria raise no real doubt as to whether that grammatical meaning is the one intended by the legislator, the legal meaning of the enactment corresponds to that grammatical meaning, and is to be applied accordingly.

Bennion, 1984, 264

Interpretation and intent

Laws are made for men of ordinary understanding, and should therefore be constructed by the ordinary rules of common sense. Their meaning is not to be sought for in metaphysical subtleties, which may mean everything or nothing at pleasure.

Jefferson, –/1948, 106

in constructing ... all written instruments, the grammatical and ordinary sense of the words is to be adhered to, unless that would lead to some absurdity or some repugnance or inconsistency with the rest of the instrument, in which case the grammatical and ordinary sense of the words may be modified, so as to avoid that absurdity and inconsistency, but no further.

Grey & others v Pearson & others, 1857

In general, statutes are presumed to use words in their popular sense .... Where, indeed, technical words are used in reference to a technical subject, they are primarily interpreted in the sense in which they are understood in the science, art, or business in which they have acquired it; but that meaning is rejected as soon as the judicial mind is satisfied that another is more agreeable to the object and intention .... that sense of the words is to be adopted which best harmonizes with the context, and promotes in the fullest manner the policy and object of the legislature.

Maxwell, 1883, 69, 333

The meaning which words ought to be understood to bear is not to be ascertained by any process akin to speculation: the primary duty of a court of law is to find the natural meaning of the words used in the context in which they occur, that context including any other phrases in the act which may throw light on the sense in which the makers of the act used the words in dispute.

Re Macmannaway, 1951

We are not the slaves of words but their masters. We sit here to give them their natural and ordinary meaning in the context in which we find them. [per Lord Denning M R]

Allen v Thorn Electrical Industries Ltd, 1967

In determining the meaning of any word or phrase in a statute the first question to ask always is what is the natural or ordinary meaning of that word or phrase in its context in the statute. It is only when that meaning leads to some result which cannot reasonably be supposed to have been the intention of the legislature that it is proper to look for some other possible meaning of the word or phrase. [per Lord Reid]

Pinner v Everett, 1969

It is a rule of law (... the commonsense construction rule) that when considering, in relation to the facts of the instant case, which of the opposing constructions of the enactment would give effect to the legislative intention, the court should presume that the legislator intended commonsense to be used in construing the enactment.

Bennion, 1984, 266

267 Commercial morality

> A merchant wishing that his worth be great
> Must always act according as is right;
> And let him be a man of long foresight,
> And never fail his promises to keep.
> ....   Further he must write
> Accounts well-kept and free from oversight.
>
> Compagni, 14c/1955, 425

It is generally said that today [good] faith abides with merchants and men-at-arms .... Neither kings nor princes nor any [other] rank of men enjoy as much reputation or credit as a good merchant. Hence, a merchant's [reputation and credit] serve him readily for cash, while those of others do not .... And whereas a simple and plain receipt of a merchant is valid even without witnesses, the rulers and any other people are not believed without an instrument and strong cautions.

Cotrugli, 1458/1955, 418

There is much reason to fear, that the standard of commercial morality must be of small estimation in the sight of many, when we discover that the most obvious and necessary duty of a trader's life, I mean the obligation to keep a methodical record of all his dealings, is so constantly neglected. It is a matter of almost daily occurrence, when a trader becomes bankrupt, to find that his books have been badly kept .... The consequence is serious, both to the bankrupt and to creditors, for after an adjudication of bankruptcy, when the trader should immediately be able to devote his attention to the preparation of his balance sheet, much delay, inconvenience, and expense is incurred in making up books, or in raising new accounts, and which in general are very unsatisfactory to creditors. It is incumbent therefore upon the Court, to be continually inculcating the great importance of regularity in bookkeeping .... [Commissioner in Bankruptcy]

Holroyd, c1850/1862, viii

Commercial morality is limited and fenced in by so many customs of trade and secret understandings that it has come to mean something very different from what the plain significance of the words would imply .... the adjective, commercial, is more qualifying even than adjectives generally are, and not only modifies but actually changes the sense of the word with which it is united. Commercial morality and commercial honor are fine-sounding terms; too often in the present day they are like the tale

> Told by an idiot, full of sound and fury,
> Signifying nothing.
>
> *Accountant*, editorial, 1875, 2

[In industry and trade] there is no corporate body set above all the members of a profession to maintain some sort of unity, to serve as the repository of traditions and common practices and see that they are observed at need. There is no organ of this description, because it can only be the expression of a life common to a group, and the group has no life in common . . . . this lack of organization in the business professions has one consequence of the greatest moment: that is, that in this whole sphere of social life, no professional ethics exist.

Durkheim, c1900/1957, 9

In modern business too high a standard of honest and intellectual integrity is, and must remain, a handicap . . . . in the last resort it is the balance sheet which must come first, and if in matters of policy and practice a conflict arises between profit and intellectual candour, it is implicit in the structure of private enterprise that for continuity alone profit must win. Intellectual and practical integrity are the basis of many businesses, just so long as they pay; . . . . Such a process necessarily results in a survival of the less intellectually scrupulous and creates a tradition at variance with ideals of social justice.

Chance, 1933, 107

Our civilization is dependent for its very existence on commerce, and a high standard of commercial morality . . . .

Thompson, 1937, 188

Financial institutions, industrial and commercial companies, all publish accounts knowing them to be incorrect and often with the deliberate intention to deceive, frequently from the most honest motives.

Ashley, 1941, 395

intellectual dishonesty . . . . is a creeping disease and its spread goes almost unnoticed . . . . The habit of using words to conceal rather than to make clear; of using words with the intention of an audience understanding one thing, when detailed analysis of the words shows a different meaning – these habits, if persisted in, pervert the thought of the speaker till he is no more capable of thinking straight than he is of speaking straight.

O'Brien, 1976, 736

During the post-war decade some 50 billions of new securities were floated in the United States. Fully half . . . have become worthless. These cold figures spell tragedy in the lives of thousands of individuals who invested their life savings . . . in these worthless securities. The flotation of such a mass of essentially fraudulent securities was made possible because of the complete abandonment by many underwriters and dealers of fair, honest and prudent dealing that should have been basic to the encouragement of investment in any enterprise. [Report No 85, 73d Congress, First Session]

US Congress, 1959/1969, 209

268 Groups and group behavior

if it is asserted that the French nation and the Roman Church literally have all the characteristics of those we ordinarily call persons . . . we are dealing with the kind of statement which is believed because it is absurd. Groups are not begot through the union of father and mother, they do not suck their mother's milk, do not play children's games, do not spend weary hours in school, do not work for wages, strike for shorter hours, and do not suffer the trials and joys of anxious parenthood. Having no sense organs, they cannot in any strict sense of the word be said to have sensations or feelings, and it is not literally true to say that they feel praise or blame, hope or disappointment, love, hunger, colds, toothaches, ennui, the creaking of old age, or the perplexities of a world that to the honest mind must always contain unsolved and perhaps insoluble problems.

Cohen, 1931/1964, 388

in order to have a useful theory of relations among aggregates [in the social sciences], it is necessary that they be defined in a manner derived from the theory of individual behavior.

Arrow, 1951, 134

Through the learning of a culture . . . men are able to predict each other's behavior most of the time and gauge their own behavior to the predicted behavior of others . . . . There is thus no need to posit a group mind or folk soul to explain concerted behavior or social integration, as some psychologists . . . have done.

Rose, 1962, 9

the belief in the empirical existence of social wholes or collectives, which may be called naïve collectivism, has to be replaced by the demand that social phenomena, including collectives, should be analyzed in terms of individuals and their actions and relations.

Popper, 1972, 341

Group morality

In the clearly dishonest cases a purpose is accomplished by giving the signs employed the characteristics of statements with syntactical or semantical dimensions, so that they seem to be rationally demonstrated or empirically supported when in fact they are neither . . . . a purpose that cannot fully stand the light of scrutiny expresses itself in a form suitable for other purposes; aggressive acts of individuals and social groups often drape themselves in the mantle of morality, and the declared purpose is often not the real one. A peculiarly intellectualistic justification of dishonesty in the use of signs is to deny that truth has any other component than the pragmatical, so that any sign which furthers the interest of the user is said to be true.

Morris, 1955/1962, 118

When a member is dependent on the group for bolstering his feelings of self-confidence, he tends to exercise self-censorship over his misgivings. The greater the dependence, the stronger will be the motivation to adhere to the group's norms . . . . Each individual in the group feels himself to be under an injunction to avoid making penetrating criticisms that might bring on a clash with fellow members and destroy the unity of the group . . . . each member avoids interfering with an emerging consensus by assuring himself that the opposing arguments he had in mind must be erroneous or that his misgivings are too unimportant to be worth mentioning.

Janis, 1972, 205

[On decision or policy making groups] The members' firm belief in the inherent morality of their group and their use of undifferentiated negative stereotypes of opponents enable them to minimize decision conflicts between ethical values and expediency, especially when they are inclined to resort to violence. The shared belief that "we are a wise and good group" inclines them to use group concurrence as a major criterion to judge the morality as well as the efficacy of any policy under discussion. "Since our group's objectives are good," the members feel, "any means we decide to use must be good". This shared assumption helps the members avoid feelings of shame or guilt about decisions that may violate their personal code of ethical behavior. Negative stereotypes of the enemy enhance their sense of moral rightness as well as their pride in the lofty mission of the in-group.

Janis, 1972, 204

I find that the oddest and perhaps the most corrupt exercise of secrecy is secrecy about one's moral position: esoteric ethics. It is practised by all groups that have one set of moral principles for public consumption and another for themselves. Esoteric ethics allows groups to follow strictly self-serving and subjective calculations. Conspiratorial groups routinely adopt such a double standard, but its appeal goes far beyond such groups.

Bok, 1983/1989, 112

See also 176, 825

269 Ethics

Tzu-kung asked saying, Is there any single saying that one can act upon all day and every day? The Master said, Perhaps the saying about consideration: "Never do to others what you would not like them to do to you."

Confucius (551–479BC), –/1971, xv:23

A prudent ruler ought not to keep faith when by so doing it would be against his interest, and when the reasons which made him bind himself no longer exist. If men were all good, this precept would not be a good one; but as they are bad, and would not observe their faith with you, so you are not bound to keep faith with them.

Machiavelli, c1519/1954, 101

Ethics, . . . in as far as it is the art of directing a man's actions [in matters such as none but himself are interested in], may be termed the art of discharging one's duty to one's self: and the quality [manifested] is that of prudence . . . . Ethics, . . . in as far as it is the art of directing a man's actions [in such matters as may affect the interests of those about him], may be termed the art of discharging one's duty to one's neighbor. Now the happiness of one's neighbor may be consulted . . . 1. by forbearing to diminish it [. . . probity . . .] ; 2. . . . by studying to increase it [. . . beneficence . . .] The only interests which a man at all times and upon all occasions is sure to find adequate motives for consulting, are his own. Notwithstanding this, there are no occasions in which a man has not some motives for consulting the happiness of other men . . . . the purely social motive of sympathy or benevolence . . . . the semi-social motives of love of society and love of reputation.

Bentham, 1843, I:143

From a sociological point of view an ethical standard is one to which men attribute a certain type of value and which, by virtue of this belief, they treat as a valid norm governing their action.

Weber, c1920/1947, 118

The only rule that an ethics can present is that an individual should rationally deal with all the values that are found in a specific problem . . . . The problem itself defines the values [and the interests involved].

Mead, 1934/1962, 388

It is the privilege of man's moral genius, expressed by inspired individuals, to advance ethical axioms which are so comprehensive and so well founded that men will accept them as grounded in the vast mass of their individual emotional experiences. Ethical axioms are founded and tested not very differently from the axioms of science . . . . Truth is what stands the test of experience.

Einstein, 1950/1953, 780

every man's rationale contains certain propositions which combine in themselves two characters: they are value judgments, and they play the role of very powerful motives. In the form in which they usually occur in consciousness, they are known by various names; we call them a man's standards, his ideals, the rules of conduct he tries to follow, or his moral code. More often than not they are what we mean when we speak of a man's philosophy . . . . To deny the power of these motives, the influence they can exercise upon our actions, is like denying that water flows downhill.

Bergmann, 1951, 209

ethics and ethical language can be regarded as part of the process whereby, as members of a community, we moderate our impulses and adjust our demands so as to reconcile them as far as possible with those of our fellows . . . . the function of ethics is to reconcile the independent aims and wills of a community of people . . . .

Toulmin, 1958, 132, 170

See also 985, 986

270 Firms and Organizations

271 Organizations

a formal organization . . . is a system of consciously coordinated activities or forces of two or more persons.

Barnard, 1938, 81

organizations are interacting entities in which the desires of the individual, the group and the organization are in a continued state of adaptation.

Pfiffner & Sherwood, 1960, 407

most organizations are simply legal fictions which serve as a nexus for a set of contracting relationships among individuals.

Jensen & Meckling, 1976, 310

the enterprise must be seen as a coalition of individuals and groups of which top management represents only one part . . . and in which a whole range of aspirations are continually juggled and balanced.

Parker, 1976, 5

the corporation can be thought of as a legal artifact designed to provide a contractual focus for its activities in the market place, whose contracts are entered into by corporate officers who act as agents of the stockholders.

Butterworth & others, 1981, 9

I believe it is productive to define an organization as a legal entity that serves as a nexus for a complex set of contracts (written and unwritten) among disparate individuals. The multilateral contracts . . . that characterize market relations are supplemented within the organization by . . . unilateral contracts [of cooperating agents] with the legal entity . . . .

Jensen, 1983, 326

272 Organizational equilibrium and survival

If the individual [participant in a cooperative system] finds his motives being satisfied by what he does, he continues his cooperative effort; otherwise he does not . . . . Thus, the efficiency of a cooperative system is its capacity to maintain itself by the individual satisfactions it affords. This may be called its capacity of equilibrium, ...

Barnard, 1938, 57

Simplifying . . . we may say that the entrepreneur seeks profit . . . , the employees seek wages, and the customers find . . . the exchange of money for products attractive. The entrepreneur gains the right to dispose of the employees' time by entering into employment contracts with them; he obtains funds to pay wages by entering into sales contracts with the customers. If these two sets of contracts are sufficiently advantageous, the entrepreneur makes a profit and . . . the organization remains in existence.

Simon, 1949, 17

the goals of a business firm are a series of more or less independent constraints imposed on the organization through a process of bargaining among potential coalition members and elaborated over time in response to short run pressures . . . . the firm is, in fact, a coalition of participants with disparate demands, changing foci of attention, and limited ability to attend to all organizational demands simultaneously.

Cyert & March, 1963, 43

The coalition within the organization for a business may include managers, workers, stockholders, customers, and so on. In other words, all the individuals who have some stake in that particular organization may in one way or another affect the goals of the organization . . . . every organization is continually undergoing the test of new demands, the test to see how these new demands conform to existing policy and, in general, pushing the policy toward new dimensions. In some sense, therefore, the goals of the organization are never completely consistent at any particular point of time.

Cohen & Cyert, 1965, 331

[The firm may be described] as a temporary coalition in a state of unstable equilibrium. It is a temporary coalition by virtue of the changing composition of its participants. Individual customers, workers, creditors and shareholders may come and go; so long as the contributions of those who go are replaced by contributions of persons of the same or alternative classes, the organization will survive. It is in unstable equilibrium by virtue of the flux of wants made known in the market place, of the changes in the quantity and quality of other organizations, and of changes in the satisfactions expected by participants.

Chambers, 1967c, 16

Everyone's relationship with the corporation – stockholders, executives, employees – rests on a contract which they can terminate at will, and which they may attempt to renegotiate from time to time either individually or collectively.

Jay, 1969, 216

The firm ... serves as a focus for a complex process in which the conflicting objectives of individuals (some of whom may represent other organizations) are brought into equilibrium within a framework of contractual relations.

Jensen & Meckling, 1976, 311

273 Firms as systems

Routine is the god of every social system; it is the seventh heaven of business, the essential component in the success of every factory, the ideal of every statesman. The social machine should run like clockwork .... it is the beginning of wisdom to understand that social life is founded upon routine .... Society requires stability, foresight itself presupposes stability, and stability is the product of routine.

Whitehead, 1933/1948, 110

Every social system is a functioning entity. That is, it is a system of interdependent structures and processes such that it tends to maintain a relative stability and distinctiveness of pattern and behavior as an entity by contrast with its – social or other – environment, and with it a relative independence from environmental forces.

Parsons, 1942/1963, 143

[The firm is] ... a series of integrated offices, in which are a number of obligations and privileges closely defined by limited and specific rules. Each of these offices contains an area of imputed competence and responsibility. Authority, the power to control which derives from an acknowledged status, inheres in the office and not in the particular person who performs the official role.

Kluckholm & Murray, 1950, 283

The simplest theory of the firm is to assume that there is a homeostasis of the balance sheet – that there is some desired quantity of all the various items in the balance sheet, and that any disturbance of this structure sets in motion forces which will restore the *status quo*.

Boulding, 1950/1962, 27

the small group ... is a social system reacting with its environment as a self-adjusting organization of response whose parts are mutually interdependent. What acts, and what reacts, is not a single part or function of the social system, nor any combination of parts or functions, but the system as a whole, a totality whose mutual interdependence *is* the system. Cause and effect disappear; what must be looked for is the resultants of complexes of interacting forces. The group is a dynamic social equilibrium. It sets up its own responses organically, determines its own measures of control, derives its own possibilities of adaptation, elaboration and change.

De Voto, 1951/1959, xv

Our theoretical model for the understanding of organizations is that of an energic input-output system in which the energic return from the output reactivates the system. Social organizations are flagrantly open systems in that the input of energies and the conversion of output into further energic input consist of transactions between the organization and its environment.

Katz & Kahn, 1966/1978, 20

An open system is one that receives matter and energy from its environment and passes matter and energy to its environment. The open system is oriented toward life and growth. Biological, psychological, and social systems follow an open model . . . . The system possesses qualities of wholeness, interdependence, hierarchy, self-regulation, environmental interchange, equilibrium, adaptability and equifinality [ability to reach a given final state in many ways and from many different starting points].

Littlejohn, 1983, 29, 32

274 The firm as an adaptive concern

Going concern – a business actually operating and in working order. The term is generally applied to a concern of which a transfer of ownership can be effected without any interruption of the business which is being carried on . . . .

Dawson, 1904, 189

Business operation means a constant process of shifting in both property and equity items.

Paton, 1917, 25

Going concern: a concern in operation. The expression is also used in reference to the sale of an undertaking without any stoppage of business.

Pixley, 1926, 1:520

Successes in enterprise seem to attend freedom to alter operating policy rather than accurate forecasts of prices.

Canning, 1931, 163

Capitalism . . . is by nature a form or method of economic change and not only never is but never can be stationary . . . . The fundamental impulse that sets and keeps the capitalist engine in motion comes from the new consumers' goods, the new methods of production or transportation, the new markets, the new forms of industrial organization that capitalist enterprise creates . . . . [The] process of creative destruction is the essential fact about capitalism.

Schumpeter, 1947, 82

Regardless of how professors of economic theory write their books or draw their demand and cost curves, the chief concern of the successful businessman is that of watching daily the moves of his competitors and the possible or prospective changes in mood or habit of prospective customers. Every new move made by a competitor or customer makes imperative some new move or considered adjustment in his own business to meet the new contingency.

McCracken, 1948, 28

it is far from true that all business enterprises have indefinitely long lives . . . . the history of business risks and fatalities is such as to remind us more of death than immortality.

Wilcox & Greer, 1950, 493

the [decision making] machinery in all but a few of the firms [studied] appears to be sufficiently fluid and flexible to permit speedy adaptation of plans to new and unforeseen conditions . . . . Firm capital investment plans are typically limited to a few months. Quick and unpredicted changes in such plans are the order of the day.

Heller, 1951, 98

Successful management is continually modifying the composition of the capital in a company in attempting to increase the income potential in the face of changing tax situations, wages, product demand, technology, interest rates, and so on.

Trumbull, 1958, 28

Probably the best example of an [exceedingly complex probabilistic] industrial system . . . is the company itself . . . . The company is certainly not alive, but it has to behave very much like a living organism. It is essential to the company that it develops techniques for survival in a changing environment: it must adapt itself to its economic, commercial, social and political surroundings, and it must learn from experience.

Beer, 1959, 17

a business unit . . . has some of the features of separate cooperating instruments and organisms. Though the unit as such may continue in existence for a long period, its separate machines, plants, properties, financiers, investors and other contributors may change or be changed as the market values of their separate contributions to the goals of the unit change. Consequently the contemporary market value of any feature of the unit is the relevant basis of any system the purpose of which is to inform the actions of participants.

Chambers, 1960a, 142

[Profit] maximization is a continuous process. Although the firm plans for a considerable period into the future, these plans are usually flexible and are subject to modification as expectations or circumstances change. Making these modifications is the principal function of the management of a going concern.

Edwards & Bell, 1961, 38

so long as the environment of the firm is unstable (and unpredictably unstable), the heart of the theory [of the behavior of the firm] must be the process of short run adaptive reactions.

Cyert & March, 1963, 100

Profitability and survivability derive in the last analysis from adaptation to the marketplace. The greater the attention management directs inwardly on the organization, the less attention it gives to the outside world. People become preoccupied with contemplating their own navels. They are taught to beat themselves, to go on economic diets. To be sure contemplation and control are highly important, but such self-preoccupation is more characteristic of monks than merchants.

Levinson, 1970, 143

the firm today is not the same firm as it was last year .... Firms change their technologies, factor intensities, operating structures, financing mix, market penetration, product outputs, activity diversifications, and expansion policies ....

Vickers, 1981, 174

275 The conventional accounting view of the firm as a going concern

Manufacturers and traders do not construct business premises or lay down special plant in the intent of a short period .... the method of treatment for annual accounting is as of a going concern .... Matter and things fixed in a permanent working position must not be treated in accounts as following the fluctuations of the market, for it is not a trading item that is in question, such as stock in trade, which can be sold any day without interruption to the works.

Guthrie, 1883, 7

The accountant ... assumes that the business with which he is dealing is a going concern. This ... assumption ... is largely one of convenience .... The going concern rather than the seriously embarrassed or insolvent business is the normal case.

Paton, 1922/1962, 478

It is assumed that the business is a going concern. Generally we mean that the firm will continue to buy and sell goods with a view toward a profit thoughout an indefinite future ....

Nelson, 1942, 132

The continuity convention involves a great deal more than mere extension of corporate existence .... it includes assumptions such as: .... that the operations reflected in the accounting statements will be continued in substantially the same terms as in the past ... ; that the economic and technological factors which are relevant to the operations will continue to exert their influence in a substantially unaltered fashion; and that ... there will be no change in the basic objectives, policies or strategic plans of the management.

Vatter, 1947, 5

A profit-seeking undertaking using wasting assets is, and for accounting purposes must always be treated as, a going concern; and a going concern will apply its wasting assets to the purposes for which they were acquired, and will not act as a dealer in the purchase and sale of such property for profit.

Leake, 1948, 2–3

The assumption underlying accounting principles . . . is that the business will continue indefinitely . . . . Accounting policies, such as those relating to depreciation and intangibles, are based on the assumption . . . .

Blough, 1956, 13

The going concern concept assumes the continuance of the general enterprise situation. In the absence of evidence to the contrary, the entity is viewed as remaining in operation indefinitely . . . . the assets of the enterprise are expected to have continuing usefulness for the general purpose for which they were acquired, and its liabilities are expected to be paid at maturity.

AAA, 1957a/1957b, 2

it is assumed that the business entity has continuity of life . . . . Properties used by the entity are deemed to have been irrevocably dedicated to the carrying on of its purposes . . . . The liquidation or market values of such properties at the time of statement preparation is, therefore, of secondary importance for statement presentation purposes.

Owen, 1958, 70

"Going concern" implies indefinite continuance of the accounting entity under scrutiny . . . . the business will not be liquidated within a span of time necessary to carry out present contractual commitments or to use up assets according to the plans and expectations presently held.

Grady, 1965, 28

Accounting reports are prepared on the assumption that the business unit . . . will continue to operate in its usual manner, performing the same general business functions for which it has invested in present plant and equipment . . . .

Pyle & White, 1966, 825

Companies (less so, shareholders, except by selling shares!) just do not adapt. Physical factors and other realities prevent such action.

Penman, 1970, 338

For accounting purposes a business is assumed to remain in operation long enough for its current plans to be carried out.

Davidson & others, 1977, 27

The continuity (or going concern) assumption postulates indefinite continuing existence (at least up to the planning horizon) of the accounting entity . . . [it] is common to all accounting valuation systems.

Ma & Mathews, 1979, 152

276 Communication essential to organizations

without communication there can be no organization, for there is no possibility then of the group influencing the behavior of the individual .... the specialization of decision making functions is largely dependent upon the possibility of developing adequate channels of communication to and from decision centers.
Simon, 1949, 154, 171

Social organization without communication is impossible.
Miller, 1951/1963

the first task of any organization is to ensure that its right hand knows what its left hand is doing at least sufficiently to ensure that they do not frustrate each other ....
Vickers, 1955, 82

An organization might almost be defined as a structure of roles tied together with lines of communication.
Boulding, 1956/1961, 27

The main task of the staff is to collect and transmit information outside the line channels, which will give the executive in the upper ranks of the hierarchy some independent check on the general state of the organization. This is the main function of accountants, statisticians, market research men, spies, intelligence officers, stool pigeons, secret police, papal legates, ambassadors, and so on .... In the first place, there is need for information about the environment of the organization beyond what is received by members at the end of the line .... The second function of staff organization is to check on the information received up the filter of the hierarchy.
Boulding, 1963, 148

to exercise command over resources is to act economically, that is, to make a choice between alternative uses of the resources .... everybody who has resources to deploy [in business, government and other settings] is a commander in the sense in which the word is here used .... Accounting reports are reports by commanders ... at one level of command to commanders at a higher level, so to speak, along a whole chain of command .... to enable decisions to be made ... by commanders.
Goldberg, 1965, 164, 167

the essential binding element of groups and organizations is information sharing. Without sending and receiving messages, groups and organizations would not exist.
Littlejohn, 1983, 261

Organizational memory

Since an organization is not an organism the only memory is possesses, in the proper sense of the term, is the collective memory of its participants. This is insufficient for organization purposes, first, because what is in one man's mind is not

269

necessarily available to other members of the organization, and second, because when an individual leaves an organization the organization loses that part of its memory. Hence, organizations, to a far greater extent than individuals, need artificial memories . . . records systems, correspondence and other files, libraries, and follow up systems.

Simon, 1949, 166

[In organizations] the memory is contained in all of the enduring records such as accounting ledgers, correspondence files, statistical tabulations, or production reports.

Pfiffner & Sherwood, 1960, 301

A formal record is the surest safeguard against faulty recollection . . . and hence against the misinterpretation of past experiences . . . . An organization . . . has no natural memory other than in the form of the memories of its agents. As agents may be assigned different functions from time to time and as agents may . . . terminate their association with it, the organization will lose the advantage of its accumulated experience unless it augments the memories of its agents for the time being with a formal records system. For an organization as such its records are its memory . . . . all original communications and records should be adequate to enable them subsequently to be placed in their original time and environmental context.

Chambers, 1964c, 16

See also 214

277 Feedback

Whenever there is an appraisal involving a rule as to better or as to needed action, there is an end to be reached; the appraisal is a valuation of things with respect to their serviceability or usefulness . . . . In every case, except those of sheer instinct and complete trial and error, there are involved observation of actual materials and estimate of their potential force in production of a particular result. There is always some observation of the outcome attained in comparison and contrast with that intended . . . . It thus makes possible a better judgment in the future as to their fitness and usefulness.

Dewey, 1939/1960, 23

when we desire a motion to follow a given pattern the difference between this pattern and the actually performed motion is used as a new input to cause the part regulated to move in such a way as to bring its motion closer to that given by the pattern.

Wiener, 1948/1961, 6

control of a machine on the basis of its actual performance rather than its expected performance is known as feedback, and involves sensory members which are actuated by motor members and perform the function of tell-tales or monitors – that is, of elements which indicate a performance.

Wiener, 1950/1954, 24

Having stated our expectations at the start of a period, we test them at its end by comparing actual with expected results, attempting to infer therefrom whether our initial diagnosis of forces and their strength was correct.

Lachmann, 1956, 24

Essential to feedback is the notion that the flow of information is actually having a reciprocating effect on behavior . . . . This circular pattern [loop] involves the flow of information to the point of action, a flow back to the point of decision with information on the action, and then a return to the point of action with new information and perhaps instructions.

Pfiffner & Sherwood, 1960, 299

The regulated system must possess certain control guidelines. The control center must know what environmental conditions to respond to and how . . . . Negative feedback is an error message indicating deviation; the system adjusts by reducing or counteracting the deviation . . . . A system can also respond by amplifying or maintaining deviation. When this happens, the feedback is said to be positive . . . . At some points [in a complex system] the feedback loops are positive, at other points negative.

Littlejohn, 1983, 34

See also 056

Responses to feedback

It is very important to keep in mind what the subject is motivated to do when knowledge of performance increases his motivation. Often he is motivated to score higher, not necessarily to learn the task faster and better. He may then resort to taking advantage of weaknesses in the apparatus, learning habits which are of no value or actually lead to poorer performance when he later attempts to learn a similar task.

Ammons, 1956, 286

The main pecularities of human beings, considered as variables in a system seem to me to be two; they have extraordinary and growing powers on the one hand to predict the future course of events and on the other to alter it. The first is the gift of science, the second of technology. Science teaches us the law and enables us to predict and obey. Technology uses the law and enables us to alter and exploit. These two are clearly likely to have opposite effects. The first should make men the most adaptable of creatures; the second makes them the least ready to adapt, for, when they encounter a limitation, their tendency is not to adapt to it but to alter the limitation.

Vickers, 1968/1970, 40

See also 237

278 Company directors and managers as agents

What is the position of directors of a public company? They are merely agents of the company. The company itself ... can only act through directors, and the case is, as regards those directors, merely the ordinary case of principal and agent. [per Cairns L C]

Ferguson v Wilson, 1866

The directors are the mere trustees or agents of the company – trustees of the company's money and property – agents in the transactions which they enter into on behalf of the company. [per Lord Selbourne L C]

Great Eastern Railway Co v Turner, 1872

To my mind the distinction between a director and a trustee is an essential distinction founded on the very nature of things. A trustee is a man who is the owner of the property and deals with it as principal .... A director never enters into a contract for himself, but ... for his principal ... the company .... [per James L J]

Smith v Anderson, 1880

Directors are agents of the company; but not mere agents. The director, if he be a shareholder, is himself a member of the body of which he is agent. He manages for himself and others. He is a managing partner. The company cannot act in its own person, for it has no person; it can only act through directors. Directors are described sometimes as agents, sometimes as trustees, sometimes as managing partners. But each of these expressions is used, not as exhaustive of their powers or responsibilities, but as indicating useful points of view from which they may for the moment and for the particular purpose be considered. It is not meant that they belong to the class, but that it is useful for the purpose of the moment to observe that they fall *pro tanto* within the principles which govern that class .... The directors of a company fill a double character. They are (i) agents of the company, and (ii) trustees for the shareholders of the powers committed to them.

Buckley, 1930, 724, 726

Because management is concerned with the enterprise as a whole, the welfare of any component must be sacrificed when necessary. The easiest to sacrifice is the stockholder .... The appropriate rate of dividend .... may be the customary rate or an amount sufficient to attract new money when needed, or an estimated percentage of invested capital. However decided, the resulting amount is arbitrary being based upon formula and judgment.

Knauth, 1948, 159

A corporation, although it . . . is a legal person, is not a human person and cannot act for itself . . . . Individual directors are not, themselves, agents of the corporation because they normally do not act independently but only as members of the group . . . . The officers are merely agents of the corporation and are subject to the control of the board of directors.

Votaw, 1965, 54, 55, 63

Between the company and the board and the officers there is an agency relationship, but there is none between the company and the members or between the members *inter se* . . . . the authority of the directors to bind the company as its agents normally depends on their acting collectively as a board . . . .

Gower, 1969, 127, 517

Company managers as fiduciaries

[The directors] are trustees for the company not for the individual shareholders. [Flitcroft's case]

Exchange Banking Company, In re, 1882

Although the courts have not classed corporate managers as fiduciaries, their responsibilities and duties to shareholders are actually fiduciary in character.

Whitney, 1940, 308

Many . . . have observed that the position of management in modern business corporations is closely akin to that of a trustee. While this may not be true in a strict legal sense, it is fair to say that management is in a fiduciary capacity ethically and actually.

Carson, 1949b, 161

to describe directors as trustees seems today to be neither strictly correct nor invariably helpful. In truth, directors are agents of the company rather than trustees of it or its property. But as agents they stand in a fiduciary relationship to their principal, the company. The duties of good faith which this fiduciary relationship imposes are virtually identical with those imposed on trustees . . . . their duties of good faith are owed by each director individually . . . . the fiduciary duties are owed to the company and the company alone.

Gower & others, 1979, 571–573

279 The subordinate position of shareholders

The corporation itself is the sole owner of its assets. It continually sells and mortgages them and the stockholders, as such, have no word in the matter. None of the attributes of title to the corporate assets is included among the rights of shareholders.
Robbins, 1929, 78

the interests of ownership and control [of corporations] are in large measure opposed if the interests of the latter grow primarily out of the desire for personal monetary gain.
Berle & Means, 1932, 123

The only practical way in which an investor can today give expression to his conclusions in regard to the management of a corporation in which he is interested is by retaining, increasing or disposing of his investment, and accounts are mainly valuable to him in so far as they afford guidance in determining which of these courses he will pursue.
May, 1943, 78

As a claimant to income, the stockholder is in an uncomfortable position. He may no longer with accuracy be regarded as the residuary owner, for the surplus reverts to the enterprise as a whole.
Knauth, 1948, 159

in the overwhelmingly important field of corporate enterprise, the nominal owner, that is, the shareholder, is becoming more and more powerless. He turns into a mere recipient of dividends, often barely distinguishable from the bond or debenture holder.
Friedman, 1951, 14

the shareholder is not the owner in the sense of proprietor. He is not a co-owner of net assets. He has no right *in rem*, but stands in a contractual relation to the company .... his main right rests in his claim to a share in the profits ... [and], in case the company is wound up, to a refund of the original capital contribution [and to share in other surpluses].
Forell, 1956, 411

Generally, the primary duty of the director is to the corporation and not to the shareholders.
Votaw, 1965, 58

the fiduciary duties [of directors] are owed to the company and to the company alone .... the directors owe no duties to the individual members as such .... the directors must act ... in what they believe to be the best interests of the company.
Gower, 1969, 517, 520

Far too often management only reveals to the shareholders important relevant information about the company when it is trying to fight off a takeover bid.

Samuels, 1969, 619

The shareholders, the theoretical owners of industry, are still a pathetically ineffective army; directors can bamboozle them with phoney accounts, and write each other fat service contracts to make sure they are not sacked.

Sampson, 1971, 657

a director is an agent, who casts his vote to decide in what manner his principal shall act through the collective agency of the board of directors; a shareholder who casts his vote in general meeting is not casting it as an agent of the company in any shape or form. His act, therefore, in voting as he pleases, cannot in any way be regarded as an act of the company. [per Walton J.]

Northern Counties Securities v Jackson & Steeple Ltd, 1974

280 Financial Publicity

281 Secrecy

it is obviously a most effective protection for legitimate secrets that it shall be universally understood and expected that those who ask questions which they have no right to ask will have lies told them.

Sidgwick, 1874/1962, 318

the administration of external politics, being in the nature of an enterprise in chicane and coercion, is necessarily furtive, runs forever on sharp practice, carefully withholds information that might be useful to the enemy, and habitually gives out information with intent to deceive. In effect, external politics is a blend of war and business and combines the peculiar traits of both. So the shadow of external politics covers also the management of domestic affairs, with the result that the authorities of the democratic commonwealths habitually go about their work under a cover of reticence tempered with prevarication.

Veblen, 1923/1964, 29

The euphoria of secrecy goes to the head very much like the euphoria of gadgets. I have known men, prudent in other respects, who became drunk with it. It induces an unbalancing sense of power. It is not of consequence whether one is hugging to oneself a secret about one's own side or about the other. It is not uncommon to run across men, superficially commonplace and unextravagant, who are letting their judgment run wild because they are hoarding a secret about the other side – quite forgetting that someone on the other side, almost indistinguishable from themselves, is hoarding a precisely similar secret about them. It takes a very strong head to keep secrets for years, and not go slightly mad.

Snow, 1962, 65

Secrecy is approved in many aspects of life, which is another way of saying that privacy is thought to be desirable. I doubt that anyone is opposed to all types of privacy . . . . Legal and political discussions of secrecy, including those pertaining to insider trading, while not always ignoring efficiency, have focused on questions of equity and morality – who is harmed and who is benefited.

Demsetz, 1969, 11

Government cannot govern without information. Where, as they often do, corporations see some proposed government action as a threat to their interests, one of the most effective weapons to combat that action is to deprive the government of the infornation it needs if it is to act, or even to provide false, incomplete, or distorted information that is designed to lead to inaction or to action favorable to corporate interests.

Stevenson, 1980, 59

Conflicts over secrecy . . . are conflicts over power: the power that comes through controlling the flow of information.

Bok, 1983/1989, 19

Secrecy for plans is needed, not only to protect their formulation but also to develop them, perhaps to change them, at times to execute them, even to give them up . . . . Secrecy guards projects that require creativity and prolonged work; the tentative and the fragile, unfinished tasks, probes and bargaining of all kinds . . . . Secrecy about plans and their execution . . . allows unpredictability and surprise.

Bok, 1983/1989, 23

282 Privacy or secrecy in financial matters

Unfortunately, there are many who keep their books in duplicate, showing one to the buyer and the other to the seller. What is worse, they swear and perjure themselves upon them. How wrongly they act! However, if they must present their books to an officer [for authentication] (such as the consuls in the employ of the city of Perosa) they cannot so easily lie and defraud.

Pacioli, 1494/1963, 38

965. With reference to the balance sheet, you would have it made public to the shareholders, I presume? – Certainly . . . . *966.* Would you not have the balance sheet registered with the registrar of joint stock companies? – No; if you did that, one half of the trading companies that I know would . . . endeavor to get out of the Act of Parliament as fast as they could. . . . *967.* . . . I have half a dozen cases in my eyes now of companies which never could have been formed if I had not given a positive assurance that there was no obligation to publish their profits and balance sheets.

Morris (solicitor), 1877, BPP, 1877

Private firms are largely indebted to the secrecy of their transactions for the undamaged credit which they often retain during periods of extremely bad trade.

Accountant, Anon, 1881, 3

Corporations which are secretive about their accounts, or which issue statements not certified to, have only themselves to blame if they are made the victims of hostile legislation.

Montgomery, 1912/1976, 22

The bogy of the competitor as an excuse for withholding information is on occasions ridden hard; on the other hand critics are sometimes apt to forget that the owners of a so-called public company are a group of private individuals the internal working and details of whose joint business are entitled to the same protection and freedom from publicity as is enjoyed by a private firm.

Kettle, 1939, 478

The principal reasons why corporate managers were so secretive with regard to their companies' financial affairs were four in number: there was no tradition of publicity, for no one would have thought of asking individual proprietors, partners or early family owners to divulge such information; management believed the public had no right to information on these matters; managers feared that by revealing financial information they would unwittingly assist their competitors; and to many the doctrine of *caveat emptor* seemed as applicable to buyers of securities as to purchasers of horses.

Hawkins, 1963, 141

the inclination of many owners and managers through the years has been in the direction of minimizing or concealing assets, and there has also long been in evidence the contrary inclination on the part of some people to maximize or overstate representations of available property.

Paton, 1963, 51

In Europe at least, financial information still has some status value; it has long been reserved to the owner of the business and his trusted bookkeeper, and has been taboo to other people; this magic is not yet fully removed.

Hofstede, 1969, 27

There is a natural reluctance, of course, on the part of business people to disclose more than they have to disclose; they are afraid of competition, for instance, but I believe this [standardized disclosure] is a small sacrifice to make if we can have the confidence of the investing public that the accounts and the accounting in this country are as good as human capacity can make them . . . . .

Leach, 1970, 32

When the Bank [of England] was nationalized in 1946 . . . . the Act made no provision for the Bank to publish its accounts, and since then, through its smokescreens and its city connections, the Bank has managed to evade close scrutiny by the Treasury, and still more by Parliament. It is the most remarkable example of secrecy defeating democracy.

Sampson, 1971, 546

Private or secret accounts

A Sienese mercantile and banking company in the late 13th century kept a] *livro dei chapitali*, to which were presumably posted all confidential entries concerning the partners' equity and, perhaps, the salaries of the factors, or employees; . . . . [A Florentine company, the Alberti company, at least during the period 1302–29, kept a] *libro segreto*, or secret account book [which] usually contained data on the distribution of capital and profits . . . . Because of the confidential nature of this information it is quite understandable why the *libro segreto*, in Italian companies, was usually kept by one of the partners himself and stored away in a locked chest to which employees had no access.

de Roover, 1956, 122, 124

Such as are disposed to keep the quaterne [ledger] in their own custody (be it either a master himself, or one that is appointed over other in the house, whereby the substance may be kept secret, except unto the said master or keeper of the accounts, as for divers considerations some men have good cause no less than so to do), they may bind their inventory . . . in the foremost end of their quaterne . . . .

Peele, 1553, ch xi

The inventory [of properties and debts owing and owed] is a part or book . . . . [which] the master may hold secretly unto himself if it please him . . . and by this manner no man shall understand or know his estate, but himself only, or such as he shall appoint to keep the said books, which is very requisite among merchants.

Weddington, 1567/1963, 36

How to begin your journal . . . . first of all, you are to enter the parcels of the inventory, viz the present estate and wealth of the merchant, except you intend to have the same written apart in a book by itself (as some use to do) that your first stock may be only known to yourself.

Carpenter, 1632, 6

It is an erroneous objection to systematic books, that they cannot be kept without making known the entire capital of the proprietor. If he desire privacy on this point, he has merely to exclude from the books all accounts not belonging to his floating stock; as estates, buildings, funded property, loans on security, private accounts with bankers &c . . . . A private ledger, with a few annual entries, will enable him to systematize all the branches of his property into one capital . . . .

Cronhelm, 1818/1978, 37

If the business is of such a nature as to make it advisable to prevent the employees from obtaining connected information concerning its various phases, the general ledger is relieved of all the facts which it is desired to keep secret. The vital data are kept in a private ledger which is posted by the head of the concern, the auditor, or a confidential clerk, from the results of the books of original entry.

Esquerré, 1914, 116

the private ledger [may contain] only the capital and drawing accounts. In practice, however, this ledger, which is provided with a lock and key and is sometimes kept by the chief clerk or accountant who occupies a confidential post, often includes other accounts of a private nature, such as loans, ... the bank balance, and the stock. Without knowing the value of the stock at the commencement and at the end of a period, it would be impossible for any clerk to arrive at the gross or net profit, even though he had access to all the other information. An earlier method of division of accounts ... still to be found ... is to keep all the nominal and real accounts in the private ledger. Another method is to keep all the expense accounts in a nominal ledger, and to put all the real or property accounts ... into the private ledger.

Carter, 1923, 218

It is a frequent practice to keep certain accounts secret from all but a few responsible higher officials – such accounts being capital, fixed assets, reserves, profit and loss, taxation, directors' fees, commissions, dividends, and so on. This can be done by segregating the relevant accounts in the private ledger which is kept by one of the higher officials.

Pickles & Dunkerley, 1950, 241

283 Financial publicity by companies as *quid pro quo*

The major concept underpinning these safeguards [of the interests of creditors, under the *Anonymous Partnership Act* of 1792, Ireland] was publicity. In an age of *laissez-faire*, men were thought to be the best judges of their own self interest. It was felt that, provided they were made aware of the nature of the concern to which they were proposing to give credit, the dangers inherent in limited liability could be largely contained. Indeed it was sometimes argued that such publicity was more useful to creditors than the personal liability of the proprietors of a firm.

French, 1990, 20

[Formula advanced for incorporation with limited liability]: limited liability; paid up capital; perfect publicity.

Clay, 1836/1936, 69

The law is warranted in requiring from all joint stock associations with limited responsibility ... that such accounts should be kept, accessible to individuals, and if needful, published to the world, as shall render it possible to ascertain at any time the existing state of the company's affairs . . . the fidelity of such accounts being safeguarded by sufficient penalties.

Mill, 1848/1940, 900

Many intolerable evils arising from the operations of corporations can be aired only when the public have full information concerning all their doings . . . .The government grants privileges to corporations and should protect against their abuse. No business whose management is secret is entitled to the privileges of incorporation. ["Recommendation as to publicity", US Industrial Commission, Final report, 1902]

Phillips, 1902/1986, 3, 4

Stockholders are entitled to adequate information . . . . incorporation is a privilege. The people grant to a private body the ineffable enjoyment of immortality, of succession, of impersonality, and, greatest of all, of limited liability . . . . The grant . . . abrogates many . . . formerly existent safeguards which must of course be offset by new provisions at law.

Ripley, 1927, 165

There is a growing feeling and acknowledgment that the information conveyed by the balance sheets of public companies is a public concern, and that such companies, having been granted certain rights and privileges, accordingly have certain obligations to the public.

Macpherson, 1934, 92

the control of business enterprises conducted in the form of public companies requires the publication of adequate and intelligible accounts and . . . this is but one return for the privilege of limited liability.

Bray & Sheasby, 1944/1949, 2

The price that joint stock companies paid under the [English] Companies Acts for the privileges of free transferability of shares and of limited liability of shareholders . . . . included [financial] publicity.

Storey, 1964, 13

The principle since the [UK Companies] Act of 1844 has been that incorporation by registration entailed publicity, although often one of the privileges obtainable through that procedure, namely limited liability, was, as being the paramount privilege of a registered company, singled out, with the result that the principle was expressed as being that limited liability entailed publicity.

Marshall, 1968, 23

284 Financial disclosure, in principle

nothing is easier than for an individual trader to conceal the extent of his engagements . . . . On the contrary, the *société anonyme* neither can nor ought to borrow without the fact becoming known to all the world – directors, clerks, shareholders and the public. Its operations partake, in some respects, of the nature of those of governments. The light of day penetrates in every direction, and there can be no secrets from those who seek the information.

Coquelin, 1843/1848, 902

Publicity is the best check against fraud . . . .

Economist, 1879, 446

The larger corporations – the so-called trusts – should be required to publish annually a properly audited report, showing in reasonable detail their assets and liabilities, with profit or loss; such report and audit under oath to be subject to government inspection. The purpose of such publicity is to encourage competition when profits become excessive, thus protecting consumers against too high prices and to guard the interests of employees by a knowledge of the financial condition of the business in which they are employed. [Report to Congress]

Industrial Commission (US), 1900/1963, 146

The right of inspection [of books of account] rests upon the proposition that those in charge of the corporation are merely the agents of the stockholders who are the real owners of the property.

Guthrie v Harkness, 1905

the business belongs to the stockholders and they are entitled to all the information about it that it is possible to give them.

Walton, 1909, 468

It would seem to be axiomatic that when a business organization offers its securities to the general public it should make available to the public complete information regarding its financial history, its personnel, the character and trend of its sales and profits, and its present financial position as expressed in a balance sheet. If there is any danger that competitors may profit by the publication of all these facts, it is possible that the public should not be asked to participate in its earnings.

AR, editorial, 1932, 214

So long as private business seeks capital, either on a credit or stock basis, from the public, the public is not only entitled to but has the right to demand those financial facts which must be the basis for intelligent dealing in the securities offered. The withholding of information generally accepted as necessary to sound investment, providing such information might affect a decision, is in the nature of a fraud.

Porter & Fiske, 1935, 197

The courts have generally held that a *bona fide* stockholder has the same right to full information as a partner in a private business.

Graham & Dodd, 1951, 66

Financial statements should disclose all information necessary to make the statements not misleading. This doctrine relates to such things as form, content, parenthetical comments, and notes to the financial statements.

Powell, 1964a/1970, 224

The principle of full or adequate disclosure is simply stated as the requirement that accounting statements and reports disclose that information which is necessary to make them not misleading.

Patillo, 1965, 91

The social conventions and legal rights we have established to protect personal privacy are founded on human values and human traits shared by the members of every society. Corporations – and other organizations – can make no direct claim to the benefits of those social and legal rules, for their fictional "personalities" do not partake of the characteristics wherein the rules find their basis.

Stevenson, 1980, 51

285 Disclosure held not to be inimical

1279 ... to what extent might it be detrimental to the *bona fide* shareholders to have all the company's transactions disclosed in open court? – I am of the opinion that where the transactions are *bona fide*, there cannot be any disadvantage, however great the publicity may be and however easily attainable by each shareholder. *1280* You think a disclosure of the way in which the money of the company has been employed would, under no circumstances, be disadvantageous? – None whatever.

C D (merchant), 1843, *BPP, 1844*

The balance sheets ought to be sent [to all shareholders], or be open to inspection; and there is no weight whatever in the fear which has been expressed, that any company has anything to fear by the disclosure of any fact required by the balance sheet [in the proposed statute]. I can state most positively that not only would it do no injury to any one of the companies for which we are auditors, but I do not know a company to which it would not be of advantage. [#1957]

Chadwick, 1877, *BPP, 1877*

The usual reply to such a suggestion [less indefinite annual reports] is that the company cannot afford to publish valuable trade secrets .... But .... stockholders ... ought to be informed concerning the true condition of their company .... it is not at all certain that valuable trade secrets need be divulged ....

Mitchell, 1907/1986, 402

full publicity of the affairs of corporations would be beneficial not only to the public but to the corporations themselves .... where corporations with large affairs have become the prey of politicians ... these corporations ... should forgo certain of their rights of privacy, and I believe they would be willing to accept the counter-effect of publicity by making known to the public the condition of their affairs in such terms as cannot be misunderstood.

Sells, 1911, 349

the modern world being what in fact it is, most companies have in operation a system of intelligence, adequate to provide them with all requisite information with regard to their competitors.

Samuel, 1933/1982, 162

that accurate disclosure will queer a company's pitch, by giving away information to competitors which can be used against its own interests . . . . is a specious argument . . . . if a company is doing less well than before, the first people to be aware of this fact are always its competitors.

Parkinson, 1937, 874

We do not believe that, if fully informed, shareholders would press for excessive dividends and we are in favor of as much disclosure as practicable.

Cohen Committee (UK), 1945

Is there a board of directors prepared to admit that it does not know its competitors' capabilities?

Accountant, editorial, 1954, 204

I am convinced that, in general, disclosure does no harm to companies. The few cases where it might be possible to show that disclosure has done harm are far outnumbered by those where it has done no harm, and are outweighed by the more informed judgments that shareholders have been able to make.

Smith, 1968, 166

286 Disclosure as policy, not as accounting principle

The 1844 (UK) *Joint Stock Companies Act* had required companies to file an audited balance sheet with the Registrar, and the 1855 *Limited Liability Act* even gave the Board of Trade the right to approve the auditors chosen by a company. However, both these acts were repealed in 1856; and from then until 1900, companies were under no obligation either to produce or file accounts or to employ auditors. The 1900 *Companies Act* reimposed the audit requirement, still for the balance sheet only; and from 1908, the audited balance sheet had once more to be filed with the Registrar. Not until 1929 was a profit and loss account required for shareholders, and not until 1948 did it have to be audited and filed . . . . But then, as now, many companies . . . included in their articles Table A from the 1862 *Companies Act*, which retained many of the features of the (repealed) 1844 and 1855 Acts. In particular, Table A required that a balance sheet and income and expenditure statement be laid before the annual general meeting and that every shareholder receive a copy of that balance sheet.

Mason, 1981, 129

I would like to question whether disclosure is a matter of accounting principle. If we take the term "the truth, the whole truth, and nothing but the truth", adequate disclosure would seem to fall under the category of "the whole truth". There may however be some question whether this is a principle of accounting or a maxim of law or of ethics or morality.

Broad, 1942, 35

Disclosure is to be considered as a matter of managerial policy, not a matter of accounting doctrine . . . . disclosure is the outcome of the action or agitation of interest groups . . . in the community; it is the response of management to the demands of other groups.

Chambers, 1950, 353

The principle of full and fair disclosure to stockholders has been embraced by a high and steadily increasing percentage of modern corporate managements, and it has been adopted as a national policy. This principle is the overriding tenet of the communication aspect of the accounting function.

Bevis, 1965, 151

287 Supplementary information

Footnotes

If any significant change in accounting principle or practice . . . has been made . . . , a statement thereof shall be given in a note to the appropriate statement, and if the change or adjustment substantially affects proper comparison with the preceding fiscal period, the necessary explanation.

SEC, 1941, ASR 21

Unusual items important enough to distort comparisons materially should be sufficiently clearly disclosed to make it possible to give due weight to them. Any significant changes in accounting principles or procedures should not only be disclosed, but their effect should be shown. Any significant departures from generally accepted principles or procedures should be fully stated, together with the means of appraising their effect upon the statement.

Rorem & Kerrigan, 1942, 556–7

U S Steel practically never found it necessary to use explanatory notes in connection with its financial statements prior to 1939.

Claire, 1945, 50

A footnote is a disclosure by management of pertinent information which it is not feasible or customary to incorporate in the statements themselves . . . . From the point of view of management, a footnote may be a solution by which unwanted changes of the proposed statement may be avoided. From the point of view of the auditor, a footnote may be a solution by which the company makes sufficient disclosure so that the necessity of taking an exception in his report is avoided.

Bullock, 1956, 40, 44

If the principle is adopted that fair presentation is met by footnote disclosure, we must also then admit that the entire set of financial statements could be presented solely by footnotes. The difference is only a matter of degree.

Spacek, 1968, 61

I picked up a set of accounts quite at random the other day, and the accounts consisted of two pages of accounts and no less than 12 pages of notes, quite apart from six more pages of financial information. This example would be fairly typical of company reporting in 1969 . . . .

Whinney, 1969, 896

"Go ahead and have your appraisal [of property, plant and equipment] made, and we'll disclose the additional value in a footnote", I essay. The client looks at me contemptuously, "Who reads footnotes? . . . ."

Landman, 1971, 81

The disclosure policy [of the SEC] carried with it several unfortunate limitations. It permitted the absurdity of voluminous footnotes, which, although they presumably revealed the necessary information, allowed accountants to include provisos indicating that they had little faith in the information itself or in the style of its presentation.

Chatov, 1975, 177

Supplementary statements

It would perhaps not be unreasonable to urge that the accountant should be held responsible for the preparation of supplementary statements at the end of each period designed to show – by making proper allowance for the change in the value of money – the true relation between the current statement and the one immediately preceding (or a series of earlier statements) . . . . it would seem that any supplementary statements which might be prepared by the accountant should be couched in terms of individual price movements, with little or no reference to any precise calculation of the movement of prices in general.

Paton, 1922/1962, 428–9

under certain conditions the income or loss reported by conventional accounting procedure may not reflect the true change in economic status . . . . At the most what is needed is a special report supplementing the usual periodic statements and designed to trace the main effects of general price movements upon the affairs of the enterprise.

> Paton & Littleton, 1940, 139, 141

After several years of discussion [of accounting for price changes and inflation] . . . it now appears that changes will be introduced not in the basic financial statement but by supplementary disclosure. Perhaps the rate of change and the uncertainty caused by inflation make a comprehensive departure from historical costs just too large a step for the preparers and users of financial reports to take at one time.

> Alexander, 1981, 8:17

I propose that in addition to full [current cost] accounts a balance sheet prepared under [realizable value] principles should also be presented.

> Lyne, 1981, 235

See also 217, 793

288 Interpretation dependent on knowledge of accounting rules or policies

one must interpret accounts with knowledge not only of the [accounting] policy [of a firm] but of the sort of judgment that is behind them.

> Cole, 1921, 339

it seems to me highly desirable that the reports and accounts of corporations should be made more fully explanatory, so that investors and others interested will know generally what methods of accounting have been followed and be in a position to appraise the value of the resulting figures accordingly.

> May, 1932, 343

The financial statements of a corporation are seldom really informative to the reader who does not possess a knowledge of the accounting policies governing their preparation . . . . A statement of the major accounting policies of a corporation has an importance equal to that of the financial statements themselves, since neither is complete without the other.

> Andersen, 1935, 336

I think that the [Companies] Act might well include a requirement that each company, or at least each public company, should file annually with the Registrar a "Statement of Accounting Procedures" at the time of publication of its annual accounts . . . . designed to explain the bases and assumptions on which the less certain of the figures in the accounts had been calculated.

> Edey, 1960/1980, 192

Disclosure is useful; but if intelligent interpretation of the disclosed items depends upon a thorough knowledge of the subtleties of accounting theory, the objective of disclosure, i.e. to promote intelligent decision making, may be largely forfeited.

Hayes, 1965, 757

When financial statements are issued purporting to present fairly financial position, changes in financial position, and results of operations in accordance with generally accepted accounting principles, a description of all significant accounting policies of the reporting entity should be included as an integral part of the financial statements.

AICPA, 1972b, APBO22

At the Commission [SEC] . . . we are giving serious consideration to requiring that all prospectuses carry a textual exposition under the title Accounting Policies, or something of the sort. This would be designed to elucidate on the financial statements, make them more meaningful, indicate underlying assumptions and changes in method and their significance and generally aid in the interpretation of financial data.

Casey, 1972a, 44

Publication of accounting rules or policies

the principal objects which this [AIA] Committee thinks the NYSE should . . . do its best gradually to achieve [include] . . . . to make no attempt to restrict the right of corporations to select detailed methods of accounting deemed by them to be best suited to the requirements of their business; but . . . to ask each listed corporation to cause a statement of the methods of accounting and reporting employed by it to be formulated in sufficient detail to be a guide to its accounting department; to have such statement adopted by its board so as to be binding on its accounting officers; and to furnish such statement to the Exchange and make it available to any stockholder on request and upon payment, if desired, of a reasonable fee.

AIA, 1932

For a banker, stockholder, or any nonexpert in accounting to accept that solution [full statement of the accounting methods employed in the annual report of each company], and successfully appraise the distinctions between the diverse presentations that will result, is not, in my opinion, a reasonable expectation.

Stans, 1950, 211

The accounting policies followed for dealing with items which are judged material or critical in determining profit or loss for the year and in stating the financial position should be disclosed by way of note to the accounts. The explanations should be clear, fair, and as brief as possible consistent with those objects . . . . The use of these concepts [going concern, accruals, consistency, prudence] is not necessarily self-evident from an examination of accounts, but they have such general acceptance that they call for no explanation in published accounts and their observation is presumed unless stated otherwise.

ASSC, 1971b, SSAP2

Accounting policies encompass the many principles, bases, conventions, rules, and procedures adopted by managements in preparing financial statements. There are many different accounting policies in use even in relation to the same subject and judgment is required in selecting those which, in the circumstances of the enterprise, are best suited to present properly its financial position and the results of its operations . . . . Financial statements should include clear and concise disclosure of all significant accounting policies which have been used.

IASC, 1974, IAS1

the notes on the accounts must set out information in respect of the valuation methods applied to the various items in the annual accounts, and the methods employed in calculating the valuation adjustments.

EEC, 1978, 4th Directive

financial reporting often provides information that depends on, or is affected by, management's estimates and judgment. Investors, creditors and others are aided in evaluating estimates and judgmental information by explanations of underlying assumptions or methods used, including disclosure of significant uncertainties about principal underlying assumptions or estimates.

FASB, 1978, SFAC1

A closer look at any accounting policy, as published, will reveal just how useless an exercise it is for a reader with limited financial expertise to read these [financial] statements . . . . Each company goes through the motions of publishing its own accounting policies, but in essence they are all the same; the exercise has degenerated, on the face of it, to a recitation of tribal incantations, familiar to the few and informative to no one.

Lothian, 1978, 43

A summary of accounting policies, so or similarly described, shall form the initial section of the notes in the accounts . . . . The summary . . . shall describe all material accounting policies which have been applied . . . . subject to the exception that where the accrual basis or going concern basis has been used, those bases need not be described.

ASRB, 1985a, ASRB1001

289 Projections and predictions

In attempting to discharge their reporting responsibilities to stockholders and others, corporate management should consider disclosure of their short term plans.

Backer, 1966a/1966b, 452

A record of past events is insufficient by itself [for reporting on the effective use of resources]. Some indication of the firm's potential at the end of the accounting period is also required . . . . the firm's potential should be indicated by the provision of a projected funds statement. It is then open to each individual to form his own opinion of the value of the firm.

Rayman, 1970, 426

accounting reports . . . should incorporate a full forecast of the cash flow and profits for the next year, and a report by the auditors on the variances (and the reasons for them) between the forecasts in the previous year's report and the actual results. The accounts might also contain, but in far less detail, a five year forecast of cash and profits.

Briston, 1974, 50

Cautions on predictions

every specific statement about the future, and every specific statement embodying estimates or expectations about the future, is excluded from the category of objective statements; for as the future is not yet present, no such statement can be tested.

Chambers, 1964b, 269

profit forecasts necessarily depend on subjective judgments and are to a greater or lesser extent, according to the nature of the business, subject to numerous and substantial inherent uncertainties, which increase markedly the further forward in time the forecasts stretch . . . . there is no question of their being audited . . . .

ICAEW, 1969b, 629

It has been the Commission's long standing policy not to permit projections and predictions in prospectuses and reports filed with the [SEC] . . . . A real danger exists . . . that projections . . . would be accorded a greater measure of validity by the unsophisticated than they would deserve.

SEC, 1969, 96

Independent auditors . . . . tend to resist any movement towards data reporting that focuses on projections of the future and therefore does not lend itself to objective verification.

Olson, 1977, 68

the publication of formal authorised forecasts puts the cart before the horse. The correct way of proceeding is to let the investor reach his own view of the worth of a company and its future by reading its accounts. By all means, let us have the prophecies of the chairman, but the wise investor should be encouraged to set them in context against the realities of the present as disclosed in the accounts.

Davison, 1978, 91

It is difficult to generalize about the effects of providing general access to documents concerned with future plans (except to say that a great deal less would be written down); but it is certain that such a rule would be perceived as grossly unfair in a society in which competition is as much a part of the cultural norm as it is in ours. Moreover, from the standpoint of public policy there seems to be very little reason to establish such a rule.

Stevenson, 1980, 49

See also 174, 184

290 Mandatory Corporate Financial Publicity

291 Financial publicity as element of a fair securities market

This Exchange recommends to the various corporations whose securities are here dealt in, that they shall print, publish and distribute to shareholders, at least fifteen days prior to annual meetings, a full report of their operations during the preceding fiscal year; together with complete and detailed statements of all income and expenditures, and a balance sheet showing their financial condition at the close of the given period. And this Exchange urges the stockholders of the several corporations to take such action as may be necessary for the accomplishment of this recommendation.

NYSE, 1895/1965, 16

Our great exchanges . . . can perform their proper function of making true prices, consonant with valuation, only when there is [adequate financial] disclosure. This is . . . the ultimate defense of publicity.

Ripley, 1927, 169

There is . . . an obligation upon us to insist that every issue of new securities to be sold in interstate commerce shall be accompanied by full publicity and information, and that no essentially important element attending the issue shall be concealed from the buying public. This proposal adds to the ancient rule of *caveat emptor* the further doctrine, Let the seller also beware.

Roosevelt, 1933/1970, 35

The duty of disclosure stems from the necessity of preventing a corporate insider from utilizing his position to take unfair advantage of the uninformed (outsider). It is an attempt to provide some degree of equalization of bargaining position, in that outsiders may exercise an informed judgment in any such transaction. [per Judge Leahy]

Speed v Transamerica Corporation, 1951

Disclosure is the cornerstone of Federal securities regulation. It is the great safeguard that governs conduct of corporate managements in many of their activities. It is the best bulwark against reckless corporate publicity and irresponsible recommendation and sale of securities.

SEC, 1963, 35

The purpose of disclosure is to place the investor in a position to make an informed judgment on the merits of a security, and to provide a basis for comparing that security with others issued by companies in the same or different industries. Essentially this purpose is achieved through the furnishing of financial information which provides a uniform pattern of reporting based on understood and generally accepted accounting practices.

Cary, 1963/1964, 281

the more information that is available and the more widely spread the information is, the less will be the likelihood of insiders using information to their advantage.

ICAS, 1988, 31

See also 283, 284, 286

292 Mandatory quality of financial statements of companies

Jurisdictions on UK pattern

the directors of such company shall cause the books of the company to be balanced, and a full and fair balance sheet to be made up; .... (s 35)

UK *Joint Stock Companies Act*, 1844

The directors shall cause true accounts to be kept .... The auditors shall make a report to the shareholders ... [stating] whether in their opinion the balance sheet is a full and fair balance sheet ... properly drawn up so as to exhibit a true and correct view of the state of the company's affairs .... [Model company regulations, Table B]

UK *Joint Stock Companies Act*, 1856

The auditors shall make a report to the members upon the balance sheet and accounts, and in every such report they shall state whether, in their opinion, the balance sheet is a full and fair balance sheet, containing the particulars required by these regulations, and properly drawn up so as to exhibit a true and correct view of the state of the company's affairs, and in case they have called for explanations or information from the directors, whether such explanations or information have been given by the directors, and whether they have been satisfactory; .... [First Schedule, Table A]

UK *Companies Act*, 1862

[Every report of auditors] shall state whether, in their opinion, the balance sheet referred to in the report is properly drawn up so as to exhibit a true and correct view of the state of the company's affairs as shown by the books of the company, ... (s 23)

UK *Companies Act, 1900*

the auditors shall make a report to the shareholders on the accounts examined by them, and on every balance sheet laid before the company in general meeting during their tenure of office, and the report shall state (a) whether or not they have obtained all the information and explanations they have required; and (b) whether, in their opinion, the report is properly drawn up so as to exhibit a true and correct view of the state of the company's affairs according to the best of their information and the explanations given to them, and as shown by the books of the company.

UK *Companies (Consolidation) Act,*
1908

The auditors shall make a report to the members on the accounts examined by them . . . and the report shall state . . . whether, in their opinion, the balance sheet referred to in the report is properly drawn up so as to exhibit a true and correct view of the state of the company's affairs according to the best of their information and the explanations given to them, and as shown by the books of the company. (s 134)

UK *Companies Act, 1929*

Every balance sheet of a company shall give a true and fair view of the state of affairs of the company as at the end of its financial year, and every profit and loss account of a company shall give a true and fair view of the profit or loss of the company for the financial year. (s 149)

UK *Companies Act, 1948*

Every company and the directors and managers thereof shall cause to be kept . . . such accounting and other records as will sufficiently explain the transactions and financial position of the company and enable true and fair profit and loss accounts and balance sheets . . . to be prepared from time to time . . . .

Australian Companies Acts, 1961

The annual acounts shall give a true and fair view of the company's assets, liabilities, financial position and profit or loss.

EEC, 1978, 4th Directive

Without affecting the generality of the preceding provisions of this section, the directors of a company shall ensure that the accounts of the company . . . are made out in accordance with applicable approved accounting standards. ["approved" by the Accounting Standards Review Board established under the *National Companies and Securities Commission Act, 1979– *]

Australian *Companies Act, 1981*

Jurisdictions on USA pattern

An Act to provide full and fair disclosure of the character of securities sold in interstate and foreign commerce and through the mails, and to prevent fraud in the sale thereof . . . . [title of Act]

US *Securities Act*, 1933

[Concluding paragraph required by FTC (later SEC) in public accountants' reports] Subject to the foregoing comments, we have, after reasonable investigation, reasonable grounds to believe, and do believe, at the date of this certificate, that the statements contained in the attached balance sheets and in the attached profit and loss statements truly and fairly reflect the application of accepted accounting practices to the facts disclosed by our investigation, and that there is no omission to state a material fact required to be stated therein or necessary to make the statements therein not misleading.

FTC, 1934/1939, 17

The requirement of full and fair disclosure. The effect of this is not merely to insist that each item as answered [in the registration forms of the Securities and Exchange Commission] state the full truth, but that all the items answered fully in this sense must not give a misleading picture of the enterprise as a whole. [The Commission's opinion in a 1935 case] makes explicit the mandate implicit in the Act that the whole truth should be told. No subtle distinctions ought to avoid the clear necessity that those seeking other people's money should be completely frank about the enterprise in which the investor is urged to participate.

MacChesney & O'Brien, 1937, 134

the "character of securities" is in large measure revealed in the financial information about the company issuing the securities, as developed in its accounting statements.

Sanders, 1937, 191

293 Explication of "true and fair (or correct) view" – UK pattern

Natural or common meaning

True. Conformable to fact; correct; exact; actual; genuine; honest . . . . In one sense, that only is "true" which is conformable to the actual state of things. In that sense a statement is "untrue" which does not express things exactly as they are. But in another and broader sense the word "true" is often used as a synonym of "honest", sincere", not "fraudulent".

Black's law dictionary, 1951, 1679

Fair. Equitable as a basis for exchange; reasonable; a fair value.

Black's law dictionary, 1951, 713

An act relating to the public highways (13 Geo III, c.78, 1773) provided for the appointment of local managers empowered to levy assessments, fines and penalties. The surveyor was to keep "one or more book or books in which he shall fairly enter a just, true and fair account of all such money as shall have come to his hands"..... On the quality of the final general account, ... [the majority of seventy deeds of settlement of banking firms, 1827–1843] stipulated: full true and explicit statement and balance sheet, 29; fair accurate and just statement and account, 26 .... The objects of the accounts specifications were, in the majority of cases, expressed in the form, "so that the real state of affairs may plainly appear", or "for fully (truly, etc.) manifesting the state of affairs."

Chambers & Wolnizer, 1991, 199, 203

[It] seems implicit in the act [UK *Companies Act, 1948*] that the scales are to be fairly held between the interests of the company as a commercial undertaking and the interests of all who are concerned with its accounts, the shareholders and creditors at the date of the accounts, potential members of either class, the directors, and, in exceptional cases, the economic interests of the community.

Campbell, 1950, 270

What represents "fair" in respect of the presentation of accounts ... is a matter of judgment .... However, the terms of reference of any audit require that the auditor satisfy himself as to the fairness of the financial statements presented to him and that they conform to ascertainable facts.

Gutteridge, 1965, 38

The Oxford Dictionary defines true as consistent with fact; representing the thing as it is; and fair as equitable, impartial. If true and fair were to be judged purely on its dictionary meaning there would be one unique balance sheet only at any one time, and there would be no room for misunderstanding and misinterpretation.

Horrocks, 1967, 568

Any thinking accountant is almost certain to agree that no financial accounts present a true view in the sense that is normally understood by reasonable right-minded people.

McMonnies, 1967, 73

Other meanings

without intending to deceive the shareholders, or to act in any way dishonestly, it is quite possible for the directors and officers of a company to present the balance sheet in a more favorable light than is warranted by the facts .... while it would be very improper for the directors to intentionally deceive their co-partners in any particular, yet in many instances it would be very unfair to themselves and to the shareholders, as well as very impolitic, to either overstate the liabilities or to under-estimate the assets.

Pixley, 1881/1976, 130

A true and fair view implies that all statutory and other essential information is not only available but is presented in a form in which it can be properly and readily appreciated.

Kettle, 1948/1950, 117

A true and fair view implies appropriate classification and grouping of the items [in the balance sheet] .... A true and fair view also implies the consistent application of generally accepted principles.

ICAEW, 1958a, N18

The words, true and fair, have a technical legal meaning, as did their predecessor, true and correct. They do not mean absolute accuracy with one possible right answer like a sum in arithmetic. They recognize the inherent elements of judgment, and in effect, they say "the accounts follow the rules appropriate to this case".

Irish, 1966, 172

I can find little reason to suppose that all auditors would agree on whether or not any particular set of annual accounts present a true and fair view. Indeed the evidence of the past decade or so makes it abundantly clear that "true and fair" is a personal standard. It is judgmental.

Chastney, 1975, 681

[Comment on IASG ED18, 1976] We have already taken steps to preserve the meaning of the phrase ["true and fair"] in the present situation by adding the words "under the historical cost convention" to it − so that the context in which the words are being used currently is made clear and specific. Under a current cost accounting convention, the words, "under the current cost convention", would surely be added for a limited time to the "true and fair" phrase so that its meaning would be assimilated and understood in its new context .... While [under CCA] there will be more subjectivity in arriving at fairer figures for profit measurement or balance sheet values, there will, hopefully, be many financial items and narrative descriptions which should still be subjected to the test of being true.

Richards, 1977, 280

"True and fair view" is ... a legal concept and the question of whether accounts comply [with this test] can be authoritatively decided only by a court .... [True and fair] is an abstraction or philosophical concept expressed in simple English. The law uses many similar concepts, of which "reasonable care" is perhaps the most familiar example. It is a common feature of such concepts that there is seldom any difficulty in understanding what they mean but frequent controversy over their application to particular facts .... The courts have never attempted to define "true and fair" .... [Opinion of Counsel to ASC]

Hoffmann & Arden, 1983, 154, 155

Accounts will not be true and fair unless the information they contain is sufficient in quantity and quality to satisfy the reasonable expectations of the readers to whom they are addressed .... But the expectations of the readers will have been molded by the practices of accountants because by and large they will expect to get what they ordinarily get and that in turn will depend upon the normal practices of accountants. For these reasons, the courts will treat compliance with accepted accounting principles as *prima facie* evidence that the accounts are true and fair. Equally, deviation from accepted principles will be *prima facie* evidence that they are not. [Opinion of Counsel to ASC]

Hoffmann & Arden, 1983, 155

a true and fair view in relation to accounts or group accounts means a representation which affords those who might reasonably be expected to refer to those accounts (including holders or prospective purchasers of shares, debentures, notes or other interests, and creditors or prospective creditors) information which is relevant to the decisions which may be made by those persons in relation to the purchase, sale or other action in connection with their securities or interests.

Walker, 1984a, 28

See also 207, 266

Explication of "fair presentation", "present fairly" – USA pattern

The phrase "presents fairly" was first used by the CICA in 1959 in Bulletin No. 17: "In the form of auditor's report recommended originally, the expression 'exhibit a true and correct view' was used . . . . The Committee believes that this expression might be interpreted as implying a degree of exactitude which is nonexistent, and therefore recommends that . . . the words should be replaced by the more general expression 'present fairly'".

Eckel, 1973, 41

Quality accounting requires a fair presentation of economic facts, without bias for or against any partisan interest, whether that interest is the management, the investor, the lender, the consumer, the government or the politician.

Spacek, 1968, 62

There is a real question whether many users of financial statements understand the auditor's intent in the phrase, fairly presents in accordance with generally accepted accounting principles, or are aware of the accounting alternatives that exist . . . . A more important question is whether it is fair for users of financial statements to be put in a position of having to understand the nuances of the term, generally accepted accounting principles, in order to get meaning from a term such as fairly presents.

Olson, 1970, 43

in order for statements to present fairly the financial position and results of operations of a business, the statements must be factual, they must fully disclose all essential information, and they may not be misleading to the average reader.

Stettler, 1970, 14

Fair presentation means that there has been fair disclosure of all relevant facts. A fact is considered relevant if there is reason to believe that the people who use the financial statements, and who are reasonably well informed about financial matters, will be influenced by the information.

Anderson & others, 1974, 113

Present fairly: to set forth information that is unbiased, unlikely to be misinterpreted, and relevant to concerned users.

NAA, 1974, 21

The auditor's opinion that financial statements present fairly an entity's financial position in conformity with generally accepted accounting principles should be based on his judgment as to whether (a) the accounting principles selected and applied have general acceptance ... ; (b) the accounting principles are appropriate in the circumstances ... ; (c) the financial statements, including the related notes, are informative of matters that may affect their use, understanding and interpretation ... ; (d) the information presented ... is classified and summarized in a reasonable manner ... ; and (e) the financial statements reflect the underlying events and transactions in a manner that presents the financial position, results of operations, and changes in financial position stated within a range of ... limits that are reasonable and practicable to attain in financial statements.

AICPA, 1975, AU411

Present fairly. The auditor does not state that the statements are true and correct. Financial statements necessarily are the result of estimates and approximations. Their precision cannot be absolute. On the other hand, the auditor can conclude that the statements are free from material misstatements and omissions.

Willingham & Carmichael, 1975, 7

To permit all auditors to judge in a consistent manner whether financial statements present fairly, there must be a standard against which those judgments can be made; generally accepted accounting principles provide such a standard.

CICA Handbook, 1979, 5400

294 Fairness in financial communication

The procedures, rules and techniques of accounting must afford equitable treatment of all interests actually and potentially involved in the financial situations covered by accounts .... Accounting rules, procedures and techniques should be fair, unbiased and impartial. They should not serve a special interest.

Scott, 1941, 342

The fairest possible presentation of periodic net income, with neither material over-statement or understatement, is important, since the results of operations are significant not only to prospective buyers of an interest in the enterprise but also to prospective sellers.

AIA, 1953a/1961, ARB43, 7

Financial reports must present fairly enterprise information to all segments of society .... With such a presentation those segments are able to formulate judgments or take actions with respect to their special interests .... Fairness to all parties ... is ... the single basic standard of accounting ....

Patillo, 1965, 50, 60

the disclosure requirements of the securities laws require "nothing more than a disclosure of basic facts so that outsiders may draw upon their own evaluative experience in reaching their own investment decisions with knowledge equal to that of the insiders". [Appellate Court]

Gulf & Western ... v Great A & P Tea Co ..., 1973/1978, 27

Fairness is a quality that should underlie the preparation of financial statements, but it is not a property that can be objectively measured by the auditor.

Cohen Commission, 1977, 13

Indeterminate connotation of true and fair

"There isn't such a reasonable fellow in the world, to hear him talk. He never wants anything but what's right and fair; only when you come to settle what's right and fair, it's everything that he wants, and nothing that you want. And that's his idea of a compromise ...."

Hughes, *Tom Brown's Schooldays,*
1857/1896, 205

[The test of fairness] turns out to be almost, if not entirely, subjective – with no objective criteria .... what is fair or fair and reasonable depends mostly on the factors that motivate the individual applying the test.

Werntz, 1963/1968, 110

in the standard report of the auditor, he generally says that financial statements "present fairly" in conformity with generally accepted accounting principles – and so on. What does the auditor mean by the quoted words? Is he saying: (1) that the statements are fair *and* in accordance with generally accepted accounting principles; or (2) that they are fair *because* they are in accordance with generally accepted accounting principles; or (3) that they are fair only *to the extent* that generally accepted accounting principles are fair; or (4) that whatever the generally accepted accounting principles may be, the *presentation* of them is fair?

AICPA, 1965, 13–14

Auditors will tell you that true and fair is a technical term which means complying with sound accounting principles; but they are unable to agree on what are the principles and they are not quite sure whether the statements should be fair to the present shareholders, including those who are intending to sell their shares, or to creditors or to debenture holders or fair to prospective investors.

Horrocks, 1967, 568

Once the view is accepted that the words true and fair must be understood otherwise than in accordance with their ordinary literal meaning it follows inevitably, in my view, that their invocation as criteria for the verification of accounts becomes largely meaningless. Within certain flexible extremities, true and fair can mean very much what directors and auditors want them to mean.

Ryan, 1967, 106

The investment community is being made expensively aware that "true and fair" means no more than "that's one way of looking at it" . . . .

Marley, 1970, 11

there are so many alternative views which can justifiably be regarded as true and fair that the words have almost lost their meaning.

Rayman, 1970, 423

Fairness is an empty box, and the sooner we bury the term, the better off we will be.

Nelson, 1976, 12

Although it has been in use for almost thirty years, "true and fair" has never been exactly defined, but it is a moot point whether any replacement could be drafted more definitely – or even whether such definition would be desirable.

Pearse, 1977, 92

We have studied the extensive literature on the significance of the words used in the auditor's report . . . . Our study persuaded us that efforts to analyze, interpret, or improve the understanding of current terminology are not fruitful . . . . we recommend that the phrase "present fairly" be deleted from the auditor's report.

Cohen Commission, 1978, 14

There are no reported cases in which the courts have defined true and fair specifically . . . .

Taylor & Turley, 1986, 53

the concept of true and fair . . . . has never been authoritatively defined by either the accounting profession or the courts.

McGregor, 1992, 69

295 Disclosure accepted *in lieu* of invariant rules

In some cases it is possible to differentiate certain usages as bad, some methods as involving incorrect principles. But this is not always true and when in doubt there is no ultimate arbiter to whom appeal can confidently be made. In this dilemma it has, therefore, seemed advisable to show the existing variations rather than to attempt to formulate rigid rules.

Hatfield, 1916/1976, vi

The more practical alternative [to the selection by competent authority of detailed rules which would become binding on all corporations of a given class] would be to leave every corporation free to choose its own methods of accounting [within limits] . . . but require disclosure of the methods employed and consistency in their application from year to year.

AIA, 1932

[The SEC] is willing to pass financial statements which may be deficient in setting forth accepted accounting practice provided the certifying accountant clearly points out the deficiency and states what the effect would be had more acceptable practice been followed. Its reasoning for this treatment results from the fact that it is administering a disclosure rather than a regulatory act . . . .

Smith, 1935, 331

the Commission [SEC] has in its accounting regulations not sought to prescribe accounting methods, but has prescribed full disclosure of whatever methods the company has chosen to adopt.

Sanders, 1937, 204

with respect to financial statements . . . . filed with this Commission . . . . where there is a difference of opinion between the Commission and the registrant as to the proper principles of accounting to be followed, disclosure will be accepted *in lieu* of correction . . . only if the points involved are such that there is substantial authoritative support for the practices followed by the registrant and the position of the Commission has not previously been expressed . . . .

SEC, 1938a, ASR4

[Methods of dealing with] price level changes in financial statements, both as to inventories and plant and equipment, constitutes too complex a problem to be solved by any single accounting prescription . . . . The accounting profession should give its primary attention to providing adequate standards of disclosure.

Grady, 1952, 566

The Institute [ICAEW] recognized that the presentation of a true and fair view would not necessarily be impaired by the use of other methods [than the recommended method of dealing with government grants], providing there was adequate disclosure and consistency of treatment.

Bleasdale, 1972, 550

296 Materiality of information

Where the market values of securities are less than the book values, save where the variation is so small as to be trivial, a reserve for loss in value on the balance sheet date must be set up.

Federal Reserve Board, 1917, 274

The term, material, when used to qualify a requirement for the furnishing of information as to any subject, limits the information required to those matters as to which an average prudent investor ought reasonably to be informed before purchasing the security registered.

SEC, 1970a, Reg. S-X

A statement, fact, or item is material if, giving full consideration to the surrounding circumstances as they exist at the time, it is of such a nature that its disclosure, or the method of treating it, would be likely to influence or make a difference in the judgment and conduct of a reasonable person. The same tests apply to such words as significant, consequential, or important.

Dohr, 1950b, 56

the doctrine of materiality specifies that items of little or no consequence may be dealt with as expediency may suggest.

Powell, 1964a/1970, 225

Materiality is not a basic postulate of accounting theory. Rather, it represents a practical convention. Where the difference between the theoretical treatment of an item and a more practical treatment of that item is immaterial in amount, the item is frequently recorded the easiest way . . . .

Spiller, 1964, 858

In an accounting sense . . . a matter is material if its nondisclosure, misstatement or omission would be likely to distort the view given by the accounts or other statement under consideration.

ICAEW, 1968c, 116–7

A material fact is a fact to which an average, reasonably prudent person would attach importance in determining a course of conduct to be taken or followed upon learning the fact, such as in deciding whether or not to buy or sell stock, or to lend or refuse to lend money, or to cancel a loan.

United States v Simon, 1969

materiality means that precision in recognition, classification and valuation are not to be carried beyond the point where the information that results costs more than it is worth.

Anderson & others, 1974, 294

297 Materiality criteria

Although theoretically two qualified accountants should reach the same decision as to the materiality of a given item, in practice opinions are sometimes exactly opposite even though all the surrounding circumstances are known to both . . . . Personal judgment will always be needed for making materiality decisions . . . .
Woolsey, 1954, 750

it is suggested that materiality for balance sheet accounts be defined as follows: no item exceeding 5 per cent of its related total may be considered immaterial . . . . for income statement accounts: no item exceeding 2 per cent of gross profit on sales may be considered immaterial.
Hylton, 1961, 64

Materiality normally turns upon the relation between the amount of the item in question and the amount of some appropriate basis of comparison – for example, net income. The selection and use of such criteria call for the exercise of judgment in the highest degree.
Hicks, 1962, 64

The interpretation of what is material is a matter for the exercise of professional judgment based on experience and the requirement to give a true and fair view.
ICAEW, 1968c, 107

neither an accounting principle nor its effective application should be based on a percentage, because principles cannot possibly be determined in that manner . . . . Arbitrary percentages and prescribed periods of time used in the determination or application of accounting principles are usually the result of a compromise, which is not based on any principle.
Catlett, 1969, 64

Financial statements should disclose all items which are material enough to affect evaluations or decisions.
IASC, 1974, IAS1

no unique fixed materiality standard for an item can exist even for a given user if the standard is stated as a magnitude of the item.
Ro, 1982, 407

298 Nondisclosure notwithstanding disclosure rules

White Knight: I'll tell thee everything I can;
            There's little to relate.
Carroll, *Through the looking glass*, Ch viii

The wording of the *Companies Act, 1908*, created a loophole which permitted evasion of the spirit of the law. It required that a statement in the form of a balance sheet "made up to such date as may be specified in the statement" be filed with the Registrar of Companies. As a result, some companies continued to file the same statement year after year. To close this loophole, the *Companies Act, 1929*, required that the date of the balance sheet to be filed be not more than nine months preceding the annual general meeting.

Hein, 1962/1978, 205

The legally permitted practices resulting in the obfuscation of the truth by directors under the aegis of the auditor's certificate [include]: (a) The use of technical terminology which, though conveying one meaning to the auditors and directors, is yet quite capable of conveying a very different meaning to investors and even financial experts. (b) The lumping together . . . of numerous assets . . . [without] information as to the constituent items and their respective values. (c) The employment of a system of valuation which, while academically or historically accurate, fails to tally with values under existing conditions. . . . (e) The employment behind the backs of shareholders of the technique of secret reserves . . . .

Samuel, 1933/1982, 243

a list of the more common deficiencies which it has been found necessary to cite in connection with financial data included in registration statements filed with this Commission . . . . Accountants' certificates [12 items] . . . . Consolidated financial statements [6 items] . . . . Assets [19 items] . . . . Liabilities [6 items] . . . . Capital stock [3 items] . . . . Surplus [6 items] . . . . Profit and loss statements [13 items] . . . . [Various schedules, 21 items]

SEC, 1938b, ASR7

in Great Britain. Far too often do accounts go as far as they can in the way of concealment of things which the shareholders would certainly be very interested to know . . . . The paraphernalia of nonscience – concealment of management remuneration, alleged conservatism in stock valuation, inscrutable treatment of taxation liabilities, and the like – are sufficiently well known . . . .

Norris, 1946, 121

possible motivations for less than optimal disclosure policies [include]: 1. The self-preservation motive which usually takes the form of manipulating the financial reports to cover up an inadequate earnings performance . . . . 2. The motive reflected in a desire to maintain continued access to bank and other loan markets . . . . 3. A desire to remove the vulnerability of the company to unfriendly takeover bids . . . . 4. A political motive which usually takes the form of adopting accounting interpretations to reduce reported earnings . . . . 5. The motivation to obtain or maintain a high multiple for a common stock in order to facilitate acquisitions through exchange of stock. 6. The motivation of management-shareholders to show earnings results that will facilitate disposal of all or part of their holdings at favorable prices.

Hayes, 1972, 79

Managers, shareholders, auditors and standard setters all derive benefits from selective financial misrepresentation . . . . loose financial reporting standards . . . . [that provide] managers with [reported] income timing latitude . . . . decision makers in both [private and public] sectors learned that clever manipulation of the surrogates – financial accounting data – could be utilized to perpetrate wealth transfers or circumvent social controls.

Revsine, 1991, 17, 23

299 Comment on mandatory disclosure

Nearly all legislation is in the nature of a leveling process, and if you view with regret the leveling down of the standards you have created, you must realize that may be only a small price to pay if the act has resulted in a much greater leveling up [of less satisfactory practices].

May, 1937, 19

The objection that statutory minima may become maxima does not appear to have restricted progressive companies to the minimal standards . . .

Werntz, 1940/1968, 340

statutory provision for disclosure may, if it is itself inadequate, produce less disclosure than there would have been without it.

Norris, 1946, 123

By telling directors what they must publish, we run the grave risk that the minimum information required will also be the maximum . . . . Only Parliament can see that the law designed to protect investors really works.

Accountancy, editorial, 1966, 757

The ambiguity of the provisions of the [legislation] in respect of asset valuations and profit calculations could be removed by a single clear statement of a general valuation rule . . . . for example, that: No balance sheet shall be deemed to give a true and fair view of the state of affairs of a company unless the amounts shown for the assets are the money amounts or the best available approximations to the net selling prices in the ordinary course of business of those assets in their state and condition as at the date of the balance sheet . . . . No profit and loss account shall be deemed to give a true and fair view of the profit or loss of a company unless that profit or loss is so calculated as to include the effects during the year of changes in the net selling prices of assets and of changes in the general purchasing power of the unit of account.

ASRC, 1978, 97

300 GENERAL CHARACTERISTICS OF ACCOUNTING

310 Time in Accounting

311 Accounting said to be historical in character

History terminates not in the future but in the present. The historian's task is to show how the present has come into existence; he cannot show how the future will have come into existence, for he does not know what the future will be.
Collingwood, 1946, 104

we can view the past, and achieve our understanding of the past, only through the eyes of the present .... The historian belongs not to the past but to the present.
Carr, 1962, 19, 20

The world of the historian, like the world of the scientist, is not a photographic copy of the real world, but rather a working model which enables him more or less effectively to understand it and to master it. The historian distills from the experience of the past, or from so much of the experience of the past as is accessible to him, that part which he recognizes as amenable to rational explanation and interpretation, and from it draws conclusions which may serve as a guide to action.
Carr, 1962, 97–98

If exposure to history-as-experience may lead the historian to doubt a little the precision of history-as-record, it also persuades him that history-as-record forms a basic part of the intellectual climate which shapes the actual unfolding of history in the future.
Schlesinger, 1963, 497

****

Annals or chronicles merely relate facts which have occurred; but true history groups together facts of the same tendency, in order to discover, if possible, the causes of happiness and misery, prosperity and ruin; so true bookkeeping, being a history, should group together similar values in its equations to discover the causes and effects of loss and gain.
Sprague, 1880, 2

the balance sheet is historical in character; it attempts a summary description of the financial aspects of transactions which have already taken place.
Sanders & others, 1938, 56

the statements for one year are but one instalment of what is essentially a continuous history.

AIA, 1940b, ARB6

The primary purpose of the annual accounts of a business is to present information to the proprietors, showing how their funds have been utilized and the profits derived from such use. It has long been accepted in accounting practice that a balance sheet prepared for this purpose is an historical record and not a statement of current worth . . . . Similarly a profit and loss account is an historical record.

ICAEW, 1952, N15

A report is a description of something which has happened. The accounting reports summarize the effect . . . of the transactions and events that have taken place . . . . From the viewpoint of the entity, accounting is historical only.

Raby, 1959, 456, 460

accounting may be viewed as . . . a history of the capital committed to a business venture . . . .

Hill & Gordon, 1959, 5

Accounting is transaction based because it is concerned only with those actions which were taken, not the opportunities forgone or anticipated for the future.

Marple, 1964, 113

Accounting is historical; it can report only on the past. Accounting can never succeed in picturing an enterprise wholly as of the present moment . . . . Accounting has no facility for reporting what might have been.

Littleton, 1970, 478, 480

See also 223

312 Periodical accounting summaries considered necessary

Merchants are induced, once in every year, or oftener, to balance their books; as well to show the true state of their affairs, as to determine whether their accounts have been kept with accuracy.

Lee, 1747/1982, 250

Merchants generally balance their books once a year . . . . to ascertain their gain or loss since the last balance; and exhibit the present state of their funds.

Hamilton, 1788/1982, 284

The business man requires to be constantly informed about the conditions of his business, just as he requires to be informed of the conditions and operations of the business world with which he has dealings.

Cole, 1921, 1

the necessity for some basis of interim judgment has brought about the convention of allocating costs and revenues to fiscal periods of one year in length.

Blough, 1956, 13

Management requires [periodic approximations to profit or loss] for administration and policy-making purposes. Investors ... expect them. Governmental agencies, taxing and otherwise, demand them. As a result, one of the most firmly established concepts in modern accounting is that of periodic reporting.

Owen, 1958, 69

interested parties .... demand regular reports and frequent accountings .... The investor wants to make sure that his investment is intact, first, and that it is growing in value .... Creditors ... expect periodical reports to permit them to gauge their present risk on money already committed as well as the risk of doing further business with the debtor ....

Smith & Ashburne, 1960, 57

Periodic summarization of recorded events and transactions enables the position and rate of change to be determined as a guide to further action.

Chambers, 1961, #116

innumerable decisions regarding the business must be made by management and interested outsiders throughout the period of its existence, and it is therefore necessary to prepare periodic reports on operations and financial position.

Noble & Niswonger, 1961, 331

313 The accounting period

The lord ought to command and arrange that his accounts are audited every year, not at one center, but on each manor, for there he can learn quickly the state of affairs and ascertain profit and loss.

Anon, *Seneschaucy*, c1276/1971, 293n

of the old account books which have come down to us, one was not balanced until the end of nine years, another not until twenty-seven years had elapsed. The British East India Company prepared a general balance sheet in 1665 – but not again until 1685. But during the seventeenth century the custom of business men changed and a marked step was taken by the French Ordinance of 1673 requiring a balance sheet each two years. At the present time an annual balance sheet is customary.

Hatfield, 1927/1971, 3

If the business be of such a kind, that most of the branches naturally come to an issue at a certain time of year, that time is the proper one for making the balance. Otherwise the end of the year, or the least busy time, may be chosen.

Hamilton, 1788/1982, 285

The operation of balancing accounts in a mercantile establishment generally takes place at the end of the year, or on the anniversary of the commencement of the establishment or partnership, or in particular branches of trade on the completion of the season in that particular branch . . . .
Pulling, 1850, 88

In general the accounting period is the unit of time selected for the purpose of determining and presenting the facts of income and financial condition. Its length varies in different enterprises and industries and depends upon how frequently financial statements are desired or are feasible.
Paton, 1924, 201

the principal accounting period, for almost all businesses, is one of twelve months . . . . Among companies with an annual cycle of activities not corresponding to the [calendar year] there has been a growing tendency to adopt a period ending at the recurring low point of the cycle . . . . At the end of the "natural" business year inventories are at or near a minimum level, which makes it possible to prepare statements which are affected to a relatively small degree by the complications involved in the valuation of goods on hand.
Paton & Dixon, 1958, 270

An accounting period may be defined as a period of time at the end of which a new balance sheet is prepared and statements of operations are presented.
Mason & others, 1959, 86

Rightly or wrongly, a year's activities have themselves come to be regarded as a venture . . . . in effect: We started on this periodic venture in that position; at the end of it, a year later, we were in this position; the result of our venture is the difference between this and that.
Goldberg, 1965, 103

314 Equitemporal accounting

where long series of accounts survive, it will be seen that, where they have not been regularly periodic before, they became so at some time during the eighteenth century . . . . agricultural estates, and accounts based on them, had one-year cycles, and joint stock companies and similar institutions required the regular payment of dividends and therefore the regular closing of books . . . . Most of all, however, it was practical needs which determined this regularity: that is to say, the bookkeeping assumes the coloring of being partly a tool of management, as well as a system of reckoning . . . . knowledge of the many facts thrown up by a large concern had to be systematized and regularized before it could be grasped by a single brain.
Pollard, 1968, 253

in order that the events during one interval may be profitably compared with those of another, the intervals should be equal.

Sprague, 1907/1972, 64

The chief use of any kind of record is for comparison and, in order that comparison of two statements ... may be valuable, they must cover the same standard period.

Gilman, 1917, 38

In the functioning of a business enterprise there is a rhythm of seasons and activities, a cycle of events, which furnishes a framework for compressing the flow of enterprise data into comparable time segments.

Littleton, 1953, 25

At one time accounting periods were not all of the same length; statements were prepared at the end of some logical interval such as the round-trip voyage of a ship from England to the colonies or the completion of a construction project. Modern practice requires the use of a uniform period ....

Mason & others, 1959, 86

Comparability in reporting requires that accounting reports be prepared for uniform periodic intervals.

Powell, 1964a/1970, 225

315 The period as determinant of the contents of periodical summaries

Unless care is taken to include in the economic entries of a period all that properly belongs in it and to exclude all that pertains to any other period before or after, we may greatly distort the presentation of facts so as to render it valueless; the period which has been adverse may appear prosperous at the expense of one which is actually more successful.

Sprague, 1907/1972, 69

The bookkeeper must constantly strive to enter in the current fiscal period only those items of revenue and expense which apply directly to the period.

Bentley, 1911, 190

Any period of time may constitute an accounting period .... The financial records during the period between ... balance sheet dates record every change that takes place in the elements that appear therein.

Couchman, 1924, 9

Just as the accounts should show, at the end of the fiscal period, all the income earned during the period, they should also show all the expenses incurred in earning that income.

McKinsey & Noble, 1935, 253

The relation of the income concept to the specified time interval is fundamental – and neglect of this crucial relation has been responsible for much confusion in the relevant literature. The measurement of income implies .... the possibility of measuring the results of individual participation in economic relations for an assigned interval and without regard for anything which happened before the beginning of that ... interval or for what may happen in subsequent periods. All data for measurement would be found, ideally, within the period analyzed.
Simons, 1938, 50

Transactions and other changes are attributed to the periods in which they become effective by changing the character of risks, by changing the amounts of the stock of particular assets or of equities, or by inducing changes in the values of assets or equities.
Chambers, 1961, #116

all significant measurable changes in assets and equities should be reported in the periods in which they occur.
AAA, 1964b, 709

The accounting model should measure events as they occur; ... all the events of a period and only the events of that period.
Edwards & others, 1979, 457

316 The accounting period said to be arbitrary

today business is a continuum. [However], ... accountants are asked to perform the hopeless task of taking this economic continuum, of chopping it up into arbitrary and meaningless lengths called a year, and apportioning to each such year a proper part of the cost of a building which will last fifty years, of a machine which will be used for twenty years, of a blast furnace which will last ten, and of a stock of coal bought in December which will all be consumed before spring again appears.
Hatfield, 1924, 252

Income implies the fixing of a period to be taken as the basis of measurement; it is accordingly necessary to divide the continuous trading of most enterprises into more or less arbitrary parts. Periods of twelve months are really arbitrary, as they have often little connection with the completion of transactions.
Clunies Ross, 1941a, 498

we cannot take a short period in the life of a business and describe exactly what happens within that period, no more, no less.
Peloubet, 1944/1982, 149

The life history of any undertaking is an indivisible whole .... there is an accounting convention that its life history is divisible into relatively short periods of time, and that profits or losses within each of these periods and financial position at the end of each period can and should be more or less accurately determined by the accounting process. The length of these accounting or financial periods is arbitrarily determined.

Fitzgerald, 1956a, 14

Modern accounting breaks up a continuous stream of business activity into artificial segments known as accounting periods.

Storey, 1960, 450

for accounting purposes it is necessary to divide business operations into arbitrary time periods .... to supply needed information for current decision making.

Spiller, 1964, 854

The activities of a company are continuous, whereas the period covered by the accounts is no more than an arbitrary segment of time .... The determination of amounts of income and expenditure attributable to an accounting period ... can be arrived at only by informed judgment exercised in accordance with accounting conventions.

ICAEW, 1969c, 843

dividing continuous operations into accounting periods is a convention and may have arbitrary effects.

FASB, 1978, SFAC1

317 Cash based accounting

[Cash] hath directly neither profit nor loss upon it; yet ... it is a most important account, and in some sorts of business possesseth the whole traffic; as bankers for instance, who daily fill whole pages with cash in and out. And petty traders, who make no account of sortments, but only of what they pay out and receive in; their whole account is a cash account, and yields them their profit and loss by the state of it .... the common shop trades ... have no surer account than the cash box. They take out and tell the money at certain times, and then having a cash account to charge with it, and to discharge by what they pay, readily find what their profit is; for they do not trouble themselves with species of goods, to draw a line of profit and loss upon, as merchants do ....

North, 1714/1986, 21, 77

at an early date several British courts explicitly rejected a cash concept of profit. One judge called cash statements "deceptive" (*Ex parte Ayre*, 1858). In *Rance's Case* (1870) the Court commented that it was as informative about profitability as a "sheet out of a newspaper". And in *Murray v Bush* (1873) the House of Lords said a cash statement was practically "useless" and almost completely without information content regarding a company's financial condition.

Reid, 1987, 249

It may be that the policy of a concern is to keep its books on the cash basis, that is to say, to consider as income earned only that which has been received in cash, and that, correspondingly, only expenses paid in cash constitute income disbursed . . . . Yet it is doubtful whether a single instance could be found where a business concern which claims to be on a cash basis is consistent enough to apply that basis to merchandise transactions.

Esquerré, 1914, 229

the cash basis of accounting . . . determines income without regard for the period which put forth the effort responsible for the receipts and without regard for the period which received the benefit of disbursements . . . . [The accrual basis] attempts to earmark cash receipts as the property of the period responsible for their receipt, and to earmark cash disbursements as costs of the period which benefited therefrom.

Husband, 1946, 248

The cash basis: This method treats every cash receipt and expenditure as revenue or expense in the period in which the transaction takes place. If large amounts are sporadically involved – in receipts, say, on long-term construction contracts or instalment sales, or in disbursements for supplies or a build-up of inventories – it is obvious that net income from year to year will fluctuate widely. A new or expanding business would show huge losses in earlier years, followed by large profits later.

Bevis, 1965, 31

The cash criterion of income has a strong, though often irrational foundation in business psychology. The cash basis eliminates any possibility of subsequent losses arising out of uncollectable accounts. It also provides immediate funds for continuing business activities and for distribution to equity interests.

Walker & others, 1970, 357

The cash basis of accounting means reflecting only transactions involving actual cash receipts and disbursements occurring within a given period with no attempt to record unpaid bills (or amounts) owed to or by the entity . . . . If cash comes in or goes out in a given period, it counts; if not, it does not count.

Hicks, 1981, 30

318 Accrual accounting

it is really the consumption or accretion of a right which we need to record in economic statements [i.e. profit and loss statements], not the settlement of the claim in cash.

Sprague, 1907/1972, 74

Accrual accounting is a refinement of method which makes possible a closer and more precise measurement of the real flow of economic resources than does the mere reporting of cash transactions.

Vatter, 1950, 40

Accrual accounting is based on the fundamental principle that, in order to measure properly the net income of a business for a given period of time, it is essential that all revenue earned during that period and all expenses assignable to the period be shown. This process of matching [with reference to specific periods] ... is the central goal of accounting.

Malchman & Slavin, 1961, 93

Accounting that takes into consideration income earned but not collected and expenses incurred but not paid is accrual accounting.

Vance, 1961, 377

the accrual process is a method for systematically spreading the results of two transactions, the acquisition transaction and the disposition transaction, over the time interval between the transaction dates.

Bedford, 1965, 31

the accrual basis attempts to transfer the income and expense effect of cash receipts and disbursements, other transactions, and other events from the year in which they arise to the year or years to which they more rationally relate.

Bevis, 1965, 95

The effects of transactions and other events on the assets and liabilities of a business enterprise are recognized and reported in the time periods to which they relate rather than only when cash is received or paid .... Recording these changes is necessary to determine periodic income and to measure financial position. This is the essence of accrual accounting.

AICPA, 1970c, APBS4

accrual: the recognition of events and transactions as they occur ....

Kohler, 1970, 15

the accruals concept: revenues and costs are accrued (that is, recognized as they are earned or incurred, not as money is received or paid), matched with one another so far as their relationship can be established or justifiably assumed, and dealt with in the profit and loss account of the period to which they relate; provided that where the accruals concept is inconsistent with the prudence concept ..., the latter prevails.

ASSC, 1971b, SSAP 2

Accrual accounting .... recognizes that the buying, producing, selling and other operations of an enterprise during a period ... often do not coincide with the cash receipts and payments of the period.

FASB, 1978, SFAC1

Accrual accounting endorsed

It is much more proper to value the goods on hand in conformity to the current prices: for the design of affixing any value is to point out the gain or loss; and the gain is in reality obtained so soon as the prices rise, or the loss suffered so soon as they fall.

Hamilton, 1788/1982, 285

accrued costs and obligations must be recognized if income for the period is to be determined correctly and an accurate picture of financial condition is to be drawn.

Paton, 1924, 217

From a practical as well as a theoretical point of view, both unrealized and realized profits and losses enjoy equal status. The important question is the determination of value, and this question is not answered by disregarding those changes in value that have not been translated into cash .... the current distinction made by the accounting profession between realized and unrealized profits is the sheerest nonsense .... it serves to conceal and misrepresent economic truths that an accountant should be duty bound to reveal.

MacNeal, 1939, 296

X buys 100 shares ... at 50 .... At the end of the calendar year the stock is selling at 53. Since there is an increase in the value of his holdings of $300 less commission, he has a gain of that much, ... whether he sells them or not. A sale is not necessary for the determination of his profit ... the sale represents only a conversion of assets, not the earning of a profit.

Lund, 1941, 378

Under the accrual basis .... the books are at all times more complete [than under the cash basis of accounting] and fewer adjustments are necessary before a balance sheet may be drafted from them.

Kester, 1946, 10

Economists count gains when accrued, accountants usually count gains when realized by the sale of the asset on which the gain has been made. However, accountants are frequently ... willing to accrue costs and losses in agreement with economists .... This dual standard indicates that the treatment of accruals is not dictated by the conceptual nature of income but rather by practical considerations summed up in the term conservatism. Economists' insistence on accrual stems from the fundamental idea of income as a difference between wealth at two different times.

Alexander, 1950, 55

the crux of the argument on behalf of accrual accounting rests on the premise that (1) reported income under accrual accounting rules conveys more information than a less ambitious cash flow oriented accounting system would, (2) accrual accounting is the most efficient means to convey this additional information . . . .

Beaver & Demski, 1979, 43

See also 325

319 Contemporarily dated information expected by users

The ordinary reader [of a balance sheet] assumes that here are the present values of the assets owned by the concern and here is stated the present net worth. It is argued that this is a reasonable conclusion and that accountants should not expect readers of balance sheets to discard the value concept which is generally accepted in the every day world.

Daines, 1929, 97

The layman, . . . unless he has been initiated into the mysteries of accountancy, undeniably assumes that the balance sheet is supposed to represent current values, whether it does in fact or not. And many accountants agree with him.

Jones, 1935, 171

When Congress specified "a balance sheet as of a date not more than ninety days prior to the date of filing", which balance sheet must contain no untrue statements, or omissions likely to mislead, it doubtless was thinking of the balance sheet mainly as it is customarily described in its own heading, a statement of financial condition as of a specified date; in other words a statement of present condition.

Sanders, 1937, 195

The layman who looks at these documents is often under the impression that the figures placed against the assets are their market value and that the item comprising capital can be taken to be the present worth of the business.

Edwards, 1938b, 121

Accountants have always tended to minimize the importance of current values. But . . . . users of financial statements employ market values freely and openly and are convinced that they derive value from doing so. No one but an accountant would think of questioning the appropriateness and utility of current value data.

McMullen, 1950, 485

There is always a presumption in favor of a more recent measure of accountability as against an earlier one and the presumption becomes stronger the older the historical basis is.

May, 1957, 35

What we should be aiming at is accurate realistic measurement . . . . It is impossible, I maintain, to administer any economic resource wisely without knowing at least roughly what it is worth in the prevailing state of affairs.

Paton, 1963, 51

the investor . . . . wants to know what they [fixed assets] are worth in current values.

Napper, 1964b, 636

[a realizable value] balance sheet will give to the ordinary shareholder what he believes he is receiving at present . . . . a statement of what the assets and liabilities of the company are worth if they were to be realized.

Lyne, 1981, 235

Contemporaneity of periodical information endorsed

I take it that the balance sheet should state clearly the present true value of our property, not what it was valued at by our grandfathers 40 years ago.

Waters, 1901, 894

The accounts should always show the present value of the property being used by an enterprise in producing its product, if accounting statistics are to furnish the entrepreneur with the information which shall enable him to make rational use of the economic resources at his disposal.

Paton & Stevenson, 1916/1976, 101

It is above all important that the accountant's statements present as accurately as possible a picture of current data in terms of the actual dollar as of the date of the statements.

Paton, 1922/1962, 429

there are some daring and rigidly logical accountants who declare that the function of the balance sheet is to show actual values and that this should be done even where the present value of merchandise exceeds its cost. Foremost among such accountants are Paton, Stevenson and Montgomery.

Hatfield, 1927/1971, 284

Both as background for creative planning, and as a basis for selection [of plans], accounting data should be as recent as possible to make predictions based thereon as reliable as may be.

Goetz, 1939, 154

in preparing financial statements, every accountant should endeavor to use economic values as of the date of the balance sheet, expressed in dollars as of the date of the balance sheet.

MacNeal, 1939, 112

Because each [business] problem is unique in time . . . it must be resolved in terms of the values ruling at that time, as determined by the environment . . . . The information that is relevant to the businessman is, therefore, information about here and now . . . the closest time, to the period in which his decision will be carried out, of which he can have knowledge. Contemporary values, costs or prices are the relevant magnitudes.

Chambers, 1955, 159

from a balance sheet standpoint a statement which showed the current value of the various assets owned by a corporation might have great advantages if it were practicable.

Broad, 1957, 3

financial statements in current [balance sheet dated] dollars are more relevant and more easily understood than those employing the general purchasing power of any other period. Current economic actions must take place in terms of current dollars, and restating items in current dollars expresses them in the context of current action.

AICPA, 1969, APBS3

If [financial] information is to be useful for decision making . . . , it must be provided regularly and it needs to be up to date.

Skinner, 1972b, 377

corporate reports are more useful if they contain up to date measures of value.

ASSC, 1975a, 29

there are three specific instances in which current values are required to be reported [under the UK *Companies Act, 1985*] when they are materially different from historical cost: the directors' report must report substantial differences between the book value and the market value of land (including buildings thereon); the market value of listed securities must be stated by way of a note to the balance sheet, when it differs from the amount appearing on the face of the balance sheet; and the replacement price of [merchandise] stocks should be stated in a note to the balance sheet when it is materially different from book value. These adjustments suggest that, in cases in which market values can be established with reasonable certainty, the legislators and their advisers prefer current values to historical costs, or at least attach equal importance to them.

Whittington, 1989b, 155

the reported amounts of resources and obligations of an enterprise should faithfully represent those resources and obligations at the reporting date.

AAA, 1991, 89

320 Quantification in Accounting

321 Accounting said to be concerned with value(s)

our young merchant by this time hath taken an inventory of his estate, and caused his cloths and kersies to be valued, and findeth that the hundred cloths are worth some 1200 pounds one with another, and his two hundred kersies of Devonshire 400 pounds.

Malynes, 1622, 364

Since a merchant's subject, stock, or capital consists of the money, goods, and debts which compose it, he is naturally led to consider every particular of these as accountable to him, or more properly, to his stock or capital, as a part to the whole, for its respective value; . . . .

Gordon, 1787/1986, 16

The estimated value of the property unsold is, in all such cases [all property accounts], the balance of the account.

Foster, 1849, 37

It is necessarily essential that such balance sheet should be based on the principle of showing on the one side the amount in sufficient detail of what is believed to be the value of the company's assets, and on the other side what is believed to be the amount of the company's liabilities.

Ogden, 1895, *BPP, 1895*

This [financial] condition is evidenced by the values of both property owned and debts due, which are together generally described as assets; the actual or estimated value of all liabilities; the surplus of one over the other, which represents the net worth or value; and a summary of the operations by which this net worth has been either created, increased or diminished.

Dickinson, 1914, 31

It is the function of accounting to record values, classify values and to organize and present value data in such a fashion that the owners and their representatives may utilize wisely the capital at their disposal.

Paton, 1922/1962, 7

Since accounting is concerned with everyday affairs, one of its major functions should be to record, faithfully and accurately the changes which are taking place in business both in the nature of the assets and their valuation. As long as economic forces cause changes in value, the accountant should be an impartial recorder of these changes.

Daines, 1929, 99

In reading American accounting literature, it is surprising to find how generally accounting was described at one time as a process of valuation, up to how recent a date this view was maintained, and how pronounced and rapid the change has been. In a more mature economy . . . business units become larger and enterprises more complex. Then, the valuation approach becomes impracticable and resort to cost as the primary line of approach becomes almost inevitable.

May 1943, 8

The term, asset, when used in relation to financial position has a connotation of value which cannot be ignored.

Catlett, 1969, 63

See also 255

322 Accounting said to be concerned with market values or prices

rational money accounting presupposes the existence of effective prices and not merely of fictitious prices conventionally employed for technical accounting.
Weber, c1920/1947, 179

the immediate data of accounting consist in prices (values in terms of the money unit).
Paton & Stevenson, 1917, 213

Even though market values have frequently been ignored in balance sheets, the time is coming when more attention will be paid to true values. Market value is the price at which a seller willing to sell at a fair price and a buyer willing to buy at a fair price, both having reasonable knowledge of the facts, will trade . . . .
Montgomery, 1922, 74

Since the market, through its processes of valuation, is the decisive arbiter of economic activities it is the highest authority to which accounting can turn for inventory values.
Scott, 1925, 192

The double entry system attempts to deal only with exchange values.
Rorem, 1927, 11

Accounting is concerned with price, however greatly the business man may be concerned with value [in the subjective appraisal sense] . . . . When accounting is loosed from this anchor of fact [price] it is afloat upon a sea of psychological estimates which . . . are beyond the power of accounting, as such, to express.
Littleton, 1929, 150

The market process is accepted universally as a process of valuation and the fundamental function of accounts is no less a process of valuation . . . . Those who deny that accounting is fundamentally a process of valuation thereby belittle the social significance of accounts and the social responsibility of accountants. Truly they are selling accounting short.
Scott, 1940, 509

the values of concern to accounting are those established by exchange – the prices agreed to by the two parties to the transaction.
Marple, 1964, 113

323 The objectivity of prices

A transaction to which the accounting entity is a party does not necessarily provide objective evidence; often a transaction between two parties, neither of which is the accounting entity, may be more reliable and objective.
May, 1952, 439

319

If and whenever accounting . . . loses contact with market determined facts in situations relevant to that enterprise, it has lost its primary tie to objective reality in the accounting sense.

Littleton, 1953, 182

Bargained price is the objective . . . result of a completed transaction, . . .

AAA, 1957a/1957b, 4

Current market price represents objective information with respect to the amount of cash into which the [marketable] securities may be converted.

Sprouse & Moonitz, 1962, 25

This [historical] cost allocation approach [to depreciation accounting] is said to be logically sound under the accrual concept of accounting; it is also claimed to be the most objective, since the asset dollar figure recorded in the books is in most cases the result of arm's length bargaining, and can be verified as such.

McCandless, 1965, 50

Each of these measures [market selling price and market buying price] may be objectively determined.

Bourn, 1969a, 79

See also 713

324 Arm's length dealing the basis of reliable quantification

At arm's length: beyond the reach of personal influence or control. Parties are said to deal at arm's length when each stands upon the strict letter of his rights, and conducts the business in a formal manner, without trusting to the other's fairness or integrity, and without being subject to the other's control or overmastering influence.

Black's law dictionary, 1951

In a transaction which is not the result of arm's length bargaining between genuinely independent parties, the prices should be viewed with some skepticism.

Paton & Littleton, 1940, 27

As originally used, the phrase [arm's length transaction] implied a standard or guide for measuring the reliability of money prices or values set for articles of commerce transferred between a buyer and a seller. It was believed that prices or values determined in negotiations between a buyer and a seller who are independent and unrelated most nearly represent significant values. In discussions relating to accounting matters, the phrase should be used only in this sense. It is useful only as a standard or test of the fairness of the values determined by other means.

AIA, 1946a, 441

Cost in an arm's length transaction, or a firm offer to purchase, is considered the best objective evidence of present value of properties.
Broad, 1949, 381

To recognize revenue the business must have an agreement with an outside party . . . . Another term for expressing the requirement of an outside party is to say that the transaction must be at arm's length . . . . When the parties are not dealing at arm's length, operating results and financial position may be manipulated to give an artificial result.
Anderson & others, 1974, 259

the current level of activity is measured by recognizing revenue on the basis of work done and the legitimization of the value of that work by an arm's length transaction with an outside party . . . . asset valuations are generally based on historical monetary costs incurred in arm's length transactions.
Burton, 1975, 36

If useful information is to be presented, measurements of economic value must be fair and acceptable to the full range of interested parties . . . . The objectivity of a transaction is assured by the presence of rational parties pursuing their own interests. Related parties are characterized by their lack of independence and so may not wish, or be able, to pursue their individual interests fully. Consequently, transactions between related parties cannot be relied on to provide objective measurements of value.
Metcalf, 1979, 99

The inherent accounting assumption is that transaction data reflect market prices determined in arm's length bargaining transactions.
Robertson, 1979, 503

In accounting . . . assets and liabilities generally are recorded when there is an arm's length, market transaction that is denominated in money terms.
Benston, 1982, 166

The clearest measure of value is usually the amount paid for an economic resource in a recent arm's length transaction between a knowledgeable, willing buyer and seller.
Andersen & Co, 1987, 36

325 Transaction not required to validate an accountable event or price

Now the uncertainty of the prices of things renders my share of the extent [total assets] liable to increase or decrease with them . . . . Suppose I have 2000 pounds weight of tobacco, which I value first at 50 pounds . . . suppose when I come to calculate anew, I find the tobacco, at the present rate, able to purchase more than 50 pounds ... then I am so much richer ....

Stephens, 1735, 16

If goods are sold for more than prime cost and charges, stock is thereby increased; but if for less, diminished. Hence although the goods be not actually sold, yet if their value or market price be increased or diminished, stock is likewise affected thereby. All kinds of transferable property producing rents, interests or dividends ... affect stock in two different manners: for stock is increased by the rents, interests and dividends that become due thereon; and will be either increased or decreased, according as their market price is higher or lower than it was when they were purchased.

Dodson, 1750, v

the design in affixing any value [to items of property] is to point out the gain or loss; and the gain is in reality obtained as soon as the prices rise, or the loss suffered as soon as they fall.

Morrison, 1849, 38

In order that there may be a price, it is not necessary that the exchange in question should actually take place. It may be only a contemplated exchange .... appraisal ... is simply a more or less skilful guess as to what price the article would or should fetch.

Fisher, 1906/1965, 11

the value of the finished product ready to ship is virtually selling price, regardless of the fact that an actual sale has not been effectuated.

Paton, 1922/1962, 294

It may, or it may not, be proper to limit dividends to profits realized through a sale; but it is absurd to say that if I have definite assurance (which is possible) of being able to sell at a given price, that the value is not there just as much a moment before the sale as a moment after.

Hatfield, 1930, 12

Generally, this system of income measurement [of realized, transaction-based income] is designated as the accrual system. This is a misnomer, however, since strict application of the accrual assumption would recognize income with the productive steps taken.

Husband, 1954a, 5

monetary gains and losses [from changes in the purchasing power of the monetary unit] are realized as soon as there is a change in the price level.

Hendriksen, 1961, 19

Donated assets are recorded at their cash equivalent value as of the donation date . . . . because every business resource, regardless of its origin, should be properly accounted for . . . .

Pyle & White, 1966, 826

the position of a firm is incompletely described if the only changes recorded are those marked by an exchange of assets and/or liabilities . . . . Of course it is a current event when a gain is realized through the disposition of an asset in the current period; but so too was the accrual of that gain a current event of the periods in which accrual took place.

Edwards, 1975, 238

Productive wealth is increased, and product and productive income are created, when production takes place and the value increases, not when the transaction occurs.

Bodenhorn, 1978, 16

As long as the market is active, an enterprise's participation or lack of participation in a transaction makes little difference in how well the current market price . . . represents the asset's or liability's present cash equivalent.

Johnson & Storey, 1982, 64

See also 318

326 Financial statements as representations of management

Management itself has the direct responsibility for the maintenance of an adequate and effective system of accounts, for the proper recording of transactions in the books of account and for the safeguarding of the assets of a concern. It is also charged with the primary responsibility to stockholders and to creditors for the substantial accuracy and adequacy of statements of position and results.

AIA, 1939b, 343

Financial statements are essentially the representations of management.

Stempf, 1943, 50

Whether the business is incorporated or not, the preparation and presentation of [financial] statements are the responsibility of the management.

Potter, 1951, 309

Responsibility for the accounts and financial control of a company rests upon the directors. Their statutory duties include responsibility for ensuring the maintenance of adequate records and the preparation of annual accounts showing the true and fair view required by the Act.

ICAEW, 1961, U1

Management has the responsibility for adopting sound accounting policies .... The financial statements remain the representations of management.

AICPA, 1963b, SAP33

The criterion a corporate management uses in selecting among accounting principles is the maximization of its utility or welfare .... That managements are in fact so motivated is taken as axiomatic.

Gordon, 1964, 261

Management is primarily responsible for the choice among alternative accounting principles used in compiling annual reports. Yet accounting statements are essentially reports on managerial performance. Apart from the obvious conflict of interest in such a situation, there is little assurance that management, beset by a variety of pressures to mold accounting results purposively, uses the best measurement criteria in reaching its accounting policy decisions.

Johnson, 1965, 705

Management quite properly has the primary responsibility for selection of accounting practices and presentation of financial statements.

Field, 1969, 2

The primary responsibility for the preparation and presentation of financial statements, and accordingly the selection of accounting principles used in the preparation of such statements, rests with the management of the enterprise; ....

AISG, 1969, 830

At the entity or micro level, the executives who run the business have a good deal of freedom to choose among alternative ways of presenting its operating results and its financial position.

Solomons, 1989, 1

Management responsible for valuations

the auditor .... has no power to influence the management in the exercise of their *bona fide* discretion [in the valuation and revaluation of assets].

Dicksee, 1892/1976, 136

[The layman] must realize that the determination of the values at which assets of a corporation are stated in its accounts is a function of the board of directors.

Andersen, 1935, 334

Revaluation of assets is a well established and generally accepted practice in Britain, though no longer in the USA. The execution of a revaluation, its disclosure and its incorporation in the accounts are entirely at the discretion of management. This gives rise to the ridiculous situation that the very people whose ability to influence the accounts is supposed to be minimized have in fact got wide control over the picture presented by the accounts . . . .

Finnie, 1968a, 285

The responsibility for properly determining the quantity and value of stock rests with the management of the business.

ICAEW, 1969a, 550

Management responsible for income determination

There is nothing at all in the [Companies] Acts about . . . how profits are to be reckoned; all that is left, and very properly and judiciously left, to the commercial world. It is not a subject for an act of Parliament to say how accounts are to be kept; what is to be put into a capital account, and what into an income account, is left to men of business. [per Stirling J]

Lee v Neuchatel Asphalte Co and others,
1889

Such questions as how the profit and loss account shall be made out, whether profits have been earned, and if so whether they shall be divided, are primarily business questions for the directors or shareholders to determine in accordance with the company's regulations, and provided they act honestly, and in accordance with such regulations in coming to such determination, they discharge all the obligations imposed upon them by the Act.

Buckley, 1930, 756

The directors . . . . have a large measure of control over the company's income account. So long as accounting standards are not hardened, and the law does not impose any specific canons, directors and their accountants may frame their figures, within limits, much as they choose.

Berle & Means, 1932, 202

It is sometimes urged that [the complex of practices which now go to the determination of income] are not consistent with one another. There is no obvious reason why they should be; they are consistent only with the object in view, namely, the sound determination of income in such manner as will conduce to prudent business management. In fact, accounting is the handmaid of prudent business management, which must be the final arbiter of accounting practices,

Sanders, 1939b, 573

327 Financial statements expected to be free of managerial influence

A variety of circumstances may have brought us to this [ruinous] state . . . but if you rightly examine, you will find it chiefly owing to the orators, who study to please you rather than advise for the best. [The third Philippic]

Demosthenes, BC341/1967

Disclosures made to the market ... in theory are merely informative .... In the normal case a management is supposed to be disclosing merely the facts of the situation, leaving the market to work out its own salvation, and interfering only when a somewhat obviously manipulative move is under way.

Berle & Means, 1932, 320

management must become more willing to let the accountants call a spade a spade – show things as they are rather than as management would like to see them.

Paton, 1946b/1948, 101

The assumption that management holds the authority to dictate channels of thought and methods of procedure [in accounting] is ill-advised .... [the] argument has been advanced without thinking it through.

McMullen, 1950, 483

Accounting is advisory and informative, not a managerial function .... the accountant (*qua* accountant) should not take part in management.

Davison, 1951, 304, 309

Published financial statements are reports on management; they can be meaningful only if management is unable to control their contents.

Davidson, 1963, 125

To satisfy the requirements of objective and impartial reporting on the performance of management, financial statements should be as free as possible from the influence of management.

Miller, 1964, 44

managers are subject to a number of pressures to influence externally reported measurement, partly on the basis of their own self-interest, and partly as a result of conflicting pressures from outside interests which attempt in various ways to exercise control over managers.

Johnson, 1966, 90

Management is responsible at law for many things, such as the technical characteristics of the output of the company it manages. But management does not, for that reason, select which engineering principles or laws of chemistry and physics it will apply in its own case .... The first and most important necessary condition for change [in accounting] is for the accounting profession to cease recognizing management as its master with regard to the technical content of accounting.

Moonitz, 1968, 630

the "management's statements" proposition ... contains an embryonic tendency to escape responsibility. The profession has been characterized by a fierce devotion to integrity and a jealously guarded independence. It was once claimed that the function of accounting was to tell the truth. To rely on management's statements is far removed from that attitude.

Sterling, 1968b, 593

Today, management has the responsibility for measuring and reporting its own performance. [Some] believe it is unreasonable to expect management to fulfil this public reporting responsibility objectively.

Hawkins, 1971, 6

328 Uncertainty

in any case of uncertainty as to the amount of annual charge for depreciation of machinery and other outlay [under cost allocation procedures], the higher rather than the lower rate should be taken as the safer . . . .

Guthrie, 1883, 7

Uncertain standards of measurement. We have already several times observed the lack of uniformity of method in accounts. This is due not only to differences in accounting policy, but to differences of judgment about values.

Cole, 1921, 339

Assigning costs and expenses to the same accounting period in which so-called related income is recognized is often impossible due to two uncertainties, i.e. uncertainty as to time and uncertainty as to amount.

Gilman, 1939, 127

Because of the uncertainty to which most accounting calculations are subject, consistency of treatment from period to period is desirable as a means of obtaining statistical comparability.

Moonitz, 1951/1978, 19

Uncertainty is the hallmark of business; accounting cannot and should not do other than reflect the uncertainty of the very thing it sets out to describe . . . . All assets . . . represent sources of future benefit. That is how an asset may be defined . . . . There can be no certainty that the firm will ever receive these [benefits] . . . . Liabilities likewise represent sources of future detriment, and many are subject to the same uncertainties.

Morison, 1970a, 411

most of the basic concepts and conventions underlying generally accepted accounting principles appear to have been developed to enable the accountant to deal with or avoid uncertainty. [They] . . . allow the accountant to substitute "certainty equivalents" for a direct confrontation with the uncertainties inherent in the items and events he attempts to measure . . . . Some of the important concepts and conventions that help the accountant resolve uncertainty are the doctrine of conservatism, the concept of objectivity, the going concern concept, the realization and historical cost concepts.

Dewhirst, 1971, 139

Uncertainty in accounting arises from two main sources: (1) Accounting information generally relates to entities that are expected to have continuity of existence into the future; since allocations are frequently made between past and future periods, assumptions must be made regarding the logic of these allocations and on the basis of expectations regarding the future .... (2) Accounting measurements are frequently assumed to represent monetary expressions of wealth which require estimates of uncertain future amounts.

Hendriksen, 1977, 128

Uncertainty about the outcome of future events affects the measurement of both an entity's earnings for a particular period and the measurement of its assets and liabilities at a particular date.

Cohen Commission, 1978, 23

[Under the matching process] Profit measurement is, as the result of the problems caused by changes in expectations, unlikely to be precise; the uncertainties that must exist about the benefit it is realistic to expect to receive in later years make accurate calculations impossible. Future expectations must affect the charge that is made against the revenue received in earlier years; the past, the present and the future are all relevant factors in this calculation.

Magee, 1979, 255

Uncertainty is ubiquitous, and its presence in financial statements is implied by the way that assets and liabilities are defined. Assets ... were defined as resources or rights that were expected to yield future economic benefits. Expectations imply a probability but not a certainty that they will be fulfilled. Liabilities were defined in terms that specifically referred to the uncertainty as to timing and amount of some future transfers of assets or services that liabilities oblige the entity to make. Thus all assets and some liabilities ... are tainted with uncertainty.

Solomons, 1989, 39

The element of futurity (and therefore of uncertainty) inherent in the concepts of assets and liabilities is clear from their definition [in FASB, SFAC2, 1980] as "probable future economic benefits" and "probable future sacrifices of economic benefits".

AAA, 1991, 83

330 Quality of Representations in Accounting

331 Accounting as description

This method [double entry] of keeping accounts is absolutely necessary in an extensive and complicated trade, in order that the books may exhibit in a concise and satisfactory manner what debts the merchant owes, and are owing to him; what property he is possessed of; and how much he has either gained or lost in trade.
Morrison, 1849, 43

The very word, account, means, both by present use and derivation, a tale, a story, a record. It must deal with what has happened . . . . Accounting, I think, must be objective.
Peloubet, 1935, 202

The selection among [alternative methods] . . . must be such that the individual, who uses accounting statements as a basis for legitimate judgment and action, would arrive at the same judgment and take the same action if he could study and interpret the underlying data from which the accountant has made selection.
Heaton, 1949, 471

Accounting is not an end in itself but a service function, responsible for supplying accurate, informative data to enterprise management in the form of reports that describe financial position and measure operating results. It is an important part of the language of business.
Easton & Newton, 1958, 11

Accounting figures are the shadows of real events . . . .
Goetz & Klein, 1960, 385

In a very important sense, accounting is passive. We record what has happened or at least what we think has happened. We do not, by the mere process of journalizing, create something that does not already exist. It we could create something by these means . . . we could create a favorable financial position at will.
Moonitz & Jordan, 1963, 382

Information serves as a representation of principals . . . . the primary function of accounting information is not to provide problem answers; it is to generate problem-relevant representations of principals.
Chen & Summers, 1977, 114, 115

See also 381

Accounts expected to be true descriptions

A merchant's books should exhibit the true state of his affairs: ....
                                        Kelly, 1801, 1

the affairs and transactions of the company shall be brought to a just and true balance
by the board of directors [at the end of each half year] ... and a balance sheet shall
be prepared containing a true statement of the affairs and transactions of the company,
and the net profits of the bank during the half year immediately preceding ....
                        BNSW, Deed of Settlement, 1850

a full and fair balance balance sheet must be such a balance sheet as to convey a
truthful statement as to the company's position. [per Rigby L J]
                        London and General Bank Ltd No. 2,
                        Re, 1895, 961

it is a business crime to falsify books so that the truth will not be made known to
the public whose money is invested in the business.
                        Bentley, 1911, 158

[The balance sheet] should be a document setting out the true position of the business.
                        Spicer & Pegler, 1914, 299

Accounting has to do with the truth, the whole truth, and nothing but the truth; and
it must not be affected by one's wishes, or prejudices, or notions of how things
would have been if they had been different. The problem of accounting is to show
how things actually are.
                                Cole, 1921, 278

the periodic statement of financial position and the report [of income figures] ...
should consistently reflect true pictures of current business conditions and tendencies ... if these statements are to form a basis for rational judgements ....
                                Paton, 1922/1962, 425

the underlying principle relating to presentation and classification of items and accounts
in financial statements is hardly an accounting principle at all but the moral principle
that with respect to financial statements the accountant is bound to tell the whole
truth.
                                Byrne, 1937, 376

[Accountants] are interpreters .... If interpreters do not tell the truth, or do not tell
the whole truth, or tell truths intermixed with half-truths, many people may be
deceived to their hurt.
                                MacNeal, 1939, 1

Any general impression conveyed by [an accounting report] should be a true impression . . . . No information should be omitted which, if disclosed, would materially alter the impressions given in the statement.

Rorem & Kerrigan, 1942, 556

We seek the truth in accounts. That means past transactions. We never have and never will assume to know whether or not the future price level, the future dollar, the future demand for inventories will insure sales or profitable use of facilities beyond or equal to [those at] balance sheet dates.

Montgomery, 1947, 460

See also 075, 292

Accounts expected to be not misleading

the accounts must show the truth and not be misleading or fraudulent. [per Lindley L J]

Verner v General and Commercial Investment Trust, 1894

This is one of those difficult cases . . . where a document has been put forward in order to be acted upon (prospectuses and other things) and put forward in such a form, though it stated every fact correctly fact by fact, yet the true effect of what was said was completely false and completely misleading. [Wright J, charge to the jury; the *Royal Mail* case, *Rex v Lord Kylsant & another*, 1931]

Brooks (ed), 1933, 255

all audits . . . provide an independent examination of the accounts with a view to ensuring that the directors or partners are not themselves misled and do not mislead others as to the financial position of the undertaking and the profit or loss derived from its operations.

Lawson, 1951, 305

When [financial] statements are published, ... care must be exercised to see that the statements are comprehensible to an informed reader, and that the general impression conveyed is not misleading . . . .

Moonitz & Staehling, 1952, I:469

What the accountant tells us may not be true, but if we know what he has done, we have a fair idea of what it means . . . . accounting may be untrue but it is not lies; it does not deceive because we know it does not tell the truth, and we are able to make our own adjustment in each individual case, using the results of the accountant as evidence rather than as definitive information.

Boulding, 1962, 54

331

Accounting reports should disclose that which is necessary to make them not misleading.
Moonitz, 1961, 50

the accountancy profession has a general responsibility to ensure that published financial statements provide information that is not irrelevant or misleading . . . .
ASA, 1966, 7

The object of an audit is to ensure that the accounts on which the auditor is reporting show a true and fair view and are not misleading.
Cooper, 1966, 1

Only when use of a certain accounting principle tends to mislead is its selection wrong.
Stewart, 1972, 103

332 Financial statements expected to be factual

> We debit that account which does receive;
> And that which does deliver, credit give.
> Moreover, we're obliged in each transact
> That science set forth clearly right and fact.
Snell, c1710, 1

Accountants should deal with figures as facts simply . . . . Accountants have nothing whatever to do with estimates or hopes of profit.
Worthington, 1895, 67

A balance sheet should not be a photograph of an accountant's opinion, but rather a photograph of the facts upon which his opinion is based.
Bentley, 1912a, 161

nothing written into books of account or published in reports can alter the actual facts of business . . . . The mere fact that an alternative way of stating a thing converts a profit into a loss is positive proof that one of the alternatives is wrong; for the facts cannot give the alternative of profit or loss.
Cole, 1933, 479

no wedge may properly be driven between accounting entries and financial facts.
Dohr, 1941, 205

if accounting is not a device for reflecting facts, what is it?
Accountant, editorial, 1945, 318

do not imagine that by altering the form of the account you can possibly alter the facts . . . . the moment at which the truth begins to have to be retained in an inner circle is a moment of danger . . . . no oversimplification or alteration of form can possibly alter the facts.

fforde, 1950, 514, 515

[In law] Bookkeeping entries do not produce either income or loss; nor do they create or destroy facts. The real facts as found by the court are controlling, and not the bookkeeping entries adopted by corporate accountants in reflecting the trans-actions under scrutiny.

Hills, 1957/1982, 23

Factual accounting results in financial reports which properly reflect financial position and results of operations, and in a manner comparable among companies within an industry and among companies in different industries. That is the kind of account-ing that serves the investors best. All companies follow factual accounting to some extent.

Spacek, 1964b, 70

those unfamiliar with accounting are quite naturally inclined to assume that a balance sheet is a factual statement showing what the assets are worth . . . .

Myer, 1969, 24

Observers and users [of financial statements] (including many financial analysts) who are not familiar with the institutional and historical developments of financial reporting standards use the numbers offered for total assets as if they were accurate descriptions of the total economic resources of the reporting firm.

Abdel-khalik, 1992, 12

See also 737, 935

333 Correspondence or isomorphism in accounting

The great object of bookkeeping is to show at all times . . . the merchant's net capital or present worth; and there are obviously two . . . ways in which this object may be accomplished; namely, 1. by collecting into one sum the total amount of his property, or assets, and deducting from it the total amount of his debts and liabilities; or, 2. knowing the amount of his property at any former period . . . [and] adding or deducting the amount of his gains and losses since that time. Now, it has been found necessary to use both of these methods, in order that, by arriving at the same conclusion by different processes, we may be the more confident of the accuracy of the result; or, in the case of any inaccuracy, that we may perceive the extent of the errors which have been committed.

Foster, 1843, 15

There are two ways of constructing the balance sheet: 1. By actual investigation of quantities and prices . . . . 2. By tracing the changes of values from the preceding balance sheet through the accounts . . . . In practice the two methods . . . must cooperate.

Sprague, 1907/1972, 31

the accounts should be as sensitive as possible to all price and value changes.

Paton & Stevenson, 1916/1976, 103

The appropriateness of the method chosen [for allowing for depreciation] and the equitableness of the result which it affords depend upon the degree to which the writing down of the book value corresponds with the actual change in the value of the asset from cost new to scrap value.

Scott, 1945, 311

[A] . . . condition of informed judgment is that the system of singular statements which constitute the financial statements shall have a structure which is identical with the structure of the objects or events about which those statements are made. We speak of this as the requirement of correspondence.

Chambers, 1965b, 4

McKesson-Robbins required us to perform empirical tests on quantities. I think McKesson-Robbins is the most significant theoretical advance in accounting in the 20th century because it partially transformed accounting from a calculational discipline to an empirical science. My argument, in a nutshell, is that we ought to go all the way; we ought to empirically test the dollar figures as well as the quantities.

Sterling, 1976, 54

[Isomorphism is among] the criteria for assessment of [accounting] standards . . . . two objects are said to be isomorphic if they have the same shape even though their sizes may be quite different. Thus one may be said to represent the other . . . . the more rounded and complete and accurate is the picture given by financial statements, the greater their degree of isomorphism and the more relevant and objective they are likely to be.

CICA 1980, 56

Representational faithfulness – correspondence or agreement between a measure or description and the phenomena that it purports to represent.

FASB, 1980a, SFAC2

The reliability of financial information will be determined by the degree of correspondence between what that information conveys to users and the underlying transactions and events that have occurred and been measured and displayed. Reliable information will, without bias or undue error, faithfully represent those transactions and events.

AARF & ASRB, 1990b, SAC3

334 Realism in accounting expected

A statement which can be fairly described as a statement of assets, liabilities and net worth, should include all of the assets at present values, as nearly as they can be estimated or computed by competent experts .... Investors and bankers want [such statements]. They do not want valuable assets excluded, because they did not cost anything or because the costs cannot be allocated or traced. They do not want assets listed at values which bear no relation to present realities ....
Whitney, 1940, 298

It is axiomatic that, ideally, accounting practice should reflect economic realities, and methods which contravene this principle are to that extent inaccurate.
Norris, 1945b, 208

it is the underlying realities rather than the monetary symbols which finally matter when we come to look at balance sheet statements.
Accountant, editorial, 1946c, 294

accounting language must be consistent with the facts and realities of commercial life.
Avery, 1953, 85

the goal of generally accepted accounting principles is to provide financial statement data which faithfully portray the realities of enterprise operations and financial condition.
Mautz & Sharaf, 1961, 168

One of the main problems of the accountant is, or should be, to bring his statements into as close a relation with economic reality ... as possible.
Edey, 1963, 11

The accounting statements should be financial presentations of enterprise data according to the realities of their present existence .... [so that users may] formulate accurate judgments on the basis of the information presented concerning their relative rights and interests in the enterprise.
Patillo, 1965, 77

Financial statement information must accurately reflect the economic realities of market situations or it will not contribute to conflict resolution.
Johnson & Gunn, 1974, 663

Instead of defining accounting as a process of allocating unobservable costs, we must define it as a process of keeping track of real things in the real world.
Sterling, 1976, 54

A business enterprise is engaged in economic activity using human, material and financial resources. The economic activity over a period and the economic position

at a point of time are the reality. The purpose of the accounts is to communicate to those who read them the essential features of that reality.
Flint, 1982, 15

By reality we mean that the numbers in the account should resemble, as closely as practicality permits, one or more important economic facts – not conjectures, about which reasonable and skilled people might differ widely, but facts about which the range of skilled opinion would be limited.
ICAS, 1988, 57

335 Objectivity in accounting expected

Objective ... relates to the expression of facts without distortion from personal bias. It is in contrast to subjective, a word which suggests that the personal equation – state of mind, wish, intent to deceive – may affect the result.
Paton & Littleton, 1940, 19

Objective (adj.): Having a meaning or application apart from the investigator, the peculiarities of his experience, or of the environment, and substantiated or capable of being substantiated by the findings of independent investigators.
Kohler, 1952, 287

If accounting statements are to be most useful [to groups whose interests tend to conflict with one another], they should be objective statements of facts to the greatest extent practicable.
Owen, 1958, 67

The accounts and statements should give expression, as far as possible, to facts evidenced by completed transactions and supportable by objective data.
Finney & Miller, 1961, 168

Changes in assets and liabilities, and the related effects ... should not be given formal recognition in the accounts earlier than the point of time at which they can be measured in objective terms.
Moonitz, 1961, 41

Objectivity is the requirement that the procedures adopted should result in reports that reflect the readily measurable financial facts of business operation in such a manner that any reasonably skilled accountant, given the same situation, would be able to achieve substantially the same results.
Stanley, 1965, 83

an accounting figure that has been objectively determined is one that rests on verifiable facts or events – a figure that could presumably be ascertainable by an independent auditor were he provided with the full set of reasons and underlying data.
Dixon & others, 1966, 103

financial statements should be as objective as possible in the sense that they should be based on information which is measurable and capable of independent verification.

NZR, 1976, 43

See also 713

336 Accounting information expected to be free from bias

Through bias in favor of one interest or prejudice against another, inequitable results may follow ... from financial operations involving rearrangement of investor-capital positions and of shares in earnings.

Paton & Littleton, 1940, 2

accounting information must be to the greatest possible extent unprejudiced and unbiased.

Davison, 1951, 305

Freedom from bias means that facts have been impartially determined and reported. It also means that techniques used in developing data should be free of built-in bias.

AAA, 1966, 7

The information presented should be ... neutral in that the perception of the measurer should not be biased towards the interest of any one user group. This implies the need for reporting standards which are themselves neutral as between competing interests.

ASSC, 1975a, 29

The role of financial reporting requires it to provide evenhanded, neutral or unbiased information.

FASB, 1978, SFAC1

neutrality is concerned with financial statements "telling it like it is" rather than the way a particular interest group, like management or stockholders, might like it to be.

Wolk & others, 1984, 172

See also 345

337 Accounting information expected to be independently verifiable

[Accounting measurements] must be performed by those competent to make them and must rest on evidence that is reliable and subject to verification.

Moonitz, 1961, 41

verifiability is a necessary attribute of accounting information . . . . Verifiability is that attribute of information which allows qualified individuals working independently of one another to develop essentially similar measures or conclusions from an examination of the same evidence, data or records.

AAA, 1966, 10

Objectivity in accounting refers to the use of data that are free from bias and that can be substantiated by independent investigation.

Black & others, 1967, 12

There can be little doubt that the desired product is financial disclosure which can be tried, tested and proven to be true, fair, reliable, credible and authentic. For such to be the case, financial disclosure must consist of independent information, that is, information which can be intersubjectively tested.

Wolnizer, 1978, 50

while inputs to the historic cost system may be verifiable, the subjection of these costs to allocations, and the creation of provisions [for depreciation, expected bad debts, for example], means that the outputs of the system, such as residual asset values and expense allocations, are not verifiable by reference to evidence outside the entity regarding contemporary prices and conditions.

Martin, 1984, 387

Accounting numbers will be more verifiable the closer they are to values that are determined externally in the market place . . . . For the purpose of determining or verifying balance sheet values, the relevant time [of valuation] is, of course, the date of the balance sheet.

Solomons, 1989, 34, 35

338 Completeness of information expected

Bookkeeping is the art of recording mercantile transactions in a regular and systematic manner. A merchant's books should contain every particular which relates to the affairs of the owner. They should exhibit the state of all the branches of his business; the connection of the different parts; the amount and success of the whole. They should be so full and so well arranged as to afford a ready information in every point for which they may be consulted.

Hamilton, 1788/1982, 265

a trading and profit and loss account, in order correctly to exhibit the result of the period's work, must include all the transactions for the period, in so far as they relate to that period, and exclude such transactions as took place during that period . . . in respect of a subsequent period. [under: Adjustments at balancing time]

Pixley, 1926, vol 1

Accounting data should be as complete as possible.
Bourn, 1967a, 171

Complete financial accounting information includes all financial accounting data that reasonably fulfil the requirements of the other qualitative objectives [i.e. relevance, understandability, verifiability, neutrality, timeliness, comparability].
AICPA, 1970c, APBS4

[Financial] statements must be complete for the periods covered.
Hawkins, 1971, 80

The financial statements of a business enterprise can be thought of as a representation of the resources and obligations of an enterprise and the financial flows into, out of, and within the enterprise – as a model of the enterprise. Like all models, it must abstract from much that goes on in real enterprise . . . . Before an accounting model . . . can be judged to represent an enterprise reliably, it must be determined that none of the important financial functions of the enterprise or its relationships have been lost or distorted.
FASB, 1980a, SFAC2

Completeness – The inclusion in reported information of everything material that is necessary for faithful representation of the relevant phenomena.
FASB, 1980a, SFAC2, Glossary

the information in financial statements must be complete within the bounds of materiality and cost.
IASC, 1989, Framework

To be reliable, information must . . . tell the whole truth. This ingredient may be called comprehensiveness.
Solomons, 1989, 32

339 Accuracy of information expected

It was the duty of the auditor not to confine himself merely to the task of ascertaining the arithmetical accuracy of the balance sheet, but to see that it was a true and accurate representation of the company's affairs. [per Stirling, J]
Leeds Estate Building & Investment Co
v Shepherd, 1887

Under the influence of individualistic enterprise a general policy of conservatism became a standard dogma of accounting. It has been carried over into corporate accounts. It is still defended by practitioners and teachers of accounting. However, ... In accounts, as in management, the dogma of conservatism must make way for the dogma of accuracy .... Why should we not be recklessly and unreservedly accurate?

Scott, 1931/1973, 153

the fundamental object of the profession is to ensure that in the documents which are produced a true and accurate account of the affairs of the company is given .... the law requires this, that the shareholders shall have put before them true and accurate accounts. [The Attorney General, closing speech for the prosecution; the *Royal Mail* case, *Rex v Lord Kylsant & another*, 1931]

Brooks (ed), 1933, 210, 212

Accounting has but one purpose, to set forth the results of business operations accurately and truthfully ....

Montgomery, 1938

The critical test, therefore, is whether the financial statement here, as a whole, fairly presented the financial condition of Continental as of September 30, 1962, and whether it accurately reported the operations for fiscal 1962. [Instruction to the jury]

United States v Simon, 1969

In the final analysis, an accurate conveyance of economic facts to stockholders in financial reporting is the one and only objective of public accounting reports.

Spacek, 1970a, 41

We accountants have tried to bury the word [accuracy] and, as a result, often seem to pursue the wrong goals. We ought not to be seeking income measurements that are "useful", "neutral", "uniform" or "fair". We ought to be seeking measurements that are accurate, testable in the marketplace, because accuracy is the substance of measurement. Usefulness, neutrality, uniformity, fairness are all attendants of accuracy.

Mosso, 1980, 140

See also 258

340 General Utility of Accounting

341 Financial statements expected to be intelligible

[It is necessary] that all the businessman's affairs be arranged in a systematic way [in accounts] so that he may get their particulars at a glance.

Pacioli, 1494/1963, 26

The balance sheet ... should be so clearly stated that every shareholder of ordinary intelligence can understand it. A knowledge of bookkeeping is not essential to the comprehension of a balance sheet properly drawn.

Pixley, 1881/1976, 150

Either misstatements of fact or misunderstanding of statements, or both, must result where there is not a common understanding of the language of the balance sheet on the part of those concerned.

Couchman, 1924, 3

directors, shareholders and, incidentally, the courts should have a clear, explicit explanation of the accounting facts relating to a corporation in form and language which in accordance with common sense will enable the ordinary reader, without being a technical interpreter, to determine the actual state of the company's business, prospects and value. Corporate statements and reports are for the information of the layman, not of skilled accountants . . . . the use of language and schedules, that not even skilled executives in the corporations involved could understand, would be done away with. [per Judge Jenkins]

Bethlehem-Youngstown merger injunction case, 1931, 85

Stockholders and the public are generally untrained in accounting technicalities and cannot be expected to understand and interpret highly technical statements. One of the areas requiring great improvement is that of preparing stockholders' reports with a view to avoiding the criticisms of unintelligibility and ambiguity now current.

Porter & Fiske, 1935, 197

The basic difficulty in accounting as elsewhere is that terminology is looked upon as a means of expressing one's self, whereas . . . self-expression is of litle importance in the understanding of any subject matter. The traffic officer's signal to stop was not developed for the benefit of the officer; it is significant only . . . in that it is intended to induce a certain type of response on the part of the motorist. And so it should be with accounting terms.

Dohr, 1941, 203

Published statements are prepared for laymen. The standard of correct language in published statements is correct non-technical meaning.

Whitney, 1941, 355

an accounting report can serve its purpose only if it is intelligible to the person to whom it is presented and upon whom it calls for action.

Fitzgerald, 1956b, 21

The important thing is that companies, and their accountant advisers, should provide the investor with the information he needs in a manner which is intelligible to him.

Accountancy, editorial, 1964, 671

the essential function of accounting is to provide understandable financial information about complex business activity to a wide variety of users.

Andersen & Co, 1972, 10

341

Understandability calls for the provision, in the clearest and simplest possible form, of all the information which a reasonably informed reader can use.

NZR, 1976, 44

The information [provided by financial reports] should be comprehensible to those who have a reasonable understanding of business and economic activities and are willing to study the information with reasonable diligence.

FASB, 1978, SFAC1

See also 235, 934

342 Financial information expected to be useful

by inspection of a merchant's books, by a man that hath skill, one may soon find out his wisdom and success, as well as his real worth.

North, 1714/1986, 73

It [bookkeeping] was invented because man wanted it, because he found that he could not get on without it. It is essentially utilitarian. It is not the result of the work of *dilettanti*, of men who conceived some theory and labored to prove the truth of it. It was evolved with a conscious, definite and practical object in view . . . .

Woolf, 1912, xxix

Always in the background must be the concept of usefulness.

Broad, 1957, 37

Accounting is not, and should not be, an intellectual exercise carried on for its own sake, but a service to the various parties concerned in the operation or ownership of business enterprises.

Coutts (ed), 1960a, 574

Accounting reports are useful because they can be used to control activities relating to resources and enable decisions to be made by those in a position to control them . . . .

Goldberg, 1965, 167

Accounting information must be useful . . . both inside and outside the entity concerned. It must be useful in the formulation of objectives, the making of decisions, or the direction and control of resources to accomplish objectives. The utility of information lies in its ability to reduce uncertainty about the actual state of affairs of concern to the user.

AAA, 1966, 8

accounting is utilitarian . . . a statement can be justified only by its usefulness.

Ross, 1966, 49

Reports and [SEC] registration statements should be designed to provide information of maximum utility to investors and their advisers.

SEC, 1969, 37

I think the overriding criterion [of an accounting system] should be usefulness.

Sterling, 1972, 198

the information communicated through a statement of financial position should be useful to the receivers.

Macdonald, 1974b, 268

Financial reporting should provide information that is useful to present and potential investors and creditors and other users in making rational investment, credit and similar decisions .... in assessing the amounts, timing, and uncertainty of prospective cash receipts from dividends or interest and the proceeds from the sale, redemption, or maturity of securities or loans,

FASB, 1978, SFAC1

Usefulness an ambiguous property

the extent to which one describes a practice as utilitarian depends pretty largely on one's objectives, point of view and desires. To a company that wished to show its assets at $5 million, a system of accounting which required them to be shown at the $1 million they cost or at the figure of $10 million for which they were to be sold next day would not be utilitarian.

Werntz, n.d./1968, 95

the criterion of usefulness has ... been used to justify the method resulting in the smallest tax bill, the easiest method to compute, the method permitting the greatest degree of manipulation, the method resulting in the highest net income, et cetera.

Sprouse, 1963, 691

What is judged to be "best" may be that combination of methods which: (a) yields the highest of all possible net incomes for a given year; (b) yields the highest of all possible rates of return on shareholders' equity for a given year; (c) yields the most realistic income figure, regardless of the effect of its calculation on the amounts of balance sheet figures; (d) yields the most conservative indication of results and position at any time; (e) yields a net income figure which is consistent with some preconceived rate of growth in net income over a period of years; (f) yields the least variable rate of net income to shareholders' equity over a period of years; (g) yields the most realistic income statement and balance sheet at any time (and, therefore, also over a period of years); (h) is the most widely accepted in general, or in the firm's line of business; (i) is the least likely to give rise to objections or qualified reports on the part of auditors: (j) is the easiest to justify (e.g. because it

343

is the combination used previously) . . . . there is in traditional literature and practice some warrant for each.

> Chambers, 1968b, 28

the difficulty with "usefulness" is in making its meaning precise enough to be applicable to a concrete situation.

> Sterling, 1972, 199

343 Financial reports expected to be timely

Executives need statements of financial position and earnings available promptly at the end of each operating period and, equally important, up-to-the-minute current financial and operating data.

> Porter & Fiske, 1935, 77

The value of earlier information exceeds the value of later information [of the same content] by the additional profit obtainable because managerial action, if required, can be taken sooner.

> Gregory & Atwater, 1957, 63

The greater the delay between period-end and publication of results, the less valuable is the report when it does appear, because the unknown results of the intervening period grow more interesting and important as that period extends.

> Bird, 1965, 34

financial reports . . . . must be timely to have any usefulness for management and investor decisions.

> Grady, 1965, 41

The scorekeeping function of the accountant is not only a question of keeping an accurate record of what takes place in the business, but also of informing everybody fast enough so that corrective measures can be taken if there are adverse trends.

> Bottrill, 1966, 123

The timeliness of information . . . is an important aspect of its value.

> Benston, 1969, 26

Reports should be as timely as practicable . . . .

> SEC, 1969, 37

the usefulness of accounting information is reduced, the longer is the time period between an event occurring and its being reported.

> Arnold & others, 1985, 61

Timeliness is an ancillary aspect of relevance and is defined as having information available to decision makers before it loses its capacity to influence decisions. Timeliness may refer to the elapsed time from the date of the financial statements until the date they are issued, or it may refer to the elapsed time from the date of the observation or measurement until the date of the financial statements, or both . . . . timeliness is not a quality of information *per se* . . . .

Sterling, 1985, 23

344 Relevance of information expected

The information yielded by any [formal information providing] system should be relevant to the kinds of decision the making of which it is expected to facilitate.

Chambers, 1955, 22

Relevance . . . requires that the information must bear upon or be usefully associated with actions it is designed to facilitate or results desired to be produced.

AAA, 1966, 7

If there exists a well-defined decision theory, then that theory will specify what observations are to be made or what properties are to be measured. This provides a definition of relevance: All properties that are specified by a decision theory are relevant to that theory.

Sterling, 1970b, 454

Relevant information is data, whether about the past, the present, or about other people's forecasts of the future, that a decision maker can use to improve his own predictions about the future.

Macve, 1981, 37

Information is relevant if it has the capacity to make a difference in investors', creditors', or other users' decisions. To be relevant, information about an item must have feedback value or predictive value (or both) for users [of financial statements] and must be timely.

FASB, 1984, SFAC5

For financial information to be relevant it must have value in terms of assisting users in making and evaluating decisions about the allocation of scarce resources and in assessing the rendering of accountability by preparers . . . . it must assist them [users] in making predictions about future situations and in forming expectations, and/or it must play a confirmatory role in respect of their past evaluations.

AARF & ASRB, 1990b, SAC3

345 Neutrality of information expected

the uses made [by diverse parties] of accounting information require that accounting should ... be neutral with respect to the wishes and claims of contributing
parties [to a firm].

> Chambers, 1952, 217

Neutrality. Neutral financial accounting information is directed toward the common
needs of users and is independent of presumptions about particular needs and desires
of specific users of the information.

> AICPA, 1970c, APBS4

The information presented should be ... neutral as between competing interests.

> ASSC, 1975a, 29

Simply because information has an effect on human behavior does not mean that
it should not seek to be neutral as between different desired modes of behavior.
Unless it is as neutral as the accountant can make it, it is difficult to see how it can
be relied on to guide behavior .... Information cannot be neutral ... if it is selected
or presented for the purpose of producing some chosen effect on human behavior.

> Solomons, 1978, 70

Neutrality – absence in reported information of bias intended to attain a predetermined result or to induce a particular mode of behavior.

> FASB, 1980a, SFAC2

The view which is given of profit or loss and state of affairs, to the extent to which
this can be given in annual accounts, must be true and fair in relation to the interests
of these parties [buyers and sellers of securities]. This means that the information
has to be adequate for the needs of any one party but also that it has to be evenhanded as between parties.

> Flint, 1982, 25

See also 336

346 Consistency

consistency ... safeguards accounting measurements from both the errors of whim
and fancy and premeditated misrepresentation.

> Bray, 1953, 5

In order to be consistent, similar material items should be handled uniformly within
a given period and from period to period. Change from one accepted method of
accounting to another may be desirable but disclosure of such change and its net
effects is necessary because the handling has not been consistent.

> Berryman, 1960, 78

Comparability and the legitimacy of inferences depend on the consistency of the use of concepts and methods.

Chambers, 1961, #116

Intertemporal consistency expected

Within quite wide limits, it is relatively unimportant to the investor what precise rules or conventions are adopted by a corporation reporting its earnings if he knows what method is being followed and is assured that it is followed consistently from year to year.

AIA, 1932

In view of the variety of approved methods which may be adopted in applying accounting principles, and in recognition of the effect which such choice may have on the financial and earnings picture, we have during the last few years come to emphasize strongly the importance of consistency in the use of the method selected.

Broad, 1937, 183

While it is not in many cases of great importance which of several alternative accounting rules is applied in a given situation, it is essential that, once having adopted a certain procedure, it be consistently adhered to in preparing the accounts over a period of time.

Byrne, 1937, 372

The doctrine of consistency, so far as the accountant is concerned, refers to one particular accounting entity and its application is considered satisfactory when the entity's accounting methods, practices or usages which have some background of general acceptance remain unchanged from period to period.

Gilman, 1939, 238

Why do we want consistency? To be able to visualize trends in the significant components of the accounting entity, to be able to measure differences in them, and to know that the trends or differences are real (i.e. reflecting actual business and economic events) and are not an illusion.

Moonitz, 1961, 44

accounting policies and procedures should be the same over a succession of accounting periods.

Ladd, 1963, 41

consistency [of application of generally accepted accounting principles] adds greatly to the usefulness and comparability of the financial statements as between periods.

Grady, 1965, 31

For accounting measurements to serve as indices to make possible useful analyses through time, the measurement and reporting practices must be consistently applied.

This . . . should relate to basic concepts . . . to the terminology and . . . to the format of reports.

AAA, 1966, 18

Consistency in accounting methods from year to year is . . . necessary to avoid confusing the reader and to enable proper evaluation of trends.

Skinner, 1972b, 33

Endorsement of consistency qualified

an erroneous basis of valuation consistently adopted year after year, even if that basis be a conservative one and really below true cost, may result in large and unexpected discrepancies between the profits shown in different periods . . . . thus entirely upsetting all the calculations and estimates of the managers.

Dickinson, 1914, 95

[The accountant] does not believe that the doctrine of consistency is offended when he adopts a certain method for one client and a different method for another. Nor does he consider it inconsistent to adopt the valuation rule of cost or market and at the same time submit comparative profit and loss statements which have been distorted thereby. The accountant does not consider it inconsistent to apply the convention of realization to gains without applying it to costs, expenses and losses.

Gilman, 1939, 238

accounting, like the common law, should have elements of flexibility and adaptability as well as of stability. Therefore, there can be no absolute rule of consistency, but only a general admonition that consistency should normally be maintained, and . . . any significant departure therefrom and its effects should be adequately disclosed.

May, 1943, 45

The basis of stating inventories must be consistently applied and should be disclosed in the financial statements; whenever a significant change is made therein, there should be disclosure of its nature and, if material, the effect on income.

AIA, 1947a, ARB29

Consistency provides assurance that . . . comparability will be achieved by requiring uniform and compatible recording and presenting of financial data . . . . consistency does not assure the integrity of the data itself. It does not counterbalance theoretical deficiencies or prevent distortions in reported incomes.

Backer, 1955a/1955b, 213

Unless principles are applied consistently from year to year, comparisons from one year to the next are meaningless . . . . [If] changes in principles [are] made . . . . the differences must be clearly disclosed if they might have an important bearing on the conclusions to be drawn from making comparisons with statements of prior years.

Blough, 1956, 24

Consistency should be maintained between the statements . . . of successive periods . . . . If a change [in procedure] of material consequence is made, the fact should be mentioned and the effect . . . indicated, if determinable . . . . it would be most unfortunate if the stated net income of a business could be determined by the whim or fancy, and particularly by the changing whim or fancy, of those directing its affairs.

Finney & Miller, 1961, 168, 170

financial statements are considered to be means through which a corporation's point of view is made known. As a corporation moves from one stage of development to another, changes in accounting procedure are needed so as to depict its changes in outlook and strategy . . . . The use of alternative accounting procedures is thus consistent with the corporation's object of survival.

Li, 1963, 55

the objective of consistency in all types of public reports might be better accomplished by a full and detailed disclosure of the measurement methods and procedures used in developing accounting information for public reports.

Bedford & Iino, 1968, 458

In case of doubt, a transaction shall be treated in the same manner as other transactions reasonably considered to be of the same class; and working rules shall not be changed arbitrarily and without notice of the effects of the change to those who use the accounts.

Lee, 1973, 16

347 Interfirm and intertemporal comparability of information expected

In order that financial statements may be compared satisfactorily it is essential that the underlying treatments of costs, expenses and revenues be substantially uniform.

Paton (ed), 1944, 29

Reporting practices should be followed which facilitate comparisons over time and among enterprises.

Illinois, 1964, 31

The writers of the 'thirties had been vague about why uniformity of accounting principles was desirable and were often wont to defend or condemn uniformity *per se*. In the post-war period, accountants were quite specific in identifying comparability of statements as the major factor requiring standardized principles, terminology, methods, etc.

Storey, 1964, 38

An investor not only must know how his company is doing, but he should be in a position to compare his company's operations with those of other companies in the same industry or even in different industries .... the accounting profession finds itself caught between the financial analyst who seeks a utopia of complete comparability and managements who want complete flexibility in the presentation of the financial data .... management has a greater stake in the cause of comparability than anyone else, because greater comparability increases usefulness, which is in turn an essential ingredient in public confidence.

Stone, 1968, 53

The Accounting Principles Board .... ranks comparability among the most important of the objectives of accounting ... and is attempting to narrow areas of difference in accounting practices that are not justified by differences in circumstances.

AICPA, 1970c, APBS4

The information [given in the corporate report] should be expressed in terms which enable the user to compare the entity's results over time and with other similar entities.

ASSC, 1975a, 29

Since comparing alternative investment or lending opportunities is an essential part of most investment or lending decisions, investors and creditors desire financial statement information that is comparable, both for single enterprises over time and between enterprises at the same time. They therefore rank comparability among the most important qualities of useful financial information.

FASB, 1976b, 161

The operating results and financial position of one year should be comparable with those of prior and subsequent years. The financial statements of one company should be comparable with those of another company in the same industry as well as with those of firms in other industries.

Edwards & others, 1979, 457

The users of general purpose financial reports need to be able to compare aspects of an entity at one time and over time, and between entities at one time and over time. This implies that the measurement and display of transactions and events need to be carried out in a consistent manner throughout an entity, and over time for that entity, and that there is consistency between entities in these regards.

AARF & ASRB, 1990b, SAC3

348 Interfirm uniformity of accounting endorsed

the advantage obtained by uniformity of valuation, not only in the successive balance sheets of particular organizations, but also in the comparison of the balance sheets of various organizations, is so great that it should not be violated save in most unusual circumstances.

Couchman, 1924, 46

Uniformity is a necessary basis of social organization.

Scott, 1931/1973, 161

Presumably no accountant would now question the necessity for uniformity in disclosure, uniformity in sequence and grouping, uniformity in the choice and use of terms, and so far as is reasonably practicable uniformity in the accounting conventions of profit measurement and balance sheet valuation . . .

Accountant, editorial, 1946a, 346

Although selection of the method should be made on the basis of the individual circumstances, it is obvious that financial statements will be more useful if uniform methods of inventory pricing are adopted by all companies within a given industry.

AIA, 1947a, ARB29

The readers [of annual reports] should not have to, and most of them could not, evaluate the effect of alternative accounting principles or conventions simply on the basis of disclosure [of the methods used]. A reader should, and has a right to, assume that the correct method of recording a transaction was followed, and that corresponding transactions are handled in the same way by all companies. Thus he has the right to make comparisons without having to assume the difficult, if not impossible, responsibility of making mental *pro forma* adjustment to make the figures comparable.

Spacek, 1958b, 370

Where various alternative methods of measuring an economic activity exist, . . . the best available one [should] be used uniformly within a firm, by different firms, and, to the extent practicable, by different industries. This uniformity refers to consistent classification and terminology as well as consistent measurement . . . . Basically . . . uniformity is necessary for effective communication.

AAA, 1966, 17

uniformity in accounting statements is an important prerequisite to successful communication . . . .

Macdonald, 1974a, 31

349 Posited trade-off of stipulated characteristics

accounting must not only be significant but practicable. Objectives desirable in themselves have sometimes to be sacrificed to considerations of practicality and convenience.

May, 1949b, 258

Both the minimum conformity required with any one of the standards [relevance, verifiability, freedom from bias, quantifiability] and rates of substitution (trade-off) among the four standards are conditioned by the circumstances .... As with ... the standards, there exist reasonable trade-off rates [for the guidelines, appropriateness to expected use, disclosure of significant relationships, inclusion of environmental information, uniformity of practices within and among entities, consistency of practices through time].

AAA, 1966, 10, 18

Increased relevance may mean less objectivity and uniformity; increasing reporting classifications and disclosing budget plans may make financial reports more complex. Some trade-off between the objectives of simplicity and economic realism will be necessary.

Davidson, 1969, 29

In translating [the main principles of an accounting system] into detailed accounting practices there are certain qualitative factors to be borne in mind. [... objectivity, realism, prudence, comparability, consistency, intelligibility, ease and economy in preparation]. These are qualifications which should ideally be possessed by any accounting system .... They are, however, to some extent mutually inconsistent and a satisfactory compromise between them has to be worked out. The view on what is a satisfactory compromise may vary between different people or groups.

Sandilands, 1975, 62

The various qualities or characteristics of useful financial statement information sometimes conflict with or reinforce each other. Potential conflicts are numerous because almost any quality may conflict with almost any other quality. For example, the most relevant information may be unverifiable, subjective, difficult to understand, biased, noncomparable, unmeasurable, and so on .... Accountants recognize many of the conflicts between qualities of useful information and commonly make trade-offs. [examples given: relevance v. reliability; relevance v. comparability; relevance v. understandability]

FASB, 1976b, 163

Once we recognize the need for a variety of information, we face the problems of trading off relevance against reliability, cost against benefit, and, possibly, the interests of one class of user against those of another.

Whittington, 1981b, 251

Accounting exists to provide information useful for making decisions. To be useful, information must be helpful in evaluating the various alternative courses of action. The information must also be reliable .... Unfortunately, some of the most relevant information is highly unreliable .... At some point, then, a trade-off must take place between the desirable qualities of relevance and reliability. Where this trade-off occurs depends on the requirements of the recipient of the information.

Martin, 1984, 102

Decision usefulness requires both relevance and reliability. Neither can be traded for the other because they perform different roles in the decision process. Relevance refers to the connection of the phenomena to the decision. Reliability refers to the connection of the phenomena to the representation.

Sterling, 1985, 30

three criteria ... determine the usefulness of the information .... relevance, reliability and cost-effectiveness. Frequently, a subjective trade-off among these criteria is necessary.

Andersen & Co, 1987, 15

In practice a balancing, or trade-off, between qualitative characteristics is often necessary .... The relative importance of the characteristics in different cases is a matter of professional judgment.

IASC, 1989, Framework

Timeliness may sometimes conflict with reliability .... Thus a trade-off may have to be made between timeliness and reliability .... The principal qualities of information ..., relevance, representational faithfulness and verifiability, are not absolutes. Always it is a matter of seeking more rather than less, and sometimes more of one quality can be obtained only by sacrificing some of another .... the problem of maximizing the usefulness of information [involves] making trades among the various qualities that together add up to usefulness.

Solomons, 1989, 31, 38–9

350 Financial Information Processing

351 Single entry bookkeeping

Double entry ... possesses a completeness and proof of the accounts .... single entry is short and simple, but imperfect and unsatisfactory; whilst double entry is complete and systematic, but laborious and complicated .... Single entry is incapable of proof, because it attends exclusively to the personal accounts, omitting one or more of the accounts of merchandise, bills, cash or stock.

Cronhelm, 1818/1978, vi

Single entry is the most simple and concise method, but it is imperfect, as it contains personal accounts only. The ledger, kept on this plan, affords to the owner a knowledge of what debts are due to him, and of what he owes to others, but it exhibits no account of the quantities of goods bought and sold, nor of the stock in hand. This mode of keeping books is best adapted to retail business, in which the articles sold are small and numerous.

Morrison, 1825, 15

Single entry chiefly records transactions of persons who buy or sell on credit . . . . by single entry I cannot tell what goods are unsold, or my profits or losses by my books only . . . . bookkeeping by single entry is essentially defective, as it affords no method of ascertaining the state of a merchant's affairs without taking stock – a task which is both laborious and liable to error, and which, at best, affords no adequate means of preventing embezzlement or detecting fraud; but these objects are attained by double entry, perhaps as effectually as human ingenuity can devise; for here accounts are opened for goods as well as for persons; and thus the owner can tell at any time what quantity is or ought to be unsold, by the inspection of his books only, without taking stock.

Kelly, 1839, 2, 4, 5

Single entry only records the transactions so far as they affect persons, and consequently personal ledgers are, strictly speaking, the only books necessary; . . . . To ascertain the profit or loss for any stated time a person who keeps his books by single entry must . . . prepare a statement of affairs showing his assets [as valued or estimated] and liabilities at the commencement [and end] of such period.

Jenkinson, 1910, 31

The purpose of single entry bookkeeping is to record all the transactions of a business, but to keep running ledger accounts with persons only; that is to say, with the proprietor . . . his customers, and . . . his creditors. To other invested values, not found in the ledger but ascertainable by . . . analysis of . . . books . . . or through periodical inventories, is left the duty of reflecting, at the end of the accounting period, the increases and decreases which they have individually received or suffered.

Esquerré, 1914, 54

Under single entry accounting, a comparison of the balance sheet position from one period to another was the only means available for the computation of income. In such circumstances it would have been natural to think of a periodical restatement of the assets in terms of current values. In point of fact this was not commonly done; even under single entry the common practice was to state assets at cost with necessary modification in the case of the inventories.

Sanders, 1939b, 573

352 Charge:discharge accounting

The only big business of [England in the thirteenth and fourteenth centuries] was the management of the nobles' estates . . . . The management of the noblemen's manors was delegated to stewards or bailiffs. The relationship between baron and bailiff was that of principal and agent . . . . Although [the steward] might possess, control and dispose of various kinds and amounts of assets, he did so only through delegated authority. The property itself was not his; he held no lawful title to any of it . . . . The steward was put *in charge* of property, of incomes, of expenditures; he was *charged* with whatever he was made responsible for. A *charge* was something to be explained; a satisfactorily explained charge was called a *discharge*. When the steward could satisfactorily explain how he had disposed of his responsibilities, he was *discharged* of what he had been previously charged.

Littleton, 1926, 68, 69

annual summary accounts for the Sussex ironworks between 1541 and 1573 . . . . are typical of their period, laid out on a charge and discharge system. The charge consisted of the previous year's surplus, small sales of iron, receipts from other estate officials or the Sidneys themselves, and income from rents and agricultural sales. The discharge comprised expenditure on operating the works, but this section also contains household and agricultural items.

Crossley (ed), 1975, 1

The keeping of all books of accounts, by this way of charge and discharge, is not that which taketh away from one without restoring to another either more or less in value. But it is that art of equality, which restoreth just as much as it taketh from another, without partiality; and therefore it may be fitly compared to a pair of balances.

Carpenter, 1632, 1

[By the method of debtor and creditor] all the Drs and Crs are declared; for that person or thing which takes, is made Dr, that is, stands charged; and that person or thing which delivers or parts from, is the Cr or discharged.

North, 1714/1986, 12

The art of Italian bookkeeping is called bookkeeping by double entry, because there must be two entries; the first being a charging of a person, money or goods; and the second, a discharging of a person, money, or goods.

Anon, 1737/1984, 41

The Cromwell [household] accounts . . . . are set out in two parts: the charge, consisting of arrears [which seems to mean debtors' opening balances] and receipts, and the discharge, consisting of payments made by the steward . . . . In the annual accounts a balance is struck by subtracting the discharge from the charge, leaving a sum which . . . represents what the head of the household would expect the steward to account for.

Myatt-Price, 1956, 106

The master and steward system was based on the notion of stewardship of the servant towards the proprietor or, later, the firm. As it had developed in the Tudor period, after which it did not change essentially until the end of the eighteenth century, it was based on double entry bookkeeping, but of a peculiar kind: on the debit side was the "charge", or all the receipts of the agent on behalf of his master, at first both in money and in kind, but by the end of the period in money only; and on the credit side the "discharge", or all the payments made, including the contributions towards the upkeep of the master's household, and cash payments to him, leaving as balance usually cash still in the hands of the agent, or, more rarely, the sum due to the agent from his master.

Pollard, 1968, 246

353 Personification of accounts

there is little doubt that the first ledger accounts were those showing personal debt relationships between merchants. With the development of the double entry system, the terms debtor [Dr] and creditor [Cr] were extended first to accounts of objects (real accounts) and later to abstract classifications (nominal accounts).

Jackson, 1956, 295

Entries which in Pacioli's treatise were in the form "Per Cash, a Capital" after translation took the form "Money oweth to Thomas Lee" in Oldcastle's manual. Money was given a theoretically independent personal existence. [s.c. H Oldcastle, *A briefe instruction and maner how to keepe books of accompts* . . ., London, 1588; first published 1543]

Jackson, 1956, 296

Whereas I said before, that the things received must owe, I mean thereby that the goods bought, or money received of any man, must in all parcels be made debtor, (that is to say) to owe unto the parties of whom it is received or bought.

Peele, 1569/1956, 297

great merchants . . . will keep or frame an account for themselves, and make their warehouses . . . debitor, because the warehouse is trusted with the wares or commodities . . . . In like manner (because their moneys are laid up or locked in a chest, which they call cash), they will therefore imagine this Cash to be a person whom they have trusted . . . .

Malynes, 1622, 364

Let it be supposed that the account of Stock [i.e. capital] is a real person employed to take care of my estate and to render an account of the improvement he has made of it. In a like manner, Cash, and all other accounts which I may have occasion to keep, may be considered as persons employed by Stock to take care of that part of my estate with which they are entrusted, and to render an account thereof to Stock. Then Cash, or the person entrusted with the care of my money, owes to Stock so much as he is entrusted with. Upon this hypothesis every transaction must be considered as though it had been transacted between persons who managed affairs for me . . . . Profit and Loss – This account may be considered as a person who is to take all the profits arising from the business and make good all the losses. Hence every account which exhibits gain or loss is to adjust with Profit and Loss, and Profit and Loss is to adjust with Stock, or the person whom I employ to take care of my estate. Balance – This account may be considered as a person who is to take possession of all my effects and debts, and whatever is owing to me by other persons on adjusting their accounts, for which he stands accountable; and therefore Balance is made debtor to every account it takes anything from; and Balance, or the person supposed, is also to make good all the demands against my estate.

Clark, 1732/1852, 14

Now observe that each of those particulars your inventory does consist of are ...
made debtor to stock [i.e. capital] in your ledger, because they are in effect so many
stewards to whom you intrust your estate, and each of them are accountable to you
for their several parts of it.

Hayes, 1731/1956, 298

The application of these terms [debtor and creditor] is originally personal; but it is
extended by analogy to every part of property, and to the whole capital itself.

Cronhelm, 1818/1978, 6

The accounts are kept as if every different sort of account belonged to a separate
person, and had an interest of its own, which every transaction promotes or injures.
If the student finds that it helps him, he may imagine a clerk to every account: one
to take charge of, and regulate, the actual cash; another for the bills which the
house is to receive when due ... and so on .... All these clerks (or accounts)
belonging to one merchant, must account to him in the end – must either produce
all they have taken in charge, or relieve themselves by showing to whom it went.
For all that they have received, ... they are bound, or are debtors; for everything
which has passed out of charge, ... they are unbound, or are creditors .... To
whom are all these parties (or accounts) bound, and from whom are they released?
Undoubtedly the merchant himself, or, more properly, the balance clerk ....

de Morgan, 1846/1861, 181–2

[Guiseppe Cerboni, in 1872] advanced the theory that the business represents the
aggregate of the persons who are intrusted with the wealth of the proprietor, or who
have intrusted the proprietor with part of their wealth. Hence, instead of debiting
and crediting accounts, he suggested debits and credits to the cashier, the store-
keeper, the manager of the building, the mortgagee, the banker, etc.

Esquerré, 1914, 80

the whole business is supposed to be carried on by clerks. There is supposed to be
a clerk called Capital or Stock who represents the owner of the business (or the
Firm). There is supposed to be a clerk called Cash who takes charge of the money.
There is supposed to be a clerk called Bank .... a clerk called Bills Receivable .... a clerk called Profit and Loss .... These clerks mind their own business
and do not interfere with another's department. Thus, if perchance Goods receives
some money, he instantly hands it over to Cash because he himself has no business
with money.

Collier, 1884/1956, 299

Observe that the accounts always balance – and thus may be made to prove anything;
if you throw 100 pounds into the sea, the sea becomes your debtor for that amount,
it would appear in the balance sheet accordingly, and you appear as neither richer
nor poorer for the transaction.

Cayley, 1894, 19

The property does not *owe* Mr Jones anything; it *belongs* to him.

Sprague, 1907/1972, 34

Debit (from the Latin *debet*, he owes) means, in accounting, not merely that something is owed, but that a definite person (or personified property or force) is responsible for some value . . . . Credit (from the Latin *credit*, he entrusts) means . . . a definite person (or personified property or force) has granted some definite value . . . . when an account takes a responsibility (that is, becomes accountable for something), debit it; and when an account puts a responsibility somewhere else (which is sometimes getting rid of accountability previously undertaken), credit it.

Cole, 1908, 9

354 Double entry bookkeeping said to be based on property rights

It is a primary axiom of the exact sciences that the whole is equal to the sum of its parts; and on this foundation rests the whole superstructure of bookkeeping. It considers property as a whole composed of various parts: the stock account regards the whole capital; the money, merchandise and personal accounts record the component parts.

Cronhelm, 1818/1978, 4

Wealth and property . . . are correlative terms. Wealth is the concrete thing owned; property is the abstract right of ownership. The two concepts mutually imply each other. There can be no wealth without property rights applying to it, nor property rights without wealth to which they apply . . . . By double entry is meant the record of every double-faced event pertaining to a particular person, whether it be a trans-action of that person with another or an interaction between the various categories of capital within his own possession.

Fisher, 1906/1965, 22, 159

The financial statistics of a business enterprise can . . . be listed in two fundamen-tally distinct and numerically equal classes – property and equities; . . . the essence of the double entry system of keeping accounts consists in the separation of the members of the equation – properties equals equities – and the maintaining of that equality.

Paton, 1917, 11

The basis of double entry is a realization that in modern business there are no assets lying about without claimants. To everything having value some one is a claimant.

Cole, 1921, 7

the sum total of the several kinds of property will always be equal to the the sum total of claims by some one to those properties . . . . [To give expression to this] is the function of modern account keeping. Double entry bookkeeping means the organized instrumentality for executing this function.

Littleton, 1933/1966, 25, 27

The assets are the economic resources of the enterprise and the equities represent the sources of the funds – and the legal rights – reflected in total assets . . . . Thus the basic relationship of accounting data is found in the equation of values, assets equal equities.

Paton & Dixon, 1958, 35–6

Double entry bookkeeping requires that two records be kept of wealth, one showing the form of the wealth and one showing the ownership equity in that wealth.

Sands, 1963, 12

There is a duality in accounting which arises out of the recognition which accounting affords of the two aspects of capital – its forms and the rights to it . . . . double entry accounting, by recognizing both the forms of and the rights to capital, enables the accountant to measure the increase or decrease of total capital by time periods while preserving a running record of capital forms and capital rights.

Marple, 1964, 112

355 Double entry bookkeeping said to be based otherwise than on property rights

The art of Italian bookkeeping is called bookkeeping by double entry, because there must be two entries; the first being a charging of a person, money, or goods; and the second, a discharging of a person, money or goods. [139]

Anon, 1737/1984, 41

By double entry is meant that the sum is twice entered . . . . Thus, for every debit, there is a corresponding credit, and *vice versa*. And the total amounts of debits and credits are equilibrated by each other.

Jackson, 1827/1896, 4

Bookkeeping by double entry means, that for every sum entered on the one side of an account in the ledger, the same sum or amount must be entered on the opposite side of some other account or accounts.

Morrison, 1849, 43

Double entry bookkeeping consists in keeping trace of the coequal receipt and disbursement of values, and showing the twofold result of their exchanges.

Folsom, 1873/1976, 318

The [double entry] system is based on the doctrine of equilibrium, that is to say that tendency supposed to be inherent in the nature of things, which makes them seek to maintain a harmonious balance among their sundry elements. Business is amenable to the doctrine of equilibrium.

Esquerré, 1914, 69

Every transaction that results in a transfer of money or money's worth involves a twofold aspect, (a) the yielding of a benefit, and (b) the receiving of that benefit . . . . The giving and receiving, however, take place between accounts and in the same set of books . . . . to have a complete record of each transaction, there must be a double entry.

Carter, 1923, 4

The [double entry] system takes advantage of the fact that every transaction may be considered from two aspects . . . .

Moore, 1937, 2

What double entry does is to combine the possibility of both measures of income and the measure of proprietorship within the one system, and it is this potentiality that is the distinctive feature of a coherent system of double entry bookkeeping.

Goldberg, 1965, 218

the bookkeeping process involves a system that embraces two equal, opposing, contrasting, initially independent elements, neither of which can be conceived as existing without the other or as having an importance greater or less than that of the other. We call these elements debit and credit.

Kohler, 1965a, 34

what makes the double entry system double is not the double classification (assets = equity) that is often described in accounting literature but rather the cost principle, which recognizes the causal relationship between an asset acquired and an asset forgone. In this sense, the double entry system and the historical cost principle . . . have a logical connection since one is a form developed to express the other.

Ijiri, 1967, 107

all transactions . . . have two aspects, one recording the acquisition of a resource, the other recording the source used to finance the acquisition. These two aspects of any transaction are represented by twin (or double) entries in the books of account – hence the term double entry bookkeeping

Arnold & others, 1985, 98

356 Double entry as an organizing principle

The method by double entry, as complex in most counting houses as it is obscure, hath something mysterious implied even in its very name. And surely there never was a more infamous and cunningly devised system ever formed, though not intended to be so originally . . . . few arguments will be necessary to prove to the conviction of every candid mind, that it only tends to cover in secrecy the worst of purposes, by systematic art. The principles of this system are, that for every occurrence in trade there must be made a double entry; so that the debit and credit, or both sides of the ledger, may balance . . . . But will this prove, as it ought, that the amount of every entry in the day book is contained in the ledger, and that every transaction is posted to its proper account? .... it is very easy to make a ledger wear the appearance of correctness, which, at the same time, may contain errors or erroneous statements on every page, or entries made in some particular account on purpose to deceive! .... Would two pictures being exactly alike prove that they were a correct copy of the original?

Jones, 1796/1978, 22

The chief use of a statement which balances is the smug satisfaction it affords to the bookkeeper. It does not signify accurate or trustworthy accounts. Many of the flagrantly false accounts which I have seen were in perfect balance and so far as looks were concerned could not have been improved. I can't emphasize too strongly the importance of getting at the substance of a balance sheet and subordinating its form.

Montgomery, 1919, 7

the double entry record is a subordinate form of statistical technique.

Scott, 1926, 20

Accountancy students are normally taught by the textbooks to regard double entry bookkeeping as the foundation on which the rest of the structure is built. It must, however, be clear that this statistical technique can never add anything to the original data, though it may well present that data in such a way that information becomes available which would not otherwise be disclosed.

Edwards, 1938b, 13

As used in the bookkeeping technique, the device [double entry] is unquestionably a worthy one. The difficulty lies in the fact that the accountant has allowed the device to influence his philosophy ....

Dohr, 1941, 201

Double entry is a wonderful servant but a bad master.

Solomons, 1948/1950, 365

the double entry system ... must be regarded as a technical device which facilitates the recording, classifying and summarizing of financial data .... in the past too great satisfaction has been derived from the result of a process which, while accurate within limits, will be of very limited value unless one is aware of the methods that have been adopted in the gathering, measuring, and determining of the data employed.

Johnston, 1949, 65

double entry is a valuable technique of combined recording and analysis; but it is only a technique. It is no more the whole of accounting than a gardening spade is the whole of horticulture.

May, 1955a, 42

The basic concepts in accounting are not dependent upon the double entry system of recording. Any discussion of recording techniques should be based upon clear ideas of the fundamental concepts that remain the same regardless of the form of written records.

Staubus, 1956, 294

Double entry is basically a classifying device of considerable efficacy, adaptability and versatility. As such the system itself does not determine what transactions or items should fall within its sway . . . . [it] has little, if any, influence on profit calculations and balance sheet valuations . . . . all the system does in this field is to ensure consistency between the profit calculation and net changes in recorded asset values.

Yamey, 1956, 11

357 The accounting identity

The equilibrium of debtors and creditors [debits and credits] . . . we may justly lay . . . down as the fundamental principle of bookkeeping – a principle not of art or invention, but of science and discovery; not of mere expediency, but of absolute necessity, and inseparable from the nature of accounts.

Cronhelm, 1818/1978, 10

That the whole is equal to the sum of its parts . . . is an axiom in mathematics; and this axiom constitutes the basis of double entry . . . . the stock account exhibits the whole capital, taken collectively; the money, personal and merchandise accounts exhibit the parts of which the capital is composed. Hence there must necessarily and inevitably be a constant equality between the stock account on the one hand and all the remaining accounts on the other.

Foster, 1843, 15

All the operations of double entry bookkeeping are transformations of the following equation:

what I have + what I trust = what I owe + what I am worth,

or symbolically written,

$H + T = O + X$

Sprague, 1880, 2

these two classes of facts, property and equities, will always be numerically equal, for they are merely different aspects of the same thing.

Paton, 1917, 9

All statements of financial position express the fundamental fact that

What I own + What I claim = What I owe + What I am worth . . . .

or Assets = Liabilities + Capital.

Gundelfinger, 1924, 331

One cannot have capital without having obtained it from some source; nor can there be assets without claimants. The relationship is frequently expressed as an equation, either

Business capital = Sources of business capital, or

Assets = Liabilities (debts) + Net worth (proprietorship) . . . .

the only possible types of business transactions are those involving (a) asset changes, (b) liability changes, (c) net worth changes . . . . every transaction must consist of two or more of these changes in opposing aspects . . . . there are only nine combinations of change possible.

Porter & Fiske, 1935, 21, 52

The equation [assets – liabilities = proprietorship] is a value equation. Each of the three terms . . . is expressed in terms of money used as a standard or common denominator of value . . . . expressing money's worth according to some criterion or set of criteria with respect to proper valuation.

Moonitz & Staehling, 1952, I:44

all of the assets of the business, at any point in time, are subject to the claims of debt holders or owners. This relationship, which is commonly known as the accounting equation, may be expressed in the following form:

Assets = Liabilities + Ownership interest

Arnold & others, 1985, 100

360 Information Processing Orientations

361 Alternative processing orientations

It is, I think, a fundamental error to regard double entry bookkeeping as anything more than a very useful technique; and even as a technique, its usefulness has been impaired since the concept of income as an increase in net worth has given way to the concept of income as an excess of revenues over costs. Under the older concept of income a single analysis yielded both a series of statements of financial position and analyses of the elements of change from which the income account could be prepared. At the present time the analysis yields a detailed income statement, but what is still called the balance sheet is now a collection of heterogeneous residuals. [letter to R J C of Aug 15, 1956]

May, 1956

Some people view earnings as a measure of increase in net resources of a business enterprise during a period [the asset and liability view] . . . . Articulation of the statements of earnings and financial position is an integral part of the asset and liability view . . . . Articulation makes measurement of earnings and measurement of increases and decreases in assets and liabilities parts of the same measurement, and . . . earnings are the dependent variable . . . . Some people . . . . define earnings primarily in terms of the difference between revenues and expenses for a period [the revenue and expense view] . . . . They commonly describe financial accounting,

363

and especially earnings measurement, as a process of matching costs with revenues .... Advocates of the revenue and expense view emphasize that the resulting list of assets, liabilities, etc. makes no representation that it reflects the wealth of the enterprise.

FASB, 1976b, 38–40

One approach, called revenue-expense .... places primacy on the income statement, principles of income recognition, and rules of income measurement. Assets and liabilities are defined, recognized, and measured as a byproduct of revenues and expense. The other approach is called asset-liability .... Emphasis is placed on the definition, recognition, and measurement of assets and liabilities. Income is defined, recognized, and measured as a byproduct of asset and liability measurement.

Wolk & others, 1984, 259

a difference of opinion ... has divided accountants for decades about the nature of profit and how it should be measured .... the revenue and expense view sees profit (or loss) for a period as the difference between revenues for the period and the expenses of earning those revenues. The process of matching costs and revenues usually involves numerous allocations of costs among activities and also among periods .... the asset and liability view sees profit (or loss) as the change in the net worth of the entity attributable to the period excluding the effects of contributions or withdrawals of capital by the owners. On this view, profit or loss is the difference between the excess of assets over liabilities [at the end] of the period and the excess at the beginning of the period.

Solomons, 1989, 16

Cutting the process of income determination loose from a strict relationship to changes in owners' equity, as the revenue and expense approach does, removes the discipline of having to show that all the debits and credits in the profit and loss account represent real transactions or the effects on the business of real outside events and conditions .... it would increase the subjectivity of income determination. It opens the door to all kinds of income smoothing; and in general it leaves management freer to decide what goes into the profit and loss account and what goes into the balance sheet, for deferred debits and credits that are not assets and liabilities ... are as readily admissible to the balance sheet as those that are. That may well be the reason why preparers of financial statements generally favor the revenue and expense view .... On the other side ..., one of the principal objections raised against the asset and liability view is that it tends to make profit a more volatile figure than the other approach .... The answer to that is that volatility is a fact of life, and it is not the accountant's job to pretend otherwise.

Solomons, 1989, 17–18

The asset-liability view depends on definitions of assets and liabilities to define earnings, whereas the revenue-expense view depends on definitions of revenues and expenses and matching .... [Under the asset-liability view, earnings] can be rigorously defined only in terms of changes in net resources. Under the revenue-expense view, earnings are the difference between revenues and expenses [which] . . . may include items necessary to match costs with revenues, even if they do not represent changes in net resources.

Robinson, 1991, 110

See also 424, 425, 604

362 Posited primacy of financial position and the balance sheet

The balance sheet may certainly be said to be the most important statement of any which can be laid before the shareholders, as, if properly drawn up, it shows the exact financial position of the company.

Pixley, 1881/1976, 129

The balance sheet is the most important financial statement.

Paton & Stevenson, 1918/1978, 201

The balance sheet . . . is the basic technical statement, and from this standpoint . . . it outranks the income sheet in importance . . . . The balance sheet is also the most widely used and highly developed accounting statement.

Paton, 1924, 477

In the structure of modern financial life, the balance sheet is becoming increasingly the chief foundation stone.

Kester, 1933, 1

To the majority of business men, bankers and investors, the balance sheet is the most important single report prepared by the accountant . . . . The banker uses it as a basis for credit; the investor, as a basis for investment; and the business man, as a basis for control of his business.

Porter & Fiske, 1935, 242

Proprietorship (P) is the dependent variable [in the basic equation], derived from the subtraction of liabilities from assets. One consequence of this characteristic is that logically we must always reason from facts with respect to A [assets] and L [liabilities] to facts with respect to P, but never the other way around.

Moonitz & Staehling, 1952, I:43

It has been popular in recent years to maximize the importance of the income statement . . . . There is, however, some evidence that the pendulum is gradually swinging in the other direction, partially through the insistence of credit men that earning power is not the sole factor of importance in credit granting . . . and . . . because the balance sheet is still an integral part of the presentation of a company's financial affairs.

Werntz, 1953b, 569

the balance sheet embodies the most fundamental elements of accounting theory, from which the essential elements contained in the income statement are necessarily derived. Indeed, the income statement can properly be described as merely a summary of one class of transactions resulting in changes in one balance sheet account.

Sprouse, 1971, 90

Financial reporting for solvency evaluation is the forgotten half of financial reporting.

Heath & Rosenfield, 1979, 49

363 The income statement as connecting link

The income statement is a connecting link between two balance sheets.

Scott, 1925, 30

Linking the balance sheet at the beginning of the period with that at its close is the statement of income operations . . . .

Kester, 1946, 79

For years we have thought of the income statement as connecting successive balance sheets.

Mautz, 1952, 82

The profit and loss account is a valuable connecting link between one balance sheet and the next . . . .

Jones, 1970, 561

The position taken here . . . amounts to holding that the basic accounting process is reflected in the succession of periodic position statements, with accompanying and connecting income reports.

Paton & Paton, 1971, 17

364 Posited primacy of income and the income account

a well kept profit and loss account was of far more value in regard to the condition of a company than any balance sheet ever constructed, more especially as it appeared that in the case of the balance sheet some of the legitimate assets could not be shown. [reported]

Welton, 1894, 1042

It is probably fairly well recognized by intelligent investors today that the earning capacity is the fact of crucial importance in the valuation of an industrial enterprise, and that therefore the income account is usually far more important than the balance sheet.

AIA, 1932

The early choice of the balance sheet as the main statement tends to place finance above operations; and finance, in turn, looks upon value in exchange as basic. Why should the balance sheet . . . have come to occupy first place in public accounting when the income statement (wherein value for exchange could not be at issue) would seem to be the natural summary of the chief data of a business enterprise?

Littleton, 1935b, 270

the past half dozen years have witnessed a shift in accounting emphasis from the balance sheet to the profit and loss viewpoint.

Gilman, 1939, iii

The primary purpose of accounting . . . is the measurement of periodic income by means of a systematic process of matching costs and revenues.

Paton & Littleton, 1940, 123

Perhaps the most significant change of all is the shift of emphasis from the balance sheet to the income account, and particularly to the income account as a guide to earning capacity rather than as an indication of accretions to disposable income.

May, 1943, 5

We consider that the profit and loss account is as important as, if not more important than, the balance sheet, since the trend of profits is the best indication of the prosperity of the company and the value of the assets depends largely on the maintenance of the business as a going concern.

Cohen Committee (UK), 1945

accountants now think more of producing as accurate a profit and loss account as possible, with a balance sheet as a by-product, rather than of producing a balance sheet with a profit and loss account as a by-product.

de Paula, 1949, 9

The modern emphasis on enterprise income rather than solvency suggests that reporting on management's stewardship is now better done through the income statement than the balance sheet.

Littleton, 1953, 21

Income is an important index of economic progress, and its determination is the principal object in accounting today.

Backer, 1955a/1955b, 209

accountants bent on belittling the balance sheet . . . . – [a group] which includes most of our leading writers – . . . . tend to dismiss the balance sheet as a mere appendage of the revenue account – a mausoleum for the unwanted costs that the double entry system throws up as regrettable by-products.

Baxter, 1962, vi

today, the prime objective of accounting is income measurement .... a reasonable measurement can be achieved by the systematic matching of costs and related revenues.

Mulcahy, 1963, 8

The information presented in an income statement is usually considered the most important information provided by financial accounting because profitability is a paramount concern to those interested in the economic activities of the enterprise.

AICPA, 1970c, APBS4

by the end of the 1930s the older approach to financial reporting was largely overturned, and the foundations of present day accounting theory were firmly established .... the emphasis of accounting in the 1930s began to switch away from valuation, and towards rules to ensure: no recognition of income or gain before confirmation by actual transactions; a fair matching of costs and revenues to determine earned income properly .... As a result the focus of accounting theory shifted from the balance sheet to the income statement, from asset and liability valuation procedures to revenue and cost allocation procedures.

Skinner, 1972b, 39

The primary focus of financial reporting is information about ... earnings and its components.

FASB, 1978, SFAC1

365 The balance sheet as connecting link

While the profit and loss account shows the results of business operations, the balance sheet takes over the task of accounting for all incomplete transactions involving receipts, payments, revenue and expenditure .... such items remain in the balance sheet ... until they have become both revenue and receipt, or expenditure and payment; then they disappear.

Schmalenbach, 1919/1959, 53

The balance sheet ... serves as a means of carrying forward unamortized acquisition prices, the not yet deducted costs; it stands as a connecting link that joins successive income statements into a picture of the income stream. This conception of the balance sheet has no place for valuation in the sense of subjective judgment of utility, probable replacement price or sales price.

Littleton, 1939, 60

The result of this [increased recognition of the significance of the income statement] ... is a tendency to regard the balance sheet as the connecting link between successive income statements and as the vehicle for the distribution of charges and credits between them. Important as this concept is, however, it should not obscure the fact that the balance sheet has significant uses of its own.

AIA, 1939a, ARB1

The balance sheets are ... simply the connecting links of a series of income statements.

Dohr, 1942, 218

a balance sheet serves the essential purpose of connecting profit and loss accounts; it is the link between successive income statements ....

Accountant, editorial, 1946c, 294

The balance sheet ... provides a connecting link between successive statements of profit and loss.

Mulcahy, 1963, 6

most of the amounts on the balance sheet are residual figures, ... the resultants of decisions which have been made from the point of view of the income statement.

Graham, 1965, 661

The term financial position is often used to mean the balance sheet as it is drawn from accounting ledgers and based on current accounting conventions and accounting practice. As a result, the statement of financial position is a residual statement – a step between two income statements. As such it provides little information because it lacks interpretability.

Hendriksen, 1982, 255

366 The complementarity of the financial statements

As unto the bow the cord is,
And unto the man is woman,
So unto the income statement
Is the statement of condition
Useless each without the other.

Wilcox, 1941a, 76

The absolute figure [net profit] by itself is meaningless. It only derives meaning by comparison with .... the capital employed in earning it .... The postulated primacy of the income statement is thus a myth. Internal and external parties using net profit as a measure of general performance ... are obliged to link it with some more satisfactory measure than paid up capital or the par value of ordinary share capital. A statement such as the balance sheet can provide this measure. The income statement and the balance sheet are thus equally necessary for informed action.

Chambers, 1957, 565

The relative importance of the income statement and the balance sheet is sometimes the subject of debate. Earlier the balance sheet was given the greater emphasis. Currently, emphasis is placed on the income statement. The debate is fruitless .... an income statement [may] exhibit marked achievement while its accompanying balance sheet exhibits weak financial structure .... The two statements ... are to be viewed as presenting necessary parts of an integrated whole; they complement each other.

Husband, 1960, 479

despite the ascendancy of the importance of the income statement from the security analyst's and creditor's point of view, the auditing emphasis . . . should still be on the balance sheet. An auditor's assurance of a valid opinion on the income statement is greater if he concentrates on the balance sheets at both ends of the period than if he devotes the equivalent time to the income statement.

Defliese, 1962, 43

Earning power is the most important fact in assaying the performance of any business undertaking . . . . It is necessary to link earnings to resources employed before any conclusion as to degree of success can be formed.

Paton, 1963, 61

the financial statements are complementary to each other, rather than one subordinate to the other.

Patillo, 1965, 48

the balance sheet and the income statement are only two parts of the same process – they are each an integral part of the measurement of income. We can never measure income sensibly without reference to assets and liabilities . . . . To disparage the balance sheet is to disparage the income statement, too.

Smyth, 1968, 157

I have often heard it stated that the income statement has more significance than the balance sheet. This statement is a fallacy. The two statements go hand in glove and they are articulate. If one is biased, equally the other must be biased.

Somekh, 1972, 87

367 Financial statements necessarily articulated

the proof of bookkeeping by double entry consists of two methods of ascertaining what you are worth: the one from a view of your present effects and debts; the other, from your former stock, allowance being made for your profits and losses; and both will correspond if the books be correct.

Morrison, 1825, 47

Double entry bookkeeping is such that receipts and payments which are not closed off to the income account are carried forward and . . . appear in the balance sheet. Hence the decision as to what to disclose in the balance sheet is essentially the same as the decision as to what to put in the income account . . . . for income measurement we cannot distinguish between the importance of the two documents.

Edwards, 1938b, 289

The income account is not more fundamental than the balance sheet. It cannot be so because balance sheet valuations are generally another aspect of income measurements.

Nelson, 1942, 141

under a double entry bookkeeping system income may be measured either by a comparison of successive balance sheets or by an analysis of transactions, one method being used as a check on the other.

May, 1943, 215

the balance sheet and the profit and loss statement are essential, coordinate elements in an integrated structure; neither, therefore, is a mere link in the preparation of the other .... each theory of asset valuation necessarily has inherent within it a theory of income, and each theory of income has inherent within it a theory of asset valuation.

Storey, 1958/1978, 5, 30

The results of the accounting process are expressed in a set of fundamentally related financial statements which articulate with each other and rest upon the same underlying data.

Moonitz, 1961, 27

Profit can always be defined, in some sense, to mean an increase in net worth. The calculation of profit, that is to say, always involves the calculation of net worth from the position statements of two successive periods .... This may not be obvious to accounting students trained to draft income statements before balance sheets. But the costs and revenues in the former statement are all implicit in the changes in the latter, and are measured by these changes.

Boulding, 1962, 49

[Many people] feel that net income is the most important figure, and they seem to believe, contrary to logic, that you can have a realistic figure for net income without necessarily having realistic balance sheet values. This is absurd .... since balance sheet values result from an accumulation of income figures, either both statements are realistically stated or neither is.

Ross, 1969, 153

The rigorous disciplines of the double entry accounting system demonstrate that there is a close, intimate and articulated relationship between the income statement and the balance sheet. Valuation rules in the balance sheet have their implications for the income account, and the matching process in the income account determines the values and equities shown in the balance sheet.

Stamp, 1971, 281

Although we sometimes attempt to separate the question of how to value assets from the question of how to measure income, the two are, in fact, inextricably intertwined. This is indicated by the fact that we often say that our financial statements articulate .... Thus, when one talks about different methods of valuation, and the conflicts between them, one is also at the same time talking about conflicts in income measurement.

Sterling, 1972, 201

The financial statements of an entity are a fundamentally related set that articulate with each other and derive from the same underlying data.

FASB, 1984, SFAC5

See also 613

368 Articulation of financial statements said to be unnecessary

In my view, stock [inventory] is not necessarily valued for the balance sheet on the same basis as it is valued for the trading account.

Bigg, 1946, 210

The determination of income based on current cost does not necessarily imply that the balance sheet should be correspondingly revised to reflect assets and proprietorship at present values. I doubt the advisability of constantly adjusting book values in the books or on the balance sheet to a current cost or present value basis.

Graham, 1949, 26

Must the accounting profession accept without question the subordinate position to which the balance sheet has been relegated by the development of income statement theory? Is there anything inherent in the situation which forbids the reinvigoration of the balance sheet by cutting it loose from income statement practice, reconciling perhaps through surplus reserves?

McMullen, 1950, 484

We find no logical reason why external reports should be expected to balance or articulate with each other. In fact, we find that forced balancing and articulation have frequently restricted the presentation of relevant information.

AAA, 1969, 118

The structural approach to accounting theory, which treats balance-sheet income statement articulation as axiomatic, seriously limits the search for more useful information constructs.

Rappaport, 1971, 113

there is no necessity for an interdependent income and financial position statement. On the contrary the burden of our argument is that these two statements fulfil their functions appreciably better if they are each based on different data [the income statement on replacement prices, the balance sheet on current cash equivalents].

Macdonald, 1974a, 130

Under the ... method dubbed lifo/fifo, a company would use lifo to measure cost of goods sold in its income statement and fifo to report inventories in its balance sheet .... proponents of lifo/fifo contend that this method produces more realistic financial information than lifo or fifo.

Bohan & Rubin, 1986, 106

370 Processing Dicta

371 Recognition in accounting

Losses should be recognized and reported in the period of their occurrence and gains should be recognized in the period in which they are realized.

Kester, 1946, 43

Conservatism encourages the recognition of all losses that have occurred or are likely to occur but does not acknowledge gains until actually realized .... In reality, however, it has often tended to create distortions in income and the shifting of profits from one period to another.

Backer, 1955a/1955b, 212

the recognition of unrealized revenues and losses ... makes the accuracy of the accounting record depend to a significant extent on future events .... Clearly, however, if unrealized revenues and losses are to be brought into account, the estimates must be based on observed phenomena, such as commodity price lists or market quotations, and not on mere subjective hopes, aspirations, and fears.

Mathews, 1962, 120

Recognition is primarily a problem of deciding what constitutes reasonable, verifiable evidence; it hinges on objective measurement.

Horngren, 1965, 325

A transaction arises from the recognition within an organization of an event or condition, following as the consequence of (1) the acceptance of responsibility for its initiation, propriety, execution, and correctness, (2) the incidence of the completed event or observed condition, (3) the ascertainment of the money amount involved, (4) the administrative review of supporting data that supply evidence of component elements, (5) the determination of its effect on specific accounts, and (6) its formal absorption in the records.

Kohler, 1965a, 26

An asset is an economic good that the accountant has decided to report to investors; often the decision to report a good is designated the accountant's recognizing the good as an asset, and one speaks of this as asset recognition.

Thomas & Basu, 1972, 41

Recognition is the process of formally recording or incorporating an item into the financial statements of an entity .... Recognition attempts to represent or depict in financial statements the effects on an entity of real world economic things and events.

Johnson & Storey, 1982, 2

Recognition addresses the fundamental accounting question: which phenomena should be represented on financial statements? .... Recognition tests are for the purpose of deciding which words and numerals should be displayed and which should not be displayed.

Sterling, 1985, 84, 2

An item should be recognized in financial statements if: (a) it conforms to the definition of an asset or liability ... ; and (b) its magnitude as specified by the accounting model being used can be measured and verified with reasonable certainty; and (c) the magnitude so arrived at is material in amount.

Solomons, 1989, 43

See also 372, 623

372 Conservatism in accounting

Conservatism, as used in accounting, ordinarily means any action which tends to keep down the value of assets, which understates rather than exaggerates the showing of profits.

Hatfield, 1927/1971, 99

By conservatism is meant an attitude which strives to avoid the overstatement of the proprietorship of an enterprise. It leads to a relatively low valuation of assets, with a relatively high valuation of liabilities .... The notion that conservatism is a desirable feature of accounting valuation is more than a mere assumption; it is a conviction.

Rorem, 1928, 291

the principle of conservatism, the tendency to record the least favorable [from the standpoint of the business] of two or more alternatives .... It represents, perhaps, an attempt to offset the natural optimism of the business man by accepting the most pessimistic of two or more possibilities.

Bell & Graham, 1936, 311

Losses, if probable, even though not actually incurred, should be provided for in arriving at net income.

Byrne, 1937, 372

the question of what is and what is not conservative .... must depend upon a consideration of three factors taken in conjunction, namely, (1) the policy determining the original charges to property, (2) the policy determining the amount of actual maintenance done, and the allocation of this between property and expense accounts, (3) the rates of depreciation charged. It is possible for a company to be conservative in one of these respects and extravagant in another, with the net result of following an approximately sound policy. While, therefore, the responsible accountant will wish to develop a sound treatment for each of these matters considered separately, the essential thing is that all three of them in combination constitute sound practice.

Sanders & others, 1938, 61

The doctrine of conservatism as applied to the income statement recognizes income only after realization in terms of cash or its substantial equivalent and provides not only for realized but also for probable costs, expenses and losses.

Montgomery & others, 1949, 427

Conservatism in accounting consists principally of counting gains only when realized but anticipating costs and losses as soon as possible.

Alexander, 1950, 55

A most important accounting doctrine in effect on accounting statements is the doctrine of conservatism, viz. that statements should be prepared in such a way as not to overstate profits or financial strength, nor to understate losses. It is motivated by the business maxim of prudence, of being always on the safe side, and can be defended from the standpoint of the owner or the creditor.

Fitzgerald, 1956a, 16

Businessmen in their quest for optimum profit attempt ... to maximize revenues and to minimize expenses. Accountants, however, seem to follow the opposite pattern when measuring a firm's performance. I suggest that when accountants measure revenues they minimeasure them, and that when they measure expenses they maximeasure them. The net effect of this optimeasurement is a deferral in the recognition of income. Optimeasurement will be recognized immediately to encompass the notion of accounting conservatism.

Jacobsen, 1963, 286

Conservatism is .... a quality of judgment to be exercised in evaluating the uncertainties and risks present in a business entity to assure that reasonable provisions are made for potential losses in the realization of recorded assets and in the settlement of actual and contingent liabilities.

Grady, 1965, 35

In case of doubt, that treatment shall be adopted which minimizes the reported figure of profit and/or asset valuation, or maximizes the reported figure of loss and/or liability valuation.

Lee, 1973, 16

Prudence

the whole object of the business is to convert these items [floating assets] into cash at the earliest possible moment .... any shrinkage [in intrinsic value] that may have taken place must consequently be regarded as a realized loss .... *Per contra* appreciations in the value of these floating assets might with equal propriety be credited to revenue, but as ... there must always be doubt as to whether such appreciation has actually occurred, it is only prudent to postpone taking credit for the assumed profit until such time as it has been actually earned.

Dicksee, 1903a, 5

Assets are often, by reason of prudence, estimated, and stated to be estimated, at less than their probable real value. The purpose of the balance sheet is primarily to show that the financial position of the company is at least as good as there stated, not to show that it is not or may not be better. [per Wrenbury L J]

Newton v Birmingham Small Arms Co Ltd, 1906

Accountants have been reproached for their conservatism but in so far as such conservatism has sought to safeguard the long term financial stability of business enterprise it has been itself a factor making for economic well being.

Bray, 1947, 23

the profit disclosed by a profit and loss statement must be interpreted in the light of accounting concepts of profit, and must be regarded as an expression of opinions which have been formed with special care for financial prudence ....

Fitzgerald & Fitzgerald, 1948, 16

the concept of prudence: revenue and profits are not anticipated but are recognized ... only when realized in the form either of cash or of other assets the ultimate cash realization of which can be assessed with reasonable certainty; provision is made for all known liabilities (expenses and losses) whether the amount of these is known with certainty or is a best estimate in the light of the information available.

ASSC, 1971b, SSAP2

valuation must be made on a prudent basis, and in particular: only profits made at the balance date may be included, account must be taken of all foreseeable liabilities and potential losses ... [arising earlier than the balance date], account must be taken of all depreciation ....

EEC, 1978, 4 Directive

The amount of any item shall be determined on a prudent basis, and in particular, (a) only profits realized at the balance sheet date shall be included in the profit and loss account; and (b) all liabilities and losses which have arisen or are likely to arise in respect of the financial year to which the accounts relate or a previous financial year shall be taken into account, including those which only become apparent between

the balance sheet date and the date on which it is signed on behalf of the board
of directors .... [Schedule 1]

UK *Companies Act,* 1981

Objections to conservatism (or prudence)

The accountant transcends the conservatism of the proverb, "Do not count your
chickens before they are hatched", saying, "Here are a lot of chickens already safely
hatched, but for the love of Mike use discretion and do not count them all, for
perhaps some will die".

Hatfield, 1927/1971, 256

You can always be conservative in a balance sheet; you can never be consistently
conservative in income accounts. It is mathematically impossible.

Peloubet, 1938/1982, 356

The extraordinary and grotesque mixing of ideas of financial prudence and the scientific job of taking a measurement has ... a firm hold on the mind of the average
accountant .... to the extent that he is, in his opinion, prudent in preparing accounts,
he is, in my view, lacking in prudence .... he is avoiding the truth ....

Norris, 1939, 846

conservatism, to the extent of understatement now, generally means overstatement
in the future. Thus overzealous attempts at conservatism are not only harmful in
their immediate misleading effects, but also involve more deception to follow.

Wilcox & Hassler, 1941, 311

Conservatism in the statement of results of operations in the past may lead to overstatement of the profits of a later period.

May, 1943, 24

The most objectionable and obstructive tradition of accounting is conservatism, so
called.

Paton, 1948, 279

The justification offered for hiding profits is often that shareholders, if they knew
the true profits, would make irresponsible claims and thus jeopardize future earnings.
This may be so, but the other half of the argument rests on an assumption of managerial infallibility and omniscience not often borne out by the facts.

Lachmann, 1956, 93

The overthrow of conservatism as an accounting doctrine does not necessarily mean
that it should cease to operate as a commercial or financial policy. In its own financial
sphere conservatism is a perfectly legitimate procedure.

Mathews, 1962, 118

conservatism is not a useful or valid principle in accounting. The basic criterion used to decide the superiority of one method over another should be that of accuracy. If accounting is to serve a useful purpose the information it seeks to convey should be as accurate as possible. Conservatism should have no place in accounting theory; caution is a matter of policy, not of principle.

Wixley, 1967, 436

Conservatism . . . is basically biased. Conservatism may protect potential investors at the expense of present stockholders. It seeks to protect the purchaser and the lender, but disregards the interests of the seller and the borrower.

Andersen & Co, 1972, 37

There is a real danger that this attitude [conservatism] may introduce bias into financial statements, thereby diminishing their usefulness and conflicting with the need to produce a realistic view.

NZR, 1976, 44

three major weaknesses of the prudence concept: (1) it assists management to suppress profits . . . ; (2) it is theoretically unsound, clashing as it does with many other . . . fundamental concepts . . . ; and (3) it is interpreted in a highly inconsistent manner throughout the standards published so far, sometimes harshly, sometimes liberally.

Lothian, 1982, 409

prudence is a chacteristic of persons, not of information. It does not belong to a list of fundamental accounting concepts.

Solomons, 1989, 41

373 Substance and form

We cannot exhibit matter without form, or form without matter: . . .

Whewell, 1860, 465

Consolidated balance sheets and income accounts represent an effort to look through form to substance: . . . .

Staub, 1929/1982, 657

Managerial actions, of course, rest largely upon the supposed amounts of earned surplus and net income. Hence, when these amounts are decidedly wrong [as in conventional accounting consequential on inflation or deflation], actions pertaining to dividends, expansion, wages, employment, and so on become, likewise, decidedly wrong. Then business fails to satisfy the needs of society at large to the extent that it might, and the people as a whole are penalized just because accounting chooses to rest on form instead of substance.

Sweeney, 1936/1964, 160

Financial accounting emphasizes the economic substance of events even though the legal form may differ from the economic substance . . . . so that information provided better reflects the economic activities represented.

AICPA, 1970c, APBS4

The guidelines for reporting information should be expressed so that substance, not form, governs. The Study Group, in framing definitions and objectives, has attempted to follow this principle. For example, ... the test for realization of sacrifices and benefits stresses probabilities rather than a formal event such as a sale. The definition of assets also highlights the substantive question of the presence of future benefits, regardless of the formality of ownership rights. The substantive economic characteristic, not the legal or technical form, should establish the accounting for transactions and other events.

AICPA, 1973, 57

Generally accepted accounting principles recognize the importance of recording transactions in accordance with their substance. The auditor should consider whether the substance of transactions differs materially from their form.

AICPA, 1975, AU411

[In accounting today] . . . business substance rather than legal form must predominate in the analysis of transactions and the determination of the accounting to be followed for them.

Burton, 1975, 36

Transactions and other events should be accounted for and presented in accordance with their substance and financial reality and not merely with their legal form.

IASC, 1974, IAS1

Financial statements should report the substance of economic events, even if their substance differs from their legal form.

Anthony, 1983, 62

If financial information is to be both relevant and reliable, it is necessary that the substance rather than the form of transactions and events be reported. The concept of relevance indicates the type of information with which general purpose financial reporting should be concerned, and this will not always be consistent with legal or contrived form.

AARF & ASRB, 1989, SAC3

374 Convenience, simplicity, etc. as desiderata

in an ordinary concern the various items in, say, a plant and machinery account are constantly undergoing change, by the addition, renewal, or sale of the various items included therein, and in such cases the employment of a fixed rate of depreciation on the diminishing value is the most convenient method.

Jenkinson, 1910, 77

the time honored straight line method [of calculating depreciation], the principal merit of which is convenience.

JA, editorial, 1949, 271

the increasing emphasis on cost as distinct from value originally was based partly ... upon convenience and practicality and partly upon recognition of the increased importance of the income statement as an indication of earning capacity.

Broad, 1949, 383

[The] straight line basis .... of allocation [for depreciation] has the great advantage of simplicity and ease of application; it is easy to understand, therefore, why it is the method most commonly used.

Dohr, 1950a, 117

If the expense of a period is easiest to determine objectively, the related and applicable revenue will be matched to the expense; or if the period's revenue is easiest to determine objectively, the related and applicable expense will be matched to the revenue. The clue to matching expense and revenue in the income statement may therefore come from either factor.

Littleton, 1953, 68

Consideration of convenience must enter into any decision [on income account charges under inflation] and it may well be argued that if the value of money is only going to fluctuate around a norm, the gain in equity to be derived from putting exhaustion charges on a current price level basis is not sufficient to justify the inconvenience of a change [from prevalent practice].

May, 1955b, 701

A convention, as distinct from an axiom, may be said to exist when it is known that an alternative, equally logical rule or procedure is available but is not used because of considerations of habit, cost, time or convenience.

Kohler, 1952, 118

the matching concept is easier to apply in practice than some other alternatives, such as a periodic revaluation of all business assets.

Spiller, 1964, 853

Among the least impressive but by no means least important of such influences [on the measurement of cost] is that of bookkeeping convenience.

Gordon & Shillinglaw, 1969, 299

The prudence concept is easy to interpret and demands a very low judgmental input from accountants. Rather than having to weigh up evidence and apply professional judgment, accountants simply disallow the recognition of many incomplete economic events which would have the effect of increasing reported profit and asset position .... [For the same reason] it is easier still for the auditors to verify!

Lothian, 1982, 409

The predominant use of cost in arriving at a dollar measure is an example of choosing one attribute instead of another because of its ease of measurement.

Carrington & Howitt, 1983, 28

[Historical cost] can be justified by its convenience.

Baxter, 1989, 37

375 Expedience as desideratum

Conservatism and expediency are to be commended at all times, and are useful offsets to the tendency of business men to fool themselves – to overstate assets and profits and to understate liabilities and losses. But there should be no secrecy about conservatism and expediency.

Montgomery, 1922, I:144

Accounts, I suggest, are prepared for a practical purpose and not to satisfy the minds of accountancy purists. Let us guard against becoming the slaves of theory .... personally I am prepared to sacrifice theoretical principles upon the altar of practical expediency.

de Paula, 1934, 857

to start from a basis of expediency and to work toward the ideal only as expediency might dictate .... is the historical course which accountancy has followed, and its practical effect is to put a premium on expediency and not on ideals. If expediency seems to lead away from ideals, the tendency is to change the ideals themselves by inventing theories which justify the practices necessitated by expediency.

MacNeal, 1939, 175

the character of the conventional rules evolved for measuring profits is arbitrary. For if they are to serve their purpose they must necessarily be definite, understandable, and simple enough to pass into practical administration. It follows then that logic will often be sacrificed to expedience and administrative convenience, and it is clearly possible that rules evolved in this manner may prove in practice far less well-adapted to abnormal than normal conditions.

Moon, 1948, 23

up to the present time many of the decisions rendered on [matching] ... have been based to a large extent upon what may be called practical considerations, conservatism and expediency.

Newlove & Garner, 1951, I:416

Often these [generally accepted accounting] principles have resulted from the gradual widespread acceptance of approaches used by one or a few businesses to solve their problems of accounting for new situations. Too often these principles have resulted more from practical expedience rather than from reasoned logic.

Black & others, 1967, 12

Under the rule of expediency accounting, one starts off with the result in mind which the interested parties may regard as palatable (if not desirable) and then determines the write offs – if any – in a way which will produce that objective. It is not usually difficult to work out the most plausible (even quasi-scientific) justification afterwards, and with luck no one will ask you anyway! It is this very manipulative trait ... which constitutes the real challenge to the drafters of both company law and accounting standards. It is a challenge which has not so far been squarely faced.

Woolf, 1974, 106

376 Circumstances as desiderata

When challenged with the fact that there are so many alternative methods of valuation [of inventories] accountants generally answer that the basis to be adopted depends upon the circumstances. This, however, is surely evasion of the issue.

de Paula, 1937, 489

The Committee on Accounting Procedure while indicating that " ... selection of the method of [inventory valuation] should be made on the basis of the individual circumstances ... " makes no attempt to define or describe what those circumstances comprise; ....

Young, 1957, 203

The circumstances of each business should determine the basis which is appropriate and the method of computation which should be adopted in determining cost [of stock in trade and work in progress] and the part thereof, if any, which should be written off.

ICAEW, 1960, N22

The need is not for uniformity without regard to circumstances. Rather it is the elimination of variations [in accounting principles] which cannot be justified by differences in circumstances ....

Jennings, 1964, 31

What do we mean by differences in circumstances? Does this expression encompass differences in the degree of management optimism or differences in financial policy ...?

Flynn, 1965, 634

While it is clear that circumstances do vary and that different circumstances call for different accounting treatments, it is not clear how one distinguishes among circumstances and chooses among accounting treatments. What is a circumstance in which a departure from customary practice is permissible? How much of a departure is tolerable?

Powell, 1965, 681

this issue of uniformity v. flexibility is a phony issue . . . . surely it is logical to argue that the use of alternative accounting methods should reflect real differences in circumstances . . . . an apparent alternative application of an accounting method is not really an alternative if it can be shown to reflect real differences in the circumstances of the event or transaction.

Skinner, 1966, 163

Two reasons I would rule out as being totally unacceptable: (a) We chose this principle because we have always done so; (b) We chose this principle because it was appropriate to the circumstances.

Morison, 1970b, 470

Generally, no significant differences in economic circumstances were consistently found among firms which use different methods of inventory pricing . . . .

Chasteen, 1971, 508

Once it has been decided that financial information is, in general terms, capable of being classified as relevant and reliable, it is necessary to consider the information in the context of the individual circumstances of the reporting entity in question.

AARF & ASRB, 1990b, SAC3

377 Economy as desideratum

accounting procedures should be kept as simple and economical to operate as is consistent with their efficient functioning and production of genuinely needed information.

Carrington & Battersby, 1963, 47

Materiality . . . . strict adherence to a principle is not required where the increased accuracy in the accounting reports as a result of adhering is not sufficient to justify the increased cost of compliance.

Pyle & White, 1966, 825

The system should be convenient to apply, be capable of yielding frequent measurements and be reasonably cheap.

Finnie, 1968a, 280

It should not require a disproportionate amount of effort and expense by companies to prepare their annual accounts.

Sandilands, 1975, 66

a precise calculus of costs and benefits is out of reach . . . . the cost [of better accounting], initially borne by the preparers, will gradually be diffused, in part by being passed on in the form of higher prices to consumers of whatever it is that the preparers sell. The benefits of better reporting will be diffused among present and potential investors, creditors, and many others. It is unrealistic to suppose that reliable cost-benefit calculations in this field will ever be possible.

Solomons, 1989, 38

A major difficulty facing preparers, auditors, standard setters and others is whether the cost of providing certain financial information exceeds the benefits to be derived from its provision . . . . There is no universally accepted methodology for measuring costs and benefits of financial information.

AARF & ASRB, 1990b, SAC3

378 Suspense accounts

If there is a great fall in values, so that the assets are no longer worth what they cost, they should only be entered in the balance sheet at their present value, and the deficiency should, if possible, be charged to profit and loss. If this is impossible the deficiency should be charged to a suspense account of some sort, so that shareholders may see clearly how much of their capital has been lost.

Wade, 1886, 695

Occasionally it happens that a business cannot at once determine the disposition of some property acquired and dislikes to give it even temporarily a wrong name; yet it is desirable for the acquisition to be in some way recorded in the books. For this suspense account, designating uncertain disposition, is serviceable.

Cole, 1921, 106

Suspense account: an account raised for the reception of items which cannot for any reason be allocated to their correct account, or items held over until disputes, etc, in connection with them are settled . . . .

Pixley, 1926, 2:914

[When] I tried to teach accounting . . . . suspense was a favorite word. It appeared on either side of the balance sheet depending on which side needed it most.

Montgomery, 1937a, 279

If [a loan is obtained in a foreign currency and] the foreign currency subsequently appreciates . . . , the liability should be brought in at the new current rate, but there is no justification for writing up the asset [acquired by means of it]. Instead a suspense balance may be brought into the balance sheet as an asset for the amount of the capital loss arising on the writing up of the liability.

Taylor & Perry, 1952, 190

380 Financial Summaries

381 Information processing; accounts

all systems of bookkeeping endeavor ... to give in some accessible way when needed the most minute information, and, on the other hand, to give the broadest and most comprehensive information.

Sprague, 1901/1984, #1

The task of the accountant may be described generally as that of analysis and correlation of various figures so that the important facts about a business, both the details and the larger meanings, may appear in their proper light and emphasis.

Cole, 1921, 6

The processes of accounting .... [include] .... summarization of the formal record [of external financial transactions and internal operations]. . . ; preparation, from the summarized record, of financial statements in such a form that relationships between various classes of financial obligations and resources are shown; ....

Fitzgerald & Schumer, 1952, 7

One of the tasks of accounting is to reduce the tremendous mass of detailed information contained in a company's business papers to manageable and understandable proportions.

Mautz & Sharaf, 1961, 170

See also 233

Accounts

Accompt, or account. A mercantile term for a collection of several particular sums ready cast up; whereby the profit or loss upon any particular commodity, or the balance due from a person, may be evidently and truly discovered.

Rolt, 1761

An account is a systematic record of financial facts of a similar or opposite tendency, leading to a conclusion.

Sprague, 1901/1984, #1

Speaking generally, an account is not merely – or even substantially – a collection of figures or calculations, but a narrative of the doings of the accounting party . . . .
Dicksee, 1905a, 147

An account is a ledger record, in summarized form, of all the transactions that have taken place with the particular person or thing specified . . . .
Carter, 1923, 3

account: A formal record of a particular type of transaction expressed in money or other unit of measurement and kept in a ledger.
Kohler, 1952, 5

382 Classification

The bases of classification which may be applied to subdivisions of [assets, liabilities, proprietorship, income and expense, are] 1. Intended uses or purposes of the objects or transactions . . . . 2. Inherent qualities or properties of the objects or transactions . . . . 3. Administrative responsibility for the objects or transactions . . . . 4. Financial appropriations or ventures (funds) . . . .
Rorem & Kerrigan, 1942, 494–5

the whole process of accounting is one of classification by stages so that significantly classified information may be prepared and presented.
Fitzgerald & Schumer, 1952, 13

Accountants are indeed concerned with moral right and wrong . . . . there is a morality in right classification and deceit in wrong classification. Bad classification and inadequate disclosure are basically involved in practically all examples of high level business immorality and fraud . . . .
Littleton, 1953, 184

all classifications are man-made; none exist in nature, but are imposed by us on the material we are examining. Classification is in large part a device for defining more sharply the subject matter under discussion.
Moonitz & Staehling, 1952, I:467

there is a sense in which the whole process of accounting may be regarded as a system of classification.
Mathews, 1962, 4

See also 212

Elementary classification of accounts

Personal accounts are limited to such with whom we deal upon mutual trust and credit . . . . Real accounts; the design of these being to know what's on hand at any time, and what's gained or lost; . . . the particular accounts of what quantities and value are from time to time received and disposed of . . . . [Imaginary accounts include stock [capital], profit and loss, and balance accounts.]

Malcolm, 1731, 9

Personal accounts are the mutual transactions between another and me . . . . Real accounts are my real property, either in my possession or in the hands of others. Imaginary accounts [include profit and loss account, partnership . . . .]

Quin, 1776, 9

the books should contain . . . . the debts which are owing to the owner, and the debts which he owes to others [called personal accounts] . . . . the goods and other articles of property which belonged to him . . . and the quantity and value which still remains in his possession [called real accounts] . . . . the amount of his stock when the books were opened; the profits he has obtained, and the losses he has suffered since; and the amount of his stock at present [sometimes called fictitious accounts].

Hamilton, 1788/1982, 265ff

Real accounts are the accounts of effects or things which may be a person's property . . . . Personal accounts are the accounts of the persons we deal with . . . . Imaginary accounts are fictitious titles invented to represent the merchant himself and to record such gains and losses as cannot be ascribed to any real or personal account . . . .

Jackson, 1809, 9

The division of accounts into personal, real and fictitious is one of the most ludicrous that ever enlivened the gravity of the scientific page. Are the personal accounts unreal? or, rather, are they something neither real nor fictitious? Is the stock or proprietor's account a mere fiction? Are the accounts of profit and loss of the same romantic nature? . . . . The proprietor may reasonably expect to find something substantial in his stock account; but the professors of bookkeeping, faithful to the Berkleian theory, gravely assure him that it is all fictitious and imaginary.

Cronhelm, 1818/1978, 27

There are two main divisions of accounts: (1) Personal accounts comprise both debtors and creditors . . . . (2) Impersonal accounts . . . (a) Real or property accounts are those that refer to assets . . . . (b) Nominal accounts are those that relate to gains and losses . . . .

Carter, 1923, 3

383 Trial balance

A trial balance of the ledger should be prepared by folding a sheet of paper length-wise and recording the debit account balances on the left, and the credit account balances on the right. By summing, it is seen whether the debit balances equal the credit balances and whether the ledger is in order.
                              Pacioli, 1494/1963, 102

The true nature of the trial balance was . . . set forth in the book *Indirizzo degli Economi*, published at Mantua in 1586 by the Genoese Benedictine monk, Don Angelo Pietra . . . . Only the balances of open accounts are used, and the equality of debits and credits is determined for the sole purpose of proving whether the ledger is in balance, which is the correct function of the trial balance . . . .
                              Peragallo, 1941, 452

The trial balance is of two sorts: The first is a survey . . . of the ledger accounts . . . . The second sort . . . is seen when all unsold wares and outlandish moneys are rated [priced]: all abatements, as likewise gains and losses, are known.
                              Dafforne, 1684, 46

The first thing to be done in balancing the books, after taking an inventory of the goods on hand at their market prices, is to prove the accuracy of the ledger entries, by forming what is called a trial balance, the design of which is to ascertain if any errors have been committed in posting . . . . For this purpose prepare a sheet of paper as follows:- Write the titles [of the accounts] in the centre [of two money columns], and place the total sum of the debtor side of each account in the left, and the total sum of the creditor side in the right hand money column; add the two columns, and if no mistake has been committed in posting, the [aggregate] amounts will correspond.
                              Foster, 1843, I:33

The balance shown by the trial balance having been adjusted by the closing entries giving effect to the valuations of stock, unexpired charges, reserves, and other particulars, the balances remaining are assets . . . and liabilities . . . .
                              Lisle, 1903–04, I:203

A trial balance is nothing but a list of the open accounts in the ledger with an extension opposite the name of each account showing the amount of the debit or credit balance . . . . A failure [of the trial balance] to prove [i.e. to yield equal aggregates] shows that there is at least one error somewhere; but it may mean a dozen errors.
                              Cole, 1908, 34, 37

The function of the trial balance is primarily to furnish a test of clerical accuracy.
                              Paton & Stevenson, 1916/1976, 54

Trial balance: a statement of the balances standing in the books for the purpose of testing the accuracy of the entries, the basic rule being that the sum of the debits must equal the sum of the credits.

Pixley, 1926, 2:929

384 Periodical accounting adjustments

Adjustments at balancing time . . . . include various items that must be charged or allowed for, before ascertaining the net profit. Outstanding liabilities and accruing income must be brought into account, expenses prepaid and unexpired income and expenditure must be apportioned, provision must be made for depreciation of assets, while reserves must be created for any expected gains and losses.

Carter, 1923, 37

Periodic valuations . . . [are] . . . required to supplement the facts presented in the trial balance . . . . [For inventories] physical quantities must first be ascertained and . . . by means of a rational system of pricing, must be translated into value terms . . . . an appropriate allowance must be made each period to measure the decline in value which has taken place in all depreciable properties used in production. Such an allowance may be determined by periodical inspection and appraisal, or it may be the expression of a systematic policy of apportionment based on estimates of service life, salvage value, and other data.

Paton, 1924, 217

bookkeeping convenience and lack of adequate information quite commonly result in a failure to record as they occur certain classes of transactions. The effect of these transactions must be included in the trial balance [by adjusting entries] before it is suitable for use as a basis for preparation of the statements . . . . The transactions covered by such entries may be classified into three groups: accruals, not previously recorded because of bookkeeping convenience; estimates of costs of goods or services received during the period but not billed until after the close of the period; and costs of goods and prepaid services used, not previously recorded because of insufficient information or bookkeeping convenience.

Porter & Fiske, 1935, 141

Changes are taking place every day. The discounted note daily becomes more valuable, interest on both receivables and payables accrues from day to day as do rent, wages, etc, supplies are daily being consumed, machinery and plant are gradually being worn out. But it would be a foolish expenditure of energy to make daily entries in the ledger to record these changes . . . . Notice is taken of them only when a money payment is involved or at the close of a fiscal period when it is thought desirable to remedy defects in the ledger and to make as correct a statement as possible. At that time . . . adjusting entries are made which will bring into the ledger the total effect of these daily occurring changes.

Hatfield & others, 1940, 114

Adjusting entries are not a logically necessary part of a bookkeeping system. They arise usually from a deliberate choice to defer the analysis and recording of certain changes ... until the end of the period, a choice ordinarily dictated by considerations of expediency and convenience, only rarely by necessity. [Adjusting entries are made, for example, for prepayments, accrued amounts receivable, amounts received under contracts in advance of performance, accrued amounts payable, and corrections of discovered errors.]

> Moonitz & Staehling, 1952, I:62–66

It is impracticable and sometimes impossible to record the day to day changes in some accounts .... Adjusting entries are made at the close of each accounting period prior to the preparation of financial statements. These entries (1) adjust the mixed accounts [balances to be divided between the past and future periods] and (2) bring on to the books information not previously recorded ....

> Malchman & Slavin, 1961, 94

Balance day adjustments are of four main kinds: 1. Transactions which have been recorded ... during the current period, but which relate wholly or partly to subsequent accounting periods; 2. Transactions which have occurred during the current period, but which for some reason have not been recorded ... prior to balance day; 3. Allocations to the current period of its share of the original cost of fixed assets – depreciation; and 4. Provisions for anticipated revenue, costs or losses arising out of the current period's operations, the exact amounts of which cannot be determined at balance day.

> Mathews, 1962, 64

[Book] entries, which have to be made to bring the asset and equity accounts into agreement with the facts of the situation as of the date of the prospective accounting reports, are called adjusting entries.

> Bierman, 1963c, 57

financial statements drawn directly from the account balances [resulting from the recording of transactions] ... would be incomplete ... because certain kinds of facts have not yet been reflected in the accounts. The entries [required] ... are known as adjusting entries .... They fall into six categories: 1. amortization of capitalized costs; 2. accrual of unrecorded liabilities; 3. recognition of unrecorded assets; 4. deferral of revenues; 5. correction of measurement errors; 6. correction of bookkeeping errors and omissions.

> Gordon & Shillinglaw, 1969, 160

385 The balance account or sheet

the balance account [after all necessary transfers to profit and loss] will contain the particulars of my effects and debts; the difference between the two sides, being my net capital or deficiency, must be adjusted with Stock; and if the difference of Stock and balance agree, all is right; – this is the touchstone of accounts. Thus the value of my estate is ascertained in two different ways: – one is by the Stock account, which contains the value at first setting out, and the profits added to it, which gives its improved value; the other is by collecting my effects and debts into one total, and taking from thence the total of the debts I owe, which also gives the present value of my estate.

Clark, 1732/1852, 15

Upon one or more sheets of paper, ruled in the form of the ledger, open an account for balance; and on another . . . open an account for profit and loss; . . . . carry the articles of gain or loss in any one of them [the separate accounts] to the profit and loss sheet . . . . carry the articles that remain to one or other of the sides of the balance account . . . . Then add up the Dr sides of the profit and loss sheet, and the profit and loss account in the ledger [i.e. for gains and losses entered there during the period] into one sum [and likewise for the Cr sides] . . . and carry the difference to the stock account [which has the opening balances of assets and liabilities] . . . which is closed by charging it Dr to balance . . . when the proper entry is made in balance account, both sides will be equal, unless some mistake has been committed . . . the balance sheet must close itself.

Gordon, 1787/1986, 56

In order to balance the books – the profit and loss on the accounts in the ledger are . . . posted to the Dr and Cr side of the profit and loss in the ledger. The balance of this account is then carried to stock account, and shows the gain or loss on the business. The balance of all the accounts, except stock, are next . . . carried . . . to balance account in the ledger, in a similar manner. The difference between the debit and credit of this account, should, if the books are accurate, correspond exactly to the balance of stock, by which this last is finally closed, and is the amount of your capital. [No reference is made to balance sheet.]

Mitchell, 1796/1978, 210

To make a general balance, or close the ledger . . . an account must be opened for profit and loss, and another for balance, which are generally first made upon loose sheets of paper, called the balance and profit and loss sheets . . . . Some book-keepers insert the particulars of these accounts in the ledger . . . others insert them at the end of the journal . . . . The articles of the balance sheet generally supply materials for a new inventory in opening another set of books: . . . .

Kelly, 1801, 12, 36, 37

When all the accounts have been adjusted [for posting errors, if any] the ledger is said to be balanced. This operation is simply the collection of the scattered balances into one general result, called the balance sheet . . . . proceed to close the books. The items of gain and loss are to be transferred . . . to profit and loss [account]; and then the difference between the two sides shows the net gain or loss; and to close profit and loss transfer this difference to stock [i.e. capital account]. In order to preserve the equilibrium of debtors and creditors in closing the remaining accounts it is necessary to open another account in the ledger under the title, balance, to which the balances of the several accounts forming the assets and liabilities of the

concern are to be transferred, and entered in the same manner as in the balance sheet. The difference between the two sides of the balance account is transferred to stock and then all the accounts will be equilibrated, and they are closed by setting down the equal sums opposite to each other.
Foster, 1843, I:33

The balance sheet . . . is for the purpose of exhibiting the closing of the accounts out of the books instead of in the books.
Sheriff, 1852, 122

balance account . . . is generally opened at the closing of books to exhibit the aggregate resources and liabilities [including the liability to the proprietor] of the firm. If balance account is not opened then the balances of resources and liabilities are brought down on the resource or liability side of the account closed . . . . Balance . . . . is not a regular ledger account.
Soulé, 1903/1976, 65, 79

Balance account – an account in the ledger to which, as at the date of closing the books, all the balances of the other accounts are carried in summarized form, so that the whole of the accounts may be balanced off. The modern practice, however, is to discard the balance account and bring down each balance in its appropriate place . . . for the succeeding period.
Dawson, 1904, 40

[Considering the development of double entry bookkeeping –] A distinction must be drawn between a balance account drawn up on the basis of the account balances appearing in the ledger, and a balance account incorporating the facts as revealed by an actual inventory where the possessions of the firm are examined and valued. The former may be called a crude or book balance and the latter an inventory balance. The former does not necessarily or usually show the true condition of the enterprise but only a list of ledger balances; the latter shows the present value of the firm's property . . . . The former statement is the product of the double entry system; the latter may be used in connection with any system, and if used in conjunction with double entry it is superimposed on the books of account and must be tied in with the double entry records.
Yamey, 1940, 336

386 Balance sheet format

[An illustrative balance sheet gives in detail what the balance account gives in summary. Assets are shown on the left hand side.]
Hamilton, 1788/1982, 319

the balance account or balance sheet receives all the balances of the ledger, which . . . must be equal; the balance account, therefore, can have no balance. The account which may be copied verbatim into the ledger without the intervention of the journal, shows at a glance the state of the house. On its Dr side it contains all the assets; and on its Cr side the liabilities, the difference between the two being the stock which balances the balance account, and this closes the books.

Henderson, 1841, 22

The assets, or balances in favor of the concern, are placed on the Dr or left hand side of the balance sheet, and the liabilities on the Cr or right hand side, the difference is the net capital or present worth.

Foster, 1843, I:33

The following statement shows how the assets and liabilities were treated by authors of works on bookkeeping prior to 1859. After that date [following the form prescribed by Table A of the *Companies Act 1862*] the authors of works on bookkeeping published in the UK in most cases adopt the method of placing liabilities on the left side:-

MODE OF PLACING ASSETS AND LIABILITIES IN BALANCE SHEETS

Author.	Date.	Title of Work.	Description of Statement or Account.	Method of Placing.	
				Left-hand Side	Right-hand Side
S. Monteage . .	1708	Debtor and Creditor made East	Balance	Assets	Liabilities
A. Malcolm . .	1718	Arithmetick and Book-Keeping	Balance	Assets	Liabilities
William Webster	1721	Essay on Book-keeping	Balance	Assets	Liabilities
A. Malcolm . .	1731	Book-Keeping	Balance	Assets	Liabilities
John Mair . . .	1800	Book-keeping Modernised	Balance Account	Assets	Liabilities
T. Dilworth . .	1801	The Young Book-Keeper's Assistant	Balance	Assets	Liabilities
W. Lorrain . .	1807	Book-keeping by Double Entry	Balance	Assets	Liabilities
Chas. Hutton. .	1810	A Complete Treatise on Book-keeping	Balance	Assets	Liabilities
Rees *Cyclopedia* .	1819	Article on Book-Keeping	Balance	Assets	Liabilities
J. Morrison . .	1820	Practical Book-keeping	Balance Account	Assets	Liabilities
P. Kelly	1821	The Elements of Book-keeping	Balance	Assets	Liabilities
J. P. Corg . . .	1839	Practical Treatise on Accounts	Balance Account	Assets	Liabilities
C. Morrison . .	1843	Practical Book-keeping	Balance Account	Assets	Liabilities
J. Caldecott . .	1850	Practical Guide to Book-keeping	Balance Account	Assets	Liabilities
B. F. Foster . .	1852	Double Entry Elucidated	Balance Sheet	Assets	Liabilities
G. H. Boulter .	1857	A Course of Book-keeping by Double Entry	Balance	Assets	Liabilities
W. Inglis . . .	1858	Book-keeping	Balance Sheet	Liadilities	Assets
James Haddon .	1859	Rudimentary Book-keeping	Balance Accounts	Assets	Liabilities

Lisle, 1903–04, I:206

the advocates of the continental form of balance sheet, in which the assets and liabilities are respectively enumerated on the same sides as they appear in the ledger, have theoretically the better of the argument, and the concurrence of the civilized world, barring England. The advocates of the English form, however, seem to have . . . effected the crystallization and adoption of their preference in the matter by means of the *Companies Act* of 1862 . . . and other acts of parliament, thereby placing the whole body of chartered accountants . . . in a fix, from which it seems they cannot extricate themselves. As the advocates of untenable theories are noto-riously the most stubborn, there is little doubt that for years to come the English will adhere to their form of balance sheet . . . .

Broaker & Chapman, 1897/1978, 91

387 The double account system

the practice of public utility companies to publish statements of capital receipts and payments [was followed] long before the double account system was prescribed for public utility corporations, beginning with the railways in 1868.

Edwards, 1980, 244

[By the *Regulation of Railways Act* of 1868, railway companies were required to prepare and distribute uniform accounts including an account of receipts and expen-diture on capital account (capital account, for short) and a general balance sheet beginning with the unspent balance on capital account. Schedules to the Act]

UK *Regulation of Railways Act, 1868*

By the term double account system I understand the necessary condition to be that the assets of a company are kept in two separate parts or funds: the one, the capital account, comprising the capital raised and the assets to which . . . [it] has been applied, and any outstanding liabilities on this account; the other, revenue account, in which the assets representing the earnings of the company, and any liabilities incurred in connection with the earnings are contained. In order to constitute the two accounts, the assets must be capable of being individually earmarked as respec-tively either on capital account or revenue account, and the two accounts can be separated only to such extent as the assets are capable of being so separately earmarked.

Cooper, 1888, 741

Certain parliamentary companies, constituted for the purpose of undertaking certain definite public works are . . . required to adopt [what] is called the double account system. It being required that all capital raised by these companies shall be expended in the construction of the public works . . . a special form of account [was to be used] in which all monies expended in the construction of the works is separated from the general balance sheet. Now, in order that this account (the capital expen-diture account) might perpetually show that – and how – the capital authorized to be raised had actually been spent only upon the authorized purposes . . . it was necessary that the actual amount expended on the works alone be debited to the account, regardless of any fluctuations in value that might afterwards occur. It would, of course, have been easy for the legislature to have provided that any fluctuation that might occur should be duly allowed for in the general balance sheet; but having regard to the fact that no such fluctuation could in any way practically affect the company, so long as it carried on business, and bearing in mind also the fact that it was contemplated that the company should *permanently* carry on business, it would appear that all consideration of these fluctuations was considered superfluous.

Dicksee, 1892/1976, 118

The double account system is probably the creation of lawyers, rather than of accountants, and its object would appear to be to direct special attention to the importance of keeping a strict account of the expenditure of moneys received by the creation of fixed liabilities; that is to say, from the issue of capital to shareholders or debentureholders .... This idea [the double account system], ingenious as it undoubtedly is, would appear to have emanated from a lawyer rather than an accountant. One seems to trace in it the well known affection of the Chancery Division for a cash statement, as well as its rooted distrust of all accounts framed on any other basis ....

Dicksee, 1903a, 126

Under the double account system, a more marked line is drawn between capital and revenue. In a sense, every increase in the value of a company's assets is a profit, or more properly a gain – that is, the company is so much the richer, but it is not a "profit arising from the business of the company," so as to be available – in the view of the advocates of this system – for purposes of dividend. Profits in this sense are the excess of revenue receipts over expenses properly chargeable to revenue account. Hence for the purpose of ascertaining profits for dividend, capital account and revenue account must be treated as separate accounts, accretions to capital must be disregarded, and the credit balance of revenue account is alone applicable for dividend. If there has been loss on revenue account there is no profit until that loss has been made good, but not so in the case of loss on capital account. Dividend may be paid without providing for such loss.

Manson, 1903–04, II:162

The double account system is a system of accounting adopted by companies where the capital is contributed by the shareholders for a specific purpose, e.g. the construction of a railway, or purchase of an electric light, gas or water undertaking .... the balance sheet is divided into two parts ... the first part consisting of ... the capital account showing on the credit side the total amount received to date on account of shares, debentures and premiums on shares; and on the debit side the expenditure to date of such capital receipts in constructing and acquiring the system. Only the balance of the capital account is shown in the general balance sheet [the second part] ....

Jenkinson, 1910, 47

Under the double account system, the balance sheet is divided into two parts, the first part, called the capital account, dealing with the fixed or permanent assets and the capital and debentures subscribed, and the second part, called the general balance sheet, dealing with the floating assets and floating liabilities .... In the double account system, the assets are not written down in the capital account, but appear thereon at cost.

Carter, 1923, 909

In the case of certain companies registered under special acts of parliament, particularly railways, gas works, electric lighting, and similar concerns formed to undertake public works, the capital receipts must be shown in juxtaposition to the "capital expenditure" in an account called the receipts and expenditures on capital account. The reason for this is that the capital receipts have been obtained for a specific purpose and the account is designed to show how these receipts have been got and how expended, and also the balance, if any, still in hand available for further development . . . . the balance of the capital account is carried to the general balance sheet . . . .

Pixley, 1926, I:283

The theory underlying it [the double account form of balance sheet] is that every business enterprise is divided into a financing branch and an operating branch. The financing branch is charged with the duty of raising capital, investing it in the permanent assets of the business, and turning over the balance to the operating branch for use as working capital. The operating branch invests the working capital in merchandise, or whatever is to be used in operating the business, and accounts therefor periodically to the finance branch.

Reiter, 1926/1976, 23

the double account form of balance sheet has had a considerable and perhaps baleful influence on the legal interpretation of accounts. It has indeed been argued that the placing of the capital in a separate account involves the principle that changes therein cannot affect the profit and loss appearing in the balance sheet . . . . the isolation of capital assets and capital liabilities in the capital account has a tendency to cause them to be considered as isolated in fact . . . . [it] seems to encourage the idea that the capital account, or at least the plant purchased with receipts from capital, have little or nothing to do with the profits exhibited in the balance sheet. The inference is easily drawn that there can be a loss in the value of the capital assets which would affect only the capital account and which would leave the profits of the year undisturbed.

Hatfield, 1927/1971, 8, 247

400 FINANCIAL POSITION AND ITS ELEMENTS

410 Financial Position

411 Inventory: estate: stock

The inventory or estate of all such goods as unto me . . . pertain, and also what I owe, or what I ought to make answer unto, at this present . . . .

Peele, 1553, n p

The end of bookwriting is to give contentment to the bookowner, and to show him (or them whom they do concern) at all times, and in every degree, how his estate standeth in the so written books . . . .

Dafforne, 1635, 4

this method . . . . sets before thee the true state of every man's account with thee, and thy account with them . . . . it shows a perfect reason for the increase and decrease in one's estate; . . . .

Monteage, 1682, Preface

[The ledger] is the mirror of a man's estate, wherein is brought together upon their several accounts all the dispersed journal parcels; so when all is transported in that book, you can see upon every man's account what he owes to you, or you to him, and upon the goods account what you have bought and sold.

Colinson, 1683, 2

as to the state of the whole [of our affairs], since the whole is nothing but all the parts taken together, the state of it can be known only by collecting the states of the several parts in a complete inventory, or account of all one's effects and debts; the difference of which is the final state of the whole, showing what one's free estate is worth, or what the debts exceed the effects.

Malcolm, 1731, 3

The first thing necessary towards keeping books in the Italian way is to take an inventory of your estate; that is to say, to take an exact and particular account of all those things your estate consists in; as ready money, houses, lands, parts of ships, shares in the public funds, annuities, bonds, goods &c, expressing their quantity and value, together with what debts are due to you; all these particulars being so many several branches, the whole together make up your estate which we call stock.

Hayes, 1741, 4

Stock is the aggregate or total of the Accountant's estate, or effects, whatever be the nature or kind of the particulars . . . . if the creditor side of the account of stock exceeds the debtor, the balance will show how much the Accountant is worth, when all his debts are paid; and, on the contrary, if the debtor side thereof exceeds the creditor, the balance will show how much he is in debt, more than his effects will pay. [accountant = party to whose affairs the accounts relate]

Dodson, 1750, ii, iii

The word stock, in the mercantile meaning of the term, as used in accounts, comprehends every thing possessed by the firm at a given time. The stock account contains upon its credit side all the lands, houses, leases, fixtures, engines, merchandise and credits of the firm; and its debts and liabilities upon its debit side . . . . the balance between the credit and debit sides of the stock account is exactly the net property of the firm.

Cory, 1839, 90

412 Occurrence of term, financial position

. . . We have carefully checked the various balances, which we also found correct, and we have no hesitation in expressing our entire satisfaction at the present financial position of the Bank. [Audit report, December]

Commercial Banking Company of Sydney
Ltd, 1849

A balance sheet shall be made out and laid before each ordinary general meeting . . . and such balance sheet shall contain a summary of the property and liabilities . . . arranged under proper distinguishing heads so as to present an accurate and comprehensive view of the financial position of the company. [Articles of association, 1866]

Oxford Benefit Building and Investment
Society, In re, 1886/1986, 147

[Of a Cornish heiress] . . . she had hardly ever given a thought to her financial position.

Braddon, 1883, *Mount Royal*, 11

the object of a company's balance sheet is to enable its shareholders to obtain a definite and correct idea as to the financial position of the company, and recognizing this principle . . . . a balance sheet which states these assets [security investments of a bank] as being worth some £600,000 less than the market price of the day can hardly be said to "properly reveal the financial position of the undertaking as upon the date named".

Accountant, editorial, 1895, 75

A reserve fund is a sum set aside out of divisible profits, and retained in hand for the purpose of strengthening the financial position of the undertaking.

Dicksee, 1903c, 51

Another object [of a balance sheet, incidental to showing the amount of distributable profit] is to show . . . the general financial position and stability of the undertaking.

Carter, 1910b, 561

If books of account are kept outside Great Britain, there shall be sent to, and kept at a place in Great Britain . . . such accounts and returns . . . so kept as will disclose with reasonable accuracy the financial position of that business . . . and will enable to be prepared . . . the company's balance sheet, its profit and loss account or income and expenditure account . . . [Table A]

UK Companies Act, 1948

A company shall (a) keep such accounting records as correctly record and explain the transactions of the company . . . and the financial position of the company, and (b) keep its accounting records in such a manner as will enable (i) the preparation from time to time of true and fair accounts of the company, and (ii) the accounts of the company to be conveniently and properly audited in accordance with this Act.

Australian Companies Act, 1981

413 Explication of "state of affairs" or financial position

what is meant by that state of our affairs . . . is this . . . . For persons; what every person owes me, or I owe them. For things; what quantity (and value) of every kind is upon hand; with the gain or loss upon that subject, within the time of the account. What is here expressed is what we call the final state of the account (or of our affairs) relating to persons and things . . . .

Malcolm, 1731, 2

Stock is a term used to represent the name of the merchant or owner of the books. On the Dr side is entered the amount of the debts which he owed when the books were opened; and on the Cr side the amount of the cash, goods, debts and other property then belonging to him. The difference between the Dr and Cr sides shows his net stock, or the state of his affairs, ... [or the] net of his estate.

Kelly, 1801, 7, 13

At the time of balancing . . . . every account [of clerks in charge of cash, merchandise, bills receivable, bills payable, and profit and loss] except Stock is closed, and the bookkeeper can say to the merchant – "Such is your position, supposing you retire from business this day, and are able to sell your goods at their present valuation, and to collect all that is owing to you, and to pay all you owe. Look at the balance sheet; it shows a surplus of so much, which it returns to your capital account. Here is your capital account, the credit side of which shows all that you possess, and the debit side all that you owe; the difference is your net capital, of which the balance sheet gives the particulars; consequently your account of capital ought to be debited, and the balance account credited, for the amount of surplus carried to the capital or stock account." In re-opening the accounts [the merchant] orders his clerks to resume their functions, and makes each personal account debtor for that which is owed before the balance . . . .

Isler, 1810/1852, 22

the balance sheet shows at one view the entire result of business, the exact situation of affairs, or, in the brief and pertinent phrase, how we stand. The balance sheet shows in what manner our capital is invested, what is the nature of the claims against us, from what sources our gain generally arose, and what speculations terminated in loss.

Marsh, 1835/1988, 201

To make up a balance sheet the trader must collect upon its debit side all the debts due to him, the cash in hand which he will take from his cash book, and the value of the goods on hand, which he has already ascertained by examination; and upon the credit side he will place the debts he owes; and the balance of this gives the state of his affairs – that is his net property, which must of course be equal to the amount of his property when he commenced, plus the intermediate profit; and consequently this balance sheet, or state of affairs, must balance the stock account.

Cory, 1839, 48

From the summary of trade [a digest of transactions], the true state of affairs can be seen at all times . . . .

Calculator, 1843, Introduction

The statement of financial position discloses asset composition and capital structure. Such information is relevant to the appraisal of the firm's stability and the soundness of its financial policies.

AAA, 1964a, 694

Users of accounts need to be informed about the nature and amount of the company's assets and liabilities and to be able to form an opinion on liquidity, solvency, fixed asset investment, working capital, financial position and general financial strength. These are the aspects of the "state of affairs" which the balance sheet is expected to disclose.

Flint, 1982, 11

The statement of financial position provides an indication of financial strength . . . the ability of a business enterprise to meet its obligations . . . . the enterprise's potential to generate future economic resources . . . . By disclosing the nature of the economic resources, the statement facilitates an assessment of the short term and long term risks the enterprise faces.

Andersen & Co, 1987, 17

See also 012

414 Financial position described with reference to assets and equities

[There are] two kinds of property directly contrary in their natures; . . . positive property, consisting of goods, cash, bills receivable and debts receivable . . . . negative property, consisting of bills payable and debts payable. And as these two kinds of property mutually destroy [offset] each other, it is evident that the stock, or entire capital, must always be equal to the difference between them, and be of the same nature as that which preponderates . . . . The proprietor is solvent [where the positive exceeds the negative]. The proprietor is . . . insolvent [where the negative exceeds the positive].
Cronhelm, 1818/1978, 5

A complete representation of financial condition requires the exhibition of both resources and rights or equities in resources.
Paton, 1924, 31

Financial position is basically a matter of financial resources compared with financial obligations.
Dohr, 1941, 201

Financial position, as it is reflected by the records and accounts . . . , is revealed in a presentation of the assets and liabilities of the enterprise.
AIA, 1947b, ARB 30

A complete description of the status of an organization at a point in time requires a list of its liabilities and proprietorship (its equities) as well as its assets, and these are shown in the balance sheet or statement of financial position.
Gordon & Shillinglaw, 1964, 5

The financial position, or status, of an accounting entity at any given point in time is shown by two factors, its assets and its equities.
Black & others, 1967, 29

The financial position of an enterprise at a particular time comprises its assets, liabilities and owners' equity and the relationship among them, plus those contingencies, commitments, and other financial matters that pertain to the entity at that time and are required to be disclosed under generally accepted accounting principles. The financial position of an enterprise is presented in the balance sheet and in notes to the financial statements.
AICPA, 1970c, APBS4

Theoretically, the basic objective of the financial position statement is to report how much the firm's assets are worth and how much the firm owes as of the date of the statement. This is the only logical definition of the term financial position . . . .
                                    Fertig & others, 1971, 512

A statement of financial position provides information about an entity's assets, liabilities, and equity and their relationships to each other at a moment of time.
                                    FASB, 1984, SFAC5

See also 352

415 Financial position otherwise described

actual financial condition . . . . is evidenced by the values of both property owned and debts due . . . ; the actual or estimated value of all liabilities; the surplus of one over the other, which represents the net worth or value; and a summary of the operations by which this net worth has been either created, increased or diminished.
                                    Dickinson, 1914, 31

Financial position:Money and legal claims thereto, namely
        Cash   = Money
        Debtors   = Money claimable by the business
        Creditors   = Money claimable from the business . . . .
Financial position, then has only cash, debts and liabilities as constituents . . . .
                                    Norris, 1946, 23

The financial position of a company . . . can be meaningfully demonstrated only if values are used. A company's debt-paying power, liquidity, stability, deferred charges available for future operations, etc, should be reflected in statements of financial position. To attain these objectives, values must be used which are verifiable, understandable to the user, and most of all pertinent to the purpose which the statement is to serve.
                                    Kollaritsch, 1965, 57

Financial position is the capacity of an entity at a point of time to engage in indirect exchanges; it is represented by the relationship between the monetary properties of the means in possession and the monetary properties of the obligations of an entity.
                                    Chambers, 1966a, 101

Since, by definition, an asset is a positive item of wealth and a liability is a negative item of wealth, the financial position (equation) of an enterprise is, in a sense, a wealth assessment.
                                    May & others, 1975, 160

financial position [is] an entity's cash flow potentials, their distribution over time, the relationships between their positive and negative elements, and their risk and uncertainty attributes. Assets and liabilities are parts of a firm's financial position.

Staubus, 1977, 122

The concept of financial position in general terms is synonymous with wealth as it refers to how well off the firm is at a particular date. But more specifically it embraces consideration of the value and liquidity of the firm's assets, in relation to the value and maturity dates of its liabilities. The measure of financial position is needed to help assess the firm's ability to meet its liabilities as they fall due for repayment, i.e. to assess its short-run liquidity and long-run solvency; to help determine its future borrowing capacity; to provide a measure of the resources currently owned by the firm and which are available for use in its future operations; and to determine the rate of return on investment which is required to evaluate the financial side of the business. This information is required by all users of financial reports.

Barton, 1984, 92

416 Financial position said to be undefined

Curiously enough, neither the writers on accounts nor the accountants seem to have given much thought to defining either term [financial position or financial condition].

Canning, 1929a, 179

The [Tentative Statement of Accounting Principles – AAA, 1936] puts the showing of financial condition as a prime object of accounting, but nowhere explains what the term means. Some earlier accountants seem to mean by the term, an exhibit of the relative position of assets and liabilities, leading up to the 2:1 rule, and the acid test. That is a possible concept if accounting is showing present values. But is does not apply in a system which rejects present values and considers costs [as the AAA statement does].

Hatfield, 1937, unpubl

financial position is not an absolute which has been precisely defined or is readily apparent.

Burton, 1975, 32

The term [financial position] is used in the [Canada Business Corporations Act, 1975] and other [Canadian] sources. But it is nowhere defined . . . . Likewise there is no definition of results of operations of a period under report.

Chambers & Falk, 1985, 16

420 The Balance Sheet

421 The balance sheet as summary of property and liabilities

What does the balance sheet exhibit? All the property and debts of the concern; consequently the net capital; all the profits and losses, therefore the gain.

Sheriff, 1852, 123

a balance sheet shall be made out in every year and laid before the company in general meeting, and such balance sheet shall contain a summary of the property and liabilities of the company . . . . [Table A]

UK *Companies Act*, 1862

The balance sheet of proprietorship is a summing-up at some particular time of all the elements that constitute the wealth of some person or collection of persons.

Sprague, 1907/1972, 30

The function of the asset side of a balance sheet should be to exhibit a classified summary of the valuable possessions of a business. The total value of these possessions should equal the total wealth owned by the business as of the date of the balance sheet.

MacNeal, 1939, 271

422 The balance sheet as representation of state or state of affairs

A merchant's books should exhibit the true state of his affairs: . . . .

Kelly, 1801, 1

the affairs and transactions of the company shall be brought to a just and true balance by the board of directors [at the end of each half year] . . . and a balance sheet shall be prepared containing a true statement of the affairs and transactions of the company, and the net profits of the bank during the half year immediately preceding . . . .

BNSW, Deed of Settlement, 1850

The auditors shall make a report to the members upon the balance sheet and accounts, and . . . shall state whether, in their opinion, the balance sheet is a full and fair balance sheet, containing the particulars required by these regulations, and properly drawn up so as to exhibit a true and correct view of the state of the company's affairs . . . . [Table A]

UK *Companies Act*, 1862

A balance sheet is intended to show the position of affairs of a continuing business at a given moment of time; and its function is . . . to show the financial position of the business – i.e. the resources it has available to meet its current liabilities.

Dicksee, 1909b, 194

Balance sheet: a statement made by merchants and others to show the true state of a particular business. A balance sheet should exhibit all the balances of debits and credits, also the value of merchandise, and the result of the whole.

Bouvier's law dictionary, 1914, I:317

See also 413

423 The balance sheet as representation of financial position

in our opinion, the balance sheet is properly drawn up so as to show the true financial position of the corporation and its subsidiary companies, and . . . the relative income account is a fair and correct statement of the net earnings for the fiscal year.

U S Steel Corporation, Audit report, 1902

The balance sheet of a business is prepared for the purpose of showing the financial condition of the concern at a particular moment of time, and should be so classified and arranged as to give the clearest and fullest idea of the financial position of the business.

Lisle, 1903–04, I:203

A balance sheet may be defined as a statement showing in summary form the various debit and credit balances standing in the books at any given date (after collecting into one account, called the profit and loss account, all balances relating to revenue), the items in the balance sheet being so grouped and classified as to show the financial position of the concern at the date of the statement.

Jenkinson, 1910, 9

The accounts of a corporation should be prepared so that the auditor can certify that the balance sheet represents the true financial position of the company, and that the profit and loss account is a fair statement of the result of the company's operations.

Webster, 1919, 258

Balance sheet: A statement of the financial position of an undertaking at a specified date, prepared from books kept by double entry, showing on the one side the assets and on the other side the liabilities and the accountabilities . . . .

AIA, 1931a, 22

While the balance sheet is sometimes nothing more than its name implies – a mere list of balances – the ideal to be aimed at in its preparation is to present as clear and as faithful a picture as possible of the company's position on a given date.

Moore, 1937, 29

Certainly the reader of a statement expects the title to inform him as to the content of the statement, and just as certainly the term balance sheet does not inform

him . . . . Away with such gibberish! Let us call the statement what it is! I suggest the title, statement of financial position.
Franklin, 1944, 56

The balance sheet then is a statement of financial position . . . and it is true only for a given moment of time.
Kester, 1946, 12

We first ruled out "condition" in a possible title for the statement – on the grounds that it conveyed ideas of realizable value and, possibly, liquidation. This left us with "position" as the best alternative we could think of – and recalled to mind that several years ago the public accounting profession had standardized on that description in its opinions on corporate statements. At the same time the profession had discontinued use of the qualifying adjective "financial" – on the grounds, I believe, that it was thought to be a factor contributing to the fallacy that the balance sheet presented realizable values. Nevertheless, we felt that the title would not be as helpfully descriptive if the adjective were omitted and we, therefore, adopted "financial position".
Blackie, 1947, 201

in 1946 published reports [of 13 US companies, 9 described the balance sheet as a statement of financial position, 4 as a statement of financial condition].
Williams, 1947, 313

the balance sheet or position statement . . . . shows the financial position of assets and equities as of a given date.
Vatter, 1950, 34

To describe it as a statement of financial position tells little about the balance sheet. It would be much more appropriate to refer to it as a statement of the sources and composition of company capital.
Marple, 1962, 57

The balance sheet as representation of financial condition

in our opinion the statement of combined assets and liabilities submitted herewith reflects the true financial condition at December 31, 1909, and that the accompanying statement of profits is correct.
International Harvester Company, Audit report, 1909/1986, 77

It is the function of a balance sheet to disclose the true financial condition of a business enterprise as of a particular moment of time. It should be a snapshot.
Noone, 1910, 241

A balance sheet is a statement of the assets, liabilities and net worth of a business at a particular time . . . . a picture of the financial condition of a business . . . .

Bentley, 1911, 50

the balance sheet is a financial statement purporting to show the true financial condition of the concern at a given date.

Esquerré, 1915, 156

The balance sheet attempts to display . . . the true financial condition at a given date of some individual or other financial unit.

Couchman, 1924, 3

The balance sheet is a statement of financial condition. The income sheet, on the other hand, is a statement of financial progress.

Daniels, 1934/1980, 7

a balance sheet is usually prepared for the purpose of showing to all concerned the financial condition of the business as a going concern.

Sanders & others, 1938, 55

The balance sheet presents data related to a company's financial condition as of a specific time, based on the conventions and generally accepted principles of accounting.

Hawkins, 1971, 80

The balance sheet as representation of financial status

The balance sheet gives a cross-section picture of the firm's status at the close of the year's business.

Scott, 1925, 27

The balance sheet is the general financial summary of economic status.

Rorem, 1928, 431

The statement of financial position provides information which describes the financial standing of a company at a given instant in time . . . . a snapshot of the financial status of the company.

Rossell & Frasure, 1967, 13

The balance sheet is a statement of the financial status of the firm as recorded by the accountant. It gives a picture of the financial affairs of a firm at a particular moment in time . . . . [It is] also known as a statement of financial position or position statement . . . . It should be noted that the balance sheet reflects the status of a firm's accounting records and may not measure the current economic condition of an enterprise.

Bierman & Drebin, 1968, 18

424 The balance sheet expected to be a statement of dated values

A balance sheet is not necessarily, or in fact usually, what so many believe . . . a statement of liabilities and assets using the latter word in the sense of representing the saleable or market value of each heading or item that appears thereon.
> Pixley, 1910, 448

the balance sheet is not a capital account showing, as a matter of history, how the capital contributed has been applied in the past, but a living account showing the true financial position of the company at its date, and the difference in amount between the assets on the one hand and the debts, liabilities, and paid up capital, on the other hand.
> Palmer, 1912, I:875

There is . . . quite a widespread impression – among persons who have not reasoned matters out – that all assets appear, or should appear, in a properly drawn up balance sheet at their realizable worth at the date which such balance sheet bears.
> Plender, 1932, 206

there are many who would like to see the balance sheet show current values. They would also like to be able to deduce from the annual accounts whether or not real capital is being preserved. That is not and cannot be the function of the balance sheet. If information like that is useful we must devise other means of getting it, such as through special supplementary statements. As a matter of fact this happens nearly every time when a company goes to its bankers for finance or converts to a public company.
> Irish, 1950, 219

Every accountant must, at some time in his life, have wondered why it is not customary for a balance sheet to show the true present value of all the assets.
> Wimble, 1952, 127

the belief that a balance sheet is a statement of realizable values is fairly widely held.
> Ballantyne, 1957, 98

The average man in the street (and woman) imagines that a balance sheet shows the true worth of the assets of a company . . . .
> Anderson, 1961, 332

Whatever accountants may say about the function and purport of a balance sheet, it is, in practice, used very widely as a valuation statement. Notwithstanding all the outpourings that have taken place in accounting literature with a view to convincing people that this document is merely a historical by-product of the matching procedure and that it does not purport to convey any sort of picture of current values of assets, . . . balance sheets are used, almost universally, as instruments for the purposes of placing valuations upon businesses, shares or parts of a business.

Goldberg, 1965, 325

How long will it be before a rational method of presenting accounts is devised and adopted which will result in the assets being represented by amounts which correspond with what the vast majority of lay shareholders already believe to be the case, i.e. current market values?

Ryan, 1967, 105

Academics should bear in mind that to most investors and nonaccountants a balance sheet should reflect the net realizable value of assets. Nothing will change that belief.

Troy, 1982, 3

The balance sheet held to be a statement of dated values

[The deed of the company provides that the directors] "shall . . . make or cause to be made out a full, true and explicit statement and balance sheet, exhibiting the debts and credits of the company, and the amount and nature of the capital and property thereof, and the then fair value of the same estimated by the directors as nearly as may be, and to the best of their judgment; and . . . all other matters and things requisite for fully, truly and explicitly manifesting the state of the affairs of the company". Now, this clause admits of no doubt; nothing could be plainer or better framed. The company are to keep a true account of their transactions . . . and are to exhibit the actual value of the property. [per Lord Chancellor, Court of Appeal]

Holme, Ex parte, 1852

a balance sheet, in order to prove of real utility, should consist, not only of a classification of the balances in the books, but also a valuation of those balances, and in order that the shareholders should be able to form a judgment of the truth of the balance sheet, the source or method of valuation should . . . be attached to the various items . . . . In cases where it is difficult or impossible to value the assets, then there should be set forth on the face of the balance sheet some such statement as that "the asset is taken at cost" or "its value cannot be accurately ascertained".

Whinney, 1895, *BPP, 1895*

a provident balance sheet ought to be drawn up in the light of the possibility of the trading concern becoming insolvent.

Parfitt, 1907, 155

If the balance sheet fails to indicate values, it is useless for interpretation . . . . To say to the reader of the balance sheet that he may convert a multitude of different costs incurred in different economic climates to amounts which have relevance to his problems represents an abrogation of the responsibilities of the accountant . . . . it is in fact impossible for many readers to make such conversions.

Benninger, 1955, 298

It is quite extraordinary what intellectual contortions some of our best pundits have gone through in an attempt to maintain that the balance sheet is not a valuation statement . . . : But if we measure income correctly . . . then surely the balance sheet . . . must correctly represent the residual value. If it does not, then the income must be wrongly stated . . . .

Ross, 1969, 35

a financial position at a specified date is a real world state which cannot be properly described by amounts invested at some time prior to that date.

Wells, 1970, 481

425 The conventional balance sheet held not to be a statement of dated financial position

the balance sheet of a large modern corporation does not and should not be expected to represent an attempt to show present values of the assets and liabilities of the corporation.

AIA, 1932

Accountants know that some of the items listed below the caption, "Assets", have no present or future realizable value, they know that some very valuable assets are not listed, they know that the amounts in the value columns are not correct values on the balance sheet date, and they know that this part of the statement will be misinterpreted by most of the investors who read it.

Whitney, 1940, 300

the balance sheet should provide the answer to the question, "What have you done with all our money?" . . . . The valuation view of the balance sheet can be abandoned. The balance sheet becomes, as an account of stewardship, merely a record of moneys received and spent . . . . Procedures such as the revaluation of fixed assets become irelevant and misleading, as indeed they always are, and to regard upward revaluations as providing a source of profit becomes nonsense, as indeed it always was.

Davison, 1951, 52

A balance sheet is . . . mainly an historical document which does not purport to show the realizable value of assets such as goodwill, land, buildings, plant and machinery . . . [and] stock in trade. Thus a balance sheet is not a statement of the net worth of the undertaking and this is normally so even where there has been a revaluation of assets and the balance sheet amounts are based on the revaluation instead of on cost.

ICAEW, 1958a, N18

I am confident that no group of responsible public accountants would deliberately encourage the impression that one of its [the balance sheet's] objectives was to achieve an accurate portrayal of financial position.

Jennings, 1958, 33

financial position or balance sheet statements do not purport to show either present values of assets to the enterprise or values which might be realized in liquidation.

Grady, 1962, 73

Deferred debits and credits

it is frequently necessary to include in balance sheets, upon the assets side, items that possess no intrinsic value, or upon the liabilities side, items that do not in any real sense represent liabilities.

Dicksee, 1903b, 474

As the grouped balances placed on the . . . liability side of the balance sheet include certain items which are not liabilities, and the grouped balances placed on the . . . assets side . . . include certain items which are not assets, it is quite evident that though an auditor may properly certify the correctness of the balance sheet containing such items, the statement itself does not, at first view, afford such information to a financial expert as is necessary to make himself thoroughly acquainted with the position of the commercial concern engaging his attention.

Pixley, 1906, 512

Suspense debits; consisting of discount on bonds, expenses of organization or other extraordinary losses or expenses which it is desired to write off to income account over a period of years . . . . Suspense credits: consisting of items which will eventually become credits to income or surplus but cannot be at present adjusted.

Dickinson, 1914, 34–5

A most helpful accounting concept . . . considers non-cash assets as being equivalent to deferred charges. Its helpfulness lies in the fact that it eliminates the factors of tangibility and intangibility and also the confusion between economic values, resale values, and accounting values . . . . it is not generally recognized that all assets except cash may be considered deferred charges, i.e. some are deferred charges against future income, others [accounts receivable] are deferred charges to cash.

Gilman, 1939, 297–8

A balance sheet is never a complete statement of the financial position of a firm . . . . Many of the figures shown for assets are only those parts of original costs which are to be charged to future operations. It is only in this special sense that a balance sheet can be called a statement of financial condition.

Mason & Davidson, 1953, 29

A new definition for the general balance sheet ... is long overdue .... It would make clear that [its function] is not to reveal the financial position, but rather it is to show the deferred charges and the unconsumed or unapportioned values for future operations and their financing.

Kollaritsch, 1960, 488

the balance sheet, in addition to the three traditional categories [assets, liabilities and equities] includes two ... categories for the purpose of accommodating the matching of costs and revenues in the income statement: 1. A deferred credit category ... serving as a means of holding in suspense an item of revenue until the period it is considered realized; 2. A deferred charge category ... – the term is used broadly to include inventory and depreciable assets – ... serving as a means of holding in suspense an item of expense until the period in which it is recognized.

Coughlan, 1965, 266

See also 445, 636

426 The balance sheet a summary of account balances

the balance sheet ... is a summarized statement of ledger balances at any particular date that represent assets and liabilities .... if only for the reason that these ledger balances relate to uncompleted transactions of a going concern, they are – or at least the majority of them are – in the nature of things incapable of absolute verification.

Dicksee, 1903b, 471

A balance sheet is simply what its name implies, a sheet or collection of balances, and is really a statement in abstract form of the debtor balances and the creditor balances of the ledger or ledgers, after the elimination of such balances as have been transferred to the revenue or profit and loss account.

Pixley, 1910, 448

a balance sheet is a summary of the ledger balances at a given date .... A balance sheet does not show ... or purport to show, what some investors imagine – namely that all the assets are capable of being converted into cash and will realize the balance sheet figures .... The balance sheet should substantially represent the position, as far as it is possible to ascertain it, of a company as a going concern ....

Plender, 1910, 477

A balance sheet is frequently termed a statement of liabilities and assets, but this definition is incomplete, as in many cases items are included on the liabilities side which are not strictly speaking liabilities ... while on the assets side such items may appear as accumulated loss ..., expenditure carried forward not represented by available assets, &c. A balance sheet may therefore be more properly defined

as a classified summary of the balances remaining in a set of books after those relating to profit and loss have been collected into one account, ...
Spicer & Pegler, 1914, 398

A balance sheet is a statement prepared from the books of a concern showing the debit and credit balances thereof, whether actual assets and liabilities or not, and the balance, whether capital, reserve or profit, at a given date. An alternative definition . . . a statement . . . setting forth the various assets and liabilities of the concern as at this date. It is also described as a classified summary of the debit and credit balances existing in the ledger after the profit and loss account has been constructed . . . . [because it] often contains items which cannot, strictly speaking, be characterized either as assets or as liabilities.
Carter, 1923, 42

Accountants . . . . have never pretended that [a balance sheet] was anything but what it purported to be – a balance sheet, lineal descendant of the balance account to which it was once the custom to transfer the whole of the unclosed balances in a ledger at certain intervals.
AA, Anon, 1936, 74

Balance sheet: a tabular statement or summary of balances (debit and credit) carried forward after an actual or constructive closing of books of account kept by double entry methods according to the rules or principles of accounting.
AIA, 1941c, ARB 9

There is nothing magical about a balance sheet; it is merely a list of the balances remaining in the books at a specified point in time. Over the years it has become accepted as a sort of photograph depicting the condition of a business at a particular date. But if it is a photograph it is a very distorted one.
Accountancy, editorial, 1964, 670

In reality, [a balance sheet] is nothing more than a hotchpotch of balances – most of which are valued on different but quite rational bases – remaining in the ledger once a true and fair profit or loss has been struck.
Leask, 1969, 28

The statement of position shows how the business stands at [a stated date] in terms of the costs that are still applicable to future operations (assets) and the obligations that are to be met sometime in the future (equities).
Vatter, 1971, 43

427 The balance sheet and the value of the firm

the value of a business as a whole cannot be found through the addition of the values of its assets irrespective of whether cost or market or any other value is used.
Schmalenbach, 1919/1959, 30

There is nothing whatsoever in accepted accounting procedure (though there are some mistaken statements in the writings on accounting) to support the notion that accountants are trying to find any figure for the capital value of enterprises.

Canning, 1929b, 6

Since only quick assets are ordinarily displayed at their cash or market value, it follows that the balance sheet is not an inventory of the values of assets in that sense. Neither does the balance sheet show the value of the entire enterprise. These points are behind a recent tendency to relegate the balance sheet to a position of secondary importance in reports to stockholders.

Daniels, 1934/1980, 32

Accounting does not purport to provide information on the total value of a business. It seeks to provide data from which the total value of a business can be determined by others .... information about the value of the separable resources ... used to produce earnings; ....

Hinton, 1973, 35

the total of the balance sheet cannot be the value of the business.

Macve, 1981, 27

The balance sheet is not intended to give the directors' valuation or any other valuation of the undertaking; ....

Flint, 1982, 12

A statement of financial position does not purport to show the value of a business enterprise.

FASB, 1984, SFAC5

See also 145

428 Balance sheet and statement of affairs

whether the company be solvent or insolvent, the valuation of the assets must be made on the footing of the company being a going concern. [per Jessel M R]

Frank Mills Mining Company, In re,
1883

the functions of a balance sheet and a statement of affairs [may be referred to] in synonymous terms as regards a going concern ... for both are intended to afford, as on a specified date, a fair view of the financial position of the concerns to which they respectively refer.

Dawson, 1900, 131

A balance sheet is a concise statement compiled from the books of a concern which have been kept by double entry .... A similar statement when not prepared from books kept by double entry is called a statement of affairs, a state of affairs, or a statement of assets and liabilities.

Lisle, 1903–04, I:203

[Among the advantages of an audit] An accurate statement of affairs together with a profit and loss account, showing how this position was reached, is prepared by a disinterested expert.

Montgomery, 1912/1976, 18

Statement of affairs . . . . a statement of the bankrupt's assets and liabilities . . . . The general purpose of such statement is to show in detail and in total the financial state of the debtor's affairs, the amount (if any) by which creditors' claims exceed the estimated value of the assets . . . .

Reid (ed), 1956, 1103

principles generally accepted for ordinary purposes must be departed from . . . in statements [of affairs of organizations] which [are] insolvent or bankrupt or in danger of becoming so . . . . [The creditors] are vitally interested in knowing how much the assets of the enterprise are likely to produce in liquidation . . . . cost goes out of the window and estimated realizable value, whether above or below cost, takes its place.

Broad, 1957, 32

A statement of affairs, arising from a prospective bankruptcy or liquidation, differs from a balance sheet chiefly in the use of estimated realizable and estimated ranking amounts for all items of an asset and liability character respectively; they are matched nonetheless, with specific matching between such items as secured creditors and the estimated value of the secured property.

Goldberg, 1965, 97

The prescribed form of the report [required on appointment of an official manager for the benefit of creditors] provides for a listing of all assets at . . . cost or net book value, and a listing in parallel of their estimated realizable values. [The form provides for the aggregation only of the realizable values.] . . . . It is of interest that the [Australian Companies] Code uses the same words ["true and fair view of the state of affairs"] in respect of financial statements required annually of companies as going concerns, of companies on the appointment of official managers, periodically of official managers, and on the commencement of a creditors' voluntary winding up. There seems to be little ground for doubting that the references to state of affairs and financial position in these settings relate to the same thing – a statement of assets, liabilities and equity in terms of up to date money equivalents.

Chambers, 1986, 269

429 Retrospective and prospective functions of the balance sheet

The uses to which a balance sheet as a whole are commonly put are four: (1) determining solvency, in which case the assets must be taken at the value at which they could be converted for the purpose of paying debt; (2) determining the advisability of lending the business money or giving it credit . . . , in which case the lender is concerned . . . with the assets soon available for paying the debt; (3) determining the value of the assets not for liquidation but for the uses of a going concern, so that one may see the present value of what is now utilized in the business; and (4) determining what is now actually invested in the business by its owners, irrespective of what the same property or an equally effective property would cost today and of what it would bring today if liquidated.

Cole, 1921, 313

the balance sheet has a dual significance . . . . it is a report of stewardship, an accounting in the legal sense for the assets turned over by equityholders . . . . [and] . . . . a kind of starting point from which to view the future course of events; the charge and discharge type of statement does not fit this situation at all.

Vatter, 1947, 59

the statement of financial position is the truly dynamic accounting report . . . . The statement of financial position marks the threshold of the future.

Ashburne, 1962, 475

[A] significant aspect of accounting realism is that accounting data reflect enterprise experience . . . . Such recorded experience is useful because it serves as the springboard for new managerial decisions and as a factual basis for appraising prior managerial decisions.

Littleton & Zimmerman, 1962, 193

The historical statement of financial position provides a useful starting point for subjective estimates about the future.

Black & others, 1967, 295

The balance sheet . . . . (a) shows the breakdown of permanent capital employed between debenture and loan capital, preferred capital, ordinary share capital, and reserves. This gives an indication of the possible form of future financing. (b) It reveals the strength or weakness of the working capital position. (c) It provides a method of checking the validity of the earnings reported in the profit and loss account. (d) It provides data to show the true success or prosperity of the business by computing the amount earned on invested capital. (e) It supplies the basis for analyzing the source of income. (f) It supplies the basis for long term study of the relationship between earning power and asset values and the development of the group's financial structure over the years.

Titcomb, 1970, 156

an important consideration in establishing and achieving the objectives of financial statements is that the information be as useful as possible to investors and others in appraising the future prospects of a business.

Andersen & Co, 1972, 9

The concern of users [of balance sheets] is for the future as well as for the past. The "state of affairs" must, therefore, be interpreted in that context, providing information to enable expectations about the future to be formed as well as opinions about the past.

Flint, 1982, 12

See also 058, 181, 182

430 Property, Resources, Assets

431 Assets as property

The assets of a business consist of all the property and rights belonging to the business which have a money value.

Lisle, 1899, 67

Resources, assets or effects are the property of all kinds possessing value and belonging to a firm, corporation or individual.

Soulé, 1903/1976, 23

Assets: All the stock in trade, cash, and all available property belonging to a merchant or company.

Bouvier's law dictionary, 1914, I:259

If instead of assets and liabilities, property and equities were used, there would be less danger of misunderstanding and bad accounting practice.

Paton, 1917, 10

Assets is a term used in accountancy to cover all property owned, all legal rights to collect property and all prepaid rights to service.

Couchman, 1924, 28

Assets: The entire property of a person, partnership, corporation, association or estate available for or subject to the payment of debts.

AIA, 1931a, 10

In accounting, the term assets means the same thing as the term property. Anything of value which a business may own is an asset of the business.

Bell & Graham, 1936, 3

The assets of a business enterprise comprise all its properties or resources. In general, three conditions apply to the listing of items as assets, (1) that the business in question owns them, (2) that the business has acquired them at a cost, and (3) that they are of value to the business.

Sanders and others, 1938, 58

The assets or economic resources of an enterprise are its rights in property, both tangible and intangible.

AAA, 1948/1957b, 14

Assets as presently owned objects and rights

The several items which constitute the merchant's entire capital are called assets or effects; . . . .

Foster, 1843, I:17

the correspondence between property and wealth is a contemporaneous correspondence. That is to say, the existing property rights are rights to existing wealth . . . . it is impossible to have a right to any future wealth which is not also a right to some present wealth as a means of securing that future wealth.

Fisher, 1906/1965, 32–3

The assets of the balance sheet consist solely of material factors outside of the proprietor, or of rights over others; in other words, of material things now in possession and of material things which shall be in possession.

Sprague, 1907/1972, 36

The assets of a business are anything of value belonging to it . . . .

Bentley, 1911, 22

An asset can be defined as any consideration, material or otherwise, owned by a specific business enterprise and of value to that enterprise.

Paton & Stevenson, 1920/1978, 18

Assets are the resources owned by the business entity, both tangible and intangible, the value of which can be objectively determined.

Bierman, 1963c, 20

Assets are things of value [which] . . . the business must have acquired the right to use or control . . . . Things may have value . . . . as purchasing power . . . . [as] a money claim . . . . [as convertible] to cash or to a money claim . . . . [as offering] some potential benefits, or rights, or services to the owner.

Finney & Miller, 1968, 3

Assets – economic resources of an enterprise that are recognized and measured in conformity with generally accepted accounting principles. Assets also include certain deferred charges that are not resources, but that are recognized and measured in conformity with generally accepted accounting principles.

AICPA, 1970c, APBS4

The assets of an entity are economic resources which have been obtained as a result of past transactions or events and to which that entity has legal rights.

ASRB, 1985b, R100

See also 264

432 Assets as exchangeable property

we are not aware who was responsible in the first instance for the dissemination of the idea that the term, assets, meant realizable property, but whatever the history of this misconception may be, it is undoubtedly responsible for a good many of the loose ideas entertained by the general public, and also by lawyers, on accounting subjects.

Accountant, editorial, 1908, 918

in 1890 the Supreme Court ... changed the definition of property from physical things having only use-value to the exchange value of anything .... Property is anything that can be bought and sold. Assets are the present exchange value of things that can be sold in the future, or whose products can be sold in the future .... Assets ... includes everything that can be sold.

Commons, 1924/1959, 14, 158

Capital can exist only in exchangeable value, and therefore capital can only be fixed by maintaining investments, in some form or other, at an exchangeable value equal to the fixed capital.

Leake, 1912/1976, 18

An asset is any severable means in possession of an entity [where means are scarce objects having utility].

Chambers, 1966a, 56, 120

An economic resource ... is defined as an element of wealth that possesses ... utility, scarcity and exchangeability .... exchangeability means that an economic resource is separable from a business as a whole and that it has value in and of itself – that it is not solely dependent on the fortunes of the particular business enterprise to which the resource is attached.

Hinton, 1972, 56

We need a simple definition. How about defining assets as cash, contractual claims to cash, and things that can be sold for cash? That definition would do away with goodwill, pre-opening costs, employee training costs, and other junk now called assets .... Abstractions – probable future economic benefits – cannot be sold for cash. Only real things can be sold for cash. Only real things can be assets.

Schuetze, 1991, 116

See also 151, 152, 153

433 Assets defined with reference to spending or debt-paying power

Assets. The effects of a deceased person, wherewith the heir or executor is to satisfy his debts.

Rolt's *Dictionary*, 1761

Assets, (Fr. *assez*, *i.e. satis*) Goods enough to discharge the burden which is cast upon the executor or heir, in satisfying the debts and legacies of the testator or ancestor.

Tomlins, *The law dictionary*, 1820

Assets – The word means, literally, sufficient. Originally, the use of the word was confined to property which an executor or heir could apply to the discharge of the debts and legacies due from the estate of a deceased person .... The term as used in business now means all available property and rights which can be applied in satisfaction of liabilities, or which can be turned into money or money's worth.

Lisle, 1903–04, I:147

Assets – property available for the payment of the debts of a deceased person; commercially, the stock in trade, land, buildings, machinery, tools, book debts, cash, &c, of a trader.

Dawson, 1904, 33

Many persons habitually use the word assets for any item which may appear on the . . . [assets] side of the balance sheet, but I do not agree with that interpretation of the word .... the term as used in business now means all available property and rights which can be applied in satisfaction of liabilities, or which can be turned into money or money's worth.

Pixley, 1906, 512

The word asset comes from the French word *assez* or from the Provençal *assatz*, both meaning enough or sufficient. Commenting upon assets, Blackstone says that "the term receives its name because its possession is sufficient to render the executor or administrator liable to discharge the debts and legacies of the deceased person, so far as the assets may be sufficient for the purpose." .... The term assets . . . means, for a going concern: that which is owned and invested in the business; that which is earned . . . and constitutes a collectable claim; that which has been expended for the benefit of future periods.

Esquerré, 1914, 135

assets are the entire property of all sorts, of a person, association, or corporation applicable or subject to the payment of debts.

Kester, 1922, I:14

"assets" (a singular noun) originally meant a sufficiency of property to meet an obligation; then by extension it was used in the plural to mean the property itself, still with the question of sufficiency in mind. Since it was applied in relation to debts and legacies, the measure of an asset was of course its estimated realizable value. Thence it came into use in double entry balance sheets in which the "values" of assets are not necessarily measured by worth, as they were in the old single entry statements of net worth.

AIA, 1940c, ARB7

Assets. The word, though more generally used to denote everything which comes to the representatives of a deceased person, yet is by no means confined to that use, but has come to signify everything which can be made available for the payment of debts, whether belonging to the estate of a deceased person or not . . . . we always use this word when we speak of the means which a party has, as compared with his liabilities or debts.

Black's law dictionary, 1951, 151

Enterprise status describes the interrelationship between enterprise assets and enterprise equities, taking into account the availability of the assets to meet the liabilities and other demands on enterprise assets as they fall due.

Illinois, 1964, 21

Assets (Norm.-Fr. *assetz*; Lat. *satis*; Fr. *assez*; . . .), property available for the payment of the debts of a person or corporation . . .

Jowitt's dictionary of English law, 1977, I:144

See also 152, 156

434 Assets as costs or unamortized outlays

it may even be correct to include among assets items representing the cost of some good to one who has no real property right therein. For instance, the money paid by a railroad company to improve a street giving access to its station . . . .

Hatfield, 1909, 75

an asset may fairly be defined as an expenditure upon a remunerative object . . . .

Dicksee, 1910, 265

[There are some] expenditures for services from which the benefit is not exhausted for a long period . . . . [such as] the expenditure of stripping overburden in the case of certain kinds of mining properties . . . . It is common practice in such a case to

421

carry the costs of stripping on the balance sheet as a deferred debit item. It . . . is really neither an expense nor a loss, but rather an asset . . . . it should be charged as an expense currently, either in proportion to the weight of ore mined or revenue received . . . .

Paton & Stevenson, 1918/1978, 230

the organization expense of a corporation . . . . is not property owned nor legal rights to property, nor does it strictly represent a prepaid service . . . . Nevertheless, it is accepted by accountants as a proper asset, if other treatment would result in a violation of any accounting principle.

Couchman, 1924, 28

An asset is an expense the benefits from which have not yet been received. An expense in turn is a used up or dissipated asset.

Kohler & Morrison, 1926, 66

assets are but expense in suspense . . . .

Littleton, 1934, 346

A current accounting dictum, which has received wide approval among accounting leaders in both teaching and practice, runs to the effect that accounting is not fundamentally a process of valuation but is rather a systematic record of historical costs. In a meeting of accounting teachers a few months ago one of the speakers advanced the suggestion that we abandon the term assets and substitute for it "unamortized costs". It is a bit hard to see how cash, accrued income and an investment in government bonds would fit into the proposed terminology . . . .

Scott, 1940, 507

Asset (as a balance sheet heading): a thing represented by a debit balance (other than a deficit) that is or would be properly carried forward upon a closing of books of account kept by double entry methods, according to the rules or principles of accounting . . . [on the grounds] that it represents either a property right or value acquired, or an expenditure made which has created a property right, or which is properly applicable to the future. Thus, plant, accounts receivable, inventory, and a deferred charge are all assets in balance sheet classification . . . . The last named is not an asset in the popular sense, but if it may be carried forward as a proper charge against future income, then in an accounting sense . . . it is an asset.

AIA, 1941c, ARB9

Unexpired costs (assets) are those which are applicable to the production of future revenues.

AICPA, 1957/1961, ATB4

On the allocation of cost principle . . . there is merit in carrying forward some expenditures which are expected to benefit future periods . . . . However, since the values created in both advertising campaigns and research are apt to be problematical, . . . it would be less confusing if such deferrals were made only . . . [where] there were strong expectations of future benefits.

Ross, 1969, 136

A balance sheet may fairly carry forward as an asset any measurable cost that demonstrably gives rise to future benefits, even though no saleable asset or right exists. Similarly, it should count as a liability any obligation likely to give rise to future costs, even though no legal liability to specific persons exists.

Skinner, 1972b, 376

under the historical cost approach, the amount of assets in the balance sheet is represented by costs which have not yet been matched against revenues.

Arnold & others, 1985, 148

435 Assets as service potentials

An asset is any future service in money . . . or convertible into money . . . the beneficial interest in which is legally or equitably secured to some person or set of persons. Such a service is an asset only to that person or set of persons to whom it runs . . . . Much of the failure to interpret the work of the accountant is due to the supposition that he is primarily concerned with objects and the valuation of objects rather than with services of objects and persons and the valuation of those services.

Canning, 1929a, 22, 187

Every asset of a business . . . is in essence a storage of service and the degree of service which can be rendered by each asset is valued in terms of . . . the money which may be derived by exchanging the goods or services produced on the market.

Kelley, 1935, 51

Service is the significant element behind the accounts, that is, service potentialities, which, when exchanged, bring still other service potentialities into the enterprise.

Paton & Littleton, 1940, 13

Assets are economic resources devoted to business purposes within a specific accounting entity; they are aggregates of service potentials available for or beneficial to expected operations.

AAA, 1957a/1957b, 3

Assets represent expected future economic benefits, rights to which have been acquired by the enterprise as a result of some current or past transaction.

Sprouse & Moonitz, 1962, 8

All assets, whatever the basis on which they are stated in the accounts, represent sources of future benefit. That is how an asset may be defined . . . . There can be no certainty that the firm will ever receive these [benefits], or that the eventual benefit it does receive will equal the expected one.

> Morison, 1971, 18

Asset – a future benefit or service potential, recognized in accounting only when a transaction has occurred.

> Davidson & others, 1977, 9

The earlier concept of asset as resources owned by the entity has been replaced in most definitions by a concept of control. Control exists when the entity has an inalienable right to the enjoyment of specific future benefits.

> Martin, 1984, 312

Assets are probable future economic benefits obtained or controlled by a particular entity as a result of past transactions or events . . . . assets may be acquired at a cost and they may be tangible, exchangeable, or legally enforceable. However, these features are not essential characteristics of assets . . . . assets may be acquired without cost, they may be intangible, and although not exchangeable they may be usable by the entity in producing or distributing other goods and services.

> FASB, 1985, SFAC6

Assets are service potential or future economic benefits controlled by the entity as a result of past transactions or other past events.

> AARF & AASB, 1992, SAC4

See also 255

436 Treatment of assets as costs or service potentials challenged

the future service potential value of an asset [being a subjective value] is unacceptable for financial statements.

> Kollaritsch, 1965, 59

A given (nonmonetary) good in possession may simultaneously have four kinds of service potential. It may be able to produce a certain quantity of a class of products . . . . It may serve as a liquidity reserve; it may be sold if any circumstance, such as a liquidity crisis or a change in output composition, justifies its sale. It may serve as part of a borrowing base . . . . And it may serve as a hedge against inflation, to the extent that its resale price rises as the general level of prices rises . . . . It is at least curious that only the first of these is commonly noticed, and that it is a physical, not a financial, notion. And it is curious that a physical capacity test is used in respect of the magnitude of an item which is to appear in a statement of financial characteristics . . . . The three last mentioned aspects of service potential are . . . all financial. Now, if there are four such aspects, is it possible to assign any amount to an asset which will represent the sum of these service potentials? I can imagine none, and I have never seen an attempt to establish such an amount.

Chambers, 1975a, 100

assets themselves are often defined as bundles of expected future benefits or service potentials. Such definitions are future-oriented, however, and since we view accounting as being comprised of measurements of present and past conditions, ... we prefer to regard assets as those things having current value ....

Edwards & others, 1979, 67

It is high time for us to stop talking (and thinking) about assets as costs in accounts, to start thinking about them as resources that benefit an enterprise, and to ask whether the descriptions and numbers that we put in financial statements represent something that is really there rather than merely entries in accounts.

Storey, 1981, 3

[Citing, by way of example, ten utterances of AICPA committees and the FASB, identifying costs as assets] I refer to this as the cost-*per se*-is-the-asset syndrome .... [It tolerates the inclusion, as assets, of a wide range of account balances that are not] real things, exchangeable things [and enjoins the exclusion of some things that are real and exchangeable things] .... I suggest that standard setters take another look at the definition.

Schuetze, 1993, 68–70

440 Asset Classes

441 Current, circulating or floating assets

[A recent inquiry by the author revealed that six of the older firms of public accountants] were able to name the approximate dates ... when they first began to utilize subtotals for current assets and current liabilities in their accounting practice. [The dates were 1898, 1905, 1906, 1907, 1910, before 1914.]

Foulke, 1945, 183

Floating assets are those which may be sold or realized without interfering with the plant or machinery of a business or its business operations, as cash, goods, customers' accounts and bills receivable. So far as floating assets are available as funds out of which current obligations may be met, they form the working capital of a business.

Lisle, 1899, 67

Floating assets ... are either (a) those acquired for the purpose of resale at a profit, benefit to the possessor arising only when realization takes place; e.g. stock in trade; or (b) those representing an incomplete stage in the conversion into cash; e.g. book debts, bills receivable, etc.; or (c) cash.

Jenkinson, 1910, 11

Floating assets – also known as current assets and quick assets – are those ever-changing assets resulting from the carrying on of the business – such as cash, accounts receivable, notes receivable, merchandise on hand, etc.

Bentley, 1911, 22

The current assets are called quick or floating, or liquid or working. The author prefers the term, current, for those assets which represent cash or items which will or should be converted into cash during the current operations of the business . . . . The intention [of the term] when related to a going business is to include all items of a cash or realizable nature as distinguished from fixed or unrealizable assets.

Montgomery, 1922, I:75

The first section [of the balance sheet] might be termed the circulating capital section, since at one time the funds of the business are tied up in a stock of goods, later the goods are sold and there is an account receivable substituted, and then the account is paid, after which the cycle is ready to begin again. The assets engaged in this short cycle are readily convertible into cash and are known as current, liquid or quick assets.

Guthmann, 1925/29, 52

Current assets . . . cash, accounts and notes receivable from outsiders and inventories of stock in trade, which in the regular course of business will be readily and quickly realized, together with such additional assets as may readily be converted into cash without impairing the business or enterprise . . . .

AIA, 1931a, 12

[Current assets are] those assets which are necessary to the operating cycle – exclusive of land and facilities – together with those assets which may be regarded as temporary investments of working capital and automatically will, or promptly can, be converted into free cash without impairing continuity and safety of operations.

Herrick, 1944, 54

current assets . . . all of those assets from which current creditors expect, in the normal course of business operations, to secure liquidation of their claims.

Kester, 1946, 46

the term current assets is used to designate cash and other assets or resources commonly identified as those which are reasonably expected to be realized in cash or sold or consumed during the normal operating cycle of the business.

AIA, 1947b, ARB30

Many years ago someone, whose identity is now probably unknown but who was evidently far in advance of his contemporaries, propounded the astounding paradox that a ship being built on the stocks in a shipbuilder's yard is a floating asset, whereas a completed ship afloat on the ocean is a fixed asset.

Davis, 1953, 37

current assets ... Cash and other assets which are expected to be converted into cash in the ordinary course of business within one year or within such longer period as constitutes the normal operating cycle of a business.

Fitzgerald, 1956a, 52

Current assets may be defined as: cash and other assets which will be converted to the status of cash or which will be consumed within the next year .... Current assets are the assets that creditors/ primarily look to for the payment of debts for they are the type most readily convertible into cash. They include stock in trade, cash, sundry debtors and other receivables. Prepaid expenses are also usually shown as current assets ....

Yorston & others, 1965, 1:25

442 Liquid (quick) assets

The term quick assets includes cash and such other items as can presumably be quickly turned into cash, such as inventories of material and merchandise, bills and accounts receivable, securities owned, etc.

Leamy, 1918, 162

Liquid assets are those that are readily available to discharge liabilities, such as cash; or that can easily be turned into money, such as gilt edged securities, bills receivable, etc.

Carter, 1923, 2

quick assets ... includes those current assets which can and will be quickly converted.

AIA, 1931a, 12

Liquid assets are those which are already in a state in which they can be used directly to meet obligations or which can be converted into such state almost immediately with little, if any, loss in value.

Goldberg, 1939/1948, 44

The quick assets are cash, readily realizable investments which are not hypothecated ... and current book debts ....

Fitzgerald, 1956a, 68

443 Fixed or noncurrent assets

assets may generally be divided into two classes: 1. those *with* which it [a company] carries on business, and (2) those *in* which it carries on business; the former may be named permanent assets, the latter floating assets.

Dicksee, 1892/1976, 120

Fixed assets are those which represent capital sunk in a business in the form of plant, machinery or ground, such as buildings, railway lines and all fixed machinery.

Lisle, 1899, 67

Fixed capital is wealth expended in land, houses, factories, mills, machinery, tools, and other things not intended to be exchanged or sold, but to be employed in the production of additional wealth.

Bithell, 1903, 55

The fixed assets are those which are of value only as far as they are serviceable to the business by their employment in the work of transforming the floating assets . . . .

Walton, 1909, 455

Fixed assets . . . are either (a) fixed or permanent, i.e. acquired for the purpose of being retained in the business, a profit being made from use and occupation and not from resale; e.g. land, buildings, plant, machinery, loose tools, etc.; or wasting, i.e. gradually consumed in the process of earning profits; e.g. quarry, mine, etc.

Jenkinson, 1910, 11

When a business . . . . acquires title to [fixed assets] with which to run the business, these things are purchased with the idea that they will be used permanently, or until those of a wasting character are worn out or replaced by improved, larger or more attractive things of the same nature.

Bentley, 1912b, 321

A fixed asset is one that will remain an economic factor within the particular business for at least two and usually five or more accounting periods . . . . which may or will with relative difficulty, or only in a roundabout fashion, be liquidated . . . .[and which] is absorbed by expense charges more slowly [than current assets].

Paton, 1924, 259

fixed assets . . . . those assets which may be retained for a long term of years, or indefinitely.

Guthmann, 1925/1929, 53

Fixed assets . . . have the fundamental characteristic that they are held with the object of earning revenue and not for the purpose of sale in the ordinary course of business.

ICAEW, 1945a, N9

Fixed assets may be regarded as those assets . . . which are of a permanent nature, and are definitely held for the purpose of earning revenue and not with a view to resale . . . . Goodwill . . . . is definitely a fixed asset notwithstanding its intangibility.

Pickles, 1974, 0578

Capital assets

Capital assets [include land and improvements, buildings, plant, equipment, patterns, dies, patents, goodwill, franchises, etc]
Dickinson, 1914, 75

By capital assets is here meant the permanent plant of the corporation, presumably purchased with the proceeds of the capital liabilities – that is, the stock and bonds.
Hatfield, 1916/1976, 46

Fixed assets: This term is synonymous with capital assets in undertakings in which capital is employed for the purpose of producing revenue, but it may also refer to tangible assets in undertakings where there is no proprietary accountability, e.g., hospitals . . . . The term "fixed assets" denotes a fixity of purpose or intent to continue use or possession. It does not refer to the immobility of an asset, which is the distinct characteristic of "fixtures".
AIA, 1931a, 13

444 Fixed assets indeterminate

The line of demarcation between fixed and circulating capital is so ill-defined that many writers object to the distinction.
Bithell, 1903, 55

If a certain department requires, to operate satisfactorily, a given amount of material on the machines and if the factory as a whole needs a certain minimum reserve of raw material, it would seem that these amounts of material are as definitely part of the fixed assets of the company as are the machines.
Peloubet, 1929, 568

though the distinction [between fixed and current assets] is regarded as vital, no one has been able to devise a precise rule for deciding which assets are fixed and which are current.
Norris, 1949b, 616

Those who oppose disclosure of estimated current value of inventories . . . . consider lifo inventories to be similar to fixed assets in that their values are not to be realized through disposal in the near future; hence information as to their current or replacement values is of limited significance.
AIA, 1949a, 220

There is no real distinction between current and fixed assets – the one type lasts longer than the other, but in the economic sense both (to plagiarize Recommendation [N9] of the Institute [ICAEW] and to reach an opposite conclusion) "have

429

the fundamental characteristic that they are not held with the object of earning revenue but for the purpose of sale in the ordinary course of business".
Bird, 1951, 103

I have never quite understood what was meant by the qualification, fixed, as applied to assets ... [and by] the fundamental dictinction between fixed and current assets .... Insofar as the major portion of the inventory of an enterprise does constitute a fixed asset necessary to the continuation of effective operations, it is my view that it should be classified as such in the balance sheet.
Bray, 1951, 358, 360

both the distinction between fixed and current assets and the terms by which the two classes are described have had and are having serious effects on the study of accounting and on accounting practice ... they ought to be abandoned.
Fitzgerald, 1951, 92

there is no such thing as a fixed asset.
Davis, 1953, 29

One can no more determine whether current or noncurrent assets provided the cash generated by operations than he can determine which blade of the scissors cut the cloth, for both were clearly necessary .... The current practice of identifying assets and liabilities as current and noncurrent should be discontinued.
Heath, 1978a, 17, 8

there is no unique rule for determining whether a particular asset should be classified as fixed or current.
Arnold & others, 1985, 92

445 Intangible and fictitious assets

The assets of a company may be divided into two classes: actual and fictitious .... the latter consist of the amounts representing the expenditure in acquiring the goodwill of a business, in the formation of the company, &c.
Pixley, 1881/1976, 139

in general, money actually expended for any purpose whatever except in the purchase of property is a nominal or fictitious asset ... incapable of paying anything ....
Cayley, 1894, 15

Whenever money or money's worth goes out of my business without anything tangible coming back to me for it, it is a dead loss, and one entry for it must be made on the Dr side of profit and loss.
Dyer, 1897/1984, 6

Fictitious assets . . . consist of expenditure unrepresented by any tangible assets, but which remain as outstanding debit balances after closing the books; e.g. expenditure spread over a term of years, such as preliminary expenses, or losses.

Jenkinson, 1910, 11

Fictitious assets are merely bookkeeping devices to preserve a balance of the books, and to permit the increment of profits for the year to be displayed without influence from the business transacted in previous years.

Page, 1916, 251

Fictitious assets are those that represent intangible expenditure; such as preliminary expenses, a debit balance of profit and loss, or value which cannot be realized . . . .

Carter, 1923, 3

Fictitious assets are merely debit balances not written off; that is, items of expenditure or losses of an unusual character which are not recoupable . . . .

Pickles, 1974, 0578

intangible assets . . . may be defined as expenditure incurred by an organization in return for which it receives nothing immediately tangible or physical, but which may result in the receipt of benefits beyond the accounting period in which the expenditure arises.

Arnold & others, 1985, 161

Deferred charges

Assets, deferred: That portion of expense items which is applicable to the period subsequent to the closing date. A better term wold be "deferred charges" or "deferred expenses" inasmuch as the charge to the operation is the thing deferred and not the asset value.

AIA, 1931a, 12

Assets also include certain deferred charges that are not resources but that are recognized and measured in conformity with generally accepted accounting principles. Note: Deferred charges from income tax allocation are an example of deferred charges that are not resources . . . .

AICPA, 1970c, APBS4

there are many types of items that might be found in the . . . deferred charge category in financial statements . . . . organization costs . . . . debt issuance costs . . . . market research . . . advertising and promotion . . . . start up and preopening costs . . . . relocation and rearrangement . . . .

Charles, 1981, 21.12ff

See also 425, 636

446 Goodwill, as potential or expectation

Lord Lucan tells a very good story, which, if not precisely exact, is certainly characteristical: that when the sale of Thrale's brewery was going forward, Johnson appeared bustling about, with an inkhorn and pen in his buttonhole like an exciseman; and on being asked what he really considered to be the value of the property which was to be disposed of, answered, "We are not here to sell a parcel of boilers and vats, but the potentiality of growing rich beyond the dreams of avarice."
Boswell, 1783/1867, 410

The goodwill which has been the subject of sale is nothing more than the probability that the old customers will resort to the old place. [per Lord Eldon]
Cruttwell v Lye, 1810

the amount by which the total of the values of the various physical properties within the enterprise, inventoried unit by unit, falls short of the legitimate asset total for the entire business, expresses the intangible asset [goodwill] value . . . . Goodwill . . . expresses the value of an excess earning power. It represents the capitalization of the peculiar rights and advantages enjoyed by the supramarginal enterprise. Evidently, then, if goodwill were completely recognized as an asset in the accounts of all businesses in a given industry all unusual rates of return would be thereby annihilated.
Paton, 1922/1962, 310, 317

Ware of a company with a huge item of goodwill on its balance sheet . . . . Goodwill . . . is the outward expression of inward unsubstantiality.
Ripley, 1927, 192

this kind of exchangeable value [commercial goodwill] is peculiar for it is based on nothing more substantial than future probabilities and possibilities; . . . .
Leake, 1929a, 31

Goodwill is not a resource or property right that is consumed or utilized in the production of earnings. Rather, it is a result of earnings, or of the expectations of them, as appraised by investors. Goodwill has no existence or life separate from the business. Goodwill value . . . . has no reliable or continuing relation to costs incurred in its creation, its purchase, or its maintenance.
Catlett & Olson, 1968, 107

Goodwill is not an acceptable asset for inclusion in financial statements because it reflects a judgment derived in part from those financial statements.
Spacek, 1970a, 48

goodwill means the future benefits from unidentifiable assets.
ASRB, 1988/1991, ASRB1013

See also 154

447 Goodwill, other aspects

What is goodwill? It is a thing very easy to describe, very difficult to define. It is the benefit and advantage of the good name, reputation and connection of a business. [per Lord Macnaughten]

Inland Revenue Commissioners v Muller Ltd, 1901

Goodwill represents the present worth or capitalized value of the estimated future earnings of an established enterprise in excess of the normal results that it might be reasonably assumed would be realized by a similar undertaking established new.

Yang, 1927, 88

Goodwill, when it appears in the balance sheet at all, is but a master valuation account – a catch-all into which is thrown both an unenumerated series of items that have the economic, though not necessarily the legal, properties of assets, and an undistributed list of undervaluations of those items listed as assets. It is the valuation account *par excellence*. It cannot under any circumstances be called an asset, unless that term is confessedly meant to include at least two kinds of things which have no common attribute peculiar to them.

Canning, 1929a, 42

goodwill represents . . . . nothing which exists, and is not real capital . . . . All such intangibles as goodwill . . . should be wholly eliminated . . . and their constantly shifting exchangeable values would be determined from day to day, as they really are now, on the stock exchanges . . . or . . . the "higgling of the market".

Leake, 1935, 779

There has never been any excuse for regarding goodwill as a "nothing" because of its intangibility . . . . For deceased estate purposes, the accountant has had to value goodwill, and he should be equally prepared and qualified to value it for purposes of a current value balance sheet.

Byrd, 1974, 434

Not only do accountants have strongly held and differing views about the best treatment of goodwill in balance sheets, but there is not even a consensus as to its nature.

Unwin & Simon, 1981, 118

It is usual for the value of a business as a whole to differ from the value of its separable net assets. The difference which may be positive or negative, is described as goodwill. Goodwill is . . . by definition incapable of realization separately from the business as a whole . . . . the value of goodwill has no reliable or predictable relationship to any costs which may have been incurred; individual intangible factors which may contribute to goodwill cannot be valued; the value of goodwill may fluctuate widely . . . over relatively short periods of time; and the assessment of the value of goodwill is highly subjective . . . . unique to the valuer and to the specific point in time at which it is measured, and is valid only at that time, and in the circumstances then prevailing.

ASC, 1984b, SSAP22

Goodwill may be regarded in broad terms as the difference between the total value of an organization as a single entity and the sum of the value of its individual net assets ... excluding goodwill.

Arnold & others, 1985, 162

See also 483

448 Dubious financial significance of intangibles

In the balance sheets of nearly all companies are to be found, included on the credit side amongst the assets, balances of expenditure accounts which cannot be said to be represented by realizable assets . . . . amounts paid for the goodwill of a business, preliminary or formation expenses of a company, establishment of agencies &c. In the event of the company going into liquidation it is evident that these items . . . will not turn out to be realizable assets, and it is therefore desirable, at any rate in some instances, to extinguish these accounts, either gradually or by charging the whole amount against the revenue of the first year.

Pixley, 1897/1978, 62

to include in ... the balance sheet mere expectancies would be to introduce items the value of which is highly speculative among items the value of which can be measured with greater reliability.

Canning, 1929a, 20

When actual consideration has been paid for goodwill, it should appear in the company's balance sheet long enough to create a record of that fact in the history of the company . . . . After that, nobody seems to regret its disappearance . . . .

Sanders & others, 1938, 14

The books of a business . . . . are not designed to record the present speculative value of its future expectations or probabilities. Men and corporations may pay money for such expectations and probabilities, but this does not cause them to become balance sheet assets . . . . Goodwill is an estimate of the future . . . . It can be created by propaganda and destroyed by a rumor. More frequently than not its value will be both unknown and unascertainable . . . . In the writer's opinion goodwill should have no place in any balance sheet.

MacNeal, 1939, 236

intangible assets, deferred items, etc . . . . seldom have any real place in the financial statements. They are . . . stray debits and credits for which a home had to be found. I cannot believe that in most instances they afford information on which investments are made or liquidated. There is no reason why Mr. Pacioli should not record them on his ledger, but our [suggested] statements would no longer purport to display all that is on that ledger.

Caffyn, 1948, 151

The loss of goodwill as a balance sheet asset is deemed of no importance, because accountants and financial analysts have come to regard such intangibles with suspicion and to automatically disregard them in computing net worth.

Kripke, 1961/1968, 83

little if any weight should be given [by the investor] to the figures at which intangible assets appear on the balance sheet.

Graham & McGolrick, 1964, 34

Any goodwill or intangible assets appearing in the balance sheet will normally be eliminated in making the calculation [of net asset value per share].

Napper, 1964a, 872

the intangibles cannot be sold without contemplating the sale of the enterprise as a whole, because they do not generally inhere in, or attach to, specific components but to the entire enterprise as a going concern . . . . their valuation necessarily warrants the valuation of the entire business . . . . the attempts of earlier writers like Dicksee, Leake and Cutforth who sought to value goodwill as a separate asset were not well founded.

Lall, 1969, 322

Intangibles as offset to equity

In balance sheets prepared for credit purposes, [goodwill] is sometimes omitted from the asset side and is brought over as a deduction from the proprietorship or net worth.

Couchman, 1924, 139

On the balance sheet recommended by the Federal Reserve Board . . . the intangible assets, so far as they are represented by goodwill, are shown as a deduction from the surplus.

McKinsey, 1925, 164

The investor, viewing the balance sheet as a statement of net assets, will disregard these "fictitious" items [intangible assets]. He will write them off by deducting the figure attributed to them from the total capital and reserves . . . . In a modern vertical form of balance sheet, goodwill arising on consolidation is often deducted from the capital and reserves . . . . why should we not deduct goodwill and other intangible assets in the same way?

Napper, 1964b, 636

The amount assigned to purchased goodwill represents a disbursement of existing resources, or of proceeds of stock issued . . . , in anticipation of future earnings. The expenditure should be accounted for as a reduction of stockholders' equity . . . . [This] is consistent in principle with existing practices of accounting for internally developed or nonpurchased goodwill.

Catlett & Olson, 1968, 106

accounting for purchased goodwill by a reduction in shareholders' equity reflects the facts of the transaction . . . . The amounts so deducted should be presented as a continuing and cumulative deduction from shareholders' equity to ensure continuing stewardship for the amounts spent.

Hinton, 1973, 35

[To write off the purchase consideration for goodwill] as soon as it is acquired implies that the goodwill never existed or that it was valueless at that date. Where, however, the goodwill is reflected as a separate item as a deduction from the shareholders' equity, this method of disclosure does comply with the requirements of accounting for goodwill.

Macintosh, 1974, 32

Because . . . goodwill . . . cannot be sold except in a sale of the whole business, [and] it is (conventionally) not shown in the balance sheet if internally generated, and because of the fugitive nature of any valuation of it, . . . goodwill should be written off on acquisition.

Westwick, 1981, 43

See also 688

449 Monetary and nonmonetary items

[Money assets] Property rights that are defined in terms of a fixed number of pounds . . . . Almost all liabilities . . . obey the same rules. [Nonmoney assets] Property rights that are not defined in terms of a fixed number of pounds, so that their current market value is free to move . . . .

Baxter, 1949/1978, 5

A balance sheet account is monetary if it consists of cash or if it represents a claim to or an obligation to pay a fixed sum of money. All other balance sheet accounts are nonmonetary.

Jones, 1956, 9

The importance of the distinction lies in the fact that monetary assets and nonmonetary assets are subject to quite different risks. Holdings of monetary assets are subject to the risk of changes in the purchasing power of money . . . . Nonmonetary assets are subject also . . . to the risks of changes in customers' preferences, in technology, and in the demands, therefore, for both producers' goods and their products.

Chambers, 1966a, 196

The generally accepted rules for [conversion of foreign currency amounts to domestic currency] .... recognize the important distinction between (a) those items in the balance sheet which are money or claims to money, in the form of cash on hand or receivable or payable, and (b) those which are ... other forms of wealth, for example plant, stock in trade and unexpired services, which are only expressed in terms of money for accounting purposes.

ICAEW, 1968e, 6

Assets and liabilities are called monetary ... if their amounts are fixed by contract or otherwise in terms of numbers of dollars regardless of changes in specific prices or in the general price level .... Holders of monetary assets and liabilities gain or lose general purchasing power during inflation or deflation simply as a result of general price level changes.

AICPA, 1969, APBS3

A monetary good ... is either money (cash) or a right to receive cash, such as a debt owed the firm by some individual or some other business .... Usually [the right] must be a legally enforceable right to receive a specific amount of cash at a specific time .... Any goods that are not monetary are called ... nonmonetary goods.

Thomas & Basu, 1972, 42

Monetary items are claims (assets) or obligations (liabilities) to a fixed number of dollars .... not altered by changes in the value of the dollar or changes in the costs or prices of individual goods .... Nonmonetary items are those whose prices are not fixed in number of dollars.

Backer, 1973, 114

Monetary items are those whose amounts are fixed, by contract or otherwise, in terms of numbers of pounds, regardless of changes in general price levels. Examples ... are cash, debtors, creditors and loan capital .... Nonmonetary items include such assets as stock, plant and buildings .... The equity interest is ... neither a monetary nor a nonmonetary item.

ASSC, 1973, ED8

Monetary assets are claims to a fixed number of dollars, and they remain unchanged in dollar terms irrespective of changes in the purchasing power of the dollar and changes in market prices .... Nonmonetary assets comprise all assets which are not claims to a fixed number of dollars.

Barton, 1984, 455

450 Liabilities

451 Liabilities described as dated debts

The liabilities of a business consist of all sums due to outside creditors as distinguished from the sums due to partners or shareholders.
Lisle, 1899, 67

The liabilities of a business include all debts owed by it, and such other obligations as it is legally liable for – such as mortgages payable, outstanding bonds, notes payable, accounts payable, accrued taxes, accrued interest, etc.
Bentley, 1911, 22

Strictly speaking, a liability is a debt or an amount owed to some one who has a right of action at law.
Guthmann, 1925/1929, 21

Liabilities – the property rights vested in persons who merely loan assets for use in the business; they are creditors.
Rorem, 1928, 22

A liability is a service, valuable in money, which a proprietor is under an existing legal (or equitable) duty to render to a second person . . . .
Canning, 1929a, 56

The liabilities of a business represent what it owes . . . .
Bell & Graham, 1936, 3

The interests or equities of creditors (liabilities) are claims against the entity arising from past activities or events which, in the usual case, require for their satisfaction the expenditure of corporate resources.
AAA, 1957a/1957b, 7

Perhaps the leading features distinguishing liabilities, broadly viewed, are the following: (1) They are nonowner equities, claims, interests, or asset reservations. (2) They generally involve future asset expenditures for their settlement. (3) They should relate to assets already recognized.
Trumbull, 1963, 46

A liability is any amount which a business is legally bound to pay. It is a claim by an outsider on the assets of a business.
Garbutt (ed), 1969, 0107

452 Liabilities described with reference to future settlement

A liability is an obligation to pay money to a creditor in the future.

Kelley, 1941, 512

The liabilities of a business enterprise are its obligations to convey assets or perform services, obligations resulting from past or current transactions and requiring settlement in the future.

Sprouse & Moonitz, 1962, 37

A liability is a claim against the entity by a creditor, arising from a past transaction and requiring that at some future time the entity pay a sum of money or some other resource or perform a service.

Black & others, 1967, 30

Liabilities are probable future sacrifices of economic benefits arising from present obligations of a particular entity to transfer assets or provide services to other entities in the future as a result of past transactions or events.

FASB, 1980b, SFAC3

A liability is the future sacrifice of economic benefits that an entity may be required to make in satisfaction of a present obligation to transfer assets or provide services to other entities as a result of past transactions and events.

Kerr, 1984, 25

Some items that are recorded as liabilities . . . are not legal debts if a debt is given its usual legal definition of a sum of money due from one person to another. The provision for taxation payable is recorded as a liability before the legal debt is assessed and dividends payable are reported as a liability before they are ratified at meetings of shareholders. Liabilities also include other provisions for future payments assumed to be related to the activities of current and past periods, but for which there is some uncertainty about the amount to be paid. Provisions are made for future warranty service, even though no legal debt will be established unless the product requires warranty service. These liabilities are not legal debts at the present time . . . . Since liabilities are not necessarily legal debts, they are defined as obligations to make payments or render services in the future.

Martin, 1984, 358

Liabilities are the future sacrifices of service potential or future economic benefits that the entity is presently obliged to make to other entities as a result of past transactions or other past events.

AARF & AASB, 1992, SAC4

Liability provisions

For the purposes of this schedule ... the expression "provision" shall ... mean any amount ... retained by way of providing for any known liability of which the amount cannot be determined with substantial accuracy; ... and in this paragraph the expression "liability" shall include all liabilities in respect of expenditure contracted for and all disputed or contingent liabilities. [Eighth schedule]

UK *Companies Act*, 1948

The term provision is now generally applied to either (a) an amount charged against income (in the course of matching revenue with cost) or set aside out of profits to meet estimated liabilities; or (b) an amount so charged or set aside to meet specific commitments or known contingencies.

Fitzgerald & Schumer, 1952, 71

Liability "reserve" accounts arise particularly where one or both of the following conditions is present: (1) the amount is uncertain and must be estimated; (2) the specific party or parties to whom payment will be made cannot yet be designated.

Paton & Dixon, 1958, 673

A provision for a specific purpose is one that has been created by a charge made against profits (i.e. before arriving at the net profit or loss) in order to provide for an anticipated expense or loss attributable to the current year, the amount of which can only be estimated.

Jones, 1970, 223

453 Liabilities – other descriptions

While the asset side contains concrete actualities, the other side deals with the distribution of these actualities among those who have the title to them and those who hold claims against them, the liabilities. In algebraic language we may say that liabilities are negative assets and that proprietorship is measured by the algebraic sum of all the assets positive and negative.

Sprague, 1907/1972, 49

Liabilities, that is, debts of any kind, may ... be considered as negative goods, the assets being positive goods .... But just as in algebraic equations a negative term in one member may be transferred to the other member thereby becoming positive, so in the bookkeeping equation the form is ordinarily
Goods $10,000 = Proprietorship $5,000 + Debts $5,000.

Hatfield, 1909, 14

Liability (as a balance sheet heading): a thing represented by a credit balance that is or would be properly carried forward upon a closing of books of account kept by double entry methods, according to the rules or principles of accounting, provided such credit balance is not in effect a negative balance applicable to an asset. Thus the word is used broadly to comprise not only . . . debts or obligations . . . , but also credit balances to be accounted for which do not involve the debtor and creditor relation.

AIA, 1941c, ARB9

Liabilities – economic obligations of an enterprise that are recognized and measured in conformity with generally accepted accounting principles. Liabilities also include certain deferred credits that are not obligations but that are recognized and measured in conformity with generally accepted accounting principles.

AICPA, 1970c, APBS4

A liability is a negative present value of an anticipated actual or constructive cash flow, other than distributions to owners, where any discretion with respect to the flow is restricted by legal or other compelling sanctions and where the activity that gives rise to the flow is completed or otherwise has progressed to a determinative stage.

Ma & Miller, 1978, 260

454 Liabilities described as capital

As capital, they [liabilities] represent that portion of the total capital which has been furnished by others, or loan capital.

Sprague, 1907/1972, 49

The term, capitalization, has many uses, as total issue of capital stock, total investment – capital stock and bonds issued, and book figure of assets.

Cole, 1921, 312

the fixed liabilities and owners' interests are frequently called the capital liabilities, although the latter is not an actual liability.

Guthmann, 1925/1929, 53

Though the law still maintains the conception of a sharp dividing line recognizing the bondholder as a lender of capital and the stockholder as a quasi-partner in the enterprise, economically the positions of the two have drawn together. Consequently, security holders may be regarded as a hierarchy of individuals all of whom have supplied capital to the enterprise, and all of whom, expect a return from it.

Berle & Means, 1932, 279

The amounts of capital provided by the firm's creditors are called its liabilities . . . .

Gordon & Shillinglaw, 1964, 5

In accordance with the entity concept of the business enterprise, both stockholders and holders of long term debt are considered equally as investors of permanent capital . . . . income to investors includes the interest on debt, dividends to preferred and common stockholders, and the undivided remainder . . . . income taxes are treated as expenses.

Hendriksen, 1977, 168

Entity capital can be defined as all of the long term capital of the business (i.e. loan capital in addition to proprietors' net worth) . . . .

Whittington, 1984, 149

See also 195, 465

455 Current liabilities

Floating liabilities are those claims by creditors which will have to be met within a short period.

Lisle, 1906, 67

Floating liabilities, also known as current liabilities, are those resulting from the routine conduct of the business, and include all liabilities except those classed as fixed.

Bentley, 1911, 23

Current liabilities are . . . those which will mature within twelve months from the date of the balance sheet . . . .

Kester, 1946, 45

The term current liabilities is used principally to identify and designate debts or obligations, the liquidation or payment of which is reasonably expected to require the use of existing resources properly classifiable as current assets, or the creation of other current liabilities.

AIA, 1947b, ARB30

A current liability is a legally enforceable debt or obligation that normally will be paid within one year of the balance date.

Kennedy, 1948, 44

456 Fixed, long term or deferred liabilities

Fixed liabilities are those permanent obligations of a concern which are not usually paid off till the concern is would up, such as debenture debt and mortgages.

Lisle, 1906, 67

Fixed liabilities include all liens on fixed assets, such as mortgages, mortgage bonds, debenture bonds and any other long time obligations.

Bentley, 1911, 22

It is customary to classify a liability as fixed, instead of current, if it does not come due within a year.

Guthmann, 1925/1929, 53

There can be no clear line of demarcation between long time debts and short time debts. A commonly drawn line is however to classify as long time debts all those which run for more than one year . . . . The use of the term deferred liabilities to describe some obligation maturing in the distant future is unsatisfactory.

Hatfield, 1927/1971, 224, 225

A fixed liability is a legally enforceable debt or obligation that normally will not be paid within one year of the balance sheet date.

Kennedy, 1948, 47

457 Contingent liabilities

Contingent liability – a liability which will only exist definitely upon the happening of some event which may or may not happen.

Dawson, 1904, 85

contingent liabilities . . . liabilities for which the proprietor may be held under certain contingencies but which he never expects to have to meet . . .

Hatfield, 1927/1971, 234

It is not enough that a balance sheet show what must be paid – it should set forth with as much particularity as possible what may have to be paid. It is the duty of an auditor to discover and report upon liabilities of every description, not only ascertained debts but possible debts. Contingent liabilities . . . should appear as footnotes on the liability side of the balance sheet. Contingent liabilities [include indorsements, guaranties, unfulfilled contracts, taxes, damages, liability for real estate bonds and mortgages] . . . [A similar provision appeared in Federal Reserve Board, 1917]

Federal Reserve Board (US), 1929, 16

A contingent liability is a liability that may arise as a result of certain past actions. As of the balance sheet date there is no actual liability of determinable amount.

Kennedy, 1948, 46

[Contingent liability] . . . a possible liability of presently determinable or indeterminable amount which arises from past circumstances or actions and may or may not become a legal obligation in the future . . . . The method most often used to disclose the existence of contingent liabilities in the balance sheet is an explanatory note.

Montgomery & others, 1949, 363, 374

A contingent liability is a responsibility in money or money's worth to another person, which may or will become a definite liability on the happening of some event following a transaction already entered into . . . . in relation to the balance sheet, the term . . . also includes any primary liability of which the amount cannot reasonably be estimated . . . at the date of the balance sheet . . . . The note as to a contingent liability should constitute part of the balance sheet . . . as a note to any related asset . . . or as a note on the liabilities side above the balance sheet totals.

Taylor & Perry, 1952, 141ff

A contingent liability will become an actual liability only if some future event occurs. Thus, if a company admits that it is liable for breach of contract, but is disputing the amount of damages . . . , then the company's liability is actual and not contingent, and can at least be estimated. If, however, the company denies that it is liable for breach of contract, but the other party is pursuing his claim, then the company's liability is contingent only, since it depends on the success or otherwise of the other party's claim.

Keenan, 1980, 91

A contingent liability is a potential liability that can develop into a real liability if a possible subsequent event occurs.

Needles & others, 1984, 377

458 Executory contracts

A contract is said to be executory so long as anything remains to be done under it by any party, and executed when it has been wholly performed by all parties.

Halsbury's laws of England, 1974 ed, 9:82

If B has contracted to make goods and deliver them to A, and if no goods have been delivered and no payments made, there is no asset arising from this contract on the books of either A or B, nor is there any liability shown either . . . . [Where] one party [A] has performed in larger proportion than the other . . . . the accountants recognize an asset of A.

Canning, 1929a, 18, 19

one schedule, schedule of material contractual commitments, may be the report to provide full and adequate disclosure of those activities [such as leasing] which do not logically belong on the balance sheet.

Zises, 1961, 44

If the mutual promises to perform [of the parties to a lease contract] are considered to have value, it would seem the entity is obligated to account for such value, and thus an immediate change has occurred in the asset-equity status of the enterprise.

Alvin, 1963, 42

[An executory contract] an agreement between two or more parties in which no party has yet performed any of the acts required of him by the agreement.

Birnberg, 1965, 814

the view that capitalized lease rentals essentially represent a debt obligation seems to be of questionable validity . . . . a recognition of a balance sheet liability implicit in lease contracts is not of major importance for investment analysis purposes.

Hayes, 1965, 770

Agreements for the exchange of resources in the future that at present are unfulfilled commitments on both sides are not recorded until one of the parties at least partially fulfills its commitment, except that (1) some leases and (2) losses on firm commitments are recorded.

AICPA, 1970c, APBS4

Contracts, the two sides of which are proportionately unperformed, should not be recognized.

Anthony, 1983, 181

459 Accounting for long term leases

when it is clearly evident that the transaction involved is in substance a purchase [i.e. when a lease is made subject to subsequent purchase of the property for a nominal sum . . . or. . .], then the leased property should be included among the assets of the lessee with suitable accounting for the corresponding liabilities and for the related charges in the income statement.

AIA, 1949b, ARB38

The capitalization technique [for rentals under long term leases] . . . endeavors to equate leasing with debt, tries to provide a figure which is assumed to be the amount of liability . . . . Leasing always differs from debt in its economic effect upon the lessee in one or more of [five stated respects].

Zises, 1961, 38

Notes to financial statements [should include] . . . . commitments that will govern the level of a certain type of expenditure for a considerable period into the future. e.g. under long term leases.

CICA, 1964, Bull 20

if we want to predict a firm's future cash flows, then footnote disclosure of the expected lease payments is likely to be more useful to users of financial statements than any other figure we can contrive.

Thornton, 1976, 41

A lease is a contract between a lessor and a lessee for the hire of a specific asset . . . . A finance lease is a lease that transfers substantially all the risks and rewards of ownership of an asset to the lessee . . . . An operating lease is a lease other than a finance lease . . . . A hire purchase contract is a contract for the hire of an asset which . . . [gives] the hirer an option to acquire legal title to the asset upon the fulfilment of certain conditions . . . . a finance lease should be recorded in the balance sheet of a lessee as an asset and as an obligation to pay future rentals. At the inception . . . the sum to be recorded both as an asset and as a liability should be the present value of the minimum lease payments, derived by discounting them at the interest implicit in the lease . . . . Rentals payable should be apportioned between the finance charge and the outstanding obligation for future amounts payable . . . . The rental under an operating lease should be charged on a straight line basis over the lease term . . . unless another systematic and rational basis is more appropriate.

ASC, 1984a, SSAP21

460 Equity, Ownership, Proprietorship, Capital

461 Equities generally as rights or claims

All equities which have contractual rights to assets as either income or principal are liabilities; the equities which have residual rights to assets constitute proprietorship.

Paton & Stevenson, 1918/1978, 248

Liabilities and proprietorship are very similar in their basic characteristics; they both represent property rights.

Rorem, 1928, 22

Equities are sources of and claims to the assets of an enterprise, and may be further categorized as (a) liabilities, that is, creditor equities the amounts of which are fixed by contract between the firm and the claimants; and (b) proprietorship, that is ownership equities, the total amount of which equals the sum of all assets less the sum of all liabilities.

Hill & Gordon, 1959, 22

Equities represent rights or claims to assets and we speak of external equities (or liabilities) representing the rights of creditors and internal equities (or proprietorship) representing the rights or claims of the owners of the enterprise. Equity holders are the sources from which a business derives the funds invested in its assets.

Yorston & others, 1965, 1:17

462 Equities (or proprietorship) as interests or rights in or claims against the assets of firms

To observe strictly the legal fiction in the case of an incorporated enterprise one should say, not equities in assets, but equities in the enterprise. A stockholder, for

example, has no claim or title to any specific asset. From the standpoint of accounting, however, it is no serious error to say that an equity, in every case, is virtually
a right in assets.

Paton & Stevenson, 1918/1978, 20

proprietorship is merely the residual ownership of the stockholders or partners in
an enterprise after the creditors' interests have been deducted from total assets.

Paton, 1924, 293

Proprietorship consists of the entire beneficial interest of a holder of a set of assets
in those assets . . . . Net proprietorship . . . . is the difference found by subtracting
the summation of the liabilities from the amount of the proprietorhsip.

Canning, 1929a, 55

The interests or equities of stockholders represent residual claims to corporate assets,
although particular classes of stock may, by contractual arrangement, be assigned
different priorities.

AAA, 1957a/1957b, 7

a residual equity [in an entity] is a right to receive any services that the entity is
capable of providing in excess of those required to satisfy the definite enforceable
rights of related parties. In a business firm, this right commonly resides in the . . .
common stockholders . . . . [but it falls to the next ranking creditors] when the traditional residual equity group is wiped out.

Staubus, 1961, 19

Owners' equity is represented by the amount of the residual interest in the assets
of an enterprise.

Sprouse & Moonitz, 1962, 54

The residual or owners' interest is the interest in the economic resources of an
enterprise that remains after deducting economic obligations. It is the interest of
those who bear the ultimate risks and uncertainties and receive the ultimate benefits
of enterprise operations.

AICPA, 1970c, APBS4

Entity equity is the difference between total assets and the sum of liabilities plus
shareholder equity [= direct contributions plus accrued interest on these funds]. Its
principal source is the entity's operating activities.

Anthony, 1983, 94

In a business enterprise, the equity is the ownership interest. It stems from ownership
rights . . . and involves a relation between an enterprise and its owners as owners . . . . Since equity ranks after liabilities as a claim to or interest in the assets of
the enterprise, it is a residual interest . . . .

FASB, 1985, SFAC6

463 Owners' equity as paid in or legal capital

The meaning of the word capital is different from that of the word stock. When persons enter into partnership it is usual to fix upon a certain sum, which shall thenceforth constitute the capital of the firm; and each partner brings in such a proportional part of this capital ... as may be agreed on between themselves. The sum, or the value of the effects [at a valuation or estimate] which each partner brings in ... constitutes his capital, or capital stock as it is sometimes called, in the concern.

Cory, 1839, 90

There is, perhaps, at this day no better established rule of law than that the capital stock of a moneyed corporation, whether it be a banking, insurance, mining or manufacturing company, is to be treated and deemed as a trust fund for the purpose of securing the payment of the debts of the corporation .... The capital stock being, as I said, a trust fund, the first duty of the officers of the bank is to keep this fund intact and unimpaired. [per Blodgett J]

Main v Mills, 1874

Some seven men form an Association
(If possible, all Peers and Baronets),
They start off with a public declaration
To what extent they mean to pay their debts.
That's called their capital: if they are wary
They will not quote it at a sum immense.
The figure's immaterial – it may vary
From eighteen million down to eighteenpence.

Gilbert, *Utopia Ltd*, 1893

Considering all assets as capital, the proprietorship is that portion (in value) of the capital which the proprietor furnishes as distinguished from ... the liabilities.

Sprague, 1907/1972, 53

As usually held in the law, the legal capital is the dollar amount which stands to the credit of the capital stock account .... This amount ... may not be returned to the owners [as dividend] unless the business goes through a partial or complete liquidation .... This concept of the legal capital as a protective device for the benefit of creditors is basic in all corporate law .... the amount designated as legal capital ... is the foundation of [a corporation's] credit life; it is the residuum of protection for creditors.

Kester, 1946, 423, 470

Paid in capital is measured by the cash, or the fair market value of other assets or services, contributed by stockholders or by persons acting in a capacity other than that of stockholders or creditors, or by the amount of liabilities discharged upon the transfer of an equity from a creditor to a stockholder status.

AAA, 1948/1957b, 16

In the beginnings of corporate organization . . . . the aggregate par amount [of shares] was regarded as legal capital – the buffer or cushion set up to protect creditors. Since the corporation enjoyed the special right of limited liability, creditors had to rely solely on present or future corporate assets for satisfaction of their claims. The requirement of a certain amount of legal capital protected creditors to that extent, by placing assets to the amount of the legal capital "in trust" to protect the creditors from loss.

Vatter, 1955, 374

Nominal capital is capital measured in terms of the number of units of account as of the date of its investment.

Eckel, 1964, 139

The legal definition of capital is . . . derived from the early common law notion that capital is a "trust fund" or safeguard for creditors and investors required by law in return for the privilege of limited liability . . . . Since the principal emphasis of the law has always been to assure the existence and to prohibit the distribution or impairment of legal capital, . . . a statute which authorized payment of dividends out of "net profits" or "surplus profits" so that "capital should not be impaired" was generally construed to mean that the amount of assets in excess of liabilities plus legal capital was freely distributable, unless some specific prohibition were set forth as to paid in or capital surplus.

Hackney, 1973, 299

The principles applicable to accounting for transactions in equity securities are few and relatively simple . . . . A transaction in an equity security is recorded at the amount of the consideration a corporation receives or distributes for the security. The consideration equals the cash or fair value of other assets that a corporation receives or distributes . . . . The fair value of other assets . . . is measured by the fair value of the security unless an estimated value of the asset is more reasonably determinable. The fair value of an equity security as a measure of consideration is based on market prices of the stock . . . .

Melcher, 1973, 137

Owners' equity as capital and surplus

The basis of accountancy is the fundamental economic concept of the distinction between capital and income . . . . capital may be briefly described as the money or assets they [stockholders] have invested in the corporation, and income as the increment resulting from the use of the capital . . . . Unfortunately, in attempting to reconcile with this fundamental idea the numerous statutory and legal doctrines . . . we have wandered into a maze of intricacies which obscure the underlying facts . . . . I would like to make a plea for a return to first principles. I would like to see the amounts contributed by stockholders considered as capital regardless of the form of the contribution.

Broad, 1938, 281

as the measure of protection offered the creditors of limited liability corporations . . . . corporation law needs no complicated array of stock and surplus
accounts . . . . Perhaps a single net worth account to represent the whole residual
equity would suffice . . . . Does the protection of creditors necessarily depend upon
limiting withdrawals to profits? . . . . As far as creditors are concerned, does it matter
whether capital is lost or withdrawn, provided they are still protected by an ample
margin?

Littleton, 1938, 83

Stockholders' interest is the investment of the owners in the enterprise, consisting
of paid in capital and retained income.

AAA, 1948/1957b, 16

from an economic point of view any subdivision of the original stockholders' investment contribution between par and excess of par or between stated value and excess
of stated value is utterly spurious.

Sprouse, 1960, 251

Proprietorship – the financial interest of the owner or owners of a concern, arising
from original investments in it and any profits left to accumulate in it.

Vance, 1961, 7

the common stockholders' equity on the balance sheet is only a residual figure
needed to balance the accounting equation for it appears to have no apparent usefulness to the investor in making his investment decision. So long as this is the
case, any attempt to subdivide the common shareholders' equity is unnecessary.

Birnberg, 1964, 968

All proprietorship accounts are basically and fundamentally homogeneous, identical,
and completely interchangeable. Proprietorship is a quantity only, a calculated or
derived difference between [the totals of] assets and liabilities, and therefore can
have no natural or normal subdivisions . . . . With the apparent (but not real) exception
of the par value of capital stock, proprietorship data are not independently determinable.

Moonitz & Jordan, 1963, II:141

Historical statistics on the cumulative amount of income earned but not distributed
may well be useful . . . as indices of past growth, conservatism in paying dividends,
and accordingly, financing from within. For many companies, however, . . . portions
of retained earnings have been capitalized in connection with stock distributions to
stockholders, acquisitions and mergers for stock and the like. The significance of
amounts of reported retained earnings has been impaired accordingly . . . . the entire
common stockholders' equity is the corporation's capital. Distinctions among capital
stock, capital surplus and retained earnings are not, for most large corporations,
useful to anybody.

Bevis, 1965, 61

The owners' equity in an enterprise consists of capital they have contributed and the cumulative comprehensive income of the enterprise that the owners have left in the business.

Andersen & Co, 1984, 67

464 Capital as equity of owners or stockholders in business assets

The form and manner of keeping a solemn inventory . . . . Then gather together the whole sum of your ready money, debts and goods, and therefrom subtract the total sum of your creditors, and the remainder is the net rest, substance or capital of the owner to be put in a traffic, etc.

Mellis, 1588, ch 3

Capital is . . . the surplus of assets over liabilities, or the measure of the indebtedness of a business to the owners in respect of money invested in the business and accumulated profits.

Lisle, 1903–04, I:203

For the purpose of the balance sheet, the word capital is used to describe the claim or equity of the owner or proprietors in the assets of the enterprise. In the case of a corporation, this equity or claim of the stockholders is represented by the capital stock, surplus amd surplus reserves. Other terms often used with the same meaning are proprietorship and net worth.

Kelley, 1941, 512

In corporate accounting, capital is the recorded stockholder equity in the assets of the enterprise.

AIA, 1945a, 264

Capital is the term used by accountants to describe the owners' equity in a business. It is represented by the excess of total assets over total liabilities.

Montgomery & others, 1949, 378

[In the accounts of a person, A,] the net value of all A's property after what he owes to other people has been deducted . . . . [is] A's ownership interest. Other terms that can be used are wealth, capital, ownership claim, equity.

Edey, 1963, 13

Stockholders' equity, often referred to as shareholders' equity, capital, or net worth, represents the excess of the company's assets over its liabilities.

Rossell & Frasure, 1967, 304

Equity is the residual interest in the assets of an entity that remains after deducting its liabilities [from its assets]. In a business enterprise, the equity is the ownership interest.

FASB, 1980b, SFAC3

465 Capital as a liability

The balance sheet is . . . the balance sheet of the business, and not of the proprietor. That is why capital is shown as a liability, being a debt due by the business to the proprietor of it.

Carter, 1923, 44

the old idea of a proprietor as one insider with specific and simple obligations to outsiders called creditors will no longer serve; for certain types of creditors instead of being really outsiders are partly inside the business and partake of the nature of proprietors. For this reason I venture to think that there is more value than [Canning] seems to assign to it of the concept of a "fictitious person", such as the corporation considered as a bookkeeping entity. This "person" is the sole proprietor and its liabilities include stocks as well as bonds . . . . the residual element in the balance sheet is a true liability, a liability to stockholders.

Fisher, 1930b, 613

Liability (as a balance sheet heading): a thing represented by a credit balance . . . . the word is used broadly to comprise . . . . liabilities in the popular sense of debts or obligations . . . [and] also . . . . capital stock, deferred credits to income and surplus . . . .

AIA, 1941c, ARB9

Net worth may be considered a technical liability from a bookkeeping standpoint. It is a liability to a legal entity such as to a proprietor, to partners, or to the stockholders who own the stock of a corporation.

Foulke, 1945, 106

In corporate organization, . . . treatment of preferred stock as contractual capital, closely akin to borrowed funds, is generally desirable, as this will facilitate disclosure of the earning power of the layer of true risk capital . . . .

Paton, 1963, 64

The entity theory made the business the focus of accounting. All transactions were interpreted from the viewpoint of the business. Assets belonged to the business rather than to the owners and liabilities were owed by the business rather than the owners . . . . From the business's viewpoint the owners were simply the providers of finance in much the same way as lenders and suppliers (creditors) who provided finance under different terms.

Henderson & Peirson, 1983, 53

See also 195, 454

466 The amount of capital as the amount of net assets

The difference between the assets and liabilities, at any time, is called his [the merchant's] net capital or present worth.

Foster, 1843, I:17

Broadly stated, capital is the surplus of assets over liabilities, whether that surplus be derived from trading or investment.

Accountant, Anon, 1882, 4

I understand the capital in a business, equally of a company, a partnership, or an individual, to be the sum by which the assets exceed in value the liabilities.

Cooper, 1888, 741

Capital is the excess of assets [property] over liabilities, the excess of what I have and have owing to me over what I owe.

Dyer, 1897, 11

The capital of a business concern at a particular moment of time may be defined, for purposes of accounting, as the surplus of the assets of the concern over the liabilities to the creditors of the concern.

Lisle, 1899, 68

The distinction between liabilities to creditors and other liabilities [to owners of capital] gives us the familiar balance sheet equation: Assets – Liabilities = Capital. Capital ... is the value of the rights of any given person (or institution) or group of persons (or institutions) in a particular asset or assets. The rights of any given group have a value which is equal to the total worth of the assets less the value of the rights of the rest of the creditors.

Edwards, 1938b, 81

467 Capital as amount of aggregate assets

Capital means the entire amount of what you now possess.

Pacioli, 1494/1963, 45

Capital is the total value of the resources of a firm or individual. Net capital or present worth is the excess of the resources over the liabilities at the close of business or at any time during business.

Soulé, 1903/1976, 23

The capital of a concern is the total amount of the property and assets employed therein, contributed partly by the proprietor and partly by those who have chosen to give him credit; and the capital of the proprietor in that concern is the surplus of the property and assets over the liabilities to third parties.

Dawson, 1904, 65

The total of the properties [assets] is also the total of the capital of the enterprise, and the equities express the equitable distribution of this total – the legal relationships connecting this wealth and certain individuals or interests, the division of ownership.

Paton, 1922/1962, 45

In bookkeeping, the capital of a business is the sum total of its assets; and the capital of the proprietor of the business is the surplus or excess of assets over liabilities.

Carter, 1923, 2

Business capital and business assets are synonymous.

Porter & Fiske, 1935, 16

Capital in its most general sense means a store of wealth from the use of which the owner hopes to obtain additional wealth. The capital of a business consists of all its property or assets, both fixed and current.

Sanders & others, 1938, 11

The single most important task of accounting is determining the value of the various resources or of the capital of the corporation. (. . . A corporation's capital is the aggregate of all its resources . . . .)

Ladd, 1963, 50

[capital being] all the items on the left hand side of the balance sheet, . . . an entity's capital is its wealth.

Anthony, 1983, 175

468 Retained earnings, undivided profits, surplus

Earned surplus: The balance of net profits, including income and gains of a corporation from the date of incorporation . . . after deducting losses and after deducting distributions to stockholders and transfers to capital stock accounts when made out of such surplus.

AIA, 1941c, ARB9

the subcommittee [on terminology] recommends that . . . . the use of the term surplus (whether standing alone or in such combinations as capital surplus, paid in surplus, earned surplus, appraisal surplus, etc) be discontinued . . . . [and] be replaced by terms which will indicate source, such as retained income, retained earnings, accumulated earnings, or earnings retained for use in the business . . . .

AIA, 1949d, ARB39

From the entity point of view . . . . retained earnings constitute part of the corporate entity's equity in itself.

Husband, 1954b, 555

Retained earnings, often still called earned surplus, represents that portion of the company's total net earnings over the years of its existence which has ... [been] reinvested in the business.

Rossell & Frasure, 1967, 310

470 Reserves

471 Reserves generally

A reserve may be defined as a provision charged against profits with a view to covering an expected loss .... A reserve created to cover loss through the deterioration in the value of any specific class of asset should, as a rule, be shown in the balance sheet, not as a liability, but as a deduction from the particular asset in respect of which it has been created .... a reserve ... created to cover a general loss in respect of all assets ... must appear as a liability in the balance sheet.

Dicksee, 1903c, 47, 48

A reserve has long been recognized as the amount by which the assets of a concern exceed the sum of its paid up capital and liabilities. Such a definition, however, might be more accurately applied to the surplus of a concern .... For the purpose of ascertaining the extent of a surplus the assets may be taken at the *bona fide* value of a company's property as a going concern. The liabilities are taken upon that basis, and it is only reasonable that the assets should be similarly treated.

Dawson, 1904, 428

The term, reserve, is used to indicate (1) a certain type of asset (as in banking), (2) a deduction from an asset to bring it to an appropriate valuation, (3) a liability, (4) an item falling in the area between liabilities and proprietary capital, and (5) a subdivision of proprietary capital.

Dohr, 1941, 204

The term, reserve, ... is a multiple-use word, having at least three distinct meanings. Reserve account balances may represent any of the following: (1) liabilities; (2) offsets to particular or group asset balances; (3) appropriated or segregated surplus.

Paton, 1943/1982, 58

the term, reserve, is used in four senses ... 1 ... to describe (a) a deduction which is made from the face amount ... or the book value of an asset ... valuation reserves .... 2 ... to indicate an estimate of an admitted liability of uncertain amount .... 3 ... to indicate a variety of charges set forth in the income statement .... 4 ... to indicate that an undivided or unidentified portion of the net assets is being held ... for a special [designated] purpose .... it is recommended that the use of the term, reserve, in accounting be limited to the last of the four senses ....

AIA, 1948, ARB34

In general usage, outside of accounting, a reserve is a fund of cash or other assets .... In accounting the term has been used to caption a variety of balance sheet items including segregated retained income, segregated assets, asset valuation and asset amortization amounts, and liabilities .... The committee believes ... that the popular understanding of financial statements, and the thinking of the profession, would be promoted by abandoning the term.

AAA, 1950/1957b, 19–20

The expression, reserve, is now properly used only to signify a sum set aside out of profits for a ... general purpose; that is, it does not relate specifically to some known loss or expense that has already been incurred. It covers possible losses or expenses, either present or future, but not actual losses or expenses, for which suitable provision must always be made.

Northcott & Forsyth, 1949, 105

A reserve is that portion of a company's profits ... which is retained for future use. It consists of appropriations from profits and other surpluses which have been earned in the past, i.e. amounts which are not designed to meet any liability, contingency, commitment or diminution in value of assets known to exist as at the date of the balance sheet.

Jones, 1970, 225

472 Reserve accounts or funds

The profits ... to be divided ... in any year shall not exceed the prescribed rate [for the undertaking], or where no rate is prescribed [ten per cent per annum] .... the excess beyond the sum necessary for such purpose shall from time to time be invested in government or other securities ... in order that the same may accumulate at compound interest until the fund so formed amounts to the prescribed sum, or if no sum be prescribed, a sum equal to one-tenth of the nominal capital ..., which sum shall form a reserved fund to answer any deficiency which may at any time happen in the amount of divisible profits, or to meet any extraordinary claim or demand ....

UK *Gas Works Clauses Act*, 1847

The directors may, before recommending any dividend, set aside out of the profits of the company such sum as they think proper as a reserved fund to meet contingencies, or for equalizing dividends, or for repairing, or maintaining, the works connected with the business of the company, or any part thereof; and the directors may invest the sum so set apart as a reserved fund upon such securities as they, with the sanction of the company, may select. [Table B, Model articles of association]

UK *Companies Act* 1856

A reserve fund is neither more nor less than an accumulation of profits which might have been distributed by the company in the form of dividends, but which it has

been considered more expedient to retain as a provision against unforeseen contingencies . . . . A reserve fund is . . . undivided profits, and it is impossible to say
it is specifically represented by any asset.

Dicksee, 1897, 89–90

A reserve fund . . . . differs from a reserve in that it is impossible to create a reserve
fund save out of divisible profits; whereas a reserve may be provided even during
periods when a loss has been sustained. A reserve fund is but a portion of the credit
balance of the profit and loss account, which has been specially earmarked as being
reserved . . . . If those profits have been absorbed in subsequent losses, the reserve
fund automatically ceases to exist . . . . the popular view that a reserve fund is only
"real" when represented by specific investments outside the business, of a corresponding value, is entirely misconceived.

Dicksee, 1903c, 51

Reserves. The results of corporate operations are characteristically summarized and
reflected in earned surplus account . . . . The resultant balance . . . may then be (a)
reclassified to reflect corporate policy, contractual agreements, or the recognition of
future uncertainties, or (b) used as the legal basis for distributions to proprietors.

Moonitz & Staehling, 1952, II:121

473 Variety of "reserves"

The word, reserve, at this time [prior to 1910 in Canada] was indiscriminately applied
to asset valuation accounts, liabilities and appropriations to retained earnings. These
accounts tended to be grouped under the liability side of the balance sheet – their
more common names being general reserve, investment reserve, insurance reserve,
contingent account, suspense, replacement reserve, rest reserve, depreciation reserve
and inventory reserve.

Murphy, 1988, 79

Three kinds of items may be found on the balance sheet under the title of reserves:
1 . . . reserves for taxes and similar items which are not reserves in the proper
sense, but instead are accrued liabilities . . . . 2 . . . reserves which represent the
estimated decrease in the value of assets, such as reserves for depreciation and
reserves for bad debts. These should be shown . . . as deductions from the assets
to which they pertain . . . . [They] may properly be called valuation reserves . . . .
3 . . . reserves which represent surplus that has been set aside for a certain length
of time for a specific purpose, and which later will be carried back to surplus account.

McKinsey, 1925, 165

At least five kinds of reserves occur [in present day accounting practice], and some
of them are so unlike that they may almost be said to be contradictions . . . . [They
are] (1) a mere indication of an overvaluation of assets shown on the other side of
the balance sheet, as an allowance for depreciation . . . ; (2) a provision for something
inevitable to be met in the future but properly chargeable to the past, as a provision

for income taxes; (3) a provision for probable losses in the future . . . ; (4) a provision for possible losses in the future . . . ; (5) straight earned surplus earmarked against distribution as dividends.

Cole, 1933, 488–9

A specific reserve represents a sum charged against profits to provide for a known contingency, the exact amount of which . . . cannot be ascertained and has, therefore, to be estimated, such as reserves for bad debts, discounts, depreciation, future repairs and renewals, disputed claims, etc . . . . A general reserve represents sums set aside out of profits, to provide against unknown future contingencies, to increase the working capital, to equalize dividends, or merely to strengthen the financial position of the concern. A general reserve presupposes a profit and is an appropriation of profits.

de Paula, 1935, 116–7

Any amount set aside to finance replacements (whether of fixed or current assets) at enhanced costs, should not be treated as a provision which must be made before profit for the year can be ascertained, but as a transfer to reserve.

ICAEW, 1949, 37

The following are capital reserves . . . : capital redemption reserve fund, share premium account, profits prior to incorporation, and a reserve arising from an unrealized appreciation in value of fixed assets . . . as a result of a revaluation of assets. The following are revenue reserves: general reserve, dividend equalization reserve . . . and the balance carried forward on profit and loss account.

Northcott & Forsyth, 1949, 292

Capital reserves, for accounting purposes, comprise all amounts, other than those falling under the heading "contributed capital", which are treated as not available for withdrawal by the proprietors . . . . Revenue reserves comprise all retained income treated as available for withdrawal by the proprietors . . . .

ICAEW & NIESR, 1951, 18

three kinds of accounts which are often called reserves: 1. valuation accounts or reserves . . . correctly shown as deductions from the appropriate assets . . . . 2. liability accounts or reserves . . . which show the estimated amount of the firm's liability on the obligation indicated . . . . 3. surplus reserves which . . . are appropriations of earned surplus.

Easton & Newton, 1958, 323

I believe that in removing the distinction between capital and revenue reserves, the 1967 Companies Act relieved us of an entirely irrelevant division . . . .

Corbett, 1972, 383

Traditionally reserves created from profits have been called revenue reserves. Reserves created from other sources have been referred to as capital reserves. However, such distinction is purely conventional . . . .

Gaffikin, 1993, 563

474 Secret, hidden or undisclosed reserves

The placing of values upon inventories below the proper figures – cost or market whichever is the lower – constitutes a secret reserve. The same may be said of any other assets, the accounts covering which have actually been reduced below their intrinsic value. Securities purchased at a low cost which subsequently rise in value form a common source of secret reserves, as the prudent business man is loath to anticipate profits by writing up the value of such assets.

Knight, 1908, 199

A secret reserve is a surplus the existence of which is not shown on the balance sheet . . . . Secret reserves are made . . . by excessive depreciation of assets . . . . by undervaluation or omission of assets . . . . by creating unnecessary or excessive reserves for bad debts . . . . by charging capital expenditure to revenue . . . .

Carter, 1923, 625

This term [secret reserves] is used to denote the existence of proprietary equities concealed through the undervaluation or omission of assets or the overstatement or inclusion of fictitious liabilities . . . . charging cost of additions to maintenance . . . . creation of excessive depreciation and other allowances . . . . understatement of inventory values . . . . secret writing down of assets . . . .

Montgomery, 1934, 431ff

An undisclosed reserve is commonly created by using profits to write down more than is necessary such assets as investments, freehold and leasehold property or plant and machinery; by creating excessive provisions for bad debts or other contingencies; by charging capital expenditure to revenue; or by undervaluing stock in trade.

Cohen Committee, 1945

Hidden reserves are represented by the difference between cost or adjusted cost of an asset as reflected on the balance sheet and the net realizable value of that asset as determined on a going concern basis. Hidden reserves can also exist if certain assets are not recorded on the books of a company.

Bradish, 1965, 763

Secret reserves, commonly referred to as inner reserves, are brought about by (1) understatement or omission of assets, fixed or current (by charging capital expenditure to revenue) and/or (2) creation of excessive provisions, or overstatement of liabilities.

Jones, 1970, 253

[Undisclosed reserves include] 1. Hidden reserves, where an item of profit is . . . described in such a manner as to indicate a liability . . . . 2. Inner reserves, where a provision . . . to cover exceptional and abnormal losses . . . is not openly disclosed . . . . 3. Secret reserves [arising from] excessive depreciation . . . . undervaluation or understatement of an asset . . . . permanent appreciation of a fixed asset . . . .

Pickles, 1974, 0719

475 Posited objects of secret reserves

The object of all secret reserves is to equalize dividends, or to equalize apparent profits . . . .

Dicksee, 1905b/1976, 194

(1) [Secret reserves] promote financial stability. Extraordinary losses may be met out of such undisclosed or hidden surpluses . . . preventing the dividend being reduced and public confidence shaken . . . . (2) They enable a normal rate of dividend to be maintained . . . because they enable unduly fluctuating profits to be manipulated, and steady, progressive results to be shown. (3) They advance the interests of the undertaking . . . . huge profits can be concealed from business rivals, whereas the publication of such profits would stimulate competition, and perhaps injure the company's trade.

Carter, 1923, 626

Some boards of directors think that stockholders as a class must not have full information for their own good; therefore . . . the profits of good years are not fully disclosed and dividends are continued through the unprofitable periods. Banks and trust companies assume this patriarchal attitude more frequently than do industrial corporations.

Montgomery, 1934, 434

Secret reserves are created for one of two reasons: (a) intent to deceive or (b) paternalism of directors.

Newlove & Garner, 1951, 1:128

See also 733, 737

476 Objections to secret reserves

The ideal goal of accounting is exact accuracy, and a hidden surplus is in its very term a confession of an inexact balance sheet.

Hatfield, 1904(p 32)/1978

Those who defend the establishment of a secret reserve seem to look upon the bank or company as an unchanging entity, and claim that it is better to conceal abnormally large profits in one year so as to provide against the necessity of showing unusually large losses in another year .... In the case of a company whose stock is somewhat scattered ... it seems impossible to find any justification for the practice.

Walton, 1909, 466

(1) The shareholders have not a full knowledge of the company's affairs .... (2) Secret reserves .... can ... be used to conceal losses arising from bad management or reckless speculation. (3) Concealment of facts and manipulation of figures are bad in principle .... Suspicions may be aroused which will weaken or destroy confidence in the management much more quickly than a policy of straightforward dealing, ...

Carter, 1923, 626

Hidden reserves may be useful for the manager of an enterprise who wants to cover mismanagement, but they are strictly to be rejected from the viewpoint of the shareholders. For the purposes of equalizing losses occurring during business cycles, open reserves may be used just as well .... The hidden reserve is to be rejected also because it favors the falsification of stock exchange prices.

Schmidt, 1930/1982, 504

there may be very great evils if those who have the control and management of the companies ... have very large portions of the company's assets left in the secret disposition of the managing authority .... it may be the subject of almost intolerable abuse. Such a system may cover up negligence, irregularities and almost breaches of faith. It is said to be a matter of domestic concern between the company and the shareholders, but if the shareholders do not know and cannot know what the position is, how can they form any view about it at all? [Wright J, charge to the jury; *Royal Mail* case, *Rex v Lord Kylsant & another*, 1931]

Brooks (ed), 1933, 223

The objections urged against undisclosed reserves can be summarized as follows. As the assets are undervalued or the liabilities overstated, the balance sheet does not present a true picture of the state of the company's affairs; the balance of profits disclosed as available for dividends is diminished, and the market value of the shares may accordingly be lower than it might otherwise be; and the creation, existence or use of reserves, known only to the directors, may place them in an invidious position when buying or selling the shares. On the other hand, if there is no detailed disclosure in the profit and loss account, undisclosed reserves accumulated in past periods may be used to swell the profits in years when the company is faring badly, and the shareholders may be misled into thinking that the company is making profits when such is not the case.

Cohen Committee (UK), 1945

I believe that the disclosure of secret reserves built up by valuing land and buildings at cost is the most urgent accounting problem facing the profession today.

Napper, 1964b, 642

477 Ambivalent attitudes towards secret reserves

I am of the opinion that what are known as secret reserves are right and proper, and tend toward the maintenance of the company as a permanent institution, and that, in fact, without those reserves it is quite impossible, having regard to the fluctuation of both financial and trading operations, for any company to exist beyond a very limited period. At the same time, these reserves must be honestly made and in the interests of the company.

Pixley, 1904, 410

The practice of creating [secret] reserves is favored by some accountants and condemned by others .... in the long run it would have to be left to those who controlled the financial affairs of a business as to whether or not secret reserves should be created.

Carter, 1923, 627

Secret reserves or inner reserves are in certain cases desirable and in many cases essential. In the Council's opinion all such reserves should be included in the balance sheet items and no company by its articles should be allowed to contract itself out of this obligation.

ICAEW, 1925

The chief criticism of banks' [financial] statements [Canada, 1960–61] relates to their notorious secret reserves. All banks have these but the amounts involved and the treatment accorded to them only become obvious when an unusual change occurs .... two banks in the 1961 year ... returned to undivided profits substantial amounts of secret reserves no longer required.

Coutts (ed), 1962b, 601

480 Group Accounts

481 Legal entities and groups

For a time many lawyers were opposed to the presentation of consolidated accounts by companies to their stockholders, but the leading lawyers engaged in corporation practice have long since recognized that the technical legal situation is less important to stockholders and the public than the substantial position and have accordingly accepted the principle of consolidated accounts.

Webster, 1919, 259

No company with branches ever thinks of publishing a balance sheet showing the amounts owing to or by those branches . . . . And yet, when the branch . . . becomes, legally, a separate entity . . . doubts and questions arise as to the desirability of consolidating the subsidiary's figures with those of the parent company. Where there is control there should be consolidation.

Readman, 1942, 132

While a group of companies is recognized by the [UK *Companies Act*], the attribute of legal entity is not conferred upon the group as such; it remains with each separate company within the group. Creditors can look for satisfaction of their debts only to the assets of the one company to which they have extended credit. It may be, of course, that a company will help a financially embarrassed subsidiary, but it is not bound to do so. A creditor is on safer ground if he assumes that the holding company will cut its losses . . . .

Jones, 1970, 120

a group is not a legal entity capable of issuing shares, owning assets and owing liabilities. It cannot have a state of affairs, nor earn profits, in the sense that legally constituted companies or corporations can. It cannot sue or be sued. To assign certain operations or transactions to one company in a group, so that their consequences may fall on that company without affecting the others, is indeed one of the reasons for creating or acquiring subsidiaries. No creditor of a member-company of any group can have recourse to the assets of any other member-company except by separate contract entered into or guarantee given by that other member-company. It is thus misleading to imply that a group can have a state of affairs or can earn profits. And since there can be no such state of affairs and no such profits, in any sense equal to or analogous to the state of affairs and the profit of a properly con- stituted company, no set of consolidated statements can give a true and fair view of anything.

ASRC, 1978, 124

"Economic entity" means a group comprising the investor [company], its subsid- iaries, and the investor's ownership interest in its associated companies.

ICAA & ASA, 1983/1987, AAS14

See also 047, 048

Associated companies

An associated company is a company not being a subsidiary of the investing group or company in which (a) the interest of the investing group or company is effec- tively that of a partner in a joint venture or consortium and the investing group or company is in a position to exercise a significant influence over the company in which the investment is made; or (b) the interest of the investing group or company is for the long term and is substantial . . . . Significant influence . . . essentially involves participation in the financial and operating policy decisions of that company ... but not necessarily control of those policies,

ASC, 1971/1982, SSAP1

"Associated company" means an investee [company], not being a subsidiary company of the investor [company], over which the investor has significant influence.

ICAA & ASA, 1983/1987, AAS14

See also 489

482 Combinations as purchases and poolings of interests

For accounting purposes, the distinction between a pooling of interests and a purchase is to be found in the attendant circumstances rather than in the legal designation as a merger or a consolidation . . . . In a pooling of interests, all or substantially all of the equity interests in predecessor corporations continue, as such, in the surviving corporation . . . . In a purchase ... part or all of the ownership of the acquired corporation is eliminated.

AIA, 1950b, ARB40

if one corporate party to a combination is quite small in comparison with another, the transaction could scarcely be regarded as a true merger.

Wilcox, 1950, 103

A combination brings the assets of two or more companies under single ownership and control. In certain instances the combination involves a change in original ownership, as, for example, when assets of one company are sold for cash to another. However, in other instances, ... assets of a company are transferred to another in exchange for stock that offers the original ownership a continued interest in and control of assets. A combination that involves the elimination of an important part of the original ownership is designated as a combination by purchase. A combination that involves a continuation of substantially all of the orginal ownership is designated as a combination by pooling of interests.

Karrenbrock & Simons, 1961, 274

the description of the merger as a pooling or purchase depends on the accounting entries made rather than on the circumstances, the real business events, surrounding the merger itself.

Moonitz, 1968, 629

Purchase or pooling is a pseudo-problem. It arises from the pervading influence of a desire to adhere to the conventional accounting system. Nonhomogeneity of the bases of asset book values is a characteristic of the historical cost technique. It is not peculiar to the accounting for business combinations.

Clarke, 1972, 139

483 Accounting for combinations as purchases

When a combination is deemed to be a purchase the assets purchased should be recorded on the books of the acquiring company at cost, measured in money or the fair value of the property acquired, whichever is most clearly evident.
AIA, 1950b, ARB40

Under purchase accounting, a business combination is viewed as a purchase . . . . the fair value of the consideration exchanged is measured and accounted for in the statements of the continuing or resulting enterprise. The separable resources and property rights of the acquired or absorbed company are recorded at their fair values at the time of the transaction . . . . The difference between the total consideration given . . . and the value of its separable resources and property rights (less liabilities) is generally referred to as goodwill. Goodwill is recorded as an asset on the balance sheet of the continuing enterprise . . . .
Olson, 1969/1973, 110

The purchase method accounts for a business combination as the acquisition of one company by another. The acquiring company records at its cost the acquired assets less liabilities assumed. A difference between the cost of an acquired company and the sum of the fair values of tangible and identifiable intangible assets less liabilities is recorded as goodwill. The reported income of an acquiring corporation includes the operations of the acquired company after acquisition, based on the cost to the acquiring corporation.
AICPA, 1970a, APBO16

recognition is given to the market value of the securities issued by the acquiring company, and this requires explicit recognition of goodwill for the excess of the purchase price over the recorded net assets of the acquired company.
Coleman, 1970, 96

Where a business combination is accounted for as an acquisition, the fair value of the purchase consideration should, for the purpose of consolidated financial statements, be allocated between the underlying net tangible assets and intangible assets other than goodwill, on the basis of the fair value to the acquiring company . . . . Any difference beween the fair value of the consideration and the aggregate of the fair values of the separable net assets . . . will represent goodwill . . . .
ASC, 1985, SSAP23

The theory supporting the purchase method holds that in each business combination one company acquires one or more other companies. The acquirer continues; the acquired disappear. The history of the combined enterprise is the history of the acquirer. Its acquisition of the acquired is accounted for as is the acquisition by a company of any other assets.
Rosenfield & Rubin, 1985, 244

Purchased goodwill

The excess of the cost of an acquired company over the sum of identifiable net assets, usually called goodwill, is the most common unidentifiable intangible asset .... Solving the [accounting] problem ... is complicated by the characteristics of an intangible asset: its lack of physical qualities makes evidence of its existence elusive, its value is often difficult to estimate, and its useful life may be indeterminable.

AICPA, 1970b, APBO17

purchased goodwill ... is an investment by the buying enterprise in a group of intangible resources of the selling company that are of a rather elusive nature. As an investment asset, it should be carried at an unamortized amount in the balance sheet as long as there is no evidence that its value has been impaired or that its term of existence has become limited.

Eiteman, 1971, 48

The excess of the purchase price over the net book value of a [purchased] subsidiary's assets should be allocated to the specific assets purchased (excluding goodwill) on the basis of their going concern market values, and only the balance should be shown as goodwill.

Gilbert, 1971, 255

the vexed question of accounting for purchased goodwill would disappear if it were accepted that the evaluation of goodwill was an investor function to be determined in part on the basis of information ... in the financial statements but not to be included therein ....

Hinton, 1972, 57

Purchased goodwill (positive or negative) is established when a business combination is accounted for as an acquisition; it includes goodwill arising on consolidation, and on the acquisition of an interest in an associated company or of an unincorporated business .... There is no difference in character between purchased goodwill and nonpurchased goodwill. However, the value of purchased goodwill, although arising from a subjective valuation of the business, is established as a fact at a particular point in time by a market transaction .... Purchased goodwill [when positive] should normally be eliminated from the accounts immediately on acquisition against reserves.

ASC, 1984b, SSAP22

Goodwill which is purchased by the company shall be measured as the excess of the cost of acquisition incurred by the company over the fair value of the identifiable net assets acquired .... To the extent that the cost of acquisition ... exceeds the fair value of the identifiable net assets acquired, but the difference does not constitute goodwill, such difference shall be charged to the profit and loss account immediately.

ASRB, 1988/1991, ASRB1013

Negative goodwill

Three methods of handling the problem [where the stock of subsidiary corporations is bought at less than the book value of net assets] are: (1) to consider an element of negative goodwill; that is, that the goodwill acquired in the purchase of other companies is to be diminished; (2) to show upon the consolidated balance sheet a capital surplus, due to the fact that a greater value of assets has been acquired than the amount of par value of stocks issued therefor; (3) to introduce into the balance sheet a valuation account entitled possibly, reserve representing overvaluation of assets of subsidiaries . . . . the conception of negative goodwill is a rather difficult one and accountants are inclined to apply it with but a halting and imperfect consistency.

Hatfield, 1927/1971, 449

When book value of the subsidiary's stock exceeds the cost thereof to the holding company, the balance arising from the consolidation is a credit. Like consolidated goodwill it is a balancing item, which is created by the consolidated statement device, and the same conclusion stated with respect to consolidated goodwill applies; namely, it should not be merged with other items in the consolidated balance sheet.

Daniels, 1934/1980, 110

When the price paid by the parent company for a controlling interest in another company is less than the book value of the corresponding equity of the subsidiary, in accordance with recognized practice only that part of the book value of the subsidiary equal to the price paid by the parent is eliminated, the excess usually being reflected in the consolidated balance sheet as capital surplus . . . . or offset against any positive goodwill . . . .

Kester, 1946, 476, 584

The values attributable to the separate resources and property rights [of an acquired company] may exceed the value of the business as a whole . . . . the consideration given is presumably less than the fair value of the net resources and property rights acquired; the difference is often referred to as negative goodwill . . . . negative goodwill should be recorded as a liability for special expenditures which may be needed to improve profitability; if no special expenditures are contemplated, the amount should be added to capital surplus or retained earnings . . . .

Catlett & Olson, 1968, 99, 112

Negative goodwill . . . arises when the purchase consideration given for an acquired business is less than the current value of the net resources when separately valued . . . . Negative goodwill is considered to be a negative asset, or . . . a contra-assets account or assets valuation account . . . . it is considered that it is the exact logical counterpart of positive purchased goodwill, and . . . that the accounting treatment of purchased goodwill (positive or negative) should be exactly the same.

Berry, 1975, 55

negative goodwill should be credited directly to reserves.

ASC, 1984, SSAP22

484 Accounting for combinations as poolings of interests

In a merger there is a pooling or commingling of the rights of the various security holders, the assets, liabilities and operations of the merging corporations being combined . . . . the application of sound accounting methods to [such] a merger . . . results . . . in the single arithmetical addition of assets, liabilities, and net worth . . . . [including] earned surplus . . . .

Black, 1947, 215

When a combination is deemed to be a pooling of interests, the necessity for a new basis of accountability does not arise. The book values of the assets of the constituent companies, when stated in conformity with generally accepted accounting principles and appropriately adjusted when deemed necessary to place them on a uniform basis, should be carried forward; and retained incomes of the constituent companies may be carried forward.

AIA, 1950b, ARB40

Pooling of interests accounting views a business combination . . . as a marriage of the constituents to the transaction. No new basis of accountability is established. The amounts at which assets and liabilities are recorded in the accounts of both or all predecessor companies are simply carried forward to the accounts of the continuing or resulting enterprise. There is no accounting . . . for the fair value (at the time of the transaction) of the separable resources and property rights of the absorbed business. There is no accounting for goodwill [on purchase] . . . .

Olson, 1969/1973, 110

The pooling of interests method accounts for a business combination as the uniting of the ownership interests of two or more companies by exchange of equity securities. No acquisition is recognized because the combination is accomplished without disbursing resources of the constituents. Ownership interests continue and the former bases of accounting are retained.

AICPA, 1970a, APBO16

no recognition is given to the market value of the [acquisition] transaction; rather the financial reports of the two companies as taken from the accounting records are simply combined as though the two companies had always been together.

Coleman, 1970, 96

A business combination may be accounted for as a merger if . . . (a) . . . [it] results from an offer to the holders of all equity shares . . . and (b) the offeror has secured . . . a holding of (i) at least 90% of all equity shares . . . and (ii) the shares carrying at least 90% of the votes of the offeree, and (c) . . . and (d) . . . . In merger accounting, it is not necessary to adjust the carrying values of the assets and liabilities of the subsidiary to fair value either in its own books or on consolidation.

ASC, 1985, SSAP23

The theory supporting the pooling of interests method holds that the method reflects an amalgamation of two streams, previously running separately and presently running together, neither one augmented or diminished by their joining. The history of the amalgamated stream becomes, therefore, the sum of the histories of its tributaries .... The pooling of interests method generally produces higher reported net income and more conservative balance sheets than the purchase method.

Rosenfield & Rubin, 1985, 244

Fair value pooling

[Where] ... the asset values on the books of a corporation, a party to a merger, are so substantially unrealistic that they would materially impair the usefulness of subsequent financial statements .... a merger is an especially appropriate occasion for any useful revaluation for which there exists authoritative accounting support applicable in the circumstances.

Wilcox, 1950, 106

[Objection] ... to the varying asset bases resulting from purchase accounting for combinations ... [might be averted]. The acquiring company's assets might be stated on a current value basis to coincide with the basis of the newly acquired assets rather than recording the new assets on a basis that existed on a different entity's records.

Wyatt, 1963, 82

485 Group accounting alternatives

four methods of presenting the accounts of holding companies .... are : (i) To publish only the holding company's balance sheet and profit and loss account, treating the interest in subsidiary companies as an investment in the balance sheet and including in the profits the dividends actually received .... (ii) To publish the balance sheet and profit and loss account of the holding company as in (i) and to present simultaneously either the separate balance sheets and profit and loss accounts of all the subsidiary companies; or (iii) As a separate statement a summary of the assets and liabilities of all the subsidiary undertakings taken together. (iv) To publish either separately or along with the holding company's balance sheet (as in (i)) a consolidated balance sheet of the whole undertaking amalgamating the assets and liabilities of all the subsidiaries with those of the holding company and a consolidated profit and loss account embracing the profits and losses of all the companies.

Garnsey, 1923, 16

Sir Arthur Whinney . . . urges that the correct method of presenting investments in subsidiaries in a holding company's balance sheet is to value them on a basis which indicates the sum to which the parent company is entitled after prior claims have been made. The information . . . should be supplemented by the publication of the balance sheets of the subsidiary companies with that of the holding company. [reported in editorial, *Accountant*, Aug 8]

Whinney, 1925, 203

With an affiliated group of companies . . . two alternatives presented themselves prior to the development of consolidated statements. One was to present a balance sheet and income account of the parent company only . . . . The other alternative was to present such parent company statements and supplement them with balance sheets and income accounts of all the subsidiaries. The first . . . left undisclosed too much information . . . . The second . . . would give more information . . . [but] would throw too great a burden on the recipient of the statements.

Staub, 1929/1982, 654

There are, generally speaking, three methods of presenting [information additional to the legal accounts], . . . viz: (i) By the publication simultaneously of the separate balance sheets and profit and loss accounts of all the subsidiary companies. (ii) By the publication of a statement giving a summary of the aggregate assets and liabilities of all the subsidiary undertakings taken together. (iii) By the publication of a statement in the form of a consolidated balance sheet of the whole undertaking, amalgamating the assets and liabilities of all the subsidiaries (and sub-subsidiaries) with those of the holding company and a consolidated profit and loss account embracing the profits and losses of all the companies.

Robson, 1936, 30

486 Objects of consolidated financial statements

The object of a consolidated balance sheet is to show the true financial position of a company and its subsidiary companies with regard to the outside public; consequently all intercompany holdings of stock and all intercompany balances of every kind should be eliminated in the consolidated balance sheet.

Webster, 1919, 262

a correctly drawn up consolidated balance sheet and income account are frankly and plainly statistical statements, or if we do not like this description we may say that they are the representation of an economic unit rather than a statement of assets on the one hand and the various claims against those assets on the other.

Peloubet, 1933, 228

[There are] . . . two basic attitudes toward the affiliate relationship . . . . first . . . since the companies are separate legal entities, accounts reflecting intercompany amounts should show no evidence of the relationship, and that intercompany transactions should be regarded as arm's length in character . . . . second . . . the peculiar relationship existing among affiliates gives rise to the necessity for special handling of intercompany accounts and transactions on the books of the companies involved. This view is based on the well-founded suspicion that transactions between affiliates are not likely to be at arm's length. Both, of course, take the position that, theoretically, the consolidated statements should reflect the effects of all transactions as though they were in fact those of one company.

Childs, 1949, 47

The purpose of consolidated statements is to present, primarily for the benefit of the shareholders and creditors of the parent company, the results of operations and the financial position of a parent company and its subsidiaries essentially as if the group were a single company with one or more branches or divisions. There is a presumption that consolidated statements are more meaningful than separate statements and that they are usually necessary for a fair presentation when one of the companies in the group directly or indirectly has a controlling financial interest in the other companies.

AICPA, 1959b/1961, ARB51

Consolidated statements are prepared for the purpose of reporting the position and activities of a group of companies operated under a common control. They are intended to reflect the facts with respect to an economic rather than a legal unit.

Wixon (ed), 1962, 23:1

A consolidated balance sheet is based upon a combination of separate balance sheets of the constituent corporations. It shows how the consolidated business entity stands with respect to the outside world, all internal intercompany asset items, intercompany liability items, and intercompany owners' equity items being eliminated. A consolidated balance sheet supplements but does not supplant the balance sheets of the constituent individual corporations, and creditors and owners must look to the individual corporations in asserting their rights . . . . A consolidated income statement is based on a combination of the separate income statements of the constituent corporations, with all intercompany transactions, such as intercompany purchases and intercompany sales, being eliminated.

Coleman, 1970, 95

The underlying object of consolidated accounts is . . . to show in one profit and loss account and one balance sheet the results and state of affairs respectively of the holding company and its subsidiaries, as if the whole group was constituted as one company, operating through one or more branches.

Jones, 1970, 119

It is generally accepted that consolidated financial statements are usually the best means of achieving the objective of group accounts which is to give a true and fair view of the profit and loss and of the state of affairs of the group . . . . the same principles apply to consolidated financial statements as would apply to the financial statements of a single entity.

ASC, 1978a, SSAP14

Consolidated financial statements present the financial affairs of a consolidated group of companies united for economic activity by common control.

Rosenfield & Rubin, 1985, 5

Criteria for inclusion in a group

criteria which some observers have considered to be wholly or partially determinative of ... whether to include or exclude a particular subsidiary in consolidation .... degree of control, degree of ownership, type of business, operating relations, peculiar characteristics of the subsidiary, and the purpose for which the consolidated statement will be used. These are not mutually exclusive but instead overlap to a considerable degree.

Werntz, 1941/1968, 550

On the whole the present inquiry into the standards commonly employed to define the area of consolidation has resulted in the commonplace finding that accountants must exercise judgment. It was found impossible ... to formulate a workable standard merely on the basis of the size of a parent company's holding of subsidiaries' shares. Even less objective is the use of controlling influence as a guide. Similarity of operations, geographical concentration, and consistency of treatment proved useful as partial standards but with too many exceptions and qualifications to warrant isolating them for exclusive attention.

Moonitz, 1951/1978, 39

when to prepare consolidated financial statements ... whenever centralized control exists, based on stock ownership, over an integrated area of operations conducted by two or more separate corporations .... Integration, as used here, implies that the subsidiary is in actuality a department or branch of the parent, performing functions which the parent could conduct, if it so desired, through a department or branch instead of through another corporation.

Moonitz & Staehling, 1952, II:199, 198

The usual condition for a controlling financial interest is ownership of a majority voting interest, and, therefore, as a general rule ownership by one company, directly or indirectly, of over fifty per cent of the outstanding voting shares of another company is a condition pointing toward consolidation. However, there are exceptions to this general rule.

AICPA, 1959b/1961, ARB51

[It] is suggested as a helpful basis for establishing the existence of a group: 1. Emphasis on the economic realities of business organization [dependence, and central unified management] rather than legalistic concepts of ownership would be a useful first step .... 2 .... It would be appropriate to consolidate accounts only for those group members in respect of which the unified management can effectively control the assets and activities for the benefit of those participators in the dominant under-taking to whom they report.

Shaw, 1976, 76

A subsidiary should be excluded from consolidation if: (a) its activities are so dis-similar from those of other companies within the group that consolidated financial statements would be misleading and that information for the holding company's shareholders and other users of the statements would be better provided by pre-senting separate financial statements for such a subsidiary; or (b) . . . . ; or (c) . . . . ; or (d) . . . .

ASC, 1978a, SSAP14

487 Adjustments on consolidation

all intercompany accounts within the group must be eliminated . . . . Intercompany profits in inventories . . . must be eliminated . . . . [Where a minority interest exists, should] only the intercompany profit on that portion of consolidated inventories applicable to the minority interest be eliminated from the consolidated surplus or should the entire intercompany profit in inventories be eliminated? There are theo-retical arguments for the former method but in practice the latter is a more con-servative method.

Montgomery, 1934, 605

In consolidating the accounts all inter-company indebtedness must be set off and not included in the assets and liabilities of the consolidated balance sheet, as it is the primary purpose of the latter to show the financial position of the affiliated group of companies to the public or outside world and not to each other.

Robson, 1936, 134

The leading principle in the technique of preparing consolidated statements is the elimination of all evidences of intercompany relationships . . . . In essence this requires a shift in viewpoint from that of a legal abstraction – the business corporation – to that of an accounting abstraction – the effective business unit. The shift must be made, and it must be complete.

Moonitz, 1951/1978, 84

The elimination of intercompany markups in assets should be complete . . . . The practice of reflecting a minority interest's share of unrealized intercompany profit as if realized, while widely accepted, conflicts with the underlying purpose of con-solidated statements as herein contemplated, namely, to reflect the activities of a group of companies as though they constituted a single unit.

AAA, 1954a/1957b, 45

In the preparation of consolidated statements, intercompany balances and transactions should be eliminated. This includes intercompany open account balances, security holdings, sales and purchases, interest, dividends, etc.

AICPA, 1959b/1961, ARB51

The basic adjustments required [in the preparation of group accounts] include the following: (a) substitution of the appropriate accounting values for the net assets of the subsidiary for the book value in the holding company's accounts of its shareholding in the subsidiary, (b) elimination of balances due to and by companies within the same group ..., (c) elimination of profits on transactions within the group where the profit is as yet unrealized by a final transaction between the group as a whole and a third party ....

Shaw (ed), 1973, 3

As each of the member-companies of a group is a legally separate entity ..., there is no merit in setting off balances between debtor-members and creditor-members of a group, as if consolidated accounts were the accounts of a legally accountable entity .... the elimination presupposes that the debtor-companies are ready, willing and able to meet the claims of creditor-companies. The presupposition may, in fact, be false. But if the two balances are set off, no reader of the balance sheet is on notice to question the possibility of the (undisclosed) liability being met.

ASRC, 1978, 125

The intercompany [or intragroup] amounts ... removed by adjustments and eliminations in consolidation .... are: intercompany stock-holdings .... intercompany receivables and payables .... intercompany sales, purchases, fees, rents, interest, and the like .... inter-company profits .... intercompany dividends ....

Rosenfield & Rubin, 1985, 4

Minority interests on consolidation

[For subsidiaries not wholly owned, the method generally used is] to include in the consolidated balance sheet the entire assets and liabilities ... [of the group], and to set up on the liabilities side of the balance sheet the amount of the net assets of subsidiaries ... which is applicable to the minority stock. The amount may be inserted in the balance sheet [between the consolidated liabilities] and the capital of the parent company, or grouped with the capital items of the parent company ....

Staub, 1929/1982, 668

According to the "combined" view, the minority interest is a proprietary interest, that is, part of the capital and surplus. According to the majority interest view, it is essentially a liability. A compromise view ... lists [the minority interest] immediately preceding capital stock, but after the liabilities.

Daniels, 1934/1980, 111

If the holding company does not own the whole of the capital of the subsidiary companies the separate [aggregative] statement and the consolidated balance sheet [as required] . . . should show as a liability the total interests of all outside shareholders.

Robson, 1936, 31

There are two definitions of the term, consolidated profit or loss: (1) the individual profit or loss of the parent company adjusted by the majority's portions of the undistributed profits or of the losses of subsidiaries; (2) the difference between the total income and expenses of the group of affiliates as a unit regardless of the presence . . . of minority interests. Under the first, the consolidated profit or loss is imputable to the stockholders of the parent company only; under the second, it is distributable between the majority and minority . . . interests.

Childs, 1949, 140

a minority interest should not affect the determination of the magnitude of consolidated assets, debts, or total capital. This is exemplified by the treatment accorded consolidated goodwill and intercompany markups in assets. In these cases it is recommended that the values assigned be determined without consideration of the size of the minority interest. This treatment is necessary to relate the consolidated statement to a specific entity, the area of integrated operations. To permit the value of consolidated inventories and cost of goods sold, for example, to be in part a function of the size of the minority interests is to make the resultant magnitudes refer to two entities – the consolidated group and the subsidiary selling the commodities. This is both illogical and unnecessary; for consolidated assets and debts, a minority may be treated in the same manner as a controlling interest, which is tantamount to saying that its existence is ignored.

Moonitz, 1951/1978, 76

The tendency to view minority interest as a liability is clearly undesirable and the practice is logically indefensible. No obligation, as that term is used in connection with debts, exists to pay off the outside shareholders . . . . Minority interest in consolidated capital [net assets] may not be interpreted as a proportionate interest in the group . . . . [it] will vary with the profitability of closed transactions initiated by the subsidiary and concluded with persons outside the group.

Moonitz, 1951/1978, 79

Minority interest is reported on the consolidated balance sheet in a number of different ways in practice. This balance is sometimes reported as a liability. Occasionally one finds it included as a part of capital. However, in most instances minority interest is excluded from both liability and capital classifications and reported under a separate heading between the liabilities and the parent company capital. One can find no theoretical support for viewing the interest of minority stockholders as a liability.

Karrenbrock & Simons, 1961, 314

Goodwill on consolidation

Writers on the subject of consolidation frequently imply that the excess of cost over equity [in the book value of net assets of a subsidiary on acquisition], a debit amount, should be shown on the consolidated balance sheet in only one way, e.g. as consolidation goodwill . . . . In none of some two hundred reports to the SEC, examined by the author in this connection, was the term goodwill used to describe the excess of cost over equity on the face of the consolidated balance sheet. It was, however, sometimes so characterized in the notes . . . . A more usual treatment is to include the excess in the consolidated fixed assets . . . . Or the excess may be charged to capital surplus . . . . an excess of equity over cost emerges in consolidation when the parent's book equity in the subsidiary's net assets at acquisition is greater than the cost of the stock. It has frequently been called negative goodwill or consolidation capital surplus . . . . Or the excess may be deducted from goodwill or other intangibles on the consolidated balance sheet.

Childs, 1949, 88–91

The net difference between the price paid for the shares acquired by the holding company and the monetary amount of the proportion of the net assets of the subsidiary underlying such shareholding at the date it was acquired, is usually reported as goodwill on consolidation if a debit, and as a capital reserve if a credit.

Bowra & Clarke, 1973, 43

[In merger accounting, on consolidation, where the carrying value of the investment in a subsidiary] is less than the nominal value of the shares transferred, the difference should be treated as a reserve arising on consolidation. Where the carrying value is greater . . . the difference should be treated on consolidation as a reduction of reserves.

ASC, 1985, SSAP23

488 Comment on consolidated statements

opposition to the consolidated balance sheet is somewhat general. The fundamental fact is no doubt that the conglomeration of assets does not tend to the enlightenment of either shareholder or creditor.

Accountant, editorial, 1925, 203

Consolidated balance sheets are never satisfactory; they are neither fish, flesh nor fowl.

Leake, 1925/1972, 129

This anomalous document [the consolidated balance sheet] is a balance sheet of a non-existent entity; it combines the debts of one corporation with the assets of another legally distinct corporation; it lists indiscriminately assets which belong to a given corporation with those which do not.

Hatfield, 1927b, 278

in the United States .... the presentation of consolidated statements alone is the rule .... Consolidated balance sheets inadequately disclose the position of creditors .... [and have other drawbacks] .... the device of consolidated statements, in its present stage of development, does not constitute a substitute for the legal financial statements of holding companies and their subsidiaries.

Daniels, 1934/1980, 10

Consolidation accounting is one of the areas in which recognized principles are few, divergent principles many, and undeveloped sectors large .... Published financial statements ... scarcely ever disclose any of the many difficult problems which frequently, if not customarily, arise in their preparation.

Werntz, 1941/1968, 541

The consolidated statement has almost no legal status in the sense that it is a required report [in the US]. Only two government regulatory agencies (the Securities and Exchange Commission and the Interstate Commerce Commission) require – usually – the consolidated statements of a reporting company and its subsidiaries to be filed in addition to the individual statements of the company. And, generally speaking, an agency will not accept a consolidated statement in lieu of an individual statement of a parent company. Likewise, only one state (California) has by statute indicated its approval of the use of consolidated statements in place of the individual statements of a parent company for the purpose of the annual report of that company.

Childs, 1949, 12

consolidated statements are *as if* reports; they are in effect based on an assumption contrary to fact. Actually the parent company and each of the affiliates is a distinct corporation in its own right ...

Paton & Dixon, 1958, 725

the Reid Murray reports and accounts were in law free to conceal and in fact not infrequently did conceal losses of huge proportions suffered by individual subsidiaries by setting them off against large profits which were said to have been made by other subsidiaries. [Report of an investigation]

Reid Murray Holdings, 1966, 36

Consolidated statements have been criticized on the following grounds: (a) Since the group is not a legal entity it cannot own assets or incur liabilities. (b) [A consolidated balance sheet] includes the assets and liabilities of the constituent companies as if they are those of one entity. (c) It is not possible to ascertain from a consolidated statement which of the constituent companies are solvent and which are insolvent, which are earning profits and which are incurring losses. (d) Many indicators of solvency, profitability and capital safety have no significance when related to the analysis of group financial statements.

Bowra & Clarke, 1973, 16

By 1940 consolidated reports had become an accepted vehicle for corporate reporting .... But ... uncertainty [about what those statements were intended to show] was reflected in an array of inconsistent and confused practices and rules. Since

1940 this confusion has continued .... In the early 1940s American writers were virtually unanimous that consolidated statements were not, by themselves, sufficient disclosures .... However, the stock exchanges, the financial press and the accounting profession have placed greater emphasis on consolidated statements than on parent company reports, so that consolidated statements have nevertheless become the primary vehicle for corporate financial reporting .... Accountants have come to accept the case for total consolidation of holding company and subsidiaries and now permit only a few exceptions to this rule .... What was originally intended as an analogy (showing related companies "as if" they were a single organization) has become a rigid framework for consolidation practice .... despite the fact that individuals buy shares in or lend money to individual corporations, not to "groups" .... the law has not recognized groups of companies as the primary unit of organization and accountability.

Walker, 1978a, 386–7

See also 048

489 Equity accounting

In the UK, equity accounting was regarded as a substitute for consolidated statements by some observers in the 1920s .... In the US .... texts by Finney (1922), Newlove (1926 and 1948), Lewis (1942), Noble *et al* (1941) and Mason (1942) all alluded to equity accounting.

Walker, 1978b, 107

[Holding company earnings from shares in subsidiaries] The question may be raised whether or not increased book value of a share on the issuer's books can ever become a generally satisfactory measure of gross financial income or earnings to the holder. Probably it cannot .... [But the author believes] that in many present instances, the enhanced book value of stock in the issuer's books is a better, more convenient and timely measure than are dividend receipts.

Canning, 1929a, 115

[Under the equity method of accounting for an investment in a subsidiary], profits are said to accrue to and losses to be attributable to the parent in the period earned or sustained by the subsidiary .... Since such "income" is unrealized to the parent, the amount is usually closed to a special surplus account, where it remains unavailable for distribution by the parent.

Childs, 1949, 109

Equity accounting means the practice of bringing into the accounts of the investor the share of earnings attributable to the investor's interest as opposed to bringing in dividends on a received or receivable basis.

Jackman, 1970, 4

The equity method [of accounting for unconsolidated subsidiaries, corporate joint ventures and other investments of 20% or more of the voting stock of an investee]. The investor initially records an investment in the stock of an investee at cost, and adjusts the carrying amount of the investment to recognize the investor's share of the earnings or losses of the investee after the date of acquisition. The amount of the adjustment is included in the determination of the net income by the investor .... [Under the cost method, an investor] records the investment ... at cost, and recognizes as income dividends received .... [In specified circumstances the equity method should be followed.]

AICPA, 1971a, APBO18

The aggregation of the purchase price paid for shares in the associated companies and a proportion of the unappropriated profits of those companies results in an uninterpretable total. It fails to provide either a representation of the market price of the shares or a monetary measure of the net assets of the associated companies. The aggregation is absurd since the component numbers do not represent any homogeneous property. The same defect is inherent in conventionally prepared financial statements; the consolidation of those financial statements can only represent a compounding of the defects.

Clarke, 1971, 9

The basic notion in equity accounting is that the investment [in an associated company] should be stated in the parent company's accounts (or consolidated accounts) at an amount equal to that portion of the book value of the net assets of the associated company, which bears the same relationship to the total book value of the net assets, as does the proportion of the parent's shareholding bear to the total issued shares of the associated company.

Bowra & Clarke, 1973, 159

the equity method of accounting departs from the traditional concept that profits must be realized before they can be recognized.

Gray, 1974, 10

Equity method ... A method of accounting under which the investment in a company is shown in the consolidated balance sheet at: (a) the cost of the investment; and (b) the investing company or group's share of the post-acquisition retained profits and reserves of the company; less (c) any amount written off in respect of (a) and (b); and under which the investing company accounts separately in its profit and loss account for its share of the profits before tax, taxation and extraordinary items of the company concerned. This method is usually applied to associated companies ....

ASC, 1978a, SSAP14

the general features of the equity method [of accounting for investments in associated companies] are: (a) an investment in the shares of another company is usually brought to account at cost; (b) the carrying amount of the investment is increased or decreased to recognize the investor's share of post-acquisition profits or losses

479

of the associated company . . . subject to adjustments to eliminate the effects of intercompany transactions; (c) the investor's share of post-acquisition profits or losses of the associated company . . . is included in the investor's profits or losses . . . . [The equity method may be implemented] (a) . . . by entries in the accounting records of the investor as a separate legal entity . . . . (b) . . . in the consolidated financial statements of the investor . . . . (c) . . . through equity supplementary statements . . . .

ICAA & ASA, 1983/1987, AAS14

490 Funds Statements

491 Funds statements described

In 1863 . . . The Northern Central Railroad issued a " . . . summary of the financial transactions of the company . . . . " It listed the January 1 cash balance and three principal "receipts" in one column, and the December 31 cash balance plus the main outlays for expenditures and assets in another column. The Assam Company in England prepared a similar report for the year ending March 31, 1862. American Bell Telephone Company included a "Cash statement" in its annual report for [1881 . . . . giving a sub-total] for operating expenses. This idea of separating annually recurring items . . . from infrequent financial outlays has continued into present practice.

Rosen & DeCoster, 1969, 125

By making a comparison [of successive balance sheets], tabulating the increases and decreases of resources and liabilities, we can see from what sources all receipts came and to what destination all expenditures went. In making this tabulation, we may well give any one of three titles to each column. Let us call the first column credits, or receipts or "where got"; the second column we may call debits, or expenditures or "where gone".

Cole, 1908, 98

A statement of the sources and applications of funds, also known as a funds statement, is a technical device designed to analyze the changes in the financial condition of a business enterprise between two dates.

Foulke, 1945, 469

The funds statement . . . [is] a condensed report of how the activities of the business have been financed, and how the financial resources have been used, during the period covered by the statement.

Mason, 1961, 48

the funds statement . . . . explains the change in working capital from one point of time to another. A variant of the funds statement shows the sources and applications

of cash rather than working capital . . . . This report . . . helps explain why [e.g.] despite the presence of high earnings, dividends cannot be increased . . . .
Bierman, 1963c, 309

The statement of source and application of funds shall summarize the sources from which funds or working capital have been obtained and their disposition . . . . As a minimum, the following shall be reported: (a) Sources of funds: current operations . . . . sale of noncurrent assets . . . . issuance of debt securities . . . . issuance or sale of capital stock (b) Disposition of funds: purchase of noncurrent assets . . . . redemption or repayment of debt securities . . . . redemption or purchase of capital stock . . . . dividends (c) Increase (decrease) in net funds or working capital.
SEC, 1970a, Reg. S-X

In view of the broadened concept of the funds statement adopted in this opinion, the Board has recommended that the title of the statement be changed to "Statement of changes in financial position" . . . . The statement of each reporting entity should disclose all important aspects of its financing and investing activities regardless of whether cash or other elements of working capital are directly affected. For example, acquisitions of property by issuance of securities or in exchange for other property, and conversions of long term debt or preferred stock to common stock, should be appropriately reflected in the statement.
AICPA, 1971b, APBO19

A funds statement should show the sources from which funds have flowed into the company and the way in which they have been used. It should show clearly the funds generated or absorbed by the operations of the business and the manner in which any resulting surplus of liquid assets has been applied or any deficiency of such assets has been financed, distinguishing the long term from the short term. The statement should distinguish the use of funds for the purchase of new fixed assets from funds used in increasing the working capital of the company.
ASSC, 1975c, SSAP10

492 The rationale of funds statements

The statement of sources and applications of funds gives a clear answer to the question of what has become of the net profits . . . .
Foulke, 1945, 470

The source and application of funds statement . . . . draws attention to the importance of working capital elements in business organizations . . . . It provides an answer to the question of "cost *versus* value" in the asset accounts . . . . Among other things it supplies an answer to the question: What happened to the profit?
Carson, 1949b, 159

Information about the sources from which a company obtains funds and the uses to which such funds are put may be useful for a variety of purposes affecting both operating and investment decisions. Some of this information is evident from the financial statements. The statement of source and application of funds is helpful because it presents other information which ordinarily cannot be obtained from the financial statements and because it presents articulated information about the flow of funds.

AICPA, 1963c, APBO3

a review of the literature supporting the publication of funds statements [revealed the following suggested aims of the statement] .... to represent changes in a firm's financial policies .... to depict how a firm's resources have been applied during a period .... to represent changes in the pattern of a firm's investments .... to provide an indication of a firm's capacity to maintain an investment program (or other activities) with resources derived from business operations .... to depict changes in a firm's liquidity .... to indicate the significance of dividend payments *vis-à-vis* other distributions, to represent capacity to pay dividends ....

Walker, 1984b, 130

493 Variants of the funds statement

The funds statement ... [may be] a cash flow statement .... [or a] summary of changes in working capital .... [or a summary of all sources and applications of financial resources during a period].

Mason, 1961, 50ff

The fact that funds analysis has not made more headway may be attributable to the absence of a definition of funds which is generally accepted. There is, in fact, a variety of definitions ranging over the whole spectrum of liquidity, from cash at one extreme to total resources at the other, with compromises like working capital somewhere in between.

Rayman, 1970, 423

Funds can be defined in a variety of ways. The three basic concepts are cash (often including short term borrowing and "near cash" short term investments ...), working capital, and total resources.

Egginton & Morris, 1974, 332

As long as certain types of transactions are disclosed in the required way, apparently any, all, or no underlying concept of funds is appropriate. [comment on APBO19]

Spiller & Virgil, 1974, 115

494 General publication of funds statements endorsed

The funds statement should be treated as a major financial statement. It should be presented in all annual reports of corporations .... The statement should be broad enough in scope and in its concept of funds to make it a report of all financial management operations.

Mason, 1961, 90

The [Accounting Principles] Board believes that a statement of source and application of funds should be presented as supplementary information in financial reports . . . . The concept of funds . . . should be consistent with the purpose of the statement . . . . for presentation in annual reports, a concept broader than that of working capital should be used which can be . . . defined as all financial resources . . . .

AICPA, 1963c, APBO3

The funds statement should be adopted as one of the standard financial statements, along with the balance sheet, income and surplus statement.

Smith, 1964, 94

A statement of changes in financial position should be included as an integral part of the financial statements.

IASC, 1977, IAS7

495 Comment on funds statements

experts . . . . probably have little need of the convoluted explanation of movements in balance sheet totals that seem to comprise the accepted method of presenting the source and application of funds statement, while [the general run of individual shareholders] are more likely to find such a document to be of considerable complexity and beyond their ability to comprehend.

Goch, 1976, 40

The liquidity report [funds statement or cash flow statement] must not be considered an alternative to the profit and loss account but an essential bridge between that account and the balance sheet.

Mitchell, 1976, 12

Let's scrap the funds statement.

Heath, 1978b, 94

The shortcomings of the products of conventional accounting have given rise to the publication . . . of other supplementary statements . . . . The case for funds statements acknowledges, if tacitly, the importance of knowledge of movements in genuine money amounts . . . . The most direct indication of [the capacity to pay interest on and to repay debts] is the relationship of debt to the money equivalents of assets . . . from time to time. Even the information in conventional accounts and a funds statement in combination will not yield this straightforward product of continuously contemporary accounting.

Chambers, 1986, 214

496 Cash flow – interpretation

Like some other fashions in accounting the term "cash flow" is a new emphasis on a familiar principle. It came into prominence in the United States of America during the last decade and appears to have entered the vocabulary of accounting through its usage by financial analysts and subsequently in company reports.

Hain, 1965, 123

Cash flow in financial analysis means net income after adding back expense items which do not currently use funds, such as depreciation.

Mason, 1961, 42

In the traditional accounting sense, cash flow refers to all of the receipts and all of the disbursements of cash. The other use of the term ... is synonymous with the phrase, funds provided from operations, as the phrase is used in relation to the funds statement.

Fess & Weygandt, 1969, 52

A statement of cash flows so titled shall be prepared ... and shall be included in the accounts or consolidated accounts .... cash means cash on hand and cash equivalents; cash equivalents means highly liquid investments ... and [certain] borrowings which are integral to the cash management function ... ; cash flows means cash movements resulting from transactions with parties external to the company ....

AASB, 1991, AASB1026

497 Posited utility of cash flow information

cash flow as the amount of assets or funds made available after meeting the current requirements of revenue earning operations .... can be used effectively as one of the major factors in judging, for example, the ability to meet debt retirement requirements, to maintain regular dividends, and to finance replacement and expansion costs.

Mason, 1961, 42

By adding the depreciation deduction back to income, it is often possible to obtain a more clear indication of the economic progress of a company. This is particularly useful when year to year or firm to firm comparisons are to be made .... this figure does not represent cash flow in the literal sense of the term .... However, it does provide a method of reducing the effects of a major inconsistency in accounting practice.

Drebin, 1964, 27

The distrust for the net income figure as a measure of profitability apparently has arisen because of the lack of uniformity in accounting methods, especially in the handling of nonfund transactions. Security analysts have, therefore, apparently reverted to such crude measures as cash flow to normalize the effect of the variances which occur because alternative accounting methods are followed by different companies.

Fess & Weygandt, 1969, 56

See also 193

498 Cash flow statements

Cash flow statements focus on the cash inflows and cash outflows, whereas funds flow statements are addressed to the analysis and uses of working capital.

Glautier & Underdown, 1976, 177

the cash flow statement bypasses the problem of uncertainty, and removes all need for valuation . . . . The statement cannot, however, replace the functions of the profit and loss account.

Magee, 1979, 295

See also 786, 787

499 Cautions on use of cash flow information

In no sense can the amount of cash flow or cash income be considered as a substitute for or an improvement upon the net income, properly determined, as an indication of the results of operations or the change in financial position.

Mason, 1961, 42

instead of studying various ways and terminology for presenting cash flow statements, I think the profession is called upon to report to companies, to analysts, to stockholders, and the exchanges, that cash flow figures are dangerous and misleading and the profession will have no part of them.

Seidman, 1961, 31

500 DATED VALUATION OF ASSETS AND EQUITIES

500 Valuation

501 Early references to dated valuation

[Example of opening inventory] I find in ready money of diverse countries . . . [so much] of every sort, etc, naming the number and value . . . . I find in rings and jewels of gold so many . . . with their weight and value in sterling money estimated . . . .

> Mellis, 1588, Ch 3

how to begin the new books . . . . for the true worth and value [of two manors, and of several houses and goods, three separate amounts] . . . . for the value of two ships . . . according to estimation, worth with all appurtenances and furniture [one amount].

> Dafforne, 1684, Journal B

The Black-boy in Fleet Street, London [a property], is debtor to stock [capital], and is for a lease thereof taken for the term of 40 years, dated the 28 of March, 1630, &c which cost me 106 pounds, &c which I now value at 160 pounds. [extract from example]

> Carpenter, 1632, 98

In transferring [to profit and loss] the loss or gain on ships, for instance, it is sufficient to leave a balance equal to their present estimated value, and whatever surplus appears on either side of the account should then be transferred to profit and loss. The same method should also be observed with respect to real estates, whenever the accounts are made up and settled to a particular period.

> Booth, 1789, 164

in proceeding with each year's balance the company's whole stock in trade shall first be taken at such valuation as in the opinion of the partners is fair and reasonable . . . .

> Newton Bernie & Company, 1837, Contract

It is a universal principle among merchants in keeping their books, both at the commencement and at every rest in the progress of business, to affix to all the articles of stock their values in money, for without this they would be unable at any time to ascertain their profits and losses. And as estimates and allowances are yearly made for wear and tear, for accidents, for the alteration in the value of the leases and patents by the effluxion of time, and of funded property by the fluctuations of the funds, and the like, the whole system depends upon this practice of valuation.

Cory, 1839, 337

In making the general balance, the residue of funded property, houses, lands, furniture, ships, or goods unsold, is here set down at the first cost; but in real business, it is more correct and satisfactory to enter such balances at their actual value, and to debit or credit profit and loss for the difference between their present worth and prime cost. Such a valuation becomes necessary when any change takes place in the firm of a house, or in the terms of copartnership; . . . .

Kelly, 1839, 126

from time to time . . . . the value of the property stock and effects of the company shall be ascertained by a valuation thereof to be made by [two named independent persons engaged in the same trade]. [Minute of copartnery]

Campbell and Christie, 1845

See also 511, 541, 542, 543

502 Valuation generally

In the accounting treatises [of the 17th and 18th centuries] three alternative treatments of fixed assets and the income from them can be distinguished. First, the net income (receipts less payments other than the cost of the asset) is transferred to the profit and loss account, the asset being carried forward at cost. Second, the balance of the account is carried forward, that is, the original cost plus expenses less receipts is carried forward with no entry to profit and loss account. Third, the asset is revalued and its new value is carried forward, the difference left on the account, whether gain or loss, being taken to profit and loss account. The three bases of valuation may conveniently be called the cost, arithmetic balance, and revaluation bases respectively.

Yamey, 1963, 197

it is customary to adopt more or less arbitrary rules for valuing assets each year in order to arrive at a profit that can be accepted for practical purposes.

Carter, 1910b, 561

Real value can only be determined by conversion through sale and reduction of the proceeds to cash.

Page, 1916, 243

The best definition of value is purchasing power.

Montgomery, 1927, 206

Measurement of phenomena is the problem attacked by the accountant under the head of valuation.

Rorem, 1927, 10

It can probably be agreed that one of the objectives of accounting should be to record, accurately and fearlessly, the entire facts with respect to present financial conditions. In so doing, may it not also be agreed that accountants should adopt a basis of valuation – if one can be found – which is theoretically consistent and logical, which is intelligible, reasonable, and easily understood by the ordinary person, which furnishes current and up to date information, and which permits objective verification . . . . ?

Daines, 1929, 97

most of the rules of valuation which the accountant applies to the fixed assets of a business, and which he uses primarily for the purpose of measuring income, cannot be construed even as serious attempts to measure values. Instead they are devices for amortizing the original costs of the assets over their period of useful life.

Bonbright, 1937/1965, 906

By [the valuation convention] nonhomogeneous assets and claims to assets are translated into financial equivalents or money values . . . . valuation is no more than a convenient method of symbolizing . . . . Essentially all that the convention of valuation really accomplishes is substitution . . . . The dollar symbol which represents an asset in the accounting equation theoretically remains unchanged as long as the physical asset itself remains unchanged. When the quantity of that asset . . . is actually reduced, then the financial symbol is proportionately altered.

Gilman, 1939, 26, 56, 247

Surely it is time for the accountants of the world to agree on some term other than valuation to describe a monetary ascription that is not a measure of worth.

May, 1951, 252

Valuation as such is not exclusively an accounting matter, and fund theory takes no position in this area.

Vatter, 1956, 122

Accounting is a discipline without any cohesive, unified theory of valuation.

Sterling, 1967, 131

In the early decades of this century, accounting principles were aimed principally at the valuation of assets, with the view that a balance sheet was intended to show the worth-value of assets compared with liabilities and that all increase in net worth (stockholders' equity) was deemed profits.

Hackney, 1973, 303

503 Items to be valued severally

Bookkeeping is the art of keeping accounts (i.e. recording the transactions) of one's affairs, in such a manner that the true state of any part, or of the whole, may be thereby known with the greatest clearness and despatch.

Malcolm, 1731, 1

the whole capital, and every one of its parts, must have a distinct account.

Cronhelm, 1818/1978, vi

Bookkeeping is the art of recording property in such a manner as to show its whole value collectively, and also the value of each of its component parts.

Foster, 1843, 13

Two things have to be accomplished [at the end of a financial period]; first, we wish to discover in the case of each item of property – both commodities and services – that has been purchased during the period or was on hand at the beginning of the period to what extent there has been a value expiration . . . ; second, what is the actual balance on hand at the moment of time in the case of each property item.

Paton & Stevenson, 1916/1976, 61

all recorded events affecting a specific financial obligation or a specific resource are gathered together in a group or class, known as a ledger account, relating to that specific obligation or resource . . . .

Fitzgerald & Schumer, 1952, 7

the overall process of valuation in accounting . . . is concerned with providing information about the financial position and performance of an entity . . . by the preparation of financial reports which depict the individual resources and the individual commitments of an entity . . . . in some situations [takeovers, mergers, liquidations], shareholders, creditors and other interested parties may consider that estimates of the value of the business . . . are relevant to the decisions they confront . . . . But even in these contexts . . . [those parties] would have some regard to the alternative of disposing of the entity's resources in some other manner, so that information concerning the value of individual asset or liability items would also be relevant to those decisions.

ASRB, 1985c, R101

504 Accountants said not to be valuers

it cannot be too strongly impressed on the public mind that accountants are not valuers.

Hasluck, 1895, 231

it is impossible for an expert in accounts alone to certify as to the accuracy of the valuation of stock in trade; he is not, of course, a valuer, but this does not seem to preclude his making such general inquiry, and giving such consideration to the matter as would enable him to form a very sound opinion as to the propriety of the figures presented to him.

Accountant, Anon, 1896, 51

an auditor cannot possibly value the assets of all the businesses whose accounts he audits. This valuation must be carried out by the partners, directors or other responsible officials.

de Paula, 1914, 73

Neither the valuation of the income and expense in a particular period, nor the valuation of the future available services is, in the first instance, the business of the professional accountant. It is the affair, rather, of the proprietor acting through the managers of the enterprise. The accountant comes in as an expert, disinterested, responsible principal to express a judgment of the validity and reliability of the manager's valuations.

Canning, 1929a, 317

Technically speaking, . . . [valuation] is not an accounting problem though the accountant has to reckon with it so often that it necessarily becomes a part of his practice. Specifically, the accountant has to check up on other people's valuations.

Berle & Fisher, 1932, 575

Accounting has a record function, not a valuation function . . . . values are too momentary and too subjective [for use in financial statements].

Littleton, 1929, 153

the accountant cannot make valuations . . . . Valuation in any true or important sense is not a matter for the accountant . . . .

Peloubet, 1935, 208, 209

The accountant is not a valuer and he does not, for the most part, concern himself with present values . . . .

Dohr, 1944, 195

505 Optional valuations

though these subjects [houses and ships] do not really keep up their value, yet I would continue them at their first value [first cost] till they were disposed of, or lost; or you may choose to state them at another value from time to time, as you think they are then really worth.

Malcolm, 1731, 90

Cast up all your goods bought and those sold, of what kind soever, in each account of goods; and see whether all goods bought be sold, or not; and if any remain unsold, value them as they cost you, or according to the market price, ready money; and bear the nett rest to balance Dr. [137]

Anon, 1737/1984, 41

If part [of the goods or other property] be on hand, enter the value of it (estimated at prime cost, or at the current prices) to the Dr side of the balance sheet, and then ascertain the gain or loss on the part sold, which enter on the proper side of the profit and loss account.

Morrison, 1825, 46

To ascertain what property he [every merchant] has in hand, he must accurately inspect all the articles of his stock, and fix an estimated value upon them according to the market prices at which he would at that moment be content to purchase them; or if they are articles of his own manufacture, at the lowest price at which he is content to dispose of them.

Cory, 1839, 21

We might measure the value of an asset by its purchase price (historic cost basis), by its discounted expected net revenues, by the potential of its liquidation yield, or many other variations and combinations.

Mattessich, 1964, 79

Investments held by investment trust companies should be regarded as fixed assets. They should preferably be stated in the balance sheet at either: (a) cost (or revaluation at a later date) with a note of the market value; or (b) market value (including the value estimated by the directors in the case of unquoted investments).

ICAEW, 1968d, 217

The value of an asset (or group of assets) or a liability (or group of liabilities) at any time is equal to its present cash consequence (which is the same as its future cash consequences discounted to the present or its past cash consequences accumulated to the present).

Johnson & Storey, 1982, 37

506 Book value

in a balance sheet none of these items [leasehold property, minerals, patent rights, and even the factory or the ship in the case of a manufacturing or shipowning company] ought to be regarded as more than book figures . . . . these parts of capital outlay mainly depend for such value as they possess on the concern being kept going and being productive of profit. Only when the railway is to be abandoned or the iron work to be discontinued does it become important to consider whether and what value for other uses may attach to the land and materials remaining.

Welton, 1890, 679

Book value – the amount appearing from time to time in the books of a concern as the "value" of a particular asset or group of assets. It generally represents (1) the actual and direct cost, or (2) the cost (whether direct or indirect, original or additional), or (3) either of the foregoing less the amounts that would have been written off by way of depreciation . . . . Sometimes the book value of an asset is a nominal amount which is obviously not the real value . . . .
Dawson, 1904, 57

by book value we understand, not any arbitrary value that may be entered upon the books of the company, but the value as predicated upon the market value of the assets of the company, after deducting its liabilities.
Steeg v Leopold Weil B & I Co,
1910/1955

[With reference to book value] . . . good accounting itself does not purport to require that assets be valued at their value in any accepted sense of this word.
Bonbright, 1937/1965, 1058

Value as used in accounts signifies the amount at which an item is stated, in accordance with the accounting rules or principles relating to that item. Generally book or balance sheet values represent cost to the accounting unit or some modification thereof; but sometimes they are determined in other ways, as for instance on the basis of market values or cost of replacement, in which cases the basis should be indicated in financial statements.
AIA, 1941c, ARB9

Such terms as book value are common in accounting literature, but by book value we do not mean value at all. We mean rather the dollar amount at which accounting conventions require us to record an item on the books, a dollar amount often at complete variance from any conception of value.
Franklin, 1944, 58

The word value in this combination [book value] is clearly misleading to lay persons and certainly has confused the courts; it is a term which is, in fact, misleading in all accounting senses except when intended to mean actual value or market value.
Stans & Goedert, 1955, 46

Book value is the amount shown on accounting records or related financial statements at or as of the date when the determination is made, after adjustments necessary to reflect (1) correction of errors, and (2) the application of accounting practices which have been consistently followed . . . . In view of the fact that the intent of the parties to arrangements involving sale or transfer of business interests should govern, and the foregoing definition may not reflect such intent, the committee recommends that the term, book value, be avoided.
AICPA, 1956/1961, ATB3

The book value ... of a security is in most cases a rather artificial value. It is assumed that if the company were to liquidate, it would receive in cash the value at which its various tangible assets are carried on the books .... The book value really measures, ... not what the stockholders could get out ..., but rather what they have put into the business ....

Graham & McGolrick, 1964, 39

book value ... simply means the amount at which an asset is shown in the ledger, and hence in the balance sheet.

Yorston & others, 1965, I:24

510 Valuation Based on Initial Cost

511 Valuation at nominal, initial or unamortized cost

The debit side of all accounts of goods ... is what they stand me of prime cost and charges ....

Macghie, 1718, 49

In accounts of goods .... When only part are sold, then first carry the remainder to balance at prime cost, and afterwards charge the goods Dr to, or Cr by, profit and loss for the gain or loss on what are sold.

Webster, 1718/1779, xiii

when any thing becomes mine, I consider it as a subject which owes, or is account-able to me for, such a sum of money as it has cost me ... for, in effect, 'tis the same thing to me as if some person owed me this money .... Again, when it is given away ... it may easily be conceived to have thereby discharged so much of the former charge .... If the money value is greater or lesser than the charge, it comes under the notion of gain or loss.

Malcolm, 1731, 13

[Balancing the ledger accounts] .... where anything [of goods] remains on hand, it is first set down on the left side by charging balance with it at prime cost, or the original value; after which the whole account must be equalled by profit and loss.

Hutton, 1788, 182

If sales be not finished, close the account by a double balance, mentioning your share of the first cost in one line, and your share of charges in another line under it ....

Jackson, 1809, 20

At least nine-tenths of the writers before 1840 advocated the valuation of stocks at cost, or, as it was sometimes called, at prime cost.

Yamey, 1940, 337

the valuation of goods on hand .... in actual business, ... is found by stocktaking .... It should always be journalized as a transaction; as if the goods left unsold had actually been all sold at cost price .... the selling price entirely ignored.
Dyer, 1897/1984, 44

the actual cost basis [for balance sheet valuations] gives us a definite thing, a matter of available knowledge independent of external fluctuations, and it involves no extra work of entry – that is, the natural entry is that on the cost basis.
Cole, 1921, 319

Universal adoption of the cost basis would afford a greater degree of comparability than now exists in published statements .... Moreover, cost is generally understood, and if accountants educate the public to appreciate the fact that book values represent cost and depreciated cost, not market or replacement values, there can be little possibility of misinterpreting financial statements and also less opportunity of misrepresentation short of actual falsification.
Daniels, 1934/1980, 39

The view that a balance sheet fixed asset should represent, not the market value of that asset or its earning capacity value, but the unabsorbed portion of an original cost of the asset is sound accountancy, and moreover is founded upon logical principle.
AA, Anon, 1936, 75

The American Accounting Association, whose membership is mainly in the academic field, sought [in the 1930s] to erect the practice of carrying capital assets at cost into a cost principle.
May, 1948b, 17

Although circumstances sometimes justify departures, the general basis for historical accounting for business corporations is cost to the present entity.
Grady, 1965, 27

The essential features [of double entry bookkeeping] have remained unchanged since Paciolo described the system in use in Italy in 1494. The basic process is to analyze each transaction twice – once from the point of view of the amount invested and once from the point of view of the source of the funds involved .... Herein lies the fundamental reason that assets are shown at cost in traditional financial statements. Double entry bookkeeping reflects the amount invested in the assets. Deviation from cost requires modification of the basic structure.
Raymond, 1965, 40

Historical cost valuation is the only valuation method which includes, as an integral part of its valuation procedure structured on the double entry bookkeeping system, the essential requirement ... that every actual change in the resources of an entity be recorded by relating inputs and outputs so that it can be traced and identified whenever necessary.
Ijiri, 1971, 13

See also 134

512 Cost or unamortized cost said to be a going concern valuation

Where the object of stocktaking is for the purpose of being incorporated in the accounts of a going concern, the goods should be priced at cost, on the footing that the business is a going concern.

Lisle, 1899, 53

so long as it is reasonable to assume the continuity of the business, the correct thing is not to attempt to show the realizable value [of fixed assets] . . . but rather to show such expenditure *as* expenditure, subject to the fact that insofar as it will not last forever its cost must be apportioned as fairly as possible, and charged against the profits earned in successive years, in order to arrive at the true working expenses and the true net profit of each year.

Dicksee, 1909b, 195

We are dealing with enterprises which are continuing in business, and of which a forced sale or liquidation is not contemplated, so that in attempting to fix the net value to a concern of its fixed assets we may say that, as a general rule, the correct basis is cost, less adequate depreciation for wear, tear and obsolescence.

Montgomery, 1912/1976, 119

Fixed assets are valued on the basis of cost [i.e. less depreciation] . . . . this represents the present value of such assets to the particular undertaking as a going concern . . . . Current market value and break up value are disregarded, as these do not affect the working lives of the particular assets at all . . . .

de Paula, 1914, 71

The inventory [of enterprise assets] should be on the basis of the value of the assets to the present holders as a "going concern". The proper value is that which they have to the holding concern, and not that which they might have to other persons . . . . [A fixed asset's] services are presumably perpetual and undiminishing; the value to the company was, in the first instance, represented by its full cost price; its services, and hence its value to the going concern, are the same as before. It is therefore proper to continue in the inventory the cost price of the land quite irrespective of changes in its market value whether that be greater or less than the cost. The market price, evidently, can never be realized as long as the land is still used as a factory site, the abandonment of the factory means ordinarily that the enterprise ceases to be a going concern.

Hatfield, 1916/1976, 80–82

The common commercial view of the going concern value of industrial plant in use is that value is based upon the unexpired capital outlay on the plant . . . .

Leake, 1929b, 798

The accountant . . . deals primarily with the administration of the affairs of the continuing business institution and accordingly emphasizes the flow of costs and the interpretation of assets as balances of unamortized costs.

Paton & Littleton, 1940, 10

It is customary to assume that a business entity has a reasonable expectation of continuing in business at a profit for an indefinite period of time. This assumption that an enterprise is a going concern provides much of the justification for recording plant assets at acquisition cost and depreciating them in a systematic manner without reference to their current realizable values.

Noble & Niswonger, 1961, 329

it is customary to show land used for business purposes at cost [and many fixed assets at cost less depreciation]. For a going concern that intends to continue using such property for business purposes, current market value is not particularly relevant.

Finney & Miller, 1968, 238

no logical relationship between the going concern concept and historical cost was ever demonstrated.

Fremgen, 1968, 654

[The value of fixed assets] to the business as a going concern depends on their earning power. But obviously it is not feasible for the accountant to measure the assets in accordance with the fluctuation of earnings. For this reason the conventional methods of measurement that have been adopted [based on historical costs] are the only feasible ones.

Myer, 1969, 32

513 Costs said to attach to assets

The accountant in general assumes that work in process . . . and finished stock are worth for balance sheet purposes the sum of the labor, material, and other costs expended in getting these results. He assumes that in some mysterious manner the values of these original commodities and services . . . pass over into and inhere in the object for which they were utilized. This is clearly an application of a cost theory of value to the internal conditions of the specific enterprise . . . . So far as price determination is concerned this is, of course, unsound in most cases.

Paton, 1922/1962, 491–2

it is a basic concept of accounting that costs can be marshalled into new groups that possess real significance. It is as if costs had a power of cohesion when properly brought into contact . . . . Ideally, all costs incurred should be viewed as ultimately clinging to definite items of goods sold or services rendered.

Paton & Littleton, 1940, 13

It is important . . . to distinguish between historical cost and embodied cost. Historical cost is a cost event occurring at a particular moment of time. Embodied cost persists through a period of time. My watch may have cost $50 some years ago. That is a definite historical fact, a closed transaction. But when as an accountant I conceive of fifty dollars as embodied in the watch I endow it with a kind of magic power; namely the power to transmit that cost to other goods and services. If the watch is used to time a production process, it is assumed that a portion of the embodied cost is transferred to the new product.

Jones, 1941/1965, 296

[The accountant] assumes (implicitly) that when money has been spent or contracted to be spent to acquire things, the money has not necessarily and inevitably been spent or contracted to be spent as it has, leaving the business with the things acquired, but that the things acquired carry the money with them, and that bits of the things flowing into different departments or products of the business carry bits of money with them, or that bits of the life period or assumed life period of the things acquired carry bits of the money with them; and that the money in question has not been wholly spent so long as any of the things acquired and still possessed has one of the bits of money attached to it. These bits of money are costs. These costs are carefully distinguished from values . . . .

Thirlby, 1946, 42

a cost element entered in the account records can be treated as though it is divisible into minute particles . . . such particles are mobile and . . . several such particles can be combined or assembled to form a new cost aggregate.

Owen, 1958, 73

Cost cohesion – It is assumed that as the physical factors of production are united to form new utility, the costs of each of these factors unite in the same way as their physical counterparts.

Dilley, 1960, 542

A basic concept of accounting is that the costs of services attach to the product and that the costs can be allocated, traced, and finally matched against the revenue produced by the sale of the product.

Anderson & others, 1974, 56

Product expenses are resource costs . . . that logically attach to products.

May & others, 1975, 105

Costs combine in the same fashion as physical factors combine in the production process . . . . This convention is . . . [an important aspect] of the rationalization of the use of historical cost.

Tilley, 1975, 193

514 Interpretations of cost – general

Cost incurred is measured by cash outlay or the fair market value of considerations other than cash. Where productive factors or other resources are acquired by donation or some similar process fair market value at the date of acquisition ... becomes the basic measure.

AAA, 1941/1957b, 53

Cost, in accounting, is a historical record of liabilities incurred expressed in units of money, which have been allocated to specific properties or transactions, and to various fiscal periods. Like other aspects of accounting, costs give a false impression of accuracy ....

Wilcox, 1941b/1982, 101

Cost means cost in cash or its equivalent.

Montgomery & others, 1949, 255

Cost is the amount, measured in money, of cash expended, or other property transferred, capital stock issued, services performed, or a liability incurred, in consideration of goods or services received or to be received.

AICPA, 1957/1961, ATB4

The amount of money paid, or the value of a liability assumed, or the money value imputed to any resource given up or transformed, necessarily in the provision of any asset other than money or a fixed claim thereto, may be regarded as the cost of such asset.

Lee, 1973, 13

Cost: The measured amount of economic sacrifice or effort, measured in terms of the cash or cash equivalent required to be given up, of performing an act.

NAA, 1974, 6

The Member States may permit the purchase price or production cost of stocks of goods of the same category and all fungible items including investments to be calculated either on the basis of weighted average prices or by the first in, first out (fifo) method, the last in, first out (lifo) method, or some similar method.

EEC, 1978, 4th Directive

515 Interpretations of cost – inventories

For variant interpretations of cost see 650

Interpretations of cost – durables

It is desirable for the wasting fixed assets to be stated at cost, or, in case this is not possible, at reproduction cost; and . . . that the available reserves for depreciation be shown separately as deductions from their correlative asset accounts.
Bentley, 1912b, 324

when one sets a value on a fixed asset one attempts to measure in terms of money the service which will be rendered by the asset in the future . . . . The impossibility of predicting the future course of market prices . . . . [obliges the accountant to fall] back on the . . . assumption that the value of the asset is equal to its money cost, less a deduction to provide for that proportion of its power to render service which has been used up.
Kelley, 1935, 51

it is good practice to charge to property accounts not only the original and direct acquisition costs but also all costs of installation, and all expenses necessary to bring the equipment to the point of being an earning asset.
Sanders & others, 1938, 60

The cost of purchased units [of plant] is the net price paid, on a cash basis, plus freight or other transportation charges and cost of installing and placing in condition to serve. The cost of special foundations and supports is a part of total plant cost but may not always be classed as equipment . . . . The cost of constructed units includes – in addition to direct material and labor – charges for surveying, designing, insurance, supervision, etc.
Paton & Paton, 1952, 188

All expenditures connected with the [transportation,] assembling, installing, and testing [of plant assets] are logically viewed as a part of asset cost.
Meigs & others, 1978, 477

Where an item of property, plant and equipment is acquired in exchange or in part exchange for another asset, the cost of the asset acquired should be recorded either at fair value or at the net carrying amount of the asset given up . . . . fair value may be determined by reference either to the asset given up or the asset acquired, which ever is the more clearly evident.
IASC, 1982, IAS16

On depreciation and appreciation, see 660

516 Valuation at price indexed cost

Adjusted historical cost is a definite objective concept – historical dollar cost adjusted to a current dollar basis by the application of a broadly accepted index of general

499

prices . . . . Under this concept net income is that portion of revenue not required to maintain intact the generalized, overall purchasing power of the capital investment – not just its dollar amount.

Graham, 1952/1984, 84

when applying a general price index to historical cost, we are substituting a purchasing power postulate for the monetary postulate. The purchasing power postulate is the assumption that a specified general price index shows the course of the value of money.

Kerr, 1956, 142

All items of plant and equipment in service, or held in stand-by status, should be recorded at cost of acquisition or construction, with appropriate modification for the effect of the changing dollar either in the primary statements or in supplementary statements.

Sprouse & Moonitz, 1962, 57

Restatement of nonmonetary items [in general price level accounting] does not introduce current values or replacement costs . . . . Restatement merely presents the cost in a unit which represents the general purchasing power of the dollar at [the balance sheet date].

AICPA, 1969, APBS3

a balance sheet prepared under present GAAP emphasizes historical cost. After general price level restatement of that balance sheet, the relationship emphasized is still historical cost, although the standard has been changed from units of money to units of general purchasing power. Current value accounting on the other hand changes the relationship emphasized from historical cost to a current value relationship.

Rosenfield, 1972, 66

520 Valuation at Replacement Cost or Price

521 Replacement cost – of assets

The replacement or reproduction cost . . . of an economic good is the market price for which one can obtain the economic good in question on the day of real or assumed replacement. Actual purchase or replacement is unessential; it is only essential that purchases could be made at the specific price at the time of evaluation. It is also unessential whether or not replacement or reproduction is under consideration. Both can be imaginary.

Schmidt, 1930, 239

replacement price [of raw materials and supplies] is determined on the basis of current quotations for the quantities usually purchased in regular trade channels. This is generally accepted as constituting market . . . . damaged and obsolete materials, scrap and similar items should always be valued on the basis of expected net proceeds of realization . . . .

Stans, 1946, 103

The present value of a thing is . . . the price at which an identical thing can be purchased, regardless of how much more or less its value happened to be at the time it was acquired. Present wealth must be measured by reference to present values.

Sands, 1963, 12

To the economist, the value of an item to a firm or individual is the amount that the firm or individual is willing to pay for it . . . . Since a business concern normally buys goods and services only for the revenues expected from their sale or use, in an economic sense a gain or loss occurs on every purchase. This gain or loss is equal to the difference between the purchase price of the asset and the value of the future receipts the firm expects to obtain from the sale or use of the asset.

Gordon & Shillinglaw, 1964, 237–8

Replacement cost balance sheet values represent the amount that a firm would have to pay, as of the balance sheet date, in order to replace the assets shown in the statement or to satisfy reported liabilities.

Revsine, 1973, 68

522 Replacement cost – of service or operating capacity

the significant replacement cost is the cost of providing the existing capacity to produce in terms of the most up to date methods available.

Paton & Paton, 1952, 325

A corporation's capital may . . . be defined as a stock of productive capacity . . . . In this view, the value of any particular resource or the value of all resources is represented by the amount of money currently required to replace them.

Ladd, 1963, 54

The current basis recommended is current cost of replacement of the services represented in the resources and commitments of the entity.

AAA, 1966, 31

It is essential . . . to interpret current replacement cost not as the cost of replacing the actual physical asset used by the firm but as the cost of currently acquiring the services provided by the asset.

Parker & Harcourt, 1969, 19

The net current replacement cost of an asset is that part of the gross current replacement cost which reflects its unexpired service potential.

IASG, 1976, ED18

replacement cost is the lowest amount that would have to be paid in the normal course of business to obtain a new asset of equivalent operating or productive capability.

SEC, 1976b, SAB7

Replacement cost represents the cost, in current dollars, of replacing the productive capacity of an existing asset.

Goldschmidt & Admon, 1977, 49

523 Replacement cost – other interpretations

Replacement cost refers to the cost of an asset of equivalent expected earning power, without regard to technical aspects, such as size, proportions, type of material, etc.

Rorem, 1929, 170

Replacement cost . . . "means all things to all men". It has been variously described as (1) what an identical asset *would* cost currently; (2) what an identical asset *will* probably cost at the time of replacement; (3) what the "equivalent" of the asset *would* cost currently, "equivalent" being none too clearly defined; (4) what it *has already* cost to replace the asset, e.g. lifo; (5) historical cost adjusted by specific price indexes – many narrowly specialized indexes, or a few, or just one index specific to all of the expenditures of a company, or even of an industry. All of these varieties of replacement cost are based on the concept that net income is the excess of revenue over some measure of the current cost of replacing the physical capital (assets and services) consumed in producing that revenue . . . .

Graham, 1952/1984, 84–5

Replacement cost – The cost required to replace the service capacity of an existing asset. Physical replacement of an identical asset is not required . . . . The current cost of replacing an asset in physical form if the asset is held for sale but in service capacity if the asset is used in operations.

NAA, 1974, 23

The current entry price of an asset, including fringe acquisition costs such as transportation and commissions, is a widely used measurement method . . . . Several methods of calculating replacement cost of plant assets are used: 1. Direct pricing by obtaining a quotation for the specific model of asset on hand. 2. Indexing of historical cost, using the percentage change in a specific price index for the type of asset being measured. 3.Unit pricing of the basic physical feature of the asset . . . . 4. Functional pricing in cases where the model of asset held is no longer in production but a new model which will perform the same function is available. If the new asset has a different productive capacity, the relative capacities of the old and the new must be taken into consideration.

Staubus, 1977, 148–9

524 Replacement cost valuation endorsed

take an exact inventory of the goods on hand, as far as can be done; and affix a moderate value to each article, according to the current prices at the time; such a value as the owner would be willing at present to buy for.

Hamilton, 1788/1982, 285

To ascertain what property he actually has in hand, he must accurately inspect all the articles of his stock, and fix an estimated value upon them according to the market prices at which he would at that moment be content to purchase them; or, if they are articles of his own manufacture, at the lowest price at which he is content to dispose of them.

Pulling, 1850, 24

replacement cost is the basic value which properly expresses business capital and income.

Rorem, 1929, 167

A balance sheet which is based upon replacement costs tells the owner what value his individual items of property have in the market on the date of the balance sheet .... the price at which he could repurchase similar goods at that moment. If the selling price is lower .... another sale of the same kind should not be attempted .... From this it follows that replacement costs as of the day of sale must be the fundamental values for profit and loss calculation.

Schmidt, 1930, 239

The policy behind the replacement value interpretation [of market, in the lower of cost and market rule] is clearly to leave the field open for the making of normal profits during the ensuing financial period.

Byrd, 1950, 310

The use of replacement cost (as a practical substitute for the theoretically correct present worth) in measuring value would meet many requirements for accounting for the contemporary large corporation .... It would make the balance sheet a much more meaningful statement of the capital currently committed to the corporation and thus make possible a reasonable assessment of the effectiveness with which the capital is being employed.

Ladd, 1963, 62

For economic resources that do not represent direct claims to cash ... measurements based on current replacement cost provide the best basis for evaluating financial position and predicting sustained earning power.

Sprouse, 1966b, 113

[In replacement price accounting] ... we are trying to give the investor a picture of the position he would buy into, and we are trying to state the assets of a company for this purpose as though it were going to compete with other companies .... at prices which would place the company on an equal position with competitors.

Ross, 1969, 35, 127

525 Replacement cost as a going concern valuation

Replacement value and cost [are] ... possible general rules for valuation. Either may express going concern value.

Daniels, 1934/1980, 31

the assumption of an indefinite life provides ... a reason for thinking in terms of replacements and replacement costs .... a concept of net income based upon replacement costs is entirely compatible with the going concern postulate.

Carson, 1949a, 35

In order for a business enterprise to continue indefinitely ... its store of productive factors must be replenished as they are exhausted. In measuring financial position, the value of productive resources is what it would cost to acquire them today.

Sprouse, 1966b, 113

Selling prices must be high enough to provide the enterprise with ... enough funds to replace used resources in order to safeguard the continuity of the enterprise .... Under this principle ... the cost of the used resources is actually the cost to replace them ....

Bakker, 1974, 2

The capital maintenance concept underlying current value accounting is that of maintaining intact the productive capacity of the business .... Maintenance of productive capacity is a necessary attribute of the going concern. By maintaining its monetary and physical assets intact from internally generated funds, the business avoids ... serious financial and operating problems ....

Barton, 1975, 447

530 Valuation at Current Cost

531 Interpretation of current cost

The current cost of an asset for which the actual outlay was made on a prior date is the cost of the current outlay of resources required to produce the asset. Current cost, therefore, coincides with the cost of replacement by manufacture.

Gordon, 1953, 375

Current cost – the cost currently of acquiring the inputs which the firm used to produce the asset being valued. [As distinguished from] Present cost – the cost currently of acquiring the asset being valued.

Edwards & Bell, 1961, 79

[In the context of measuring a firm's operating efficiency in terms of current cost] . . . replacement cost means the current cost to replace the service potential of fixed assets used up in the production of income rather than the current cost of alternative replacement assets.

Popoff, 1973, 11

The current cost of inventory owned by an enterprise is the current cost of purchasing the goods concerned or the current cost of the resources required to produce the goods concerned (including an allowance for current overhead costs . . .) whichever would be applicable in the circumstances of the enterprise . . . . The current cost of plant, property and equipment owned by an enterprise is the current cost of acquiring the same service potential (indicated by operating costs and physical output capacity) as embodied by the asset owned.

FASB, 1979, SFAS33

532 Current cost as a going concern valuation

In effect, [in current cost accounting] we accept the traditional going concern convention in accounting, which is based upon the assumption that the firm is a continuing long run entity with an established set of assets and an established production process.

Edwards & Bell, 1961, 275

current cost . . . . is appropriate [as a measurement basis for the preparation of financial statements] where the entity is viewed as a going concern . . . .

NZSA, 1983, SSAP1

533 Determination of current cost

Under a current cost basis of valuation, the assets carried forward from the prior period are raised (lowered) to their current cost. This requires no change in the monetary assets and liabilities, since the dollar prices of these assets are invariant over time. Each nonmonetary asset carried forward is adjusted to current cost with the index number appropriate to the account. The gains or losses on the assets carried forward are called capital gains, and they are not taken to net worth through the regular income statement.

Gordon, 1953, 373

Where there is an established market for assets of like kind and condition, quoted prices provide the most objective evidence of current cost . . . . Where there is no

505

established market ... current cost may be estimated by reference to the purchase price of assets which provide equivalent service capacity. The purchase price of such substitute assets should be adjusted for differences in operating characteristics such as cost, capacity, and quality. In other cases, adjustment of historical cost by the use of specified price indexes may provide acceptable approximations of current cost. Appraisals are acceptable only if they are based on the above methods of estimating current cost. Whenever there is no objective method of determining the current cost of obtaining the same or equivalent services, depreciated acquisition cost should continue as the basis of valuation.

AAA, 1964a, 695

The current cost of an asset is the lower of (a) its net current replacement cost; and (b) its recoverable amount, that is, the higher of (i) its net realizable value, and (ii) the amount recoverable from its future use (i.e. its economic value) .... The net current replacement cost of an item of plant and machinery is ... the asset's gross current replacement cost ... [reduced] by an accumulated depreciation provision based on (i) the gross current replacement cost; (ii) the proportion of the asset's useful economic life which has expired; and (iii) the depreciation method adopted for the asset.

ASC, 1986, 59, 63

The most convenient method of calculating the gross current replacement cost of an item of plant and machinery is normally by applying a relevant index to the existing book value. Indices are averages and so can be used for blocks of similar assets .... [Official] or generally recognized privately compiled indices may be used.

ASC, 1986, 63

540 Valuation at Market Price, Value in Exchange, Selling Price, Exit Value, Net Realizable Value

541 Valuation at market price (buying or selling not specified)

[Accounts of the period 1436–1440 of Jachomo Badoer, a Venetian merchant trading throughout the Levant, Black Sea and the Mediterranean basin, indicate that] Badoer was not troubled by problems of valuation. Market value is the one he used, though at times he is called upon to estimate the value of wares subject to customs duties, which was determined in accord with customs officials. The intent, of course, was to estimate the market value of the merchandise at the time of the tax. Badoer also uses estimated values when transactions cannot be consummated in the market.

Peragallo, 1980, 99

[On taking inventory] – Debit Mechini ginger . . . credit capital for so many packages weighing so many pounds, in my store or at my house, which according to current prices I value at so many ducats per hundred . . . .

Pacioli, 1494/1963, 56

for the whole quantity [of goods] remaining unsold, [value] the same at the present market price, or at the price they cost you . . . . If only part of the goods be sold . . . [value] those goods that remain by you unsold at the price they cost you, or at the market price. *N.B.* It is usual with merchants, when they make a general balance of their books, to value the goods they have by them at the market price they then go at, at the time of their balancing, but some do not so.

Hayes, 1741, 79

In an account of real property . . . if the whole be on hand, enter the present value on the debit side of the balance sheet (at current prices, recognizing profit or loss).

Enc Britannica, 1810, IV, "Bookkeeping"

taking an inventory of the goods on hand at their market prices . . . . Accounts of merchandise . . . . houses, lands, &c . . . . property in the funds . . . . ships . . . . contain on the Dr side the value of the property at the time of opening the books, and on the Cr side . . . the value of what remains unsold at the time of balancing.

Foster, 1843, I:33, II:11

the basic solvency formula which has formed the framework of [Massachusetts] insurance company balance sheets since that time [1847]:

Assets – Liabilities + Capital stock = Legal surplus.

Assets were listed at market value . . . .

Raymond, 1965, 41

In the above [illustrative] inventory, the several articles are set down at first cost, although it is obvious this practice in actual business may often prove fallacious; for it is not the first cost, but the present price of the article, especially if that be less than the cost, that must be taken into consideration: . . . .

Morrison, 1849, 38

In order to arrive at a balance, the first thing a merchant or trader does . . . is to ascertain the amount of his property . . . by examination, weighing, pricing, &c, according to the current market price, the various articles of merchandise of which his stock consists.

Pulling, 1850, 89

[As for] companies whose business depends on their periodically showing to their constituents and the public their sound and unquestionable financial position, . . . while . . . nothing could be more reprehensible than for directors of a bank to deceive their shareholders and the customers, by stating its securities at a value they know they do not possess, yet they would naturally, as competitors for public patronage, desire to set forth the assets at their fair market value, and to this the auditor cannot raise any objection.

Pixley, 1881/1976, 130

Even though market values have frequently been ignored in balance sheets, the time is coming when more attention will be paid to true values. Market value is the price at which a seller willing to sell at a fair price and a buyer willing to buy at a fair price, both having reasonable knowledge of the facts, will trade.

Montgomery, 1922, I:74

Present market price has the advantage of always being up to date. It is accurate where cost would not be so .... the figure to be used is the present market price according to the best evidence at hand. This is no rule of thumb. None is needed. None is desirable .... As long as business enterprise is subject to the regulation of the market, accounting cannot faithfully .... present financial affairs in as trustworthy and accurate a manner as possible .... unless it looks to the market as its guide.

Scott, 1925, 193–198

market price is in reality a price equidistant from the high bid and the low offer, and ... this market price can be in error only to the extent that not all the facts may be known regarding the high bid and the low offer .... Economic values should be determined from both bid and offer prices whenever these are available .... the value of a thing is not what it could be sold for if it were offered for sale. Its value is what it is being bought and sold for or, if it is not being bought and sold, its logical price under the ratio of supply and demand that actually exists.

MacNeal, 1939, 142, 143

The ideal measure of resources is current exchange value. This is not the same as either liquidation value or market replacement cost, though these set lower and upper limits respectively, and can often be used to measure value.

Philips, 1963b, 708

The essence of wealth is value .... If accounting is to provide adequate measurements of tangible wealth and income .... The simple results of asset exchanges ... must be supplemented ... with estimates of the extent to which the market values of all assets and liabilities have changed.

Sands, 1963, 9, 92

The directors' report ... shall also, if ... the market value [of interests in land] differs substantially from the amount at which they are included in the balance sheet and the difference is, in the opinion of the directors, of such significance as to require that the attention of members ... or of holders of debentures ... should be drawn thereto, indicate the difference with such degree of precision as is practicable. [s16(1)(a)]

UK *Companies Act*, 1967

Most decision makers appear to prefer up to date market values over the market values of assets at their acquisiton dates (historical cost) as exemplified most clearly by investors requiring current market values of assets when making decisions to buy or sell shares in mutual funds.

Staubus, 1972, 40

The current market price of an asset in an active market shows, among other things, the amounts of cash that are: (a) presently obtainable from selling the asset and (b) presently required to obtain another, similar asset . . . . (c) presently obtainable from borrowing against the asset. Moreover, current market price is . . . a good surrogate for (d) the present value of cash obtainable in the future from holding or using the asset . . . .

Johnson & Storey, 1982, 63

542 Valuation at value in exchange or selling price

By the assistance of this money, everyone might compare what he had with the things of his neighbor . . . . thus, such a thing of my own is worth 20 pounds, that is, people will give so much for it; and such a thing of another man's is worth 20 pounds, consequently mine is equal to his in value.

Stephens, 1735, 2

In accounts of goods or other property . . . . If the whole be still on hand, enter the present value on the Dr of the balance sheet; and if this be different from the prime cost, charges included, enter the difference in the proper side of the profit and loss sheet . . . . The sum is the whole return that will be obtained if the rest of the goods be sold at estimated value; . . . .

Hamilton, 1788/1982, 285

the directors . . . shall cause to be provided and kept . . . all necessary and proper books of account . . . and shall twice in every year . . . take and make up a fair, accurate, and just statement and account of the stock and capital of the company . . . and of the profits . . . and the losses . . . ; and in each such stocktaking reference shall be had to the then value of the funded and all other property of the company, which shall be estimated, not at the cost, but at the then selling price thereof; so that the real state of the affairs of the company may in such statement plainly appear. [Deed of settlement]

Huddersfield Banking Company, 1827

In estimating the value of the property belonging to the company at the end of each year with a view to striking the annual balance due care shall be taken that the realizable worth of the property at the time, so far as the same can be ascertained, shall be made the basis of such valuations. [Amalgamation agreement]

James Finlay & Company, 1858

From the beginning of the use of the Commercial Code [in Germany] the principle of disposal values ruled almost universally as the basis of valuation; this included sales value, liquidation value, and exchange value. This was the general legal view held by the German courts. But not without opposition.

Weigmann, 1932, 103

the value of property is determined by its purchasing power.

Sadler & Rowe, 1894/1986, 2

it seems clear that if a bank balance sheet is to serve any useful purpose, it is only to be done by placing upon its assets those values which it is known, or reasonably expected, that they would realize within the period named.

Accountant, editorial, 1895, 76

I see no reason why we should not take into the assets the stock (whether shares, produce or goods) at its fair market value; that is, the value at which it could be sold on the day and for which a ready purchaser could be found. And even if it is only by so doing that a profit can be shown, I say I can see no legal reason why such profit should not be distributed as a dividend.

Marshall, 1895, 495

The market value of an asset is a thing we can understand . . . . the value of capital is mainly based on the realizable values of assets.

Carter, 1910a, 126

If [a balance sheet] is to possess real value it must unequivocally declare the state of affairs at the date to which the accounts are made up, and investments should in all cases be valued as at that date . . . . Shareholders have the right to be told precisely what their assets will realize at the end of the financial year. [cited from *The financial news*]

Accountant, 1921, 789

The liquidation value [of assets] is of significance to the creditor. He makes a loan looking to the assets as security. Hence there is some tendency, noticeable though not dominant, to insist that assets should be revalued at what they would bring.

Hatfield, 1927/1971, 74

Assets are the sources of future services and in so far as it is anticipated that these services will be valuable the right to them will command a present price, which price is the worth of the asset . . . . While it is easy to show that the purchasing power test of value is well understood and generally accepted, no accountant has stated, so far as the writer is aware, an alternative proposition and shown it to be useful.

Edwards, 1938b, 81, 289

wheat may be as valid an asset in support of gain as cash. Wheat in fact might be a more acceptable asset than cash, for if a farmer holds his wheat he is in fact valuing it (off the accounting record) above current market value. Hence in this instance valuation at market price does not lack conservatism; it is in fact the best measure of value.

Bowers, 1941, 145

The appraisal balance sheet . . . . Each accounting balance sheet entry . . . . is weighed, as far as possible, in terms of the present exchange money value. In creating this appraisal balance sheet out of the accounting balance sheet, two procedures are necessary: 1. The elimination of certain balances which appear on the accounting balance sheet . . . because they have no apparent and immediate exchange value. 2. The specific valuation, in terms of current realizable money value, of each ledger balance as it appears in one or the other summary columns of the accounting balance sheet.

Dewing, 1953, I:524

The saleable value of assets reflects the price that other people are prepared to pay for those assets. In the ultimate analysis this price reflects the degree of usefulness that the community attaches to the assets . . . . If directors fail to earn something approaching market rate of return on figures approximating to the market value of the resources they control they are in effect reducing the level of the national income below what the market in general thinks it could be. Such a situation should be made apparent . . . .

Edey, 1960/1980, 201

The most important determination [of asset value] to be made generally is the measurement of significance in the market, i.e. the determination of market value . . . . the market value of property is what it will bring. So widespread is the use of this concept that in many cases it is indicated by the use of the term, value, without any qualifying adjective.

Dohr & others, 1964, 87

selling prices . . . . are necessary to define market alternatives, they express the investment required to hold assets and they are a component of a risk indicator. . For all of these reasons, I conclude that the items on a balance sheet should be valued at their present selling prices. Since income is defined as the difference between wealth (net worth) at two points of time, it follows that the income statement would be an explanation of the changes in the exit values on two successive balance sheets.

Sterling, 1972, 208

Valuation at money equivalent or cash equivalent

When we speak of an object as possessing a certain money value, we express the measure of its purported equivalent in money.

Gundelfinger, 1924, 335

for the purpose of determining the amount to be declared and paid as a dividend, it is necessary that the true value of the assets in cash, and not the mere book value, should be ascertained.

> Cannon et al v Wiscessett Mills Co. et al, 1928

Important as buildings may be for the activities of the human beings who inhabit them, this importance has no place in the statement of account, unless [it] can somehow be given a money value equivalent.

> Dewing, 1953, I:517

the single financial property which is uniformly relevant at a point of time for all possible future actions in markets is the market selling price or realizable price of any or all goods held. Realizable price may be described as current cash equivalent.

> Chambers, 1966a, 92

To an accountant, value is simply the appropriate cash equivalent for any asset involved in the accounting process.

> Ross, 1969, 2

543 Valuation of inventories at selling price

[Matthaus Schwarz, chief accountant of the business of the Fuggers, designed a method of bookkeeping (c.1550) under which the] profit is determined by comparing two statements of capital at two different moments in time. The merchandise inventory is valued at "what it will bring in".

> ten Have, 1972/1976, 47

Fix some definite value which should be no more or less than the property could be sold for . . . . if you value what you have unsold at a price for which you could sell it, and carry the same to the credit side of the merchandise account, the difference in the footing would be gain.

> Harris, 1842/1933, 151

[On farm accounts] I . . . believe that livestock and farm products may be safely inventoried at market prices, and gross profit computed to include profits by increase figured on the same basis, otherwise it would seem difficult to provide a balance sheet showing the condition of a business at a given moment of time.

> Finlay, 1914, 49

It is customary to condemn unreservedly the practice of inventorying goods or commodities at selling prices . . . . If we define good accounting practice to be that which is followed by good accountants, we find many precedents for valuing inventories at selling prices. We find balance sheets of well-managed and prosperous concerns certified to by leading accountants, in which the statement appears that inventories are valued at selling prices. Under the circumstances we are forced to the conclusion that it may be good accounting practice.

Montgomery, 1922, I:147

[Under extractive lines] Whenever the product is a staple such as wheat, petroleum, copper, sugar, or the like, it may with reason be urged that income should be accounted for in terms of physical output rather than in terms of delivery and title passing [i.e. at net selling value. The same principle applies to gold mining and farm produce].

Paton, 1924, 592

The Federal Trade Commission in 1920 squarely criticized [the great meat packing concerns for showing] their inventories as invariably appraised on a market basis when sound accounting principles required a basis of cost.

Ripley, 1927, 191

Unrealized profit should not be credited to income account . . . . An exception to the general rule may be made in respect of inventories in industries (such as the packing house industry) in which, owing to the impossibility of determining costs, it is a trade custom to take inventories at net selling prices, which may exceed cost. [Exhibit I]

AIA, 1932

we may find precedents for valuing inventories at selling prices [examples given: for mining companies, gold, silver, copper, lead and other metals; for packing companies, fresh meats and other products; for oil companies, crude oil and refined products; for sugar companies, sugar and molasses]. Perhaps the test always lies in full disclosure . . . . if the inventory is clearly shown to be at selling prices, the chief cause for criticism has been removed. There may be anticipation of profits, but there is no deception. If there is good reason for this basis of value, the other objections likewise are removed.

Montgomery, 1934, 223

The market quotation [realizable value] of the merchandise produced finds proper application as the test of income in a number of cases in the agricultural and extractive industries. In these industries there is commonly a ready market for the product. No effort or important expense is necessary to accomplish the sale. [References to a number of agricultural and mineral products, and to companies in those industries]

Lund, 1941, 374

Only in exceptional cases may inventories properly be stated above cost . . . . precious metals having a fixed monetary value, with no expense of marketing, may be stated at such monetary value. Any other exceptions must be justifiable by the characteristics of fungibility, immediate marketability at quoted market prices, and inability to determine approximate costs . . . .

Stans, 1946, 106

Any inventory is worth what the quantity of goods actually on hand will bring on the market at orderly sale . . . .

Moonitz, 1953, 690

In some types of businesses, such as tea and rubber producing companies and some mining companies, it is a recognized practice to bring stocks of products into account at the prices realized subsequent to the balance sheet date, less only selling costs. By this means the whole of the profit is shown in the period in which the crop is reaped or the minerals won. This basis has come to be accepted as customary in the industries concerned.

ICAEW, 1960, N22

544 Valuation of security holdings at selling price

[After endorsing the representation of assets at their fair market value] As a matter of prudence, however, [the auditor] might suggest the cost price being inserted in the balance sheet, supposing the securities have not depreciated in value, and it being stated, in a footnote, the actual market value at the date on which the balance sheet is made out.

Pixley, 1881/1976, 130

As the whole theory of these security holdings [temporary investments] lies in their availability, they should be priced at their fair market valuation as on the balance sheet date, irrespective of cost. Otherwise they cannot be considered as the equivalent of cash.

Montgomery, 1912/1976, 115

Balance sheet valuation of temporary investments at market, or in other words, at present realizable values, is logical inasmuch as the item is of considerable interest to creditors.

Daniels, 1934/1980, 50

As a current asset, marketable investments become a part of the showing of solvency – of particular interest to creditors. Accordingly their cash realizable value, i.e. their market value, represents their debt-paying ability and is, therefore, an appropriate measure for solvency purposes. However, the use of any other measure than cost injects elements of profit and loss. As a prudent basis for the measurement of profits . . . . the lower of cost or market formula will be used to measure the dollar amount of the asset to be carried forward . . . . giving . . . market value by means of a parenthetic footnote.

Kester, 1946, 118

Marketable securities are usually considered as good as cash .... The net price [that a marketable security] can be sold for determines the funds available for alternatives. Thus, its current market price, not its sunk cost, should be used [in financial statements].

Corbin, 1964, 255

reporting of investments in common stock at market value (or at approximate fair value if market value is not available) is considered to meet most clearly the objective of reporting the economic consequences of holding the investment.

AICPA, 1971a, APBO18

The focus on mark-to-market accounting for investment securities reflects the emerging conceptual focus on the balance sheet, on the critical nature of asset and liability measurements if balance sheets are to reflect faithfully the resources and obligations of the reporting entity. While this focus is of equal concern for unregulated entities and for nonfinancial entities, it is vital for the partially regulated financial institutions.

Wyatt, 1991, 83

Property of investment and like companies

The accounting problems of investment trusts, ... all corporations the business of which consists of owning or trading in the securities of other corporations for purposes other than control, are so special that the committee will, at the appropriate time, issue a statement devoted to them. In the meantime the general pronouncements of the committee should not be regarded as necessarily applicable to investment trusts.

AIA, 1939a, ARB1

Value based companies comprise: (a) authorized insurers; (b) property investment and property dealing companies; and (c) investment trust companies, unit trusts and other similar long term investment entities.

ASC, 1986, 144

****

it has now become common practice [for investment trusts] to integrate the presentation of realized profits and unrealized appreciation. In the case of a large proportion of the investment trusts, the principal financial statement is based on market value of the assets.

Werntz, 1953b, 560

In the case of certain types of investment trusts, perhaps the most useful item of information to stockholders is the market value of the investments .... The practice accordingly developed ... to reflect the investments at cost with the quoted market value shown parenthetically, or to take them in at market value, showing cost parenthetically. It is recognized as proper here to reflect unrealized appreciation in the

balance sheet, even though it is a departure from the cost basis ... and the reason is that a balance sheet so prepared is more useful to the parties interested.
Broad, 1957, 32

Market value at a particular date ... is capable of reasonably precise definition ... and is more relevant for use when calculating the asset value per share and measuring income yield. Investments may therefore appropriately be stated in the accounts of investment trust companies at market value as an alternative to their being stated at cost or revaluation with their market value stated merely as a note.
ICAEW, 1968a, N28

the authors of the guide [Audits of personal financial statements, AICPA, June 1968] erred in putting primary emphasis on historical cost. It seems to me that a personal statement of assets and liabilities is more appropriately compared to that of an investment company than to the usual commercial enterprise. In the case of investment companies, it is well established that a current value basis is preferable – in practice as well as in theory.
Trueblood, 1969, 22

The balance sheets of open end [management investment] companies shall reflect all assets at value, showing cost parenthetically. The balance sheets of closed end companies shall either (1) reflect all assets at cost, showing value parenthetically, or (2) reflect all assets at value, showing cost parenthetically. [Rule 6–02–6]
SEC, 1970a, Reg S-X

Unlike industrial and commercial corporations ... a mutual fund offers its shares at a price equivalent to net asset value plus, in most cases, a sales or load charge, and offers to redeem outstanding shares at net asset value (in some cases, less a redemption charge). Accordingly, the correct calculation of net asset value – not only for financial statement purposes, but on a daily basis – is of the utmost importance. .... [It is required] that assets be stated at fair value based upon market quotations or, in their absence, the next best indication of value (which may be the opinion of management in certain cases).
Tiedemann, 1970, 31–33

This statement requires investment properties to be included in the balance sheet at open market value .... an investment property is an interest in land and/or buildings (a) in respect of which construction work and development have been completed; and (b) which is held for its investment potential, any rental income being negotiated at arm's length [with specified exemptions].
ASC, SSAP19, 1981

545 Net realizable value (prospective) described

Net realizable value of inventory is a measurement of expected revenue less costs of completion and disposal.
AAA, 1964b, 707

Net realizable value can be defined as the amount which it is estimated, as on the balance sheet date, will be realized from disposal of stock in the ordinary course of business, either in its existing condition or as incorporated in the product normally sold, after allowing for all expenditure to be incurred on or before disposal.

ICAEW, 1969a, 551

The net realizable value of an asset is defined as the maximum net amount which can be realized from the disposal of that asset within a short period of time (not a forced sale situation, ...) .... the selling price less disposition costs including tax effects discounted to the point of measurement.

Bedford & McKeown, 1972, 333

Realizable value – the amount of net cash or cash equivalent that could be obtained by orderly sale in the near future of resources in their present form.

NAA, 1974, 22

Net realizable value: the actual or estimated selling price (net of trade but before settlement discounts), less all further costs to completion and all costs to be incurred in marketing, selling and distributing.

ASSC, 1975b, SSAP9

Expected exit value (net realizable value) is distinguishable from current exit value because expected exit value is based on expected future sales proceeds or other events whereas current exit value is based on current disposable value, albeit disposable value in an orderly liquidation of the asset in question.

FASB, 1976b, 205

net realizable value. Selling price of an item less reasonable further costs to make the item ready for sale and to sell it.

Davidson & others, 1977, 36

Valuation at net realizable value

As a general rule, the amount at which all assets are stated in the balance sheet – except where a special statutory provision to the contrary obtains – should be regulated by the realizable value of such assets on the basis of a going concern.

Dicksee, 1908, 194

the same principle should apply to all of the different types of stock [inventory] and the only principle which, it seems to me, can be applied is the net realizable value in the form of finished products.

de Paula, 1937, 489

The matching of revenues with costs by valuing inventories at net realizable value is a desirable alternative to the matching of costs with revenues under the present realization convention. First, it is theoretically acceptable .... Second, the number of arbitrary allocations necessary to determine periodic net income is reduced to a minimum . . . . Third, the data emerging are more valid . . . than comparable data furnished by present accounting methods . . . . in making informed decisions about the future of the enterprise . . . . Net realizable value is related to the future . . . . It never produces poorer income figures, and it always produces better balance sheet figures.

Storey, 1958/1978, 181

Inventories which are readily saleable at known prices with readily predictable costs of disposal should be recorded at net realizable value, and the related revenue taken up at the same time.

Sprouse & Moonitz, 1962, 57

since the net realizable value reflects the amount of cash that can reasonably be expected to be realized in the sale of the inventories in the normal course of business, it would seem to more closely reflect the true position of inventories as an item of working capital.

Mulcahy, 1963, 19

It is quite possible to argue that economic income arises from the processes of production and merchandising rather than from sales and that the sale, as signaled by delivery of goods or service, is a secondary rather than the primary aspect of revenue recognition. Those who take this position would show inventories at their net realizable value – the revenue to be obtained on delivery, less the costs incident to delivery and collection efforts.

Vatter, 1971, 362

Net realizable value is widely used in practice. Accounts receivable, for example, are valued at realizable value . . . . The lower of cost or market valuation of inventories frequently relies on net realizable value in computing market value. Even the estimation of salvage value in computing historical cost depreciation purports to be a realizable value.

Bedford & McKeown, 1972, 336

The cash surrender value [of a life insurance policy on a principal officer of a firm named as beneficiary] is an asset to the firm.

Keller, 1977, 14:29

The [Canada *Business Corporations Act*, 1975] refers to a number of situations in which a company may make payments to acquire its own shares . . . to redeem shares . . . to reduce its capital . . . to pay dividends . . . to acquire shares of certain dissenting shareholders . . . . In these cases it is provided that no such payment shall be made if there are reasonable grounds for believing that (a) the corporation is, or would after the payment be, unable to pay its liabilities as they become due, or (b) the realizable value of the corporation's assets would, after the payment, be less than the aggregate of its liabilities (in some of the above cases) or the aggregate of its liabilities and stated capital (in other cases).

Chambers & Falk, 1985, 16

[Conclusion from a survey] . . . persons with no prior [learning] of accounting tend to use cash flows and/or net realizable values in the income statement; and persons with prior [learning] tend to use historic costs in both statements . . . . In the case of those with no prior [learning], . . . learning causes cash flow and net realizable value accounting to be abandoned for allocated historic costs in most cases.

Lee, 1984, 135

net realizable values . . . . are the values which the assets could be sold for, if disposed of in an orderly fashion, near the time of the account . . . . we advocate the use of net realizable value as a relevant basis for helping to appraise an entity's financial wealth.

ICAS, 1988, 58, 61

546 Exit value

Exit values . . . . opportunity costs – values that could currently be realized if assets (whether finished goods, semifinished goods, or raw materials) were sold (without further processing) outside the firm at the best prices immediately obtainable.

Edwards & Bell, 1961, 79

Exit value is the proceeds that could be obtained from selling an asset (in the case of an asset) or the payment needed to discharge an obligation (in the case of a liability or stock equity), net of transaction costs.

Ronen, 1974, 152

The current exit value of an asset is the amount of cash that could be obtained currently by selling it under conditions of orderly liquidation [of assets]. Ideally, that attribute is measured by quoted market prices for assets of a similar kind and condition.

FASB, 1976b, 204

exit value. The proceeds that would be received if assets were disposed of in an arm's length transaction; current selling price; net realizable value.

Davidson & others, 1977, 23

Exit value differs from net realizable value in that [for example, in the case of a crude oil deposit] in the latter we are required to deduct lifting costs, transportation expenses, and the normal profit margin from the refinery price of the crude. What is sought in exit value accounting is the immediate sale price of the oil as is. Thus, the exit value of the deposit will be different from the net realizable value of the oil.

Sterling, 1979, 220

Exit valuation denotes the selling price that can be received from the firm's assets when sold through a process of orderly liquidation. Orderly liquidation refers to a situation in which the firm continues operations – as opposed to the larger discounts arising in forced liquidation circumstances.

Wolk & others, 1984, 356

547 Market selling price etc. as going concern value

The value obtaining on the day of valuation for going concerns is, I think, the only sound and safe way of determining the amount. It is what property would fetch, not what it cost, that settles value . . . . We have, I apprehend, to make up accounts . . . as things stand today, and let tomorrow look after itself.

Harris, 1883, 9, 10

valuation . . . as a going concern . . . at such a price as a willing purchaser would be prepared to give. That is to say, the assets should be written down from time to time to provide effectively for depreciation.

Dicksee, 1909a, 192

Those who say that the selling price of fixed assets, being of no significance to a going concern, should be disregarded in revaluations, should, by that same token, maintain that to a concern engaged in selling merchandise the price at which it can be sold is the significant one.

Hatfield, 1927/1971, 99

Market value: . . . . Under this meaning [of value] property does not have value unless it can be sold to some other person – and the valuation is determined by the sum obtained on sale. This is probably the meaning accountancy writers intend when they refer to the going concern valuation of a business.

Battersby, 1949, 122

if a firm does not replace its assets, it cannot continue – it will cease being a going concern after the present assets are sold (inventory), or wear out, or become obsolete (depreciable asset). Since exit values of owned assets are necessary for the replacement decision and since replacement is necessary for the continuity of the firm, exit values are necessary for the going concern. Exit valuation does not imply liquidation of the firm.

Sterling, 1979, 121

548 Fair value and fair market value

Fair value [and Fair valuation]. Present market value; such sum as the property will sell for to a purchaser desiring to buy, the owner wishing to sell; such a price as a capable and diligent business man could presently obtain from the property after conferring with those accustomed to buy such property . . . .

Black's law dictionary, 1951, 718

We hold . . . that the basis of all calculation as to the reasonableness of rates to be charged by a corporation maintaining a public highway under legislative sanction must be the fair value of the property being used by it for the convenience of the public.

Smyth v Ames, 1898

All the assets included in a balance sheet should be stated at their fair value . . . .

Lisle, 1903–04, I:208

the fair market value of assets [other than money] paid in is the proper basis for their book value . . . . The fair value of property received in an exchange is the selling price of the property given in exchange; and the fair value (of the property received) thenceforth becomes its cost.

Kohler & Morrison, 1926, 225, 288

Banks have long required personal balance sheets from their personal borrowers and from guarantors . . . . In most instances, the forms provided . . . for reporting upon their financial position have provided specifically for reporting assets at fair market value, without regard to historical cost . . . . [This method] has been used almost exclusively by investment companies and stock brokers.

Pitt & Tang, 1968/1970, 247

As a general principle, the current fair value of an issue of securities being valued by the board of directors [of a registered investment company] would appear to be the amount which the owner might reasonably expect to receive for them upon their current sale.

SEC, 1970b, ASR118

[Fair values of assets] . . . amounts estimated to be recoverable under the economic and political conditions of ownership and use at the date of issuance of the balance sheet.

Spacek, 1970b/1973, 45

Fair value is the approximation of exchange price in transfers in which money or money claims are not involved. Similar exchanges are used to approximate what the exchange price would have been if an exchange for money had taken place,

AICPA, 1970c, APBS4

Fair value is the amount for which an asset could be exchanged between a knowledgeable, willing buyer and a knowledgeable, willing seller in an arm's length transaction.

IASC, 1982, IAS16

In a market economy, the value of an economic resource is the price it commands in exchange. We call this fair market value. The fair market value of an economic resource may be indicated by its cost, by a market price, by a cost to reproduce a similar product or service, or by reference to values of other economic resources that would provide comparable services.

Andersen & Co, 1984, 19

550 Valuation at Net Present (Discounted) Value

551 Valuation at net present value, discounted value or capitalized value

Perhaps the most trustworthy value is that which is established by capitalizing the use of the property to be valued. It is almost the sole criterion of those who buy and sell property.

Montgomery, 1927, 206–7

the capitalization of the income producing value of the net assets . . . . is impractical [as a basis for valuing individual assets], since . . . the earnings of a business are the joint products of all the assets, conditions and services which the business possesses and uses. It is impossible, therefore, to impute on the basis of total earnings any particular value to any given asset.

Daines, 1929, 98

from the standpoint of the going concern, a theoretically sound principle might prescribe that assets be valued on the basis of the present (discounted) value of the future services or receipts which they will produce . . . and . . . that liabilities be listed at the present (discounted) value of the future payments which they require to be made. Not only would such a principle be practically impossible to apply with respect to many types of assets, but it would require constant changes in the values recorded.

Bell & Graham, 1937, 310

the value of an asset to a firm is the present value of the expected net receipts which can be attributed to the use of the asset.

Nolan, 1955, 2

Where sufficiently definite verifiable evidence is available to permit the valuation of an asset on one or more bases, the basis to be used is the one considered to yield the closest approximation to the discounted value of the asset's future cash flows.

Lemke, 1966a, 40

the choice of a measurement method to apply to a particular asset for financial reporting purposes should be made on the basis of two criteria: (1) the proximity of the measurement method to the ideal of maximum time-adjusted cash potential. . . , and (2) availability of a reliable reading of the particular type of evidence (measurement method) chosen.

Staubus, 1967, 660

The going concern value of an asset is the present worth of the future cash flows that the asset may be expected to generate.

Fremgen, 1968, 655

the true value of debtors at balance sheet date is the book value discounted back from collection date . . . . trade creditors should be discounted from the date they are payable.

Greener, 1969b, 348

pure value is a psychic phenomenon not always based on utility and . . . all value is subjective in nature . . . . the most nearly perfect basis for achieving correct values is a discounted flow method.

Williams, 1969, 33, 40

Discounted cash flows: a valuation basis quantifying specific assets and liabilities, or the enterprise as a whole, by discounting all expected cash flows at a rate reflecting both time values and risks.

AICPA, 1973, 41

Present [discounted] values measure the (estimated) values-in-use of assets, i.e. their cash flow values from the future use of assets in the operating activities of the business.

Barton, 1984, 528

See also 785

552 Net present value not a singular or unique value

A theory of value based on discounted future expectations is faced with the problem that . . . there is no certainty about the future, so that expectations about the future become subjective and must vary [from person to person].

Finnie, 1968b, 345

there is no single, true discounted value. Instead there are many true discounted values – probably as many true discounted values as there are participants in the market.

Sterling, 1979, 132

Most assets of business enterprises have more than a single cash flow potential, even to a single enterprise. For example, an asset that can be either sold or used . . .

has at least two cash flow potentials . . . . Many assets have several cash flow potentials because they have several uses. For example, milk . . . . steel ingots . . . .
Johnson & Storey, 1982, 95

553 Confusion of dated value and prospective value

this conception of value [i.e. discounted net proceeds of services to be derived from an asset] is an abstraction which yields but limited practical basis for quantification. Consequently, the measurement of assets is commonly made by more feasible methods [at or based on initial cost].
AAA, 1957a/1957b, 4

the accountant . . . cannot avoid making certain projections about the future. This is implicit, in fact, in an evaluation process. The act of valuation, Janus-like, has two faces. On the one hand, we value assets by past cost, sometimes compounded; on the other hand, we value them at discounted future receipts. The former is what we can most easily find out; the latter, however, is the truly significant figure.
Boulding, 1962, 52

The value of an asset is the money equivalent of its service potentials. Conceptually, this is the sum of the future market prices of all streams of service to be derived, discounted by probability and interest factors to their present worths. However this conception of value is an abstraction which yields but limited practical basis for quantification. Consequently, the measurement of assets is commonly made by other more feasible methods [for nonmonetary assets, mainly cost or derivatives of cost].
Dohr & others, 1964, 98

Theoretically we should define the sum of the assets of a firm to be equal to the present value of the future net cash flows that will be generated by the firm . . . . as a compromise with the unattainable but correct procedure described above . . . . use market value . . . . or economic value . . . . [or adjusted cost].
Bierman, 1965, 34

[An enterprise may be valued] by valuing the individual assets and liabilities in terms of their acquisition cost . . . . [by] capitalization of earning power . . . . by a summation of the various asset values after appraisal . . . . by adjusting the original cost valuations incurred at various times by some uniform dollar amount.
Bedford & others, 1967, 152

The concept of value. The economic value of an asset is the maximum amount that the firm would be willing to pay for it. This amount depends on what the firm expects to be able to do with it . . . . Value, in other words, depends on three factors: (1) the amount of anticipated future cash flows, (2) their timing, and (3) the interest rate. The lower the expectation, the more distant the timing, or the higher the interest rate, the less valuable the asset will be. Value may also be represented by the amount the firm could obtain by selling its assets. This sale price is seldom a good measure of the asset's value to the firm, however, because few firms are likely to keep many assets that are worth no more to the firm than their market value. Continued ownership of an asset implies that its present value to the owner exceeds its market value, which is its apparent value to outsiders. [per G Sh]

Enc Britannica, 1981, I:38

treating the two systems [present value accounting and *ex post* accounting] as alternatives confuses the information required for decisions with the realized consequences of those decisions . . . .

Barton, 1984, 540

Although information about value in that pure form [present value of future cash flows] is often not available for individual assets and liabilities, even on an estimated basis, some surrogate, such as current market price, frequently is.

Andersen & Co, 1987, 15

See also 147

560 Hybrid Valuation Schemes

561 The lower of cost and market rule

You will not find [the cost or market price rule for valuing inventory] in accounting literature before the mid-nineteenth century, for before that time consistent valuation at cost seems to have been the rule.

Solomons, 1961, 377

a sound rule to follow in regard to the valuation of both manufactured and unmanufactured stocks is to take them at cost, or at the market value of the goods purchased, whichever is the lower of the two.

Accountant, editorial, 1890b, 665

the ordinary rule for profit and loss purposes, that stock in trade should be valued at cost price or market price (whichever be the lower), is one that is more generally recognized among accountants than among traders and manufacturers.

Accountant, editorial, 1899, 1226

The general rule for valuing stock is to take cost or market price whichever is lower. Speaking generally, on no account must a value in excess of the cost price be taken. The reason for this is that profits must not be anticipated. A profit is not made until the goods are actually sold . . . .

Walbank, 1903–04, VI:167

It is . . . generally recognized as a correct accounting principle that, if the cost value of the inventory exceeds the market value, a reserve should be created to bring it down to the latter value, while on the other hand, if the market value exceeds the cost, no credit should be taken for the profits until they are realized by an actual sale.

Dickinson, 1914, 94

Stock should be valued at cost or market price [realizable value], whichever is lower at the date of the balance sheet. In no case should the value be higher than cost, even though the market value has risen, as this would result in taking profit before the sale is effected and the profit earned.

Spicer & Pegler, 1914, 171

valuation of use elements should never be in excess of cost and . . . valuation of exchange elements should never exceed either cost or market value.

Gundelfinger, 1924, 347

an asset acquired for permanent use should never be valued in excess of cost, whereas an asset acquired for consumption, sale or exchange should never exceed in balance sheet value either cost or market value.

Reiter, 1926/1976, 14

The valuation principle [under current value accounting] consists of replacement cost and net proceeds, which ever is lower, and is a variant of the conventional accounting rule of cost (historical cost) and market, whichever is lower.

Bakker, 1974, 3

Inventories should be valued at the lower of historical cost and net realizable value.

IASC, 1975, IAS2

562 Interpretation of market in the lower of cost and market rule

Only one principle of the monetary valuation of current assets has withstood the test of time and the criticisms of financial authorities . . . . the general rule of cost or market [cash to be realized], whichever is lower, is applicable to all current assets . . . . Good accounting . . . favors the substitution of replacement cost [of inventories] for cost where the market is declining.

Kohler & Morrison, 1926, 284, 304

The orthodox principle is that inventories should be valued on the basis of the lower of cost or market value . . . . there are two schools of thought, the first holding that the market value represents the replacement cost . . . the second holding that the market value represents the estimated net amounts that the goods would realize.

de Paula, 1937, 488

As used in the phrase lower of cost or market the term market means current replacement cost (by purchase or by reproduction, as the case may be) except that (1) market should not exceed the net realizable value (i.e. estimated selling price in the ordinary course of business less reasonably predictable costs of completion and disposal) and (2) market should not be less than net realizable value reduced by an allowance for an approximately normal profit margin.

AIA, 1947a, ARB 29

When inventories are valued on the basis of market . . . . Each item in the ending inventory is valued on the basis of the replacement price of the particular items in the volume in which they are usually purchased by the business.

Kennedy, 1948, 113

Market, as used in the phrase, cost or market, whichever is lower, is interpreted to mean the replacement cost of the goods on the inventory date.

Noble & Niswonger, 1961, 243

the cost rule in operation becomes a rule of cost (less depreciation, if applicable) not in excess of net realizable value.

Moonitz & Jordan, 1963, I:169

The market value of stock [in the lower of cost and market price valuation rule] can be taken as (i) the replacement value . . . . (ii) the net realizable value [of completed stock, less costs of completion] . . . . (iii) the net realizable value . . . less the normal profit margin.

Garbutt (ed), 1969, 0705

In the UK market value is generally regarded as being the equivalent of net realizable value, and most UK companies now certify that stock is valued at the lower of cost and net realizable value.

Kirkman, 1974, 79

for the purposes of the lower of cost or market test, market is defined as replacement cost subject to a ceiling value of net realizable value and a floor value of net realizable value minus a normal profit margin.

Dearden & Shank, 1975, 109

563 Valuation at lowest of cost, replacement price and net realizable value

The nearest approach to a general rule for the valuation of current assets is that they be stated at (a) cost, or (b) current replacement values, or (c) realizable values, whichever is lowest.

Sanders & others, 1938, 70

The portion of the original cost of each class of . . . inventories to be carried forward as applicable to future operations should be not more than the least of (a) actual cost . . . , (b) current replacement cost . . . , (c) net realization value.

Greer, 1956, 12

At the end of an accounting period any asset (other than money) which is expected to be realized in money in the ordinary course of business within the next account-ing period shall be valued at the lowest of historical cost, current realizable value (less any further expenditure needed to effect realization), or current replacement cost (on the terms on which it is usual for the firm to acquire such assets), or of such of these three values as may be applicable.

Lee, 1973, 15

564 Optional applications of the lower of cost and market rule

[There are three alternative applications of the rule;] (1) to consider each article in stock separately; (2) to group articles in categories having regard to their similarity or interchangeability; or (3) to consider the aggregate cost of the total stock in trade in relation to its total market value.

ICAEW, 1945b, N10

There are three alternatives available [in application of the cost or market rule] . . . to apply the rule to each item . . . , to the total of the inventory, or on the basis of some intermediate subdivisions of the inventory.

Stans, 1946, 104

Depending on the character and composition of the inventory, the rule of cost or market, whichever is lower may properly be applied either directly to each item or to the total of the inventory (or, in some cases, to the total of the components of each major category). The method should be that which most clearly reflects periodic income.

AIA, 1947a, ARB29

There are three basic methods of valuing inventories at the lower of cost or market, as follows: (1) the item by item method, (2) the major category method, and (3) the total inventory method.

Needles & others, 1984, 405

565 Objections to valuation at lower of cost and market

The inventory of a trading concern should be valued at cost . . . . [Referring to valuation at lower than cost –] Accounting is not interested in what would happen "if", but in what has actually happened; and since the goods unsold were purchased at a certain price, the profits realized are to be measured by comparing that price with the proceeds. To reduce the inventory to a value lower than cost is to add to the cost of the goods sold during the period . . . [a] result [which] is contrary to the truth.

Esquerré, 1914, 171

the rule of "cost or market, whichever is lower" renders impossible a true and accurate balance sheet whenever market values substantially exceed cost.

Montgomery, 1922, I:144

The rule [cost or market price, whichever is the lower of the two] is more to be commended for its conservatism than for its logic.

Guthmann, 1925/1929, 20

The main justification for the cost or market basis seems to be its claim to conservatism. This is urged on the score of both the balance sheet and the income sheet . . . . But . . . . What is conservative in this respect as regards one fiscal period is equally unconservative as regards the following period . . . . There is the further point that it is notoriously inconsistent [resulting in a mixture of cost and market prices and reversals of practice from period to period].

Daniels, 1934/1980, 64

Many corporations, even the more progressive, content themselves with a mere statement that inventories are carried at cost or market, whichever is lower. Yet this leaves large areas of the unknown and unguessable.

Jones, 1935/1975, 584

No writer has ever been able to find a single definite point supporting the proposition that cost or market, whichever is the lower is a sound accounting rule . . . . in this rule inconsistency is made a virtue . . . . it opens the door to the use of cost inventories in one period, a shift to market values in the next, and so on . . . . The rule assumes that current market values are important to the creditor, proprietor or manager, only when they happen to be less than costs . . . . The rule is not conservative, in that the understatement (as compared with cost) of operating net in the current period is matched by overstatement in the following period or periods.

Paton, 1938, 202

Cost or market whichever is lower is not a proper method of inventory evaluation, since it results in exhibiting an item as a cost which does not represent cash spent or to be spent in obtaining the cash received or to be received from the period's sales.

Husband, 1946, 249

[The lower of cost and market rule] is not consistent with or supported by the traditional realization concept.

Paton & Paton, 1971, 125

529

566 Differential valuation of current and fixed assets

a particular inventory and valuation of the company's effects and of the debts owing to the company shall be made out prior to each balance, the value of the effects being to be fixed as near as may be at the rates they would bring at a public sale and of the work in hand in a finished or unfinished state being to be rated at the prime cost thereof .... [Contract of copartnery]

St Rollox Foundry Co, 1830

The justification for valuing works and plant on different principles to stock in trade ... is derived from commercial usage or custom, which custom in turn is based on reason and commonsense.

Cooper, 1888, 745

as long as a reasonable basis of depreciating the assets is arrived at and continued in good faith, it is quite unnecessary to take into consideration any possibility of the fixed assets of a company fluctuating in value from time to time. With regard to the floating assets, however, it is important that the actual values at the time should be taken into consideration, as these assets are only held by the company for the purposes of their being converted into cash as soon as possible, and therefore it is their cash values that should be taken, and not their cost.

Dicksee, 1897, 98

In general it is considered legitimate to continue fixed assets at their cost despite a subsequent decline in their value. But in valuing circulating assets regard must be had to current values, although there is some question whether the market value, even of circulating assets, can be accepted where that exceeds the original cost.

Hatfield, 1909, 81

[Fixed] assets should be shown in the balance sheet at cost price, less any depreciation that may have taken place .... The valuation of floating assets should be at cost or market price, whichever is the lower at the date of the balance sheet.

Spicer & Pegler, 1914, 351, 133

In general, [if] ... current assets for sale [are] taken at cost or market, whichever is lower, current assets for collection [are] taken at estimated collectability, and agents of production ... [are] taken at cost .... we have a point of departure for ... converting the balance sheet into a statement of realizable assets and payable liabilities as a test of either ultimate or immediate solvency.

Cole, 1921, 339

The general principle of valuation ... for the current assets may be stated as a valuation on the basis of cash-realizable values .... The long term creditor, mortgagee, or bondholder desires to know the sufficiency of the values which are the security for his loan. As a usual thing valuation of the fixed assets is, therefore, based on original cost.

Kester, 1924(p 11)/1978

Fixed assets are to be valued on a cost basis, but this rule is not to be applied to current assets .... Current assets are held for the express purpose of sale .... The present market value, to some extent, is an index of what they will bring.

Hatfield & others, 1940, 343

The suggestion that asset valuation should ... be related to asset classification [following Dicksee's distinction between permanent and floating assets, 1892] appears to have been an attempt to extend the application of the double account procedures [of statutory companies of the public utility variety] to registered companies.

Walker, 1974, 288

See also 444

567 Valuation at value to the owner

The value to be assigned to the several elements entering into the determination of the capital of a given business entity are the values which they severally possess to that particular entity at the moment of time for which the capital is determined .... the purposes for which they are severally intended at the given point of time must always be taken into consideration.

Gundelfinger, 1924, 338

Limperg's own value theory ... culminated in the following valuation rule: The value of a commodity is its realizable value or its replacement value, but always the lower of the two. As to the realizable value, a distinction should be made with regard to factors of production between the direct and the indirect realizable value [proceeds to be realized in the normal course of business]; of these two the higher is always relevant.

Burgert, 1972, 112

Let NRV = the net realizable value of the asset; PV = present value of expected net receipts from the asset; RC = [depreciated] replacement cost of the asset; VO = the asset's value to the owner. Then

[VO = NRV if RC > NRV > PV
VO = RC if NRV > PV and > RC
VO = RC if NRV < PV and PV > RC
VO = PV if NRV < PV and PV < RC
VO = lower of RC and PV if NRV < PV]

Solomons, 1966, 125

Value to the firm = replacement cost, except where replacement cost > present value or replacement cost > net realizable value, when value to the firm = present value or net realizable value, whichever is the greater.

Parker & Harcourt, 1969, 18

the value of an asset to the firm is equal to the lower of its netback value and its replacement cost . . . [where] netback value [is] the higher of economic value [present value of expected net receipts] and net realizable value.

Stamp, 1971, 285

if the cash flows from an asset are measured against the best alternative available to the owner, their discounted net present value equals the value of that asset to its owner.

Wright, 1973, 24

the value of an asset to a company is its written down current replacement cost (current purchase price), except in situations where the written down current replacement cost is higher than both the economic value [discounted value of expected net receipts] and the net realizable value in which case the value of the asset to the company is the economic value or the net realizable value whichever is the higher.

Sandilands, 1975, 60

The value to the business of an item of stock and work in progress [under current cost accounting] is the lower of current replacement cost and net realizable value.

IASG, 1976, ED18

If any asset . . . is essential to the continuance of operations, its worth to the enterprise is the cost to replace the same operating capacity which it provides . . . . the current cost of replacement. If the asset is not essential to the continued operations of the enterprise, it is worth no more than its sale price.

NZR, 1976, 93

Value to the business is: (a) the net current replacement cost; or, if a permanent diminution to below net replacement cost has been recognized, (b) recoverable amount . . . . [which] is the greater of the net realizable value of an asset and, where applicable, the amount recoverable from its further use.

ASC, 1980b, SSAP16

Value to the business, a concept integrating economic value and net realizable value with current cost, is a basis for the approach used in SFAS33, "Financial reporting and changing prices" . . . . The value of an asset to the business can . . . be described as its current cost, except when both net realizable value and the present value of its future cash flows are higher than current cost.

Alexander, 1981, 8:14, 15

Deprival value as value to the owner

The value of a property to its owner is identical in amount with the adverse value of the entire loss, direct and indirect, that the owner might expect to suffer if he were to be deprived of the property.

Bonbright, 1937/1965, 71

deprival value can be defined as the lower of replacement cost or expected direct benefits. Replacement cost must be interpreted in the light of cost avoidance or postponement; and expected direct benefits means the higher of services in use and of scrap value.

Baxter, 1971, 36

The CCA concept of value is that of value to the business. The value to the business of a company's assets is identical in amount with the adverse value of the entire loss, direct and indirect, that the company might expect to suffer if it were deprived of those assets (i.e. the value to the business is equal to its deprival value). The value to the business of an asset is [as given in 567, Sandilands, 1975, above].

IASG, 1976, ED18

Value to the owner in accounting challenged

as value to the owner is specific to, assessable by, and strictly an opinion of the owner, it can have no significance as financial fact to investors or creditors.

Chambers, 1971, 72

the concept of deprival value was not developed in, nor is it applicable to, the context of valuing assets owned.

Macdonald, 1974b, 269

value to the owner has never been demonstrated to arise out of a particular information requirement of a potential user of annual reports (other than that of an insurer).

Whittington, 1981a, 19

570 Valuation of Various Assets and Liabilities

571 Valuation of liabilities at dated contractual amount

The account for bonds is . . . always exact since it expresses a legal relation. The corporation can only be obliged to pay back the bonds in terms of nominal [money units].

Wasserman, 1931, 5

all liabilities should be exhibited at amounts representing their legal claims on the possessions of a business . . . .

MacNeal, 1939, 275

indebtedness is a contractual obligation from the moment it is incurred, even though not payable until some future time. No matter how long the term of the debt, its face amount is the obligation, and it continues so to exist until discharged.

Staub, 1942, 9

Ordinarily liabilities are fixed or readily determinable in amount, as stated or implied in the contract, and hence there is no serious problem of valuation or measurement . . . .

Paton (ed), 1944, 884

To adjust liabilities because of changes in prices at which obligations may be traded . . . attempts to introduce the market place's ongoing overall evaluation of the business into the balance sheet . . . . [But a] liability is a liability until is it discharged . . . . The company's economic resources are not enhanced by changes in the market value of its outstanding securities, whether debt or stock . . . . The debtor cannot cancel or in any way reduce his liability until he pays his debt, or his indebtedness is cancelled through legal proceedings or bankruptcy.

Andersen & Co, 1972, 58

572 Valuation of liabilities at present (discounted) value

in the case of long term debt, the liability is properly measured by the present (discounted) value of all future payments to be made under the contract . . . . Ordinarily the pertinent rate of interest for determining present value is the yield rate of interest at the date of issue (also called the effective rate or market rate), which may differ from the nominal or coupon rate in the contract itself.

Sprouse & Moonitz, 1962, 39

As assets are stated at their current value, it is only logical that liabilities should be stated at current value too. This step would involve an important and highly contentious departure from current accounting conventions. It would mean that long term liabilities should be discounted to present value.

Ross, 1969, 67

In measuring the amount to be reported for a liability, the future amount of the obligation should ordinarily be discounted at the interest rate implicit in the amount of funds received.

Anthony, 1983, 188

See also 550

573 Valuation of liabilities at market price

it is not appropriate to adjust liabilities because of subsequent changes in the market's evaluation of those liabilities. To change liabilities because of changes in the market rates at which a particular security may be [traded] . . . goes beyond the accounting function and tends to introduce the market place's ongoing evaluation of the business into the financial statements.

Hinton, 1972, 57

The amount of the liabilities represents the claims of creditors against the assets of the firm. The claims of creditors against the assets of the firm do not become the less (or the greater) as a consequence of transactions between bondholders.

Chambers, 1974b, 132

Where the bonds [of a company] are traded on the market, the appropriate measure of their current cash equivalent is the market price. Where they are not traded . . . the appropriate measure of their current cash equivalent is the amount the creditors are prepared to accept . . . or the amount the borrower has to offer a financial specialist to divest himself (the borrower) of the liability, whichever is the lower of the two amounts.

Ma, 1974, 126

the real liability of . . . debt declines during its lifetime by the decline in the value of the currency in that period . . . . the greater part of the benefit to the borrower . . . takes place as soon as there is an increase in the rate of inflation . . . . [this could be reflected] if long term debt were brought into the . . . balance sheet at market value, and the capital adjustment on this in each year were taken into the profit and loss account.

Thompson, 1974, 49

The use of NRV [net realizable value] . . . applies to liabilities . . . . The market value will be the figure for which the liability can be bought in.

ICAS, 1988, 66

574 Valuation of receivables

before striking the balance there shall be put to the debit of the profit and loss account and the credit of suspense account fifteen per cent on the amount of the debts owing to the company at such balance, these debts embracing the amount of all open accounts remaining to be settled . . . the sum . . . being to cover the risk of bad debts, loss of interest and expenses in the collection of payment . . . and when any bad debt is made and the amount thereof ascertained it shall be immediately transferred to the debit of the profit and loss account . . . . [Contract of copartnery]

St Rollox Foundry Co, 1830

an allowance shall be made on the debts due to the company to cover the expenses of their collection and to cover bad and doubtful debts . . . . [Minutes of copartnery]

Campbell & Christie, 1845

there shall be a deduction made of ten per cent from the amount of the debts due to the company on open account, and of five per cent on all debts due by current bills or on balance of accounts current so as to cover the risk of bad debts, discounts, interest, and expenses of collection. [Partnership agreement]

A & I Inglis, 1868

The book value of accounts receivable is exact. This account is based upon contractual agreements with the customers of the firm who agreed to pay a definite sum .... No matter ... how high the general level of prices goes, they cannot be obliged to pay more than the stipulated amount.

Wasserman, 1931, 4

The initial charge for notes and drafts receivable may be set up in the accounts on three principal bases: (1) face amount; (2) sum due at maturity; (3) discounted or market value .... The initial value of notes and bills [receivable] carrying no interest ... is less than face value – by an amount roughly representing a satisfactory interest charge. In other words, such notes are really interest-bearing, and strictly accurate accounting for income and financial condition during the life of the note requires the recognition of this "interest" as such.

Paton (ed), 1944, 434

Is it right to include in a balance sheet at its face value ... a debt which is not receivable until a year hence? The answer clearly seems to be that the amount of the debt should be reduced by a year's discount to bring it back to its true present value. [The same applies to long term liabilities.]

Beaton, 1968, 292

the appropriate current cash equivalent of receivables is given by the sale price of the entire inventory of debtors' accounts to a commercial factor corporation.

Ma, 1974, 125

Valuation describes the process of estimating the cash to be realized on the receivables. This requires a provision for uncollectible accounts, or bad debts – a customer's default on a legitimate obligation .... Estimates of bad debts should be periodically recorded among costs and expenses (not as revenue reductions) at the time revenue is recognized, with appropriate adjustments based on ongoing evaluations of accounts outstanding.

Peterson, 1981, 18.9, 10

575 Foreign assets and liabilities: conversion and translation

Because Americans do not think in terms of pesos, pounds, and francs, we need to have them translated into the language of dollars. When we receive a foreign balance sheet, we "translate" the foreign words into the kind we use, and the operation we perform on the foreign currency figures is analogous. We "translate" them into the currency in which we are accustomed to think.

Chinlund, 1936, 120

Translate and convert are terms with a distinctly different meaning.

NAA, 1960, 13

Translation is an accounting process in which amounts measured in one scale of measurement are converted to amounts stated in another scale of measurement by following the rules of translation . . . . Units in two monetary scales, such as dollars and pounds, are related by the foreign exchange rate.

Rosenfield, 1971, 61

Although the term, conversion, better describes changing a unit of measure than the term, translation, conversion is also commonly used to mean the exchange of one money for another. Continued use of the term, translation, instead of conversion, is justified to avoid confusing the two meanings.

Lorensen, 1972b, 49

The issue in the treatment of foreign operations in general purchasing power financial statements is whether the financial statements of foreign branches or subsidiaries should be restated for foreign inflation or for domestic inflation . . . . whether the foreign statements should (a) first be restated for foreign inflation and then translated, or (b) first be translated and then be restated for domestic inflation . . . . the translate-restate method [is] . . . the method required by APBS3 . . . . The working guide to the preparation of general purchasing power financial statements [under PSSAP7] published by the ICAEW . . . . indicates that translate-restate should be used if the temporal approach to the translation of foreign accounts is adopted, and restate-translate should be used if the closing rate approach is adopted . . . . The different rates of inflation in different countries will . . . cause the two methods to produce significantly different results.

Rosenfield, 1975a, 37

Translation is the process whereby financial data denominated in one currency are expressed in terms of another currency.

ASC, 1980a, ED27

The temporal (heterotemporal) method

where the exchange rate is subject to violent fluctuations . . . . the accounts are converted at different rates . . . (1) Remittances at the actual rate of the day when made or cashed. (2) Fixed assets . . . at the rate of the day when purchased. Fixed liabilities . . . at the rate ruling on the day they were incurred. (3) Floating assets and liabilities at the current rate of exchange on the date of balancing the books. (4) Revenue items . . . at the average rate for the year or period.

Carter, 1923, 685

Foreign currency on hand and cash on deposit in foreign countries usually should be valued in the balance sheet at the rate of exchange current at the date of the balance sheet . . . . Fixed assets in foreign countries should be converted into dollars at the rates prevailing when such assets were acquired or constructed.

Montgomery, 1934, 134, 284

Fixed assets, permanent investments, and long term receivables should be translated into dollars at the rates prevailing when such assets were acquired or constructed . . . .
Cash, accounts receivable, and other current assets, unless covered by forward exchange contracts, should be translated at the rate of exchange prevailing on the date of the balance sheet . . . . Current liabilities payable in foreign currency should be translated at the rate of exchange in force on the date of the balance sheet. Long term liabilities and capital stock stated in foreign currency should . . . be translated . . . at the rates of exchange prevailing when they were originally incurred or issued.

AIA, 1953a/1961, ARB43

The [optional] historical rate basis – Fixed assets . . . [and the aggregate provision for depreciation], at the rate of exchange ruling when these assets were acquired . . . . All other assets and current liabilities . . . [and long term liabilities] at the rate ruling at the end of the period . . . . [profits and losses at historical or average rates]

ICAS, 1970, 416

the temporal principle of translation . . . . Money and receivables and payables measured in amounts promised should be translated at the foreign exchange rate in effect at the balance sheet date. Assets and liabilities measured at money prices should be translated at the foreign exchange rate in effect at the dates to which the money prices pertain.

Lorensen, 1972a, 19

under [the temporal] method, assets, liabilities, revenues and expenses are translated at the rate of exchange ruling at the date on which the amount recorded in the financial statements was established. At the balance sheet date any assets or liabilities which are carried at current values are retranslated at the closing rate.

ASC, 1980a, ED27

The temporal principle is that translation rates should be determined by the measurement basis. Balances carried at historic cost will be translated using the relevant historic cost rate; balances carried at present or future values will be translated at the closing rate.

Nobes, 1980, 422

The current/noncurrent method

The fixed assets and liabilities may safely be taken at the actual figure that they cost in English money – that is to say . . . at the rate of exchange of the day when they were incurred. The floating assets and liabilities must, however, be extended at the rate of exchange ruling at the date of balancing . . . . The revenue items . . . are not figures in respect of any one day . . . . adopt the average rate of exchange ruling during that period . . . .

Dicksee, 1897, 33

In the case of foreign branches which keep a complete set of books in the currency of the country [of operations] .... The items in the [branch] trial balance are converted into sterling thus: (1) Fixed assets may be taken at the figure they actually cost, the [exchange] rate at the date of purchase being taken .... (2) Floating assets and liabilities are taken at the current rate of exchange .... (3) Revenue items should be taken at (i) average rate for the period; or (ii) rate when transaction took place; or (iii) normal rate.

Jenkinson, 1910, 214

[Foreign transactions and balances] Revenue items should be converted either at the average rate of exchange for the period covered, or at the current rate ruling at the date when the same were effected .... Assets and liabilities of a fixed or permanent nature should be converted at the rate ruling at the date when they were assumed .... Floating assets and liabilities ... should be converted at the current rate ruling at the date of the account.

Pixley, 1926, I:272

Fixed assets should be converted into dollars at the rates prevailing when such assets were acquired or constructed .... Cash, accounts receivable and other ... current assets [and current liabilities] should be converted at the rate of exchange prevailing on the date of the balance sheet .... Long term liabilities should ... be converted ... at the rate of exchange prevailing when the liability was actually contracted.

AIA, 1931/1984, 472

The recognized rules of balance sheet valuation – cost for fixed items and present value for current items – yield the following [for consolidation of foreign subsidiaries]: 1. Current assets and current liabilities at rate of exchange on date of balance sheet. 2. Fixed liabilities at rate of exchange when incurred. 3. Fixed assets at rate of exchange when acquired. 4. Income sheet at current or average rate of exchange.

Daniels, 1934/1980, 56

For balance sheet purposes .... the [foreign] currency value of [foreign] fixed assets will be converted into sterling at the rate ruling when the asset was purchased .... If [in respect of foreign currency loans] the foreign currency subsequently appreciates in terms of sterling, the liability should be brought in at the new current rate .... Cash and liquid assets [and floating liabilities] will be converted at the rate ruling at the date of the balance sheet.

Taylor & Perry, 1952, 190

In general, the following methods should be used for balance sheet accounts: Current assets (except inventories) and current liabilities – translate at the rate of exchange current on the balance sheet date .... Inventories – historical rates of exchange should be used .... Long term accounts receivable – the traditional method ... is to use historical rates of exchange .... Fixed assets, accumulated depreciation, ... provisions for depreciation and amortization – translate at historical rates .... Long term liabilities – the traditional method is to translate at the rate prevailing when the debt was incurred .... Capital stock, capital surplus and paid in surplus – translate at [the historical rate] .... In general, items in the income account should be translated at the average monthly rate of exchange ....

Smith, 1961, 457

A ... company that uses the current/noncurrent distinction translates current assets and liabilities of foreign subsidiaries at the foreign exchange rate in effect at the balance sheet date ..., and ... noncurrent [items] at the foreign exchange rates in effect when the [items] were acquired or otherwise recorded ....

Lorensen, 1972a, 29

Under the current/noncurrent method, the current assets and current liabilities of the foreign subsidiary are translated into dollars at the exchange rate that existed on the balance sheet date. Noncurrent assets and liabilities are translated into dollars at the rate that existed on the date that the asset was acquired or the liability incurred.

Dearden & Shank, 1975, 331

The current/noncurrent method uses closing rates for current assets and liabilities, and the relevant historic rates for others.

Nobes, 1980, 421

The monetary/nonmonetary method

[In respect of foreign balances] when changes in money values are being studied, the significant line of demarcation in the balance sheet does not lie between current and fixed items, but between (a) rights and obligations that are defined in terms of money (including even preference shares), and (b) forms of wealth whose money value can alter freely.

Baxter & Yamey, 1951, 119

The translation date [exchange] rate should be applied to asset and liability items in the money-value category, with non-money-value assets being translated by use of the acquisition date exchange rate. The principal effect of this recommendation, in contrast with conventional technique, is to remove inventory items from the current rate category and to require translation of long-term receivables and payables at the translation date (current) rate.

Hepworth, 1956, 203

The coincidence of results between the temporal principle and the monetary/nonmonetary method is due solely to the nature of the accounting principles that are presently accepted – assets and liabilities are measured on bases that coincide with their classifications as monetary and nonmonetary. The results of the temporal principle and the monetary/nonmonetary method would differ significantly under other accounting principles that would require monetary assets and liabilities to be measured at money prices in effect at dates other than the balance sheet date, or would require nonmonetary assets and liabilities to be measured at money prices in effect at dates other than those at which they were acquired.

Lorensen, 1972b 54

All monetary assets and liabilities are translated at the current exchange rates . . . . Nonmonetary assets and liabilities are translated at the rates that existed at the time of acquisition or when incurred.

Dearden & Shank, 1975, 334

The monetary/nonmonetary method uses closing rates for monetary assets and liabilities, and the historic rates relevant to the date the balance was established for other balances.

Nobes, 1980, 421

The current rate method

there can be no question that the balance sheet and profit and loss account, prepared on the basis of the local [foreign] assets and liabilities being the equivalent of pounds sterling measured by the ruling rate of exchange of the day, must represent its position as on that day.

Plumb, 1891, 259

The [optional] closing rate basis – All balance sheet items [and profits and losses] are converted . . . at the closing rate of exchange . . . .

ICAS, 1970, 416

The current rate method, as the name implies, involves the translation of all assets and liabilities at current rates.

Dearden & Shank, 1975, 334

Under this [the closing rate/net investment] method all the amounts in the balance sheet of a foreign subsidiary company should be translated into the reporting currency of the holding company using the rate of exchange ruling at the balance sheet date. Amounts in the profit and loss account should be translated at an average rate for the accounting period.

ASC, 1980a, ED27

An entity's functional currency is the currency of the primary economic environment in which the entity operates . . . . All elements of financial statements shall be translated by using a current exchange rate. For assets and liabilities, the exchange rate at the balance sheet date . . . . For revenues, expenses, gains and losses . . . an appropriately weighted average exchange rate may be used . . . . Transactions: (a) At the date the transaction is recognized, each asset, liability, revenue, expense, gain or loss arising from the transaction shall be measured and recorded in the functional currency of the recording entity by use of the exchange rate in effect at that date. (b) At each balance date, recorded balances that are denominated in a currency other than the functional currency of the recording entity shall be adjusted to reflect the current exchange rate.

FASB, 1982, SFAS52

576 Valuation of intangibles

The amount at which goodwill is stated in a balance sheet is never supposed to represent either its maximum or its minimum value; no one who thought of buying a business would be in the least influenced by the amount at which the goodwill is stated in the accounts; in short, the amount is absolutely meaningless.

Dicksee, 1892/1976, 127

the real test as to a patent's value is perhaps seldom its cost .... This figure is likely to bear no relation whatever to reasonable value once the particular device has proved its merit. There is at least something to be said in such cases for the proposition that selling value, *bona fide* market value, is the most valid basis for accounting entries.

Paton, 1922/1962, 32

There is a theory ... that an organization may calculate the amount of goodwill by capitalizing at a certain rate the amount by which the net profits for a term of years exceed a given percentage of the net investment .... in this calculation there are three arbitrary factors ... the percentage used for capitalization ... the period of time ... the percentage of investment to be allowed as a deduction before capitalization.

Couchman, 1924, 133

The values of intangibles bear no definite relation to the costs of their development.

Yang, 1927, 13

A member of my staff, who is studying for his Final, asked me the other day, "What is the value of goodwill?" I replied, "What some fool can be made to pay for it."

Gittens, 1938, 451

goodwill has no accounting significance except in terms of an earning capacity which is estimated to be above normal. A price is paid for goodwill ... [for that reason].

Walker, 1953, 213

Any valuation of goodwill involves an attempt to assign some current value to a stream of future earnings. As such goodwill has no place in an accounting fabric which seeks to provide information on the separable resources owned.

Hinton, 1973, 35

See also 445–448

580 Annual and Occasional Valuations

581 Periodical valuation

all three valuation bases [for fixed assets – cost, arithmetical balance and revaluation] are to be found in [eight ledgers of seven businessmen and one partnership running between 1665 and 1774] .... there was no aversion to the upward and downward revaluation of fixed assets ... nor was there meticulous concern with the distinction between capital and revenue elements .... there was no consistent or rigorous application of any clear concept of profit or income, or of any single set of accounting procedures.

Yamey, 1963, 197–8

Revaluations [of capital assets] are valuable to adjust insurance schedules, etc, but are not so scientific from an accounting standpoint as cost and depreciation.
Montgomery, 1906, 497

an annual appraisal of these [fixed assets] based on current market values, would probably produce such distortion in the profit and loss accounts as to make them utterly worthless and misleading, besides making the balance sheet unreliable, an appraisal being always the result of an individual opinion, while original cost is an undeniable fact.
Parton, 1917/1988, 72

[Periodical revaluation] is adopted [for such assets as] horses, casks, bottles, packages, loose tools, patterns, models, moulds, trade marks, copyrights, investments, etc.
Carter, 1923, 616

In an earlier age, when capital assets were inconsiderable and business units in general smaller and less complex than they are today, it was possible to value assets with comparative ease and accuracy and to measure the progress made from year to year by annual valuations .... this has become increasingly impracticable .... Any consideration of the accounts of a large business enterprise of today must start from the premise that an annual valuation of the assets is neither practical nor desirable.
AIA, 1932

It would in most cases be impractical and expensive to revalue the fixed assets every year on an appraisal basis; and even if it were possible it would not necessarily be significant information, since there are other factors entering into the determination of the value of a going industrial concern, including the capitalized present worth of its estimated future earnings.
BAPC, 1934/1939, 54

Present procedure is unsatisfactory in that it permits periodic revaluation of assets, up or down, in accordance with present price levels and expected business developments. Occasional uncoordinated "appraisals" produce in the average financial statements a hodge-podge of unrelated values of no explicable significance to the ordinary investor . . . .

AAA, 1936/1957b, 61

A purpose of [asset] valuations [as a response to inflation] is to disclose the cost of fixed assets . . . in terms of current prices (or current price levels) and, thus, provide a more uniform basis for intercompany comparisons and a more realistic measure of capitalization . . .

Scapens, 1953, 11

To require a periodical revaluation of fixed assets would, in our opinion, be to impose a most onerous duty on companies and require them to give information which we think would often be worthless and misleading. [#353]

Jenkins Committee, 1962, 138

See also 319, 540, 613

582 Accounting for asset appreciation

A balance sheet should be a statement of fact; and if, at any periodical revaluation, the assets are found to have appreciated, it seems to me to be advisable – if not necessary – that this increase be clearly shown in the accounts by writing up the value of the respective assets and crediting the total of the appreciation to a special reserve account.

Accountant, Anon, 1901, 920

when general or trade conditions bring about a real permanent increase in values, or when errors have been made in calculating depreciation . . . an adjustment of book values to conform to the real conservative values . . . is legitimate.

Herr, 1906, 13

there are causes at work, particularly in young and growing communities, which may render a statement prepared on the basis of cost of capital assets misleading and even prejudicial to the proper interest of present owners . . . . there are well known cases in which by far the larger part of the ultimate profits of a corporation over a long series of years has been due . . . to the large unearned increment on its capital assets. This condition . . . is frequently met by means of careful appraisals of all properties, the resulting increase (or possible decrease) being . . . shown as entirely distinct from the operating results.

Dickinson, 1914, 80

appreciation in the value of fixed assets is now so widely permitted by accountants ... that it may be said that the accountant has abandoned a strict adherence to his original cost less depreciation and depletion views.

Daines, 1929, 99

We cannot agree ... that appreciation should not be recognized in the books of account. To take the position that closed transactions only are entitled to recognition is to narrow the function of accounting unduly and gainsay many of the well-settled practices.

Wildman, 1930, 34

There are ... instances in which good accounting practice does recognize appreciation of assets, This is done in regard to meat products, where inventory value is based on selling price modified by certain deductions, in malting operations, in long term contracts such as shipbuilding, and in certain jurisdictions in regard to securities, or even commodities publicly quoted in exchanges.

Hatfield, 1942/1947, 35

Frequently, appreciation is recorded by writing up the book value of assets to reflect the present sound values. The present sound value of a property is its reproduction cost new, less the accumulated depreciation on the replacement cost basis. Current appraised values may be placed on the books to provide a basis: for a higher credit rating; for issuing bonds and stocks; for writing off a deficit; for issuing stock dividends; for showing the current financial condition to prospective investors; for reorganization; for the sale or consolidation of the business; for insurance purposes; and for furnishing data for governmental taxation.

Kennedy, 1948, 126

[The writing up of fixed assets may] be appropriate and desirable in certain special circumstances, such as where a subsidiary is acquired and the assets are written up to reflect the cost to the acquiring company, or where subscriptions for new capital are invited on the basis of a current valuation of the assets. Apart from such special purposes, the writing up of assets appears to be suitable only for the readjustment of all balance sheets by government action as part of a process of stabilizing a currency.

ICAEW, 1952, N15

The inclination to write things down to market has been strong enough to cause practitioners to overcome the practical problems. To write things up would be no more difficult, and thus the only thing lacking is the inclination to do so.

Sterling, 1968a, 499

The revaluation of a class of noncurrent assets shall not result in the carrying amount [net book value] of any asset within that class exceeding its recoverable amount [net cash inflows arising from its continued use and subsequent disposal].

ASRB, 1987/1991, ASRB1010

See also 668, 669

583 Asset revaluation

For fuller occasional satisfaction [than is given by cost allocation] prudent manufacturers will periodically call in professional valuers . . . not necessarily annually,
but perhaps every three, seven or ten years . . . . But every valuation so taken . . .
should be made with regard to normal cost rather than to the value on the day of
the valuation.

Guthrie, 1883, 7

Take the case of a brewery built on inexpensive land in London fifty or a hundred
years ago. The value has multiplied ten or twenty times. I say there is no legal
objection, and certainly no objection on the ground of prudence, to the directors
showing the enhanced value of the brewery in their accounts . . . . The proprietors'
interests will become of greater marketable value, the credit of the concern will
become greater from showing enhanced value, and debentures would be more readily
issued upon the security of the property.

Cooper, 1891, 14

no wise man of business would write up such assets [as buildings] and attempt to
show a profit this way . . . . probably the wisest course is to have all machinery
revalued every five years and readjust the reserves or the amount written off accordingly.

Eddis & Tindall, 1904/1988, 68

accounting deals primarily with the value representations of things; the use of physical
facts in accounting statistics is entirely subordinate . . . . It is sometimes objected
that, if a factory site, for example, appreciates, it does not add anything to the
physical efficiency of the site for manufacturing purposes; hence it should not be
considered in the accounts. This objection is not valid . . . . [The] fact should be
recognized in the accounts in order that the entrepreneur realize the situation, and
either make more efficient use of the property or move the enterprise as soon as
feasible to a cheaper site.

Paton & Stevenson, 1916/1976, 14, 104

The occasions for revaluations which give rise to estimated increases in values are
various . . . . to bring out a bond issue . . . . to offer an issue of preferred stock . . . .
to overcome a deficit in capital, thus preparing the way for future declarations of
dividends payable in cash . . . . to use the restated value as a basis for depreciation
and thus increase the charge for depreciation against earnings.

Wildman, 1928, 397

I do not think that any useful purpose can generally be achieved by revaluing fixed assets.

Anderson, 1961, 334

Revaluation of fixed assets occurs within the framework of historical cost accounting, and is accepted as compatible with, and part of, the historical cost method.
Lissiman, 1975, 23

[Of 1456 companies] listed at some time on the Melbourne Stock Exchange from 1950 to 1975 .... 835 ... made 1905 upward revaluations of fixed assets over the period.
Leech & others, 1978, 354

In historical cost statements, fixed assets are stated at an amount in excess of cost which is determined at irregular intervals – as required or predominant practice, in 28 countries; as minority practice, in 16 countries. The matter was reported to be "not applicable" to 11 countries, including Austria, Germany, Japan, Switzerland, United States. The survey covered 64 countries. [digested]
Price Waterhouse International, 1979,
#40

Where a non-current asset is to be revalued the entire class of assets to which the asset belongs should normally be revalued .... The revaluation of a class of non-current assets should not result in the carrying amount for that class being greater than the aggregate amount that is expected to be recovered from the continued use and, where applicable, disposal of the assets within that class. A downwards revaluation ... should be undertaken only when the carrying amount is greater than the amount that is expected to be recovered from [continued use and disposal]; that is its recoverable amount. In this situation the asset should be revalued to its recoverable amount .... Carrying amount ... means [book value at a particular date, net of accumulated depreciation].
ICAA & ASA, 1981/1991, AAS10

584 Upward revaluation rejected

the suggestion that the appreciation in value of fixed assets ... should be given effect to in the accounts, and the profits shown thereby inflated, is entirely opposed to law and to all principles of sound finance.
Accountant, editorial, 1901, 894

There is no warrant for writing up the value of [a fixed asset] so as to show a profit, unless possibly the enhanced value is due to the building of a new railroad track or other transportation facility that ... has conferred a distinct and direct benefit on the business; and even then the advisability of such a course would be very doubtful
....
Walton, 1909, 455

revaluations of properties from period to period .... would complicate unnecessarily the routine accounting procedures.
Graham, 1934/1988, 114

In ordinary circumstances ... there is no justification for adjusting the books of account to reflect an unrealized increase in asset values ....
Cranstoun, 1938, 70

revaluations ... do violence to every proper conception of the function of accounts in recording the history of a business enterprise.
Greer, 1938c, 291

Appreciation normally should not be reflected on the books of account of corporations. ... when such appreciation has been entered in the books, income should be charged with depreciation computed on the new and higher values.
AIA, 1940a, ARB5

In America, the emphasis on [market] valuation was in earlier years far greater than in England, and it is only in very recent years that the propriety of recording appreciation on books of account has been questioned.
May, 1943, 90

585 Quasi-reorganization

If a corporation elects to bring about a legitimate restatement of its assets, stock and surplus through readjustment, and thus avail itself of the permission to relieve its future income account or earned surplus account of charges which should otherwise be made thereagainst, it should make a clear report to the stockholders of the restatements proposed to be made, and obtain their formal consent.
AIA, 1939c, ARB3

The restatement of capital and absorption of an operating deficit with stockholder approval but without the creation of a new corporate entity has been termed a quasi-reorganization.
Werntz, 1939/1968, 118

Quasi-reorganization, as an accounting concept, was originated quite recently ....
there must be a revaluation of assets ... [and adjustments of capital and surplus accounts] .... In effect, the procedures generally result in new value representations in the corporate accounts. These representations become, in a sense, the revised costs upon which the accounting for the investment and stewardship ... will be based.
Blough, 1945, 106

the procedures of a reorganization and a quasi-reorganization ... [recognize that] ... it is necessary at times, and under proper circumstances, to acknowledge a fresh or new start for the corporate enterprise .... the carrying values of the assets after the new start should be based upon monetary values which are the most significant at the time of the fresh start. These values are those which willing buyers and willing sellers would recognize as proper when actual transactions take place in comparable circumstances. [attr by G O May to CAP, Oct 20, 1945]

AIA, 1945b/1957, 34

The accounting reorganization, or quasi, is the necessary safety valve in a structure of accounting generally based on cost. It furnishes a means under which a corporation may restate its accounts, and provide a new basis of income measurement, without undergoing an actual legal reorganization.

Paton, 1946a, 199

It has . . . been the generally accepted accounting practice in the case of a quasi-reorganization – a new start – that after the reorganization assets should be stated at a fair and not unduly conservative value, whether above or below cost.

Broad, 1949, 385

The need for the quasi-reorganization came about during the depression. Times were poor. Corporations needed a means of obtaining a fresh start. Assets were overvalued on the historical cost basis, and fixed charges . . . on the cost basis were widely burdensome on income. Corporations also needed a means of writing off their heavy deficits. The quasi-reorganization provided the means. By obtaining approval of the stockholders, management could write off overvalued assets and deficits against the capital accounts . . . . The first accounting action taken in regard to quasi-reorganization was made in 1934 by the American Institute of Accountants.

Burleson, 1953, 12

the quasi-reorganization procedure has been applied generally only to entities in financial difficulties . . . to eliminate an accumulated deficit and to adjust asset values to a more realistic basis. The entity is given a fresh start . . . . There does not appear to be any logical reason, however, to limit the quasi-reorganization procedure to [that] situation.

Wyatt, 1963, 85

The term quasi-reorganization denotes a procedure equivalent to an accounting fresh start. A company with a debit balance in retained earnings starts over with a zero balance rather than a deficit. A quasi-reorganization involves a reclassification of a deficit in retained earnings to paid in capital, and may also include a restatement of the carrying values of assets and liabilities to reflect current values.

Gibson, 1988, 83

590 Heterogeneous Valuations

591 Grounds for a single (uniform) valuation rule

it is not easy to see why if an incoming shareholder, who is misled by overvaluation, is entitled to damages against directors to whom he was a stranger, an outgoing

shareholder, whose paid agent in a sense the directors are, is not entitled to recover the loss occasioned by having sold his shares below their real value, owing to under representation of the company's position.
Cooper, 1888, 744

private [unincorporated] firms are under no statutory requirement to retain the whole of their undertaking intact; the double account principle does not therefore apply to the accounts of private traders . . . . the double account principle of stating values might be employed [by companies] (but for the fact that a registered company is under no obligation to retain possession of any of its assets), ... [and] the fact that no particular assets can claim to be considered more permanent than the rest . . . . The amount, therefore, at which *all* assets are stated in balance sheets . . . should be regulated by the value of such assets.
Dicksee, 1892/1976, 120

Either an undervaluation or an overvaluation of the assets may prejudice those interested in the accounts, and we must therefore see that we obtain a reasonable ground for believing not only that such assets exist, but, that in the interests of all concerned, the accounts disclose such assets at a proper and fair valuation at the time of the audit.
Payne, 1892, 142

[On conventional accounting] A million sets of mutually exclusive [valuation] rules each giving a true and fair view of a company's state of affairs and its profits! This is absurd. Where there are so many possible rules there are in effect no rules, and where there are no rules there can be no correspondence, no general comprehensibility, no language – a set of signs maybe, but no language. It is as if there were a million people with different foot rules, or a million motorists with different road rules. Reason and order are deposed and chaos is enthroned in their place.
Chambers, 1965b, 16

See also 257

592 The utility of a single valuation rule rejected

To emphasize some one basis of valuation is not necessarily objective, for every valuation is related to the situation in which it is made and the purpose which it is to serve. True objectivity would seem better served by recognizing different bases of valuation as alternatives that may have special significance to some and less significance to other readers, since the situations and problems involved are different.
Vatter, 1947, 67, n.40

The committee is of the opinion that no single concept of value will suffice . . . , and concludes that multiple measurements should be reported in general purpose statements to meet a reasonably wide range of needs.
AAA, 1966, 22

Value in accounting, as in the world of business portrayed by accounting, has more than one dimension, and attempts to confine it to a single dimension, such as current replacement cost or market selling price, will produce data that are just as arbitrary and misleading as unadjusted historical cost data.

Mathews, 1968, 516

where there is more than one ownership interest, as in the case of a limited company, the statement of a single balance sheet value is ... untenable in principle. For it ignores the possibility that individual assessments of a given situation may differ.

Rayman, 1970, 426

The specific user approach [to the choice of asset valuation rules] rests on the belief that no one measurement system is necessarily relevant to a wide range of decision makers.

Revsine, 1973, 19

593 Heterogeneous valuations and their aggregation tolerated

In the balance sheet of a going concern, after a number of years of operation, some of the items will be found to represent the original cost; others, market value; others so-called cost; some, cost plus profit; while others, such as depreciation, are based upon estimates.

Stockwell, 1925, 172

The truthful balance sheet .... marketable assets valued at market price, nonmarketable reproducible assets valued at replacement cost, and occasional nonmarketable, nonreproducible assets valued at original cost.

MacNeal, 1939, 189

Financial reports to external users may appropriately include in the current cost column some assets stated at recently determined current cost, other assets at older estimates of current cost, and still others at original transaction price, where verifiability of the other kinds of information varies among the assets.

AAA, 1966, 28

Assets must be stated in terms which measure their current value .... for example, values based on earning power, on appraisal, on replacement value, or on up to date market price. In each case it is a matter of judgment as to which procedure should be used in valuing an asset.

Ross, 1969, 66

Most textbooks consider the assets *seriatim* and often insulate the discussion. The result is different valuation methods for different assets. We could find the same author proposing the following: 1. Undiscounted future receipts (accounts and notes receivable). 2. Discounted future receipts (bonds receivable). 3. Current market price (agricultural commodities). 4. Lower of cost or market (inventories). 5. Unamortized purchase price (organizational expenses, land). 6. Amortized purchase price (equipment). 7. Market price at date of gift (donated assets). 8. Market price at date of legal action (some or all of the assets at time of quasi-reorganization or partnership formation). 9. Zero (advertising and research costs). 10. Constant (exchange rate applied to foreign subsidiary assets).

Sterling, 1970a, 248

the objectives of financial statements cannot be best served by the exclusive use of a single valuation basis . . . . different valuation bases are preferable for different assets and liabilities. That means that financial statements might contain data based on a combination of valuation bases.

AICPA, 1973, 41

There is no mathematical impropriety in aggregating replacement costs, or discounted present values or even mixtures of the two, denominated in current pounds, although there may well be an economic (or accounting) problem in interpreting the aggregate . . . .

Whittington, 1983b, 319

[Under GAAP, or prevalent accounting standards] each asset measure is contaminated by a mixture of actions and allocations that are subject to managerial discretion, competing objectives, and policies. The reported book values are often balances of arbitrary upward or downward adjustments that rarely describe what the firm expects to earn from using the asset. Thus, the sum of these numbers, reported as total assets, becomes a conglomeration of heterogeneous measurement bases, values, methods, mechanical adjustments and calculations . . . . Yet . . . we continue to ascribe a semantic content to this sum in itself and to consider it a basis to which other numbers, such as profits or other subsets of assets, can be meaningfully related.

Abdel-khalik, 1992, 12

See also 257

594 Heterogeneous and heterotemporal aggregation illustrated

Sears Holdings . . . 1968 published accounts [showed]: BSC Footwear Group . . . Freeholds and leaseholds not containing a rent review clause operative before January 1, 1993 are at professional valuations . . . at December 31, 1967. The basis of the valuations was market value assuming vacant possession . . . . The other leaseholds, some of which were previously included at professional valuations, have been included at cost. Lewis's/Selfridge Store Group . . . at professional valuations . . . in 1966 . . . , with subsequent additions at cost. The basis of the valuations was market value assuming present use excluding any value attributable to goodwill. Shipyard . . . at professional valuations made in 1954 with subsequent additions at cost.

Greener, 1969a, 170

the 1968 accounts of Whitbread & Co Ltd showed freehold and leasehold properties as follows: revalued 1960, 10 million pounds; revalued 1961, 10 million;
revalued 1962, 29 million; revalued 1963, 2 million; revalued 1964, 11 million;
revalued 1965, 11 million; revalued 1966, 4 million; revalued 1967, 10 million;
revalued 1968, 26 million; additions after dates of valuation, at cost, 18 million;
pre-1948 book values or subsequent cost, 5 million; total 136 million.

Greener, 1969a,170

The 1970 balance sheet of Dunlop Australia Ltd showed "freehold and leasehold
land and buildings" as $59.5 million, with details provided in a note as follows [in
$millions, rounded]: Deemed value 1962, $0.7 Valuations 1949–63, $4.6; Valua-
tions at July 5 1963, $20.7; Valuations 1968–69, $6.1; Net additions at cost, $29.2;
Less provision for depreciation, $1.8; Total as per balance sheet $59.5. Aggregation
of measures representing different properties of an object [deemed value, dated valuations, cost] can produce no sensible total. Further, numbers added may represent
different money scales . . . . 1949 dollars, 1962 dollars, and 1970 dollars. The total
refers to dollars of no particular purchasing power, and on this ground also is not
interpretable.

Birkett & Walker, 1974, 185

600 INCOME AND INCOME CALCULATION

600 Income Concepts

601 Vagueness of the notion of income

It is a peculiar fact that while all business is carried on for the purpose of securing profits, while the distribution of profits is continually the subject of controversy in the courts, while the ascertainment of profits enters largely into the discussion of every economist, the term is still vaguely and loosely used and without definition by either economist, man of affairs, jurist or accountant.

Hatfield, 1927/1971, 241

The accountants have no complete philosophical system of thought about income; nor is there evidence that they have ever greatly felt the need for one.

Canning, 1929a, 160

Accounting at present lacks an income concept.

Edwards, 1938b, 290

Income is an abstract concept of an imprecise character; allocation of income to short periods of time is achieved by conventions which are a compromise between theory and practicality. To evolve out of these elements a determination of income which will serve all purposes and be readily understandable is beyond the power of man.

May 1948b, 15

The principal differences among the bewildering number of concepts of income that can be conceived can be narrowed down to three major issues. These are the real *versus* the money measure, inclusion *versus* exclusion of capital gains, and accrual *versus* realization as the criterion for timing of a gain or loss. If decisions were reached on these three major issues, almost every one of the many controversial points concerning the measurement of income could be settled.

Alexander, 1950, 94

the question, What is the business income for a year of a corporation?, is one that may be said to bear a fairly close analogy to the question, What is the color of the chameleon? For income, like color, is dependent on external conditions, and a matter of imperceptible gradations from one extreme to the other. And the corporation has in relation to income an even greater capacity for adaptation than the chameleon has in relation to color.

AIA, 1952, 18

the profession . . . should now accept . . . the necessity of explaining what the accounting concept of income really is . . . and what is the nature of the risks that accounting income may never in fact be realized and thus become available for consumption.

Fitzgerald & Schumer, 1952, 196

Fund theory has no concept of income because there is no recipient for such gains or sufferer of losses.

Vatter, 1956, 122

my own guess is that, so far as the history of accounting is concerned, the next twenty-five years may subsequently be seen to have been the twilight of income measurement.

Solomons, 1961, 383

Enterprise income is a many-sided concept. There is no such thing as *the* concept of income.

Lee, 1974, 189

accounting resembles a game. That is, its results cannot be independently verified, as least not in the satisfying way of some other disciplines . . . . measurement in accounting is not measurement in the usual sense of the word. It is not the application of measurement techniques to something that exists apart from those techniques. We do not walk up to income and slap a yardstick against it. Accounting income exists solely as a product of the techniques for measuring it.

Gerboth, 1987, 97

Reported income . . . . is a metaphor.

Thornton, 1988, 9

the concept of earnings is one of the most frequently used and one of the most ill-defined concepts in our accounting vocabulary.

AAA, 1991, 83

602 Income said to be a subjective or conventional notion

income is a concept; not something absolute but, in part at least, a matter of definition or convention.

Broad, 1954, 582

In accountancy the term profit has no absolute meaning. It is simply a measurement of the success or failure of a business to achieve what it has set out to achieve. The measurement is a subjective one in so far as it depends upon the view taken as to

555

what the business has in fact set out to achieve. Thus the term profit as used by accountants can never have that absolute meaning which lawyers, economists and revenue officials seek to attribute to it.

> Morison, 1962, 662

Income is an artifact .... income in any case is an artificial construct.

> Revsine, 1971, 480, 482

Profit for the year is a practical business concept used as a guide for prudent decision making by companies. It may usefully be defined as the amount of the total gains arising in the year that may prudently be regarded as distributable. It is thus a subjective concept, since inevitably there will be differences of opinion on how far gains arising in any given year may prudently be distributed.

> Sandilands, 1975, 28

expense and revenue are both subjective concepts, as is, therefore, profit (net income) or loss.

> Most, 1977a, 290

Profit is always a convention ....

> Clayton, 1978, 531

profit is a creature of definition ....

> French, 1978, 619

The true income hypothesis ... is not a promising approach to policy choices. Accounting income is not an observable phenomenon – it has no real world referent in an accounting environment characterized by uncertainty. The economic reality that accountants seek to portray is subject to multiple interpretations. This ambiguity, of course, is the source of the choice problem.

> Carter, 1981, 110

Income is a matter of definition – an artificial construct.

> Skinner, 1982, 125

603 A single concept of income contemplated

Income is not only the most vital concept in economic science, it is also the simplest and most fundamental.

> Canning, 1929b, 8

During the long evolution of accounting there has been developed a very dependable technique of calculating interim profits.

> Littleton, 1937, 59

it is not too much to ask that the net income of different companies, and even different industries, be predicated on common concepts, so that it may be assumed to be of the same essential nature.

JA, editorial, 1947b, 442

With each month that passes, it becomes more and more desirable that accountants and economists should find an agreed definition of what profits are.

Economist, 1951, 212

different users of accounting data will find different figures relevant to their purposes . . . . This need for variety of data does not, however, imply a need for variety of income concepts . . . . Insofar as accountants attempt to report financial position and income, it is necessary to have a meaningful single concept of income.

Philips, 1963a, 20, 25

there is a need for one overall general concept of income . . . .

Bedford, 1965, 8

[One complaint about present modes of accounting] is that the financial statements produced by accountants do not, in certain important respects, reflect economic facts. This is sometimes explained by claiming that the economist's concept of income is different from the accountant's; but any notion that there are two useful and legitimate ways of looking at the operations of an enterprise simply will not do. The economist and the accountant do have different points of view . . . . But it does not follow from this that there should be two types of statement.

Ross, 1969, 7

I believe . . . that there should only be one figure for net income.

Ross, 1972, 31

604 Enterprise net income and income to financial supporters

If the corporation were viewed as merely an aggregation of individual investors, it would be consistent to hold that the earnings of the enterprise belonged to the shareholders from the moment of original realization . . . . Gains and losses are changes in enterprise assets, not in proprietors' assets or in stockholders' assets.

Paton & Littleton, 1940, 8, 9

The income of a company is not the income of the individual shareholders, and any relationship is dependent upon the directors' recommendations to pay dividends.

Couldery & Sheppard, 1955, 295

Interest charges, income taxes and true profit-sharing distributions are not determinants of enterprise net income. In determining income to shareholders, however, interest charges, income taxes, profit-sharing distributions . . . are properly included.

AAA, 1957a/1957b, 5

periodic net income may be defined as the amount of the increase in the equities of all those who have provided capital to the business and have claims upon income, including creditor-investors and senior stockholders, such increase being measured by the excess of total revenues over applicable expenses, losses and taxes.

Paton & Dixon, 1958, 95

gains and losses from . . . . the holding of monetary assets and monetary current liabilities [during inflation or deflation] should be included in the computation of net income to the enterprise . . . . The gains and losses from the holding of long term debt . . . . should be included in the computation of net income to stockholders.

Hendriksen, 1961, 19

Interest charges are considered to be an expense of operations, but dividends . . . are considered to be a distribution of income under the proprietary theory. Both interest and dividends would be distributions of income under the entity theory. Contemporary accounting practice in the reporting of income thus conforms to the proprietary theory. But in the basic equation that assets equal equities, the concept of the accounting unit as a separate distinct entity prevails.

Bedford & others, 1967, 12

If an entity view is adopted, interest becomes an appropriation of profit rather than an expense; . . . . the cost of debt finance is not a cost to the business as such, but an appropriation of its income to satisfy the claims of debt-providers (and thus a cost to the common stockholders) . . . .

Archer & Peasnell, 1984, 112

See also 046

605 A single concept of income not desirable or not possible

the measurement of income is not the sole, or even the most important, aim of accounting; in fact, there are grounds for the belief that the accountant has over-emphasized and overworked the notion of income far past the point of diminishing returns. It is impossible to present a single income figure that will begin to meet all the demands which will be made upon it . . . .

Vatter, 1947, 35

It is manifest that no single method of implementation of a single concept of income can in itself meet all the needs of those who use income determinations as a guide to action of one sort or another. The point that income is defined differently for different purposes emerges from any discussion of economic, legal, or accounting history of the problem.

AIA, 1952, 107

for different purposes we need different concepts of income, and in each case a choice must be made as to the concept which is relevant to the use to be made of the income determination.

Kerr, 1956, 146

I believe that this idea of a unique concept of business surplus is a will-o'-the-wisp. It seems to me that further progress in relation to the price level problem – and indeed in many other important problems of accounting – depends on the recognition that alternative concepts may be needed for different purposes. It then remains to decide on the appropriate concept for each purpose and to consider whether or not the concept can be – or should be – measured within the double entry framework of accounts.

Mathews, 1960, 8

The fact that accounting data can serve many purposes suggests that it may be a serious mistake to restrict accounts to the kind of data from which but one profit concept can be developed.

Edwards & Bell, 1961, 110

[A] wide range of profit figures . . . can result from adopting different concepts of profit and capital . . . . [Of the five sets of concepts considered] the highest figure of profit . . . is almost double the lowest . . . . they are all equally "correct". It is impossible to say in the abstract that one of the five figures is "right" and the others are "wrong" since all are right within their own assumptions. The company in our example might legitimately show its profit on any one of the five bases.

Sandilands, 1975, 39

The first requirement for progress is to rid ourselves of the notion that there is a single measure of profit suitable for all purposes and for all users of accounts . . . . There are all sorts of purposes for which a measure of profit or gain is required: for management accounting, for the calculation of return on capital employed, for wage negotiations, for pricing policy, for dividend distribution policy, in the calculation of . . . earnings yields, for investment analysis, for determining the inflation corrected gain in the shareholders' interest, and as a basis for company taxation. One has only to list these purposes . . . . to realize that no single measure of profit will be suitable for them all; . . . .

Kennedy, 1978/1986, 188

There is no unambiguous or correct definition of income and value on which to base measures of profit and net assets.

Macve, 1981, 9

no one income and wealth measurement system can suit all types of decision making, financial performance and position evaluation, stewardship purposes, etc; . . . the system adopted should be tailored to suit the end uses of the information.

Barton, 1984, 521

There isn't one income number that will do for all purposes, and I think to pretend otherwise flies in the face of reality. We can report several income numbers and talk about what they're useful for.

Weil, 1984, 96

in a realistic setting of imperfect and incomplete markets, no single true income measure exists which will satisfy all needs.

Tippett & Whittington, 1988, 77

See also 255

610 Income or Profit

611 Income as gain

Gain. The profit, or lucre, a person reaps from his commerce, trade, employment, or industry, which may be either honorable or infamous, lawful or illicit . . . . in regard to the private gain of the merchant, it is all that part of the price of his goods in which his sale exceeds his purchase; and this difference of the price is paid by the consumer.

Rolt's Dictionary, 1761

Income. The gain which proceeds from property, labor, or business. It is applied particularly to individuals . . . . The word is sometimes considered synonymous with profits, the gain as between receipts and payments; . . . .

Bouvier's law dictionary, 1914, 1527

Here we have the essential matter; not a gain accruing to capital, not a growth or increment of value in the investment; but a gain, a profit, something of exchangeable value proceeding from the property, severed from the capital however invested or employed, and coming in, being derived, that is received or drawn by the recipient . . . for his separate use, benefit and disposal: – that is income derived from property. [per Justice Pitney]

Eisner v Macomber, 1920

Ordinarily, profit is traced simply to a difference in prices (cost and selling) . . . .

Littleton, 1928, 284

The [US Supreme] Court's definition conforms closely to the accounting concept, and is, therefore, appropriate for adoption by accountants for general use as well as for tax purposes. The . . . definition reads: Income may be defined as the gain derived from capital, from labor, or from both combined, provided it be understood to include profit gained through a sale or conversion of capital assets . . . . [<i>Eisner v Macomber</i>, 1920]

AIA, 1941c, ARB9

When a company is developing rapidly, as was true of both Canada and the United States in the early years of this century, investment is made for appreciation and not for a steady return of income. In this stage, the balance sheet has a significance it does not have in a more mature economy. After things settle down the measurement of income, rather than the appreciation of assets, becomes the criterion of success in business ventures.

Smyth, 1953, 204

let us not . . . forget the plain meaning of profit – the difference between buying prices and selling prices.

Bennett, 1972, 219

the accountant has adopted what might be called a transactions approach to income measurement. He recognizes as income only those increases in wealth that can be substantiated from data pertaining to actual transactions that have taken place with persons outside the firm. In such systems, income is measured when work is performed for an outside customer, when goods are delivered, or when the customer is billed. [per G Sh]

Enc Britannica, 1981, I:38

612 Income or profit as increment in wealth

I consider equally of an individual, or of a partnership, or of a . . . company, that every increment to capital [net assets] is profit, and every diminution, loss . . . and inversely I consider every profit as an increase, and every loss a diminution of the real capital.

Cooper, 1888, 741

profit must be increase of capital and nothing else, and . . . the value of capital is mainly based on the realizable values of assets.

Carter, 1910a, 127

Increase in wealth – which is measured in the accounts by the net revenue figure – is the purpose of the business enterprise from the standpoint of the individual owners.

Paton & Stevenson, 1918/1978, 220

Income is the increment in wealth arising from the use of capital wealth and from services rendered.

Sanders & others, 1938, 11

A profit is an increase in net wealth.

MacNeal, 1939, 295

As every profit is in essence an increase in capital, so every loss is a decrease . . . .

Clunies Ross, 1941b, 575

Income . . . is wealth at the end of the period minus wealth at the beginning of the period . . . .

Sands, 1963, 39

Net income may be defined as an increase in wealth from profit-seeking activities during a particular period of time.

Corbin, 1964, 48

The change . . . in wealth which results from the activity of a business is called income.

Black & others, 1967, 57

In an economic sense, income can be thought of as the increase in wealth experienced during a period.

Skousen & others, 1981, 163

Profit, i.e. income, in any given period must, if it is to earn that name, be represented by an increase in wealth, i.e. capital, over that same period.

Greener, 1982, 77

Income as increment in net assets

Profits [of the Alberti company of Florence in the early 14th century] were determined by deducting total liabilities and invested capital from total assets including receivables, goods in stock, and cash in hand.

de Roover, 1956, 125

If the total assets of a business are valued at the commencement [and at the end] of the year, the difference between [the net assets at the two dates], subject to any appropriations of profit or adjustments of capital, is the profit [or loss] for the period.

Spicer & Pegler, 1914, 351

For the unincorporated concern as well as for the corporation, it is the accountant's natural instinct to conceive of business property as belonging to the entity, and of income as asset increment.

Paton & Littleton, 1940, 9

The income of an enterprise is the increase in its net assets (assets less liabilities) measured by the excess of revenue over expense.

AAA, 1948/1957b, 14

the most important feature of profit . . . is that it has to be found to exist . . . as an increase in net assets if it is to mean anything sensible, and the only thing that can make profit have sense is that it is available to the proprietors to live on.

Mutton, 1962, 409

once earned, income exists only as increased net assets . . . .
Dohr & others, 1964, 133

the most useful picture of earnings is . . . the picture which shows . . . . how fast the economic wealth of the enterprise is growing (or is decreasing) . . . . our concept of income must be based on an increase in net assets . . . .
Ross, 1969, 43

Income as increment in owners' equity

The net worth of the proprietor at a given time, when compared with his net worth at a different date, will show the increase or decrease in his wealth – or his profit or loss during the interim.
Lafrentz, 1906, 482

If the balance sheets at the beginning and end of a period are theoretically and practically accurate, and show the true financial position at those dates, the increase or decrease of surplus, after allowing for distribution of profit during the interval, represents the true profit or loss for the period . . . .
Dickinson, 1914, 74

Profit in the accounting sense is the amount by which assets have increased as a result of doing business, and hence it is the increase of proprietors' claim to assets . . . .
Cole, 1921, 263

The figure of income . . . . expresses the amount of resources which may be drawn upon . . . to meet interest charges, income taxes, and dividend appropriations without impairment of capital and surplus as of the beginning of the period.
Paton & Littleton, 1940, 48

Net profit (earnings, income) or net loss for an accounting period is the increase (decrease) in owners' equity, assuming no changes [by way of additional contributed capital] and no distribution to the owners.
Sprouse & Moonitz, 1962, 9

the proprietary view of the business . . . . the business as a financial fund administered by the managers for the benefit of the proprietors, who provide the finance. On this view . . . a profit is an increase in the wealth of the proprietors.
Whittington, 1983a/1986, 9

To the accountant, net income equals revenues minus expenses . . . . Net income is the net increase in owner's equity resulting from the operations of the company.
Needles & others, 1984, 99

See also 160

613 Income calculation from periodical asset valuations

I think that we have arrived at a very clear perception of the principle upon which the directors and the company were bound to act in ascertaining such [divisible] net profits. The first step would be to make good the capital by taking stock and putting a value upon all the assets of the company, of whatever nature, and deducting therefrom all the liabilities (including amongst those liabilities the amount of contributed capital), and the surplus, if any, then remaining of the gross receipts would be net profit. [per Kindersley V C]

Binney v The Ince Hall Coal and Cannel Company, 1866

I have no doubt, in valuing partnership assets an increase or decrease in the value of an article is treated, and properly treated, as part of the profit or loss at the end of the year. It is the duty of a partnership to ascertain in any way it can the value of the assets; and any diminution in the selling value is a loss and any increase in the selling value is a profit, and is dealt with accordingly. [per Vice Chancellor – Chancery]

Salisbury v Metropolitan Railway Company (2), 1870

In order to ascertain the profits earned and divisible at any time, the balance sheet must contain a fair statement of the liabilities of the company, including its paid up capital; and, on the other hand, a fair or more properly *bona fide* valuation of assets, the balance, if in favor of the company, being profits. These profits may . . . be represented by obligations of debtors, often secured, and by direct securities over property. They are not the less profits fairly realized and divisible because they exist in that form and have not been received in cash. [per Lord Shand]

City of Glasgow Bank v Mackinnon, 1882

The word profits has, in my opinion, a well-defined legal meaning, and this meaning coincides with the fundamental conception of profits in general parlance . . . .profits implies a comparison between the state of a business at two specific dates usually separated by an interval of a year. The fundamental meaning is the amount of gain made by the business during the year. This can only be ascertained by a comparison of the assets of the business at the two dates. For practical purposes these assets, in calculating profits, must be evaluated and not merely enumerated . . . . Even if the assets were identical at the two periods it would by no means follow that there had been neither gain nor loss, because the market value – the value in exchange – of these assets might have altered greatly in the meanwhile . . . . the strict meaning of the word profit is rarely observed in drawing up the accounts of firms or companies. These are domestic documents designed for the practical guidance of those interested . . . . But though there is a wide field for variation of practice in these estimations of profit in the domestic documents of a firm or company, this liberty ceases at once when the rights of third parties intervene . . . . In the absence of special stipulations to the contrary profits, in cases where the rights of third parties come in, mean actual profits, and they must be calculated as closely as possible in accordance with the fundamental conception or definition to which I have referred. [per Fletcher-Moulton, L J]

Spanish Prospecting Co Ltd, In re The,
1910, 576

In the widest possible view, profits may be stated as the realized increment in value of the whole amount invested in an undertaking; and, conversely, loss is the realized decrement in such value. Inasmuch, however, as the ultimate realization of the original investment is from the nature of things deferred for a long period of years, during which partial realizations are continually taking place, it becomes necessary to fall back on estimates of value at certain definite periods, and to consider as profit or loss the estimated increase or decrease between any two such periods. This method would permit any business concern to revalue periodically the whole of its assets and liabilities, and to record the difference between its surplus so ascertained at the commencement and the end of the year as its profit or loss, respectively; and provided that this estimate were fairly and reasonably made, there would be no objection to such a course.

Dickinson. 1914, 67

The profits of a year can be accurately shown without an elaborate set of books, all that is necessary being a carefully prepared annual inventory. The herdsman telling the tale of his sheep, the miser counting over his hoard, compares the figures of a preceding period and learns what has been his annual increase.

Hatfield, 1916/1976, 274

Every profitable transaction must automatically result in an increase of the profit shown by the profit and loss account, and in an exactly corresponding increase in the net amount of assets which the firm holds. Where, on the other hand, a transaction results in a loss, the profit shown by the profit and loss account is diminished, and to a corresponding extent net assets disappear. These statements are so thoroughly true that it would be feasible to measure profit by ascertaining the net surplus of assets over liabilities at successive points of time and (after adjusting introductions and withdrawals of capital) taking the difference between the two results to represent the profit or loss of the intervening period. [substantially similar in 1968, Magee, ed.]

Rowland & Magee, 1934, 281

Fifty years ago it was not unusual for an enterprise or an individual to value the assets at the beginning and again at the end of the year and, after allowing for withdrawals, to regard the difference as income for the year. This concept was undoubtedly useful at the time . . . the hope for appreciation was a major factor in investment . . . . [This method] became inexpedient . . . under the changed economic conditions [i.e. of large investments in corporations in new, varied and expensive assets].

Broad, 1954, 582

Financial accounting has evolved during the past century from the point where a balance sheet consisted of an inventory or listing of assets and liabilities, with profit or loss calculated by reference to the increase or decrease in net worth from one year to another. The process of accounting is now largely concerned with the correct matching of costs against income, and the balance has become, in the eyes of some, a collection of residuals.

Leach, 1962, 237

If the [merchant] adventurer finished [an expedition] with more pounds . . . than he invested in the venture, the surplus was profit . . . . yesterday's adventurer and today's corporation have the same essential characteristic. The objective of every trading activity is still to end that activity with more money than was invested in it.

Slimmings, 1974, 211

See also 366, 367

614 Capital maintenance a condition of the emergence of income

Net income is either (a) what is left over at the end of a period after the real value of capital has been maintained, or (b) what is left over at the end of a period after such dispositions have been made as will maintain the real income flow.

Edey, 1949, 76

That there is no income (net) until capital has been maintained out of the revenue yielded by the same capital is a fundamental consideration . . . . what is important in income determination is not the maintenance of specific assets, but the maintenance of the overall capital of the firm.

Trumbull, 1958, 26

the concept of capital maintenance provides a benchmark that can be used to establish whether or not income has been earned. Capital is a stock of wealth represented in accounting by the measured amount of net assets . . . . If actual capital is more [at the end than at the beginning of a period], income has been earned – income is the difference between the actual amount of net assets and the amount that represents the maintenance of capital.

Carsberg, 1982, 60

The concept of maintaining capital intact . . . is the benchmark for the definition and measurement of income.

Barton, 1984, 90

To have income is to have an increment of capital; to have a loss is to have lost some capital. Capital maintenance and income are interdependent building blocks of financial accounting. All other notions either derive from or build on those foundation stones . . . . Financial accounting cannot, of course, assure that capital is maintained. It can only report whether the aggregate return includes any income or, if it does not, that there has been a loss of capital . . . . [Business income] is anything left over after capital is maintained.

Gellein, 1987, 59–61

See also 163

615 Varied interpretations of capital maintenance

See, for nominal capital maintenance, 714
for physical capital maintenance, 753, 754
for purchasing power maintenance, 774

What is it to replace or maintain property that has been exhausted? Is it to maintain the power to produce commodities and services; is it to maintain the productivity in value of commodities and services; is it to maintain the market value of the assets; is it to maintain the earning capacity, or profit-producing capacity; or is it to maintain the value invested or locked up in the plant?

Cole, 1921, 311

[Maintenance of capital may be interpreted as]: 1. Maintenance of actual physical, material capital . . . preservation of the same amount of material, physical objects . . . . 2. Maintenance of nominal capital – i.e. of a value measured by the worth of the price index of a single good or service, usually money . . . . 3. Maintenance of individual real capital . . . preservation of the original absolute command exercised by the capital over the goods and services of most importance to the particular concern . . . . [4] Maintenance of general real capital is effected by preservation of general purchasing power.

Sweeney, 1930, 279–283

it seems best to regard net debtors and cash as comprising a separate part of the business, i.e. as the financial side as contrasted with the manufacturing and trading side . . . . [or] as forming part of a separate business with different ideas on maintaining capital . . . . A net creditor position should also be ignored.

Lacey, 1952, 80, 81, 83

The . . . proposed pattern of profit measurement can now be summarized – 1. For fixed assets, capital is deemed to be maintained intact on a net value basis, the revalued depreciation being regarded conventionally as reinvested in other real assets . . . . 2. For stocks, capital is treated as requiring to be maintained intact to the extent of the volume of stocks actually carried at the balance sheet date. 3. For other assets, capital is regarded as requiring to be maintained intact only in conventional money terms.

Lacey, 1952, 87

there are strong practical grounds for accepting accounting procedures designed to maintain the real value of capital invested in physical assets, but it is difficult to justify accounting procedures designed to preserve the purchasing power of cash resources and money claims .... Physical asssets are valued in terms of money merely for accounting convenience, whereas cash and other liquid assets, debtors' balances, creditors' balances, etc. are claims to money and nothing else. By definition they do not represent claims to real resources .... the wider question of avoiding losses in purchasing power arising from inflation ... is not an accounting problem.

Mathews & Grant, 1958, 22

The capital maintenance concept on which periodic present value income is based .... does not refer to keeping a stock of capital resources intact ... but to keeping intact a stream of expected income earning power.

Barton, 1974, 675

Conventional historical cost accounting is based on maintaining money capital .... Current purchasing power accounting is based on maintaining purchasing power capital .... Replacement cost accounting is based on maintaining specific physical assets ....

Myddelton, 1974, 46

The distributable funds [or business capacity maintenance] approach .... is different from physical capacity or financial capital maintenance. Business capacity maintenance recognizes that a continuing enterprise has distributable funds available only after it provides for the maintenance of that portion of its operating capability financed by shareholders' equity .... Business capacity, in contrast with the notion of physical capacity, includes not only productive facilities but also the company's increased net working capital requirements.

Rappaport, 1979, 39

income can be regarded as equal to the maximum amount of cash that someone could spend in a period while expecting to remain equally well off in the sense of being able to spend the same amount per period in subsequent periods.

Carsberg, 1982, 65

The two approaches [to capital maintenance in periods of changing prices can be described] in terms of the entity approach (physical capital maintenance) and the proprietary approach (financial capital maintenance). The entity approach is concerned with the specific prices of the assets held by the entity. The proprietary approach, on the other hand, is concerned with the maintenance of the wealth of the proprietors of the business, regarding capital as a fund belonging to them and to be maintained relative to a general index, which might be thought to be more relevant to their spending habits.

Whittington, 1984, 149

Capital can ... be viewed in financial terms. Here the capital of a business is viewed as a fund attributable to shareholders and profit is the difference between the opening and closing fund .... There are two variants: capital in terms of nominal units of

purchasing power . . . and capital in terms of a fund of general purchasing power
. . . .

ASC, 1986, 23

Financial capital maintenance – purchasing power basis. Under this concept, capital is considered to be the purchasing power inherent in the net resources at any point in time.

Skinner, 1987, 541

616 Capital erosion

profits calculated by ordinary accounting processes are swollen under inflation by sums which, economically considered, are capital rather than income. An excess profits tax begins to acquire some of the characteristics of a capital levy, a rather bad sort of capital levy.

Hicks & others, 1941, 57

The high tax rates, combined with the present rules [for computing taxable profits], are steadily eating into the capital resources of industry, and the owners are losing a part, a very considerable part, of their equity in the business.

CSR, 1950, 1

Inflation itself, we suggest, is the disease that is affecting the whole economic life of the nation, and one of the symptoms is the erosion of industrial capital.

Accountant, editorial, 1952, 563

The impact of rising prices and of high taxation is leading to an eating up of capital. There is an erosion of capital in the guise of profit – whether it be distributed or retained.

Latham, 1952, 144

During an inflationary period . . . investment at the level of conventional depreciation charges will not purchase the new assets required for maintaining stable production. If the pre-inflation dividend policy is continued, the company's asset position will deteriorate in real (productive) terms, although in money terms stability will be maintained . . . . Equity erosion occurs when the company's real value (purchasing power) of equity declines over time.

Goldschmidt & Admon, 1977, 194, 196

Erosion of physical capital (or erosion of operating capability) may be regarded as the failure to retain sufficient financial resources to acquire assets needed to maintain the capacity of the enterprise to provide a constant supply of goods and services. The concept of physical capital erosion may be linked to a concept of distributable income where distributable income is defined as the amount of cash that may be distributed without reducing the operating capability of the enterprise.

FASB, 1979, SFAS33

Business accounting is made deceptive by inflation. Illusory profits on inventories, and likewise illusory profits due to depreciation rules that allow [one] to take into account only original cost instead of replacement cost of plant and equipment, grossly exaggerate true earnings. Taxes and dividends are paid from possibly nonexistent profits.

Wallich, 1979, 32

Some businesses are actually paying dividends out of capital . . . . A recent *Business week* article [March 19, 1979] summed up the situation by stating that "fully one third of the earnings that companies reported for 1978 were an illusion – gains created by inflation and out of date accounting methods".

Williams, 1979, 73

By matching current revenues with costs incurred at an earlier date at lower prices, profits are distorted, and distributions may cause capital to be eroded.

Solomons, 1989, 50

617 Whole life income alone considered determinate

No profit can be . . . definitely stated until the business is actually wound up and all the assets are realized in cash.

Walton, 1909, 454

It is seldom possible to tell the exact profit made by an undertaking until it has been finally wound up and its assets distributed.

Carter, 1910b, 562

a final measure of gross income that is a fact and that describes a state of affairs in the real world does inevitably result from the accountant's procedure both (a) when the relation of any person to an enterprise ceases in reality, and (b) when any enterprise is wound up. All measures of income for periods [shorter than these] are approximate indexes only.

Canning, 1929a, 124

Profits are accurately and definitely determinable only when a business ceases and is liquidated. Profits of a going concern are always estimates.

Kester, 1933, 494

accurate determination of [periodical] profit is utterly impossible for the large well-managed corporation with an indefinite life tenure.

Gilman, 1939, 75

Business earnings are fundamentally indeterminate short of the total life of the business venture. Any interim calculation of earnings is, therefore, an estimate.

Robnett & others, 1951, 509

On a cash to cash basis, and embracing the entire life of the business, income is readily measured .... comparison of the cash invested and the cash from dissolution discloses the amount of income.

Smith & Ashburne, 1960, 57

A complete and accurate picture of the degree of success achieved by an enterprise cannot be obtained until it discontinues operations and converts its assets into cash.

Noble & Niswonger, 1961, 331

it is possible to determine the profit or loss of a business accurately only over the complete period of its existence ....

Beacham, 1964, 13

A completely factual set of accounting reports containing no estimates based on future events can be prepared only after the firm's life has come to an end.

Barton, 1984, 58

618 Conjecture in periodical income determination

much of the accounting for profit and loss of a past period involves forecasting. When we lead receipts [accrue], we forecast the amount to be collected. When we lag disbursements, we forecast, among other things, the number of service units to be had and their total cost.

Nelson, 1942, 140

It seems very doubtful if any significant income figure for the current year can be developed by taking future activities into account. However important it may be for a firm to plan the financing of its future capital expenditures, it is hard to believe that a charge to provide for such future needs is a legitimate factor in the computation of current income.

Coutts (ed), 1961, 65

in measuring net income, the accountant must make assumptions regarding the life expectancy of most assets.

Needles & others, 1984, 102

Financial reporting, at the present time, does not make statements about the future, though the going concern concept, one of its basic postulates, requires it to make a number of assumptions about the future in order to depict the present and the past.

Solomons, 1989, 12

See also 252, 328

619 Identification of income components said to be desirable

methods could, and should, be developed . . . so that the results of activities, measured in units of equal purchasing power, and the effects of changes in value of the monetary unit would be reflected separately in an integrated presentation which would also produce statements of financial position more broadly meaningful than the orthodox balance sheet of today.

AIA, 1952, 105

the probability of rational action will be increased by any device which designates the real sources of income .... The income statement should specify gain from operations, gain (or loss, ...) from incidental sources, and gain (or loss) from variations in the purchasing power of the currency.

Chambers, 1952b, 262

The conduct of most businesses ... involves three basic speculations: (1) speculation specifically related to the provision of a goods or service utility; (2) speculation in the changing value of money; (3) speculation in the changing economic value of the items which constitute the tools of business conduct. Accounting seldom measures and expresses separately the success or failure realized in each of the indicated speculations .... For managerial purposes and for the purpose of better judging the business' achievement, separate measurement and emphasis are desirable.

Husband, 1960, 211

The measurement and reporting of current income should provide a basis for prediction of future earnings. To facilitate the predictive process, reported current income should include: (1) the result of ordinary operations, (2) catastrophic losses and discovery of assets, and (3) holding gains and losses.

AAA, 1964a, 693

620 Receipts and Revenues

621 Revenue

Revenue receipts, or income, are the profits arising from the sales, discounts received, commission earned, interest on any investment, transfer fees, etc.

Carter, 1923, 250

Revenue is a generic term for (a) the amount of assets received or liabilities liquidated in the sale of the products or services of an enterprise, (b) the gain from sales or exchanges of assets other than stock in trade, and (c) the gain from advantageous settlements of liabilities. Revenue does not arise from a gift.

AAA, 1948/1957b, 15

Revenues are the gross amounts of increases in owners' equity derived from profit-seeking activities.

Corbin, 1964, 48

Normally revenue is measured in terms of the amount of cash or cash equivalent received from customers on the date revenue is recognized. Cash equivalent refers to the amount of cash into which the item received . . . could be converted on the date the revenue is recognized.

Bedford, 1965, 98

Revenue is an inflow of assets in the form of cash, receivables or other property from customers and clients, and is related primarily to the disposal of goods and the rendering of services.

Finney & Miller, 1968, 243

Revenues are the values of goods and services transferred to external parties in exchange for cash or a promise of a future cash inflow, and are measured by cash inflows either received or expected.

Anderson & others, 1974, 46

Revenues are inflows or other enhancements of assets of an entity or settlements of its liabilities (or a combination of both) during a period from delivering or producing goods, rendering services, or other activities that constitute the entity's ongoing major or central operations.

FASB, 1980b, SFAC3

Revenues are increases in the interest of residual equity holders in an entity arising other than by contributions [of residual equity holders].

ASRB, 1985b, R100

622 Capital receipts

capital receipts are sums contributed to an undertaking and intended to be permanently left in that undertaking for the sake of enabling it to carry on its business.

Dicksee, 1903a, 7

Capital receipts comprise any additional capital paid in by partners, or, in the case of a joint stock company, any sums received from shareholders or debentureholders, any loans, the proceeds of sale of any of the assets.

Carter, 1923, 250

The capital receipts consist of sums obtained on account of (a) share capital; (b) capital stock; (c) debentures; (d) debenture stock; (e) mortgages; (f) loans; (g) premiums on shares, stock or debentures.

Pixley, 1926, I:283

623 Revenue recognition

The most theoretically correct concept of the income account is that charges or credits to it accrue from day to day, and this concept is applied wherever it is practicable to do so – as in the case of rent or interest. In many more cases, however, its application is impracticable, and the income charge or credit is deemed to arise when a transaction takes place . . . .

May, 1937/1978, 22

The recognition of revenue [may occur on the making of a sale, on the receipt of cash, on the completion of production, on accretion of value prior to completion of production, and on appreciation of property values].

Backer, 1955a/1955b, 239ff

[Among the occasions of revenue recognition are] . . . the sale of goods or services . . . . the receipt of cash . . . . contract completion . . . . percentage of completion . . . . production [of farm products].

Moonitz & Jordan, 1963, I:173ff

[Revenue may be recognized] . . . at the time of sale . . . . at the time the sales price is collected . . . . at the time the product is completed . . . . proportionately over performance of contracts.

Grady, 1965, 76ff

Revenue recognition [may be related to] production . . . . passage of time . . . . price changes . . . . delivery of product . . . . collection of cash . . . . accretion [physical increase] . . . . appreciation . . . . discovery . . . . donations . . . .

Dixon & others, 1966, 102ff

Revenue is recognized when three tests are met: the revenue is captured; the revenue is measurable; the revenue is earned . . . . revenue might be recognized: 1. at the time a product or service is produced; 2. at the time of sale; 3. at the time cash is collected.

Thomas, 1977, 12:6, 9

According to the revenue recognition principle, revenues are usually recorded when . . . (1) . . . a sale has been made or a service has been performed, and (2) an exchange has taken place.

Skousen & others, 1981, 168

Accountants are loath to recognize revenue unless there is an arm's length market transaction.

Henderson & Peirson, 1983, 121

Revenue recognition refers to the point in the operating cycle of transactions at which it is considered that the revenue from operating activity has been earned . . . .

There are five events in the normal cycle . . . acquisition of resources . . . production of the goods . . . receipt of customer order . . . delivery of the goods . . . cash collection . . . . each of the events could be used [as the point of recognizing revenue] in appropriate circumstances.

Barton, 1984, 217

Revenue recognition at the date of production . . . . at the date of cash receipt . . . .

Arnold & others, 1985, 108

624 Realization as event or process

There are many equivalents of cash which are now recognized legally as constructive cash-receipt; there are many kinds of accrual . . . . Income must be objectively measured by such a device as (1) a completed transaction between parties of independent interest, (2) apportionment between fiscal periods on an objectively determinable basis, . . . (3) reference to price in a market of a certain recognized character . . . . a tentative definition of realization can be offered. Realization may be defined as the act or condition of placing a value increment into disposable form.

Bowers, 1941, 154

The essential meaning of realization is that a change in an asset or liability has become sufficiently definite and objective to warrant recognition in the accounts.

AAA, 1957a/1957b, 3

according to the [AAA, 1957] definition, we can speak of the realization of a cost, of a cost transfer, of an expense, of a loss, of revenue and income, of a capital contribution, of a capital withdrawal, of an investnment, of a liability liquidation, or of a loan. Each of these is the result of a change in an asset or liability. Each of these changes is realized when the change becomes sufficiently definite and objective to warrant recognition in the accounts . . . . For an item to be sufficiently definite, it must appear unlikely to be reversed. We may say it must appear to have permanence . . . . In his [the accountant's] opinion the item must be such that it is unlikely to be cancelled, revoked, or lost in the foreseeable future.

Windal, 1961, 252

gain or loss is realized only through sale and is measured by the difference between selling price established at the time of sale and purchase price established at the time of acquisition.

Gordon & Shillinglaw, 1964, 47

Realization in the most precise sense means the process of converting noncash resources and rights into money and is most precisely used in accounting and financial reporting to refer to sales of assets for cash or claims to cash. The related terms realized and unrealized therefore identify revenues or gains or losses on assets sold and unsold respectively.

FASB, 1985, SFAC6

625 Point of revenue realization

The accountant assumes . . . . that expense accrues but that net revenue or profit suddenly appears, full-blown, on some specific occasion, commonly that of the sale.
                                    Paton, 1922/1962, 493

if we have sold . . . goods for cash, then the profit is a realized one; but if we have sold these goods on credit, then the profit exists only on paper, and will not be realized until the debt is paid.
                                    Carter, 1923, 610

Revenue is realized when title to the product passes or when the service is performed . . . . Revenue can then be reported in the period in which the moment of realization falls.
                                    Smith & Ashburne, 1960, 62

The point of sale is generally regarded as the point of revenue realization because . . . it is the point at which the amount of revenue is, in the normal case, objectively determinable from a sale price acceptable to both parties.
                                    Finney & Miller, 1961, 174

When it is a question of choice of time for recording the completion of a goods transaction, the accountant asks for security, i.e. the probability of the definitive conclusion of the occurrence. Therefore he is unwilling to include receipts before they manifest themselves in money or its equivalent.
                                    Hansen, 1962, 77

The realization principle. Accomplishment (revenue) should be recognized in the period when the prices to be received for products and services provided by the enterprise (1) become reasonably certain and (2) have been earned by the enterprise . . . . [i.e. when] a legally enforceable sale of a product or completion of a service has taken place.
                                    May & others, 1975, 100

626 Comment on the realization test

Suppose that an individual owns a bond and that it advances in value. The profit has been realized in the ordinary accounting sense although a sale has not been made. All accruals are, of course, based on "unrealized" transactions.
                                    Paton & Stevenson, 1918/1978, 464

Accountants favor [applying] the test of completion and practical realization to income [revenue] but not to costs, losses and expense, because it is otherwise impossible to match expenditures incurred . . . with such income or . . . because of . . . conservatism.
                                    Gilman, 1939, 609

One of the most obvious and important of economic truths is the fact that a profit is an increase in net wealth .... The notion that the validity of a profit depends upon its being realized is childish, untrue, and in complete opposition to the realities of modern business procedure.

MacNeal, 1939, 295

Present usage is normally said to be that profits arise when realized. But for some reason, not recorded in history, "realized" does not mean what it says: it apparently means converted into debt, whether or not that debt is converted into cash. In other words, profit arises on delivery of goods. But this principle is not applied universally; it is very common, for instance, for some part of profit to be taken on partly completed contract work. The profession has no principle on which such work in progress should be valued, it merely imposes a maximum on the whim of the business man.

Norris, 1939, 846

the realization postulate was not accepted prior to the First World War [1914–1918].

AIA, 1952, 23

The ... postulate of realization is that profit or loss can only be shown on the basis of a completed transaction. The argument is that until the transaction is completed and the profit or loss realized, the amount is indeterminate. This is true, as far as exactness is concerned. But it is not true in an economic or commercial sense .... Indeed, realization may never take place, in view of the postulate of permanence .... Is not the postulate of realization based on a fallacious theory of exactness?

Knauth, 1957, 31

Assume that a portfolio of securities appreciates. Can it be said, in all honesty, that such appreciation is not recognized because of fear of a subsequent market decline? Is the requirement of a completed transaction a convenient excuse? After all, under an accrual system of accounting, there are exceptions to the completed transaction postulate. Recognition of profits and losses on long term contracts is but one case in point.

Bastable, 1959, 54

The realization convention is usually justified on the basis of conservatism .... Without a single exception, the 72 security analysts interviewed expressed opposition to the recognition of income before a sale takes place.

Backer, 1970, 155, 163

Wealth and income are generated when values change. The actual transaction is an exchange of objects of equal value; no wealth is affected. This flies in the face of the realization principle, which should be discarded because it is logically inconsistent with the preparation of periodical financial statements.

Bodenhorn, 1978, 5

realization is not an essential characteristic of accounting income but rather merely a convenient criterion for recognition that may be abandoned when considered appropriate.

Skinner, 1987, 47

See also 325, 694

630 Expenditures and Expenses

631 Revenue expenditures

Revenue expenditures . . . are such as must be incurred in order that advantage may be taken of the earning capacity of the enterprise, or in order that such capacity may be maintained at the required standard.

Esquerré, 1914, 226

Revenue expenditure . . . expenditure incurred in replacements, repairs, renewals, depreciation . . . current expenses of carrying on the business . . . .

Carter, 1923, 248

An expenditure which merely maintains an asset in the same state of operating efficiency as before . . . is an expense. An expenditure which increases the normal operating efficiency . . . is an asset.

Kohler & Morrison, 1926, 314

a revenue expenditure is one that results in an addition to an expense account . . . . Revenue expenditures benefit a current period and are made for the purpose of maintaining the asset in satisfactory operating condition.

Malchman & Slavin, 1961, 354

Revenue expenditure is all expenditure incurred in carrying on the business, and maintaining the capital assets in a state of efficiency.

Woolf, 1973, 75

Revenue expenditure . . . is such outlay as is necessary for the maintenance of earning capacity . . . and the normal total cost [of conducting business operations].

Pickles, 1974, 0801

expenditures treated as expenses of the current period are called revenue expenditures.

Meigs & others, 1978, 477

632 Capital expenditures

Items of outlay which are actual additions to, or extensions of, property, and which increase thereby the permanent value or influence the power of production, should, without doubt, come under the head of capital expenditure; while those which represent repairs, replacement, or general upholding of property, should be regarded as revenue expenditure.

Whatley, 1893, 1

Capital expenditure is that expenditure *bona fide* incurred for the sake of acquiring, extending, or completing the equipment of the undertaking, with a view to placing it upon a revenue earning basis, or to improve its revenue earning capacity . . . . Capital expenditure is represented by assets – fixed or floating.

Dicksee, 1903a, 7

the term [capital expenditures] appears to apply to such expenses as, in the aggregate, . . . represent the cost of the increased earning capacity of the enterprise as a whole or of particular parts thereof, which has been secured over the earning capacity known to exist before the said expenses were incurred.

Esquerré, 1914, 226

Capital expenditure comprises all expenditure incurred in acquiring assets for the purpose of earning income, or increasing the earning capacity of a business; . . . land and buildings . . . plant and machinery . . . .

Carter, 1923, 248

At the time of organization of a business, the capital contributed by the owner is expended to acquire the necessary assets with which to carry on the business. A fundamental distinction must be made between expenditures for the purchase and installation of the assets themselves and expenditures for expenses in connection with their repair, maintenance and upkeep . . . . The expenditures for expenses . . . are subtractions from profits and proprietorship, while asset expenditures constitute an exchange of the asset cash for some other asset, which exchange has no effect on proprietorship.

Kester, 1917/1939, 130

A capital expenditure should be defined in terms of economic behavior, rather than in terms of accounting convention or tax law. The criterion, then is the flexibility of the commitment involved, that is, the rate of turnover into cash.

Dean, 1952, 4

Accounting proceeds on the assumption that the distinction between capital and revenue is purely one of time . . . . "capital expenditure" is a misnomer and can mean only one thing to an accountant: expenditure which is applicable to more than one accounting period . . . . The source of such expenditure is in this respect irrelevant – . . . contributed capital, . . . undistributed income capital, loan capital or creditor capital.

Most, 1959, 635

A capital expenditure is one that results in an addition to an asset account . . . . Capital expenditures are in the nature of major alterations, additions, replacements and betterments or improvements which are significant in amount and which benefit future periods . . . . the expenditure is referred to as being capitalized.

Malchman & Slavin, 1961, 354

Capital expenditure may be said to be all expenditure incurred for the purpose of acquiring assets of a permanent nature, by means of which to carry on the business, or for the purpose of increasing the earning capacity of the business.

Woolf, 1973, 75

The total cost of a plant asset is the cash outlay, or its equivalent, made to acquire the asset and put it in operating condition . . . . Initial expenditures that are included in the cost of assets are called capital expenditures, and such expenditures are commonly said to be capitalized . . . . The theoretical test to distinguish a capital from a revenue expenditure is simple: Have the services acquired been entirely consumed within the current period, or will there be a carryover of beneficial services into future periods?

Meigs & others, 1978, 476–7

633 Expenditure on durables considered as prepaid expenses

so long as it is reasonable to assume the continuity of the business, the correct thing is not to attempt to show the realizable value [of fixed assets] . . . but rather to show such expenditure *as* expenditure subject to the fact that in so far as it will not last for ever its cost must be apportioned as fairly as possible, and charged against the profits earned in successive years . . . .

Dicksee, 1910, 195

Whatever amount is paid for a machine is in reality a prepayment for the service which the machine is expected to render. The cost of this service is deducted periodically in the form of depreciation from the gross income of the periods receiving the service.

Couchman, 1924, 121

Most of the fixed assets are, strictly speaking, deferred charges to expense, being gradually charged to expense by the periodic depreciation charge.

McKinsey, 1925, 164

[Property and plant] assets are really in the nature of a deferred charge against the future income they will help to produce . . . . the property accounts . . . should show the cost of the property.

Sanders & others, 1938, 59

From an accounting point of view, an investment in plant and equipment with a limited useful life constitutes a deferred charge to operations, a prepaid expense. As the services constituting the asset are used up or expire from lack of use, a corresponding portion of the investment is transferred from the plant and equipment account to operations.

Moonitz & Jordan, 1963, I:378

over the whole life of a business, all expenditure is revenue expenditure and fixed assets are merely costs held in suspense from one artificial period to another.

Beacham, 1964, 47

The purchase of an asset, generally, is nothing more than a payment in advance for an expense.

Pickles, 1974, 0701

See also 443

634 Revenue and capital expenditures indistinguishable

Most of the errors of principle that are perpetrated in practice arise from the lack of ability, or lack of desire, to strictly discriminate between capital and revenue items.

Dicksee, 1907, 3

in ordinary commercial undertakings the difference between [capital expenditures and charges against revenue] is not diametrical. The machine, the tool, the raw material are all alike expenses of producing commodities. All are operating expenses, provided a long enough field of operation is taken into view. [*Electric railway journal, Oct 16, 1915, p 800*]

Hatfield, 1915/1978

A capital expenditure is one, the usefulness of which is expected to extend over several accounting periods. If the accounting period were increased from the customary year to a decade, most of what is now treated as capital expenditure would become chargeable to income; while if the period were reduced to a day, much of what is now treated as current maintenance would become capital expenditure.

May, 1937/1978, 6

there is no absolute line between capital and revenue expenditure, the classification to be adopted being related to a more or less conventional decision as to depreciation procedure and the size of the asset unit adopted for this purpose.

Norris, 1949a, 128

there is no sharp or fundamental distinction between [capital expenditure and current expenditure]. What is termed capital or current depends essentially on the practice – a practice which is unavoidable – of drawing up accounts covering relatively short periods of time. If the direct benefits resulting from some particular class of expenditure are exhausted during the same accounting period in which they are made, then the expenditure is regarded as current expenditure; if not, as capital expenditure. In the long run, if one takes as a single period a succession of accounting periods, so-called capital expenditure becomes indistinguishable from current expenditure.

Walker, 1955, 360

in the long run, all expenditure is revenue expenditure and all income is revenue income. Were the periods of account long enough, costs and sales of capital equipment would appear in the profit and loss account.

Greener, 1974a, 40

See also 444

635 Capitalization of expenditures

everything necessary to acquire fixed assets in place and ready to operate should be capitalized; that is, charged to the asset account.

Goetz & Klein, 1960, 308

In effect the accounting period assumption results in a classification of transactions into current and capital; transactions or parts of transactions not related to the current period are capitalized.

Mathews, 1962, 63

Certain kinds of expenditures may at the option of the company be treated either as current expense or capital expense. In the latter case the expenditure appears on the balance sheet as an asset, which is generally written off gradually over a period of years.

Graham & McGolrick, 1964, 88

[Capitalization policies] generally provide for the capitalization of costs only where they have the effect of enlarging physical dimensions, increasing productivity in some substantial way, lengthening future life, lowering future costs, or involving major replacements.

Kohler, 1965a, 83

as a practising security analyst, I take exception to [the view that] accounting opinions [professional prescriptions] should be formulated to encompass the capitalization of increased amounts of deferred research and development expenditures, training costs and advertising expenditures. Empirical evidence indicates that permissive deferral of R&D expenditures and related items is an area that is being much abused.

O'glove, 1970, 28

Conceptually, current expenditures for research and development, advertising, training, and similar activities should be capitalized because the central purpose of capitalization is to hold on the balance sheet expenditures that are made for future benefit.

Anthony, 1973, 42

The verb, to capitalize, is often used among accountants. It means simply that the acquisition cost of a service is recognized and recorded as an asset or deferred cost.

Anderson & others, 1974, 339

636 Deferred expenditure or charges

expenditure . . . primarily of a revenue nature, but the benefit of which is not exhausted during the period covered by the profit and loss account . . . . may be conveniently termed deferred revenue expenditure, and it may be carried forward and written off within the period during which the benefit from it is likely to be felt . . . .

Spicer & Pegler, 1914, 130

The common element . . . in both [deferred charges and prepaid expenses] is that they are all amounts held in suspense, to be charged as expenses in subsequent fiscal periods; in the meantime they are carried as assets in the balance sheet . . . . Prepaid expenses are mostly of short duration, are for services not yet received, but to be received in the near future, and are usually parts of ordinary recurring expenses . . . . Deferred charges, on the other hand, generally are of longer duration, and are for services already received though the benefits from them may accrue into the future; often they do not constitute parts of regular expenses, and sometimes are abnormal losses which it is not yet convenient to write off. [They] include discount and expense on bonds, organization expense, experimental expense, developmental expense, . . . unusual losses carried forward to future fiscal periods.

Sanders & others, 1938, 75

Prepayments arise [where] . . . payment is made in advance of the receipt or utilization of goods and services . . . . The term deferred charge is sometimes used to describe prepayments. The cost of any asset which will be consumed in production is a deferred charge to future operations; the more permanent the asset, therefore, the more appropriate the use of the expression, deferred. Prepaid expenses is sometimes used as a substitute term but this too is subject to objection since many of the fixed assets may also be considered, in a sense, to be prepaid expenses.

Wixon (ed), 1962, 11:59

The argument for deferred revenue expenditure is neither that the charge to profits in each year is right, nor that the amount carried forward in the balance sheet is right, but that the results of the year in which the expenditure was incurred would have been misleading without it . . . . When is an item big enough to call for spreading in this way? How long . . . should the period of spreading be? . . . . there are no general answers to these questions; they depend on accepted practice . . . and indeed on the habitual views of the parties deciding them.

Morison, 1974, 356

See also 425, 445

637 Expenses

Any expenditure would be an expense if the period of operation were long enough . . . . Expenses are the costs incurred in getting certain incomes or in getting the incomes of a certain period.

Bell & Graham, 1936, 15

the word, expense, has been given many divergent meanings. Sometimes it is used as synonymous with cost, that is, as a generic term which has no technical meaning without the addition of qualifying words. More often it is used to refer to cost of services (as against cost of tangible goods) or specifically to those service costs which are incidental to the selling, administration and financial aspects of business operation. Another use of the term includes costs assignable to a particular quantity of revenue . . . . But as an accounting concept many would agree that expense in the sense of overall cost of revenue or profit determinant is much more significant than any other usage of the term . . . .

Chow, 1939, 340

Expense is the cost of assets or portions thereof deducted from revenue in the measurement of income. These deductions arise through a current expenditure of cash, a total or partial expiration of asset cost, or the incurrence of a liability. Expense consists of operating costs – deductions that have a traceable association with the production of revenue, and losses – deductions that have no such association.

AAA, 1948/1957b, 15

Those costs that are applicable to present revenues are called expenses; those applicable to future revenues are denoted as assets.

Spiller, 1964, 853

Expense is the cost of the services used up to provide the recognized revenue.

Bedford, 1965, 101

Expenses are the value of services consumed in the process of producing revenues and are measured in terms of the cash disbursements necessary to acquire the services.

Anderson & others, 1974, 54

Product expenses are recognized as expenses in the period in which the particular product is sold. But if [the consumption of a resource] cannot be specifically identified with a unit of present or future revenue, its cost is recognized as an expense in the period in which it is consumed or sacrificed. Such costs . . . are called period expenses.

May & others, 1975, 105

Expenses are outflows or other using up of assets or incurrences of liabilities (or a combination of both) during a period from delivering or producing goods, rendering services, or carrying out other activities that constitute the entity's ongoing major or central operations.

FASB, 1980b, SFAC3

Expenses are costs that are applicable to the current accounting period.

Anthony, 1983, 122

Expenses are consumptions or losses of service potential or future economic benefits in the form of reductions in assets or increases in liabilities of the entity, other than those relating to distributions to owners, that result in a decrease in equity during the reporting period.

AARF & AASB, 1992, SAC4

638 Expenses as expired costs

The term expired capital outlay is an exact definition of that which the word depreciation is intended to imply when used in its commercial sense, and the general adoption of this term would avoid the common mistakes arising from a natural belief that depreciation covers at least all that which is opposite to appreciation.

Leake, 1912/1976, 12

The terms, expired cost and expense, are . . . rather similar in nature, both being closely identified with the production of gross revenue. The distinction between them lies mainly in the source of the original charge giving rise to the item. If the original charge is first reportable as an asset, such as inventories and fixed assets, the amount of the asset matched against periodic revenue would be the expired cost item. If, on the other hand, the original charge has no asset quality at the time of its incurrence, such as many types of repairs, salaries and wages, taxes, delivery charges, and advertising, the amount matched against periodic revenue would be an expense item.

Newlove & Garner, 1951, 1:417

Expense in its broadest sense includes all expired costs which are deductible from revenues.

AICPA, 1957/1961, ATB4

585

Cost expires when title to a commodity is given up, when a service is given, when an asset is used up, or as time passes.

Smith & Ashburne, 1960, 64

Cost expirations are of two classes; expenses and lost costs . . . . both are deducted from revenue in determining the profitability of an enterprise.

Finney & Miller, 1968, 246

Expired product costs, or cost of goods sold . . . . are recorded as expenses in the period in which the costs were incurred . . . . Expired period costs [are] costs expiring this period that were incurred for the purpose of making possible the earning of revenue.

Fertig & others, 1971, 243

640 Matching, Allocation and Amortization in Income Calculation

641 Income as resultant of effort and accomplishment

Costs are considered as measuring effort, revenues as measuring accomplishment.

Paton & Littleton, 1940, 15

An accounting statement of profit . . . . is an attempt to measure in money terms, during an arbitrary short period of time, current exertions and benefits, current efforts and accomplishments . . . .

Accountant, editorial, 1946b, 250

Current accomplishment, measured in terms of revenue, must be matched against the effort . . . expended to achieve that accomplishment.

Barton, 1955, 92

costs constitute one measure of business effort, and revenues represent accomplishments coming from those efforts.

AAA, 1965c, 368

the result of an activity is the difference between . . . accomplishment and effort . . . . [In accounting, accomplishment] is measured by the realization principle . . . . accomplishment equals sales . . . . the effort is to be matched with the accomplishment, and thus the matching principle determines the amount of effort expended to produce the result.

Arnold & others, 1985, 85

642 Income calculation as matching costs with revenues

The first rule . . . with regard to the accrual or allocation of incomes and expenses is that they must apply to the same operations so that the resultant net figure will be, so far as it goes, a trustworthy index of the success or failure of those operations. A second rule . . . is that from the total incomes of any period there should be deducted all expenses which are costs of obtaining those incomes.
Scott, 1925, 52

interested parties need test readings [of the outcomes of business activity] from time to time in order to gauge the progress made. By means of accounting we seek to provide these test readings by a periodic matching of the costs and revenues that have flowed past "the meter" in an interval of time.
Paton & Littleton, 1940, 14

The use of the terms profit and profit and loss account suggests the important truth that gain is usually a difference and must be measured by matching costs and expenses against revenue.
May, 1943, 26

we can never complete a structure of accepted principles of accounting without basing such principles upon a logical, consistent convention of matching costs with revenues . . . .
Gilman, 1944, 115

Perhaps the greatest advance ever made in explaining accounting theory is the concept that the preparation of a profit and loss account is a process of matching cost with income.
Fitzgerald, 1948, 46

With the change from increased net worth to the realization test of income [*circa* 1920 in the United States], it became common to speak of income determination as being essentially a process of matching costs and revenues.
AIA, 1952, 28

income determination by matching cost and revenue has, for 500 years, been the central feature of double entry.
Littleton, 1953, 27

The matching concept is really the accounting theory of profit determination.
Barton, 1955, 92

the matching of costs (expenses) with revenues [means] that expense charges within the life span of an enterprise should, insofar as possible, be assigned to the accounting periods within which their related revenues have been recognized.
Dixon & others, 1966, 125

The income determination process in accounting is a matter of matching, or asso-ciating, revenues with related expenses . . . . it is imperative that revenues and related expenses be reported in the same period . . . . If revenue is deferred because it is regarded as not yet earned, all elements of . . . expense related to such deferred revenue must be deferred also, in order to achieve a proper matching and a proper determination of income for the period.

Finney & Miller, 1968, 248

Costs recorded in the accounts should be matched with revenues for the purpose of determining income of individual accounting periods in a manner which best reflects the cause and effect relationship existing between costs and revenues.

Skinner, 1972b, 3

Insofar as possible, the total sacrifices made in all periods to produce and sell a particular product or service should be recognized as expense in the period in which the revenue from the same product or service is recognized.

May & others, 1975, 102

the matching process requires that firstly the revenue of the period should be iden-tified, and subsequently the appropriate costs should be attached to it, that is, the costs incurred in producing the goods and services sold should be matched against or deducted from the revenue they have produced.

Magee, 1979, 252

Income calculation as matching costs with realized revenues

Income is measured by matching revenues realized against costs consumed or expired, in accordance with the cost principle.

AAA, 1941/1957b, 55

Because of the divisible, mobile, adhesive characteristics of cost, directly identi-fiable costs can be accumulated in the accounting records in terms of units of product or service. When the unit then reaches the point at which revenue is to be rec-ognized as realized, these accumulated costs are obviously to be matched against that revenue.

Owen, 1958, 74

Determination of net income for a period is a process of requiring costs to be matched with realized revenues of the period.

Smith & Ashburne, 1960, 64

According to the matching concept, the statement of profit and loss reports the revenues realized and the costs absorbed or expired during the current accounting period. The balance sheet reports the balances of incurred costs which are appli-cable to future operations . . . .

Mulcahy, 1963, 5

Matching is the process of comparing an entity's effort or expense ... to its ... realized revenue .... The accountant first applies the ... requirements for revenue realization to determine the amount of revenue for the accounting period. Next he determines the cost of services used up to produce that amount of realized revenue. He then compares the two and calculates income.

Anderson & others, 1974, 118

643 Matching costs with revenues challenged

the ideal of matching costs and income is disregarded by this common practice of recognizing unrealized losses due to decreases in replacement price.

Gilman, 1939, 130

The definition of income accounting as substantially a process of matching costs against related revenues has had strong support in academic accounting circles and is, therefore, widely accepted among the new entrants to the accounting profession. The definition, however, does not stand the test of practical experience .... the allocation of costs to accounting periods is based on conventions, some highly arbitrary in character and some permitting alternative methods that may produce widely different results.

May, 1949a, 13

The cardinal virtue claimed for the principle of matching costs and revenues is that it results in determinations that are objective and verifiable .... [But] only in part are costs matched against revenues, and matching gives an inadequate indication of what is actually done .... what transactions or what acquisition prices shall govern the determination is a matter either of convention or of subjective choice; hence income determination is by no means as objective or as factual a process as one might be led to suppose.

AIA, 1952, 28

The matching of cost and revenue has grown during the past fifteen or twenty years into a cardinal principle of accounting. We have learned to postpone or accelerate either cost or revenue, as the case might require, in order to get all the elements of a single transaction into the same period.

Myers, 1959, 528

Any income concept involves periodic matching – that is, assignment of the recognition of value changes to time periods. The objection is not to this general notion, but rather to the idea that a theory of income can be constructed around the association of specific costs with specific revenues. Matching is necessary because of the currently accepted concept of realization, not because matching itself is a concept of income.

Philips, 1963a, 15

the cost matching notion suffers from considerable confusion in its application. [Its] ... value amortization procedures .... are nearly always mathematical abstractions. Instead of reflecting the extent to which an asset has declined in exchange value, they frequently tend to reflect some notion of intrinsic value which is different from measurable exchange value, and some overriding sense of fairness, which requires that equal physical services should have assigned to them equal physical costs, regardless of what happens to their market values.

Sands, 1963, 45

Capital costs are ... neatly and systematically disposed of [by assuming a useful life for the assets and writing them off over such assumed period] and, in the process, the accountant gets around to persuading himself that his basic function is to match costs against revenues. He thus sidetracks problems of valuation by announcing that the purpose of accounting is not valuation at all, but rather the matching of costs and revenues .... this is simply an evasion of his manifest responsibility ....

Ross, 1966, 92

For a long time I've wished that the [1940] Paton and Littleton monograph (*An introduction to corporate accounting standards*) had never been written, or had gone out of print twenty five years or so ago. Listening to Bob Sprouse take issue with the matching gospel, which the P & L monograph helped to foster, confirmed my dissatisfaction with this publication.

Paton, 1971, x

the matching concept, based as it is on the preeminence of the income statement and relying heavily on subjective notions of correctness, applicability and propriety, is responsible for those unique accounting products that one so frequently finds in today's sheet of balances: deferred charges that are not assets and deferred credits that are not liabilities.

Sprouse, 1971, 93

644 Allocation

Accounts are a record of fact, and that which is incapable of separation in fact, cannot be separated by accounts.

Cooper, 1888, 743

An accounting allocation divides a monetary magnitude among recipients (inputs to the firm, accounting periods, and so forth) .... most of financial accounting's allocations are arbitrary, and this renders them useless for the general purposes which financial accounting attempts to serve.

Thomas, 1971, 472

The idea that accounting is a process of allocating costs crystallized in the 1930s. We made the concept of asset synonymous with unexpired cost and the concept of expense synonymous with expired cost. There were various methods of calculating expired and unexpired cost; we could allocate the costs by different conventional methods. This cost allocation idea is now firmly entrenched .... These concepts are not concerned with real things in the real world.

Sterling, 1976, 54

Allocation is the accounting process of assigning or distributing an amount according to a plan or formula .... examples ... include assigning manufacturing costs to production departments ... and thence to units of product ..., apportioning the cost of a basket purchase to the individual assets acquired on the basis of their market values, and spreading the cost of an insurance policy or a building to two or more periods.

FASB, 1985, SFAC6

Cost allocation is an inescapable problem in nearly every organization and in nearly every facet of accounting .... four purposes for allocating costs: economic decisions, motivation, income and asset measurement for external parties, and cost justification or reimbursement.

Horngren & Foster, 1987, 410

Allocation is the process of disaggregating a value which can only be directly attributed to a whole chain of events or to an entire asset complex ... and assigning portions of this value to parts of the chain of events or parts of the firm.

Ma & others, 1987, 232

See also 037

645 Temporal allocation

Once at least in every year the directors shall lay before the company in general meeting a statement of the income and expenditure .... The statement so made shall show ... the amount of gross income, distinguishing the several sources ..., and the amount of gross expenditure .... Every item of expenditure fairly chargeable against the year's income shall be brought into account so that a just balance of profit and loss may be laid before the meeting; and in cases where any item of expenditure which may in fairness be distributed over several years has been incurred in any one year, the whole amount of such item shall be stated, with the addition of the reasons why only a portion of such expenditure is charged against the income of the year. [Table B, Model articles of association. Also UK *Companies Act 1862*, First Schedule, Table A]

UK *Joint Stock Companies Act 1856*

there is absolutely no authority for a company to spread expenditure of any one year over succeeding years, unless expressly authorized by the articles of association.

Pixley, 1897/1978, 80

The balance sheet values of both fixed assets and stock are ... based on the ... assumption that the business will continue as a going concern .... although there may be every indication that in reality the business is tottering .... For balance sheet purposes ... expenditure may be apportioned in a balance sheet between the year under review and future years, just as if the business were certain to continue.
Carter, 1910b, 563

All income and all expenses should be correctly allocated to the periods to which they apply. In this way, the net income of the period under consideration will be properly ascertained.
Sanders & others, 1938, 25

Periodic remeasurements of recorded amounts are made to effect an equitable allocation of such amounts to the periods benefited by them.
Kester, 1946, 43

Apportionments [of income and expenditure] are based on certain well-established rules, conventions and doctrines of accounting, in the formulation of which conservatism (in its derived sense of caution) has been the over-riding consideration.
Fitzgerald & Fitzgerald, 1948, 16

Certainty assumption – It must be assumed that the future is known to the firm for certain. Only then can the allocation of costs and revenues among past, present and future periods be certain. This is necessary if the operations of a continuing firm are to be measured accurately for fiscal periods.
Edwards & Bell, 1961, 7

the determination of income is purely a matter of timing – the allocation of expense and revenue to the proper accounting period.
Graham, 1965, 660

Apportioning cost outlays between cost expirations and cost residues .... may be done ... by making computations of cost expirations (expenses) and accepting the remainder as cost residues (assets) .... [or *vice versa*].
Finney & Miller, 1968, 246

Viewed purely as a problem in measurement, the allocation of joint costs to reporting periods for matching with revenues has no meaningful solution.
Backer, 1970, 85

Prior to 1940 there was no mention of matching expenses and revenues and revenues were determined by reference to periods of time .... Paton and Littleton introduced the matching principle in 1940 ....
Most, 1977a, 287

if a resource is used for several accounting periods, the amount of its cost assigned to any one period should be in proportion to the estimated benefits provided in that period.

Anthony, 1983, 131

See also 613

646 Product and process allocation

It sometimes happens that two different commodities have what may be termed a joint cost of production . . . . Cost of production does not determine their prices, but the sum of their prices. A principle is wanting to apportion the expenses of production between the two.

Mill, 1848/1940, 569

The most common method of attaching burden . . . (contrasted with blanket methods [labor hours, wages and prime cost]) utilizes a machine rate . . . . all costs connected with land and buildings are gathered . . . ; this space cost is then apportioned to various departments . . . on square feet or cubic feet of space occupied; the shop share of space cost is then apportioned among the machines . . . in the shop; the total power costs are . . . apportioned among machines on the basis of horse-power consumption; then costs peculiar to each machine . . . are calculated . . . ; the sum of all such costs for each machine . . . is then divided by the number of working hours for the period used for figuring costs (usually a year), and the quotient is . . . the rate to be charged per hour for all product making use of this machine.

Cole, 1921, 396

in the course of a recent inspection of electrolytic caustic soda and chlorine plants . . . . The joint costs of the process up to the point of the split off of the chlorine from the soda were found to be distributed . . . . in several different ratios: 50–50, 40–60, 60–40, 39.008–35.46 (the atomic weights of sodium hydroxide and chlorine), and 56.73 to 43.27. The pseudo-mathematical precision of the last ratio had its origin in a criterion no more scientific than that of distributing the joint costs so that both the caustic and the chlorine would earn an equal book profit.

Kreps, 1930, 426

As soon as any elements other than direct material and direct labor enter into the cost of a product or article, we leave the realm of fact and certainty and enter that of opinion.

Peloubet, 1938/1982, 338

indirect manufacturing costs cannot be traced to specific orders. Indirect costs are accumulated by departments and then allocated to the jobs in process by some method of distribution that seems to charge each order with its rightful share. This involves finding a relationship between indirect manufacturing costs and some factor that can be measured by jobs. This factor might be units manufactured, material cost, labor cost, or machine hours . . . . an indirect manufacturing costs application rate . . . [may be based on] . . . maximum capacity . . . practical capacity . . . normal capacity . . . expected actual capacity for a single year . . .

> Crowningshield, 1962, 83, 175

accountants use a number of necessarily arbitrary bases for assigning overhead to units produced. Among the commonly used bases are direct labor dollars, direct labor hours, machine hours, direct labor and material costs, and contribution margin (selling price less direct costs).

> Benston, 1982, 175

indirect costs of an accounting period should be allocated to cost objects in proportion to the amount of these costs that each cost object caused. If a causal relationship cannot be established, another equitable basis of allocation should be used.

> Anthony, 1983, 131

Top managers may resort to seemingly arbitrary cost allocations, ranging from zero to a high price above full cost. Why? Because the allocation is used as a major means of getting subordinates to behave as desired by top managers.

> Horngren & Foster, 1987, 422

647 Allocation defended

Though it is true that distribution of joint costs is usually more or less arbitrary, . . . there is always a way to approximate a correct distribution, and a distribution based on a reasonable approximation is far better than one wholly arbitrary.

> Cole, 1921, 392

Despite the apparent strength of the . . . arguments against the practice of allocating overhead expenses, the fact remains that allocation is very common . . . . We should . . . expect to find that, if the logic of the practice were shaky, many businesses would have noticed bad results and vigorous criticism would have followed. But the reverse is the case . . . . many of the most successful and profitable enterprises rely on costing methods that involve allocation, and attribute their prosperity at least in part to such systems.

> Baxter, 1938, 634

Manifestly, when a laborious process of manufacture and sale culminates in the delivery of the product at a profit, that profit is not attributable, except conventionally, to the moment when the sale or delivery occurred. The accounting convention which makes such an attribution is justified only by its demonstrated practical utility.

> May, 1943, 30

For the purpose of making management decisions, arbitrary allocations of overhead to the various divisions of a company are useful because management understands that they are arbitrary and not precise. But stockholders and potential investors could easily be misled by published statements indicating that a particular product line had contributed exactly X dollars of profit or loss.

JA, editorial, 1966, 34

the fact that accounting allocations are arbitrary does not prove that accounting information is useless.

Wolk & others, 1984, 206

648 Allocation held to be unnecessary or misleading

There is nothing in business experience, or in the training of experts, which enables a man to say to what extent service life will be impaired by the operation of a single year, or of a series of years less than the service life . . . . [Justice Brandeis, dissenting]

United Railways and Electric Co v West, 1930

It may be protested that unless arbitrary allocations of departmental expenses are made it is impossible to see which department is paying best and should be expanded. This is untrue, as we test the profitability of increased output by examining marginal variations in cost and revenue. In other words, we compare increments to cost with increments to revenue, rather than totals or averages.

Edwards, 1937/1973, 83

To find the most profitable mix of products we need to equate marginal cost and marginal revenue for each product. There is no allocation of joint costs involved directly in this procedure; it has all been taken into account in calculating marginal cost.

Walters, 1960, 419

If we shift attention to decisions, then we must shift from making arbitrary allocations, since the allocations will not be the basis of decisions.

Bierman, 1963a, 63

Decision making, inventory valuation, income determination, budgeting and so on can all be accomplished without the allocation of overhead costs.

Barton, 1965, 125

In the general case . . . corporate net profits will not suffer if corporate fixed expenses are left unallocated.

Solomons, 1965, 73

Accountants, economists, and even lawyers have grappled time and again with the problem of dividing joint costs in a manner which would result in a meaningful separate cost for each joint product. The absence of success is not due to lack of effort or ingenuity but to the impossibility of the act.

Field, 1969, 90

accountants at present either amortize the costs of nonmonetary assets in an arbitrary manner, or else allocate these costs in a pattern which conforms to the pattern of the input's effects on income (or to a corresponding pattern of cash flow effects) .... the accountant first allocates income to one or more individual inputs, then uses the resulting pattern of income effects to determine a second allocation pattern, whereby the cost of the nonmonetary input is allocated to one or more years .... all of these approaches [of present allocation theory] lead to arbitrary effects if inputs interact. The accountant's allocation problem here is similar to that of one who would allocate the services of a watch to its individual parts. It is always mechanically possible to conduct some kind of allocation, but the results are apt to be meaningless.

Thomas, 1969, xiii

A great variety of individuals are affected by financial statements, and their financial interests are in conflict .... Thus, if inputs interact, financial accounting's arbitrary allocations are bound to be unsatisfactory to a large percentage of the individuals affected by the allocations.

Thomas & Basu, 1972, 322

allocated costs are not required for purposes of decision making.

Dopuch & others, 1974, 568

allocations must almost always be incorrigible – that is to say, they can neither be refuted nor verified.

Thomas, 1975, 66

For anyone engaged in cost control, the conclusion is as short as it is absolute: Thou shalt not apportion.

Harper, 1980, 87

Since there is no objective definition of systematic and rational allocation, some form of exit value may be the best approach in determining what proportion of the carrying amount of long term assets should be charged against operations during a particular reporting period.

Kay, 1981, 7.43

649 Amortization

The process of eliminating part or all of goodwill is called amortization, a term which applies to the reduction of value of any intangible asset.

Kohler & Morrison, 1926, 324

The basic idea suggested by this word [amortization] is that of reducing, redeeming or liquidating the amount of an account already in existence. In finance and accounting this word means the gradual extinguishment of an asset, a liability or a nominal account by prorating the amount of it over the period during which it will exist or its benefit will be realized.

AIA, 1931a, 9

we have used the term "amortization" to describe the processes by which the recorded valuations of assets may be allocated equitably and rationally to operations over the periods in which the assets make useful contributions to the enterprise.

Robnett & others, 1951, 345

amortization: 1. the gradual extinguishment of any amount over a period of time, as, the retirement of a debt by serial payments to the creditor or into a sinking fund; the periodic writedown of an unexpired insurance premium or bond premium. 2. A reduction in the book value of a fixed asset: a generic term for the depreciation, depletion, writedown, or writeoff of a limited life asset or group of such assets . . . .

Kohler, 1952, 26

Amortization is the accounting practice of assigning to or reassigning among the accounts, in a systematic way over several fiscal periods, an amount related to a fixed base.

Singer, 1957, 412

Amortization often is used as a general term to cover depreciation, depletion and write-downs of certain other assets.

Malchman & Slavin, 1961, 355

[The] process of transferring debits [from asset accounts to operations] . . . is usually called amortization when applied to patents, trade marks, and leaseholds, the so-called intangible assets.

Moonitz & Jordan, 1963, I:378

amortization . . . is the accounting process of reducing an amount by periodic payments or write downs . . . . examples include recognizing expenses for depreciation . . ., insurance and . . . earned subscription revenues.

FASB, 1985, SFAC6

See also 662

650 Inventory Charges

651 Cost flow assumptions

Cost for inventory purposes may be determined under any one of several presently acceptable methods of assuming the flow of cost factors (such as fifo, average, lifo or base stock), although the method which in application most closely fulfils the objective of correct income determination should be employed.

Stans, 1946, 105

We will reach more realistic conclusions as to the merits of different methods of allocating inventory costs between periods if we consider them to reflect assumptions regarding the flow of costs not necessarily related to the goods.

Blough, 1948, 206

The cost to be matched against revenue from a sale may not be the identified cost of the specific item which is sold .... Cost for inventory purposes may be determined under any one of several assumptions as to the flow of cost factors (such as first in first out, average, and last in first out); the major objective in selecting a method should be to choose the one which, under the circumstances, most clearly reflects periodic income.

AIA, 1947a, ARB29

There are a number of assumptions concerning the flow of costs that might be made. The ones that have received the greatest attention are: 1 ... that cost flow coincides with the physical flow of goods .... 2 ... that costs flow so that the resulting charge to income gives an income figure that reflects the change in disposable cash .... 3 ... that costs flow so that the resulting charge to income gives an income figure that minimizes the variations in reported income from year to year .... 4 ... that costs flow so that inventories are carried at the lowest cost for which some justification can be found .... 5 ... that costs flow so as to minimize the effect of inflation on reported profits .... 6 ... that cost flow should be determined in such a manner that no unrealized profits will be recorded .... 7 ... that the cost flow should result in the appearance of replacement cost or current cost on the income statement.

Coughlan, 1957, 435

Some assumption of the flow of units and related costs is ... necessary to assign appropriate acquisition costs (1) to the units sold during an accounting period and (2) to units remaining on hand in inventory at the end of the period .... the use of differing assumptions of cost flow may result in substantially different income determinations and asset valuations in circumstances which are substantively the same ....

Barden, 1973, 148, 74

when identical items are bought and sold, it is often impossible to tell which items have been sold and which are still in inventory .... [A cost flow assumption is made.] .... the assumed cost flow may or may not be the same as the actual goods flow .... Several assumed cost flows are acceptable under generally accepted accounting principles. In fact, it is sometimes preferable to use an assumed cost flow that bears no relationship to goods flow because it gives a better estimate of income ....

Needles & others, 1984, 399

In many organizations it is not possible to identify which particular items of stock have in fact been sold .... This problem is resolved by making an assumption about the physical flow of stock in a business .... the three most common [assumptions] are first in first out (fifo), last in first out (lifo) and weighted average.

Arnold & others, 1985, 184

Goods flow describes the actual physical movement of goods in the firm's operations .... Cost flow is the real or assumed association of unit costs with goods either sold or on hand. The assumed cost flow does not always reflect the actual goods flow .... 1. In a physical sense, specific identification best presents actual cost of goods sold. 2. Weighted average can best be associated with business operations in which like goods are commingled. 3. Fifo probably represents most accurately the actual goods flow for most firms. 4. Lifo represents the least plausible goods flow for most businesses ....

Gaffikin, 1993, 366, 370

652 Identified (actual) cost

Under this [specific identification] method each lot of material purchased or manufactured is separately identified and recorded, and marked off in the records when sold or otherwise disposed of. It is, therefore, possible to identify the goods on hand at the end of the period and obtain their exact cost from the records. This method clearly requires that each unit be physically identifiable .... The method is especially appropriate when purchases are made to cover firm sales orders. [Research department]

AIA, 1940d, 328

The most realistic procedure ... [for cost determination], would be a system of labelling or tagging each unit or particle of cost incurred in such a manner that it could be specifically traced and identified at any subsequent point in its journey – long or short – through the area of business operation .... such a procedure is impossible or impracticable .... [in respect of] fungible goods like standard liquids and other commodities that are so handled and stored that each acquisition becomes an unidentifiable element of the stock on hand.

Paton & Paton, 1952, 59

actual cost is another way of saying historical cost .... Actual costs are not to be confused with facts .... so-called actual costs contain estimates for such items as depreciation .... In part, actual costs are predetermined costs.

Crowningshield, 1962, 13

Specific identification of costs is practicable and desirable only if the inventory items are not interchangeable and are acquired or produced as units that are identifiable throughout the production and merchandising operations.

Barden, 1973, 148

An obvious way to account for inventory is through specific identification via physical observation or the labelling of items in stock with individual numbers or codes. Such an approach is easy and economically justifiable for relatively expensive merchandise like custom artwork and diamond jewellery .... specific identification requires the linkage of individual inventory items with the exact purchase costs of each unit.

Horngren, 1984, 274

653 Average cost

The average cost is recomputed after each purchase as total cost of inventory plus purchase cost of additions, divided by total units on hand and purchased. It is thus a moving average cost.

Porter & Fiske, 1935, 379

the cost of the goods on hand at the end of a period is assumed to be the weighted average of the inventory cost of the goods on hand at the beginning of the period and of all goods purchased during the period .... [Research department]

AIA, 1940d, 328

Cost is computed by averaging the amount at which stock is brought forward at the beginning of a period with the cost of stock acquired during the period; consumption in the period is then deducted at the average cost thus ascertained. The periodical rests for calculating the average are as frequent as the circumstances and nature of the business require and permit. In times of rising price levels this method [average cost] tends to give a lower amount than the cost of unsold stock ascertained on a first in, first out basis and in times of falling prices a higher amount.

ICAEW, 1960, N22

The average cost method draws costs from a common pool made up of several prices. Under the moving average method, a new average cost is computed after each purchase by dividing the total cost of the material on hand by the number of units in the inventory.

Crowningshield, 1962, 119

the term, average cost, includes two different methods. One, weighted average, is computed by dividing the total cost of beginning inventory plus purchases by the total number of units included in these two categories. The second, moving average, requires computation of a new average cost after each acquisition .... the methods do not sharply reflect the effects of price changes, weighted average being poorer in this respect than moving average.

Wixon (ed), 1962, 12.27–28

Practically all unit product cost determinations in manufacturing operations involve some degree of averaging, batching, or pooling of input costs during some specific period as part of the allocation of costs to the period's production.

Barden, 1973, 77

654 First in first out (fifo)

The first in, first out method calls for the issuance of materials at the unit cost of the oldest lot until that lot is exhausted, and then at the unit cost of the next oldest lot, and so on. The inventory is therefore taken at the unit costs of the newest lots.

Porter & Fiske, 1935, 380

This [fifo] basis assumes that goods sold or consumed were those which had been longest on hand and that the quantity held in stock represents the latest purchases. It has the effect of valuing unsold stock in a reasonably close relation to replacement price.

ICAEW, 1945b, N10

As a general rule, on a rising price market, the fifo profit calculation will always be greater than the lifo calculation; and on a falling price market the fifo profit calculation will always be the lower.

Parkinson, 1950, 211

A company which is on the fifo basis for inventory purposes will, during a period of inflation, include in its monetary profits a gain which in large part reflects only the reduced purchasing power of the dollar. A company which uses the lifo basis to a large extent excludes such profits.

Broad, 1952, 308

Under the fifo method, costs follow the physical flow of the material .... The inventory is priced at the latest costs.

Crowningshield, 1962, 117

When cost factor prices rise, fifo causes cost of sales to lag behind current market prices because charges reflect the earliest incurred costs. On the other hand, the closing inventory contains the most recent costs. If selling prices of a company's products keep pace with the prices of input cost factors, reported profits are increased by matching costs incurred at a lower price level with sales made at a higher price level. When cost factor prices fall, the effect on cost of sales and profit is reversed.

Backer, 1970, 97

The first in first out assumption of cost flow is recognized intuitively as being generally consistent with the physical flow of material and production processes and with the physical flow of products and goods in most merchandising operations.

Barden, 1973, 76

655 Base stock

Some writers recommended the systematic use of the "normal inventory" method as a means of securing truer accounting statements, more appropriate taxes and dividends, and greater safety in the efforts to preserve capital . . . . This method was a variant of the well known "base stock" method. It was used in Sweden as early as 1800 . . . . It came . . . to be used in not only Europe . . . but also in the United States . . . .

Sweeney, 1936/1964, 169–170

In certain businesses the original investment in inventories has every investment characteristic of a fixed asset . . . . [The books and financial statements of such businesses] should show their inventories on a basis of normal stocks at fixed prices so that the management and public may get a true view of the position of the company and its realized, distributable net income, unaffected by any marking up or down of a fixed asset.

Peloubet, 1929/1982, 573

the base stock method . . . that part of the stock which is regarded as being the normal quantity necessary for the effective operation of the business is carried in the accounts at a low basic price and is retained at that price irrespective of market fluctuations.

Lawson, 1951, 312

In some businesses the minimum quantity of raw materials or other goods, without which they cannot operate their plant or conduct their operations, is treated as being a fixed asset which is under constant renewal by charges to revenue; that part of their stock (the base stock) is therefore carried forward not at its cost at the date of the accounts but at the cost of the original quantity of stock with which the business commenced operation. In old established businesses the amount will be based on prices paid for stocks acquired many years previously and many times replaced.

ICAEW, N22, 1960

Lifo evolved from the base stock method which has long been used in Great Britain . . . . The base stock method differs from lifo principally in that the base stock method treats a portion of the inventory as a permanent asset which is stated at constant and largely arbitrary cost.

Backer, 1970, 98

Base stock: the calculation of the cost of stocks and work in progress on the basis that a fixed unit value is ascribed to a predetermined number of units of stock, any excess over this number being valued on the basis of some other method.

ASSC, 1975b, SSAP9

Base stock assumes that a minimum quantity of stock valued at the cost ruling at the time the method was first adopted, must be held in order to carry on the business

.... this stock ... should be considered as a fixed asset, as essential as the [processing plant] itself, except that its actual physical composition is always changing .... [Its effect is to secure] matching current costs against the related current revenue.

Hardy, 1976, 181

656 Last in first out (lifo)

The prime purpose of the last in, first out principle ... is to bring about, in the determination of profits in the financial accounts, a substantial correlation between sales prices and those raw material prices which have been directly causative of such sales prices.

AIA, 1936a/1948a, 110

About the same time [1930s], the Petroleum Institute sought recognition of the practice of carrying inventories on what is called the ... lifo basis. This was accepted in the Revenue Act of 1938 as one measure of cost on condition that it was used also in the taxpayer's general financial accounts.

May, 1948b, 17

Lifo neither came into being nor obtained its present prominence as a result of inflationary conditions. It was used by several large and representative enterprises in the 1920s and earlier, not under that particular name but as a type of base stock ....

Peloubet, 1948, 299

The base stock method was disallowed [for tax purposes in the US in 1930] because it contained an arbitrary price applied to an arbitrary quantity. Lifo, which in effect legalizes the base stock idea, defines the acceptable quantity as the quantity on hand at the end of the year equal to the beginning quantity and calls for pricing that quantity at cost.

McAnly, 1953, 694

[The popularity of lifo] rests solely on the unique provision of the Internal Revenue Code requiring the use of lifo in all published statements and reports if a taxpayer wishes to use lifo for tax purposes.

Moonitz, 1953, 690

When cost factor prices rise, lifo causes cost of sales to be charged with the most recent or highest costs .... lifo ... tends to normalize or smooth income fluctuations induced by fluctuations in factor prices where other cost flow methods are used .... Lifo came into widespread use with the period of rising prices which began with World War II after changes in the US tax law made the method permissible for determining taxable income.

Backer, 1970, 98

The last in first out assumption of cost flow is seldom justified as following the physical flow of merchanise. Year end inventory quantities that equal those on hand at the beginning of the year are priced at the beginning of the year cost basis. Year end quantities that exceed those at the beginning of the year are priced at a basis reflecting current year cost incurrence. The effect on income is to match latest incurred production or merchandise cost against the current year's sales revenue.

Barden, 1973, 76

Lifo and the cost rule

the choice between lifo and fifo is still a choice between historical cost methods . . . [not] a valuation at current prices.

Dean, 1951, 23

the lifo convention . . . . says nothing about any costs that have not actually been incurred . . . . the lifo principle is not a replacement or current cost principle; lifo merely rearranges the costs actually incurred without undertaking to anticipate any future costs of replacement.

McNair & Hersum, 1952, 332

Under existing tax regulations, lifo is a cost method; a taxpayer who elects lifo must stay on lifo.

Moonitz, 1953, 685

lifo implies a departure from cost incurred in favor of replacement cost of current cost. Nevertheless, the departure has been accomplished in such a manner that students of inventory accounting are apparently convinced that no departure from cost incurred is involved.

Coughlan, 1957, 434

The essence of lifo is that it allocates historical cost in a special way, but note carefuly that it is historical cost that is allocated.

Lindsay & Sametz, 1963, 137

Probably all can agree that it is not really proper to characterize lifo as an historical cost method of inventory valuation. In fact, it is not an inventory valuation method at all; it is ordinarily advocated only as a method of measuring the cost of goods sold.

Sprouse, 1963, 693

lifo . . . . is inconsistent with the principles of historic cost accounting, which endeavor to measure historic costs rather than current costs.

Martin, 1984, 316

Posited merits of lifo

The significance of the recognition [by Congress in the 1939 revenue act] of the last in first out method .... [is that it shows] profits as realized rather than as indicated by marking up and marking down quantities of inventories permanently carried .... [showing] as nearly as may be only such profits as are actually realized.

Peloubet, 1939/1982, 75

for inventory accounting the current cost position (at least as approximated by lifo) does not charge income with more than the actual dollar costs incurred by the business. It simply reallocates the order in which purchases and other inventory costs are charged against sales.

Butters, 1949, 138

there appears to be general support at the present time for the view that the lifo procedure represents a practical way of matching current revenues with current costs.

Broad, 1950b, 231

Lifo ... tends to wash out the paper profits that result from comparing a closing inventory with an equal opening inventory stated at different prices.

Dean, 1951, 23

The attraction of lifo is that it matches current sales revenue with current, or very recent, costs of items sold, thus ensuring that reported profits make due allowance for the replacement of inventories without fresh infusions of capital.

Carscallen, 1977, 28

Critical comment on lifo

Lifo seems to us to be perilously like an attempt to reflect things as one would like them to be rather than as they are. In effect it charges production with a figure approximating to the cost of replacing the goods that production consumes and is not disturbed if, in consequence, the balance sheet carries for ever the cost of goods purchased on the first day when business was opened. If we correctly interpret the conception, it carries the double account view of accounting into the whole field of assets, both current and fixed.

Accountant, editorial, 1945, 318

the adoption of lifo has involved acceptance of the view that a meaningless figure in the balance sheet (for inventories) is not too high a price to pay for a more informative income figure ....

May, 1947b, 456

To justify the lifo method on the basis of the flow of goods, or even on a flow of costs, is pure sophistry. It is an abortive attempt to appear to remain on a past cost basis while actually departing from it in favor of current costs.
Graham, 1949, 23

The salient effect of lifo is the smoothing of reported profits in the face of continued changes in prices.
Moonitz, 1953, 690, 686

The Federal income tax is, more than any other factor, responsible for the wide adoption of lifo, with its attendant calamitous effect on the balance sheet.
Taggart, 1953, 301

If you tell me you are for lifo because it reduces taxes ... I will respect that for an honest opinion. If you tell me you are for lifo because it is an income smoothing device ... I recognize the usefulness of averages. I cannot respect the logic of the argument that lifo results in a more realistic, more accurate, more truthful, or more factual presentation of periodic business financial information.
Johnson, 1954, 26

Replacement cost has been widely adopted for accounting purposes. Lifo and accelerated amortization are the means by which replacement cost methods are introduced into the income statement. The price of paying lip service to original cost has been the meaningless balance sheet that resulted.
Coughlan, 1957, 466

Although lifo improves the measurement of profit, it results in a balance sheet figure for inventories that can severely distort the apparent financial position of the company.
Carscallen, 1977, 28

lifo ... provides a proxy for current values in the income statement but erroneous values in the balance sheet, and fifo ... yields the reverse.
Rutherford & Boys, 1977, 261

657 Other cost-based methods

Highest in, first out

Hifo, the highest in, first out method, is a modification of lifo .... It uses the highest lot cost in inventory in costing out sales, regardless of price trends, and thereby tends to reflect remaining inventories at the lowest cost. In certain mining, refining and processing industries it finds some acceptance ....
Stempf, 1943/1947, 337

The hifo method is based on the generally acceptable idea that every enterprise must try to get rid of the heaviest risks as quickly as possible by charging out the most expensive items first . . . .

JA, Anon, 1947, 337

Retail inventory method

[The retail method] consists in compiling the inventory at retail and determining cost of goods on hand through a deduction based on records of markups, markdowns, and other adjustments.

Paton (ed), 1944, 574

[The adjusted selling price] method is widely used in retail businesses. The cost of stock is estimated by calculating it in the first instance at selling prices and then deducting an amount equal to the normal margin of gross profit on such stocks . . . . The calculations under this method may be made for individual items or groups of items or by departments.

ICAEW, 1960, N22

In department store type operations, specific identification of merchandise costs becomes impracticable because of large volumes of merchandise sold in small quantities at varying rates of turnover . . . . The retail inventory method . . . . consists essentially of the accumulation of the retail selling value of all items entering into the departmental merchandising operations in a manner that enables a reduction of the retail amounts of sales output and remaining inventories to a cost basis through the application of average departmental gross mark up percentages.

Barden, 1973, 153

The retail method is essentially an averaging method that results in a valuation at cost or market, whichever is lower . . . . the cost of the ending inventory can be determined without reference to detailed purchase information . . . and without the necessity of a physical inventory at cost. Basically, the only requirement is the computation of the relationship of cost to retail price and the application of this percentage to the retail inventory as indicated by the company's inventory records, periodically verified by actual count.

Bohan & Styczenski, 1981, 19.20

660 Depreciation and Appreciation

661 Causes of depreciation

Much depends upon the character of the business or class of trade; whether it be financial, commercial or manufacturing: in the one, the depreciation will arise principally from shrinkage or falling off in market value of the securities and investments; while in the others, property such as plant . . . etc. will form the more important items upon which depreciation, in the way of wear and tear, will have to be calculated.

Whatley, 1893, 23

this fall [in exchangeable value of industrial plant, depreciation] is due to natural decay, wear and tear, and obsolescence, and to all or any of these causes.

Leake, 1912/1976, 77

The value of all physical property tends to decrease owing to such causes as use, abuse, oxidation, deterioration, disintegration, inadequacy, obsolescence and even change of ownership . . . . Since the passing of physical property is inevitable, provision for its loss should be made from . . . profits. The accounting term used to denote this charge . . . is depreciation.

Wildman, 1914/1980, 129

Depreciation may be due to wear and tear, decrepitude, obsolescence, inadequacy, accidents, diseases, or diminution of supply of the object in question . . . . exhaustion of mineral deposits . . . . the passage of time.

Reiter, 1926/1976, 15

Depreciation, in its true business and accounting sense, means the decrease in value of fixed assets due to expiration of time, wear and tear, obsolescence and inadequacy.

Grady, 1938/1982, 13

there is often a real distinction (not, unfortunately, observed by accountants) between economic life and physical life. Only the former is of interest to investors, It is not age that obsoletes capital assets, but the accumulation of competing assets. Shifts in demand are perhaps the most visible and obvious cause of changes in the scarcity of capital assets . . . but the shifts in supply resulting from the formation of new assets are the most predictable and the most relentless.

Traynor, 1976, 4

Depreciation is a measure of the wearing out, consumption or other loss of value of a fixed asset whether arising from use, effluxion of time or obsolescence through technology and market changes. Depreciation should be allocated to accounting periods so as to charge a fair proportion to each accounting period during the expected useful life of the asset.

ASC, 1977, SSAP12

Such a metaphor [that fixed assets or their value are consumed] is not merely inept; it is positively misleading, because it gives the impression that the main cause of depreciation is to do with the use of the asset, whereas in most cases the main cause is external to such use . . . . mainly by external technological progress [in electricity generation, shipping, oil refining, the chemical industry, gas supply, the pharmaceutical industry, spinning and weaving, food processing, printing (the list is long). . . .]

Rudd, 1979, 54

662 Depreciation as decline in market price or value in exchange

The direct way of determining the depreciation or appreciation of the assets of an undertaking would *prima facie* appear to be by means of a revaluation of all the properties at periodical times . . . . But this method would in the majority of trades lead to such enormous fluctuations in the profit and loss account, especially if based upon the market prices of the properties . . . that, except in a few trades, it would be impracticable.

Garcke & Fells, 1893/1976, 98

In its true commercial sense the word depreciation means fall in exchangeable value of wasting assets, computed on the basis of cost expired during the period of their use in seeking profits, increase, or other advantage.

Leake, 1912/1976, 9

a machine after ten years of use may . . . perform the same kind of work as at the beginning, yet its usefulness to the organization may have passed away and its value, therefore, has decreased from cost price to whatever price may be obtained for it. This decrease in value is usually referred to as depreciation.

Couchman, 1924, 49

In its true commercial sense the word, depreciation, means fall in exchangeable value of wasting assets, computed on the basis of cost expired during the period of their use in seeking profits, increase of value, or other advantage.

Pixley, 1926, I:399

In the popular and literal sense the word [depreciation] signifies a shrinkage in value (that is to say in exchange value) but in accounting it has a quasi-technical meaning subtly though completely different.

Smails, 1927, 104

If a depreciation method is to be helpful, it must show . . . how much of the firm's wealth is consumed in a period and how much remains at the end . . . . this is precisely what is done by the market for worn assets.

Baxter, 1971, 31

Depreciation is the decline in the exit value of productive assets.

Sterling, 1979, 75

Depreciation as decline in value or wealth

Depreciation . . . . in respect of capital . . . is the measure, as between an earlier and a later date, of the reduction in value of any given property.

Guthrie, 1903–04, II:357

Depreciation is the loss of value in physical property, tangible or intangible in form, resulting from the action of physical and non-physical agencies.
Mann, 1917, 107

Depreciation is the gradual decrease in value of an asset from any cause.
Carter, 1923, 600

Allowance for the depreciation of an asset .... is a method by which the cost of the change from value new to scrap value is distributed over the service life of an asset.
Scott, 1925, 210

The calculation of depreciation may be accomplished without double entry book-keeping by revaluing the particular asset; and in the isolated instances where depreciation appears in early accounts and textbooks such depreciation represents value declines determined in that way.
Yamey, 1940, 340

the commonsense approach to depreciation views it not as an item in the accounting record but as an objective phenomenon – as a change in the value of assets which takes place regardless of whether or not it is reflected in the accounts.
Scott, 1945, 313

When a fixed asset is acquired it represents a stock of future services to the owning corporation. That stock of services is drawn upon as the asset is used .... Since accounting must be based on money equivalents or values, it is most convenient to refer to this phenomenon as decline in value.
Ladd, 1963, 83

Depreciation is simply the diminution in value of an asset from any cause by reason of its use.
Beacham, 1964, 46

Depreciation may be defined as the permanent and continuing diminution in the quality, quantity, or value of an asset.
Pickles, 1974, 0701

Depreciation is the measure of the wearing out, consumption or other loss of value of a fixed asset whether arising from use, effluxion of time or obsolescence through technology and market changes.
ASC, 1977, SSAP12

Depreciation not used, in accounting, of decline in value

any association of depreciation with evaluation should be avoided .... Depreciation is the prime cost of the service rendered by a fixed asset during any accounting period and is in the same ratio to the original cost of the asset as is the quantity of service rendered during that accounting period to the total service of which the asset is estimated to be capable.

Smails, 1927, 105

to explain depreciation as a part of the cost of the equipment now to be "attached" to the product and taken by the customer .... is more rational than the valuation of assets explanation of depreciation.

Littleton, 1934, 344

Depreciation, as used in accounting, means the exhaustion of service units embodied in fixed assets. Despite its etymological derivation, it does not refer to a decline in market price, nor to the deterioration of merchandise on hand.

Hatfield & others, 1940, 304

Definitions which imply that depreciation for the year is a measurement, expressed in monetary terms, of the physical deterioration or of the decline in value within the year, or, indeed, of anything that actually occurs within the period, are unacceptable.

AIA, 1943, ARB 20

Depreciation is the decline in plant capital during a given interval resulting from the expiration of service content or remaining useful life.

Trumbull, 1958, 26

The term depreciation literally means decline in value .... [But it is] not the object of depreciation accounting to measure resale value or value in exchange of fixed assets.

Moonitz & Jordan, 1963, I:378

Depreciation reflects the estimated expiration of service potential of the asset.

AAA, 1964a, 695

Depreciation is basically expired utility ....

Kohler, 1965a, 78

Some assets give up their services gradually rather than all at once. Such assets are reported on the balance sheet at their original cost, less an allowance for depreciation. The allowance for depreciation represents the cost of the portion of the asset's anticipated lifetime services that has already been used up. To measure this, the accountant must try to predict both how long the asset will continue to provide useful services and how much of its potential to provide these services will be used up in any one period. [per G Sh]

Enc Britannica, 1981, I:38

depreciation is not a process of valuation .... through an advantageous buy and specific market conditions, the market value of a building may rise. Nevertheless, depreciation must continue to be recorded because it is the result of an allocation, not a valuation process. Eventually the building will wear out or become obsolete regardless of interim fluctuations in market value.

Needles & others, 1984, 462

Depreciation accounting as cost amortization

[The amount written off for depreciation] is usually a percentage on the cost . . . , the object being to charge the revenue account of the period with a proper sum for the usage of the plant and for the balance to represent its present value.

Pixley, 1881/1976, 118

If the realizable value at the end of the assumed period of life is to be assumed [in depreciation calculations], why is not this, the principle of valuation, to apply at every rest or period throughout the life? . . . . such would not be a true system of interim assessment . . . . the method of treatment is as of a going concern. Otherwise . . . a depreciation of 50 per cent would probably not be sufficient to represent the realizable value at the end of the first year. Manifestly the career of the business contemplated must have an assumed term, and the cost of the consumption of machinery and other erections must be attributed to the whole term assumed.

Guthrie, 1883, 7

The function of depreciation is recognized by most accountants as the provision of the means for spreading equitably the cost of comparatively long-lived assets . . . . at the time of abandonment the cost of the asset shall as nearly as possible have been charged off as expense under some systematic method.

Daniels, 1933, 303

The accountant's valuation of physical assets at any given point of time involves the determination of what part of original cost should be written off to reflect consumed, expired or lost usefulness, and what part should be carried forward as reasonably applicable to future operations.

AAA, 1936/1957b, 61

The term depreciation, in its most significant use, designates the expiration of the cost of buildings and equipment in the course of business operation.

Paton, 1941, 256

Depreciation accounting . . . aims to distribute the cost or other basic value of tangible capital assets over the estimated useful life of the unit . . . in a systematic and rational manner . . . . the meaning of the word [depreciation] is sharply distinguished from the sense of fall in value in which the word is employed in common usage and in respect of some assets (e.g. marketable securities) in accounting.

AIA, 1943, ARB20

the usual over-concrete view of asset figures has led many to think of a depreciation charge as being an allowance for diminution in market value rather than the amortization of expenditure incurred . . . . The use of the word depreciation is responsible for this. The word seems to relate to market value. The market value of a building will sometimes appreciate and sometimes depreciate . . . . in this sense depreciation is not a continuous process. Periodical depreciation of a figure of cost is an absurdity; had the word amortization been more generally used by accountants, it might have prevented market value from becoming a factor occasionally invoked in the charging (or rather, not charging) of capital expenditures to revenue.

Norris, 1946, 49

The accepted view of depreciation regards it as a process of cost allocation.

Coutts (ed), 1960b, 53

depreciation takes place even when plant is functioning perfectly and even if its realizable value rises to many times its original cost. The charge for depreciation is intended . . . to allocate to successive periods a proportionate part of the cost which cannot be wholly charged against the revenue of the period in which it is actually incurred.

Beacham, 1964, 46

Fixed assets are normally recorded in the books at cost and periodical allowances made for that cost; this allowance is the depreciation, amortization or depletion.

Garbutt (ed), 1969, 0601

Depreciation is the allocation of the depreciable amount of an asset over its estimated useful life . . . . Depreciable amount of a depreciable asset is its historical cost or other amount substituted for historical cost in the financial statements, less the estimated residual value.

IASC, 1976, IAS4

Provision for depreciation of fixed assets having a finite useful life should be made by allocating the cost (or revalued amount) less estimated residual values of the assets as fairly as possible to the periods expected to benefit from their use. Where there is a revision of the estimated useful life of an asset, the unamortized cost should be charged over the revised remaining useful life. However, if at any time the unamortized cost of an asset is seen to be irrecoverable in full, it should be written down immediately to the estimated recoverable amount which should be charged over the remaining useful life.

ASC, 1977, SSAP12

663 Depreciation charges related to nominal capital maintenance

the ordinary [cost based] depreciation method is concerned with maintenance of nominal, monetary capital; the stabilized type with preservation of real, economic capital; and the reproductive cost type with keeping physical, material capital intact.

Sweeney, 1931, 174

A further purpose [of the accounting provision for depreciation] is to maintain the capital investment intact.

Sanders & others, 1938, 31

The view is frequently held that the chief purpose of depreciation and the necessity for considering it are to maintain intact the amount of the original capital invested.

Kester, 1946, 258

See also 714

Depreciation charges related to maintenance of "real capital"

[Management must] recognize that successful and continuous operation requires the recovery of the physical plant which must be replaced in the future. In other words, the real capital invested measured in terms of the prevailing price level must be maintained.

Hull, 1927, 305

Depreciation based on reproductive cost is . . . objectionable. The fundamental reason . . . is that such a method endeavors to maintain visible, instead of real, economic, general purchasing power, capital. Consequently, the result may be physically to preserve capital whose worth in the general system of values is itself declining or rising.

Sweeney, 1931, 173

To charge depreciation on the replacement cost of assets, even when the assets are not going to be replaced, is simply a rough and ready way of maintaining real capital intact, and not just money capital.

Solomons, 1948/1950, 365

The [recommended] principles relating to the maintenance of real capital [include the following]: . . . Provision for the replacement of [tangible or nonmonetary] assets and materials should be made by a charge included in the costs of the sale of goods or the provision of services . . . . The replacement cost used for calculating the amount charged in costs should be the current (or notional) cost of replacement . . . . Any failure on the part of previous charges to provide the full current replacement cost should be made good by an appropriation of profit.

ICWA, 1952, 61

The owners of a business, when originally subscribing to it or when subsequently increasing their subscriptions out of profits, take up the ownership of physical assets. It is reasonable therefore that their interest should be kept equal in real value to that of the assets they have owned. This does not imply that the physical assets must be kept intact. It does mean that, since the deduction from current revenue should be sufficient to maintain the real value of those assets, the charge for their use in any operating period must be computed on present values.

Little, 1952, 860

Ideally, the depreciation charge should maintain intact the real capital resources, or productive capacity of the enterprise. However, this may be difficult if prices rise continually over a number of accounting periods. To maintain the real value of capital it would be necessary to base depreciation on the replacement value at the time when the asset is replaced. This is not known in advance, and the only practicable alternative would be to [charge in any period]: (a) depreciation based on the current replacement value of the asset; plus (b) the amount by which previous depreciation charges . . . have been insufficient to provide for replacement on the basis of current values . . . . [But to include (b)] would seriously distort the measurement of current income . . . . For purposes of estimating current income, therefore, depreciation must be restricted to (a) above.

Mathews & Grant, 1958, 11

See also 753

664 Depreciation charges said to be related to replacement

Inasmuch as any machine or building . . . is bound to eventually arrive at the point when it . . . either requires entire reconstruction or is fit only for the junk heap . . . it is self-evident that its cost should have been all charged off against operating, or what is equivalent thereto, a reserve sufficient for its renewal or replacement set up, by the time its usefulness has expired.

Staub, 1909, 403

if the whole of the profits of a business are withdrawn without providing for the loss arising through depreciation, no moneys will be accumulated out of revenue during the life of the asset for the purpose of replacement. When such replacement becomes necessary, fresh capital will have to be provided for the purpose.

Spicer & Pegler, 1914, 135

Unless assets are depreciated . . . on the balance sheet their value will be overstated . . . . Secondly . . . loss . . . through wear and tear is undoubtedly a loss incurred in the earning of . . . income . . . . Thirdly, if depreciation is not provided for by charges against revenue, additional capital would have to be raised whenever the necessity of replacing the asset arose.

Carter, 1923, 600

in view of the fact that all businesses are, or are intended to be continuing concerns, it is the provision of replacement funds that is the important aspect of the depreciation provision . . . . If the value of money (. . . in terms of the goods it will purchase) remains stable . . . the funds available as a result of the recovery of original cost will be sufficient to replace the asset; but where inflation occurs . . . these funds will not be sufficient for replacement . . . .

Humphreys, 1940, 644

Depreciation and replacement as distinct phenomena

Charging depreciation does not necessarily provide for the replacement of the wasting article – it simply means that there has been a decline in the value of certain assets; consequently, if the capital is to be kept intact, there must be an increase in some of the others.

Parton, 1911/1988, 140

It is a common custom to describe the annual provision for depreciation . . . as a provision for future renewals, as though it has reference to the future; but this is surely a misconception. The annual provision for depreciation has nothing to do with the future but relates solely to the past. It is a replacement of capital in respect of past capital outlay expired . . . .

Leake, 1912/1976, 76

The measure most commonly invoked, when it is proposed to adjust depreciation for inflation, is command over the same kind or kinds of goods that are currently undergoing depreciation . . . . The proper measure of purchasing power for our purpose is not power for self-duplication [replacement in kind]; it is power to command goods and services generally . . . . In our view, the goal [of depreciation policy] is recovery of capital, not physical replacement of the asset. Depreciation policy has nothing to do with the subsequent expenditure or reinvestment of the funds recovered.

Terborgh, 1947/1962, 327

The replacement of machinery or any other asset is a financial problem, not a question of profit determination.

Irish, 1948, 409

The provision of funds for replacement is a matter of business policy quite unconnected with annual charges for depreciation.

Ashley, 1950, 174

Depreciation and replacement are essentially independent phenomena, related only by the fact that replacement would not be necessary if assets did not depreciate.

Jones, 1956, 80

expenses and decisions to replace should not be linked to each other . . . because depreciation charges are made long before replacement occurs and replacement itself seldom means replacement in kind because of technological change . . . .

Edwards & Bell, 1961, 162

The actual replacement of fixed assets is essentially a financial and investment problem not necessarily related to the depreciation charges made against income in the past.

Popoff, 1973, 11

665 Depreciation distinguished from price fluctuations

[Whole life depreciation of industrial plant is] wholly unaffected by fluctuations in the market price of similar property during the period of its use.

Leake, 1912/1976, 77

The term depreciation is usually understood to convey permanent shrinkage in value. Temporary shrinkage in value has been termed fluctuation.

Spicer & Pegler, 1914, 137

Depreciation denotes a permanent decrease in value; fluctuation indicates merely a temporary decrease or increase in value; . . . .

Carter, 1923, 600

depreciation must be differentiated from fluctuation, not only because the latter is temporary, but because it may signify an increase in the value of an asset. Speaking generally, the question of fluctuation confines itself to the money value aspect.

Pickles, 1974, 701

Price fluctuations to be disregarded

fluctuation is something altogether apart from profit and loss, being merely an accidental variation (owing to external causes) in the value of certain property owned, but not traded in: to carry the amount of such variation to profit and loss account would be to disturb and obscure the results of actual trading, and so render statistical comparison difficult, if not impossible. On no account, therefore, should the results of fluctuations affect the profit and loss account.

Dicksee, 1892/1976, 121

where an asset has been purchased for the purpose of producing an income, and not for the purpose of resale, it comes clearly under the head of fixed assets, and no fluctuations can have any bearing on its book value.

Teichmann, 1906, 102

The justification for . . . ignoring fluctuations in the value of capital assets is that these assets have been acquired, and are being retained permanently, not with a view to their eventually being realized at a profit in the ordinary course of business, but with a view to their being used for the purpose of enabling trading profits to be made in other ways.

Dicksee, 1911, 5

in writing off depreciation, no regard need be taken to fluctuation in the market price of similar plant, whether such price be either up or down. The particular plant is held as a fixed asset, and is not held with a view to resale, but with a view to earning income by the use thereof during its working life. Therefore, as a going concern, all that is necessary . . . is that the net cost should be written off over the working life . . . . the earning capacity of the particular plant is absolutely unaffected by the market price of similar machinery . . . .
de Paula, 1912, 905–6

it is ordinarily improper to alter the original cost to show either appreciation or depreciation in value where the change arises from fluctuations in market price, except in the case of depreciated inventories . . . .
Guthmann, 1925/1929, 20

The justification for ignoring fluctuations in exchange value of fixed assets lies . . . in the fact that as the cost of the service rendered from time to time is set off against the current market value of those services (as reflected in the selling price of the commodity produced) the realized portion of the rise or fall in exchange value is automatically and equitably amortized and adjusted in the proprietorship account.
Smails, 1927, 105

The amount which a particular asset will bring on the market is usually regarded as its value; . . . . It is not customary, in the case of a fixed asset, to change its book value because of an increase or decrease in its market value. It is customary to continue charging depreciation according to the original cost and the use value.
Bell & Graham, 1936, 322

The market values of similar machinery may be disregarded; for the plant of a manufacturer is held solely for the purpose of manufacturing for the whole of such asset's working life, and this period is unaffected by fluctuations in prices. The break up or realizable values are also disregarded, for this asset is not held with a view to resale.
de Paula, 1942, 148

666 Formal methods of charging or providing for depreciation

[Among other methods] by charging to revenue each year . . . the difference between the book value of the asset and its actual value at the present time, as ascertained by a revaluation made by an expert valuer. This . . . method, while theoretically the most perfect, as enabling the assets to be brought into the balance sheet on a more theoretically correct basis of valuation, is as a rule very defective in practice, on account of the uneven sums that it charges against revenues from year to year in respect of practically identical services . . . .
Dicksee, 1911, 256

In assessing annual depreciation ... by far the nearest approach to accuracy will be obtained by estimating the whole life period ... of each class of industrial plant, with due regard to all known facts, as well as future probabilities, and distributing the cost, less estimated scrap value, to future revenue accounts, in equal instalments over each year of that estimated whole life period.

Leake, 1912/1976, 73

the principal methods of providing for depreciation, where it is desired that the amount set aside should be accumulated in the business [are]: the fixed instalment system, or straight line method . . . . the reducing instalment system . . . . the annuity system . . . . Where it is desirable to accumulate moneys outside the business, . . . the principal methods [are]: the depreciation fund system . . . . the insurance policy system . . . . In cases where the nature of the asset renders it difficult to provide for depreciation on a mathematical basis, revaluation should be resorted to.

Spicer & Pegler, 1914, 137

To determine the amount to be written off annually there are several methods at hand, namely, the fixed percentage, the fractional method with weighted years, declining balance unscientific, declining balance scientific, sinking fund and revaluation . . . . at best depreciation is only an estimate.

Wildman, 1914/1980, 129

There are seven different methods of charging or providing for depreciation: – (1) fixed instalment method. (2) diminishing or reducing balance method. (3) annuity system. (4) depreciation fund method. (5) insurance policy system. (6) revaluation process. (7) to charge one sum to cover repairs, renewals and depreciation.

Carter, 1923, 601

The principal methods used in the United States in providing for the exhaustion of property are, briefly, . . . 1. retirement and renewal method followed by most railroads . . . . 2. retirement reserve method followed by a considerable portion of the public utility industry . . . . 3. the straight line method . . . probably more generally used in the United States than any other method . . . . 4. the production method . . . [provisions being] made a function of units produced . . . . 5. the sinking fund method . . . based upon the expected life of the property . . . [and] compound inteest . . . . 6. the diminishing balance method . . . used more widely in England than in America . . . .

Grady, 1938/1982, 13

667 Conventional depreciation methods conjectural and arbitrary

Depreciation was not regularly and periodically charged to profits by most firms during the nineteenth century. During this period there is no evidence that indicates [that] any sustained effort was made to charge the cost of an asset to profits during the time in which the asset was in use. Provision for depreciation would sometimes be made for a year or two but these charges were frequently discontinued or were made only in "good" years. In addition, the bookkeeping methods employed enabled the amounts actually charged to depreciation to be restored to profits.

Brief, 1964/1976, 178

"Fourteenth of March, I *think* it was," the Mad Hatter said.
"Fifteenth," said the March Hare.
"Sixteenth," said the Dormouse.
"Write that down," the King said to the jury; and the jury eagerly wrote down all three dates on their slates, and then added them up, and reduced the answer to shillings and pence.
I think that is how depreciation charges are calculated . . . .

Fabricant, 1948/1982, 20

For the past hundred years, accountants have been searching for the true depreciation method which would allocate the cost of a machine over its lifetime in accordance with the rate at which it is actually being used up. They have reluctantly concluded that there is no true depreciation method, and that all the methods used or proposed are merely conventions, the choice between which is a matter of convenience.

Lutz & Lutz, 1951, 7

Depreciation means different things to different people . . . . As a concept, depreciation may be broadened or narrowed to support almost any reasonable theory by merely constructing a definition which describes the idea held by the particular writer.

Parker, 1959, 427

all these methods are conventional and arbitrary . . . . there is no one ultimately right way to establish the true amount of depreciation.

Ross, 1966, 43

present accounting literature includes five main kinds of approaches to depreciation . . . . Insofar as cost accumulation and matching involve allocation of nonmonetary economic goods, these allocations presently are almost always arbitrary; no general solution to this problem is possible within the framework of present allocation theory and present conventional rules.

Thomas, 1969, 25, 77

the usual rule of thumb methods [of calculating depreciation charges] use estimates of life span and scrap proceeds; and, in fact, they rely also on sweeping assumptions about the future – all the more dangerous because they have never been spelled out.

Baxter, 1975, 149

Before the true depreciable cost can be determined, an estimate of the scrap or trade-in value of the asset must be made. This estimate involves a forecast or prediction both as to length of service life and as to future prices.

Moonitz & Jordan, 1963, I:386

The accountants . . . often end up settling on whatever method of depreciation has been accepted for tax purposes . . . . it is not unusual to find precision machine tools actively in use 30 to 40 years after they have been acquired . . . . [compared with] Internal Revenue Service "guideline lives" of 12 years and IRS "asset depreciation range" minimum of 9.5 years for companies in the metal fabricating industry.

Rickover, 1973/1977, 1716, 1717

an examination of the plant register of one of [a chemical] company's main operations revealed 53% of the items of plant still in use were fully written off. On an insured value basis these zero book value assets accounted for 38% of the total.

Peasnell, 1977, 129

All methods [of calculating depreciation] are equally arbitrary, whether based on years of useful life, units of output, hours of production or even estimated net revenues.

Most, 1977a, 289

668 Appreciation

The argument may be urged that there is a certain appreciation of values which offsets . . . depreciation. Such a claim as applied to a statement of current operations, is, of course, absurd and will hardly be considered seriously by an accountant.

Montgomery, 1904/1980, 132

An appreciation may and usually does take place because of a change of ownership [of an asset as it passes along a distribution chain] . . . . Changes in general or trade conditions will also produce appreciation of values.

Herr, 1906, 2

A rise in the cost of replacement . . . . This is appreciation.

Paton, 1918/1976, 44

Since value and price are constantly changing, either from changes in the relative value of goods or from changes in the value of money, it is almost physically impossible for accounting to keep a record of all of them. The accounting records show values that were true at one particular time, but which are not continuously true. The increasing attention being paid to the problem of accounting for appreciation is partly due to the attempt to make accounting continuously exact instead of historically exact.

Carpenter, 1930, 10

Appreciation is an accretion to the value of an asset not attributable to an expenditure but rather to a present or prospective increase in its relative financial productiveness ... We cannot agree ... that appreciation should not be recognized in the books of account. To take the position that closed transactions only are entitled to recognition is to narrow the function of accounting unduly and gainsay many of the well-settled practices.

Wildman, 1930, 3, 34

stabilized accounting .... prefers to limit the meaning of appreciation to an increase in the general purchasing power that the particular asset can command, or, in other words, to a growth in the individual value of the asset greater than that experienced by all goods in general.

Sweeney, 1932, 115

Appreciation .... 5. rise in exchangeable value.

SOED, 1936

Appreciation ... means a permanent increase in the value of an asset,

Garbutt (ed), 1969, 0602

See also 582

669 Appreciation regarded as gain or profit

In *Robinson v Ashton* (20 Eq. 28) Sir G Jessel said: "the rise or fall in value of fixed plant or real estate belonging to a partnership was as much profit or loss of the partnership as anything else".

Cooper, 1888, 744

It would ... appear that there is no legal objection to a revaluation of assets caused by a fluctuation (upwards) in value, and that, even where these assets are what the court ... has called capital assets, the resultant increase is profit available for dividend.

Dicksee, 1892/1976, 135

every appreciation of assets is a profit, and every depreciation a loss; and in many private concerns this method, technically known as single entry, of ascertaining profits has been regularly adopted for years without bad results.

Dickinson, 1904, 172

Net revenue due to appreciation is just as available [for dividend appropriations] as is net revenue tied up in any asset other than cash .... Ignoring the appreciation of unsold assets which results in an understatement of assets and a corresponding misstatement of equities is simply another method of building up secret reserves;

and it is essentially as misleading a practice as the charging of capital outlays to expense.

> Paton & Stevenson, 1918/1978, 467, 469

The difference arising from the revaluation [of assets, if a loss,] is debited to profit and loss account and credited to the asset account. If . . . a profit, . . . such appreciation is credited to profit and loss account and debited to the asset account.

> Carter, 1923, 616

If a company acquires assets and with them carries on business, every increment in value, whether by way of appreciation of the assets or by way of profit earned in employing them, is in some sense profit. The corporation is so much the richer, actually or potentially, whether the additional wealth arises from appreciation of assets or by fruit produced by their employment.

> Buckley, 1930, 757

The objection to recording appreciation because it is a vague estimate applies just as truly to depreciation.

> Hatfield, 1930, 33

if a feasible plan could be devised whereby a corporation could have an appraisal of its property legally established and recognized . . . no objection should be made to the subsequent declaration of dividends out of the appreciation surplus which resulted from booking the appraised value.

> Mason, 1932, 63

Since 1945 some [UK] companies have begun to restate the accounting values of their fixed assets from time to time . . . . The unrealized gain on revaluation is not, however, carried to profit and loss account as in eighteenth century accounting; instead, it is treated as a credit balance which is not available as profit for distribution to shareholders.

> Yamey, 1961, 758

Accounting for the historical cost of marketable securities held by investment trusts . . . is no longer the prevailing accounting practice . . . . most accountants have proved to be willing to embrace the recognition of unrealized appreciation. The discouraging feature is that they have not insisted on the recognition of appreciation of marketable securities held by all types of firms.

> Sprouse, 1963, 694

On the conservatism convention, appreciation may be ignored until assets are sold and the profit is realized in hard cash. In practice, this may make a balance sheet highly misleading.

> Garbutt (ed), 1969, 0602

Objection to treatment of appreciation as gain or profit

In order to arrive at the true profits of the business the depreciation must be debited, while the appreciation must not be credited. The reason for this is obvious. Depreciation is a working expense and an integral part of the cost of production, without which no revenue can be earned, whereas the incidental appreciation of a fixed asset (even so far as it can be legitimately regarded as a profit at all) is not a profit derived from the carrying on of the business of the undertaking.

Accountant, editorial, 1901, 894

under no circumstances should appreciation in the value of fixed assets be credited to revenue, while appreciation in the value of floating assets should under normal circumstances not be taken credit for until actual realization.

Dicksee, 1903a, 6

The market value [of an investment in securities] is not an investment value but a commercial one; it is the price at which the investor could withdraw his investment, but until he has done so, he has not profited by its rise, or lost by its fall. So long as he retains his investment, the market value does not affect him nor should it enter into his accounts. It is valuable information, however, from time to time, if he has the privilege of changing investments, or the necessity of realizing.

Sprague, 1904/1984, 74

if fixed assets . . . rise in value, and the increase is taken into account, it represents an unrealized profit which may never accrue.

Spicer & Pegler, 1914, 351

Generally speaking, the appreciation of fixed assets should be ignored . . . . There may, however, be circumstances in which these assets may be written up to their appreciated value . . . . In cases in which it is decided to write up the value of fixed assets, the enhanced value should not be credited to profit and loss account to be used for dividend purposes, although there is no illegality in such a procedure. The auditor should . . . strongly object to its distribution as dividend, both on the ground that it is financially unsound, and that it is a capital profit. Floating assets which have appreciated should not be written up. They should always appear in the books at cost prices . . . . until realized . . . . [The enhanced receipts will] then be credited to the trading account, and thus become available for appropriation to dividend or other purposes.

Pixley, 1926, I:49

The recognition of appreciation in accounts generally is unsound from the point of view of economics . . . . Appreciation should not be recognized unless it is justified by newly discovered value, or by increased value in use. Value in exchange does not justify its recognition . . . . Appreciation may not be shown as having given rise to surplus of any character, without danger of being misleading. Appreciation should not be given effect in a balance sheet, except as an estimate of unrealized value, in the nature of a reserve which may be shown either on the side of the liabilities

or as a deduction from the corresponding asset. If shown on the side of the liabilities, it should appear above the capital section of the balance sheet, and in any event should be described as unrealized appreciation, unearned appreciation or ... some caption equally clear and accurate.
Wildman, 1928, 405

the part of the "profit" represented by the rise in unit stock [inventory] values is capital and should not be distributed or included in the yield upon which the transfer price of shares is based ....
Lacey, 1945, 59

there is no objection ... to a *bona fide* writing up of fixed assets to their present value and to crediting the increase to a capital reserve. Such capital reserve may be applied in paying up bonus shares, but not in paying a cash bonus.
Holt, 1950, 96

to place depreciation charges on a current cost basis .... the accounts [should be] adjusted as though an ordinary revaluation were involved. However, instead of a credit to a surplus account, a capital adjustment account should be employed. This capital adjustment account is not a profit, realized or unrealized .... [it] should be closed into the permanent capital stock or stated capital accounts ....
Moonitz & Jordan, 1963, I:412

When property, plant and equipment is revalued upwards, any accumulated depreciation existing at the date of the revaluation should not be credited to income.
IASC, 1982, IAS16

See also 325

670 Losses and Gains from Inflation and Deflation

671 Accounting for inflation and deflation necessary

inflation is not without its effect upon accounting. Since accounting attempts to interpret the results of business operations in terms of prices, to show at given periods, the financial situation of a business in terms of prices, and since the only calculus which it employs is cast likewise in prices and the only values with which it deals are price values, the rapid increase in prices [in France, 1919–1927] rendered the results of ordinary accounting methods unsatisfactory.
Wasserman, 1931, 2

Nor ... [are the reasons against recording appraisals] a denial of the desirability in times of a steadily rising or steadily falling price level, of a periodical revaluation of fixed assets designed to bring the fixed asset values into line with those employed by newer concerns in the industry and so to adjust depreciation charges that selling prices of the product may be fixed neither too high nor too low for competitive purposes.

Smails, 1933/1988, 99

under conditions of inflation, the fact that prices in general are higher at the time of sale than they were when some at least of the costs were incurred automatically swells the profits . . . calculated [by accounting methods]. Profits rise, not in proportion to the rise in prices, but more than in proportion; because they are calculated as a difference between selling prices (measured at one level of prices) and costs (measured at a lower level).

Hicks & others, 1941, 57

If the method of determining profits currently employed is to be continued, it would seem desirable that a form of presentation should be adopted which will result in the profits from ordinary operations of business being sharply distinguished from the accretion to purely monetary resources which results from a fall in the value of money.

May, 1949b, 260

During the past two decades a sharp clash of opinions has developed, with ever-increasing intensity, regarding this vital problem [accounting in relation to changes in the purchasing power of money]. On the one hand there are the economists, the industrialists, and an increasing section of the accountancy profession, who point out the limitations of the significance of accounts prepared on the generally accepted basis, known as historical cost, and put forward alternative principles and procedures designed to overcome these limitations. On the other hand, an important section of accountants . . . see great difficulties and complexities in the way of the adoption of a new conception of profit.

Accountant, editorial, 1952, 561

Solution of the problem of price level changes cannot be allowed to wait until popular understanding of accounting concepts is perfected.

Fitzgerald & Schumer, 1952, 186

business income has two components . . . one reflecting the results of business activities measured in units of substantially equal purchasing power, and the other reflecting the results of changes in the purchasing power of the monetary unit on the final determination of income.

Knauth & May, 1952, 294

In these days the equitable distribution, between labor and capital, of the rewards of industry, is a matter of growing importance in promoting and maintaining good and cooperative relations between labor and capital . . . . the publication of figures of profit which are unreal . . . and inflated by the inclusion of elements of capital loss [due to cost-based accounting] result in giving a distorted picture of the relative rewards .... The effect on the mind of labor of the publication of [such artificially inflated] profit figures ... cannot be lightly disregarded.

Latham, 1952, 144

the following limitations in our present [cost-based accounting] must be faced [in an inflationary environment]: (a) Profits as measured by reference to out of date costs are inflated by merely holding nonmoney assets during a period of rising prices while the loss from holding money assets is not recognized. (b) No account is required by management of their success in conserving the real wealth of the undertaking .... (d) The measurement of the return on the investment ... is distorted because the resources employed are not valued contemporaneously with the return.

Brown, 1972, 91

It is not possible for outsiders to estimate accurately the effects of inflation on companies. Only the directors of a company possess enough information to produce accurate figures.

Cutler & Westwick, 1973, 15

May I leave one ... question for those who argue that [the effects of] inflation can be measured by using different indices for different kinds of businesses? Inflation is like measles; it is the same disease for everyone who catches it. Different people react to it differently; some get it worse than others. But how is the state of the patients to be measured and compared if temperatures are taken with thermometers which register differently from one another?

Parker, 1975, 428

surely it would be preferable, for purposes of comparison, to make approximate adjustments based on imperfect data rather than maintain the fiction that the size of the unit of account is unchanged. The retail price index, with all its imperfections, is widely used in economic discussions as a general indicator of changes in the value or purchasing power of the pound.

Temple, 1978, 309

the need for disclosure of the impact of inflation on corporate performance is simply no longer open to serious debate. The question is not whether it should be disclosed, but how.

Williams, 1978a, 83

See also 126, 127

672 Inflation accounting said to be related to nonmonetary assets only

In brief, the problem of inflation, as it touches on accounting procedures, is the problem of a rational accounting for inventories and tangible fixed assets.

Moonitz, 1948, 139

I would suggest that there are valid reasons for treating debtors and cash (and other financial assets) as not involving adjustment for price changes . . . . for the community as a whole, cash, debtors and creditors cancel out, and what is primarily needed is a correction for errors which distort income as viewed by the whole community.
Lacey, 1952, 80

It is my opinion that the whole problem of changing money values as a question of accounting measurement should be limited to real or physical assets.
Bray, 1953, 34

there are strong practical grounds for businesses maintaining intact the capital invested in physical assets. However, I do not believe there is any case at all for accounting procedures designed to preserve the purchasing power of cash resources and money claims.
Mathews, 1955, 196

In order to derive a measure of current income, income determined on the basis of current prices, these two items [depreciation and the opening stock element in cost of goods sold] need to be revalued in terms of current prices.
Grant & Mathews, 1957, 145

673 Purchasing power gains and losses associated with monetary items only

in times of rising price levels, borrowed money produces a gain in purchasing power; monetary assets will lose purchasing power; and if funds are invested in fixed assets, purchasing power is retained until such assets are consumed or converted into money assets.
Wilk, 1960, 34

General price level gains and losses arise from holding monetary items. On the other hand, nonmonetary items are generally stated in terms of the general purchasing power of the dollar at the time they were acquired. Holding nonmonetary items does not give rise to general price level gains and losses.
AICPA, 1969, APBS3

Gains and losses result from holding these [monetary] items during periods of price level change . . . . Gains and losses do not accrue through the holding of nonmonetary items.
Mueller, 1970, 31

Holders of monetary assets lose general purchasing power during a period of inflation. Possessors of monetary liabilities gain during inflation . . . . Holders of nonmonetary items neither gain nor lose purchasing power during inflation.
ASSC, 1971b, SSAP2

holding monetary items when a change in the general price level occurs results in a monetary gain or loss, while the holding of nonmonetary items does not result in any gain or loss.

Backer, 1973, 115

in times of inflation, monetary or nominal assets generate a loss .... a company, in times of inflation, makes an inflation profit when the monetary liabilities exceed the monetary assets.

Bakker, 1974, 49

if money or the equivalent is held during a period of inflation, there will inevitably be losses in purchasing power. Conversely there are very definite benefits to be obtained by getting into debt in a period of inflation, as the amount eventually repaid will not have the same purchasing power as the amount originally borrowed.

Kirkman, 1974, 86

Holders of monetary assets lose general purchasing power during a period of inflation .... A company with a material excess on average over the year of long- and short-term debt ... over debtors and cash will show, in its supplementary current purchasing power statement, a gain in purchasing power during the year. This is a real gain to the equity shareholders .... The retention of the historical cost concept requires that holders of nonmonetary assets are assumed neither to gain nor to lose purchasing power by reason only of changes in the purchasing power of the pound.

ASSC, 1974c, PSSAP7

during a period of inflation, companies holding monetary assets such as cash or receivables lose purchasing power, and companies with monetary liabilities such as accounts or notes payable gain purchasing power. This phenomenon does not occur with nonmonetary assets and liabilities .... [the value of which] increases or decreases in response to demand in the market place.

Skousen & others, 1981, 239

Purchasing power gains and losses arise as a result of holding net monetary assets or liabilities during a period when the price level changes.

Wolk & others, 1984, 357

Preferred stock to be treated as a monetary item

there is no reason to maintain the original purchasing power of preference capital since it is only entitled to a portion of the company's assets equivalent to the nominal value of such preference shares. Capital maintenance reserve will therefore be restricted to maintaining the purchasing power of ordinary capital.

Wilk, 1960, 80

The preferred stock account ... should ordinarily be treated as a monetary item and the purchasing power gain or loss should be computed in the same manner as that of a monetary liability. The result during a period of rising prices is that the loss in purchasing power of the preferred stockholders' claim becomes an increase in common stockholders' equity.

AICPA, 1963a, ARS6

674 Purchasing power gain or loss on long term debt

the gains or losses from changes in the burden of debt as price levels rise or fall influence greatly the distribution of purchasing power. For that reason these gains or losses must find a place in a discussion of the economic measurement of business income.

Fabricant, 1948/1982, 22

Depression times are times when all other values are falling .... The only thing whose value is rising is money. The real burden of debt is rising, as is the real advantage of being a creditor.

Crowther, 1949, 121

as far as the firm itself is concerned there is no profit on ... items of long term debt when prices are rising – and no loss when prices are falling. All of these long term debt items form part of the permanent capital of the firm in the same way as do amounts contributed by shareholders.

Gynther, 1966, 140

It has been argued that the gain on long term borrowing should not be shown as profit in the supplementary statement because it might not be possible to distribute it without raising additional finance. This argument, however, confuses the measurement of profitability with the measurement of liquidity.

ASSC, 1974c, PSSAP7

as the monetary debt declines in purchasing power and a gain occurs, that gain has been realized in the only sense in which it will ever be realized – through a decline in purchasing power, not through its eventual disposition .... It may be objectively measured immediately by means of an index measuring such changes in the value of the dollar. Conversion of the debt, i.e. repayment, creates no further objectivity.

Boersma, 1975a, 26

Debentures are a fixed obligation .... [under inflation] with the passage of time, the debt burden decreases.

Kirkby, 1975, 42

The entity does not make a gain from debt capital under rising prices.

Mumford, 1977, 375

Inflation makes a money liability less burdensome, and so gives a gain on owing money to those who are in debt.

Baxter, 1984, 59

675 Purchasing power gains and losses said to be associated with all items

Decline in the value of money, which is synonymous with a rise in the general price level, affects all financial items . . . .

Bowers, 1945, 425

[In the event of inflation] profits should first be computed in dollars. Sufficient dollars should then be transferred from profits to capital to offset the shrinkage of the dollar capital previously contributed. These dollars should be credited to a capital price adjustment account and deducted at the bottom of the profit and loss statement in somewhat the same way as . . . the income tax . . . . Any credit balance in the capital price adjustment account would be added on the balance sheet as one more item of capital and surplus.

Freeman, 1948, 114

[The 1971 paper of the UK ASSC affirms:] "Holders of nonmonetary items neither gain nor lose purchasing power during inflation". It seems to me this could only be true on the thoroughly unrealistic assumption that the prices of all commodities tend to move with the general price index.

Ross, 1972, 31

See also 127, 774, 777

676 Realized and unrealized gains and losses of purchasing power

A distinction is sometimes made between realized and unrealized losses and gains on monetary accounts . . . . it is often maintained that a purchasing power loss or gain is unrealized until cash is spent or a liability is paid. This concept . . . puts the emphasis upon cash receipts and disbursements rather than on . . . accrual accounting. The gains and losses have accrued in much the same sense that interest has accrued . . . . If we are willing to recognize revenue on the basis of a receivable, we should be willing to recognize a loss or gain in purchasing power on the same basis.

AICPA, 1963a, ARS6

gain on long term liabilities [under inflation] should not be put [in the income statement] until the loan is repaid; . . . .

Baxter, 1984, 68

See also 325

680 Transfer Payments and Quasi-expenses

681 Transfer payments (in economics)

[In national income accounting, items that are not deductible for taxation purposes] would be considered a disposition of assets by the firm, not a current allocation of the market value of production. Although business transfer payments are a part of gross and net national product, they are not included as a part of national income, since they do not represent payments made to the factors of production.

Ruggles, 1949, 116–117

[in national product accounting] . . . transfer payments . . . are movements from one sector [of the community] to another for purposes other than reimbursement of factors of production.

Powelson, 1955, 349

National income accounts record . . . (a) the value of production in a given period . . . [the sum of the values of consumption and investment], (b) the value of command over resources flowing to the factors of production during the same period, that is, of income; (c) certain other transfers of command over resources representing net accretions to given groups of transactors though not passing in exchange for currently produced goods and services – for example, taxes, interest on government debt, and social security benefits.

Edey & Peacock, 1959, 16

The sums received [from government] by private persons in national insurance benefits, national assistance, family allowances, interest on the national debt, and so on, are undoubtedly part of their income. But they are paid out of the incomes of other persons who make national insurance contributions or pay taxes. They are transferred from one set of incomes to the other set without any service being rendered in exchange.

Cairncross, 1960, 400

Much government expenditure goes on what is called transfer payments. These are payments made not in return for any goods or services. They transfer money from one person or group to another without adding to total production. Public welfare, old age, unemployment and disability payments are all examples of transfer payments . . . . [It is standard practice to deduct] transfer payments from both our revenue and expenditure figures for the central authorities [in calculating national flows of income].

Lipsey, 1972, 428, 451

See also 159

682 Grants received

[Of five methods considered by a committee of the ICAS, a majority of the committee favored the] transfer of the grant to capital reserve (less a proportion transferred to taxation equalization account and brought back to profit and loss account over the life of the asset as an offset against the extra tax suffered by reason of the reduced writing down allowance).

ICAS, 1966, 696

a company which receives [an] investment grant and bases its depreciation charge on the net cost ... will be relieving its profit and loss account of a substantial proportion of the charge for depreciation .... will ultimately convert the capital receipt of grant into additional revenue profits available for dividend .... will considerably gear up its return on capital employed .... may easily give a misleading impression of its performance .... the important thing for accountants is to reflect accurately the accounting implications of fiscal policy. This, I believe, is best done by accounting for all assets and depreciation on the basis of full cost and regarding investment and other grants as a capital receipt forming part of the permanent capital of the company.

TAM, Anon, 1966, 290, 294

it seems prudent that the charge for depreciation ... should be calculated on the gross, and not the net, value of fixed assets .... logic, accounting principle and commercial prudence all support the case for crediting investment grants to a capital reserve.

Peddie, 1966, 406

Investment grants [by government] should be treated as a form of deferred credit which should be reflected in the profit and loss account over the estimated useful lives of the assets .... Either of the following treatments is appropriate: (a) grants should be applied in reduction of the purchase price of the assets to which they relate, with a consequential reduction in the amounts charged to revenue by way of depreciation of the assets or writing off the relevant expenditure .... or, (b) assets should be shown in the balance sheet before deduction of grants and the grants shown in the liabilities section, separate from capital and reserves, as a deferred credit pending transfer to profit and loss account at a rate consistent with that at which the relevant depreciation charge is computed.

ICAEW, 1967, N24

Four of the methods used [in dealing with government grants in respect of capital expenditures on new assets, were]: (1) asset values not reduced – (a) immediate credit to profit and loss account .... (b) deferred credit .... (c) capital reserve .... (2) deduction from asset value ....

Bleasdale, 1972, 550

Grants [from government] relating to fixed assets should be credited to revenue over the expected useful life of the asset. This may be achieved by (a) reducing the cost of the acquisition of the fixed asset by the amount of the grant; or (b) treating the amount of the grant as a deferred credit, a proportion of which is transferred to revenue annually.

ASSC, 1974a, SSAP4

When a government grant is received or receivable in relation to research and development costs which have been deferred, the grant should be deducted from the carrying amount . . . . Where [the costs have been written off] . . . the grant should be credited to the profit and loss account.

AARF, 1983, AAS13

Gifts and donations received

When property is donated to a business as an outright . . . gift, it should theoretically not give rise to any entry. The value parted with having been zero, the value received is also zero. On the other hand, this treatment is undesirable, since it results in the entity's possession of an asset with which it is not formally charged. It therefore becomes necessary to assign some arbitrary value to the donated asset. Such value may be the nominal amount of $1 merely for the purpose of establishing a record, or it may be some estimated basis of market value. Under any of these conditions there is no realization . . . . accountants generally agree that a donated asset, while it does result in an increase in the indebtedness of the entity to the proprietor, does not result in realized income . . . . If the property is subsequently sold, then income is realized . . . .

Gilman, 1939, 111

Donations in the form of cash, or of claims which will automatically be converted into cash without the need for an intervening sales transaction, are properly to be treated as a form of revenue. When the donation is in the form of fixed assets some question may exist as to proper treatment. Three choices are available: (1) the fair market value of the donated asset may be credited to a special surplus account; (2) the credit may be made to a special income account for the year and be reported as such; (3) the credit may be apportioned to the periods during which the asset is used. Using the last alternative in connection with a depreciable asset, the asset itself would be shown at fair market value in a memorandum account only; depreciation would be charged to operations in the usual manner with the offsetting credit going to a special income account . . . . Resources are occasionally acquired by donation . . . and bequest or inheritance . . . . The prevailing opinion is that income is not realized by such happenings.

Paton (ed), 1944, 168, 198

In the case of a gift without any "strings" attached to it, no entry is absolutely required since there has been no exchange of values. Since the business firm has, however, an additional resource in its possession, some record should be made of the fact. The dollar amount used in this transaction might be some nominal sum, such as $1, or some larger figure closely approximating the fair market value.

Assuming that the donated asset is a physical or intangible one not constituting a claim for cash, there is clearly no realization of revenue involved. The credit for whatever amount decided upon should be to the donated surplus account.

Newlove & Garner, 1951, I:406

Business firms are occasionally the recipients of donations such as the gift of a tract of land as an inducement to locate in a particular community. In general such transactions are preferably viewed as capital contributions rather than as revenue, and should be reflected in a special paid-in capital account.

Wixon (ed), 1962, 5.9

683 Income taxes held not to be in the nature of expenses

Theoretically, income taxes are not costs, for they constitute a sharing of profits with the government . . . .

Cole, 1921, 291

Taxes do not represent a payment for definite commodities, services or conditions . . . . The payment is coerced . . . . The government's contribution to the success of the particular business is a factor entirely outside market laws. Taxes are in no sense a price for specific services. Taxes in general are not apportioned in accordance with benefit received. Hence we cannot view tax payments as measuring the value of services received and, later, a cost of production or expense.

Paton, 1922/1962, 179

In view of the . . . economic, legal and practical aspects of the situation . . . the logical conclusion is that, in the final analysis, income taxes are a distribution of profits and not expense . . . .

Seeger, 1924, 108

If there is no net income, there is no income tax . . . . We shall, therefore, treat income taxes as a share of the Federal and . . . state governments in the net income of a corporation – an income distribution rather than an expense.

Mason & Davidson, 1953, 168

Taxes are a somewhat anomalous element in business finance. Taxes are coerced; . . . they can hardly be said to measure the value of services received and utilized in production. Taxes therefore are not strictly congruous with ordinary expenses. However taxes are clearly a deduction from or charge against revenues in the process of determining net income.

Paton, 1955, 99

If income taxes were treated as a distribution of income, after the manner of dividends, most of the problems associated with the reporting of income taxes would disappear . . . .

Moonitz, 1957, 175

a dollar of corporate income tax differs from a dollar of corporate wages in that the former is paid only if period revenues exceed period costs. In this respect, the tax dollar is suspiciously like the dividend dollar.

Hill, 1957, 357

An income tax is a revenue deduction that is peculiarly different from an expense. Typically, an increase in expenses results in an increase in revenues . . . . An increase in taxes does not bring about an increase in revenues.

Drinkwater & Edwards, 1965, 580

Income taxes do not have any of the . . . characteristics of expenses – they are not incurred by management in anticipation of future benefits, and they are not costs of facilities used up to earn the period's revenue . . . . Income tax is a compulsory levy on all those companies whose operations yield taxable income, and as such it is a charge on the profits of the company, and not a charge on revenue earned. Because the charge is an obligatory one, it is more accurate to describe it as an expropriation of profits . . . than as an appropriation.

Barton, 1970, 6, 9

684 Income taxes held to be in the nature of expenses

Income taxes are an expense which should be allocated, when necessary and practicable, to income and other accounts, as other expenses are allocated.

AIA, 1944, ARB23

When the present income tax was first levied in 1913 . . . . Payment by the corporation resulted in a relief from taxation to the stockholder when income was distributed in dividends. The [relief] . . . constituted a justification for the treatment of the tax as falling in an intermediate classification between pure expenses and distributions . . . . In 1936 . . . . relief to stockholders was ended, and the corporation tax became a pure expense of the corporation.

May, 1945, 124

from the accounting standpoint, it [a deferred debit or charge to income tax expense] is definitely an advance payment, a payment of an expense related to net income that will be reported on the income statements of future periods. As such it would seem to qualify as a legitimate asset.

Graham, 1959a, 19

Income taxes are an expense of business enterprises earning income subject to tax.

AICPA, 1967, APBO11

Timing differences

Timing differences. Differences between the periods in which transactions affect taxable income and the periods in which they enter into the determination of pretax accounting income. Timing differences originate in one period and reverse or turn around in one or more subsequent periods . . . . Four types of transactions are identifiable which give rise to timing differences . . . . Interpretations of the nature of timing differences are diverse, with the result that three basic methods of interperiod allocation of income taxes have developed and been adopted in practice . . . . the deferred method . . . . the liability method . . . . and the net of tax method . . . . [Allocation may be partial, or comprehensive.]

AICPA, 1967, APBO11

Timing differences are differences between profits as computed for taxation purposes and profits as stated in financial statements which result from the inclusion of items of income and expenditure in taxation computations in periods different from those in which they are included in financial statements. Timing differences originate in one period and are capable of reversal in one or more subsequent periods . . . . Deferred taxation is the taxation attributable to timing differences.

ASC, 1978b, SSAP15

[APB] Opinion 11 [1967] used the term timing differences for differences between the years in which transactions affect taxable income and the years in which they enter into the determination of pretax financial income . . . . All such differences collectively are referred to as temporary differences in this statement.

FASB, 1987, SFAS96

685 Tax allocation endorsed

Income taxes are an expense that should be allocated, when necessary and practicable, to income and other accounts, as other expenses are allocated. What the income statement should reflect under this head . . . is the expense properly allocable to the income included in the income statement for the year.

AIA, 1944, ARB23

There may be situations in which the declining balance method [or the sum of the years' digits method] is adopted for tax purposes but other appropriate methods are followed for financial accounting purposes. In such cases it may be that accounting recognition should be given to deferred income taxes. However, the committee is of the opinion that, in the ordinary situation, deferred income taxes need not be recognized in the accounts unless it is reasonably certain that the reduction in taxes during the earlier years of use of the . . . method . . . is merely deferment of income taxes until a relatively few years later, and then only if the amounts are clearly material.

AIA, 1954, ARB44

Most asset values would shrink substantially, and in some cases would disappear almost entirely, if continued operation at a profit were not anticipated. Does it not follow logically that both of these deferred amounts [deferred charges and deferred credits to income tax expense] are legitimate, even though their realization depends upon future taxable income?

Graham, 1959a, 15

If income taxes are considered an expense, they must be charged against revenues in the same way as other expenses, that is, the taxes incurred in earning income must be charged against that income in the same year the income is recognized in the accounts.

Sands, 1959, 584

Interperiod tax allocation is an integral part of the determination of income tax expense, and income tax expense should include the tax effects of revenue and expense transactions included in the determination of pretax accounting income.

AICPA, 1967, APBO11

The corporation tax charge [in the profit and loss account] should be based on the accounting profit without regard to the fact that some items are allocated to other periods for taxation purposes . . . . A deferred taxation account should be established and maintained at current rates of taxation whenever there exists material taxation liabilities which may crystallize at some future date on profits and losses already brought into account.

ICAEW, 1968b, 77–79

The objective in accounting for income taxes on an accrual basis is to recognize the amount of current and deferred taxes payable or refundable at the date of the financial statements (a) as a result of all events that have been recognized in the financial statements and (b) as measured by the provisions of enacted tax laws.

FASB, 1987, SFAS96

686 Tax allocation rejected

continuing differences between reported and taxable business earnings are to be expected . . . . Since such differences are often significant . . . they should be disclosed. Disclosure is sometimes accomplished by recording the differences as prepayments . . . or accruals . . . . However, these items do not present the usual characteristics of assets or liabilities; the possible future offsets are often subject to unusual uncertainties; and treatment on an accrual basis is in many cases unduly complicated . . . . and is therefore undesirable.

AAA, 1957a/1957b, 6

Under the tax allocation procedure [where accelerated depreciation is used for tax purposes and straight line depreciation for reporting, we are] faced with the necessity of forecasting, not only the future tax rates and earnings levels, but also the pattern of future acquisitions of depreciable assets [for the calculation of the liability for future tax payments].

Hill, 1957, 359

For the most part the committee was concerned originally [in devising ARB23] with specific, nonrecurring transactions of a material and extraordinary nature . . . . It is regrettable . . . that the committee is currently suggesting that the tax allocation principle be applied on a long range basis . . . . no corporation should be required to provide for income taxes by charges to income of amounts in excess of the legal liability therefor . . . .

Johns, 1958, 42, 50

Interperiod income tax allocation . . . cannot improve the matching process, nor can it improve the usefulness of the income statement.

Li, 1961, 268

From the theoretical aspects of the nature of taxes, the matching principle, and the going concern concept, the arguments for tax allocation appear to be without adequate support.

Drinkwater & Edwards, 1965, 581

The [AICPA] approach to accounting for income taxes [i.e. favoring tax allocation] is a curious departure from its philosophy in dealing with other contingencies which businesses face . . . . It [tax allocation] is a form of income smoothing otherwise almost universally abhorred by accountants as well as bankers and reasonable businessmen.

Bevis, 1968, 40

I wonder how useful deferred tax liabilities are in accounts. There have been so many changes in tax depreciation allowances [over the past twenty years] that any concept of normal tax is out of the question.

Myddelton, 1968, 157

This whole business of trying to estimate future taxes and future tax benefits is an exercise in futility . . . . No one knows what the rates are going to be next year or five years from now or the applicability of losses . . . .

Lorenzen, 1972, 5

I do not like hypothetical, as-if accounting. Deferred tax accounting is hypothetical, as-if accounting.

Schuetze, 1991, 115

687 Tax allocation "assets" and "liabilities"

The so-called liability held to result from a current underpayment of the period income tax does not fit the common definition of a creditor claim . . . . No one owes

639

anyone anything in the presently accepted sense of the word liability . . . . The prepaid income tax presumed to arise from an overpayment presents similar conceptual difficulties.

Hill, 1957, 358

[Treating] income taxes on an accrual basis, and [letting] the tax follow the income – if revenue subject to tax in some period is recognized in the records, the corresponding tax liability is also recognized; if expense is permitted as a tax deduction in some period, the related benefit is reflected in the records.

Moonitz, 1957, 177

As applied to liberalized depreciation [for tax purposes] . . . . there is obviously no deferral of tax liability – there is no tax liability to defer.

Dohr, 1959, 19

A provision for income taxes is a period debit to profit and loss. No part of such a provision is allocable to future periods of income because the allocation lacks the proof of either a legal liability or a current asset (i.e. inventory) value.

Johnson, 1961, 83

Deferred taxation dealt with in the profit and loss account should be shown separately as a component of the total tax charge or credit in the profit and loss account or by way of note to the financial statements . . . . Deferred taxation account balances should be shown separately in the balance sheet and described as deferred taxation.

ASC, 1978b, SSAP15

Deferred taxes should not be carried as liabilities. The government defines the tax base and the accountants should not generate liabilities on the basis of their ideas about what the tax base should have been.

Bodenhorn, 1978, 5

A current or deferred tax liability or asset is recognized for the current or deferred tax consequences of all events that have been recognized in the financial statements . . . . A deferred tax liability or asset shall be adjusted for the effect of a change in tax law or rates.

FASB, 1987, SFAS96

688 Amortization of intangibles, including goodwill

as goodwill is an asset distinctly paid for by shareholders and represented in their capital on the opposite side of the balance sheet, profits should not be subject to a charge for its reduction or extinction.

Browne, 1902, 1342

It may be safely stated that capital outlay on the purchase of goodwill inevitably expires year by year, whether the profits of an undertaking are increasing or decreasing .... It is urged against the writing off of the cost of goodwill – and often it is a fact – that the goodwill of a prosperous undertaking ... is worth no less now than it was when it was purchased ten or twenty years ago. The question is asked: Why, therefore, should the goodwill be written off? The answer is that the present goodwill is, in the main, not the goodwill which was bought ten or twenty years ago.

Leake, 1921, 77, 78

In Canada, there are several options available at present for dealing with combination goodwill: (1) goodwill can be left on the books unamortized, (2) it can be amortized systematically over a reasonable period in the future, and (3) it can be written off immediately against surplus.

Dewhirst, 1972, 42

By reason of its unique nature and its unseverability, goodwill may well be a benefit held in trust by management for present and future owners. Should it be treated in the same manner that a trust company reports its "assets under administration" with an offsetting equity segregation? No amortization would be required until management or the market forced recognition of impairment.

Stewart, 1972, 107

Amortization assumes that purchased goodwill is susceptible of separable measurement after purchase .... This is a fiction .... any capitalization-amortization approach is in reality completely arbitrary .... Proper matching of costs and revenue calls only for amortization of those assets that can be related to earnings on some realistic and systematic basis.

Hinton, 1973, 33

Systematic amortization

By order of the General Court [of the East India Company] in June 1733, £10,000 p.a. was written off the payment recorded in the account entitled "Prolongation of the company's right to an exclusive trade & perpetuity of their corporate capacity".

Yamey, 1961, 759

It appears to me that the period within which the price paid for goodwill should be replaced out of revenue ought, to a large extent, at least, to be regulated by the number of years' purchase of the profits which the price represents.

More, 1891, 286

In the case of goodwill the number of years' profits which have been purchased determines the number of years over which goodwill shall be charged off.

Gilman, 1916, 195

The logical principle seems to be that the [intangible] assets should be written off during the periods for which the excess earnings were capitalized when calculating the purchase price.

Yang, 1927, 196

purchased goodwill represents an advance recognition of a debit for a portion of income that is expected to materialize later. It follows that the amount expended for goodwill should be absorbed by revenue charges – during the period implicit in the computation on which the price was based – in order that the income not paid for in advance may be measured.

Paton & Littleton, 1940, 92

Purchased goodwill that is written off to a surplus account should be debited to earned surplus. Over the period in which purchased goodwill expires, its cost should be balanced off against the realized excess incomes, if any .... If there had been some compelling justification for bringing the nonpurchased goodwill into the accounts, it might be amortized systematically over the period implicit in the original valuation.

Walker, 1953, 216

the recorded costs of intangible assets should be amortized by systematic charges to income over the periods estimated to be benefited .... The period of amortization ... should be determined from the pertinent factors ... [but] should not, however, exceed forty years.

AICPA, 1970b, APBO17

Purchased goodwill should be amortized systematically and appear as an operating expense on the income statement.

Gilbert, 1971, 255

[Purchased goodwill] shall be systematically amortized to the profit and loss account over the period of time which the benefits are expected to arise. The period ... shall not exceed twenty years.

ASRB, 1988/1991, ASRB1013

Goodwill amortization – *ad hoc*

After once placing a value [for goodwill] upon your books, if you actually have it, write it off; if not, then continue it and make a show of having it. If you have a thing, you haven't; if you haven't, you have. [from an American correspondent]

Accountant, Anon, 1913, 817

if you can write it down, you need not; if you cannot, you should!

Couchman, 1924, 138

There is usually no logical reason for writing it off. When profits are large, goodwill is a very real asset. To write it off then is not logically consistent. When profits are small, . . . it would hardly be logical to write off any amount less than its decreased value, yet the profits at such a time are rarely sufficient to stand so heroic a treatment.

Kester, 1933, 393

Many of the corporations which have amortized goodwill, purchased or nonpurchased, have not followed a policy of making regular amortization charges, often amortizing a large or small amount depending upon the ability of net profits or surplus to bear large or small charge offs.

Walker, 1953, 215

the cost of control [i.e. goodwill] . . . . is not . . . a cost of earning the profits at all, but simply the cost of the right to enjoy the profits. This view seems quite clear from British practice, various as it is; we have never treated the write off of genuine goodwill, whether immediate or delayed, as a charge against profits.

Morison, 1974, 357

690 Classification of Gains and Losses

691 Operating gains and losses

Operating profits are the return earned on the total capital used in operations. Out of these profits must be paid federal taxes, interest on borrowed money, and extraordinary losses, before the balance remaining at the disposition of stockholders is determined.

Bliss, 1923, 79

Income from sources other than the main operations of the business should be shown separately.

Sanders & others, 1938, 114

those who advocate the "current operating performance" type of income statement . . . are mindful of the particular business significance which a substantial number of the users of financial reports attach to the income statement . . . . The net income of a single year is only one of scores of factors involved in analyzing the future earnings prospects and potentialities of a business . . . . However, this group insists that the net income for the year should show as clearly as possible what happened in that year under that year's conditions, in order that sound comparisons may be made with prior years and with the performance of other companies . . . . They believe that material extraordinary charges or credits may often best be disclosed as direct adjustments of surplus.

AIA, 1947c, ARB32

Revenue is normally subdivided into: operating revenue, which is the normal revenue earned from the major activities of the business during the period in question . . . . [and] nonoperating revenue, which is all revenue which fails to meet the operating revenue criteria. [Operating and nonoperating costs and expenses may be subdivided correspondingly.]

Mathews, 1962, 47

Income from ordinary operations is important to investors in making investment decisions. This amount, when compared with cash dividends, is relevant to an appraisal of the intent of management to contract or expand operating capacity of the firm. Secondly, it facilitates predictions of future income from ordinary operations.

AAA, 1964a, 696

Operating revenues result from the company's providing its main products or services to its customers – those products or services it is in business to provide. They are reported gross . . . . Nonoperating revenues are incidental gains, such as those which result from sales of noncurrent assets and from retirements of noncurrent liabilities. They are reported net.

Thomas, 1977, 12:5

Distinction between operating and nonoperating items questioned

the ultimate distinction between operating income and charges and nonoperating gains and losses, terms having considerable currency in the accounting profession, has not been made. The former are generally defined as recurrent features of business operation, more or less normal and dependable in their incidence from year to year; the latter are generally considered to be irregular and unpredictable, more or less fortuitous and incidental. [similar in AICPA, 1961, 59]

AIA, 1947c, ARB32

In any business the whole of the assets are represented by capital, using the word capital in its widest sense . . . . Accordingly a profit on the sale of stock [merchandise] is just as much a capital profit as is that on the sale of freehold land and buildings.

Davis, 1953, 29

See also 612

692 Capital gains and losses

Capital profits and losses arise out of: (a) the acquisition, loss or sale of some fixed or capital asset, (b) a transaction affecting some capital liability, or (c) a gift or payment of funds for capital purposes.

Thompson, 1932, 156

[A profit made on the sale of part of a base stock] is the same kind of profit that you would make by selling scrap machinery or by selling an unnecessary piece of real estate. It is not an operating profit; it is a capital profit.

Peloubet, 1938/1982, 349

The underlying conception of the so-called capital gain or loss is that of the difference between the proceeds received upon the disposition of assets of the enterprise other than product over the cost or net book value of such assets.

Paton (ed), 1944, 162

A capital gain arises in accounting practice when a fixed asset is realized for an amount greater than that at which it stands in the books .... Capital losses, such as a loss on the sale of a fixed asset for less than its book amount ....

ICAEW & NIESR, 1951, 15

The terms capital gain and capital loss are often applied to the favorable or unfavorable differences resulting from transactions in assets other than the regular products of the enterprise.

Paton & Dixon, 1958, 207

In [the United States] in the early twentieth century most discussions concerning capital gains and losses were related almost exclusively to fixed (capital) assets, with many authors taking the position that such gains and losses should be closed directly to capital surplus .... In the early 1930s views on this matter began to change .... terms such as nonrecurring, fortuitous, speculative, sporadic and nonoperating were used frequently to describe capital gains and losses .... the nature of the event or happening became at least as important as the nature of the item involved (e.g. fixed assets) in determining when something was a capital gain or loss as opposed to ordinary income or loss. And the concept broadened perceptibly up to the present time.

Arnett, 1965, 54

[The idea that income and capital must be separated] was embodied in the writings of early classical economists, and came into accounting usage through business practice and several leading court decisions on distributable profits during the late nineteenth century .... there is considered to be a capital fund and an income fund which are separate from each other. The capital fund is represented by fixed assets, and the income fund by working capital. Any increase in the value of the capital fund from natural growth or price increases is treated as a capital gain and not income. This appreciation is often called a capital gain .... Growth in the working capital fund may be treated as income. However where this growth proceeds from the fixed capital, e.g. the fruit on a tree, the wool on a sheep, the crop on the land, interest on a bank deposit, it must be severed from the base property for it to be recognized. It is held that income must be detached from capital; otherwise it is capital appreciation.

Barton, 1984, 442–3

693 Holding gains and losses

Any gains which accrue to the firm as a result of . . . holding activities are capital gains. Any gains made by the firm as a result of . . . operating activities are operating profits.

Edwards & Bell, 1961, 73

Holding gains and losses relating to long-lived assets result from holding such assets during periods of value change (other than . . . from depreciation).

AAA, 1964a, 693

Since income from operations and holding gains or losses result from different causes, they can be expected to have different patterns of recurrence. Effective prediction of future income is facilitated by reporting them separately.

AAA, 1965a, 320

Realizable income . . . is the change in value of individual resources between two dates. Normally it is measured in terms of changes in the sales market price.

Bedford, 1965, 28

An increase in the price of a specific asset results in a holding gain which is measured by the difference between historical cost and current cost.

Popoff, 1973, 11

A replacement cost income concept attempts to isolate two components of earned income . . . . the results of (1) operating activities, and (2) holding activities.

Revsine, 1973, 58

Under the financial capital [maintenance] concept, if the effects of [periodical] price changes are recognized, they are called holding gains and losses and are included in return on capital. Under the physical capital concept, those changes are recognized but are called capital maintenance adjustments and are included directly in equity and are not included in return on capital.

FASB, 1980b, SFAC3

holding gains (or losses) . . . are increases (or decreases) in the replacement costs of the assets held during the current period . . . . The advocates of a physical concept of capital maintenance claim that all holding gains (both those gains related to the units sold and the gains related to the units unsold) should be excluded from income and become part of revalued capital called revaluation equity. That is, for a going concern no income can result unless the physical capital devoted to operations during the current period can be replaced.

Horngren, 1984, 634, 635

In a replacement cost system that articulates through double entry accounting, changes in replacement costs of specific assets necessarily give rise to credits or debits off-setting the recorded changes in replacement costs. These offsetting credits and debits have come to be called holding gains and holding losses . . . . To label cost increases as gains and decreases as losses may seem twisted, depending on the perspective. From a capital maintenance perspective, a cost increase is a gain because of the advantage gained in using an asset for which the actual outlay was less than the outlay for that asset would have been today, and *vice versa* for a cost decrease. In short, gains and losses measure opportunities forgone.

Gellein, 1987, 63

Operating and holding gains said to be undistinguishable

The dichotomy [current operating profit and holding gain] cannot be used for the separate evaluations of different kinds of decisions; holding and operating activities are not independent.

Drake & Dopuch, 1965, 205

It is not only venture companies who are interested in making holding gains; ordinary companies typically trade off operating profit for the prospect of realized holding gain.

Buckley, 1975, 522

There are no valid supports for the claim that the current operating profit-holding gains dichotomy does in fact possess the benefits usually ascribed to it. The dichotomy is artificial and arbitrary, and equally defensible (or indefensible) schemes of decomposing income can be readily constructed.

Prakash & Sunder, 1979, 1

From an economic point of view, income can be defined as the change in the firm's wealth during a period of time, from all sources other than the injection or withdrawal of investment funds. Income is the amount that the firm could consume during the period and still have as much real wealth at the end of the period as it had at the beginning. In concept any increase in wealth increases the wellbeing of the firm and thus fits this definition, whether it comes from the firm's use of its assets or from a holding gain. A holding gain occurs whenever an asset's market value increases. Conversely, a holding loss occurs when the market value declines. [per G Sh]

Enc Britannica, 1981, I:39

694 Realized and unrealized income or profits

Profit is not attributable to the year in which the ore is turned into market lead, but to the year in which the actual sale of the article takes place.

Accountant, Anon, 1890, 667

As a rule, the safer course in all cases must be to postpone the distribution of such increases in value, until actually realized by the sale of the property; but in any case

the real value should, I think, be stated on the face of the accounts, so that present shareholders may have their share in such enhanced value, through the increased price that such disclosure would give to the shares.
Payne, 1892, 143

Realized profits are those actually made and existing in the form of cash, as when investments have been sold for more than their book value. Where investments appreciate in value over and above their original cost, the amount of such appreciation is known as unrealized or paper profits.
Fieldhouse & Fieldhouse, 1929, 922

Up to [the point of sale] the goods belong to the merchant or manufacturer as the case may be. When the goods have been sold or accepted, the asset is changed from the asset, stock in hand, to an asset consisting of a claim against a supposedly responsible party. That change in the legal status seems to form the most appropriate marking point for the taking of a profit on the books.
Stockwell, 1925, 57

The general acceptance of this test [when sale is made] of profits is probably due in large part to the fact that it offers objective evidence of the correctness of estimated profit.
Hatfield, 1927/1971, 255

Income is the economic benefit coming in during a period of time. It consists of current income and of capital gains and losses. The general accounting habit of regarding income as though it were synonymous with realized income, although of some usefulness in practical affairs because it tends to substitute fact for fancy, should be more clearly recognized as both illogical and generally causative of the compilation of false information. All the income – realized, unrealized, and the total thereof – coming into existence during a period should be credited to that period, but the realized should continue to be separated from the unrealized.
Sweeney, 1933b, 335

The income shall include only realized profits in the period during which realized; profit is deemed to be realized when a sale in the ordinary course of business is effected, unless the circumstances are such that collection of the sale price is not reasonably assured.
Byrne, 1937, 372

By realized income is commonly meant income validated by sale, and by unrealized income, accordingly, estimated income not yet assured or realized through the fact of sale, especially appreciation.
Paton (ed), 1944, 183

The realized net income of an enterprise . . . is the change in its net assets arising out of (a) the excess or deficiency of revenue compared with related expired cost and (b) other gains or losses to the enterprise from sales, exchanges, or other conversions of assets.

AAA, 1957a/1957b, 5

The accountant ordinarily reports holding gains only when assets are sold. Such gains are said to be realized. Unrealized holding gains are seldom reported to management and are reported even less frequently to the outside public. Holding losses, on the other hand, are ordinarily reported as soon as they can be identified, whether they are realized or not. [per G Sh]

Enc Britannica, 1981, I:39

Unrealized increments not to be counted as income or profit

In an individual concern the stock should be taken at the cost price, as, although a profit might afterwards accrue from their sale, yet, at the time of taking stock, it is not realized . . . .

Jackson, 1827/1896, 96

The right principle undoubtedly is that in a manufacturing business a profit should not be considered to have been made until a sale has been effected . . . . even in [the case of raw materials and other goods which could be put upon the market and realized at their normal price] it would probably in the long run prove to be more judicious to price the commodity in the books at its cost, and only to credit profit and loss account with the profit when the sales have been effected.

Garcke & Fells, 1893/1976, 123

Profits can only be made out of the sale or exchange of one commodity for another of a definite and realizable cash value. The mere increase in the market value of an article which is not actually sold can not be considered as a profit; for the reason that the article may never be sold at that price, and the paper profit may never be realized.

Dickinson, 1914, 93

It is one of the oldest rules of financial statements to allow profit to appear only after it has been realized . . . . Therefore all unrealized changes in the value of assets must be accounted for not on profit and loss but on appreciation accounts.

Schmidt, 1930, 240

Unrealized profit should not be credited to income account of the corporation either directly or indirectly . . . .

AIA, 1932

the primary reason for using cost as a basis of accounting is that this is essential to the measurement of realized profits and to excluding unrealized profits from the income statement.

Broad, 1954, 584

The accounting principle that income should not be regarded as earned until an asset increment has been realized, or until its realization is reasonably assured, is violated if unrealized appreciation is regarded as income.

Finney & Miller, 1968, 249

Only profits realized at the balance sheet date shall be included in the profit and loss account .... [Realized profits are such profits] as fall to be treated as realized profits ... in accordance with principles generally accepted with respect to the determination for accounting purposes of realized profits. [Schedule 4]

UK *Companies Act 1985*

Critical comment on realization as income desideratum

The postulate of realization is of quite modern origin. In America at least its acceptance could not be related back to any date prior to the First World War .... [The American] corporation excise tax law of 1909 had been levied normally on the basis of receipts and payments in respect of income .... Gradually there emerged the concepts of "the completed transaction" and "cash or its equivalent" – which became embodied in the [income tax] law of 1918 .... [This and the assertion by the Supreme Court] of the realization postulate lent support to the proposition that, until realized, assets should be carried at cost, and thus contributed to the building up in accounting literature of a so-called traditional cost principle.

AIA, 1952, 21, 25

The denial that profit can exist without a sale and the simultaneous recognition of accruing interest as profit is another of the many inconsistencies in accounting practice. The exception in favor of interest probably rests upon the idea that it is definitely calculable .... But if this is a satisfactory basis of differentiation, the rule for recognizing profits should be expressed in terms of calculability or certainty rather than made dependent upon the existence of a contract.

Hatfield, 1927/1971, 257

the arbitrary choice of the sale as the point of revenue recognition is one of the major contributing factors of the difficulties of periodic income determination .... The realization convention does not eliminate or decrease the effects of uncertainty and subjectivity in accounting; it merely shifts the problem from the revenue to the cost side of the matching process.

Storey, 1958/1978, 15

the realization and matching concepts were only devised as a means of approximating increases in wealth. Unfortunately, in current accounting practice they have tended to become accepted for their own sakes, regardless of their measure of wealth income.

Sands, 1963, 41

The accounting profession has adopted a different meaning for the words "realization" and "realize" from that which appears in language commonly used by laymen
.... the term "realized profit" is a misnomer when any form of accrual accounting is being used.

Hoggett, 1973, 19, 23

See also 325, 626

695 Extraordinary items

Surplus additions and deductions. Items of unusual or extraordinary profit which do not strictly belong to the period under audit, or can not be said to be the legitimate result of the ordinary transactions of the concern, should be entered here .... Similarly, deductions should be treated.

Federal Reserve Board (US), 1917

Extraordinary expenditure, such as repairs and renewals incident to accidents or storms, are sometimes capitalized at the time with the expressed intention of spreading the loss over several years .... Quite frequently the debit balances so created are carried forward as an asset until subsequent accruals wipe out the deficit. The practice is not sound, because ... it simply results in setting up on the balance sheet accounts which are in no sense of the word assets.

Montgomery, 1912/1976, 283

Items of an exceptional or nonrecurrent nature should be dealt with in such a way as to show in the particular circumstances a true and fair view of the result of the year .... (a) ... they may be dealt with in arriving at the trading surplus or deficit and disclosed separately ... (b) they may be shown separately in the section of the account which includes other income and nontrading expenditure of the year (c) they may be shown separately after the profit after taxation (d) they may in appropriate circumstances be ... taken direct to reserve.

ICAEW, 1958a, N18

[Extraordinary events and transactions] will be of a character significantly different from the typical or customary business activities of the entity .... Examples of [their effects] ... include material gains or losses ... from (a) the sale or abandonment of plant ..., (b) the sale of an investment not acquired for resale, (c) the write-off of goodwill ..., (d) the condemnation or expropriation of properties and (e) a major devaluation of a foreign currency .... such material items, less applicable income tax effect, should be segregated, but reflected in the determination of net income.

AICPA, 1966a, APBO9

Extraordinary items ... are those items which derive from events or transactions outside the ordinary activities of the business and which are both material and expected

651

not to recur frequently or regularly . . . . [they] (less attributable taxation) should be shown separately in the profit and loss account . . . .
ASSC, 1974b, SSAP6

Unusual items should be included in net revenue; the nature and amount of each such item should be separately disclosed.I
ASC, 1978, IAS8

696 Prior period adjustments

As far as possible net income should be so determined that it will need no subsequent correction. When, however, such correction becomes necessary, it may be made through current income only if it is not so large as to distort the statement of that income; otherwise it should be made through earned surplus.
Sanders & others, 1938, 114

Adjustments related to prior periods – and thus excluded in the determination of net income for the current period – are limited to those material adjustments which (a) can be specifically identified with and directly related to the business activities of particular prior periods, and (b) are not attributable to economic events occurring subsequent to the date of the financial statements for the prior period, and (c) depend primarily on determinations by persons other than management, and (d) were not susceptible of reasonable estimation prior to such determination.
AICPA, 1966a, APBO9

Prior period adjustments are those material adjustments applicable to prior years arising from changes in accounting policies and from the correction of fundamental errors . . . . [they] should be accounted for by restating prior years . . . .
ASSC, 1974b, SSAP6

[With specified exceptions] . . . , all items of profit and loss recognized during a period, including accruals of estimated losses from loss contingencies, shall be included in the determination of net income for that period. Items of profit and loss related to the following shall be accounted for and reported as prior period adjustments and excluded from the determination of net income for the current period: a. Correction of an error in the financial statements of a prior period and b. Adjustments that result from realization of income tax benefits of pre-acquisition operating loss carryforwards of purchased subsidiaries.
FASB, 1977, SFAS16

Prior period items and the amounts of the adjustments, if any, resulting from changes in accounting policies should be either (a) reported by adjusting opening retained earnings in the financial statements for the current period and amending the comparative information in respect of prior years which is included in the financial statements, or (b) separately disclosed in the current income statement as part of net income. In either case the disclosure relating to these items should be adequate to facilitate comparisons of the figures for the periods presented.

IASC, 1978, IAS8

697 Comprehensive or all-inclusive income

Contrary to a view prevailing in the business world, current income may be increased, as well as decreased, by a change in the value of capital that continues to be used in a fixed asset capacity.

Sweeney, 1933b, 325

Proponents of the "all inclusive" type of income statement . . . . emphasize the dangers of possible manipulation of annual earnings if material extraordinary items may be omitted in the determination of income . . . . They argue that when judgment is allowed to enter the picture with respect to the inclusion or exclusion of special items, material differences in the treatment of borderline cases will develop and that there is danger that the use of "distortion" as a criterion may be a means of ratio-nalizing the normalization of earnings.

AIA, 1947c, ARS32

it is the opinion of the committee [CAP] that there should be a general presumption that all items of profit and loss recognized during the period are to be used in determining the figure reported as net income. The only possible exception to this presumption in any case would be with respect to items which in the aggregate are materially significant in relation to the company's net income and are clearly not identifiable with or do not result from the usual or typical business operations of the period.

AIA, 1947c, ARB32

the all-inclusive income statement . . . . seems to me to have several advantages. First it is simple and straightforward. Second, it furnishes a medium for appraising the performance of management over a period of time. I am old-fashioned enough to believe that one of the functions of financial statements is to present manage-ment's accounting for its fiduciary responsibilities, and I think the all-inclusive income statement is well designed to fulfil this function. Third, it contains the basic infor-mation required for the purposes of evaluating earning capacity.

Powell, 1966, 35

Comprehensive income is the change in equity of a business enterprise during a period from transactions and other events and circumstances . . . . except those resulting from investments by owners and distributions to owners.

FASB, 1985, SFAC6

Comprehensive income is the change in a business entity's net assets for a period from all sources except transactions with owners . . . . [It includes] operating income, other types of revenue/gains and expenses/losses, and prior period adjustments . . . . unrealized gains and losses from changes in the market values of noncurrent marketable equity securities, and foreign currency translation adjustments, amounts now included in owners' capital under GAAP . . . . donations from nonowner sources . . . . The increasing complexity of business, the diversity of businesses reported on, the controversial nature of the items on the FASB agenda, and the sophistication of the user community, all argue for a full, comprehensive income presentation.

Robinson, 1991, 107–109

698 Divisible income or profit

No dividend shall be payable except out of the profits arising from the business of the company. [Table B, Model articles of association]

UK *Joint Stock Companies Act, 1856*

In declaring a dividend, in my opinion, in trading concerns, the directors are entitled to put an estimate on the value of their assets from time to time, in order to ascertain whether there is or is not a surplus remaining after providing for liabilities; and where they make these valuations from time to time on a just and fair basis, and take all the precautions which ordinary prudent men of business engaged in a similar business would do, they are entitled to treat the surplus thus ascertained as profit. [Chancery: per Chitty J]

Midland Land and Investment Corporation Ltd, 1886

Where nominal or share capital is diminished in value . . . by reason of causes over which the company has no control, or by reason of its inherent nature, that diminution need not, in my opinion, be made good out of revenue. In such a case a dividend may be paid out of current annual profits . . . . It appears to me that if a contrary view were adopted it might be successfully contended that where, owing to extraneous circumstances, the capital is increased in value, that increase might be dealt with as revenue or profits, and go to increase the dividend. This is contrary to all practice, and I think contrary to principle. The capital and the revenue accounts appear to me to be distinct and separate accounts, and, for the purpose of determining profits, accretions to and diminutions of the capital are to be disregarded. [per Lopes L J]

Lee v Neuchatel Asphalte Co & others, 1889

The legal decisions on company dividends have remained a jungle for accountancy students. We can only speculate how far that jungle might have been cleared had

Dicksee and Leake discerned more clearly the particular relationship of the *Lee* and *Verner* judgments to special cases including companies for which the double account system was appropriate, rather than to the generality of business entities. Had they done so, the legal judgments about dividends which followed the *Lee* and *Verner* cases [*Lee*, a mining venture, *Verner*, in respect of an investment trust] ... might have been decided differently.

Kitchen, 1979, 290

These contracts were to deliver at a future time a product not yet made from raw material not yet purchased, with the aid of labor not yet expended. The price agreed to be paid had to cover all the possible contingencies of the market in the meanwhile, and might show a profit and ran the chance of showing a loss. When the sales actually took place they were entered in the books. But to calculate months in advance on the results of the future transactions and on such calculations to declare dividends, was to base such dividends on paper profits ... and not upon the surplus or net profits required by law. It does not seem to me that you can divide ... a hope based on an expectation of a future delivery at a favorable price of what is not yet in existence. [per Clarke J]

Hutchinson v Curtiss, 1904

it is quite likely that no legal obstacle would prevent a corporation from revaluing part of its assets and applying the excess so raised to surplus available for dividends.

Montgomery, 1912/1976, 194

The regulations of a corporation in England [under the permissible but not compulsory Table A of the *Companies Act, 1862*] provided that no dividends should be paid except out of profits arising from the business of the corporation .... the words "arising from the business of the corporation" are omitted [from table A of the *Companies (Consolidation) Act, 1908*]. This change of wording clearly expresses the present law that all profits, however arising, may be distributed as dividends, unless the regulations of the company impose any limitation thereon.

Dickinson, 1914, 69

699 The income (profit and loss) statement

Increases and decreases of wealth, so far as they arise from business conduct, are ... not recorded immediately in the accounts of proprietorship but in subordinate accounts ["economic accounts"] ... [A summary of the results of those accounts, "economic summary", is the profit and loss account] .... To present the affairs of a business concern at the close of a year in intelligible shape it is necessary to have ... : A balance sheet at the end of the period, showing the then condition. A profit and loss account for the period showing how the condition was attained.

Sprague, 1907/1972, 67, 81

The revenue account in the case of trading concerns is usually divided into two parts, the first part, which is called the trading account, showing the sales and cost of goods sold and expenses connected therewith; the second portion, which is known as the profit and loss account, only including expenditure not connected with trading, the net trading profit being transferred from the trading account to the credit.
Jenkinson, 1910, 6

The profit and loss statement is concerned only with financial and operating transactions which produce profit or loss and, further, only with such of those same transactions as occurred during the specific period covered by the report.
Porter & Fiske, 1935, 36

The income statement for any given period should, where necessary, be divided into two sections, one showing particulars of operations for the period, . . . and the other showing realized capital gains and losses and extraordinary credits and charges resulting from income realization and cost amortization not connected with the operations of the period.
AAA, 1936/1957b, 62

The income account is a total account for two classes of movements of values through the business, consumption, and production of value during a given period. The definition of expense and revenue must embrace these two phenomena and nothing more . . . . It is perhaps unfortunate that the older title, profit and loss account, has been neglected, since it directs attention to the diverse elements entering into the results of an entity during a period of time.
Most, 1977b, 279

700 ACCOUNTING SYSTEMS

710 Cost Based Systems Generally

For periodical cost based valuations, see 510
For assumption of a stable money unit, see 128

711 Origin and persistence of cost based accounting

Historical cost/nominal dollar accounting. The generally accepted method of accounting, used in the primary financial statements, based on measures of historical prices
in dollars without restatement into units, each of which has the same general purchasing power.

FASB, 1979, SFAS33

The [elements of] historical cost accounting theory . . . . are: belief in the importance of income measurement; reliance on cost as the primary basis of reporting
assets acquired for sale or use; recognition of revenue as earned based on substantial completion of effort and assurance, usually contractual, of collection of
proceeds; and recognition of expense as benefits from costs incurred or consumed.

Skinner, 1987, 56

****

history records no unwillingness quite so persistent as the unwillingness of mankind
to abandon time-honored principles.

MacNeal, 1939, 184

accounting has been predominantly a record of historical costs and incomes, and
. . . income determination has consisted of the allocation of these costs and incomes
to the appropriate periods. The majority of practitioners have done this for generations without ever thinking about it . . . in theoretical terms . . . . periodic revaluation [of all assets in terms of current prices] is in practice impossible.

Sanders, 1939b, 573

Historically the value basis [of accounting] has much support but the increased size
and complexity of business and the impracticability of annual appraisals led to its
abandonment. The acceptance of cost as the more useful basis for accounting purposes
is based on practical rather than theoretical grounds.

Broad, 1948, 18

657

the cost principle ... does not represent an old tradition that should be regarded as sacred. I believe carrying assets at a valuation (usually perhaps a conservative one) was the tradition followed when "venture accounting" was first displaced by periodical income accounting. Assets were carried at monetary values.

May, 1948a, 109

the cost rule is in large part a reaction to a world of uncertainty . . . .

Moonitz, 1951/1978, 48

The real foundation for cost seems to rest on the adoption of the realization concept . . . . If only realized profits are to be taken into income, cost becomes the yardstick for income measurement . . . . the most useful and reliable basis for accounting generally.

Broad, 1957, 32

Although some nineteenth century accountants advocated the cost principle and the related realization postulate, no consensus was reached until the twentieth century.

Brief, 1965, 23

Historical cost is an unsatisfactory basis for business income measurement. It is unrealistic in its emphasis on cost of acquisition and its assumption that prices and the value of money never change. It appears to have persisted through ... adhering to familiar traditional practices originally based on medieval bookkeeping methods rather than through any solid conviction about its worth as a method of measurement.

Finnie, 1968b, 350

the historical cost basis is essentially an accounting for cash.

Moonitz, 1970c, 13

Historical cost has been the accepted orthodoxy in published financial statements throughout the financial history of the United States.

Wolk & others, 1984, 26

Accounting conventions in our present [historical cost based] model may be responses to the lack of reliable measures of more relevant information or the inability to attain reliable measures at a reasonable cost. However, the result of following those conventions, if described accurately and measured in accordance with the convention, is information that usually is as complete and representationally faithful as is possible even though some may question the relevance of the convention and the attribute being measured.

Kirk, 1991, 137

712 Justifications of cost based accounting

financial statements which serve accountability have a particular duty to be free from arbitrariness and uncertainty. Where the accountant is presented with a choice between several possible valuations, he will choose, in case of doubt, one which is based on factual evidence rather than a mere estimation. For this reason, cost will generally be preferred to current market price.

Schmalenbach, 1919/1959, 36

Cost can usually be supported by . . . tangible evidence of . . . transactions to each of which this corporation has been a party . . . . Compare it with market or appraisal values. Can these be supported as definitely and as accurately by records of real transactions? Is it more realistic to substitute transactions to which the corporation has not been a party for those to which is has been a party? Is it realistic to substitute an estimate for a fact, if the fact is ascertainable and provable?

Couchman, 1940, 257

By basing his work on the concept of embodied cost, the accountant is able to furnish an account of stewardship, to record all costs incurred, and to trace them to their ultimate disposition.

Jones, 1941/1965, 299

The truth cannot be different from what has happened, and the pure orthodox [cost based] method is true because it does not do other than record the transactions which have taken place.

Briscoe, 1953, 677

Cost and invested value represent the investors' commitment relationship [to the business undertaking]; hence, these are the amounts to be reported to the investors up to the date when assets are sold or otherwise disposed of.

Husband, 1960, 477

[Some hold that] the main purpose for which accounting statements are produced is, and has always been, to report on the stewardship of management in handling the capital funds entrusted to its care. The best way to keep such reports unbiased is to record in the accounts only costs actually incurred in the transactions consummated by management, and the disposition of such costs.

Skinner, 1961, 54

Accounting is what it is today not so much because of the desire of accountants as because of the influence of businessmen. If those who make management and investment decisions had not found financial reports based on historical cost useful over the years, changes in accounting would long since have been made.

Mautz, 1973, 23

If the concepts financial position and performance, are themselves inherently ambiguous and nonobservable . . . , contracting parties will need to agree on some sort of state revelation technology or measurement system. We argue that the traditional accounting serves this role – that the historical cost system provides a basis for financial contracting by making assessments of marginal productivity and/or the states of nature obtaining. In this sense, accounting, rather than being a faithful representation of some underlying "true" (but unobservable) economic reality, becomes reality itself. That is, accounting constructs or defines reality for the purposes of financial contracting.

Whittred & Zimmer, 1988, 84

How could accounting reports have survived so long [if accounting practice was little more than mere ritual], we reasoned, if they cost real dollars to prepare yet had no bearing on the wealth positions of the shareholders to whom they were addressed? The fact that reports did not match exactly what this or that accounting theorist prescribed was, and still is, insufficient grounds for rejecting reports prepared under generally accepted accounting principles.

Brown, 1989, 204

713 The alleged objectivity of conventional accounting

cost . . . is generally capable of objective verification, and is free from the subjective element inherent in valuation by appraisal.

Sanders & others, 1938, 59

Recorded costs are objectively determined data; estimated current values are largely matters of opinion and for some types of cost factors are conspicuously unreliable.

Paton & Littleton, 1940, 123

It [cost] provides an objective basis for measurement and minimizes the need for subjective opinion.

Broad, 1948, 18

An important feature of the historical cost basis of preparing annual accounts is that it reduces to a minimum the extent to which accounts can be affected by the personal opinion of those responsible for them.

ICAEW, 1952, N15

Accountants have adopted cost as the measure of asset value largely because of the objectivity and verifiability of the amount, and because of the actual investment by the business.

Anton, 1956, 119

More definite and objective evidence is available for the determination of cost than for the determination of market or realizable values, which in many cases would be matters of pure conjecture.

Finney & Miller, 1958, 169

original measurement [cost] is not tinged with subjectivity. However, subjectivity is introduced when cost allocations are made.
Bastable, 1959, 54

Accounting profit has the advantage of being a more or less objective measure which may be derived by reference to the actual transactions of an enterprise.
Mathews, 1960, 9

orthodox statements prepared in compliance with the money [historical cost] convention are considered the most useful for general business purposes, since they are based on verifiable objective evidence and on a minimum of subjective speculation.
Pyle & White, 1966, 824

Historical cost is more objective and verifiable than current cost or other valuation methods based on current market price, mainly because historical cost is based on the actions actually taken by the firm while other methods are based on hypothetical actions that the firm could have taken or is likely to take in the future.
Ijiri, 1984, 19

The subjectivity of conventional accounting

it is necessary to recognize the fact that cost allocation at the best is loaded with assumption and that in many cases highly arbitrary methods of apportionment are employed in practice. Certainly it is wise not to take the results of the usual process of internal cost imputation too seriously.
Paton & Littleton, 1940, 120

when we prepare accounting statements we must realize that, whether we like it or not, they constitute a picture of something which we have formed in our own minds and for which we must accept the responsibility.
Peloubet, 1945, 394

There is an almost infinite variety of cost alternatives.
Backer, 1955a/1955b, 224

Too many of us close our eyes to the gaps in objectivity, to the clerical burdens, and to the tortuous logic of a procedure if only it relies solely on data derived directly from the accounts by conventional bookkeeping procedures.
Gordon, 1960, 609

historical cost accounts can lay no great claim to merit on grounds of objectivity.
Finnie, 1968b, 351

one has only to consider the various alternative methods which are available . . . for measurement of profit on construction contracts, determination of depreciation, allocation of costs between joint products, allocation of overheads, provision for bad

debts, amortization of deferred charges and other intangible assets, etc. to realize that even the historical cost basis itself is not as objective as we often like to think.
Stamp, 1971, 281

Accountants shudder at the non-objectivity of current values. They tend to forget just how many subjective judgments permeate the financial statements that we now prepare. Calculation of a bad debt provision, determination of an inventory's sale-ability, determination of the period during which benefits will be derived from research and development expenditures, the status of long term contracts in process, even the extent and maturity of many liabilities. All of these items and many more as well require the exercise of subjective judgment, making cost based financial statements much less objective than their proponents claim.
Stone, 1971, 147

the establishment of accounting standards will not eradicate the possibility that any out of a wide range of reported profits might reflect the profit of the past year, for there is a substantial element of subjectivity involved which can never be removed.
Briston, 1974, 50

One of the most basic and more arbitrary accounting principles is that assets are shown on the balance sheet at their cost . . . . This principle causes many problems for the user of the balance sheet. With changing price levels, the cost of an asset purchased several years ago may have no relationship to its current replacement price or its current selling value.
Dearden & Shank, 1975, 11

historic costs *qua* purchase prices are quite objective, while historic costs *qua* allocated purchase prices are quite subjective.
Sterling, 1979, 37

The role of estimate, judgment and opinion

The greatest deception men suffer is from their own opinions.
Leonardo (1452–1519)/1960, 199

under no circumstances can [balance sheets] be regarded as statements of fact, or statements which it is possible for the most skilful or impartial person to absolutely verify, in the strict sense of the term. They are but estimates which . . . may sometimes be expected to be very closely borne out by actual results in the future, but which . . . in some cases cannot reasonably be expected to afford more than a rough indi-cation of the possible course of future events.
Dicksee, 1903a, 282

Every balance sheet must be largely a matter of opinion; . . .
Dickinson, 1908, 422

It must be borne in mind that a balance sheet of any large corporation is not a statement of facts that can be demonstrated with mathematical accuracy so much as an expression of an honest and intelligent opinion.

Sterrett, 1909, 272

the assets of a business ... have to be valued for balance sheet purposes and of necessity these valuations must be based on opinion and judgment.

de Paula, 1926/1978, 123

Any presentation of the state of a corporation's business or of its prospects or of its value must therefore be an opinion, and, so far as it is a matter of accounting, an opinion based on some canons of accounting, which in turn must have their foundation in convention and practical wisdom and not in any absolute or uniform rules of logic. This is a simple truth which is too often ignored by those who should appreciate its existence and its inevitableness . . . .

JA, editorial, 1931a, 86

financial statements of industrial companies are not statistical presentations of fact . . . . While properly based on facts, these statements represent the judgments of the company's management in the application of conventional methods of stating assets and liabilities and in appropriate allocations of income and outgo items to specific periods of time . . . . [not at figures supposed to reflect present day values].

NYSE, 1939, 237

It is difficult to convey to laymen the knowledge that accounting statements are largely based on judgment, estimate, and opinion – that assets are not usually stated at amounts which reflect immediate values, that surplus has no relation to available cash, that depreciation is based on someone's guess of the useful life of an asset, and so on *ad infinitum*.

JA, editorial, 1939, 292

the balance sheet does not show financial condition . . . because the details therein are largely statements of opinion on a conventional basis rather than factual statements and therefore do not contain information which gives a definite measure of condition.

Myer, 1946, 9

The balance sheet is, and can be only, an expression of opinion as to the estimated financial position at a given point of time in the light of (a) recorded facts, (b) the unrealistic assumption that the operations of the enterprise have temporarily halted at that time, (c) estimates or approximations to fact made previously for the purpose of preparing an operating statement, and (d) forecasts of prospective happenings similarly made with the [same] primary purpose . . . .

Fitzgerald, 1956a, 26

Reasonableness cannot be an objective test [of depreciation allocations] because . . . [it] is wholly a matter of subjectively formed opinion. Everyone tends to have his

own unique concept of reasonableness and accountants would do well to abandon such terms as reasonable, equitable and fair if they wish to be objective.
McFarland, 1961, 30

the accounting process includes the use of estimates and the exercise of judgment to a significant extent. In fact these are among the most important features of accounting.
Powell, 1965, 682

[Accountancy] is a record of what a man sees. Accounts express a view, an opinion. The reporting accountant expresses an opinion on them.
Morison, 1970a, 410

The reason that manipulation and massaging [of accounts] are so easy is that old accounting chestnut – judgment . . . . Where matters of judgment exist, creative accounting opportunities exist.
Jameson, 1988, 70, 107

accounting is largely a matter of judgment.
Bosch, 1990, 124

See also 643, and *per contra*, 330

714 Capital maintenance as maintenance of nominal capital

at all events, theoretically speaking, no profits are available until provision has been made for keeping the whole of the paid up capital intact.
Dicksee, 1898, 286

Maintenance of value that is measured in money [nominal capital] ignores the probability of significant fluctuations in the worth of the measuring unit after the date when the capital was originally invested.
Sweeney, 1930, 281

[The increased net worth] notion of income is . . . identified with capital maintenance – but in an arithmetic sense only – it does not, and no concept of income should require the maintenance of a given company's resources at a particular level measured either in physical or value terms.
Edwards, 1938b, 399

Real capital is . . . generalized purchasing power . . . . Accounting, within its self-formulated framework of assumptions, postulates and standards, does not recognize real capital. The postulates of accounting that are the principal offenders in this area are the stable unit of account, the cost concept, the realization principle and the going concern concept.
Eckel, 1964, 139

Accounting calculates capital maintenance on a transaction basis, matching the cost of a good or service with the price of the asset received. It equates cost with the assets sacrificed in exchange. Cost recovery equals capital maintenance.

Illinois, 1964, 20

the amount of the shareholders' interest [at a given date, the valuation of assets being based on their costs] is regarded as the company's capital. Profit for the year is regarded as any gains arising during the year which may be distributed while maintaining the amount of the shareholders' interest in the company at the beginning of the year, which is regarded as the company's capital.

Sandilands, 1975, 32

With money capital, the bench mark used to decide whether a profit has been earned is the book value of the shareholders' interest at the start of the period.

Lewis & Pendrill, 1985, 64

financial capital maintenance means the firm has the same amount of assets in terms of money value, measured either in nominal dollars [e.g. as in historical cost accounting] or in constant [progressively redated] dollars.

Ma & others, 1987

Financial capital maintenance – monetary basis. Under this concept, capital at any point in time is the cumulative total to that point of contributions less withdrawals of resources, . . . Income for a period is simply the increase in the monetary amount of net resources over the period after allowing for [capital contributions, dividends and other distributions] in the period.

Skinner, 1987, 540

See also 615, 663

715 The irrelevance of cost based accounting

In defining a balance sheet, it was stated that its object was to show condition on a certain date, yet the asset values, generally speaking, show the cost at which they were acquired . . . . [a] variation from what would appear to be the commonsense method . . . .

Guthmann, 1925/1929, 19

Cost is only an accident. The value of an asset to a business is measured solely by the value of the use . . . . cost should not be confused with value . . . . Balance sheet valuations at cost ignore the practical, and substitute historical and sentimental measures of value . . . . What makes an investor buy? What are the controlling factors in business? Certainly among the major factors we find the intention to pay debts and to realize a profit. We cannot pay a single debt with assets at cost, nor can we sell goods at profit based on cost.

Montgomery, 1927, 207, 257

once dollars have been turned into other tangible and intangible assets, the money value invested therein ceases to have any direct bearing on their value. Value thenceforth is determined by their ability to produce income.
Daniels, 1933, 302

the past is always obtruding on our discrimination of the present. We ask not only what a thing is now worth but [also] what it did cost, often a fact interesting for deplorable reasons but utterly irrelevant to the present decision that the merchant must make – to sell it for what it is now worth or not sell it at all . . . .
Barnard, 1938, 208

the use of original cost results in both the balance sheet and the income account reflecting values which may have no natural relation to present realities.
May, 1947a, 100

The cost recovery illusion . . . . that money or capital is or can be "recovered" – fantastically – by the process of bookkeeping. Bookkeeping is simply what it purports to be, a recording process and [never could it] recover anything . . . . Cost (in its relationship to price) may . . . dictate when some action – manufacture, purchase or sale – shall *not* be done; but it seldom dictates what *shall* be done.
Blackie, 1948, 1361–2

If the balance sheet fails to indicate values, it is useless for purposes of interpretation . . . . In periods of changing prices, under conventional accounting procedures of stating assets . . . ratios become invalid.
Benninger, 1955, 298

Past costs and book values are irrelevant to all problems of economic choice.
Nolan, 1955, 8

historical costs are generally irrelevant for budgeting purposes.
Fitzgerald, 1956b, 21

Use of historical cost data for [managerial decisions] is rather like the man who wanted to go to New York but went to Chicago instead – where he didn't want to be – because someone gave him a ticket there.
Goetz & Klein, 1960, 525

Subsequent to acquisition, events may demonstrate that acquisition cost . . . no longer represents a useful measure of future benefits for a particular asset.
Sprouse & Moonitz, 1962, 26

Under the historical cost model, accounting has become increasingly divorced from economics . . . . The savings and loan crisis simply provided new evidence of existing accounting inadequacies that some had been pointing to for a number of years.
Wyatt, 1991, 83

See also 737

716 Other comment on cost based accounting

original costs can present few claims to being acceptable indices of present economic values. Originally they may have represented economic values, private prices, or accounting conventions. At a later date, however, they must necessarily be reduced to the status of representing either historical data or accounting conventions, and only by accident could either of these approximate present economic value.

MacNeal, 1939, 161

the use of concepts which see the significance of a good in past expenditure on it can only be misleading.

von Hayek, 1941, 89

The dictum that accounting is essentially a record of historical costs divorces the viewpoint of accounting from that of management.

Scott, 1945, 315

the basis for the consummation of all business transactions is market value . . . . cost is significant primarily because it approximates fair value at date of acquisition . . . . cost does not necessarily represent value at subsequent dates.

Paton, 1946a, 192

To insist on recovering historical costs is irrational, and people who obstinately insist on doing so must be phenomenally lucky to avoid the bankruptcy courts.

Stigler, 1946, 149

Cost is a significant fact at the time of purchase. It is a significant fact historically thereafter but it may lose its significance in other respects if it moves too far away from value . . . . We should not make a fetish of [cost] and bow down to it when its usefulness . . . is lost.

Broad, 1949, 388

Expenditure only has meaning as a historical datum; for the determination of value it has no function whatsoever.

Kleerekoper, 1959, 844

There is hardly a more subtle or corrupting fallacy in economics than that of misplaced concreteness as applied to values, the view that every good goes through its life with a birth certificate in the form of a price tag.

Boulding, 1950/1962, 194

The cost basis may, legalistically speaking, be more objective and may circumvent some kind of uncertainty, but in doing so it violates one of the most fundamental constituents of any value theory: the fact that value of an object or event is bound to time and circumstances.

Mattessich, 1964, 163

I have never seen a cost attach. I never hope to see one. Of those who say they have, I can't myself believe one.

Coughlan, 1965, 470

To hold management accountable in sums of money spent under conditions no longer prevailing, and in all likelihood spent by persons who are no longer managers, and sums which have no logical or discoverable relationship to a present monetary equivalent, is to fly in the face of the nature of things and to make accountability a ludicrous notion.

Chambers, 1966c, 451

Historical costs ... have absolutely no current significance to anyone.

Ross, 1966, 55

The historic cost basis of valuation is objective but arbitrary. The valuation problem is not solved; it is merely avoided.

Rayman, 1970, 423

Farewell to historic costs? [headline]

Accountant, editorial, 1974, 505

See also 737

717 Posited effects of cost based accounting on the trade cycle

Were the incomes [of fat years] fat and [of lean years] lean or only the income figures? Toward the answering of these questions the accountants' annual figures give us exactly no help at all .... if, and to the extent that, business men believe what the accountants' figures seem to say, we have a pernicious state of affairs that probably to a large extent is responsible for the violence of business fluctuations in modern times.

Canning, 1933, 61

Bookkeeping is more or less based on the assumption of a constant value of money .... durable means of production ... figure in the cost accounts at the actual cost of acquisition, and are written off on that basis. If prices rise, this procedure is illegitimate .... too little is written off, paper profits appear .... These paper profits are ... likely to add to the cumulative force of the upswing, because they stimulate borrowers and lenders to borrow and lend more. They foster the optimistic spirit prevailing during the upswing, and so the credit expansion is likely to be accelerated. This phenomenon has its exact counterpart during the downswing of the cycle.

Haberler, 1937/1946, 49

most business men have failed to realize that in periods of rising prices their reported profits are not all real .... The failure to recognize that inventory profits introduce an important fictitious element in the earnings of many corporations has been a major factor in aggravating and intensifying the ups and downs of business.

Arthur, 1939, 10, 13

The currently employed [accounting] procedures tend to accentuate fluctuations in profits, and consequently the amplitude of the oscillations in business expectations between pessimism and optimism.

Buchanan, 1941, 753

The first in first out method of charging operations for the cost of short term inventories and for allocations of longer term plant and equipment has greatly added to the height of the booms and to the depth of the busts.

Grady, 1950, 17

the disturbance to the economy arising from [cyclical] changes in the level of real investment is reinforced by the disturbance caused by the present accounting treatment of assets replaced at higher or lower costs, with the result that the uptrend is likely to run away with itself and become an unhealthy boom, whilst a downtrend is apt to develop into a deep depression.

Lacey, 1952, 19

The accountant's devotion to historic data begets cost figures that lag behind prices. In consequence, accounting profits overpaint the state of trade. The depreciation error tends to make the high price years (both before and after the peak) look better, and the low price years look worse. The stock error instead lifts profits in all years when prices are rising, and depresses profit throughout the downgrade . . . . It appears reasonable to conclude that an error so widespread and so emphatic in its rhythm must have a considerable influence on business sentiment.

Baxter, 1955, 112

Even though economic effects of large magnitude appear to be unlikely, still the greater stability of lifo dividends that is indicated might tend somewhat to temper the severity of business cycle fluctuations relative to the more fluctuating dividends reported under the fifo method. Also, the relatively larger dividend payments that are indicated with the application of the fifo method might to some degree be an aggravating influence on inflationary pressures during periods of price inflation.

Cerf, 1957, 217

In considering the effects of accounting procedures on the trade cycle ... all that can be said is that business confidence may be misplaced if it is based upon accounting profit rather than on current income. There is no ground for the belief that accounting assumptions themselves can cause business confidence to be greater in one period than in the preceding period. In making comparisons between periods, it is necessary to examine pricing policies as well as accounting procedures.

Grant & Mathews, 1957, 157

despite the fact that the majority of writers who have touched on the subject believe that accounting methodology does accentuate business fluctuations, the evidence, at present, does not support the theory.

Ray, 1960, 170

720 Practice Under Generally Accepted Accounting Principles (Conventional, Initial Cost Based Accounting)

721 Practices and principles having substantial support

It is an important part of the accountant's duty, in making his examination of financial statements, to satisfy himself that accounting practices are being followed which have substantial recognition by the accounting profession. This does not necessarily mean that all companies will observe similar or equally conservative practices.

AIA, 1936b, 4

In cases where financial statements filed with this Commission . . . are prepared in accordance with accounting principles for which there is no substantial authoritative support, such financial statements will be presumed to be misleading or inaccurate despite disclosures contained in the certificate . . . or in footnotes . . . .

SEC, 1938a, ASR4

Generally accepted accounting principles are those principles which have substantial authoritative support. Opinions of the Accounting Principles Board constitute substantial authoritative support. Substantial authoritative support can exist for accounting principles that differ from opinions of the Accounting Principles Board. [Special bulletin]

AICPA, 1964, 12

Inasmuch as generally accepted accounting principles embody a consensus, they depend heavily on notions such as general acceptance and substantial authoritative support, which have not been and probably cannot be precisely defined. There is concurrence, however, that the notions of general acceptance and substantial authoritative support relate to the propriety of the practices, as viewed by informed, intelligent, and experienced accountants in the light of the purposes and limitations of the financial accounting process. [Attributed to a committee of the AICPA Accounting Principles Board]

Armstrong, 1969, 50

Only confusion results when generally accepted accounting principles are described officially as those principles which have substantial authoritative support. An undefined term is used to define another undefined term. No one really knows what general acceptance means – by whom and to what extent.

Catlett, 1970, 47

722 Generally accepted accounting principles described

Examination of financial statements [January 1936] .... is probably the first Institute [AIA] publication in which the term "generally accepted accounting principles" appears.

Zeff, 1972, 129

reference to the phrase, generally accepted, has been a useful device for the accounting practitioner .... the device has performed the role of a *deus ex machina* for the profession, since, whenever the accountant could not reach a completely logical solution to his problems, he could refer to the consensus of the accounting profession as expressed by the generally accepted accounting principles. The consensus of the accounting profession, then, became a kind of justification for the accountant's actions.

Stanley, 1965, 7

We must recognize that our so-called generally accepted accounting principles are simply ways of producing financial statements which have, over the years, gained a measure of support.

Ross, 1966, 20

Generally accepted accounting principles encompass the conventions, rules and procedures necessary to define accepted accounting practice at a particular time. The standard of generally accepted accounting principles includes not only broad guidelines of general application, but also detailed practices and procedures. Generally accepted accounting principles are conventional – that is, they become generally accepted by agreement (often tacit agreement) rather than by formal derivation from a set of postulates or basic concepts. The principles have developed on the basis of experience, reason, custom, usage, and to a significant extent, practical necessity.

AICPA, 1970c, APBS4

Generally accepted accounting principles are relatively objective; that is they are sufficiently established so that independent auditors usually agree on their existence .... No single source of reference exists for all established accounting principles .... [The main sources are] statements and interpretations issued by the Financial Accounting Standards Board, APB opinions and AICPA accounting research bulletins .... [Other sources are] AICPA accounting interpretations, AICPA industry audit guides and accounting guides, and industry accounting practices. Depending on their relevance in the circumstances, the auditor may also wish to refer to APB statements, AICPA statements of position, pronouncements of other professional associations and regulatory agencies, such as the Securities and Exchange Commission, and accounting textbooks and articles.

AICPA, 1975, AU411

723 Generally accepted accounting principles said to be unspecified

Almost daily, principles that for years I had thought were definitely accepted among members of the profession are violated in a registration statement prepared by some accountant in whom I have high confidence. Indeed, an examination of hundreds of statements filed with our [Securities and Exchange] Commission leads one to the conclusion that, aside from the simple rules of double entry bookkeeping, there are very few principles of accounting upon which the accountants of this country are in agreement.

Blough, 1937, 31

The chief reason for the present day disagreement in the measurement of income for a given period . . . [lies] in the fact that the basic standards or principles, on which the very concept of income rests, are not agreed to and generally accepted.

Kelley, 1948, 148

While many books have been written which have sought to recite in one place a body of accounting principles, and many more articles have been written setting down certain specific principles, vast areas of disagreement exist concerning practices and procedures vital to the production of useful and understandable financial statements.

King, 1951/1980, 22

[The phrase generally accepted accounting principles] is widely used today in cases in which it is not appropriate because there is no source from which even a general idea of the principles adopted can be gained.

May, 1958, 24

The opinion paragraph of the standard form of [audit] certificate uniformly reads that the financial position and operating results are fairly presented in accordance with generally accepted accounting principles. While practically every accounting firm uses this standard wording to express its opinion on corporate financial statements, there is no general agreement as to the exact meaning of the phrase or its applicability to the variety of situations in which it is used.

Spacek, 1958a, 116

there does not exist any authoritative, comprehensive system of accounting principles.

Mautz & Sharaf, 1961, 161

Currently, a comprehensive, consistent, and generally accepted body of accounting principles does not exist in the United States.

Anthony, 1963, 100

when we independent public accountants report that financial statements are presented in conformity with generally accepted accounting principles, we cannot be sure what we mean, because the expression, generally accepted accounting principles,

has never been satisfactorily defined . . . . [Those] who issue the financial statements on which we report, and those who use them, do not know what we mean
either.

Higgins, 1963/1967, 19

The phrase "generally accepted principles" has unfortunately almost reached the
status of a cliché . . . . generally accepted accounting principles have permitted some
of the largest firms in the country to change their accounting procedures primarily
because someone else is following a particular practice. And all of this happens
without departing from principles. Under these circumstances, you may wonder just
who is doing what and to whom. The fact is . . . that the accounting profession
cannot say precisely – or perhaps even approximately – what those generally accepted
accounting principles are.

Laeri, 1966, 58

the rulebook of accounting measurements, entitled "generally accepted accounting
principles", is almost non-existent, except for the title.

Johnson, 1966, 93

the generally accepted principles of accounting have never been fully and authoritatively codified to anyone's satisfaction.

Ross, 1966, 33

The certified public accountants, of course, certify only that all is in accordance
with generally accepted accounting principles. I think that is just an euphemism for
"anything goes".

Rickover, 1974/1977, 1713

no formal, comprehensive, basic set of generally accepted accounting principles
exists.

Flegm, 1984, 27

724 Interpretation of acceptable, accepted, and generally accepted

the phrase "in accordance with accepted accounting principles" is a most indefinite
characterization of what should be a fairly definite concept. Too frequently accepted
accounting principles are simply those principles which each individual practitioner
considers acceptable in the light of his own experiences and relations with his clients.

Smith, 1935, 332

it would seem that the proper interpretation to give to the term generally accepted
principle is that it is a procedure for handling the recording and interpretation of
a particular type of business transaction so extensively followed that it may be
considered to be generally followed. If this is a proper interpretation of the term,

I am very much afraid it is difficult to name very many principles that are generally accepted.

Blough, 1937, 31

In 1934 we started . . . to express opinions in our reports as to whether the financial statements were prepared in conformity with accepted principles of accounting . . . . in 1939 the phrase was expanded to generally accepted principles of accounting, crystallizing in words the sense in which accepted had generally been used.

Broad, 1944, 186

"Generally accepted" does not mean that the principle is best; or even that it is better than others; or that it is logically and objectively derived; or that it is necessarily most useful at all times. All the term means is, literally, what it says: enough persons have adopted it to ensure its acceptance – in other words, so many other people are in the same boat, that if you adopt the principle you will not be lonely.

Lemke, 1957, 324

There is no common understanding as to "by whom" there should be general acceptance or "to what extent" it should exist. No group of accountants has been in a position to judge the degree of acceptance.

Catlett, 1960a, 38

the standard "generally accepted" – not a reasoned application from a postulate within an established frame of reference but rather justified on the ground that somebody else tried it and got away with it.

Cannon, 1962, 45

we are almost totally lacking in any definition of acceptable [rules], nor have we said by whom these rules should be accepted. It is interesting to note that acceptable does not imply use or approval . . . . if approval is not necessary for acceptance, then where is our determinant of acceptable accounting theory? The unfortunate fact is that we have been perilously close to having none at all.

Hylton, 1962, 24

The phrase, generally accepted accounting principles, has been parroted for so long that it has become almost meaningless.

Gibbs, 1970, 39

725 General acceptance an inadequate criterion for principles

I feel some danger to be inherent in the idea that profit is based purely on conventions accepted by the general body of accountants – that if a procedure is settled practice, then, *ipso facto* it is right . . . . I think we are guilty of having given too much force to common usage in building up our present day system of accounting procedure . . . .

Norris, 1945b, 208

the propriety or soundness of a financial accounting practice ... should be judged not by whether it is generally accepted by accountants or required for certain purposes by governmental bodies, but according to the reasonableness of the result it achieves in portraying realistically the financial affairs of the company . . . . an accounting practice is no sounder than the reasoning on which it is based.

Werntz, 1945/1968, 493

A few [legal] decisions purport to accept accounting conclusions solely because they are founded on generally accepted principles or practices of accounting. But, whenever an attempt has been made to induce a regulatory agency or a court to apply accounting principles merely because they are generally accepted as such, the attempt has failed.

Hills, 1957/1982, 4

Agreement as to a lot of rules on accounting principles does not meet our needs if we have no agreement on the objectives of such rules and no criteria on which to base them.

Spacek, 1958b, 369

Generally accepted accounting principles have been both adopted and rejected by the courts, the legislatures, and regulatory agencies for the determination of income.

Graham, 1965, 654

reporting must be truthful and reasonably complete within the present system . . . . So long as management uses and follows accepted accounting procedures, the certified public accountant must approve the presentation even though he does not agree with it completely. The norm for both groups – accountants and managers – should not be accepted principles, but rather, adequate reporting judged according to the needs of the shareholding public.

Garrett, 1966, 165

The first law for accountants was not in compliance with generally accepted accounting principles but, rather, full and fair disclosure, fair presentation and, if the principles did not produce this brand of disclosure, accountants could not hide behind the principles but had to go behind them and make whatever disclosures were necessary for full disclosure. In a word, "present fairly" was a concept separate from "generally accepted accounting principles" and the latter did not necessarily result in the former.

United States v Simon et al, 1969

The use of general acceptance as a standard of accountability – a standard used for more than 30 years by the accounting profession – has led to a kind of accounting by consensus and a natural evolution toward an ever lower common denominator in practice.

Olson, 1970, 44

In order to ascertain what are the correct principles [of the prevailing system of acccountancy, the court] has recourse to the evidence of accountants. That evidence is conclusive on the practice of accountants in the sense of principles on which accountants act in practice. That is a question of pure fact, but the court itself has to make a final decision as to whether that practice corresponds to the correct principles of commercial accountancy . . . . The expression, ordinary principles of commercial accountancy is, as I understand it, employed to denote what is involved in this composite process. [per Pennycuick V-C]

Odeon Associated Theatres Ltd v Jones,
1971

The policy underlying the securities laws of providing investors with all the facts needed to make intelligent investment decisions can only be accomplished if financial statements fully and fairly portray the actual financial condition of the company . . . . if application of accounting principles alone will not adequately inform investors, accountants, as well as insiders, must take pains to lay bare all the facts needed by investors to interpret the financial statements accurately. [per Chief Judge Macmahon]

Herzfeld v Laventhol et al, 1974

The accountant is using an unstable mixture of standards whose proportions can vary from engagement to engagement . . . . it is time to drop "generally accepted" from the standard short form [audit] report. These words can no longer be reconciled with today's and tomorrow's conditions. They no longer communicate. If they ever were a good choice of words, they no longer are.

Kapnick, 1974, 382

730 Features of Practice under Generally Accepted Principles

731 Inconsistency in principle and practice

It has been held that it is proper [to value inventory] on the basis of the market value if such a value is smaller than cost; but it is generally denied that a market value higher than cost can be used. If the lower value is allowed, there is no reason why the higher one should not be.

Esquerré, 1914, 171

Those who object to the recognition of profits [when assets appreciate but] no sale has taken place seldom apply this rule so as to prohibit the recognition of accruing interest as an element of profit . . . . The denial that profit can exist without a sale and the simultaneous recognition of accruing interest as profit is another of the many inconsistencies in accounting practice.

Hatfield, 1927/1971, 257

The balance sheet of a business is expected to show its ability to pay its debts. In connection with the rest of the current assets – cash, marketable securities, and the

receivables – this has dictated their dollar measurement on a cash realizable basis
. . . . It might seem desirable, therefore, to use the same basis for the measurement
of inventories. Prudent management, however, prefers to measure its inventories
. . . on such a basis as will properly measure its periodic profits. [That is usually
a cost basis.]

Kester, 1946, 168

We maintain that our accounting is a historical process but the history which our
statements summarize is a rationalized history and not the history of the items and
the events which the statements are intended to depict. We contend that cost is the
basis of record and then proceed to define cost in a manner foreign to its customary
meaning. We argue that profit realized because of increases in market value is not
profit because we need to reinvest it to restore the original goods position, in spite
of the fact that the sale which produced the profit completed the original venture
and that the reinvestment begins a new venture. We hold that losses may properly
be booked before realization takes place but gains may not be so booked . . . .

Husband, 1954a, 13

In many cases the [accounting research] bulletins [of the American Institute] allowed
a number of different alternatives – the alternatives in some cases being completely
inconsistent with one another.

Spiller, 1964, 851

conventional accounting is a collection of many different principles and practices,
which, in some cases, are mutually inconsistent.

Ijiri, 1967, 88

the present consistency principle often fails by leading to noncomparability over
time . . . .

Corbin, 1967, 639

Traditionally, the measurement of inventories at market price has only been accepted
when those prices were less than cost. The measurement of all inventories at current
market prices has usually been rejected on the grounds that (1) market prices are
not objective; (2) in many instances market prices do not exist; (3) the use of market
prices implies the recognition of unrealized gains. Of course, each of those grounds
could be refuted by referring to the traditional cost or market rule – if market prices
are sufficiently objective when they are less than cost, they must, logically, be sufficiently objective when above cost; if prices sufficient for the purpose exist in one
case, they must exist in the other; and if unrealized losses must be recognized, then
similarly so must unrealized gains.

Wells, 1970, 481

An increase in the net carrying amount arising on revaluation of property, plant and
equipment should be credited directly to shareholders' interest under the heading
of revaluation surplus, except that, to the extent that such increase is related to and
not greater than a decrease arising on revaluation previously recorded as a charge

to income, it may be credited to income. A decrease in net carrying amount arising on revaluation . . . should be charged directly to income, except that, to the extent that such a decrease is related to an increase which was previously recorded as a credit to revaluation surplus and which has not been subsequently reversed or utilized, it should be charged directly to that account.

IASC, 1982, IAS16

732 Diversity, ambiguity and variability of conventional accounting

Accounting practitioners . . . . are impressed with the difficulty of choice between equally defensible alternatives, the impossibility of exactness in measuring values and results, the inevitability of compromise and approximation.

Greer, 1938b, 213

financial statements . . . incomprehensible mixtures of present facts, historical data, and accounting conventions.

MacNeal, 1939, 184

Intelligent laymen are dissatisfied with published statements which are mysterious results of expert opinions, audited costs, out of date appraisals, and significant omissions.

Whitney, 1941, 356

It may be said that in commercial and investment banking or any business extending credit, success depends on knowing what not to believe in accounting. Few concerns go into bankruptcy or reorganization whose books do not show them to be solvent, and often profitable. [per Justice Jackson]

Federal Power Commission v Hope
National Gas Company, 1944

accounting is a very fluid practice. Accounting varies from industry to industry. In fact even among companies in the same field, practices are so diverse as to make comparisons of earnings less than meaningful. To be sure, few companies make it a habit to juggle their books. Nonetheless, there are many acknowledged alternatives by which earnings can legally be exaggerated or minimized.

Andreder, 1962/1964, 13

But how can two such diverse methods [as lifo and fifo], which produce such different net income figures and working capital ratios, be equally acceptable?

Miller, 1962, 50

In his *Inventory*, Paul Grady [1965] lists thirty sets of [two or more] alternative methods of implementing generally accepted accounting principles. [Fourteen relate to] alternatives available in situations where there are no significant differences in circumstances. [Thirteen relate to] alternatives available in situations where there

are significant differences in circumstances that in current practice are ordinarily ignored in selecting the alternatives to be employed: . . .
Graham, 1965, 669

Once in a frivolous moment I calculated that there were 2,971,332,000 different book values that could be reported for inventory.
Sterling, 1968b, 592

If accounting is a tool designed to facilitate a rational assessment of business success or failure, its techniques should give a timely and accurate representation of an enterprise's current operations, permit comparison with results in previous years, and allow comparison with other comparable enterprises. As currently practised, accounting does not always meet these expectations. On a number of key issues, generally accepted accounting principles permit a range of reporting choices that can materially alter reported company operating results. There need be no consistency in the treatment of depreciation charges, inventory evaluation, the expensing of research and development, and other factors. The specific method of reporting selected by management may be changed from one period to another. It may be said categorically that acccounting statements often are neither consistent over time nor comparable between firms.
FTC, 1969, 120

What the public at large (particularly shareholders and directors) do not seem to have realized is that behind the "true and fair view" of the auditors' report there are 101 ways of presenting the same information – each one perhaps giving quite a different figure of profit and of fixed and current assets.
Croxton-Smith, 1970, 372

[In conventional accounting] . . . Valuation adjustments, like depreciation provisions, cost allocation, and stock valuation, are included in the same accounts as the records of external transactions. Consequently, it is impossible to distinguish between the results of actual events and the effects of accounting procedures.
Rayman, 1970, 423

Accounting bases are the methods which have been developed for expressing or applying fundamental accounting concepts to financial transactions and items. By their nature accounting bases are more diverse and numerous than fundamental concepts, since they have evolved in response to the variety and complexity of types of business and business transactions, and for this reason there may justifiably exist more than one recognized basis for dealing with particular items.
ASSC, 1971b, SSAP2

[Accountants] know that a thousand different accountants, given the same facts, will come up with a thousand different sets of accounts . . . .
Jameson, 1988, 7

733 Manipulation and smoothing of reported income

although the profitability of [19th century British] railway companies was extremely sensitive to changing economic conditions, railway managers believed that shareholders required a steady dividend . . . . This led them, in many cases, to employ valuation procedures designed principally to produce a pattern of reported profit sufficient to justify the desired level of distribution – the aim was profit-smoothing on a large scale.

Edwards, 1985, 26

The loose way in which the books were kept would appear to have led the clerks of the [Eastern Counties] railway [c.1840, under the chairmanship of George Hudson, railway promoter and member of parliament] into a state of unenviable bewilderment . . . . entries were made to the credit or debit of heads of account, as the case might be, for securing nominal aggregate sums to bear out half-yearly statements . . . premiums realized on certain shares were carried to income, and the ascertained loss on other shares was carried to works [assets] . . . passenger and merchandise account were continually overstated, and entries were not made in the order in which they arose . . . .

Evans, 1859/1968, 32

On the whole, depreciation charges tend to be modified, if at all, in such a manner as to make more steady the computed annual profits.

Fabricant, 1938, 86

Normally the object of creating an undisclosed reserve is to enable a company to avoid violent fluctuations in its published profits or its dividends.

Cohen Committee, 1945, 56

An important objective of income presentation should be the avoidance of any practice that leads to income equalization.

AIA, 1947c, ARB32

Given [managerial self interest] . . . a management should within . . . the latitude allowed by accounting rules, (1) smooth reported income, and (2) smooth the rate of growth in income.

Gordon, 1964, 262

the conclusion is difficult to avoid that income equalization is the primary motive underlying the current practice of amortizing book value in excess of cost . . . , amortizing gains on sales and leasebacks . . . , and amortizing investment credits into income over a period of years.

Sprouse, 1966a, 52

Artificial smoothing represents accounting manipulations undertaken by management to smooth income. These manipulations do not represent underlying economic events or affect cash flows, but shift costs and/or revenues from one period to another.

Eckel, 1981, 29

Conceptually, smoothing can be viewed as a form of signalling whereby managers use their discretion over the choice among accounting alternatives within generally accepted accounting principles so as to minimize fluctuations of earnings over time around the trend they believe best reflects their view of investors' expectations of the company's future performance.

Givoly & Ronen, 1981, 175

the stock market ... much prefers the fantasy of smooth growth to the reality of fluctuating operational performance. It falls to the creative accountant to ensure that those fluctuations are removed by hoarding profits in the years of plenty for release in the years of famine.

Griffiths, 1986, 3

See also 475

734 Comment on conventional income calculation

It is ... obvious to all who have considered the actual conditions that face the accountant that no annual measure of income ... can be looked upon as a matter of fact. And what is set out as a measure of net income can never be supposed to be a fact in any sense at all except that it is the figure that results when the accountant has finished applying the procedure which he adopts.

Canning, 1929a, 98

ordinary accounting procedure is not suitable for indicating whether an enterprise has approached nearer the usual goal of economic activity, viz, increase in the general purchasing power of the owners' investment in the enterprise.

Sweeney, 1936/1964, 24

To entitle any interpretation of income "the accounting concept" is hazardous . . . . the rules by which accountants arrive at the annual income of a given enterprise are not self-consistent and could not be derived by deduction from any major premise as to what income means.

Bonbright, 1937/1965, 902

The significance of periodic accounting profit is ... the algebraic sum of the separate significances of the various conventions, doctrines, rules and practices which at any time constitute the common law of accounting.

Gilman, 1939, 605

In some cases, in the interests of financial prudence, the application to known facts of conservative accounting conventions may be carried to more extreme lengths than in others. For these reasons, profit and loss statements and balance sheets are conditioned both by accounting convention and by opinion and financial policy; the profit disclosed by a profit and loss statement must be interpreted in the light of accounting concepts of profit, and must be regarded as an expression of opinions which have been formed with special care for financial prudence . . . .

Fitzgerald & Fitzgerald, 1948, 16

the results shown by accounts on the basis of historical cost are not a measure of increase or decrease in wealth in terms of purchasing power; nor do the results necessarily represent the amount which can prudently be regarded as available for distribution, having regard to the financial requirements of the business. Similarly the results shown . . . are not necessarily suitable for purposes such as price fixing, wage negotiation and taxation, unless . . . due regard is paid to the amount of profit which has been retained in the business for its maintenance.

ICAEW, 1952, N15

conventional statutory and financial accounting are now totally inadequate and need a complete overhaul . . . . Given time to reflect on the doubtful validity of our accounting conventions, it would seem that, having made nonsense of profits and nonsense of capital employed, we deduce, by expressing one nonsense as a percentage of the other, a return on capital employed, by which we may compare the performance of one company's index of nonsense with that of another.

Accountant, Anon, 1964, 596, 598

Profit as we now determine and report it defies objective definition . . . . [That profit] is the consequence of observing a great number of accounting practices which we and the business community have been in the habit of following. And, this habit is the authority for their existence. These practices . . . . were adopted as patchwork compromises in bookkeeping to meet certain desired and often conflicting viewpoints at one time or another, and they have been continued regardless of changed conditions and the absence of basic objectivity. Their repetitive use is like copying last year's working papers in making this year's audit, a sure way to repeat all previous mistakes.

Spacek, 1970b/1973, 38

735 Creative or cosmetic accounting

An historian of manners might find parallels in examining the points, in different periods, at which the cosmetician's treatment of a balance sheet and a woman's face is regarded as indecent, and it may be supposed that the present time would not show up too well in such a comparison of periods.

Schmalenbach, 1919/1959, 208

The appointees [to an independent inquiry into the affairs of Pergamon Press Ltd do not] recommend any changes in the general accounting principles adopted by the group. But they do recommend very material changes in the way in which those principles have been applied . . . . The effect of the [recommended] adjustments to the 1968 accounts is: (a) to reduce the trading profits before tax . . . from £2.104 million as shown in the published accounts to £0.495 million . . . and (c) to reduce the net assets of the group at 31 December 1968 . . . from £7.034 million to £4.461 million.

Holmes, 1970, 699

In the area of accounting principles, efforts are increasingly being devoted to the codification of rules so that auditors will have the authority to veto creative accounting approaches developed by their clients.

Burton, 1971, 48

The term creative accounting is widely used to describe accepted accounting techniques which permit corporations to report financial results that may not accurately portray the substance of their business activities . . . . creative accounting is recognized as a synonym for deceptive accounting . . . . Creative accounting methods are noteworthy because they remain in use as generally accepted accounting principles, even though they have been shown to be deceptive in many cases.

Metcalf, 1977a, 188

Wages, taxes and dividends, all cash outflows, are a function of profits. Keep the profits low and this will take the steam out of the various parties who make these cash draining demands . . . . The prudence concept not only helps management in this deliberate and permanent suppression of profits; it legitimizes this activity.

Lothian, 1982, 407

Every company in the country [UK] is fiddling its profits. Every set of published accounts is based on books which have been gently cooked or completely roasted . . . . this deception is all in perfectly good taste. It is legitimate. It is creative accounting.

Griffiths, 1986, 1

Creative accounting . . . . operates within the letter both of the law and of accounting standards but it is quite clearly against the spirit of both . . . . It is essentially a process of using the rules, the flexibility provided by them and the omissions within them, to make financial statements look somewhat different from what was intended by the rule. It consists of rule-bending and loophole-seeking.

Jameson, 1988, 20

It was common [in the mid 1980s in Australia] for the so-called entrepreneurial companies to include capital profits from the sale of properties or shares . . . as operating profits . . . . on the ground that speculation was a major element in their business . . . . Some companies . . . booked unrealized capital gains as operating profit . . . . some of the transactions which gave rise to these "profits" were done with business associates or even within the same group of associated companies. The values put on the assets "sold" often looked very suspicious, with secret put and call option arrangements sometimes allowing the "buying" company to transfer the asset back to the seller at a later date – in some cases just after balance date .... It was common for companies to include their "share" of the net profits of associated companies in their own results .... There was an extensive use of 49 per cent owned companies that were not consolidated into group accounts to keep debt off a group's balance sheet and thus to give a misleading appearance of its capital structure. Associated companies and interposed trusts were also used to conceal other favorable information from the eyes of investors.

Bosch, 1990, 122–3

736 Uniformity of accounting said to be undesirable or impossible

no general rules for bookkeeping can be applied with equal elegance and utility upon all occasions.

Dunn, 1760/1965, 661

The conditions under which companies carry on their business are so numerous, the nature of the business so varied and the places at which the businesses are carried on so spread over the world, that to attempt to prescribe either a statutory form of balance sheet or what a balance sheet must disclose or that there should be in addition a profit and loss account is considered likely to do more harm than good.

ICAEW, 1925

The practices which might be most suitable for one industry will be different at times from those which are most suitable for another industry .... To some extent variations in accounting practice within a specific industry may be justified, if not necessitated, by different operating conditions .... variations in accounting practice within an individual company are sometimes warranted and made desirable by different underlying economic or operating conditions.

Broad, 1950a, 381

Uniformity of accounting method is neither expected nor necessarily desirable.

AAA, 1954b/1957b, 47

The misconception held by some, that accountants should be able to present the one true measure, has hindered progress in the reporting of financial information.

Bierman, 1963b, 502

Judgment and estimates play a substantial role in accounting on an accrual basis, which is the only useful basis for presenting statements of financial position and results of operations for complex business entities. It is axiomatic that when there is diffusion in decision making, a necessity to the free enterprise system, there is bound to be diversity in the accounting results.

Grady, 1965, 33

divergent [accounting] practices are both the outgrowth and reflection of our economic system and . . . the effort to eliminate or reduce them is not a service either to our accounting system or to the economic system it serves.

Browne, 1966, 42

Like standardization of spelling, uniformity in presentation can increase the speed of comprehension. It would, however, be a mistake to believe that it would be possible so to standardize accounting procedures that a unique figure of profit was always reported in given circumstances without detriment to the quality of the information.

Edey, 1969, 539

We are nowhere near being able to deduce from a given set of facts one single accounting treatment to the exclusion of all others.

Morison, 1970b, 468

There are overwhelming reasons which lead us to conclude that no single accounting system yet invented or to be invented will be sufficient for all industries, all purposes, and all people.

Whitman & Shubik, 1971, 72

no set of standards (applied to the accounting alternatives *per se*) exists that will always rank accounting alternatives in relation to consistent individual preferences and beliefs.

Demski, 1973, 722

Accounting is . . . not capable of rigid and uniform standardization. Accounting systems must be left free to report information in a way which reflects a high degree of utility to users and their needs, however defined, in particular situations, and this implies an element of diversity.

McCusker, 1979, 203

The diversity convention . . . . accounting procedures can differ between businesses even if those businesses are similar.

Henderson & Peirson, 1983, 83

See also 348

Potential variation in accounting outputs illustrated

I would almost undertake to draw up two balance sheets for the same company, both coming within an auditor's statutory certificate, in which practically the only recognizable items would be the name and the capital authorized and issued.

Chamberlain, 1938, 605

for this group of [20] companies, over the eight year period reviewed, the most restrictive application of these [accepted] principles with relation to profits would have produced an aggregate net profit for all the companies combined of about 125 million dollars, while the most liberal application, if consistently followed, would have produced an aggregate profit of about 275 million dollars. It is noteworthy also that none of the differences result from the difficulties of measurement of values (in which accounting judgment is considered so important); they arise exclusively from differing opinions as to what constitutes a profit.

Greer, 1938a, 29

a company which reported $3.11 [as earnings] per share, could have shown $2.86, $3.11, $3.87, $3.90, $4.12, $4.15, $4.91 or $5.16 – merely by its disposition of three items [for which alternative rules were permissible].

Werntz, 1946, 37

The president's letter [of Loew's Inc, 1957] noted that instead of the reported loss of $455,000, there would have been net earnings of $745,000 if the company had followed the accounting practices of previous years . . . . Adjustments [in respect of prior years, due in part to] changes in accounting policies in the amount of $6,307,151 (after taxes) have been charged to earned surplus.

JA, 1958, 20

[A calculation tendered in the course of a debate between two eminent practitioners at the 1960 meeting of the AICPA showed that, from the same data relating to a hypothetical firm, there could be derived financial statements which reported net incomes per share as different as $0.80 and $1.79, the difference being due solely to the specific accounting rules chosen from the battery of generally accepted rules.]

Wise, 1962, 37, 203

[By the use of different sets of accounting rules in a hypothetical case, the same basic events could be shown to have yielded a net profit as different as $624,000 and $28,000.]

Savoie, 1963, 148

In October 1967, the board of AEI forecast a profit of £10m for the year ending 31 December 1967, in the course of a takeover battle against GEC . . . . GEC gained control of AEI and in July 1968 they reported that AEI had suffered a loss of £4.5m in 1967. [Of the difference of £14.5m, it was] admitted by GEC that only £5m . . . was a matter of fact, while the remaining £9.5m was a matter of judgment regarding the selection of the accounting principles relevant for reporting the 1967 results.

Briston, 1973, 97

For the year ended March 1985 CSR reported a net loss after tax of $63 million, after charging $156 million as an extraordinary item for the full extent of the group's foreign exchange losses on overseas loans at balance date. CRA, on the other hand, reported a net profit of $22 million after charging $89 million as an operating charge for foreign exchange losses. In the balance sheet a further $200 million was deferred, representing the balance of net unrealized losses on overseas borrowing .... if CRA had used CSR's accounting policy, it would have shown a loss of something like $178 million instead of a profit of $22 million. If CSR had used CRA's accounting policy it would almost certainly have shown a substantial profit instead of a loss of $63 million.

Bosch, 1990, 124

Diversity of practices criticized

The accountants are enabled to play ball with figures to an astounding degree.

Ripley, 1927, 50

taxation is now dealt with by four methods, namely, as a capital reserve, as a revenue reserve, as a provision and as a liability shown in splendid isolation. Apparently a fifth is to be added, a contingent liability method presumably in conjunction with the first four methods. Five different answers to the one problem; and accountancy is deemed an exact science!

Harman, 1953, 47

It just doesn't make sense to tell the public that professional skill is required to determine that fifo presents the financial position better in one company and lifo in another; that one company should capitalize intangible drilling cost but another should charge it to expense; or that one company should provide for deferred tax and another does not have to: ....

Spacek, 1958a, 44

we have double-standard accounting – double standards which result in several methods of providing for depreciation, in several methods of accounting for goodwill, and in the omission of certain liabilities from the balance sheet. Yet double-standard accounting was the basis of the criticism that led to the creation of the Securities and Exchange Commission in 1933. Thus we find that the standards of accounting that created such debacles as the Insull and Hopson failures are again held in favor, and have the approval of regulatory commissions as adequate financial statements presented to investors.

Spacek, 1964b, 68

Contrary to popular belief, there are no mechanical rules that auditors and accountants automatically follow; they chiefly use their common sense – and some of them have more of it than others. But shareholders have no means of measuring it; they cannot tell ... whether two men preparing the figures for two roughly comparable companies in the same industry are using the same or wildly different mental ground rules .... The price being paid now for the unrestricted use of a host of dissimilar accounting methods is an unacceptable and unnecessary diversity, which is largely hidden from shareholders by the fact that a lot of it does not, legally, have to be disclosed.

Economist, 1970, 66

737 Posited functional unfitness of products of conventional accounting

Irrelevance to decisions

Think of the economic conception of capital as distinct from income, and then deliberate on the sorry figure that is cut in the light of it by your modern fetish of a safe or sound balance sheet, which lies in almost every line and yet is approved by you because it overstates no assets and understates no liabilities, while it has valuable premises written down to negligible figures and reserves hidden in innumerable places, or profits held up and tucked away. "The truth, the whole truth and nothing but the truth" cannot be derived from the modern balance sheet, so vaunted for its prudence, but prudence is just as possible without departing from what a balance sheet ought to be – a faithful record of the employment of the total capital invested in the business . . . . Has the shareholder who wishes to sell his shareholding no rights as to some real knowledge of the value of what he is selling?
Stamp, 1932, 776

Did not one of your fellow-craftsmen, the late Sir Mark Webster Jenkinson, say only a few years ago that "backers of horses have better information available than speculators in shares"?
Jenkinson, c1930/1938, 605

To the extent that they record past rather than current values, and to the extent that alternative bases of valuing different items are expressly permitted, financial statements prepared in accordance with generally accepted accounting principles are capable of misleading investors, creditors, and shareholders who make use of the information contained in the statements and who are not aware of the technical limitations of the statements.
ASA, 1966, 7

consistent following of acquisition cost . . . results in a logical system . . . but one which is useless for the two major objectives of a report on the past or a basis for future action.
Moonitz, 1970c, 20

to the extent that traditional historical cost accounting is a stewardship of the dollars invested in the business by its owners, it is a stewardship of a grossly inadequate standard . . . . if managers need only account for the number of dollars invested and not for the preservation of true economic capital in the face of inflation, there is no meaningful standard of stewardship.
Kripke, 1972, 97

The fundamental way in which generally accepted accounting principles fail to assist in the economic resolution of conflict is their lack of relevance to the decision problems of economic actors.
Johnson & Gunn, 1974, 651

there is very considerable agreement amongst most members of the accounting profession, important institutions and the government, that historic cost accounts are
now totally inadequate for proper financial decisions to be made from the information they contain.

Morpeth, 1977, 302

historical cost accounting is not really up to producing numbers which are necessarily appropriate for forecasting . . . . they are not very good at showing current
values, so it should not be all that surprising that they are not particularly useful
for predicting future values.

Jameson, 1988, 15

See also 715

Lack of correspondence with reality

The method . . . of valuation "at cost", unless supported or qualified by some further
statement, wraps the whole of the assets in a mist of nebulous history quite inconsistent with any effective standard of informativeness. For what the words really
mean is this: "At a particular date or dates which the directors may or may not
allow to be mentioned these assets were purchased for £xyz, but the company is
careful not to commit itself in writing to the statement that these assets are worth
this figure at present, even on a going concern valuation (let alone on a forced
realization), or that the book value even corresponds to their replacement value".
Put thus nakedly, such a purely historical valuation of the company's assets would
probably produce a somewhat unsympathetic reaction in the minds of its readers.
But the words "at cost", hallowed as they are by use, appear comfortably to lull
the mind of the shareholder.

Samuel, 1933/1982, 254–5

The financial information which corporations make public or render to the government is incomprehensible, false and misleading. Their propaganda is calculated
to keep the public under the delusion that preparation of a statement of condition
by a certified public accountant is a guarantee of truthful representation of the facts.
Nothing is further from the truth . . . .

UMW, 1946, 271

As both the world and business grow more complex the element of uncertainty in
accounting becomes greater. Therefore the tolerances within the limits of generally
accepted accounting principles inevitably become wider . . . . today it is difficult to
decide just what significance may be attached to the annual accounts of a corporation.

May, 1955a, 43

we in the financial field have adopted some practices that are so abominable that
no tough-minded executive could accept them because the practices conflicted with

economic reality. On the other hand, some executives have learned the weaknesses of accounting in portraying true economic results and, by taking advantage of those weaknesses, have produced financial statements that could be supported only by accounting fantasies called "generally accepted accounting principles".
Spacek, 1968, 62

It is clear that what we call accounting and the standard methods of accounting are of remarkably limited usefulness for purposes of figuring out what is going on in the real world of economic activity.
Manning, 1969, 85

The sanctity of cost and the related matching concepts have tended to litter balance sheets with dreams of the future – preoperating, development, advertising, research costs – on the basis that these expenditures will be matched against future revenues even though they attach to no economic resource in which there can be a viable interest or equity.
Hinton, 1972, 58

unsupplemented historical cost based data do not adequately reflect current business economics.
SEC, 1976a, ASR190

financial statements prepared according to generally accepted accounting principles are meaningless; they do not measure any known economic variable. They should ultimately be replaced by statements which measure carefully defined economic concepts . . . . cash flows, wealth (. . . the present market value of all assets less the present market value of all obligations . . .), and income (. . . the increase in wealth between two points in time, plus consumption during the time interval).
Bodenhorn, 1978, 5

Until we in this country [UK] learn that management and annual accounts prepared under the historical cost convention are no better than laudable pus, so long will a large number of our businesses move remorselessly and deservedly to the mortuary.
Benson, 1983, 51

See also 716

738 Audit of conventional accounts

statutory auditors [under the companies acts] verify very little and certify nothing.
Trigg, 1950, 43

If [the use of current market values] be unacceptable or for some unfathomable reason impractical, ought not auditors in common honesty insist that to every balance sheet they audit the directors append a legend something along the lines of the following: "The amounts appearing opposite the various items in the balance sheet are not to be taken literally. They may or may not truly represent the value of the assets to the company at the date of the balance sheet. We are unable or unwilling to disclose the true value of the assets." How long do you think that the historical cost concept would survive that treatment?

Ryan, 1967, 105

if the audit profession or most of them fail to adopt some step [e.g. to ascertain the true financial position of a company] which despite their practice was reasonably required of them, such failure does not cease to be a breach of duty because all or most of them did the same. [per Moffitt J]

Pacific Acceptance Corporation Ltd v
Forsyth & others, 1970

what the auditor really certifies (in current practice) are not the figures themselves, but the procedures by which they have been obtained . . . . once it is accepted that the professional accountant is not qualified to certify discretionary valuations, it becomes clear that conventional profit and loss statements are outside his proper area of responsibility as an auditor.

Rayman, 1970, 426

The auditing process is not a verification of the outputs; instead it is, in essence, a recalculation of the outputs and an examination of the underlying business documents in order to check on the accuracy or verity of the inputs.

Sterling, 1970b, 450

739 Accounting and corporate misdemeanors

[The operations of Ivar Kreuger, c1913–1931] had been, one might say, the greatest fraud in history . . . . Asked once to explain the secret of his success, he said . . . "There are three things. The first is silence. The second thing is more silence. The third thing is still more silence." Concealing from his associates and supporters the immense ramifications of his huge conspiracy, retaining in his hands alone the "inner" books from which accounts and balance sheets were compiled . . . . [and by] the wholesale falsification of accounts . . . . he persuaded the greatest international bankers that he was the world's most powerful man . . . .

Vallance, 1955, 164

[In 1963, an extensive speculative exercise to corner the oil futures market by Allied Crude Vegetable Oil Refining Corporation – Anthony De Angelis, president –prompted investigation by the Commodity Exchange Authority. Completely out of ready cash, Allied could not sustain the dizzy level to which its own operations had forced the prices of futures contracts. Prices plummeted; margin calls on Allied's holdings could not be met. Allied and three other De Angelis companies filed for bankruptcy. Ira Haupt & Co, the brokerage house that had financed De Angelis' margin buying, failed. The members of the NYSE contributed $10 million to make good the losses of Haupt clients. As for Allied, 1,854 milllion pounds of oil with a stated value of

$175 million, was missing. One tank, supposed to contain $3.6 million worth of soybean oil, poured out salt water for twelve days after it was tapped. Fifty-one companies which had loaned money to or deposited oil with Allied were caught: banks, merchant banks and trading companies right across the United States and some as distant as London, Bremen and Zurich. American Express, ultimate owner of Allied, was saddled with a liability of $60 million or more. – Digested]
Miller, 1965, *passim*

The methods [of accounting] to which we refer are the taking to account of total book profit upon terms sales as at the date of sale without any provision being made for bad debts, and the capitalization of holding costs [of properties under development] without adequate steps to ensure that book values were not increased beyond realizable values. We think these policies . . . were deliberately adopted . . . in order to produce accounts which would show at the earliest possible date the largest possible profit by the use of recognized accounting principles . . . . in our view the result of combining in one set of accounts a series of extreme techniques all of which maximized [reported] profits . . . was to produce grossly misleading figures.
Payne's Properties Investigation, 1965,
164

The 1961 accounts . . . combined what was plain dishonesty with misleading exploitations of recognized accounting practices . . . . in the circumstances in which the 1961 accounts were prepared many of the devices which I have called misleading exploitations of recognized accounting practices received the imprimatur of the various accountants who were auditing the accounts involved. Now it is true that some of the auditors of the companies whose affairs I have investigated were supine and gullible but most were not and I do not think that any were dishonest – and yet the accounts were approved . . . . In my opinion the investigation has shown that . . . the whole question of how company accounts ought to be prepared and presented requires urgent and critical examination.
Reid Murray Holdings Investigation,
1966, 94

[Atlantic Acceptance Corporation had grown from a group having assets of $1.2 million in 1954 to $133 million at the end of 1964. It collapsed in default of the terms of debt covenants.] For a Canadian company of this size doing business in the field of finance in times of unexampled affluence, in respect of which no sign of instability had been previously detected, and which had debt then outstanding in excess of $130,000,000 owing to lenders which included institutions regarded as the most shrewd and experienced investors in North America, suddenly to default on a routine obligation was an event which astonished the financial world. From it flowed the collapse of Atlantic Acceptance and all its subsidiaries, the bankruptcy of many companies dependent upon it, the ruin of many lives and the searching re-examination of financial practices and legislation of long standing.
Atlantic Acceptance Royal Commission
Report, 1969, 1

the Atlantic Acceptance scandal . . . . is concerned with a financial collapse involving losses of approximately $70 million. The report of the Royal Commission took four years to complete . . . . the evidence fills over 200 volumes of transcript. The Atlantic Acceptance crash [1965] has resulted in four chartered accountants being expelled by the Ontario Institute (two of them also being sentenced to jail for two years), one lawyer being disbarred by the Law Society of Upper Canada (and being sentenced to a year in jail), and the expulsion of a member of the Toronto Stock Exchange.

Stamp, 1970b, 303

as both the operating and liquidity condition of Penn Central deteriorated, its management made increasingly strenuous efforts to make a bad situation look better by maximizing reported income. An elaborate and ingenious series of steps was concocted to create or accelerate income, frequently by rearranging holdings and disposing of assets, and to avoid or defer transactions which would require reporting of loss. Accounting personnel testified that they were constantly under intense pressure from top management to accrue revenue optimistically and underaccrue expenses, losses, and reserves, to realize gain by disposing of assets and to charge losses to a merger reserve which would not take them through the income statement. Gains were reported on real estate transactions in which the realization of benefits to the company depended on operating results far into the future and in which there was little if any change in the character or amount of assets owned by Penn Central . . . . It is essential that the end result of applying accounting principles be a realistic reflection of the true situation of the company on which a report is prepared. Here, there was no adequate presentation of the fundamental reality that reported income was not of a character to make a contribution to the pressing debt maturities or liquidity needs of Penn Central, nor was it of the sort that might reasonably be expected to be evidence of continuing earning power.

Casey, 1972b, ix, x

In the private sector, business has gone through a series of damaging trends and events. In the 1960s there were the go-go managers who parlayed small companies into giant conglomerates through accounting manipulations that ultimately resulted in the bilking of hordes of small investors. These were accompanied by the spectacular collapse of a number of prominent companies, like Penn Central and Equity Funding, whose securities were thought to be outstanding investments. The management frauds and cover-ups that came to light over the last decade were the forerunners of corporate misdeeds of unimagined pervasiveness. The revelations about corporate bribes, illegal political contributions and other assorted irregularities which are currently unfolding are leading to demands for disclosure and openness that are likely to eliminate most remaining vestiges of privacy of financial information.

Olson, 1976, 82

The study was precipitated by continual revelations of previously unreported wrongdoing by major corporations, as well as a series of corporate failures and financial difficulties which have come to light in recent years. In many cases, the problems which occurred were caused or aggravated by the use of accounting practices that failed to reflect accurately the substance of corporate business activities. [Letter of transmittal of Staff Study Report]

Metcalf, 1977a, iii

The accounting profession is being battered again. The occasion this time has been the epidemic of savings and loan failures; before it was the failures of nonfinancial firms and before that the illegal political contributions and improper overseas payments. It is a fair bet that when another wave of financial rapacity and greed afflicts American sensibilities there will be another round of accountant bashing.

Sommer, 1990, 114

740 Index Adjusted Historical Cost (CPP) Accounting

[as in systems described as general price level accounting, or constant or current purchasing power (CPP) accounting]

For indexed cost valuations see also 516

741 CPP accounting described

Altogether to disregard the changing dollar does not permit the true condition of affairs to be set forth . . . . All accounts should be expressed in terms of the current dollar . . . . The value of goods varies directly as the price index . . . . The value of the dollar varies inversely as the index.

Middleditch, 1918, 115, 120

if one accepts the principle that real capital must be maintained intact out of profits . . . . cash subscribed . . . and profits subsequently ploughed back . . . would be converted to present day pounds at the index number relating to the year concerned. The aggregate excess of the amounts of present day values over book equivalents would be credited to . . . inflation reserve, and the corresponding debit could be to an account called "depreciation of sterling in the business" . . . . The excess amounts over book cost on revaluing the fixed assets [and depreciation] and stocks in the manner described [i.e. by a general price index] would be credited against the account "depreciation of sterling in the business" . . . . The debit balance left on the [latter] account would represent the amount by which the capital and profits invested in the business had depreciated in terms of the present day pound. It would therefore require to be covered by "profits" before a real profit could be found to have emerged.

Beaton, 1949, 17

The effects of price fluctuations upon financial reports should be measured in terms of the overall purchasing power of the dollar – that is, changes in the general price level as measured by a general price index. For this purpose, adjustments should not be based on either the current value or the replacement costs of specific types of capital consumed .... all statement items affected should be adjusted in a consistent manner.

AAA, 1951/1957b, 26

Two methods of ... [conversion accounting] are possible. One is to convert all figures to the comparatively stable pre-inflation pound in exactly the same way as fluctuating foreign currencies are converted to the comparatively stable home currency .... [However] .... People are naturally accustomed to think in terms of pounds of present day values. The preferable method is, therefore, probably to convert those figures in the accounts which represent pounds of the past to their equivalent values in pounds of the present. All revenue and expenditure items should be converted at the average rate of inflation ruling during the year and all balance sheet items at the rate current at the year-end. If the equity shareholders' interest is converted at the year-end rate, the resulting figure is the minimum amount at which the net assets must be maintained before any profits are revealed.

Wimble, 1952, 130

The same accounting principles used in preparing historical dollar financial statements should be used in preparing general price level financial statements except that changes in the general purchasing power of the dollar are recognized in general price level financial statements.

AICPA, 1969, APBS3

Inflation and accounts .... The essence of the proposed solution is simple .... (a) business organizations would continue to keep their records and present their financial accounts on the present historical cost basis; (b) they would also translate all or at least the principal items in the historical cost accounts from their heterogeneous mixture of £s of different vintages into £s of a uniform current purchasing power. The presentation could take one of a number of forms, varying from a simple re-conciliation of the results under the two bases to a full supplementary set of accounts restated in £s of current purchasing power.

ASSC, 1971a, 497

There are three basic CPP rules: (a) Always date monetary units. (b) Use a general index of purchasing power to translate monetary units of different dates into units of constant purchasing power. (c) Only add and subtract and compare units of the same purchasing power.

Myddelton, 1981, 93

Except for monetary assets and liabilties ... all amounts in the [conventional] financial statements will be restated in terms of the general purchasing power of the dollar at a given date, either as of the financial statement date itself or the average purchasing power of the dollar during the current year.

Wolk & others, 1984, 28

742 General object of CPP accounting

The object of the index method of adjusting accounts is to eliminate from profits the effect of fluctuations in the purchasing power of money. The method is not strictly a proposal for a change from accounting based on historical cost; it is more in the nature of a proposal for adjusting accounts which have been prepared on the basis of historical cost .... For the conversion process an index of purchasing power would be used.

ICAEW, 1952, N15

Where ... the principles of historical cost are regarded as the most suitable ..., the translation of such accounts into terms of the current value of the pound involves assessing the value of the pound as a general unit of measurement rather than as a means of acquiring particular goods and services .... the object is not to ascertain the current cost or prospective replacement cost of particular assets acquired ... nor to measure changes in the prices of particular types of assets relative to the general price level. It is to ... translate past investment at varying dates into its current monetary equivalent.

ICAEW, 1968e, 8

The basic difference between general price level and historical dollar financial statements is the unit of measure used in the statements. In general price level statements the unit of measure is ... the general purchasing power of the dollar at a specified date .... The amounts of nonmonetary items should be restated to dollars of current general purchasing power at the end of the period.

AICPA, 1969, APBS3

The objective of general price level accounting ... is to use a unit of measure that represents a single specified amount of general purchasing power.

Rosenfield, 1971, 60

The method [of general purchasing power accounting] shows the effects on annual accounts of inflation only .... It does not show changes in value due to changes in other factors ....

ASSC, 1973, ED8

General price level accounting seeks to calculate and report on the purchasing power gains and losses incurred on monetary items.

Boersma, 1975b, 7

In adjusting original transaction values for changes in general purchasing power, the purpose is to express the original sacrifice in terms of the number of current (or recent) dollars that, if spent today, would mean the forgoing of the same alternate real goods and services.

May & others, 1975, 192

RC (replacement cost accounting) is an alternative to HC (historical cost) accounting. The CPP [current purchasing power] calculations need to be made whichever of HC or RC is used .... What inflation affects is not the values (as distinct from the prices) of goods and services but the value of the money in which prices are measured.

Parker, 1975, 426

The primary objective of adjusting historical accounts for changes in the general price level is to convert monetary units (for example, dollars) reflecting varying amounts of general purchasing power into a common measuring unit reflecting a uniform amount of general purchasing power for all measurements.

Davidson & others, 1976, 5

743 Posited merits of CPP accounting

[Adjustment of accounts by use of a general price index] would enable the true state of affairs to be set forth, all accounts being stated in terms of the same unit. It would also be of value where the accounts are used for comparative purposes, as between houses in the same business ... and for the same house at different times in its business career.

Middleditch, 1918, 119

Management may properly include in periodical reports to shareholders comprehensive supplementary statements which present the effects of the fluctuation in the value of the dollar upon net income and financial position.

AAA, 1951/1957b, 27

Historical costs (adjusted for general price levels) provide a basis for accountability, a uniqueness and stability that is especially useful in reconciling various conflicts among parties involved in business activities.

Horngren, 1970, 5

CPP accounting was conceived as a means of preventing the erosion of shareholders' capital as the result of persistent and material inflation.

Edwards, 1976, 67

Adjustments of historical amounts to reflect changes in the general price level are designed ... to make the results of arithmetic operations using accounting measurements more meaningful .... to make interperiod comparisons more meaningful .... to improve the meaning and measurement of income .... to provide explicit information about the impact of inflation across firms.

Stickney, 1977, 32:4

CPP was an admirable system ... not unduly complicated and conceptually sound. It tackled the problem at its root, ensuring that every item in any set of accounts (including comparative figures) would be expressed in currency units of substantially the same value.

Denza, 1978a, 490

Constant purchasing power accounting (CPP) is a consistent method of indexing accounts by means of a general index which reflects changes in the purchasing power of money . . . . CPP is concerned with the measurement unit, not with the techniques used to value assets and liabilities. It is possible to apply CPP methods to any valuation base . . . .

Whittington, 1983a/1986, 73

744 Capital maintenance under CPP accounting

It may be argued that . . . it would be preferable to use a different index for each category of asset. To do this is, however, to fall into exactly the same fundamental error as that committed by the advocates of replacement accounting when they assume that the maintenance of physical assets ensures the maintenance of real wealth.

Wimble, 1952, 130

Under the adjusted historical cost concept of income, the original capital contributed is considered as providing a pool of purchasing power units which are invested in various forms and on realization represent another pool of purchasing power units. The capital to be maintained intact is represented by the purchasing power units in the original contribution, and this is effected when the money value of capital has increased in proportion to the general price level.

Kerr, 1956, 141

General price level adjustments by themselves . . . ensure only the preservation of real historic cost, and not of real capital.

Lemke, 1966b, 394

Current purchasing power (CPP) accounting is concerned with removing the effects that changes in the general purchasing power of money have on accounts prepared in accordance with ordinary accounting practice. It looks at the undertaking from the point of view of the purchasing power invested in it by its owners and of the maintenance of that purchasing power, but otherwise it accepts the existing conventions of financial accounting [including the use of net realizable values where the CPP value exceeds that net realizable value].

ASSC, 1974c, PSAPP7

The CPP method explicitly adjusts the company accounts for the general level of inflation by indexing items in the balance sheet against some general measure of inflation such as the retail price index [RPI]. The method in effect maintains the purchasing power of the shareholders' interest in the company. It still employs the historical cost of the assets as the basis of the calculation, but in adjusting this each year on the basis of the RPI it turns the whole monetary denominator into a "current purchasing power" unit of account rather than a "present pounds" unit of account.

Thompson, 1987, 528

745 Index adjusted historical cost (CPP) income

A restatement of the values of assets in terms of dollars which themselves have changed in value . . . does not involve taking up any unrealized profit. This type of adjustment is only a correction of the accounts so that the values are stated in terms of the new monetary unit.

Bell & Graham, 1936, 312

The object of the index method of adjusting accounts is to eliminate from profits the effect of fluctuations in the purchasing power of money . . . . Unless all items were converted into the new currency and not merely selected items such as depreciation of fixed assets and consumption of stock in trade, the account would not, in a period of rising prices, reflect the loss in purchasing power arising from the holding of assets such as investments, debtors and bank balances or the gain arising on liabilities of fixed monetary amount.

ICAEW, 1952, N15

Realized [nominal] dollar income is a measure only of dollar accomplishment . . . . Corrected [index adjusted] dollar income, on the other hand, is the measurement of realized economic accomplishment . . . . it represents the amount that can be extracted from the business without disturbance to the economic asset investment base.

Husband, 1955, 395

With an assumption of continuity, the relevant purchasing power is the power to purchase investment goods . . . . a concept of investment purchasing power is the most relevant level of purchasing power in the adjustment for price level changes.

Hendriksen, 1963, 486, 491

The general price level gain or loss in the general price level statements indicates the effects of inflation (or deflation) on the company's net holdings of monetary assets and liabilities. The company gains or loses general purchasing power as a result of holding these assets and liabilities during a period of inflation (deflation).

AICPA, 1969, APBS3

The difference between the total equity interest in the converted balance sheets at the beginning and end of the year (after allowing for dividends and the introduction of new capital) is the profit or loss for the year measured in pounds of purchasing power at the end of the year.

ASSC, 1973, ED8

746 CPP income calculation components – depreciation

Depreciation on the basis of original costs charges to operations over the useful life of the asset – recovers – the dollar capital initially invested. Depreciation on the basis of current costs charges against operations this same initial cost, measured, however, in terms of current dollars, thereby recovering the equivalent of the physical capital invested . . . . Certainly the latter provides the better measure of the actual economic sacrifice incurred.

Graham, 1949, 21

The depreciation provision in the profit and loss acount . . . requires expression in terms of current money values if it is to function as a yardstick against receipts in current values when deciding what profit has been made. A current money value for the depreciation provision can be produced by applying price indices to the original costs of assets and this is logically a very different thing from referring depreciation provisions to anticipated replacement costs.

Pakenham-Walsh, 1950, 681

Depreciation is a process of allocating the cost of property to successive accounting periods . . . . Depreciation based on original cost re-expressed in terms of current dollars of equivalent economic power as measured by a general price index produces a net income amount that should be a somewhat better basis for estimating future earning power than either . . . [original cost or anticipated cost of replacement].

Graham, 1959b, 374

747 CPP income components – purchasing power gains and losses

historical cost should continue to be the basis on which annual accounts should be prepared and, in consequence, the basis on which profits shown by such accounts are computed . . . . any amount set aside out of profits in recognition of the effects . . . [of] changes in the purchasing power of money . . . should be treated as a transfer to reserve and not as a charge in arriving at profits.

ICAEW, 1952, N15

The supplementary statement should contain separate figures, if material, . . . for the net loss or gain in purchasing power resulting from the effects of inflation on the company's net monetary assets or liabilities.

ASSC, 1973, ED8

[The general index method of adjustment] creates a new kind of profit (or loss) – on net monetary liabilities (or assets) – which cannot occur if the value of the money is assumed to be stable.

Myddelton, 1974, 46

An enterprise is required to disclose . . . . the purchasing power gain or loss on net monetary items . . . . the gain or loss . . . shall not be included in income from continuing operations . . . . The purchasing power gain or loss . . . shall be . . . found by restating in constant dollars the opening and closing balances of, and transactions in, monetary assets and liabilities . . . . [It may be measured] in average-for-the-year constant dollars or in end-of-year constant dollars . . . .

FASB, 1979, SFAS33

748 Adjustment information sources

The effects of price fluctuations upon financial reports should be measured in terms of the overall purchasing power of the dollar – that is, changes in the general price level as measured by a general price index. For this purpose, adjustments should not be based on either the current value or the replacement costs of specific types of capital consumed.

AAA, 1951/1957b, 26

The most authoritative basis at present available for measuring the general price level is that which is used by the government in estimating changes in the internal purchasing power of the pound. These estimates are based on the Consumer Price Index . . . .

ICAEW, 1968e, 9

All accounts laid before the members of listed companies in general meeting should be supported by a supplementary statement showing in terms of pounds of purchasing power at the end of the year to which the accounts relate the financial position at that date and the results for the year. The supplementary statements should be prepared by converting the basic [historical cost] accounts by the application of a general index of prices . . . .

ASSC, 1974c, PSSAP7

Historical cost/constant dollar accounting. A method of accounting based on measures of historical prices in dollars, each of which has the same general purchasing power . . . . The index used to compute information on a constant dollar basis shall be the Consumer Price Index for All Urban Consumers, published by the Bureau of Labor Statistics of the U.S. Department of Labor.

FASB, 1979, SFAS33

749 Critical comment on CPP accounting

while there is and must be a connection between present prices and anticipations of future prices, there is no necessary connection or significant value relationship between present prices and past prices.

Robbins, 1935/1969, 62

correction for changes in the general price level . . . . cannot, by itself, place the business income figures for two different periods on a par with one another and render them fully comparable. One important reason is that the various business costs set off against gross income . . . are based on heterotemporal prices . . . . The ordinary deflation [of recent amounts to constant prices] will not take care of this peculiarity of accounting figures.

Fabricant, 1950, 145

Because all prices normally do not change at a uniform rate . . . . Data which are measured in different units to begin with cannot be converted to a common basis of measurement merely by applying a common conversion factor . . . . If the accounting information system is to produce meaningful data we must recognize the effects of all price changes on business enterprise accounts, not merely the effects of changes in the general level of prices.

Mathews, 1965, 138, 147, 148

Using the same general price level index to adjust the statements of all firms assumes that the effects of price changes are uniform across firms. But . . . . some firms may experience more than average price changes, others less than average changes . . . . [and some] price movements in the opposite direction from the economy as a whole.

Revsine, 1973, 58

750 Replacement Price (Cost) Accounting (RPA)

For replacement price valuation see 520

751 Replacement price accounting (RPA) described

What we need is a method of accounting which will . . . charge against gross income the real current cost of earning that income, measured in monetary units having the same value as those in which gross income is measured . . . . In a period of rising prices, [the method] would consist essentially, whether fixed assets or current assets are concerned, of debiting profit and loss with the replacement cost of assets used up, crediting the asset accounts with the historical cost of the expired portion of the assets, and crediting the excess of replacement cost over historical cost to a capital adjustment reserve.

Solomons, 1948/1950, 367

Changes in the general price level will . . . be reflected in changes in the price of any particular good or service and therefore replacement cost implicitly includes any changes in general price levels.

Ladd, 1963, 56

The proper value at which to include an asset [in a balance sheet] is the value at which it would be purchased in a transaction between reasonably willing parties.

Ross, 1971, 10

Replacement cost accounting is not a means of adjusting for economy-wide price level changes. Instead it is a method that incorporates only those individual price changes that affect a specific firm.

Revsine, 1973, 57

The term, replacement cost accounting, has been used to describe methods of accounting which include, among others: (a) showing freehold and leasehold property at current market values; (b) showing all fixed assets and depreciation at current replacement values; (c) showing fixed assets and stock, with depreciation and cost of sales, at current replacement values; (d) as in (c), with the equity interest adjusted for the general price level change, and with monetary assets and liabilities at their original money values, with consequential adjustments to profit.

ASSC, 1974c, PSSAP7

The core of current replacement value accounting is as follows: Normal quantities of assets . . . are presented in the balance sheet at their current replacement values (net of depreciation) in terms of money. Increases in the replacement values . . . are credited to reserves and do not affect the determination of net income. The replacement values of those assets . . . at the time they are sold are charged to net income in the period of sale. Depreciation of fixed assets is based on an allocation of their current replacement values . . . . All other asset, liability, revenue and expense items are treated essentially as they are treated in the context of the historical cost system . . . .

Rosenfield, 1975b, 64

The new rule [Reg. S-X, Rule 3–17] . . . requires registrants who have inventories and gross property, plant and equipment which aggregate more than $100 million and which comprise more than 10% of total assets to disclose the estimated current replacement cost of inventories and productive capacity at the end of each fiscal year . . . and the approximate amount of cost of sales and depreciation based on replacement cost for the two most recent full fiscal years . . . .

SEC, 1976a, ASR190

752 Posited functions or objects of RPA

It is not the cost of the building or power unit or machine which is significant to the manager interested in a wise utilization of available resources. It is rather the cost of replacement which must form the basis of his reckoning.

Paton, 1918/1976, 38

Market value or cost of replacement, is a more satisfactory basis [than the orthodox basis, cost]: (a) it can be justified on the basis of economic reasoning; (b) it reflects more accurately the everchanging value facts which are encountered by business enterprises; (c) it can be introduced into the accounting records without doing violence to any accounting or legal theory of income; (d) it puts the accountant in the position

of furnishing current and up to the minute information . . . ; (e) it provides information which, for purposes of comparing operating results and formulating managerial decisions and policies, is preeminently more useful.
Daines, 1929, 102–3

a reproduction-value balance sheet has the greatest significance for understanding the economic condition of the enterprise concerned, because the total value therein is the only figure on which the earning capacity of the enterprise can be based.
Schmidt, 1930, 239

We can . . . approach the question of [stock or inventory valuation] from the point of view of maintaining intact the real capital of the firm . . . . The cost of a sale on this basis is the cost of replacement of the goods sold.
Lacey, 1952, 46

Replacement cost accounting . . . aims to show the maintenance or otherwise of the physical assets of the business rather than the maintenance of the amount of purchasing power . . . originally invested in the assets. It may therefore be regarded as management-orientated rather than shareholder-orientated, because the shareholder is likely to be concerned with the general purchasing power of his investment.
ASSC, 1974c, PSSAP7

reasons why replacement cost should be used as the basis for determining income and financial position. First, it clearly distinguishes between capital and income in measuring economic progress and points out where capital may be impaired through cost increases in specific items. Second, it helps in decisions on pricing, projecting needs for cash and capital and in assessing return on investment and managerial performance. Third, improved financial reporting will result in better investment decisions and allocations of capital resources.
Alexander, 1975, 58–9

The purpose of this rule is to provide information to investors which will assist them in obtaining an understanding of the current costs of operating the business which cannot be obtained from historical cost financial statements taken alone . . . . [And] to provide information which will enable investors to determine the current cost of inventories and productive capacity as a measure of the current economic investment in these assets existing at the balance sheet date. [Rule 3–17]
SEC, 1976c, Reg S-X

[Replacement cost acounting is favored by some] because it is more closely related to the idea of maintaining a company's productive capacity as a going concern.
Needles & others, 1984, 519

753 Capital maintenance as maintenance of substantive property

is the purpose of management merely to maintain investment in terms of dollars, and to show current costs and profits accordingly, or is it really to keep up the plant and equipment and to maintain the physical productivity of the property? .... The purpose of management certainly must be to maintain the physical plant, and to keep up production without drawing on capital funds .... when the price level has risen, the charge to operations for renewals should not be the original cost of the property retired, but the cost of new property which, in function and capacity, is required to replace the old.

Bauer, 1919, 414

In the case of the real capital of an enterprise, profit is only produced when between the beginning and end of a fiscal period an increase in the concrete property [the stock of real property including money and money due] has taken place.

Schmidt, 1930, 235

[The unimpaired capital efficiency concept of net income construes income from any property] to mean the gross receipts yielded by this property after reservation of a sufficient amount of these receipts to continue operations and also to replace the property, when it must be retired, with an equally efficient substitute.

Bonbright, 1937/1965, 906

The profit of a period ... is ... only that part of the increase in capital which, if it should be fully paid to participants, does not jeopardize the rational replacement of goods and services used in production.

Kleerekoper, 1959, 845

The reporting of a company's profits should properly reflect what is available for distribution to its shareholders, after allowing for such sums as are required to keep the business physically intact.

Merrett & Sykes, 1974, 11

The capital maintenance benchmark [in current cost accounting is] the stock of net assets of the firm .... it enables the firm to conserve its physical and financial resources without having to raise additional funds to finance a given volume of operations during a period of changing asset prices.

Barton, 1984, 479

Capital maintenance as maintenance of productive capacity or operating capability

Economists do not agree with the accounting view of the meaning of maintaining capital intact .... The economist is concerned with "real" assets and not with the monetary costs thereof or questions of proprietary interest. The economist argues that it is the productive capacity of an enterprise that must be maintained intact.

ICAW & NIESR, 1951, 30

only that part of the increase in the net assets of the enterprise which can be consumed without impairing the productive capacity of the enterprise is to be considered as profit.

> Groeneveld, 1957, 577

the crucial question is this: which of the two inflation accounting alternatives generates an income figure that reflects the amount of resource inflows that could conceivably be distributed as a dividend without impairing the physical operating level of the firm?

> Revsine & Weygandt, 1974, 76

[Operating capacity, or capability, is concerned] not so much with the operating capacity to produce the same value or the same volume of goods or services as in the past; it is [concerned] with the capacity to produce the actual goods and services being produced or capable of being produced at the particular time with the resources of the enterprise .... if operating capacity is maintained at all times, capital is maintained at all times.

> NZR, 1976, 36

State the estimated current cost of replacing (new) the productive capacity together with the current depreciated replacement cost of the productive capacity on hand .... Productive capacity is a measurement of a company's ability to produce and distribute ... within a particular time frame; ... [Rule 3–17]

> SEC, 1976b, SAB7

According to the physical productive capacity concept of capital, provision must be made for maintenance of an enterprise's productive capacity before income can be counted.

> FASB, 1978, SFAC1

the entity view of the business: its specific physical substance, either in terms of assets or that seductive but elusive concept, productive capacity, must be maintained before we recognize an increase in the value of the assets of the business as giving rise to a profit which is regarded as a suitable object for distribution ... or taxation.

> Whittington, 1983a/1986, 9

[A survey of ideas relating to the maintenance of operating capacity, covering seven countries over the period 1975–1983, yielded eight ideas of operating capacity]: physical assets .... physical assets + monetary assets (excluding ... long term monetary assets) .... physical assets + all monetary assets .... physical assets + all monetary assets less all liabilities .... physical assets + all monetary assets less liabilities (excluding long term borrowings) .... physical assets + monetary assets (generally excluding cash) less short term liabilities (generally excluding bank overdrafts) .... physical assets + monetary assets (excluding "non-fluctuating" cash less short term liabilities (excluding "non-fluctuating" bank overdrafts) . . . . physical assets + net monetary assets . . . .

Tweedie & Whittington, 1984, 286

Capital can be viewed in physical terms. Under this approach, profit is measured after provision has been made to maintain a company's physical operating capital. Operating capital . . . is usually thought of in terms of a company's ability to produce a certain volume of goods and services.

ASC, 1986, 22

Physical capital maintenance means that the firm has the same quantity of assets in terms of some physical standard, such as the same number of physical units, the capacity to produce the same volume of goods and services or the capacity to produce the same value of goods and services.

Ma & others, 1987, 482

In effect [the replacement cost] concept looks at the accounts of a business as a going concern, in terms of its ability to at least continue producing a comparable output year by year. The implied objective of the firm here is for it to maintain or increase its net worth in terms of the physical assets deployed.

Thompson, 1987, 528

See also 663

754 Critical comment on physical capital maintenance

The thesis that true capital is preserved if, and only if, the physical capital is kept intact cannot be maintained. Such a proposition would be true only if price movements were uniform and proportionate throughout all the ramifications of the economic structure, a condition which is not even approximated in the actual situation.

Paton, 1922/1962, 430

maintenance of material capital is not in harmony with the fundamental customary aim of economic endeavor, namely, to maintain original purchasing power over the general field of goods and services while, in the long run, acquiring more.

Sweeney, 1930, 279

This confusion between technical potentiality and economic value . . . we may call the fallacy of misplaced concreteness, . . . borrowing a phrase of Professor Whitehead's.

Robbins, 1935/1969, 51

Those who define depreciation . . . in terms of an exhaustion of usefulness . . . . appeal to the technical serviceability of assets which lies back of every market price attached to them. They do this in an attempt to avoid the responsibility for making monetary valuations which do not rest upon business transactions. However, they do not in fact avoid such a responsibility so long as they undertake to select proper and equitable methods of calculating depreciation. The appeal to exhaustion of technical usefulness .... is parallel to ... [insisting] upon using the technique of barter when the effective operation of a price system was available.

Scott, 1945, 311

Maintaining the physical serviceability of a given asset is to say nothing of its worth in economic terms. It is the value that constitutes the real capital and not the physical attributes.

Bowers, 1950, 154

This theory [of providing, by depreciation charges, the amount needed to meet the cost of replacement of all fixed assets as and when they wear out] is fundamentally unsound. No director of a company (or sole proprietor) will be prepared to state that fixed assets will be replaced by similar items .... Any business must retain the right to change its methods of manufacture if a more profitable method becomes available .... management must also keep the right to change its end products.

Wilk, 1960, 14

profit of a business enterprise is not what is left after the productive capacity of the enterprise has been maintained intact. I find considerable fortification of my belief when I remember what has happened to covered wagons, ice chests, sailing ships and neck to knee bathing costumes.

Mutton, 1975, 53

Operating capacity is too nebulous a concept [of capital] and, if it could be defined, too difficult to quantify, for it to be a useful concept of capital for financial reporting purposes .... operating capacity which is a physical, not a financial, concept, defies simple aggregation.

Solomons, 1989, 55

755 Replacement cost income

This replacement cost as of the day of sale tells the owner the price at which he could repurchase similar goods at that moment .... it follows that replacement costs as of the day of sale must be the fundamental values for profit and loss calculation.

Schmidt, 1930, 240

Economists ... regard the gain arising on a sale as being the difference between selling price and replacement cost, on the principle that goods consumed diminish wealth, with the consequence that no gain can arise unless this wealth is replaced .... the economists consider that an enterprise is failing to maintain its assets if it sells stock in trade without full replacement.

ICAEW & NIESR, 1951, 27

Published financial statements should be supplemented, where appropriate, by collateral notations showing the extent ... to which stated net income would have been raised or lowered had charges for (a) inventory liquidation, and (b) fixed property amortization, been computed on the basis of current replacement cost of the assets ....

Greer, 1956, 14

The essence of the CRVA [current replacement value accounting] method lies in dividing profit into two pieces: (1) operating profit, defined as revenue less the current replacement value of the assets consumed or used to produce that revenue; and (2) holding gains that result from owning physical assets that rise in value during an inflationary period .... holding gains represent earnings set aside in a valuation reserve (part of shareholders' equity) and retained to provide sufficient capital for maintaining the physical capital of the business.

Vancil, 1976, 60

The notion of maintaining operating capacity is merely a guide for profit measurement purposes and does not imply commitment to any specific action with regard to eventual replacement or future use of assets.

Tweedie, 1978, 150

The physical capital maintenance concept .... [entails that] a company only makes a profit if it has replaced (or is in a position to replace) the assets which were held at the start of the period and which have been used up in the course of the period .... [alternatively] if the company is able to maintain the same level of output.

Lewis & Pendrill, 1985, 66

756 Replacement cost income components – depreciation

there is much force in the contention that in times characterized by serious price movements fixed assets should be revalued on the basis of replacement cost and depreciation should be correspondingly adjusted so as to insure the accumulation of funds sufficient to maintain the plant from a physical or managerial standpoint.

Paton, 1924, 339

The argument here advanced in favor of basing depreciation charges upon current replacement values holds, first, that such a practice will afford a more accurate control of operations and permit more effective internal management of the individual business enterprise; and second, that it will afford a better coordination of the enterprise with its economic or business environment.

Scott, 1929, 225

Profit can only be calculated upon cost of production when the monetary unit is relatively stable .... Where money is undergoing a rapid depreciation and where

costs are rising with equal or greater rapidity, then profit must be figured on the cost of reproduction or replacement of the materials and labor sold.
Wasserman, 1931, 8

the depreciation charge each year should be based on the cost of installing in that year a plant with a life capacity of the plant actually in use. The resultant profit or loss would be the true operating profit or loss having regard to changes in the price level and improvements in the arts. If adjustment of the depreciation so charged against operations was considered desirable for financial reasons, such adjustment would be made through surplus account. Practically, however, this conclusion is of no value because of the insuperable difficulty of determining from year to year the cost of installing a plant of similar capacity.
Smails, 1936, 148

Selling prices must be high enough to provide the enterprise with . . . enough funds to replace the used resources in order to safeguard the continuity of the enterprise . . . . Under this principle . . . the cost of the used resources is actually the cost to replace them . . . .
Bakker, 1974, 2

For most capital intensive companies, a replacement cost depreciation figure is unlikely to have any significant meaning because . . . [for specifically calculated replacement costs] (a) major depreciable assets are rarely replaced on a like for like basis; (b) the time scale . . . is generally so long that estimates . . . are rarely based on anything more than crystal ball gazing; (c) the work involved . . . would be beyond the resources of many companies; (d) company engineers . . . generally have a strong vested interest in underestimation; (e) the evidence available to company engineers is normally inadequate for making credible estimates. The use of macroeconomic indices applied to historical costs is unlikely to produce meaningful results, [for] the impact of technological change is vastly different from industry to industry.
Giles, 1977, 22

Backlog depreciation

The [recommended] principles relating to the maintenance of real capital [include the following]: . . . . Provision for the replacement of [tangible or nonmonetary] assets and materials should be made by a charge included in the costs of the sale of goods or the provision of services . . . . The replacement cost used . . . should be the current (or notional) cost of replacement . . . . Any failure on the part of previous charges to provide the full current replacement cost should be made good by an appropriation of profit.
ICWA, 1952, 61

The basic theory of [the replacement cost method of dealing with fixed assets] is that one should make charges to profit and loss account to provide the amount needed to meet the cost of replacement of all fixed assets as and when they wear out . . . . this system charges not only depreciation for the year based on current cost . . . . but also makes good the backlog for the increase in replacement cost since the last accounts.

Wilk, 1960, 14

Backlog depreciation is the additional amount required to raise the sum of the accumulated depreciation at the beginning of any accounting year and the charge for depreciation for that year to the amount required to equal the difference between the gross and the net replacement cost of an asset at the end of the year . . . . backlog depreciation is charged against the related revaluation surpluses.

IASG, 1976, ED18

the total of the current cost depreciation charges over the life of the asset will not equal the replacement cost of the asset at the end of its life [and will not therefore maintain the operating capacity of a company]. The difference . . . . backlog depreciation . . . . [is] transferred to the current cost reserve rather than charged in arriving at profit.

ASC, 1986, 83

757 Posited objections to replacement cost income

The replacement theory substitutes for something certain and definite, the actual cost, a cost of reproduction which is highly speculative and conjectural and requiring frequent revision . . . . As one writer has expressed it, "The fact that the plant cannot be replaced at the same cost, but only at much more, has nothing to do with the cost of its product, but only with the cost of future product turned out by the subsequent plant." As the product goes through your factory it should be burdened with expired, not anticipated, costs.

USCC, 1929/1934, 35

the replacement cost basis for computing depreciation as an element of accrued charges has no special validity, even for the internal purposes of the entrepreneur.

Little, 1948, 78

According to [the replacement fund theory of income calculation] income should be charged with amounts such that, if they were funded, there would be in the fund at the end of the useful life of the assets an amount sufficient to replace them . . . . As a matter of fact, long lived plant assets are not replaced in kind . . . . Replacement implies a static condition in the industrial facilities of our economy which is contrary to its dynamic nature.

Wilcox & Greer, 1950, 493

any provision made out of current ventures for replacement of fixed assets should be regarded purely as a reserve put aside out of profits and not as an expense chargeable in arriving at such profits.

Kessell, 1951, 252

there is no profit and loss account logic in charging depreciation based on probable replacement costs of assets . . . . as making provision for funds to be available to replace assets is a matter for the future, it should be taken care of . . . by periodical appropriations of profit.

McMonnies, 1969, 77

A subjunctive gain or loss is the difference between the amount of a measurable property of an object at a point of time and the amount it might have been at the same point of time if prior events had been (subjunctive mood) different from what they were . . . . Net income reported under the replacement price principle is the numerical result of adding (1) . . . gains and losses from purchase and sale of assets within the period, (2) subjunctive gains and losses from assets purchased before [or during] the period . . . , and (3) subjunctive . . . gains and losses from selling assets purchased before the period. This numerical result . . . [is] an undecipherable combination [of magnitudes] . . . . Net income reported under the replacement price principle . . . is unintelligible . . . . uncorroborable . . . . irrelevant for any purpose.

Rosenfield, 1969, 789, 795

In CRVA [current replacement value accounting] . . . the zero point for a gain in terms of money is physical operating capacity at the beginning of the period. That is the natural zero point for a system that uses physical operating capacity as the standard resource. CRVA thus uses two standard resources, one [money] for relating to the various resources and the other [physical operating capacity] for defining the zero point for determining success or failure.

Rosenfield, 1975b, 68

to calculate earnings on a replacement cost basis, accountants must not only charge more depreciation; they must also adjust for differences in output and operating costs. When they have done so, they wind up in a curious dream world where companies subtract savings they did not realize from costs they did not incur to derive earnings they did not make.

Business week, editorial, 1976, 80

758 Sources and quality of replacement cost information

It is recognized that while the theory herein discussed [basing depreciation charges on replacement cost consequent upon changes in prices and price levels] may have some merit, the impossibility of accurately forecasting either the fluctuations of price levels or the term of the useful life of depreciable property and the impracticability of adjusting book values of permanent assets for every fluctuation in price levels render the plan of little practical worth.

Chenoweth, 1921, 472

there is no basis in experience which can justify predicting whether a replacement, renewal, or substitution falling in some future year will cost more or less than it would at present, or more or less than the unit cost when it was acquired. [Justice Brandeis, dissenting]

United Railways and Electric Co v West,
1930

the uncertainty of any estimate of replacement cost makes it a less desirable basis for computing depreciation than the original known cost.

Sanders & others, 1938, 22

replacement cost . . . stands condemned because it is patently impossible of objective measurement. Obviously, if the only criterion of objectivity is that someone else can recompute on the specified basis and come up with the same answer, objective measurement is easily attainable. If, however, the criterion is that another knowledgeable person can independently arrive at the same conclusion based on a reasoned application of his knowledge of the facts at hand, the impossibility of the assignment becomes apparent.

Dickens & Blackburn, 1964, 324

Among the approaches to the ascertainment of the current cost of equipment and machinery are the following: (1) Purchase price, new, on the current market, adjusted for depreciation . . . . (2) Purchase price, used, in the current market . . . . (3) In those cases where new equipment or machinery is available only in more efficient form . . . downward adjustment . . . to reflect this obsolescence in calculating current cost of the old equipment would be appropriate . . . . (4) Adjustment to current cost can be approximated through use of a specific price level index.

AAA, 1966, 75

In all [the methods described as replacement cost methods] replacement costs might be arrived at by estimating current market values or by applying specific price indices, each of which was believed to be a reasonable indicator of the replacement cost of the asset or class of assets concerned. In using a replacement cost method, therefore, a wide degree of discretion and subjective judgment enters in each separate case into the choice of the adjustment factor, and a general index for adjustment of asset values cannot be prescribed.

ASSC, 1974c, PSSAP7

To adjust conventional accounts it [RPA] uses various specific indices measuring historical changes in the prices of particular assets. This approach . . . has at least four serious drawbacks. Most businesses do not replace physical assets with their exact equivalent, due to technological and market changes; the method assumes replacement whatever the current price . . . ; it ignores monetary gains and losses; and it does not distinguish between pounds of different years.

Myddelton, 1974, 46

This study [of prices in the US steel industry] has demonstrated that within a common group of assets the price movements of specific items can vary considerably . . . . The application of a composite price index to any particular group of goods and services may therefore bear little relationship to the changes in the actual prices of the specific goods and services included in the group. Further, an industry wide index may bear little relationship to the prices of the specific goods and services used or bought by any particular company . . . . The use of indexes may, therefore distort the resulting financial statements of companies whose product mix differs from the regimen of the index.

Wolnizer, 1983, 187

759 Relevance of replacement cost valuation

[Replacement prices are] wholly outside the prior decisions and the recorded experience of [an] enterprise . . . . Facts outside of an enterprise, such as replacement prices, do have significance to management, but they can hardly be considered facts suitable for use in ledger accounts.

Littleton, 1952, 171

We may take it as an axiom that any accounting statement, to be true, must report what has happened . . . . when we allow market valuation [replacement cost] to creep in we no longer report what has happened.

Briscoe, 1953, 677

Replacement cost may have little significance if it is defined strictly in terms of a specific physical asset . . . . changes in consumer tastes or in technology since the asset was acquired may call for changes in a whole complex of jointly operating asset services.

Edey, 1974, 79

Replacement cost is only relevant when it is time to replace.

Nicholls, 1975b, 153

current replacement prices . . . . do not represent a relationship that exists between the enterprise and the world at the balance sheet date that is part of its financial position at that date . . . . The one thing above all that [an enterprise] cannot do with assets it owns is buy them . . . . Buying prices, current or otherwise, therefore do not pertain to any aspect of the assets held by the enterprise of interest or value to the enterprise.

Rosenfield, 1975b, 68

First, an existing asset may not be exactly replaceable . . . . Second, . . . no true replacement cost for either the asset or its utility can be established . . . . Third, the existing asset may be unique . . . . Fourth, changes in economic and market conditions may make it difficult to establish replacement costs for some assets . . . . Finally, the replacement cost is not relevant for . . . . obsolete or damaged . . . items.

Carscallen, 1977, 33

entry values of owned assets are irrelevant to their sale (since one must sell them for their exit values) and to their purchase (since they are already owned.)

Sterling, 1979, 124

Appraisal of replacement price accounting

Any replacement cost method utterly abandons the cost of acquisition concept . . . .
The replacement of merchandise sold is in the nature of a new venture.

Gilman, 1939, 402, 407

The adoption of "replacement cost" fixed asset and depreciation accounting . . . is not a complete answer [to the problem of dealing with the effects of inflation] . . . . it does not take into account the effect of inflation on other assets and liabilities; and . . . the use of replacement cost as the basis of adjusting for inflation may, under certain circumstances, result in the reflection in the inflation adjustment of factors other than those relating to the decline in the value of money.

Coutts (ed), 1962a, 481

Most firms do not intend to replace their capital [goods] with assets of the same type as formerly used . . . . they have an oppportunity to change their type of investment over time if changes in specific prices indicate that such a course of action would be better for the operations of the firm.

Hendriksen, 1963, 490

Whether replacement cost is used to write up or write down the inventory, it represents anticipation of what is expected to happen in a future period.

Marple, 1963, 481

A curiously metaphysical argument is used [by some] to restrict the meaning of purchasing power to purchasing power over particular assets, namely the same ones as were held before . . . . The asset mix of a real life firm is constantly changing, as the firm must adapt to changing factor prices (fixed assets, materials and services), and product prices, or perish.

Bennett, 1972, 219

if one accepts that the replacement of an asset is a new investment decision . . . then that replacement (if indeed one can call it that) is not a valid accounting fact until it has happened. In the meantime, it could be a possible economic conjecture concerning future investment.

Wilson, 1974, 172

Replacement cost valuations are useful for insurance purposes, but there are few other purposes for which it is useful to know the loss which you would suffer if deprived of an asset [under the deprival value proposal of the Sandilands report].

Kay, 1977, 301

the accounting alternatives which can be loosely grouped as "replacement cost" .... do not necessarily account for inflation, i.e. changes in the general price level. A balance sheet valued on this basis does not reflect wealth, financial position or command over goods and services. Valuation at replacement cost erroneously assumes or implies the replacement of assets. These alternatives generally imply some type of physical capital maintenance, but exactly what is to be maintained is often unclear. These alternatives match future costs with past revenues. They account both for assets owned and those not owned by the company.

Boersma, 1979, 35

760 Current Cost Accounting (CCA)

For current cost valuation see 530

761 Current cost accounting (CCA) described

the dollar remains the unit of account under current cost .... (1) the balance sheet at the close of each year reports assets at the costs prevailing during that year [not costs prevailing at the end of a period]; (2) the capital gains arising from changes in asset costs are separated from operating income; and (3) real income is readily determined by adjusting the opening net worth with a general price index.

Gordon, 1953, 374

[Current cost accounting] is not directly concerned with the preservation of the wealth of the business in terms of constant purchasing power nor does it seek to measure the effect of any decline in money values on cash, accounts receivable and similar money assets. The rise or fall in the general price level is entirely incidental to its basic philosophy .... The method postulates that holding gains or losses are outside the purview of management.

Brown, 1972, 93

Accounting that incorporates both current values and price level changes is, in our opinion, the best solution to the problem of accounting for changing prices. Such accounting reports holding gains and losses on all assets and the recognition of gain or loss on holding monetary items.

Davidson & others, 1976, 226

In deference to the known views of the accountancy bodies, the Sandilands version of current value accounting was called current cost accounting rather than replacement cost accounting.

Dewhurst, 1976, 62

The essence of the CCA system is simple: the charge against income in arriving at profit for stocks consumed and fixed assets used is based on current replacement costs and not on out of date and irrelevant historical costs. Similarly, the balance sheet shows up to date values in place of historical costs.

IASG, 1976, ED18

Some inkling of the answer which the [Sandilands] committee might have been expected to arrive at could perhaps have been obtained from a close study of the make up of its members. Some were experienced in other accounting methods. One of these was replacement costing, developed in the Netherlands in the early 20s, and since used in that country by several large companies .... The solution recommended by the Sandilands Committee was indeed a form of replacement accounting. The committee called it current cost accounting (CCA), though it differed very little from any other type of accounting based on the replacement concept.

Dewhurst, 1978, 471

In current cost accounting, wealth is the aggregate value [at buying prices] of the firm's net assets, and income is the increase in that wealth over a period after maintaining intact the initial stock of net assets of the firm .... The capital maintenance benchmark used is that of the stock of net assets of the firm rather than initial money investment or the general purchasing power of that investment .... maintenance of operating capacity.

Barton, 1984, 477, 479

762 Objects of current cost accounting

emphasis in accounting today must ... be on the development of methods and techniques which will lead to the measurement of real or current costs ... [and] ... the approximate real profit of any given concern .... for the formulation of financial policies or for the determination and control of profits and prices, information as to current costs and real profit is essential.

Johnston, 1949, 66

management may be misled by a historical cost system which does not distinguish holding gains from operating profit .... current cost accounting, by distinguishing between operating profit and holding gains, will provide important information to which management will need to react.

Sandilands, 1975, 218

the main aim of CCA is to produce a realistic measurement of profit whereas the main concern of CPP accounting is the maintenance of capital.

Edwards, 1976, 67

The historical cost accounting convention has traditionally been used as the basis for preparing accounts because of its underlying simplicity and certainty .... It has always contained the inherent inadequacy that changes in price levels over a period of years would result in accounts not reflecting current conditions .... [As consequences], not all balance sheets reveal the real value of all assets; depreciation is inadequate to replace the assets consumed during the year; the charge for the stock consumed is inadequate to replace it . . . ; the effects of holding monetary assets or owing monetary liabilities are ignored . . . . growth is exaggerated because no allowance is made for the fall in the value of the money used to measure the results; . . . capital, although maintained in money terms, may not be maintained in real terms and may be distributed . . . to the detriment of the long term viability of the business. CCA seeks to remedy these defects . . . .

Gilbert, 1976, 3–4

costs must be measured at current cost in order to provide for the maintenance of operating capability.

FASB, 1979, SFAS33

The basic objective of current cost accounts is to provide more useful information than that available from historical cost accounts alone for the guidance of the management of the business, the shareholders and others on such matters as (a) the financial viability of the business: (b) return on investment: (c) pricing policy, cost control and distribution decisions: and (d) gearing.

ASC, 1980b, SSAP16

The objective of CCA is to ensure that, having regard to changes in specific prices, the results and resources of an entity are realistically measured so as to be of maximum value to users.

ASA & ICAA, 1989, SAP1

763 Posited merits of current cost accounting

the realizable profit concept [assets being valued at realizable values] represents a more substantial departure from accepted accounting principles than does the business profit concept [assets being valued at current costs]. This important consideration is a weighty argument in favor of the accumulation of data on a current cost basis, and it is the approach that we intend to take . . .

Edwards & Bell, 1961, 109

This more realistic information [yielded by CCA] should enable a clearer picture to be obtained of the relative performance of: (a) managers and products within a company, (b) different companies, (c) different industries, and should help to lead to better decisions being taken in such areas as pricing, cost reduction, levels of remuneration, resource allocation between and within companies, dividends, gearing and borrowing levels.

IASG, 1976, ED18

Entry values and entry value rates of return are always important in evaluating decisions and in formulating new decisions. Replacement decisions cannot be made without them .... Entry values are needed to evaluate what the firm set out to do and actually did do in the period under consideration; ....

Edwards & others, 1979, 645

CCA is said to be more subjective than HCA [historical cost accounting]. So far as this is true, it is the price of greater realism.

Edey, 1982, 110

764 Asset valuations under CCA

The net current replacement cost will be the gross current replacement cost less the sum of the accumulated depreciation at the beginning of the period, backlog depreciation and the depreciation charge for the period under review. The net current replacement cost therefore reflects the diminution in the gross current replacement cost of an asset due to wear and tear and obsolescence, so that it represents the value of the unexpired service potential of the asset.

IASG, 1976, ED18

The current cost amounts of inventory and property, plant and equipment shall be measured as: a. Inventories at current cost or lower recoverable amount .... b. Property, plant and equipment ... at the current cost or lower recoverable amount of the asset's remaining service potential .... The current cost of a used asset may be measured [by reference to] a. ... the current cost of a new asset that has the same service potential as the used asset had when it was new ... and deducting an allowance for depreciation; b. ... the current cost of a used asset of the same age and in the same condition as the asset owned; c. ... the current cost of a new asset with a different service potential and adjusting for the difference in service potential ....

FASB, 1979, SFAS33

Under CCA, non-monetary assets are measured at the lower of current cost (written down, where applicable) and recoverable amount. Under CCA, monetary items are measured ... either at the amount established by a transaction or event, or, where this amount is not expected to be realized, at recoverable amount .... The recoverable amount of ... assets held for resale .... is their net realizable value .... [For other assets] it will be necessary to calculate the recoverable amount in terms of the net present value of future cash flows (including the ultimate proceeds of disposal) expected to be derived from the use of the asset .... [discounted] at an appropriate discount rate. [Guidance notes]

ASA & ICAA, 1989, SAP1

See also 530, 567

765 Current cost income

sales of the period should be charged with the current cost of the goods sold . . . . The offsetting credit should be split between two accounts. The inventory account should be credited with the original costs of the goods sold. The difference between the current cost and the original cost should be charged or credited to . . . the capital adjustment account . . . . It is an adjustment or restatement, in terms of a new level of prices, of the owner's capital investment.
Graham, 1949, 23, 25

Business income from an economic viewpoint should be determined by subtracting from sales a cost of goods sold in which the units sold are valued at current, not original, cost prices.
Fabricant, 1950, 147

Under the [current cost] method of computing profits suggested in this book, the conventional profit would be adjusted for price changes in the sense that inventory profits and losses would be excluded and depreciation would be revalorized into current money terms. Broadly speaking, this means that profits would then be regarded as the excess of the selling price over the replacement cost of the goods sold.
Lacey, 1952, 29

The object of the current value method of dealing with depreciation and stock in trade is to express charges for consumption of assets in current values and not in terms of the monetary cost of the assets consumed.
ICAEW, 1952, N15

Current income . . . is the difference between revenues and costs and expenses, all expressed in current prices.
Mathews & Grant, 1958, 167

Income from ordinary operations should represent an amount, in current dollars, which . . . is available for distribution outside the firm without contraction of the level of its operating capacity. [This income can be measured] only if the expiration of service potential is measured in terms of current cost.
AAA, 1964a, 695

the measures of current income and current funds employed [under current value accounting] may be deflated in order to express them in terms of a constant price level, and thus provide an indication as to whether the purchasing power of income or of residual equity is being maintained.
Mathews, 1968, 511

The operating profit or loss for the year of a company is its revenue less current expenses, including in those expenses the value to the business of the physical assets consumed during the year, but before interest, taxation, or extraordinary items

.... The current cost profit or loss ... is the operating profit or loss ... after accounting for interest payable and receivable, taxation and extraordinary items.

IASG, 1976, ED18

The operating capability of the business is the amount of goods and services which the business is able to supply with its existing resources in the relevant period. These resources are represented in accounting terms by the net operating assets at current cost .... Current cost operating profit is the surplus arising from the ordinary activities of the business in the period after allowing for the impact of price changes on the funds needed to continue the existing business and maintain its operating capability, whether financed by share capital or borrowing. It is calculated before interest on borrowing and taxation.

ASC, 1980b, SSAP16

766 CCA income calculation components

In measuring current income ... depreciation may be defined as the current cost of using fixed assets in producing revenue during the period. The current cost may be estimated by reference to the current replacement value of the asset .... the current cost of an identical asset, if available, or if that is not available, the cost of an asset capable of achieving similar performance .... Current cost of goods sold [during a period] may ... be defined as opening stocks plus purchases minus closing stocks, all valued at current prices of the period.

Mathews & Grant, 1958, 10, 13–14

[The current cost] system differs from the replacement cost theory in that no provision is made for any [depreciation] backlog .... It is argued ... that where the equivalent of the annual charge is invested in fixed assets, such sums will retain their value and further charges for backlog are unnecessary.

Wilk, 1960, 24

If price changes occur during the life of a fixed asset, the cumulative amount of the depreciation charges on a current cost basis will not normally equal the replacement cost of the machinery at the end of the service life .... There is no reason, however, why the cumulative charge should equal replacement cost.

Edwards & Bell, 1961, 192

No question arises of providing backlog depreciation in the profit and loss account since the basis of current cost profit is not to strike profit after providing for the replacement of assets, but rather to show profit after making a charge equal to the value to the business of the assets consumed during the year. However, in order that the cumulative depreciation figure in the balance sheet should match the difference between the gross and net value to the business of the depreciated assets, an adjustment should be made in the figure of cumulative depreciation before a transfer is made to revaluation reserve and should be retained as part of the cumulative depreciation in the balance sheet.

Sandilands, 1975, 184

The purpose of providing depreciation in current cost accounting is to match the current cost of fixed assets used up in earning revenue with the revenue and to state such assets net of accumulated depreciation at current cost . . . . [The calculation will normally be based on] the current equivalent replacement cost of new assets . . . . [A capital maintenance reserve account will be augmented by, *inter alia*, adjustments made to restate assets to current cost, and depreciation backlog should be charged to the capital maintenance reserve, not against operating profit or retained profits of prior periods.]

NZR, 1976, 113, 133

Three main adjustments to trading profit, calculated on the historical cost basis before interest, are required to arrive at current cost operating profit . . . . The depreciation adjustment allows for the impact of price changes when determining the charge against revenue for the part of fixed assets consumed in the period . . . . The cost of sales adjustment allows for the impact of price changes when determining the charge against revenues for stock consumed during the period . . . . Monetary working capital adjustment . . . should represent the amount of additional (or reduced) finance needed for monetary working capital as a result of changes in the input prices of goods and services used and financed by the business.

ASC, 1980b, SSAP16

Where a proportion of the net operating assets is financed by net borrowing, a gearing adjustment is required in arriving at the current cost operating profit attributable to shareholders. This should be calculated by (a) expressing net borrowing as a proportion of the net operating assets using average figures for the year from the current cost balance sheets; and (b) multiplying the total of the charges or credits made to allow for the impact of the price changes on the net operating assets of the business by the proportion determined at (a).

ASC, 1980b, SSAP16

767 Valuation adjustments and their disposition under CCA

A change in the value of an item of plant and machinery or other fixed asset such that the old and new values are both based on gross current replacement cost should normally be credited or charged, net of backlog depreciation, as a revaluation surplus or deficit. A change in the value of an item . . . [arising otherwise] should be credited or charged to the profit and loss account . . . .

IASG, 1976, ED18

The accounts should include a statement, by way of note, setting out prominently the gain or loss for the period of account in the shareholders' net equity interest after allowance has been made for the change in the value of money during the period . . . . by applying a general price index.

> IASG, 1976, ED18

The adjustments required to CCA (as [it is] usually expounded) are simple and may be summarized as follows: Current operating profit, add revaluation surplus . . . , deduct capital maintenance adjustment (opening owners' equity x % change in the value of the monetary unit) . . . . The task of the capital maintenance adjustment is, in a single entry, to introduce the net effects of the change in the value of the monetary unit so that the profit or loss is reported in real terms, terms which are comparable between different firms and different industries within the one country.

> Warrell, 1978, 620

The current cost balance sheet includes a reserve in addition to those included in historical cost accounts. The additional reserve may be referred to as the current cost reserve. The total reserves will include, where appropriate: (a) unrealized revaluation surpluses on fixed assets, stock and investments; and (b) realized amounts equal to the cumulative net total of the current cost adjustments, that is: (i) the depreciation adjustment (and any adjustments on the disposal of fixed assets); (ii) the two working capital adjustments; and (iii) the gearing adjustment.

> ASC, 1980b, SSAP16

When a nonmonetary asset is restated in terms of current cost . . . the credit or debit corresponding to the adjustment . . . should . . . be made to the current cost reserve. However, when it is apparent that a decrease . . . marks a permanent impairment of the utility of its operating capability to the entity, the debit should be made to the profit and loss account . . . .

> ASA & ICAA, 1989, SAP1

The current cost reserve is progressively credited or debited with adjustments generated by the various CCA measurement procedures, including: (a) restatement of non-monetary assets; (b) recognition of gains (losses) on holding monetary items; (c) recognition of gains (losses) in reinvestment ability for nonmonetary assets bought and sold on the same market; (d) bringing to account the proportion of investees' current cost reserves under the equity method of accounting; and, (e) recording of foreign currency translation adjustments. [Guidance notes]

> ASA & ICAA, 1989, SAP1

768 Adjustment information sources

The current cost of materials used . . . . is simply the quantity sold multiplied by the weighted average purchase price during the period in question.

> Edwards & Bell, 1961, 144

If . . . the statements are to reflect the situation as to physical capital maintenance, a set of indexes that measure the specific price changes that affect the individual accounts would be appropriate.

AICPA, 1963a, 6

Factual evidence for current costs can be obtained by reference to the current prices of similar commodities, by reference to price indexes for similar groups of commodities, or through expert opinion.

Popoff, 1973, 12

The net current replacement cost of an asset is derived from its gross current replacement cost, which is the lower of: (a) the current cost of a substantially identical asset in new condition, and (b) the cost of the modern equivalent asset . . . . to establish the actual gross cost of a substantially identical asset . . . . most companies will wish to use more than one of the data sources: (a) suppliers' official price lists . . . ; (b) the company's own replacement cost estimates, based on expert opinion; (c) an index compiled by the company from its own purchasing experience; (d) authorized external price indices analyzed by asset type; (e) authorized external indices analyzed by using industry . . . . To estimate the cost of the modern equivalent asset, the gross capital cost of the modern alternative asset should be adjusted by (a) the present value of any material differences in operating costs over its whole life; (b) any material differences in output capacity . . . ; (c) material differences in the total life of the modern machine, compared with the substantially identical replacement.

IASG, 1976, ED18

Enterprises may use various types of information to determine the current cost of inventory, property, plant, and equipment, cost of goods sold, and depreciation, depletion, and amortization expense . . . . [externally and internally] generated price indexes for the class of goods or services being measured; current invoice prices; vendors' price lists or other quotations or estimates; standard manufacturing costs that reflect current costs.

FASB, 1979, SFAS33

The CCA background papers on ED18 (CCA) . . . considered that the effect of technological advance on the current value of assets should be reflected in the accounts; but the real calculations are many times more subtle and complicated than . . . envisaged, and they require a detailed knowledge of the technology and engineering economies involved, together with a decade or two of responsible experience in the industry. The calculations would be very expensive to perform (with any pretension of accuracy) every year for every fixed asset, and the notion that they could be effectively audited is ludicrous.

Rudd, 1979, 54

769 Appraisal of current cost accounting

The current values [or current costs] theory maintains that the cost applicable to any given sale is the sum of the various components of that cost expressed in terms of the outlay which would be necessary at the time that such sale was completed .... [Its result] is the discarding of accounting as a record of facts and the substitution of an estimate of a notional position which would have arisen if all expenditure had taken place at the date of sale.

Wilk, 1960, 23

What is proposed [in the Sandilands report] is not an inflation accounting system at all. It does nothing to preserve the real value of the shareholder's interest, which is what the owners would expect of an inflation accounting system.

Financial Times, 1975

Failure of the [Sandilands] proposed CCA basis of accounting to recognize the decrease in value of monetary assets, and of obligations represented by monetary liabilities, in a period of continuing inflation is a matter of particular concern to banks and other financial institutions whose assets and liabilities are predominantly monetary. Current cost accounting ... requires to be supplemented by information showing changes in the purchasing power of capital invested.

Accountant, editorial, 1975b, 513

[The method] proposed by Sandilands ... makes no adjustment for changes in the general purchasing power of the monetary unit and thus eliminates the monetary gain on debt.

Vancil, 1976, 60

the reader of ED18 will search in vain for any precise statement of the objectives of current cost accounting or the interpretation to be put on the figures which emerge. He will find occasional statements of what the figures do not mean ... but he will generally have to be content with assurances that the figures are "more realistic" and "take account of inflation" in some sense which is wisely left undefined. In consequence, almost all substantive issues have been quite explicitly evaded, ... The [IASG] report is exclusively concerned with the minutiae of a system whose principles are shrouded in mystery.

Kay, 1977, 308

there is certainly a recognition of the need to adjust accounts for the effect of inflation. But CCA is not such a system; it is a system for adjusting for the specific price increases experienced by each particular business, which is a very different thing altogether .... The only approach which makes economic sense is to evaluate assets according to current cost, but make a provision for capital maintenance based on the value of money before striking a real profit figure.

Allen, 1978, 448

[Periodical accounts] are of real value only if all items in them are expressed in monetary units of the same or substantially the same value. Only when that has been achieved can one be said to have accounted for inflation .... [CCA is] not ... a system of accounting for inflation .... the [CCA] system appears to have been accepted simply because the [UK] government wanted it.

Denza, 1978b, 566

Fixed assets do not really depreciate less in geared companies than in ungeared companies; nor are the costs of sales of geared companies' stocks really less affected by inflation; hence it would be illogical to make a gearing adjustment which effectively reduces the depreciation and cost of sales adjustments compared with otherwise similar ungeared companies.

Rudd, 1979, 54

the CCA profit and loss account is in average-for-the-year pounds while the CCA balance sheet is in end-of-year pounds. Thus the two are not consistent even within a single year, let alone between years.

Myddelton, 1981, 94

It seems entirely inappropriate to use the current cost of [new style merchandise] as a basis for measuring income from selling [old style merchandise].

Milburn, 1982, 101

the members of the ICAEW do not wish any system of current cost accounting to be made compulsory. [Resolution of a special meeting, July 6, 1977, carried, 54 per cent to 46 per cent.]

Accountant, 1977, 2

770 Current Money Equivalent Accounting

> [described as cash equivalent accounting, continuously contemporary accounting, exit value accounting or net realizable value accounting.]

For valuation at market price, value in exchange, selling price, exit value, money equivalent, cash equivalent, net realizable value, see 540

771 Current money equivalent accounting described

A statement of financial position at a point of time is significant only insofar as it represents the monetary measures of assets and equities in terms of the monetary unit of prevailing purchasing power at that time, and only insofar as the monetary measures of assets are, or are approximations to, resale prices ruling at that time .... It follows that every transaction shall be recorded at the amount of the price paid, for this is the amount of the actual cash outflow or inflow consequent upon each transaction. It follows also that changes in prices of goods held shall be brought into the accounts for such goods, so that those accounts will always approximate the contemporary cash equivalents of holdings at any time and the financial position of the firm at that time. The different treatments of accounts for cash balances and goods account balances are due to the fact that the representation of money (and other monetary asset) holdings in terms of money involves a one-to-one relationship, whereas the monetary measurements of goods, their prices, are variable relationships.

Chambers, 1967a, 30

There are really two problems of inflation accounting which stem from: (1) the effects of general and particular price changes on the value of nonmonetary assets in the annual balance sheets; and (2) the effect of general price changes on the profit and loss account .... the profit is simply the difference between the real values of the shareholders' funds at the start and finish of the venture. If the monetary values are S_1 and S_2 and the general index moves from I_1 to I_2 during the venture, the real profit in end-of-venture terms is S_2-S_1 x I_2/I_1; hence the single correction to the money profit (S_2-S_1) is $S_1(I_2-I_1)/I_1$.

Rudd, 1979, 57

all assets are valued at their current realizable prices [in the normal course of business] ... and all liabilities are valued at their cash discharge values on maturity .... continuously contemporary accounting ... uses the dollar as a unit of general purchasing power, and hence incorporates a general inflation adjustment in the measure of income and capital maintenance .... real capital maintenance refers to the preservation of the general purchasing power of the initial capital investment [of a period].

Barton, 1984, 507, 509

CoCoA .... produces a balance sheet measuring the same property of each asset, its current cash equivalent, ... what the company would receive if it sold its assets individually. This informs creditors and shareholders of the cash available to the company, through sale of its assets, to meet its debts or reinvest elsewhere .... depreciation ... is based solely on the decline in the current cash equivalent of the asset .... CoCoA is not dependent upon unverifiable cost and revenue allocations .... The disclosure of net selling prices in the balance sheet reduces the possibility of a company being taken over ... for the purpose of asset-stripping .... The adjustment for changing price levels is made in one entry by indexing the opening capital by [the inflation rate] and deducting that amount from income.

Martin, 1984, 417–419

772 Object – a purchasing power accounting

Accountants are fully aware of the difference between dollar accounting and a conceivable purchasing power accounting, and would prefer, just as economists do, a purchasing power accounting.

Canning, 1929a, 196

What is needed is an adjustment of financial statements to eliminate the distorting effects of a rising general price level – in a word, purchasing power accounting.
Fabricant, 1978, 17

CoCoA [continuously contemporary accounting] concerns itself exclusively with financial aspects of business . . . . deals fully and systematically with the effects of all transactions and the effects of the two (generally counteracting) features of inflationary periods, changes in specific asset prices and changes in the general purchasing power of the money unit. The consistent use of . . . externally discovered prices makes the results realistic, capable of independent verification (objective), and subject to a minimal extent to the possibility of manipulation or innocent misrepresentation. The use of the common rule avoids the fallacies of mixed aggregation and mixed measurement.
Chambers, 1980, 62

Individuals presumably are interested in maintaining their consumption in real terms, that is, in maintaining their purchasing power. Consequently, the most relevant form of financial capital maintenance is one in which financial capital is measured in real terms . . . . the impact on income would come from differences between specific price changes and general inflation.
Carsberg, 1982, 68

773 Posited merits of current money equivalent accounting

Relevance to judgment and choice of information recipients

all assets, even though shown at depreciated historical cost in the accounting records, should be revalued at resale market or at managerial estimates of values in other uses for purposes of entering such items in comparative budgets used as a basis for managerial decision.
Goetz & Klein, 1960, 525

the present market [selling price] method of valuation is (1) relevant to all receivers, because it specifies the currently available alternatives and the ability to perform current obligations; (2) veritable, in the sense that all observers would agree to the value; (3) a measurement of an empirically meaningful dimension; (4) additive, in the sense that the sum of the parts is equal to the independent measurement of the whole; . . . .
Sterling, 1970a, 360

accounting must present information to facilitate risk assessment . . . . The larger an asset's exit value, the more flexible is the firm in employing its resources and the less dependent it is on its specific plans and operations. The specific-advantage firm is restricted in its alternatives, since its assets have zero exit values.
Ronen & Sorter, 1972, 261–262

a statement of financial position can usefully be reported so long as the resources are stated in terms of a current cash equivalent. By so doing the statement is rendered useful to those parties external to the firm . . . . The information presented is current, statistically valid and therefore open to comparison, and relevant . . . . Moreover it is information necessary to management in assessing alternative investment opportunities, for, when income is measured as a rate of return on capital valued at a current cash equivalent, this indicates the rate of return required from any alternative . . . projects.

Macdonald, 1974a, 129

Exit value accounting statements present to the user information which can be used . . . 1. To determine the liquidity of the firm . . . . 2. To appraise the effectiveness of managerial decisions involving assets . . . . 3. To estimate past economic income or predict future economic income . . . . measurement on this basis does not assume that the assets will be sold.

McKeown, 1974, 161, 162

current exit values are uniquely useful in making all judgments about the past and all decisions about the future . . . . current exit value reports . . . are explicitly designed to be allocation free.

Thomas, 1974, 113

a system based on the [net realizable values] of assets and the face values of liabilities . . . recognizes the full legal and economic position of the firm as it was at the stated date, in respect of the things it owned, the amounts it owed, and the markets in which it operates . . . . current resale prices enjoy three unique advantages over competing alternatives for inclusion in statements of *ex post* financial position and performance: 1, those prices are generally relevant; 2, they are neutral as to intention; and 3, they are objective and thus verifiable.

Gray & Wells, 1975, 94

Exit values become significant only if and when liquidation becomes an issue. It may always be an issue; clearly liquidation is one alternative a firm should always consider . . . . exit values are needed to evaluate an alternative that the firm might choose in preference to what it is currently doing,

Edwards & others, 1979, 645

the total potential receipts from the piecemeal sale of all assets is a statistic that creditors may well deem important . . . . a manager wants to know how much money he could marshal for new projects . . . by selling off assets piecemeal . . . . [sale price] can draw attention to assets that the firm would be wise to get rid of . . . . the sum of the sale prices [. . . may be] the benefit forgone by staying in business, and so an ingredient in the most momentous budget of all . . . . In short, "the single financial property which is uniformly relevant at a point of time for all future actions in markets is the market selling price or realizable price of all or any goods held." This is all very true.

Baxter, 1984, 197

Under certain restrictive conditions, economic theory does establish a clear cut objective function for project evaluation by firms. This is the maximization of current net market values .... this objective is identical to the maximization of the discounted net cash equivalent flow for the life of the project or the discounted flow of net CoCoA [continuously contemporary accounting] incomes.

Madan, 1985, 201

The conventional balance sheet .... needs to be replaced by a net wealth statement containing schedules of the realizable cash values of assets and liabilities so as to give a cash-oriented perspective to the measurement of enterprise capital ....

Mathews, 1989, 42

Technical merit

there is little prospect of more useful or informative reporting until the historical cost principle is jettisoned. Managers, investment analysts and economists want to know what assets are worth now, not what they used to be worth. If this change were made the need for separate inflation accounting would disappear.

Kay, 1973, *Financial Times*

a system of net asset valuation and cost measurement based strictly on current net realizable values, and changes in those values, would eliminate the need for many arbitrary allocation procedures now generally used. Thus, observation at periodic intervals of changes in net realizable value of a machine provides a basis for inferring periodic depreciation (or appreciation, if values are rising) without the need for an estimate of economic life or of a depreciation allocation procedure for distributing asset cost to time periods .... [and thus produces] an apparent net reduction in subjectivity.

Standish, 1976, 47

the current cash equivalent concept avoids the necessity to aggregate past, present and future prices [in balance sheets].

Hendricksen, 1977, 269

All of the input data [of the system] are historical .... there are no alternative valuation rules .... no supplementary accounts ... the possibility of confusion or misdirection from the simultaneous publication of two sets of accounts is thus averted. The [financial statements] would be in reasonably up to date terms in all respects and therefore readily interpretable, and comparable as between companies for any given date or period ... [and] between periods .... [They] would be complete in that they embrace all causes of changes in financial position and all sources of profit or loss. Companies, directors, officers and auditors would be relieved of the uncertainties, corporate and personal, which arise from the use of variant rules and conjectures.

ASRC, 1978, 12

Net realizable values represent wealth, the money's worth at a company's command, command over goods and services. Net income [so calculated] measures changes in wealth. Net realizable values are consistent with maintaining the purchasing power of a financial capital. Net realizable values best satisfy the requirements of stewardship . . . . [and are] the best basis on which to evaluate managerial responsibility. Financial statements based on market resale prices are most comparable between companies, and from period to period for the same company. These statements provide a meaningful calculation of the rate of return. Depreciation and amortization will no longer be arbitrary. Net realizable values are the only values relevant to investment decision that can reasonably be maintained in an accounting system. [Net realizable values are] properly additive . . . [A system] based on net realizable values accounts only for existing assets and events that have actually taken place. . . .

Boersma, 1979, 35

I have great difficulty understanding the strident assertion "assets are intended to be used and therefore exit values are irrelevant" that is so often encountered in the literature. People who make that assertion must be overlooking the fact that firms adapt to changing technology, changing consumer tastes, and changing prices.

Sterling, 1979, 121

[Under exit value accounting] the balance sheet becomes a huge statement of net liquidity . . . . It thus portrays the firm's adaptability or ability to shift its presently existing resources into new opportunities . . . . all of the measurements are additive because valuations are [made] at the same time point . . . and . . . of the same attribute.

Wolk & others, 1984, 30

NRV [net realizable value] is a value which is readily understandable by investors and other users of accounts . . . . Arbitrary decisions about such matters as depreciation are eliminated . . . . The amounts generated by using NRV can be added together because they are all expressed in current values . . . . [NRV is] relevant as a measure of an entity's potential adaptability . . . . The use of NRV would ensure a greater degree of comparability among the financial statements of different entities.

ICAS, 1988, 61

A series of surveys in six countries (Australia, Canada, New Zealand, Singapore, South Africa and United States) over the interval 1980–1985 suggests that accountants and non-accountants [share common understanding of wealth and financial position]. In total there were some 5700 responses, approximately half of them from accountants and half from non-accountants having more than trivial interests in the products of accounting. The responses were of substantially the same composition in all countries and as between accountants and non-accountants. Some 90 per cent of respondents were of the opinion that valuations of assets at cost less formally calculated depreciation were not indicative of wealth. Some 80–90 per cent were of the opinion that the current purchase prices (i e, replacement prices) of assets in possession were not indicative of spending power. Some 80 per cent were of the opinion that the resale prices of assets would provide better indications of wealth and financial position than initial or replacement cost valuations. [For a summary of the surveys, see Chambers & others, 1987]

Chambers, 1991, 142

774 Capital maintenance as maintenance of general purchasing power

The basis for [capital] maintenance probably most often in harmony with the customary fundamental purpose of economic activity is maintenance of absolute general purchasing power, i.e. maintenance of general real capital or simply real capital. It alone measures capital and income in such a way as to facilitate realization of the usual goal of economic effort, namely, increase of general purchasing power, and thus materially assists accounting to realize its main purpose of accurately distinguishing between capital and income.

Sweeney, 1930, 286

The economic capital of the enterprise is the value of the assets originally contributed by the stockholders. It is this value which must be maintained in terms of real purchasing power if the stockholders are not to suffer a diminution of their equity.

Jones, 1935, 184

accounting is accounting for capital – not capital in a purely monetary sense, nor in a legal sense – but in an economic sense. The capital to be accounted for must, accordingly, be the capital contributed, plus or minus the capital gained or lost through business operation, plus or minus the capital gained or lost as a result of change in price levels and money value.

Blackie, 1948, 1365

The economist takes his stand on the criterion that the physical capital should be maintained intact before striking a balance of profit . . . . the accountant seems content to hold fast to the money concept of profit, oblivious of the change in the purchasing power value of money from time to time. Yet, if it belongs to the essence of the idea of profit, that provision should first be made for maintaining the capital of a business, should we not think in terms of real capital, rather than its nominal money amount?

Moon, 1948, 23

It is true that the particular assets at present in use in a business may not in fact have to be replaced. But the capital represented by them must be recovered out of the gross proceeds from the business before that business can be said to have made a profit . . . . It is the amount of purchasing power that was originally invested that has to be recovered.

Solomons, 1948/1950, 365

I assume that general purchasing power is what most of us have in mind when we speak of keeping capital intact.

Baxter, 1949/1978, 4

The responsibility of the management to the owners is the preservation of their real capital in terms of general purchasing power and not in terms of specific assets.

Pakenham-Walsh, 1951, 12

In case of substantial monetary inflation appropriate conversion adjustments should be undertaken in order that the capital of the enterprise may be maintained in terms of the purchasing power invested by the stockholders.

Grady, 1962, 72

With real money capital . . . the bench mark used to determine whether a profit has been made is the purchasing power of the equity shareholders' interest in the company at the start of the period.

Lewis & Pendrill, 1985, 64

775 Real (current purchasing power) income

In order to give expression in one comprehensive measure to the size of these benefits [the flow of benefits called income], they are best considered as amounts of exchange value. It is simplest to base these calculations on the market prices during the period to which the estimation of income refers and subsequently to allow for changes in monetary purchasing power.

Lindahl, 1933, 399

In order to measure real income it is necessary to put both year-end and year-beginning equity into terms of dollars of equal purchasing power.

Alexander, 1950, 75

Profits are a residual in a calculation that uses dollars of many different dates . . . . To measure real profits, all of these assets must be stated in dollars of the same purchasing power.

Dean, 1951, 21

There can be no real net income in the accounting or business sense unless the full amount of purchasing power originally invested is recovered.

Jones, 1956, 53

[Under the purchasing power definition of capital] . . . . Net income would not be realized until the stock of purchasing power consumed in producing the gross income had been restored out of gross income.

Ladd, 1963, 53

Only by comparing dollar valuations which are stated in terms of dollars of the same worth can real gains and losses be separated from those caused by changes in the value of the dollar.

Stanley, 1965, 48

whether or not a company and its shareholders are, or are not, better off in terms of real financial wealth, . . . is what the concept income is supposed to measure.

Bell, 1982, 358

776 Real income calculation components

The dual effects of exchanges shall enter the accounting system as they occur and at their then monetary amounts. [The net increment is net revenue.] The dual effects of specific price changes [appreciation and depreciation] shall enter the system as they occur [or periodically.] [The net increment is a price variation adjustment.] The dual effects of changes in the general level of prices shall enter the system whenever the income of a past period is to be discovered. [The net effect is a capital maintenance adjustment.] [Periodical income is the algebraic sum of these three components.]

Chambers, 1966a, 265

Hicks' definition of income implies that business income consists of: *Plus* – net revenues which is all receipts from sales less the market value of opening inventory, less purchases plus closing inventory at market prices, less other current payments such as wages. *Minus* – depreciation of fixed assets which is the change (reduction) in market value of all assets other than inventories. *Minus* - the capital maintenance adjustment for the loss in consumer purchasing power on the market value of proprietors' equity at the beginning of the period . . . . The accounting system which comes closest to one based on Hicks' definition, and which shares its efficiency and equity properties [as a tax base], is continuously contemporary accounting . . . .

Swan, 1976, 2–4

I mean by exit value or exit value method the process of valuing assets at their immediate market selling price. Depreciation is the difference between such exit values at two dates.

Sterling, 1979, 117

When an exit value method is used, changes in value of assets held by the business are recognized as they occur; no distinction is made between gross profit on operations and holding gains and losses. Depreciation expense is not recorded, but instead the net change in exit value of property, plant and equipment is included as a component in each period's earnings statement.

Alexander, 1981, 8:11

777 Treatment of the effect of inflation and deflation

When the general level of prices changes, the maintenance of capital at t_0 is represented by transforming the measure of capital at t_0 [based on cash equivalents of assets at t_0] to its equivalent in units of the dimension [general purchasing power] prevailing at t_1. The absolute difference in the number of units representing a given capital at t_1 and t_0 is designated capital maintenance adjustment.
Chambers, 1966a, 264

both general and specific price adjustments are necessary in order to account in real terms. Abandonment of the historic cost principle involves both types of correction. General and specific price level adjustments are thus not alternatives but complements.
Lemke, 1966b, 394

Net profits for a period are the net gains in fair value of net assets during the period ... exclusive of changes in the value of old capital attributable to price level fluctuations, new capital received, and dividends paid.
Spacek, 1970b/1973, 45

If inflation has occurred, successive amounts of net assets [on a cash or money equivalent basis] will not be expressed in dollars of equal general purchasing power, and the difference between two successive amounts of net assets will be a purely nominal increment. To derive the amount of the increment expressed in dollars of general purchasing power at the end of a year, ... the nominal increment must be reduced by the loss in general purchasing power during the year in respect of the opening net assets. The adjustment is the product of the opening amount of net assets and the proportionate change in an index of changes in the general level of prices during the year. The adjustment may be described as a purchasing power adjustment, or an inflation adjustment, or a capital maintenance adjustment (since its object is to secure the calculation of a profit by reference to the general purchasing power of the opening net investment, or net assets, of any year) .... [Where there are undivided profits at the beginning of any year], the total amount of the adjustment is divided proportionately into two parts, [one for equity accounts other than undivided profits, and one for undivided profits].
ASRC, 1978, 108

778 Accessibility of market selling prices

Price-current: a list of the various articles of merchandize in the market, with the present prices annexed to each. In most of the great commercial cities and towns lists of this description are generally published once or twice a week.
Morrison, 1825, 266

The two main objections to using current values in balance sheets appear to be (a) it can't be done – and (b) it would open the door to manipulation of figures ....

In actual fact it is being done continuously by businessmen whenever balance sheet figures are used as a basis for any material decision . . . . Many companies have already adopted a policy of revaluing property and issuing shares covering the differences resulting from the revaluations.

Tomlinson, 1965, 555

Pricing of fixed assets is thought to be particularly difficult, but compare the current depreciation procedure which requires the accountant to predict a future price – salvage value – for those assets. Surely it is easier to discover the present price than the future price of the same asset.

Sterling, 1968a, 499

exit values . . . . reflect the net proceeds that would be received if the assets were to be sold separately in the ordinary course of business . . . . quantification in this case is usually reliably ascertainable.

Ronen, 1974, 15

detailed and up to date selling price information is readily available at little or no cost for all major primary products [in Australia; specifically, for wool, livestock, wheat, dairy products, sugar, dried vine fruits, coarse grains].

Wolnizer, 1977, 310

The market resale prices sought under CoCoA are not prices appropriate to sales under liquidation or duress. They are prices which give the best approximation, on the basis of independent evidence, of the money equivalents of assets in their then state and condition from time to time. There are many possible sources of indicative information. Engineers and project evaluation officers . . . . salesmen, buyers and other company officers . . . . trade papers, price lists of specialist dealers in secondhand goods . . . . Much information is available without recourse to specialist valuers. But expert estimates of resale prices (on a willing seller, willing buyer basis) may be obtained from expert valuers, either as primary information or as a check on information otherwise available.

Chambers, 1980, 52

Not only are the selling prices of steel inventories [in the US] obtainable with relative ease compared with the complexities of index-based valuation procedures, but they are more precise measures.

Wolnizer, 1983, 187

Current selling prices . . . are generally available, for finished goods . . . most raw materials . . . . general purpose plant . . . . land and general purpose buildings . . . . marketable securities . . . . [For specialized assets and work in progress the current selling price may be negligible or zero.]

Barton, 1984, 513

779 Posited objections

Selling price challenged as being liquidation value or inappropriate for going concerns or transient

As a general basis for asset valuation, liquidation value [market value] can be ruled out immediately on the ground that it has no significance to the going concern.
Daniels, 1934/1980, 31

One of the most forceful objections to the value balance sheet is that it may result in placing an undue appearance of authenticity on market values, which are always transitory and which may be based on extraordinary or unsound economic conditions.
Lynch, 1943, 242

In a well-managed and profitable business, the current worth of assets is really only of academic importance. What does matter is the ability to pay creditors and to continue profitable activity on the same scale in the future.
Irish, 1950, 219

we have to regard the business as a going concern .... In valuing its material assets, therefore, we must have regard primarily to the purpose they are intended to serve ... and not the current realizable or market values of those or similar assets.
Beacham, 1964, 13

selling price should not be used [for raw materials and work in progress] because the finished goods may subsequently become unsaleable, or may be sold only at a reduced price.
Bourn, 1967b, 323

assets not held for resale would only be valued in this way [at market selling prices] if liquidation of the firm was imminent, or in similar circumstances.
Amey, 1968, 448

1. Market prices ignore the going concern. 2. Market prices for a given asset are often difficult or impossible to attain. 3. Market prices are so heavily influenced by illogical considerations that they may not reflect expectations. 4. Market prices ignore intangibles and other assets not readily saleable. 5. Market prices require legal title, a consideration not relevant to asset valuation.
Williams, 1969, 40

A firm that values its assets at exit prices derived from markets in which the firm is normally a buyer reports unusual values – those which would obtain in a liquidation situation, at least as far as the assets being so valued are concerned. To employ such values when liquidation is not contemplated is surely misleading.

Edwards, 1975, 240

once the directors have decided that an asset is fixed (not for sale in the reasonably near future), its exit value is not relevant to the decisions of the recipient of a balance sheet.

Nobes, 1983, 77

The principal criticism of exit valuation concerns the . . . question of relevance: how useful are net realizable value measurements for fixed assets if the firm intends to keep and utilize them during the foreseeable future . . . .

Wolk & others, 1984, 30

See, *per contra*, 318, 319

Selling price valuation said to anticipate profits

As to the making a close and balance of your ledger, you may value the balances of goods as they cost you, or according to the current rates: yet it seems more reasonable to value them as they cost you; for otherwise you bring in gain and loss into your accounts, which has not yet actually happened, and may, perhaps, not happen; because you may not dispose of them at those rates.

Malcolm, 1731, 89

Profits should not be anticipated by taking into stock at the market value. It is quite uncertain when the stocks will be sold and the sale would be attended by certain expenses.

Accountant, editorial, 1890b, 665

The general mode [of valuing commodity stocks], I think, is to take the market price. This is not wise, for if the market price is above cost we are anticipating profit – an unwise thing to do. I think the safest plan is that when the market price is below cost take the market price . . . [except in the case of a wine stock of exceptionally good vintage]. It is then safe to take the market price . . . .

Bilton, 1901, 51

Some of the most common violations of accounting principles which tend to cast a rosy glow over an otherwise gloomy statement [include] . . . . the very common practice of inventorying stock on hand at selling prices . . . .

Roberts, 1906, 467

To use selling prices in taking inventories . . . is to anticipate profits.

Paton & Stevenson, 1918/1978, 464

Valuing inventories at selling price ... will result in recognition of income that is both unearned and unrealized.

Paton & Dixon, 1958, 355

See, *per contra*, 325

780 Present Value and Cash Flow Accounting

For valuation at present (discounted) value, see 550

781 Present value accounting described

Generally, discounted cash flow accounting refers to the quantification of the firm's value or wealth by discounting its expected net cash flows over a specified time period . . . . this value may be separated into specific assets and liabilities reflecting for each asset and liability the present value of the expected contributions to the cash flows of the firm . . . . the individual values would not necessarily add up to the total value of the firm.

Ronen, 1974, 150

The present value (or discounted cash flow) system ... concerns only the future . . . . [it] applies to ... the evaluation and selection [from available alternative courses of action] of policies to follow . . . . all assets and liabilities are valued according to their expected cash flows . . . . However, future net cash flows are likely to differ in amounts, timing, and duration according to each prospective venture [considered], and it is necessary to put them, on a comparable basis for a decision to be made. This is done by discounting the prospective cash flows back to the present time.

Barton, 1984, 526–8

782 Posited merits of present value accounting

That investment is most attractive which offers us the greatest present value of future receipts per dollar invested, when discounted at the going rate of interest . . . . it is growth in present value which alone appears to be significant; and since it seems to carry out the function generally attributed to income, growth in present value must be what we had better understand income to mean.

Solomons, 1961, 375

From an economic point of view this [accounting] concept of profit is very defective . . . . the accountant ought to advocate a concept of profit based on the economic theory of income. If ... managers ... [in] their choice of business policy ... must make their decisions from computations based on economic theory [i e, on the present value of prospects], . . . the annual accounts, which in principle should function as a control calculation on the business policy pursued, must appear as an economic computation, if they are to fill this role.

Hansen, 1962, 116

the most commonly used measure of wealth at a point of time is the present value of discounted future cash flows.

Burton, 1975b, 69

Present value accounting is often regarded as the ideal income and wealth measurement system as it provides all users with the information they want about the firm's future profitability and financial position . . . . the system avoids all the arbitrary interperiod allocations of the historical cost system . . . . The need for interperiod allocations is removed by discounting all future cash flows back to the present time . . . . The discounting process . . . takes account of the time value of money.

Barton, 1984, 535–6, 528

See also 145, 146

783 Financial position and balance sheet

"Ideal" meaning of financial position – With respect to procurement of funds, . . . financial position as disclosed in the balance sheet means "regarded from this date, future fund procurements by means of enterprise operations will occur to the extent of the directly valued assets. Toward the procurement of further future funds there are certain correctly, but indirectly, valued assets, future necessary services now subject to control, in the amounts set out".

Canning, 1929a, 191

A forward-looking balance sheet can be prepared for all the firm's existing assets and liabilities. The value of each item is the present value of the future cash flows attributable to it . . . . cash on hand . . . is shown at its face value; accounts receivable . . . at their [discounted] gross value . . . ; investments in securities and other assets held for resale . . . at their currently realizable value (which should equal their discounted cash flow value); . . . . Liabilities . . . are shown at the amounts to be repaid, including interest, discounted from their maturity dates back to the present time. Owners' equity then remains as the difference between the gross present value of assets and liabilities . . . .

Barton, 1984, 538

784 Present value income

the accounting ordinarily employed in business . . . . is, in fact nothing but a method of recording the items of income and their capitalization at different points of time. A merchant's balance sheet is a statement of the prospects of his business. Each item in it represents the discounted value of items he may expect later to enter in his income account. Rightly interpreted, the capital account merely represents as a whole the capitalization of expected items in the income account; . . . .

Fisher, 1906/1965, 264

income in the accounting sense, *I*, is determined by the formula

$$I = (V + or - a) - V/(1 + i)$$

[where *V* is the estimate at the beginning of the period of the value of proprietorship claims at the end of the period, *a* is the divergence between the estimates at the beginning and at the end, *i* is the rate of discount per period] . . . . This expression . . . . this formula or ideal . . . . is essentially what the accounting technique is endeavoring to determine.

Buchanan, 1940, 213

Since assets are valuable to the extent of their presumed (subjectively determined) ability to produce future net receipts, their present significance to the firm would be the present equivalent of this future stream of net receipts. It is here contended that the enhancement in this present (or discounted) value from one point in time to another, after adjusting for investments and withdrawals, is the appropriate net income to appear in corporate annual reports.

Zeff, 1962, 620

The subjective value of an asset or group of assets is the present value of the expected receipts which the resource(s) will yield . . . . the receipts expected by a person discounted at a rate of interest which that person expects to be the appropriate rate . . . . Subjective income is the change in subjective value between two dates. It may be computed either before the fact or after the fact.

Bedford, 1965, 25

Annual income [under discounted cash flow accounting] . . . is merely the difference in the value of the firm at the beginning and the end of the year.

Ronen, 1974, 150

The essential feature of present value accounting is that the usual distinction between income and capital gains is disregarded . . . . all gains made in the year, including unrealized holding gains and losses, are taken to the profit and loss account.

Sandilands, 1975, 152

An alternative method of income determination . . . may be derived from the concepts of economics. This method is based on the discounted cash flow approach . . . and relies on the use of forecasts (of future cash flows) rather than on past transactions.

Arnold & others, 1985, 270

741

Maintaining capital intact

The present value method is normally associated with a concept of capital maintenance under which no amounts are regarded as distributable until a charge has been made equal to the value of the assets consumed during the year.

Sandilands, 1975, 152

Maintaining capital intact [in the present value system] means the retention of sufficient resources to maintain the future income stream intact.

Barton, 1984, 537

785 Appraisal of present value accounting

Asset valuation

The articles of association of a limited liability company provided that no dividends should be payable except out of realized profits .... The business of the company consisted chiefly in lending money to builders on mortgages payable by instalments .... It was the practice of the directors to estimate the profits of the company available for dividend by making out an account of the liabilities and assets and treating the excess of the amount of assets over liabilities as profits. The most important item of assets in the account was "present value of repayments and value of properties in hand". This value was arrived at by calculating from year to year upon a 5 per cent annuity table the present value of the instalments of principal and interest remaining unpaid by each mortgagor. *Held*, that realized profits must be taken in its ordinary commercial sense as meaning at least profits tangible for the purpose of division, and that the directors having treated estimated profits as realized profits, and having in fact paid dividends out of capital, on the chance that sufficient profits might be made, were jointly and severally liable, as upon a breach of trust, to repay, and must repay, the sums improperly paid as dividends ....

Oxford Benefit Building and Investment Society, In re, 1886

it does not seem rational or practicable to recognize in the asset accounts of an enterprise the capitalized value of a part of its probable future income .... the revenues of the specific properties of the business world are largely indeterminate; and it would be difficult indeed to settle upon capitalization rates ....

Paton, 1922/1962, 320

whenever a stream of cash flows is jointly generated by more than one asset, the discounted services method cannot be used to value those assets individually without becoming very arbitrary .... Nothing bars its use in economic theory or investment analysis, for here the intention is to come to a single net asset value for the entire company. The approach breaks down only when we try to use it to value individual assets for balance sheet purposes.

Thomas, 1964, 1, 11

Another exercise in futility is to assume that the investor's real interest in the assets of an enterprise lies in their earning power, and to argue from this that balance sheet values should be arrived at by capitalizing income. How can we capitalize income without first determining what the income is? And how do we determine income without an appropriate amortization of asset values? To avoid this dilemma, it has been proposed that assets might be valued by capitalizing cash flow. But this would be worse still, since cash flow ties us more hopelessly than ever to transactions and ignores entirely the important non-transaction aspects of profit determination.

Ross, 1969, 35

The implicit equating of capital with capitalized value is a . . . source of confusion. A capital sum is, in all ordinary usage, a sum employed or available to be employed in an income earning prospect. It is, in effect, an input. The capitalized value of the expected net proceeds of a venture is a time and interest adjusted estimate of an output. In no sense whatever may the two ideas be equated or the two terms be used interchangeably.

Chambers, 1976, 53

the net present value concept of income is not primarily a concept of periodic income – rather it is the total income expected to be earned up to the time horizon of the firm [or the time horizon of the projects under examination] . . . . Because net present value income is primarily a measure of total income, it is not directly comparable with measures of periodic historical income.

Barton, 1984, 536

Futurity and subjectivity

A system of accounting which attempted to reflect changes in the value of an income stream in the determination of income would create an insoluble problem of circular reasoning.

May, 1957, 35

Expectations cannot be audited. Were accountants to depend solely on subjective estimates of managers, not only would manipulation of accounting results be easily accomplished but also it would be impossible to tell whether there was manipulation in a given situation.

Zeff, 1962, 621

Use value – the discounted present worth of future net receipts – ... by its very definition ... [involves] estimates made by a specific person .... there is no possibility that an application of an accounting system based on use value ... can be objective in the sense of freedom from personal bias.

Stanley, 1965, 44, 53

Economic income describes the firm's predictions of its future. It does not describe the firm's past and current success in dealing with its economic environment.

Shwayder, 1967, 34

Provision of a valuation based on discounted expectations would presumably run counter, in audited accounts, to the general ban on lending professional names to forecasts.

Finnie, 1968b, 356

Periodic present value income ... is futuristic – it is an annual average of total income expected up to the horizon and it is thereby affected by [subsequent events], by the accuracy of forecasts and by the discount rate. Periodic *ex post* income refers to the income earned from the actual market transactions and events of the past year, at least in principle .... Periodic present value income would not, therefore, appear to be the ideal income concept for accounting purposes.

Barton, 1974, 675

Present value calculations may play some part in the decision to acquire ... assets .... However, after acquisition it is seldom possible ... to determine with any degree of accuracy the future flows to be produced by an asset .... or an appropriate discount rate .... we cannot accept that present value would provide a generally acceptable basis of valuation.

NZR, 1976, 92

The figures arrived at by the economic approach [discounting the estimated future net cash flow] cannot serve for asset valuation in an accounting framework for three reasons: (1) the calculations are based on subjective judgment, (2) usually this method does not provide data on individual assets, and (3) it contradicts the main objective of the accounting system – to provide cost and income data for judging performance and determining wealth (value). Economic value is computed from projections of accounting data; using this value as an input for the accounting system ... represents circular reasoning.

Goldschmidt & Admon, 1977, 43

Because a company's economic income relates to expectations about future flows, it ... is inconsistent with important accounting reporting objectives. In particular, ... it does not provide information useful for evaluating performance in the period .... economic income is not an ideal standard by which accounting income measurement may be judged .... But the present value concept has economic significance in many decision contexts.

Ma & Mathews, 1979, 431

present value accounting relates only to the future .... is almost completely subjective .... could not possibly be used in audited published reports .... treating the two systems [present value accounting and *ex post* accounting] as alternatives confuses the information required for decisions with the realized consequences of those decisions, i.e. it confuses expectations of the results of the future with actual achievements to date.

Barton, 1984, 540

Cash Flow Accounting

786 Cash flow accounting described

If accounting is to be liberated from the arbitrary effects of asset valuation, a system of accounting must be developed in which objective records and subjective valuations are kept rigidly apart .... The system proposed .... is a system of funds accounting, from which asset valuations are completely excluded.

Rayman, 1970, 424

cash flow accounting ... is intended to describe past and projected business activity for control and decision making purposes. Its main advantage ... is that it avoids, in both its historic and forecast forms, the subjectiveness introduced into accounting by the accrual methodology .... a pattern of flows must be reported reflecting several years' activity .... to minimize the effect of exceptional inflows and outflows of cash in one particular year ....

Lee, 1972, 199

cash flow accounting ... involves the estimation and presentation of expected cash flows into the indefinite future and the assessment of future probabilities. Making such estimates and projections is part of the job of management. Whether they should be published raises knotty and weighty problems.

Edey, 1973, *Financial Times*

Under a cash flow accounting system, entries would be made in the accounts of a company when cash was received or paid out. Depreciation would be abandoned for the purpose of published accounts, and the cash spent on acquisition of fixed assets would be charged in full to the year of acquisition. Similarly the cash spent on acquisition of materials, fuel, stock and all other factors would be charged in full at the point of outgoing.

Sandilands, 1975, 156

the cash flow basis of accounting means recording not only the cash receipts and disbursements of the period (the cash basis of accounting) but also the future cash flows owed to or by the firm as the result of selling and transferring title to certain goods (the accrual basis of accounting). Both of these are "real" cash flows. To reject them would be ridiculous, particularly since the name of the game in decision making is future cash flows, and accruals are one type of future cash flow.

Hicks, 1981, 30

The genuine unexpired benefits of maintaining an asset in use can never be more than expectations. Expectations do however have a value and will be impounded in the market value of a company's shares and/or other financial instruments accordingly. Hence, capital expenditure should be treated as a cost in the period in which it is incurred and, at the end of the sequence of periods, the (multiperiod) performance of which is to be measured, the market value of a company's shares and loans should in effect be brought in as a credit. Similarly, the market value of shares and loans should be brought in on the debit side at the beginning of the sequence since, whatever happens thereafter, those values represent the cost of acquiring total ownership at the outset.

Lawson, 1981, 47

CFA [cash flow accounting] is the term used to denote a system of financial reporting which describes the financial performance of an entity in cash terms. It is based on a matching of periodic cash inflows and outflows, free of credit transactions and arbitrary accounting allocations . . . . it is a measurement and reporting system which avoids time lags and distortions. It concentrates on the liquidity and financial management of the reporting entity, and can be conceived in terms both of actual and forecast cash transactions.

Lee, 1981a, 63

787 Appraisal of cash flow accounting and reporting

a cash flow earnings figure cannot be considered a substitute for or an improvement upon the net income calculated with a proper and reasonable deduction for depreciation, depletion, amortization and the like.

Mason, 1961, 39

The measurement of financial performance (or financial reporting) on a cash flow basis . . . allows management to escape from most if not all the controversial problem areas which have bedevilled traditional accounting for the bigger part of this century.

Lawson, 1971, 40

There is . . . only one method of measuring financial performance in terms of current purchasing power, namely, a total cash flow accounting system.

Lawson, *Financial times*, 1973

Cash flow reporting as an alternative to standardization . . . . Historic cash flows represent definite events, which can be objectively measured, verified and reported. Unlike accrual accounts, they do not require subjective value measurements in respect of incomplete transactions. Cash flow statements would, therefore, be free from the biases introduced by accrual accounting valuations. Interfirm comparisons would also be aided, as all the comparative data would be prepared and published on an identical basis.

Jones, 1975, 278

Advocates of cash flow accounting believe there can be no objective correct measure of the income and financial position of a company, and that the traditional profit and loss account and balance sheet should therefore be replaced by a statement of cash flows .... It is suggested by the supporters of cash flow accounting that the separation of profitability from liquidity is a serious disadvantage of conventional accounting .... The advantages of accounting in terms of cash are: (i) The system is more objective and more easily verified than historic cost or value accounting .... (ii) The system automatically deals with the problems of changing costs and prices .... (iii) [The system] ... avoids the problem of gains or losses arising from holding monetary liabilities or assets when costs and prices are changing.

Sandilands, 1975, 156–7

The problems associated with distinctions between capital, revenue, income and expenditure, or of allocations of costs between a series of arbitrary time periods, do not arise under cash flow accounting.

Glautier & Underdown, 1976, 664

accountants usually reject immediate write off [of capital expenditures] on the grounds that it ignores the unexpired benefits of capital outlays. But ... allocating capital expenditure over the succession of periods which enjoys its use is wholly objectionable. Such allocations are inevitably arbitrary .... Written down values do not represent real world values and are in no way relevant to the returns which can be enjoyed by the shareholders and other financiers of a going concern.

Lawson, 1981, 47

CFA [cash flow accounting] and NRVA [net realizable value accounting] are both based firmly on the importance of cash as a business resource .... [Both are] allocation-free systems ....The condition of enterprise survival is greatly emphasized in CFA and NRVA .... Both systems concentrate on reporting the activity of the enterprise and its management. Neither assumes continuity of this activity, and both appear capable of providing essential information on the financial management of the reporting entity (particularly that pertaining to its liquidity).

Lee, 1981b, 163

See also 193, 496–499

790 Other Proposals and Observations

791 Multivalent accounting

accountants may discover that the last chance of preserving the traditional principles [in the face of conflicting forces] is by advocating publication of an additional statement including all assets at present values ....

Whitney, 1940, 308

it is likely that in the future several interrelated monopurpose accounting systems will replace one multipurpose establishment.

Mattessich, 1964, 9

accounting should be recognized as embodying statistical techniques capable of producing different sorts of information about the same basic events to meet varying purposes, rather than as being confined to a single, authoritative, general purpose set of statements of spurious validity for many uses. The product of the accounting process should be diversified, carefully differentiated and accurately labelled.

Carrington, 1965, 540

Reporting multiple valuations of an asset will reduce the pressure on a single valuation to serve many purposes . . . . The presentation of the historical [cost based] information alone excludes the full impact of the environment on the firm; presentation of current cost information alone obscures the record of consummated market transactions. The committee recommends that both kinds of information be presented in a multi-valued report, in which the two kinds of information appear in adjacent columns.

AAA, 1966, 29, 30

[For personal financial statements –] A two column presentation of personal financial statements is recommended as the most useful and easily understood. The first column should present financial data on the cost basis, paralleled by a second column presenting estimated values. [Editorial, *JA*, July 1968 – This can be described as an almost revolutionary proposal, since it is the first time an Institute (AICPA) committee has recommended the use of current values.]

AICPA, 1968, 29

The solution [to the problem of choice between diverse accounting systems] could quite easily be the production of multiple column statements in which the results of several of the combinations of net asset valuation methods and capital maintenance ideas are presented.

Gynther, 1971, 19

the complexities of modern economic life require both [net realizable value and current replacement cost] calculations . . . . Clearly the accounting profession must start presenting multiple valuations and make multiple disclosures in their annual public report.

Bedford & McKeown, 1972, 338

since the financial information needs of the many interested parties vary . . . , and the media by which such information is communicated can also differ considerably, accounting should be concerned with producing information in terms of different bases. Ideally, this would result in the preparation of separate statements in terms of several different models.

Johnston, 1972, 98

the adoption of current value accounting will not eliminate the necessity of maintaining records on the historical cost basis or of reporting on that basis.

Somekh, 1972, 87

[I believe that] accounting reports must show a range of values, drawn up on different bases appropriate to the needs of different users, with the figures in each group containing an indication of the likely margins of error in the measurement estimates. It seems to me to be clear that if accounting data are presented as single-valued estimates they cannot be regarded as either neutral or, indeed, useful.

Stamp, 1972b, 195

all of today's differing information requirements can never be satisfied with a single, general purpose financial statement that is in reality directed to very narrow and special interests.

Trueblood, 1972, 260

No changes are to be made in the primary financial statements; the information required by the Statement is to be presented as supplementary information in published annual reports . . . . An enterprise is required to disclose . . . information on income from continuing operations for the current fiscal year on a historical cost/constant dollar basis . . . . information on income from continuing operations for the current fiscal year on a current cost basis . . . . the current cost amounts of inventory and property, plant and equipment at the end of the fiscal year . . . . increases or decreases for the current fiscal year in the current cost amounts of inventory and property, plant and equipment, net of inflation . . . .

FASB, 1979, SFAS33

accountants must cease to believe that all of the financial complexities of a modern public corporation can be captured and portrayed by one set of figures prepared on what would necessarily be an arbitrarily selected measurement basis.

CICA, 1980, 72

I don't see why we are trying to dictate the choice of a measurement basis. Why do we want to report a primary measure, or primary income, of our own choosing and deprive society of other measures? I'm not sure we are qualified to make that choice for society. Why should we deprive them of the current cost income number, for example? Why can't we produce both and let the market decide . . .?

Abdel-khalik, 1984, 97

it is not essential to have a single capital maintenance concept: it is quite feasible to report a number of profit figures derived from different capital maintenance concepts, within a single income statement. We would advocate such a procedure not for the negative reason that we are unable to choose between a bewildering variety of competing concepts, but for the positive reason that different measures of profit may be useful for different purposes . . . . Our own view is that future developments should include the reporting of alternative [asset] valuations for certain assets where different valuation bases give materially different results.

Tweedie & Whittington, 1984, 294, 301

See also 062, 066

792 Ambivalent and supplementary accounting rejected

We recommend that accounts drawn up in accordance with the principles of current cost accounting should as soon as practicable become the basic published accounts of companies . . . . if current cost accounts were presented as supplementary statements to historic cost accounts confusion could legitimately arise as to which set of accounts showed a true and fair view . . . . We recommend, however, that at any rate for the foreseeable future the net book value of assets on a historic cost basis and the historic cost depreciation should continue to be shown in notes to the accounts.

Sandilands, 1975, 164

If the historical figures in traditional accounts provided a true and fair view, there would hardly be a need for their conversion. As far as truth and fairness are concerned, therefore, the published statutory accounts and their CPP supplement are seen to be mutually exclusive, rather than mutually supportive – the auditors, strictly, should tell us which ones they believe, since one set of figures, by definition, presents a picture which is unfair and tells a lie!

Woolf, 1975, 93

The overriding aim of agreeing on workable standards for inflation accounting is that we end up with only one set of results for the company. If we appear to produce two sets of books, we entirely undermine this attempt to achieve wider understanding of the economic facts of business life – because we appear unable to agree what those facts are.

Cadbury, 1977, 624

793 Information overload in accounting

Nor was the usefulness of the statements increased by the fact that pages and pages of footnotes to the statements and comments in the auditors' reports sought to explain the results of the idiosyncracies and gyrations of practice which went into the making of the statements. Indeed, the multitude of footnotes and explanations were in themselves sources of confusion.

Associated Gas and Electric Company, 1942/1960

Evidence is plentiful that, as more notes, explanations, supporting schedules, and breakdowns are given, the more likely it is that the average investor or stockholder will be dissuaded or discouraged from even reading the statements and supporting data, let alone studying them enough to understand them.

Werntz, 1960, 299

Two outcomes of [the] practice of over-information are apparent: (1) financial resources are misallocated, and (2) the critical factors are apt to be obscured.

Gibson, 1963, 499

what we need is a relatively few significant figures, properly calculated and clearly stated . . . . a general overall view is all that can be expected from a balance sheet and income statement . . . . Additional detail that does not affect the general picture . . . is undesirable . . . . information that is not going to be used is worse than useless; it tends to clutter up and divert.

Ross, 1966, 69

It is . . . possible that much of the prettiness of modern company reports distracts attention from their financial kernels. Increasing detail may provide further distraction.

Cramer, 1968, 23

A hypothesis might be stated with respect to present reporting practices that the greater the amount and diversity of accounting data to which the user is exposed, the greater is the potential for misunderstanding, confusion, and hindrance to rational investment action.

Fertakis, 1969, 689

too many notes to accounts do more harm than good to the layman whose interests we all seek to serve.

Waldron, 1969, 479

To disclose every detail, to columnarize, to display the same item in different ways, to reflect transactions rather than to summarize and classify, to show what the effects of an alternative accounting method would be – all of these and other disclosures are frequently nothing but cop-outs. In effect, such disclosures may represent acknowledgments of either an inability or an unwillingness to . . . provide meaningful and understandable information . . . .

Andersen & Co, 1972, 11

Each additional disclosure requirement, and each attempt . . . to provide shareholders with more information about companies . . . , inevitably makes published accounts more complicated, and hence less easy for the layman to understand.

Holmes, 1974b, 72

the scarce resource is human attention, not information. That puts a tight constraint on how much information you can pour into a system. This was the main reason why management information systems were such a disappointment; they were designed to provide information without ever asking how much information could be absorbed, or what information was relevant.

Simon, 1990, 659

See also 217, 287

800 SYSTEMATIC INQUIRY AND KNOWLEDGE

800 Science

801 Scientific knowledge

the method of science. Its fundamental hypothesis . . . is this: There are real things, whose characters are entirely independent of our opinion about them; those realities affect our senses according to regular laws, and, though our sensations are as different as our relations to the objects, yet, by taking advantage of the laws of perception, we can ascertain by reasoning how things really are, and any man, if he have sufficient experience and reason enough about it, will be led to the one true conclusion. The new conception here involved is that of reality.
Peirce, 1877/1958, 107

Science is a river with two sources . . . . The practical source is the desire to direct our actions to achieve predetermined ends . . . . The theoretical source is the desire to understand.
Whitehead, 1929/1957, 107

In the last analysis science is nothing but the effort we make to understand anything.
Ortega, 1931/1961, 23

Pure logical thinking cannot yield us any knowledge of the empirical world; all knowledge of reality starts from experience and ends in it. Propositions arrived at by purely logical means are completely empty as regards reality.
Einstein, 1935, 133

the scientific attitude . . . . On its negative side, it is freedom from control by routine, prejudice, dogma, unexamined tradition, sheer self-interest. Positively, it is the will to inquire, to examine, to discriminate, to draw conclusions only on the basis of evidence after taking pains to gather all available evidence.
Dewey, 1955/1962, 31

It is these five features – those of abstraction, generality, reliance on empirical evidence, ethical neutrality, and objectivity – which we propose to adopt as the defining characteristics of a science.
Gibson, 1960, 3

To have a science of anything is first to have recognized a domain and a set of phenomena in that domain, and second to have devised a theory whose inputs and outputs are phenomena in the domain (the first observations, the second predictions) and whose terms may describe the underlying reality of the domain.

Caws, 1972, 72

Knowledge in the objective sense is knowledge without a knower: it is knowledge without a knowing subject.

Popper, 1972, 109

Science is organized knowledge . . . . Science is, or aspires to be, deductively ordered. It parades principles, laws and other general statements from which statements about ordinary particulars follow as theorems. The sciences don't begin this way, to be sure; nor do they always end in this tidy deductively ordered form.

Medawar, 1986, 3

See also 203

802 Science as method

The unity of all science consists alone in its method, not in its material.

Pearson, 1911, 12

Science (research for uniformities among facts independently of any considerations of utility, of sentiment, or of influence on conduct).

Pareto, 1916/1963, 2015 (index)

The basic procedures of empirical science occur in daily life. Prior to his cultivation of science an individual perceives relatively stable things in space and time, describes them with the aid of symbols which record and communicate the results of observation, and explains perceptible phenomena in terms of causes.

Lenzen, 1955/1962, 281

Science is a method of approach to the entire empirical world, i.e. to the world which is susceptible of experience by man. It is furthermore an approach which does not aim at persuasion, at the finding of ultimate truth, or at conversion. It is merely a mode of analysis that permits the scientist to state propositions in the form of "if –, then – ".

Goode & Hatt, 1952, 7

science is not mathematics, but reasoning; not equipment, but inquiry.

Platt, 1962, 2

Science . . . is the attentive consideration of common experience; it is common knowledge extended and refined. Its validity is of the same order as that of ordinary perception, memory and understanding.

Santayana, 1962, 29

science is characterized by its method of formulating and testing propositions, not by its subject matter.

Blaug, 1980/1984, 12

The word science began to be used in the honorific sense by the English only in the nineteenth century . . . . Earlier it meant studies, as in classical studies . . . . Economics . . . is merely a disciplined inquiry into the market for vice or the scarcity of love. Economics is a collection of literary forms, not a science. Indeed, science is a collection of literary forms, not a science. And literary forms are scientific.

McCloskey, 1985, 54

803 Scientific method

It is necessary, first, to determine what are the principal forces in operation, and the laws in accordance with which they operate. Next comes the purely deductive stage, in which are inferred the consequences which will ensue from the operation of these forces under given conditions. Lastly, by a comparison of what has been inferred with what can be directly observed to occur, an opportunity is afforded for testing the correctness and practical adequacy of the two preceding steps, and for the suggestion of necessary qualifications.

Keynes, 1890/1930, 216

science is in reality a classification and analysis of the contents of the mind; and the scientific method consists in drawing just comparisons and inferences from the store of impresses of past sense-impressions, and from the conceptions based upon them. Not till the immediate sense-impression has reached the level of a conception, or at least a perception, does it become material for science.

Pearson, 1911, 52

Scientific method is a systematic effort to eliminate the poison of error from our common knowledge.

Cohen, 1931/1964, 79

I am not one of those who hold that there is a scientific method as such. The scientific method, as far as it is a method, is nothing more than doing one's damnedest with one's mind, no holds barred.

Bridgman, 1945, 450

the scientific method is not confined to those who are called scientists. The body of knowledge and ideas which is the product of the work of the latter is the fruit of a method which is followed by the wider body of persons who deal intelligently and openly with the objects and energies of the common environment . . . . the engineer . . . the farmer, the mechanic, and the chauffeur, as far as these men do

what they have to do with intelligent choice of means and with intelligent adaptation of means to ends, instead of in dependence upon routine and guesswork.
                                                                        Dewey, 1955/1962, 29

The method of science is not a fixed thing, it is a growing process .... Consequently scientific method, like science itself, defies definition. It is made up of a number of operations, some mental, some manual. Each of these in its time, has been found useful, first in the formulation of questions that seem urgent at any stage and then in the finding, testing and using the answers to them.
                                                                        Bernal, 1954/1969, 35

Science has been built up by some of the damnedest methods ....
                                                                        Homans, 1961, 9

The scientific method (1) postulates a model based on existing experimental observations or measurements; (2) checks the predictions of this model against further observations or measurements; (3) adjusts or replaces the model as required by the new observations or measurements. The third step leads back to the first step, and the process continues without end.
                                                                        Walker, 1963, 5

we test the concept, as we test the thing, by its implications. That is, when the concept has been built up from some experiences, we reason what behavior in other experiences should logically flow from it. If we find this behavior, we go on holding the concept as it is. If we do not ... we must go back and correct it. In this way logic and experiment are locked together in the scientific method, in a constant to and fro in which each follows the other.
                                                                        Bronowski, 1964, 40

Ask a scientist what he conceives the scientific method to be, and he will adopt an expression that is at once solemn and shifty-eyed: solemn, because he feels he ought to declare an opinion; shifty-eyed, because he is wondering how to conceal the fact that he has no opinion to declare .... The scientist is not in fact conscious of acting out a method. If a scientist is more or less successful in the enterprise he is engaged on, he attributes it to having enjoyed more or less of luck or learning or perceptiveness or flair, never to the use or misuse of a formal methodology.
                                                                        Medawar, 1969, 11, 8

The scientific method is a potentiation of common sense, exercised with a specially firm determination not to persist in error if any exertion of hand or mind can deliver us from it. Like other exploratory processes, it can be resolved into a dialogue between fact and fancy, the actual and the possible; between what could be true and what is in fact the case.
                                                                        Medawar, 1969, 59

the idea of a fixed method, or of a fixed theory of rationality, rests on too naïve a view of man and his social surroundings .... there is only one principle that can be defended under *all* circumstances and in *all* stages of human development. It is the principle: anything goes . . . . All methodologies have their limitations and the only "rule" that survives is "anything goes".

Feyerabend, 1975/1982, 27, 28, 296

anything goes . . . means that, in practice, everything stays.

Krige, 1980, 142

In many cases it is not easy to tell whether the latest accepted methods are not just the latest fad . . . . what may be considered "*the* scientific method" today may tomorrow be considered very inadequate and thus may be replaced by another accepted method.

Boland, 1982/1984, 190

See also 823–825

804 Science as a system of beliefs

Science is a body of knowledge which represents [an] . . . effort to form a concept of reality which will stand in some sort of consistent working relationship with the external world . . . . both for the sake of knowing what is going on, and to find better ways of controlling and exploiting it.

Beck, 1962, 89

The corpus of science at any moment consists of the theories that have not been disproved.

Robinson, 1962/1983, 26

the difference between science and myth [does not] lie in the fact that the one is essentially less speculative than the other. They are differently speculative . . . since myth terminates in unverifiable notions . . . while science terminates in concepts or laws . . . belonging to the same experience as those from which the theory started.

Santayana, 1962, 12

in a certain sense, science is myth-making just as religion is. You will say: But the scientific myths are so very different from the religious myths. Certainly they are different. But why are they different? Because if one adopts this critical attitude then one's myths do become different. They change; and they change in the direction of giving a better and better account of the world – of the various things which we can observe. And they also challenge us to observe things which we would never have observed without these theories or myths.

Popper, 1963/1974, 127

Science is an interconnected series of concepts and conceptual schemes that have developed as a result of experimentation and observation and are fruitful of further

experimentation and observation . . . . science is not a quest for certainty; it is rather a quest which is successful only to the degree that it is continuous.
Conant, 1964, 25

Science exists . . . as a body of universal propositions believed by scientists, in the light of which particular propositions about matters of fact are rendered intelligible and seen to be coherently related to one another.
Caws, 1967, 41

the manner in which we accept or reject scientific ideas is radically different from democratic decision procedures. We accept scientific laws and scientific facts . . . without ever having subjected them to a vote. Scientists do not subject them to a vote – at least this is what they say – and laymen certainly do not subject them to a vote.
Feyerabend, 1975/1982, 301

What myths and science have in common . . . is that both are imaginative fabrications – the difference being that myths fail the cruel examination which measures against real life that which purports to be an explanation of it.
Medawar, 1986, 90

805 The unity of science

science is a single whole . . . the divisions between its branches are largely conventional and devoid of ulterior significance.
Campbell, 1921/1952, 14

The belief that sciences must be kept in watertight compartments is widely held by philosophers, but no longer by scientists.
Henderson, 1935/1967, 73

Medicine . . . could never have advanced itself very effectively or very far. It had to wait until other branches of science were ready to solve its fundamental problems and instruct it how to act.
Topley, 1940, 21

we may look at all sciences as dove-tailed . . . as parts of one science . . . . because we cannot know anticipatively when it may be useful, and when not, to take into account all the statements together in analyzing certain correlations in a certain field.
Neurath, 1944/1962, 9

science is essentially a unity . . . . history of science teaches us again and again how the extension of our knowledge may lead to the recognition of relations between formerly unconnected groups of phenomena, the harmonious synthesis of which demands a renewed revision of the presuppositions for the unambiguous application of even our most elementary concepts.

Bohr, 1955/1962, 28

Just as theologians treat man as soul and biologists treat man as organism, so psychologists treat him as personality, economists as resources, and sociologists as members of groups. But these are only special ways of approaching the study of man – who cannot be reduced to any of them, but is understood only when all are considered.

Ross, 1962, 79

although the division of scientific knowledge into subjects is a convenience . . . the subjects themselves do not strictly speaking exist.

Pyke, 1963, 14

the domain of truth has no fixed boundaries within it. In the one world of ideas there are no barriers to trade or to travel. Each discipline may take from others techniques, concepts, laws, data, models, theories, or explanations – in short, whatever it finds useful in its own inquiries.

Kaplan, 1964, 4

consensus in any [distinct new field of study] draws its roots from several of the older major disciplines, and cannot be taught without reference to the general principles current in several of the sciences . . . . To expound merely those aspects that seem relevant to present knowledge and research problems in the narrow field is . . . to underestimate the scope of the consensus of the subject.

Ziman, 1968, 67

There are those who argue that explanation in the social sciences must be essentially different from what it is in the physical sciences. I cannot agree with them . . . . The process of explanation is the same for all the sciences, though the content of the propositions will naturally differ from science to science.

Homans, 1970, 314

810 Characteristics of Scientific Knowledge

811 The objectivity of science

Science as something existing and complete is the most objective thing known to man. But science in the making, science as an end to be pursued, is as subjective and psychologically conditioned as any other branch of human endeavor . . . .

Einstein, 1935, 139

A conscious, critical social consensus is of the essence of the idea of objectivity or truth. Moreover, a consensus regarding truth is itself by no means a mere (undisputed) fact. It rests upon value judgments as to both the competence and the moral reliability of observers and reporters. (It is no matter of a majority vote!) .... To the extent that any proposition or idea is regarded as false or as affected with uncertainty, its contents are regarded as subjective, as being in somebody's mind rather than in the objective world.

Knight, 1940, 7, 11

the intended objectivity of scientific knowledge ... requires that all statements of empirical science be capable of test by reference to evidence that is public, i.e. which can be secured by different observers and does not depend essentially on the observer.

Hempel, 1952/1960, 22

"Subjective" and "objective" properly apply not to persons and opinions but to sensations and judgments. Every person ... is necessarily subjective in all his sensations. But some of his subjective sensations are of objects, others of himself, or "subject" .... differentiating between subjective and objective ... comes down to asking oneself: "Is this an object in the outer world?" If after careful scrutiny you decide Yes, that judgment is an objective judgment.

Barzun & Graff, 1962, 145

Science is an attempt to formulate an understanding of nature which is not dependent on the individual, but can be held in common by all men. To that extent it can be objective.

Beck, 1962, 89

objectivity is closely bound up with the social aspect of scientific method, with the fact that science and scientific objectivity do not (and cannot) result from attempts of an individual scientist to be objective, but from the friendly-hostile cooperation of many scientists. Scientific objectivity can be described as the intersubjectivity of scientific method.

Popper, 1945/1966, II:217

The objectivity of science arises, not because the individual is impartial, but because many individuals are continually testing each others' theories.

Robinson, 1962/1983, 23

another name for the objective is the public.

Strawson, 1966, 151

What guarantees the objectivity of the world in which we live is that this world is common to us with other thinking beings. Through the communications that we have with other men we receive from them ready made harmonious reasonings. We know that these reasonings do not come from us and at the same time we recognize in them, because of their harmony, the work of reasonable beings like ourselves.

And as these reasonings appear to fit the world of our sensations, we think we may infer that these reasonable beings have seen the same thing as we; thus it is that we know we haven't been dreaming. It is this harmony, this quality if you will, that is the sole basis for the only reality we can ever know.

Pirsig, 1974, 268

812 Scientific truth

Reality is just itself, and it is nonsense to ask whether it be true or false. Truth is the conformation of appearance to reality .... Our purposes seek their main justification in sheer matter-of-fact .... The blunt truth that we require is the conformal correspondence of clear and distinct appearance to reality.

Whitehead, 1933/1948, 277, 288

One of the dominant characteristics of science is its rationality in the sense which is opposed to traditionalism. Scientific investigation ... is oriented to certain normative standards. One of the principal of these in the case of science is that of objective truth .... the mere fact that a proposition has been held to be true in the past is not an argument either for or against it before a scientific forum.

Parsons, 1939/1963, 36

an assertion, proposition, statement or belief, is true if, and only if, it corresponds to the facts.

Popper, 1945/1966, II:369

the necessary and sufficient conditions for knowing that something is the case are first that what one is said to know be true, secondly that one be sure of it, and thirdly that one should have the right to be sure.

Ayer, 1956, 35

The most straightforward way of defending the truth of a statement about the world of experience is to point to the state of affairs it describes; if the state of affairs corresponds to what has been asserted, everybody will agree that the statement is a true one. This kind of truth may be called empirical truth, since it depends on our experience of the world; and the view that truth consists in a correspondence with the facts is called the correspondence theory. One may also, however, point out in defense of a claim to truth that the statement in question follows from some other statement already admitted as true – .... This kind of truth may be called systematic truth, since it depends on the place of statements within a system; and the view that truth consists in fitting in with other truths is called the coherence theory.

Caws, 1965, 15

See also 207

813 Neutrality in science

It is not possible to have a scientific ethic, but it is no more possible to have an immoral science. And the reason is simple; it is, how shall I put it? for purely grammatical reasons. If the premises of a syllogism are both in the indicative, the conclusion will equally be in the indicative. In order for the conclusion to be put in the imperative, it would be necessary for at least one of the premises to be in the imperative. Now, the principles of science, the postulates of geometry, are and can only be in the indicative; experimental truths are also in this same mode, and at the foundations of science there is not, cannot be, anything else. Moreover, the most subtle dialectician can juggle with these principles as he wishes, combine them, pile them up one on the other; all that he can derive from them will be in the indicative. He will never obtain a proposition which says do this, or do not do that; that is to say a proposition which confirms or contradicts ethics.
Poincaré, 1913/1967, 154

Whenever we undertake any particular action, we have two decisions to make; we have to decide . . . what result we wish to obtain; and we have to decide . . . what action will produce the desired result . . . . Since science must always exclude from its province judgments concerning which differences are irreconcilable, it can only guide practical life in the choice of means, and not in the choice of ends.
Campbell, 1921/1952, 160

The findings of science are *per se* nonethical.
Lundberg, 1942, 53

Like physical science, behavior science with its various branches – psychology, sociology, economics, and so on – deals with facts and with facts only. Like physical science, it tries to organize its facts by means of laws and theories which are of the same logical nature as those of physical science. Unlike physical science, it concerns itself with people's motives, values, and ideals and with those facts –institutional, historical, and so on – of which such psychological facts are important ingredients. But this does not mean either that behavior science makes value judgments or that the truth of its findings is in principle dependent upon value judgments.
Bergmann, 1951, 207

The scientific sentiments are neutrality and impersonality, or in one word: objectivity.
Barzun, 1964, 85

It is commonly said that science is ethically neutral because its discoveries can be used for good or ill. This judgment confuses two meanings of the word science: the process of discovery, and what is discovered at the end of it. Of course what is discovered is neutral . . . . But the long and dedicated activity of the men who made these discoveries was not neutral: it was firmly directed and strictly judged.
Bronowski, 1967, 99

All scientific hypotheses have philosophical, social and even political undertones, which may prejudice scientists in evaluating the evidence for or against a particular hypothesis . . . . Ideological biases and special pleading of all kinds are a universal feature of scientific work for which the only remedy is the public criticism of other scientists relying on the shared professional standards of the subject.

Blaug, 1980/1984, 152

814 Coherence

A physical law is a symbolic relation whose application to concrete reality requires that a whole group of laws be known and accepted.

Duhem, 1914/1962, 168

Facts and laws, elements and system, mutually imply and support one another. If a law is comprehensive enough to cover all the relevant facts, and explains them consistently with one another, we regard it as true. This two-edged test of comprehensiveness and consistency is called the test of coherence. It is our ultimate guarantee of the certainty of either facts or theories . . . . Our knowledge becomes more certain and more difficult to overthrow as it becomes more organized into coherent systems.

Latta & Macbeath, 1956, 373

Whatever reality may be, we seem to be so made that we aspire towards an interpretation of the universe that shall hold together in a complete and reasonable scheme.

Singer, 1959/1962, 239

No scientific theory has ever provided a more striking advance in our understanding of nature than Newton's . . . . Yet the actual forecasts the theory led to were in many cases incorrect. How, then, did Newton succeed in making our celestial and tidal forecasting techniques intelligible? What does it mean to say that we now understand why our computational techniques work, in a way the Babylonians did not? We say this mainly because we now have a number of general notions and principles which make sense of the observed regularities, and in terms of which they all hang together.

Toulmin, 1963, 32

Favorable empirical evidence is inconclusive because one-sided. In effect empirical tests may show that a given hypothesis covers or fails to cover a set of data, but the most exacting empirical tests are silent concerning other desirable properties, especially the way the hypothesis fits or fails to fit the rest of the relevant knowledge.

Bunge, 1967, II:336

Scientific creativity is imagination in a straitjacket. The whole question of imagination in science is often misunderstood by people in other disciplines . . . . They overlook the fact that whatever we are allowed to imagine in science must be consistent with everything else we know.

Feynman, 1992, 324

Consensus

Science is the study of those judgments concerning which universal agreement can be obtained.

Campbell, 1921/1952, 27

One of the methods of achieving impersonality [in science] is by consensus. If all competent observers agree in their reports, it would seem to be highly probable that the personal elements have been eliminated from the report . . . . It does not preclude the possibility that all competent persons are reacting incorrectly because of some feature in contemporary culture, and there are examples . . . where consensus was ultimately shown to have been wrong.

Bridgman, 1961, 129

Science exists as a body of wide-ranging authoritative knowledge only as long as the consensus of scientists continues. It lives and grows only so long as this consensus can resolve the perpetual tension between discipline and originality.

Polanyi, 1946/1966, 16

[The concern of science] is not what men think about the world and how they consequently behave, but what they ought to think.

von Hayek, 1955/1964, 22

Suppose . . . that all scientists were charlatans . . . or . . . self-deluded . . . . Or suppose that standards of scientific reliability and significance were generally . . . debased . . . . or that the natural sciences were replaced altogether by the occult sciences based on cabalistic methods. There might still exist a consensus between the various specialists acknowledging each other as scientists . . . . But clearly, if I knew what lay behind such a consensus, I should regard it as a consensus of rogues and fools, deceiving both each other and the public – the result of an accident or a conspiracy, and in either case devoid of any true significance.

Polanyi, 1958, 218

Objectivity is the sacred cow of the scientists and with it goes a belief in the necessity for scientific literature to be impersonal. But this is a convenient myth. The literature itself belies it. For it is customary in scientific papers to interlard all assertions with references to authors . . . with titles of their works at the end. The need for ascription to persons is well recognized.

Meredith, 1966, 48

The objective of science ... is a consensus of rational opinion over the widest possible field .... a corpus of generally accepted principles develops in every technical field.

Ziman, 1968, 9, 24

The forms and constraints of scientific practice are held in place not just by the grounding in experiment but by the customs of a community more homogeneous and rule-bound than any community of artists. Scientists still speak unashamedly of reality, even in the quantum era, of objective truth, of a world independent of human construction, and they sometimes seem the last members of the intellectual universe to do so. Reality hobbles their imaginations. So does the ever more intricate assemblage of theorems, technologies, laboratory results, and mathematical formalisms that make up the body of known science.

Gleick, 1992, 325

816 The self corrective nature of science

Progress is directed at an ever closer adaptation of theory to reality.

Mach, 1908/1960, 272

To reach a theory, science observes certain facts and argues logically therefrom. The theory is submitted again to the facts. The cycle is: observation, theory, verification, more observation, and so on forever.

Homans & Curtis, 1934/1970, 21

The work of science is discipline in that its essential inventiveness is most of all dedicated to means for promptly revealing error .... Science is disciplined in its rejection of questions that cannot be answered and in its grinding pursuit of methods for answering all that can.

Oppenheimer, 1947/1957, 202

scientific procedures provide policies of such a nature that if a decision is selected wrongly the procedure will indicate the incorrectness of the wrong solution earlier or more economically than any other method.

Churchman, 1953/1961, 30

Science is a predictor mechanism in process of continual self correction.

Bronowski, 1960, 117

the self-correcting character of reason is only valuable tomorrow, never today – in the long run, never now.

Whyte, 1962/1967, 45

There is nothing distinctively scientific about the hypothetico-deductive process. It is not even distinctively intellectual. It is merely a scientific context for a much more general stratagem that underlies almost all regulative processes or processes

765

of continuous control, namely feedback, the control of performance by the consequences of the act performed .... scientific behavior can be classified as appropriately under cybernetics as under logic.

Medawar, 1969, 54

in empirical science we aspire only to approximate truths; we are under no illusion that we can find a single simple formula, or even a moderately complex one, that captures the whole truth and nothing else. We are committed to a strategy of successive approximations, and when we find discrepancies between theory and data, our first impulse to is patch rather than to rebuild from foundations.

Simon, 1976/1992, 366

representation of science as automatically and rapidly self-correcting is not justified by the historical facts .... [Alfred Wegener's] hypothesis of continental drift [put forward in 1912, was] rejected by the great majority of geologists for something like 50 years ....

Ziman, 1978, 93

817 Scientific explanation

Explanation consists merely in analyzing our complicated systems into simpler systems in such a way that we recognize in the complicated system the interplay of elements already so familiar to us that we accept them as not needing explanation.

Bridgman, 1936/1964, 63

there is nothing in the nature of an explanation in a scientific theory. Phenomena are not explained; they are merely interconnected, or described in terms of their mutual relations.

D'Abro, 1927/1950, 397

all the most important explanations are ... basically analogical – that is to say, their source is the imagination, not a book of rules, a fact which is in no way a criticism and in no way a reflection of inadequacy.

Theobald, 1968, 109

the covering law view of explanation. First, an explanation consists of a set of propositions, each proposition stating a relationship between properties of nature .... Second, the set of propositions forms a deductive system, such that the proposition to be explained, the *explicandum*, follows as a conclusion in logic from the others in the set .... Third, the propositions from which the *explicandum* follows ... [are] general propositions (sometimes called laws) and propositions introducing the given conditions within which the general propositions are to be applied .... Finally, the propositions must be contingent in the sense that data, evidence, fact are relevant to their acceptance as true or false. An explanation of a relationship is a theory of the relationship.

Homans, 1970, 313

Scientific explanation . . . connects and links phenomena with a wider range. But it is a mistake to think that this connection is like the subsumption of a generalization under a broader one . . . . The explanation which subsumes an event or class of events under a broader generalization can serve to set the stage for an explanation of the kind which shows the connection . . . . But it obviously is not equivalent to it.

Taylor, 1970, 51

820 Scientific Inquiry

821 Scientific inquiry

Man tries to make for himself in the way that suits him best a simplified and intelligible picture of the world and thus to overcome the world of experience, for which he tries to some extent to substitute this cosmos of his . . . . The supreme task of the physicist is to arrive at those elementary laws from which the cosmos can be built up by pure deduction. There is no logical path to these laws; only intuition, resting on sympathetic understanding of experience, can reach them.

Einstein, 1935, 124

In its proper and authentic sense, science is exclusively investigation: the posing of problems, working at them, and arriving at their solution. From the moment a solution is reached, all that may subsequently be done with the solution is not science – except to question it afresh, to convert it back to a problem by criticizing it, and hence to repeat the cycle of scientific investigation.

Ortega, 1946/1963, 59

The irreversible character of discovery suggests that no solution of a problem can be accredited as a discovery if it is achieved by a procedure following definite rules.

Polanyi, 1958, 123

Scientific inquiry in any field must begin not with some method taken over *a priori* from some other field, but with the character of the problems of its own field and the analysis of those problems. A subject becomes scientific not by beginning with facts, with hypothesis or some pet method brought in *a priori*, but by beginning with the peculiar character of its particular problems.

Northrop, 1959, 274

Assume that we have deliberately made it our task to live in this unknown world of ours; to adjust ourselves to it as well as we can; to take advantage of the opportunities we can find in it; and to explain it, if possible (we need not assume that it is), and as far as possible, with the help of laws and explanatory theories. If we have made this our task, then there is no more rational procedure than the method of trial and error – of conjecture and refutation; of boldly proposing theories; of trying our best to show that these are erroneous; and of accepting them tentatively if our critical efforts are unsuccessful.

Popper, 1963/1974, 51

The German [academic] system emphasized the social character of *Wissenschaft* (which included historical and classical studies as well as the natural sciences) by making sure that every new discovery or theory was thoroughly examined and exhaustively tested before admission into the consensus. The virtues that it most strongly encouraged were those of painstaking care, loving attention to detail, precision of language and of argument.

Ziman, 1968, 85

in the house of scholarship there are many mansions. In some scholars test truth by manipulating dials in soundproof laboratories. In others, they actually test it by working in the turmoil of cities, welfare centers, clinics, courts, and the like. In still others, lonely thinkers test their ideas by poring over dusty manuscripts in the hush of libraries.

Brubacher, 1982, 23

there are no methods that are intrinsically better than others; the utility of a method is always situation- and problem-specific. Researchers who specialize in one or two research strategies are especially liable to too early reification of design and likely to err in the direction of their own research skill.

Chadwick & others, 1984, 42

scientists do not make their discoveries by induction or by the practice of any other one method. "The" scientific method is therefore illusory . . . . A scientist commands a dozen different stratagems of inquiry in his approximation to the truth . . . .

Medawar, 1986, 16

See also 951

822 The subject of scientific inquiry: problems

Inquiry begins when some past belief is questioned, when a familiar solution fails, or when we do not understand some fact . . . . every scientific investigation arises from some problematic situation.

Brown & Ghiselli, 1955, 133

The scientist must . . . be concerned to understand the world and to extend the precision and scope with which it has been ordered. That commitment must, in turn, lead him to scrutinize, either for himself or through colleagues, some aspect of nature in great empirical detail. And, if that scrutiny displays pockets of apparent disorder, then these must challenge him to a new refinement of his observational techniques or to a further articulation of his theories.

Kuhn, 1962, 42

What is the general problem situation in which the scientist finds himself? He has before him a scientific problem; he wants to find a new theory capable of explaining certain experimental facts; facts which the earlier theories successfully explained; others which they could not explain; and some by which they were actually falsified. The new theory should also resolve, if possible, some theoretical difficulties (such as how to dispense with certain *ad hoc* hypotheses, or how to unify two theories.)
Popper, 1963/1974, 241

we accept the idea that the task of science is the search for truth, that is, for true theories .... Yet we also stress that truth is not the only aim of science. We want more than mere truth; what we look for is interesting truth – truth which is hard to come by.
Popper, 1963/1974, 229

The ability to see that there is a problem there at all is in part a function of the scientist's knowledge, for unless we have a certain minimum knowledge we shall not recognize a problem when we see one. But equally if not more important for science is the part played by the scientist's imagination in seeing a problem for what it is worth, in seeing its significance for science as a whole. Some problems are worth more attention than others, because in their solution the conceptual structure of science is put at risk ....
Theobald, 1968, 32

The purpose of scientific inquiry is not to compile an inventory of factual information, nor to build up a totalitarian world picture of natural laws in which every event that is not compulsory is forbidden. We should think of it rather as a logically articulated structure of justifiable beliefs about nature. It begins with a story about a possible world – a story which we invent and criticize and modify as we go along, so that it ends by being, as nearly as we can make it, a story about real life.
Medawar, 1969, 59

It is a vulgar fallacy to suppose that scientific inquiry cannot be fundamental if it threatens to become useful, or if it arises in response to problems posed by the everyday world. The real world, in fact, is perhaps the most fertile of all sources of good research questions calling for basic scientific inquiry.
Simon, 1976/1992, 344

823 Methods of inquiry

in order to estimate it [the empirical method] fairly, we must suppose it to be completely, not incompletely, empirical. We must exclude from it everything which partakes of the nature ... of a deductive operation .... The vulgar notion that the safe notions on political subjects are those of Baconian induction – that the true guide is not general reasoning, but specific experience – will one day be quoted as among the most unequivocal marks of a low state of the speculative faculties in any age in which it is accredited .... Whoever makes use of an argument of this kind, not intending to deceive, should be sent back to learn the elements of some one of the more easy physical sciences. Such reasoners ignore the fact of plurality of causes in the very case which affords the most signal example of it.

Mill, 1865/1925, 296, 298

What the precedents of physical science, rightly understood, teach the economist is to regard deduction as his principle resource; the facts furnished by observation and experience being employed, so far as circumstances permit, as the means of verifying the conclusions thus obtained, as well as, where discrepancies are found to occur between facts and his theoretical reasonings, for ascertaining the nature of the disturbing causes to which such discrepancies are due. It is in this way, and in this way only, that the appeal to experience is made in those physical sciences which have reached the deductive stage – that is to say, which in the logical character of their problems present any real analogy to economic science.

Cairnes, 1875, 84

The question of the right method of economic inquiry was not as such discussed by Adam Smith .... the support of his authority has been claimed on behalf of both the schools ... one of which describes political economy as positive, abstract and deductive, while the other describes it as ethical, realistic and inductive .... The reason for this apparent contradiction .... is to be found in Adam Smith's freedom from excess on the side either of *a priori* or of *a posteriori* reasoning. He rejected no method of inquiry that could in any way assist him in investigating the phenomena of wealth.

Keynes, 1890/1930, 9, 10

I did not begin my scientific work by conceiving a ready made system from which every truth could be deduced and into which the reality had at any price to be pressed in order to fit. This is no truly scientific way of going to work .... I have tried at every step to let my aims and methods be determined solely by the essential economic nature of the subject to be investigated .... there is much of necessity in economic life and also much of necessity in the ways of analyzing this life. The important thing is just to find out those necessities.

Cassel, 1925, 12

The scientist proceeds by the two inextricably interconnected activities of empirical investigation and logical analysis, the one ... being concerned with the behavior of facts, and the other with the language in which this is to be discussed.

Hutchison, 1938/1965, 9

There are many social scientists who ... [hold] that economic theory cannot be modeled after physics since it is a science of social, of human phenomena, has to take psychology into account, etc. Such statements are at least premature. It is without doubt reasonable to discover what has led to progress in other sciences, and to investigate whether the application of the same principles may not lead to progress in economics also. Should the need for application of different principles arise, it could be revealed only in the course of the actual development of economic theory

.... But since ... it is by no means certain that there ever will be need for entirely different scientific principles, it would be very unwise to consider anything else than the pursuit of our problems in the manner which has resulted in the establishment of physical science.

von Neumann & Morgenstern, 1944/
1980, 3

Unlike the position that exists in the physical sciences, in economics and other disciplines that deal with essentially complex phenomena, the aspects of the events to be accounted for about which we can get quantitative data are necessarily limited and may not include the important ones .... in the study of such complex phenomena as the market, which depend on the actions of many individuals, all the circumstances which will determine the outcome of a process ... will hardly ever be known or measurable. And while in the physical sciences the investigator will be able to measure what, on the basis of *prima facie* theory, he thinks important, in the social sciences often that is treated as important which happens to be accessible to measurement. This is sometimes carried to the point where it is demanded that our theories must be formulated in such terms that they refer only to measurable magnitudes .... such a demand quite arbitrarily limits the facts which are to be admitted as possible causes of the events which occur in the real world.

von Hayek, 1974/1992, 180

In both [natural science and social science], there is no "certain" substantive knowledge; only tentative hypotheses that can never be "proved", but can only fail to be rejected .... In both ... , the body of positive knowledge grows by the failure of a tentative hypothesis to predict the phenomena the hypothesis professes to explain; by the patching up of that hypothesis until someone suggests a new hypothesis that more elegantly or simply embodies the troublesome phenomena, and so on *ad infinitum*. In both, experiment is sometimes possible, sometimes not (witness meteorology). In both, no experiment is ever completely controlled, and experience often offers evidence that is the equivalent of controlled experiment. In both, there is no way to have a self-contained closed system or to avoid interaction between the observer and the observed.

Friedman, 1976/1992, 267

Comment on methods of inquiry

the questionnaire is not a scientific implement; it is only a cheap, easy and rapid method of obtaining information or non-information – one never knows which. No effort has been made to use it in experimental sciences; it is worth hardly more in education, law, and the other social sciences, for words never mean precisely the same thing to different persons, and there is no possible way of discounting poor analytic capacity or the practical joker. The post office is, therefore, no substitute for trouble and thought; ...

Flexner, 1930/1968, 125

Beware of the man of one method or one instrument, either experimental or theoretical. He tends to become method oriented rather than problem oriented; the method oriented man is shackled.

Platt, 1964, 351

The most serious yet most common symptom of this game [we psychologists play with our apparatus, our computers and models] is the glow that so many of us get from saying that a result is statistically significant. The song and dance of null hypothesis testing goes on and on – apparently endlessly .... most of us remain content to build our theoretical castles on the quicksand of merely rejecting the null hypothesis.

Dunnette, 1966, 345

the antihistorical method [in economics] leads to the development of slick technicians who know how to use computers, run massive correlations and regressions, but who do not really know which side of anyone's bread is buttered, who are incredibly ignorant of the details of economic institutions, who have ... very little sense of any reality which lies beyond their data. We seem to be producing a generation of economists now whose main preoccupation consists of analyzing data which they have not collected and who have no interest whatever in what might be called a data-reality function, that is, in what extent a set of data corresponds to any significant reality in the world. The antihistorical approach, furthermore, leads to a rejection of any information which cannot easily be fitted on to punched cards or their equivalents, and hence results in a distortion of the information input in the direction of that which can be easily quantified and away from those intangibles and imponderables which may nevertheless be an essential part of reality .... We seem to be engaged in finding out more and more numbers which mean less and less, and the parallel with the Ptolemaic epicycles is not difficult to draw.

Boulding, 1971, 232–33

Anyone who actually runs experiments or fits curves knows that they ... depend on analogies (the market is just like this demand curve), metaphysical propositions (the time series is a sample from all possible universes), and traditional authority (we have always assumed finite variance of the error term). And he knows that they too are merely supportive and probable. There is no certitude to be had, with any methodology.

McCloskey, 1985, 61

Every science is subject to the ever present danger of turning into mindless, automatic science – compute a t-statistic and a chi-square statistic, and then you're done .... What you have to fight for continually is that at least some people spend some of their time thinking.

Simon, 1990, 663

See also 803

824 Individual inquiry

I don't know what I may seem to the world, but, as to myself, I seem to have been only like a boy playing on the sea shore, and diverting myself in now and then finding a smoother pebble or a prettier shell than ordinary, whilst the great ocean of truth lay all undiscovered before me.

Newton, c1727/1964, 60

Science is fundamentally and in the end always an affair of the individual. No possible development can change that.

Harnack, 1905/1968, 119

If [said Sir Alexander Fleming] he had been, in 1928, one of a team studying sta-phylococci, he would, when a mould contaminated one of his culture plates, have "played for the side" . . . instead of following up the side track which led, by devious paths, to penicillin. The lone hand has, he said, advantages as well as the much advertised team work, but each in its own place.

Fleming, 1945, 796

the principal elements in biological research are intensely individual efforts in (a) recognizing the unexpected discovery and following it up, and (b) concentrated prolonged mental effort resulting in the birth of ideas.

Beveridge, 1950/1957, 162

research . . . is a highly personal activity. It cannot be done by groups and com-mittees.

Catlett, 1963/1973, 33

Time after time . . . it has been the work of a single scholar, doggedly holding out against the set prejudices of others, that has given us the great new idea which has advanced our knowledge . . . .

Pusey, 1964, 20

scholarship, for all its social aspects, is an intensely individual activity.

Ziman, 1968, 91

the bulk of scientific and technological innovations is this country [UK] have been attributable to independent researchers, the majority of them working without organized support.

Renshall, 1971, 648

825 Group inquiry

It would be as easy to write a poem or a symphony by a committee as to promote the study of human problems by physically arranged groups. Can really first-rate minds, working in various fields, be artificially and mechanically brought to cooperate in their study, or is anything new likely to be accomplished if ordinary persons mechanically pool their activities in a "clearing house"?

Flexner, 1930/1968, 118

committees are dangerous things that need the most careful watching. I believe that a research committee can do one useful thing, and one only. It can find the workers best fitted to attack a particular problem, bring them together, give them the facilities they need, and leave them to get on with the work.

Topley, 1940, 31

Canons of accounting could not properly be described as "principles" in the more fundamental sense of that word but might be said to be principles in the narrower sense ["methods expressed to be followed"]. It may well be that in agreeing on this word the [Special Committee on Cooperation with Stock Exchanges of the AIA, 1932] was resorting to the familiar expedient of securing unanimity by the adoption of a formula which was capable of sufficient variety in interpretation to cover the area of difference of opinion among its individual members. But the object to be sought was of major importance, and unanimity was highly desirable; its achievement was worth a minor ambiguity of this kind.

May, 1943, 42

The work of a team is important for the development of an idea already formulated, but I do not believe that a team has ever produced a new idea.

Chain, 1959, 167

Leadership in the accounting profession, as in other phases of human endeavor, is the result of the efforts of individuals. Collective action, which is necessary in the case of a group such as the APB, must necessarily result in compromise, but the wrong type of compromise can seriously impair the objectives being sought. As is well known, the larger the group, the greater the need to compromise . . . .

Catlett, 1969, 65

a committee is unable, by its nature, freely to engage and disengage from its immediate attention particular clusters of ideas in the search for worthwhile conclusions . . . . [This] requires the concentration of one mind. But a committee has not one mind. It has many minds. At any stage in the deliberations of a committee, each member will have different sets of ideas in the back of his mind, waiting to be drawn upon, and each will tend to value those ideas differently from other members. Debate follows. Sharp lines are drawn, lines which prevent the free association of ideas and lead to premature commitment. Committees are impatient with involved argument. They tend to brush aside evidence . . . . They tend to seek verbal consensus rather than understanding, and to value convergence of opinion rather than the convergence of evidence.

Chambers, 1972, 156

[In pursuit of justification, consultation with friends, elders, colleagues, peers] does not eliminate bias; nor does it question shared assumptions and fallacious reasoning.

This is especially often the case ... in professional and powerful circles, where those who might object are not given a voice, and where those considered "wise" can be those most likely to agree with the questionable scheme.
Bok, 1978/1989, 96

Committees are useful creations for obtaining decisions which satisfy the differing interests of varied groups or individuals. They produce compromises, which may be the only realistic approach in practical affairs. Such compromises may, however, be unsupportable ... [as] a best solution for any purpose.
Grinyer, 1978, 51

See also 176, 268

826 Specialization

I think ... that great harm is caused by too wide a separation of the disciplines which work toward the perfection of each individual art, and much more by the meticulous distribution of the practices of this art to different workers. The result is that men who have set the art before themselves as a goal take up one part only. They leave aside things which point toward, and are inseparable from, that end; and as a result they never accomplish anything outstanding. They never attain their proposed goal, but constantly fall short of the true essence of the art.
Vesalius, 1543/1960, 128

The man who knows only his own science, as a routine peculiar to that science, does not even know that. He has no fertility of thought, no power of quickly seizing the bearing of alien ideas. He will discover nothing, and be stupid in practical applications.
Whitehead, 1929/1957, 62

Few experts have extensive opportunity of checking up the work of every other expert; and a great deal of professional prestige is based on meretricious grounds. Reputations may be based on previous achievements which happen to have hit a shining mark by an unusually favorable turn of the wind.
Cohen, 1931/1964, 31

The specialist "knows" very well his own, tiny corner of the universe; he is radically ignorant of all the rest .... We shall have to say that he is a learned ignoramus, which is a very serious matter, as it implies that he is a person who is ignorant, not in the fashion of the ignorant man, but with all the petulance of one who is learned in his own special line.
Ortega, 1932, 123

If specialization in the sciences [or any other field] is carried to the point where exchange of ideas becomes impossible – where each man is so specialized that he can understand only himself – then specialization has become silly.

Boulding, 1941/1955, 21

In this day of specialization, all men must rely on authority in the fields of technical information. Since no one can be a specialist in everything, even specialists must defer to one another. The mechanic consults the doctor about his health, the doctor consults the mechanic on the maintenance of his car, both consult the accountant when they make out their income tax .... Source material should be given the weight due to an authority if and only if the source is (a) personally reliable, and (b) qualified as an expert.

Fearnside & Holther, 1959, 84

Every subject today confronts the tyranny of the professional .... The rampant specialism, an arbitrary and purely social evil, is not recognized for the crabbed guild spirit that it is, and few are bold enough to say that carving out a small domain and exhausting its soil affords as much chance for protected irresponsibility as for scientific thoroughness.

Barzun, 1964, 27

827 Cross-disciplinary fertilization

It is not too much to say that, in certain directions, the progress of the law is through accounting – just as a century ago, its progress lay through the custom of merchant bankers, whence comes our entire jurisprudence of banking, negotiable instruments, and what is known as the law merchant .... we need the accountant quite as much for our own enlightenment and evolution as for his own peculiar contribution. But we need the cross-fertilization as a schematic, systematic body of doctrine; and that is to be had only by guarding the manner of its growth.

Berle, 1938, 15

There is a great fertilizing and revivifying value in the contact of two scientists with each other; but this can only come when at least one of the human beings representing the science has penetrated far enough across the frontier to be able to absorb the ideas of his neighbor into an effective plan of thinking. The natural vehicle for this type of organization is a plan in which the orbit of each scientist is assigned rather by the scope of his interests than as a predetermined beat.

Wiener, 1950/1954, 126

"Mendelism was the creation of an investigator who hybridized plants and who also raised bees" (C. Zirkle, 1951). Thus ... a major discovery was the result of the combination in one and the same research work of two sources of knowledge, and of apparently independent methods and interests.

Taton, 1957, 129

major scientific progress often comes from scientists who have crossed conventional disciplinary boundaries, and have no more authority than a layman in a unfamiliar field.

Ziman, 1978, 8

828 Simultaneous discovery

before any great scientific principle receives distinct enunciation by individuals, it dwells more or less clearly in the general scientific mind. The intellectual plateau is already high, and our discoverers are then those who, like peaks above the plateau, rise a little above the general thought at the time.

Tyndall, 1870, 78

The same conception arises in the brains of two or even more men at practically the same time. In many cases the men are separated by thousands of miles, belong to entirely different nationalities, and are not even aware of each other's existence; and the differences in temperament, environment and outlook of two such men as Descartes and Fermat are striking. How can we account for this strange phenomenon? It seems as if the accumulated experience of the race at times reaches a stage where an outlet is imperative, and it is merely a matter of chance whether it fall to the lot of a single man, two men, or a whole throng of men to gather the rich overflow.

Danzig, 1930/1954, 197

It is characteristic of any branch of science entering on a phase of effective and rapid growth that it springs up almost simultaneously in many different places under the inspiration of many different men. If a pioneer has no immediate followers it is because his particular discovery has been made before its time.

Topley, 1940, 25

great discoveries often arise when the general level attained by the science of the times renders them almost inevitable.

Taton, 1957, 108

830 Conditions of Inquiry, Creation, Innovation

831 The role of observation and experience

Attention is an essential requirement of observation .... To get some agreement between observers they must be paying attention ....

George, 1936, 77, 91

scientific observation ... performs more accurately and deliberately the processes involved in ordinary observation. Thus science finds the world of knowledge not

quite uncharted but more or less mapped out. Its business is to discover deeper uniformities, more exact classifications, more comprehensive laws. This often involves correcting the analyses, classifications, and interpretations of ordinary thought.
Latta & Macbeath, 1956, 301

Every advance in methods of observation or in measuring procedures leads, within a relatively short time, to a revision of the corresponding theories, and sooner or later to the creation of new theories that are in closer correspondence with reality.
Taton, 1957, 100

Scientists are empiricists; they believe that knowledge of nature is validated only by observing nature.
Walker, 1963, vi

The empiricists were right to believe that facts and ideas are significantly connected, but they inverted the relationship. Ideas create information, not the other way round.
Roszak, 1986, 105

Personal knowledge, introspection

there seems to be little reason to suppose that a science of human conduct can be built up without reference to properly controlled introspection . . . . we cannot fully understand or conduct human life without some introspection.
Cohen, 1931/1964, 317

In economics, . . . the ultimate constituents of our fundamental generalizations are known to us by immediate acquaintance. In the natural sciences they are known only inferentially.
Robbins, 1935/1969, 105

No one questions the scientific validity of a physician's readings of his own temperature any more than we question his reading of other people's temperatures. His observations are acceptable in either case only if he communicates them to us in a language which permits us to check his findings . . . . When we develop techniques for observing and reporting "subjective" phenomena so that they can be communicated and corroborated, they are as proper objects of scientific study as any other data. "Objective" and "subjective", therefore, turn out to be not intrinsic qualities of different types of phenomena, but rather a designation of the degree to which we have developed checkable means of reporting our observations.
Lundberg, 1942, 19

The social sciences . . . are concerned with man's conscious or reflected action, actions where a person can be said to choose between various courses open to him, and here the situation is essentially different [from the natural sciences] . . . . The external stimulus which may be said to cause or occasion such actions can . . . be defined in purely physical terms. But if we tried to do so for the purposes of explaining human action, we would confine ourselves to less than we know about the situation . . . . We know . . . that in his conscious decisions man classifies external stimuli in a way which we know solely from our own subjective experience of this kind of classification . . . . It would be impossible to explain or understand human action without making use of this knowledge.

von Hayek, 1955/1964, 26

intuition . . . . is essentially a matter of grasping a situation by living through it, instead of merely noting various features of it and piecing them together. The central idea here is that if we can *be* something, we can understand it completely there and then without further fuss . . . . In simply being ourselves, we know ourselves, and from the inside. From this we can pass on to those cases where we find out about other people and the social situations in which they are placed by identifying ourselves with them . . . . we can put ourselves in their places and so appreciate what they feel . . . . it is natural to speak of this procedure as one of sympathetic understanding.

Gibson, 1960, 14

It seems to me undeniable that a valuable part of the data for behavioral science is provided by self-observation.

Kaplan, 1964, 141

All scientific investigation is initiated, in somewhat pragmatic fashion, in response to specific problems. In the social sciences the importance of starting with specific problems, such as the behavior of business firms, is perhaps even more important than in the physical sciences. One reason for this lies in the nature of many behavioral problems, which often are not objective in the sense of being based upon physical facts as in the natural sciences, but instead are derived from introspective observations. In the natural sciences, too, introspection may be an important source of discovery, However, in both, the verification of theories may be accomplished by an appeal to empirical data obtained through the senses.

McGuire, 1964, 11

introspection is a more important source of evidence for social than for natural science.

Friedman, 1976/1992, 267

832 The role of doubt

The first [precept I adopted] was never to accept anything for true which I did not clearly know to be such; that is to say, carefully to avoid precipitancy and prejudice, and to comprise nothing in my judgment than what was presented to my mind so clearly and distinctly as to exclude all ground of doubt.

Descartes, 1637/1937, 15

The first condition that has to be fulfilled by a scientist who is devoted to the investigation of natural phenomena is to preserve a complete freedom of mind based on philosophical doubt.

Bernal, 1865/1962, 180

the progress of science always depends upon our questioning the plausible, the respectably accepted, and the seemingly self-evident.

Cohen, 1931/1964, 348

Scientific method pursues the road of systematic doubt. It does not doubt all things, for this is clearly impossible. But it does question whatever lacks adequate evidence in its support.

Cohen & Nagel, 1934/1957, 394

A scientist doubts systematically everything that goes into his proof. He doubts his facts; he doubts his hypotheses; and he doubts whether they fit together as he thinks they do.

Larrabee, 1945, 317–8

It seems extraordinary that so many people who like to think of themselves as plain, down to earth, practical men should dismiss the critical examination of models as an unpractical activity. If you don't drag into the light the presuppositions of your thinking you remain simply the prisoner of whatever the reigning orthodoxy in the matter at issue happens to be. Thus the model of your age, or the model of your day, becomes your cage without you even realizing it.

Magee, 1978/1981

Presumably a good scientist accepts that his aim is to test and attack hypotheses. He functions best as a Doubting Thomas, not a believer. His knowledge of history tells him that scientific laws can never be viewed as final.

Baxter, 1979, 34

833 The role of imagination

The laws of science are ... products of the creative imagination.

Pearson, 1911, 35

though the discovery of laws depends ultimately not on fixed rules but on the imagination of highly gifted individuals, this imaginative and personal element is much more prominent in the development of theories; ....

Campbell, 1921/1952, 97

Imagination is not to be divorced from the facts; it is a way of illuminating the facts. It works by eliciting the general principles which apply to the facts, as they exist, and then by an intellectual survey of alternative possibilities which are consistent with those principles. It enables men to construct an intellectual vision of a new world, and it preserves the zest of life by the suggestion of satisfying purposes .... Fools act on imagination without knowledge; pedants act on knowledge without imagination.

Whitehead, 1929/1957, 97–98

the most simple and apparently innocent statements often do contain a wealth of significance that may have bearing on everything that we do. It requires practice, imagination, and insight to perceive that the most obvious observations ... may contain revolutionary implications.

Bridgman, 1936/1964, 6

A man who sticks to the *terra firma* of facts, that is to coincidence observations, just sticks. If he will not take the perilous plunge into the world of the imagination he will not even find many new facts.

George, 1936, 221

Major contributions to the sciences have been made only by men of imagination, and Bacon was quite wrong in supposing that the sciences could ever be developed without such men.

Presley, 1954, 91

When a situation is blocked, straight thinking must be superseded by "thinking aside" – the search for a new, auxiliary matrix which will unblock it, without having ever before been called to perform such a task. The essence of discovery is to hit upon such a matrix – as Gutenberg hit on the wine press and Kepler on the sun force.

Koestler, 1966, 163

the history of science ... has been the history of imagination controlled by evidence; and the arrangement has the great virtue that there is an acceptable procedure for the rejection of an earlier imaginative account, which leaves the contemporary imagination ... free to replace the old account with a new one.

Caws, 1967, 37

an imaginative or inspirational process enters into all scientific reasoning; it is not confined to "great" discoveries, as the more simple-minded inductivists have supposed .... Inventors speak unaffectedly about brain waves and inspirations: and what, after all, is a mechanical invention if not a solid hypothesis, the literal embodiment of a belief or opinion of which mechanical working is the test?

Medawar, 1969, 55

Science needs people who are adaptable and inventive, not rigid imitators of "established" behavioral patterns.

Feyerabend, 1975/1982, 215

The relationship of ideas to information is what we call a generalization. Generalizing might be seen as the basic action of intelligence; it takes two forms. First, when confronted with a vast shapeless welter of facts ... the mind seeks for a sensible, connecting pattern. Second, when confronted with very few facts, the mind seeks to create a pattern by enlarging upon the little it has and pointing it in the direction of a conclusion. The result in either case is some general statement which is not in the particulars, but has been imposed upon them by the imagination.

Roszak, 1986, 88

834 The role of the unusual and the anomalous

The first impulse towards a revision and reconstruction of a physical theory is nearly always given by the discovery of one or more facts which cannot be fitted into the existing theory .... Nothing is more interesting to the true theorist than a fact which directly contradicts a theory generally accepted up to that time, for this is his particular work.

Planck, 1925, 72

the irregularities in the development of any human endeavor bring out more clearly the underlying factors than do those features that it has in common with similar endeavors.

Danzig, 1930/1954, 181

Accidents to the body politic, like accidents to the physical body, often provide observations of a kind which would not be possible under normal conditions. In peaceful times we may speculate concerning the consequences of violent change. But we are naturally precluded from verifying our conclusions: we cannot upset the smooth current of things for the advancement of abstract knowledge. But when disturbance takes place, it is sometimes possible to snatch good from evil and to obtain insight into the working of processes which are normally concealed. No doubt there are dangers here .... But the dangers are clear; it is not difficult to keep them in mind and guard against them.

Robbins, 1937/1948, 5

In scientific inquiry there is scrupulous attention to exceptions and whatever appear to be exceptions. The technique of inquiry is concerned as much with effective eliminations as with noting agreements.

Dewey, 1938/1966, 181

Never neglect any appearance or any happening which seems to be out of the ordinary: more often than not it is a false alarm; but it *may* be an important truth.

Fleming, 1959, 109

As accountants, we are faced both with the great desirability of conforming to existing conventions and principles and with wondering whether the principles stated before are not subject to exceptions. But as soon as a group of such exceptions is established, there is reason also to wonder whether there is not some broader or more basic principle to be stated embracing both the existing principle and the established exceptions.

Werntz, 1955, 48

it is the exceptional phenomenon which is likely to lead to the explanation of the usual.

Beveridge, 1950/1957, 138

Discovery commences with the awareness of anomaly, i.e. with the recognition that nature has somehow violated the paradigm-induced expectations that govern normal science. It then continues with a more or less extended exploration of the area of anomaly. And it closes only when the paradigm theory has been adjusted so that the anomalous has become the expected.

Kuhn, 1962, 52

835 The role of analogy

there is no analogy, however faint, which may not be of the utmost value in suggesting experiments or observations that may lead to more positive conclusions.

Mill, 1865/1925, 368

In the course of explaining any rather abstract matter, it is an advantage to use a concrete illustration in order to make one's meaning clear . . . . When, on the other hand, a concrete illustration is used to create a conviction of the truth of whatever it illustrates, or when it implies that truth in order to deduce some new conclusions, it is no longer a mere illustration; it is then an argument from analogy . . . . analogy proves itself a reasonably good guide to conduct; it becomes dangerous, however, when the conclusions to which it points are regarded as certain and not merely as probable.

Thouless, 1930/1977, 169

In the formation of hypotheses . . . if previously established knowledge can be used in new settings, analogies must be noted and exploited . . . . We generally begin with an unanalyzed feeling of vague resemblance, which is discovered to involve an explicit analogy in structure or function only by a careful inquiry.

Cohen & Nagel, 1934/1957, 222

In the science of electricity the notion of an electric fluid was really never more than a metaphor. But it suggested many fruitful analogies, such as differences of level, direction of flow, etc. Faraday's suggestion of lines or tubes of force may have been taken by many in a more or less literal sense, but the present electron theory shows that it was a metaphor, justified in its day by the fruitful analogies to which it led.

Cohen, 1944/1961, 97

Analogy is a sort of similarity. Similar objects agree with one another in some respect, analogous objects agree in certain relations of their respective parts . . . . Inference by analogy appears to be the most common kind of conclusion, and it is possibly the most essential kind. It yields more or less plausible conjectures which may or may not be confirmed by experience and stricter reasoning.
Polya, 1945/1957, 37, 43

Although no argument by analogy is ever valid, in the sense of having its conclusion follow from its premises with logical necessity, some are more cogent than others . . . . The first criterion relevant to the appraisal of an analogical argument is the number of entities between which the analogies are said to hold . . . . A second . . . is the number of respects in which the things involved are said to be analogous . . . . A third . . . is the strength of their conclusions relative to their premises . . . . A fourth . . . has to do with the number of disanalogies or points of difference between the instances mentioned in the premises and the instance with which the conclusion is concerned . . . . Our fifth criterion . . . is that the more dissimilar the instances mentioned in the premises, the stronger is the argument . . . . [The last criterion is relevance.] In an argument by analogy, the relevant analogies are those which deal with causally related properties or circumstances.
Copi, 1953/1964, 343–348

Analogy is the assertion that things which resemble each other in some respects will resemble each other in some further respect . . . . Though generalizing by analogy is dangerous when only one or two similarities are known, it is good reasoning if the number of essential qualities known to be shared is very large.
Fearnside & Holther, 1959, 22

Scientists often find analogy suggestive and often they seek in it hints for research, but they do not regard it as a way of reasoning and still less of proof.
Singer, 1959/1962, 136

Lord Kelvin hit on the idea of the mirror galvanometer when he noticed a reflection of light on his monocle . . . . Newton saw that the moon behaved like an apple. Pasteur saw the analogy between a spoilt culture and a cow pox vaccine; Fleming saw the analogy between the action of a mould and the action of a drip from his nose. Freud, on his own account, conceived the idea of the sublimation of instincts by looking at a funny cartoon in . . . the one-time German equivalent of *Punch*.
Koestler, 1966, 200

Without analogy there might be no knowledge: the perception of analogies is a first step towards classification and generalization . . . . A first role of analogy is to suggest equivalence, without however establishing it.
Bunge, 1973, 125

836 The role of criticism, conflict and error

truth emerges more readily from error than from confusion ...
Bacon, 1620/1891, 477

The world little knows how many of the thoughts and theories which have passed
through the mind of a scientific investigator have been crushed in silence and secrecy
by his own severe criticism and adverse examination; that in the most successful
instances not a tenth of the suggestions, the hopes, the wishes, the preliminary
conclusions have been realized.
Faraday, (1791–1867)/1911, 32

[The scientific] imagination has to be a disciplined one. It has in the first place to
appreciate the whole range of facts which require to be resumed in a single statement;
and then when the law is reached ... it must be tested and criticized by its discoverer in every conceivable way, till he is certain that the imagination has not
played him false, and that his law is in real agreement with the whole group of
phenomena which it resumes.
Pearson, 1911, 31

the resolution of [scientific] revolutions is the selection by conflict within the scientific community of the fittest way to practice future science.
Kuhn, 1962, 171

My thesis is that what we call science is differentiated from the older myths not
by being something different from a myth, but by being accompanied by a second
order tradition – that of critically discussing the myth. Before, there was only the
first order tradition. A definite story was handed on .... This second order tradition
was the critical or argumentative attitude.
Popper, 1963/1974, 127

The *locus in quo* of human creativity is always on the line of intersection between
the two planes; and in the highest form of creativity between the tragic or absolute
and the trivial planes.... This interlacing of the two planes [bisociation] is found
in all great works of art, and at the origin of all great discoveries of science.
Koestler, 1966, 367

What shows a theory to be inadequate or mistaken is not, as a rule, the discovery
of a mistake in the formulation that led us to propound it; more often it is the
contradictory evidence of a new observation which we were led to make *because*
we held that theory .... "Trial and error" will not do as a description of the process
by which we devise and test hypotheses, for it carries the sense of random exploration, or of exploration according to a scheme ... which is not influenced by the
testimony of prior mistakes.
Medawar, 1969, 33, 55

Scientific criticism is a sympathetic search for insights and errors. If we seek for insights in the works of others, there is some (perhaps small) chance that we may find them and benefit from them. If we search for errors, we may help others avoid pitfalls in their research. On the contrary, if we apply a hyperbolic criticism that no scientific research could withstand, we are more apt to inhibit research than contribute to progress.

Sterling, 1979, 60

To err is not only human but also scientific.

Stigler, 1982/1992, 64

837 The role of chance

all the most noble discoveries have (if you observe) come to light, not by any gradual improvement and extension of the arts, but merely by chance . . . .

Bacon, 1620/1891, 498

more is owing to what we call chance, that is, philosophically speaking, to the observation of events arising from unknown causes, than to any proper design or preconceived theory in this business [i.e. discovery].

Priestley, c1775/1967, 210

Accidental discoveries of which popular histories of science make mention never happen except to those who have previously devoted a great deal of thought to the matter.

Cohen, 1931/1964, 17

If he [Pasteur] had not been appointed to a professorship at Lille, if the distillers and brewers of the neighborhood had not gone to him for advice, he might perhaps not have come to take an interest in fermentations, though, his genius being what it was, he would have discovered something else. Fleming [discoverer of penicillin] had for a long time been hunting for a substance which should be able to kill the pathogenic microbes without damage to the patient's cells. Pure chance depositied the substance on his bench.

Maurois, 1959, 123

luck makes sense only against a background of prior expectations.

Medawar, 1969, 33

in 1820, H C Oersted made one of the basic discoveries in physical science while giving a lecture! While he was demonstrating the electric current from one of Volta's batteries, he noticed that a compass needle that happened to be on the lecturer's desk, deflected. He had found, entirely by accident, that an electric current produces a magnetic field.

Brown, 1987, 29

Nearly all the great discoveries in chemotherapy have been made as a result of a false hypothesis or due to a so-called chance observation.

Kohn, 1989, 3

840 Facts, Generalizations, Laws

841 Facts and factual statements

For us, a fact is a receptor experience, in terms of a conceptual scheme. A receptor experience is anything observed by the five senses, by the eyes, ears, nose, and so on. As for a conceptual scheme, it is not observed by the senses, but is a frame, often a crude one, somehow constructed by the mind, by which the mind classifies sense experiences .... By logical reasoning from [facts] ... we set up theories. These theories are again submitted to the test of fact and are rejected if they fail to pass it. Theories such as these we call experimental theories.

Homans & Curtis, 1934/1970, 51–53

a scientific fact ... an item that can be tested publicly by means of approximate coincidence observations carried out by normal observers according to conventions which have proved serviceable in similar circumstances. It consists, when analyzed, of something sensed, concerning which there is a substantial agreement among independent inquirers who have not been coerced by violence or threats or indeed anything except the hard data of the experience itself.

Larrabee, 1945, 136

facts seldom occur pure, free from interpretation or ideas. We all make the familiar distinction between gathering the facts and expressing ideas, but in reality most of the facts we gather come dripping with ideas.

Barzun & Graff, 1962, 115

But what is a fact? .... to carve a something out of its environment and call it a fact is to make a judgment and to be doing it for a purpose which expresses value. It is a judgment again, charged with value, to note a relation that has not previously been shown or named. And since like other disciplines science aims at relevance, coherence, and simplicity of form, the facts and theories of science result from judgments of value. Fact and truth embody emotion as well as thought.

Barzun, 1964, 66

The facts of what the layman sees are notoriously different from the facts of what the physicist sees .... What appears problematic to the scientist will not so appear to the layman.

Theobald, 1968, 31

Facts that speak for themselves talk in a very naïve language.

Frisch, 1970/1992, 16

Observation statements . . . are always made in the language of some theory and will be as precise as the theoretical or conceptual framework that they utilize is precise.

Chalmers, 1976/1987, 29

We can never free observation from the theoretical element of interpretation. Our observational knowledge is theoretical and fallible.

Kohn, 1989, 167

See also 848

842 Generalizations

The union of facts into generalizations is the organization of knowledge . . . .

Spencer, 1861/1976, 49

There is no science but the science of the general . . . . by generalization, every fact observed enables us to predict a large number of others; only we ought not to forget that the first alone is certain, and that all the others are merely probable.

Poincaré, 1903/1952, 4, 143

among all scientific inferences there is only one of an overreaching type: that is the inductive inference. All other inferences are empty, tautological; they do not add anything new to the experiences from which they start. The inductive inference does; that is why it is the elementary form of the method of scientific discovery.

Reichenbach, 1938/1961, 365

Experience teaches us that the phenomena of a given class – economic, biological, mechanical, electrical and what not – are indeed individual occurrences each of which, as it occurs, reveals peculiarities of its own. But experience also teaches us that these individual occurrences have certain properties or aspects in common and that a tremendous economy of mental effort may be realized if we deal with these properties or aspects, and with the problems they raise, once and for all.

Schumpeter, 1954/1967, 15–16

The universal propositions which constitute the main body of science . . . are of two principal kinds, generalizations and hypotheses, the difference between them being that hypotheses contain terms not found in the vocabulary of description, while generalizations (which are generalizations of particular factual descriptions) contain only descriptive or observational terms, apart of course from grammatical or logical connectives.

Caws, 1967, 43

Induction

An inductive argument affirms, not that a certain matter of fact is so, but that relative to certain evidence there is a probability in its favor. The validity of induction, relative to the original evidence, is not upset therefore if, as a fact, the truth turns out to be otherwise. The clear apprehension of this truth profoundly modifies our attitude towards the solution of the inductive problem. The validity of the inductive method does not depend on the success of its predictions. Its repeated failure in the past may, of course, supply us with new evidence, the inclusion of which will modify the force of subsequent inductions. But the force of the old induction relative to the old evidence is untouched.

Keynes, 1921/1948, 220

There is a tradition of opposition between adherents of induction and of deduction. In my view, it would be just as sensible for the two ends of a worm to quarrel. Both observation and deduction are necessary for any knowledge worth having.

Whitehead, 1929/1957, 119

The chief characteristic of inference in the exact sciences ... is a kind of logical compulsion whereby a person who makes certain assumptions is forced, simply by doing so, to make others .... In what is called inductive thinking there is no such compulsion. The essence of the process, here, is that having put certain observations together, and having found that they make a pattern, we extrapolate this pattern indefinitely. This is technically described as proceeding from the known to the unknown, or from the particular to the universal. It is essential to inductive thinking ... that the step so described is never taken under any kind of logical compulsion.

Collingwood, 1946, 254

Based as it is on analogy and intuition and on subtle distinctions rather than geometric precision, induction attempts to divine unknown relations, and thus to establish new principles from which deductions may then be made. Clearly inductive reasoning is much bolder and much more adventurous than deductive reasoning. Deduction is certainty, at least in appearance; induction is risk. But risk is the price paid for all great achievements, and that is why induction, because it disdains established truths to venture forth into unexplored fields, may be said to be the true source of all great scientific discoveries.

de Broglie, 1962, 203

Induction, i.e. inference based on many observations, is a myth. It is neither a psychological fact, nor a fact of ordinary life, nor one of scientific procedure. The actual procedure of science is to operate with conjectures; to jump to conclusions – often after one single observation .... Repeated observations and experiments function in science as tests of our conjectures or hypotheses, i.e. as attempted refutations.

Popper, 1963/1974, 53

the principle of induction . . . is simply the most general and inclusive theory we possess . . . . But the principle of induction needs logical foundations as little as the conservation principle [of physics] needed them; and if they are not needed it hardly seems worth a great deal of effort to supply them.

Caws, 1965, 262

generations of men were in possession of the empirical facts concerning gravity long before the laws of gravity were formulated. The formulation of those laws only occurred by induction; that is, the brilliantly imaginative leap from the particular to the general.

Peasnell, 1974, 73

the philosophy of science is and has been exclusively concerned with . . . how initial conjectures are converted into scientific theories by stringing them together into a more or less tightly knit deductive structure and how these theories are then tested against observations. In short, let us not say that science is based on induction; it is based on adduction followed by deduction.

Blaug, 1980/1984, 17

843 The concrete (particular) and the abstract (general)

A science of the accidental is not even possible . . . . The accidental . . . is what occurs, but not always and of necessity, nor for the most part, and for that reason there can be no knowledge of it.

Aristotle, 4c BC/1956, 161

It is evident, that in forming most of our general ideas, if not all of them, we abstract from every particular degree of quantity and quality, and that an object ceases not to be of any particular species on account of every small alteration in its extension, duration and other properties.

Hume, 1739/1960, 17

Knowledge, in proportion as it tends more and more to be particular, ceases to be knowledge.

Newman, 1852/1905, 112

every fact may be considered from the point of view of many sciences, each of which deals with it from one side. That is just what is meant by saying that the fact is concrete, and the science abstract. The concrete means simply the embodiment of a number of general qualities or relations; the abstract means simply the selection of one of those aspects and the exclusion of the others.

Welton, 1915, 65

to be an abstraction does not mean that an entity is nothing. It merely means that its existence is only one factor of a more concrete element of nature,

Whitehead, 1920/1930, 171

You cannot think without abstractions; accordingly it is of the utmost importance to be vigilant in critically revising your modes of abstraction .... A civilization which cannot burst through its current abstractions is doomed to sterility after a very limited period of progress.

Whitehead, 1926/1938, 75

The concrete has ever preceded the abstract .... And the concrete has ever been the greatest stumbling block to the development of a science. The peculiar fascination which numbers as individuals have exerted on the mind of man from time immemorial was the main obstacle in the way of developing a collective theory of numbers, i.e. an arithmetic; just as the concrete interest in individual stars long delayed the creating of a scientific astronomy.

Danzig, 1930/1954, 57

In the rational use of ideas ... we do not deal with abstractions as a queer kind of objects in a world of their own, but with objects and events in the world around us abstractly (that is, incompletely) characterized and with what can be found out about them in terms of their known characters and behavior.

Murphy, 1943, 48

the abstract objects of thought, such as numbers, law, or perfectly straight lines, are real parts of nature (even though they exist not as particular things but as the relations or transformations of such particulars), so that none of the so-called fictions of science in any way falsifies its results .... Abstractions are real parts, phases or elements of things, or their relations.

Cohen, 1944/1961, 107

Abstraction is the price paid for generalization.

Homans, 1951/1959, 14

A hypothesis is important if it explains much by little, that is, if it abstracts the common and crucial elements from the mass of complex and detailed circumstances surrounding the phenomena to be explained and permits valid predictions on the basis of them alone. To be important, therefore, a hypothesis must be descriptively false in its assumptions; it takes account of, and accounts for, none of the attendant circumstances, since its very success shows them to be irrelevant for the phenomena to be explained.

Friedman, 1953/1966, 14

Observation in itself is meaningless unless it is combined with abstraction. Many factual details are, and should be, ignored because they are irrelevant to the observer's purpose.

McGuire, 1964, 4

See also 015, 229

844 Scientific laws

What is our idea of necessity, when we say that two objects are necessarily connected together? .... necessity is something that exists in the mind, not in objects .... Either we have no idea of necessity, or necessity is nothing but that determination of the thought to pass from causes to effects, and from effects to causes, according to their experienced union.

Hume, 1739/1960, 155, 165

Our natural laws ... consist of a series of readily utilizable propositions, indeed of propositions adopted because of their ease of practical utilization. And science itself may be considered an accumulation of instruments for the sounding out of our picture of some only practically manifest domain of facts, or for the precise delimitation of our expectation of the future.

Mach, 1908/1960, 272

To speak of a uniformity that is not uniform is to say a thing which has no meaning [#101] .... If one grants to a person who is stating a law that his law may have its exceptions, he can always meet every fact that is adduced against him with the excuse that it is an "exception", and he will never be caught in the wrong. And that is exactly what literary economists, moralists and metaphysicists do: They proclaim laws and then do what they please with them, taking advantage of indefiniteness in terms, exceptions, and other subterfuges of the kind, to bend their laws to their every wish and whim. [#1689n]

Pareto, 1916/1963, 53, 1125

Laws are propositions asserting relations which can be established by experiments or observations. The terms between which the relations are asserted consist largely or entirely of judgments of the material world, immediate or derivative, simple or complex; the relations asserted, if not always the same, have always a common feature which may be described as uniformity of association.

Campbell, 1919/1957, 38

The practical value of science arises ... from the formulation of laws. Laws predict the behavior of that external world with which our practical and everyday life is an unceasing struggle.

Campbell, 1921/1952, 158

The notion of law, that is to say, of some measure of regularity or of persistence or of recurrence, is an essential element in the urge towards technology, methodology, scholarship, and speculation. Apart from a certain smoothness in the nature of things, there can be no knowledge, no useful method, no intelligent purpose. Lacking an element of law, there remains a mere welter of details with no foothold for comparison with any other such welter, in the past, in the future, or circumambient in the present.

Whitehead, 1933/1948, 130

scientific laws are descriptions in terms of a conceptual scheme.

Homans & Curtis, 1934/1970, 25

Scientific law differs from both hypothesis and theory in that it has received sufficient verification and confirmation in fact to be accepted with little question.

Brown & Ghiselli, 1955, 161

a scientific law is a rule by which we guide our conduct and try to ensure that it shall lead to a known future.

Bronowski, 1960, 110

The laws formulated by science – the transitive figments describing the relation between fact and fact – . . . . are more real, if you will, than the facts themselves, because they are more permanent, trustworthy, and pervasive; but at the same time they are, if you will, not real at all, because they are incompatible with immediacy and alien to brute existence.

Santayana, 1962, 12

Generalizations which have been shown to the satisfaction of scientists to be true – that is, which have been accepted as such – are called laws, and in a similar way hypotheses which satisfy this condition are sometimes called principles.

Caws, 1967, 44

See also 261

845 Hypotheses

Hypothesis: a supposition or conjecture put forth to account for known facts; esp. in the sciences, a provisional supposition which accounts for known facts, and serves as a starting point for further investigation by which it may be proved or disproved.

SOED, 1936

great contributions to science are not made by those who go to nature innocent of all preconceptions but rather by those who have acquired the most knowledge and fruitful ideas on the subject of their inquiry.

Cohen, 1931/1964, 82

We cannot take a single step forward in any inquiry unless we begin with a suggested explanation or solution of the difficulty which originated it. Such tentative explanations are suggested to us by something in the subject matter and by our previous knowledge. When they are formulated as propositions they are called hypotheses.

Cohen & Nagel, 1934/1957, 200

Hypothesis may mean simply a guess, a hunch, an assumption which points to a possibly fruitful line of work. Hypothesis may mean a statement of uniformity . . . . Hypothesis, also, may mean a conceptual scheme.

Homans & Curtis, 1934/1970, 23

Science is an economy of thought only if its hypotheses sum up in a simple form a large number of facts.

Homans, 1951/1959, 16

A hypothesis is a proposition about factual and conceptual elements and their relationships that projects beyond known facts and experiences for the purpose of furthering understanding. It is a conjecture or best guess which involves a condition that has not yet been demonstrated in fact but that merits exploration.

Brown & Ghiselli, 1955, 153

No fixed lines can be drawn between theories, hypotheses and mere hunches, the differences being at best those of degree.

Machlup, 1955, 3

A fundamental hypothesis serves to bring together under a common principle of explanation vast numbers of very diverse observations, masses of data of apparently very different sort, phenomena that would otherwise seem to have nothing in common . . . . If these hypotheses are successful in the [task of tackling diverse problems] . . . and give more satisfactory results than other modes of treatment could, then we accept them and stick by them as long as there is nothing better –which may be forever.

Machlup, 1955, 9

A hypothesis, being a discursive device, gains its utmost possible validity when its discursive value is established. It is not; it merely applies; and every situation in which it is found to apply is a proof of its truth.

Santayana, 1962, 13

every recognition of a truth is preceded by an imaginative preconception of what the truth might be – by hypotheses . . . . Most of the day to day business of science consists in making observations or experiments designed to find out whether this imagined world of our hypotheses corresponds to the real one. An act of imagination, a speculative adventure, thus underlies every improvement of natural knowledge.

Medawar, 1986, 51

846 Models

We make for ourselves internal pictures or symbols of external objects, and we make them of such a kind that the necessary consequences in thought of the pictures are always the pictures of the necessary consequences in nature of the objects pictured

.... When on the basis of our accumulated previous experiences we have succeeded in constructing pictures with the desired properties, we can quickly derive by means of them, as by means of models, the consequences which in the external world would only occur in the course of a long period of time or as a result of our own intervention.

Hertz, 1899/1953, 91

To think in terms of the model is ... frequently the most convenient way of thinking about the structure of the theory, for it avoids the self-consciousness required in order to have before the mind at the same time both the set of propositions arranged in a deductive system which is the theory, and the set of sentences or formulae arranged in order which is the calculus representing the theory .... There are, however, serious dangers in the use of models .... the objects with which the model is concerned ... [may] be supposed actually to be the same as the theoretical concepts of the theory .... Thinking of scientific theories by means of models is always *as-if* thinking; hydrogen atoms behave (in certain respects) as if they were solar systems each with an electronic planet revolving round a protonic sun. But hydrogen atoms are not solar systems; it is only useful to think of them as if they were such systems if one remembers all the time that they are not. The price of the employment of models is eternal vigilance.

Braithwaite, 1953, 92–93

The essential content of the concept of model is the existence of a correspondence between the model itself and the prototype, and a single correspondence is often enough to provide a very useful model.

Walker, 1963, 3

A model, as its name implies, is a less ambitious, scaled down version of some situation or phenomenon which is the ultimate object of the analyst's concern. Because the problem with which he wishes to deal is too complex and too much beset by petty detail to permit effective analysis, he is forced to deal with a substitute problem, one which ... is close enough to the facts of the matter to permit the conclusions drawn from investigation of the model to retain some relevance for the more complicated phenomenon which the model is designed to represent.

Baumol, 1966, 90

The perfectly competitive model is useful [as a tool of economic analysis] precisely because of its power to abstract from nonessentials. The difficulty arises in its normative use, when it provides the underlying rationale for economic policy proposals .... There are two senses in which the normative use of perfect competition is incorrect. The first of these is that it costs something to remove imperfections. The second is that perfect competition is simply a description of equilibrium characteristics.

Demsetz, 1969, 3

the essential features of models [in economic science] ... are (i) drawing up a list of the variables to be considered; (ii) drawing up a list of the equations or relations the variables have to obey and (iii) testing the validity of the equations .... The advantages of models are, on one hand, that they force us to present a "complete" theory by which I mean a theory taking into account all relevant phenomena and relations and, on the other hand, the confrontation with observation, that is, reality.

Tinbergen, 1969/1992, 42

By definition, a model is not a complete and faithful rendering of reality. It is no more than an analogy or metaphor. It implies a structure of logical and mathematical relations that has many similarities with what it purports to explain, but cannot be fully identified with it.

Ziman, 1978, 23

847 Theory (singular)

Theories are merely what people say about the things they do or experience.

Pareto, 1916/1963, 2024

A theory is not formed from a single isolated fact, but from a whole series of individual propositions combined together .... each consequence of the theory is the result of the coordination of several propositions ....

Planck, 1925, 73

a hypothesis or theory consists of an assertion that certain forces are, and by implication others are not, important for a particular class of phenomena and a specification of the manner of action of the forces it asserts to be important.

Friedman, 1953/1966, 24

A scientific theory might ... be likened to a complex spatial network: Its terms are represented by the knots, while the threads connecting the latter correspond, in part, to the definitions and, in part, to the fundamental and derivative hypotheses included in the theory. The whole system floats, as it were, above the plane of observation and is anchored to it by rules of interpretation.

Hempel, 1952/1960, 36

A scientific theory is not merely a collection of objectively true statements; it also exhibits an organic structure and hierarchy such that, once we are in possession of a fundamental law or a basic hypothesis, we can deduce any number of fact statements of lesser generality ....

Kecskemeti, 1952, 211

A scientific theory is a deductive system in which observable consequences logically follow from the conjunction of observed facts with the set of the fundamental hypotheses of the system.

Braithwaite, 1953, 22

A hypothesis and a theory are alike in that they are both conceptual in nature and have as their primary function the explanation of natural events .... Hypotheses are more restricted in their coverage. Theories are more general in nature .... When there are several interrelated areas of phenomena to be explained, more than one hypothesis may be necessary to account for all of the varied phenomena. The several hypotheses are usually mutually compatible and supplementary and can be fitted together into a more inclusive and comprehensive conceptual scheme of a theory.

Brown & Ghiselli, 1955, 161

A theory is something other than myself. It may be set out on paper as a system of rules, and it is the more truly a theory the more completely it can be put down in such terms .... A theory, moreover, cannot be led astray by my personal illusions .... It has a rigid formal structure, on whose steadfastness I can depend whenever mood or desire may possess me.

Polanyi, 1958, 4

A theory of any kind, whether scientific or philosophic, is a body of propositions, and a body of propositions is a set of concepts .... A concept is a term to which a meaning has been assigned.

Northrop, 1959, 82

A theory is a complex of symbols organized to pattern the way we see things, to predict, and explain. It is more than a sum of atomic, empirical hypotheses and observation statements joined together through formal rules of logic and coordinating definitions. True, theories deal mainly with observable matters, but the relationships between the simplifications of a theory and its empirical content are only occasionally clear.

Krupp, 1961/1964, 5

The word theory is often used in the social sciences (including economics) rather loosely, to designate almost any general statement, however narrow its intended range of application may be.

Nagel, 1962/1963, 211

Theory in science is properly a completed network of facts and general statements about them. Popular usage makes theory mean the suppositions that come earlier, for which the right word is hypothesis ....

Barzun, 1964, 86

a theory consists of (1) a set of primitive terms, undefined but occasionally explained within the framework of the theory, (2) a set of definitions composed of primitive terms or other terms defined from them, (3) a set of premises, assumed as self evident or in case of empirical propositions inferred by induction, (4) a set of conclusions derived from the premises or from other conclusions of these premises.

AAA, 1971, 41

A theory is a systematic statement of the rules or principles which underlie or govern a set of phenomena. A theory may be viewed as a framework permitting the organization of ideas, the explanation of phenomena and the prediction of future behavior .... A theory ... is essentially a set of acceptable hypotheses.
Most, 1977b, 11, 15

848 Conceptual frameworks

Our coordinated knowledge, which in the general sense of the term is science, is formed by the meeting of two orders of experience. One order is constituted by the direct immediate discriminations of particular observations. The other order is constituted by our general way of conceiving the universe. They will be called the observational order and the conceptual order. The first point to remember is that the observational order is invariably interpreted in terms supplied by the conceptual order .... We inherit an observational order, namely types of things which we do in fact discriminate; and we inherit a conceptual order, namely a rough system of ideas in terms of which we do in fact interpret.
Whitehead, 1933/1948, 183

The first conceptual scheme for all the sciences is the common-sense world .... a conceptual scheme is not observed by the senses, but is a frame ... somehow constructed by the mind, by which the mind classifies sense experiences.
Homans & Curtis, 1934/1970, 27, 52

all knowledge presents itself within a conceptual framework adapted to account for previous experience .... When speaking of a conceptual framework, we refer merely to the unambiguous logical representation of the relation between experiences.
Bohr, 1958/1961, 67

The evolution of a conceptual framework for a problem means organizing our knowledge [facts and explanations] into a meaningful set of relations which will enable us to get a clear perspective of the variables at work and which will reveal modes of attack for collecting additional information .... When an explanation effects a pattern of logical constructs as a conceptual framework into which all the facts relevant to some phenomenon can be fitted, it is usually called a theory.
Brown & Ghiselli, 1955, 135, 148

in complex affairs of science one is concerned with trying to account for a variety of facts and with welding them into a conceptual scheme; one fact is not by itself sufficient to wreck the scheme. A conceptual scheme is never discarded merely because of a few stubborn facts with which it cannot be reconciled; a conceptual scheme is either modified or replaced by a better one, never abandoned with nothing left to take its place.
Conant, 1964, 173

theory is as nearly as we can make it so a replica, in constructs and language, of the real world.

Caws, 1965, 86

scientific explanation shows an event to partake of the norm in the sense that it is accounted for by the same set of factors which account for all events of this class. But in the case of scientific explanation, the norm is discovered, not given .... [The factors] have to be discovered, and their discovery involves our taking the phenomena to be explained at the right level of analysis and with the right conceptual framework. For it is only as identified and characterized in a certain way that the phenomena can be exhibited as all being variations in the same fundamental dimensions. The search for a conceptual framework, as a search for the definition of "normalcy", is therefore central to all scientific inquiry.

Taylor, 1970, 53

Copernicus' heliocentric alternative .... did offer a theory, a conceptual framework, an idea structure within which one seemed able to relate the actual behavior and appearances of the planets ... with a physical account of what sort of things such objects really were.

Hanson, 1972, 46

See also 841, 851

849 The mutability of scientific knowledge

the ephemeral nature of scientific theories takes by surprise the man of the world.

Poincaré, 1903/1952, 160

The influence of one doctrine on another makes itself felt not only in the points where they stand in agreement one with the other, but in their points of divergence as well. Aristotle owes something to Plato even when he criticizes him. If there had been no Euclidean geometry, we should perhaps never have had non-Euclidean geometries. Newton's theory of universal gravitation would probably never have existed had there not been the earlier theories that it contradicts. [note to #2142]

Pareto, 1916/1963, 1477

The laws, theories, and inferences of experimental research are as subject to rectification as are inferences based on other human activities. They are approximations getting nearer and nearer the actuality with time .... All research is based on so-called axioms and postulates, the ultimate accuracy of which may be called in question and sooner or later subjected to investigation itself.

Smith, 1929, 745

Knowledge does not keep any better than fish.

Whitehead, 1929/1957, 102

logic, mathematics, physical theory, are all only our inventions for formulating in compact and manageable form what we already know, and like all inventions do not achieve complete success in accomplishing what they were designed to do, much less in fields beyond the scope of their original design . . . .
Bridgman, 1936/1964, 136

A scientific law is not to be thought of as having an independent existence which some scientist is fortunate to stumble upon. A scientific law is not a part of nature. It is only a way of comprehending nature.
Thurstone, 1947/1961, 51

A scientific theory should not close the door to further research on a subject. No theory is ever to be considered the last and irrefutable word, and no theory should remove the problem to an untestable realm.
Beck, 1962, 77

to talk about the immutable laws of nature is meaningless . . . . science is seeking immutable laws, and may even have found some, but . . . no law, however firmly established, can ever be known to be immutable.
Caws, 1965, 83

Nature does not utter sentences. Laws and principles are the verbal formulations of men who observe certain uniformities . . . . If the laws of nature were, more correctly, described as laws of natural science, their mutability might more readily be recognized.
Chambers, 1965c, 22

Nature itself does not speak. Neither do our minds or our bodies or . . . our bodies politic. Our conversations about nature and about ourselves are conducted in whatever languages we find it possible and convenient to employ. We do not see nature or intelligence or human motivation or ideology as "it" is but only as our languages are.
Postman, 1987, 15

See also 881

850 Theory Construction

851 Facts and theories

Necessary truths are formed from our thoughts, the elements of the world within us; experiential truths are collected from things, the elements of the world without us. The truths of experience, as they appear to us in the external world, we call facts; and when we are able to find among our ideas a train which will conform themselves to the apparent facts, we call this a theory.

Whewell, 1860, 464

Facts are not obliged to govern themselves in accordance with our ideas. But our expectations *are* governed by our ideas, in particular by our conception of the facts which comprise our evidence.

Mach, 1908/1960, 272

Science is built up of facts, as a house is built of stones; but an accumulation of facts is no more a science than a heap of stones is a house . . . . Detached facts cannot therefore satisfy us, and that is why our science must be ordered, or, better still, generalized.

Poincaré, 1903/1952, 141, 143

It is by now a platitude of the scientific method that if theory without empirical evidence is unreliable, empirical inquiry without theoretical background is unfruitful.

Arrow, 1951, 132

of two forms of knowledge, we should consider as more objective that which relies to a greater measure on theory rather than on more immediate sensory experience. So that, the theory being placed like a screen between our senses and the things of which our senses otherwise would have gained a more immediate impression, we would rely increasingly on theoretical guidance for the interpretation of our experience, and would correspondingly reduce the status of our raw impressions to that of dubious and possibly misleading appearances.

Polanyi, 1958, 4

Without the hard little bits of marble which are called facts or data one cannot compose a mosaic; what matters, however, are not so much the individual bits, but the successive patterns into which you arrange them, then break them up and rearrange them.

Koestler, 1966, 236

Vast quantities of information do not add up to much serious knowledge without theories to give it meaning.

Ziman, 1968, 27

Never let yourself be goaded into taking seriously problems about words and their meanings. What must be taken seriously are questions of fact, and assertions about facts; theories and hypotheses; the problems they solve; and the problems they raise.

Popper, 1976, 19

Facing facts, we all agree, is good. In this modest sense we are all empiricists. The problem comes, and the modernist shouting begins, with the words empirical and evidence. Should it all be objective, experimental, positive, observable? Can it be? One doubts it.

McCloskey, 1985, 22

852 Terminological propriety

in science, logical distinctions are inexorable and their violation always brings retribution.

Fisher, 1906/1965, 107

the tendency to make a term cover everything prevents it from denoting anything definite.

Cohen, 1931/1964, 35

There is a well-known saying that the word firm can be declined as follows: I am firm, thou art obstinate, he is pig-headed.

Thouless, 1930/1977, 11

The language of everyday conversation is notoriously vague, and the language of even technical treatises is not always very much better. ... Many of the fatuities of actual thinking take place because the inescapable vagueness of most words makes a careful check upon one's thoughts well-nigh impossible .... To the vagueness of words their ambiguity must be added .... Serious blunders in reflective thinking occur because the meaning a word has in some context is replaced, without the fact being noticed, by an allied but different meaning.

Cohen & Nagel, 1934/1957, 224

For evil, then, as well as for good, words make us the human beings we actually are. Deprived of language we should be as dogs or monkeys. Possessing language, we are men and women able to persevere in crime no less than in heroic virtue, capable of intellectual achievements beyond the scope of any animal, but at the same time capable of systematic silliness and stupidity such as no dumb beast could ever dream of.

Huxley, 1940/1969, 5

Methodology, in the sense in which literate people use the word, is a branch of philosophy or of logic .... Semiliterates adopt the word when they are concerned neither with philosophy nor with logic, but simply with methods. Instead of statistical techniques they would say statistical methodology, and instead of research methods they love to say research methodology.

Machlup, 1962/1963, 204

See also 224, 934

853 Concepts

Concept: an idea of a class of objects; general notion.
SOED, 1936

in dealing with physical situations the operations which give meaning to our physical concepts should properly be physical operations, actually carried out. For in so restricting the possible operations, our theories reduce in the last analysis to descriptions of operations actually carried out in actual situations, and so cannot involve us in inconsistency or contradiction, since these do not occur in actual physical situations.
Bridgman, 1936/1964, 9

Physical concepts are free creations of the human mind, and are not, however it may seem, uniquely determined by the external world.
Einstein & Infeld, 1938, 33

Concepts are signs (mainly audible or visible words and symbols) pointing to invariant relations, i.e. relations which remain identical despite the variations of the material in which they are embodied.
Cohen, 1944/1961, 83

the concept of thing expresses a relatively invariant correlation of properties attributed to it . . . . the concept of objective thing is social; science is tested by social procedure. The scientific criterion of objectivity ultimately rests upon the possibility of occurrence of predicted perceptions to a society of observers.
Lenzen, 1955/1962, 312, 285

The concept or notion of anything is the thing as an object of thought. A concept is a universal, and it is generally regarded as the idea of certain common qualities, characteristics or elements which thought finds in a variety of things or kinds of things . . . . there are no concepts of individual things.
Latta & Macbeath, 1956, 22

There are two major ways in which assignment [of meanings to terms] may be made . . . . A concept by intuition is one which denotes, and the complete meaning of which is given by, something which is immediately apprehended. Blue in the sense of the sensed color is a concept by intuition . . . . A concept by postulation is one the meaning of which in whole or part is designated by the postulates of the deductive theory in which it occurs . . . . Blue in the sense of the number of a wave length in electromagnetic theory is a concept by postulation.
Northrop, 1959, 82

A concept, whether mathematic or empirical, is meaningful only if there is a decision procedure connected with it, i.e. a way of finding out whether or not the concept applies in a given case (for quantitative concepts, what their values are in given cases).

Pap, 1963, 179

To have a thought or to think about something is one fact; what this thought intends . . . is a different, usually nonmental, fact. Terms refer, concepts intend . . . . Two terms may refer to . . . the same thing. Two concepts never intend . . . the same thing

Brodbeck, 1968, 61

concepts are invented or discarded when it seems that the existing conceptual framework in terms of which we talk about the world is failing in some respect or another. No one in science invents concepts for fun. They invent them because they need them, because without them some facet of the world would go uncharted.

Theobald, 1968, 28

our concept of a real stone is a simple abstraction from the much more complex properties of stones and expresses our experience of seeing and feeling many stones. It is a metaphor which, in terms of our everyday experience, describes something far more complicated, interesting and mysterious . . . . [Thus] it is possible to arrive at quite different, even contradictory, concepts of the thing which is being observed.

Brown, 1987, 139

Constructs

An abstraction is the union of particulars into universals and occurs at all levels of science. Construction [the creation of constructs] in addition to performing this union, endows the product with suitable properties of its own; it is a creative as well as a synthetic act . . . . there exists a large area of discourse in which the word, construct, as we have employed it, is wholly synonymous with concept.

Margenau, 1950, 70–72

[Theoretical constructs] are not introduced by definitions or reduction chains based on observables; in fact they are not introduced by any piecemeal process of assigning meaning to them individually. Rather, the constructs used in a theory are introduced jointly, as it were, by setting up a theoretical system formulated in terms of them and by giving this system an experiential interpretation, which in turn confers empirical meaning on the theoretical constructs.

Hempel, 1952/1960, 32

The constructs of natural science are conceptual tools that provide a framework for keeping manifest data together in the unity of a theory. Meanings, on the other hand, are derived in a different way; they are derived by means of acts of interpretation.

Kecskemeti, 1952, 7

Meanings in the form of postulated entities, processes or relations, which the scientist conceptually invents to account for his results, are called logical constructs.

Brown & Ghiselli, 1955, 48

constructs (theoretical concepts, hypotheses, and theories) . . . . are invented or created rather than distilled (e.g. induced) from sense data, precisely because they go beyond data.

Bunge, 1967, I:190

Constructs, to be useful in a science, must possess both systematic and empirical import. By systematic import is meant simply that the construct must be such as to lend itself to multiple connections with other constructs in the structure. By empirical import is meant that the construct must be connected, either directly or through other constructs, to the observable data. One of the important concerns in science is the search for or the invention of constructs with both empirical and systematic import.

Torgerson, 1958/1967, 11

854 Definition

men imagine that their reason governs words, whilst, in fact, words react upon the understanding . . . . the great and solemn disputes of learned men often terminate in controversies about words and names, in regard to which it would be better (imitating the caution of mathematicians) to proceed more advisedly in the first place, and to bring such disputes to a regular issue by definition.

Bacon, 1620/1891, 397

Definitions . . . are like steps cut in a steep slope of ice, or shells thrown on to a greasy pavement; they give us foothold, and enable us to advance, but when we are at our journey's end we want them no longer.

Butler, 1890/1969, 13

the main objects to be kept in view in discussing and framing definitions in political economy are – (1) to make as distinct and precise as possible the conceptions that are fundamental in the science, (2) to mark those distinctions between phenomena that are of chief economic importance. In other words, our aim should be to make our ideas at once clear and appropriate.

Keynes, 1890/1930, 159

A good definition should always conform to two tests: it must be useful for scientific analysis; and it must harmonize with popular and instinctive [common sense] reasoning.

Fisher, 1906/1965, 103

Logically, definitions aim to lay bare the principal features or structure of a concept, partly in order to make it definite, to delimit it from other concepts, and partly in order to make possible a systematic exploration of the subject matter with which it deals.

Cohen & Nagel, 1934/1957, 231

The less a science has advanced, the more its terminology tends to rest on an uncritical assumption of mutual understanding. With increase of rigor this basis is replaced piecemeal by the introduction of definitions .... It is valuable to show the reducibility of any principle to another though definition of erstwhile primitives, for every such achievement reduces the number of our presuppositions and simplifies and integrates the structure of our theories.

Quine, 1936, 90, 124

One particularly harmful form of arbitrary defining arises when a test is developed to measure a poorly defined property. Then the property is defined as that which the test measures. Aside from the circularity of such a procedure, it prevents us from improving our methods of measuring the property.

Ackoff, 1953, 59

the lesson which we have received from the whole growth of the physical sciences is that the germ of fruitful development often lies just in the proper choice of definitions.

Bohr, 1958/1961, 29

When we define a word .... either (1) we are stating what we are going to mean by it [stipulative definition], or (2) we are reporting what people in general ... who use the language we are speaking ... already mean by it [reportive or lexical definition] .... It is sometimes said that a definition can be neither true nor false .... A stipulative definition does not assert that anything is or is not the case .... On the other hand, ... reportive definitions are reports of word usage, and there can be true reports and false reports. In this sense, then, definitions not only can be, but are, true or false.

Hospers, 1959, 51

Definitions of terms by reference to other terms belonging to the same language system (for example, the language of physics) are internal definitions, and one might, by using this kind of definition alone, build a whole ingrown language whose terms referred to one another but to nothing else. Definitions which go outside the language system to something else – perception, for instance – are external definitions, and they are required if the whole system is to mean anything.

Caws, 1965, 46

The traditional stock example of a vague term is the word "bald". No doubt we could so redefine this good old word that in its future correct usage it implied some specific density of, or some specific total, hair population. But this would be a silly move. For we should be exchanging a humbly serviceable tool, which we do often

806

have occasion to employ, for a shiny new piece of futile equipment, which in our normal everyday life we never should be in a position to use correctly.

Flew, 1975, 71

855 Reasoning, deductive inference

By the method *a priori* we mean . . . reasoning from an assumed hypothesis; which is not a practice confined to mathematics, but is of the essence of all science which admits of general reasoning at all. To verify the hypothesis itself, *a posteriori*, that is, to examine whether the facts of any particular case are in accordance with it, is no part of the business of science at all but of the application of science.

Mill, 1874, 143

if I wanted to be one of those ponderous scientific people . . . . what an opportunity is here . . . . In the space of 176 years the Lower Mississippi has shortened itself [by cut-offs] 242 miles . . . . Therefore, any calm person, who is not blind or idiotic, can see that in the Old Oolitic Silurian Period, just a million years ago next November, the Lower Mississippi River was upward of 1,300,000 miles long, and stuck out over the Gulf of Mexico like a fishing rod. And by the same token any person can see that 742 years from now the Lower Mississippi will be only a mile and three quarters long, and Cairo and New Orleans will have joined their streets together and be plodding comfortably along under a single mayor and a mutual board of aldermen. There is something fascinating about science. One gets such wholesome returns of conjecture out of such a trifling investment of fact.

Clemens [Mark Twain], 1883/1956, 93

logic is of two kinds: the logic of discovery and the logic of the discovered. The logic of discovery consists in the weighing of probabilities, in discarding details deemed to be irrelevant, in divining the general rules according to which events occur, and in testing hypotheses by devising suitable experiments. This is inductive logic. The logic of the discovered is the deduction of the special events which, under certain circumstances, would happen in obedience to the assumed laws of nature. Thus, when the laws are discovered or assumed, their utilization entirely depends on deductive logic.

Whitehead, 1929/1957, 61

Traditionally a statement which can be certified by reference exclusively to defined or definable meanings is called analytic; what is nonanalytic being called synthetic. And traditionally that knowledge whose correctness can be assured without reference to any particular experience of sense is called *a priori*; that which requires to be determined by sense experience being called *a posteriori* . . . . The thesis here put forward, that the *a priori* and the analytic coincide, has come to be a matter of fairly wide agreement amongst logicians in the last half-century.

Lewis, 1946, 35

The awkward fact – that reason, as we know it, is never aware of its hidden assumptions – has been too much for some philosophers and even many scientists to admit. Few have stated explicitly that their ideas were not correct, but merely the best available; that the greatest possible achievement of a single human mind, including their own, is to eliminate a few errors, while remaining blind to others.
Whyte, 1962/1967, 45

one way in which ground may be shifted, often without anyone realizing what is going on . . . . consists in responding to the falsification of a contingent proposition by covertly so reinterpreting the words in which it was originally formulated that these now become the expression of an arbitrarily made-to-measure necessary truth. This manoeuvre always involves either a high or a low redefinition of a crucial term . . . .
Flew, 1975, 57, 49

Theorems

any proposition, that is implied by another proposition or conjunction of propositions granted or previously proved within the system, is a theorem . . . . The same theorem may follow from more than one selection of premises . . . . But contradictory theorems can never follow from consistent postulates.
Langer, 1953, 186

So far as our present argument is concerned, the things (propositions) that we take for granted may be called indiscriminately either hypotheses or axioms or postulates or assumptions or even principles, and the things (propositions) that we think we have established by admissible procedure are called theorems.
Schumpeter, 1954/1967, 15

The axioms provide us with the properties to be assumed of our primitive notions, whereas the definitions provide us with the meaning of special terminology that we employ for convenience. Given these axioms and definitions, many consequences called theorems can be deduced logically.
Spencer, 1963, 312

856 Theory construction

The constitution of any physical theory results from the two-fold work of abstraction and generalization. In the first place, the mind analyzes an enormous number of concrete, diverse, complicated, particular facts, and summarizes what is common and essential to them in a law, that is, a general proposition tying together abstract notions. In the second place, the mind contemplates a whole group of laws; for this group it substitutes a very small number of extremely general judgments, referring to some very abstract ideas; it chooses these primary properties and formulates these fundamental hypotheses in such a way that all the laws belonging to the group studied can be derived by deduction that is very lengthy perhaps, but very sure. The system of hypotheses and deducible consequences, a work of abstraction, generalization and deduction, constitutes a physical theory in our definition . . . .

Duhem, 1914/1962, 55

A fool looks to the beginning, a wise man regards the end . . . . A wise man begins in the end, a fool ends in the beginning.

Polya, 1945/1957, 223

Rules of theory-building . . . . : 1. Look first at the obvious, the familiar, the common. In a science that has not established its foundations, these are the things that best repay study. 2. State the obvious in its full generality. Science is an economy of thought only if its hypotheses sum up in a simple form a large number of facts. 3. Talk about one thing at a time . . . . always use the same words when referring to the same things. 4. Cut down as far as you dare the number of things you are talking about. "As few as you may; as many as you must", is the rule governing the number of classes of fact you take into account. 5. . . . . describe systematically the relationships between the facts designated by your words. 6. Recognize that your analysis must be abstract, because it deals with only a few elements of the concrete situation . . . . do not be afraid of abstraction.

Homans, 1951/1959, 16

a theorist is not confronted by just one question, or even by a list of questions numbered off in serial order. He is faced by a tangle of wriggling, intertwined and slippery questions. Very often he has no clear idea of what his questions are until he is well on the way to answering them. He does not know, most of the time, even what is the general pattern of the theory that he is trying to construct, much less what are the precise forms and interconnections of its ingredient questions.

Ryle, 1954, 7

we must not forget that the proudest intellectual structures rest on trivialities that are entirely uninteresting in themselves.

Schumpeter, 1954/1967, 911

theories . . . do not evolve piecemeal to fit facts that were there all the time. Rather they emerge together with the facts they fit from a revolutionary reformulation of the preceding scientific tradition, a tradition within which the knowledge-mediated relationship between the scientist and nature was not quite the same.

Kuhn, 1962, 140

[Requirements for the growth of knowledge] The first requirement is this. The new theory should proceed from some simple, new, and powerful, unifying idea about some connection or relation . . . between hitherto unconnected things (such as planets and apples) or facts . . . or new theoretical entities . . . . secondly, we require that the new theory should be independently testable . . . . it must lead to the prediction

of phenomena which have not so far been observed . . . . [thirdly, we] require that
the theory should pass some new, and severe, tests.

Popper, 1963/1974, 241

Theory construction consists in breaking up objects of common sense and in reuniting
the elements in a different way.

Feyerabend, 1975/1982, 297

Theory selection

The methodology of science involves deliverances of sense as well as rules of correspondence, constructs and principles regulating constructs [theories and elements
of theories]. Having learned that the latter are not conveyed by sensory data and
yet function in guiding experience, we should call them metaphysical principles in
the modern sense of the word. Metaphysical principles, thus understood, are an
important part of all procedures which ultimately define reality . . . . [They are] . . . .
logical fertility . . . . multiple connections . . . . permanence and stability . . . . extensibility . . . . causality . . . . simplicity and elegance. . . . these requirements . . . blend
into a system which might be called the logic of theoretical science.

Margenau, 1950, 81–100

In deciding what scientific theory to adopt, . . . we apply not one but a number of
tests. The initial and most important test is that of predictive reliability . . . . The
next test is that of coherence . . . . Finally, if we have to choose between two theories
which are both reliable . . . we apply the test of convenience: the theory which
produces the results with less effort on our part is the one we prefer.

Toulmin, 1958, 95

in some areas at least, nature seems to show an inexplicable simplicity. This is a
brute fact, more or less of a bonus, which if it had not existed could not have been
expected. As a result, the working scientist learns as a matter of routine experience
that he should have faith that the more beautiful and more simple of two equally
inaccurate theories will end up being a more accurate describer of wider experience. This bit of luck vouchsafed the theorist should not be pushed too far, for the
gods punish the greedy.

Samuelson, 1964, 739

Both confirmationists and instrumentalists recognize that empirical criteria are often
insufficient for unambiguous choice among competing theories. Their solution is to
supplement the empirical criteria with other criteria. Such criteria may be placed
into four categories. The first category includes . . . . logical consistency . . . . elegance
. . . . extensibility . . . . generality . . . . multiple connectedness . . . . simplicity . . . .
The second category involves criteria which are used to evaluate the intuitive plausibility of theories . . . . realism and explanatory power . . . . A third criterion involves
the pedagogic value of theories . . . . the ability to illuminate a crucial point or to

simplify a complex problem situation . . . . A final category assesses the research
potential of theories: fruitfulness and fertility . . . .
Caldwell, 1982/1984, 231

857 Assumptions, axioms, postulates

To postulate a proposition is no more than to hope it is true . . . . [A postulate] is
the formulation of a material fact which we are not entitled to assume as a premise,
but the truth of which is requisite to the validity of an inference. Any fact, then,
which might be supposed postulated, must either be such that it would ultimately
present itself in experience, or not.
Peirce, 1892/1958, 164, 166

Axiom: a proposition that commends itself to general acceptance; a well established
or universally conceded principle; a maxim, rule, law. A self evident proposition,
not requiring demonstration, but assented to as soon as stated.

Postulate: a proposition demanded or claimed to be granted: esp. something claimed
or assumed as a basis of reasoning, discussion or belief; hence, a fundamental
condition or principle.
SOED, 1936

Axioms are simply assumptions or hypotheses, used for the purpose of system-
atizing and sometimes discovering the theorems they imply. It follows that axioms
need not be known to be true before the theorems are known, and in general the
axioms of a science are much less evident psychologically than the theorems. In
most sciences . . . the material truth of the theorems is not established by means of
first showing the material truth of the axioms. On the contrary, the material truth
of axioms is made probable by establishing empirically the truth or the probability
of the theorems.
Cohen & Nagel, 1934/1957, 132

Axioms are now held to be postulates, neither true nor false in themselves, and to
have their meaning determined by the consequences that follow because of their
implicatory relations to one another. The greatest freedom is permitted, or rather
encouraged, in laying down postulates – a freedom subject only to the condition
that they be rigorously fruitful of implied consequences.
Dewey, 1938/1966, 10

The propositions of economic theory, like all scientific theory, are obviously deductions from a series of postulates. And the chief of these postulates are all assumptions involving in some way simple and indisputable facts of experience relating
to the way in which the scarcity of goods . . . actually shows itself in the world of
reality . . . . These are not postulates the existence of whose counterpart in reality
admits of extensive dispute once their nature is fully realized. We do not need

controlled experiments to establish their validity: they are so much the stuff of our everyday experience that they have only to be stated to be recognized as obvious.

Robbins, 1935/1969, 78

All we ask of a postulate is (1) that it shall belong to the system, i.e. be expressible entirely in the language of the system [coherence]; (2) that it shall imply further propositions of the system [contributiveness]; (3) that it shall not contradict any other accepted postulate, or any proposition implied by such another postulate [consistency]; and (4) that it shall not itself be implied by other accepted postulates, jointly or singly taken [independence].

Langer, 1953, 185

An assumption of a rather general nature which is posited as a principle for an argument or for a whole system of thought, but is neither self-evident nor proved, is often called a postulate.

Machlup, 1955, 3

The axioms or postulates of a system are its assumed primary statements, from which other statements called theorems are deduced .... statements accepted without proof.

Spencer, 1963, 312

The formulation of the postulates of new models [theories] is an act of creation and is subject to no limitations of method. The scientist uses any and all means, conscious and unconscious, in the act of creation.

Walker, 1963, 5

Postulates, axioms, premises, etc, are statements of the same logical standing; they differ one from another in the ways they have come to be formulated and the degree of confidence they enjoy. We assert a postulate and take an axiom for granted, but hypotheses we merely venture to propose.

Medawar, 1969, 47

858 Theories required to be self-consistent

What ... are the conditions logically imposed on the choice of hypotheses to serve as the basis of our physical theory? These conditions are three in number .... a hypothesis shall not be self-contradictory .... the different hypotheses which are to support physics shall not contradict one another .... hypotheses shall be chosen in such a manner that from them taken as a whole mathematical deduction may draw consequences representing with a sufficient degree of approximation the totality of experimental laws.

Duhem, 1914/1962, 220

a requirement demanded of any physical theory is that it form a consistent whole. By this we mean that it be free from hypotheses *ad hoc*, postulated as and when required, to account for every new fact of experience which appears to be in conflict with our theory .... if we introduce hypotheses of that [*ad hoc*] kind we can account for anything we choose but at the same time we can predict nothing ....

D'Abro, 1927/1950, 409

The requirement of consistency plays a special role among the various requirements which a theoretical system, or an axiomatic system, must satisfy .... a self-contradictory system is uninformative. It is so because any conclusion we please can be derived from it.

Popper, 1934/1961, 91, 92

"Pure theory" affords us a sharp clear-cut language or system of definitions with which to approach the problems which the facts of the world raise .... Theoretical analysis ... compensates us, in a certain way, for the fact that our brains are not all-powerful .... pure theory, by consistent uncontradictory use of the economic vocabulary and by building up the vocabulary further, brings home to us what the implications of our definitions are.

Hutchison, 1938/1965, 34–35

the scientist's conviction ... incompatible rules for doing science cannot coexist except during revolutions when the profession's main task is to eliminate all sets but one.

Kuhn, 1962, 169

859 Simplicity and simplification

William of Occam's razor .... *Entia non sunt multiplicanda praeter necessitatem* [Entities are not to be imagined beyond necessity] .... Sir William Hamilton expresses Occam's canon in the more complete and adequate form: Neither more, nor more onerous, causes are to be assumed than are necessary to account for the phenomena. [William of Occam, c1290–1349]

Pearson, 1911, 393

To know what we think, to be masters of our own meaning, will make a solid foundation for great and weighty thought. It is most easily learned by those whose ideas are meagre and restricted; and far happier they than such as wallow in a rich mud of conceptions .... For an individual ... there can be no question that a few clear ideas are worth more than many confused ones.

Peirce, 1877/1958, 117

the procedure of the scientist ... consists in coordinating and linking together in a rational manner a number of experimental facts, with the maximum of simplicity .... As for the criterion of simplicity, ... it appears to be linked with our valuing of the expenditure of effort.

D'Abro, 1927/1950, 359

we are seeking for the simplest possible system of thought which will bind together the observed facts. By the simplest system we do not mean the one which the student will have the least trouble in assimilating, but the one which contains the fewest possible mutually independent postulates or axioms . . . .

Einstein, 1935, 140

relevant considerations [in the choice among alternative hypotheses] are suggested by the criteria of simplicity and fruitfulness . . . . A theory is simpler the less the initial knowledge needed to make a prediction within a given field of phenomena; it is more fruitful the more precise the resulting prediction, the wider the area within which the theory yields predictions, and the more additional lines for further research it suggests.

Friedman, 1953/1966, 10

In order to simulate the workings of this machine [the world], we usually describe a model made of simple units and obeying simple laws whose motions are then shown to take it to just those points in time and space where experiment can check it against the physical world.

Bronowski, 1960, 105

Simple statements, if knowledge is our object, are to be prized more highly than less simple ones because they tell us more; because their empirical content is greater; and because they are better testable.

Popper, 1934/1961, 142

If there is not a small number of principles, if there is no simplicity, there is no science . . . . The work of the scientist consists in finding simple formulae. Some may say that the scientist doesn't help us to understand anything because he oversimplifies everything. Who knows another way of understanding complicated things than by oversimplifying them?

Frank, 1957/1962, 43

Science always simplifies; its aim is not to reproduce the reality in all its complexity, but only to formulate what is essential for understanding, prediction, or control.

Kaplan, 1964, 280

Scientific knowledge is incomprehensible – i.e. cannot be grasped by the human mind – unless it can indeed be represented by a few relatively simple and coherent theories.

Ziman, 1978, 22

science has to isolate a few simple aspects of the world; . . . . conscious and cautious oversimplification, far from being an intellectual sin, is a prerequisite for investigation. We can hardly study at once all the ways in which everything is related to everything else.

Goodman, 1983, xx

860 Testability and Testing

861 The testability of hypotheses, laws and theories

it is important not to multiply hypotheses indefinitely. If we construct a theory based upon multiple hypotheses, and if experiment condemns it, which of the premises must be changed? Conversely, if the experiment succeeds, must we suppose that it has verified all these hypotheses at once? Can several unknowns be determined from a single equation?

Poincaré, 1903/1952, 151

The quality that is most important in a proposed hypothesis is testability, which depends upon whether or not deductions can be made from it in such a way that it can be definitely credited or discredited by observational tests.

Larrabee, 1945, 199

We do not take even our own observations quite seriously, or accept them as scientific observations, until we have repeated and tested them. Only by such repetitions can we convince ourselves that we are not dealing with mere isolated coincidence, but with events which, on account of their regularity and reproducibility, are in principle intersubjectively testable.

Popper, 1934/1961, 45

We all agree that scientific assertions must be formulated in an objective language. This means, among other things, that no predicate P can form part of a scientific language unless there is an objective test, performable at will by everyone, by which it can always be determined whether P applies to a thing or not.

Kecskemeti, 1952, 210

while hypotheses and theories may be freely invented and proposed in science, they can be accepted into the body of scientific knowledge only if they pass critical scrutiny, which includes in particular the checking of suitable test implications by careful observation or experiment . . . . if it has no test implications . . . . it lacks empirical import.

Hempel, 1966, 16, 30

One of the most important tasks of science is to test the laws and theories it introduces for the purpose of explanation and analysis.

Feyerabend, 1981, 2:62

862 Verification, confirmation

the final and sole decision about the usefulness of the picture [theory] lies in the condition that it represent experience as simply and accurately as possible . . . .

Experience, after all, remains the sole judge of the usefulness of a theory; from its judgment there can be no appeal; it is irrevocable.
                                                    Boltzmann, 1899/1960, 247, 248

Science is a permanent record of premises, deductions and conclusions, verified all along the line by its correspondence with facts.
                                                    Whitehead, 1929/1957, 112

Science is a system of statements based on direct experience, and controlled by experimental verification. Verification is not, however, of single statements, but of the entire system or subsystem of such statements.
                                                    Carnap, 1934, 42

The existence of a thing, the occurrence of an objective event, or any other objective state of affairs, is knowable only as it is verifiable or confirmable. And such objective facts can be verified, or confirmed as probable, only by presentations of sense.
                                                    Lewis, 1946, 203

[There are no rules to guide verification] that can be relied on in the last resort. Take the most important rules of experimental verification: reproducibility of results; agreement between determinations made by different and independent methods; fulfilment of predictions. These are powerful criteria, but I could give you examples in which they were all fulfilled and yet the statement which they seemed to confirm later turned out to be false. The most striking agreement with experiment may occasionally be revealed later to be based on mere coincidence . . . .
                                                    Polanyi, 1946/1966, 30

Verification of a theorem [by empirical testing] is dependent upon two conditions. First, we must be sure that the testing situation meets the demands of the theorem . . . . Secondly, the facts collected must correspond with the consequences stated in the theorem.
                                                    Brown & Ghiselli, 1955, 169

Verification in research and analysis may refer to many things, including the correctness of mathematical and logical arguments, the applicability of formulas and equations, the trustworthiness of reports, the authenticity of documents, the genuineness of artifacts and relics, the adequacy of reproductions, translations and paraphrases, the accuracy of historical and statistical accounts, the corroboration of reported events, the completeness in enumeration of circumstances in a concrete situation, the reproducibility of experiments, the explanatory or predictive value of generalizations.
                                                    Machlup, 1955, 1

all our knowledge has been built up communally . . . . it follows that we must be able to rely on other people; we must be able to trust their word . . . . there is a principle which binds society together, because without it the individual would be helpless to tell the true from the false. This principle is truthfulness. If we accept truth as an individual criterion, then we have also to make it the cement to hold society together . . . . there is a social nexus which alone makes verification possible . . . . the obligation to tell the truth. Thus is follows that there is a social injunction implied in the positivist and analyst method. This social axiom is that: we *ought* to act in such a way that what *is* true can be verified to be so.

Bronowski, 1964, 62

questions of analogy are not settled by deductive logic. In other words, the relation between theory and theoretical implication is deductive, but between theoretical implication and observation, nondeductive. It is this logical gap which exercises the scientific judgment. It is this gap which allows us to describe explanations as reasonable or not; which allows us to speak of them as helping us to understand . . . ; and which allows other interpretations of the observational data to be tried without the suspicion of a logical contradiction. Whether a theory fits the observations is not a question to be settled by the professional logician, but by the trained scientist with his special skill.

Theobald, 1968, 108

863 Testing of hypotheses and theories

Comparison between the conclusions of theory and the truths of experiment is . . . indispensable, since only the test of facts can give physical validity to a theory. But this test by facts should bear exclusively on the conclusions of a theory . . . .

Duhem, 1914/1962, 206

[The] shift from the question of whether a general proposition is true to the question of whether it is better founded than its rival is the key to the understanding of the role of probable and inductive reasoning.

Cohen, 1931/1964, 82

Complex phenomena in the production of which various causal chains are interlaced cannot test any theory. Such phenomena, on the contrary, become intelligible only through an interpretation in terms of theories previously developed from other sources.

von Mises, 1949, 31

Any economic theorem rigorously deduced from given postulates may be regarded as an hypothesis about the real world . . . . But theorems which say something about the actual world cannot be derived solely from postulates that do not . . . . Consequently, the postulates which by their very nature cannot be tested directly by economic experience require to be tested by testing the theorems. This is the normal method of science . . . .

Stone, 1951, 12

in the case of almost all scientific hypotheses, except the straightforward generalizations of observable facts which serve as the lowest level hypotheses in the

deductive system, complete refutation is no more possible than is complete proof. What experience can tell us is that there is something wrong somewhere in the system; but we can make our choice as to which part of the system we consider to be at fault. In almost every system it is possible to maintain any one hypothesis in the face of apparently contrary evidence at the expense of modifying the others.
Braithwaite, 1953, 19

Since no scientific hypothesis is ever completely verified, in accepting an hypothesis on the basis of evidence, the scientist must make the decision that the evidence is sufficiently strong or that the probability is sufficiently high to warrant the acceptance of the hypothesis .... How sure we must be before we accept a hypothesis depends on how serious a [consequential] mistake would be.
Rudner, 1953/1961, 32

verification in the sense most relevant to us – the testing of generalizations – is a procedure designed to find out whether a set of data of observation about a class of phenomena is obtainable and can be reconciled with a particular set of hypothetical generalizations about this class of phenomena.
Machlup, 1955, 1

A theory consists of a great number of statements which may be interlocked in a complex way. The newly discovered fact [that is contradictory to some conclusion drawn from a theory] does not tell us which of these statements is false .... Much has been said about the crucial experiment that can decide whether a certain theory must be rejected or not. A single experiment can only refute a theory if we mean by a theory a system of specified statements with no allowance for modification. But what is actually called a theory in science is never such a system.
Frank, 1955/1962, 30

What we call scientific evidence can never confirm that a theory is true; it can only confirm that it is more true than another.
Koestler, 1966, 243

testing is impossible ... where the universe itself is random and subject to no law. The movements of stock prices, for instance, have so strong a random element in them, especially in regard to relative stock prices, that anyone who detects a law in their behavior is probably as much under illusion as he who detects a law in the fall of the dice.
Boulding, 1966, 136

there are two ways in which we can examine any statement – we can try to confirm it, that is to show that it is true, or we can try to falsify it, that is to show that it is false .... science will develop only if testing is deliberately contrived so as to provide the maximum chance of a statement proving false. For then we have to think again.
Theobald, 1968, 79

The role of empiricism in science is in putting theory to the test of experience.

Brubacher, 1982, 83

864 Experiment

we must never do experiments in order to confirm our ideas but merely to check them.

Bernal, 1865/1962, 181

It is often said that experiments should be made without preconceived ideas. That is impossible.

Poincaré, 1903/1952, 143

It is the inferior observer who tries to make up for bad experiments by fancy calculations.

Ritchie, 1923, 131

experiment is nothing else than a mode of cooking the facts for the sake of exemplifying the law.

Whitehead, 1933/1948, 108

Sense-data certainly do not make up the whole, or even the major part, of a scientist's materials. The events that are given for his inspection could be faked in a dozen ways – that is, the same visible events could be made to occur, but with a different significance. We may at any time be wrong about their significance, even when no one is duping us; we may be nature's fools. Yet if we did not attribute an elaborate, purely reasoned and hypothetical history of causes to the little shivers and wiggles of our apparatus, we really could not record them as momentous results of experiments. The problem of observation is all but eclipsed by the problem of meaning .... our sense-data are primarily symbols.

Langer, 1942/1969, 20

The hypothetico-deductive approach would be little more than an exercise in logic without the modern version of trial by fire, experimentation (including scientific observation), by means of which the scientist obtains the verdict of experience.

Goldstein, 1962, 12

an experiment is only an artificial device for putting the observer in a favorable position with respect to nature – a contrivance to have things happen where they can be seen .... A crucial experiment is exactly one on which the choice between two theories hinges; it is so designed that either of two possible outcomes refutes one of the theories in question .... But even if tests are not actually feasible, so that the crucial experiment strategy breaks down, it is still possible to consider what would be observed if some ideal experimental situation could be devised .... thought experiments .... The point of a crucial experiment is that it gives new data; the limitation of a thought experiment is that it cannot give new data ....

> Caws, 1965, 52, 233

Experiments are of at least four kinds: (i) Inductive or Baconian experiments ... ("I wonder what would happen if ..."). (ii) Deductive or Kantian experiments ... ("let's see what happens if we take a different view") .... (iii) Critical or Galilean experiments: actions carried out to test a hypothesis or preconceived opinion by examining the logical consequences of holding it .... (iv) Demonstrative or Aristotelian experiments, intended to illustrate a preconceived truth and convince people of its validity.

> Medawar, 1969, 35–37

In some fields, the scientist ... is ... able to generate observations that will provide evidence for or against the hypothesis. Experimental sciences, such as chemistry and some branches of psychology, have an advantage because it is possible for them to produce relevant evidence through controlled laboratory experiments. Other sciences, such as astronomy and economics, cannot do this. They must wait for time to develop observations that may be used as evidence in testing their theories.

> Lipsey, 1972, 7

865 Mathematics and mathematical reasoning

To draw quantitative conclusions we must use the language of mathematics .... Mathematics as a tool of reasoning is necessary if we wish to draw conclusions which may be compared with experiment. So long as we are concerned only with fundamental physical ideas we may avoid the language of mathematics.

> Einstein & Infeld, 1938, 29

those who take this view [that all universals or mathematical entities are fictions] have never been able to explain why it is that mathematical fictions have proved such a fruitful way of penetrating the secrets of nature, or why so many phenomena have been discovered by means of purely mathematical methods.

> Cohen, 1944/1961, 171

The power of mathematics is no more and no less than the power of pure reason .... all abstract reasoning that is sufficiently precise and systematic constitutes mathematics.

> Kemeny, 1961, 5, 22

Mathematics can spare us the painful necessity of doing our own thinking, but we must pay for the privilege by taking pains with our thinking both before and after the mathematics comes into play.

> Kaplan, 1964, 205

pure mathematics is neutral and, when applied, it is applied to our ideas about some matter of fact, not to the facts themselves. What gets mathematicized is not a chunk of reality but some of our ideas about it.

Bunge, 1973, 131

Mathematics is invaluable in science as a strong grammar for didactic discourse; it is the ideal vehicle for precise intersubjective communication . . . . Mathematical reasoning is immensely more powerful than plain language when it comes to generating verifiable predictions, unpalatable conclusions, or unsuspected connections between known facts.

Ziman, 1978, 17

Mathematics as abstraction

mathematics studies nothing but hypotheses, and is the only science which never inquires what the actual facts are . . . .

Peirce, 1898/1958, 341

mathematics may be defined as the subject in which we never know what we are talking about, nor whether what we are saying is true.

Russell, 1901/1964, 26

Mathematics is thought moving in the sphere of complete abstraction from any particular instance of what it is talking about . . . . The certainty of mathematics depends on its complete abstract generality.

Whitehead, 1926/1938, 34, 35

It is now apparent that the concept of a universally accepted, infallible body of reasoning – the majestic mathematics of 1800 and the pride of man – is a grand illusion . . . . Proof, absolute rigor, and their ilk are will-o'-the-wisps, ideal concepts . . . .There is no rigorous definition of rigor. A proof is accepted if it obtains the endorsement of the leading specialists of the time and employs the principles that are fashionable at the moment. But no standard is universally accepted today.

Kline, 1980, 6, 315

Mathematics and statistics in economic and scientific inquiry

In my view every economic fact, whether or not it is of such a nature as to be expressed in numbers, stands in relation as cause and effect to many other facts: and since it never happens that all of them can be expressed in numbers, the application of exact numerical methods to those which can is nearly always a waste of time, while in the large majority of cases it is positively misleading; and the world would have been further on its way forward if the work had never been done at all.

Marshall, 1901/1966, 422

I know I had a growing feeling in the later years of my work at the subject [economics] that a good mathematical theorem dealing with economic hypotheses was very unlikely to be good economics: and I went more and more on the rules – (1) Use mathematics as a shorthand language, rather than as an engine of inquiry. (2) Keep to them till you have done. (3) Translate into English. (4) Then illustrate by examples that are important in real life. (5) Burn the mathematics. (6) If you can't succeed in 4, burn 3. This last I did often . . . . Mathematics used . . . by a man who is not a mathematician by nature – and I have come across a good deal of that – seems to me an unmixed evil.

Marshall, 1906/1966, 427

In psychology . . . it is easier than elsewhere to rush off to measure something without considering what it is that we are measuring, or what measurement means. In this respect some recent measurements are of the same logical type as Plato's determination that a just ruler is 729 times as happy as an unjust one.

Cohen, 1931/1964, 305

social elements seldom admit of simple addition . . . . This makes it difficult to apply the mathematical methods which have proved so fruitful in the natural sciences . . . . It is vain to expect [in the social sciences] that the crudeness of our observation and the vagueness of our fundamental categories will be cured by manipulation of the paraphernalia of statistical methods.

Cohen, 1931/1964, 353

There is no point in using exact [mathematical] methods where there is no clarity in the concepts and issues to which they are to be applied.

von Neumann & Morgenstern, 1944/
1980, 4

The blind transfer of the striving for quantitative measurements, to a field in which the specific conditions are not present which give it its basic importance in the natural sciences, is the result of an entirely unfounded prejudice. It is probably responsible for the worst aberrations and absurdities produced by scientism in the social sciences. It not only leads frequently to the selection for study of the most irrelevant aspects of the phenomena because they happen to be measurable, but also to measurements and assignments of numerical values which are absolutely meaningless.

von Hayek, 1955/1964, 51

Two rival hypotheses may sometimes be so closely related that their relative merits are positively computable; the significance tests of mathematical statistics do for us what can be done in this way. But this happens only where the really difficult intellectual problems do not arise. As soon as we broaden our view, and consider situations calling for conceptual innovations, where there are several demands to be satisfied, the idea of an evidential calculus for scientific theories becomes unrealizable.

Toulmin, 1963, 112

It is a common trait of intellectual snobbery ... to think that scientifically significant problems must always be associated with differentials and integrals, probability functions, difference equations, power series or other complicated relations ....

Mattessich, 1964, 64

Today we preach that science is not science unless it is quantitative .... Measurements and equations are supposed to sharpen thinking, but, in my observation, they more often tend to make the thinking noncausal and fuzzy. They tend to become the object of scientific manipulation instead of auxiliary tests of crucial inferences. Many – perhaps most – of the great issues of science are qualitative, not quantitative; even in physics and chemistry. Equations and measurements are useful when and only when they are related to proof; but proof or disproof comes first and is in fact strongest when it is absolutely convincing without any quantitative measurement.

Platt, 1964, 351

I have found ... that one of the chief duties of the mathematician in acting as adviser to scientists in less precise fields is to discourage them from expecting too much of mathematics. They must learn that there is no intellectual virtue (and that there is, in fact, a severe intellectual vice) in using a number of three digits when our available accuracy runs to one digit. [In a case where many specialists were involved] is was the mathematicians rather than the physiologists and the sociologists who had most to throw cold water on an overestimation of the detailed possibilities of mathematics in these other fields.

Wiener, 1956, 285

The use of the fundamental principle of reasoning and research, "other things being equal", is being attacked today by some economists who try to boost their own mathematical and statistical studies by playing down the value of general reasoning about cause and effect. They argue that science can only measure and predict. They seem to suggest that science is nothing more than a testing of hypotheses by correlation studies and that the hypothesis which can best predict by means of a measure of correlation is the nearest to the truth. This treacherous suggestion must be resisted by a clear statement that not even perfect correlation can prove a false hypothesis. In the natural sciences one studies causal relations by observing, thinking, experimenting and measuring, and one takes a great deal of trouble to make sure that in fact other things are equal. In economics, where there is little opportunity for simple controlled experiments, we use the principle "other things being equal". We assume a situation in which all independent variables remain unchanged except one, and then we think out, with the help of our knowledge of the fundamental principles of economic behavior, how the change in one independent variable would affect the total situation.

Gifford, 1968, 1093

There can be no question ... that prolonged commitment to mathematical exercises in economics can be damaging. It leads to the atrophy of judgment and intuition which are indispensable for real solutions and, on occasion, leads also to the habit of mind which simply excludes the mathematically inconvenient factors from consideration.

Galbraith, 1971, 41

The employment of low levels of weaponry, such as a critical analysis using only the English language, is considered off-side .... Too much of what goes on in economic and econometric theory is of little or no relevance to serious economic science .... Does the fact that some economists play abstract games of little relevance and others engage in meretricious quantification prevent serious economists from going about their business? The danger is that university courses in economics will become increasingly mathematical and increasingly concerned with technique to the exclusion of the subject matter itself .... The more the impression is allowed to persist that economics is an exact science, or, if not already one, then with the aid of mathematical models and the computer is about to become one, the more damage will be done to the subject when it fails to live up to exaggerated expectations.

Worswick, 1972, 83–84

It must never be forgotten that statistical argument never actually confirms a hypothesis; it can only tell us, more or less loosely, whether the data are consistent with our theoretical assumptions.

Ziman, 1978, 170

Page after page of professional economic journals are filled with mathematical formulas leading the reader from sets of more or less plausible but entirely arbitrary assumptions to precisely stated but irrelevant conclusions. Year after year economic theorists continue to produce scores of mathematical models ... without being able to advance, in any perceptible way, a systematic understanding of the structure and the operations of a real economic system.

Leontief, 1982, 104, 107

Mathematics is a very useful language, but not universally so .... attempts to use it at ... an early stage in the development of an area are often counterproductive because authors are led to assume the problem away or to define sterile "toy" problems that are mathematically tractable.

Jensen, 1983, 333

The abuse of the word "significant" in connection with statistical arguments in economics is universal. Statistical significance seems to give a criterion by which to judge whether a hypothesis is true or false. The criterion seems to be independent of any tiresome consideration of how true a hypothesis must be to be true enough. But the world does not serve up free intellectual lunches .... significance in statistics, however useful it sometimes might be, is not the same as economic significance.

McCloskey, 1985, 156

866 Convergence

even if we have succeeded in finding a satisfactory solution we may still be interested in finding another solution. We desire to convince ourselves of the validity of a theoretical result by two different derivations as we desire to perceive a material object through two different senses. Having found a proof, we wish to find another proof as we wish to touch an object after having seen it. Two proofs are better than one.

Polya, 1945/1957, 61

In general, indirect verification seems to be accomplished by examining the involvement of the suspect thing with the rest of our experience and finding whether it presents us with a picture which is consistent with what we expect . . . . The more thorough the verification, the more varied and larger in number the involvements which we examine . . . . The smaller the number of involvements, the less complete or satisfactory the verification.

Bridgman, 1961, 62

Convergence of findings by two methods with different weaknesses enhances our belief that the results are valid and not a methodological artifact.

Bouchard, 1976, 268

The initial path to a new discovery may be apparently one-dimensional with no more reliable authority than a simple causal chain. But the strategy of research is to seek alternative routes, from other starting points, to the same spot until the discovery has been incorporated unequivocally into the scientific map.

Ziman, 1978, 84

If, as claimed, proof is validation and certification, then one might think that once a proof has been accepted by a competent group of scholars, the rest of the scholarly world would be glad to take their word for it and to go on. Why do mathematicians and their students find it worthwhile to prove again and yet again (by different or new stratagems) the Pythagorean theorem or the theorems of Lebesgue or Wiener or Kolmogorov? Proof serves many purposes simultaneously. In being exposed to the scrutiny and judgment of a new audience, the proof is subject to a constant process of criticism and revalidation. Errors, ambiguities, and misunderstandings are cleared up by constant exposure. Proof is respectability. Proof is the seal of authority.

Davis & Hersh, 1981, 151

867 The explanatory power of theories

A physical theory is not an explanation. It is a system of mathematical propositions, deduced from a small number of principles, which aim to represent as simply, as completely, and as exactly, as possible a set of experimental laws.

Duhem, 1914/1962, 19

When we have succeeded in constructing some lofty scientific synthesis which takes in the facts of experience, our synthesis must always be such as to permit us to account for the facts of crude observation; for these, to the same extent as the results of ultra-precise experiment, constitute facts which must be coordinated.

D'Abro, 1927/1950, 401

what we seek in science is not merely prediction in the Friedman sense of the term – which is the prediction of the crystal ball – but prediction through explanation. Only this enables us to construct a deductive system involving the real world which can make this world intelligible to us.

Rotwein, 1961/1964, 9

a theory is to be judged by the number of factual assertions (past, present or future, categorical or hypothetical) which it supports .... makes sense of or explains .... [The merits of Newton's hypotheses] were explanatory rather than predictive. They showed us what must happen if certain conditions were fulfilled, not what must happen unqualifiedly. They thus drew attention to an intelligible pattern of relationships between apparently unrelated types of happening – the ebb and flow of tides, the appearances of comets, the fall of stones, and the motions of the planets. This nexus of regularities and connections was the thing that mattered most for Newton .... It formed a network of natural necessities, holding equally for the actual and for the unfulfilled conditions.

Toulmin, 1963, 34

explanations provide understanding, but we can predict without being able to understand, and we can understand without necessarily being able to predict. It remains true that if we can predict successfully on the basis of a certain explanation we have good reason, and perhaps the best sort of reason, for accepting the explanation.

Kaplan, 1964, 350

The astronomers of Babylon were able to make astonishingly precise predictions: they calculated the length of the year with a deviation of only 0.001 per cent from the correct value; their figures ... were the foundations on which the Ptolemaic, and later the Copernican, systems were built. Theirs was certainly an exact science; and it worked; but that does not prove the truth of their theories, which asserted that the planets were gods whose motions had a direct influence on the health of men and the fortunes of states.

Koestler, 1966, 243

The general form of all scientific explanations and predictions can be summarized thus:

> 1 Laws and theories
> 2 Initial conditions
> 3 Predictions and explanations.

Chalmers, 1976/1987, 9

See also 817

868 The predictive power of theories

Absolute precision, an altogether accurate specification of the consequences of a hypothesis, can only be found in physical theory, it cannot be expected in applied physics (any more than in applied geometry).

Mach, 1908/1960, 272

to prophesy the future we make use of the same intellectual operation that serves us to understand the past.

Ortega, 1931/1961, 24

Viewed as a body of substantive hypotheses, theory is to be judged by its predictive power for the class of phenomena which it is intended to explain. Only factual evidence can show whether it is right or wrong or, better, tentatively accepted as valid or rejected.

Friedman, 1953/1966, 8

If verification of a theory takes the form of testing whether predictions based on that theory actually come true, one might think that this can be done in economics no less than in the physical sciences. It cannot, alas, because of the non-reproducibility of the experiments or observed situations and courses of events in the economy. For, while certain types of event, or changes, recur in the economy often enough, they recur rarely under the same conditions.

Machlup, 1955, 18

In modern science, a theory is regarded as an instrument that serves towards some definite purpose. It has to be helpful in predicting future observable facts on the basis of facts that have been observed in the past and present. It should also be helpful in the construction of machines and devices that can save us time and labor.

Frank, 1961a, 22

Forecasting . . . is a craft or technology . . . . a novel and successful theory may lead to no increase in our forecasting skill; while, alternatively, a successful forecasting technique may remain for centuries without any scientific basis. In the first case, the scientific theory will not necessarily be any the worse; and, in the second, the forecasting technique will not necessarily become scientific, just because it works.

Toulmin, 1963, 36

a successful theory enables us to predict as yet unobserved events . . . . a scientific prediction . . . is a conditional statement of the form: if you do this then such and such will follow. If we wish to test any theory we confront its predictions [the implications of its assumptions] with evidence. We seek to discover if certain events have the consequences predicted by the theory.

Lipsey, 1972, 13

all theoretical sciences are predicting sciences . . . . Ordinary predictions in science are conditional. They assert that certain changes (say, of the temperature of water in a kettle) will be accompanied by other changes (say, the boiling of the water).
Popper, 1963/1974, 339

Scientific prediction is conditional prediction. A theory binds together certain variable quantities into a set of fixed attainable configurations. It allows as possible any one of these configurations, but excludes all others. But if further classes of measurements are introduced as variables into the list, . . . the set of configurations or states of affairs which can arise can be entirely altered.
Shackle, 1972, 36

Prediction and retrodiction

the predictions by which the validity of a hypothesis is tested need not be about phenomena that have not yet occurred, that is, need not be forecasts of future events; they may be about phenomena that have occurred but observations on which have not yet been made or are unknown to the person making the prediction.
Friedman, 1953/1966, 9

Logically speaking, there is no difference between prediction and retrodiction. The pattern of theory is usually hinged to certain established points . . . from which a number of other experimentally observable facts . . . are deduced. It does not matter . . . whether those other facts have already been determined; the logical fitting and the verification of the theory is just as good as if we then set down to measure them for the first time.
Ziman, 1968, 41

Predict in the scientific sense means to anticipate unobserved phenomena without regard to the temporal location of those phenomena. Thus, in science predict often refers to present phenomena. Forecast refers exclusively to anticipated phenomena that lie in the future.
Sterling, 1979, 13

869 Abandonment of theories

a scientific theory is declared invalid only if an alternative candidate is available to take its place.
Kuhn, 1962, 77

six types of case in which we should be inclined to say of a theory t_1 that it is superseded by t_2 in the sense that t_2 seems − as far as we know − to correspond better to the facts than t_1 in some sense or other.
(1) t_2 makes more precise assertions than t_1, and these more precise assertions stand up to more precise tests

(2) t_2 takes account of, and explains, more facts than t_1 (which will include for example the above case that, other things being equal, t_2's assertions are more precise)
(3) t_2 describes, or explains, the facts in more detail than t_1
(4) t_2 has passed tests which t_1 has failed to pass
(5) t_2 has suggested new experimental tests, not considered before t_2 was designed (and not suggested by t_1, and perhaps not even applicable to t_1); and t_2 has passed these tests
(6) t_2 has unified or connected various hitherto unrelated problems.

Popper, 1963/1974, 232

few theories are utterly discredited . . . . Theories are repaired more often than they are refuted . . . . Sometimes theories merely fade away . . . . More often they are merely assimilated into wider theories in which they rank as special cases.

Medawar, 1969, 30

As a generalization we can say that our theories tend to be abandoned when they are no longer useful, and that they cease to be useful when they cannot predict the consequences of actions in which we are interested better than the next best alternative.

Lipsey, 1972, 14

scientists are seldom eager to see their own children killed; usually they are anxious to show that their creations are viable. To this end they will not hesitate to protect them with *ad hoc* hypotheses.

Bunge, 1973, 28

economists fight tooth and nail when faced with an empirical refutation of a proposition in positive economics involving the asssumption of perfect competition. For what is threatened is not just that particular propositiom but the entire conception of economic "efficiency" that gives *raison d'être* to the subject of economics. No wonder that intellectual tenacity in the face of empirical refutations, the tendency to protect falsified theories by *ad hoc* immunizing stratagems, has loomed and continues to loom so large in the history of economics.

Blaug, 1980, 153

that facts, all by themselves, can jar and unseat ideas . . . . is rarely the case . . . . in the absence of a well formulated, intellectually attractive, new idea, it is remarkable how much in the way of dissonance and contradiction a dominant idea can absorb . . . . The Ptolemaic cosmology . . . had been compromised by countless contradictory observations over many generations. Still it was an internally coherent, intellectually pleasing idea; therefore, keen minds stood by the old familiar system. When there seemed to be any conflict, they simply adjusted and elaborated the idea, or restructured the observations in order to make them fit . . . . It was not until a highly imaginative constellation of ideas . . . replete with new concepts of gravitation, inertia, momentum, and matter, was created that the old system was retired.

Roszak, 1986, 90

870 Description and Prescription

871 Theory and practice

Those who are enamored of practice without science [knowledge, understanding] are like the pilot who gets into a ship without rudder or compass and who never has any certainty where he is going. Practice should always be based on sound theory . . . .
Leonardo, (1452–1519)/1980, 225

Nothing is more common than to hear from the lips of seemingly sensible men the announcement that a certain proposition may be right in theory, but it is undoubtedly wrong in practice. The relation which exists between theory and practice is not that of opposition or contrast at all . . . . Theory is meant simply to designate generalized practice, or in other words, the general principles of correct practice; practice indicates a certain method of acting, in relation to which theory points out the most excellent way.
Carmichael, n d/1843, 9

Success in practice depends on theorists who, led by other motives of exploration, have been there before, and by some good chance have hit upon the relevant ideas. By a theorist I do not mean a man who is up in the clouds, but a man whose motive for thought is the desire to formulate correctly the rules according to which events occur.
Whitehead, 1929/1957, 107

[The] connection of logic with theoretic science should warn us against the popular fallacy that a proposition may be true theoretically but not practically. Those who thus reject theory sometimes possess a sound perception but a highly inaccurate one. That which is true cannot be false, and if anything is true theoretically it is foolish to regard it as in any sense false.
Cohen, 1944/1961, 194

Theory and the comprehension of living and changing reality are not in opposition to one another. Without theory, the general aprioristic science of human action, there is no comprehension of the reality of human action.
von Mises, 1949, 38

The usefulness of any theory is an empirical matter; . . .
Caws, 1965, 284

In past epochs a man was regarded as practical if, in acting, he paid little or no attention to theory or if he relied on worn-out theories and common knowledge. Nowadays a practical man is one who acts in obeyance to decisions taken in the light of the best technical knowledge . . . . And such a technical knowledge, made up of theories, grounded rules and data, is in turn an outcome of the application of the method of science to practical problems.

Bunge, 1967, II:121

See also 949

872 Positive and imperative (normative) propositions

the imperative mood is the characteristic of art, as distinguished from science. Whatever speaks in rules or precepts, not in assertions respecting matters of fact, is art.

Mill, 1865/1925, 616

As the terms are used here, a positive science may be defined as a body of systematized knowledge concerning what is; a normative or regulatory science as a body of systematized knowledge relating to criteria of what ought to be, and concerned therefore with the ideal as distinguished from the actual; an art as a system of rules for the attainment of a given end. The object of a positive science is the establishment of uniformities, of a normative science the determination of ideals, of an art the formulation of precepts.

Keynes, 1890/1930, 34

A positive judgment is one which deals with questions of fact; it indicates that A is B (or is not B). A normative judgment is one which deals with questions of value or the desirable; it takes the form, A ought to be B (or ought not to be B).

Fraser, 1937/1947, 15

People have ideas about how reality actually is, or was, and they have ideas about how it ought to be, or ought to have been. The former we call beliefs. The latter we call valuations. A person's beliefs, that is, his knowledge, can be objectively judged to be true or false and more or less complete. His valuations – that a social situation is or was just, right, fair, desirable, or the opposite in some degree of intensity or other – cannot be judged by such objective standards as science provides. In their opinions, people express both their beliefs and their valuations. Usually people do not distinguish between what they think they know and what they like or dislike.

Myrdal, 1944, 1027

As we survey man's history, we cannot, I believe, escape the following conclusion. The motive power of a value judgment is often greatly increased when it appears within the rationale of those who hold it not under its proper logical flag as a value judgment but in the disguise of a statement of fact. A statement of this kind, that is, a value judgment disguised as, or mistaken for, a statement of fact, I shall call an "ideological statement" .... It is, I believe, open to serious doubt whether the effect on the people would have been the same had the text [of the Declaration of

Independence] read "These we hold to be self evident value judgments" instead of the clarion call "These truths we hold to be self evident".

Bergmann, 1951, 210

A positive social science must be value-free in the sense that it is not social advocacy in disguise, but not in the sense that it has nothing to say about values.

Passmore, 1953, 676

Positive sciences are sciences of fact; they endeavor to ascertain the laws in accordance with which events actually happen in the outer world or in the world of mind. Logic, ethics and aesthetics, on the other hand, are often called normative sciences, because their business is to discover certain norms or standards to which our thoughts, actions and feelings ought to conform and by means of which these thoughts, actions and feelings may be tested and pronounced to be correct or incorrect, right or wrong.

Latta & Macbeath, 1956, 9

The division of labor among different analysts according to the distinction between normative and positive propositions cannot be carried very far without depriving social science of most of its operational utility.

Millikan, 1960, 177

the semantic meaning of a statement is that state of affairs whose existence would make the statement true. The word "fact" is more current in ordinary language than the clumsy "state of affairs" .... Imperatives ... have no semantic meaning; we do not call then true or false, but obeyed or disobeyed.

Pap, 1963, 6, 9

Positivists and analysts alike believe that the words *is* and *ought* belong to different worlds, so that sentences which are constructed with *is* usually have a verifiable meaning, but sentences constructed with *ought* never have.

Bronowski, 1964, 61

A typical value judgment is the imperative statement demanding or designating a specific goal. But it would be a mistake to consider a statement of the following form a value judgment: "if goal A is pursued, then action B should be chosen". Though couched in a conditional sentence, this is a factual proposition, because it is refutable and possesses a truth value, it does not set a norm, and has to be supplemented by an imperative such as :"Goal A is to be pursued" before the theory becomes normative. Only if both these statements are available can the conclusion and policy recommendation, "Do action B", be attained.

AAA, 1971, 37

Positive statements concern what is, was or will be, and normative statements concern what ought to be .... Thus, disagreements over positive statements are appropriately handled by an appeal to the facts .... Disagreement over normative statements cannot be settled merely by an appeal to the facts .... The distinction between positive and normative follows from the fact that it is logically impossible to deduce normative statements from positive assumptions and *vice versa*.

Lipsey, 1972, 4

it is paramount in theory construction and verification to distinguish between positive and normative assertions, because "ought" statements do not, epistemologically speaking, necessarily entail "is" statements . . . . As the discipline [of accounting] progresses, it is quite possible to have the two phases synthesized, but we believe that the former [the positive] is necessarily the foundation of the latter. This is not to say that the fashionable goal-oriented deductive system is methodologically invalid . . . . a synthesis of [positive and normative phases of accounting] may come only after a logically and empirically validated frame of reference has been established.

Yu, 1976, 3

the scientific message is not prescriptive. It is not an order from a social superior, nor a moral imperative. The influence of knowledge over action arises from its power of prediction.

Ziman, 1978, 106

But how do we tell whether a given utterance is an is-statement or an ought-statement? It is clearly not to be decided by whether the sentence containing the statement is or is not grammatically formulated in the indicative mood, because there are sentences in the indicative mood, like "murder is a sin", which are thinly disguised ought-statements dressed up as is-statements.

Blaug, 1980/1984, 130

The term "positivist" in economic literature seems often to imply the upholding, in economics and the social sciences, of the "methods", criteria, and aims of the natural sciences. But the term has come to be used quite indiscriminately, as a kind of all-purpose pejorative adjective, from contrasting political directions, by epistemological anarchists as well as by dogmatists of all stripes, from Marxists to Misesists. The term, "positivist" seems especially to be directed at those who support a disciplined observance of, or emphasis on, distinctions and demarcations between normative and positive, or between prescriptive, descriptive or predictive propositions, or between definitional and empirical, or analytic, synthetic or other types of proposition.

Hutchison, 1981, 279

873 The positive, the normative, and action

if there is one thing which *is* shown by history, not less than by elementary logic, it is that historical induction, unaided by the analytical judgment, is the worst possible basis of prophecy.

Robbins, 1935/1969, 74

Scientific laws do not command people, or things, to behave under given circumstances in a particular way; they sum up the way in which people, or things, under given circumstances do behave .... they are positive, not normative .... whereas legal rules and moral precepts are sometimes disregarded or broken ... scientific laws must hold wherever the circumstances are found to which they apply. They cannot be broken; for if any case is found in which the rule they embody does not hold, the existence of this exception disproves the law as formulated.
Fraser, 1937/1947, 46

the pure scientist finds abundant motivation in the faith that only by a knowledge of what is can we make any practical programs of what ought to be. Without this foundation our utopias are futile because they may be impossible or undesirable. In short, the scientist has ample motive in his belief that only by a more perfect knowledge of the nature of his universe can man adjust himself intelligently to it.
Lundberg, 1942, 54

The statesman, when he acts scientifically and wisely, must think and operate literally in two worlds. He must know things as they are; he must also know things as they ought to be .... Scientifically grounded wise statesmanship consists of possessing scientifically verified factual theory concerning what is the case, and scientifically verified normative social theory of what ought to be the case and then achieving as much of the ideal as possible changes in the factual will permit.
Northrop, 1959, 263

Positivism lacks the driving force for serving as a leader on this road .... For its activity is essentially critical, its glance is directed backward. But progress, advancement requires new associations of ideas and new queries, not based on the results of measurements alone, but going beyond them, and toward such things the fundamental attitude of positivism is one of aloofness.
Planck, 1950, 172

The view that it is the task of the theoretical sciences to discover the unintended consequences of our actions brings these sciences very close to the experimental natural sciences .... both lead us to the formulation of practical technological rules stating what we cannot do.
Popper, 1963/1974, 342

Man masters nature not by force but by understanding. This is why science has succeeded where magic failed: because it has looked for no spell to cast over nature .... we gain our ends only with the laws of nature; we control her only by understanding her laws.
Bronowski, 1964, 19

In order to recommend a course of action to achieve an objective, we must first know whether that course of action will in fact promote the objective. Positive scientific knowledge that enables us to predict the consequences of a possible course of action is clearly a prerequisite for the normative judgment whether that course

834

of action is desirable. The road to hell is paved with good intentions, precisely because of the neglect of this rather obvious point.

Friedman, 1976/1992, 268

all propositions can be stated in normative form or in positive form . . . . The continued insistence upon avoiding normative propositions in accounting borders on the absurd . . . . all scientific propositions are normative in the sense that you can use them to achieve objectives. If you cannot use them to attain objectives, then they are useless. But the original statements of such propositions are positive.

Sterling, 1982a, 75

There is a close formal resemblance between the schema for normative reasoning and that for explanatory reasoning. In each case we are given the conclusion of a deductive argument, and we seek to find the premises from which it can be deduced. In other words, we reason in the reverse of the deductive direction. There is this difference. In explanatory reasoning, we accept the explicandum as true on the basis of observation; we terminate reverse reasoning when we have found laws and initial conditions that we likewise accept on the basis of observation. In normative reasoning, we desire that the description of a certain final state be true; and we terminate reverse reasoning when we have found laws that we accept as true and controllable initial conditions that we can make true by our actions.

Christenson, 1983, 14

874 Skill

Knowledge and proficiency . . . are thought to belong more properly to art [=science] than to experience, and artists [=scientists] are considered wiser than those who are limited to experience . . . . an artist knows the cause of a thing, while the other does not. He who has only experience knows that a thing is so, but not why it is so, whereas an artist knows the why and the wherefore. That is why a master craftsman in any trade is more highly esteemed, is considered to know more . . . than an artisan, because he understands the reason for what is done. He is said to be wiser, not indeed for what he can do, but on account of his theoretical knowledge.

Aristotle, 4cBC/1956, 52

If I know the law and act upon it, I have in my mind both the general induction and its particular application. But if I act by the ordinary billiard-player's skill, without thinking of momentum or law, there is no induction in the case.

Whewell, 1860, 241

the aim of a skilful performance is achieved by the observance of a set of rules which are not known as such to the person following them . . . . In performing a skill we are . . . acting on certain premises of which we are focally ignorant, but which we know subsidiarily as part of our mastery of that skill, and which we may get to know focally by analyzing the way we achieve success . . . .

Polanyi, 1958, 49, 162

We may . . . somewhat paradoxically, describe awareness as that experience which decreases and fades away with our increasing mastery of a skill exercised under monotonous conditions. Mastery of the code [of the skill] and stability of environment are the two factors which lead to the formation of habit; and habit formation is accompanied by a gradual dimming and darkening of the lights of awareness. On the other hand we may regard this tendency towards the progressive automatization of skills as an act of mental parsimony, as a handing down of the controls to lower levels in the hierarchy of nervous functions, enabling the higher levels to turn to more challenging tasks.

Koestler, 1966, 155

To most car drivers a car is a black box; they operate the levers and switches knowing what behavior they will induce thereby but they know little if anything about the engine and the transmission mechanism . . . . To a machine designer, on the other hand, a car and a computer are transparent or at least translucid boxes . . . . the user of a machine is supposed to treat it as a means not as an end. But it would be . . . absurd to criticize research engineers for not remaining satisfied with the external approach and for wishing to know what mechanism each switch controls. Yet that is precisely what the behaviorist (phenomenalist, positivist, black boxist) philosophy does: it derides all those who inquire into the *modus operandi* of things.

Bunge, 1973, 103

880 Advancement of Knowledge

881 The growth of knowledge

time is the greatest innovator; and if time of course alter things to the worse, and wisdom and counsel shall not alter them to the better, what shall be the end?

Bacon, 1620/1891, 397

Except at rare intervals of intellectual ferment, education in the past has been radically infected with inert ideas . . . . Every intellectual revolution which has ever stirred humanity to greatness has been a passionate protest against inert ideas.

Whitehead, 1929/1957, 13

There is no such thing as perfection in human knowledge, nor for that matter in any other human achievement. Omniscience is denied to man . . . . A scientific system is but one station in an endlessly progressing search for knowledge.

von Mises, 1949, 7

The general advance of science has, in fact, taken place in following out the solutions of problems set in the first place by actual economic necessity, and only in the second place arising out of earlier scientific ideas. At any given time there are usually a set of challenging problems like the doubling of the cubic altar at Delphi, which involved extracting a cube root, or the finding of the longitude, which led to Newton's laws, or the curing of the silkworm disease in France, which helped Pasteur to arrive at the idea of the germ theory of disease.

Bernal, 1954/1969, 39

no experience is definable without a logical frame .... any such frame may prove too narrow to comprehend new experiences .... any apparent disharmony can be removed only by an appropriate widening of the conceptual framework.

Bohr, 1958/1961, 67, 82

paradigm changes do cause scientists to see the world of their research engagement differently .... though the world does not change with a change of paradigm, the scientist afterward works in a different world.

Kuhn, 1962, 110, 120

It was supremely difficult to escape from the Aristotelian doctrine [of inertia] by merely observing things more closely, especially if you had already started off on the wrong foot .... the modern law of inertia is not the thing you would discover by mere photographic methods of observation – it required a different kind of thinking-cap, a transposition of the mind of the scientist himself .... somewhat upon the policy of picking up the opposite end of the stick.

Butterfield, 1965, 16

The growth of knowledge – or the learning process – is not a repetitive or a cumulative process but one of error elimination.

Popper, 1972, 144

Reason grants that the ideas we introduce in order to expand and to improve our knowledge may *arise* in a very disorderly way and that the *origin* of a particular point of view may depend on class prejudice, passion, personal idiosyncrasies, questions of style, and even on error, pure and simple. But it also demands that in *judging* such ideas we follow certain well-defined rules: our *evaluation* of ideas must not be invaded by irrational elements. Now, what our historical examples seem to show is this: there are situations when our most liberal judgments and our most liberal rules would have eliminated an idea or a point of view which we regard today as essential for science, and would not have permitted it to prevail – and such situations occur quite frequently. The ideas survived and they can *now* be said to be in agreement with reason. They survived because prejudice, passion, conceit, errors, sheer pigheadedness, in short because all the elements that characterize the context of discovery, *opposed* the dictates of reason and because these irrational elements were permitted to have their way. To express it differently: Copernicanism and other "'rational'" views exist today only because reason was overruled at some time in their past.

Feyerabend, 1975/1982, 154

882 Rate of change of knowledge and art

In all negotiations of difficulty, a man may not look to sow and reap at once; but must prepare business, and so ripen it by degrees.

Bacon, 1625/1907, 145

Neither thinkers nor governments effect all they intend, but in compensation they often produce important results which they did not in the least foresee. Great men and great actions are seldom wasted; they send forth a thousand influences, more effective than those which are seen; and though nine out of every ten things done, with a good purpose, by those who are in advance of their age, produce no material effect, the tenth thing produces effects twenty times as great as any one would have dreamed of predicting from it.

Mill, 1865/1925, 614

A physical theory is not the sudden product of a creation; it is the slow and progressive result of an evolution.

Duhem, 1914/1962, 221

in the year 1500 Europe knew less than Archimedes who died in the year 212BC . . . .

Whitehead, 1926/1938, 16

Harvey's views [on the circulation of the blood] were not generally accepted in the thirty years or more before Malpighi's discovery [in 1661 of capillary structures in the lungs of a frog] forced assent.

Gillispie, 1960/1967, 73

Progress in human affairs, whether in science or in history or in society, has come mainly through the bold readiness of human beings not to confine themselves to seeking piecemeal improvements in the way things are done, but to present fundamental challenges in the name of reason to the current way of doing things and to the avowed or hidden assumptions on which it rests . . . . no sane person ever believed in a kind of progress which advanced in an unbroken straight line without reverses and deviations and breaks in continuity, so that even the sharpest reverse is not necessarily fatal to the belief.

Carr, 1962, 150, 110

Though a generation is sometimes required to effect the change, scientific communities have again and again been converted to new paradigms. Furthermore these conversions occur not despite the fact that scientists are human but because they are. Though some scientists, particularly the older and more experienced ones, may resist indefinitely, most of them can be reached in one way or another. Conversions will occur a few at a time until, after the last hold-outs have died, the whole profession will again be practising under a single, but now a different, paradigm.

Kuhn, 1962, 151

The principle of unripe time – "the time is not ripe" – is that people should not do at the present moment what they think right at that moment, because the moment at which they think it right has not yet arrived.

Cornford, 1964, 24

I would not hazard a guess as to the rate of increase in knowledge in the disciplines which are basic for accountancy, but I know that in my own subject of biochemistry, the doubling time for knowledge has been between four and a half and six years. This means that in my own case knowledge of biochemistry has increased by a factor of 32 since I graduated 30 years ago; even had I learnt at that time all the biochemistry that there was to be known, it would amount to only about three per cent of present knowledge!

Webb, 1971, 9

From the time of Plato (5th century BC) to the time of Kepler (17th century AD) the paths of the planets were believed to be circular – 22 centuries to demolish a mistaken belief. Though some Greek philosophers of the 4th century BC believed in a heliocentric universe, the geocentric doctrine prevailed for over 20 centuries. Though some Greek philosophers had believed in an earth in motion, for 20 centuries the doctrine of a stationary earth persisted .... More recently, such eminent scientists as Kelvin, Mach and Rutherford held firmly to beliefs that were discarded, because disproved, within a generation of their utterance. As for technology, the following periods elapsed between the conception of the basic idea and its fruition –photography, 56 years; television, 63 years; antibiotics, 30 years; zip fasteners, 30 years; instant coffee, 22 years [S Rosen, *New York Times*, Jun 18, 1976]. In the light of this it is perhaps understandable that the emergence of an agreed, serviceable form of accounting from a trial and error stage, through speculation, experimentation and confirmation to execution, cannot be expected to occur speedily.

Chambers, 1980a, 167

Discoveries are made when the time is ripe and are then readily accepted as filling the available gaps in knowledge.

Kohn, 1989, 167

883 Impediments to the endorsement of new knowledge

there is nothing more difficult to carry out, nor more doubtful of success, nor more dangerous to handle, than to initiate a new order of things. For the reformer has enemies in all those who profit by the old order, and only lukewarm defenders in all those who would profit by the new order, this lukewarmness arising partly from fear of their adversaries, who have the laws in their favor; and partly from the incredulity of mankind, who do not truly believe in anything new until they have had actual experience of it. Thus it arises that on every opportunity for attacking the reformer, his opponents do so with the zeal of partisans, the others only defend him half-heartedly, so that between them he runs great danger.

Machiavelli, c1519/1952, 55

The slowness and difficulty with which the human race makes discoveries and its blindness to the most obvious facts, if it happens to be unprepared or unwilling to see them, should suffice to show that there is something gravely wrong about the logician's account of discovery.

Schiller, 1917, 257

the ideas of economists and political philosophers, both when they are right and when they are wrong, are more powerful than is commonly understood. Indeed the world is ruled by little else. Practical men, who believe themselves to be quite exempt from any intellectual influences, are usually the slaves of some defunct economist. Madmen in authority, who hear voices in the air, are distilling their frenzy from some academic scribbler of a few years back. I am sure that the power of vested interests is vastly exaggerated compared with the gradual encroachment of ideas. Not, indeed, immediately, but after a certain interval; for in the field of economics and political philosophy there are not many who are influenced by new theories after they are twenty five or thirty years of age, so that the ideas which civil servants and politicians and even agitators apply to current events are not likely to be the newest. But, soon or late, it is ideas, not vested interests, which are dangerous for good or evil.

Keynes, 1936/1942, 383

The mind likes a strange idea as little as the body likes a strange protein and resists it with a similar energy. It would not perhaps be too fanciful to say that a new idea is the most quickly acting antigen known to science. If we watch ourselves honestly we shall often find that we have begun to argue against a new idea even before it has been completely stated.

Trotter, 1941/1946, 186

A new scientific truth does not triumph by convincing the opponents and making them see the light, but rather because its opponents eventually die, and a new generation grows up that is familiar with it.

Planck, 1950, 33

When a person makes a decision, a corresponding behavioral element is established and his cognitions about the alternatives among which he has chosen are then consonant or dissonant with this element. All the favorable aspects of the unchosen alternatives and unfavorable aspects of the one chosen are dissonant with the choice. Consequently, the creation of dissonance is a common result of decisions. After the choice has been made, the person therefore tends, according to [Festinger's dissonance] theory, to expose himself to information that he perceives as likely to support the decision and to avoid information that is likely to favor the unchosen alternatives.

Ehrlich & others, 1957, 98

Just as truth ultimately serves to create a consensus, so in the short run does acceptability . . . . people approve most of what they best understand . . . . Because familiarity is such an important test of acceptability, the acceptable ideas have great stability.

Galbraith, 1960, 6

Men prefer service, without real allegiance, under outworn banners, to compliance with the painful effort of revising inherited principles and setting them in accord with their own deepest feelings.

Ortega, 1931/1961, 21

of all forms of mental activity, the most difficult to induce . . . is the art of handling the same bundle of data as before, but placing them in a new system of relations with one another by giving them a different framework . . . . But the supreme paradox of the scientific revolution is the fact that things which we find it easy to instil into boys at school . . . defeated the greatest intellects for centuries.

Butterfield, 1965, 13

Though one might assume that an old idea could serve as a stepping stone to something better, more often than not it hinders the acceptance and development of new ideas.

Kohn, 1989, 172

884 Conditioned thinking and fixation

The human mind gets creased into a way of seeing things. Those who have envisaged nature according to a certain point of view during much of their career rise only with difficulty to new ideas.

Lavoisier, c1777/1967, 232

Men who have an excessive faith in their theories or in their ideas are not only poorly disposed to make discoveries but they also make very poor observations. They necessarily observe with a preconceived idea and, when they have begun an experiment, they want to see in its results only a confirmation of their theory. Thus they distort observation and often neglect very important facts because they go counter to their goal.

Bernal, 1865/1962, 181

The moment one has offered an original explanation for a phenomenon which seems satisfactory, that moment affection for his intellectual child springs into existence . . . . There is an unconscious selection and magnifying of the phenomena that fall into harmony with the theory and support it, and an unconscious neglect of those that fail of coincidence. The mind lingers with pleasure upon the facts that fall happily into the embrace of the theory, and feels a natural coldness toward those that seem refractory . . . . When these biasing tendencies set in, the mind rapidly

degenerates into the partiality of paternalism . . . . From an unduly favored child, it [the theory] readily becomes master, and leads its author whithersoever it will.
Chamberlin, 1890, 93

nothing will delay the decision which should determine a fortunate reform in a physical theory more than the vanity which makes a physicist too indulgent towards his own system and too severe towards the system of another.
Duhem, 1914/1962, 218

every theory will produce a certain bias in the observer. It will direct his attention upon those facts and those features which are relevant to his theory, and more particularly, which support it. This is usually an advantage, because it helps him to select what is relevant to his inquiry from the chaos of events; but it will *pari passu* blind him to whatever does not seem to be related to, and to fit into, his theory.
Schiller, 1917, 264

Emotional attachment to views which we habitually honor, and repugnance toward those views that good people are taught to despise, hinder free scientific inquiry.
Cohen, 1931/1964, 348

Doublethink means the power of holding two contradictory beliefs in one's mind simultaneously, and accepting both of them . . . . The process has to be conscious, or it would not be carried out with sufficient precision, but it also has to be unconscious, or it would bring with it a feeling of falsity and hence of guilt . . . . To tell deliberate lies while genuinely believing in them, to forget any fact that has become inconvenient, and then, when it becomes necessary again, to draw it back from oblivion for just so long as it is needed, to deny the existence of objective reality and all the while to take account of the reality which one denies – all this is indispensably necessary.
Orwell, 1949/1955, 171

the persistent error . . . . Thinking becomes conditioned just as conditioned reflexes are formed. We may have enough data to arrive at a solution to the problem, but, once we have adopted an unprofitable line of thought, the oftener we pursue it, the harder it is for us to adopt the profitable line . . . . Thinking also becomes conditioned by learning from others by word of mouth or from reading.
Beveridge, 1950/1957, 87

The creed whose legitimacy is most easily challenged is likely to develop the strongest proselytizing impulse.
Hoffer, 1951, 108

anyone who is drunk with gadgets is a menace. Any choice he makes . . . is much more likely to be wrong than right . . . . The nearer he is to the physical presence of his own gadget, the worse his judgment is going to be. The gadget is there. It is one's own. One knows, no one can possibly know as well, all the bright ideas it contains, all the snags overcome.

Snow, 1962, 62

The chief trouble with most assertions of principle is that they lead very quickly to self-righteousness. Our feelings get involved, then out the window goes reason.

Pusey, 1964, 60

In the era of discovery . . . it may actually be advantageous not to have been well indoctrinated in the complacent fog of contradictory ideas that passes for received opinion upon the topic in question.

Ziman, 1968, 67

When we are trying to understand how certain avoidable policy errors happen to be made, we should look into the behavior of the small group of decision makers, because all the well known errors stemming from limitations of an individual and of a large organization can be greatly augmented by group processes that produce shared miscalculations . . . . Groupthink refers to the deterioration of mental efficiency, reality testing, and moral judgment that results from in-group pressures.

Janis, 1972, 7, 11

By his education, and by participation in normal science, the average research worker is heavily indoctrinated and finds great difficulty in facing the possibility that his world picture might be wrong.

Ziman, 1978, 90

See also 918

885 Vested interests and conservatism

Nor are discoveries easy to get recognized when they have been made. The persecutions to which discoverers of new truth are subjected always and everywhere (more or less) form as discreditable a chapter of human history as the persecution of moral reformers. Those may count themselves fortunate who are simply ignored. Hence everything has to be discovered over and over again. Nothing new ever enters the world, just as nothing old ever passes away, without infinite pains and after a protracted struggle.

Schiller, 1917, 256

it was Erasmus . . . who formulated the law of degeneracy – the thesis that all social institutions . . . are driven by their desire to survive into programs of self-entrenchment and self-aggrandizement in the course of which their original faiths and ideals are perverted and abandoned.

Salomon, 1949, 599

Innovations are often opposed because they are too disturbing to entrenched authority and vested interests in the widest sense of that term.

Beveridge, 1950/1957, 149

It is the true believer's ability to shut his eyes and stop his ears to facts that do not deserve to be either seen or heard which is the source of his unequaled fortitude and constancy . . . . By elevating dogma above reason, the individual's intelligence is prevented from becoming self-reliant.

Hoffer, 1951, 78, 125

The innate conservatism, or at least inertia, of professional standards has from time to time stood in the way of scientific progress. The martyrs of science have sometimes been victims of the faithful rather than of the infidels. Ignaz Semmelweiss and Georg Cantor ... were hounded by their respectable colleagues for their revolutionary ideas about puerperal fever and transfinite arithmetic . . . . Yet for every resisted scientific genius there are numberless crackpots, for every martyr to the truth there are countless victims only of their own paranoid delusions.

Kaplan, 1964, 4

One of the conspicuous handicaps [to the advancement of knowledge] is the conservatism of the scientific mind in its corporate aspect. The collective matrix of a science at a given time is determined by a kind of establishment, which includes universities, learned societies, and, more recently, the editorial offices of technical journals. Like other establishments, they are consciously or unconsciously bent on preserving the *status quo* – partly because unorthodox innovations are a threat to their authority, but also because of the deeper fear that their laboriously erected intellectual edifice might collapse under the impact. Corporate orthodoxy has been the curse of genius from Aristarchus to Galileo, to Harvey, Darwin and Freud.

Koestler, 1966, 240

new ideas meet inevitable resistance, not only from the old guard, governed by a conventional conservatism dating from the semiphilosophical or theological era, but also from the disappointed rival theorists who are reluctant to give up the hope of themselves providing the successful interpretation. These are the most dangerous critics, for they have more to lose than the simple conservatives.

Ziman, 1968, 52

[The idea of scientific continuity is] used to explain the not uncommon phenomenon of the failure of a man of genius to get acceptance for his ideas from his contemporaries, even though later generations will applaud the performance. Augustin Cournot, for example, was an important scholar in one of the leading intellectual centers of Europe, but he could not persuade economists in 1838 that the mathematical theory of maxima and minima was a useful tool for economic analysis.

Stigler, 1982/1992, 64

The most serious enemy of discovery and scientific attainment based on a new idea is dogma and authority; the accepted dogma of today may be the error of tomorrow.

Kohn, 1989, 5

886 Fear of novelty

by far the greatest obstacle to the progress of the sciences, and to the undertaking of new tasks and provinces therein, is found in the tendency of men to despair, and to suppose things impossible.

Bacon, 1620/1891, 283

if you are chronically insecure or anxious or frightened, you cling desperately to your belief system, and you are too busy defending yourself against real or imagined threats to take in information about the disbelief system.

Hayakawa, 1952/1965, 256

There is in all of us a psychological tendency to resist new ideas which come from without just as there is a psychological resistance to really radical innovations in behavior or dress. It perhaps has its origin in that inborn impulse which used to be called the herd instinct.

Beveridge, 1950/1957, 146

Poincaré, who had so much wider a mathematical background than Einstein, . . . knew all the elements required for such a synthesis [the special theory of relativity], of which he felt the urgent need and for which he laid the first foundations. Nevertheless he did not dare to explain his thoughts, and to derive all the consequences, thus missing the decisive step separating him from the real discovery of the principle of relativity.

Taton, 1957, 134

When Jenner, the father of vaccination, asked the Royal Society for permission to present his findings and ideas there, the answer was: He ought not to risk his reputation by presenting to the learned body anything which appeared so much at variance with established knowledge, and withal so incredible.

Kohn, 1989, 7

887 Disputation

Myself when young did eagerly frequent
Doctor and Saint, and heard great argument
About it and about: but evermore
Came out by the same door as in I went.

Omar Khayyam, d.1123, xxvii

where reason is not, its place is taken by clamor.

Leonardo, d.1519/1980, 5

in learning, where there is much controversy, there is many times little inquiry.

Bacon, 1605/1930, 140

it quite naturally happens that those who believe too much in their own theories do not sufficiently believe in the theories of others. Then the dominant idea of these condemners of others is to find fault with the theories of the latter and to seek to contradict them . . . . They are doing experiments only in order to destroy a theory instead of doing them in order to look for truth. They also make poor observations because they take into the results of their experiments only what fits their purpose, by neglecting what is unrelated to it, and by very carefully avoiding whatever might go in the direction of the idea they wish to combat.

Bernal, 1865/1962, 181

The objects of scientific thought being the passionless laws and phenomena of external nature, one might suppose that their investigation and discussion would be completely withdrawn from the region of the feelings, and pursued by the cold dry light of intellect alone. This, however, is not always the case. Man carries his heart with him into all his works. You cannot separate the moral and emotional from the intellectual; and thus it is that the discussion of a point in science may rise to the heat of a battlefield.

Tyndall, 1870, 73

Men who accept different ideals and paradigms have really no common theoretical terms in which to discuss their problems fruitfully. They will not even have the same problem: events which are phenomena [things to be explained] in one man's eyes will be passed over by the other as perfectly natural.

Toulmin, 1963, 57

888 Obscurantism

[The Director of Hatcheries and Conditioning:] Imagine the folly of allowing people to play elaborate games which do nothing whatever to increase consumption. It's madness. Nowadays the Controllers won't approve of any new game unless it can be shown that it requires at least as much apparatus as the most complicated of existing games.

Huxley, 1932/1966, 20

It has become conventional among students of fiscal policy . . . to dissemble any underlying social philosophy and to maintain a pretense of rigorous, objective analysis untinctured by mere ethical considerations . . . . Having been told that sentiments are contraband in the realm of science, they religiously eschew a few proscribed phrases, clutter up title pages and introductory chapters with pious references to the science of public finance, and then write monumental discourses upon their own prejudices and preconceptions.

Simons, 1938, 1

Whereas the function of research is to test social theory by observation of reality, the function of agitprop [agitation and propaganda] is to make reality appear to conform to The Ideology. One does not consult the man who wears the shoe to learn where it pinches; one tells him that it must pinch now to fit better later – or that it doesn't really pinch at all.

Lerner, 1960, 24

All economic regularities that have no common sense core that you can explain to your wife will soon fail.

Samuelson, 1963, 235

Although he may seem to be using the very latest and most powerful methods, and has learned to avoid obvious mistakes of technique, algebraic errors, etc, the [graduate school student] is not conditioned to watch out for the logical hiatus, the falsely excluded middle, the verbal ambiguity, the divergent mathematical formula, the alternative explanation. Turgidity and verbosity stuffed with technical jargon may mask the problem to be solved, and the nature of the proposed solution may be muffled under a blanket of half-meaningful, solemn and portentous sentences.

Ziman, 1968, 90

889 Diversions and distractions

the particular phenomena of the arts and nature are but a handful compared with the figments of the wit, after they have been separated and abstracted from the evidence of things.

Bacon, 1620/1891, 291

The fear that the conquests of science may shortly leave research nothing to do vanishes before the new Alexanders, who have discovered in the inane and trivial inexhaustible worlds to conquer.

Flexner, 1930/1968, 155

Theories come into fashion and theories go out of fashion, but the facts connected with them stay.

George, 1936, 218

When reality becomes unbearable, the mind must withdraw from it and create a world of artificial perfection.

Koestler, 1959/1964, 59

all the great mechanical brains, translating machines, learning machines. chess-playing machines, perceiving machines, etc, accounts of which fill our press, owe their "reality" to a failure to use the subjunctive mood. The game is played as follows: First, it is asserted that except for trivial engineering details, a program for a machine is equivalent to a machine. The flow chart for a program is equated to a program. And finally, the statement that a flow chart could be written for a non-existent program for a nonexistent machine establishes the existence of the machine. In just this way Uttley's "Conditioned Reflex Machine", Rosenblatt's "Perceptron", Simon, Shaw & Newell's "General Problem Solver" and many other nonexistent devices have been named in the literature and are referred to as though they existed.

Taube, 1961, 59

I find it difficult to understand, particularly in periods of transition and uncertainty, how much fashion plays a role in science, scarcely inferior to the one it plays in women's dress. (letter)

Einstein, –/1962, 154

We find in the history of science as many fashions, crazes and schools as in the history of literature or interior decoration.

Koestler, 1966, 248

folderol – those practices characterized by excessive ornamentation, nonsensical and unnecessary actions, trifles and essentially useless and wasteful fiddle-faddle – [including] tendencies to be fixated on theories, methods and points of view, conducting little studies with great precision, attaching dramatic but unnecessary trappings to experiments, asking unimportant or irrelevant questions, grantsmanship, coining new names for old concepts, fixation on methods and apparatus, seeking to prove rather than test theories, and myriad other methodological ceremonies conducted in the name of rigorous research.

Dunnette, 1966, 343

a high degree of confirmation can be obtained by tampering either with the hypothesis or experience. In fact any of the following tricks would enhance a degree of confirmation to practically any desired extent: (i) reinterpreting unfavorable evidence as favorable by introducing *ad hoc* hypotheses; (ii) reformulating the hypothesis in a loose (semantically weak) way so that it will span almost any evidence; (iii) disregarding (hiding) unfavorable evidence, i.e. selecting the data; (iv) subjecting the hypothesis to slack tests.

Bunge, 1967, II:323

Science is not immune from fashion – a sure sign of its socio-psychological nature .... the climate of professional opinion at any one moment is as important as the genius of individuals in determining the intellectual history of the subject.

Ziman, 1968, 17, 53

late 20th century science has given up all philosophical pretensions and has become a powerful *business* that shapes the mentality of its practitioners. Good payment, good standing with the boss and the colleagues in their "unit" are the chief aims of these human ants who excel in the solution of tiny problems but who cannot make sense of anything transcending their domain of competence.

Feyerabend, 1975/1982, 188

Flockthink . . . . the sheeplike and enthusiastic adoption of half-baked solutions to half-understood problems which fleetingly catch the public fancy.

Hildreth, 1977, 7

Sectarianism is a natural social tendency that cannot be entirely eliminated even in the world of objective knowledge, but it can claim no legitimacy, nor permanent institutional form, within the research community.

Ziman, 1978, 134

The journals abound with papers that apply regression analysis to every conceivable economic problem, but it is no secret that success in such endeavors frequently relies on "cookbook econometrics": express a hypothesis in terms of an equation, estimate a variety of forms for that equation, select the best fit, discard the rest, and then adjust the theoretical argument to rationalize the hypothesis that is being tested . . . . Empirical work that fails utterly to discriminate between competing explanations quickly degenerates into mindless instrumentation and it is not too much to say that the bulk of empirical work in modern economics is guilty on that score.

Blaug, 1980/1984, 257

890 Science, Art, Technology and Philosophy

891 Science as art

Our aesthetic judgment demands harmony between the representation and the represented, and in this sense science is often more artistic than modern art.

Pearson, 1911, 17

Nothing could be more absurd than the attempt to distinguish between science and art. Science is the noblest of the arts and men of science the most artistic of all artists. For science, like art, seeks to attain aesthetic satisfaction through the perceptions of the senses; and science, like art, is limited by the impositions of the material world on which it works.

Campbell, 1919/1957, 227

By some the scientist is regarded as a man who, working by well tried rules of logic and experiment, has made himself independent of artistry or intuition. This is entirely false. The really great scientist is always a great artist . . . . By some the artist is regarded as a man who owes little or nothing to working hypotheses or experimental tests. This is an even more dangerous fallacy.

Topley, 1940, 37

scientific investigation, as distinct from the theoretical content of any given branch of science, is a practical art. It is not learnt out of books, but by imitation and experience.

Ziman, 1968, 7

people don't learn how to do research or how to make discoveries by reading about scientific method in books. The most important things about scientific method are usually learned by example, by following someone who knows how to do research.

Brown, 1987, 13

892 Science and technology

Those who fall in love with practice without science are like a sailor who enters a ship withour a helm or a compass, and who can never be certain whither he is going.

Leonardo (1452–1519), –/1960, 162

Science is theory, art is practice. It is not always necessary that science should be reduced to practice, or become art, yet every art is dependent upon science for its truth and certainty.

Foster, 1843, 8

every science is evolved out of its corresponding art. It results from the necessity we are under . . . of reaching the abstract by way of the concrete, that there must be practice and an accruing experience with its empirical generalization, before there can be science.

Spencer, 1861/1976, 61

Now, the reasons of a maxim of policy, or of any other rule of art, can be no other than the theorems of the corresponding science . . . . The art proposes to itself an end to be attained, defines the end, and hands it over to the science. The science receives it, considers it as a phenomenon or effect to be studied, and having investigated its causes and conditions, sends it back to art with a theorem of the combination of circumstances by which it could be produced. Art then examines those combinations of circumstances, and according as any of them are or are not in human power, pronounces the end attainable or not. The only one of the premises, therefore, which art supplies is the original major premise, which asserts that the attainment of the given end is desirable. Science then lends to art the proposition . . . that the performance of certain actions will attain the end. From these premises art concludes that the performance of these actions is desirable, and finding that it is also practicable, converts the theorem into a rule or principle.

Mill, 1865/1925, 616

There is no need to argue over the priority of science as against technology, or the reverse. Both may best be interpreted as phases of one process; as aspects of one cultural development. Our habit of dividing our activities into the two processes of discovering truth and then applying it, or of applying it and then doscovering it, rests upon abstractions from the actual process.

Scott, 1931/1973, 127

anything worth thinking about has consequences in the practical order and . . . anything in the practical order may suggest something that is worth thinking about.

Hutchins, 1953/1964, 63

A technique is an individually acquired and socially secured way of doing something; a science is a way of understanding how to do it in order to do it better.

Bernal, 1954/1969, I:47

In our historic era empirical science criticizes, augments and systematizes practical experience. The science of one generation becomes incorporated in the technology of the succeeding one. Science and practice cooperate in the adjustment of man to his environment.

Lenzen, 1955/1962, 281

The practical arts for a long time ran ahead of science; only in very recent years have scientific discoveries affected practice to a greater extent than practice has affected science.

Conant, 1964, 39

A theory may have a bearing on action either because it provides knowledge regarding the objects of action, e.g. machines, or because it is concerned with action itself, e.g. with the decisions that precede and steer the manufacture or use of machines . . . . Both are technological theories . . . . Looked at from a practical angle, technological theories are richer than the theories of science, in that, far from being limited to accounting for what may or does, did or will happen regardless of what the decision maker does, they are concerned with finding out what ought to be done in order to bring about, prevent or just change the pace of events or their course in a preassigned way. In a conceptual sense, the theories of technology are definitely poorer than those of pure science . . . because the practical man . . . wants to know how things within his reach can be made to work for him, rather than how things of any kind really are.

Bunge, 1967, II:122, 123

We can often say, of two explanations of a given phenomenon, that they are compatible but that one is more basic than the other, for it appeals to deeper level laws which themselves can be used to explain the laws invoked in the shallower account . . . . the stronger kind lays the basis for an advance in technology since, in showing the differences between outcomes, it also gives us information which can be used, if the techniques are available, to control the outcome . . . . It enables us also to bring about new, as yet nonexistent outcomes . . . .

Taylor, 1970, 52

893 Science and philosophy

Our [physical] theories have as their sole aim the economical condensation and classification of empirical laws; they are autonomous and independent of any metaphysical system .... [or] philosophical doctrine.

Duhem, 1914/1962, 219

most investigators prefer to say that pure science has nothing to do with ultimate philosophy. The purpose of science is to ascertain facts and its method is to determine relations and express them in equations .... Science solves the problems it sets itself by leaving the observer wholly outside the experiment and submitting its results to all observers. To the extent that there is a method, it is that of the open secret – each man closeted with nature but all invited to look.

Barzun, 1964, 85

philosophic isms are the grave of inquiry, for they have got all the answers, whereas research, either scientific or philosophic, consists of wrestling with problems rejecting dogmatic strictures.

Bunge, 1967, II:357

not one of those whom we recognize as great methodologists was a practising scientist himself. Francis Bacon was a lawyer and man of affairs .... John Stuart Mill was ... a political theorist and a sociologist in the modern sense .... William Whewell .... did not practice science nor add to it .... Karl Pearson was a mathematician; Stanley Jevons and John Maynard Keynes were economists; C S Peirce was, as Karl Popper is, a great philosopher.

Medawar, 1969, 9

Unless he has been got at by philosophy, the average bench scientist is quite prepared to swear that his branch of science is just commonsense.

Ziman, 1978, 124

894 Inquiry and practice

lookers-on many times see more than gamesters.

Bacon, 1625/1907, 147

Invention, though it can be cultivated, cannot be reduced to rule; there is no science which will enable a man to bethink himself of that which will suit his purpose. But when he *has* thought of something, science can tell him whether that which he has thought of will suit his purpose or not. The inquirer or arguer must be guided by his own knowledge and sagacity in the choice of the inductions out of which he will construct his argument. But the validity of the argument when constructed depends on principles and must be tried by tests which are the same for all descriptions of inquiries, whether the result be to give A an estate, or to enrich science with a new general truth.

Mill, 1865/1925, 186

Now, in order that a modification of historical consciousness may reach the mass, it must have previously influenced the choice minority. The members of the latter are of two classes: men of action and men of contemplative nature. There is no doubt that the new tendencies, not yet at their full strength, will be perceived by the contemplative natures earlier than by the active. The preoccupation of the moment prevents the man of action from feeling the first vague stirrings of the breeze that is not yet ready to fill the sails of his practical temperament. It is in the realm of pure thought, therefore, that the earliest faint signs of the coming age can be traced.

Ortega, 1931/1961, 26

Science, upon entering into a profession, must be detached from its place in pure science, to be organized upon a new center and a new principle, as professional technics.

Ortega, 1946/1963, 63

It is hard to master the intellectual content of a profession while one is practising it. The demands of active professional life are not favorable to study and reflection. On the other hand, universities are not well adapted to teaching the tricks of trades. And it is unwise for them to make the attempt.

Hutchins, 1953/1964, 39

Nobody in his senses would expect a born seer to *do*. That much is generally acknowledged. But it is equally ridiculous to suppose that a dashing and triumphant doer can really *see*. It must not be assumed that power and wisdom are the same thing.

Priestley, 1955

The advantage of the man over the child is an advantage of experience (in the sense of practice) and of education, and the scientist enjoys a similar advantage over the ordinary man. He has had practice in recognition and discrimination, and he has learned to classify and define. He is thus able to do what the ordinary man is quite incapable of doing in similar circumstances, namely to write down what he sees explicitly and unambiguously.

Caws, 1965, 73

The expertise of the scholar is primarily expertise at analysis. The elegance of scholarly results is measured by their public verifiability, their comprehensiveness, their simplicity. To achieve these goals, one must invest large amounts of time. In the world of action, however, elegance tends to elude one's grasp because time may be of the essence. The decision maker would like elegant analyses on which to act, but there is seldom time enough. The scholar must not become polarized by this difference into criticizing the man of action for sloppy analysis, nor the man of action into accusing the scholar of living in an ivory tower.

Brubacher, 1982, 24

See also 954

900 ACCOUNTING BELIEFS AND KNOWLEDGE

910 Accounting Practices, Procedures and Rules

911 Accounting procedures said to be based on practical considerations or opinions

One of the unfortunate things about the profession of accountancy is the absence of any supreme tribunal which can pass on questions about which there is an honest difference of opinion, and can render a decision which will be binding on individual practitioners . . . . it is left to each individual to be a law unto himself, and the result is a mass of conflicting opinions on many subjects, each one of which receives its value principally from the reputation of the person holding it, or the more or less convincing way in which he can express it.

Walton, 1909, 452

In one important respect bookkeeping differs from other sciences, in that it is not in the least theoretical, but essentially and fundamentally practical. It is based upon expediency, and upon the actual needs and requirements of everyday life.

Woolf, 1912, xxix

In accounting there is no person or academy whose pronouncement can be accepted as having unquestioned authority. Those who write on the subject must, in general, express opinions and formulate arguments rather than render decisions.

Hatfield, 1927/1971, viii

So-called principles of accounting are not of the same character as the fixed laws of the natural world but principles in the secondary sense of "rules adopted or professed as a guide to action", so that they are neither inevitable nor immutable, but depend for their right to continued recognition upon continued usefulness for the purposes for which accounts are mainly employed.

May, 1938, 8

We are a very young profession . . . . the profession developed upon purely individualistic lines. Each one of us, having passed our final examinations, went our several ways and built up our own individual code of principles.

de Paula, 1946, 39

See also 021, 713

912 Accounting principles said to be derived from experience

[Accountancy] can not function merely as a code of fixed rules, for it is constantly modified by the principles which are developed as a composite of the best and most enlightened business experience.

Andersen, 1935, 332

Initially, accounting rules are mere postulates derived from experience and reason. Only after they have proved useful, and become generally accepted, do they become principles of accounting.

AIA, 1940c, ARB7

The Committee on Accounting Procedure has emphasized the fact that accounting rules and principles are founded not on abstract theories or logic, but on utility.

May, 1942, 35

Good experience becomes accepted practice . . . . If the action (practice) is verbally associated with a justifying reason (theory), we have a framework of associated ideas which can readily be converted into a statement of an end or objective in association with a means of attaining that end. This form of statement of accounting ideas deserves the name "principle of accounting".

Littleton, 1953, 186

Financial statements are based on conventions derived from experience. These conventions represent the accountant's best efforts to meet recognized needs in the most useful manner.

AAA, 1957a/1957b, 2

Accounting principles are not laws in the sense of the laws of physics and chemistry. Rather they are broad rules for accounting action distilled from the best accounting practice and experience and adopted by the accounting profession as guides to its practice.

Pyle & White, 1966, 822

913 Rules and ritual

A rule to be useful should be simple – the more simple the rule the better it is; because it is to be applied by a person ignorant in the science. A rule should be devoid of exceptions; for where one exception is apparent, many more may exist undiscovered. A rule should not be an accidental coincidence, but an independent truth, and that truth self evident to common sense. In proportion as the number of rules, principles and divisions in a science is augmented, the memory becomes charged, and the reason discharged from the study. The less we depend on our rational faculties the more liable we are to err. When the rules are numerous, it is no small task to decide when to accept one as a guide or when to reject the same – which rule to use and which not to use.

Marsh, 1835/1988, 187

Between a mind of rules and a mind of principles, there exists a difference such as that between a confused heap of materials and the same materials organized into a complete whole, with all its parts bound together.

Spencer, 1861/1976, 49

In the manual arts, where the requisite conditions [of attaining a given end] are not numerous ... rules may often be safely acted upon by persons who know nothing more than the rule. But in the complicated affairs of life, and still more in those of states and societies, rules cannot be relied on without constantly referring back to the scientific law on which they are founded.

Mill, 1865/1925, 617

To discover that somebody or everybody accepts a certain rule is to discover an empirical fact. But no rule as such, is an empirical proposition, whether it is or is not accepted by anybody. Rules differ from empirical propositions, and, equally, from logical propositions such as entailments. A rule can be accepted, and then satisfied, or violated. Indeed only a rule can be so treated. An empirical or logical proposition cannot.

Körner, 1959, 5

the accountant must give some kind of an answer to the question "What profits have been earned?" .... on the basis of knowledge about the future which he cannot possibly have. Under these circumstances, it is not surprising that the economist regards much accounting procedure as in the nature of ritual. To call these procedures ritualistic is in no way to deny or decry their validity. Ritual is always the proper response when a man has to give an answer to a question, the answer to which he cannot really know. Ritual under these circumstances .... is comforting .... and it is also an answer sufficient for action.

Boulding, 1962, 53

The danger of ritual is that it may sometimes be too good a substitute for the solution of a problem and may actually prevent its solution. Ritual is fine for insoluble problems but it is very bad for soluble problems.

Boulding, 1963, 95

Conventions of many kinds, political, social and academic, many times serve more of a ritual function than the function of exchanging information or achieving some instrumental goal .... What is called a report may better serve as an incantation .... Three characteristics of most rituals are most important: the rituals must be performed with others (immediately or symbolically present); they must be performed on some occasion; and they must be performed with special care to details.

Condon, 1966, 103, 102

The principal [functional requisites of rules] are: 1. an indication of the circumstances in which the rule is applicable; 2. an indication of that which ought, or may, or must be, or not be, concluded or decided; 3. an indication of the type of inference contemplated, whether under the rule it is permitted, required or prohibited; 4. an indication that the statement is indeed designed to function as a rule or inference-warrant . . . . obscure or vague rules, no less than obscure road signs or faded maps, fail as tools for guidance. They evidently fail also when there are clearly contradictory rules or rules which it is impossible to follow.

Gottlieb, 1968, 39, 41

Rule is used here to mean a general prescription guiding conduct or action in a given type of situation . . . . (a) A rule is prescriptive, that is to say it is concerned with ought (not), may (not) or can (not), in relation to behavior, rather than with factual description of behavior. (b) A rule is general in that it is concerned with types of behavior in types of situation or circumstances; a prescription governing a unique event is not a rule. (c) Rules guide behavior, that is to say, activities, acts or omissions.

Twining & Miers, 1976, 48

rules tell us, very broadly, what to do, or how to act, in order to bring about certain objects or ends, either with regard to physical things, or with regard to ourselves, or with regard to other persons, especially where our actions impinge on them beneficially or detrimentally.

Stoljar, 1980, 1

An outstanding feature of normative (moral as well as legal) rules is that they are susceptible to, in fact even encourage, exceptions, quite unlike scientific or technical principles which describe or picture the world as it is, so that an exception would directly and falsifiably challenge this picture.

Stoljar, 1980, 115

[On statutory interpretation] A rule binds, but a principle guides . . . . If an enactment incorporates a rule, it makes that rule binding in relation to the purposes of the act. But if it attracts a principle it leaves scope for flexible application. The clue is given by this. General principles of law and public policy underlie and support the rules laid down by the whole body of legislation. If it were not so the rules would be merely arbitrary.

Bennion, 1984, 285

See also 261, 262, 844, 870

914 Accounting principles as rules

Accounting principles comprise at least all those rules, techniques, basic procedures or methods, and the broad principles of right and propriety in economic relations, both within the business unit and between the unit and outsiders, in accordance with which the accounting work of the business unit should be carried on.

Kester, 1946, 3

"A general law or rule adopted or professed as a guide to action; a settled ground or basis of conduct or practice" .... This ... comes nearest to describing what most accountants, especially practising public accountants, mean by the word principle.

AIA, 1940c, ARB7

In the opinion of accountants generally, accounting principles are not principles of nature but rules of human behavior. They are not inherent in nature to be discovered by man but are developed by man. They are, therefore, not immutable and they need to be changed to meet changing needs. They are designed for the greatest usefulness of those who need to rely upon accounting.

Blough, 1956, 1

Calling rules and procedures principles may be good packaging technique, but it may constitute a mislabeling of our product and lead to confusion in our development of accounting theory and in the minds of readers of audited financial reports.

Gaa, 1961, 47

Even such an apparently rational activity as accounting turns out upon examination to have large elements of ritual within it; the basic problems of the accountant are fundamentally insoluble, as they involve information about the future that is not accessible to him. A great deal of accounting technique, therefore, is an attempt to ensure that all accountants will come out with the same answer, whether it is the right answer or not.

Boulding, 1963, 95

The word "principles" may have certain philosophic overtones, but in accounting the so-called principles are in point of fact simply sound and safe rules drawn from the best commercial practice.

Ross, 1966, 33

The term, accounting principle, has been in use since the turn of the century and has been used variously, without much regard to precise definition, to denote both broad guidelines and detailed practices and procedures. It also suffers from the implication ... that it represents a universal and immutable law – which plainly is not appropriate to accounting.

Lee, 1975, 25

915 Practices described as accounting policies

the lack of uniformity of method in accounts . . . . is due not only to differences of accounting policy, but to differences of judgment about values. Much accounting is more a matter of judgment than of application of predetermined fixed standards.
Cole, 1921, 339

certain broad accounting policies, such as those referring to conservatism, disclosure, consistency, and materiality, ...
Gilman, 1939, 186

My dictionary defines the word, principle, as "a law or doctrine from which others are derived". That does not imply that in accounting our principles must be upon the most conservative basis. I think that in this connection there has been loose thinking and that we have intermixed accounting principles with financial policy. We are directly concerned with principles but the proprietors of a business are solely responsible for financial policy.
de Paula, 1947, 54

The only conceivable accounting policy is a policy of providing comprehensive and relevant information.
Chambers, 1964a, 185

Accounting policies are principles expanded and adapted to the needs of a particular organization . . . .
Kohler, 1965a, 11

Accounting policies are the specific accounting bases [methods for expressing or applying fundamental accounting concepts] selected and consistently followed by a business enterprise as being, in the opinion of the management, appropriate to its circumstances and best suited to present fairly its results and financial position.
ASSC, 1971b, SSAP2

The uncertainties which surround many business transactions should be recognized by the application of prudence in the selection of the particular accounting policies to be used.
NZSA, 1983, SSAP1

916 Diverse influences on accounting rules and procedures

Inconsistencies and fallacies in accounting are the results of indifference, vacillation, ignorance, expediency, casuistry or dishonesty of purpose. Indifference, vacillation or ignorance may produce either or both, but where expediency, casuistry or dishonesty of purpose govern, principle does not abide in accounting or other human activity, and the inevitable result is fallacy.
Dunn, 1916, 599

Every administrative body has a specific job to do, and serves a special interest. That is why it is there. Its views on accounting, accordingly, are conditioned by its desire to reach that result, rather than by any interest in the healthy growth of accounting as a whole . . . . There is always the danger, where accounting rules are made by specialized administrative tribunals, that the resulting body of doctrine may be lop-sided, if not positively dangerous.

Berle, 1938, 11

Accounting practices at present are based in a large measure upon the ethics and opinions of respectable accountants . . .

Sanders & others, 1938, xii

Accounting procedures have in the main been the result of common agreement between accountants, though they have to some extent, and particularly in recent years, been influenced by laws or regulations.

May, 1943, 3

administrative agencies have been a significant influence on the development of accounting during most of the last half century . . . . However, to the extent that they have curtailed freedom of thought on accounting matters or have forced accounting into outdated molds or have required observance of principles well suited for limited purposes but ill suited for most uses, their influence must be regarded as hurtful.

Werntz, 1953a, 95

As for relying on the income tax regulations to support accounting theory, this illogical and reprehensible practice has existed longer and has more influence than most accountants care to admit . . . . There is no logical reason, except that of convenience, for accounting income to equal taxable income. Accounting income should attempt to measure economic growth, or the lack of it, while the income tax computation is designed as a means of determining the amount of an immediate tax payment . . . . goals entirely foreign to accounting purposes, such as economic regulation and political favoritism . . . have important bearing on the content of the income tax laws.

Hylton, 1962, 23

There seems to be general agreement that the primary responsibility for the preparation and content of financial statements rests with the management of the issuing company. Yet the accounting profession, governmental agencies, and stock exchanges are prescribing accounting and reporting rules which must be followed by managements.

Catlett, 1970, 45

A set of accounting principles will not evolve as a natural process from the practices of the business community. The forces at work in that community, particularly on

the part of management, argue against constraints of any kind, including accounting rules.
Moonitz, 1970b, 64

Published accounts are a hotch potch. They contain a host of items which governments of one complexion or another have seen as desirable public knowledge . . . . which the stock exchange has decided companies ought to disclose . . . . [and] which [standards committees have] recommended should be disclosed.
Holmes, 1974c, 46

I believe that over the years the SEC, the academics, the issuers and the auditors have succumbed to the siren song of the users . . . . But designing a financial report that would substantially reduce the incidence of bad decisions is an impossible task and ignores the tremendous complexity of the decision making process and the vagaries of the future.
Olson, 1977, 71

917 Accounting development said to be evolutionary

"Brief history of the evolution of bookkeeping" [introduction]
Soulé, 1903/1976, 14

the first part of the book is a brief reconstruction of the long evolutionary struggle to devise and perfect a tool of expression and measurement – proprietary double entry bookkeeping.
Littleton, 1933/1966, preface

Financial accounting is still in the process of evolution. Out of a study and comparison of methods evolved in meeting varying needs in different fields, there should emerge principles, procedures, and forms of presentation that will make accounting in all fields more useful for the purposes which it is designed to serve.
AIA, 1946b, 440

To some extent, accounting will always be evolving to meet the needs of our society. However, reliance on evolution is frequently used as an excuse for not taking any significant action on a professional basis . . . . Evolution and usage do not guarantee progress.
Catlett, 1964, 39

As a result of many years of experience, there has evolved a body of general guides to accounting, referred to as generally accepted accounting principles.
Black & others, 1967, 12

[Some hold] that progress [in accounting] can be made only by evolution of practices through usage and acceptance and that improvements will emerge by the irresistible force of their desirability. Neither history nor human nature supports this line of reasoning. In fact, evolution does not produce such a result, and this is one of the reasons that so much government regulation exists today.

Catlett, 1969, 62

Although the term generally accepted accounting principles has been used for years, there is no official list of such principles. The reason is that accounting principles have evolved over the years.

Dearden & Shank, 1975, 187

918 Tradition

To explain a thing by tradition is a very easy matter; for among the many legends that exist or can be invented if necessary one can readily be found that, in view of some resemblance more or less distant, some accord of sentiments more or less vague can be made to fit the thing for which an "explanation" is sought. [#1447]

Pareto, 1916/1963, 918

Professions first appear as customary activities largely modified by detached strains of theory. Theories are often wrong; and some of the earlier professional doctrines erred grievously and were maintained tenaciously. Doctrines emerged as plausible deductions, and survived as the wisdom of ancestors. Thus the older professional practice was rooted upon custom, though it was turning towards the intellectual sunlight.

Whitehead, 1933/1948, 77

Traditional accounting has taken it [cost price] without reflection as the principal basis of balance sheet valuation. In the face of its many deficiencies . . . its dominant place in the balance sheet was not the result of the highest grade of reflective consideration but was rather due to more or less thoughtless imitation.

Schmidt, 1930, 239

Many accountants . . . follow the precedent of other accountants or the opinions of recognized authorities in whom they have confidence without reasoning the problem through to their own satisfaction. You all know how precedents of this kind may become established. An accountant has a peculiar situation that he thinks may best be treated by some digression from what he himself considers to be the best practice under normal circumstances. Again, a very positive and valued client has taken a position contrary to the accountant's best judgment but, in the particular case, the accountant, because he thinks the principle at stake is not sufficiently important to cause him to withdraw, accedes to the wishes of his client. After a few cases of this kind by reputable firms, some accountant, hurried in a job, accepts such precedent without giving careful thought to the problem. Subsequently, some textbook writer relates the practice as an example of a procedure followed in some instances and this is, in turn, cited by others in support of the practice. Thus a large body of precedent is established for a procedure that was firstly reluctantly undertaken as an exception.

Blough, 1937, 32

I believe that we have developed the habit of talking of practices as resting on historical or traditional bases when they have no such foundation, and, what is even more important, we have failed to recognize that a philosophy can be built up only by repeated critical examination of accepted postulates and traditions in the light of changing conditions.

May, 1950b, 45

The continued utilization of ideas with little or no conscious reference to their real merit, but with past usage being the basic force for continuation, is a prime requisite of a tradition.

Wyatt, 1956, 396

See also 205, 883, 884, 885

920 Guiding Dicta

921 An accounting viewpoint posited

income is the earning flowing from the work done; it is the consequence of a prior outlay made with intent to generate income. From the businessman's point of view, and hence the point of view also of accounting theory, the key to this doctrine is the word, intent.

Littleton, 1937, 58

It is the insistence upon these elements [the realization test for revenues, but not for costs and expenses] which distinguishes the accounting concepts of income and profit.

Gilman, 1939, 609

The words value and valuation are [here] used . . . in their accounting sense of the amount at which an item is stated. They do not necessarily relate to the worth of the item. [Research department]

AIA, 1941b, 296

uniformity in the treatment of other than routine transactions is not always attainable because there may be a question whether the resemblance or the difference between transactions is the more significant from an accounting standpoint.

May, 1943, 258

Accounting has considered its own logic and its own concepts as of greater importance than statutory permissions or requirements. It has adopted the consolidated statement of earnings for a parent and its subsidiary companies, in spite of the lack of legal support; it has its own concepts for distinguishing between earnings and capital; and, finally, is has emphasized fairness of presentation of earnings to avoid misleading inferences instead of a legal concept of earnings.

Bailey, 1948b, 690

The accountant . . . has sometimes regarded himself as not necessarily forming a part of the solar system. He is a thing apart, weaving spells and writing things in books, all on his own methods, evolved, some of them, in the fifteenth century, and he is inclined to think that what he says goes, in so far as his own art is concerned. The management should ensure, to my mind, that the accountant comes down to earth . . . . he should ensure, where accounting facts are presented, that they are presented with due regard to the facts of the real world outside.

Davison, 1950, 589

the Institute's correspondence with the New York Stock Exchange formally enunciated . . . for the first time, a basic principle or concept that had been well recognized for some time in accounting practice. For corporate accounting the measurement of income by a process of valuation was formally discarded in favor of the realization concept ["Unrealized profit should not be credited to income account . . . . Profit is deemed to be realized when a sale in the ordinary course of business is effected . . . ."] . . . . These concepts are so all pervasive in accounting practice that their expression may be regarded as a fundamental step in defining income from an accounting standpoint.

Broad, 1954, 583

there exists a fair amount of confusion relative to what an asset is from an accounting point of view.

Bierman, 1965, 33

From the accountant's point of view, since the enterprise is to be kept continuously alive for the greatest length of time, financial and accounting policies automatically dictate that everything done is to be directed towards maintaining such continuity of activity; in other words, a policy will be undertaken conducive to nourishing the business for as long as possible.

Yorston & others, 1965, I:12

Finally we get to the current practice of qualifying the [auditor's] declaration by referring to fair presentation "in accordance with generally accepted accounting principles consistently applied." . . . . Here we begin to encounter the concept of a distinctively accountant's view of profit and value – a view largely ritualistic.

Ross, 1966, 45, 46

In extant accounting . . . . Assets are expired costs . . . . Liabilities are credit balances . . . which do not refer to proprietorship. Hence, assets and liabilities are technical terms whose operational meaning in any particular case depends upon the particular methods used in matching costs and revenues, for they are the residuals of the process.

Whittred & Zimmer, 1988, 81

The appropriate measurement basis for an asset will depend upon the model of accounting being applied.

AARF & AASB, 1992, SAC4

922 Principles, and accounting principles

Nothing can be so dangerous as principles ... taken up without questioning or examination; .... If therefore those that pass for principles are not certain, ... but are only made so to us by blind assent, we are liable to be misled by them; and instead of being guided into truth, we shall, by principles, be only confirmed in mistake and error.

Locke, 1700/1979, IV:xii

If by principles we mean general propositions which may occasionally be applied to particular cases, who is without them? But on the other hand what merit is there in having them? They are indeterminate maxims, which we never learn justly to apply .... If ... we must have principles .... [it is implied] that we ought to have made a diligent study of particular truths, and to have ascended by different abstractions up to universal propositions .... To say that a man has such principles, is giving to understand that he has a thorough knowledge of the arts and sciences which he makes his study, and that in everything he proceeds with the utmost clearness and precision.

de Condillac, 1756, 73, 74

these arts [navigation, surveying, engineering and the like] depend for their certainty and success upon the truth of the rules whereby the several operations are performed; and the truth of the rules depends on the previous reasoning or science: these truths constitute what are called the principles of the science .... if we wish to make a learner understand, clearly and fully any ... rules ... we must begin by unfolding the principles upon which those rules are founded, the truths from which they are deduced.

Foster, 1843, 9

A principle may be defined as a fundamental truth used as a basis of reasoning; a convention is merely a generally accepted practice, which may or may not be based on reasoned analysis.

Fitzgerald, 1938, 103

Modern juristic analysis shows law operating through four distinct categories – principles, standards, concepts and rules. It is a *principle* of public policy that those who exercise a public calling should not take an unfair advantage of their position. One formulation of this principle is the *rule* that a common carrier must not charge more than a reasonable rate. This rule contains within itself a *concept* (common carrier) and also a *standard* (reasonable rate). A principle is the broad reason which lies at the basis of a rule of law; . . . .

Paton G W, 1946, 176

Accounting principles

It used to be not uncommon for the accountant who had been unable to persuade his client to adopt the accounting treatment that he favored, to urge as a last resort that it was called for by "accounting principles". Often he would have had difficulty in defining the "principle" and saying how, why, and when it became one. But the method was effective, especially in dealing with those (of whom there were many) who regarded accounting as an esoteric but well established body of learning and chose to bow to its authority rather than display their ignorance of its rules. Obviously, the word "principle" was an essential part of the technique; "convention" would have been quite ineffective.

May, 1943, 37

what has frequently been spoken of as accounting principles includes a conglomeration of accounting practices, procedures, policies, methods and conventions relating both to the construction of accounts and their presentation; and . . . there seems to be general agreement among the commentators that the difficulty of any attempt to formulate so-called principles or prescribed rules and regulations on accounting matters is that the field is so large and the conditions encountered so diverse that few, if any, sweeping generalizations can safely be adopted.

Byerly, 1937, 94

Accounting principles . . . are the fundamental concepts on which accounting, as an organized body of knowledge, rests. Like the axioms of geometry, they are few in number and general in terms; they possess the distinguishing characteristic of a compelling and coercive nature, and they are the foundation upon which the superstructure of accounting rules, practices and conventions is built.

Byrne, 1937, 372

The frank admission that there are no principles of accounting will leave the accounting profession in the more defensible position of being guided by general doctrines, specific conventions, and various rules, practices, methods, and standards derived from the relationship between accounting and other fields, which by the test of experience have been proved practical and reasonable. By such admission the accountant will be relieved of that embarrassment and awkwardness which results from trying to justify a proposition as a principle of accounting because it is based upon a principle of mathematics, or because it is derived from a principle of economics, or because it is required by statute or edict.

Gilman, 1939, 257

standardization of accounting principles . . . . What I have in mind as principles are those similarities between the financial statements of different companies that enable us . . . to speak of balance sheets and profit and loss statements as generic terms and . . . to expect that the reader of those statements will obtain the information we seek to convey without in each case first making a comprehensive and detailed study of all the methods and policies pursued in their preparation.

Werntz, 1939/1968, 440

Accounting principles can be defined if we stop trying to make accounting into a world of its own for a group of highly trained technicians and, instead, mold it into a tool to convey to the public salient and important facts which will serve them as a guide for establishing a course to follow.

Spacek, 1958c, 44

First, . . . accounting principles are not comparable with those in the natural sciences, in that they cannot be established by laboratory experimentation. Secondly, [they] are not determined by law or by government directive, nor should they be . . . . They must be developed in harmony with the assumptions and doctrines of accounting and the logical reasoning which considers the requirements and objectives of all parties . . . . Thirdly, accounting principles are deductive reasoning on which practices are based. They are the source rather than the result of accounting practices.

Dilley, 1960, 544

principles of accounting must be established by reasoning.

Spacek, 1964a, 282

See also 943

Dicta or ideas described as principles

the broad principles to be laid down . . . should be few in number . . . . Presumably the list would include . . . . 1. Unrealized profit should not be credited to income account . . . . 2. Capital surplus, however created, should not be used to relieve the income account . . . . 3. [Preacquisition] earned surplus of a subsidiary company . . . does not form a part of the consolidated earned surplus . . . . 4. [Dividends on treasury stock] . . . should not be treated as a credit to the income account . . . . 5. Notes or accounts receivable from officers, employees or affiliated companies must be shown separately . . . . [Exhibit I]

AIA, 1932

a statement [of accounting principles] would include: (1) Accounting is essentially the allocation of historical costs and revenues to . . . fiscal periods. (2) The investment in . . . plant should be charged against operations over the useful life of the plant . . . . (4) The income shall include only realized profits . . . . (5) Losses, if probable, even though not actually incurred, should be provided for in arriving at net income . . . . (8) While it is not in many cases of great importance which of several alternative accounting rules is applied in a given situation, it is essential that, once having adopted a certain procedure, it be consistently adhered to in preparing the accounts over a period of time.

Byrne, 1937, 372

It seems to me that principles are few; perhaps, at most, five in number . . . . the familiar idea of double entry . . . . the unit of organized activity . . . . the standpoint of continuing entities . . . . accounting methods must be consistently employed . . . . a formal principle of accounting design which is expressed by a set of fundamentally related accounts . . . .

Bray, 1953, 4

Principles – matching principle . . . . revenue recognition principle . . . . expense recognition principle . . . . seem the most fundamental.

Dilley, 1960, 544

principles or guidelines that the accountant follows in recording transaction data . . . . (1) the historical cost principle, (2) the revenue realization principle, (3) the matching principle, (4) the consistency principle, (5) the full disclosure principle, and (6) the objectivity principle.

Kieso & Weygandt, 1974, 25

The business entity principle . . . . The continuity or going concern principle . . . .The monetary principle . . . .The revenue realization principle . . . . The cost principle . . . . the matching principle . . . . The objectivity principle . . . . The consistency principle . . . . The disclosure principle . . . .

Meigs & others, 1978, 13ff

[The UK *Companies Act 1985*] specifies four fundamental accounting principles . . . . the going concern assumption, consistency in application of accounting policies, prudence, and the accruals principle.

Whittington, 1989b, 155

923 Accounting doctrines

it is legitimate to adopt "doctrine" as referring to a general statement of accounting or reporting policy as evidenced by the words materiality, disclosure, conservatism and consistency . . . .

Gilman, 1939, 186

A doctrine is a belief, deliberately taught or promulgated. As applied to accounting records, it is a method or rule laid down by instructors and others as to what a particular practice should be, and how it should be done; . . . .

Reid (ed), 1956, 6

an accounting doctrine is a belief that a given practice should be followed . . . . a dogma inculcated by teachers of accounting, textbook writers or authoritative associations of accountants.

Fitzgerald, 1956a, 8

Within the framework of assumptions there exist several taught or recommended conformities which are thought to be desirable policies in keeping accounts and preparing financial statements. These conformities, called doctrines, serve as a guide to the manner in which principles and rules should be applied in accounting practice . . . . doctrines are advocated policies as to how to record and report accounting data.

Dilley, 1960, 542

There is also [beside conventions] a group of concepts which apply more to attitudes of mind in carrying the [accounting] process into effect. They are usually referred to as doctrines, because they are based on a normative or ethical belief as to what is right, thus differing somewhat in emphasis from the more practical expediency expressed in the conventions.

Carrington & Battersby, 1963, 45

Dicta described as doctrines

there are four doctrines of accounting . . . . conservatism . . . . consistency . . . . disclosure . . . . materiality . . . .

Gilman, 1939, 231

The accounting doctrines . . . [include] . . . disclosure . . . . consistency . . . . conservatism . . . . materiality . . . . matching costs with income . . . .

Reid (ed), 1956, 7

Doctrines . . . . conservatism . . . . consistency . . . . verifiable, objective evidence . . . . full disclosure . . . . materiality . . . .

Dilley, 1960, 542

The doctine of conservatism . . . . of disclosure . . . . of consistency . . . . of materiality . . . . of objectivity . . . . of comparability . . . . of economy . . . .

Carrington & Battersby, 1963, 45ff

The most important doctrines . . . are conservatism, consistency, materiality and fair disclosure.

Anderson & others, 1974, 293

924 Accounting said to be conventional

For commercial purposes, . . . assets are valued according to certain conventional rules, and the profit or loss arrived at in this way is considered sufficiently near and accurate for ordinary business purposes . . . .

de Paula, 1914, 70

balance sheets are necessarily to a large extent historical and conventional in character . . . .

AIA, 1932

accounting is necessarily in large part conventional, . . . accounts are required for many different purposes, and . . . the same conventions are not equally appropriate for all the different purposes for which accounts are required.

May, 1940, 15

As a language, accounting is essentially conventional in nature, a body of convention rather than of logic. A convention is a practice that rests for its usefulness on its general acceptance.

Cannon, 1955, 60

Financial statements are based on conventions derived from experience. These conventions represent the accountant's best efforts to meet recognized needs in the most useful manner.

AAA, 1957a/1957b, 2

Earnings [in accounting] . . . are based on conventions . . . .

AICPA, 1973, 22

the belief that most of the difficulties with respect to financial reporting stem from our failure to establish a basic set of principles or a conceptual framework of accounting [is a myth]. This notion that there are certain basic truths which await our discovery overlooks the fact that financial accounting standards are simply conventions derived from experience and through general acceptance.

Olson, 1977, 69

See also 263, 918

Conventions and accounting conventions

general agreement, tacit understanding, common or general consent are common elements of a convention . . . . In reasonable accord with [this] is the use of the word convention in accounting.

Gilman, 1939, 184

A convention is something which, although it may be widely or even universally recognized as a basis for procedure, is nevertheless really a more or less arbitrary creation of manmade conditions . . . . accounting conventions . . . . represent axioms or assumptions underlying and pervading the accounting procedures.
Goldberg, 1948, 235

A convention is a customary rule, regulation or requirement that is more or less arbitrarily established by common consent or tacit understanding.
Littleton, 1953, 142

A convention of accounting is an accounting practice based on general understanding that the practice should be followed.
Fitzgerald, 1956a, 8

Convention – A statement or rule of practice which, by common consent, express or implied, is employed in the solution of a given class of problems, or guides behavior in a certain kind of situation.
Kohler, 1952, 118

One may . . . at least suggest the possibility that the basically subjective origin of these conventions has been lost sight of and that they have become dogma not because of any inherent validity but simply because of general and continued usage.
Ladd, 1963, 41

[In accounting discourse] the term, convention, is applied to statements of fact, to statements contrary to fact, to conclusions from argument, and to propositions of other kinds. Looseness of this kind can only mean that what is designated as a convention is itself quite arbitrarily determined. Without pure rote learning and indoctrination one cannot know what "accounting convention" means.
Chambers, 1964a, 184

all sciences have need for some conventions, but these are relatively unimportant matters. For example, an inch is defined by convention to be a certain length. It could have just as easily been defined as some other length, and that fact is what makes it a relatively unimportant matter. The selection of a particular convention is an arbitrary choice. Therefore, conventions are things that are decreed, not debated . . . . Although arbitrary, conventions, once decreed, must be followed consistently.
Sterling, 1975b, 30

We prefer to use the term, accounting conventions [rather than accounting principles, postulates of accounting, accounting concepts or accounting standards], so as to stress that the ground rules of financial accounting are not the subject of immutable law, but are based on consensus . . . . [and] to underline the freedom which accountants have enjoyed in determining their own rules.
Glautier & Underdown, 1976, 56

A convention is something which depends for its force on a wide measure of popular acceptance, so that truth according to this or that convention is *ex hypothesi* a departure from absolute truth. In such circumstances, continuing references to "a true and fair view" tend to import a misleading semblance of certainty into a number of grey areas which are inevitably matters of judgment.

Accountant, editorial, 1978, 301

Dicta or ideas described as conventions

There are . . . certain conventions which are well known and are generally admitted to represent fundamental assumptions . . . . the entity [as the subject of accounts] . . . . valuation . . . . accounting period . . . . [and] other conventions which are commonly accepted and seldom questioned.

Gilman, 1939, 245ff

[Accounting conventions include] entity convention . . . . continuity convention . . . . accounting period convention . . . . valuation or monetary convention . . . . cost convention . . . . historical record convention . . . . multiple personality convention . . . .

Goldberg, 1948, 235

the accounting conventions are . . . the entity convention . . . . the historical record convention . . . . the constant money value convention . . . . the equities or algebraic convention . . . . the continuity of activity or going concern convention . . . . the accounting period convention . . . . the arithmetic convention . . . .

Reid (ed), 1956, 4

The valuation convention . . . . entity convention . . . . accounting period convention . . . . historical cost convention . . . . constant money value convention . . . . continuity or going concern convention . . . . compliance with legal requirements convention . . . .

Carrington & Battersby, 1963, 41ff

Accounting conventions . . . . the implicit assumption that the real value or purchasing power of the monetary unit remains constant . . . . an accounting period . . . . the business as a going concern . . . . [prudence, i.e.] Any bias in . . . estimates should be in the direction of understating profits and generally of not putting too optimistic an interpretation on the facts.

Beacham, 1964, 12

Among these [generally accepted] conventions are the following: . . . the business entity . . . . the entity a going concern . . . . matching of costs and revenues . . . . verifiable objective evidence . . . . a stable monetary unit . . . . conservatism . . . . intertemporal consistency . . . . periodical accounting . . . . materiality . . . . revenue realization.

Bierman, 1965, 3

14 basic conventions .... enforceable private property rights .... business entity .... going concern .... monetary .... accounting period .... consistency .... historical cost .... realization .... matching of costs and revenues .... dual aspect .... reliability of evidence .... disclosure .... conservatism .... materiality ....

Hawkins, 1971, 57ff

Principal conventions of generally accepted accounting principles – business entity .... going concern or continuity .... acccounting period .... monetary valuation .... cost as economic significance .... cost cohesion .... constant value of money .... historical record .... historical cost ....

Tilley, 1975, 191

... entity .... money measurement .... going concern .... cost .... realization .... accrual .... matching .... periodicity .... consistency .... conservatism ....

Glautier & Underdown, 1976, 58ff

The entity convention .... going concern convention .... monetary convention .... consistency .... diversity .... conservatism .... objectivity .... materiality .... accounting period ....

Henderson & Peirson, 1983, 77ff

925 Accounting postulates, assumptions, axioms

Axiom: A general statement the truth of which is not questioned; a postulate; a principle which is itself incapable of proof but is assumed to be true in order to proceed with or test the consistency of a line of reasoning .... Since by definition axioms are not directly examined or criticized for their truth value, the critical study of axioms is directed at their consistency, independence, completeness and fecundity .... In an applied field, such as accounting, the axioms are identical with propositions which belong equally to other disciplines .... [such as] (a) an economic unit has an identity apart from other economic units; (b) the life of a typical economic unit extends indefinitely into the future; (c) ....

Kohler, 1952, 43

Postulates are few in number and are the basic assumptions on which principles rest .... A fairly broad set of coordinated accounting principles should be formulated on the basis of the postulates.

AICPA, 1958, 63

Assumptions are the postulates or suppositions which are generally taken for granted without proof; they outline the basic framework within which accounting functions.

Dilley, 1960, 545

The reason we need to agree upon the postulates and principles of accounting is to provide a unifying and internally consistent logical basis for financial statements.

We need to narrow the areas of difference in reporting on similar events. We need assurance that what appears in the statements reflects real occurrences in the business entity and not simply changes or differences in accounting technique.

Cannon, 1962, 42

the entity or going concern assumption, the basic equation of assets and equities, the matching of costs and revenues, the assumption of a stable measuring unit, the realization assumption, etc. are some well known axioms of accounting.

Spencer, 1963, 312

Dicta or ideas described as assumptions or postulates

The postulates of accounting . . . . the business entity . . . . the going concern . . . . the balance sheet equation . . . . financial condition and the balance sheet . . . . cost gives actual value for purposes of initial statement . . . . value [of inputs] attaches to the result . . . . costs accrue . . . . sequences . . . .

Paton, 1922/1962, 471ff

Perhaps the three most fundamental postulates of accounting presently accepted are: 1. that the entire income from sale arises at the moment when realization is deemed to take place; 2. that fluctuations in value of the monetary unit . . . may properly be ignored; 3. that in the absence of actual evidence to the contrary, the prospective life of the enterprise may be deemed to be indefinitely long.

May, 1950a, 387

The basic assumptions of the theory relating to accounting are . . . 1. The firm or business exists to earn income. 2. The firm is a continuous entity (intends to live indefinitely). 3. The future is uncertain.

Morgan, 1953, 23

Assumptions . . . . business entity . . . . going concern . . . . accounting period . . . . monetary valuation . . . . cost as economic significance . . . . cost cohesion . . . . constant value of monetary unit . . . .

Dilley, 1960, 540

Basic postulates . . . . A. The environment . . . . quantification . . . . exchange . . . . entities . . . . time period . . . . unit of measure . . . . B. The field of accounting . . . . financial statements . . . . market prices . . . . entities . . . . tentativeness . . . . C. The imperatives . . . . continuity . . . . objectivity . . . . consistency . . . . stable unit . . . . disclosure . . . .

Moonitz, 1961, *passim*

some of the postulates or assumptions which might form the theoretical framework for the currently existing accounting [income measurement] model . . . . matching

875

costs and revenues .... entity concept .... going concern postulate .... concept
of the accounting period .... monetary postulate .... recognition postulate ....
Spiller, 1964, 852ff

The framework of traditional accounting is based on a number of assumptions.
Among others .... 1. A profit motive .... 2. A rational management .... 3. Cost
is a reasonable and objective measure of value at acquisition .... 4. The existence
of a profit plan ....5. Continuity [of the firm] .... 6. Experience has a tendency
to be repeated ....
Mobley, 1967, 114

fundamental accounting asssumptions: (a) going concern .... (b) consistency ...
[of accounting policies] from one period to another. (c) accrual ....
IASC, 1974, IAS1

Four basic assumptions that seem to underlie the financial accounting structure are
(1) an economic entity assumption, (2) a going concern assumption, (3) a monetary
unit assumption, and (4) a periodicity assumption.
Kieso & Weygandt, 1974, 22ff

926 Dicta or ideas described as basic concepts or features

Underlying the conventions of accounting are a number of concepts: business entity,
enterprise continuity, money measurement, and realization.
AAA, 1957a/1957b, 2

Basic accounting concepts .... The business unit (entity) .... The going concern
.... Stable monetary unit .... The cost concept .... Periodic matching of cost and
revenue ....
Malchman & Slavin, 1961, 20

There are seven basic concepts in accounting .... modified by three conventions.
The concepts are – the business entity .... money as a common denominator ....
the cost concept .... the going concern concept .... the dual aspect concept ....
the accrual concept .... the realization concept .... [The conventions are] conservatism .... consistency .... materiality ....
Garbutt (ed), 1969, 0101ff

The basic features of financial accounting .... are: accounting entity .... going
concern .... measurement of economic resources and obligations .... time periods
.... measurement in terms of money .... accrual .... exchange price .... approximation .... judgment .... general purpose financial information .... fundamentally related financial statements .... substance over form .... materiality ....
AICPA, 1970c, APBS4

Nine basic concepts underlying generally accepted accounting principles . . . . business entity . . . . going concern . . . . historical dollar accounting . . . . realization . . . . use of estimates and exercise of judgment . . . . consistency between periods for the same entity . . . . diversity of accounting among independent entities . . . . conservatism . . . . materiality . . . .

Coleman, 1970, 13ff

Fundamental accounting concepts are here defined as broad basic assumptions which underlie the periodic financial statements of business enterprises. It is expedient to single out for special mention four in particular: the going concern concept . . . . the accruals concept . . . . the consistency concept . . . . the prudence concept. . . .

ASSC, 1971b, SSAP2

Basic theoretical concepts in managerial accounting . . . . separate entity . . . . going concern . . . . right to private property . . . . reliability of data . . . . monetary expression . . . . cost basis . . . . realization . . . . conservatism . . . . matching of costs and revenues . . . . consistency . . . . materiality . . . . timeliness and estimates . . . . capital/income distinction . . . . impartiality . . . . dual effects – double entry . . . . form and substance . . . .

Flegm, 1984, 32ff

927 Diversity of description of dominant ideas

Instead of repeating the trite but, eminently pertinent quotation from Humpty Dumpty regarding the meaning of words, I quote a somewhat less familiar authority, Mr Dooley. In his description of expert testimony in the Luetgert case, he reports the expert as testifying: I made lab'ratory experiments in an i'r'n basin with bichloride of gool, which I will call soup stock, an' coal tar, which I will call i'r'n filings. I then packed it in ice which I will call glue, an' rock-salt which I will call fried eggs an' obtained a dark queer solution which is a cure f'r freckles which I will call antimony, or doughnuts or anny thing I blamed please.

Somewhat similarly the [AAA] Committee on Principles might almost say: I put in a much disputed dictum [valuation of property at cost] which I will call a fundamental axiom, then I added twenty unrelated statements which I call corollaries an' obtained a dark queer solution of accounting problems which I will call a Tentative Statement, which is a cure for all accounting difficulties, which I will call rules, or principles, or a hodge-podge of unrelated values of no explicable significance, or anny thing I blamed please.

Hatfield, 1937, unpubl

With sublime disregard of lexicography, accountants speak of principles, tenets, doctrines, rules and conventions as if they were synonymous.

Gilman, 1939, 169

In these fields [accounting and business law] there are no principles, in the more fundamental sense of that word, on which we can build; and the distinctions between laws, rules, standards, and conventions lie not in their nature but in the kind of sanctions by which they are enforced.

May, 1943, 3

Terms such as axiom, postulate, principle, standard, procedure, canon, and rule, among others, are widely used, but with no general agreement as to their precise meaning.

Moonitz, 1961, 1

the failure to define precisely a term as basic as "principles" is, of course, related to the larger problem of terminology. Accountants have been extremely careless in this matter, and the situation has degenerated to such a state that it is doubtful whether accountants really understand each other. The formulation of a set of precise terms is a prerequisite to development in any field of endeavor. Until it is accomplished, accounting will be hamstrung.

Storey, 1964, 62

the writer has come across the following [words used with the same meaning as principles]: assumptions, axioms, canons, concepts, conventions, criteria, descriptions, doctrines, facts of life, hypotheses, maxims, objectives, premises, postulates, practices, precepts, propositions, requirements, tenets, theorems.

McMonnies, 1967, 74

Textbooks refer variously to accounting principles, postulates of accounting, accounting concepts and accounting standards to describe those basic points of agreement on which accounting theory and practice are founded.

Glautier & Underdown, 1976, 56

In [a] broad sense, rule is a term for the genus of which precepts, regulations, rules of thumb, conventions, principles, guiding standards and even maxims are examples.

Twining & Miers, 1976, 49

The first sentence of the explanatory note to SSAP2 says : "In accounting usage terms such as accounting principles, practices, rules, conventions, methods or procedures have often been treated as interchangeable". That is very true, and it is a great pity. If our thinking was woolly enough to treat all these terms as being virtually synonymous, it is hardly surprising that we did not communicate successfully with people outside the profession.

Slimmings, 1981, 19

930 Variance, Flexibility and Conflict of Principles

931 The mutability and flexibility of principles

Accounting rules or principles must be flexible and in continuous process of evolution.
JA, editorial, 1938, 92

Accounting ... should be adaptable, but not to the extent of serving one set of interests at the expense of another, nor to the extent of being unintelligible to the reader not acquainted with the specific adaptations used. Rules and standards should not be rigid nor be regarded as ends in themselves, but enough stability should be preserved in accounting conventions so that the reasonably informed reader will be able to find his way about and will not feel that he is lost in a strange house.
Wilcox & Hassler, 1941, 312

accounting conventions [are to be considered], not as something fixed and unalterable, but as something that, like the law, should have elements of stability and of flexibility.
May, 1943, 9

Action in accounting does not rest on immutable laws.
Littleton, 1953, 170

"You know, Mr Rearden, there are no absolute standards. We can't go by rigid principles, we've got to be flexible, we've got to adjust to the reality of the day and act on the expediency of the moment."

"Run along, punk. Go and try to pour a ton of steel without rigid principles on the expediency of the moment."
Rand, *Atlas shrugged*, 1959, 343

one of the fundamental reasons for advocating flexibility [during the 1930s] was to facilitate catering by the accountants to client needs. The rationale of the accountants was highly compatible with the interests of their clients – and, therefore, with their own interests as well. It is a rationale that explains much of the tenacity with which the accounting profession traditionally fights any challenge to the notion of flexibility in the application of accounting principles.
Chatov, 1975, 173

932 Rules said to be subject to exceptions and variations in application

It is common for works on bookkeeping to be free from any thing like rational instruction or explanation .... they embrace many rules, principles, divisions and classifications; but it can easily be shown that the rules are encumbered with numberless exceptions, that the principles are entirely imaginary and do not exist in the subject; and that the classifications are entirely useless in the study or practice, and afford not the least assistance to the learner, but rather tend to confuse and disgust him.

> Marsh, 1835/1988, 187

The accountant . . . should always have in mind the possibility of there being exceptions to even the best established rules. Accountancy is essentially a profession of common sense and good business judgment, which should be exercised, of course, with constant regard to accounting principles and sound financial and legal theories . . . but which should never attach to theories so much weight as to enforce them at the sacrifice of substantial justice.

> May, 1906, 32

The existence of a body of generally accepted accounting principles does not mean that there is only one proper accounting treatment for every situation with which the accountant must deal. For many situations there are available a number of treatments which are in accord with generally accepted principles . . . . it is not the essential nature of a principle to forbid all courses of action save one . . . .

> Sanders & others, 1938, 5

principle, as applied to accounting rules of practice, . . . does not connote a law of that high order from which there is no appeal. An accounting principle is not a principle in the sense that it admits of no . . . conflict with other principles.

> AIA, 1940c, ARB7

While objective standards, and not the opinion of the individual, are thus the deciding factor, there nevertheless still remains ample scope for the exercise of professional judgment; in determining, for example, what principle or standard applies in particular circumstances where a choice is possible; or in deciding the manner or extent to which it is to be applied.

> Broad, 1944, 186

933 Conflicts of principle, doctrine and convention

Conservatism often conflicts with the convention of the going concern. This occurs when values are so conservatively stated as to make them equivalent to liquidation values . . . . Conservatism also may conflict with the doctrine of disclosure . . . . Conservatism is opposed to consistency, this conflict being particularly evident in the effect of the cost or market rule on earnings. Conservatism also conflicts with that desirable but often unattainable accounting ideal of matching costs with income.

> Gilman, 1939, 235

a philosophy of accounting which treats values created altogether differently from exactly similar values acquired by purchase is in need of revision.

> May, 1957, 35

A profit should not be anticipated [in valuing inventories] .... In some businesses it may be appropriate to use special bases, including some which depart from the rule that profit should not be anticipated.

ICAEW, 1960, N22

In any practical art there is a continual clash between the three guiding aims of objectivity (or certainty), significance (or relevance) and simplicity. In financial accounting ... objectivity is .... of utmost if not prime importance, and simplicity is also an acknowledged goal. But in managerial accounting, ... relevance or significance will be the major goal and hence techniques and concepts which depend to a greater extent on subjective opinion may be and are selected. Thus reports prepared for a particular purpose are likely to have limitations if required or used for any other purpose: ....

Johnston, 1961, 32

accounting principles ... sometimes conflict with each other. For example, conservatism predicates the use of the cost principle, despite the fact that, during inflation, market values may yield a much more accurate picture of a firm's assets. Consistency, as a principle, requires that the same method of accounting be used from period to period, even though recurring errors in estimating depreciation, and so forth, ought to be corrected under the principle of full disclosure.

Corbin, 1964, 241

there is a fundamental conflict between the criterion of objectivity and the criterion of usefulness.

Anthony, 1966, 261

It is possible for accounting information to possess high degrees of relevance and verifiability and yet be biased in favor of some parties and detrimental to others. This bias may result from use of inappropriate techniques or it may be of a personal nature.

AAA, 1966, 11

The depreciation method which a firm chooses should meet the general criteria of objectivity, usefulness, and feasibility. Unfortunately, these criteria are often competitive rather than complementary. Sometimes the accounting method which would be most useful to statement readers in appraising business performance and planning future action is not sufficiently objective to be dependable. Likewise, it may not be practicable to obtain useful or objective accounting information.

Black & others, 1967, 506

One of the dilemmas facing the APB or any other organization which tries to develop improved accounting principles is the problem of usefulness vs verifiability. Since the AICPA committees, government agencies, and stock exchanges have generally been influenced by enforcement problems and the possible danger of abuses, verifiability has tended to win out over usefulness .... continued adherence to the cost basis and many of the realization rules may be more influenced by verifiability than by usefulness in meeting today's needs.

Catlett, 1969, 64

934 Terminological propriety

to collate and arrange accounting words and phrases and show in connection with each the varying usages to which they are put .... This committee will not attempt to determine the correct or even the preferable usage where more than one is in existence. [Charge to a special committee on accounting terminology of the American Association of Public Accountants (AAPA), precursor of the AICPA]

AAPA, 1909/1972, 112

The undertaking of American accountants to give uniformity to the meaning of the technical terms they employ in their profession is laudable.

Gerstenberg, 1910, 201

accounting terminology is marked by the following defects:- (a) a lack of uniformity in the sense in which similar or like words or terms are used by different accountants or by different schools of accountants; (b) a professional use – or misuse – of words and terms in a sense which is foreign to the accepted connotation of those words and terms in everyday speech; (c) the use of several different terms to express the same idea, many of the terms containing words which have been coined with little respect for philological principles; and generally (d) a lack of precision in the use of language.

Fitzgerald, 1936, 133

an improved terminology is always to be desired; a mere change in terminology may bring new problems without solving the old ones.

Moonitz & Staehling, 1952, II:121

uniformity of meaning of words and numbers used in accounting is essential.

AAA, 1966, 13

Many of the problems of accounting theory could be ... dissolved if only we took the trouble to define our terms more precisely.

Walters, 1967, 198

[In the case of a contract] if it is unambiguously clear what each task and each payment is to be, and if one of the parties does not invoke methods of imposing his will on the other party which are foreign to the contract itself, then the determination of whether the bargain is equitable may safely be left to the judgment of the two contracting parties. If it is manifestly inequitable, at least one of the contracting parties may be supposed to be in the position of being able to reject the bargain altogether. What, however, they cannot be expected to settle with any justice among themselves is the meaning of a bargain if the terms employed have no established significance, ...

Wiener, 1950/1954, 106

See also 852

Terminological inexactitude in discourse

It is a singular and unaccountable fact, that there are in the various old systems of bookkeeping, many terms and forms of expression that are never used, and are even unknown, in the language of commercial intercourse.

Marsh, 1835/1988, 188

The ancient misfortune which bequeathed us this term, depreciation, is responsible for much of the maltreatment of this cost. This has happened because depreciation ostensibly connotes diminution of value. Whilst most accountants do in fact regard it as amortization of cost, accounting practice has been colored by considerations of value changes . . . . by depreciation the accountant does not mean what he says; he uses the word in a special sense and does not normally (at least consciously) connect it with value fluctuation.

Norris, 1945a, 103

The accountant's definitions are unbelievably fuzzy. Typically, he does not have a clear cut conception of the nature of the income he attempts so obstinately to measure.

Devine, 1951, 60

Our accounting profession has been in the habit of employing ostensibly descriptive adjectives – one is tempted to say – *ad nauseam* . . . . acceptable, adequate, advantageous, appropriate, desirable, material, meaningful, permissible, practicable, preferable, proper, rational, realistic, reasonable, significant, sound, systematic, useful . . . . fair and logical . . . . in their ordinary undefined use by accountants they are freely interchangeable . . . . purely decorative in their effect.

Kohler, 1965b, 38

This ["accounting principles"] . . . is an example of using an expression which sounds as if it means something of weighty import and in fact means virtually nothing. Its origin is wholly transatlantic, but it has been taken up and bandied about all over the world, meaning in the mouth of each utterer exactly what he wants it to mean.

McMonnies, 1967, 73

If [by the term, depreciation] we mean allocation of cost, let us say so; if we mean loss of value or intend to convey some notion of replacement, let us use phrases which will convey our meaning and our intention; if we mean physical deterioration, let us be specific in our expression. Let us excise depreciation from the

883

vocabulary of accounting, except perhaps in the context of purchasing power, where there is an economic rather than an accounting usage of the word.

Goldberg, 1969, 664

terms of convenience are by no means unusual in accounting language . . . . [There are] capital expenditure, revenue expenditure and the no man's land called deferred revenue expenditure . . . . [There are] assets which are neither fixed nor current and items which are neither monetary nor nonmonetary . . . .

Woolf, 1974, 106

Our trouble as accountants is that we allow ourselves to be taken up by the latest catchword and do not stop to ask ourselves what misunderstandings we are introducing to the future by using loose and inaccurate language.

Coad, 1977, 466

As the definition has broadened [from a narrow legal orientation to a broader concept of economic resources], the boundary around what is and what is not an asset has become hazy and ambiguous.

Wolk & others, 1984, 266

Obscurity in financial communications

[In accounting] the ordinary language of the market place has been used in senses the market place knew not of, and in senses varying with different accountants.

Hatfield, 1927b, 271

Stockholders and the public are generally untrained in accounting technicalities and cannot be expected to understand and interpret highly technical statements. One of the areas requiring great improvement is that of preparing stockholders' reports with a view to avoiding the criticism of unintelligibility and ambiguity now current.

Porter & Fiske, 1935, 197

No greater criticism can be levelled against the professional accountant than the widely held view that accounts presented in double entry form are incomprehensible to any except the expert.

Accountant, Anon, 1939, 255

Much effort had . . . been expended in seeking correct or sound accounting principles. Correct and sound, however, have a way of adapting themselves to the objectives their users have in mind . . . . The interests of the public investor . . . have in many cases been accorded only slight weight.

Werntz, 1939/1968, 435

What accountant is not familar with the questions of the uninstructed layman who wants to know why it is that capital is a liability and why revenue deficiency is an asset? .... these questions reveal that the terms liability and asset as unqualified [balance sheet] headings are defective.

Bray & Sheasby, 1944/1949, 3

Unless accounting terminology is going to wind up in the madhouse, it would seem to me imperative that public accountants, bankers, controllers, and public relations men get together on the study of the whole problem of the semantics of financial reports, and arrive at a new terminology .... We need words that will mean the same thing to the CPA, the truck driver, the steel worker, and the controller .... words that no union organizer, no political leader, no prophet of a new economic panacea, can distort or misuse.

Knowlton, 1947, 366

When accountants' terminology loses touch with common meaning it becomes at best a verbal exercise and at worst meaningless doubletalk. [Chairman, SEC]

Caffrey, 1948, 225

[The consequence of following the provisions of the *Companies Act, 1948*] is often an elaboration of particulars, as well as a mass of explanatory notes, which, while of great value to the expert, ... cannot readily be assimilated or understood by those lacking an expert knowledge of accounting methods.

Alban, 1949b, 139

To the average investor or creditor – the man on the Clapham omnibus – they [accounts in general and those of companies in particular] are cryptograms which he is incapable of solving.

Gower, 1954, 439

The language in the annual reports is fuzzy, the footnotes verbose, and the terminology imprecise.

Powell, 1962/1964, 13

accounting is the language not of business but of accountants ....

Stone, 1971, 149

For many years, the accounts of major public companies have been couched – perhaps because of the age-endowed shibboleths and mysteries of the accounting profession – in terms that even members of that profession have problems in justifying, and that can hardly be said to be models of succinct statement.

Greener, 1974b, 734

much of every profession's technical language simply does not stand up to close scrutiny. Much of it [the technical language of accounting] is bogus, existing only to impress the innocent and unwary; much of it is not essential, cannot be justified on practical grounds and fulfils no purpose except possibly as a kind of masonic glue between different members of our profession . . . . the user [of financial statements] with limited financial expertise may find our language at best confusing and at worst incomprehensible.

Lothian, 1978, 42

See also 224

935 Recourse to fictions

many of the accounting errors that have been made by courts, lawyers, economists and business men have been due to their failure to realize the fictional element in accounting conventions.

Gilman, 1939, 245

cost or market, whichever is lower . . . . and other cost bases, such as average, or first in first out, or last in first out, or base stock, or any others, have for their purpose the allocation of historical costs between past and future periods. Each method is based on a particular fiction, and no one of these fictions ever quite exists, in fact.

Wilcox, 1941b/1982, 101

the monetary postulate [assumption of the stability of the monetary unit] is an obvious fiction.

AIA, 1952, 46

What is the prime requisite is not to value the inventories, but to measure the proper charge in respect of the consumption or disposition of inventoriable goods; and the same holds true with respect to the charge for exhaustion. For either purpose a fiction may be a more acceptable basis than a purely factual one . . . . in America . . . the identification method is rejected in the case of fungible goods because of the obvious opportunity for manipulation of profits that it affords. This is a case in which a fiction is a better guide than a fact. Lifo and fifo are both fictions.

May, 1955b, 701

assumed stability in the monetary unit is an obvious fiction – a fiction which is acceptable only if, by following it rather than some other assumption, more useful results can be obtained.

Spiller, 1964, 854

The literature of accounting . . . contains much that has no counterpart in the real world.

Coughlan, 1965, 127

The group, as such, . . . is a commercial fiction.

Burgess, 1966, 542

While many writers have gravely pointed out that allocation may be misleading, none has managed to indicate when they would not be misleading. The answer is, of course, never. All these allocations are fictions.
Walker, 1968, 32

A good deal of accounting, as currently practised, has a mystical quality. Depreciation methods, inventory valuations, arbitrary distinctions between capital and revenue, overhead allocations, and joint product costing are examples of procedures that fall into this category. So also do profit centers and transfer prices. Revenue which is not revenue, transfer prices which are not prices, and profit centers which do not earn a profit, are mystical inventions. They are fictions which cannot serve as a basis for action.
Wells, 1968, 180

As long as you use a whole set of fictions called depreciation and amortization to determine income, you are going to get irrelevant information.
Sterling, 1980, 105

936 Education of investors advanced as antidote to accounting limitations

[A major task] is to educate the public in regard to the significance of accounts, their value and their unavoidable limitations.
AIA, 1932

One of the most important problems involved in this question of corporate reporting is that of educating the rank and file of investors to an appreciation of the character of balance sheets and income statements, and especially of their unavoidable limitations.
Sanders, 1934, 203

[There exists] the problem of educating the public as to the meaning and fundamental limitations of accounting statements.
Andersen, 1935, 332

Any attempt to modify existing accounting methods with the avowed intent of minimizing cyclical variations in business profits . . . would encounter vigorous opposition . . . . perhaps the only practicable alternative is to teach business men and the public at large what profit figures mean and what they do not mean, what inferences they support and what reject, what questions they throw no light on at all.
Buchanan, 1941, 753

The correct solution of this problem lies in the education of the public in the problems of business economics and the way in which they are affected by changes in money values. This requires not a revision of accounting statements but a thoroughgoing exposition of their significance as stated.
Greer, 1948, 131

every effort should be made to educate all those involved in financial reporting in the reasons accounting principles are the way they are.

Skinner, 1972a, 19

The public is confused about the difference between the information auditors provide in statements and information outside those statements . . . . In short a gap exists between reality and what accounting statements tell us . . . . we should do a better job of educating people about what the numbers really mean.

Williams, 1980a, 124

We should do our best to educate them [the public] that the balance sheet does not represent values, it cannot represent values, amd it doesn't purport to represent values. And we shouldn't call it a statement of financial position. We should call it a balance sheet, which is what it is.

Anthony, 1984, 106

To date, the profession's response to the expectations gap [see 098 *supra*] has been varied but revolves around one basic theme: Educate the public. In other words, it's the other side's fault. This version of the classic *caveat emptor* doctrine . . . suggests that financial statement users – be they investment bankers, physicians, homemakers, or social workers – should educate themselves about the subtle nuances of generally accepted auditing standards and the limitations inherent therein. The public, on the other hand, has precious little interest in such arcana and typically views the audit certificate as saying that the product has no hidden defects, the profits are genuine, and the reported assets really exist.

Kaplan, 1987, 3

perhaps more efforts should be undertaken to educate individuals as to the [intended meaning of the term, generally accepted accounting principles] rather than towards developing a substitute phrase.

McEnroe, 1991, 162

937 Accounting theory as rationalization

If we view the term broadly, theory can properly be called a body of doctrine. It is an area of beliefs, explanations, justifications related to an area of practice.

Littleton, 1953, 175

acceptance of the sale [rather than accrual] as the basis of income measurement . . . . is illustrative of the application of a degree of rationalization to the process of income measurement . . . . Rationalizations of one sort or another influence . . . the matching process . . . . [the concurrent endorsement of different cost flow assumptions] . . . . the use of the cost or market, whichever is lower, method of evaluation . . . . depreciation procedures . . . . Accounting appears to have among its leaders a most respectable and capable group of Philadelphia lawyers . . . . Rationalization has been built upon rationalization to the point where its acceptance is question-able.

Husband, 1954a, 3–14

A . . . proposition that should be laid to rest is that the purpose of accounting prin-ciples is to justify accounting practice. The literature of accounting is replete with so-called accounting theory which is nothing more than an attempt to rationalize the *status quo*.

Storey, 1964, 64

justification for an alternative accounting method is too easy. Citation from an article in a respected professional journal or an example from a published financial statement has been considered sufficient support in innumerable instances. I am afraid that it may be true that CPAs too often search the literature and published financial state-ments with the objective of finding justification for the use of a method they privately hold to be inferior. Their acquiescence thus adds another example in support of the inferior method.

Miller, 1964, 44

Accounting theory has increasingly served not to develop practice that ought to be implemented but rather to rationalize practice after it has been adopted. One result, in my opinion, is that accounting theory has increasingly lost much of the internal consistency that it once possessed and accounting practice has increasingly become characterized by attempts to juxtapose irreconcilable methods, each supported by a so-called theoretical justification. Since almost anything can be called theory in that context, accounting theory is of little help in solving many accounting problems.

Storey, 1972, 113

accounting theories have always served a justification role . . . . The predominant function of accounting theories is now to supply excuses which satisfy the demand created by the political process . . . .

Watts & Zimmerman, 1979, 300

938 Accounting thought said to lack systematic development

many of these fundamental propositions [of accounting] are incapable of any complete proof or demonstration. Indeed, some of them can be disproved from the standpoint of literal accuracy . . . . They are largely assumptions of expediency, without which it would be impossible for the accountant to proceed . . . . the entire structure of accounts and the recognized system of procedures is based upon assumptions.

Paton, 1922/1962, 499

Accounting . . . . needs above all else the formulation of sound theories, which can be crystallized into clear terminology. Progress in the other sciences has for its milestones a series of formulated theories, comprehensive and significant. [Astronomy, chemistry, biology, engineering, cited as examples]

Hatfield, 1927b, 272–3

Our difficulty with present accounting theory lies not in the existing differences of opinion but in the lack of any sense of direction in which we should be moving to make accounting . . . a primary, accurate, and dependable source of information for all who are seeking reliable data about the operations of a given financial entity.

Hylton, 1962, 27

Why does the accounting profession appear to be almost adamant in opposing the elimination of double-standard accounting? Because of the vested interests . . . of the professional accountants who approve, and of the companies which use, double-standard accounting. These vested interests also create the recognized authorities that sustain the acceptance of the double-standard. Thus the circular action from vested interests to acceptance and then back to vested interests for authority to sustain them. Like three imbibers leaning against one another, they hold each other up.

Spacek, 1964b, 70

After many years of effort no statement of accounting principles has been prepared on which accountants, financial statement users, and tax administrators can rely.

Cohen, 1966, 37

Development of accounting theory in recent years has failed to achieve results commensurate with the effort . . . . Inadequate methodology has led to a confusing vocabulary of terms and to theoretical structures which fail to meet the requirements of logic.

Buckley & others, 1968, 283

Accounting thought has developed for many years on an *ad hoc* basis, in which particular practical problems of the moment have been observed and analyzed in isolation in order to find a useful practical solution. The unfortunate result has been the inevitable stockpiling of accounting methods, procedures and rules, often totally unrelated and inconsistent with one another, and often completely lacking the support of a justifying theoretical structure – the inventory of methods etc. being available for use in a variety of different situations, irrespective of the individual problems which gave rise to particular methods in the first instance.

Lee, 1971, 243

While we may lack theory in accounting, we have an abundance of theorizing – i.e. statements of opinion . . . . Unfortunately, these opinions are often called theories, and so we may tend to mistakenly believe that we have an abundance of theory.

Caplan, 1972, 46, 50

After forty years of discussion there is still no comprehensive, integrated statement of concepts on which accountants and statement readers can agree and rely. There is still no consensus as to the exact meaning of the standard audit opinion that financial statements present the results of operations fairly in accordance with generally accepted accounting principles. One result is that accounting methods have changed much more slowly than has the accounting environment. And the profession has not solved its basic problems of disclosure, consistency and statement comparability.

Chatfield, 1977, 302

939 A unified theory said to be unattainable

I must confess that a man is guilty of unpardonable arrogance who concludes, because an argument has escaped his own investigation, that therefore it does not really exist. I must also confess that, though all the learned, for several ages, should have employed themselves in fruitless search on any subject, it may still, perhaps, be rash to conclude positively that the subject must, therefore, pass all human comprehension.

Hume, 1777/1978, IV:ii

A surprising number of accountants still believe that there is a true set of principles, that is, one figure for an asset's value or a firm's income is the true figure.

Gordon, 1964, 259

the great debate in accounting is hardly ever concerned with the logical and mechanical processes of accounting but rather revolves constantly around the socially significant and value-laden concepts of the discipline, such as fairness, disclosure, impartiality, objectivity and materiality . . . . when social concepts are concerned there are no universal truths or general laws.

Bernstein, 1965, 34

the truth in inventory valuation has never been discovered, nor will any solution be found through research and discovery; there is no "unknown" to be sought, nor any likelihood that the brain of some budding genius will suddenly provide the long-awaited key to unlock the mystery.

Roy & MacNeill, 1967, 56

The objects of criticism which have been identified in recent years – determination of profit; valuation . . . ; calculation of depreciation – are among the most documented areas of accounting literature. It is highly unlikely that the one principle which will apply uniquely to all or any of them lies waiting to be discovered.

Most, 1969, 684

no single governing theory of financial accounting is rich enough to encompass the full range of user-environment specifications effectively; . . . .

AAA, 1977, 1

Our view is that there is no theoretical basis for preferring one set of techniques over another and no basis for presuming *a priori* that either set leads to more informative values of accounting numbers.

Gonedes & Dopuch, 1979, 391

not only is there no generally accepted accounting theory to justify accounting standards, there never will be one.

Watts & Zimmerman, 1979, 301

we should abandon the chimera that we can ever establish a unified conceptual framework for accounting that will measure operations and value the net financial position of a firm in an uncertain world with incomplete markets.

Kaplan, 1980, 183

The contingency approach to management accounting is based on the premise that there is no universally appropriate accounting system which applies equally to all organizations in all circumstances.

Otley, 1980, 413

940 Accounting Theory

941 Accounting and other disciplined pursuits

There is in accountancy a curious absence of any pronounced tendency toward research and scientific development. Unlike the medical and engineering professions, where laboratory work frequently precedes the practical application, accountancy has been shaped almost entirely by outward circumstances. Accounting thought has lain dormant for generations at a time, arousing itself sluggishly for self improvement only after it is been kicked awake.

Carman, 1936, 348

If accounting had to do with phenomena that could be objectively and accurately measured, such as the motion of the planets or the behavior of gases under given conditions of pressure and temperature, calculations based on accounting data could be made which would result in accurate predictions, but accounting data are not of this nature. They are the expression of human purpose, will, or intention, and so far it has been impossible to reduce these human elements to any rules which may be universally and objectively applied.

Peloubet, 1945, 394

One test of a science is the ability to predict future events. The physical and natural sciences can meet this test, but the social sciences, and accountancy in particular, cannot meet this test if exact prediction is required, because of the many variable factors involved in the future course of an economic enterprise.

Kelley, 1948, 151

accounting theory cannot justifiably be said to consist of scientific explanations. There are no immutable laws of accountancy comparable to the immutable laws of nature.

Littleton, 1953, 135

Accounting is not formulated with reference to, nor does it stand on, general truths or the operation of natural or general laws.

Smith & Ashburne, 1960, 1

It would be incorrect to suggest that the rules which establish whether a given accounting procedure is acceptable or unacceptable are in the nature of principles like those found in physics or chemistry. Accounting principles are more properly associated with such terms as concepts, conventions and standards. It is important to remember that accounting principles are man-made, in contrast to natural law.

Finney & Miller, 1961, 165

what is, in my opinion, a sterile approach to the development of accounting . . . . is the attempt to describe the broad and varied field of accounting practice as a system of logic like geometry in which all principles are deduced from a few axioms and postulates such as reliance on objective evidence.

McFarland, 1961, 29

In the search for a comprehensive statement of accounting principles which can achieve general acceptance, it should always be remembered that such principles can neither be derived from natural laws nor tested by scientific experiment. They are strictly man-made.

JA, editorial, 1965, 27

If, in truth, a practitioner of the accounting art is a truthseeker, he is confronted by a host of uncertainties. There are no natural laws of accounting which he can employ, only conventions validated by experience, estimates born of human judgments, guidelines developed by his professional societies.

Lawler, 1968, 88

accounting principles are intellectual concepts. They are not subject to the kinds of proof that are applied to laws of physical science. So legitimate differences of opinion within the profession itself are virtually inevitable.

Stone, 1968, 53

Financial accounting and reporting are not grounded in natural laws as are the physical sciences, but must rest on a set of conventions or standards designed to achieve what are perceived to be the desired objectives of financial accounting and reporting.

AICPA, 1972a, 19

in accounting as well as in economics, concepts of income and wealth are not descriptive, but normative; not objective, but subjective; and not unique, but manifold . . . . In light of current knowledge, the word "true", its derivatives, its synonyms, and its antonyms have no legitimate meaning in describing income and wealth – in accounting as well as in economics.

Gerboth, 1973, 478

here is the notable feature which sets accounting off from other professions. Medicine and dentistry are rooted in the natural laws of the biological sciences. Engineering and architecture are rooted in the natural laws of the physical sciences. Law is rooted in prescriptions by the state which create social laws. Accounting, however, insofar as it is "self-regulated", has no external referent. It is an entirely human construct, and its "principles" represent contractual restraint among its practitioners as to what they will say and how they will say it.

Kripke, 1980, 99

Unlike the natural sciences, where the laws are embedded in the natural environment, so that we can discover them but not make them, . . . accounting standards are man-made efforts to control a man-made environment and they must be flexible enough to adapt to changes in this environment.

Stamp, 1981b, 218

Unfortunately, truth from an accounting perspective is not an empirical fact to be discovered; it is a subjective understanding to be manufactured and agreed upon.

Ingram & Rayburn, 1989, 59

See also 844, 849

942 Accounting said to be ideally or potentially scientific

the science of accounting is the real basis on which our entire commercial and credit structure is built . . . . I believe that accounting is, or should be, a science – not a system of ethics but an exact science, amenable to definite laws, constructed on definite axioms, and capable, in proper practice, of producing definite and exact results . . . . I also maintain that it is within your power to make it an exact science. You can do this by adopting and putting in practice a system of fundamental principles so clearly and exactly defined that they will admit of no material latitude in their interpretation, so exactly defined that the optimism, or the pessimism, or the individual prejudice of the accountant, will not be brought into the operation at all. The accountant will then be concerned only with the determination of the facts, and not at all with their interpretation.

Smith, 1912, 244, 249

"The commonly accepted proof that a body of organized knowledge has attained the rank of an established science is the coercive or compelling character of the generalizations to which it gives rise and which come to be known as scientific laws (principles)" (H C Adams, *American railway accounting*) . . . . The principles of accounting are also characterized by their coercive or compelling quality because inherent in accounting principles are business laws which must be obeyed if in the long run the enterprise is to survive.

Byrne, 1937, 370

There is an excessive tendency to applaud the virtues of common sense and let theory alone. It cannot be emphasized too strongly that accountancy is a science; common sense is needed in its application, but as complementary to, not in substitution of, logical method.

Norris, 1939, 846

The accountancy profession sets up standard procedures as models for general adoption, and tests them in the same way as a scientist does his hypothesis. They are tested in practice and constantly modified and approved and gradually out of them emerge principles which are general laws serving as guides to action.

Chancellor, 1950, 59

it is not the quantitative element, or the degree of precision in measuring phenomena which distinguishes science or scientific inquiry; rather it is the rigor with which a knowledge of qualities, states and relationships is pursued that entitles a study to be called scientific .... In short, accounting differs in no material particular from other fields which are subject to scientific study. Not all the methods of the natural sciences may be appropriate to the study of accounting, but the attitude toward the subject matter can be essentially the same.

Chambers, 1960b, 35

Accountancy is not merely a collection of techniques and procedures to be learned by rule; it is an intellectually demanding academic discipline with a central body of theory derived from the social and economic objectives and relevance of accounting – albeit that the theory is at present unsatisfactory and as yet incomplete, too little understood and not wholly recognized.

Flint, 1966, 645

Accounting ought to be deductive. Every branch of knowledge ought to be. A mathematical treatment is the developed form of every science because, as a branch of logic, it is both clear and exact; it allows the greatest number of possible conclusions to be drawn from the observed data and hence permits the greatest number of possible predictions to be made .... If accountancy is the quantified representation of economic reality I can see no reason in principle why a strictly mathematical model should not one day be constructed.

Morison, 1970b, 467

it is foolish to expect our principles to be immutable in the sense of, say, the second law of thermodynamics. On the other hand, I do believe that it will be possible to achieve uniformity of theoretical and conceptual foundations in much the same way that Darwin and his successors have been able to bring order out of chaos in the life sciences.

Stamp, 1972a, 64

895

The primary problem of accounting is that our figures do not have empirical referents
.... I remember [the McKesson-Robbins case] as resulting in the most important
improvement in accounting in this century. It was a significant, albeit unrecognized,
theoretical advance because it partially transformed accounting into an empirical
science. Prior to the trial, empirical testing of asset quantities was not a generally
accepted auditing standard. Instead of looking at the assets, the auditors looked at
the accounts and records.

Sterling, 1979, 213

See also 022

943 Accounting principles expected to be invariant

The qualifications "usually" and "seldom" will not do in mathematics and accounts.
Principles are principles, and deviations can only be excused by the minuteness of
the deviation in a particular case.

Sprague, 1906, 296

accounting principles, if sound, do not change with their application to any particular form of accounts ....

Lybrand, 1908, 32

The principles of accounting remain the same, and about them there should be no
substantial disagreement; as to the body of accounting rules, practices and conventions derived from those principles, there may well be differences of opinion as
to their validity in a particular case.

Byrne, 1937, 370

Tests for principles. Varying statutes test ... are principles of accounting the same
regardless of law and judicial decisions? .... all accounting propositions which are
related to or derived from statute, ukase or decision are rules rather than principles.
Varying proprietorship test ... are principles of accounting the same regardless of
the form of proprietorship? If the answer to this is in the affirmative, propositions
which apply solely to one rather than all forms of proprietorship must be eliminated
as principles .... Varying industries test ... do principles of accounting remain the
same regardless of the type of activity recorded? If so, then all propositions which
do not apply equally to banks, mining companies, manufacturers, governmental
units, hospitals and farms must be rules rather than principles.

Gilman, 1939, 251

There is a demand for the development of a harmonious body of accounting rules
or principles.

May, 1942, 35

accounting principles are not something to be laid down by authority; they are
logical (perhaps scientific) notions capable of being deduced from the economic

structure of industry and trade so that whilst authority, in the shape of the Institute [ICAEW] Council or otherwise, can do much to bring us nearer to the ascertainment and use of correct principles, it cannot lay down principles.

Norris, 1945b, 208

Principle envisages a fundamental truth or proposition of universal application. It may also suggest a general law or rule adopted or professed as a guide to action; a settled ground or basis of conduct or practice. The fact is that, as yet, none of our so-called principles measures up fully to those standards.

Irish, 1948, 401

I prefer to think of a principle as a fundamental concept and not as a rule to guide conduct . . . . Rules, practices, conventions and procedures may change, but principles ought to prevail.

Bray, 1951, 353

If I were required to say what I thought were fixed and unchangeable principles of accounting, I would say there were three – consistency, materiality and disclosure.

Peloubet, 1959, 24

Accounting principles deal with the recording and reporting practices of a typical business or other organization, as dictated by established conventions or by widely accepted professional fiat; they have universal application.

Kohler, 1965a, 11

Legal requirements may vary from one territory to another; true accounting principles ought not to.

Smith, 1972, 181

944 Posited types of theory

Accountants ought to measure something and then communicate that measurement to the people who will make the decisions. Under this interpretation [of accounting theory construction], the outputs of the accounting system are the inputs to decision theories. This interpretation focuses on decision theories, in contrast to the psychological interpretation which focuses on decision makers.

Sterling, 1970b, 454

expressions like entity theory, fund theory, replacement value theory, events theory, etc, might be considered misnomers, as they do not refer to the construction of a whole theory, but to the annunciation of individual hypotheses or other specific theory aspects.

Mattessich, 1980, 158

if positive theory means anything, it refers not to "what is" but to "what can be". Normative theory does tell us what "ought to be" but in a specific sense. For a theory to be normative, it needs a value judgment for its closure.

Schreuder, 1984, 214

Accounting theories may be categorized broadly as either normative (prescriptive) or positive (descriptive). Normative theories are concerned with what ought to be, and positive theories with what actually happens. It follows that normative theories are based largely on value judgments, whereas positive theories are not . . . . Empirical methods are used to test positive theories, by comparing the results predicted by the model with what is observed to happen in the real world. Normative theories cannot be tested empirically because they are not intended to predict actual outcomes.

Arnold, 1989, 15

Theory as to "what accountants do"

One of the most elementary though disregarded of distinctions is that between the scientist and his science. Science is created by the scientist, but about nature, not about himself.

Gillispie, 1960/1967, 150

One way [of thinking of accounting theory] is to consider the theory as the many explanations, reasons, justifications which will help us understand why accountancy (technology and profession) is what it is . . . . theory as explanations, reasons, justifications, does not contemplate producing "a" theory . . . .

Littleton, 1956, 363

Probably the most ancient and pervasive method of accounting theory construction is to observe accountants' actions and then rationalize those actions by subsuming them under generalized principles. The result is not a theory about accounting or a theory about the things accounted for; instead it is a theory about accountants.

Sterling, 1970b, 449

the explanation of something in accounting must start with observations outside accounting . . . . a hypothesis which relies on observations of what accountants do in order to explain why they do it is of little use in theory construction.

Most, 1977b, 16

Chemical theory consists of propositions about the behavior of chemical entities (molecules and atoms) not about the behavior of chemists.

Christenson, 1983, 6

Conventions, doctrines, concepts, postulates, principles and rules are all confirmed hypotheses about accounting practice. How they are labelled seems to be of little importance. A set of confirmed hypotheses collectively comprises a general scientific theory of accounting. Together the set of confirmed hypotheses purports to explain what accountants do . . . . The conventions of accounting were made explicit by careful observation of accounting practices. In other words, the conventions were discovered by researchers using the scientific method. The resulting descriptions of conventional accounting behavior can, therefore, be labelled as scientific theories.

Henderson & Peirson, 1983, 55, 91

The objective of accounting theory is to explain and predict accounting practice . . . . theory as we describe it yields no prescriptions for accounting practice . . . . It is designed to explain and predict which firms will and which firms will not use a particular method of valuing assets, but it says nothing as to which method a firm should use.

Watts & Zimmerman, 1896, 2, 7

945 Posited characteristics of accounting theory

Accounting theory is here conceived to be a coherent, coordinated, consistent body of doctrine which may be compactly expressed in the form of standards if desired.

Paton & Littleton, 1940, ix

the reader of a [financial] statement should be able to assume that, in the absence of clear indications to the contrary, certain basic principles or standards have been followed. To achieve this end, a unified and coordinated body of accounting theory is required.

AAA, 1941/1957b, 53

the development and use of a comprehensive code of accounting principles . . . and of greater uniformity and of less latitude in present techniques may well be pre-requisites to any complex development of new tools to measure economic income . . . . There is always a logical order in building. Windows are not fitted until walls have been built and ceilings are not constructed before floors. The planning and blueprinting is geared accordingly. By the same token, it is more logical that we complete a sound framework for financial reporting before we attempt to attach to it complex modifications [in income reporting] that will collapse the entire structure because they leave too many unconnected and weak parts.

Stans, 1949, 5, 14

the term "theory" is usually applied to the whole apparatus, extending from the primitive statements and rules for transforming them to other acceptable sentences, to the construction of axioms, definitions, classes, etc, with empirical content, and to the accumulated theorems that have been proved. If the theory is . . . a reason-ably accurate characterization, its resulting models and related abstractions may be used for description, explanation, and perhaps prediction.

Devine, 1960, 391

A theory in accounting is a definition or rule for the measurement of income, wealth, etc. at some level of generality and the arguments that support the use of the definition . . . . The investigator is free to adopt the definitions that suit his purpose, and his theory is true or false depending on whether or not other objective investigators confirm the statements or predictions of his theory concerning the variables in question.
Gordon, 1960, 618

Theory needs to be tested in the light of experience and common sense, just as practice needs to be considered in the light of logic and reason. The statement . . . that a given procedure is theoretically sound but practically unfeasible is a contradiction. If the indicated result is impracticable, the theory upon which it is based is invalid and should be restudied. Thus practice tends to refine and improve theory, just as theory helps to solve practical problems.
Powell, 1961, 29

accounting theory consists of the reasoning and logic used to justify, or to arrive at, a method, procedure or rule . . . . rules themselves are not theory; rather they are, or should be, the result of applied theory.
Hylton, 1962, 22

My notion of an accounting theory is that it clearly articulates the "why", "what" and "how" aspects of accounting reports, supporting each stage by reference to available evidence and to reasoned argument.
Grinyer, 1985, 15

At the structural level, a theoretical system [of measurement and valuation] is required to be logically rigorous and internally consistent. At the semantic level, the system output must provide a true interpretation of the real world. At the behavioral level, the information must be relevant for decision making . . . .
Ma & others, 1987, 473

946 Conceptual frameworks in accounting

Every science, methodology, or other body of knowledge is oriented to some conceptual structure – a pattern of ideas brought together to form a consistent whole or a frame of reference to which is related the operational content of that field. Without some such integrating structure, procedures are but senseless ritual without reason or substance; progress is but a fortunate combination of circumstances; research is but fumbling in the dark; and the dissemination of knowledge is a cumbersome process, if indeed there is any "knowledge" to convey.
Vatter, 1947, 1

principles distilled from practice are capable of leading so far and no further. A point is reached at which principles of this type become meaningless unless and until a conceptual framework is developed which gives meaning to the procedures followed, or points out that the procedures followed do not make sense and should be replaced by others which do. Building a conceptual framework, which will be at once both the reasoning underlying procedures and a standard by which procedures are judged is a long run process.

Storey, 1964, 60

for the establishment of accounting principles . . . a conceptual framework must be constructed, including concepts of income and value which will result in measurements relevant to the observed needs of users . . . .

Stamp, 1970d, 102

It is often said by critics that the fundamental weakness of the approach hitherto taken by the profession in the setting of accounting standards has been the absence of a consistent logically developed and empirically tested conceptual framework. Such a framework would proceed from clear assumptions as to the information needs of those considered to be the prime users of financial statements. It would define the purposes of financial statements consistent with such needs. It would define the main concepts employed in the construction of financial statements, such as assets, liabilities, revenue, expense, profit. It would define the bases for measuring each of those elements. It would deal with such matters as capital maintenance and the realization rule.

Feller, 1974, 396

A conceptual framework is a constitution, a coherent set of interrelated objectives and fundamentals that can lead to consistent standards and that prescribes the nature, function, and limits of financial accounting and financial statements. The objectives identify the goals and purposes of accounting. The fundamentals are the underlying concepts that guide the selection of events to be accounted for, the measurement of those events, and the means of summarizing and communicating them to interested parties.

FASB, 1976a, 2

The attempt to develop an agreed conceptual framework is an attempt to establish a common framework of theory that will both identify the important basic questions to be asked, and, it is hoped, produce substantial areas of agreement about how the answers are to be found, so that it will become clearer how individual accounting problems should be resolved than is the case at present.

Macve, 1981, 22

In essence, a conceptual framework comprises a set of basic principles that command general support and can be used to help with detailed decisions by increasing the likelihood of consistency and reducing the costs of analysis. In financial reporting, a conceptual framework is expected to help with decisions by standard setters and others about how accounting measurements should be made, what information should be included in published reports, and how the information should be displayed.

Carsberg, 1984, 25

The major role of the conceptual framework is ultimately to enhance the likelihood of acceptability of statements to be proposed. The more plausible the logic and the more compelling the facts, the greater the chance of winning the support of diverse interests.

> Horngren, 1984, 731

Essentially, [a conceptual framework for accounting and financial reporting] is an interrelated structure of propositions and observations that helps us explain financial reporting practices or deduce what they ought to be.

> Skinner, 1987, 628

Appraisal of frameworks

The adoption of a conceptual framework that serves as the logical point of departure for an authoritative derivation of financial accounting standards is implicitly based on the anachronistic view that accounting is essentially a field dedicated to the search for "true income" and "true wealth", and, once discovered, the truth will become compellingly apparent to all but the unenlightened.

> Rappaport, 1977, 92

not only do we lack an agreed conceptual framework from which all standards can be developed; we have no clear idea of whether we really want one, nor of what we would expect it to do if we had one.

> *Accountancy*, editorial, 1979b, 1

A conceptual framework is a *sine qua non*; we need one whether we have accounting standards or not.

> Stamp, 1981b, 216

There is no need for a conceptual framework beyond what has served the profession for nearly 50 years.

> Flegm, 1984, 249

the view of most British researchers remains that attempts to seek to base the authority for accounting standards on an agreed conceptual framework are bound to fail.

> Hopwood & Bromwich, 1984, 147

There isn't going to be one conceptual framework that's going to solve all the problems.

> Weil, 1984, 60

See also 848

947 Accounting theory construction

As the value of an art can only be known by its end, so the only way to get a distinct and clear notion of the art [of bookkeeping] and to understand thoroughly its principles and rules, is to get first a just and complete notion of the design and end of it; . . . .

Malcolm, 1731, 2

The author, in compiling this theory, has endeavored to render it scientific; he has therefore defined all the terms used in the method, has made use of several known truths, equivalent to axioms, and has defined one thing to be granted; which done, the precepts given for conducting the operative part are shown to be founded on the above principles and the whole process, from the inventory to the balance, will appear to be the result of sound reason and judgment.

Dodson, 1750, VI

Accounting theory first appeared in the nineteenth century, and there followed an epidemic of so-called systems of bookkeeping – most of them fantastic and utterly useless for practical purposes.

Montgomery, 1938

As a branch of mathematical and classificatory science, the principles of accountancy may be determined by *a priori* reasoning, and do not depend upon the customs and traditions which surround the art.

Sprague, 1907/1972, ix

the first order of business in constructing a theoretical system for a service function is to establish the purpose and objectives of the function . . . . Once this first step is taken, we have a framework that lets us investigate and conduct research in terms of carefully constructed objectives.

Devine, 1960, 399

a theory of accounting, in the sense of it being a theory of what to measure or account for, can be constructed from the specifications of the broader theories of economic decisions.

Sterling, 1970b, 457

See also 856

948 Sources of postulates of an accounting theory

The onus or rather the privilege that rests upon the accountant is to exploit to the utmost for the benefit of his own special work the instruments of thought and action accumulated by all other workers, no matter in what field.

Branford, 1903–04, I:29

Accountancy, to my mind, is not only applied mathematics, but also applied economics. The accountant must know the theory of value in order to properly understand his profession . . . . we find mathematics and economics going hand in hand in aid of the accountant . . . . The themes of the economist, such as capital, profit, income, expenditure, value, property, labor, are the terms employed here.
Lafrentz, 1906, 480, 483

The conduct of business enterprise is the source from which accounting theory takes its rise.
Scott, 1926, 19

There is reason to fear that some in authority have . . . a misunderstanding of the nature of accounting; this is the only conclusion which can be drawn from their tendency to expect business to conform to an accounting pattern rather than the reverse.
Montgomery, 1938

The social pattern is the matrix from which all social sciences spring.
Eggleston, 1941, 120

The statement of this principle [usefulness] . . . . provides a basis for accounting outside itself. We do not have to start with emphasis on the distinction between capital and income, or verifiable objective evidence, or anything else chosen from within accounting itself. The field of business is the objective world in which accounting exists. Accounting may be treated much as a science in this world.
Wilcox & Hassler, 1941, 309

Accounting theory is very closely related to . . . . jurisprudence . . . . to business management . . . . to economics . . . . to government and to statistics and to logic and to mathematics in certain ways and by certain ties.
Chambers, 1950, 338

there is no accounting theory as such . . . accounting is a scientific method – the statistical tool of the business man . . . . the economic theory of the firm and the behavior of the business man [is] the true theory that [lies] behind the practice of accounting.
Morgan, 1953, 32

All of financial accounting – principles, objectives, and basic features – is grounded in the environment of business enterprises.
AICPA, 1970c, APBS4

To date, writings [on accounting principles] have been primarily cast in a data-oriented mold . . . . The area will not be mastered in any sense scientifically until accountants argue backwards from the uses of information.
Simmonds, 1972, 22

As I see it, accounting principles are a synthesis; they represent the conglomeration of sociology, history, economics, communications, philosophy, law, mathematics, taxation . . . . Accounting principles draw from every conceivable discipline – certainly every one among the behavioral sciences.

Briloff, 1981, 257

accounting objectives, methods and procedures will derive from the social values and standards of society . . . . Accounting is, therefore, interactive with not only political economy but also law, social philosophy, industrial sociology, political theory, administrative theory, organizational theory and psychology.

Flint & Shaw, 1981, 135

949 Accounting theory and practice

The conflict between theory and practice is a false one, for practice to be sound should be related to sound theories.

Hatfield, 1939/1982, 5

theory which cannot stand the acid test of practice is not good theory, and . . . practice which is not compatible with sound logic and reasoning is not good practice . . . . there is no fundamental conflict between good theory and good practice.

Queenan, 1962, 33

The statement sometimes made that a given procedure is theoretically sound but practically unfeasible is a contradiction. If the indicated result is impracticable, the theory upon which it is based is invalid and should be restudied. Thus practice tends to refine and improve theory, just as theory helps to solve practical problems.

Powell, 1964b, 42

practicality cannot make correct that which is logically untenable . . . .

Simon, 1968, 414

See also 871

950 Accounting Research

951 Research generally

See also Section 800 *passim*

Research is fundamentally a state of mind involving continued reexamination of doctrines and axioms upon which current thought and action are based. It is, therefore, critical of existing practices.

Smith, 1929, 742

[Research] is a quiet, painstaking effort on the part of an individual himself . . . to reach the truth, the severest that the human mind, with all available apparatus and resources, is capable of making at the moment. The subject matter must be serious or have serious implications; the object must be disinterested; no matter how closely the outcome may affect wealth, income or appetite, the observer must preserve an objective attitude.

Flexner, 1930/1968, 126

Scientific research is not itself a science; it is still an art or craft . . . . There is a very useful place in research for vague thinking. New ideas do not suddenly appear with no initial vague brooding over the subject. Although a new idea in definite form seems suddenly to flash through the mind, the thinker seems to go through an earlier stage of vague thinking, when he could not express to others what he is thinking. Vagueness has its place in research technique and thought, but not in the written or spoken expositions intended to be considered seriously by more than the author.

George, 1936, 29

More discoveries have arisen from intense observation of very limited material than from statistics applied to large groups . . . . only by being familiar with the usual can we notice something as being unusual or unexplained.

Beveridge, 1950/1957, 140

There is only one paramount reason for studying anything but the multiplication table. Either you are so interested in a subject that you cannot let it alone, or you are not. In the end it is a matter of intellectual passion.

Homans, 1951/1959, 2

The essential feature of a strategy of discovery lies in determining the sequence of choice of problems to solve. Now it is in fact very much more difficult to see a problem than to find a solution for it. The former requires imagination, the latter only ingenuity.

Bernal, 1954/1969, I:39

The world will go on somehow . . . . It will go on best, however, if among us there are men who have stood apart, who have refused to be anxious or too much concerned, who were cool and inquiring and had their eyes on a longer past and a longer future. By their example they can remind us that the passing moment is only a moment; by their loyalty they will have cherished those things which only the dis-interested mind can use.

Lippmann, –/1963, 491

progress is dependent not only upon research directly germane to the profession but also upon discoveries in cognate fields.

Roy & MacNeill, 1967, 53

It is right that the campus should no longer be an ivory tower. But there must still be ivory towers on the campus, places where scholars can do work which may seem irrelevant and even pedantic, without having to feel apologetic about it. And they must be free to do it at their own pace and style, even if this does not produce a flow of published work each year. A university which does not offer its faculty and students opportunities for this kind of solitude and detachment is failing in one of its duties to society. ["Ivory towers in tomorrow's world"]

Ashby, 1967, 421

The dynamic of research does not derive from an abstract metaphysics, nor from conscious adherence to a normative code; it is driven by the psycho-social tensions between critical and creative roles, between competition and cooperation.

Ziman, 1978, 59

great scientific breakthroughs are never assembled piecemeal from lint-picking research. At times, limited, fine-grained investigation may succeed in raising important doubts about a scientific theory; but it must at least have that theory before it as a target or baseline. Without some master idea that serves that function, one would not know where to begin looking for facts. Science is structured inquiry, and the structures that guide its progress are ideas.

Roszak, 1986, 102

952 Accounting research

few accounting issues have the merits of good whisky of improving with age. In fact they frequently deteriorate with time, and become more complex and much more difficult to deal with.

Phillippe, 1964, 223

Accounting research must be philosophical or methodological, must revolve around such questions as fairness, utility, relevance, equity, questions to which there are no "right" answers.

Roy & MacNeill, 1967, 56

We accountants do not resolve issues, we abandon them, ... we debate them loud and long . . . . until another issue comes along that is more current and more controversial, and then we forget the former issue . . . . The explanation for our inability to resolve issues is to be found in the way we conceive issues. We conceive of the issues in such a way that they are in principle unresolvable . . . . We phrase the questions in a way that prohibits answers. We define our problems so that the very definition precludes the possibility of a solution.

Sterling, 1975b, 28

Because accounting is pragmatic and can be justified only in terms of its usefulness in the real world, the test of what is valid and appropriate in accounting must relate to real world phenomena and behavior.
Caplan, 1972, 50

(Bearing in mind that method and methodology have quite different meanings): Is accounting, like physics a couple of hundred years ago, a science in search of a methodology, or is accounting research a methodology in search of a science? . . . I get the feeling that the second is closer to the truth.
Caws, 1972, 72

the objects of accounting research may be characterized as the relationship between economic events of an entity and information recorded and reported about them.
Ijiri, 1972, 60

Paton [e.g. 1922/1962] was the first to search for the analytical and empirical premises on which accounting rests . . . .
Mattessich, 1980, 159

In our research endeavors the academic community finds our presumptive first-rate intellects constrained to demonstrate their competence as second-rate financial analysts, applying third-rate mathematical methodology to fourth-rate data contained in various computerized data banks compiled by fifth-rate accounting drones. As a consequence the leading journals, wherein accounting academics are compelled to publish lest they perish, demonstrate intensified mathematical sophistication, with diminished contact with the real world.
Briloff, 1984, 509

Accounting research involves the collection and analysis of facts, the development of principles, the collection of information concerning accounting statements of all kinds, the uses to which that information is put and the role and behavior of accountants and those who are affected by the information they provide.
Arnold, 1989, 3

953 Modes of inquiry

We must . . . adapt our methods of enquiry to the nature of the ideas we examine, and the truth we search after.
Locke, 1700/1979, IV:xii

Since [in accounting theory] we are concerned with the choice among measurement rules and not with describing or predicting the behavior of the variables that are to be measured, there appears to be little room for empirical research.
Gordon, 1960, 607

real breakthroughs in accounting theory are more likely to come from ... individuals working more or less alone, on what are now considered the fringes of accounting and uninhibited by considerations of accounting practice, than from committees concerned with specific practical problems.

Storey, 1964, 62

theoretical research in accountancy ... should not be centered in a person or firm then actively engaged in the practical pursuit of accountancy. To the extent that the Institute [AICPA] has determined on such a centering for its research program we believe that it has embarked on a practice inimical to the research objectives of the profession .... [Research], especially that research relating to the probing of the theoretical infrastructure or the special body of knowledge which the accountant professes to know better than anyone else .... should be within the universities .... only the universities are presently capable of avoiding the inner contradictions which are considered to be indigenous to the centering of research in the major accounting firms and the Institute.

Briloff, 1967, 102

When one looks at some of the empirical studies which have been carried out so far, one is surprised to find how many of them have not really been concerned with real world situations. Questions which should have been put to businessmen and managers have been put to students in the classroom because they were more easily available. Managerial decisions which should have been observed under real working conditions have been simulated by gaming situations, where no important consequences to the player could be expected to result from his success or failure in the game.

Solomons, 1970, 16

We accountants have a tendency to allow our course [in research] to be influenced by the fickle winds of fashion.

Sterling, 1990, 132

See also 823–825

954 Research and practice

We do not expect practising accountants to be social scientists any more than we expect practising physicians to be physical or natural scientists .... Practitioners are not expected to do research .... They are expected to make use of the research performed by the scientists ... and, where possible, to feed back to those scientists case studies and empirical data that will help the scientist to extend the bounds of human knowledge.

Mautz, 1963, 319

There is, at present, in my opinion, a much bigger gap between the academic research-ers and the practising members of the accounting profession than in any other pro-fession that I know – including law, medicine and engineering.
Bevis, 1966, 39

Einstein expressed over and over again the thought that one should not couple the quest for knowledge with a bread-and-butter profession, but that research should be done as a private spare time occupation .... He believed that only in this way could one preserve one's independence.
Born, 1971, 107

A study of the US experience suggests that the academic literature has had remark-ably little impact on the the writings of practitioners and upon the policies of the American Institute or the SEC. Too often, accounting theory is invoked more as a tactic to buttress one's preconceived notions rather than as a genuine arbiter of contending views. This circumstance, which is hardly unique to the United States .... surely places accounting, as a professional calling, below both law and medicine.
Zeff, 1974, 177

research has to be free from the pressures which professions are likely to impose.
Feyerabend, 1975/1982, 219

Current problems of immediate concern to practising accountants have attracted little interest among academic researchers .... concern with the enhancement of research methodology has tended to displace concern with the problems of the pro-fession .... The resulting contribution of academic research to improvement in professional practice has been less than is desirable.
Cohen Commission, 1978, 87

Does accounting research matter (have an impact on accounting practice)? ... Yes – but not much.
Henderson & Peirson, 1978, 32

Researchers are liable to insinuate that practitioners are irrational and out-dated; practitioners are liable to accuse researchers of irrelevance and abstraction.
Dent & others, 1984, 233

Research in other academic pursuits has generally resulted in cycles of innovation which have substantially advanced the fields .... Accounting research has developed during [the past generation], but primarily in the sophistication of methodologies used rather than in the significance of the results obtained either for practice or for education .... Academic success ... has been related to the use of increasingly sophisticated techniques appraised by a small group who control the academic journals and apply high but limiting standards.
Burton & Sack, 1991, 121, 122

See also 894

960 Accounting Standards

961 Grounds for standard setting

although it is possible to make false or imperfect accounts . . . yet whenever such a practice or omission is known, that person, who is guilty of it, is to all merchants and tradesmen detestable to the last degree; and if he insists on the advantage, as infamous as a common thief; and being never after trusted, or dealt with by any of them, is from thenceforth (in his reputation) cracked, and soon after (probably) bankrupt, and broke; so sacred a thing is it to keep books of accounts in time, and with the utmost rigor of truth and justice, in the matter and form of them.

North, 1714/1986, 45

the principle adopted by any company in the distribution of its expenditure between the two [capital and revenue] accounts is of comparatively minor importance, provided that the system pursued be distinctly avowed and understood by the shareholders. It is the deception practised upon unwary proprietors by avowing one rule and clandestinely acting upon another, that has produced so much discredit and disaster. [leading article]

Morning Chronicle (London), 1845/ 1936, 112

a shareholder selling upon the faith of an undervalued balance sheet has at least as much ground for complaint as a shareholder buying upon an overvalued balance sheet – especially when the departure from absolute truth is deliberate and intentional.

Accountant, editorial, 1895, 76

To give a practical example of the evils which may arise from a too prudent policy [on asset valuation] . . . some years ago . . . one of the directors of a small company gradually purchased – on the basis of the annual balance sheets – over five-sixths of the issued shares. Then by means of a revaluation of the assets and the flotation of a new company, this astute gentleman reaped a rich harvest, in which the original shareholders would no doubt have participated had the balance sheets shown the assets at their true value.

Accountant, Anon, 1901, 920

The outcome of a contest between a board of directors and a professional auditor as to what ought or ought not to appear in a balance sheet and the nature of the auditor's report thereon depends very largely upon the auditor's strength of character. If by nature he be weak, his report may reflect his weakness; if, on the other hand, he be strong and reliable, his certificate will embody his personal characteristics. It is impossible to obtain an inviolable safeguard against the weakness of human nature.

Martin, 1922, 27

I have been impressed in this case as to both companies, with the divergence of accounting practices and the arbitrary technical treatment of accounting items. These have resulted here in much difficulty of understanding and in use of time, and made what should be a comparatively simple valuation of two similar projects a complex mathematical problem of incommensurable quantities .... From this I deduce that action should be taken ... for the purposes of setting up uniform standards of comparison of accounts, earnings and values for the guidance and necessary knowledge of directors and shareholders, as well as of the investors generally. [per Judge Jenkins]
Bethlehem-Youngstown merger injunction, 1931, 85

by inviting a committee of men from the universities of the country to make an independent and impartial study of [accounting principles] .... it is hoped that there may be established a body of principles which will become useful in unifying thought and which by its acceptance will serve to standardize accounting practices. [letter of invitation to the Sanders-Hatfield-Moore committee by the Haskins & Sells Foundation, 1935]
Sanders & others, 1938, xi

In 1942 the Council of the Institute [ICAEW] commenced to issue a series of recommendations upon "accounting principles" .... it was the first time that we accountants attempted to think out, upon a corporate basis, our problems .... In the past we developed upon a purely individualistic basis, we each laid down our own code of principles and hence our practice showed wide difference in method and in the form in which accounts were presented.
de Paula, 1947, 52

The general purpose of standards [of measurement is] to be able to assert that x has property y at time t in such a manner that the information contained in the assertion can be used in a wide number of other conditions and times to enable many different kinds of people to make decisions.
Churchman, 1959/1962, 89

All too easily accountants play in with the directors to prevent the true facts about companies coming to light .... The battle for disclosure will need more than a new definition of accountants' principles; it may in the end need legislation to allow shareholders to compel the accountants to work in their interests.
Sampson, 1971, 508

users of financial statements need world-wide accounting standards so that they can be assured that the financial statements of all companies, regardless of the countries in which they are domiciled, will be comparable and will reflect economic facts.
Hauworth, 1973, 23

As an educated guess, I would suspect that the number of cases against accountants that either have been resolved or are still pending exceeds 300. (Harvey Kapnick in a recent issue of *Business week* put the number at 500.) The number of lawsuits is greatly in excess of that. This, of course, includes claims ranging from a few hundred dollars to the multi-million dollar open-ended Securities Act claims. Although it is impossible to assess with any degree of certitude the total amounts sought by these complaints, it is fair to say that it is several billion dollars. For example, on paper the claims growing out of the Penn Central litigation are several hundred million dollars and one complaint in Equity Funding seeks $2.5 billion.

Liggio, 1974b, 119

Accounting standards are necessary because insiders are accountable to outsiders, and financial reports (one medium of accountability) should therefore be prepared on a basis that strikes the right balance between the conflicting interests of all the different groups that have a stake in the affairs of a reporting enterprise.

Stamp, 1982, 124

962 Objects of accounting standards

there is scarcely any likelihood that two professional auditors today would, with respect to the accounts of an undertaking of any considerable magnitude, show the same net result of profit .... It is extremely important that an effort be made to establish standards which will appeal to those responsible for the stating of accounts as scientific and reasonable.

Montgomery, 1912/1976, 181

diversity of practice may continue as new practices are adopted before old ones are completely discarded. The principal objective of the [Committee on Accounting Procedures] has been to narrow areas of difference and inconsistency in accounting practices ....

AIA, 1953a/1961, 8

The general purpose of the [AICPA] in the field of financial accounting should be to advance the written expression of what constitutes generally accepted accounting principles .... [which] means continuing effort to determine appropriate practice and to narrow the areas of difference and inconsistency in practice.

AICPA, 1958, 62

It is the Council's intention to advance accounting standards along the following lines: narrowing the areas of difference and variety in accounting practice .... disclosure of accounting bases .... disclosure of departures from established definitive accounting standards ....

ICAEW, 1969c, 842

Standard accounts seem desirable because so many readers are too inexpert to detect shortcomings and omissions. Further, the accountant may, because of pressure by powerful directors, be in no position to embark on a cool and judicious quest for truth; a stern code will then strengthen him more than one that leaves him scope for judgment . . . .

Baxter, 1972, 387

the use of accounting standards is an attempt (a) to minimize any unnecessary flexibility which may exist in accounting practice; and (b) to increase uniformity in the measurement of accounting information in order to enable its user to make adequate comparisons between companies.

Lee, 1975, 26

the personal judgment school . . . favors leaving it to boards of directors . . . to decide the practices which will best communicate the states of affairs of their companies . . . . We have followed it in the past and it has become discredited . . . . the standard practice proponents . . . say that unless companies report alike you cannot compare them in order to judge their performance and standing . . . . equivalent treatments under circumstances that are not equivalent should show up just that and ought, other things being equal, to disclose which business entity is in the more favorable position.

McMonnies, 1977, 165

963 Qualities expected of endorsed methods and standards

A standard is an agreed upon criterion of what is proper practice in a given situation; a basis for comparison and judgment; a point of departure when variation is justifiable by the circumstances and reported as such. Standards are not designed to confine practice within rigid limits but rather to serve as guideposts to truth, honesty and fair dealing . . . . they direct a high but attainable level of performance, without precluding justifiable departures and variations in the procedures employed.

Littleton, 1953, 143

statements to be issued by the [proposed Accounting Principles] Board would be regarded as an authoritative written expression of what constitutes generally accepted accounting principles . . . . [They] would be framed in relation to basic postulates and broad principles.

AICPA, 1958, 68

Accounting standards . . . . should be more closely defined, permit of fewer variations, and be more readily recognizable to investors. This task is being undertaken by the Chartered Accountants Institutes – it means five years' hard work – . . . .

Leach, 1970, 31

rather than eliminate all but one method of reflecting depreciation and all but one method for pricing inventories, [in the US] careful studies, hopefully, will determine the specific circumstances under which each one of several methods will produce the most meaningful results.

Layton, 1971, 114

The accounting profession should not tolerate or advocate an "either-or" position on alternative procedures because of some uncertainty concerning which alternative is best. It should make a single choice among the alternatives, even though some practitioners may dissent from the choice, in the interests of improved consistency and comparability.

Hayes, 1972, 86

accounting standards should apply to all companies – not just to listed ones or those over a certain size . . . . standards are an essential contributor to a true and fair view . . . . standards should ideally specify a single accounting treatment, rather than allow alternatives . . . . Once alternatives are allowed, comparability – one of the main reasons from the user's point of view for having standards – is undermined.

Percy, 1979, 46

964 Choice of a mode, style or system of accounting

Accounting must be dominated by an orderly body of accounting thought consistently applied on the basis of objective information.

Bailey, 1948a, 18

What form should accounting take? This appears to involve questions of value . . . . But is the appearance of a value question illusory? Admittedly the objectives, wants, tastes of persons and organizations differ; but given any set of objectives, wants, tastes . . . , the problem of accounting is to inform adequately (but subject to the limits of accounting) the actions by which objectives are pursued or wants and tastes are satisfied.

Chambers, 1960b, 39

Suppose that mankind knew nothing about final accounts, and had now to invent them *de novo*. Can anyone seriously contend that managers and investors would ask for historical data? Surely they would instead ask for various up to date figures to show: 1. how the firm's wealth has grown recently – as a test of efficiency in buying and selling assets and in operating them; and 2. the current nature and value of the net assets – as a test, e.g. of the adequacy of the income:capital ratio.

Baxter, 1964, 34

Accounting practices that enable management to manipulate the measure of income of a period are inferior to accounting practices that avoid the possibility of manipulation . . . . To stabilize the real income of a firm may be a worthwhile objective to management . . . , but the stabilization of income by accounting tricks is not desirable. Investors have a right to know that income fluctuates.

Bierman, 1965, 191

Accounting as it exists today is largely data-oriented. It starts with certain data in mind and is concerned with its recording, analysis and presentation. A data-orientation, however, does not answer, nor even ask, the really important question as to why data should be collected . . . in the first place . . . . The opposite of a data-orientation in this sense is an information orientation . . . . the first question [then] becomes " . . . what information might change the decision?" rather than "what information can be extracted from these data?"

Simmonds, 1972, 17

965 Antipathy to standardization and regulation

many a manufacturer and many a merchant believes that [despite scientific management principles and standardization] he must bring about the fruition of his own personal plans in his own individual way, and that he is the only competent judge of his own policies. Consequently statements and reports relating to the financial condition of a going business concern . . . . cannot be reduced to rules and methods, any more than they can be imprisoned within the narrow confines of standardized forms.

Esquerré, 1927, 3

standardization of accounting practice or procedure . . . would mean the substitution of fixed rules for opinion and discretion . . . . If we had been standardized or unionized at any time during [the past] fifty years, I am sure we would have lost one of our choicest possessions – independence to express our convictions in each particular case submitted to us, and most cases differ from every other case.

Montgomery, 1937b, 345

there is a danger that the establishment of uniformity may lead to crystallization . . . . The tyranny of tradition is present . . . in nearly all fields . . . . it may grow on us [accountants] if we don't watch out.

Wilcox, 1945, 181

There exists in the accounting profession a strong tendency toward freedom of decision by the individual in the acceptance or nonacceptance of accounting methods . . . . This spirit of independence is strongly advocated and jealously defended. To speak in favor of standardization, enforced conformity through regulation, or regimentation generally, is regarded as a form of professional treason.

Young, 1957, 202

We have an example in this country of the effect of the promulgation of fixed accounting rules by authority – the Interstate Commerce Commission. It is I think generally agreed among accountants that the rigidity of the rules of the Commission has in the last few years forced the railroads to prepare accounts which are not only uninformative but which are positively misleading. It is hard to imagine any other result when an authoritative body has the responsibility of making definite rules for anything so subject to change and variation as the business enterprises for which accountants prepare financial statements.

Peloubet, 1959, 25

neither comparability among financial statements nor any other interests of investors are better served ... by centrally promulgated uniform accounting rules.
Bevis, 1966, 37

It may at some time become clear beyond question that standard setting cannot be left in private hands. But that time is not yet. Until it is shown without doubt that this task must be entrusted to government, we strongly prefer to keep it where it is.
AICPA, 1972a, 23

Practitioners of the thirties self-servingly equated comprehensive rules of financial reporting with rigid, foolish and arbitrary directives enforced by hostile and incompetent bureaucrats. This ideological commitment became ritualized in the fight over the control of accounting principles, and persisted thereafter.
Chatov, 1975, 174

A good scientist accepts that principles must be regarded as tentative. His knowledge of history strengthens this view: sooner or later, principles are likely to be improved on, if not refuted. Only god-like creatures know where truth lies. It follows that *ex cathedra* pronouncements by human authority are pretentious, and inevitably must sometimes be wrong.
Baxter, 1981, 8

if a company needs to get around some accounting pronouncement, the letter of the edict may be twisted to derive a result that is at odds with its spirit. Such excessive literalism then leads to ever more explicit rules in a process rapidly resembling the development of the Internal Revenue Code.
Kaplan, 1987, 7

966 Regulation by law and administrative agencies

I think I can say unequivocally that the temper of the present Commission [SEC] is to permit the accountants to draw up for themselves what they shall consider accepted accounting principles. If the practitioners, after sufficient time has elapsed, have not come to some substantial agreement as to what are or should be considered accepted principles and practices, we may well expect the Commission's staff accountants to prepare and the Commission to publish what it shall demand in the way of such practices .... If this project is to be undertaken by a governmental body, I know of no such body more capable, more sincere or more impartial than the present Securities and Exchange Commission.
Smith, 1935, 327, 332

it cannot be that there are no real standards in accounting. It seems to me that one great difficulty has been that there has been no body which had the authority to fix and maintain standards. I believe that such a body now exists in the Securities and

Exchange Commission . . . . I think the purpose of accounting is to account – not to present opinions of value. [Healy was one of the original members of the SEC.]
Healy, 1938, 5, 6

[Under the administration of the SEC] most questions of accounting are settled by the star-chamber process [in respect of particular corporations] . . . . Now this, it is submitted, is not a satisfactory state of affairs. Specifically, (1) Decisions so made are not recorded or available to others as a guide of conduct or a basis of informed criticism and comment; (2) They are by no means necessarily uniform, reasoned, systematic, or grounded in anything other than the feeling of the examining staff; (3) They are not reviewed by any competent authority, nor susceptible of being so; and (4) There is no procedure leading to the conclusion that such decisions are valid precedent rather than purely arbitrary determination, depending on the capability and integrity of the Commission staff at any given moment.
Berle, 1938, 12

Independent accountants and auditors should become neutral corporate financial reporters. Thus, to the maximum extent practicable, the SEC should prescribe by rule a framework of uniform accounting principles. In instances where uniformity is not practicable, the SEC should require the independent auditor to attest that the accounting principles selected by management represent financial data most fairly. He should also prescribe supplemental data to permit a translation from one set of assumptions to another, thereby permitting comparability among companies in a particular industry.
Moss Committee, 1976, 51–52

Accounting was Congress' most important charge to the Commission [SEC] and represented the Commission's greatest opportunity to be of use to the investor . . . . The determination of what accounting should mean is the SEC's most important job – too important to be left to others . . . . The Commission's failure to consider the purposes and nature of financial accounting led to forty years' stagnation of accounting thought within the practising profession.
Kripke, 1979, 142, 153, 147

Congressional concerns about the accounting profession have been recorded and repeated time and again during the past few years. The lack of uniformity in generally accepted accounting principles and standards, management fraud and illegal political contributions escaping the detection of accounting firms, financial failures of corporate giants following the publication of unqualified financial statements by Big Eight auditors, and the accelerating trend toward concentration of the profession . . . are some of these concerns.
Nelligan, 1980, 113

[Response of a former chief accountant of the SEC to a question: why has the SEC chosen to delegate to the profession power over accounting and reporting procedures used by public companies?] In 1933 the American Institute of Accountants couldn't pull itself together to testify at hearings on what became the Securities Act.

.... Arthur Carter ... then the president of the New York State Society of CPAs ... was the only accountant to do so. He rebutted those senators who thought the government ought to hire an army of auditors to audit all public companies. He saved the day. Because of Carter's testimony, reliance on the auditor and auditor independence were written into the securities acts.

Barr, 1988, 79

it was Congress that instigated the Savings and Loan [regulatory accounting] rules that kept insolvent associations open in the early 1980s and thereby deferred (and worsened) the problem.

Revsine, 1991, 25

See also 916

967 Professional self-regulation

The essential features derived from British practice [of the proposals of the Special Committee on cooperation with the stock exchanges of the AIA, 1932] were: (1) each company was to choose its own accounting methods, (2) the companies were to disclose clearly the nature of the methods and procedures used, (3) the statements were to be put forth as representations of management, and (4) the public accountant would certify whether the methods used were acceptable, ... consistently followed, and ... properly reflected in the statements.

Storey, 1964, 14

With the widespread recognition of the importance of accounting in solving present day problems of government and industry, practitioners and teachers of accounting have an unparalleled opportunity to make a constructive contribution. If we fail the lawyers of the Securities and Exchange Commission and other government agencies will do it for us.

Barr, 1938, 323

It seems desirable that the profession formulate its own rules and standards, rather than leave their development to chance or government legislation.

Greer, 1938b, 221

We should take a decided stand ... in the formulation of and obtaining the acceptance of proper accounting principles, rather than yield this leadership to governmental regulatory agencies, who do not have the basis of experience which must, of necessity, provide the foundation for the determination of such principles.

Olive, 1943, 464

the companies acts .... should state that accounting principles are those principles which are defined and promulgated from time to time by the Accounting Standards Steering Committee and ratified by the Institute of Chartered Accountants, and that standards so defined have the force of law just as if they appeared as part of the act itself.

Stamp, 1970c, 628

1. Neither the Committee on Accounting Procedure nor the Accounting Principles Board issued a binding statement of accounting principles in over thirty years of continuous activity in the area. 2. Neither agency adopted a set of terms with related definitions, e.g. "cost", "asset", "revenue" .... 6 The buffeting the Board [APB] took in its attempt to resolve difficult issues led it, in later years, to avoid them, and concentrate instead in compiling a record by issuing opinions on less controversial topics.

Moonitz, 1974, 28

[Comment on a statement of professional bodies on compliance with accounting standards] There is thus no attempt to require mandatory compliance with the standards – what is mandatory (for members) is the disclosure and explanation of departures, with an unequivocal comment from the auditor. This leaves the user of the accounts in the position where he has information on which he can make up his own mind.

Balmford, 1977, 554

It is unrealistic ... to expect that the objectives which the professional bodies seek to achieve through the issue of standards, viz. the improvement of the quality and uniformity of reporting, can be achieved through efforts of the profession alone.

Ryan, 1977, 561

I have sometimes felt that a major obstacle to progress in accounting principles has been that those generally accepted principles have been enunciated by auditors who were more concerned with auditability than economic reality.

Davidson, 1978, 206

It is a safe bet that some 90% of accountants are not excessively fond of government. Their political philosophy holds that the state should interfere little in the affairs of good citizens, and that state controls soon reach a point at which they do more harm than good. Such men would scoff at the notion that, by entrusting difficult problems to political authority, we bring the millenium closer. Yet these men are now happily erecting and submitting to an extra form of authority within their own profession. They hungrily demand more controls over their daily work, and do not doubt that the outcome will be good. Is this not a puzzling paradox?

Baxter, 1979, 25–6

[The step of imposing an obligation on members of the accounting profession to ensure that financial reports comply with statements of accounting concepts and accounting standards] has been taken by the accounting profession because it provides an explicit financial reporting framework in accordance with which a preparer can prepare and present a financial report, and against which an auditor can form an independent opinion on the financial report. In doing so it provides a greater degree of certainty as to what is a desirable standard of financial reporting.

McGregor, 1992, 70

970 Standard Setting

971 Development on the legal pattern

there is urgent need of an "accounts division" of the High Court of Justice being established, under a judge who had undergone a special training in some chartered accountant's office, and who was in fact an expert in questions relating to figures and accounts of any description.

Accountant, editorial, 1890a, 420

In the majority of [common law] cases where a new precedent is established, the process is obviously that of applying existing acknowledged principles to a new set of facts. The principles, it may be, give no explicit answer to the question put. It does not follow that they give no answer at all. By a process of deduction, by argument from analogy, the existing principles may be made to yield a new principle, which is new because never stated before, but which in another sense is not new because it was already involved in what was already acknowledged. Just in the same way the conclusions of a science may be involved in its premises, and yet when first made constitute something new, an addition to what was before acknowledged. Even where a decision does not follow a definite logical process from acknowledged principles, it has not the arbitrary character of legislation. In the absence of clear precedents which might govern a question, we find judges relying on such considerations as the opinions of legal writers, . . . the law of other modern countries, the Roman Law, principles of natural justice or public policy.

Geldart, 1911/1933, 23

As a judicial adjunct to the security and exchange commission a board of financial review should be formed to serve as a court of arbitration of such disagreements as may arise between licensed auditors and their clients . . . . A group of interested, earnest specialists, such as would be chosen for this court, would build up in a relatively short time a most useful body of sound and authoritative precedents related to specific situations. This would afford an exceptional basis for shaping that body of doctrine called principles of good accounting and sound finance into a well coordinated form, ...

Littleton, 1935a, 288–9

It should be within the realm of possibility to create a Board of Accounting Appeals to which accounting questions could be referred . . . . It ought not to follow the doctrine of *stare decisis* as do common law courts; that is, precedent should not be binding. Rather we ought to borrow from the experience of our European friends who practice the Roman law, and follow the system by which the writers, the scholars, the commentators, are as persuasive authority as are the decisions of the group itself.

Berle, 1938, 14

I believe the preferable way of eliminating alternative principles [is] the establishment of a court of accounting principles. From a professional point of view, we need the case method of arriving at decisions on accounting principles .... We now have no satisfactory method of challenging what are presently regarded as accepted principles of accounting .... This must be corrected; and as I see it the court of accounting principles would do so.

Spacek, 1958b, 375

The statement is sometimes made that evolution in accounting should proceed in somewhat the same manner as evolution in common law. This analogy is not a good one because common law is determined by independent judges (without clients) and juries in a court system – with testimony, cross examination, filing of briefs, written decisions and a public record. There is nothing comparable to this in the field of accounting.

Catlett, 1964, 39

[The idea that] accounting principles must be developed on a case-by-case basis, as are the principles of common law [should be discarded]. The analogy is a poor one .... The common law is formulated by judges who have ceased to be members of the legal profession .... Unless accountants are willing to set up similar machinery – an accounting court composed of judges who have severed all relationships with clients and firms ... – they should stop using the analogy.

Storey, 1964, 64

The lack of training and knowledge in accounting on the part of SEC commissioners, plus their ingrained reliance as lawyers on precedent, has always provided the basis for their supporting the *ad hoc* development of accounting principles by a private group.

Chatov, 1975, 178

accounting standards should evolve in response to environmental changes in the same way as the common law.

Stamp, 1982, 124

972 Standard setting said to be a political process

In common with other essentially political activities, accounting rule-making must overcome as its chief obstacle not the inscrutability of nature, but rather the conflict between interest groups .... a politicization of accounting rule making was not only inevitable but just. In a society committed to democratic legitimization of authority, only politically responsive institutions have the right to command others to obey their rules.

Gerboth, 1973, 479, 481

My hypothesis is that the setting of accounting standards is as much a product of political action as of flawless logic or empirical findings. Why? Because the setting of standards is a social decision. Standards place restrictions on behavior; therefore they must be accepted by the affected parties. Acceptance may be forced or voluntary or some of both. In a democratic society, getting acceptance is an exceedingly complicated process that requires skillful marketing in a political arena.

Horngren, 1973, 61

in practice as well as in theory, the social welfare impact of accounting reports apparently is recognized. Therefore it is no surprise that the [Financial Accounting Standards Board] is a political body and, consequently, that the process of selecting [an] acceptable accounting alternative is a political process.

May & Sundem, 1976, 750

in the final analysis the responsibility of mediating conflicting values in our society rests with Congress rather than with any private sector or organization. Congress, on the other hand, is not presently equipped to deal effectively with the complex disclosure and measurement issues in contemporary corporate reporting. It has, in fact, delegated accounting standard setting to the SEC and other federal agencies. The SEC in turn has delegated some of its power to the FASB. In brief, no single organization has both the technical competence to deal with the complex measurement and disclosure issues and the social legitimacy to assess and resolve conflicts among competing interests. Indeed, as one moves down the Congress-SEC-FASB hierarchy, one observes increasing technical competence and decreasing social legitimacy.

Rappaport, 1977, 89

Why is there a need for participation by parties outside the accounting profession in the accounting standard setting process? Probably the major reason for the need for representation is that accounting standards have economic consequences . . . . Since standards affect resources allocation and income distribution, many people believe that the standard setting process should be a representative democratic process. After all, few people would accept, say, [that] monetary or fiscal policy should be determined by a private, non-representative group.

Hines, 1983, 24

Probably the most effective way of influencing the course of a tribunal's decisions is through the selection of its members, either generally or for particular matters. Clearly, those who have the power of initial appointment of the members of the tribunal have the opportunity to select persons who are favorably disposed towards one line of thinking rather than another.

Mills, 1984, 328

973 Standard setting expected to be apolitical

If it ever became accepted that accounting might be used to achieve other than purely measurement ends, faith in it would be destroyed just as faith in speedometers would be destroyed once it was realized that they were subject to falsification for the purpose of influencing driving habits.

Solomons, 1978, 69

If it becomes accepted or expected that accounting principles are determined or modified in order to secure purposes other than economic measurement ... we assume a grave risk that confidence in the credibility of our financial information system will be undermined.

Williams, 1978b, 69

Accounting standards are subject to Murphy's law of thermodynamics: things get worse under pressure, especially political pressure .... The thermodynamic reference is particularly apt because politics is essentially a thermodynamic process – the generation of power through the application of hot air.

Mosso, 1980, 128

Nothing could undermine the credibility of financial reporting among users more than knowledge that the amount of information released in financial reports has been determined by political horse trading or that the information itself may have been biased by standard-setters' opinions as to what is good for people to know. Rather, accounting standards must be neutral to be believable.

Skinner, 1987, 662

974 Standard setting

The Accounting Standards Steering Committee (ASSC) came into being on 1 January 1970 .... The ASSC was a self-regulatory private sector body, sponsored by the three chartered institutes [English, Scottish and Irish], dominated by accountants in public practice, and relying for its authority on its disciplinary powers over individual members of its constituent bodies who were preparers or users of accounts. The ASSC became the Accounting Standards Committee (ASC) in 1975 .... The Consultative Committee of Accountancy Bodies (CCAB) which controls ASC is now sponsored by all six of the leading accountancy bodies ....

Whittington, 1989a, 195

We keep kidding ouselves to the effect that we [accountants] and management are on the same side. This is a myth. Management wants to win; it wants to show increased earnings; it wants to have a good report card. The objective of the public accountant is, or ought to be, to tell it like it is. Given these opposing interests, it

seems clear to me that we ought to get management out of the business of establishing accounting principles, especially when the main principle that they want to
establish is one of diversity or flexibility.

Sterling, 1973a, 65

The work of Britain's own Accounting Standards Steering Committee has not escaped
attack from those who believe that the profession is attempting, through its effective
monopoly of the statutory audit function, to usurp the authority of Parliament.

Accountant, editorial, 1975a, 61

Usually they [standards] consist of three parts: (a) A description of the problem to
be tackled; (b) a reasoned discussion (possibly exploring fundamental theory) of
ways of solving the problem. Then, in the light of the decision on theory: (c) The
prescribed solution . . . . If a standard confines itself to (a) and (c), it may or may
not be a useful rule of action; at least it can be judged by how it works. When it
includes (b), it incurs two extra risks: its reasoning may be false, and it will impede
other attempts to reach truth.

Baxter, 1979, 30–31

The standard setting process as a negotiation creates a dilemma for the profession:
it assumes that the professional accounting bodies are attempting to represent the
views and interests of their own members and at the same time to act as rule makers
in the wider public interest.

TAM, editorial, 1982, 350

The choice of accounting measurement or valuation procedures remains a matter of
some controversy . . . . any guidelines governing the application of valuation procedures would be highly contentious and the Board does not intend to attempt such
a task at this stage.

ASRB, 1985c, R101

giving preparers [top management and chief financial officers of companies] a stronger
position in the process [of standard setting] might be like using a fox to guard the
henhouse.

Miller, 1985, 30

while the ASC has not ignored theory altogether, it remains true that it has not
approached standard setting from the point of view of a coherent theoretical
framework. No statement of what the ASC sees as the purpose and nature of financial
reporting has ever been produced.

Taylor & Turley, 1986, 80

975 Dual or differential standards

dual standards for audits . . . [one level for smaller, and another for larger, companies]
would only serve to confuse the reader . . . . using such words as "we have audited

the above accounts in accordance with the standards applicable to this class of company", . . . raises a question in the mind of the reader as to what standards are being applied.

Davison, 1978, 94

This [current cost accounting] standard applies to all annual financial statements . . . other than those of entities falling within the categories listed below: (a) entities which do not have any class of share or loan capital listed on the stock exchange and satisfy at least two of the following three criteria: (i) they have a turnover of less than £5,000,000 per annum; (ii) their balance sheet total at the commencement of the relevant accounting period is less than £2,500,000 as shown in the historical cost accounts; and (iii) the average number of their employees . . . is less than 250; (b) wholly owned subsidiaries . . . ; (c) authorized insurers, property investment and dealing entities . . . ; investment trust companies, unit trusts and other similar long term investment entities; entities whose long term primary financial objective is other than to achieve an operating profit . . . [such as] charities, building societies, friendly societies, trade unions and pension funds.

ASC, 1980b, SSAP16

We [the technical issues committee of the private companies practice section of the AICPA] do not believe . . . that exempting private companies from accounting standards that are not relevant or cost-effective for them is the same as establishing two sets of GAAP.

AICPA, 1982, 9

Adoption of dual standards could . . . destroy our credibility with the financial world . . . . Bankers and other lenders would be presented with income statements that upset the financial community, cause problems with terms of loan indentures and other contracts . . . . Are proponents of dual standards of the opinion that private companies don't have financing needs? . . . I believe that adoption of dual measurement standards is against the best interests of our clients, the financial community and the profession.

Kaplan, 1982, 65

The [UK *Companies Act, 1985*] contains two sets of accounting rules, the historical cost accounting rules and the alternative accounting rules. The latter rules apply when a historical cost basis is not used for valuation purposes and, in practice, many companies use a mixture of historical cost and current valuation.

Whittington, 1989b, 155

Differential reporting relates to the imposition of different statutory and professional reporting requirements for different categories of reporting entities . . . . Examples of different categories are large versus small entities, public as opposed to private companies, or some combination of legal structure and size . . . . A popular argument is that the relatively high cost of compliance for small firms warrants differential reporting requirements.

Holmes & others, 1991, 126, 131

976 Comment on quality of professional dicta

[The first three bulletins of the AIA Committee on Accounting Procedure] have succeeded in being little more than attempts to explain and justify practices existing among professional accountants.

Kohler, 1939, 453

accounting societies appear to be content to recommend what they think the general body of business will bear, a salutary attitude in building up an accounting practice but hardly commendable when aimed at social and economic improvement, which should be one of the aims of a professional society.

Stacey, 1954, 118

the concepts and principles set forth in this statement are based upon ineffective foundations, along the lines of the following: (1) vague generalizations which are noncontroversial but serve no useful purpose; (2) circular reasoning, with undefined terms being defined by other undefined terms, such as the description of assets and liabilities as those items "recognized and measured in conformity with generally accepted accounting principles"; and (3) reverse logic, by summarizing a wide variety of customs and practices, many of which need to be changed and improved, and then rationalizing back to principles that presumably support what now exists. [attributed to G R Catlett]

AICPA, 1970c, APBS4

Detailed rules are made to plug loopholes inherent in broad general standards . . . . [They are] sometimes thought to provide a safe haven for an accountant who follows them. In law suits against accountants, the defendant typically seeks to establish as a defense his adherence to professional standards . . . . The accounting profession seems to oppose an increase in authority and favor a decrease in responsibility. Statements on auditing procedures often seem to be designed to reduce responsibility – to provide a rule which if followed will free the accountant of further responsibility. Much the same design appears to be built into Accounting Principles Board opinions.

Savoie, 1973, 75

To the careful reader of professional pronouncements it will be obvious that there are inconsistencies within and between statements of accounting standards; different treatments are prescribed for events or transactions which, when ordered acccording to logical criteria, would appear to fall within the same category. In some important aspects such framework as exists is sadly out of tune with the actual environment in which accounting as a function has to perform.

Feller, 1974, 396

The results of the Commission's [SEC's] 1938 decision, by a 3 to 2 vote, to rely primarily on the private accounting profession to establish accounting principles has been disappointing at best. In 1940 the Committee on Accounting Procedure (CAP) was established by the . . . American Institute of Accountants. The CAP dealt almost exclusively with the articulation of existing accounting practices and pragmatic solutions to specific accounting problems. Little effort was devoted to the development of a rational conceptual structure. The AICPA finally reacted to the CAP's failures by creating the Accounting Principles Board (APB) in 1959. The APB folded in the early 1970s, after destroying its credibility as an organization capable of resolving financial reporting controversies. Its failure to set down hard and fast rules about merger accounting until October 1970, after billions of dollars had been accounted for by inadequate and often misleading methods, brought condemnations from public investors, financial analysts, academicians, accountants, and the Congress .... In the wake of the APB's disintegration, the AICPA created the Financial Accounting Standards Board (FASB). Instead of reacting to the the dismal record of the FASB's predecessor boards by reversing its 1938 decision, the SEC continued to recognize the standards, principles, and practices promulgated by the private sector through the FASB .... Considering the FASB's record, the SEC's continued reliance on the private accounting profession is questionable.

Moss Committee, 1976, 31–336

In all of these documents [of AAA, AICPA, FASB, CICA] the authors have avoided stating propositions that imply radical changes from current accounting practice. Rather, the trend has been to use undefined terms such as "information useful to investors and creditors" (AICPA, 1973) and "relevance to users' needs" (CICA, 1980). .... As one might expect, none of these studies has had any discernible effect on actual accounting practice.

Butterworth & others, 1981, 8

unprecedented make-believe and illusion have been the hallmark of professional prescriptions [for dealing with inflation in accounts]. What has been said to account for the financial effects of price and price level changes has neither done so, nor been capable of doing so; what has been said to support the professional prescriptions has often been part of a grand illusion; what has been presented to be a measurement of general purchasing power gains or losses has usually not been a measurement of general purchasing power gains or losses; and what has been passed off as a measure of specific purchasing power gains and losses invariably has not been a measurement of purchasing power gains or losses of any variety.

Clarke, 1984, 106

[The ASC's] publications have attempted to resolve difficult problems by categorical assertions, rather than by careful argument leading to considered judgments and recommendations. The outcome of this process is statements which sometimes lack internal coherence, are often mutually inconsistent, and seem to reflect political pressures to a greater extent than logic. In my view the fundamental reason for the difficulties I have identified is the ASC's failure to adopt a clearly articulated theory for accounting.

Grinyer, 1985, 14

977 Comment on quality of accounting standards

The accounting information that the SEC requires is, on the whole, not relevant for investors . . . . the insistence on traditional, historically-based accounting contributes to the lack of usefulness of financial reports.
Benston, 1969, 73

The establishment of accounting standards will not eradicate the possibility that any out of a wide range of reported profits might reflect the profit of the past year, for there is a substantial element of subjectivity involved which can never be removed.
Briston, 1974, 50

Despite accounting standards, there are still too many ways in which the same sort of transaction can be handled by different companies; and what is worse, it is too easy for directors with grasshopper minds to change their companies' accounting policies.
Holmes, 1975, 57

I have observed the ways in which it [FASB] has avoided the critical issues, vacillated on other controversial matters, and handed out special dispensations in order to obtain a consensus for a particular standard. I expected much, much more from a select body endowed with presumptive independence and supposedly possessed of intellectual might, integrity and intrepidity. In short, we have had a surfeit of compromise, of the vulgar pragmatism, of pussy-footing and inching along.
Briloff, 1976, 32

The FASB has accomplished virtually nothing toward resolving the fundamental problems plaguing the profession. These include the plethora of optional "generally accepted" accounting principles (GAAPs), the ambiguities inherent in many of those principles, and the manifestations of private accountants' lack of independence with respect to their corporate clients.
Moss Committee, 1976, 32

The most striking inconsistency [in UK SSAPs] . . . derives from the failure to define a profit concept . . . . Many standards . . . appear to be based on the matching concept of profits. Others . . . are founded on a periodic wealth measurement based profit concept. The two approaches seem to me to be incompatible.
Grinyer, 1978, 52

[The ASC] has apparently been unable to decide on a consistent approach to measuring profit; some standards depend on a direct matching of costs and revenues, . . . while others try to make accurate balance sheet measurements of wealth . . . . vacillation between different principles is most clearly shown in the ASC's successive attempts to introduce a deferred tax standard . . . . Some standards lean heavily on the prudence concept . . . while some do not . . . . Conflicts also arise in matters of substance

versus form, historical cost versus current valuation, in whether items of a similar nature should be considered individually or in aggregate, and so on.
Paterson & Smith, 1979, 54

a variety of income measures are either directly required by [FASB] SFAS33 or can be computed from the required disclosures. Some of these income measures imply a capital maintenance concept [one, physical capital maintenance; three, financial capital maintenance; one, a hybrid which combines physical capital maintenance for nonmonetary items and financial capital maintenance for monetary items; and there are four income figure choices where no clear capital maintenance concept is applicable], and, of course, each income measure implies a different [income] concept.
Livingstone & Weil, 1982, 228

those who advocate a conceptual framework for accounting would argue that present standards say far too little about underlying objectives and basic principles; and many responsible preparers of accounts would argue that standards impose too many rigid regulations.
TAM, editorial, 1982, 350

The reason why [creative accounting] has survived and thrived is that the system of accounting standards is itself designed to encourage an element of flexibility. The standards are not intended, despite their name, to lay down specific treatments, but rather to narrow down the range of options .... this leaves a system which gives the impression of laying down uniform standards but in practice it merely endorses the differing accounting treatments which are available.
Griffiths, 1986, 8

978 Comment on standard setting

We tend to meet any new situation by reorganizing and a wonderful method it can be for creating the illusion of progress while producing confusion, inefficiency and demoralization.
Roman citizen, AD60/1971, 43

Social reformers as a rule . . . fail to notice, or at least they disregard, the fact that individuals entertain different opinions with regard to utility, and that they do so because they get the data they require from their own sentiments. They say, and believe, that they are solving an objective problem: "What is the *best* form for a society?" Actually they are solving a subjective problem: "What form of society best fits my sentiments?" The reformer, of course, is certain that his sentiments have to be shared by all honest men and that they are not merely excellent in themselves but are also in the highest degree beneficial to society. Unfortunately that belief in no way alters the realities. [#2145]
Pareto, 1916/1963, 1477

Routine is the god of every social system; it is the seventh heaven of business . . . .
But when the adequate routine is established, intelligence vanishes, and the system
is maintained by a coordination of conditioned reflexes.
Whitehead, 1933/1948, 110

The Council of the AICPA recently adopted the position that . . . departures from
APB Opinions . . . must be reported . . . . Probably the effect will be felt most by
the APB itself, in that it will be more cautious than otherwise in stepping out ahead
of current accounting thought and practice in an attempt to set direction and pace.
Bevis, 1965, 190

If the accounting profession were to become completely subjected to a rule-making
body, or in fact to become a rule-making body itself, the results might well be to
force accountants to spend most of their time "looking for loopholes" whereby
satisfactory procedures may be followed despite prohibitive rules, and I could not
be convinced that "loophole looking" is in the best interests of the profession or
the public generally.
Gutteridge, 1965, 33

There is something faintly ridiculous about a profession formulating technical
standards for more than eight years without tackling two of its biggest problems
. . . . as accountants, we have not seriously attempted to define profit, nor have we
drawn a clear distinction between capital and revenue.
Accountancy, editorial, 1978, 1

once statutory treatment of an item is achieved, it is rarely challenged in the sense
of a reversal towards greater freedom of presentation. Recommendations concerning items already statutorily defined and required are generally in the direction of
redefining the requirement in the light of current trends.
Hain, 1978, 242

From 1968 through 1971, the APB struggled with the accounting for business combinations . . . . [In the upshot, the] APB, appearing almost as a pawn in a game of
political chess, disenchanted many of its supporters as it abandoned positions of
principle in favor of an embarrassing series of pressure-induced compromises.
Zeff, 1978, 59

[Speaking as] a specialist user of accounts, . . . the ASC seems to have lost its way
in recent years, which was perhaps to be expected as a group of unpaid part-time
people got involved in increasingly complex areas and came up against powerful
and conflicting pressure groups.
Percy, 1979, 48

The combination of the SEC's abdication of authority to prescribe accounting rules
in favor of action by the profession and the profession's reluctance to move toward
that end has left the development of "generally accepted accounting principles" in
a vacuum in which "flexibility" (read "general acceptance of just about anything")

has reigned. It is only recently, under the smart of the embarrassing performance of the profession during the "go-go years" of the late sixties, that some progress has been made.

Stevenson, 1980, 98

Setting standards primarily by assertion requires muscle for compliance, whereas conceptually based standards have a built-in persuasiveness. The APB's problems stemmed more from a missing anchor than from conflicts of interest and part time attention.

Gellein, 1981, 2–9

the erosion of that sense of personal responsibility which is the essence of professionalism [is among the prices paid for accounting opportunism] .... opportunistic exploitation of gaps in accounting rules exerts its own price in the form of still more rules, each more tedious than the one before. In 14 years, the FASB alone has churned out more than 90 statements, nearly 40 interpretations and more than 40 technical bulletins .... this ever-thickening scatter of rules has made it hard for practitioners to move .... Equally obstructive is the sometimes appalling level of detail to which the rules have descended .... Their scope often shrinks nearly to the level of individual transactions .... Such hemidemisemiquavers of the rules can distract attention from the larger purposes the rules are supposed to serve.

Gerboth, 1987, 98

Highly specific instructions . . . invite legalistic structuring of transactions to evade the intent of the standard. Such evasions lead, in turn, to further detailed standards and technical interpretations. These contribute to the burden of standards overload and, incidentally, increase the likelihood that literal interpretation of the rules will, in particular cases, produce results that do not pass the test of common sense.

Skinner, 1987, 515

the advent of accounting standard setting radically transformed the nature of accounting .... [The present crisis] is characterized by four fundamental problems that cannot be resolved in a scientifically acceptable manner within the context of the double entry accounting paradigm. These are that (1) accounting is inherently arbitrary . . . (2) accounting has been politicized . . . (3) rational selection of normative accounting standards is impossible . . . and (4) the role of accounting scholars has been to supply "excuses" to competing groups seeking to influence accounting standards to further their own interests.

Cushing, 1989, 37

The accounting standard setting process is in deep trouble, possibly in such deep trouble that our present structure is irretrievably lost to us. After seventeen years, the Financial Accounting Standards Board lies dead in the water beset by critics on all sides .... The Board has not been able to lead its various constituencies in an identifiable direction. It has joined its predecessors in its inability to construct and sell a meaningful conceptual framework, and it has therefore found it difficult to develop standards which flow from an accepted vision.

Burton & Sack, 1990, 117

Over the last twenty years no profession has subjected itself to more studies than has the accounting profession. [Committees of 1972, 1973, 1976, 1986, 1987, 1990 cited.] . . . . Out of the Trueblood and Wheat Committees came the FASB . . . . Notwithstanding all this the profession continues to be harried by litigation . . . , charges of ineptitude and insufficient independence from high places in government, public suspicion of its credibility, demands that the accounting standard setting process be reformed, and blame for every financial catastrophe . . . . The time may be ripe for . . . a national commission on auditing and accounting, one hopefully organized by the AICPA and other interested organizations rather than the government . . . . The commission should include accounting professionals, of course, lawyers, business people, government officials . . . , academics, users of financial statements, and others with a concern for the continued integrity and viability of an independent accounting profession.

Sommer, 1990, 114ff

Steps have . . . been taken, within the last three years, to strengthen the audit system through the establishment of a new regulatory framework. The Financial Reporting Council and its associated bodies – the Accounting Standards Board, the Urgent Issues Task Force, and the Financial Reporting Review Panel – have been set up to improve and tighten accounting standards, to deal with problem areas as they emerge, and to examine departures by individual companies from the statutory requirements and accounting standards.

Cadbury Committee, 1992, 36

979 Regulation and the regulated

Regulatory commissions often seem to work more in the interests of the regulated than of those they are supposed to protect, for the simple reason that they are so much in closer contact with the former.

Kuhn, 1963, 681

if nearly a century of regulatory history tells us anything [about the relationship between business and government], it is that the rules-making agencies of government are almost invariably captured by the industries they are established to control. Thus the ICC becomes the protector and promoter of the railways; the FPC, the ally of private rather than public power; the FCC, unable to define any standard of "public interest" that might cut seriously into the profits of the broadcasting industry; the CAB, an agency whose primary aim is to limit competition among the airlines; the Pentagon, a guardian of the health of its client corporations; even the SEC, . . . an agency characterized by a philosophy of benign neglect.

Heilbroner, 1972, 239

Two main theories of economic regulation have been proposed. One is the public interest theory . . . . that [government] regulation is supplied in response to the demand of the public for the correction of inefficient or inequitable market practices . . . . The second theory is the capture theory . . . . that regulation is supplied in response to the demands of interest groups struggling among themselves to maximize the incomes of their members . . . . This theory . . . singles out a particular interest group – the regulated firms – as prevailing in the struggle to influence regulation, and it predicts a regular sequence, in which the original purposes of a regulatory program are later thwarted through the efforts of the interest groups.

Posner, 1974, 335–342

Capture is said to occur if the regulated interest controls the regulation and the regulatory agency; or if the regulated parties succeed in coordinating the regulatory body's activities with their activities so that their private interest is satisfied; or if the regulated party somehow manages to neutralize or ensure nonperformance (or mediocre performance) by the regulatory body; or if in a subtle process of inter-action with the regulators the regulated party succeeds (perhaps not even deliber-ately) in coopting the regulators into seeing things from their own perspective and thus giving them the regulation they want; or if, quite independently of the formal or conscious desires of either the regulators or the regulated parties, the basic reward system leads neither venal nor incompetent regulators inevitably to a community of interests with the regulated party.

Mitnick, 1980, 95

The ASRB's early history can be considered a case study in regulatory capture . . . . During 1984–5 the profession had ensured the nonperformance of the ASRB; by the beginning of 1986 the profession had managed to influence the procedures, the priorities and the output of the Board. It was controlling both the regulations and the regulatory agency; it had managed to achieve coordination of the ASRB's activi-ties with the AARF's activities; and it appears to have influenced new appointments so that virtually all members of the Board might reasonably be expected to have some community of interests with the professional associations. The ASRB had been captured by the profession, within only 24 months.

Walker, 1987, 282

Financial reporting rules in both the private and public sectors are often arbitrary, complicated, and misleading. Most critics view this situation as accidental, a result of bad judgment by standard setters and regulators. By contrast, this paper advances the hypothesis that the problem is not accidental, but instead results from contrived and flexible reporting rules promulgated by standard setters who have been "captured" by the intended regulatees and others involved in the financial reporting process.

Revsine, 1991, 16

980 The Accountancy Profession

981 Professions generally

Sir Patrick Cullen: All professions are conspiracies against the laity.
Shaw, 1906, The Doctor's Dilemma, I

The ancient professions of law and medicine stand near the center [of those vocations called professions]. The practitioners, by virtue of prolonged and specialized intellectual training, have acquired a technique which enables them to render a specialized service to the community. This service they perform for a fixed remuneration whether by way of fee or salary. They develop a sense of responsibility for the technique which they manifest in their concern for the competence and honor of the practitioners as a whole – a concern which is sometimes shared with the state. They build up associations, upon which they erect, with or without the cooperation of the state, machinery for imposing tests of competence and enforcing the observance of certain standards of conduct .... It is the existence of specialized intellectual techniques, acquired as the result of prolonged training, which gives rise to professionalism and accounts for its peculiar features.
Carr-Saunders & Wilson, 1933/1964, 284

there are at least three characteristics that every legitimate profession should have. These are the rendering of a service, a certain psychological unity on the part of at least a considerable group of those who render it, and the recognition by them of certain ethical principles that should govern their conduct.
Custis, 1933, 4

the term profession means an avocation whose activities are subjected to theoretical analysis and are modified by theoretical conclusions derived from that analysis. This analysis has regard to the purposes of the avocation and to the adaptation of the activities for the attainment of those purposes. Such criticism must be founded upon some understanding of the nature of the things involved in those activities, so that the results of action can be foreseen. Thus foresight based upon theory, and theory based upon understanding of the nature of things, are essential to a profession .... The antithesis of a profession is an avocation based upon customary activities and modified by the trial and error of individual practice. Such an avocation is a craft ....
Whitehead, 1933/1948, 73, 74

A profession is a vocation whose practice is founded upon an understanding of the theoretical structure of some department of learning or science, and upon the abilities accompanying such understanding. This understanding and these abilities are applied to the vital practical affairs of man. The practices of the profession are modified by knowledge of a generalized nature and by the accumulated wisdom and experience of mankind, which serve to correct the errors of specialism. The profession, serving

the vital needs of man, considers its first ethical imperative to be altruistic service to the client.
Cogan, 1953, 49

Professional behavior may be defined in terms of four essential attributes: a high degree of generalized and systematic knowledge; primary orientation to the community interest rather than to individual self-interest; a high degree of self-control of behavior through codes of ethics . . . and through voluntary associations organized and operated by the work specialists themselves; and a system of rewards (monetary and honorary) that is primarily a set of symbols of work achievement and thus ends in themselves, not means to some end of individual self-interest.
Barber, 1963, 672

Essential features [of a profession] are: (a) A profession involves a skill based on theoretical knowledge. (b) The skill requires training and education. (c) The professional must demonstrate competence by passing a test. (d) Integrity is maintained by adherence to a code of conduct. (e) The service is for the public good. (f) The profession is organized.
Millerson, 1964, 4

all professions seem to possess: (1) systematic theory, (2) authority, (3) community sanction, (4) ethical codes, and (5) a culture.
Greenwood, 1966, 10

These well-established professions [medicine, theology and law] have common characteristics: Each renders essential services to society. Each is governed by ethical principles which emphasize the virtues of self-subordination, honesty, probity, devotion to the welfare of those served. Each has requirements for admission to the profession which are regulated by law. Each has procedures for disciplining those whose conduct violates ethical standards. Each depends upon a body of specialized knowledge acquired through formal education. Each has developed a language of its own, in its more sophisticated forms understandable only to the initiated.
Roy & MacNeill, 1967, 31

A profession is a vocation of the highest standing; it calls on its members to serve (no doubt for reward) the public by offering to them highly technical and always confidential advice and services, which require a different standard of conduct from the tradesman. [per Lord Upjohn]
Pharmaceutical Society . . . v Dickson,
1968, 703

It is the practitioner who decides upon the client's needs, and the occupation will be classified as less professional if the client imposes his own judgment.
Goode, 1969, 278

[Among the characteristics of a true profession] Its rules, sanctions and standards are imposed in order to enhance the level of service to the public, not to protect the selfish interests of the members of the profession.

Benson, 1981, 45

Most authorities agree that a profession is characterized by four important elements: a specialized body of knowledge taught in a formal and certifiable manner; a commitment to social purposes (good ones) that justify the profession's existence; the capacity to regulate itself, often with the sanction of the law for those who violate acceptable norms of behavior; status and prestige of above-average ranking in society.

Cottell & Perlin, 1990, 18

982 Accountancy profession

In England it appears to have been the *Companies Act* of 1862 and the *Bankruptcy Act* of 1869 which caused the emergence of the professional accountant in independent practice. The 1869 *Bankruptcy Act* abolished the Official Receiver and provided for the appointment of receivers by the creditors, who generally appointed an accountant; while the 1862 *Companies Act*, in giving impetus to the formation of joint stock trading companies, created a demand for professional accountants to act as auditors and liquidators.

Carr-Saunders & Wilson, 1933/1964, 210

Has it ever struck you, gentlemen, to inquire how it is that only in this kingdom does accountancy flourish; and why there is no corresponding profession on the continent, or even in America?

Carter, 1882, 9

The profession of accounting has become established on a par with law, medicine and other learned professions.

Bauer, 1948, I:406

three aspects of public accounting mark its practitioners as professional men. (1) Professional accountants have equipped themselves with suitable technical knowledge and appropriate skills; (2) they render their service in an atmosphere of ethical and economic independence; (3) public recognition has been given to the fact that the public interest is involved in the practitioner's character and in the results of his work.

Littleton, 1953, 110

In the mid-nineteenth century, English law created the independent auditor as a protection to stockholders against the incompetence or malfeasance of the managements to whom the investors had entrusted their money. With the acceptance of responsibility to investors as well as to the employer, the accountant-auditor assumed the mantle of professionalism. He became a "public accountant", accepting a responsibility to the public as well as to the client who paid his fee.

Carey, 1969, I:5

The emerging or marginal profession is an occupation which is not so clearly high or so clearly low on both ... generalized knowledge and community orientation that its status is clearly defined by itself and others .... Library work, social work, pharmacy and accountancy are all examples of the emerging or marginal profession ... because the knowledge on which their occupational performance is based is not highly developed, the codes they construct are full of vague generalities, and therefore hard for the individual practitioner to apply in concrete cases. The emerging profession is also unable to construct the machinery of interpretation and enforcement of its codes that exists in established professions.

Barber, 1963, 675

Members of our Institute [ICAEW] profess a competence to render a service which is of more than ordinary value and complexity. They profess a willingness to place their obligations to others – to the public, including those who retain and employ them, to the profession itself and to their colleagues – ahead of their own immediate self-interest. They profess integrity and objectivity, adherence to proper technical and professional standards, courtesy, and conduct consistent with the good reputation of the profession and the Institute.

Grenside, 1975, 507

983 Professional knowledge and skill

Effective knowledge is professionalized knowledge, supported by a restricted acquaintance with useful subjects subservient to it. This situation has its dangers. Each profession makes progress, but it is progress in its own groove. Now to be mentally in a groove is to live in contemplating a given set of abstractions. The groove prevents straying across country, and the abstraction abstracts from something to which no further attention is paid. But there is no groove of abstractions which is adequate for the comprehension of human life .... The remainder of life is treated superficially, with the imperfect categories of thought derived from one profession.

Whitehead, 1926/1938, 228

the existence of the code [of professional ethics] proclaims that in return for the faith which the public reposes in members of the profession, they accept certain obligations to behave in a way that will be beneficial to the public .... [Those who rely on the service of a professional practitioner] have to trust him, since they cannot appraise the quality of his product.

Carey, 1956, 4

A profession delivers esoteric services .... Professionals profess. They profess to know better than others the nature of certain matters, and to know better than their clients what ails them or their affairs. This is the essence of the professional idea and the professional claim . . . . Since the professional does profess, he asks that he be trusted. The client is not a true judge of the value of the services he receives; . . . . Only the professional can say when his colleague makes a mistake . . . . Every profession considers itself the proper body to set the terms in which some aspect of society, life or nature, is to be thought of, and to define the general lines, or even the details, of public policy concerning it.

Hughes, 1963, 655–7

The professional is expected to think objectively and inquiringly about matters which may be, for laymen, subject to orthodoxy and sentiment which limit intellectual exploration. Further, a person, in his professional capacity, may be expected and required to think objectively about matters which he himself would find it painful to approach in that way when they affected him personally. This why it is unfair to ask the physician to heal himself, the priest to shrive himself, or the teacher to be a perfect parent.

Hughes, 1963, 656

There is a very important sense in which the professional practitioner in our society exercises authority . . . . the area of professional authority is limited to a particular technically defined sphere . . . . A professional man is held to be an authority only in his own field.

Parsons, 1942/1963, 38

A nonprofessional occupation has customers; a professional occupation has clients. What is the difference? A customer determines what services and/or commodities he wants, and he shops around until he finds them. His freedom of decision rests upon the premise that he has the capacity to appraise his own needs and to judge the potential of the service or of the commodity to satisfy them . . . . In a professional relationship, however, the professional dictates what is good or evil for the client, who has no choice but to accede to professional judgment. Here the premise is that, because he lacks the requisite theoretical background, the client cannot diagnose his own needs or discriminate among the range of possibilities for meeting them. Nor . . . able to evaluate the caliber of the professional service he receives.

Greenwood, 1966, 12

With respect to knowledge, seven major characteristics affect the acceptance of an occupation as a profession. They are: 1. Ideally, the knowledge and skills should be abstract and organized into a codified body of principles. 2. The knowledge should be applicable, or thought to be applicable, to the concrete problems of living . . . . 3. The society or its relevant members should believe that the knowledge can actually solve these problems . . . . 4. Members of the society should also accept as proper that these problems be given over to some occupational group for solution . . . . 5. The profession itself should help to create, organize and transmit the knowledge. 6. The profession should be accepted as the final arbiter in any disputes over the validity of any technical solution lying within its area of supposed competence. 7. The amount of knowledge and skills and the difficulty of acquiring them should be great enough that the members of the society view the profession as possessing a kind of mystery that is not given to the ordinary man to acquire, by his own efforts or even with help.

Goode, 1969, 277

984 Customary professional constraints

In addition to training and experience, there are two most important principles upon which the position and reputation of the public accountant rest. The first is what may be called the doctrine of personal responsibility. He alone is responsible to his clients for the results of his work . . . . The second principle is that of absolute secrecy regarding all matters which may come before him in the course of his business.

Dickinson, 1902, 745

The characteristic feature of professional self-government is the development within its organization of rules of conduct which are enforced on its members . . . . These rules relate either to the conduct of professional men to each other, or to their conduct towards the community in general. The rules relating to the conduct of members *inter se* generally forbid competition and advertisement, discourage the adoption of unorthodox views, and prevent the association with unqualified persons of their own profession, and even qualified persons of allied professions.

Crew, 1925, 365

The rules of professional conduct of the accounting profession are in part a pledge to the public that in consideration of public confidence the profession will protect the public interest, and in part a code of behavior designed to protect the profession itself against the selfish interests of individual members.

Carey, 1946, 2

Every profession has practices which it bars. Amongst the commonest of these are advertising, poaching and undercutting. These activities which are considered in the business world to be laudable examples of enterprise – so much so that their restraint is *prima facie* contrary to public policy – have always been considered offensive professionally. [per Devlin J]

Hughes v Architects' Registration Council,
1957

Those seeking the advice of a professional man are entitled to expect of him the highest standards of ethical conduct. This means that the professional man must submit to some restraints of trade, such . . . as a prohibition against advertising and a refusal, by undercutting or otherwise, to snatch work from another practitioner . . . . The restraints on professional men are justifiable in law for they are necessary not only in the interests of the profession but also in the interests of the public, who trust to the peculiarly high standing and integrity of a profession to serve it well. [per Lord Upjohn]

Pharmaceutical Society ... v Dickson,
1968, 703

Mixed engagements – potential conflict of interest

concentration of attention on the problem of self interest with its related false dichotomy of concrete egoistic and altruistic motives, has served seriously to obscure the importance of ... other elements, notably rationality, specificity of function and universalism [in the complex balance of diverse social forces found in professional activities and business and bureaucratic administration].

Parsons, 1942/1963, 48

A member who is engaged in the practice of public accounting shall not concurrently engage in any business or occupation which .... detracts from the public image of the profession ... or, impairs the member's objectivity in rendering professional services to clients ... or, serves as a feeder to the member's public accounting practice ... or, requires extensive personal solicitation ... or, inherently involves responsibilities which are likely to conflict with the member's responsibility to others arising out of the client-CPA relationship. [ET Rule 504]

AICPA, 1973/1976

Loyalty to the truth – embodied in the very notion of objectivity – is fundamental to accounting. But .... While auditing may be the bread and butter of an acccounting organization, increasingly we find that consulting is where profits lie in the accounting profession. In fact, concern has frequently been expressed that competitive pressure, particularly price competition, is reducing the audit to a mere commodity. With pride in a quality audit and the attending external and internal rewards in danger of extinction, the audit could be reduced to nothing more than a means to entry for lucrative management advisory service work.

Cottell & Perlin, 1990, 77

In the aftermath of the savings and loan crisis of 1988–1989 .... the Federal Home Loan Bank Board initiated ten lawsuits against accounting firms that had audited the books of failed savings banks. Three of the nation's top [public accounting] firms were among the defendants. The congressional General Accounting Office, having examined eleven failed savings units in the Dallas, Texas, district, found that in six cases auditors had failed "to meet professional standards". The chairman of the House Banking Committee stated to accounting industry leaders that the auditors of the savings units were "derelict in their responsibility to sound early alarms about impending disasters". It is impossible to know ... the extent of complicity in the role of accounting firms in the savings and loan crisis.

Cottell & Perlin, 1990, 83

See also 093

985 Professional ethics

The distinctive feature of this kind of morals [professional ethics] and what differentiates it from other branches of ethics, is the sort of unconcern with which the public consciousness regards it . . . . The transgressions which have only to do with the practice of the profession, come in merely for a rather vague censure outside the professional field. They count as venial . . . . a bookkeeper who is complacent about the rules of scrupulous accounting . . . does not give the impression of a guilty person, although he is treated as such in the organization to which he belongs . . . . [Professional ethics] cannot be of deep concern to the common consciousness precisely because they are not common to all members of the society . . . . This is why public sentiment is only mildly shocked by transgression of this kind.

Durkheim, c1900/1957, 5

Professional ethics are concerned with moral directives which guide the relationship between the professional and others. They are designed to distinguish right from wrong action. Professional ethics are composed of rules and etiquette. Rules are obligatory customs, which may be implicit or explicit codes enforced by a recognized authority. Etiquette is a loose form of permissive conventions observed generally, but not enforced by any central authority, though a breach can lead to censure by colleagues.

Millerson, 1964, 149

There are three levels of professional responsibility: legal, ethical and moral. The legal responsibilities . . . . are the minimum which society imposes upon those who are given the honor of professional recognition, and the privilege of self-discipline . . . . codes of ethics are a reflection of the groups' sense of social responsibility. They are an expression of what a profession stands for . . . . moral responsibilities . . . are self-imposed by individuals, and often call for a standard of behavior even higher than that of the ethical requirements.

Carey, 1957/1964, 134

The code of the consultant professions . . . . reflects the four different aspects of consultant professionalism: 1. Rules arising from the fact that an expertise is involved . . . . 2. Rules arising from frequent concern with intimate personal matters . . . . 3. Rules arising from frequent concern with property of great value . . . . 4. Rules arising from the fact that the profession is a brotherhood of long standing.

Bennion, 1969, 29

986 Ethics – accountancy profession

The position of the company auditor is one of peculiar delicacy, for though he is appointed as the "watchdog" of the shareholders, he must yet work in close and constant cooperation with the board. It is essential, therefore, that, where the interests of the shareholders demand it, he should feel himself able to resist pressures that may be brought to bear on him, in regard either to the form of his certificate or to the manner in which the accounts are presented. Accordingly it has become part of the unwritten code of the profession that an auditor who is unable to agree with his directors upon a point of principle is under a duty to resign.

Carr-Saunders & Wilson, 1933/1964, 221

It is because it is believed by the investors and others who rely on his certificate that he is both competent and loyal to the truth, that it has value; and out of this fact arises a definite obligation to them. He is false to this obligation if, through any fault of his, the certificate misrepresents the facts.

Custis, 1933, 18

Eternal vigilance is the price of accounting as well as of liberty .... Let's fight for honest accounting, clear statements and full disclosure of all essential facts .... Let's fight for easily understood accounting terms. Let's fight weasel words. Let's fight bunk whenever and wherever it appears.

Montgomery, 1937c, 81, 92

In general, the code of professional ethics may be summarized as requiring that the accountant deal with his client, his fellow accountant, and with the public in a spirit of fairness and honesty, and in a manner in keeping with the dignity of his profession.

Graham, 1939, 262

[To] whom do these professional people [accountants] owe a duty? They owe the duty, of course, to their employer or client; and also I think to any third person to whom they themselves show the accounts, or to whom they know their employer is going to show the accounts, so as to induce him to invest money or take some other action on them .... In my opinion accountants owe a duty of care not only to their own clients, but also to all those whom they know will rely on their accounts in the transactions for which these accounts are prepared. [per Denning L J]

Candler v Crane, Christmas & Co, 1951

Professional ethics form a small part of a complex system of discipline which civilized society has imposed on itself through laws, customs, moral standards, social etiquette .... A code of professional ethics signifies voluntary assumption of the obligation of self-discipline above and beyond the requirements of the law.

Carey, 1956, 3

the profession in the United Kingdom has no written code of ethics. We regard it as essential that a public accountant shall be honest with himself and with others, a man of integrity, character and common sense, that he shall do unto others as he would that they should do to him and that he shall do all he can to maintain the esteem in which his profession is held by the public; ....

Robson, 1957, 87

Chartered accountants in our modern society are the every day custodians of the businessman's conscience. Judges, lawyers and ministers may in various aspects

become involved with it but not in the same way as an accountant who ... is concerned continually with a variety of small ethical problems ... [and problems] sometimes of frightening size, which should be solved in terms of right and wrong.
CanCA, editorial, 1960, 228

The reliance of the public and the business community on sound financial reporting and advice on business affairs imposes on the accounting profession an obligation to maintain high standards of technical competence, morality and integrity. To this end a member or associate of the American Institute of Certified Public Accountants shall at all times maintain independence of thought and action, hold the affairs of his client in strict confidence, strive continuously to improve his professional skills, observe generally accepted auditing standards, promote sound and informative financial reporting, uphold the dignity and honor of the accounting profession and maintain high standards of personal conduct.
AICPA, 1969a

The most ruthless of commercial operators, and the most cynical, cannot get very far if professional men [the auditor, the actuary, the lawyer] will not serve him, if the certificates and the advice and the comments are critical or revealing.
Boyd-Carpenter, 1973, 240

How well does the accounting profession measure up on the dimensions of public service performance and effective self-regulation? Not very well, according to a recent ... [U S Senate report]. ... [The Big Eight firms] often seem to care more about the interests of the corporations than the public welfare. They identify with the corporations rather than the public and join them in lobbying efforts against congressional efforts to reform accounting and corporate reporting standards. Through their domination of the accounting standards boards, the Big Eight practice what they call "creative accounting", that is, they adopt standards that have been labelled by outsiders as being so flexible that corporations sometimes seem to be able to call profits losses, and losses profits, depending on which label is most profitable and least taxable. In a considerable number of cases that have later been publicly exposed, accounting firms have aided corporations in deceiving the public and the government.
Barber, 1978, 610

Ethical behavior. An accountant should conduct himself in a manner consistent with the good reputation of the profession and refrain from any conduct which might bring discredit to the profession.
International Federation of Accountants, 1979, 78

by certifying the public reports that collectively depict a corporation's financial status, the independent auditor assumes a public responsibility transcending any employment relationship with the client. The independent public accountant performing this special function owes ultimate allegiance to the corporation's creditors and stockholders, as well as to the investing public. This public watchdog function demands that the accountant maintain total independence from the client at all times and requires complete fidelity to the public trust. [Per Chief Justice Burger]

United States v Arthur Young & Co et al, 1984

See also 269

987 Professional associations

Since . . . society as a whole feels no concern in professional ethics, it is imperative that there be special groups in the society, within which these morals may be evolved, and whose business it is to see that they be observed . . . . Each branch of professional ethics being the product of the professional group, its nature will be that of the group . . . . professional ethics will be the more developed, and the more advanced in their operation, the greater the stability and the better the organization of the professional groups themselves.

Durkheim, c1900/1957, 7

Professional associations are stabilizing elements in society. They engender modes of life, habits of thought and standards of judgment which render them centers of resistance to crude forces which threaten steady and peaceful evolution.

Carr-Saunders & Wilson, 1933/1964, 497

That the profession of Accountants, to which the Petitioners belong, is of long standing and great respectability . . . : That the business of Accountant . . . is varied and extensive, embracing all matters of account, and requiring for its proper execution, not merely thorough knowledge of . . . the province of the Actuary, but an intimate acquaintance with the general principles of law . . . : That Accountants [in various specified capacities] . . . . have duties to perform, not only of the highest responsibility . . . but which require, in those who undertake them, great experience in business, very considerable knowledge of law, and other qualifications which can only be attained by a liberal education: . . . that the Petitioners conceive that it would . . . conduce much to the benefit of the public if the Petitioners . . . were united into a body corporate and politic, having a common seal, with power to make rules and bye-laws for the qualification and admission of members and otherwise. [Petition for incorporation by Royal Charter by the Society of Accountants of Edinburgh, 1854]

ICAS, 1954, 23

Discipline

The preparation and certification of exhibits, statements, schedules or other forms of accountancy work, containing an essential misstatement of a fact or omission therefrom of such a fact as would amount to an essential misstatement or a failure to put investors on notice in respect of an essential or material fact not specifically shown in the balance sheet itself shall be, *ipso facto*, cause for expulsion, or for such other discipline as the Council may impose upon proper presentation of proof that such misstatement was either wilful or the result of such gross negligence as to be inexcusable.

AIA, 1931b, 155–6

The enumeration of [AICPA] rules of ethical conduct does not define further "sound and informative financial reporting". [The rules proscribe] a failure to disclose a known material fact, a failure to report any material misstatement, and a failure to direct attention to any material departure from generally accepted accounting principles. These nebulous statements hardly provide a sound basis for enforcement of ethical standards . . . . Surveillance is also inadequate.

Scott, 1972, 111

As a professional body, we enjoy the freedom of self-regulation and self-discipline . . . . there are those . . . who question the efficacy and even the desirability of self-regulation in today's environment. This challenge to the general concept of self-regulation makes it imperative that we always keep ahead of the game . . . .

Grenside, 1975, 507

The extension of the authority of the government executive must sooner or later endanger the right of the professions to order their own affairs. It has been a characteristic of most professional organizations that they are self-regulating: they control the conditions of entry – education, training and examinations; they maintain discipline and ethics; they develop, monitor and enforce the standards to which their members work; and they seek to foster and preserve that independence, integrity and sense of responsibility which is the mark of a true profession.

Wright, 1975, 789

Secrecy of proceedings and results, failure to address significant problems, and inaction during litigation are weaknesses in the state and professional disciplinary mechanism.

Cohen Commission, 1977, 140

There is no way in which a firm can be disciplined. You can investigate the actions of individual members, but not those of the firm itself. You can punish an individual, but not the firm . . . .

Accountancy, editorial 1979a, 1

A spate of Department of Trade inspectors' reports published at that time [1976] in the wake of a few financial scandals triggered off a crisis of public confidence in the competence and independence of accountants . . . and auditors . . . . The government expressed concern about the professional bodies' apparent inability to discipline their members for bad professional work . . . . in October 1976, the then Secretary of State for Trade . . . warned . . . that unless the profession took steps to "put its house in order", regulation by statute would be difficult to avoid.

Holmes, 1979, 5

988 Advancement of knowledge and skill

I hold every man a debtor to his profession; from the which as men of course do
seek to receive countenance and profit, so ought they of duty to endeavor themselves, by way of amends, to be a help and ornament thereunto.

Bacon (1561–1626)/1819, iv:10

the most effectual method which any class of men can adopt for securing their
political rights, and advancing their professional standing, consists not in disputation and warm argument, but in a steady and persevering attention to intellectual
improvement, and the establishment of such regulations as are calculated to ensure
collective privileges by increasing the amount of individual merit.

Bell, 1842/1964, 53

There is a real need . . . [in accountancy] for sustained academic study and research
. . . . but so far as I am aware, the Institute and the Society have not directly concerned
themselves with the academic study of accountancy or research work . . . .

de Paula, 1927, 31

A professional man has one foot in the academic world and the other in the world
of affairs; the academic knows what is theoretically possible, the professional man
knows what is possible in practice, or at least he is in a position to discover what
is possible and to make it known. This is his unique province for observation, and
it is here that he can contribute to knowledge.

Carr-Saunders & Wilson, 1933, 485

There is . . . one very definite contribution which practising accountants can and
should make to their profession. They should furnish accountancy with a scientific
literature . . . .These writings should develop not only sound practice and procedure
in accounting, but – much more important – they should present a scientific theory
and a genuine philosophy for the whole subject.

Jackson, 1933, 133

Is a profession which takes pride only in "being practical", in "getting on with the
work", which appears to shrink from being thought "academic" (and can even assume
that this implies some contradiction), and which is not prepared to make the sacrifices necessary to improve its own efficiency, really worthy to retain its place
among the learned professions?

Woodifield, 1935, 261

Among the vocations brought into prominence by the industrial revolution, accountancy was the only one whose growth in stature was for the most part unaccompanied by sustained research, either by its members or by its professional organizations.

Stacey, 1954, 219

It is significant that in America the accountants responsible for the public companies
supervised by the Securities and Exchange Commission indulge in more ferocious

argument and much more serious thought about the need to develop and define sensible accounting principles [than in the UK]. It is fair to say, indeed, that they have more to contend with – the inconsistencies of American company accounts are notoriously the despair of investors. But one does not have to agree with those who press for extensive standardization to believe that accountancy in Britain could become more efficient and its job more relevant if it scrapped the old textbooks and set out to define its aims and methods in twentieth century language . . . . it is the accountant's field itself that needs defining – what he is best suited to do in the world today as well as how he can do it better.

Economist, 1964, 805

the dynamics of all professions is the *status quo*. The ability to come together and provide leadership for change is extremely difficult for any group to undertake on its own.

Williams, 1980a, 124

Consider . . . the effects of state certification of accountants on the profession's ability to change. Certification ensures that prospective students are subject to a particular socialization process. This . . . instils in them common value sets and ways of thinking. Upon completing their training, new accountants then must comply with a code of ethics that governs their conduct. There is increasing recognition that some of those rules inhibit the free functioning of the market . . . . restrict the flow of new ideas into the market place.

Milne & Weber, 1981, 204

See also 885

989 Comment on the professions

It sometimes appears that professional ethics operate as a code of self-limitation against contributing to the embarrassment of colleagues by discovering too much that they themselves might have found out.

Lasswell, 1960, 96

The casuistry of accountants has long ceased to be comical; it is now a matter of grave concern. Until the day comes when the man on the omnibus can pick up an account of the dealings in his money by his stewards [company directors] and fully understand the implications of what is written therein, the accounting profession will still be in debt to society.

Greener, 1975, 42

Everywhere in the United States the professions have reached new heights of social power and prestige. Everywhere, because of the power of their special knowledge, they are of increasing consequence in the lives of individuals and in the affairs of groups, the polity and society as a whole. Yet everywhere they are also in trouble, criticized for their selfishness, their public irresponsibility, their lack of effective self-control, and for their resistance to requests for more lay participation in the vital decisions professionals make affecting laymen.

Barber, 1978, 599

codes of ethics function all too often as shields; their abstraction allows many to adhere to them while continuing their ordinary practices. In business as well as in those professions that have already developed codes, much more is needed. The codes must be but the starting point for a broad inquiry into the ethical quandaries encountered at work. Lay persons, and especially those affected by the professional practices, such as customers and patients , must be included in these efforts, and must sit on regulatory commissions. Methods of disciplining those who infringe the guidelines must be given teeth and enforced.

Bok, 1978/1989, 246

When *The Wall Street Journal* began using the term "accounting industry", I wrote them a letter of objection. Now I wouldn't dare, because I'm afraid the label is all too accurate. [attributed to a retired partner of a Big Eight firm of CPAs who was a leader of the profession when he was active]

Zeff, 1987, 65

990 Accounting Training and Education

991 Education generally

When a man teaches something he does not know to somebody else who has no aptitude for it, and gives him a certificate of proficiency, the latter has completed the education of a gentleman.

Shaw, 1903/1948, 273

Do not teach too many subjects . . . . What you do teach, teach thoroughly . . . . Let the main ideas which are introduced into a child's education be few and important, and let them be thrown into every combination possible.

Whitehead, 1929/1957, 14

the primary aim of thought and action is to satisfy [man's] needs and to preserve his life . . . . It is the duty of a teacher of science to impart to his listeners knowledge which will prove useful in their professions. . . .

Schrödinger, 1935/1957, 27, 29

there is an enormous vacuum where until a few decades ago there was the substance of education. And with what is that vacuum filled: it is filled with the elective, eclectic, the specialized, the accidental and incidental improvisations and spontaneous curiosities of teachers and students. There is no common faith, no common body of principle, no common moral and intellectual discipline. Yet the graduates of these modern schools are expected to form a civilized community. They are expected to govern themselves. They are expected to have a social conscience. They are expected to arrive by discussion at common purposes.

Lippmann, 1941, 187

The test of a successful education is not the amount of knowledge that a pupil takes away from school, but his appetite to know and his capacity to learn . . . . Too many leave school with the appetite killed and the mind loaded with undigested lumps of information. The good schoolmaster is known by the number of valuable subjects that he declines to teach.

Livingstone, 1941/1960, 29

Education comes into being . . . when the knowledge which has to be acquired is out of proportion to the capacity to learn. Today, more than ever before, the profusion of cultural and technical possessions is such that it threatens to bring a catastrophe upon mankind, in as much as every generation is finding it more nearly impossible to assimilate it. It is urgent therefore for us to base our science of teaching, its methods and institutions, upon the plain, humble principle that the child or youth who is to be the learner cannot learn all we should like him to know – the principle of economy in education . . . . We must pick out that which appears as strictly necessary for the life of the man who is now a student . . . . What remains, having been judged strictly necessary, must be further reduced to what the student can really learn with thoroughness and understanding.

Ortega, 1946/1963, 55–57

See also 206

992 Post-secondary education

If . . . a practical end must be assigned to a university course, I say it is that of training good members of society . . . . a university training is the great ordinary means to a great but ordinary end; it aims at raising the intellectual tone of society, at cultivating the public mind, at purifying the national taste, at supplying true principles to popular enthusiasm and fixed aims to popular aspiration . . . . It is the education which gives a man a clear conscious view of his own opinions and judgments, a truth in developing them, an eloquence in expressing them, and a force in urging them. It teaches him to see things as they are, to go right to the point, to disentangle a skein of thought, to detect what is sophistical, and to discard what is irrelevant.

Newman, 1852/1905, 177

I should accept any practical subject which can be made a serious intellectual pursuit, if by doing so I could advance practical knowledge and increase intellectual training. Thus, for instance, the whole system of accounting, or as it is sometimes called with a sneering connotation "bookkeeping", I should make an element in all such curricula. The theory of accounting is as strictly a scientific subject as the theory

of political economy itself, and steady application to this subject offers a stimulating and valuable mental discipline. [before the American Economic Association]
James, 1900/1938, 133

A well-planned university course is a study of the wide sweep of generality .... The really useful training yields a comprehension of a few general principles with a thorough grounding in the way they apply to a variety of concrete details .... The function of a university is to enable you to shed details in favor of principles.
Whitehead, 1929/1957, 38

Ideals are in the custody of universities. Universities are morally and intellectually bound to be honest and consistent. They can plead nothing in extenuation if they mislead.
Flexner, 1930/1968, 129

I should describe a university as an association or corporation of scholars and teachers engaged in acquiring, communicating or advancing knowledge, pursuing in a liberal spirit the various sciences which are a preparation for the professions or higher occupations of life .... it is safer to say not that its purpose or object is the professions, which may appear too utilitarian, but that it does in fact prepare for the professions by pursuing the sciences on which those professions are founded.
Alexander, 1931, 337

The principle of economy, which amounts to the determination to see things as they are and not as a Utopian illusion, has led us to define the primary mission of the university in this wise: 1. The university, in the strict sense, is to mean that institution which teaches the ordinary student to be a cultured person and a good member of a profession. 2. The university will not tolerate in its program any false pretense: it will profess to require of the student only what actually can be required of him. 3. It will consequently avoid causing the ordinary student to waste part of his time in pretending that he is going to be a scientist. To this end, scientific investigation proper is to be eliminated from the core or minimum of the university. 4. The cultural disciplines and the professional studies will be offered in a rationalized form based on the best pedagogy – systematic, synthetic and complete – and not in the form which science would prefer, if it were left to itself: special problems, samples of science, and experimentation. 5. The selection of professors will depend not on their rank as investigators but on their talent for synthesis and their gift for teaching.
Ortega, 1946/1963, 73

A modern university has two principal activities – teaching and research. The first part of its obligation is to keep knowledge alive, usable and growing: the other essential part is to help prepare young people for responsible living and for all the great callings of life.
Pusey, 1964, 18

951

The American graduate school gives a professional polish to the language and techniques of research. By taking formal training up to the very edge of the unknown, by teaching the most up to date methods and the latest discoveries, the young scientist is acquainted with the current consensus almost before it has been achieved . . . . But it also lends itself dreadfully to the sway of fashion. A new idea, not fully worked out or universally accepted as public knowledge, is often taught a little too dogmatically by enthusiastic champions to not very critical students . . . . the natural swing of opinion, interest and undiscriminating acceptance is reinforced by the too rapid incorporation of half-baked and speculative notions into the canon of the graduate school curriculum.

Ziman, 1968, 89

while the university is the guardian of our culture and the transmitter of much that is good from the past, it is also the watchdog over those who can stand apart and criticize, and analyze and create . . . .

Webb, 1971, 10

One of the roles of the academic arm of a profession is to serve as the conscience of the profession.

Cohen Commission, 1978, 86

993 Professional training – general

At no time have universities been restricted to pure abstract learning. The University of Salerno in Italy, the earliest of European universities, was devoted to medicine. In England, at Cambridge, in the year 1316, a college was founded for the special purpose of providing "clerks for the King's service". Universities have trained clergy. medical men, lawyers. engineers. Business is now a highly intellectualized vocation, so it fits well into the series.

Whitehead, 1929/1957, 96

The amount of routine knowledge required may be very considerable in these cases [midwifery, nursing, the merchant navy, and mine management], but it need not be founded upon fundamental study in any field of knowledge. On the other hand, doctors, dentists, and others must study the sciences upon which their techniques rest. They cannot otherwise be efficient . . . . Between these extremes there are many professions, such as accountancy, the position of which is difficult to determine.

Carr-Saunders & Wilson, 1933/1964, 376

A practical art comes . . . in its very nature to be strongly conservative, reluctant to accept the new, still more reluctant to give up the old; it will teach by precept and example of the master, by apprenticeship; it will embody its lore in traditional dogma and in rule of thumb. Its ideal of success will thus be fulfilled as much by a given course of conduct having been correctly carried out as by its object having been attained.

Trotter, 1941/1946, 169

The teaching of the professions and the search for truth must be separated. They must be clearly distinguished one from the other, both in the minds of the professors and in the minds of the students. For their present confusion is an impediment to science. Granted, the apprenticeship to some professions includes as a very important element the mastery of the systematized content of numerous sciences; but this content is the end result of investigation, and not the investigation itself. As a general principle, the normal student is not an apprentice to science. The physician is learning to effect cures, and as a physician he need not go beyond that. For his purpose he needs to know the system of physiology current in his day, but he need not be, and in fact cannot be expected to be, a trained physiologist .... If a man has the calling to be a physician and nothing more, let him not dabble in science. He will but turn science into mediocrity. It is enough, in fact it is everything, that he is a good physician.

Ortega, 1946/1963, 60–61

Professional education in colonial times [in the US] . . . was largely apprenticeship in character. Not till the nineteenth century was education for the professions to be had to any considerable extent in formal schools and not till the latter part of this century were these schools raised to university grade.

Brubacher & Rudy, 1958, 196

Vocations and professions seem to be inherently concerned with the particular. The practice of a technology or a profession is essentially an art. As such it can best be learned in the context of its practice – that is, on the job. Thus, the place to learn commerce is in the countinghouse; . . . .

Brubacher, 1982, 82

Professional training – accounting

any one can call himself a public accountant or an "expert" accountant without having a single qualification for the profession . . . .

Montgomery, 1905, 30

in my opinion the present system of education is far from satisfactory. The practical work of the average articled clerk is devoted mainly to routine checking, which is of little educational value, and the theoretical studies of the great proportion of students are conducted by the professional crammers. No doubt the results are satisfactory from an examination point of view, but from the point of view of the education of the future members of a great profession the present position . . . is capable of considerable improvement.

de Paula, 1927, 31

953

The present [UK] system by which the articled clerk is expected to give the whole of his time in the day ... for practical work, with a few weeks off before the examination is, in my view, unsatisfactory .... My own view is that the five year period [of articles] should be allocated 50% to full time practical work and 50%to full time theoretical work.

de Paula, 1944/1964, 45

It is my view that both academics and practitioners each have a substantial but separate contribution to make to the education of the effective accountant. Without reference to a theoretical framework, decision rules employed in practice become arbitrary ....

Skerratt, 1981, 126

994 Technical and liberal education

In a scheme of professional training for accounting, as for other specialized occupations, the use of theory is not only to provide principles of occupational action – a scientific ground-plan of professional conduct – but also to provide a corrective for the illusions of specialism. The theory or science corresponding to a given art not only provides technical sanctions for practical rules, but also discloses the relationship of the art and its practitioners to the rest of the world. It is a proof of inadequacy and unsoundness if its theory does not tend to correct the bias of social narrowness and selfishness which is a customary outgrowth of specialized occupations.

Branford, 1903–04, I:39

Technical education should be based upon a general knowledge of literature and the mathematical, mechanical, political and physical sciences.

Soulé, 1903/1976, 19

The antithesis between a technical and a liberal education is fallacious. There can be no adequate technical education which is not liberal, and no liberal education which is not technical: that is, no education which does not impart both technique and intellectual vision.

Whitehead, 1929/1957, 58

What makes [university study for the professions] ... academic is its liberal spirit which can be cultivated as well ... in natural science and technology as in the subjects such as literature ... or the moral sciences which used to monopolize the name of liberal subjects. Liberality is a spirit of pursuit, not a choice of subject.

Alexander, 1931, 341

There has never seemed to me to be any necessary conflict between a good and broad education and an adequate vocational training. (Vice Chancellor, University of Lancaster; reported)

Carter, 1977, 59

995 General object and mode of accounting education

though bookkeeping has commonly been treated of and taught by way of rote, or arbitrary rules, without showing the reason for them; yet . . . the subject is of great utility, is now introduced and taught in all our academies which qualify youth for business, requires no inconsiderable knowledge of numbers, and is capable of being treated in a rational manner . . . . [preface]

Donn, 1765/1956, 302

When the numerous arbitrary and irrational rules shall cease to be resorted to by the ignorant, are expunged from the science, and discarded from the institutions of learning by the wise, then will bookkeeping advance to a status among the first branches of necessary knowledge, and be taught with the first.

Marsh, 1835/1988, 186

It seems unaccountable that a process of [bookkeeping] instruction so inadequate, so unscientific, so entirely dogmatical, should have been permitted to pass so long unnoticed. In the whole range of education there is not a similar example of such a loose application of language; such an utter disregard of everything like rational investigation. Bookkeeping has indeed been called a science; but it is impossible to conceive that the term could be seriously applied to mere exemplifications without theory or principle.

Foster, 1843, 7

The ordinary mode of teaching bookkeeping is to commence by copying from some popular treatise a series of transactions, such as receipts, payments, purchases, sales, consignments and the like. After being wearied, *secundum artem*, with this work, the student is made to construct a journal; that is, to narrate under what heads in the ledger the respective items are to be placed, the substance of his instruction being that "the thing received is debtor to the thing delivered"; but as to the object of making one thing debtor to another, he must be totally ignorant; for every journal entry has reference to the ledger, and the ledger is a sealed book to him. His whole progress through the journal is, therefore, a blind process of guessing; and when, ultimately, he transfers these items to the ledger, and balances his books, he does so more like an automaton than a rational being.

Foster, 1846/1956, 305

Accountancy is a proper subject for a university course because the subjects required for the accountant can be systematized and taught just as can the principles of the law or of mathematics required for engineering or those of medicine. Every calling which becomes a profession of an advanced character must rest on definite and fixed principles, rather than on the rule of thumb. When these principles reach a certain high point of development they constitute a body of knowledge or a science which can be imparted by scientific teaching methods more quickly and to greater advantage than by compelling each individual to begin at the beginning and learn all those principles through the long process of experience.

Young, 1905(p 417)/1978

955

Accounting and auditing courses should emphasize principles and theory more than techniques, and such technical education as is given should be not of a mechanical nature but simply illustrate the application of principles and theory. The technical part of accountancy should be learned in internship programs . . . . The term professional implies that a man has qualified for the society of educated men . . . that he is more concerned with ideas than things . . . that he has developed habits and powers of logical thought.

Perry, 1948, 474

There is not time in a college course for everything, and the details of specialized technical training can be secured after graduation, on the job, and along the specific lines called for in the situation in which the young graduate finds himself . . . . but the cultural background, the broad general training in business organization and management, the ability to analyze complex situations, the capacity to think without confusion clearly, must be developed in his college courses: . . . .

Graham, 1950, 49

accountancy should be established as a thoroughly respectable subject for study and research at university level . . . . It tends at some [UK] universities to be something of a Cinderella, at others it may not even be regarded as respectable for inclusion in degree studies.

Nelson, 1964, 230

Until the last decade the main method of study for the examinations of the profession was by means of correspondence courses . . . . The one-year full time course for articled clerks was the first bold step forward in educational policy, inaugurated by a UK professional body, when in 1966 the ICAEW placed the formative year of accountancy education in the hands of the educators.

Lewis & Stitt, 1972, 211

Except for some theologies, I don't know of any other discipline that perceives its duty to be the passing along of accepted practices.

Sterling, 1973b, 49

Dr Carter [chairman of the UK Advisory Board of University Education] stressed the distinction between the professional accountant who offered substantial advice or made major decisions, and the technician who developed the raw material. He did not accept that one educational process could produce both . . . . All the accountancy bodies had been accepting students whose aspirations should not be encouraged to go beyond technician status, and he was afraid that, unless some distinction was made, too low a standard could be set for the real professionals. [reported]

Carter, 1974, 394

for accountancy to be a legitimate field of study in colleges and universities and for accountancy to be acknowledged as a legitimate learned profession, something

more fundamental and enduring than facile application of an increasingly comprehensive set of detailed rules and procedures must be at its foundation.

Sprouse, 1988, 121

996 Educational curricula, and teachers

There needs little observation to know that the manner in which merchants' accounts
are taught in the generality of schools is tedious, defective and unsatisfactory. The
pupil is disgusted, because the systems adopted are incomprehensible, or so perplexed
with difficulties that the reason is fettered, and all attempts at deductions from the
premises are futile, and so much labor lost. [Review of a bookkeeping textbook]

The Times, 1845/1956, 304

The present state of university training for accountancy ... is still far from satisfactory. To judge by public curricula, relatively too much emphasis is given to
routine accounting procedure and too little to substantive problems with which the
student will have to deal as a principal when he is ten years out of school.

Canning, 1929a, 329

Want of contact with the universities may also be advanced to explain the small
amount of study interest exhibited by the accountants, who have been accused by
economists of missing great opportunities. It is not surprising that they should miss
them when, in the course of preparation for entry to the profession they have made
no study of economics or of any other fundamental field of investigation pursued
in universities.

Carr-Saunders & Wilson, 1933/1964,
484

Ideally the scope of accountancy education embraces all subjects and matters relating
directly or indirectly to the production, acquisition, conservation or transfer of valuable
property or services by individuals or associations of individuals. Therefore it includes
the known facts as to all forms of transactions, as to all classes of value, in all kinds
of business, and in addition, it embraces the relation to accountancy of the material
sciences, law, economics, finance, ethics and logic.

Webster, 1934/1939, 258

Accounting is the leading form of the communication and control language of business,
and it would seem to follow that accountants should be at home among the concepts
of psychology, sociology, and the behavioral sciences in general. The truth is that
accountants have almost no such knowledge, have developed little rapport with
these related fields, and have made some fantastically naïve behavioral assumptions
(along with some reasonably astute ones).

Devine, c1960/1985, I:57

Recommendations by authority on matters of accounting theory may in the short
run seem unmixed blessings. In the end, however, they will probably do harm.

They are likely to yield little fresh knowledge . . . . They are likely to weaken the education of accountants; the conversion of the subject into cut and dried rules, approved by authority and not to be lightly questioned, threatens to reduce its value as a subject of liberal education almost to nil. They are likely to narrow the scope for individual thought and judgment; and a group of men who resign their hard problems to others must eventually give up all claim to be a learned profession.
Baxter, 1962, 427

most accountants know too little about economics . . . . This is a matter to which our programs of professional education must give greater attention . . . .
Stewart, 1962, 487

the accountant's education . . . certainly should include economics, history, political science, psychology, natural science, physical science and a foreign language . . . . The accountant's formal university level education must include such courses as psychology, anthropology, sociology, political science and organization theory . . . . operations research must become the concern of accountants . . . . the accountant [should] be thoroughly grounded in linear algebra, with special emphasis on the theory of matrices and determinants . . . . a working facility with the fundamentals of integral and differential calculus is desirable . . . . the accountant of the future must be thoroughly grounded in [electronic data processing] techniques . . . . accountants need a background in statistics that emphasizes the mathematical theory of probability and sampling theory . . . . He needs to be intimately acquainted with the finance function, the production function and the marketing function . . . . He must comprehend the total environment of the business, including the legal, regulatory, cultural, political and social environments in which it operates, as well as the internal forces in the organization.
TIMS Committee, 1964, 81–2

[From 1900] to the present day, accounting instruction has been over-fractionated into many, often overlapping, specialties and has often been directed more toward first-job performance than toward the theory and fundamentals which are necessary for long run professional competence . . . . The beginning CPA must . . . have a conceptual grasp of accounting, its interdisciplinary aspects, the environment in which it functions, and of those bodies of knowledge which are ancillary to its central purpose [the humanities, logic and ethics, economics, behavioral science, law, mathematics, statistics, probability, the functional fields of business].
Roy & MacNeill, 1967, 46, 21

Research is isolated from [accounting] education [and] practice . . . . My suggestion is that educators teach research results as *the desired state* and teach accepted practices as *the current state*. Adoption of this suggestion ought to lessen the resistance to reform within the profession and lessen the tendency to reason by contradiction.
Sterling, 1973b, 52

the role of opinion and judgment has been permitted to outweigh the role of knowledge in the teaching and practice of accounting . . . . the characteristics of money, prices and inflation are commonly misunderstood, and are not taken into consideration in the teaching of accounting and in the revision of accounting practices .... the fundamental conditions of aggregation and relation have been almost completely disregarded in traditional accounting education and practice .... these misunderstandings and omissions will be eradicated only by more comprehensive and more exact treatment, in the educational process, of the fundamentals mentioned.

Chambers, 1977/1986, II:271

How scrupulously honest are [educational institutions] in setting an example ... ? To what extent, and in what disciplines, are deceptive techniques actually taught to students? .... Colleges and universities, as well as nursing schools, police academies, military academies, accounting schools, and many others need to consider how moral choice can best be studied and what standards can be expected, as well as upheld.

Bok, 1978/1989, 247

The study of standards now plays a big part in any accounting curriculum. They must have a profound influence on students, just when they are at their most impressionable and uncritical. You have only to look at an up to date text book to see how much weight is given to official pronouncements, how little to the economic reality that accounts are supposed to show .... learning by rote replaces reason; the good student of today is he who can parrot most rules. On this spare diet, accounting students are not likely to develop the habits of reasoning and scepticism that education should instil.

Baxter, 1981, 10

At least four distinct but related classes of knowledge may be identified as being essential to the exercise of professional skill. [1] Knowledge of the nature of mercantile and financial affairs .... [2] Knowledge of the elements of choice in financial matters .... [3] Knowledge of measurement, quantification and instrumentation .... [4] Knowledge of the conditions of objective communication ....

Wolnizer, 1987, 163–170

Teachers

Most of you know that many universities in the United States are now teaching or trying to teach accountancy. One of the reasons that I can only say that the universities are "trying to teach" accountancy is that few men are trained to be teachers ... and universities have found it an almost impossible task in the past 10 years to find men who can teach accounting. Those who knew it couldn't teach, and those who could teach didn't know. [Before the Michigan Political Science Association]

Hatfield, 1903/1938, 134

He who can, does. He who cannot, teaches.

Shaw, 1903/1948, 274

criticizing the teacher with a theoretical proclivity was an old pastime, as witness the fun the dramatist Aristophanes poked at Socrates, one of the greatest teachers of them all.

Brubacher & Rudy, 1958, 211

In part, the decline of professional accounting education [in U S colleges] results from a schism within accounting academe itself. A state of cold war exists between *avant garde* and traditional faculty. Failure to influence professional accounting and/or accountants leads the *avant garde* to direct their attentions elsewhere, primarily toward management accounting, information systems and other exotic areas. Failure to understand the motives, objectives or methodologies of the *avant garde* leads the traditionals to man their shrinking bastions in a last ditch defense of the old empire. The inflexible posture of the traditionalists at some schools has led to the total abandonment of professional accounting education . . . .

Buckley, 1970, 43

Many academics have hobby horses which they ride to death without true regard for practicality and economic viability.

Danby, 1970, 36

"Teachers" using grades and the fear of failure mold the brains of the young until they have lost every ounce of imagination they might once have possessed . . . . the first and most pressing problem is to get education out of the hands of "professional educators".

Feyerabend, 1975/1982, 217

The academic community, which had a substantial concern with the profession and financial accounting in the 1930s, has moved in recent years heavily toward managerial accounting or financial analysis with a mathematical emphasis. This tendency has been accentuated by the recent trend of business academics, including accounting faculty, to obtain the PhD degree directly after undergraduate work, without business experience.

Cohen Commission, 1978, 86

University departments of accounting contain too many mathematicians, economists and behavioral scientists who have turned to teaching accounting as a way of staying within the university system as a comfortable way of life, even though their qualifications would not have obtained for them a university post within their own disciplines.

Accountants record (UK), editorial, 1983, 3

Most accounting faculty base their course content on information gained through secondary sources – usually textbooks and sometimes standards. They frequently lack other significant, continuing sources of information about the realities of the practising environment.

Big Eight, 1989/1992, 86

Practitioners and educators alike deplore the proliferation of accounting and auditing standards, rules and regulations. I see no way to blame accounting educators for that phenomenon . . . . Accounting educators must take the lion's share of the blame, however, for imposing all those rules on their poor, defenceless students.

Sprouse, 1989, 107

997 Academic indoctrination

What sometimes enrages me and always disappoints and grieves me is the preference of great schools of learning for the derivative as opposed to the original, for the conventional and thin which can be duplicated in many copies rather than the new and powerful, and for arid correctness and limitation of scope and method rather than for universal newness and beauty, wherever it may be seen.

Wiener, 1950/1954, 135

The price of training is always a certain trained incapacity: the more we know how to do something, the harder it is to learn to do it differently . . . .

Kaplan, 1964, 29

Many psychology graduate students today . . . live for a period of from 3 to 8 years in an environment that enforces and reinforces the learning of a particular approach, a narrow point of view or a set of pet methodologies which come to define for them the things they will pursue as psychologists.

Dunnette, 1966, 349

The graduate school often has an atmosphere of the broiler house, of forced feeding. The course work is too rich a diet, and the knowledge it contains has been jelled too soon. The method of examination tends to make the student credulous, and distrustful of his own powers of comprehension . . . ; he does not learn early enough that Homer can nod. He does not acquire that deep suspicion, counter-suggestibility and independence of mind that are so essential in scientific work . . . . The graduate school, by its mechanization of learning, has thrown its philosophy out of the window.

Ziman, 1968, 91

[On surveys of users of accounting information] . . . users may be conditioned to the data that they receive . . . in at least two ways. First, as students in business training curricula, the prospective users are introduced to generally accepted accounting principles and the financial statements that result . . . . they are taught manipulative operations . . . that utilize accounting data as a means for evaluating enterprise performance and prospects. In short, users are generally indoctrinated concerning the relevance and utility of traditionally disseminated information. Second, this formal conditioning is continuously reinforced by each external report that users receive.

Revsine, 1973, 50

The initial grounding in science which people receive today conditions them to repeat what from teacher and textbook they have learnt to be right and proper, and inhibits them from direct observation and description.

Stansfield, 1975/1989, 167

See also 206

998 Books and authors

[Many] writers on bookkeeping before 1800 . . . [were not] narrow specialists. [There were] authorities on algebra . . . , on navigation, on optics, a commissioner to settle the foreign exchange, the author of the French code of 1763 . . . Savary, ... astronomers, a French grammarian, an authority on gunpowder, and the historian of the Baptist church . . . . There is Simon Stevin [Dutch polymath]. . . . There was Charles Hutton, a colliery boy, who became teacher of mathematics at eighteen and later professor at the royal academy at Woolwich . . . . There was Robert Hamilton, who . . . was professor first of natural philosophy and later of mathematics at Aberdeen . . . . [Since 1800 there was] Augustus de Morgan [professor of mathematics at Dublin] . . . . And . . . Arthur Cayley . . . professor of mathematics at Cambridge . . . .

Hatfield, 1924, 248–9

The writers on this business [bookkeeping] strictly copied from each other, not daring to differ in opinion from a schoolmaster, who never knew the fundamental elements of commerce, nor even what he assumed to teach of it; for those who have a competent commercial knowledge seldom became authors, well knowing the emoluments of the practic part of the art.

Quin, 1776, 5

The most generally approved [tracts on accounting] are those of Dodson, Weston, Donn, Hutton, Hamilton, Gordon, Dowling, and Jackson. It is remarkable that all the foregoing authors were either schoolmasters or teachers . . . . the works themselves evidently show that those writers, in general, followed each others' plans, and took their documents from printed books more than from real business.

Kelly, 1801, vii

authors have treated bookkeeping very superficially; they have not explained it as a rational science – not addressed themselves to the reason, but only to the eye. They have mistaken the proper method of simplification, or else considered it unnecessary; for they have invariably confined their attention to the forms of account books or the number, when they should have investigated the principles of the science, erased superfluous and redundant rules, amalgamated the many divisions into which it has been divided, and thereby presented to the mind something like unity.

Marsh, 1835/1988, 186

Coming now to the subject of technical literature, by which term we mean the works of professional accountants written for the profession, we have to confess that no such works of any prominence, published in the United States, have come to our notice. There have, indeed, been works claiming to be of such character, which upon examination show that they were written merely to sell, and while running into high page numbers and treating in an imaginary sort of way with a variety of businesses, contain but a repetition of simple detail under different names, and altogether fail to realize the stupendous hopes excited by the promises contained in their voluminous indices. We are therefore compelled to go abroad for high grade technical literature, and happily we find that which we are seeking in the accountancy literature of Great Britain, where for years past the profession has occupied an exalted plane, attracted to itself the finest intellects, and developed a galaxy of writers of marked ability.

> Broaker & Chapman, 1897/1978, 185

The appointment of British-based firms as auditors of US corporations around the turn of the century, and the on-going immigration of British-trained accountants both contributed to the importation of ideas. The English journal, *The Accountant*, was widely read in the US .... three of the four [books, said by MacNeal to have "exerted a dominating influence on the formation of current American accounting thought"] bore close links with the UK literature. Dickinson [*Accounting practice and procedure*, 1914] was an English chartered accountant who worked in the USA between 1901 and 1911 .... Hatfield's textbook [*Modern accounting*, 1916] drew heavily from overseas literature (and particularly from Dicksee's *Auditing*) .... Montgomery had produced American editions of Dicksee's *Auditing* (1905 and 1909) before publishing another version [*Auditing theory and practice*] under his own name in 1912 ....

> Walker, 1978a, 166–7

Whenever a textbook is written of real educational worth, you may be quite certain that some reviewer will say that it will be difficult to teach from it. Of course it will be difficult to teach from it. If it were easy, the book ought to be burned; for it cannot be educational.

> Whitehead, 1929/1957, 16

much of the literature of accounting is of passing value only. As compared with other fields of learning, it is woefully lacking in scientific method and scholarly handling.

> Jackson, 1933, 133

We think the student would still do well to imbibe his theory from such American writers as Hatfield, Paton or Rorem, whose works, in our opinion, contain a surer theoretical foundation than do any of the English texts with which we are conversant.

> Smails, 1935, 367

much patient honesty in presentation ... has come to naught because the authors did not have a deep enough understanding of the subject they are presenting.

> Bruner, 1960, 22

It seems to me . . . that one of the biggest obstacles that must be overcome by these authors [in the university accountancy faculties] is to resist the urge to equate learning with the esoteric jargon that some of them use.

Goch, 1969, 398

As a working accountant I try to keep abreast of the main stream of academic thinking, but the overriding impression I get from reading the output of many academic accountants is the sheer tedium of their prose . . . . I cannot for the life of me understand why it is that when a man takes up a lecturing career he feels impelled to adopt all the trappings of the new accounting gobbledegook . . . . Unless they want to be condemned forever to taking in each other's verbal washing, they have got to learn to communicate their ideas to their real audience – the broad mass of accountants – in good, plain, English.

Goch, 1970, 56

more than occasionally the questions being addressed in manuscripts seem to be contrived in order that novel research methods might be given some exercise. When modeling problems, researchers seem to be more affected by technical develop-ments in the literature than by their potential to explain phenomena. So often it seems that manuscripts are the result of methods in search of questions, rather than questions in search of methods. [on retirement from editorship of *AR*]

Zeff, 1983, 134

Perhaps the most conspicuous index of accounting educators' response to the pro-liferation of accounting pronouncements in a climate of conformity is the increas-ing girth of the intermediate accounting textbooks . . . . The hefty textbooks have come to resemble encyclopaedic handbooks . . . . Quite a number of the most complex pronouncements . . . are covered in mind-numbing detail. When standard setters make important alterations in standards . . . [the change] is, more often than not, unaccompanied by any substantive discussion of its historical development . . . . Typically, the authors do not point out contradictions between inconsistent standards, even when they both appear in the same chapter . . . .

Zeff, 1989, 165

See also 889

999 Educators and the advancement of the profession

For years it [the profession] has failed to see the problems before it: problems for the complexity of which it alone has been responsible . . . . To instructors of account-ing, this condition of affairs should offer a challenge. Now, more than ever, the voice of enlightened opinion within the profession is needed. Shall we as accoun-tants recognize that the responsibilities of the profession are large, particularly to third persons? Or shall we drift as we have done in the past, waiting, at first hopefully and now fearfully, for someone else to tell us what to do? Is it impossible for us to take any initial responsibility for defining our accountability to the business and financial world and to the investing public?

AR, editorial, 1934, 334

No problem can be studied seriously short of analyzing it into a series of abstractions. Unless the higher learning provides a place for long term research and unhurried meditation which transcends immediate and utilitarian demands, not even practical concerns will prosper.

Brubacher & Rudy, 1958, 210

"For goodness sake, what has happened to *The Accounting Review*? Most of us, and here I include academic types as well as practitioners, find this foreign language magazine almost impossible to read .... I cite this as an illustration of how far apart academic and applied accounting have become.

Mautz, 1974, 356

universities do not exist merely to produce holders of degrees. They exist also for research ... ; for the dissemination of the results of that research ... ; and for the provision of a forum for a continuing dialogue between the thinkers and the doers. Engineering, law, medicine and other disciplines owe much to academic research. Why is the same not true of accountancy? ... many accountants ... would say that accountancy is such an intensely practical subject that it neither needs nor lends itself to that kind of fundamental thought which is the mark of an academic discipline. *Accountancy* believes they are wrong.

Accountancy, editorial, 1975, 1

During the hectic years of the 1960s, when conventional accounting concepts were sometimes distorted as a basis for the inflation of earnings and share prices, most members of the academic community remained silent. The academic community failed to provide the intellectual leadership and criticism that might have stimulated corrective actions.

Cohen Commission, 1978, 86

I have always been concerned – and somewhat bewildered – by the fact that academia, although making many contributions, has not always provided the accounting profession with the significant ongoing expertise, criticism, innovation, creative ideas – and academic conscience – that it has provided, for example, to the professions of law and medicine. Many of the most crucial issues now before the profession – including independence, measurement, relevance, reliability, audit technology, display of information, economic consequences, summary indicators, and particularly the conceptual framework – are subjects which can greatly benefit from the unique contributions and perspectives associated with scholarly research and thought.

Williams, 1980b/1981, 260

When we look at today's accounting textbooks and courses, we find thicker tomes and syllabi crammed with additional pronouncements and institutional changes, but there is little evidence of fundamental change . . . . The impact of accounting research on courses is negligible. Its impact on the practice of accounting is less.

Burton & Sack, 1991, 122

Source Index

A & I Inglis, 1868, Partnership agreement, UGD69/1/1, 574

AA, Anon, 1936, Mar, 426, 511

AAA, 1936/1957b, "A tentative statement of accounting principles . . . ", s.c. AAA 1957b, 037, 581, 662, 699; 1941/1957b, "Accounting principles underlying corporate financial statements", s.c. AAA 1957b, 514, 642, 945; 1948/1957b, "Accounting concepts and standards underlying corporate financial statements", s.c. AAA 1957b, 255, 431, 463, 612, 621, 637; 1950/1957b, "Reserves and retained income", s.c. AAA 1957b, 471; 1951/1957b, "Price level changes . . .", s.c. AAA 1957b, 741, 743, 748; 1954a/1957b, "Consolidated financial statements", s.c. AAA 1957b, 047, 487; 1954b/1957b, "Standards of disclosure . . .", s.c. AAA 1957b, 736; 1957a/1957b, "Accounting and reporting standards for corporate financial statements", 1957 revision, s.c. AAA 1957b, 033, 041, 131, 146, 254, 255, 275, 323, 435, 451, 462, 553, 604, 624, 686, 694, 912, 924, 926; 1957b, *Accounting and reporting standards for corporate financial statements and preceding statements and supplements*

AAA, 1964a, *AR*, Jul, [land, buildings and equipment], 057, 194, 413, 533, 619, 662, 691, 693, 765; 1964b, *AR*, Jul, [inventory measurement], 315, 545; 1965a, *AR*, Apr, [realization] 693; 1965b, *AR*, Apr, [entity], 049; 1965c, *AR*, Apr, [matching], 641; 1966, *A statement of basic accounting theory*, 016, 051, 068, 336, 337, 342, 344, 346, 348, 349, 522, 592, 593, 758, 791, 933, 934; 1969, *AR Supp*, "Report of . . . Committee on external reporting", 243, 368; 1971, *AR Supp*, "Report of the Committee on accounting measurement", 246, 252, 847, 872; 1972, *AR Supp*, "Report of the Committee on basic auditing concepts", 034, 093; 1973, *A statement of basic auditing concepts* (SAR 6), 081; 1977, *Statement on accounting theory and theory acceptance*, 939; 1991, *AccHor*, Sep, "Report of Committee on accounting and auditing measurement, 1989-90", 252, 319, 328, 601

AAPA (American Association of Public Accountants), 1909/1972, s.c. Zeff, 1972, 934

AARF, 1983, AAS13 [R & D costs], 682

AARF & AASB, 1992, SAC4, [elements of financial statements] , 435, 452, 637, 921

AARF & ASRB, 1990a, SAC2, [objective of financial reporting], 072; 1990b, SAC3, [characteristics of financial information], 333, 344, 347, 373, 376, 377

AASB, 1991, AASB1026, [cash flows], 496

Abdel-khalik A R, 1984, in Sherman (ed), 1984, 791; 1992, *The messy culture of GAAP . . . .*, Sydney, AFFUS, 148, 332, 593

Accountancy, editorial, 1964, Aug, 341, 426; 1966, Nov, 299; 1975, Jan, 999; 1978, Oct, 978; 1979a, Jan, 987; 1979b, Aug, 946

Accountant, Anon, 1881, Sep 24, 282; 1882, Nov 25, 466; 1890, Dec 6, 694; 1892, Jun 11, 099; 1896, Jan 18, 504; 1900, Apr 14, 101; 1901, Aug 24, 582, 961; 1913, Dec 6, 688; 1938, Feb 12, 001; 1939, Feb 25, 934; 1964, Nov 14, 734

Accountant, editorial, 1875, Feb 6, 001, 099, 267; 1876, Jul 22, 001; 1878, Nov 16, 082; 1881, Apr 23, 091; 1890a, Aug 9, 971; 1890b, Dec 6, 561, 779; 1892, Jun 18, 001; 1895, Jan 26, 412, 542, 961; 1899, Dec 23, 561; 1901, Aug 17, 584, 669; 1907, Apr 20, 091; 1908, Jun 27, 432; 1925, Aug 8, 488; 1945, Jun 30, 332, 656; 1946a, Jun 22, 348; 1946b, Nov 16, 641; 1946c, Dec 7, 257, 334, 365; 1952, May 31, 616, 671; 1954, Aug 21, 285; 1973, Feb 1, 095; 1974, Apr 25, 716; 1975a, Jan 16, 974; 1975b, Nov 6, 769; 1978, Mar 9, 924

Accountant, non-editorial; 1921, Jun 18, 542; 1977, Jul 7, 769

Accountants record, (UK), editorial, 1983, Jun/Jul, 996

Ackoff R L, 1953, *The design of social research*, Chicago, UCP, 854

Ackoff with S K Gupta & J S Minas, 1962, *Scientific method: optimizing applied research decisions*, NY, Wiley, 241, 242, 243, 248

"Adam Smith", 1967/1969, *The money game*, NY, Dell, 001

AIA, 1931a *Accounting terminology* [report of a special committee], 086, 423, 431, 441, 442, 443, 445, 649; 1931b, Rules of professional conduct, in A P Richardson, *The ethics of a profession*, NY, Century, 987;1931/1984, Memorandum, s.c. Zeff & Moonitz (eds), 1984, 575; 1932, "Report of the Special Committee on cooperation with the stock exchanges of the American Institute of Accountants. . .", Sep, s.c. May, 1943, 051,

Baxter & S Davidson (eds), 1962, *Studies in accounting theory*, London, Sweet & Maxwell; 1977, *Studies in accounting*, London, ICAEW

Baxter & B S Yamey, 1951, *AccRes*, Apr, 575

Beacham R H S, 1964, *Commercial accounting*, London, U of London P, 617, 633, 662, 779, 924

Beaton D C, 1949, *Acct*, Jan 8, 741; 1968, *Acct*, Mar 2, 574

Beaver W H & J S Demski, 1979, *AR*, Jan, 318

Beaver, J W Kennelly & W M Voss, 1968, *AR*, Oct, 057

Beck S D, 1962, *The simplicity of science*, Harmondsworth, Penguin, 211, 804, 811, 849

Bedford N M, 1957, *AR*, Jan, 138; 1965, *Income determination theory*, Reading, Mass, Addison-Wesley, 318, 603, 621, 637, 693, 784; 1988, *AHJ*, Fall, 016

Bedford & V Baladouni, 1962, *AR*, Oct, 231

Bedford & T Iino, 1968, *AR*, Jul, 346

Bedford & J C McKeown, 1972, *AR*, Apr, 191, 545, 791

Bedford, K W Perry & A R Wyatt, 1967, *Advanced accounting, an organizational approach*, NY, Wiley, 045, 172, 553, 604

Beer S, 1959, *Cybernetics and management*, London, English Universities P, 274; 1972, *Brain of the firm*, Harmondsworth, Penguin, 171, 217, 233

Bell J, 1842/1964, s.c. Millerson, 1964, 988

Bell P W, 1982, *TAM*, Oct, 775

Bell S & W J Graham, 1936, *Theory and practice of accounting*, Chicago, American Technical Society; 372, 431, 451, 551, 637, 665, 745

Bellman H, 1938, *Acct*, Apr 30

Bennet J (*The American system of practical bookkeeping*, NY, Collins, 1842) and B F Foster (*The origin and progress of bookkeeping*, London, Souter, 1852), repr 1976, NY, Arno P

Bennett A H M, 1972, *Acct*, Feb 17, 611, 759

Bennett R J, 1912, *JA*, Jul, 095

Benninger L J, 1955, in Backer (ed), 1955b, 424, 715

Bennion F A R, 1969, *Professional ethics*, London, Knight, 985; 1984, *Statutory interpretation*, London, Butterworth, 266, 913

Benson H A (Lord), 1981, *JA*, Feb, 981; 1983, s.c. *CAA*, Feb, 737

Benston G J, 1969, in Manne (ed), 1969, 139, 343, 977; 1982, in *The Antitrust Bulletin*, Spring, 071, 146, 164, 324, 646

Bentham J, 1843, *The works of Jeremy Bentham*, Bowing (ed), 1835/1843, repr NY, Russell, 1962, 269

Bentley H C, 1911, *The science of accounts*, NY, Ronald, 043, 315, 331, 423, 431, 441, 451, 455, 456; 1912a, *JA*, March, 332; 1912b, May, 443, 515

Berger C, 1977, *Communication quarterly*, Winter, 217

Bergmann G, 1947/1953, in Feigl & Brodbeck (eds), 1953, 243; 1951, *Ethics*, Apr, 189, 269, 813, 872

Berle A A, 1938, *AR*, Mar, 265, 827, 916, 966, 971

Berle & F S Fisher, 1932, *Columbia law review*, April, 504

Berle & G C Means, 1932, *The modern corporation and private property*, NY, Macmillan, 279, 326, 327, 454

Berlo D K, 1960, *The process of communication*, NY, Holt Rinehart, 231, 232, 234, 235, 238

Bernal C, 1865/1962, *An introduction to experimental medicine*, s.c. Duhem, 1914/1962, 832, 864, 884, 887

Bernal J D, 1954/1969, *Science in history*, v. 1, Harmondsworth, Penguin, 803, 881, 892, 951

Bernstein L, 1965, *JA*, Dec, 022, 939

Berry R N, 1975, *Accy*, Sep, 483

Berryman R G, 1960, *AR*, Jan, 093, 346

Bethlehem Youngstown merger case, 1931, s.c. *JA*, editorial, Feb, 1931, 341, 961

Beveridge W I B, 1950/1957, *The art of scientific investigation*, rev ed, NY, Random House, 204, 824, 834, 884, 885, 886, 951

Bevis H W, 1962, *JA*, Feb, 016, 082, 085; 1965, *Corporate financial reporting in a competitive economy*, NY, Macmillan, 057, 286, 317, 318, 463, 978; 1966, *JA*, Jul, 954, 965; 1968, *JA*, Oct, 686

Bierman H, 1963a, *Topics in cost accounting and decisions*, NY, McGraw-Hill, 648; 1963b, *AR*, July, 251, 736; 1963c, *Financial and managerial accounting*, NY, Macmillan, 255, 384, 431, 491; 1965, *Financial accounting theory*, NY, Macmillan, 553, 921, 924, 964; 1974, *AR*, Jul, 059

Bierman & A R Drebin, 1968, *Financial accounting: an introduction*, NY, Macmillan, 423

Big Eight (US professional firms), 1989/1992, *Perspectives on education . . . .*, 1989, NY, s.c. C W Mulford, D B Smith, D E Stout, M S Stone & T R Weirich, *AccHor*, Dec, 1992, 996

Bigg W W, 1946, *Acct*, Oct 26, 368

Bilton R, 1901, *Acct*, Jan 12, 779

Binney v The Ince Hall Coal and Cannel Company, (1866), 35 L J Ch 363, 613

Bird F A, L F Davidson & C H Smith, 1974, *AR*, Apr, 046

Bird P A, 1965, *Acct*, Jan 9, 343

Bird R, 1951, *Acct*, Feb 3, 444

Birkett W P & R G Walker, 1974, *JBFA*, Summer, 594

Birnberg J G, 1964, *AR*, Oct, 463; 1965, *AR*, Oct, 458

Birnberg & N Dopuch, 1963, *JA*, Feb, 035

Bithell R, 1903, *A counting house dictionary*, London, Routledge, 001, 443, 444

Black H A, J E Champion & R G Brown, 1967, *Accounting in business decisions*, EC,

Byrd K F, 1950, *JA*, April, 524; 1974, *Acct*, Oct 3, 447

Cadbury A, 1977, *Acct*, Nov 17, 792
Cadbury Committee, 1992, *Report of the Committee on the financial aspects of corporate governance*, London, Gee, 978
Caffrey J J, 1948, s.c. *Acct*, Sep 18, 934
Caffyn H R, 1948, *JA*, Aug, 448
Cairncross A, 1960, *Introduction to economics*, London, Butterworth, 124, 141, 681; 1969, *Economic j*, Dec, 174
Cairnes J E, 1875, *The character and logical method of political economy*, London, Macmillan, 823
Calculator, 1843, *Counting house manual*, London, Simpkin Marshall, 413
Caldwell B, 1982/1984, *Beyond positivism: economic methodology in the twentieth century*, London, Allen & Unwin, 856
Campbell N R, 1919/1957, *Physics, the elements*, 1919, repr as *Foundations of science*, NY, Dover, 1957, 187, 243, 247, 844, 891; 1921/1952, *What is science?*, 1921, repr, NY, Dover, 1952, 203, 204, 205, 222, 245, 247, 805, 813, 815, 833, 844
Campbell W G, 1950, *Acct*, Sep 16, 293
Campbell & Christie, 1845, Minutes of copartnery, UGD152/1/3, 501, 574
Campfield W L, 1958, *AA*, Mar, 035
CanCA, editorial, 1919, Jan, s.c. Murphy, 1988, 192; 1960, Mar, 986
Candler v Crane, Christmas & Co, [1951] 2 K B 164, 986
Canning J B, 1929a, *The economics of accountancy*, NY, Ronald, 043, 066, 101, 145, 248, 254, 257, 416, 435, 447, 448, 451, 458, 462, 489, 504, 601, 617, 734, 772, 783, 996; 1929b, *AR*, Mar, 101, 146, 174, 427, 603; 1931, *AR*, Sep, 274; 1933, *Econometrica*, I(1933), 717; 1937/1971, 001
Cannon A M, 1952, *AR*, Oct, 227; 1955, *JA*, Mar, 235, 924; 1962, *JA*, Feb, 038, 259, 724, 925
Cannon et al v Wiscesset Mills Co et al, 1928, 195 S C 119, 114 S E 344, s.c. *AR*, Mar, 1930, [symposium], 542
Caplan E H, 1972, in Sterling (ed), 1972, 938, 952
Carden's case, 1938, *Commissioner of Taxes (South Australia) and the Executor Trustee and Agency Co of South Australia Ltd, 63 C L R 108*, s.c. Ryan, 1974, 265
Carey J L, 1946, *Professional ethics of public accountants*, NY, AIA, 984; 1956, *Professional ethics of certified public accountants*, NY, AIA, 983, 986; 1957/1964, *NYCPA*, Aug 1957, s.c. Ray (ed), 1964, 985; 1969, *The rise of the accounting profession*, NY, AICPA, 095, 982
Carey (ed), 1962, *The accounting profession: where is it headed?*, NY, AICPA, 036
Carman L A, 1936, *JA*, May, 941
Carmichael, n d /1843, s.c. Foster, 1843, 871

Carnap R, 1934, *The unity of science*, London, Kegan Paul, 022, 862
Carpenter C C, 1930, *AR*, Mar, 668
Carpenter J, 1632, *A most excellent instruction for the exact and perfect keeping merchants bookes of accounts . . .*, London, Boler, 282, 352, 501
Carr E H, 1962, *What is history?*, London, Macmillan, 206, 233, 311, 882
Carrel A, 1935/1948, *Man, the unknown*, West Drayton, Pelican, 222
Carrington A S, 1965, *Acct*, Apr 24, 791
Carrington & G B Battersby, 1963, *Accounting*, Christchurch, Whitcomb & Tombs, 265, 377, 923, 924
Carrington & G Howitt, 1983, *Financial information systems*, Carlton, Victoria, Pitman, 065, 182, 188, 255, 374
Carroll L, *Through the looking glass*, 298
Carr-Saunders A M & P A Wilson, 1933/1964, *The professions*, Oxford, OUP, repr London, Frank Cass, 981, 982, 986, 987, 988, 993, 996
Carsberg B, 1982, in Sterling & Lemke (eds), 1982, 614, 615, 772; 1984, in Carsberg & Dev (eds), 1984, 946
Carsberg & S Dev (eds), 1984, *External financial reporting*, London, Prentice-Hall International
Carsberg, A Hope & R W Scapens, 1974, *ABR*, Summer, 057
Carscallen M P, 1977, in Chippindale & Defliese (eds), 1977, 163, 656, 759
Carson A B, 1949a, *JA*, Jan, 525; 1949b, *AR*, Apr, 278, 492
Carter C F, 1972, in Carter & J L Ford (eds), *Uncertainty and expectation in economics*, Oxford, Blackwell, 187, 189; 1974, *Acct*, Sep 26, 995; 1977, *Acct*, Jul 14, 994
Carter E, 1882, *Acct*, Oct 21, 982
Carter E M, 1910a, *Acct*, Jan 22, 542, 612; 1910b, *Acct*, Oct, 22, 143, 252, 412, 502, 617, 645
Carter R N, 1923, *Advanced accounts*, London, Pitman, 023, 192, 282, 355, 381, 382, 384, 387, 426, 442, 445, 465, 467, 474, 475, 476, 477, 575, 581, 621, 622, 625, 631, 632, 662, 664, 665, 666, 669
Carter W K, 1981, *AR*, Jan, 602
Carver T N, 1926, *The distribution of wealth*, NY, Macmillan, 142
Cary W, 1963/1964, s.c. Spacek, 1964a, 291
Casey W J, 1972a, *JA*, Jun, 288; 1972b, SEC staff report, *The financial collapse of The Penn Central Company*, Washington, USGPO, 739
Cassel G, 1925, *Fundamental thoughts in economics*, London, Unwin, 172, 823
Catlett G R, 1960a, *JA*, Mar, 724; 1960b, *JA*, Oct, 021; 1963/1973, in Catlett & Olson, 1973, 824; 1964, *JA*, Dec, 917, 971; 1969, *JA*, Oct, 297, 321, 825, 917, 933; 1970, *JBF*, Winter, 721, 916
Catlett & N O Olson, 1968, *Accounting for goodwill*, (ARS10), AICPA, 446, 448, 483; 1973, *In pursuit of professional goals*, Chicago, Andersen & Co

158; 1950/1957, *A discussion of money*, s.c. Olivecrona, 1957, 115

Couldery F A J & A J G Sheppard, 1955, *Acct*, Mar 12, 604

Cournot A, 1838/1963, *The mathematical principles of the theory of wealth*, s.c. trans N T Bacon (1897), Irwin, 1963, 151

Coutts W B (ed), 1960a, *CanCA*, Jun, 342; 1960b, *CanCA*, 662; 1961, *CanCA*, Jan, 618; 1962a, *CanCA*, May, 759; 1962b, *CanCA*, Jun, 477

Cramer J J, 1968, *Abacus*, Aug, 793

Cranstoun W D, 1938, *JA*, Jan, 584

Craswell A T, 1984, in Gaffikin (ed), 1984, 097

Crew A, 1925, *CanCA*, May, 984

Cronhelm F W, 1818/1978, *Double entry by single*, London, Longman Hurst, repr NY, Arno P, 1978, 012, 042, 255, 282, 351, 353, 354, 357, 382, 414, 503

Croome H, 1956, *Introduction to money*, London, Methuen, 112, 115

Crossley D W (ed), 1975, *Sidney Ironworks accounts, 1541–1573*, London, Camden fourth series, v.15, Royal Historical Society, 001, 352

Crowningshield G R, 1962, *Cost accounting*, Boston, Houghton Mifflin, 646, 652, 653, 654

Crowther G, 1949, *An outline of money*, London, Nelson, 125, 137, 674

Croxton-Smith C, 1970, *Acct*, Sep 17, 732

Cruttwell v Lye, 1810, *17 Ves 335*, 446

CSR (Colonial Sugar Refining Co Ltd), 1950, *Capital erosion and the Income Tax Assessment Act*, Sydney, booklet, 257, 616

Cushing B E, 1989, *AHJ*, Dec, 978

Custis V, 1933, in Vawter lectures, 1933, 981, 986

Cutler R S & C A Westwick, 1973, *Accy*, Mar, 671

Cyert R M & J G March, 1963, *A behavioral theory of the firm*, EC, Prentice-Hall, 272, 274

D'Abro A, 1927/1950, *The evolution of scientific thought – from Newton to Einstein*, NY, Dover, 1950, 258, 817, 858, 859, 867

Dafforne R, 1635, *The Merchants Mirrour . . .*, London, Bourne, 411; 1684, same title, London, Horne, 383, 501

Daines H C, 1929, *AR*, Jun, 319, 321, 502, 551, 582, 752

Danby P W, 1970, *CAA*, Jul, 095, 996

Daniels M B, 1933, *AR*, Dec, 662, 715; 1934/1980, *Corporation financial statements*, Ann Arbor, U of Michigan, repr NY, Arno P, 1980, 148, 423, 427, 483, 487, 488, 511, 525, 544, 565, 575, 779

Danto A & S Morgenbesser (eds), 1960, *Philosophy of science*, Cleveland, World Publishing

Danzig T, 1930/1954, *Number, the language of science*, Garden City, Doubleday, 828, 834, 843

Davidson S, 1963, *JAR*, Autumn, 327; 1969, *JA*, Dec, 349; 1978, in A R Abdel-Khalik & T F Keller (eds), *Impact of accounting research on*

practice and disclosure, Durham, Duke U P, 1978, 967

Davidson, J S Schindler, C P Stickney & R L Weil, 1977, *Accounting, the language of business*, Glen Ridge, Horton, 275, 435, 545, 546

Davidson, Stickney & Weil, 1976, *Inflation accounting*, NY, McGraw-Hill, 742, 761

Davidson & Weil (eds), 1977, *Handbook of modern accounting*, NY, McGraw-Hill

Davis B J, 1953, *Inflation, its treatment in accounts*, London, Gee, 157, 441, 444, 691

Davis P J & R Hersh, 1981, *The mathematical experience*, Brighton, Harvester P, 866

Davison E H, 1950, s.c. *Rydge's* (Sydney), Jun, 921; 1951, *Acct*, Mar 31, 327, 336, 425

Davison I H, 1978, *Accy*, Jan, 289, 975

Dawson S S, 1900, *Acct*, Feb 3, 428; 1904, *The accountant's compendium*, London, Gee, 274, 385, 433, 457, 467, 471, 506

Dean J, 1951, *Managerial economics*, NY, Prentice-Hall, 101, 164, 165, 186, 656, 775; 1952, *Capital budgeting*, NY, Columbia U P, 632

Dearden J & J Shank, 1975, *Financial accounting and reporting*, EC, Prentice-Hall, 192, 562, 575, 713, 917

de Broglie L, 1962, *New perspectives in physics*, trans A J Pomerans, NY, Basic Books, 842

de Condillac É B (1714–1780), 1756, *An essay on the origin of human knowledge*, trans T Nugent, London, Nourse, 011, 214, 217, 225, 922; –/1967, s.c. Gillispie, 1960/1967, 215

Defliese P L, 1962, *JA*, Oct, 366

Defoe D, 1726, *The complete English tradesman*, London, Rivington, 001, 032

Delaware General Corporation Laws, 1974, *8 Del Code Ann #220(b)*, s.c. Stevenson, 1980, 074

DeMaris E J, 1963, *AR*, Jan, 035

de Morgan A, 1846/1861, *Elements of arithmetic*, London, Walton & Maberly, 353

Demosthenes, BC341/1967, *Demosthenes' orations*, J Warrington (ed), London, Dent, 1967, 327

Demsetz H, 1969, in Manne (ed), 1969, 068, 281, 846

Demski J S, 1973, *AR*, Oct, 736

Denny and Company, 1862, Partnership contract, UGD70/1, 073

Dent J, M Ezzamel & M Bevin, 1984, in Hopwood & Schreuder (eds), 1984, 954

Denza J, 1978a, *Acct*, Apr 13, 743; 1978b, *Acct*, Oct 26, 769

de Paula F R M, 1912, *Acct*, Jun 15, 665; 1914, *The principles of auditing*, London, Pitman: 504, 512, 924; 1926/1978, in de Paula, *Developments in accounting*, 1948, London, Pitman, repr 1978, NY, Arno P, 192, 259, 713; 1927, *Acct*, Jan 1, 988, 993; 1934, *Acct*, Dec 15, 375; 1935, *The principles and practice of auditing*, Melbourne, Pitman, 473; 1937, *Acct*, Apr 3, 376, 545, 562; 1942, 7 ed of 1935 title, 665; 1944/1964, s.c. K F Byrd, *CanCA*,

Jan, 1964, 993; 1946, *Acct*, Jul 27, 911; 1947,
Acct, Jan 25, 915, 961; 1948, *Acct*, June 5, 066

de Paula F C, 1949, *Acct*, Jul 2, 364

de Roover R, 1956, in Littleton & Yamey (eds),
1956, 282, 612

Descartes R, 1637/1937, *A discourse on method*,
trans J Veitch, London, Dent, 1937, 205, 261,
832

de Ste Croix G M, 1956, in Littleton & Yamey
(eds), 1956, 071

Devine C T, 1951, *California Certified Public
Accountant*, Nov, 934; 1960, *AR*, Jul, 945,
947; c1960/1985, *Essays in accounting theory*,
AAA, 1985, 996; 1963, *JAR*, Autumn, 066

De Voto B, 1951/1959, in Homans, 1951/1959,
273

Dewey J, 1938/1966, *Logic: the theory of inquiry*,
NY, Holt, Rinehart, 202, 222, 234, 834, 857;
1939/1960, *Theory of valuation*, UCP, 145,
182, 277; 1955/1962, in Neurath & others
(eds), 801, 803

Dewhirst J, 1971, *CanCA*, Aug. 328; 1972, *CanCA*,
Sep, 688

Dewhurst J, 1976, *Acct*, Jul 15, 761; 1978, *Acct*,
Oct 12, 761

Dewing A S, 1920, *The financial policy of
corporations*, NY, Ronald, 015; 1953, same
title, 074, 542

Dickens C, 1850, *David Copperfield*, 001;
1855, *The works of Charles Dickens*,
v.XIX, n.d, NY, Bigelow Brown,
001

Dickens R L & J O Blackburn, 1964, *AR*, Apr,
758

Dickinson A L, 1902, *Acct*, Jul 26, 984; 1904,
in *Official record of the proceedings of the
congress of accountants* (St Louis), NY,
Wilkinson, 669; 1906, *JA*, Apr, 047; 1908,
JA, Oct, 713; 1914, *Accounting practice and
procedure*, NY, Ronald P, 097, 163, 321,
346, 415, 425, 443, 561, 582, 612, 613, 694,
698

Dicksee L R, 1892/1976, *Auditing*, London, Gee,
repr NY, Arno P, 1976, 326, 387, 443, 576,
591, 665, 669; 1897, *Bookkeeping for company
secretaries*, London, Gee, 472, 566, 575;
1898, *Auditing*, London, Gee, 714; 1903a,
Advanced accounting, London, Gee, 372, 387,
622, 632, 669, 713; 1903b, *Acct*, Apr 4, 032,
425, 426; 1903c, *Depreciation, reserves, and
reserve funds*, London, Gee, 412, 471, 472;
1905a, *Acct*, Feb 4, 001, 072, 381; 1905b/1976,
Auditing, Authorized American edition, R H
Montgomery (ed), repr NY, Arno P, 1976,
475; 1907, *Advanced accounting*, London, Gee,
634; 1908, *Auditing*, 8 ed, London, Gee, 545;
1909a, *Advanced accounting*, London, Gee,
083, 547; 1909b, *Auditing*, London, Gee, 8 ed,
422, 512; 1910, *Auditing*, London, Gee, 434,
633 ; 1911, *Advanced accounting*, London,
Gee, 665, 666; 1930, *The accountants' journal*,
Mar, 236

Dilley D R, 1960, *CanCA*, Jun, 128, 513, 922, 923,
925

Dixon R L, S R Hepworth & W A Paton Jr, 1966,
Essentials of accounting, NY, Macmillan, 191,
335, 623, 642

Dodson J, 1750, *The accountant, or the method
of accounting deduced from clear principles*,
London, Nourse, 325, 411, 947

Dohr J L, 1941, *JA*, Mar, 145, 236, 253, 332,
341, 356, 414, 471; 1942, *JA*, Mar, 365; 1944,
JA, Mar, 255, 504; 1950a, *JA*, Feb, 256, 374;
1950b, *JA*, Jul, 296; 1953, *JA*, Aug, 181; 1959,
JA, Feb, 687

Dohr, E L Phillips, G C Thompson & W C
Warren, 1964, *Accounting and the law*,
Brooklyn, Foundation P, 195, 542, 553, 612

Donaldson G, 1969, *Strategy for financial mobility*,
Boston, Harvard College, 196

Donn B, 1765/1956, *The accountant and
geometrician*, London, Johnson, s.c. Jackson,
1956, 995

Dopuch N, J B Birnberg & J Demski, 1974,
Cost accounting, NY, Harcourt, Brace &
Jovanovich, 191, 648

Dopuch N & L Revsine (eds), 1973, *Accounting
research, 1960–1970*, CIERA

Dorfman R, 1964, *The price system*, EC,
Prentice-Hall, 136

Drake D F & N Dopuch, 1965, *JAR*, Autumn,
693

Drebin A R, 1964, *JAR*, Winter, 497

Drinkwater D & J D Edwards, 1965, *AR*, Jul, 683,
686

DuBrul S, 1925/1964, *Management and
administration*, Dec 1925, s.c. Sweeney,
1936/1964, 256

Duhem P, 1914/1962, *The aim and structure
of physical theory*, trans P P Wiener, NY,
Atheneum, 1962, 221, 245, 814, 856, 858, 863,
867, 882, 884, 893

Duncan H D, 1968, *Communication and social
order*, London, OUP, 235

Duncan J C, 1909, *JA*, Feb, 022, 054

Dunn H A, 1916, *Acct*, Dec 23, 916

Dunn S, 1760/1965, *The new method of
bookkeeping*, London, s.c. H P Hain, *AA*, Dec
1965, 736

Dunnette M D, 1966, *American psychologist*, Apr,
823, 889, 997

Durkheim E, c1900/1957, *Professional ethics
and civic morals*, trans C Brookfield,
London, Routledge & Kegan Paul, 267, 985,
987

Dyer S, 1897/1984, *A commonsense method of
double entry bookkeeping. . .*, Part I, London,
Philip, repr NY, Garland, 1984, 445, 466,
511

Easton E E & B L Newton, 1958, *Accounting
and the analysis of financial data*, NY,
McGraw-Hill, 094, 331, 473

Eaton M, 1955, *JA*, Feb, 023

E B M Co Ltd v Dominion Bank [1937] 3 All E R, 043

Eckel L G, 1964, *CanCA*, Feb, 463, 714; 1973, *CA Mag*, 095, 293

Eckel N, 1981, *Abacus*, Jun, 733

Economist, 1879, Apr 19, 284; 1951, Jan 27, 603; 1964, Nov 21, 001, 055, 988; 1966, Jan 1, 097; 1970, Feb 28, 736

Eddis W C & W B Tindall, 1904/1988, *Manufacturers' accounts*, Toronto, Eddis & Tindall, s.c. Murphy, 1988, 583

Edey H C, 1949, *Acct*, Jan 29, 154, 614; 1951, *AccRes*, Apr, 252; 1960/1980, s.c. Edwards (ed), 1980, 067, 288, 542; 1963, *Introduction to accounting*, London, Hutchinson, 334, 464; 1969, *Acct*, Oct 25, 736; 1973, *Financial Times*, Aug 14, 786; 1974, in Edey & Yamey (eds), 1974, 759; 1978, *Accy*, Oct, 066, 252; 1982, *Accy*, Aug, 763

Edey & A T Peacock, 1959, *National income and social accounting*, London, Hutchinson, 681

Edey & B S Yamey (eds), 1974, *Debits, credits, finance and profits*, London, Sweet & Maxwell

Edwards E O, 1975, *AR*, Apr, 325, 779

Edwards & P W Bell, 1961, *The theory and measurement of business income*, Berkeley, U of California P, 052, 056, 186, 274, 531, 532, 546, 605, 645, 646, 693, 763, 766, 768

Edwards, Bell & L T Johnson, 1979, *Accounting for economic events*, Houston, Scholars Book, 044, 062, 192, 194, 315, 347, 436, 763, 773

Edwards J R, 1976, *Acct*, Jan 15, 743, 762; 1980, *ABR*, Spring, 387; 1985, *Abacus*, Mar, 733

Edwards J R (ed), 1980, *British company legislation and company accounts, 1844–1976*, 2 vols, NY, Arno P; 1986, *Legal regulation of British company accounts, 1836–1900*, 2 vols, NY, Garland

Edwards R S, 1937/1973, in Buchanan & Thirlby (eds), 1973, 648; 1938a, *Acct*, Apr 23, 129; 1938b, *Acct*, Jul 2, 162, 254, 356; Jul 16, 045, 145, 466, 542; Jul 23, 319; Jul 30, 183; Aug 27, 367, 542, 601; Sep 3, 136; Sep 17, 714

EEC (European Economic Community), 1978, *Fourth directive*, 288, 292, 372, 514

Egginton D A & R C Morris, 1974, *Acct*, Sep 12, 493

Eggleston F W, 1941, *The search for a social philosophy*, Melbourne, Melbourne U P, 948

Ehrlich D, I Guttman & P Schonbach, 1957, *J of abnormal and social psychology*, v 54, 883

Einstein A, 1901/1987, *The collected papers of Albert Einstein*, trans A Beck, Princeton U P, Princeton, 205; 1935, *The world as I see it*, London, Lane & Bodley Head, 801, 811, 821, 859; 1950/1953, in Feigl & Brodbeck (eds), 1953, 269; –/1962, s.c. de Broglie, 1962, 889

Einstein & L Infeld, 1938, *The evolution of physics*, Cambridge, CUP, 853, 865

Eisner v Macomber, 1919, *[1919] 252 US 189*, 611

Eiteman D S, 1971, *JA*, Mar, 483

Eliot T S, 1935/1963, *Collected poems 1909–1962*, London, Faber & Faber, 226

Ellett et al v Klein et al, 1927, *District Court E D Pennsylvania, No. 1321*, 001

Encyclopaedia Britannica, 1810, 4 ed, Edinburgh, s.c. Brief, 1964/1976, 541; 1981, 15 ed, Chicago, 034, 553, 611, 662, 693, 694

Esquerré P-J, 1914, *The applied theory of accounts*, NY, Ronald, 282, 317, 351, 353, 355, 433, 565, 631, 632, 731; 1915, same title, 423; 1927, *Accounting*, NY, Ronald, 965

Etzioni A (ed), 1969, *The semi-professions and their organization*, NY, Free P

Evans D M, 1859/1968, *Facts, failures and frauds*, London, Groombridge, repr NY, Kelley, 1968, 001, 733

Exchange Banking Company, In re, (Flitcroft's case), 1882, *(1882) 21 Ch D 519*, s.c. Reid, 1986, 278

Fabricant S, 1938, *Capital consumption and adjustment*, New York, National Bureau of Economic Research, 733; 1948/1982, in Zeff (ed), 1982, 667, 674; 1950, in AIA, 1950, 749, 765; 1976, in Fabricant, 1982, 126; 1978, in Fabricant, 1982, 254, 772; 1982, *Studies in social and private accounting*, NY, Garland

Fagerberg D, 1971, *JA*, Apr, 035

Faraday M, (1791–1867), s.c. Pearson, 1911, 836

FASB, 1974, Discussion memorandum, *Reporting the effects of general price level changes in financial statements*, 127; 1976a, *Scope and implications of the conceptual framework project*, in 1976b, 946; 1976b, Discussion memorandum, *Conceptual framework for financial accounting and reporting: elements of financial statements and their measurement*, 347, 349, 361, 545, 546; 1977, SFAS16 [prior period adjustments], 696; 1978, SFAC1 [accounting concepts], 033, 035, 052, 061, 062, 067, 072, 252, 288, 316, 318, 336, 341, 342, 364, 753; 1979, SFAS33 [reporting and changing prices], 531, 616, 711, 747, 748, 762, 764, 768, 791; 1980a, SFAC2, 056, 181, 333, 338, 345; 1980b, SFAC3, 452, 464, 621, 637, 693; 1982, SFAS52 [foreign currency translation], 575; 1984, SFAC5, 255, 344, 367, 414, 427; 1985, SFAC6, 435, 462, 624, 644, 649, 697; 1987, SFAS96 [income taxes], 684, 685, 687

Fawcett H, 1883, *Manual of political economy*, London, Macmillan, 113, 142, 151, 155

Fayol H, 1916/1949, *General and industrial management*, London, Pitman, 054

FBI (Federation of British Industries, UK), 1951, *The effects of inflation on industrial capital resources*, booklet, 129, 198

Fearnside W W & W B Holther, 1959, *Fallacy, the counterfeit of argument*, EC, Prentice-Hall, 213, 826, 835

Federal Power Commission v Hope National Gas Company (1944) 51 PUR (NS), s.c. R W Pinger, *AR*, 1954, Oct, 732

Federal Reserve Board (US), 1917, *Federal Reserve Bulletin*, Apr 1, [for professional origin of document, see Zeff, 1972, 114], 082, 095, 296, 695; 1929, *Verification of financial statements*, pamphlet, 457

Feigl H & M Brodbeck (eds), 1953, *Readings in the philosophy of science*, NY, Appleton-Century-Crofts

Feller B, 1974, *AA*, Aug, 946, 976

Fen Lands Act 1773, 13 Geo III, c.45, 072, 074

Ferguson v Wilson, 1866, *(1866) 2 Ch App 77*, 278

Fertakis J P, 1969, *AR*, Oct, 015, 793

Fertig P E, D F Istvan & H J Mottice, 1971, *Using financial information*, NY, Harcourt Brace Jovanovich, 414, 638

Fess P E & J J Weygandt, 1969, *JA*, Aug, 496, 497

Festinger, L, 1957/1962, *A theory of cognitive dissonance*, London, Tavistock, 238; 1963, in Schramm (ed), 1963, 201

Fetter F A, 1937, *AR*, Mar, 045, 156, 157, 158

Feyerabend P K, 1975/1982, *Against method*, London, Verso, 226, 803, 804, 833, 856, 881, 889, 954, 996; 1981, *Problems of empiricism*, Cambridge, CUP, 861

Feynman R, 1992, in Gleick, 1992, 814

fforde A, 1950, *Acct*, Nov 18, 332

Field R E, 1969, *Financial reporting in the extractive industries* (ARS11), NY, AICPA, 326, 648

Fieldhouse A & E E Fieldhouse, 1929, *The student's complete commercial bookkeeping*, 37 ed, Huddersfield, Fieldhouse, 032, 143, 694

Financial Times (London), 1975, Sep 5, 769

Finlay & Co Ltd, 1941, *Acct*, Feb 21, 1942, 096

Finlay W B, 1914, *JA*, Jul, 543

Finney H A & H E Miller, 1958, *Principles of accounting – intermediate*, EC, Prentice-Hall, 713; 1961, same title, 335, 346, 625, 941; 1968, *Principles of financial accounting*, EC, Prentice-Hall, 128, 134, 431, 512, 621, 638, 642, 645, 694

Finnie J, 1968a, *TAM*, Jun, 061, 326, 377; 1968b, *TAM*, Jul, 552, 711, 713, 785

Firmin P A, 1957, *AR*, Oct, 072

Fisher I, 1906/1965, *The nature of capital and income*, repr NY, Kelley, 1965, 131, 147, 151, 152, 153, 154, 194, 324, 325, 354, 431, 784, 852, 854; 1912, *The purchasing power of money*, NY, Macmillan, 112, 124; 1920, *Stabilizing the dollar*, NY, Macmillan, 126; 1929, *The money illusion*, London, Allen & Unwin, 113; 1930a, *The theory of interest*, NY, Macmillan, 145; 1930b, *AER*, Dec, 146, 255, 465

Fitzgerald A A, 1936, in *Proceedings of the Australasian congress on accounting, 1936*, Melbourne, Congress, 934; 1938, *AA*, Mar, 922; 1948, *AA*, Feb, 642; 1951, *AA*, Mar, 444; 1956a, *Analysis and interpretation of financial and operating statements*, Sydney, Butterworth, 192, 316, 372, 441, 442, 713, 923, 924; 1956b, *AA*, Jan, 341, 715

Fitzgerald (ed), 1957, *Fitzgerald's Accounting, stage 1*, Sydney, Butterworth

Fitzgerald & G E Fitzgerald, 1948, *Form and content of published financial statements*, Sydney, Butterworth, 372, 645, 734

Fitzgerald & L A Schumer, 1952, *Classification in accounting*, Sydney, Butterworth, 381, 382, 452, 503, 601, 671

Flegm E H, 1984, *Accounting: how to meet the challenges of relevance and regulation*, NY, Wiley, 723, 926, 946

Fleming A, 1945, *Nature*, Jun 30, 824; 1959, in Maurois, 1959, 834

Flew A, 1975, *Thinking about thinking*, Glasgow, Fontana/Collins, 202, 214, 215, 854, 855

Flexner A, 1930/1968, *Universities: American, English, German*, NY, OUP, 823, 825, 889, 951, 992

Flint D, 1966, *TAM*, Aug, 942, 1982, *A true and fair view in company accounts*, London, Gee, 334, 345, 413, 427, 429

Flint & J C Shaw, 1981, in Bromwich & Hopwood (eds), 1981, 948

Flynn T D, 1965, *LCP*, Duke U, Autumn, 376

Folsom E G, 1873/1976, *The logic of accounts*, NY, Barnes, 1873, repr NY, Arno P, 1976, 133, 143, 355

Fomento (Sterling Area) Ltd v Selsdon Fountain Pen Co Ltd, [1958] 1 All E L R, 11, 091

Forell S R, 1956, *AA*, Oct, 279

Forrester J W, 1968, *Management science*, Mar, 175

Foster B F, 1843, *Double entry elucidated*, London, Souter & Law, 081, 333, 357, 383, 385, 386, 431, 466, 503, 541, 892, 922, 995; 1849, same title, 321; 1846/1956, *Remarks on the ordinary modes of teaching writing and bookkeeping*, London, s.c. Jackson, 1956, 995; 1852/1976, *The origin and progress of bookkeeping*, London, Souter, 1852, repr in Bennet & Foster, NY, Arno P, 1976, 011

Foster G, 1978, *Financial statement analysis*, EC, Prentice-Hall, 192

Foulke R A, 1945, *Practical financial statement analysis*, NY, McGraw-Hill, 061, 064, 192, 227, 441, 465, 491, 492

Frank J, 1930/1963, *Law and the modern mind*, NY, Doubleday, 182, 213

Frank J N, 1939, *JA*, Nov, 191

Frank P G, 1955/1962, in Neurath & others (eds), 1955/1962, 228, 863; 1957/1962, *Philosophy of science*, EC, Prentice-Hall, 203, 859; 1961a, in Frank (ed), 1961b, 868

Frank (ed), 1961b, *The validation of scientific theories*, NY, Collier

Frank Mills Mining Company, In re, 1883, *(1883) 23 Ch D App 52*, 428

Franklin W H, 1944, *NACA Bull*, Sep, 423, 506

Llewellyn K N, 1930/1960, *The bramble bush*, Dobbs Ferry, NY, Oceana Publications, 262

Lloyd D, 1964, *The idea of law*, Harmondsworth, Penguin, 204, 262, 263

Locke J, 1693/1970, *Some thoughts concerning education*, London, Churchill, repr Menston, Scolar P, 1970, 001; 1700/1979, *An essay concerning human understanding*, P H Nidditch (ed), London, OUP, 922, 953

London and General Bank Ltd, ex parte Theobald (no.2), Re, 1895, *[1895–99] All E R*, 091, 097, 331

Lopez R S & I W Raymond (eds), 1955, *Medieval trade in the Mediterranean world*, London, OUP

Lorensen L, 1972a, *Reporting foreign operations of US companies in US dollars* (ARS12), AICPA, 575; 1972b, *JA*, Aug, 575

Lorenzen F, 1972, *CanCA*, Jul, 686

Lorig A N, 1964, *AR*, Jul, 042, 045

Lothian N, 1978, *Accy*, Nov, 288, 934; 1982, *TAM*, Nov, 372, 374, 735

Louderback J G, 1971, *AR*, Apr, 184

Louwers P C, 1972, *TAM*, Nov, 067

Loveday A, 1933, in Akerman & others, 1933, 188

Lowe E A, 1970, *JBF*, Summer, 144

Lund R I, 1941, *AR*, Dec, 318, 543

Lundberg G A, 1942, *Social research*, NY, Longmans Green, 813, 831, 873

Lutz F & V Lutz, 1951, *The theory of investment of the firm*, Princeton, Princeton U P, 189, 667

Lybrand W M, 1908, *JA*, Nov, 943

Lynch J F, 1943, *JA*, Sep, 779

Lyne S, 1981, *TAM*, Jul, 287, 319

Lyttleton O, 1953, *Acct*, Nov 28, 001

Ma R, 1974, *Abacus*, Dec, 573, 574

Ma & R L Mathews, 1979, *The accounting framework*, Melbourne, Longman Cheshire, 256, 275, 785; 1987, Ma, Mathews & J Macmullen, rev ed same title, 068, 154, 192, 257, 644, 714, 753, 945

Ma & M C Miller, 1978, *ABR*, Autumn, 453

MacChesney B & R H O'Brien, 1937, *LCP*, Apr, 292

Macdonald G, 1974a, *Profit measurement: alternatives to historical cost*, London, Haymarket Publishing, 233, 348, 368, 773; 1974b, *ABR*, Autumn, 342, 567

Macdonald & B A Rutherford (eds), 1989, *Accounts, accounting and accountability*, London, van Nostrand & ICAEW

Macghie A, 1718, *The principles of bookkeeping explained*, Edinburgh, Rachel Hill, 511

Mach E, 1908/1960, in Danto & Morgenbesser (eds), 1960, 197, 258, 261, 816, 844, 851, 868

Machiavelli N, c1519/1952, *The prince*, NY, Mentor, 1952, 269, 883; 1521/1990, s.c. P Zagorin, *Ways of lying*, Cambridge, Harvard U P, 1990, 224

Machlup F, 1955, *Southern economic j*, Jul, 845, 857, 862, 863, 868; 1962/1963, *AEA papers* (1962, publ 1963), 852

Macintosh J C C, 1974, *Accy*, Nov, 448

Macmannaway, Re, 1951, *[1951] A C 161*, 266

MacNeal K, 1939, *Truth in accounting*, Philadelphia, U of Pennsylvania P, 132, 143, 194, 227, 318, 319, 331, 375, 421, 448, 541, 571, 593, 612, 626, 711, 716, 732

Macpherson L G, 1934, *CanCA*, Jan, 283

Macve R, 1981, *A conceptual framework for financial accounting and reporting*, London, ICAEW, 062, 066, 344, 427, 605, 946

Madan D B, 1985, *Abacus*, Sep, 773

Magee B, 1978/1981, s.c. Flint & Shaw, 1981, 832

Magee C C, 1979, *Framework of accounting*, Plymouth, Macdonald & Evans, 328, 498, 642

Main v Mills, 1874, *Fed Cas 506, no 8974*, (Wisconsin), s.c. Reid (ed), 1988, 463

Mair J, 1793, *Bookkeeping methodiz'd*, 6 ed, Edinburgh, Bell & others, 033

Malchman L H & A Slavin, 1961, *Foundations of accounting for managerial control*, NY, Holt Rinehart, 318, 384, 631, 632, 649, 926

Malcolm A, 1731, *A treatise of bookkeeping, or Merchants accounts*, London, Osborn, 382, 411, 413, 503, 505, 511, 779, 947

Malynes G, 1622, *Consuetudo, vel lex mercatoria, or The ancient law merchant*, London, Islip, 321, 353

Manchester City News, 1892/1972, Mar 23, s c H P Hain, *AA*, July 1972, 001

Mann O G, 1917, *JA*, Feb, 662

Manne H G (ed), 1969, *Economic policy and the regulation of corporate securities*, American Enterprise Institute for Public Policy Research, Washington, D.C.

Manning B A, 1969, in Manne (ed), 1969, 737

Manson E, 1903–1904, in Lisle (ed), 1903–1904, 387

March J G & H A Simon, 1958, *Organizations*, NY, Wiley, 237

Margenau H, 1950, *The nature of physical reality*, NY, McGraw-Hill, 243, 244, 252, 853, 856; 1959/1962, in Churchman & Ratoosh (eds), 1959/1962, 241

Marley C, 1970, *JBF*, Winter, 052, 294

Marple R P, 1962, *JA*, Nov, 031, 423; 1963, *AR*, Jul, 759; 1964, *Toward a basic accounting philosophy*, NY, NAA, 155, 311, 322, 354

Marsh C C, 1835/1988, "A lecture on the study of bookkeeping", repr *AHJ*, Fall, 1988, 001, 012, 013, 413, 913, 932, 934, 995, 998; 1864, *The theory and practice of bank bookkeeping and joint stock accounts*, 4 ed, NY, Appleton, 001

Marshall A, 1887/1966, letter, in A C Pigou (ed), 1925, *Memorials of Alfred Marshall*, London, Macmillan, repr NY, Kelley, 1966, 116; 1890/1920, *Principles of economics*, London, Macmillan, 113, 151, 153, 155, 161, 228; 1901/1966, letter, in Pigou (ed), 1966 (above), 865; 1906/1966, letter in Pigou (ed),

Source Index

Moscovici S, 1981, in J P Forgas, 1981, *Social cognition*, London, Academic P, 225

Moss Committee, 1976, Report of US Congress subcommittee on oversight and investigation (chairman J E Moss), *Federal regulation and regulatory reform*, Washington, USGPO, 966, 976, 977

Mosso D, 1980, in Buckley & Weston (eds), 1980, 139, 252, 339, 973

Most K S, 1959, *Acct*, Dec 26, 632; 1969, *Acct*, Nov 20, 939; 1977a, *ABR*, Autumn, 602, 645, 667; 1977b, *Accounting theory*, Columbus, Grid Inc, 144, 699, 847, 944

Mueller F, 1970, in Zaidi (ed), 1970, 673

Mueller G G & C H Smith (eds), 1970, *Accounting: a book of readings*, NY, Holt Rinehart

Mulcahy G, 1963, *Use and meaning of "market" in inventory valuation*, Toronto, CICA, 364, 365, 545, 642

Mumford M J, 1977, *CertAcc*, Dec, 674

Mun T, 1664/1949, *England's treasure by forraign trade*, London, Clark, repr 1949, Oxford, Blackwell, 001

Munn N L, 1961, *Psychology*, Boston, Houghton Mifflin, 204, 215

Murphy A E, 1943, *The uses of reason*, NY, Macmillan, 231, 843

Murphy G J, 1988, *The evolution of selected annual corporate reporting practices in Canada 1900-1970*, NY, Garland, 473

Mutton A R, 1962, *AA*, Aug, 254, 612; 1975, *CAA*, Nov, 754

Myatt-Price E M, 1956, in Littleton & Yamey (eds), 1956, 352

Myddelton D R, 1968, *Acct*, Aug 3, 686; 1974, *Acct*, Jul 11, 615, 747, 758; 1981, in Leach & Stamp (eds), 1981, 257, 741, 769

Myer J N, 1946, *AR*, Jan, 713; 1969, *Financial statement analysis*, EC, Prentice-Hall, 332, 512

Myers J H, 1959, *AR*, Oct, 643

Myrdal G, 1944, *An American dilemma*, NY, Harper, 872

NAA, 1959, *Return on capital as a guide to managerial decisions*, NY, 191; 1960, *NAA research report no. 36*, Mar, 575; 1974, *Accounting terminology*, 293, 514, 523, 545

Nagel E, 1932/1960, in Danto & Morgenbesser (eds), 1960, 247; 1962/1963, *AEA papers*, 847

Napper D, 1964a, *Accy*, Oct, 448; 1964b, *Acct*, Nov 21, 319, 448, 476

Nau C H, 1924, *JA*, Jan, 064

Needles B E, H R Anderson & J C Caldwell, 1984, *Principles of accounting*, Boston, Houghton Mifflin, 036, 128, 191, 192, 195, 254, 457, 564, 612, 618, 651, 662, 752

Nelligan J L, 1980, in Buckley & Weston (eds), 1980, 966

Nelson B, 1964, *Acct*, Aug 22, 995

Nelson C L, 1976, *Business week*, Mar 8, 294

Nelson E G, 1935, *AR*, Dec, 057; 1942, *AR*, Apr, 275, 367, 618

Nelson G K, 1966, *AR*, Jan, 145

Neurath O, 1944/1962, *Foundations of the social sciences*, Chicago, UCP, 805

Neurath O, R Carnap & C Morris (eds), 1955/1962, *International encyclopedia of unified science*, Vol 1, Chicago, UCP

Newbold G D, 1970, *Business finance*, London, Harrap, 191

Newlove G H & S P Garner, 1951, *Advanced accounting*, Boston, Heath, 046, 375, 475, 638, 682

Newman J H, 1852/1905, *The idea of a university*, London, Longmans Green, 843, 992

Newman B, 1964, *Auditing*, NY, Wiley, 093

Newton Bernie & Company, 1837, Partnership contract, UGD152/1/2, 073, 501

Newton C R, 1972/1977, *General principles of law*, London, Sweet & Maxwell, 263

Newton I, c1727/1964, s.c. Spence, c1735/1964, 824

Newton v Birmingham Small Arms Co Ltd, 1906, *[1906] 2 Ch 378*, 372

Nicholls F A, 1975a, *CertAcc*, Feb, 193; 1975b, *CertAcc*, Mar, 759

Nobel lectures, 1992, Economic science, 1969–1980, 1981–1990, Singapore, World Scientific Publishing

Nobes C W, 1980, *ABR*, Autumn, 575; 1983, *Abacus*, Jun, 779

Noble H S & C R Niswonger, 1961, *Accounting principles*, Cincinnati, South-Western, 041, 128, 145, 312, 512, 562, 617

Nolan F E, 1955, *AccRes*, Jan, 551, 715

Noone J, 1910, *JA*, Aug, 423

Norris H, 1939, *Acct*, 372, 626, 942; 1945a, *Acct*, Mar 3, 934; 1945b, *Acct*, Apr 28, 334, 725, 943; 1945c, *Economica*, Aug, 037; 1946, *Accounting theory*, London, Pitman, 298, 299, 415, 662; 1949a, *AccRes*, Jul, 634; 1949b, *Acct*, Dec 10, 444

North R, 1714/1986, *The gentleman accomptant*, London; repr NY, Garland, 1986, 001, 022, 075, 155, 198, 317, 342, 352, 961

Northcott L J & C S Forsyth, 1949, *Practical bookkeeping and accountancy*, London, Odhams, 471, 473

Northern Counties Securities v Jackson & Steeple Ltd, 1974, *[1974] 1 W L R 1133*, 279

Northrop F C S, 1959, *The logic of the sciences and the humanities*, NY, Meridian, 821, 847, 853, 873

Nussbaum F L, 1937, *A history of the economic institutions of modern Europe*, NY, Crofts, 012, 157

NYSE, 1895/1965, s.c. Bevis, 1965, 291; 1939, Report of Subcommittee of Committee on Stock List, 1939, *JA*, Oct, 713

NZR, *Report of the Committee of inquiry into inflation accounting*, (I L M Richardson, chairman), 1976, Government Printer, Wellington, 335, 341, 372, 567, 753, 766, 785

063, 251; 1941, *Advanced accounting*, NY,
Macmillan, 138, 195, 662; 1943/1982, in Zeff
(ed), 1982, 471; 1946a, *JA*, Mar, 585, 716;
1946b/1948, s.c. *JA*, Aug 1948, 327; 1948, *JA*,
Apr, 372; 1955, *Essentials of accounting*, NY,
Macmillan, 683; 1963, *JAR*, Spring, 191, 257,
282, 319, 366, 465; 1971, in Stone (ed), 1971,
643

Paton (ed), 1944, *Accountants' handbook*, NY,
Ronald P, 347, 571, 574, 657, 682, 692, 694

Paton & R L Dixon, 1958, *Essentials of
accounting*, NY, Macmillan, 131, 313, 354,
452, 488, 604, 692, 779

Paton & A C Littleton, 1940, *An introduction to
corporate accounting standards*, AAA, 042,
052, 128, 145, 287, 324, 335, 336, 364, 435,
512, 513, 604, 612, 641, 642, 688, 713, 945

Paton & W A Paton Jr, 1952, *Asset accounting*,
NY, Macmillan, 129, 515, 522, 652; 1955,
Corporation accounts and statements, NY,
Macmillan, 129; 1971, *Assets – accounting and
administration*, n p, Roberts & Roehl, 127,
255, 363, 565

Paton & R A Stevenson, 1916/1976, *Principles of
accounting*, Ann Arbor, Ann Arbor P, repr
NY, Arno, 1976, 255, 319, 333, 383, 503,
583; 1917, same title, Ann Arbor, Wahr, 014,
022, 253, 322; 1918/1978, same title, NY,
Macmillan, repr NY, Garland, 1978, 362, 434,
461, 462, 612, 626, 669, 779; 1920/1978, same
title, repr NY, Arno P, 431

Paterson R & D Smith, 1979, *Accy*, Aug, 977

Patterson N, 1683, in Colinson, 1683, 001

Payne A W, 1892, *Acct*, Feb 13, 591, 694

Payne's Properties, 1965, *Interim report of an
investigation into the affairs of Payne's
Properties Pty Ltd . . . .* , Government Printer,
Melbourne, 739

Pearcy J, 1971, *TAM*, Jul, 125

Pearse D, 1977, *CertAcc*, Apr, 294

Pearson K, 1911, *The grammar of science*, London,
Black, 202, 802, 803, 833, 836, 859, 891

Peasnell K V, 1974, *ABR*, Winter, 056, 842; 1977,
Abacus, Dec, 667

Peddie R, 1966, *TAM*, May, 682

Peele J, 1553, *The maner and forme how to kepe a
perfecte reconyng . . .* , London, Grafton, 282,
411; 1569/1956, *The pathwaye to perfectnes in
th'accomptes of debitour and creditour . . .* ,
s.c. Jackson, 1956, 353

Peirce C S, 1868, 1877, 1892, 1898, s.c. P P Wiener
(ed), *Values in a universe of chance*, NY,
Doubleday, 1958, 202, 204, 205, 221, 801, 857,
859, 865

Peloubet M E, 1929, in *International Congress
on Accounting 1929*, NY, repr NY, Garland,
1982, 444, 655; 1933, *Acct*, Aug 5, 486; 1935,
JA, Mar, 141, 144, 331, 504; 1938/1982, in
AIA, 1938/1982, 372, 646, 692; 1939/1982, in
Zeff (ed), 1982, 656; 1944/1982, in Zeff (ed),
1982, 316; 1945, *AR*, Oct, 015, 713, 941; 1948,
JA, Apr, 656; 1959, *JA*, Mar, 943, 965

Pen J, 1966, *Harmony and conflict in modern
society*, NY, McGraw-Hill, 136

Penman S H, 1970, *AR*, Apr, 275

Pepys S, 1666/1930, *The diary of Samuel Pepys*, H
B Wheatley (ed), London, Bell, 001

Peragallo E, 1938, *Origin and evolution of double
entry bookkeeping*, NY, American Institute
Publishing, 001, 023; 1941, *JA*, Nov, 383;
1980, *ABR*, no 37A, 541

Percy K, 1979, *Accy*, Jul, 963, 978

Perry D P, 1948, *JA*, Dec, 995

Perry R B, 1909/1937, *The moral economy*, NY,
Scribner's Sons, 207

Peterson C E, 1981, in Burton & others (eds),
1981, 574

Pfiffner J M & F P Sherwood, 1960,
Administrative organization, EC, Prentice-Hall,
188, 237, 238, 271, 276, 277

*Pharmaceutical Society of Great Britain & another
v Dickson*, 1968, *[1968] 2 All E R 686*, 981,
984

Philips G E, 1963a, *AR*, Jan, 164, 603, 643; 1963b,
AR, Oct, 541

Phillips T W, 1902/1986, s.c. Brief (ed), 1986, 283

Phillippe G L, 1964, *CanCA*, Mar, 952

Pickles W, 1974, *Accountancy*, London, Pitman,
443, 445, 474, 631, 633, 662, 665

Pickles & G W Dunkerley, 1950, *Accountancy*,
London, Pitman, 282

Pigou A C, 1941, *Economica*, Aug, 159

Pinner v Everett, 1969, *[1969] All E R 257*, 266

Pirsig R M, 1974, *Zen and the art of motor cycle
maintenance*, NY, Morrow, 811

Pitt J F & E P Tang, 1968/1970, s.c. Mueller &
Smith (eds), 1970, 548

Pixley F W, 1881/1976, *Auditors: their duties
and responsibilities . . .* , London, Effingham
Wilson, repr NY, Arno P, 1976, 083, 092,
293, 341, 362, 445, 541, 544, 662; 1897/1978,
The profession of a chartered accountant,
London, Good, repr NY, Arno P, 1978,
448, 645; 1904, International congress of
accountants, s.c. J P Joplin, *JA*, Dec 1914,
477; 1906, *Acct*, Oct 27, 425, 433; 1910,
Auditors: . . . . , 10 ed, London, Gee, 424,
426; 1926, *The accountant's dictionary*,
London, Pitman, 2 ed, 274, 338, 378, 383,
387, 575, 622, 662, 669

Planck M, 1925, *A survey of physics*, trans R
Jones & D H Williams, London, Methuen,
834, 847; 1950, *Scientific autobiography
and other papers*, trans F Gaynor, London,
Williams & Norgate, 203, 221, 873,
883

Plate Glass Manufacturers Act 1773, (*13 Geo III, c
38*), 074

Platt J R, 1962, *The excitement of science*, Boston,
Houghton Mifflin, 802; 1964, *Science*, Oct 16,
823, 865

Plender W, 1910, *Acct*, Oct 8, 426; 1932, *Acct*, Feb
13, 424

Plumb H A, 1891, *Acct*, Apr 4, 575

Source Index

Subject Index

References are to section numbers

Subject Index

Subject Index

Substance and form, 373
Substantial support, of principles, 721
Supplementary statements, 287
Surplus, 463, 469
Suspense accounts, 378
Symbols, 221

Tax allocation, 685–687
Taxation, 683–687; as expense, 684; as transfer
    payment, 681
Teaching, 996
Technology and science, 892
Terminological obscurity, 927, 934
Terminological propriety, 852, 934
Testability of propositions, theories, 861
Testing of theories, 863
Theorems, 855
Theory, 847, 849; and practice, 871, 949;
    explanatory power, 867; predictive power, 868
Theory construction, 850; in accounting, 947
Theory selection, 856; supercession, 869
Thinking, 215, 830, 842
Time in accounting, 310
Timeliness of information, 343
Trade cycle and accounting, 717
Trade off of information characteristics, 349
Tradition, 205; in accounting, 918
Transactions, 131–133; accounting for, 032, 033
Transfer payments, 681
Translation of foreign balances, 575
Trial balance, 383
True accounts, 292
True and fair view, 292, 293
Truth, 207, 812
Truthfulness in accounting, 075, 292, 293, 331

Unamortized costs, as assets, 434; as valuation
    basis, 510
Uncertainty of future, 174
Uncertainty in accounting, 328
Uniformity in accounting, 348, 736
Unity of science, 805
University education, 992

Unpredictability of future, 174, 187
Usefulness of accounting information, 342

Valuation, of assets and liabilities, 500;
    conjectural, 550; dated, 142, 143, 147,
    501, 553; itemized, 503; optional, 505;
    periodical, 581; prospective, 145, 146, 147,
    553, 785; responsibility of management, 326;
    revaluation, 583, 584; subjective, 132, 144
Valuation as preference ranking, 185
Valuation bases, cash equivalent, 542; cost, 510;
    current cost, 530, 764; differential, 566; exit
    value, 546; fair value, 548; heterogeneous, 593;
    hybrid, 560; indexed cost, 516; market price,
    541; money equivalent, 542; net present value,
    550; net realizable value, 545; replacement
    price, 520, 759; selling price, 542, 543, 544;
    uniform, 591, 592; value in exchange, 540,
    542; value to owner, 567
Value(s); accounting outputs as, 321; book, 506;
    capitalized, 146, 551; dated, 142, 424, 501;
    diverse meanings, 141; market, 541; measured
    attribute, 255; personal, 132, 144
Value in exchange, 142, 143; measured attribute,
    255; valuation basis, 540
Value in use, 148; see also Prospective value
Value of the firm, 427; see also Prospective value
Value to the owner, 567
Verifiability, 337
Verification, audit as, 082, 086; in science, 862,
    866
Volatility of context of choice, 173

Wealth, as dated purchasing power, 152; as
    exchangeable means, 151; as expectations,
    154; excludes intrinsic properties, 153;
    representation in accounting, 031; see also
    Capital
Words, as signs, 222; interpretation, 266; jargon,
    226
Working capital, 192

Yield, 191